The Oxford Handbook of Organizational Citizenship Behavior

OXFORD LIBRARY OF PSYCHOLOGY

AREA EDITORS:

Clinical Psychology
David H. Barlow

Cognitive Neuroscience
Kevin N. Ochsner and Stephen M. Kosslyn

Cognitive Psychology
Daniel Reisberg

Counseling Psychology
Elizabeth M. Altmaier and Jo-Ida C. Hansen

Developmental Psychology
Philip David Zelazo

Health Psychology
Howard S. Friedman

History of Psychology
David B. Baker

Methods and Measurement
Todd D. Little

Neuropsychology
Kenneth M. Adams

Organizational Psychology
Steve W. J. Kozlowski

Personality and Social Psychology
Kay Deaux and Mark Snyder

OXFORD LIBRARY OF PSYCHOLOGY

The Oxford Handbook of Organizational Citizenship Behavior

Edited by

Philip M. Podsakoff

Scott B. MacKenzie

Nathan P. Podsakoff

OXFORD
UNIVERSITY PRESS

OXFORD
UNIVERSITY PRESS

Oxford University Press is a department of the University of Oxford. It furthers the University's objective of excellence in research, scholarship, and education by publishing worldwide. Oxford is a registered trade mark of Oxford University Press in the UK and certain other countries.

Published in the United States of America by Oxford University Press
198 Madison Avenue, New York, NY 10016, United States of America.

Library of Congress Cataloging-in-Publication Data
Names: Podsakoff, Philip M., editor. | MacKenzie, Scott B., 1954– editor. |
Podsakoff, Nathan P., editor.
Title: The Oxford handbook of organizational citizenship behavior / edited by
Philip M. Podsakoff, Scott B. MacKenzie, Nathan P. Podsakoff.
Description: New York : Oxford University Press, [2018] |
Series: Oxford library of psychology | Includes bibliographical references and index.
Identifiers: LCCN 2017044643 | ISBN 9780190219000 (hardcover : alk. paper)
Subjects: LCSH: Organizational behavior. | Organizational effectiveness. |
Psychology, Industrial.
Classification: LCC HD58.7 .O94185 2018 | DDC 302.3/5—dc23
LC record available at https://lccn.loc.gov/2017044643

9 8 7 6 5 4 3 2 1

Printed by Sheridan Books, Inc., United States of America

SHORT CONTENTS

ABOUT THE EDITORS

Philip M. Podsakoff

Philip M. Podsakoff is the Hyatt and Ceci Brown Chair of Business at the Warrington College of Business at the University of Florida. He received his doctoral degree at Indiana University, and he taught at The Ohio State University and Indiana University before joining the faculty at the University of Florida. Professor Podsakoff is a Fellow of the Society for Industrial and Organizational Psychology (SIOP) and the Academy of Management Association; past chair of the Research Methods Group of the Academy of Management; a recipient of the Academy of Management Research Methods Division's Distinguished Career Award; a co-recipient of the SIOP William A. Owens Scholarly Achievement Award; and a co-recipient of *The Leadership Quarterly's* Decennial Influential Article Award. He has published over 75 articles in organizational behavior, management, marketing, psychology, and MIS journals.

Scott B. MacKenzie

Scott B. MacKenzie is the Neal Gilliatt Chair and Professor of Marketing at the Kelley School of Business at Indiana University. He is the author of over 70 widely cited articles on organizational citizenship behavior, leadership, and research methodology published in leading marketing, management, and MIS journals. In addition, he is a previous winner of the Society for Industrial and Organizational Psychology's William A. Owens Scholarly Achievement Award, the American Marketing Association's Harold H. Maynard Award, *The Leadership Quarterly's* Decennial Influential Article Award, and Honorable Mention in the Association for Consumer Research's Robert Ferber Award competition.

Nathan P. Podsakoff

Nathan P. Podsakoff is a Robbins Fellow in the Eller College of Management at the University of Arizona. He received his Ph.D. from the University of Florida and his A.B. from Princeton University. His research has been published in management, psychology, and MIS outlets. He is a recipient of the Society for Industrial and Organizational Psychology's William A. Owens Scholarly Achievement Award and the Early Career Achievement Award from the Academy of Management's Research Methods Division. He has also served as an Associate Editor for *Personnel Psychology*.

CONTRIBUTORS

Tammy D. Allen
Department of Psychology
University of South Florida
Tampa, FL, USA

Tom Bellairs
Department of Management
University of Alabama
Tusacaloosa, AL, USA

Diane M. Bergeron
Weatherhead School of Management
Case Western Reserve University
Cleveland, OH, USA

Mark C. Bolino
Price College of Business
University of Oklahoma
Norman, OK, USA

Daniel J. Brass
LINKS Center for Social Network Analysis
University of Kentucky
Lexington, KY, USA

Holly Brower
School of Business
Wake Forest University
Winston-Salem, NC, USA

Evan A. Bruno
Department of Management and Organizations
Cornell University
Ithaca, NY, USA

Claudia Buengeler
Department of Human Resources
Kiel University
Kiel, Germany

Ethan R. Burris
Mc Combs School of Business
The University of Texas at Austin
Austin, TX, USA

Andrea E. Caldwell
School of Business
The University of Texas at Austin
Austin, TX, USA

Goran Calic
DeGroote School of Business
McMaster University
Ontario, Canada

Nichelle C. Carpenter
Darla Moore School of Business
Department of Management
University of South Carolina
Columbia, SC, USA

Joseph A. Carpini
The Business School
University of Western Australia
Perth, Australia

Chiachi Chang
Department of Management
London School of Economics
London, England, UK

Chu-Hsiang (Daisy) Chang
Department of Psychology
Michigan State University
East Lansing, MI, USA

Dan S. Chiaburu
Mays Business School
Texas A&M University
College Station, TX, USA

Jacqueline A-M. Coyle-Shapiro
Department of Management
London School of Economics
London, England, UK

Russell Cropanzano
Leeds School of Business
University of Colorado at Boulder
Boulder, CO, USA

Reeshad S. Dalal
Department of Psychology
George Mason University
Fairfax, VA, USA

James R. Detert
Darden School of Business
University of Virginia
Charlottesville, VA, USA

Marjo-Riitta Diehl
EBS Business School
Oestrich-Winkel, Germany

Anat Drach-Zahavy
Faculty of Health and Welfare Sciences
University of Haifa
Haifa, Israel

P. Christopher Earley
UTS Business School
University of Technology
Sydney, Australia

Mark G. Ehrhart
University of Central Florida
Orlando, FL, USA

Ulrike Fasbender
University of Central Florida
Orlando, FL, USA

Michael Frese
National University of Singapore
Singapore

Kamalika Ghosh
Department of Psychology
Rice University
Houston, TX, USA

Steven Grover
Department of Management
University of Otago
Otago, New Zealand

Sarah Haidar
College of Business Administration
University of Alabama in Huntsville
Huntsville, AL, USA

Jonathon Halbesleben
Department of Management
University of Alabama
Tusacaloosa, AL, USA

Brooks C. Holtom
McDonough School of Business
Georgetown University
Washington, DC, USA

Seulki "Rachel" Jang
Department of Psychology
University of South Florida
Tampa, FL, USA

Russell E. Johnson
Eli Broad School of Management
Michigan State University
East Lansing, MI, USA

Timothy A. Judge
Max M. Fisher College of Business
Ohio State University
Columbus, OH, USA

Harrison J. Kell
Department of Psychology and Human Development
Vanderbilt University
Nashville, TN, USA

Anthony C. Klotz
College of Business
University of Oregon
Eugene, OR, USA

Joel Koopman
Texas A&M University
TX, USA

Amy L. Kristof-Brown
Tippie College of Business
University of Iowa
Iowa City, IA, USA

Anna C. Lennard
Eli Broad School of Management
Michigan State University
East Lansing, MI, USA

Jeffery A. LePine
W.P. Carey School of Business
Arizona State University
Phoenix, AZ, USA

Christina S. Li
Tippie College of Business
University of Iowa
Iowa City, IA, USA

Wen-Dong Li
Department of Management
CUHK Business School
The Chinese University of Hong Kong
Hong Kong, China

Scott B. MacKenzie
Kelley School of Business
Indiana University
Bloomington, IN, USA

Sophia V. Marinova
College of Business Administration
University of Alabama in Huntsville
Huntsville, AL, USA

Michelle P. Martin
Educational Testing Service
Princeton, NJ, USA

Tomas M. Martinez
Eller College of Management
University of Arizona
Tucson, AZ, USA

Fadel K. Matta
Department of Management
University of Georgia
Athens, GA, USA

Timothy D. Maynes
School of Management
University of Buffalo
Buffalo, NY, USA

Robert Moorman
Department of Business Leadership
Elon University
Elon, NC, USA

Elizabeth W. Morrison
Stern School of Business
New York University
New York, NY, USA

Stephan J. Motowidlo
Department of Psychology
Rice University
Houston, TX, USA

Daniel W. Newton
W.P. Carey School of Business
Arizona State University
Phoenix, AZ, USA

In-Sue Oh
Fox School of Business
Temple University
Philadelphia, PA, USA

Dennis W. Organ
Kelley School of Business
Indiana University
Bloomington, IN, USA

Sharon K. Parker
The Business School
University of Western Australia
Perth, Australia

Liana G. Passantino
Eli Broad School of Management
Michigan State University
East Lansing, MI, USA

Ronald F. Piccolo
College of Business Administration
University of Central Florida
Orlando, FL, USA

Nathan P. Podsakoff
Eller College of Management
University of Arizona
Tucson, AZ, USA

Philip M. Podsakoff
Warrington College of Business Administration
University of Florida
Gainesville, FL, USA

Christopher C. Rosen
Sam M. Walton School of Business
University of Arkansas
Fayetteville, AR, USA

Deborah E. Rupp
Department of Psychological Sciences
Purdue University
West Lafayette, IN, USA

Benjamin Schneider
Center for Effective Organizations
University of Maryland
College Park, MD, USA

Brent A. Scott
Eli Broad College of Business
Michigan State University
East Lansing, MI, USA

Tomoki Sekiguchi
Graduate School of Management
Kyoto University
Kyoto, Japan

Ruodan Shao
Asper School of Business
University of Manitoba
Winnipeg, Manitoba, Canada

Anit Somech
Department of Educational Leadership and Policy
University of Haifa
Haifa, Israel

Trevor M. Spoelma
University of New Mexico
Albuquerque, NM, USA

Phillip S. Thompson
Weatherhead School of Management
Case Western Reserve University
Cleveland, OH, USA

Meghan A. Thornton-Lugo
College of Business
University of Texas at San Antonio
San Antonio, TX, USA

William H. Turnley
College of Business Administration
Kansas State University
Manhattan, KS, USA

Linn Van Dyne
Eli Broad School of Management
Michigan State University
East Lansing, MI, USA

Chantal van Esch
Weatherhead School of Management
Case Western Reserve University
Cleveland, OH, USA

Mo Wang
Warrington College of Business Administration
University of Florida
Gainesville, FL, USA

Steven W. Whiting
College of Business Administration
University of Central Florida
Orlando, FL, USA

Eric J. Yochum
Sam M. Walton School of Business
University of Arkansas
Fayetteville, AR, USA

Yujie Zhan
School of Business and Economic
Wilfrid Laurier University
Waterloo, Ontario, Canada

TABLE OF CONTENTS

CHAPTER

1 Organizational Citizenship Behavior: Introduction and Overview of the *Handbook*

Philip M. Podsakoff, Scott B. MacKenzie, *and* Nathan P. Podsakoff

Abstract

This chapter provides an introduction and overview to the *Handbook of Organizational Citizenship Behavior*. It begins with a brief discussion of how organizational citizenship behavior (OCB) was traditionally defined and then explores the reasons why this concept has gained so much attention in the past three decades. Following this, we provide an overview of the *Handbook*. Specifically, the *Handbook* is organized into four sections: the history and meaning of organizational citizenship behavior; the consequences of OCB, the antecedents of OCB, and moving forward. Finally, we provide a brief description of the contents of the chapters in each of these sections.

Key Words: organizational citizenship behavior, OCB, antecedents of OCB, consequences of OCB, extra-role behavior

The purpose of this *Handbook* is to provide a broad and interdisciplinary review of state-of-the-art research on organizational citizenship behavior (OCB) and related constructs such as contextual performance, prosocial behavior, voice behavior, and proactive behavior in the workplace. Chapters will address the conceptualization of OCB; the antecedents and consequences of this behavior; and the methodological and measurement issues that are common when studying OCB. In addition, this book will focus on pushing future scholarship in these and related areas by identifying substantive questions, methods, and issues for future research. The overarching goal of this *Handbook* is to offer a single resource that will inform and inspire scholars, students, and practitioners of the origins of this construct, the current state of research on this topic, and potentially exciting avenues for future exploration. As such, it is designed to meet the needs of a broad spectrum of researchers and advanced undergraduate and graduate students in a variety of disciplines, including management, organizational behavior, human resources management, industrial and organizational psychology, as well as those interested in studying citizenship behavior in a variety of organizational contexts, including marketing, nursing, engineering, sports, and education.

Motivation for the *Handbook*

There are several reasons why we believe a book that summarizes the current state of research on OCB is needed. Since the OCB concept was first developed and reported in two articles in the early 1980s (Bateman & Organ, 1983; Smith, Organ, & Near, 1983), the amount of interest paid to OCBs has dramatically increased. As indicated in Figure 1.1, of the over 4,900 articles published in the literature on OCB and related constructs from 1983 to 2017, approximately 83% have been published within the past 10 years and over half (51%) have been published in the just the past 5 years (Web of Knowledge, 2018). In addition, some of the most highly cited articles in the field of management and Industrial/Organizational psychology have focused on OCB. Therefore, the publication of this *Handbook* comes at a time when OCB research is

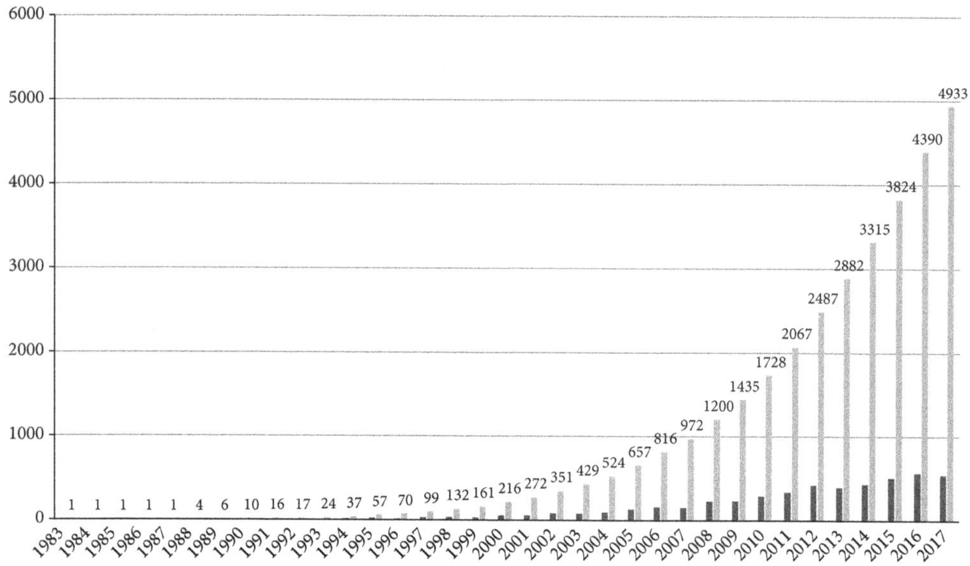

Figure 1.1 Plot of yearly and cumulative publications on organizational citizenship behaviors and related constructs.
Note: The keywords used for this search were as follows: extra role behavior, extra-role behaviors, organizational citizenship behavior, organizational citizenship behaviors, organizational citizenship performance, contextual performance, employee voice behavior, proactive organizational behavior, prosocial organizational behavior, and organizational spontaneity.

accelerating rapidly in popularity and having a major impact on researchers.

Second, along with task performance and counterproductive work behaviors, citizenship behavior is universally recognized as an essential part of the employee performance domain (e.g., Rotundo & Sackett, 2002). For example, numerous researchers have shown (e.g., Allen & Rush, 1998; Johnson, Erez, Kiker, & Motowidlo, 2002; MacKenzie, Podsakoff, & Fetter, 1991, 1993; Podsakoff, MacKenzie, Paine, & Bachrach, 2000) that when evaluating employees, managers give a considerable amount of weight to OCBs. Indeed, a meta-analysis by Podsakoff, Whiting, Podsakoff, and Blume (2009) indicates that OCB has about the same impact as task performance on managerial evaluations of employee performance. Moreover, several studies have shown that OCBs influence managers' reward allocation decisions. In view of this, interest in examining these behaviors is not likely to fade.

Related to the earlier discussion, OCB has become an important measure of a leader's effectiveness. For example, several leadership researchers have argued that to be effective leaders must "lift ordinary people to extraordinary heights" (Boal & Bryson, 1988, p. 11) and cause followers to "do more than they are expected to do" (Yukl, 1989, p. 272) and "perform beyond the level of expectations" (Bass, 1985). As noted by Podsakoff, MacKenzie, Moorman, and Fetter (1990), because OCBs are extra-role behaviors that are typically not part of a follower's role requirements, they are perhaps the premier example of going the extra mile and performing above and beyond the call of duty that is to be found in the literature (Bolino & Turnley, 2003; Organ, 1988; Organ, Podsakoff, & MacKenzie, 2006).

Fourth, OCB are now recognized as a major determinant of group/unit/organizational effectiveness and success. Indeed, Podsakoff, Podsakoff, MacKenzie, Maynes, and Spoelma's (2014) recent review of the literature indicates that OCB has been found to be related to the quantity and quality of unit performance, goal achievement, speed of task performance, efficiency, product quality, customer satisfaction, service quality, market performance, sales revenue, operating costs, and profitability. In view of the many beneficial effects of OCB on organizational success, it appears that the substantial weight that managers give to OCB when evaluating employee performance is not misplaced.

Fifth, the widespread interest in OCBs is no longer confined to research in the area of organizational behavior but has expanded into many other disciplines. Indeed, a testament to the growing interest in OCB is that, in addition to articles in the business disciplines (management, industrial-labor relations, economics, marketing, operations research, hospitality management, etc.), research on OCB has also been published in the fields of ethics, ergonomics, information sciences, computer science, public administration, social work, criminology, social psychology, sociology, political science, anthropology, communications, sports science, environmental studies, engineering, health care services, psychiatry, and nursing (Web of Knowledge, 2018).

Finally, it is also important to note that interest in OCBs is not an exclusively American phenomenon but extends to other countries as well (cf. Farh, Earley, & Lin, 1997; Farh, Zhong, & Organ, 2004; Gelfand, Erez, & Aycan, 2007). Indeed, research indicates that OCBs also have important effects at both the individual and organizational level in many other cultures, including China, Taiwan, Korea, Japan, Singapore, Australia, India, Turkey, Israel, Iran, Nigeria, Brazil, Russia, and the European Union. For example, in a major study involving 741 managers and 2,111 subordinates in 18 countries representing all major cultural regions of the world, Reiche et al. (2014) found that OCB indirectly influenced the trustworthy behavior of managers and that this individual-level effect was moderated by the collectivism of the culture. Similarly, Yen and Niehoff (2004) report significant relationships between OCB and several organizational-level measures of effectiveness, including labor costs, average profit, and protecting company resources in a sample of Taiwanese banks.

Overview of the *Handbook*

Part One—The History and Meaning of Organizational Citizenship Behavior

The chapters in this section of the *Handbook* provide a description of historical and contemporary research related to the topic of OCB. In addition, this section provides in-depth discussions of the conceptualization of the various dimensions of OCB, and of the similarities and differences between OCB and other related constructs. This section begins with a chapter on the historical development of the concept of OCB written by Dennis Organ, who is widely considered to be the father of OCB. Following this chapter, there are several chapters which distinguish OCB from related constructs. Chapter 3 discusses how OCB compares to other aspects of work performance and fits within broader models of individual work performance. Chapter 4 compares and contrasts OCB with job engagement and concludes that there are clear conceptual differences between the two constructs and that each of them plays an important role in explaining how psychological states and contextual factors combine to influence job performance. Chapter 5 draws on evolutionary psychology to understand the different biological roots of OCB helping and proactive behavior and argues that this is the key to distinguishing these behaviors. Chapter 6 examines whether OCB and counterproductive work behavior are opposite ends of a single continuum or different constructs. Using evidence from a variety of different sources, the authors conclude that these two constructs are relatively independent from each other, and this suggests many different avenues for future research. The final chapter in this section (Chapter 7) explores the factors that influence whether employees perceive OCB as an integral part of their role requirements or as being discretionary in nature.

Part Two—Consequences of Organizational Citizenship Behavior

Undoubtedly one of the major reasons for the interest in OCB is the impact it has been found to have on individual- and organizational-level outcomes. The chapters in this section of the *Handbook* summarize research on the consequences of OCB. Chapter 8 provides a review of the empirical research on the effects of OCB on organizational-level and individual-level outcomes, and also discusses the mediators and moderators of these relationships. Chapter 9 examines how OCB influences career outcomes (e.g., salary, financial rewards, promotions, advancement speed, etc.) and provides an agenda for future research in this area. Chapter 10 explores the dark side of OCB by examining how helping behavior can sometimes harm the intended beneficiaries of these behaviors. Chapter 11 continues this discussion by highlighting additional unintended negative consequences of OCB experienced by those who exhibit them and/or by the organization/work group itself.

Part Three—Antecedents of Organizational Citizenship Behavior

Given the many beneficial effects of OCBs, it is not surprising that a major portion of the research has focused on understanding the antecedents of these behaviors. Some of the chapters in this section highlight the many dispositional, motivational, and attitudinal causes of OCB that have been identified in the literature. For example, Chapter 12 provides an integrative review of the relationship between the Big Five personality traits and OCB. Chapter 13 examines the extent to which gender is or is not related to OCB. The primary motives for exhibiting OCB that have been identified in the literature (prosocial values, organizational concern, and impression management) are examined in Chapter 14. Chapter 15 focuses on organizational justice, which has been found to be one of the most important antecedents of OCB. And finally, the complex interplay between trust and OCB is examined in Chapter 16.

The remaining chapters in this section highlight the leadership, group, and organizational factors that influence OCB. Research on the relationship between leadership and OCB is examined in Chapter 17. Chapter 18 recognizes that organizational actors do not exist in isolation and are embedded in networks of social relationships that influence the performance of OCB and proposes a model of how OCBs diffuse throughout these social networks. Chapter 19 reviews the theoretical foundations of several types of employee-organizational relationships (EOR) and examines the empirical evidence linking EORs to employees' OCB. Chapter 20 explores the question of whether people who experience a better fit in their environment exhibit more OCB and finds that the answer depends on both the nature of the types of fit and the types of OCB in question. Chapter 21 discusses the direction of causality between job embeddedness and OCB and suggests that the different dimensions and foci of job embeddedness may activate different motives for exhibiting citizenship behavior which manifest themselves in distinct forms of OCB. The final chapter in this section (Chapter 22) examines citizenship behavior from a cross-cultural perspective and provides a framework to aid in the understanding of how cultural frames influence the engagement and display of OCB.

Part Four—Moving Forward

In the final section of the *Handbook*, the authors provide their insights into several important methodological and conceptual issues related to the study of OCB and highlight important avenues for future research. Chapter 23 reviews the measurement and methodological practices commonly used in the OCB domain and provides concrete recommendations for improving future research. Chapter 24 argues that although the vast majority of OCB research uses a between-subjects design, much can be gained in future research by using a within-subjects level of analysis. Chapter 25 focuses on the impact of unit-level antecedents of individual-level OCBs and the factors that mediate and moderate these effects. The next two chapters consider the future of two of the most common forms of OCB. Chapter 26 reviews prior conceptualizations of helping behavior and related behaviors and proposes an integrative framework of helping processes organized around the key decisions of whether to seek help, help when asked, offer help, and accept help when offered. Recognizing that most scholars have focused on the barriers that prevent employees from voicing their ideas, Chapter 27 explores various strategies to encourage employees to speak up and the conditions that determine which of these strategies may be particularly relevant and effective in a given situation. Chapter 28 highlights the distinctive features of service organizations, discusses how these characteristics shape the nature of OCB in this unique context, and proposes an integrated typology for better understanding OCB in service organizations. Chapter 29 continues the focus on service organizations by exploring how the prosocial implicit trait policies of employees relate to basic personality traits and their citizenship behavior in these contexts. Chapter 30 argues that the concept of citizenship behavior is fundamental to three major retirement activities (postretirement employment, family support, and community support), identifies the antecedents and consequences of OCB in these contexts, and proposes important avenues for future research in this domain. Finally, Chapter 31 provides a summary of many of the important issues raised in this *Handbook* and recommends areas for future research.

References

Allen, T. D., & Rush, M. C. (1998). The effects of organizational citizenship behavior on performance judgments: A field study and a laboratory experiment. *Journal of Applied Psychology, 83*, 247–260.

Bass, B. M. (1985). *Leadership and performance beyond expectation*. New York, NY: Free Press.

Bateman, T. S., & Organ, D. W. (1983). Job satisfaction and the good soldier: The relationship between affect and employee "citizenship." *Academy of Management Journal, 26*, 587–595.

Boal, K. B., & Bryson, J. M. (1988). Charismatic leadership: A phenomenological and structural approach. In J. G. Hunt, B. R. Baliga, H. P. Dachler, & C. A. Schriesheim (Eds.), *Emerging leadership vistas* (pp. 5–28). Lexington, MA: Lexington Books.

Bolino, M. C., & Turnley, W. H. (2003). Going the extra mile: Cultivating and managing employee citizenship behavior. *Academy of Management Executive, 17*, 60–71.

Farh, J. L., Earley, P. C., & Lin, S. C. (1997). Impetus for action: A cultural analysis of justice and organizational

citizenship behavior in Chinese society. *Administrative Science Quarterly, 42*, 421–444.
Farh, J. L., Zhong, C. B., & Organ, D. W. (2004). Organizational citizenship behavior in the People's Republic of China. *Organization Science, 15*, 241–253.
Gelfand, M., Erez, M., & Aycan, Z. (2007). Cross-cultural organizational behavior. *Annual Review of Psychology, 58*, 479–514.
Johnson, D. E., Erez, A., Kiker, D. S., & Motowidlo, S. J. (2002). Liking and attributions of motives as mediators of the relationships between individuals' reputations, helpful behaviors, and raters' reward decisions. *Journal of Applied Psychology, 87*, 808–815.
MacKenzie, S. B., Podsakoff, P. M., & Fetter, R. (1991). Organizational citizenship behavior and objective productivity as determinants of managerial evaluations of salespersons' performance. *Organizational Behavior and Human Decision Processes, 50*, 1–28.
MacKenzie, S. B., Podsakoff, P. M. & Fetter, R. (1993). The impact of organizational citizenship behavior on evaluations of salesperson performance. *Journal of Marketing, 57*, 70–80.
Organ, D. W. (1988). Organizational citizenship behavior: *The good soldier syndrome.* Lexington, MA: Lexington Books.
Organ, D. W., Podsakoff, P. M., & MacKenzie, S. B. (2006). *Organizational citizenship behavior: Its nature, antecedents and consequences.* Thousand Oaks, CA: Sage.
Podsakoff, P. M., MacKenzie, S. B., Moorman, R. H., & Fetter, R. (1990). Transformational leader behaviors and their effects on followers' trust in leader, satisfaction, and organizational citizenship behaviors. *Leadership Quarterly, 1*, 107–142.
Podsakoff, P. M., MacKenzie, S. B., Paine, J. B., & Bachrach, D. G. (2000). Organizational citizenship behaviors: A critical review of the theoretical and empirical literature and suggestions for future research. *Journal of Management, 26*, 513–563.
Podsakoff, P. M., Podsakoff, N. P., MacKenzie, S. B., Maynes, T. D. & Spoelma, T. M. (2014). Consequences of unit-level organizational citizenship behaviors: A review and recommendations for future research. *Journal of Organizational Behavior, 35*, S87–S119.
Podsakoff, P. M., Whiting, S. W., Podsakoff, N. P., & Blume, B. D. (2009) Individual- and organizational-level consequences of organizational citizenship behaviors: A meta-analysis. *Journal of Applied Psychology, 94*, 122–141.
Reiche, B. S., Cardona, P., Lee, Y.-T., Canela, M. Á., Akinnukawe, E., Briscoe, J. P., ... Wilkinson, H. (2014). Why do managers engage in trustworthy behavior? A multilevel cross-cultural study in 18 countries. *Personnel Psychology, 67*, 61–98.
Rotundo, M., & Sackett, P. R. (2002). The relative importance of task, citizenship, and counterproductive performance to global ratings of job performance: A policy-capturing approach. *Journal of Applied Psychology, 87*, 66–80.
Smith, C. A., Organ, D. W., & Near, J. P. (1983). Organizational citizenship behavior: Its nature and antecedents. *Journal of Applied Psychology, 68*, 655–663.
Web of Knowledge. (2016). Keyword search conducted in the *Institute of Scientific Information's Web of Knowledge* on July 18, 2016.
Yen, H. R., & Niehoff, B. P. (2004). Organizational citizenship behaviors and organizational effectiveness: Examining relationships in Taiwanese banks. *Journal of Applied Social Psychology, 34*, 1617–1637.
Yukl, G. A. (1989). Managerial leadership: A review of theory and research. *Yearly Review of Management, 15*, 251–289.

CHAPTER

2 The Roots of Organizational Citizenship Behavior

Dennis W. Organ

Abstract

This chapter traces the development of organizational citizenship behavior (OCB) back to related constructs discussed by scholars, such as Weber, Barnard, Roethlisberger and Dickson, and Katz and Kahn, in management and organization theory from the early 20th century onward. We look at the pros and cons of the proposition that job satisfaction is a causal factor with respect to members' contributions to organizational performance, what forms these contributions take, the rival hypotheses that could be consistent with the empirical data, the extent to which OCB has generalizability and meaning across cultures, and the issue of whether OCB at some levels and forms might have undesired effects on organizations and their members. We also take note of a closely related construct, "contextual performance," which has emphasized the effects of personality on certain discretionary individual contributions to organizational effectiveness.

Key Words: job satisfaction, performance, organizational citizenship behavior, OCB, contextual performance

The term "organizational citizenship behavior" (OCB) is, of course, of quite recent vintage, dating from the late 1980s. However, one suspects that related ideas have been given expression down through the ages. "Beyond the call of duty" harks back at least to the 18th century, probably originating in military contexts and thereafter eventually finding its way into the civilian sector. Even farther back, by a couple of millennia or more, the Greeks had much to say about the kinds of behavior expected of citizens of the city-state. Graham (1986) has provided an instructive exposition of the relevance of those ideas to what we have come to call OCB.

However, for most of recorded history, the work contributions of the rank and file were evoked by specific orders and commands—lift that barge, tote that bale—with well-understood consequences if those orders were ignored. It seems unlikely that many foot soldiers, slaves, serfs, or minions of kings thought about what they might contribute by "going the extra mile." What they were most concerned about was avoiding the consequences of not doing what they were told to do. Otherwise, people responded to the strains of necessity and survival.

OCB is about the types of discretionary behavior and contributions that are not explicitly associated with the specific job requirements. This, of course, logically assumes that such specific requirements exist, are known, and probably documented. That leads us to what we often refer to as "bureaucracies" or "formal organizations." Such organizations originally developed in governments at various levels—nation, state, colony, city—and then private commercial organizations, particularly those of more than middling size, took on many of the features of the bureaucratic form. With this development came such now-familiar practices as job descriptions, specifications of employee rights and responsibilities, contracts, performance appraisals, and incentive plans. Principles judged useful, if not necessary, were unity of command (everyone has a boss but no more than one) and span of control (there is an upper limit to the number of people one boss can manage, with such limits partly determined by the dominant technology, but in any event the limit was generally assumed to be on the low side).

German sociologist Max Weber (1947) provided the earliest fully articulated model of the bureaucratic organization, noting its defining characteristics, its strengths, and potential weaknesses. One of the salient characteristics he ascribed to it was its impersonality. But the other side of the coin, regarded by Weber as a weakness, was the absence of recognition of the informal organization. One might infer from this that a pure bureaucracy does not deem as relevant any cooperative relationships among members unless they were already foreseen and specified as necessary parts of their formal roles.

More immediately relevant to our purposes here is the work of Chester Barnard, especially in his *Functions of the Executive* (1938). Barnard had a long and successful career as an administrator with the Bell System, as well as several large public and philanthropic organizations. In his correspondence with Fritz Roethlisberger at Harvard, he frequently exchanged observations and opinions about the nature of large organizations. Barnard characterized an organization as a "cooperative system." Such a system has a formal structure, to be sure, but inevitably the informal organization arises as well, and often with such informal organization, modes of cooperation that go beyond those that the formal structure dictates.

Barnard postulated that a formal organization must achieve both "effectiveness" and "efficiency." "Effectiveness" refers to the successful operation of the major functions of the formal organization as it seeks to attain its goals—whether such goals are financial and economic, as in business firms; providing public services, as in governmental organizations; or mitigating a pressing social problem, as many nongovernmental, charitable organizations. "Efficiency," on the other hand, is the curious name Barnard gave to the degree of satisfaction that organization members gain as recompense for contributing to the attainment of organizational effectiveness. Such recompense goes beyond purely economic largesse. Barnard argued that effectiveness and efficiency go hand in hand—that the rank and file will fully cooperate in the system only to the extent that their own goals and motives are served.

Barnard argued that the "willingness" of members to contribute efforts to the cooperative system was "indispensable." He described this notion of willingness as something different from "effectiveness" or "ability," and regarded it as something like a disposition to go beyond the formal duties or role requirements of the individual member.

Daniel Katz and Robert Kahn (1966) extended and more fully articulated the concept of organization as an open system. In particular, they specified the different classes of behaviors that such a system requires in order to attain effectiveness. The system must attract and hold people in the system; ensure that members reliably perform the tasks formally associated with the positions they hold; and encourage spontaneous behaviors beyond formal role prescriptions when such behaviors facilitate, directly or indirectly, the attainment of effectiveness in pursuit of formal goals. Katz and Kahn noted that the three classes of behavior are mainly driven by different motivational methods. Attracting and holding members are functions of "system rewards" that accrue to members as a function of membership in the system; "instrumental" or incentive rewards motivate task performance and productivity beyond the satisfactory level, whereas "spontaneous" cooperation (performing beyond formal role requirements) is motivated by a sense that one has full "citizenship" in the system.

When alternatives or modifications to the fully developed bureaucratic form of organization were proposed, they generally addressed those cases in which bureaucracy had become dysfunctional in achieving what Barnard had called "effectiveness," that is, goal attainment in terms of return on investment or, in the case of nonprofits, achieving the results in those conditions and aims that provided their reason for existence. One such modification was "management by objectives, or MBO" (e.g., Odiorne, 1965). The idea was that top management should set specific, challenging goals for the organization as a whole and then proceed to break these down into subgoals for each functional area or department, and from there to the individual level. The emphasis was on specific operational goals to be achieved by designated dates. The assumption was that any criterion not susceptible to reasonably precise measures should not factor into the reward system. Informal modes of cooperation would have little prospect for recompense. This is not to suggest that some organizations did not improve their functioning for some period of time, but the potential was there for long-term problems to develop if the dominant focus became solely on those contributions amenable to precise measures and neglected those forms of contributions not on the scorecard. The inherent difficulty of specifying and quantifying the "spontaneous cooperation" posed by Katz and Kahn, as we shall see, presents serious challenges to researchers and managers who would endeavor to elicit it as a form of contribution by individual members.

The Satisfaction-Performance Riddle

Roethlisberger and Dickson's (1939) account of the famed Hawthorn studies documented the extensive forms and effects of the "informal organization," which pervaded the formal system and gave rise to informal status hierarchies and various forms of "sentiment" in the workplace—often, but certainly not invariably, providing value-added contributions to efficiency and effectiveness (to use Barnard's terminology). Because of the attention Roethlisberger and Dickson gave to sentiments—which we would probably translate in today's terms as attitudes or job satisfaction—and because their work is believed to have ushered in management's focus on "human relations," the work has come to be associated with the idea that "satisfaction causes productivity." But one looks in vain for such a statement in their volume.

Nonetheless, the satisfaction-leads-to-productivity hypothesis gained purchase among some later students and practitioners of management, particularly those with a "human relations" bias. However, when formal studies finally began to put this idea to empirical test, results showed little statistical relationship between the two variables (e.g., Viteles, 1953; Brayfield & Crockett, 1955).

The generally accepted view among academic and professional psychologists and management scholars became one of turning the causal arrow around. This was the approach of Lawler and Porter (1967), who thought it more plausible that job satisfaction was the result of the rewards that employees derived from the organization—whether they be extrinsic rewards such as pay and benefits derived from membership in the system, the intrinsic rewards flowing from effort and accomplishment of the work, or the social rewards provided by the informal organization. As Porter and Lawler noted, quite often these various forms of reward would not necessarily bear a close correspondence with the work productivity of individuals. For example, pay might be more closely related to formal status, years of tenure, or labor market imperatives than determined by level of individual productivity. Therefore, if rewards create satisfaction, but rewards are only loosely connected to individual productivity, then we should not expect satisfaction and productivity to bear much in the way of a statistical association.

Yet opinion polls of practicing managers, as well as union leaders, continued to express agreement with the notion that "a satisfied worker is a productive worker." Perhaps those groups endorse that proposition as a matter of faith rather than observation, or they hold to it because it provides a "rational" justification for them to do things that their people seem to appreciate.

But another explanation could be that many managers include more in their concept of "productivity" or "performance" than measurable output. Maybe they add to it what Katz and Kahn defined as "spontaneous" contributions, especially those that go beyond the narrow definition of the task or job description, more than just the productivity that provides the direct connection to bonus pay for the individual.

This was the musing that prompted Organ (1977) to suggest that what managers really mean when they say "a happy worker is a productive worker" is not about measurable physical or monetary results, but rather the more qualitative gestures that help sustain the "cooperative" system. Later, someone else—and I'm honestly not sure who it was—offered the term "organizational citizenship behavior" (OCB) to refer to these more qualitative contributions to the cooperative system.

At the most general, all-encompassing level, OCB can be defined as the set of behaviors that sustain or enhance the cooperative system of the organization but are not systematically or generally recorded in the formal system of the organization or tied in any consistent way to specific rewards. Immediately, however, we run into some challenges for both practice and research.

First, we have to define more precisely what classes of behavior qualify as OCB. This, in itself, is a double-barreled challenge. We have to come up with a parsimonious taxonomy of behaviors that—in one fashion or another—collectively and logically bear some relationship to organizational effectiveness. Such behaviors must also be under the control of the individual, such that he or she has the discretion of opting not to perform the behavior in question, that is, would not be penalized by the formal system for its omission.

Second, much of what we are calling OCB would not generally be addressed in the formal archives of the organization. Measures of task performance pertaining to the formal job description are sometimes available in the information system of the firm, but spontaneous forms of either individual or group OCB are seldom recorded, other than perhaps in the memories of coworkers, supervisors, or customers; researchers would need to tap those memories with their own devices.

Construction of a measure of OCB must be preceded by some explicit—and ideally not too numerous—contributions, however humble, that follow logically from the broad conception of what we mean by "citizenship" behaviors. First, we require that the behaviors in question must be within the discretion of the individual member. We take this requirement to imply that the person can choose either to carry out that behavior or elect not to do so, and in particular that choosing not to do so would not generally place the individual in harm's way, that is, rebuke from a supervisor, loss of some privilege, a lower rating of core job performance, or assignment to some kind of probationary status. Second, the individual in question must not have reason to think that carrying out the behavior would—even if observed—have a direct and timely connection to benefits mediated by the formal organization; that is, the individual would not expect the behavior in and of itself to have an effect on formal performance appraisals or other benefits, such as wages or salary or bonus pay, that might be contingent on formal appraisals.

We do not require that the behavior in question never meet with some positive consequences. Indeed, we can well imagine that individuals who habitually perform such positive behaviors might generate a reputation for such behaviors and elicit respect and expressions of approval from coworkers, supervisors, or customers, and thereby ultimately be recognized as worthy of enhanced status and/or compensation. The point is that such positive outcomes are not foreseen by the individual in any short-term or contractual sense.

Finally, we impose the requirement that the behavior, if it is to be regarded as OCB, must be susceptible to the view that, if performed by a sufficient number of members, such behavior would render the larger organization capable of a higher level of performance and effectiveness in achieving its goals—or, at the very least, significantly more capable of that than would be the case if such positive behaviors were rarely exhibited.

Some naysayers might object that formal job descriptions and performance appraisals often include items that sound much like our description of OCB. For example, some job descriptions might include items pertaining to collegiality, for example, "interact cooperatively with coworkers," and an appraisal form might include an item such as "respected by colleagues" or "sets a good example for others." However, such expectations connote behavior that resists quantification and precise measurement. Rating people on such criteria is more likely to depend on reputational effects, which in turn arise over a considerable period of time, during which impressions are formed—by coworkers, clients, and managers—and during such time do not meet with any immediate or guaranteed recompense.

Ultimately, we must concede that there is often a fine line between what is construed as OCB and what would be described as "doing one's job." Rather, we do well to think in terms of a continuum, anchored on one end by "pure productivity" that can be measured objectively and rewarded on a formulaic basis, and an opposite pole representing "pure OCB" that defies quantification or a contractual expression. Between those poles are contributions that represent more or less semblance to "individual productivity" or "going beyond what is required."

One could argue that individuals vary in the degree of breadth in their subjective view of what their job or role includes; that is, what we call "citizenship behavior" might include forms of contribution that individuals see part and parcel of what they see as their job description (Morrison, 1994). Still, if individuals vary in the extent to which they include OCB in their personal definition of the job and thus proceed to practice it in the process of discharging what they view as incumbent upon them, then we would still be interested in how this enlarged, subjectively viewed sense of job comes about and what contributions derive from it.

We might do well by not trying, at the present stage of theory development, to seek an ironclad precise definition of the OCB concept. Indeed, Kaplan (1964), an historian and philosopher of science, suggested that we should avoid "premature" closure in how precisely we define constructs in the behavioral sciences, reminding us that in the physical sciences, our present conceptions of theoretical constructs often evolved as the stream of empirical evidence continued and led to reinterpretation of how we should think about those constructs. We suspect that, even more so in the social and behavioral sciences, we should give our constructs some room to breathe.

Measures of Organizational Citizenship Behavior

To develop a measure of OCB for empirical research, what we require is a manageable collection of varied exemplars that are consistent with how we have defined OCB. The first two versions of OCB measures, and the first two studies to examine predictors of OCB, appeared in Bateman and Organ (1983) and Smith, Organ, and Near (1983). Analysis of the scales used in those studies yielded two factors. One of these was referred to as "altruism," because the statements that loaded on this factor pertained to help provided to a colleague or coworker, whether that help was unsolicited or responded to a request for help. The help could take the form of aiding the colleague with a task by some means, such as coaching, working together to handle a big job or catch up with the flow of work, and offering encouragement and reassurance. More recently, this factor has been labeled "OCB-I (Williams & Anderson, 1991)," because the items have to do with OCB directed to individuals. We would add to that interpretation that much of what falls under the rubric of OCB-I represents informal types of OCB, because they are often spontaneous and seldom recorded, and thus difficult to use as a criterion for precise evaluation of an individual's contributions.

A different factor in the analysis, which was initially referred to as "conscientiousness," seemed to have in common a more organizationally relevant focus rather than targeting a particular individual. Some examples of items loading on this dimension or factor were exemplary records of attendance and punctuality, maintaining a clean and orderly environment, and involvement—when appropriate—in off-hours organizational programs and projects that sustain and enhance the organization's reputation in the community. Some of the items, such as attendance and punctuality, are more likely to be captured in the formal information system of the firm; others, if not recorded, are more apt to catch the attention of the supervisor and informal expressions of gratitude.

Another dimension that could be discerned in factor analyses of the early studies seemed to have in common several items describing what members *don't* exhibit. For example: Don't rail against real or imagined slights; don't fuss about temporary loss of privileges and conveniences; don't overload the system with grievances, formal or otherwise; don't foul the atmosphere with negative comments about coworkers. The notion of "sportsmanship"—the idea of "rolling with the punches," accepting the fact that "in each life some rain must fall," "accentuating the positive and eliminating the negative"—seemed to qualify as a form of OCB.

"Courtesy" came out of the analysis as a factor that had to do more with the actions that organization members take to prevent problems. This factor includes such gestures as giving colleagues advance notice about some development that they might need to prepare for, using common resources in a fashion that leaves them problem-free for those who use them later—for example, reloading paper into the copier.

The fifth and final dimension to be added to most of the measures intended to capture OCB was "voice." This factor did not emerge from some of the early studies because there it was not proffered as a separate form of OCB distinguishable from the others and thus did not include items that might capture it. This seems surprising, given that Katz and Khan (1966, 1978) had explicitly recognized it as a form of "spontaneous cooperation." By means of voice, organizations gather feedback about their effectiveness with respect to their environments of clients and competitors, the community, and of course problems that members feel with respect to inequities and dysfunctional processes and procedures. No doubt some members might exercise "voice" for selfish reasons, but one suspects that competent managers can usually know when to discount the source and when to take seriously the potential value of following up on the intuitively credible and important instances in which members "speak up."

Predictors of Organizational Citizenship Behavior

Now that we have defined OCB and proceeded therewith to develop a measure of it, what would we do with it? If it can be measured, and if we believe that it is a positive factor for organizational effectiveness, should we not proceed to muse over some of the most intuitively plausible forces acting upon OCB?

Recall that Barnard (1938) distinguished "effectiveness" from "efficiency." The distinction corresponds to the organization's ability to achieve its collective goals, whereas "efficiency" pertains to the degree to which members satisfy their own needs and positive outcomes in exchange for contributing to the achievement of the collective's goals.

Katz and Kahn (1966, 1978) emphasized the value of spontaneous, nonspecified, extra-role behaviors by members that serve the larger interests of the organization. They reasoned that the propensity to engage in such behaviors was determined by their sense of "citizenship" in the larger collective. While they did not elaborate very strenuously or explicitly upon how this sense of citizenship develops, the overall tone of their discussion suggests that it involves "fair dealing," respect from the formal leadership, and indications by the leaders of concern for their welfare. If we blend Katz and Kahn's thinking with that of Barnard, we come up with what we usually think of as "job satisfaction"—that is, a propensity to describe in positive tones how the organization treats them.

Thus, the early empirical work on OCB tested the proposition that measures of job satisfaction among the rank and file would correlate positively with measures of OCB, and do so to a greater extent than measures of productivity or narrowly defined in-role performance.

Rather than examine all relevant studies, we take note of an early meta-analysis by Organ and Ryan (1995) of 28 studies, the results of which were reported between 1983 and 1995. The raw weighted average correlation between job satisfaction and the "altruism" (helping) dimension of OCB was .24. Correcting for reliability of the measures, the estimated population correlation coefficient was .28; the 95% confidence interval of this estimate was .26 to .31. For the "conscientiousness" factor, the estimated population coefficient was .28. By comparison, previous meta-analyses of the relationship between satisfaction and productivity or task performance yielded a 95% confidence interval of .13 to .17.

We should note that other studies during and after the 1995 meta-analysis looked at affectively toned measures—for example, of perceived organizational supportiveness, leader supportiveness, affective commitment, perceived fairness—that probably capture much of the same variance as job satisfaction. Podsakoff, MacKenzie, Paine, and Bachrach (2000) conducted a meta-analysis of the results of OCB studies that included these other affectively loaded measures, and they found comparable estimate population coefficients in the range of .24 to .28 for each of the OCB dimensions, except Civic Virtue (defined largely by the "voice" dimension of OCB), where the estimated coefficient was .09–.15. If we assume, not unreasonably, that some nontrivial proportion of voice functions to articulate grievances and criticisms, then we would not expect this dimension of OCB to correlate as strongly as the others with job satisfaction.

We conclude, then, that something like a generalized propensity of the workforce to describe their environment in positive terms, and to describe themselves as generally pleased with that environment, are more apt to go beyond the formal task requirements of their job in what they contribute to the "cooperative system." What is not so apparent from what we have reviewed thus far is just what is it that is "in" satisfaction that accounts for this relationship.

Affect Versus Cognition

Measures of job satisfaction are sometimes referred to as measures of job attitudes. The instruments used to measure job satisfaction are often called "attitude surveys." Furthermore, social psychologists have for many years described attitudes as having cognitive, affective, and behavioral components. In other words, attitudes pertain to mixtures of what we know or believe, how we feel about the referents of such knowledge or beliefs, and the tendency to respond to the objects of such knowledge or beliefs in a positive or negative manner.

If we apply this conceptual schema of job attitudes to the work environment, it seems reasonable to think of the cognitive dimension as pertaining to what one has come to know or believe about that environment—the coworkers, management, the policies, the pay system, its reputation in the community. Especially important among these referents of knowledge and beliefs is, we believe, the "fairness" of the organization, especially the beliefs about the fairness of pay and benefits, supervisory treatment, and rules that apply to the workplace. The greater the extent to which these attributes of the organization are judged to be fair, the more likely that individuals will feel and express some degree of positive affect about the organization, and the more likely they will express some of this affect in fashions that are positive or beneficial behaviors with respect to the organization and its management. Conversely, cognitions or beliefs about the organization that are predominantly negative will tend to inhibit spontaneous, nontask gestures that benefit the collective enterprise.

We must, however, take note of the recognition among social psychologists that attitudes manifest a "strain toward consistency." There is a tendency among us all not only toward "rationality"—meaning that we let our knowledge (cognitions) guide our behavior and emotions—but also toward "rationalizing." If we act in ways that are negative toward some entity, we will sometimes try to justify that negativity by reference to negative beliefs about that entity, and with those beliefs, negative feelings. With respect to OCB, to put it bluntly, those who, for whatever reason, do as little as possible could try to justify that posture. That could take the form of a bias toward seeing the organization as not deserving spontaneous cooperation with the collective order, because it has not treated them equitably.

Having noted that positive affect and cognition are not independent of each other, neither are they one and the same (Zajonc, 1980), and we have some basis for thinking that measures of job satisfaction capture more of the cognitive dimension (beliefs) than they reflect affect (negative versus positive feelings) (Andrews & Withey, 1976; Campbell, 1976).

Campbell (1976), drawing from a series of surveys using measures of subjective well-being, concluded that measures of satisfaction—whether with life or the job—and measures of happiness do not behave the same way when looking at other variables they are associated with. Some of the items on their measures asked respondents to report their level of happiness; other items asked about satisfaction. The scores from these item groups indeed correlated in the range of .50–.60. But there are some interesting twists. For example, older groups tend to express greater satisfaction than their younger counterparts, but the younger respondents express the greater happiness. Widowed men and women score above the mean on life satisfaction and below the mean on happiness. Moreover, national surveys of job satisfaction generally find that job satisfaction is positively correlated with age.

Finally, many standardized job satisfaction measures require the respondent to "do some cognitive work." That is, the format of these measures requires the subject to focus on specific aspects of work; others require the subject to make a comparison of how these specific aspects at the present job compare to what he or she had expected, or what was experienced at one or more other organizations, or what he or she had heard about other places of work.

In light of these findings and considerations, we favor a stance at this point to think of perceived fairness—that is, the more cognitive dimension of job attitudes—as the factor that more likely predicts OCB at either the individual or group level. When we assert this, we do not mean to suggest that the individual or group must believe that the workplace is always fair to everyone; we doubt that such a condition is possible in a collective group in which external constraints and demands would inevitably make it impossible to meet those demands without some regrettable fallout on some individuals or groups. As we often hear, "life is unfair." Rather, we think what matters is that the individuals involved believe that the larger collective is something like a "microcosm of the just world," in which the longer term dynamic is toward fairness. That is, unfair outcomes will be noted and, in the fullness of time, corrected by those with the means and authority to do so.

Organizational Citizenship Behavior and Organizational Effectiveness

As noted earlier, the interest in OCB from the start was the idea that it was more likely than individual productivity to be a function of job satisfaction. But we also ventured the hypothesis that OCB on the part of the workforce as a whole would have positive effects on the organization's performance. At the outset, this hypothesis was tentatively put forth as plausible belief. However, in order to justify further inquiry into nature and antecedents of OCB, one could not overlook the value of empirical tests of the relationship between collective OCB and overall organizational performance.

Putting this issue to empirical test is no trivial enterprise. What we would be doing is setting the unit of measurement at the level of the organization. To have even modest statistical power, we would require probably 25 or more organizations. Furthermore, the organizations within that group must share at least one objective criterion of effectiveness, preferably more. Finally, there must be comparability among the organizations selected in terms of the relevant time intervals.

One approach to dealing with this problem takes the form of studying small but semiautonomous units of chain-type organizations, as are found in quite a few retail firms and restaurants. Walz and Niehoff (2000) studied a chain of 30 limited-menu restaurants. A particular advantage of such a research plan is that one could presume that some factors—such as average pay levels, demographics of the workforce, hours and conditions of work—could be regarded as a constant factor across the organizations, or at worst, generate some random variation unrelated to the variables of interest. They found significant positive relationships between the OCB dimension of helping behavior and such dependent variables as operating efficiency, quantitative feedback from customers—registering their satisfaction with service, food, and ambience—and an index of quality of performance.

Koys (2001) also followed the strategy of comparing independent subsets of a larger organization, but with a longitudinal design, in order to determine if earlier OCB predicted later effectiveness better than opposite direction of causality. The results of his analyses were consistent with the conclusion that OCB was the driver of unit-level effectiveness.

Subsequently, Podsakoff, Whiting, Podsakoff, and Blume (2009) conducted a meta-analysis of 38 studies that investigated OCB and organization-level outcomes, with varied criteria such as productivity, reduced costs, and customer satisfaction. The estimated population correlations between unit-level OCB and "positive" criteria ranged from .15 (for unit profitability) to .47 for subjective or reputational measures of effectiveness. For "negative" criteria (staff turnover and operating costs), the correlations were negative; that is, higher unit-level OCB was associated with lower turnover and costs. The authors also noted that time-lagged correlations between earlier OCB and later outcomes were generally stronger than those associated with same-time measures.

Subsequent chapters in this volume will report the results of more recent studies and meta-analyses of the connections between OCB and various criteria of organizational effectiveness. As you will see from these accounts, there is reason to think that the relationship between OCB and some such criteria is not so direct and straightforward as initially assumed. The relationship in some instances seems to hinge on the moderating effect of other factors.

Organizational Citizenship Behavior and Organizational Efficiency

The presumption at the outset of work on OCB was that the sorts of behaviors defined by the concept operationalizing it would have something to do with how well organizations function. The actual items that comprise measures of OCB sound much like what we would assume to be the profile of a healthy, efficient enterprise. Indeed, even to suggest that such behaviors make organizations function better could be considered a truism.

However, the tautology resemblance is less troubling if we at least surmise *why or how* such behaviors benefit the larger collective. Organ, Podsakoff, and MacKenzie (2006) have articulated some reasoning along such lines. First, some forms of OCB represent *added resources.* For example, someone who takes the time to help a new hire learn some operations is providing additional inputs to those not otherwise forthcoming in the mix of organizational resources. Second, OCB serves to economize on the use of resources already at the organization's disposal. This might be illustrated by the staff member who steps into the breach to resolve conflict or prevent conflict from taking its toll on the stamina of colleagues or draining the time and energy of managers who have to become referees. Similarly, timely suggestions in the appropriate tone and forum often provide the means of reducing waste of materials, money, and time. Furthermore, Williamson (1975) argues that the very reason for the existence of organizations is that they minimize the extent and cost of transactions needed to negotiate or contract for the inputs they require. Absent OCB, much effort would be diverted into ascertaining what benefits would derive from each and every efficacious input. An organization that inspires trust and cultivates an environment in which fairness can be assumed does not have to negotiate for some of the contributions it receives from the workforce, and it can rely on reputational effects to identify those who can and do contribute beyond the most narrow interpretations of the job description.

Contextual Performance

We noted early on that, for quite some time, the research community in organizational psychology and management did not find much support for the "folk wisdom" hypothesis that job satisfaction had a causal link to job performance or productivity. Only when we looked at a different dependent variable—OCB—did we begin to see indications of the salubrious effect of job satisfaction on organizational effectiveness.

Folk wisdom had also held to the notion that individual personality had a nontrivial influence on job performance. Eventually, serious reviews of the empirical literature failed to provide strong or consistent support for this idea. Although few observers doubted the relationship between cognitive abilities (as measured by intelligence tests) and individual performance, that was considered a different sort of factor from temperament.

However, in recent years, thanks to the conceptual and empirical work that went into Project Alpha (e.g., Borman and Motowidlo, 1993, 1997), we now find renewed respect for the effects of personality in the workplace. Borman and Motowidlo, much like those who contributed to the work on OCB, made a distinction between task performance and contextual performance. The latter focused not on productivity, but the contributions that individuals made to the socioemotional climate of the work group.

Borman and Motowidlo's construct and measure of contextual performance (CP) overlaps somewhat with, but is not identical to, what we have called OCB. In particular, they did not see CP as totally distinct from job or task performance, nor did they define it so as to separate it from any kind of contractual reward. Rather, they define it as the contributions that individuals and groups make to the socioemotional climate in which problems are solved or prevented, innovative improvements are conceived and implemented, and support enlisted for the missions of the collective order. The similarity to OCB is that such contributions resist precise articulation, and therefore do not often lend themselves to precise quantification.

The work on CP was guided by the conviction that dimensions of personality were of greater relevance to performance than one would conclude from the previous empirical literature on that question. That literature seemed to make a powerful argument against the more commonly held view that an individual's personality had an important bearing on how productive and effective that individual was at a particular job. However, Borman and Motowidlo argued that the effects of personality would manifest themselves more in how they affected the social and emotional "context" within which work took place.

There is an interesting parallel between the programs of research on OCB and CP. OCB research concerned itself with the effects of job satisfaction or job attitudes; CP examined the influence of personality dimensions. Both programs—which began and continued largely independently of each other—were concerned with the distinction between job performance in terms of the tasks and productivity versus contributions of a more discretionary and spontaneous form.

In a sense, the two programs complement each other. One of them reasserts the importance of job attitudes; the other importance of personality. These two domains have in common the generally held belief that they influence behavior when there are no strong external factors that drive behavior. Strong social pressures and prospects of substantial reward or punishment for specific behaviors usually overrule attitudes and temperament as the decisive factors. When external pressures, prods, and incentives are weak or absent, attitudes and temperament come to the fore.

The research program on personality and CP drew from the "Big Five" framework, defined by five factors: Extraversion, Neuroticism, Conscientiousness, Agreeableness, and Openness to Experience (McCrae and Costa, 1987). We might well expect—as Borman and Motowidlo have found—that the trait "conscientiousness" would predict some degree of "conscientious work behavior" that goes beyond the formal job description, at least with respect to attendance, punctuality, doing their "homework," and maintaining a neat and organized workplace. Neuroticism, connoting as it does frequent experience of negative affect, could very well have a negative effect on perceptions of fairness and difficulty in sustaining the bonds of teamwork or the camaraderie in which "altruism" or "helping" take place. And, indeed, Motowidlo and Van Scotter (1994) and Motowidlo (2000) find such empirical relationships.

If we think in terms of "state" and "trait" and either OCB or CP, we might ponder causal models in which personality factors have an indirect effect on OCB, via job satisfaction and/or positive affect.

We might find that it will be difficult to disentangle the causal strands among personality, job satisfaction, and OCB. Evidence suggests that both personality and job satisfaction appear to have a genetic base. Studies of twins separated at birth and brought together in adulthood find that their traits and job satisfaction are more similar than is true of non-twin siblings (Arvey, Bouchard, Segal, & Abraham, 1989). The first reported meta-analysis of personality traits, job satisfaction, and OCB (Organ & Ryan, 1995) generally found job attitudes more strongly related than personality to OCB. However, we should note that the Big Five factor of conscientiousness was found to have an estimated population correlation of .30 with "generalized compliance." Thus, people who describe themselves as above average in tendencies toward self-discipline, planfulness, and striving for achievement are in fact regarded that way by peers and superiors as more regular in attendance, more observant of formal rules and policies, less likely to waste time or materials, and more goal-oriented. And perhaps such individuals report more job satisfaction because their conduct earns respect of coworkers and superiors.

Is the Construct of Organizational Citizenship Behavior Relevant in Other Cultures?

The early studies of OCB were almost entirely conducted in the United States. The question arises as to whether the concept has heuristic or applied value in countries with different cultures.

Hofstede's (1984) empirically derived framework for comparing dominant cultures in various geographic regions indicates that the United States, relative to other countries, stands out as highly individualistic (as opposed to collectivist), highly masculine in tone, manifests a considerable tolerance for uncertainty, and is low-to-medium in power distance.

These differences might well condition the matrix of specific forms of OCB that would be understood in cultures that pose a quite different profile of Hostede's dimensions. In cultures marked as very high in power distance, it might be quite risky to go beyond specific instructions in order to deal with a situation that the individual thinks needs correcting. Also, a culture that predisposes individuals to avoid ambiguity whenever possible would have the effect of not relying on the future recompense for contributions above and beyond instructions or job description. On the other hand, a more collectivist culture would, one suspects, condition work groups to provide much reciprocal give and take among themselves.

In one of the earliest studies on cultural variations in OCB, Farh, Zhong, and Organ (2004) provided employees and managers with a general definition of OCB and asked them to provide examples of that definition in their places of employment. The descriptions of OCB that they provided were content-analyzed and yielded a set of factors somewhat different from what had emerged from studies in North America. For example, the factor "social welfare participation," referring to voluntary work in the community, stood out strongly, but especially so in state-owned enterprises. Analysis also revealed a factor pertaining to self-study and acquisition of new skills. Emphasis on interpersonal harmony in the work group also came out loud and clear—not surprising in a strongly collectivistic culture.

The findings from Farh et al. suggest that the construct of OCB has potential relevance to a broad continuum of cultures—obviously, the culture of the People's Republic of China differs considerably on Hofstede's dimensions from the United States, particularly in individualism-collectivism and power distance. However, what OCB research in other cultures is likely to require is development of some degree of cultural relevance in the measuring instruments that pertain to the values, behaviors, and forms that individuals perceive as exemplars of OCB in their contexts.

Is There a Downside to Organizational Citizenship Behavior?

As we have documented in the preceding pages, there is reason to believe that OCB has potential positive effects for the individual in the form of noncontractual benefits, whether in the form of eventual pay increases, favorable treatment by managers or officers (in terms of latitude and range of personal discretion), or informal status and reputation among colleagues. However, "can there be too much of a good thing"? Might there arise some inflection point at which the time, energy, and concern about OCB has negative fallout?

One could argue that an individual might get so caught up in many forms of well-intended involvement in helping coworkers and taking on other functions outside the core job requirements, that productivity and performance in fulfillment of those core tasks would suffer. However, the empirical findings generally reveal that OCB is positively, not negatively correlated with in-role job performance and productivity measures.

Perhaps more likely is the phenomenon in which attempts to maintain a high level of productivity and excellence in the core job definition, while maintaining a mode of very active OCB, could lead to overload, with negative fallout on one's health, work–family conflicts, and other indications of stress. Bolino and Turnley (2005) have presented evidence that, at some levels of OCB, these problems can arise.

Bolino (1999) also has suggested that some portion of OCB might also be used as a tool for ingratiating one's self with superiors. Perhaps so. But a less-than-admirable motive or intent does not necessarily rule out the possible value of the actions. Also, such Machiavellian striving would, we think, be selective in terms of the time and context in which it occurs. For example, OCB intended to ingratiate would likely appear when the boss is around and not so much when the boss is elsewhere. Peer ratings would probably reveal if OCB is strategic and calculated. Nonetheless, the issue merits further scrutiny.

Conclusion

As the reader has doubtless surmised, much effort has gone into building and testing a rather substantial conceptual framework about OCB. Still, many issues remain unresolved with regard to empirical identification of antecedents and consequences of OCB, as well as the conceptual clarity of fully fleshed-out causal models that would articulate moderator and mediator variables. For example, we have seen how national culture bears upon our identification of the relevant forms of OCB. Perhaps we should ponder whether the type or purpose of the organization also tends toward a strong, defining culture that would define different forms of OCB. Consider how the culture of a large health care organization might pose a hierarchy of forms of OCB much different from a large retail chain. Read on in subsequent chapters for what recent, cutting-edge theory and research has to say about some of these issues.

References

Andrews, F. M., & Withey, S. B. (1976). *Social indicators of well being.* New York, NY: Academic Press.

Arvey, R. D., Bouchard, T. J., Segal, N. L., & Abraham, L. M. (1989). Job satisfaction: Environmental and genetic components. *Journal of Applied Psychology, 74*, 187–192.

Barnard, C. I. (1938). *The functions of the executive.* Cambridge, MA: Harvard University Press.

Bateman, T. S., & Organ, D. W. (1983). Job satisfaction and the good soldier: The relationship between affect and employee "citizenship." *Academy of Management Journal, 26*, 587–595.

Bolino, M. C. (1999). Citizenship and impression management: Good soldiers or good actors. *Academy of Management Review, 24*, 82–98.

Bolino, M. C., & Turnley, W. H. (2005). The personal costs of citizenship behavior: The relationship between individual initiative and role overload, job stress, and work–family conflict. *Journal of Applied Psychology, 90*, 740–748.

Borman, W. C., & Motowidlo, S. J. (1993). Expanding the criterion domain to include elements of contextual performance. In N. Schmitt, W. C. Borman, & Associates (Eds.), *Personnel selection in organizations*, pp. 71–98. San Francisco, CA: Jossey-Bass.

Borman, W. C., & Motowidlo, S. J. (1997). Task performance and contextual performance: The meaning for personnel selection research. *Human Performance, 10*, 99–109.

Brayfield, A. H., & Crockett, W. H. (1955). Employee attitudes and employee performance. *Psychological Bulletin, 38*, 393–420.

Campbell, A. (1976). Subjective measures of well being. *American Psychologist, 31*, 117–124.

Farh, J. I., Zhong, C. B., & Organ, D. W. (2004). Organizational citizenship behavior in the People's Republic of China. *Organization Science, 15*, 241–253.

Graham, J. W. (1986). Organizational citizenship behavior informed by political theory. Paper presented at the Annual Meeting of the Academy of Management, Chicago, Illinois.

Hofstede, G. (1984). *Culture's consequences.* Newbury Park, CA: Sage.

Kaplan, A. (1964). *The conduct of inquiry: Methodology for behavioral science.* San Francisco, CA: Chandler.

Katz, D., & Kahn, R. L. (1966). *The social psychology of organizations.* New York, NY: Wiley.

Katz, D., & Kahn, R. L. (1978). *The social psychology of organizations.* (2nd ed.) New York, NY: Wiley.

Koys, D. J. (2001). The effects of employee satisfaction, organizational citizenship behavior, and turnover on organizational effectiveness: A unit-level, longitudinal study. *Personnel Psychology, 54*, 101–114.

Lawler, E. E., III, & Porter, L. W. (1967). The effect of performance on job satisfaction. *Industrial Relations, 7*, 20–28.

McCrae, R. R., & Costa, P. T., Jr. (1987). Validation of the five-factor model of personality across instruments and observers, *Personality and Social Psychology, 52*, 81–90.

Morrison, E. W. (1994). Role definitions and organizational citizenship behavior: The importance of the employee perspective. *Academy of Management Journal, 37*, 1543–1567.

Motowidlo, S. J. (2000). Some basic issues related to contextual performance and organizational citizenship behavior in human behavior. *Human Resource Management Review, 10*, 115–126.

Motowidlo, S. J., & Van Scotter, J. R. (1994). Evidence that task-performance should be distinguished from contextual performance. *Journal of Applied Psychology, 79*, 475–480.

Odiorne, G. S. (1965). *Management by objectives: A system of managerial leadership.* New York, NY: Pitman Publishing.

Organ, D. W. (1977). A reappraisal and reinterpretation of the satisfaction-causes-performance hypothesis. *Academy of Management Review, 2*, 46–53.

Organ, D. W., Podsakoff, P. M., & MacKenzie, S. B. (2006). *Organizational citizenship behavior: Its nature, antecedents and consequences.* Thousand Oaks, CA: Sage.

Organ, D. W., & Ryan, K. 1995. A meta-analytic review of attitudinal and dispositional predictors of organizational citizenship behavior. *Personnel Psychology, 48*, 775–802.

Podsakoff, N. P., Whiting, S. W., Podsakoff, P. M., & Blume, B. D. (2009) Individual- and organizational-level consequences of organizational citizenship behaviors: A meta-analysis. *Journal of Applied Psychology, 94*, 122–141.

Podsakoff, P. M., MacKenzie, S. B., Paine, J., & Bachrach, D. G. (2000). Organizational citizenship behaviors: A critical review of the theoretical and empirical literature and suggestions for future research. *Journal of Management 2000 Yearly Review, 26*, 513–563.

Roethlisberger, F. J., & Dickson, W. J. (1939). *Management and the worker.* New York, NY: Wiley & Sons.

Smith, C. A., Organ, D. W., & Near, J. P. (1983). Organizational citizenship behavior: Its nature and antecedents. *Journal of Applied Psychology, 68*, 653–663.

Viteles, M. S. (1953). *Motivation and morale in industry.* New York, NY: Norton.

Walz, S. M., & Niehoff, B. P. (2000). Organizational citizenship behaviors: Their relationship to organizational effectiveness. *Journal of Hospitality & Tourism Research, 24*, 301–319.

Weber, M. (1947). *The theory of social and economic organization*. Oxford, UK: Gerth and Mills.

Williams, L. J., & Anderson, S. E. (1991). Job satisfaction and organizational commitment as predictors of organizational citizenship and in-role behaviors. *Journal of Management, 17*, 601–617.

Williamson, O. E. (1975). *Markets and hierarchies*. New York: Free Press.

Zajonc, R. B. (1980). Feeling and thinking: Preferences need no inferences. *American Psychologist, 35*, 151–175.

CHAPTER

3

The Bigger Picture: How Organizational Citizenship Behaviors Fit Within a Broader Conceptualization of Work Performance

Joseph A. Carpini *and* Sharon K. Parker

Abstract

Scholars have identified numerous forms of individual work performance, including core task, adaptive, proactive, and citizenship. Although the diversity of performance constructs has contributed to breadth, it has also resulted in a fragmented literature that, at times, operates in theoretical silos. As such, the overarching purpose of this chapter is to consider how organizational citizenship behavior (OCB) constructs relate to, and can fit within, broader models of individual work performance. We begin with a brief history of work performance concepts and review five integrative models of individual performance, culminating with the presentation of the Griffin, Neal, and Parker (2007) model. We use the latter to assess systematically whether and how OCB concepts relate to other performance concepts. We highlight constructs that fit readily within the Griffin et al. framework, in addition to constructs that do not. We conclude with five recommendations.

Key Words: individual performance, organizational citizenship behavior, proficiency, adaptivity, proactivity

Individual work performance refers to work behavior by an individual that generates value for the organization (Campbell, McCloy, Oppler, & Sager, 1993). For almost a century, individual work performance has been a central topic for researchers and practitioners (Henderschott, 1917; Viswesvaran & Ones, 2000). Nevertheless, in the past several decades, the work context has changed dramatically (Griffin, Neal, & Parker, 2007). Scholars have argued that the modern workplace requires a broader conceptualization of work performance to capture all aspects of behavior that positively contribute to the attainment of organizational goals (Griffin et al., 2007; Murphy & Jackson, 1999). In response, researchers have developed and investigated a bourgeoning array of conceptualizations of individual performance, including core-task or "in-role" performance (Campbell et al., 1993; Morrison, 1994), adaptive performance (Berg, Wrzesniewski, & Dutton, 2010; Pulakos et al., 2002), proactive performance (Crant, 2000; Parker, Williams, & Turner, 2006), and citizenship behaviors (Organ, 1988; Podsakoff, Whiting, Podsakoff, & Blume, 2009) or "contextual" performance (Borman & Motowidlo, 1993).

The emergence of multiple performance concepts has ensured that research captures the full range of behavior that is likely to be critical for effective organizations. But there is a benefit in understanding how these types of performance are similar or different to each other, and how they interrelate. With a few exceptions that we discuss later, the focus of most research on performance has largely been on the antecedents and consequences of a specific category of performance, rather than on synthesizing across types of performance (Campbell, 2012), resulting in rather discrete literatures with separate reviews and meta-analyses that ignore commonalities between constructs (Sackett, 2002). Synthesis across constructs enables the identification of common or distinct motivational processes and antecedents as well as consequences. If the literature is overly compartmentalized, such theoretical development is inhibited.

To aid with this synthesis, the objective of this chapter is to identify where organizational citizenship behaviors "fit" in relation to other individual-level performance concepts. We consider multiple types of citizenship behaviors (Borman & Motowidlo, 1993; Borman et al., 2001; Johnson, 2003; Organ, Podsakoff, & Podsakoff, 2006), highlighting key dimensions as well as categorical structures. We then relate citizenship behaviors to work performance concepts more broadly, using the integrative performance model developed by Griffin et al. (2007). Our synthesis is limited to individual-level behaviors that generate value for organizations, including how individual behaviors contribute to team or higher level performance outcomes (e.g., Bartram, 2005). Performance concepts at the team level, such as team effectiveness (e.g., Marks, Mathieu, & Zaccaro, 2001) or at the organizational level (e.g., Venkatraman & Ramanujam, 1986), such as company return on investment, are not the focus here. We also exclude work behaviors, even if they are individual level, that do not generate value for organizations (e.g., counterproductive behaviors; Carpini, Parker, & Griffin, 2017).

Our chapter proceeds as follows. First, we provide a brief history of the individual performance domain. Second, we recap on integrative individual performance models. Third, we assess whether and how OCB constructs can be encompassed within the existing Griffin et al. (2007) framework. This analysis extends the Griffin et al. framework because it explicitly maps OCBs into the model and includes new OCB constructs. Finally, we conclude with six recommendations derived from our analysis.

A Brief History of Performance Concepts

Individual work performance has been a central topic within industrial and organizational psychology for almost a century (Henderschott, 1917). Scientific investigation of individual work performance has been approached from two broad perspectives. The first perspective, fuelled by the research executed in response to World War 1, has focused almost uniquely on the prediction of job performance using ability and personality tests. Performance during this time was synonymous with outcome measures such as productivity, efficiency, training time, quality, work samples, accidents, tenure, and ratings (Austin & Villanova, 1992). The second perspective, which emerged in the 1960s and which is our focus here, sought to understand the nature of job performance, such as identifying its dimensionality (Van Dyne, Graham, & Dienesch, 1994).

Within this perspective, the work of Katz (1964) had a profound impact, largely due to the distinguishing of "in-role" and "extra-role" behaviors. In-role behavior was defined as the extent to which individuals carry out their assigned roles (formally outlined in the job description) to a minimum standard of both quantity and quality. But Katz also argued for a set of neglected requirements that fall outside the traditional boundaries of one's role but are none the less instrumental in attaining organizational goals—which were coined "extra-role" behaviors. Katz identified seven key extra-role behaviors: innovative and spontaneous behavior, cooperation, protection, constructive ideas, self-training, and favorable attitude. This distinction between in-role and extra-role behaviors continues to be influential (Chiaburu & Baker, 2006; Van Dyne & LePine, 1998), and many of the seven constructs introduced in Katz's article have grown into streams of research (e.g., cooperation is reflected in contemporary definitions of helping found in the literature). With this said, the distinction between in-role and extra-role behavior has been argued to not be as clear-cut as Katz proposed. Morrison (1994), for instance, demonstrated that the extent to which behaviors are in-role or extra-role depends on how broadly employees define their work roles.

Building on the work of Katz (1964), the concept of organizational citizenship behavior (OCB) was introduced. OCB is defined as discretionary behavior that goes above and beyond the formal requirements of a given role (Bateman & Organ, 1983) and "lubricate[s] the social machinery of the organization" (Smith, Organ, & Near, 1983, p. 654). In an initial study by Bateman and Organ, the authors developed a 30-item instrument of OCB including behaviors such as compliance, altruism, dependability, cooperation, and punctuality. Results using cross-lagged analysis demonstrated a strong relationship between employee job satisfaction and citizenship behaviors. Further refining the OCB construct, Smith and colleagues (1983) developed a 16-item, two-factor measure of citizenship behavior that focused on altruism (helping) as well as generalized compliance. Recently, N. P. Podsakoff, Podsakoff, MacKenzie, Maynes, and Spoelma, (2014) highlighted 37 OCB-like constructs in the literature, attesting to the fervor with which this construct has been investigated.

Next, based on research from developmental and social psychology, came the introduction of prosocial organizational behavior (Brief & Motowidlo, 1986, p. 711), or behavior "performed by a member of an organization, directed toward an individual, group, or organization with whom he or she interacts while carrying out his or her organizational role, and performed with the intention of promoting the welfare of the individual, group, or organization toward which it is directed." The authors presented eleven different types of functional and two types of dysfunctional prosocial organizational behavior. Brief and Motowidlo distinguished between various types of helping behavior, as well as including additional behaviors such as principled organizational dissent and voice, putting in extra effort, loyalty, and organizational compliance.

Building on the work of their predecessors, Borman and Motowidlo (1993) presented a two-dimensional model of individual performance. The first dimension, task performance, reflects the proficiency with which an individual executes the role-prescribed parts of his or her job and includes behaviors such as job-specific and non-job-specific task proficiency (Campbell et al., 1993) or what Katz (1964) would consider "in-role." The second dimension, contextual performance, lent heavily on the existing OCB and prosocial organizational behavior literatures and was defined as those behaviors that do not directly support the technical core of the organization, but rather contribute to the organization, social, and psychological environment. Behaviors belonging to the contextual performance factor are similar to those described by Campbell et al.'s (1993) facilitating peer and team performance dimension and include helping, cooperating, and following rules. Borman and Motowidlo (1993) argued that, while cognitive ability is a strong antecedent of task performance, individual motivation and personality are key antecedents of contextual performance. Motowidlo and Van Scotter (1994) tested the model in a sample of 421 U.S. Air Force mechanics. Using multisource supervisor ratings of performance, the authors found that both task and contextual performance contributed uniquely to ratings of overall job performance.

In a further extension, Borman and Motowidlo (1997) developed a taxonomy of contextual performance that included five factors: (1) persisting with enthusiasm and extra effort, (2) volunteering to carry out task activities that are not formally part of own job, (3) helping and cooperating with others, (4) following organizational rules and procedures, and (5) endorsing, supporting, and defending organizational objectives. The authors found that personality was correlated to a greater extent with contextual performance as opposed to overall performance. In a further expansion, Conway's (1999) meta-analysis showed that peers weighed contextual performance more in rendering an overall performance rating, as opposed to supervisors who attended to task performance more in determining overall performance. Borman and Motowidlo's (1993) model continues to attract empirical attention (e.g., Christian, Garza, & Slaughter, 2011). In a recent meta-analysis, Carpenter, Berry, and Houston (2014) included contextual and extra-role performance as general types of OCBs.

The turn of the century saw a dramatic increase in research related to OCBs (Podsakoff, MacKenzie, Paine, & Bachrach, 2000) as well as other performance constructs, notably adaptivity. Turbulent global economies, advances in technology, widespread organizational restructuring, and other such change have all contributed to a growing interest in adaptive performance (Schmitt & Chan, 2014). While some scholars argued adaptive performance was already captured under other performance constructs (e.g., task performance and contextual performance; Borman & Motowidlo, 1993; Campbell et al., 1993), others argued it represents a distinct form of individual performance (Baard, Rench, & Kozlowski, 2014). Adopting the latter perspective, Pulakos, Arad, Donovan, and Plamondon (2000) developed a taxonomy of individual adaptive work performance with eight types of adaptivity: (1) solving problems creatively, (2) dealing with uncertain and unpredictable work situations, (3) learning work tasks, technologies, and procedures, (4) demonstrating interpersonal adaptivity, (5) demonstrating cultural adaptivity, (6) demonstrating physical oriented adaptivity, (7) handling emergencies or crisis situations, and (8) handling work stress. Factor analyses supported an eight-factor Job Adaptability Inventory. Additional evidence showed concurrent and criterion-related validities of the eight-factor model (Pulakos et al., 2002).

Around the same time as this focus on adaptivity, the performance literature was undergoing a parallel shift with the emergence of constructs focused on individual agency at work, that is, behaviors exhibited by employees that are anticipatory and proactive instead of reactive (Grant & Ashford, 2008). Some authors proposed specific constructs such as taking charge (Morrison & Phelps, 1999), helping, and voice (Van Dyne & LePine, 1998) as extra-role behaviors, while others sought to distinguish these behaviors more clearly by using labels such as proactive behavior (Crant, 2000; Parker et al., 2006) and personal initiative (Frese & Fay, 2001). Crant (2000, p. 436) defined proactive behavior "as taking initiative in improving current circumstances or creating new ones; it involves challenging the status quo rather than passively adapting to present conditions." While several definitions of proactive behavior have been offered (e.g., Crant, 2000; Grant & Ashford, 2008), it is generally accepted that three key characteristics distinguish proactive behavior from others types of individual performance: the self-starting nature of the behavior, that the behavior is anticipatory and future-focused as opposed to reactive, and that the behavior is intended to change the situation and/or oneself (Parker et al., 2006).

Proactive work behaviors have attracted a great deal of scholarship; however, this research stream is fragmented (Thomas, Whitman, & Viswesvaran, 2010). Several syntheses of the proactive literature exist. For example, Crant (2000) proposed two general classifications of proactivity: (1) general proactive behaviors or attitudes, including role-based self-efficacy, proactive personality, taking charge, and personal initiative, as well as (2) context-specific proactive behaviors, including socialization, feedback seeking, innovation, coping with stress, and issue selling. Parker and Collins (2010) also sought to integrate and differentiate the various forms of proactive behavior. Using a sample of 622 managers, the authors found evidence for three higher order factors. The first factor, proactive work behavior, contained taking charge, voice, individual innovation, and problem prevention. The second factor, proactive person-environment-fit behavior, included feedback inquiry, feedback monitoring, job change negotiation, and career initiative. The final factor, proactive strategic behavior, included strategic scanning and issue selling.

In sum, Katz (1964, p. 132) ignited a revolution in the performance literature by putting the spotlight on a "neglected set of requirements consist[ing] of those actions not specified by role prescriptions which nevertheless facilitate the accomplishment of organizational goals." This seminal work was followed by the introduction of OCBs (Organ, 1997; Smith, Organ, & Near, 1983), contextual performance, and both adaptive (Pulakos et al., 2000) and proactive behavior (Crant, 2000). However, most of these performance models have been domain specific. Next we turn to more integrative perspectives.

A handful of models have attempted to synthesize the broader domain of individual work performance. Here we outline, in chronological order, five integrative models that we believe have made particularly noteworthy contributions.

Campbell's Taxonomy of Major Performance Components

Building on research conducted in a military context during the late 1980s, Campbell and colleagues (1993) presented an eight-factor hierarchical model of individual job performance. The purpose of the model was to describe a meaningful and invariant latent factor structure of performance that distinguished between types of performance and avoided an overgeneralized general factor (Campbell & Wiernik, 2015).

The first factor is job-specific task proficiency, reflecting the classic definition of technical or "core" task performance. For example, on a hospital ward, drug administration is a job-specific (or core) task for a nurse, while drug preparation is a core task for a pharmacist. The second factor, non-job-specific task proficiency, includes tasks that are expected of employees across a wide range of jobs. Within a hospital setting, it is expected that all staff should be prepared to perform basic first aid and CPR should the need arise. The third factor, written and oral communication proficiency, refers to the proficiency with which one communicates with others in both written and spoken form. The fourth factor, demonstrating effort, reflects the consistency with which an individual exerts effort daily and the frequency with which an individual exerts extra effort, as well as a general willingness to persist under adverse circumstances. The fifth factor, maintaining personal discipline, is defined by the absence of undesirable negative behaviors such as substance abuse at work, excessive absenteeism, and deviation from established procedures. The sixth factor, facilitating peer and team performance, is concerned with the extent to which individuals support and help peers. The seventh factor, supervision and leadership, includes interpersonal behaviors exhibited by leaders within an organization intended to influence subordinates. The final dimension is management and administration, which includes behaviors such as articulating goals, obtaining, allocating resources, and being an ambassador for the unit. While the last two dimensions are specified for those holding management and supervisory positions, Campbell et al. (1993)

suggest that job-specific task proficiency, demonstrating effort, and maintenance of personal discipline are critical components of every job.

In 2012, Campbell revised the taxonomy to reflect advances in the performance literature. The main changes were the elimination of the non-job-specific task proficiency, the addition of a peer/team management dimension, and redefining of the previous "maintaining personal discipline" dimension. The latter was originally defined by the absence of behavior but was reconceptualized into a counterproductive work behavior dimension that captures individual and organizationally directed deviant behaviors.

One challenge with the Campbell et al. (1993; Campbell, 2012) taxonomy is that little empirical data have supported the eight-factor structure. Also the definition of performance provided by Campbell and Wiernik (2015, p. 48) as "things that people actually do, actions they take, that contribute to the organization's goals" arguably should preclude counterproductive work behaviors as these behaviors *detract* from the attainment of goals.

The Role-Based Performance Scale

Welbourne, Johnson, and Erez (1998) derived a model of performance that extends beyond the traditional focus on job role behaviors through the synthesis of role theory and identity theory. The authors proposed five "roles," each of which can be performed more or less effectively. The first role, the "job role," captures the traditional view of individual performance as the content of one's formal job description. This role is measured by the quantity and quality of work output, accuracy of work, and customer service (both internal and external). The decision to include output measures is inconsistent with arguments that performance should be defined as behaviors under the control of the individual (Campbell et al., 1993; Campbell, 2012). The "organization role" relates to the OCB literature and concerns behavior that goes above and beyond the normal call of duty for the betterment of the organization. The "career role" concerns the extent to which an individual obtains the necessary skills to successfully progress through the organization. This role uses several outcome measures, including "obtaining personal career goals" and "making progress in his/her career"—both of which are difficult to purely attribute to the individual's behavior. It is also possible that career progression will require an employee to exit the organization in order to advance, which might be detrimental to the organization. The fourth role, the "innovator" role, focuses on coming up with new ideas, working to implement ideas, finding improved ways to do things, and creating better processes and routines. This role is very similar to proactive performance concepts. Finally, acknowledging the growing reliance on teams within organizations, Welbourne and colleagues (1998) proposed the "team role," defined by teamwork and cooperation with coworkers. The four items included in this measure are similar to what Podsakoff et al. (2014) classified as "affiliation-oriented OCB."

Welbourne and colleagues (1998) provided empirical evidence of the distinctiveness of the five roles using self-evaluations, manager ratings, archival personnel data (e.g., current salary and salary increases), and organization characteristics (e.g., gainsharing). The model presented by Welbourne et al. (1998) has been used in several studies. For example, Wallace and colleagues (2009) found hindrance demands to be negatively related to both job and organization roles, while challenge demands were only weakly positively related to job roles. Interestingly, in a study executed by Chen, Kirkman, Kanfer, Allen, and Rosen (2007), the authors found that the job, team, and organization roles were indistinguishable from one another. Overall, research utilizing this framework has largely focused on a single role (e.g., Bauer, Erdogan, Liden, & Wayne, 2006; Wang & Howell, 2010), has not distinguished between the roles and simply used an aggregate variable (e.g., Chen & Klimoski, 2003), or has failed to replicate the factor structure (e.g., Chen et al. 2007).

Integrated Hierarchical Taxonomy of Individual Performance

Johnson (2003) presented an integrative hierarchical taxonomy of individual work performance, defined as "behavior that is relevant to the goals of the organization and can be measured in terms of the level of the individual's contribution to those goals" (p. 88). Johnson's model encompasses, at the highest level, task performance, citizenship performance, and adaptive performance. Following these three general dimensions are several second-level dimensions composed of specific behaviors.

Task performance is defined by the five facets presented in the Campbell et al. (1993) model, along with two facets of the conscientious initiative argued to be essential in task performance, namely learning work tasks, technologies, and procedures, as well as demonstrate effort. The citizenship performance dimension is a synthesis of several models yielding three subfacets, including organizational support, personal support, and four behaviors classified under the conscientious initiative dimension (demonstrate effort, handling work stress, showing initiative, and engaging in self-development). Johnson (2003) integrated Pulakos et al.'s (2000) handling work stress dimension as an essential component of all three subfacets of organizational citizenship identified in the model. A defining contribution of this model is the inclusion of adaptive performance (defined by a single subdimension, dealing with uncertain and unpredictable work situations) as a distinct dimension.

The overarching purpose of Johnson's integrative taxonomy of individual performance was to provide a framework to link individual personality traits with specific performance dimensions. Although the taxonomy has not been empirically validated, it remains an important step in the theoretical development connecting individual differences and various types of personality building on the seminal work of Barrick and Mount (1991).

Great Eight Competencies

There is a global trend toward the use of competency models, with over 50% of all Fortune 500 companies reporting they use them (Mansfield, 2005). While there is still no consensus regarding the definition of a competency (Campbell & Wiernik, 2015), it has been argued that competencies are concerned with *how* work is accomplished, as opposed to simply what is accomplished (Catano, Darr, & Campbell, 2007). Working within this framework, Bartram (2005) presented a hierarchical model of individual work performance. The model was derived using factor analysis and validated in a meta-analysis of 29 studies (N = 4,861 individuals across 10 countries) executed by the SHL consulting group.

Beginning at the highest level, the author identified eight distinct general competencies: (1) leading/deciding, (2) supporting/cooperating, (3) interacting/presenting, (4) analyzing/interpreting, (5) creating/conceptualizing, (6) organizing/executing, (7) adapting/coping, and (8) enterprising/performing. Next are 20 competency dimensions. At the lowest level, there are 112 competency components making up the 20 dimensions.

Interestingly, when the eight competencies were submitted to principle-components analysis (PCA), only two general factors emerged. The first factor was made up of analyzing/interpreting, creating/conceptualizing, organizing/executing, enterprising/performing, and leading/deciding, and the second factor included supporting/cooperating and adapting/coping. The interacting/presenting competency had cross-loadings on both factors. These results echo to some extent Borman and Motowidlo's (1993) identification of two general factors: task and contextual performance. Although this competency-based model of individual work performance has been well cited, there is a dearth of research testing details of the model. One exception is a study by Lievens, Sanchez, Bartram, and Brown (2010), who challenged the assertion that variance in incumbents' competency ratings within the same occupation is random error. Results of their study of 192 incumbents across 64 occupations suggest that approximately 25% of observed variance in competency ratings within the same occupation is related to job characteristics, including ambiguity, autonomy, interdependence, and routinization.

Griffin et al.'s Context-Based Dimensions and Forms of Individual Performance

Griffin, Neal, and Parker (2007) drew on role theory to develop an integrative model of work performance. They theorized that performance can be synthesized according to two overarching dimensions that, in turn, reflect the contextual variables of uncertainty and interdependence. The first dimension focuses on differences in form (proficiency, adaptivity, and proactivity) which relate to the level of uncertainty in an organizational environment. As uncertainty in an organization increases, the requirements of a given role become more dynamic and ambiguous (thus, adaptive and proactive forms of individual performance become increasingly important), whereas in low-uncertainty environments the formal requirements of a given job (i.e., proficiency) take precedence. It is important to note that the forms of performance are not argued to be mutually exclusive, but rather their relative importance reflects the degree of uncertainty in the environment. The second dimension, the target of contribution (individual task, team member, and organization member), relates to the level of interdependence in the organizational environment. Interdependence relates to the link between individual performance and effectiveness, such that when interdependence is low, the link is simple; however, when interdependence is high, the link is more complex as it involves the behavior of other individuals within the organization (Griffin et al., 2007).

The two dimensions together form a matrix yielding nine categories of performance (see Table 3.1): individual task proficiency, team member proficiency, organization member proficiency, individual task adaptivity, team member adaptivity, organization member adaptivity, individual task proactivity, team member proactivity, and organization member proactivity. Griffin et al. presented factorial evidence for these nine dimensions, as well as evidence that different antecedents relate to the various dimensions in distinct and meaningful ways. For example, as hypothesized by the authors, openness to change was related to individual, team, and organizational member

Table 3.1 Adapted Griffin et al. (2007) Model Overview

		Level of Uncertainty		
		Proficiency Behaviors that can be formalized and anticipated in advance.	***Adaptivity*** "Behaviors in which individuals cope with, respond to, and or/ support changes"[1]	***Proactivity*** Agentic and self-starting, change-oriented, and future-focused behavior
Level of Interdependence	**Individual Task Behaviors**	**Individual Task Proficiency** "that reflect the degree to which an employee meets the known expectations and requirements of his or her role as an individual."[1]	**Individual Task Adaptivity** "reflects the degree to which individuals cope with, respond to, and/ or support changes that affect their roles as individuals."[1]	**Individual Task Proactivity** "extent to which individuals engage in self-starting, future-oriented behavior to change their individual work situations, their individual work roles, or themselves."[2]
	Team Member Behaviors	**Team Member Proficiency** "behaviors that can be formalized and are embedded in a team or group . . . (or) the degree to which an individual meets the expectations and requirements of his or her role as a member of a team"[1]	**Team Member Adaptivity** "reflects the degree to which individuals cope with, respond to, and/ or support changes that affect their roles as members of a team."[1]	**Team Member Proactivity** "extent to which individuals engage in self-starting, future-oriented behavior to change their a team's situation or the way the team works."[2]
	Organization Member Behaviors	**Organization Member Proficiency** "reflects the degree to which an individual meets the expectations and requirements of his or her role as a member of an organization."[1]	**Organization Member Adaptivity** "reflects the degree to which individuals cope with, respond to, and/ or support changes that affect their roles as organization members."[2]	**Organization Member Proactivity** "extent to which individuals engage in self-starting, future-oriented behavior to change his or her organization and/or the way the organization works."[2]

All quotes from Griffin et al. (2007).
[1] = p. 331.
[2] = p. 332.

adaptivity; role breadth self-efficacy was related to proactivity; organizational commitment was related to all organization member performances; and role clarity was positively related to individual task proficiency. Further evidence was reported by Neal, Yeo, Koy, and Xiao (2011), who found that the Big Five personality traits related to the various performance dimensions in distinct ways. For example, openness was positively related to individual and organizational proactivity, but negatively related to both team and organizational proficiency. The authors also reported that, while openness was positively related to proactivity, agreeableness was negatively related to this outcome, consistent with its inherently challenging nature (Morrison & Phelps, 1999). This model has been utilized in subsequent research by other scholars (Griffin, Parker, & Mason, 2010; Leroy, Anseel, Gardner, & Sels, 2012; Strauss, Griffin, & Rafferty, 2009).

Although the Griffin et al. model might appear not to include OCBs, the authors argued OCBs do fit when individual performance is conceptualized within a broader perspective. Some citizenship behaviors are conceptualized as forms of proficiency—notably as team member proficiency and organizational member proficiency—because these behaviors can be anticipated and predicted in advance whenever there is interdependency in work. Thus, for example, helping and related interpersonal citizenship behaviors were conceptualized as forms of team member proficiency because they will typically be required when individuals work in teams. Likewise, organizational loyalty was conceptualized as an example of organization member proficiency because this behavior can be anticipated as important in advance. We elaborate this perspective on how a greater breadth of OCB constructs might fit into the model in the next section.

One important contribution of this model, apart from its comprehensiveness, is its clear link to the context—a link that is largely ignored in other performance models (Austin & Villanova, 1992). A critical challenge of integrative performance models has been the balancing of construct measurement and context sensitivity. Indeed, Bailey (1983) argued performance criteria are context dependent and Johns (2006) advanced the notion that context is a critical, albeit often overlooked, aspect of organizational behavior. Taken together, this means creating overly generic models may fail to measure important aspects of within-context behavior, while overly specific models might be incompatible, thus undermining our ability to generalize findings across studies (Austin & Villanova, 1992). Furthermore, the model circumvents problems with classifying whether behaviors are "in-role" or "extra-role" (see Morrison, 1994); instead, the model considers only the behavior itself in relation to the two dimensions previously discussed. A final advantage of this model is its recognition that work behaviors can have different targets; in this case, the individual set of tasks, the team, and the organization. The distinction between individual, team, and organizational member behaviors echoes work by Campbell et al. (1990) that distinguished between organization-wide or job-specific performance dimensions, as well as work by Williams and Anderson (1991), who classified OCBs as benefiting individuals (e.g., coworkers) or the organization.

Summary

The integrative performance models have assisted in the development of overarching perspectives, but they have mostly been independent of context, and the behaviors remain ambiguous in their targets. The Griffin, Neal, and Parker (2007) model, in contrast, links behavior to both context and target. Hence, it is the framework for our analysis.

An Integrative Approach: Organizational Citizenship Behaviors Within a Broader Performance Framework

In this section, our goal is to assess whether and how OCBs fit into Griffin et al.'s (2007) integrative model of work performance. Although Griffin et al. included OCBs in their model, their analysis was partial as they did not systematically consider the full breadth of OCB concepts, nor were all of these concepts explicitly mapped into the framework. In addition, since the publication of the Griffin et al. model, there have been new conceptualizations of OCBs (e.g., change-oriented citizenship; Chiaburu, Lorinkova, & Van Dyne, 2013) and new concepts (e.g., promotive and prohibitive voice; Liang, Farh, & Farh, 2012). We structure our synthesis by form of contribution (proficiency, adaptivity, and proactivity), systematically examining the three levels of contribution (individual, team, organizational) within each form. Table 3.2 summarizes the results of this synthesis.

Proficiency

INDIVIDUAL TASK PROFICIENCY

Griffin and colleagues (2007) defined individual task proficiency as behaviors "that reflect the degree

Table 3.2 Synthesis of Organizational Citizenship Behavior Constructs Into the Griffin et al. (2007) Performance Model

	Proficiency	Adaptivity	Proactivity
Individual Task Behaviors	Compliance to Organizational Rules and Procedures Compliance/Generalized Compliance Conscientiousness Individual Initiative* Job Dedication* OCB+ Organizational Obedience Persisting With Enthusiasm and Extra Effort Personal Industry Protecting the Organization Protection of Company Resources Sportsmanship*+* Voluntary Performance of Task Activities*	Sportsmanship*+	Making Constructive Suggestions+ Taking Charge+ Voice+ Voluntary Performance of Task Activities*
Team Member Behaviors	Altruism Altruism toward Colleagues Cheerleading Courtesy Helping* Interpersonal Facilitation Interpersonal Harmony Interpersonal Helping OCB+ OCB-I OCB-Supervisor* Peacemaking Sportsmanship*+*	OCB-Supervisor Sportsmanship*+*	Individual Initiative Issue Selling+ Making Constructive Suggestions+ OCB-Supervisor* Organizational Participation*+* Taking Charge+ Voice+
Organization Member Behaviors	Altruism—Distant Civic Virtue Endorsement, Support, and Defence of the Organization+ Involvement Keeping Up [with changes] Loyal Boosterism OCB+ OCB-O Organizational Identification* Organizational Loyalty Organizational Participation*+* Promotion of Company Image Sportsmanship*+* Spreading Goodwill	Sportsmanship*+	Advocacy Participation Issue Selling+ Organizational Identification* Organizational Participation*+* Principled Dissent Suggesting Organizational Improvements Taking Charge+ Voice+ Whistle Blowing

* Constructs that cover multiple forms of individual performance (proficiency, adaptivity, proactivity).

+ Constructs contributing at multiple levels (individual, team, organization).

to which an employee meets the known expectations and requirements of his or her role as an individual" (p. 331). Individual task proficiency is closely related to existing constructs such as "task performance" (Borman & Motowidlo, 1993), "job specific," "non-job-specific" performance, "demonstrating effort," "written and oral communication" (Campbell et al., 1993), "job role behavior" (Welbourne et al., 1998), and "task performance" (Johnson, 2003), as well as subfacets of Bartram's (2005) "interacting and presenting," "analyzing and interpreting," "organizing and executing," and "enterprising and performing" competencies.

The factor of "persisting with enthusiasm and extra effort as necessary to complete own task activities successfully" presented in Borman and Motowidlo's (1997) taxonomy of contextual performance also falls within this category; that is, high persistence and effort to do one's own tasks effectively reflect a high level of individual task proficiency. Individual effort and persistence are also evident in OCB constructs such as personal industry (Moorman & Blakely, 1995), job dedication (Van Scotter & Motowidlo, 1996), and individual initiative (Organ et al., 2006). The operational definitions and scales for these constructs include paying close attention to important details, completing work with few errors, meeting deadlines, and persisting with difficult work; all of which are individual task proficiency behaviors. Additionally, constructs stressing the adherence to established rules and procedures fit the definition of individual task proficiency; such behaviors are often formalized in job descriptions and codes of conduct. Examples of constructs falling into this category include organizational obedience (Van Dyne et al., 1994), compliance/compliance to organizational rules and procedures (Borman & Motowidlo, 1993), protection of company resources (Farh, Earley, & Lin, 1997), and some aspects of sportsmanship (e.g., avoiding excessive complaining and grievances; Organ, 1988).

Another theme found in several OCB constructs is attendance and punctuality, including the constructs of job dedication (e.g., puts in extra hours; Van Scotter & Motowidlo, 1996), personal industry (e.g., rarely misses work; Moorman, Blakely, & Niehoff, 1998), compliance (attendance at work is above the norm; Smith et al., 1983), and conscientiousness (e.g., often arrives early and starts to work immediately; Farh et al., 1997; e.g., took extra breaks; Podsakoff, MacKenzie, Moorman, & Fetter, 1990). Orderliness is a further theme found in the OCB literature. Bateman and Organ (1983) included housecleaning (e.g., makes sure that things are neat) in their initial measure of OCB, and a similar item is found in the organizational obedience measure used by Van Dyne, Graham, and Dienesch (1994). We suggest that all these constructs can be seen as high levels of individual task proficiency: The value of these behaviors exists regardless of the degree of interdependence and uncertainty in the environment.

Empirical evidence supports the idea that some constructs traditionally seen as OCB can be seen as indicative of individual task proficiency. Drawing on the Griffin et al. model, Neal, Yeo, Koy, and Xiao (2011) showed that conscientiousness was the strongest personality predictor of individual task proficiency. Similarly, in their review, Organ et al. (2006) reported an average corrected correlation of .21 between conscientiousness and OCB. These results are very similar to the results reported by Barrick and Mount (1991; see also Barrick, Parks, & Mount, 2005), who found an average correlation of .23 between conscientiousness and job proficiency. Finally, meta-analytic findings support the argument that OCBs are strongly correlated with task performance (.60 ± .04; Hoffman, Blair, Meriac, & Woehr, 2007).

TEAM MEMBER PROFICIENCY

Katz (1964) argued, "The patterned activity which makes up an organization is so intrinsically a co-operative set of interrelationships, that we are not aware of the co-operative nexus any more than we are of any habitual behavior like walking" (p. 132). Indeed, this observation remains highly relevant in modern organizations; as work has become increasingly interdependent, complex, and dynamic, task completion increasingly requires the cooperation of coworkers (Van der Vegt & Van de Vliert, 2005). Griffin and colleagues argued that, when work is interdependent, this—by definition—requires coordination and cooperation across individuals. Hence, such behaviors are predictable and anticipated, thus constituting a form of proficiency—which they labeled as team member proficiency. Team member proficiency is defined as "behaviors that can be formalized and are embedded in a team or group . . . (or) the degree to which an individual meets the expectations and requirements of his or her role as a member of a team" (Griffin et al., 2007, p. 331). This construct is conceptually similar to several performance constructs such as "facilitating peer and team performance" (Campbell et al.,

1993); "supporting and cooperating" (Bartram, 2005); "personal support" (Borman, Penner, Allen, & Motowidlo, 2001); "assisting co-workers with job-related matters" (Brief & Motowidlo, 1986), and the "team role" within Welbourne et al.'s (1998) integrative model.

The OCB literature has also recognized the importance of individual-level OCBs when tasks are interdependent (Organ, 1988; Podsakoff & MacKenzie, 1997). Several studies have sought to understand the relationship between OCBs and performance under varying levels of interdependence, including Bachrach, Powell, Bendoly, and Richey (2006), Van der Vegt and Van de Vliert (2005), and Van der Vegt, Van de Vliert, and Oosterhof (2003). In this section we review OCB constructs contributing to the maintenance and reinforcement of the status quo through positive social interaction (Choi, 2007).

Much research has examined helping others as a type of OCB (Organ et al., 2006; N. P. Podsakoff et al., 2014; P. M. Podsakoff et al., 2000; Van Dyne & LePine, 1998). Relevant constructs include "OCB-Individual" (Williams & Anderson, 1991), "OCB-Supervisor" (Rupp & Cropanzano, 2002), "interpersonal helping" (Moorman & Blakely, 1995), and "altruism" (Becker & Vance, 1993; Smith et al., 1983). Example items capture behaviors such as helping coworkers who have been absent, helping individuals who have heavy workloads, or helping those who encounter a work-related problem (e.g., Smith et al., 1983). Related OCB constructs that reflect behaviors that encourage interpersonal cooperation and the facilitation of work-related tasks include courtesy (Podsakoff et al., 2000), "peacekeeping," "cheerleading" (Podsakoff & MacKenzie, 1994), "interpersonal harmony" (Farh et al., 1997), and "interpersonal facilitation" (Van Scotter & Motowidlo, 1996). At the scale level, there is overlap between the various items that capture behavior such as trying to avoid creating problems or additional work for others (Organ et al., 2006), encouraging others (Podsakoff & MacKenzie, 1994), and taking a personal interest in others (Williams & Anderson, 1991).

Taken together, our synthesis of affiliative (Choi, 2007) and helping (Organ et al., 2006) OCBs is consistent with the meta-analytic findings of LePine, Erez, and Johnson (2002), who concluded that many of the existing OCB constructs (e.g., altruism, courtesy, and sportsmanship) represent a general tendency toward cooperation and help. Furthermore, the items used to assess team member proficiency by Griffin and colleagues (2007) are very similar to those used by OCB scholars. The Griffin et al. items are "provided help to coworkers when asked, or needed," "coordinated your work with coworkers," and "communicated effectively with your coworkers" (p. 337). Bachrach, Bendoly, and Podsakoff (2001) argued that "both helping behavior and civic virtue are generally described in terms of those activities or behaviors that team members can perform to make their team or organization more effective" (p. 1291). Furthermore, Morrison (1994) demonstrated 64% of surveyed clerical workers believed helping/altruistic behaviors part of their roles at the hospital. As such, in reviewing the operational definitions for each construct as well as their respective scales, we contend that the aforementioned OCB constructs represent forms of team member proficiency: The behaviors are readily anticipated to be required in interdependent work arrangements (Nielsen, Bachrach, Sundstrom, & Halfhill, 2012).

ORGANIZATION MEMBER PROFICIENCY

Organization member proficiency behaviors "reflect the degree to which an individual meets the expectations and requirements of his or her role as a member of an organization" (Griffin et al., 2007, p. 331). This category is conceptually similar to "organizational support" (Johnson, 2003), "organizational role behavior" (Welbourne et al., 1998), and "complying with organizational values, policies, and regulations" (Brief & Motowidlo, 1986). Griffin and colleagues argued organization member proficiency is also conceptually similar to "loyalty" and "civic virtue" (Podsakoff et al., 2000). For example, they observed, "In the case of a nurse, behaviors such as defending organizational reputation and participating in organizational committees would be considered organization member proficiency . . . our definition does not require these types of behaviors to be discretionary, as these contributions are often expected, particularly when work systems are highly interdependent" (p. 331). Findings support this theorizing. For example, Griffin et al. found affective organizational commitment was positively related to organization member proficiency, and Becker and Kernan (2003) found affective organizational commitment explained a significant amount of variance in loyal boosterism.

We expand this preliminary synthesis to include additional OCB constructs. There are several OCB constructs representing loyalty. Organizational loyalty represents behaviors exhibited by employees to promote a positive image of the organization to outsiders, protect and defend the organization, and refraining from voluntary turnover (Organ et al., 2006). In their synthesis of the OCB literature, Organ et al. (2006) argue "spreading goodwill" (e.g., speaking kindly of the organization; George & Jones, 1997), "loyal boosterism" (Podsakoff et al., 2014), and "promoting the company's image" (Moorman, Blakely & Niehoff, 1998) represent facets of organizational loyalty. We also include "altruism—distant" (Becker & Vance, 1993) in this category as it is an extension of spreading goodwill by assisting targets outside of one's department. While conceptually similar to helping, the target of the behavior is external to the work unit or team. We extend the synthesis by Organ et al. (2006) to suggest that the aforementioned OCBs, regardless of whether they are discretionary or not, are most often expected of employees and are often inherent when tasks are interdependent (Griffin et al., 2007). The scales that have been developed to assess organizational loyalty are very similar to the items Griffin and colleagues used to assess organization member proficiency.

Similarly there are several OCB constructs emphasizing participation in organizational affairs and governance (Graham, 1991). Constructs such as "organizational participation" (Van Dyne et al., 1994), "civic virtue" (Organ, 1988), and "organizational identification" (Farh et al., 1997) all emphasize taking interest in organizational affairs and governance, attending discretionary meetings, and keeping informed, which we see as expected behaviors when part of an organization.

Overall, our synthesis of the OCB literature suggests seven of the twelve (58%) key OCB constructs Podsakoff et al. (2014) reviewed can be categorized as affiliation-oriented OCB directed at the organization or as organizational member proficiency.

Summary

In sum, we suggest several OCBs can be conceptualized as forms of proficiency. Interestingly, our analysis of the OCB literature within the broader Griffin et al. (2007) conceptualization of proficiency yields similar results as those presented by Coleman and Borman (2000). Coleman and Borman utilized cluster analysis to identify a higher order factor structure among OCB constructs. Results of their analyses resulted in three distinct clusters. The first cluster was job/task conscientiousness, which included aspects related to exerting extra effort, dedication, and persistence. These results are consistent with our arguments that these constructs are conceptually similar and are related to an employee's specific task performance (individual task proficiency). The second cluster, interpersonal citizenship performance, included altruism and behaviors related to cooperation and facilitation. These results support our grouping of these constructs as team member proficiency. The final cluster, organizational citizenship performance, included compliance with rules, policies, and procedures, and loyalty. These empirical results are also consistent with our synthesis and classification of these OCB constructs as organizational contributions. While the authors considered a narrower set of OCB constructs than the present analyses, these results bolster the arguments presented earlier. Finally, as noted earlier, Morrison (1994) provided empirical evidence that many OCB constructs are perceived by employees as part of their jobs, further supporting their classification as forms of proficiency.

Adaptivity

Evolutions in technology, structure, and job assignments are all examples of external changes requiring adaptivity in the workplace (Chan, 2001). Griffin et al. (2007) defined adaptivity as "the degree to which individuals cope with, respond to, and/or support changes that affect their roles" (pp. 331–332), including their roles as individuals, members of a team, and members of an organization. This definition is narrower than that provided by Hesketh and Neal (1999), which included both behaviors and capacity for the behaviors, as well as Baard et al. (2014), who include cognitive, motivational, and affective elements. Consistent with the meaning of performance, we focus on adaptivity as behavior (Campbell & Wiernik, 2015).

Conceptually the definition provided by Griffin and colleagues is similar to the essential element of "dealing with uncertain and unpredictable work situations" (Johnson, 2003, p. 95) present in the Pulakos et al. (2000) model of adaptive performance and integrated within the multidimensional model presented by Johnson (2003). Several of the eight dimensions of adaptive performance identified by Pulakos et al. (2000) fit within this definition of individual task adaptivity, including "handling emergencies or crisis situations," "handling work stress," "solving problems creatively," "dealing with uncertain and unpredictable work situations," "learning work tasks, technologies, and procedures," and "demonstrating physically oriented adaptability." Additionally, several of

Bartram's (2005) competency dimensions fit in the adaptivity concept, including "coping with stress" and "maintaining emotional self-control," "dealing with ambiguity," and "learning quickly."

In our review of the OCB literature, we found both "sportsmanship" (Organ, et al 2006) and "OCB-supervisor" (Rupp & Cropanzano, 2002) to contain behaviors that fit within the definition of individual adaptivity. Specifically, Organ defined sportsmanship as "a willingness to tolerate the inevitable inconveniences and impositions of work without complaining" (1990, p. 96). This definition has since been broadened to include behaviors such as maintaining a positive attitude, "even when things do not go their way, are not offended when others do not follow their suggestions, are willing to sacrifice their personal interests for the good of the work group, and do not take the rejection of their ideas personally" (Podsakoff et al., 2000, p. 517). Podsakoff et al. (2000) reported job satisfaction, trust in leader, and organizational commitment, transformational leadership, and the articulation of a vision to be positive antecedents of sportsmanship. The findings related to vision are consistent with research conducted by Griffin et al. (2010), who found the articulation of a strong vision fostered adaptive behaviors in subordinates. Interestingly, the literature examining the consequences of sportsmanship are mixed (e.g., MacKenzie, Podsakoff, & Rich, 2001; Walz & Niehoff, 2000) or null (e.g., MacKenzie, Podsakoff, & Fetter, 1991; MacKenzie, Podsakoff, & Paine, 1999; Podsakoff et al., 2000). Given the broad definition of sportsmanship, it does not fit neatly as an individual-, team-, or organization-level contribution, although we do see it as being quite close to the concept of adaptivity.

One of the core elements of sportsmanship is the ability of an employee to simply "get on with it" regardless of changes that affect his or her individual tasks (Bachrach et al., 2001). This core element is consistent with the Pulakos et al. (2000) definition of adaptivity, as well as the Griffin et al. definition of individual member adaptivity. For example, the medical staff working in a new hospital have had to demonstrate adaptivity in coping with numerous changes in their core tasks; surgeons have had to adapt to different instrument sets, nurses to new protocols, and administrative staff to new patient workflows (Carpini, Parker, & Flemming, 2015). A "good sport" (Organ et al., 2006) would adapt to these changes without engaging in excessive amounts of complaining (Bachrach et al., 2001) and may even demonstrate leadership in getting colleagues to adapt.

While sportsmanship contains elements of individual task adaptivity, we agree with Marinova, Moon, and Van Dyne (2010) and Podsakoff et al. (2014) that the crux of sportsmanship is its interpersonal/affiliation-orientation. As a team-level contribution, sportsmanship is conceptually similar to the "demonstrating interpersonal adaptability" and "demonstrating cultural adaptability" dimensions present in the Pulakos et al. (2000) model. As a team-level contribution, research indicates sportsmanship has a positive effect on group performance when task interdependence is high, but there is no observable effect when interdependence is low (Nielsen et al., 2012). The authors propose that sportsmanship contributes to unit/team performance due to the reduction of complaining, which may result in emotional contagion, demotivation, and reduced effort.

The same arguments presented for sportsmanship as a team-level contribution can also be extended to include sportsmanship as an organization member contribution. The item "always finds fault with what the agency/company is doing" (Organ et al. 2006) includes a clear referent to the organization. Although there is scant research on sportsmanship (particularly contributing to the organization), one exception is Walz and Niehoff (2000), who found when employees demonstrated sportsmanship, the organization had significantly lower food cost and customer complaints, supporting our proposition that individual sportsmanship can function as an organization-level contribution.

The second OCB construct that we see as related to adaptivity is OCB-supervisor (OCBS). OCBS is an interpersonal construct defined as "helping behavior that benefits the supervisor" and is grounded in social exchange theory (Lemmon & Wayne, 2015, p. 129). The interpersonal/helping core of OCBS positions the construct as a team-level input (Rupp & Cropanzano, 2002). Interestingly, at the item level this construct also has an additional dimension which is not apparent in the construct definition—adapting to changing demands. Klein and Pierce (2001) defined team adaptivity as "teams that are able to make the necessary modifications in order to meet new challenges" (p. 4). Indeed, when considering the supervisor as a critical element of the team, the items assessing OCBS fit Klein and Pierce's definition of adaptivity: "helps when you [the supervisor] have a heavy workload" and "accepts added responsibility when you [the supervisor] are absent" (Rupp & Cropanzano, 2002, p. 942). OCBS is also conceptually similar to "adapting to the team" and "supporting others," which are part of the Bartram (2005) competency model. The addition of OCBS as a form of adaptivity benefiting the team contributes an additional dimension to the Pulakos et al. (2000) model. Finally, the contextual conditions under which an employee must behave adaptively has been a point of contention (Jundt, Shoss, & Huang, 2014); thus, positioning OCBS within this space contributes an additional link between contextual changes (in this case, a shift in workload demands at the supervisor level) and subordinate adaptive performance.

Proactivity

Greater uncertainty in the work environment due to macro change (e.g., global economies, evolving industry demands; Grant & Parker, 2009), meso change (e.g., flattening of organizational and team structures; Parker, 2000), and micro change (e.g., dynamic work roles; Crant, 2000) is having a profound impact on organizations and their members. To remain competitive in such a dynamic environment, organizational members must be proactive by initiating changes in anticipation of new challenges and opportunities (Crant, 2000). Proactivity scholars have argued that all types of behaviors (e.g., safety, citizenship) can be exhibited more or less proactively (Frese & Fay, 2001; Griffin et al., 2007). Proactive behavior is characterized by its agentic, self-starting, change-oriented, and future focused nature (Parker & Collins, 2010).. Examples of individual proactive work behavior constructs include taking charge (Morrison & Phelps, 1999), voice (Van Dyne & LePine, 1998), innovator role (Welbourne et al., 1998), proactive behavior (Crant, 2000), and individual/personal initiative (Frese, Kring, Soose, & Zempel, 1996; Moorman & Blakely, 1995), as well as both innovating and seeking and initiating change (Bartram, 2005). These constructs encapsulate proactive behaviors that contribute at multiple levels of the organization (individual, team, organizational) and provide general measures of individual proactive behavior at work (Tornau & Frese, 2013). For example, the innovator role includes "coming up with new ideas" and "finding improved ways to do things" (Welbourne et al., 1998, p. 554), both of which could occur in relation to one's tasks (individual task proactivity), how one's team functions (team member proactivity), or how one's organization functions (organization member proactivity). Research has found positive relationships between proactive work behavior and various outcomes, including task performance (Thompson, 2005), career progression (Seibert, Kraimer, & Crant, 2001), and job satisfaction (Thomas et al., 2010), and it is argued to be a critical ingredient for organizational success (Parker, 2000).

Van Dyne et al. (1995) proposed the classification of OCB constructs as either affiliation oriented or challenge oriented. While affiliation-oriented OCBs are concerned with maintaining the status quo (see team member proficiency), challenge-oriented OCBs are intrinsically geared toward challenging the status quo in order to yield organizationally functional outcomes (Podsakoff et al., 2014). Building on the synthesis by Podsakoff et al. (2014), who classified OCBs as either affiliative or challenge, we review OCB constructs falling within the challenge-oriented OCB category. We begin by reviewing OCB constructs that fit within the Griffin et al. framework, and then proceed to consider taking charge and voice as two constructs, sometimes considered as OCBs, that have garnered a great deal of research and span multiple levels of contribution. We also note that proactive work behavior is distinct from "change-oriented citizenship behavior" (COCB; Choi, 2007). Although the latter is defined as "proactive," the items include adaptive performance (Chiaburu et al., 2013) and, as we have previously discussed, we consider adaptive performance to be a separate performance dimension.

INDIVIDUAL TASK PROACTIVITY

Individual task proactivity refers to proactive behavior intended to change individual work situations or work roles (Griffin et al., 2007). Constructs such as constructive ideas (Katz, 1964), and task revision (Staw & Boettger, 1990) are examples of individual proactive behaviors. For example, a hospital porter can proactively negotiate more challenging tasks (task and work responsibilities i-deals) or could assist nursing staff by taking responsibility for some administrative tasks (changing scope and type of job tasks, job crafting). These behaviors are similar to what Borman and Motowidlo (1993) considered as voluntary performance of task activities.

Individual proactive work behavior is distinct from constructs such as "conscientiousness" and "personal industry" (Podsakoff et al., 2000) found in the OCB literature because these constructs reflect effort and persistence without stipulating the behavior as self-starting. Furthermore, individual task proactivity is also distinct from "pro-self" proactive behavior, which includes career initiatives such as self-training and career development (Belschak & Den Hartog, 2016).

TEAM MEMBER PROACTIVITY

Team member proactivity refers to proactive behaviors that "change a team's situation or the way the team works" (Griffin et al., 2007, p. 332). Authors including as Grant and Ashford (2008) as well as Belschak and Den Hartog (2010) have postulated the potential for proactive behavior to be directed at peers and the team. For example, Belschak and Den Hartog (2010) introduced "prosocial proactive behavior" as a construct denoting proactive behavior, including proactively helping peers and socializing a newcomer. Additionally, voice (Van Dyne & LePine, 1998) and both promotive and preventative voice (Liang et al., 2012) are measured as team-level contributions with the items using the work unit as the referent, although the behavior can conceptually apply at the organizational level as well. Sample items include "this particular co-worker develops and makes recommendations concerning issues that affect this work group" (Van Dyne & LePine, 1998, p. 112) and "raise suggestions to improve the unit's working procedure" (promotive voice; Liang et al., 2012, p. 79). Additionally, aspects of organizational participation fit within team member proactivity (e.g., "frequently makes creative suggestions to coworkers"; Van Dyne et al., 1994, p. 781). Finally, individual initiative fits well within the team member proactivity category and is defined as "communication to others in the workplace to improve individual and group performance" (Moorman, Blakely, & Niehoff, 1998, p. 353). A sample item for individual initiative is "frequently communicates to co-workers suggestions on how the group can improve" (Moorman & Blakley, 1995, p. 132). Given the target referent are coworkers and the group, these behaviors constitute forms of team member proactivity.

ORGANIZATION MEMBER PROACTIVITY

Organization member proactivity reflects proactive behavior intended to change the organization. Constructs such as principled dissent, advocacy participation (Van Dyne et al., 1994), whistle-blowing (Near & Miceli, 1985), suggesting procedural, administrative, or organizational improvements, and objecting to improper directives, procedures, or policies (Brief & Motowidlo, 1986), all of which have been argued to be subtypes of voice (Klaas, Olson-Buchanan, & Ward, 2012), are forms of organization member proactivity. Additionally, organizational participation contains elements of organization member proactivity (e.g., "keeps well informed where opinion might benefit organization"; Van Dyne et al. 1994, p. 781). Consistent with the empirical findings of Parker and Collins (2010), we consider issue selling a form of organization member proactivity. Finally, organizational identification (Farh et al., 1997) also includes a voice element in the form of making suggestions for improvement.

To our knowledge, the Griffin et al. (2007) measure of organizational member proactivity is one of the only validated measures of proactive behavior using the organization as a referent throughout (e.g., "made suggestions to improve the overall effectiveness of the organization," p. 337). The majority of the proactive behavior scales used (e.g., voice and taking charge) contain items at the organizational level but also include items at other levels of contribution, thus clouding the level of contribution. It is evident that voice and taking charge (two of the most highly researched challenge-oriented OCBs; Podsakoff et al. 2014) are difficult to differentiate by level of contribution because operational definitions and measurement tools do not explicitly consider this issue. In the next section we build on our previous review of proactive constructs in reviewing both taking charge and voice as two important proactive constructs that span multiple levels of contribution.

TAKING CHARGE

Taking charge is defined as "voluntary and constructive efforts to effect organizationally functional change with respect to how work is executed" (Parker & Collins, 2010, p. 637). Research examining taking charge has largely focused on its antecedents (e.g., Fuller, Marler, & Hester, 2012). Relatively few studies have examined the relationship between taking charge and performance; however, a meta-analysis executed by Thomas et al. (2010) found a positive correlation with overall performance across four studies.

The operational definition for taking charge does not specify levels of contributions as defined by Griffin and colleagues, although an analysis of the scale items provides insights. A couple of the items capture individual task proactivity (e.g., "this person often tries to adopt improved procedures for doing his or her job" Morrison & Phelps, 1999, p. 410) as well as team member proactivity (e.g., "This person often tries to bring about improved procedures for the work unit or department"). There are also several items with the organization as the referent (e.g., "this person often tries to change organizational rules or policies that are non-productive or counterproductive") as well as several without a referent (e.g., "This person often tries to eliminate redundant or unnecessary procedures"). Taken together, taking charge does not fit neatly within the Griffin et al. framework and instead includes proactive contributions directed toward all of the levels.

VOICE

Voice is the most highly researched challenge-oriented OCB (Podsakoff et al., 2014). Several definitions of voice exist. We adopt the integrative definition by Bashshur and Oc (2015), who operationalized voice as "the discretionary or formal expression of ideas, opinions, suggestions, or alternative approaches directed to a specific target inside or outside of the organization with the intent to change an objectionable state of affairs and to improve the current functioning of the organization, group, or individual" (p. 1531). This definition encompasses the critical "proactive" component of voice and is unique in the fact that it acknowledges the potential multilevel contribution of voice. Overall, research examining voice has demonstrated it has positive outcomes for individuals, groups, and organizations (Morrison, 2014; Thomas et al., 2010). With this said, an important caveat is that the positive outcomes associated with employee voice may become negative when voice is ignored (Hunton, Price, & Hall, 1996) or when voice exceeds its constructive capacity (MacKenzie, Podsakoff, & Podsakoff, 2011).

Within the OCB literature, there are several constructs that can be argued to be forms of voice. For example, scholars have argued that voice, grievance filing, whistle-blowing, informal complaints, issue selling, upward-feedback, and participation in suggestion systems can all be classified as types of voice (Bashshur & Oc, 2015; Klaas et al., 2012). Building on the synthesis by Podsakoff et al. (2014) and our own review of the OCB literature, we extend the integration of constructs further. We contend that constructs including creative suggestions (Katz, 1964), making constructive suggestions (George & Jones, 1997), civic virtue (referring to voice; Van Dyne & LePine, 1998), principled dissent, advocacy participation (Van Dyne et al. 1994), and organizational identification (Farh et al., 1997) all represent forms of voice, some of which are unique in their form, focus, and identifiability (Klaas et al., 2012), while others lack discernible characteristics. For example, constructs such as "making constructive suggestions" (George & Jones, 1997), "suggesting procedural, administrative, or organizational improvements" (Brief & Motowidlo, 1986), and "making creative suggestions" (Katz, 1964) are all similar constructs.

In sum, we find that the challenge-oriented OCBs identified by Podsakoff et al. (2014) can be classified as proactive behaviors, some of which fit neatly into the Griffin et al. model (e.g., individual initiative, advocacy participation) and some of which do not (e.g., voice, taking charge). Additionally, we highlight that constructs generally not considered change-oriented, including helping, organizational identification, OCB-supervisor, and individual initiative, have proactive elements.

Summary, Discussion, and Future Directions

The performance literature has largely evolved as separate streams of research (e.g., OCBs, proficiency, adaptivity, proactivity; Campbell & Wiernik, 2015), all attempting to understand individual behavior at work but doing so through different lenses. These various streams collectively provide enormous insights into the topic of performance as well as specific behaviors. Nevertheless, scholars in the different perspectives have rarely included alternative perspectives in their research, resulting in a somewhat fragmented literature (Austin & Villanova, 1992). The purpose of this chapter was to integrate the OCB literature within a broader framework of individual performance. In this section, we first summarize our approach and findings. Second, we make five recommendations for future research.

Summary of Approach and Findings

In order to achieve our goal, we briefly reviewed the history of the individual performance literature and provided overviews of five multidimensional models of individual performance. The review of the five models resulted in us selecting the Griffin et al. (2007) model as the framework for our synthesis due to its comprehensiveness as it integrates the level of contribution of each behavior reflecting degrees of interdependence (individual, team, organizational) and it also accounts for environmental uncertainty by proposing different forms of behavior (proficiency, adaptivity, proactivity).

In the second part of the chapter we systematically integrated the various performance constructs into the Griffin et al. framework, focusing especially on how OCB concepts fit within this model. We executed our synthesis lending heavily on construct definitions and the items used to assess each construct. Our synthesis and integration demonstrated that many OCB constructs can be considered as forms of individual proficiency (e.g., individual initiative, job dedication), team member proficiency (e.g., OCB-I, helping, courtesy), and organization member proficiency (e.g., OCB-O, civic virtue, loyal boosterism). Only sportsmanship fit best as an adaptive behavior and several other constructs were classified within proactivity (e.g., voice, taking charge, issue selling). Our analysis highlighted the relative dearth in adaptive performance constructs and the opportunity for both theoretical and empirical work in this area. Integrating challenge-oriented OCB constructs into the model demonstrated that taking charge and voice tend to be ambiguous in their level of contribution (individual, team, organization), whereas other more fine-grained constructs (e.g., issue selling and individual initiative) have a clearer intended target. Finally, classifying the vast majority of challenge- and change-oriented OCBs as proactive behaviors is consistent with the controversial and interpersonally risky aspect of these behaviors (Chiaburu et al., 2013; Choi, 2007; Van Dyne, Cummings, & McLean Parks, 1995).

Overall, we were mostly successful in categorizing the various OCB concepts into the overarching Griffin et al. model, suggesting this is a useful framework for considering various types of performance. Of course, the model is not perfect, and there are gaps. But our analysis helps to address one of the most important issues in the field, which is construct proliferation, or "the accumulation of ostensibly different but potentially identical constructs representing organizational phenomena" (Shaffer, DeGeest, & Li, 2016, p. 80). It is a cause for concern as it threatens theoretical parsimony and impedes the accumulation of knowledge (Le, Schmidt, Harter, & Lauver, 2010). Construct proliferation is not a new concern in the OCB space: In their meta-analysis of the OCB literature, LePine and colleagues (2002) found over 40 OCB construct measures and Podsakoff et al. (2014) included 37 OCB constructs in their review. While a breadth of constructs is necessary for mapping out a conceptual space (Whetten, 1989), such diversity can be a double-edged sword (Organ et al., 2006). We hope that our mapping on of OCB concepts into a broader literature helps to secure the benefits of having diverse concepts while also allowing for integration.

Recommendations for Future Research

In conducting our analysis, we identified a number of recommendations for future research.

First, we propose that researchers use our synthesis or others like it to situate performance constructs within a broader conceptualization of individual work performance. As we have previously noted, many of the OCB constructs fit well within the overarching Griffin et al. model, which we believe is an important contribution as it accurately captures the complexity of the performance literature while simultaneously facilitating cohesion and clarity. By situating performance constructs within a broader framework, we connect OCB constructs with the work context, something that has been a pervasive and often lamented issue in the performance literature (Austin & Villanova, 1992; Johns, 2006). The Griffin et al. model facilitates the link between performance constructs and the work context as it accounts for both the level of interdependence as well as uncertainty in distinguishing behavior.

In terms of interdependence, the advance by Williams and Anderson (1991) in recognizing different foci of OCBs is further expanded on in the present synthesis by classifying multiple OCB constructs as types of individual task proficiency. That is, while Williams and Anderson identified individuals and organizations as potential targets of OCBs, we contend many OCBs are directed at the individual's tasks. As such, we contend that the present synthesis extends previous work and recognizes several of the behaviors previously argued to be OCBs are often formalized and highly predictable in the work context. Indeed, recent surveys of employers in both the United States and Australia demonstrate the ability to work in a team structure is among the top three qualities employers seek in job applicants (Graduate Careers Australia, 2014; National Association of Colleges and Employers, 2015), suggesting cooperative behaviors are no longer viewed as "extra" but rather are essential ingredients for organizational success.

Our synthesis also revealed a growing number of agentic, change-oriented, and future-focused behaviors within the OCB literature (Parker et al. 2006; Van Dyne et al. 1995), which is an accurate reflection of the evolving work context, one that is increasingly characterized by uncertainty (Grant & Parker, 2009). While the vast majority of OCB constructs reviewed fit within the proficiency category, some recent OCB constructs appear to fit within the proactive category (e.g., voice and taking charge). By classifying OCBs within the broader performance framework and accounting for levels of uncertainty, we are able to highlight areas of convergence between the OCB and proactivity literatures, thus supporting the accumulation of knowledge.

Finally, situating OCBs within the Griffin et al. framework allows for a greater understanding of the nomological network underlying performance constructs. There have been repeated calls for scholarship aimed at fleshing out the nomological network across the performance literatures (Parker & Collins, 2010; Spitzmuller, Van Dyne, & Ilies, 2008; Thomas et al., 2010; Van Dyne et al., 1995). While our review is by no means definitive, we expect those behaviors classified together to share more commonalities than differences in terms of both their antecedents and consequences. For example, OCBs categorized as team member proficiency (e.g., helping, courtesy) should be more similar to one another than constructs classified as team member proactivity (e.g., voice). As such, we provide a framework in which future scholars can explore the relationships between constructs.

> ***Recommendation 1.*** *Scholars should leverage this synthesis to better understand the antecedents and outcomes of multiple important work behaviors, ultimately drawing the disparate performance literatures more closely together.*

The second issue we alert researchers to concerns the dimensionality of OCB. Since the introduction of OCBs in the early 1980s, research in this domain has grown tremendously and there have been several refinements to the definition of OCB (Podsakoff et al., 2000). Smith, Organ and Near (1983) first defined OCB in terms of discretionary "spontaneous charitable acts to specific others, as well as more impersonal prosocial conduct" that are outside the formal reward systems (p. 654). However, in light of increasing conceptual complexity and evolving organizational contexts, Organ (1997) advocated an updated definition of OCBs as "performance that supports the social and psychological environment in which task performance takes place" (p. 95). In essence, OCBs appear to be primarily concerned with affiliative and promotive behaviors that reinforce the psychosocial work environment (Organ, 1988; Podsakoff et al., 2014). Hence, by definition, OCBs exclude challenging and controversial behaviors. However, recent developments within the OCB literature include the introduction of challenge-oriented (Van Dyne et al., 1995) and change-oriented (Choi, 2007) OCBs. Based on our synthesis and integration, we suggest that challenge- and change-oriented behaviors might be more usefully considered as proactive work behaviors.

Challenge-oriented OCBs are defined as those behaviors that challenge the status quo (Van Dyne et al., 1995). Although voice has been the most highly researched construct within the challenge-oriented OCB category, other constructs including taking charge and issue selling are included (Podsakoff et al., 2014). Similarly, change-oriented OCBs are defined as "proactive actions aimed at identifying and implementing changes in work processes, products, and services" (Chiaburu et al., 2013, p. 292). The authors argue voice, adaptive performance, personal initiative, and taking charge are all forms of change-oriented OCBs. As one can see, there is a great deal of conceptual overlap between challenge- and change-oriented OCBs and little, if any, existing evidence to support the distinction between these constructs. Perhaps the only discernible difference between change- and challenge-oriented OCBs is that the former includes adaptive performance while the latter is very similar to the proactivity literature (Crant, 2000; Grant & Ashford, 2008).

In meta-analyses conducted by Chiaburu, Oh, Berry, Li, and Gardner (2011) and Chiaburu et al. (2013), the authors contend that the expansion of the OCB construct to include change-oriented OCBs addresses a dearth in the literature related to "good-change-agent employee behaviors" (Chiaburu et al., 2013, p. 1141). However, there are two pertinent issues: First, the authors include adaptive performance behaviors along with proactive behaviors in their measurement of change-oriented OCBs, which we and others have argued are distinct performance dimensions (Griffin et al., 2007; Pulakos et al., 2000). Second, and related, not all change is equal such that there is a fundamental difference between adapting to a change in the environment (adaptivity; Baard et al., 2014) and instigating the change oneself (proactive behavior; Parker et al., 2006). Van Dyne et al. (1995) advocated for OCB scholars to discard challenge-oriented OCBs as these behaviors did not conform to the operational definition of OCB as affiliative and nonchallenging. We concur with Van Dyne and colleagues' call and suggest that challenge-oriented OCBs and change-oriented OCBs might more usefully be considered as proactive behaviors and—for some of the constructs—adaptive behaviors. Thus:

Recommendation 2. Challenge- and change-oriented OCB dimensions can be usefully considered as examples of proactive performance (and to some extent adaptive performance), and it will be helpful to situate these dimensions within these performance literatures.

The third issue that became apparent in executing our synthesis is that of *chameleon items*—the same or highly similar items that shift between different constructs, even though the constructs are intended to be discrete from one another. For example, conscientiousness, personal industry, and job dedication all contain highly similar items. The three scales contain multiple items related to low error rates and high quality outputs as well as items capturing punctuality, and a general willingness to take on difficult work assignments. A similar pattern is found when comparing the items used to assess personal initiative (Moorman et al., 1998) and voice (Van Dyne & LePine, 1998). Where constructs are operationalized differently but simultaneously draw on a similar pool of items, one must be cautious of the "jangle fallacy" (Kelley, 1927), which occurs when two ostensibly distinct psychological constructs appear different by virtue of their names but in essence represent the same basic phenomena. As such, we extend the recommendations of Shaffer et al. (2016) to include the need for researchers to examine scale items as part of their literature search and their assessment of construct discriminate validity. We recommend:

Recommendation 3. In establishing new measures of performance constructs, scholars should examine item similarity with existing measures to ensure the content is sufficiently different from existing measures.

While construct proliferation requires attention, we also believe the performance literature requires expansion and refinement in certain areas. One major benefit of integrating the existing OCB literature into the Griffin et al. model is the ability to discern the type of behavior based on the level of uncertainty as well as the level of contribution (see Table 3.2 for review). As described previously, several constructs (e.g., helping and organizational identification) fit in multiple performance categories (proficiency, adaptivity, proactivity), and several concepts (e.g., voice, taking charge, sportsmanship) are ambiguous in regard to their target contribution (individual, team, organization). Although we do not contend that all constructs must neatly fit within a single cell of the Griffin et al. model, we do see an opportunity for additional theoretical and empirical work. For example, we would suggest scholars consider adaptive forms of sportsmanship at the individual, team, and organizational member levels. This may include reactive items such as "maintained a positive attitude despite changes in your core tasks" (individual member adaptivity), "even when your ideas were not actioned, you respected decisions made by the group" (team member adaptivity), and "responded constructively to organizational changes" (organizational member adaptivity; items modified from Organ et al., 2006 and Griffin et al., 2007).

Additionally, several scholars have argued all behaviors can be performed more or less proactively (Crant, 2000; Parker & Collins, 2010), including OCBs. For example, helping is one of the most highly researched OCB constructs (Podsakoff et al., 2014) and offers significant theoretical opportunity. Much of the existing research positions helping as a form of team member proficiency; however, we would argue it can be executed in both a proficient and proactive manner. Proficient helping may include items such as "assists coworkers after they have been absent" (modified from Rupp & Cropanzano, 2002). On the other hand, proactive helping, operationalized as offering help to others before they need to ask for it through organizationally functional change (adapted from Frese & Fay, 2001), might include items such as "this person adopts improved procedures to alleviate work for others" (adopted from Morrison & Phelps, 1999) or "offer team members help when it might be needed."

The responsible expansion of performance constructs, which includes clear concept definitions (Podsakoff, MacKenzie, & Podsakoff, 2016), will answer calls for additional research devoted to explaining and understanding individual performance (Campbell & Wiernik, 2015). As such, we recommend:

Recommendation 4. Scholars should consider expanding constructs to fill relevant gaps in the individual performance literature.

The fifth issue that became apparent is antithetical items (or reverse-scored items; Dalal, 2005). The use of items assessing OCB constructs through reverse scoring results in what might now be considered counterproductive work behaviors (CWBs). There are several OCB constructs that are assessed using antithetical items such as conscientiousness (e.g., "took undeserved breaks"; Podsakoff et al., 1990), sportsmanship (e.g., "consumes a lot of time complaining about trivial matters"; Organ, 1988), organizational loyalty and obedience (e.g., "sometimes misses work for no good reason"; Van Dyne et al., 1994), and organizational participation (e.g., "difficulty coopering with others on projects"; Graham, 1991). When antithetical items are used for construct measurement, the distinctions between OCBs and CWBs begins to blur, causing conceptual issues. Spector, Bauer, and Fox (2010) demonstrated that the use of antithetical items in assessing OCBs was problematic as it inflated the observed relationship between OCBs and CWBs. Additionally, antithetical items are also problematic as they are inconsistent with the operational definition of individual performance advanced by Campbell et al. (1993). Given the majority of the antithetical items are about refraining from certain behavior and therefore are, in fact, the lack of the target behavior, these items might not accurately represent the performance construct.

One example is that of sportsmanship (Organ, 1990). The original definition of sportsmanship was dominated by antithetical statements that focused on what an employee does *not* do as opposed to what an employee does, "avoid complaining, petty grievances, railing against real or imagined slights, and making federal cases out of small potatoes" (Organ, 1988, p. 11). Even recent redefinitions of the construct (e.g., Organ et al., 2006) still rely on antithetical statements such as "not [being] offended when others do not follow their suggestions" (p. 308). Hence, while we consider the core idea of sportsmanship as an adaptive behavior, this construct requires more conceptual work. This might also explain why sportsmanship is the least researched OCB construct (Podsakoff et al., 2000). Scholars studying sportsmanship should attempt to define and measure the construct in terms of observable behavior, consistent with the essence of individual performance which is behavior itself—"performance means to do and act" (Frese & Fay, 2001, p. 173). Thus:

> ***Recommendation 5.*** *Scholars should reduce the use of antithetical items in studying individual performance as it may impact the observed relationships between variables. Constructs should be defined in terms of behavior, not the lack thereof.*

Conclusion

In sum, Swales (1986, p. 85) argued, "In the history of science and scholarship, we find numerous examples of related research streams that advance without awareness of one another." While the performance literature is no exception to Swales' observation, we hope that our analysis and recommendations will help to address this issue in the performance literature and ultimately contribute to a more coherent body of knowledge.

Acknowledgments

This research is supported by a doctoral fellowship from the Social Sciences and Research Council of Canada (752-2013-1861) to the first author and by an Australian Research Council grant to the second author. The ideas presented are those of the authors and are not necessarily endorsed by the funding agencies. Portions of this chapter were presented at the 31st Annual Conference of the Society for Industrial and Organizational Psychology (SIOP), Anaheim, CA.

References

Austin, J. T., & Villanova, P. (1992). The criterion problem: 1917–1992. *Journal of Applied Psychology, 77*(6), 836–874.

Baard, S. K., Rench, T. A., & Kozlowski, S. W. J. (2014). Performance adaptation: A theoretical integration and review. *Journal of Management, 40*(1), 48–99. doi:10.1177/0149206313488210

Bachrach, D. G., Bendoly, E., & Podsakoff, P. M. (2001). Attributions of the "causes" of group performance as an alternative explanation of the relationship between organizational citizenship behavior and organizational performance. *Journal of Applied Psychology, 86*(6), 1285–1293. doi:10.1037//0021-9010.86.6.1285

Bachrach, D. G., Powell, B. C., Bendoly, E., & Richey, R. G. (2006). Organizational citizenship behavior and performance evaluations: Exploring the impact of task interdependence. *The Journal of Applied Psychology, 91*(1), 193–201. doi:10.1037/0021-9010.91.1.193

Bailey, C. T. (1983). *The measurement of job performance.* Aldershot, England: Gower Press.

Barrick, M. R., & Mount, M. K. (1991). The Big Five personality dimensions and job performance: A meta-analysis. *Personnel Psychology, 44*(1), 1–26. doi:10.1111/j.1744-6570.1991.tb00688.x

Barrick, M. R., Parks, L., & Mount, M. K. (2005). Self-monitoring as a moderator of the relationships between personality traits and performance. *Personnel Psychology, 58*(3), 745–767.

Bartram, D. (2005). The Great Eight competencies: A criterion-centric approach to validation. *The Journal of Applied Psychology, 90*(6), 1185–1203. doi:10.1037/0021-9010.90.6.1185

Bashshur, M. R., & Oc, B. (2015). When voice matters: A multilevel review of the impact of voice in organizations. *Journal of Management, 41*(5), 1530–1554. doi:10.1177/0149206314558302

Bateman, T. S., & Organ, D. W. (1983). Job satisfaction and the good soldier: The relationship between affect and employee "citizenship." *Academy of Management Journal, 26*(4), 587–595. Retrieved from www.jstor.org/stable/255908

Bauer, T. N., Erdogan, B., Liden, R. C., & Wayne, S. J. (2006). A longitudinal study of the moderating role of extraversion: Leader-member exchange, performance, and turnover during new executive development. *Journal of Applied Psychology, 91*(2), 298–310. doi: 10.1037/0021-9010.91.2.298

Becker, T. E., & Kernan, M. C. (2003). Matching commitment to supervisors and organizations to in-role and extra-role performance matching commitment to supervisors and organizations to in-role and extra-role performance. *Human Performance, 16*(4), 327–348. doi:10.1207/S15327043HUP1604_1

Becker, T. E., & Vance, R. J. (1993). Construct validity of three types of organizational citizenship behavior: An illustration of the direct product model with refinements. *Journal of Management, 19*(3), 663–682.

Belschak, F. D., & Den Hartog, D. N. (2010). Pro-self, pro-social, and pro-organizational foci of proactive behaviour: Differential antecedents and consequences. *Journal of Occupational and Organizational Psychology, 83*(2), 475–498. doi:10.1348/096317909X439208

Belschak, F. D., & Den Hartog, D. N. (2016). Foci of proactivity. In S. K. Parker & U. K. Bindl (Eds.), *Proactivity at work: Making things happen in organizations* (*Organization and Management Series*). Melbourne, Australia: Routledge, Taylor & Francis Group.

Berg, J. M., Wrzesniewski, A. M. Y., & Dutton, J. E. (2010). Perceiving and responding to challenges in job crafting at different ranks: When proactivity requires adaptivity. *Journal of Organizational Behavior, 31*(2–3), 158–186. doi:10.1002/job.645

Borman, W. C., Buck, D. E., Handson, M. A., Motowidlo, S. J., Stark, S., & Drasgow, F. (2001). An examination of the comparative reliability, validity, and accuracy of performance ratings made using computerized adaptive rating scales. *Journal of Applied Psychology, 86*(5), 965–973. doi:10.1037//0021-9010.86.5.965

Borman, W. C., & Motowidlo, S. J. (1993). Expanding the criterion domain to include elements of contextual performance. In N. Schmitt & W. C. Borman (Eds.), *Personnel selection in organizations* (pp. 71–97). San Francisco, CA: Jossey-Bass Publishers.

Borman, W. C., & Motowidlo, S. J. (1997). Task performance and contextual performance: The meaning for personnel selection research. *Human Performance, 10*(2), 99–109.

Borman, W. C., Penner, L. A., Allen, T. D., & Motowidlo, S. J. (2001). Personality predictors of citizenship performance. *International Journal of Selection and Assessment, 9*(1/2), 52–69.

Brief, A. P., & Motowidlo, S. J. (1986). Prosocial organizational behavior. *Academy of Management Journal, 11*(4), 710–725. Retrieved from www.jstor.org/stable/258391

Campbell, J. P. (2012). Behavior, performance, and effectiveness in the twenty-first century. In S. Kozlowski (Ed.), *The Oxford handbook of organizational psychology* (pp. 159–196). New York, NY: Oxford University Press.

Campbell, C. H., Ford, P., Rumsey, M. G., Pulakos, E. D., Borman, W. C., Felker, D. B., . . . Riegelhaupt, B. J. (1990). Development of multiple job performance measures in a representative sample of jobs. *Personnel Psychology, 43*(2), 277–300.

Campbell, J. P., McCloy, R. A., Oppler, S. H., & Sager, C. E. (1993). A theory of performance. In N. Schmitt & W. C. Borman (Eds.), *Personnel selection in organizations* (pp. 35–69). San Francisco, CA: Jossey-Bass.

Campbell, J. P., & Wiernik, B. M. (2015). The modeling and assessment of work performance. *Annual Review of Organizational Psychology and Organizational Behavior, 2*(1), 47–74. doi:10.1146/annurev-orgpsych-032414-111427

Carpenter, N. C., Berry, C. M., & Houston, L. (2014). A meta-analytic comparison of self-reported and other-reported organizational citizenship behavior. *Journal of Organizational Behavior, 35*(4), 547–574. doi:10.1002/job.1909

Carpini, J. A., Parker, S. K., & Flemming, A. S. F. (2015). Communication in the operating theatre: Working smarter across professional boundaries. In *Royal Australasian College of Surgeons Tri-State (NT, WA, SA) Annual Scientific Meeting*. Darwin, Northern Territory, Australia.

Carpini, J. A., Parker, S. K., & Griffin, M. A. (2017). A look back and a leap forward: A review and synthesis of the individual work performance literature. *Academy of Management Annals, 11*(2), 20.

Catano, V. M., Darr, W., & Campbell, C. A. (2007). Performance appraisal of behavior-based competencies: A reliable and valid procedure. *Personnel Psychology, 60*(1), 201–230.

Chan, D. (2001). Understanding adaptation to changes in the work environment: Integrating individual difference and learning perspectives. In G. R. Ferris (Ed.), *Research in personnel and human resources management* (pp. 1–42). Greenwich, CN: JAI Press INC. Retrieved from http://ink.library.smu.edu.sg/soss_research/216/

Chen, G., Kirkman, B. L., Kanfer, R., Allen, D., & Rosen, B. (2007). A multilevel study of leadership, empowerment, and performance in teams. *The Journal of Applied Psychology, 92*(2), 331–346. doi:10.1037/0021-9010.92.2.331

Chen, G., & Klimoski, R. J. (2003). The impact of expectations on newcomer performance in teams as mediated by work characteristics, social exchanges, and empowerment. *The Academy of Management Journal, 46*(5), 591–607. doi: 10.2307/30040651

Chiaburu, D. S., & Baker, V. L. (2006). Extra-role behaviors challenging the status-quo: Validity and antecedents of taking charge behaviors. *Journal of Managerial Psychology, 21*(7), 620–637. doi:10.1108/02683940610690178

Chiaburu, D. S., Lorinkova, N. M., & Van Dyne, L. (2013). Employees' social context and change-oriented citizenship: A meta-analysis of leader, coworker, and organizational influences. *Group & Organization Management, 38*(3), 291–333. doi:10.1177/1059601113476736

Chiaburu, D. S., Oh, I.-S., Berry, C. M., Li, N., & Gardner, R. G. (2011). The five-factor model of personality traits and organizational citizenship behaviors: A meta-analysis. *The Journal of Applied Psychology, 96*(6), 1140–1166. doi:10.1037/a0024004

Choi, J. N. (2007). Change-oriented organizational citizenship behavior: Effects of work environment characteristics and intervening psychological processes. *Journal of Organizational Behavior, 28*(4), 467–484. doi:10.1002/job.433

Christian, M. S., Garza, A. S., & Slaughter Jerel. E. (2011). Work engagement: A quantitative review and test of its relations with task and contextual performance. *Personnel Psychology, 64*(1), 89–136. doi:10.1111/j.1744-6570.2010.01203.x

Coleman, V. I., & Borman, W. C. (2000). Investigating the underlying structure of the citizenship performance domain. *Human Resource Management Review, 10*(1), 25–44.

Conway, J. M. (1999). Distinguishing contextual performance from task performance for managerial jobs. *Journal of Applied Psychology, 84*(1), 3–13.

Crant, J. M. (2000). Proactive behavior in organizations. *Journal of Management, 26*(3), 435–462. doi:10.1177/014920630002600304

Dalal, R. S. (2005). A meta-analysis of the relationship between organizational citizenship behavior and counterproductive work behavior. *The Journal of Applied Psychology, 90*(6), 1241–1255. doi:10.1037/0021-9010.90.6.1241

Farh, J.-L., Earley, C., & Lin, S.-C. (1997). Impetus for Action: A cultural analysis of justice and organizational citizenship behavior in Chinese society. *Administrative Science Quarterly, 42*(3), 421–444. doi:10.2307/2393733

Frese, M., & Fay, D. (2001). Personal initiative: An active performance concept for work in the 21st century. *Research in Organizational Behavior, 23*, 133–187. doi:10.1016/S0191-3085(01)23005-6

Frese, M., Kring, W., Soose, A., & Zempel, J. (1996). Personal initiative at work: Differences between East and West Germany. *Academy of Management Journal, 39*(1), 37–63.

Fuller, J. B., Marler, L. E., & Hester, K. (2012). Bridge building within the province of proactivity. *Journal of Organizational Behavior, 33*(8), 1053–1070. doi:10.1002/job

George, J. M., & Jones, G. R. (1997). Organizational spontaneity in context. *Human Performance, 10*(2), 153–170. doi:10.1207/s15327043hup1002

Graduate Careers Australia Ltd. (2014). *2014 Employers' Perspectives on Graduate Recruitment in Australia.* (2014). Melbourne, VIC, Australia.

Graham, J. W. (1991). An essay on organizational citizenship gehavior. *Employee Responsibilities and Rights Journal, 4*(4), 249–270.

Grant, A. M., & Ashford, S. J. (2008). The dynamics of proactivity at work. *Research in Organizational Behavior, 28*, 3–34. doi:10.1016/j.riob.2008.04.002

Grant, A. M., & Parker, S. K. (2009). Redesigning work design theories: The rise of relational and proactive perspectives. *The Academy of Management Annals, 3*(1), 317–375. doi:10.1080/19416520903047327

Griffin, M. A., Neal, A., & Parker, S. K. (2007). A new model of work role performance: Positive behavior in uncertain and interdependent contexts. *Academy of Management Journal, 50*(2), 327–347. doi:10.5465/AMJ.2007.24634438

Griffin, M. A, Parker, S. K., & Mason, C. M. (2010). Leader vision and the development of adaptive and proactive performance: A longitudinal study. *The Journal of Applied Psychology, 95*(1), 174–182. doi:10.1037/a0017263

Henderschott, F. C. (1917). Psychology and business. *Journal of Applied Psychology, 1*(3), 214–219.

Hesketh, B., & Neal, A. (1999). Technology and performance. In D. R. Ilgen & E. D. Pulakos (Eds.), *The changing nature of performance: Implications for staffing, motivation, and development* (pp. 21–55). Brisbane: Wiley. Retrieved from https://books.google.com.au/books/about/The_Changing_Nature_of_Performance.html?id=P3NhQgAACAAJ&redir_esc=y

Hoffman, B. J., Blair, C. A., Meriac, J. P., & Woehr, D. J. (2007). Expanding the criterion domain? A quantitative review of the OCB literature. *The Journal of Applied Psychology, 92*(2), 555–66. doi:10.1037/0021-9010.92.2.555

Hunton, J. E., Price, K. H., & Hall, T. W. (1996). A field experiment examining the effects of membership in voting majority and minority subgroups and the ameliorating effects of postdecisional voice. *Journal of Applied Psychology, 81*(6), 806–812.

National Association of Colleges and Employers (2015). *Job Outlook 2015.* Bethlehem, PA: National Association of Colleges and Employers. Retried from: www.naceweb.org.

Johns, G. (2006). The essential impact of context on organizational behavior. *Academy of Management Review, 31*(2), 386–408. doi:10.2307/20159208

Johnson, J. (2003). Toward a better understanding of the relationship between personality and individual job performance. In M. R. Barrick & R. A. Mount. (Eds.), *Personality and work: Reconsidering the role of personality in organizations* (pp. 83–120). San Francisco, CA: Jossey-Bass.

Jundt, D. K., Shoss, M. K., & Huang, J. L. (2014). Individual adaptive performance in organizations: A review. *Journal of Organizational Behavior, 36*(S1), S53–S71. doi:10.1002/job

Katz, D. (1964). The motivational basis of organizational behavior. *Behavioral Science, 9*(2), 131–146.

Kelley, E. L. (1927). *Interpretation of educational measurements.* Yonkers, NY: World.

Klaas, B. S., Olson-Buchanan, J. B., & Ward, A.-K. (2012). The determinants of alternative forms of workplace voice: An integrative perspective. *Journal of Management, 38*(1), 314–345. doi:10.1177/0149206311423823

Klein, G., & Pierce, L. (2001). *Adaptive teams.* Fairborn, OH: Klien Associates Inc. Retrieved from http://oai.dtic.mil/oai/oai?verb=getRecord&metadataPrefix=html&identifier=ADA467743

Le, H., Schmidt, F. L., Harter, J. K., & Lauver, K. J. (2010). The problem of empirical redundancy of constructs in organizational research: An empirical investigation. *Organizational Behavior and Human Decision Processes, 112*(2), 112–125. doi:10.1016/j.obhdp.2010.02.003

Lemmon, G., & Wayne, S. J. (2015). Underlying motives of organizational citizenship behavior: Comparing egoistic and altruistic motivations. *Journal of Leadership & Organizational Studies, 22*(2), 129–148. doi:10.1177/1548051814535638

LePine, J. a., Erez, A., & Johnson, D. E. (2002). The nature and dimensionality of organizational citizenship behavior: A critical review and meta-analysis. *Journal of Applied Psychology, 87*(1), 52–65. doi:10.1037//0021-9010.87.1.52

Leroy, H., Anseel, F., Gardner, W. L., & Sels, L. (2012). Authentic leadership, authentic followership, basic need satisfaction, and work role performance: A cross-level study. *Journal of Management, 41*(6), 1677–1697. doi:10.1177/0149206312457822

Liang, J., Farh, C. I. C., & Farh, J.-L. (2012). Psychological antecedents of promotive and prohibitive voice: A two-wave examination. *Academy of Management Journal, 55*(1), 71–92.

Lievens, F., Sanchez, J. I., Bartram, D., & Brown, A. (2010). Lack of consensus among competency ratings of the same occupation: Noise or substance? *The Journal of Applied Psychology, 95*(3), 562–71. doi:10.1037/a0018035

MacKenzie, S.B., Podsakoff, P.M. & Fetter, R. (1991). Organizational citizenship behavior and objective productivity as determinants of managerial evaluations of salespersons' performance. *Organizational Behavior and Human Decision Processes, 50*(1), 123–150.

MacKenzie, S. B., Podsakoff, P. M., & Paine, J. B. (1999). Do citizenship behaviors matter more for managers than for salespeople? *Journal of the Academy of Marketing Science, 27*(4), 396–410.

MacKenzie, S.B., Podsakoff, P. M., & Podsakoff, N. P. (2011). Challenge-oriented organizational citizenship behaviors and organizational effectiveness: Do challenge-oriented behaviors really have an impact on the organization's bottom line? *Personnel Psychology, 64*(3), 559–592.

MacKenzie, S. B., Podsakoff, P. M., & Rich, G. A. (2001). Transformational and transactional leadership and salesperson performance. *Journal of the Academy of Marketing Science, 29*(2), 115–134.

Mansfield, R. S. (2005). *Practical questions in building competency models.* Fort Lauderdale: Workitect Inc. Retrieved from www.workitect.com

Marinova, S. V., Moon, H., & Van Dyne, L. (2010). Are all good soldier behaviors the same? Supporting multidimensionality of organizational citizenship behaviors based on rewards and roles. *Human Relations, 63*(10), 1463–1485. doi:10.1177/0018726709359432

Marks, M. A., Mathieu, J. E., & Zaccaro, S. J. (2001). A temporally based framework and taxonomy of team processes. *Academy of Management Review, 26*(3), 365–376. doi: 10.5465/AMR.2001.4845785

Moorman, R. H., & Blakely, G. L. (1995). Individualism-Collectivism as an individual difference predictor of organizational citizenship behavior. *Journal of Organizational Behavior, 16*(2), 127–142. Retrieved from www.jstor.org/stable/3004081

Moorman, R. H., Blakely, G. L., & Niehoff, B. P. (1998). Does perceived organizational support mediate the relationship between procedural justice and organizational citizenship behavior? *Academy of Management Journal, 41*(3), 351–357. Retrieved from www.jstor.org/stable/256913

Morrison, E. W. (1994). Role definitions and organizational citizenship behavior: The importance of the employee's perspective. *Academy of Management Journal, 37*(6), 1543–1567. doi:10.2307/256798

Morrison, E. W. (2014). Employee voice and silence. *Annual Review of Organizational Psychology and Organizational Behavior, 1*(1), 173–197. doi:10.1146/annurev- orgpsych-031413-091328

Morrison, E. W., & Phelps, C. C. (1999). Taking charge at work: Extrarole efforts to initiate workplace change. *Academy of Management Journal, 42*(4), 403–419. Retrieved from www.jstor.org/stable/257011

Motowidlo, S. J., & Scotter, J. R. Van. (1994). Evidence that task performance should be distinguished from contextual performance. *Journal of Applied Psychology, 79*(4), 475–480.

Murphy, P. R., & Jackson, S. E. (1999). Managing work role performance: Challenges for twenty-first century organizations and their employees. In D. R. Ilgen & E. D. Pulakos (Eds.), *The changing nature of performance: Implications for staffing, motivation, and development* (pp. 325–365). San Francisco, CA: Jossey-Bass.

Neal, A., Yeo, G., Koy, A., & Xiao, T. (2011). Predicting the form and direction of work role performance from the Big 5 model of personality traits. *Journal of Organizational Behavior, 33*(2), 175–192. doi:10.1002/job.742

Near, J. P., & Miceli, M. P. (1985). Organizational dissidence: The case of whistle-blowing. *Journal of Business Ethics, 4*(1), 1–16.

Nielsen, T. M., Bachrach, D. G., Sundstrom, E., & Halfhill, T. R. (2012). Utility of OCB: Organizational citizenship behavior and group performance in a resource allocation framework. *Journal of Management, 38*(2), 668–694. doi:10.1177/0149206309356326

Organ, D. W. (1988). *Organizational citizenship behavior: The good soldier syndrome.* Lexington, MA: Lexington Books.

Organ, D. W. (1997). Organizational citizenship behavior: It's construct clean-up time. *Human Performance, 10*(2), 85–97.

Organ, D. W., Podsakoff, P. M., & Podsakoff, N. P. (2006). *Organizational citizenship behavior: Its nature, antecedents, and consequences* (pp. 243–317). SAGE Publications.

Parker, S. K. (2000). From passive to proactive motivation: The importance of flexible role orientations and role breadth self-efficacy. *Applied Psychology: An International Review, 49*(3), 447–469.

Parker, S. K., & Collins, C. G. (2010). Taking stock: Integrating and differentiating multiple proactive behaviors. *Journal of Management, 36*(3), 633–662. doi:10.1177/0149206308321554

Parker, S. K., Williams, H. M., & Turner, N. (2006). Modeling the antecedents of proactive behavior at work. *The Journal of Applied Psychology, 91*(3), 636–52. doi:10.1037/0021-9010.91.3.636

Podsakoff, P. M., & MacKenzie, S. B. (1994). Organizational citizenship behaviors and sale unit effectiveness. *Journal of Marketing Research, 31*(3), 351–363.

Podsakoff, P. M., & MacKenzie, S. B. (1997). Impact of organizational citizenship behavior on organizational performance: A review and suggestion for future research impact of organizational citizenship behavior on organizational performance: A review and suggestions for future research. *Human Performance, 10*(2), 133–151. doi:10.1207/s15327043hup1002_5

Podsakoff, P. M., MacKenzie, S. B., Moorman, R. H., & Fetter, R. (1990). Transformational leader behaviors and their effects on followers' trust in leader, satisfaction, and organizational citizenship behaviors. *The Leadership Quarterly, 1*(2), 107–142. doi:10.1016/1048-9843(90)90009-7

Podsakoff, P. M., MacKenzie, S. B., Paine, J. B., & Bachrach, D. G. (2000). Organizational citizenship behaviors: A critical review of the theoretical and empirical literature and suggestions for future research. *Journal of Management, 26*(3), 513–563. doi:10.1177/014920630002600307

Podsakoff, P. M., MacKenzie, S. B., & Podsakoff, N. P. (2016). Recommendations for creating better concept definitions in the organizational, behavioral, and social sciences. *Organizational Research Methods, 19*(2), 159–203. doi: 10.1177/1094428115624965

Podsakoff, N. P., Podsakoff, P. M., MacKenzie, S. B., Maynes, T. D., & Spoelma, T. M. (2014). Consequences of unit-level organizational citizenship behaviors: A review and recommendations for future research. *Journal of Organizational Behavior, 119*(S1), 87–119. doi:10.1002/job.1911

Podsakoff, N. P., Whiting, S. W., Podsakoff, P. M., & Blume, B. D. (2009). Individual- and organizational-level consequences of organizational citizenship behaviors: A meta-analysis. *The Journal of Applied Psychology, 94*(1), 122–141. doi:10.1037/a0013079

Pulakos, E. D., Arad, S., Donovan, M. A., & Plamondon, K. E. (2000). Adaptability in the workplace: Development of a taxonomy of adaptive performance. *Journal of Applied Psychology, 83*(4), 612–624. doi:10.103///0021-9010.85.4.612

Pulakos, E. D., Schmitt, N., Dorsey, D. W., Arad, S., Hedge, J. W., & Borman, W. C. (2002). Predicting adaptive performance: Further tests of a model of adaptability. *Human Performance, 15*(4), 299–323.

Rupp, D. E., & Cropanzano, R. (2002). The mediating effects of social exchange relationships in predicting workplace outcomes from multifoci organizational justice. *Organizational Behavior and Human Decision Processes, 89*(1), 925–946.

Sackett, P. R. (2002). The structure of counterproductive work behaviors: Dimensionality and relationships with facets of job performance 1. *International Journal of Selection and Assessment, 10*(1/2), 5–11.

Schmitt, N., & Chan, D. (2014). Adapting to rapid changes. In D. Chan (Ed.), *Individual adaptability to changes at work: New directions in research* (*Organization and Management Series*; pp. 3–17). Florence, SC: Taylor and Francis.

Seibert, S. E., Kraimer, M. L., & Crant, J. M. (2001). What do proactive people do? A longitudinal model linking proactive personality and career success. *Personnel Psychology, 54*(4), 845–874.

Shaffer, J. A., DeGeest, D., & Li, A. (2016). Tackling the problem of construct proliferation: A guide to assessing the discriminant validity of conceptually related constructs. *Organizational Research Methods, 19*(1), 80–110. doi:10.1177/1094428115598239

Smith, C. A., Organ, D. W., & Near, J. P. (1983). Organizational citizenship behavior : Its nature and antecedents. *Journal of Applied Psychology, 68*(4), 653–663.

Spector, P. E., Bauer, J. a, & Fox, S. (2010). Measurement artifacts in the assessment of counterproductive work behavior and organizational citizenship behavior: Do we know what we think we know? *The Journal of Applied Psychology, 95*(4), 781–90. doi:10.1037/a0019477

Spitzmuller, M., Van Dyne, L., & Ilies, R. (2008). Organizational citizenship behavior: A review and extension of its nomological network. In *The SAGE handbook of organizational behavior* (*volume 1—Micro approaches*) (pp. 106–123). New York, NY: SAGE Publications.

Staw, B. M., & Boettger, R. D. (1990). Task revision: A neglected form of work performance. *Academy of Management Journal, 33*(3), 534–559.

Strauss, K., Griffin, M. A., & Rafferty, A. E. (2009). Proactivity directed toward the team and organization: The role of leadership, commitment and role-breadth self-efficacy. *British Journal of Management, 20*(3), 279–291. doi:10.1111/j.1467-8551.2008.00590.x

Swales, J. (1986). Citation analysis and discourse analysis. *Applied Linguistics, 7*(1), 41–56.

Thomas, J. P., Whitman, D. S., & Viswesvaran, C. (2010). Employee proactivity in organizations: A comparative meta-analysis of emergent proactive constructs. *Journal of Occupational and Organizational Psychology, 83*(2), 275–300. doi:10.1348/096317910XS02359

Thompson, J. A. (2005). Proactive personality and job performance: A social capital perspective. *The Journal of Applied Psychology, 90*(5), 1011–1017. doi:10.1037/0021-9010.90.5.1011

Tornau, K., & Frese, M. (2013). Construct clean-up in proactivity research: A meta-analysis on the nomological net of work-related proactivity concepts and their incremental validities. *Applied Psychology, 62*(1), 44–96. doi:10.1111/j.1464-0597.2012.00514.x

Van der Vegt, G. S., & Van de Vliert, E. (2005). Effects of perceived skill dissimilarity and task interdependence on helping in work teams. *Journal of Management, 31*(1), 73–89. doi:10.1177/0149206304271382

Van der Vegt, G. S., Van de Vliert, E., & Oosterhof, A. (2003). Informational dissimilarity and organizational citizenship behavior: The role of intrateam interdependence and team identification. *Academy of Management Journal, 46*(6), 715–727. Retrieved from www.jstor.org/stable/30040663

Van Dyne, L., Cummings, L. L., & McLean Parks, J. (1995). Extra-role behaviors: In pursuit of construct and definitional clarity (A bridge over muddied waters). In L. L. Cummings & B. M. Staw (Eds.), *Research in organizational behavior: An annual series of analytical essays and critical reviews* (pp. 215–285). Greenwich, CT: JAI Press Inc.

Van Dyne, L., & LePine, J. A. (1998). Helping and voice extra-role behaviors: Evidence of construct and predictive validity. *Academy of Management Journal, 41*(1), 108–119.

Van Dyne, L., Graham, J. W., & Dienesch, R. M. (1994). Organizational citizenship behavior: Construct redefinition, measurement, and validation. *Academy of Management Journal, 37*(4), 765–802.

Van Scotter, J. R., & Motowidlo, S. J. (1996). Interpersonal facilitation and job dedication as separate facets of contextual performance. *Journal of Applied Psychology, 81*(5), 525–531.

Venkatraman, N., & Ramanujam, V. (1986). Measurement of business performance in strategy research: A comparison of approaches. *Academy of Management, 11*(4), 801–814.

Viswesvaran, C., & Ones, D. S. (2000). Perspectives on models of job performance. *International Journal of Selection and Assessment, 8*(4), 216–226.

Wallace, J. C., Edwards, B. D., Arnold, T., Frazier, M. L., & Finch, D. M. (2009). Work stressors, role-based performance, and the moderating influence of organizational support. *The Journal of Applied Psychology, 94*(1), 254–262. doi:10.1037/a0013090

Walz, S. M., & Niehoff, B. P. (2000). Organizational citizenship behaviors: Their relationship to organizational effectiveness. *Journal of Hospitality & Tourism Research, 24*(3), 301–319.

Wang, Z-H., & Howell, J. M. (2010). Exploring the dual-level effects of transformational leadership on followers. *Journal of Applied Psychology, 95*(6), 1134–1144. doi: 10.1037/a0020754

Welbourne, T. M., Johnson, D. E., & Erez, A. (1998). The role-based performance scale: Validity analysis of a theory-based measure. *Academy of Management Journal, 41*(5), 540–555. Retrieved from www.jstor.org/stable/256941

Whetten, D. A. (1989). What constitutes a theoretical contribution? *Academy of Management Journal, 14*(4), 490–495.

Williams, L. J., & Anderson, S. E. (1991). Job satisfaction and organizational commitment as predictors of organizational citizenship and in-role behaviors. *Journal of Management, 17*(3), 601–617.

CHAPTER

4

Organizational Citizenship Behavior and Job Engagement: "You Gotta Keep 'em Separated!"

Daniel W. Newton *and* Jeffery A. LePine

Abstract

Scholars largely agree that organizational citizenship behavior (OCB) is a behavioral construct that promotes individual performance and, in the aggregate, unit and organizational functioning and effectiveness. However, there are some views of the OCB construct that blur its conceptual lines with other constructs, thus limiting the theoretical, empirical, and practical insights we can draw from our research. In this chapter, we offer a counterpoint to the idea that the OCB and engagement constructs are largely redundant and that they should be combined. We first describe the nature of the two concepts and identify similarities and core distinctions. We then position OCB and engagement in a general framework that clarifies how and under what conditions they are related more or less strongly. Finally, we offer a road map for future research based on insights gleaned from considering associations and theoretical gaps among the two constructs' dimensions.

Key Words: organizational citizenship behavior, engagement, OCB, behavioral construct, individual performance

Scholars have studied *organizational citizenship behavior* (OCB), defined as individual behaviors that contribute to the maintenance and enhancement of the social and psychological context that enable individuals' task work (Organ, 1997), for over three decades (Smith, Organ, & Near, 1983). As a popular construct in organizational behavior and I/O psychology, a significant amount of research on OCB has accumulated, the results of which have been summarized in numerous articles, books, book chapters, and meta-analyses (e.g., Organ, 1988; Organ, Podsakoff, & MacKenzie, 2006; Organ & Ryan, 1995; Podsakoff, Ahearne, & MacKenzie, 1997; Podsakoff, MacKenzie, Paine, & Bachrach, 2000; Podsakoff, Whiting, Podsakoff, & Blume, 2009). Authors of this research have demonstrated that OCB is influenced by a wide array of antecedents, including personality traits, job attitudes, job cognitions, leadership, and other contextual factors (Organ, 1988; Organ & Ryan, 1995; Podsakoff et al., 1997, 2009). Additionally, scholars have demonstrated linkages between OCB and important outcomes such as job performance or various forms of withdrawal (e.g., turnover intentions, absenteeism, and turnover; Podsakoff et al., 2009).

OCB is most often viewed as a broad behavioral construct insofar as it reflects a wide range of individually and organizationally focused activities that promote social functioning and a positive psychological work climate (Organ, 1988, 1997). Moreover, to the extent that OCB contributes positively—albeit indirectly—to organizational effectiveness, it can be viewed as an important contributor to job performance (Borman & Motowidlo, 1993), or the value of the aggregated contributions of employee activities over some defined time period that contribute directly and indirectly to the accomplishment of organizational goals (Motowidlo, Borman, & Schmit, 1997). There are advantages to a broad view of OCB in accounting for the commonality inherent in a range of functionally similar work activities that together serve to reflect an important aspect of job performance. However, we believe that the breadth of OCB can be taken too far. An *overly* broad view of OCB will yield reduced precision in the meaning of the construct and make it more difficult to draw conceptual and empirical distinctions between OCB and its causes and consequences. This will be especially true if the causes and consequences of OCB are also conceptualized broadly.

Perhaps the blurring of constructs can be best exemplified by considering the idea that OCB is the same as *engagement*, which has been broadly characterized as "the simultaneous employment and expression of a person's "preferred self" in task behaviors that promote connections to work and to others, personal presence (physical, cognitive, and emotional) and active, full performances" (Kahn, 1990, p. 700). Macey and Schneider (2008) recognized this breadth and suggested that engagement is an umbrella construct that can manifest as a state, a trait, or a behavior that blends affective energy and discretionary effort. Indeed, the behavioral component of Macey and Schneider's notion of engagement bears a striking resemblance to OCB. In a similar vein, Harrison, Newman, and colleagues have argued with their attitude-engagement model (Harrison, Newman, & Roth, 2006; Newman & Harrison, 2008; Newman, Joseph, Sparkman, & Carpenter, 2011) that engagement can be thought of as a higher order multidimensional effectiveness construct with underlying dimensions captured by task performance, OCB, and withdrawal. The thrust of the arguments supporting this merger of constructs, in essence, is that engagement and OCB suffer from the jangle fallacy, in that the two are distinct only by their label when in fact they are conceptually similar (Newman et al., 2011).

We believe that these overly broad views of OCB and engagement, and the idea that they should be considered one in the same, inhibit growth in our theoretical and empirical understanding. Merging engagement and OCB blurs distinct motivational and behavioral phenomena, and it limits our understanding of how they might function jointly in more elaborate models of individual and organizational behavior. In this chapter we advance an alternative conceptual lens—one in which the two constructs are separate but functionally related—to provide for improved theoretical and empirical insight. To this end, we draw on a contemporary view of engagement as the willingness to employ and express one's personal energies in one's work (Rich, LePine, & Crawford, 2010). With this view in mind, we can distinguish the behavior of employees (i.e., OCB or other performance-related constructs) with the underlying motivational force (i.e., engagement), and by doing so, we can expand our understanding of the processes and mechanisms that link the two constructs to each other and to other constructs.

The purposes of the chapter, therefore, are to clarify the unique nature of OCB and engagement, and to outline the benefits of maintaining their distinctiveness in regard to theory and research. We begin by delineating the two constructs conceptually and empirically through a review of the relevant aspects of the OCB and engagement literatures. In our review, we describe the nature of the OCB and engagement constructs, and we make clear distinctions between the two. From there we offer a general conceptual framework that explains how and under what conditions OCB and engagement are related. We conclude with a road map for future theory and research that links specific dimensions of OCB (Organ, 1988; Podsakoff, MacKenzie, Moorman, & Fetter, 1990) to specific dimensions of engagement (Kahn, 1990; Rich et al., 2010). In the end, we hope that this chapter will lead scholars to heed the lyrics of The Offspring song, referenced in the title of this chapter, and keep OCB and engagement separated (Holland, 1994, track 7).

Distinctiveness of Organizational Citizenship Behavior and Engagement

The Nature of Organizational Citizenship Behavior

Scholars have long recognized the importance of spontaneous innovative actions of employees that extend beyond defined work roles (Barnard, 1938; Katz, 1964; Katz & Kahn, 1978) and that "lubricate the social machinery of organizations" (Bateman & Organ, 1983, p. 588). In 1983, Smith et al. coined the term "organizational citizenship behavior," or OCB, to represent instances of these behaviors. Organ (1988) later referred to OCB as an "individual behavior that is discretionary, not directly or explicitly recognized by the formal reward system, and that in the aggregate promotes the effective functioning of the organization" (Organ, 1988, p. 4). The problem of delineating activities that are discretionary from those that are not discretionary, as well as those that are formally rewarded from those that are not formally rewarded, prompted further refinement to OCB's definition that eventually shifted it to more closely align with the construct of contextual performance (Borman & Motowidlo, 1993; Motowidlo et al., 1997; Organ, 1997; Podsakoff et al., 2009). Specifically, OCB came to refer to employee behaviors that "maintain the broader organizational, social, and psychological environment in which the technical core must function" (Motowidlo et al., 1997, p. 75).

Although there seems to be general agreement regarding the definition of OCB, there is lesser consensus regarding the nature of the construct's underlying behavioral dimensions. When they asked lower level managers to identify instances when employees engaged in helpful but unrequired job behaviors, Smith et al. (1983) found that the behaviors consisted of two primary factors: altruism and generalized compliance. A few years later, Organ (1988) expanded the number of essential facets of OCB to five: altruism, courtesy, sportsmanship, civic virtue, and conscientiousness. *Altruism* captures behaviors intended to help and assist others. *Courtesy* refers to small interpersonal acts that signal respect and the willingness to cooperate. *Sportsmanship* refers to maintaining a positive attitude at work, not complaining to others, and tolerating undesirable inconveniences. *Civic virtue* refers to the acceptance of responsibility to be involved in maintaining and supporting the management and governance of the organization. Finally, *conscientiousness* includes a consistent pattern of going above and beyond organizational expectations. This framework, together with the measure developed and validated by Podsakoff and his colleagues (1990), has dominated the organizational behavior landscape for the last 25 years. However, scholars have offered alternatives. For example, Van Dyne, Graham, and Dienesch (1994) adopted a political philosophy lens and suggested that OCB consists of obedience, loyalty, social participation, advocacy participation, and functional participation. Coleman and Borman (2000) noted commonalities in items and dimensions across the various OCB-related measures and found support for three broad dimensions: interpersonal citizenship performance (i.e., OCB-I), organizational citizenship performance (i.e., OCB-O), and job/task citizenship performance (i.e., conscientious extra effort and persistent enthusiasm for completing task activities).

There also appears to be some inconsistency in the literature in regard to how the behavioral dimensions are positioned relative to the more general OCB construct. Some scholars have focused their research on relationships with the specific dimensions of OCB (e.g., Moorman, 1991; Podsakoff, MacKenzie, & Bommer, 1996) or OCBs, whereas others have focused on the more general OCB construct itself (e.g., Allen & Rush, 1998; Deckop, Mangel, & Cirka, 1999). Although it is beyond the scope of the present work to overview the advantages and disadvantages of the two approaches to OCB, researchers have found that the specific dimensions are strongly correlated, functionally similar, and load onto the same general OCB factor (Hoffman, Blair, Meriac, & Woehr, 2007; LePine, Erez, & Johnson, 2002), Accordingly, it has been suggested that if the conceptual logic in a theoretical effort or empirical piece refers to the broad OCB construct, and if there are no arguments that distinguish the functioning of the dimensions, then it may be most appropriate to consider the dimensions in concert as indicators of OCB rather than as separate OCB variables (LePine et al., 2002). As we will suggest later in this this manuscript, there may be value in revisiting the dimensionality of OCB in an effort to enhance our understanding of the relationship between OCB and engagement, another multidimensional construct.

The Nature of Engagement

Although our discussion has focused predominantly on the nature of OCB and its dimensions, the majority of OCB research has focused on its antecedents. In fact, a great deal of this research has examined factors that might motivate employees to contribute to their organizations through activities reflected in OCB. The motivational construct of engagement is an excellent example of a variable that might serve this focus. That engagement has commanded significant practitioner and scholarly attention (e.g., Crawford, Rich, Buckman, & Bergeron, 2014; Kruse, 2012) is understandable given that the concept relates positively to job satisfaction, organizational commitment, autonomy, social support, task performance, and, most relevant to our focus here, organizational citizenship behavior (Christian, Garza, & Slaughter, 2011).

Our theoretical grounding of engagement is based on the work of Kahn (1990), who employed grounded theory methods to conceptualize employee engagement in motivational terms. Kahn found that, under certain conditions, employees harness themselves to their work roles by employing their physical, cognitive, and emotional energies to the various activities involved in their work roles. In other words, engaged employees are those who are willing to channel their physical, cognitive, and emotional energy to their jobs simultaneously—what Ashforth and Humphrey (1995) have described as investing personal energy from the "hands, head, and heart" (p. 110).

Consistent with this thinking, Rich and his colleagues (2010) suggested that Kahn's (1990) notion of engagement involved three distinct motivational dimensions. The first dimension, *physical engagement*, refers to the willingness to allocate actual bodily effort and physical resources to role-related activities. Physical engagement is reflected in the intensity with which employees complete their work and involve themselves in work-related activities. The second dimension, *cognitive engagement*, refers to the degree of mental focus and attention individuals give to their work. Individuals who are cognitively engaged are mentally absorbed in their role activities, concentrate on what they are doing, and are vigilant for opportunities to enhance role performance. Finally, *emotional engagement* reflects the level of emotional energies and resources individuals are willing to commit to their roles. Emotionally engaged individuals are energetic and enthusiastic about their work, proud of their work accomplishments, and interested and positive about tasks they perform. We should note here that this interpretation of Kahn's (1990) conceptualization of engagement as motivation is quite different than the characterization offered by other engagement scholars who have described engagement as a job attitude that taps a general work condition (e.g., Harter, Schmidt, Agrawal, & Plowman, 2013), as the positive antipode of burnout (e.g., Llorens, Bakker, Schaufeli, & Salanova, 2006; Maslach, Schaufeli, & Leiter, 2001), or as an affective-cognitive state that reflects well-being and is reflected in the dimensions of vigor, dedication, and absorption (e.g., Schaufeli, Salanova, Gonzalez-Roma, & Bakker, 2002).

Distinguishing Organizational Citizenship Behavior and Engagement

As we noted earlier, OCB and engagement have been conceptualized in different ways; therefore, it should not be surprising that scholars have different views regarding how the concepts might be related. Indeed, as we briefly discussed in the introduction, some have recently suggested that the constructs are essentially redundant and should be combined in some way. For example, Macey and Schneider (2008) argued that engagement could be defined as a state, a trait, or a behavior that refers to the degree to which an employee goes above and beyond job requirements. Obviously, this behavioral aspect of engagement is synonymous with how we think of OCB. Following from this, the behaviors that have been identified as reflecting OCB would be the very same behaviors that reflect engagement. As another example of the blurring between OCB and engagement, Harrison, Newman, and colleagues have argued that engagement is the outcome of an overall job attitude, and it can be conceptualized as a higher order effectiveness construct reflecting task performance, OCB, and withdrawal (Harrison et al., 2006; Newman & Harrison, 2008). These authors have argued that engagement should be distinguished from general job attitudes, and—if viewed as a behavioral provision of time and energy into one's work role—is reflected in the variance shared in an overarching model of job performance including OCB. From this perspective, therefore, engagement refers to a broad performance construct of which OCB is a major element. Although the proposed parsimony of frameworks such as these that merge OCB and engagement may appear desirable, positioning these concepts as indicators of the same overarching construct may obscure important conceptual distinctions. Furthermore, and more generally, viewing OCB and engagement as functionally equivalent paints an incomplete picture of more complex phenomena and may limit theoretical advances in our understanding of employee work behavior.

At its core, OCB is a *behavioral* construct that reflects the degree to which an individual acts in ways that tend to enhance the social and psychological functioning of an organization. As such, OCB reflects affiliative responses to opportunities an individual has to help a coworker, respond to a request for information with courtesy, attend an extra meeting, be a good sport when things do not go well or as planned, and accomplish work with extra diligence and care. In contrast, engagement is a *motivational* construct that reflects an individual's willingness to channel and apply personal resources to the full set of demands that are believed to comprise one's work role. The two constructs are clearly related insofar as they reflect positive qualities and contributions of individual employees, and also because highly engaged individuals are more likely to perceive a more expansive role that includes OCB-related activities. We should emphasize here that we are not only suggesting that engagement and OCB are distinct but also that engagement precedes OCB in a causal sense. This perspective aligns with a general understanding of motivation, which can be thought of as a set of energetic forces that leads to work-related behavior as a consequence of individual and environmental influences (e.g., Latham & Pinder, 2005; Pinder, 2008). If an individual is engaged—whether caused by individual disposition, empowering leadership, or organizational factors that instill feelings of meaningfulness, safety, or availability—internal energies may be allocated to work and contextual activities in a way that aligns with how the role is understood and internalized by the individual. Given that engagement may be reflected in an understanding of the work role as being quite expansive, and thus including OCB-like activities (e.g., Kahn, 1990), the association between the two constructs is positive.

However, given that there are differences among individuals in their understanding of their roles, as well as in opportunities to exhibit OCB, the relationship is substantially less than perfect. Indeed, it is easy to think of coworkers who are very engaged in their jobs, but who do not engage in much organizational citizenship. This may occur when individuals are so engrossed and absorbed in aspects of their work that their attention is diverted from their social environment, or they fail to notice ways they can get involved in and contribute to the organization. It is also easy to think of coworkers who may seem disengaged in their jobs but are considered to be good organizational citizens. This scenario may play out in monotonous or menial independent jobs where individuals seek fulfillment through social attachment and the energy that accompanies positive interdependent activities such as helping coworkers (e.g., Ashforth & Mael, 1989; Baumeister & Leary, 1995; McGrath & Kelly, 1986). Taken together, research has shown that OCB and engagement share only 12% of their variance (Christian et al., 2011). By way of comparison, the strength of the association between OCB and engagement is about the same as the relationship between engagement and leader–member exchange ($R^2 = .10$), social support ($R^2 = .10$), feedback ($R^2 = .11$), and autonomy ($R^2 = .15$; Christian et al., 2011). Obviously, no one would argue that OCB is the same thing as these four constructs.

In the next section, we turn to a more refined view of the relationship between engagement and OCB, and the role these constructs play in a broader understanding of organizational behavior. Specifically, we propose a model that describes how engagement and OCB together provide a more complete understanding of the relationship between a wide variety of individual and organizational antecedents on the one hand, and employee performance on the other. Our model also accounts for an important factor that influences the relationship between engagement and OCB and, therefore, moderates the association between the set of antecedents and job performance. Considering this boundary condition, and the integrative model more generally, may help resolve and clarify important distinctions between OCB and engagement, as well as enhance our understanding regarding how the two constructs are causally connected.

An Integrative Model of Organizational Citizenship Behavior and Engagement

A significant amount of research on both OCB and engagement has focused on antecedents and outcomes. This research has been summarized in meta-analyses and narrative reviews of each construct (e.g., Christian et al., 2011; Harter et al., 2013; Organ, 1988; Organ & Ryan, 1995; Podsakoff et al., 1997, 2009). However, given our view that engagement and OCB are causally related, it may be useful to consider how the literature could be integrated to produce a more systematic and comprehensive understanding of the relationships that have been considered. Although there are a number of different conceptual lenses we could use as a basis for our theoretical model, we draw from Kahn's theory of personal engagement (1990). This theory incorporates elements of other well-known theories in organizational behavior (e.g., Hackman & Oldham, 1980), and it examines a wide array of antecedents and outcomes that have been considered in both the engagement and OCB literatures. Our model, depicted in Figure 4.1, proposes that engagement and OCB are jointly responsible for transmitting the effects of individual and contextual factors to influence job performance.

In his inductive work, Kahn (1990) found that three separate psychological conditions emerged that, when present, stimulated individuals' engagement in their work and, when not present, led individuals to disengage in their work. The three antecedents are *meaningfulness* (i.e., what employees do that makes a difference in their organization), *safety* (i.e., the security individuals feel such that they can take initiative without fear of negative consequences), and *availability* (i.e., whether individuals possess the know-how to do their work, or know where to obtain resources to improve task knowledge and functioning). Kahn identified several

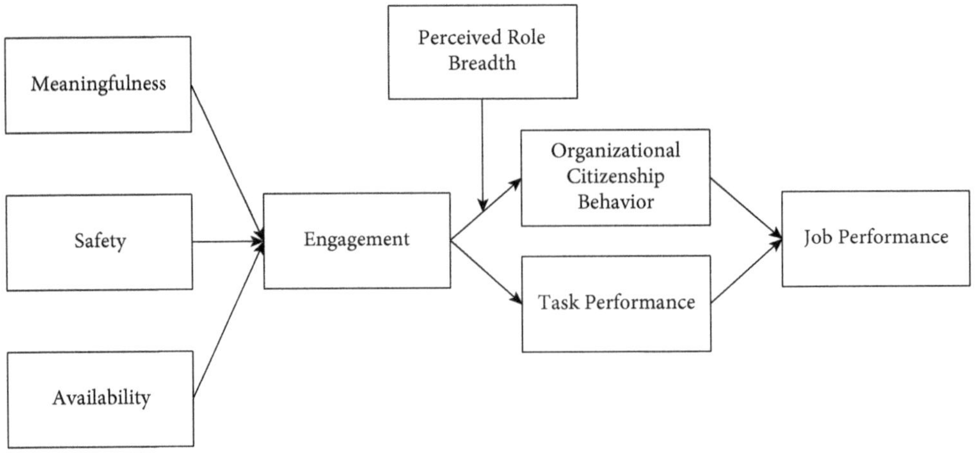

Figure 4.1 Integrative model of engagement and organizational citizenship behavior.

different individual and organizational factors that are associated with engagement by virtue of their influence on these three psychological conditions.

Employees derive feelings of meaningfulness from characteristics of the task (e.g., whether the task is challenging, creative, or provides autonomy), characteristics of the role that resonate with employees and help them feel important, and social interactions that enhance dignity and create valuable structures of social support (Kahn, 1990). When these factors are present, employees tend to feel engaged because they feel what they do is important and that their inputs and perspective are worthwhile. Second, feelings of safety are derived from interpersonal relationships that foster trust, group and intergroup dynamics that create safe spaces for expression, management style and processes that are supportive and strengthen employees' resilience, and organizational norms that reinforce positive work behaviors. When employees feel safe, they are more likely to extend all their energies into their work because they feel less vulnerable. Third and finally, feelings of availability are influenced by perceptions that one has the resources and capabilities to cope with the demands necessary to perform effectively. Employees who possess the capabilities and requisite resources needed for full and effective role performances will tend to be more engaged because they feel greater availability.

We suggest further that the psychological states of meaningfulness, safety, and availability will influence job performance because they foster OCB and task performance through engagement. That is, these psychological conditions enhance the perceived value of an individual to the organization because they inspire a willingness to devote a full array of personal energies to the work role, thus enhancing contextually focused and task-focused activities that are appreciated as contributions to organizational effectiveness. Although this might seem to be a somewhat long causal chain, there are strong conceptual rationales for this process. For example, if engagement is the simultaneous expression and presence of physical, cognitive, and emotional energies that promote connections to the organization and others, then it follows that engaged employees will tend to go beyond their job descriptions to enact behaviors that strengthen and support the organization (OCB-O) and other individuals in the organization (OCB-I; Williams & Anderson, 1991) more so than individuals who are not engaged. Moreover, engaged employees invest more effort and energy in their work tasks than those who are less engaged, in addition to approaching their task work with higher levels of persistence and vigilance. Consequently, employee engagement is likely translated into increased effectiveness generally and in the performance of specific tasks (Christian et al., 2011). Because engaged employees are more likely to be involved and interpersonally connected in their work, such employees are also likely to be extra conscientious in their tasks, help coworkers, and attend meetings to keep up with organizational happenings. Similarly, OCB exhibited from engaged employees builds and strengthens social relationships with coworkers, which facilitates the effective completion of work that results in higher evaluations of job performance. Of course, the individual relationships and the component stages of mediation have been explored and supported previously in empirical research. For example, researchers have established relationships between job characteristics and job performance (Fried & Ferris, 1987; Humphrey, Nahrgang, & Morgeson, 2007). As another example, Rich et al. (2010) demonstrated that the factors reflecting meaningfulness, safety, and availability influence OCB and task performance through engagement. Finally, there is compelling evidence that OCB and task performance influence overall job performance (Podsakoff et al., 2009).

As shown in Figure 4.1, our integrative model also includes a key factor that influences the relationship between engagement and OCB. Drawing from the work on the relationship between perceived role breadth and OCB (e.g., Graen, 1976; Morrison, 1994), we argue that when individuals perceive that their roles are broad and relatively open to enlargement, they are more likely to respond with OCB when they are highly engaged. However, when individuals have a narrower view of their role, or when they view their role as consisting of well-defined elements, engagement will likely translate into investments of more personal energy into these specific role elements or perhaps into completely different roles. The underlying rationale for this moderation is that engaged individuals allocate their personal energies to all aspects of a role (Kahn, 1990). The larger the perceived role, the more likely it is that the role will include the belief that OCB is part of the role, and following from this, the more likely it is that the energies inspired by engagement will be allocated to enact OCB.

Of course, following through with this logic suggests that perceived role breadth may moderate the entire meditational chain. That is, role breadth may influence the degree to which engagement and OCB explain the relationships between meaningfulness, safety, and availability on the one hand, and job performance on the other. When employees see their roles as relatively broad, such a view may enhance the meaning individuals can derive from their work because they may sense greater autonomy to perform and control their work (McAllister, Kamdar, Morrison, & Turban, 2007). Furthermore, individuals' sense of safety may also be enhanced with perceptions of larger work roles because the increased role breadth adds a buffering space that allows them to take initiative with an added sense of security. Finally, availability is also likely to be heightened with increased perceived role breadth because a larger role may provide greater access or touch points with others in the organization to acquire needed and important knowledge, skills, and abilities that facilitate the completion of job requirements. In summary and more specifically, we propose that the indirect relationships of the three psychological states (i.e., meaningfulness, safety, and availability) and job performance attributable to engagement and OCB will be stronger when perceived role breadth is high, and the indirect relationships attributable to engagement and OCB will be weaker when perceived role breadth is low.

Dimensionality and Future Research

Thus far we have presented an integrated view of OCB and engagement. Next we turn to implications for future research. Although we could have focused our discussion on how the integrated model could be expanded to include a more comprehensive set of antecedents (additional variables that influence meaningfulness, safety, and availability), moderating conditions (variables that influence the association between engagement and OCB), or outcomes (other aspects of employee effectiveness), we will instead focus on an issue we feel is more fundamental. That is, we will next consider how our model illuminates new and important insights to the OCB and engagement constructs.

Construct Decomposition

In this chapter we have outlined broad conceptual arguments regarding why engagement and OCB are distinct but related. We now turn to consider how the relationship between these two broad constructs can be understood in terms of the connections among the more specific facets of each construct. We specifically suggest that by decomposing the constructs and considering relationships of the narrower dimensions, it is possible to pinpoint areas where both constructs can be developed in future research. To this end, we draw upon the five dimensions of OCB suggested by Organ (1988) and the three dimensions of engagement suggested by Rich and colleagues (2010). We readily acknowledge that there may not be complete consensus regarding these frameworks; however, they have been used extensively in the literature and offer a platform to discuss connections that other scholars may find insightful.

To understand how engagement and OCB may be linked through the constructs' dimensions, we now briefly consider how the willingness to invest physical, cognitive, and emotional energies into one's role could differentially enhance the tendency to exhibit altruism, courtesy, sportsmanship, civic virtue, or conscientiousness. For instance, physical engagement might have its strongest impact on an individual's conscientiousness. Employees who are physically engaged in their work activities will tend to put forth significant effort and intensity in completing their tasks, and they will tend to work hard and do more than is asked in order to help the organization meet its goals. Similarly, cognitive engagement could be particularly relevant to civic virtue. Individuals who are cognitively engaged tend to think about better ways of accomplishing their work and strategizing, and therefore would experience greater involvement in matters that affect the organization. Finally, there appear to be obvious connections between emotional engagement and courtesy and altruism. When employees feel energy in and are enthusiastic about their work, they will likely be more receptive to the emotional appeal to assist others by proactively doing good and by providing extra care or compassionate assistance. Although future research could consider and empirically test how the specific motivational dimensions of engagement are related to the specific behavioral dimensions of OCB, the purpose of this discussion here is to explore how the content of the engagement construct could be used to identify areas of deficiency in the OCB construct, and how the content of the OCB construct could identify areas of deficiency in the engagement construct.

With respect to the former issue, it seems reasonable to propose that the OCB construct could be expanded to include employee activities that are reflected in smooth transitions between role activities that require different mixes of physical, cognitive, and emotional energies. Indeed, a cornerstone of Kahn's (1990) theory of engagement is that engaged individuals willingly invest their energies to meet whatever demands are required for effective role performance, and that by extension, the ability to adapt and transition between various role demands is crucial. Indeed, Kahn described how engaged architects transitioned from work tasks such as drafting, which requires physical and cognitive engagement, to other tasks such as interacting with and helping customers that require emotional engagement, all at a moment's notice. Note here that we are not reiterating the importance of any specific task or socially related activity, but rather, the ease and flexibility with which an individual is able to step away from one task to the next without causing stress that might impinge on the social and psychological work context. This ability to adapt (Pulakos, Arad, Donovan, & Plamondon, 2000) or shift gears effectively between different facets of a job (Louis & Sutton, 1991) appears to be consistent with the definition of OCB insofar as it involves behavior that is relatively discretionary and facilitates the social context in which task work is performed (Bateman & Organ, 1983).

With regard to how dimensions of OCB might be used to expand our understanding of engagement, it is instructive to consider that the majority of the OCB dimensions are socially focused. This is perhaps most obvious for the dimensions of altruism and courtesy. These dimensions convey cooperativeness, respect, empathy, and benevolence, and they are explicitly interpersonal. Moreover, to the extent that sportsmanship reflects tolerance for negative workplace occurrences and the withholding of negative feelings and complaints that might otherwise upset interpersonal relationships, it can also be viewed as a socially focused behavior. Interestingly, however, energies that might reflect the willingness to invest in these types of socially focused behaviors are not directly considered in the conceptualization or measurement of the engagement construct. Yet Kahn did describe how engaged individuals are driven to enact behaviors that "promote connections to work and to *others*" (p. 700, our italics). There is, however, no explicit reference to engagement as including the willingness to invest one's social energies, which might be defined as internal resources that individuals use to understand and manage their own emotions and behavior, as well as the emotions and behavior of others, to facilitate cooperation and mutual dependencies.

Theoretical and Research Implications

Now that we have outlined our conceptual framework and identified some implications, we now turn to the steps researchers could take to examine or explore some of the ideas that we have advanced. First and most obviously, researchers may need to re-examine our measures of engagement and OCB to ensure that they are consistent with their definitions and do not overlap with the other construct. Measures of engagement should not reference specific activities reflected by OCB, but instead they should focus on the willingness to invest personal energies in the work role. For example, "At my work, I always persevere, even when things do not go well" (Schaufeli & Bakker, 2003) is a commonly used engagement item. Unfortunately, this item also seems to overlap with the conscientiousness dimension of OCB. Similarly, measures of OCB should focus on activities and behaviors that contribute indirectly to organizational effectiveness rather than the general allocation of personal energies at work. As an example item, "Persisting with enthusiasm on own job" (Coleman & Borman, 2000) is intended to tap citizenship behavior; however, it appears to overlap with the facet of engagement concerned with the allocation of emotional energies. Although the prospect of re-examining the content validity of well-established scales will not be welcome news to scholars who do research on OCB and engagement, the results of such efforts may be necessary to produce new and important insights.

Second, research could be conducted that more thoroughly examines the conceptual framework we offer in this chapter. The result of such research would not only help us better understand the nature and functioning of OCB and engagement, but it would also provide a more comprehensive explanation for why individual and contextual factors associated with meaningfulness, safety, and availability influence job performance. A challenge here is that the constructs in our model are typically measured in a way that would result in common method variance (e.g., Podsakoff, MacKenzie, Lee, & Podsakoff, 2003). This would be particularly true of the relationship between the three psychological states and engagement, which are typically self-reports, and OCB, task performance, and job performance, which are typically supervisor reports. Although it may be possible to mitigate this issue with ratings from coworkers or significant others, there are practical challenges to such designs. Moreover, the failure of any single source to respond to a survey results in the case being excluded from analysis.

Finally, to the extent that *role flexibility* and the *investment of social energies* could emerge as dimensions of OCB and engagement (respectively), measures for these dimensions would have to be created and validated (e.g., Hinkin, 1995, 1998). The resulting scale development process should take care to maintain the distinction between OCB and engagement. Sample items for role flexibility or role adaptability could include "I transition between different facets of my job without creating a disruption in the workflow" and "I shift between tasks in a way that does not cause problems for my coworkers." Sample items for the investment of social energies could include "I try to understand how my coworkers are feeling" and "I think about how my actions are going to influence my peers."

Summary and Some Caveats

The purpose of this chapter has been to clarify the nature of OCB and engagement, and to describe some advantages in keeping the constructs separated. We readily acknowledge the dangers of the jangle fallacy as well as the benefits of parsimony that might be afforded by combining engagement and OCB. However, there are clear conceptual differences in the two constructs, and each construct plays a role in helping us understand how psychological states informed by individual and contextual factors come to influence job performance. Moreover, we illustrated in this chapter how a fine-grained analysis of the constructs can benefit our theoretical understanding. The following propositions summarize our ideas more explicitly.

1. *Engagement and OCB are related but distinct constructs.*
2. *Engagement has a positive influence on OCB.*
3. *The associations between meaningfulness, safety, and availability (and by extension, antecedents of these three psychological conditions) and job performance are mediated—at least in part—by engagement and, in turn, OCB and task performance.*
4. *The indirect effects through OCB implied in the previous proposition are moderated by perceived role breadth such that the indirect relationship is stronger when individuals perceive their roles broadly and weaker when individuals perceive their roles narrowly.*
5. *An integrated view of engagement and OCB into narrower dimensions suggests that both constructs could be expanded:*

    a. *Multidimensional models of OCB that include activities such as altruism, courtesy, sportsmanship, conscientiousness, and civic virtue could be supplemented to include role flexibility or role adaptability.*

    b. *Multidimensional models of engagement that include the investment of one's physical, cognitive, and emotional energies could be supplemented to include the investment of social energies.*

We note that engagement and OCB, and the role they play in explaining job performance effects, are much more complex than we have depicted in this chapter. For example, we did not discuss how supervisors' beliefs regarding the relative importance of OCB and task performance could influence the relationships in our model. Engaged employees who perceive high role breadth may tend to engage in high levels of OCB, but the energy invested in these activities may not result in positive performance evaluations if their supervisors place more weight on employees' task performance. Consistent with this idea, researchers could begin to investigate the role of alignment between supervisor role expectations and employee role perceptions to better understand associations among engagement, OCB, task performance, and overall job performance. As another example, we did not discuss many of the other behavioral aspects of job performance that are likely to be inspired by engagement. In this regard, constructs such as voice, adaptability, and counterproductive behavior could be considered in future research. Moreover, we did not mention certain third variables that may provide alternative explanations regarding why engagement and OCB might be positively correlated. Individual differences in personality and dispositional affect should certainly be considered in empirical research on this relationship to address potential concerns regarding endogeneity. Finally, we completely ignored feedback loops and nonrecursive paths that might be present. For example, acts of OCB may trigger reciprocity, which may in turn be engaging because receiving OCB enhances psychological conditions of meaningfulness, safety, and availability. Possibilities such as this could be considered in theoretical and empirical efforts to enhance our understanding of employee effectiveness. In the end, our goal for this chapter is rather modest. Rather than trying to present a comprehensive accounting of OCB and engagement, our overarching objective is to offer a general conceptual lens that supports the idea that OCB and engagement are distinct and, in doing so, to identify opportunities for future research and theory building.

References

Allen, T. D., & Rush, M. C. (1998). The effects of organizational citizenship behavior on performance judgments: A field study and a laboratory experiment. *Journal of Applied Psychology, 83*(2), 247–260. doi:10.1037/0021-9010.83.2.247

Ashforth, B. E., & Humphrey, R. H. (1995). Emotion in the workplace: A reappraisal. *Human Relations, 48*(2), 97–125. doi:10.1177/001872679504800201

Ashforth, B. E., & Mael, F. (1989). Social identity theory and the organization. *Academy of Management Review, 14*(1), 20–39. doi:10.5465/AMR.1989.4278999

Barnard, C. I. (1938). *The functions of the executive*. Cambridge, MA: Harvard University Press.

Bateman, T. S., & Organ, D. W. (1983). Job satisfaction and the good soldier: The relationship between affect and employee "citizenship." *Academy of Management Journal, 26*(4), 587–595. doi:10.2307/255908

Baumeister, R. F., & Leary, M. R. (1995). The need to belong: Desire for interpersonal attachments as a fundamental human motivation. *Psychological Bulletin, 117*, 497–529. doi:10.1037/0033-2909.117.3.497

Borman, W. C., & Motowidlo, S. J. (1993). Expanding the criterion domain to include elements of contextual performance. In N. Schmitt & W. C. Borman (Eds.), *Personnel selection in organizations* (pp. 71–98). San Francisco, CA: Jossey-Bass.

Christian, M. S., Garza, A. S., & Slaughter, J. E. (2011). Work engagement: A quantitative review and test of its relations with task and contextual performance. *Personnel Psychology, 64*(1), 89–136. doi:10.1111/j.1744-6570.2010.01203.x

Coleman, V. I., & Borman, W. C. (2000). Investigating the underlying structure of the citizenship performance domain. *Human Resource Management Review, 10*(1), 25–44. doi:10.1016/S1053-4822(99)00037-6

Crawford, E. R., Rich, B. L., Buckman, B., & Bergeron, J. (2014). The antecedents and drivers of employee engagement. In C. Truss, R. Delbridge, K. Alfes, A. Shantz, & E. Soane (Eds.), *Employee engagement in theory and practice* (pp. 57–81). London, England: Routledge.

Deckop, J. R., Mangel, R., & Cirka, C. C. (1999). Getting more than you pay for: Organizational citizenship behavior and pay-for-performance plans. *Academy of Management Journal, 42*(4), 420–428. doi:10.2307/257012

Fried, Y., & Ferris, G. R. (1987). The validity of the job characteristics model: A review and meta-analysis. *Personnel Psychology, 40*(2), 287–322. doi:10.1111/j.1744-6570.1987.tb00605.x

Graen, G. (1976). Role-making processes within complex organizations. In M. D. Dunnette (Ed.), *Handbook of industrial and organizational psychology* (pp. 1201–1245). Chicago, IL: Rand McNally.

Hackman, J. R., & Oldham, G. R. (1980). *Work redesign*. Reading, MA: Addison-Wesley.

Harrison, D. A., Newman, D. A., & Roth, P. L. (2006). How important are job attitudes? Meta-analytic comparisons of integrative behavioral outcomes and time sequences. *Academy of Management Journal, 49*(2), 305–325. doi:10.5465/AMJ.2006.20786077

Harter, J. K., Schmidt, F. L., Agrawal, S, & Plowman, S. K. (2013). *The relationship between engagement at work and organizational outcomes: 2012 Q12 meta-analysis.* Retrieved from Gallup, Inc. website: http://employeeengagement.com/wp-content/uploads/2013/04/2012-Q12-Meta-Analysis-Research-Paper.pdf

Hinkin, T. R. (1995). A review of scale development practices in the study of organizations. *Journal of Management, 21*(5), 967–988. doi:10.1177/014920639502100509

Hinkin, T. R. (1998). A brief tutorial on the development of measures for use in survey questionnaires. *Organizational Research Methods, 1*(1), 104–121. doi:10.1177/109442819800100106

Hoffman, B. J., Blair, C. A., Meriac, J. P., & Woehr, D. J. (2007). Expanding the criterion domain? A quantitative review of the OCB literature. *Journal of Applied Psychology, 92*(2), 555–566. doi:10.1037/0021-9010.92.2.555

Holland, D. (1994). Come out and play. On *Smash* [CD]. Los Angeles, CA: Epitaph Records.

Humphrey, S. E., Nahrgang, J. D., & Morgeson, F. P. (2007). Integrating motivational, social, and contextual work design features: A meta-analytic summary and theoretical extension of the work design literature. *Journal of Applied Psychology, 92*(5), 1332–1356. doi:10.1037/0021-9010.92.5.1332

Kahn, W. A. (1990). Psychological conditions of personal engagement and disengagement at work. *Academy of Management Journal, 33*(4), 692–724. doi:10.2307/256287

Katz, D. (1964). The motivational basis of organizational behavior. *Behavioral Science, 9*(2), 131–146. doi:10.1002/bs.3830090206

Katz, D., & Kahn, R. L. (1978). *The social psychology of organizations* (2nd ed.). New York, NY: John Wiley & Sons.

Kruse, K. 2012. What is employee engagement? Retrieved December 2, 2014, from http://www.forbes.com/sites/kevinkruse/2012/06/22/employee-engagement-what-and-why.

Latham, G. P., & Pinder, C. C. (2005). Work motivation theory and research at the dawn of the twenty-first century. *Annual Review of Psychology, 56*, 485–516. doi:10.1146/annurev.psych.55.090902.142105

LePine, J. A., Erez, A., & Johnson, D. E. (2002). The nature and dimensionality of organizational citizenship behavior: A critical review and meta-analysis. *Journal of Applied Psychology, 87*(1), 52–65. doi:10.1037/0021-9010.87.1.52

Llorens, S., Bakker, A. B., Schaufeli, W., & Salanova, M. (2006). Testing the robustness of the job demands-resources model. *International Journal of Stress Management, 13*(3), 378. doi:10.1037/1072-5245.13.3.378

Louis, M. R., & Sutton, R. I. (1991). Switching cognitive gears: From habits of mind to active thinking. *Human Relations, 44*(1), 55–76. doi:10.1177/001872679104400104

Macey, W. H., & Schneider, B. (2008). The meaning of employee engagement. *Industrial and Organizational Psychology, 1*(1), 3–30. doi:10.1111/j.1754-9434.2007.0002.x

Maslach, C., Schaufeli, W. B., & Leiter, M. P. (2001). Job burnout. *Annual Review of Psychology, 52*, 397–422. doi:10.1146/annurev.psych.52.1.397

McAllister, D. J., Kamdar, D., Morrison, E. W., & Turban, D. B. (2007). Disentangling role perceptions: How perceived role breadth, discretion, instrumentality, and efficacy relate to helping and taking charge. *Journal of Applied Psychology, 92*(5), 1200–1211. doi:10.1037/0021-9010.92.5.1200

McGrath, J. E., & Kelly, J. R. (1986). *Time and human interaction: Toward a social psychology of time.* New York, NY: Guilford Press.

Moorman, R. H. (1991). Relationship between organizational justice and organizational citizenship behaviors: Do fairness perceptions influence employee citizenship? *Journal of Applied Psychology, 76*(6), 845–855. doi:10.1037/0021-9010.76.6.845

Morrison, E. W. (1994). Role definitions and organizational citizenship behavior: The importance of the employee's perspective. *Academy of Management Journal, 37*(6), 1543–1567. doi:10.2307/256798

Motowidlo, S. J., Borman, W. C., & Schmit, M. J. (1997). A theory of individual differences in task and contextual performance. *Human Performance, 10*(2), 71–83. doi:10.1207/s15327043hup1002_1

Newman, D. A., & Harrison, D. A. (2008). Been there, bottled that: Are state and behavioral work engagement new and useful construct "Wines"? *Industrial and Organizational Psychology, 1*(1), 31–35. doi:10.1111/j.1754-9434.2007.00003.x

Newman, D. A., Joseph, D. L., Sparkman, T. E., & Carpenter, N. C. (2011). Invited reaction: The work cognition inventory: Initial evidence of construct validity. *Human Resource Development Quarterly, 22*(1), 37–47. doi:10.1002/hrdq.20065

Organ, D. W. (1988). *Organizational citizenship behavior: The good soldier syndrome.* Lexington, MA: Lexington Books.

Organ, D. W. (1997). Organizational citizenship behavior: It's construct clean-up time. *Human Performance, 10*(2), 85–97. doi:10.1207/s15327043hup1002_2

Organ, D. W., Podsakoff, P. M., & MacKenzie, S. B. (2006). *Organizational citizenship behavior: Its nature, antecedents, and consequences.* Thousand Oaks, CA: Sage Publications.

Organ, D. W., & Ryan, K. (1995). A meta-analytic review of attitudinal and dispositional predictors of organizational citizenship behavior. *Personnel Psychology, 48*(4), 775–802. doi:10.1111/j.1744-6570.1995.tb01781.x

Pinder, C. C. (2008). *Work motivation in organizational behavior.* New York, NY: Psychology Press.

Podsakoff, P. M., Ahearne, M., & MacKenzie, S. B. (1997). Organizational citizenship behavior and the quantity and quality of work group performance. *Journal of Applied Psychology, 82*(2), 262–270. doi:10.1037/0021-9010.82.2.262

Podsakoff, P., MacKenzie, S. B., & Bommer, W. H. (1996). Transformational leader behaviors and substitutes for leadership as determinants of employee satisfaction, commitment, trust, and organizational citizenship behaviors. *Journal of Management, 22*(2), 259–298. doi:10.1177/014920639602200204

Podsakoff, P. M., MacKenzie, S. B., Lee, J. Y., & Podsakoff, N. P. (2003). Common method biases in behavioral research: A critical review of the literature and recommended remedies. *Journal of Applied Psychology, 88*(5), 879–903. doi:10.1037/0021-9101.88.5.879

Podsakoff, P. M., MacKenzie, S. B., Moorman, R. H., & Fetter, R. (1990). Transformational leader behaviors and their effects on followers' trust in leader, satisfaction, and organizational citizenship behaviors. *Leadership Quarterly, 1*(2), 107–142. doi:10.1016/1048-9843(90)90009-7

Podsakoff, P. M., MacKenzie, S. B., Paine, J. B., & Bachrach, D. G. (2000). Organizational citizenship behaviors: A critical review of the theoretical and empirical literature and suggestions for future research. *Journal of Management, 26*(3), 513–563. doi:10.1177/014920630002600307

Podsakoff, N. P., Whiting, S. W., Podsakoff, P. M., & Blume, B. D. (2009). Individual- and organizational-level consequences of organizational citizenship behaviors: A meta-analysis. *Journal of Applied Psychology, 94*(1), 122–141. doi:10.1037/a0013079

Pulakos, E. D., Arad, S., Donovan, M. A., & Plamondon, K. E. (2000). Adaptability in the workplace: Development of a taxonomy of adaptive performance. *Journal of Applied Psychology, 85*(4), 612–624. doi:10.1037/0021-9010.85.4.612

Rich, B. L., LePine, J. A., & Crawford, E. R. (2010). Job engagement: Antecedents and effects on job performance. *Academy of Management Journal, 53*(3), 617–635. doi:10.5465/AMJ.2010.51468988

Schaufeli, W. B., & Bakker, A. B. (2003). *Test manual for the Utrecht Work Engagement Scale.* Utrecht, the Netherlands: Utrecht University. Retrieved May 17, 2016 from http://www.wilmarschaufeli.nl/

Schaufeli, W. B., Salanova, M., González-Romá, V., & Bakker, A. B. (2002). The measurement of engagement and burnout: A two sample confirmatory factor analytic approach. *Journal of Happiness Studies, 3*(1), 71–92. doi:10.1023/A:1015630930326

Smith, C., Organ, D. W., & Near, J. P. (1983). Organizational citizenship behavior: Its nature and antecedents. *Journal of Applied Psychology, 68*(4), 653–663. doi:10.1037/0021-9010.68.4.653

Van Dyne, L., Graham, J. W., & Dienesch, R. M. (1994). Organizational citizenship behavior: Construct redefinition, measurement, and validation. *Academy of Management Journal, 37*(4), 765–802. doi:10.2307/256600

Williams, L. J., & Anderson, S. E. (1991). Job satisfaction and organizational commitment as predictors of organizational citizenship and in-role behaviors. *Journal of Management, 17*(3), 601–617. doi:10.1177/014920639101700305

CHAPTER

5

Distinguishing Proactivity From Citizenship Behavior: Similarities and Differences

Wen-Dong Li, Michael Frese, *and* Sarah Haidar

Abstract

Organizational citizenship behavior (OCB) and proactivity have garnered a great deal of research attention recently. Some scholars have subsumed proactivity under the concept of OCB because both concepts are based on discretionary behaviors. In this chapter, we want to summarize reasons to differentiate OCB from proactivity. We do this by showing that their functions are different even when they may be correlated, that there are different evolutionary paths for the development of OCB and proactivity, and that there are different biological components. At the same time, we argue that both OCB and proactivity have important evolutionary functions for humans, allowing humans to become a dominate animal in the world. We hope this chapter can spur more research on the intersection between the two constructs.

Key Words: OCB, proactivity, helping, evolution, agency, communion, genetics

The last three decades have witnessed a surge of research interests in organizational citizenship behaviors and proactivity, the latter of which encompasses both proactive personality and proactive behaviors (Bateman & Crant, 1993; Bateman & Organ, 1983; Bindl & Parker, 2010; Frese & Fay, 2001; Grant & Ashford, 2008; Organ, Podsakoff, & Podsakoff, 2011). There is no question that organizational citizenship behavior (OCB) and proactive behavior are important phenomena at work. It is our thesis in this chapter that both concepts show some overlap but also need to be clearly distinguished. We shall argue that both have deep evolutionary roots but, at the same time, that they have developed in the evolution for different purposes.

The increased attention on OCB and proactivity in research and practice is due to the changing nature of work with an emphasis on service, and dealing with a fast-paced business world and ever more quickly developing innovations. Thus, modern work is full of uncertainty, challenges, and interdependence, which necessitate employees to go above and beyond the call of duty and embrace more work responsibilities by engaging in more spontaneous behaviors to enhance employee and organizational effectiveness (Griffin, Neal, & Parker, 2007; Katz & Kahn, 1978). Indeed, both OCB and proactivity have been demonstrated in previous empirical research to be positively correlated with employee job performance (N. P. Podsakoff, Whiting, Podsakoff, & Blume, 2009; Tornau & Frese, 2013), and even organizational-level performance outcomes (Baer & Frese, 2003; Glaub, Frese, Fischer, & Hoppe, 2014; MacKenzie, Podsakoff, & Podsakoff, 2011; Podsakoff, Ahearne, & MacKenzie, 1997).

Briefly, OCB's centerpiece is discretionary helping behavior that is not explicitly required by the work role (Organ, 1988). Proactivity also encompasses discretionary and extra-role behaviors; however, such behaviors refer to self-starting behaviors that are future oriented and persistent in the face of obstacles (Frese & Fay, 2001). A defining characteristic of proactivity is that it concentrates on making things happen and requires personal agency, even overcoming obstacles. There are various concepts that belong to the family of proactivity, such as personal initiative (Frese & Fay, 2001), proactive personality (Bateman & Crant, 1993), or taking charge (Morrison, 1994), as well as voice (Van Dyne & LePine, 1998). There are differences whether they emphasize personality (e.g., proactive personality) or behavior (e.g., personal initiative) or whether they are more implementation oriented (e.g., both taking charge and personal initiative) or more related to signaling a need for change (e.g., voice). However, they all share the earlier definition in broad strokes (Bindl & Parker, 2010; Grant & Ashford, 2008). Tornau and Frese (2013) argued on the basis of their meta-analysis that it is best to clearly differentiate between proactive personality (which can be captured by the scale of proactive personality and the scale of personal initiative personality) and proactive behavior (consisting of personal initiative behavior, taking charge, and voice). Table 5.1 provides an overview of the definitions and the differentiations within proactivity (Tornau & Frese, 2013, p. 47).

The increased attention on OCB and proactivity in research and practice is due to the changing nature of work, with an emphasis on service, and dealing with a fast-paced business world and ever more quickly developing innovations. Thus, modern work is full of uncertainty, challenges, and interdependence, which necessitate that employees go above and beyond the call of duty and embrace more work responsibilities by engaging in more spontaneous behaviors to enhance employee and organizational effectiveness (Griffin, Neal, & Parker, 2007; Katz & Kahn, 1978). Indeed, both OCB and proactivity have been demonstrated in previous empirical research to be positively correlated with employee job performance (N. P. Podsakoff, Whiting, Podsakoff, & Blume, 2009; Tornau & Frese, 2013) and even organizational-level performance outcomes (e.g., MacKenzie, Podsakoff, & Podsakoff, 2011; Podsakoff, Ahearne, & MacKenzie, 1997).

We endeavor to highlight the differences between proactivity and OCB in this chapter. We are aware that the conceptual domain of OCB has recently been substantially broadened from its original conceptualization and operationalization (e.g., Moon, Van Dyne, & Wrobel, 2005; Podsakoff, MacKenzie, Paine, & Bachrach, 2000; Spitzmuller, Van Dyne, & Ilies, 2008). It now includes a good part of proactivity as well. Even one of us wrote an article arguing that personal initiative was one form of OCB (Speier & Frese, 1997). However, we now concur with Bindl and Parker (2010) that it is useful and necessary to differentiate the two concepts (see also McAllister, Kamdar, Morrison, & Turban, 2007).

This is how we would like to proceed in this chapter: First, we perform a thought experiment and show how easily one can fill all four dimensions of a 2 x 2 figure (Figure 5.1) that includes high and low OCB and proactivity. In doing so, we also draw upon the social psychological literature on agency and communion, which serves as an important theoretical foundation in examining the relationship between OCB and proactivity. Second, we speculate on the different evolutionary functions of proactivity and OCB. Third, we show and partly speculate that there are different hormonal systems underlying proactivity and OCB. Finally, we present that there is an empirical overlap between OCB and proactivity and discuss why that is possible.

A 2 x 2 Figure of Proactivity and Organizational Citizenship Behavior

Before we present the 2 x 2 figure, we need to explain why there are good historical reasons to focus on one particular type of OCB, namely the *helping/altruism* dimension instead of challenge-oriented citizenship behaviors. First, in his seminal book, *The Functions of the Executive*, which is a pivotal basis for Organ's original work on the conceptualization of OCB (Organ et al., 2011), Barnard (1938) raised the importance of the "willingness of persons to contribute efforts to the cooperative system" (p. 83). The emphasis was essentially on cooperation (rather than change-oriented behaviors). Thus, the original conceptualization of OCB centered on the willingness to cooperate. Related to this, Organ (1988) originally conceptualized citizenship behavior as altruistic and prosocial in nature, and as such, helping/altruism was one of the two factors in the original OCB research (Smith, Organ, & Near, 1983). Third, in their influential paper, Van Dyne et al. (1995) provided the following suggestion to future OCB research: "The conceptual definition and subsequent operationalizations of Organizational Citizenship Behavior (OCB) should focus on citizenship behavior that is affiliative and promotive [e.g., helping] and should not include challenging/prohibitive, challenging/promotive, or affiliative/prohibitive behaviors" (p. 274). Fourth, Organ has repeatedly argued that OCB is important for the smooth functioning of

Table 5.1 Definitions and Differences Among Proactivity Constructs

Concept	Original Definition	Dominant Operationalization	Sample Items
Personal initiative/ personality	Self-rated personal initiative, defined as self-started, future- and change-oriented, and persistent behaviors; essentially, it is the same as proactive personality (Frese & Fay, 2001; Tornau & Frese, 2013)	Self-rating	I actively attack problems.
Personal initiative/ behavior	"Personal initiative is work behavior characterized by its self-starting nature, its proactive approach, and by being persistent in overcoming difficulties that arise in the pursuit of a goal" (Frese & Fay, 2001, p. 134).	Interview:	Worker says he or she changed something at work; Interviewer prompts whether it was (a) his or her own idea and (b) future oriented. If so, code it as personal initiative.
		Overcoming barriers	How many barriers were overcome and was this was an active approach?
		Retrospective initiative	Have you introduced work changes last year? (Code how much energy went into the activity and how much did the activity go beyond job descriptions.)
		Peer, supervisor-rating	Others rate behaviors on the self- report personal initiative scale. For instance, whenever there is a chance to get actively involved, this person takes it.
Proactive personality	"relative stable tendency to effect environmental change" (Bateman & Crant, 1993, p. 105)	Self-rating	I am constantly on the lookout for new ways to improve my life.
Taking charge	"Taking Charge entails voluntary and constructive efforts, by individual employees, to effect organizationally functional change with respect to how work is executed within the contexts of their jobs, work units, or organizations" (Morrison & Phelps, 1999, p. 403).	Peer-/supervisor-rating	This person often tries to change how his or her job is executed in order to be more effective.
Voice	"promotive behavior that emphasizes expression of constructive challenge intended to improve rather than merely criticize. Voice is making innovative suggestions for change and recommending modifications to standard procedures even when others disagree" (Van Dyne & LePine, 1998, p. 109)	Peer-/supervisor-rating	This person develops and makes recommendations concerning issues that affect the work group.

	Low OCB	High OCB
High Proactivity	Shows no helping, may be callous; however, provides ideas and improves organization's long term well-being, as well as career	Helps without being asked, suggesting new ideas both to group as well as boss directed toward improving team and organization as well as helping others' well-being (e.g., proactive helping)
Low Proactivity	Person neither helps nor is concerned about organization's long-term well-being and career; disengaged person	Person reacts to pleas of help but does not volunteer help (e.g., reactive helping)

Figure 5.1 A conceptual model of the relationship between proactivity and organizational citizenship behavior (OCB).

the organization; in contrast, proactivity can often have disruptive effects in organizations. In our view, expanding the definition of a construct (e.g., encompassing change-oriented behaviors as part of OCB) may result in unnecessary confusion and less clarity to the very nature of the construct. Based on the aforementioned reasoning, we decided to concentrate on helping as the core manifestation of OCB. In this chapter, by OCB we mean affiliative citizenship behaviors (i.e., helping) that may enhance the smooth functioning of the organization, if not otherwise noted. Thus, in essence, OCB is about the smooth social functioning of a team/tribe/organization, whereas proactivity is about the long-term, self-starting behavior that overcomes barriers to achieve long-term agentic goals. The latter may sometimes upset the smooth functioning of a team/tribe/organization in the present in order to improve the long-term functioning and the change of environment.

One important objective of this chapter is to offer a more nuanced and refined model clarifying the relationship between proactivity and OCB. Toward this goal, we draw upon research on the agency–communion framework. *Agency* and *communion* were two terms coined by Bakan (1966) as two fundamental modalities of human existence. Agency is manifested as "self-protection, self-assertion and self-expansion" and "the urge to master [the world and people]." Thus, agency bears substantial overlap with proactivity in terms of obtaining mastery over the outside world. Communion, on the other hand, is typically related to "being at one with other organisms" and "noncontractual cooperation" (Bakan, 1966, p. 15). Thus, communion overlaps largely with OCB in its emphasis on cooperation. This agency–communion framework is very similar to those adopted in other areas of psychology, such as Hogan's socioanalytic theory (e.g., the two fundamental dimensions of personality: getting ahead and getting along, Hogan, 1982; Hogan & Blickle, 2013), the higher order factors of the Big Five personality traits (alpha and beta factors; Digman, 1997), and the competence and warmth dimensions in social judgments (Abele, Cuddy, Judd, & Yzerbyt, 2008; Judd, James-Hawkins, Yzerbyt, & Kashima, 2005). Moreover, it has been theorized that agency and communion have been formed over millennia in order to meet two core life challenges: acquiring mastery of the environment and other people, and connecting with others (Ybarra et al., 2008). Such theorizing shares a great deal with our reasoning on the evolutionary basis of proactivity and OCB. Thus, this framework has widely been adopted in various streams of research in psychology.

Given that the core of proactivity is human agency and the heart of OCB is helping, the agency–communion framework seems to fit nicely for the purpose of refining the relationship between proactivity and OCB. Following Wiggins (1991), we treat proactivity and OCB as two independent constructs and provide a conceptual model to represent their relationship (Figure 5.1). As depicted in Figure 5.1, four different situations (cells) are generated based on the levels of proactivity and OCB: 2 (high versus low levels of OCB) x 2 (high versus low levels of proactivity).

The most important function of this figure is to make it obvious that one can easily think of examples for each of the four situations in the figure. This by itself speaks to the necessity to separate the two dimensions: OCB, which leads to the smooth functioning of the organization; and proactivity, which refers to self-started initiatives to improve work and organizing work for better future functioning.

However, each cell may be more or less probable depending upon the environment. Thus, while some cells may appear highly frequent, others may be less so. This is partly due to possible selection effects within certain organizations or even across most organizations. For example, completely non-altruistic people are less frequently employed, and completely passive individuals are less frequently hired or retained. Once differential cell frequencies appear, a sizable but not high correlation may become apparent between proactivity and OCB even if they are conceptually distinguishable.

High Proactivity and High Organizational Citizenship Behavior

High levels of proactivity and OCB probably generate the most ideal and beneficial situation for organizations. There are many examples for such a case. One is proactive helping, defined as helping behaviors that "originate from within the helper on the basis of active efforts to satisfy personal needs" (Spitzmuller & Van Dyne, 2013, p. 565). Such proactive helping behaviors are initiated by the agentic person and are driven by the helper's personal motives. This term is very similar to the reconceptualization of giving, defined as "prosocial behaviors in which one willingly engages" (Cain, Dana, & Newman, 2014, p. 505). Similarly, volunteering is also a good manifestation of this case in which proactivity and OCB are both high. "Volunteering involves prosocial action in an organizational context, which is planned and that continues for an extended period" (Penner, Dovidio, Piliavin, & Schroeder, 2005, p. 375). That is probably an important reason why researchers have observed positive relationships between volunteering and job meaningfulness, job absorption, and job performance (Rodell, 2013). Another example is the study by Grant, Parker, and Collins (2009), showing that the beneficial influences of proactive behaviors (e.g., taking charge and voice) on supervisors' performance ratings were contingent on employees' prosocial motives. Across two studies, they observed that the positive relationships between proactive behaviors and performance ratings only held for those employees with high levels of prosocial motives. This research showcases the importance of high agency and high communion for the benefits of employees in terms of securing favorable job performance ratings.

High Proactivity and Low Organizational Citizenship Behavior

Although it is ideal to have both high levels of proactivity and OCB, one possible combination is high proactivity and low OCB. Researchers in the field of proactivity have long recognized the possibility that proactivity is not always welcomed by coworkers and even supervisors (Frese & Fay, 2001; Grant & Ashford, 2008). One reason could be that high proactivity is sometimes accompanied with low levels of OCB. Bakan (1966) also stressed that either high levels of agency or communion alone may lead to negative outcomes. The so-called unmitigated agency has been used to refer to the case in which agency is taken to the extreme without communion. For example, Kim and Glomb (2010) examined the relationship between intelligence (an important predictor of agency/proactivity; Fay and Frese, 2001) and victimization, that is, whether smart people are more likely to be victimized by others. They found a positive relationship between the two constructs. Moreover, they also observed that this positive relationship was more pronounced among those people who scored high on agency traits (i.e., dominance or extraversion), and it was less pronounced among those who were high on communion traits (i.e., community/agreeableness). In a follow-up study, Kim and Glomb (2014) further looked into the mediating mechanisms in the relationship between agency (as reflected in high levels of performance) and victimization. They found that high performers tended to be envied by other people, which in turn fostered victimization. Such research demonstrates some adverse effects that may result from high levels of proactivity and low levels of OCB.

Low Proactivity and High Organizational Citizenship Behavior

In extending Bakan's (1966) work, Helgeson (1994) pointed out that, similar to unmitigated agency, communion in the absence of agency (unmitigated communion) may also be harmful. Helgeson argued that "An exaggerated focus on connection and concern with the preservation of relationships can be harmful if it undermines physical and psychological caring for oneself" (p. 417). Related to this, Cain et al (2014) coined the term of "giving in," defined as "prosocial behavior in which one reluctantly engages, often in response to social pressure or obligation" (p. 505). This is similar to a more refined conceptualization of helping, reactive helping, which refers to helping behavior performed in the context of a social exchange in response to others' needs and which is triggered by the environment, not by the helper (Spitzmuller & Van Dyne, 2013). Another related concept is job creep, which has been developed to refer to the situation in which extrarole behaviors (e.g., helping) gradually become part of expected behaviors by colleagues or supervisors (Van Dyne & Ellis, 2004). In other words, job incumbents are forced to expand their role requirements to include such behaviors originally regarded as above and beyond the call of duty. Although this is an important research topic, to our knowledge, there has been little research on this issue.

Low Proactivity and Low Organizational Citizenship Behavior

This scenario represents a situation in which both proactivity and OCB are low. Probably no manager or organization would like to see employees who do not take initiative and engage in no OCB either. However, it is likely that this category exists. Popular literature often reports that there is a high degree of disengagement at the workplace (Bruch & Ghoshal, 2002, 2004). Moreover, there is clearly a high degree of variance in the organizational climate of supporting personal initiative (Baer & Frese, 2003).

Differential Evolutionary Roots and Functions of Proactivity and Organizational Citizenship Behavior

We draw upon evolutionary psychology (Buss, 2008) in clarifying the origins of OCB and proactivity, and we propose that both OCB and proactivity are likely to be important for evolutionary purposes. Moreover, we argue that humans are uniquely strong on both of these characteristics—altruism and social concern, as well as agentic and long-term change of the environment. "The genus Homo is estimated to be about 2.5 million years old and for most of their existence, hominids lived in small, kin-based bands on the African savannah, adopting a nomadic hunter-gatherer lifestyle" (van Vugt, Hogan, & Kaiser, 2008, p. 183) This requires the development of group-oriented approaches to assure survival and reproduction. The cooperative nature of OCB enables various matters within a group to run smoothly, and it promotes timely reactions to danger and development of good routines. In this regard, OCB may be the first and foremost function of evolution. On the other hand, proactivity is more about challenging the status quo, which may sometimes disrupt the smooth functioning of a group. Proactivity is also related to the exploration of new physical or intellectual territories (e.g., what is behind the next mountain; how can I predict the weather). The development of novel tools and technology is crucial to proactivity in this sense, because it renders change and exploration possible. It is very interesting that the development of human tools is also estimated to have a history within the range of 2.5 or 2.6 million years (Festinger, 1983). Thus, it seems plausible that tool use may serve as a prima facie example of the proactive agentic nature of humans.

Evolutionary psychology highlights the importance of evolved psychological mechanisms because such mechanisms help to solve specific survival or reproduction problems that have faced humans repeatedly in the evolutionary history. Humans may have developed numerous evolved psychological mechanisms. Such specific and complex evolved psychological mechanisms may provide humans with the advantage of ensuring that the social behavior of teams, tribes, and families functions smoothly. At the same time, without long-term future thinking and preparing for potential catastrophes now and without being interested in developing new ideas and improving tools and their use, human beings would have suffered and may not have survived. Thus, two major evolved psychological mechanisms for survival include OCB and proactivity.

Altruistic/prosocial behavior or helping "represents a broad category of acts that are defined by some significant segment of society and/or one's social group as generally beneficial to other people" (Penner et al., 2005, p. 366). Such behaviors represent "costly acts that confer economic benefits on other individuals" (Fehr & Fischbacher, 2003, p. 785). A critical question in this line of inquiry on altruistic/prosocial behavior often arises: Why do individuals engage in behaviors that are beneficial to other people (e.g., not necessarily to the helper)? Indeed, this question has puzzled researchers, including economists and social psychology, for decades. From an evolutionary perspective, helping others seems irrational because helping oneself is more directly useful to promote one's chance for survival and reproduction during human evolution (in the sense of the selfish gene; Dawkins, 1976; Hamilton, 1964; Trivers, 1971). Over years of research, researchers have proposed several theoretical explanations for this puzzle. The first possible reason is that, through extended human evolution, altruistic behavior may have evolved in order to aid extended family members when they are in need (i.e., kinship selection), because family members also carry similar genetic materials and thus assisting them will also enhance the chance for help providers' genes to transmit from one generation to another. Simply put, helping others such as one's extended family members may also be evolutionally logical in terms of aiding the transmission of one's genes to later generations. Second, helping may have been retained through human evolution because help receivers may return the favor to help providers at some later point in time (i.e., reciprocal altruism). The beauty of reciprocal helping is that both the help provider and the help receiver can benefit from such behaviors. Such mutual helping behavior engenders evolutionary advantages of survival and development for both help providers and help receivers. As a result, the groups with higher levels of mutual helping behavior tend to have greater fitness to the ever-changing environment and thus have a much greater chance to survive and reproduce their genetic materials in the evolution process. In this vein, helping behavior may have been selected and retained during the long process of human evolution to enhance group survival and reproduction.

Similarly, proactivity may have been formed through human evolution as well (Arvey, Li, & Wang, 2016; Li, 2011). As a manifestation of human agency, proactivity represents humans' unique capability to change the environment (Frese & Zapf, 1994). In his influential book, Bakan (1966) asserted that "the objective of agency is mastery [of the world and people]" (p. 60). Thus, proactivity may be manifested in numerous forms, including achieving high levels of status and customizing the surrounding environment. In the history of human evolution, human agency may have been one factor that contributed to humans' migration out of Africa into other continents (cf. Buss, 2008). In addition, researchers have proposed that foresight and planning, a core element of proactivity to implement changes in the environment, is one defining feature that distinguishes humans from other animals (Suddendorf & Corballis, 2007). In particular, using foresight and planning together with tools seems to be uniquely human (although there are some other performers of tool use such as chimpanzees) (Dolgin, 1985; Schurig, 1985).

Tool use and the development of technology make it possible for humans to deal with specific defects. From an evolutionary perspective, humans are somewhat defective social animals—they are neither exceptionally strong, fast, nor equipped with very good senses (hearing, eyesight, night vision, smelling) or special physical skills, such as climbing or flying. They are also not perfectly shielded from outside danger (e.g., compared to turtles or chameleons), and they have the added disadvantage of a long childhood and long dependency of children on adults, which reduce the chances to reproduce quickly enough. In other words, tool use and the development of technology provided humans with unique advantages for survival and reproduction. Through work and working in which systematic and social organization of tool use takes place, humans could survive in spite of their biological defects. Eventually, tool use has spurred the development of specialized languages, writing, and formidable tools that extend human strength, intellectual capacity, reach, and theoretical penetration. In this way, the human form of tool use has led to dominance over all other species and dominance over the nature (for better or worse).

Thus, humans are to some extent flawed social animals from a biological point of view. With evolution, humans did not get faster, stronger, or anything resembling that. In contrast, human evolution did the exact opposite: It handicapped the early humans (Festinger, 1983). As Festinger (1983) pointed out about the humans of 2–5 million years ago: "Speed of movement, for example, . . . would have been a highly advantageous thing for any animal. Bipedalism greatly reduced the speed of movement . . . . Almost any four-legged animal can run faster than a man" (pp. 4–5). And later he adds: "An extraordinary variety of uses were invented for the arms and hands—and invented is the key word" (p. 5). The hand became a multipurpose instrument. To quote Festinger (1983) again: "They used their hands to manipulate tools . . . excavations in Ethiopia have revealed that about 2.6 million years ago humans were manufacturing stone tools deliberately, creating sharp edges" (pp. 10 and 12). Although other animals also use tools and even manufacture them, Festinger (1983) adds: "It should also be simultaneously clear that there is an enormous difference of degree, both in the variety of tool uses and in the dependence of tools for survival, between the human and other animals" (p. 12).

Different Hormones Possibly Responsible for Proactivity and Organizational Citizenship Behavior

Hormones play a crucial role in contributing to helping related behaviors, including cooperation and prosocial behaviors. Two that are often studied in previous research are oxytocin and vasopressin (Arvey, Wang, Song, & Li, 2014; Ebstein, Knafo, Mankuta, Chew, & Lai, 2012). Variations of oxytocin and vasopressin existed approximately 700 million years ago and have also been found to modulate social behaviors for both humans and animals, such as social bonding and attachment (Donaldson & Young, 2008). Oxytocin was initially called a "female reproductive hormone," because of its influences in parental care and nurturing (Lee, Macbeth, Pagani, & Young, 2009). It was also termed the "hormone of love" due to its role in social bonding (Carter, 2014). Recently, experimental research reveals the role of oxytocin in modulating trust and cooperation. For example, it was reported that intranasal oxytocin gives rise to increased amounts of money that an investor is willing to allocate to his or her "trustee" (Kosfeld, Heinrichs, Zak, Fischbacher, & Fehr, 2005). This result only held when the trustee was allowed to return some money back to the investor, but not for the situation when the return of money to the investor was determined randomly. Another study found that when an investor was betrayed by getting little money returned by the trustee, the discovery of betrayal only led to a decrease of further investment for the placebo control group, but not for the group with the oxytocin treatment (Baumgartner, Heinrichs, Vonlanthen, Fischbacher, & Fehr, 2008). Molecular genetic research found that the receptor gene for oxytocin was significantly related to empathy (Rodrigues, Saslow, Garcia, John, & Keltner, 2009), one important affective variable associated with prosocial behaviors. This gene was also found to be linked with important psychological resources, such as optimism, mastery, and self-esteem (Saphire-Bernstein, Way, Kim, Sherman, & Taylor, 2011). Compared to oxytocin, vasopressin has been studied less. But similar patterns of results have been obtained for this hormone as well. For instance, research found that vasopressin changed the perceptions of friendliness of facial expression (Thompson, George, Walton, Orr, & Benson, 2006).

For proactivity, two hormonal systems may be of particular importance: dopamine and testosterone. One form of biological foundation that undergirds human agency/proactivity is the dopamine system, which is involved in human reward, approach, and motivation systems (Depue & Collins, 1999). In support of this argument, researchers have found that a dopamine transporter gene, DAT1, is significantly related to proactive personality, defined as an individual's tendency to alter the environment (Li et al., 2015). Dopamine receptor genes, such as DRD4, have also been reported to be linked to approach-related traits and behaviors, such as novelty taking (Benjamin et al., 1996; Ebstein et al., 1996; Munafò, Yalcin, Willis-Owen, & Flint, 2008), and entrepreneurship (Nicolaou, Shane, Adi, Mangino, & Harris, 2011) and involved in job changes (Chi, Li, Wang, & Song, 2016). DRD4 was also found to be related to job satisfaction (Song, Li, & Arvey, 2011), which has been regarded as an important consequence of proactivity (Fay & Sonnentag, 2002).

Human agency/proactivity may also be related to status achieving, because after he or she has achieved a high level of status in the society, one can have more control over other people and perhaps also the surroundings. Potentially, people with a high degree of proactivity may also be seen as effective and are, therefore, provided higher status. Hormones play a significant role in "the development and expression of social status" (Cummins, 2005, p. 678). For example, testosterone has been proposed to contribute to humans' striving for status (Buss, 2008). Testosterone is connected to risk taking for males (Mazur & Booth, 2014). For example, high levels of testosterone is linked to risk-taking behaviors (Stenstrom, Saad, Nepomuceno, & Mendenhall, 2011), risk-taking decisions (Garbarino, Slonim, & Sydnor, 2011), aggression (Hönekopp, 2011), and risk preference and long-term profitability of male traders (Coates, Gurnell, & Rustichini, 2009). Moreover, testosterone is related to proactive career choices, such as entrepreneurship (Bönte, Procher, & Urbig, in press).

More recent data reveal that the effect of testosterone (at least prenatal testosterone) may depend on other conditioning variables. One study showed that entrepreneurs with a high level of exposure to prenatal testosterone were more successful, but this relationship was significant only for those who also showed a high level of need for achievement (Unger, Rauch, Weis, & Frese, 2015). The authors argued that testosterone may be a form of unregulated energy, whereas the achievement motive provides the direction and regulation for this energy.

The evidence seems to support the argument that testosterone is an important form of biological foundation for proactivity. Interestingly, the causation direction between proactivity and the level of testosterone may go both ways. Change in social status may enhance testosterone levels, and change in testosterone levels may also generate alteration in social status. For example, research shows that male winners of competitive games elevated their levels of testosterone compared to losers (Booth, Shelley, Mazur, Tharp, & Kittok, 1989). In contrast, animal studies demonstrate that after low-ranking cows were treated with testosterone, their ranking within the group of cows rose; moreover, when the treatment was stopped, their rank sank to the previous low levels (Bouissou, 1978).

In summary, human agency/proactivity may be a product of human evolution. In stressing this important notion, Bandura (2001) wrote:

> People are not only reactors to selection pressures, but they are producers of new ones at an increasingly dizzying pace. Through agentic action, people devise ways of adapting flexibly to remarkably diverse geographic, climatic and social environments; they figure out ways to circumvent physical and environmental constraints, redesign and construct environments to their liking, create styles of behavior that enable them to realize desired outcomes, and pass on the effective ones to others by social modeling and other experiential modes of influence. By these inventive means, people improve their odds in the fitness survival game. (p. 22)

Why Is There Empirical Overlap Between Proactivity and Organizational Citizenship Behavior?

Although OCB and proactivity are distinct from each other, they also share some similarities. Conceptually, they are two different constructs. Judging from their definitions, a fundamental feature of OCB is providing assistance to others, either colleagues or supervisors. Helping may be completely reactive or proactive (Spitzmuller & Van Dyne, 2013). Proactivity, on the other hand, is a manifestation of human agency to gain mastery over the environment and other people. Such change-oriented behaviors may "rock the boat," and thus proactivity may not be welcomed by coworkers or supervisors (Frese & Fay, 2001; Seibert, Kraimer, & Crant, 2001). In this section, we will discuss why there is empirical overlap between OCB and proactivity.

OCB and proactivity may share similar antecedents. Some individual difference variables (personality traits and general mental ability) have been theorized and investigated as critical predictors of both OCB and proactivity. To initiate positive changes in the environments, individuals need cognitive abilities to detect problems in the environment and come up with novel solutions to such problems. Moreover, positive changes of the environment and the person often require individuals to overcome numerous obstacles and barriers and reflections of strategies and effective actions (Bindl & Parker, 2010; Frese & Fay, 2001). All such activities necessitate high levels of cognitive abilities and skills. Indeed, a meta-analytic study found that general mental ability was significantly related to proactive behaviors (i.e., personal initiative; corrected $r = .25$; Tornau & Frese, 2013, p. 66). Cognitive abilities have not been suggested to be related to OCB, and, indeed, research shows that there is no significant correlation between cognitive abilities and OCB (Chiaburu, Oh, Berry, Li, & Gardner, 2011; Organ, 1988). See Table 5.2 for

Table 5.2 Differences and Similarities in the Antecedents and Consequences of Organizational Citizenship Behavior (OCB) and Proactive Behavior

	Antecedents		Outcomes
	Individual Differences	Organizational Variables	
OCB	Big Five personality traits	Transformational leadership, LMX, abusive supervision, coworker support	Individual job performance, organizational effectiveness
Proactive behavior	General mental abilities, Big Five personality traits, self-efficacy, need for cognition, attachment styles	Transformational leadership, coworker relationship	Individual job performance

a summary of the similarities and differences for antecedents and outcomes of OCB and proactive behaviors.

However, personality traits have been suggested to be more important in shaping OCB than task performance (Organ, 1988). The most recent meta-analytic study on the relationship between personality and OCB (Chiaburu et al., 2011) found that all the Big Five personality traits were related to individually directed OCB (OCB-I; encompassing altruism, helping, courtesy, interpersonal facilitation, and personal support) with corrected correlations ranging from .10 to .21. There are also clear relationships between the Big Five with proactive behavior: Extraversion and conscientiousness were most important in predicting proactive behaviors (Tornau & Frese, 2013). Agreeableness was not an important predictor of proactivity (Tornau & Frese, 2013). Note that proactive personality was found to be more strongly related to proactive behaviors as reported in this meta-analytic study, with corrected correlations ranging from .28 to .53. Such evidence provides support to the notion that proactive personality is a compound personality trait for people to engage in proactive behaviors (Bateman & Crant, 1993). Lastly, self-efficacy, need for cognition, and attachment styles have recently been examined as important individual difference variables driving proactivity (Frese, Garst, & Fay, 2007; Wu & Parker, 2012; Wu, Parker, & De Jong, 2014).

Organizational contextual variables have also been studied as enabling factors that facilitate OCB and proactivity. Previous research looked at leadership variables, such as transformational leadership (Piccolo & Colquitt, 2006; Wang, Oh, Courtright, & Colbert, 2011), LMX (Dulebohn, Bommer, Liden, Brouer, & Ferris, 2012; Ilies, Nahrgang, & Morgeson, 2007), abusive supervision (Zellars, Tepper, & Duffy, 2002), and organizational culture (Li, Wang, Taylor, Shi, & He, 2008) precursors of OCB. In addition, coworker relationships (e.g., coworker support and coworker antagonism) have also been examined as predictors of OCB (Chiaburu & Harrison, 2008). Similarly, leadership and coworker relationships have also been shown to be related to proactivity (Li, Fay, Frese, Harms, & Gao, 2014). For instance, management openness to change was found to give rise to taking charge (Morrison & Phelps, 1999). Transformational leadership (Den Hartog & Belschak, 2012) and LMX (Dulebohn et al., 2012) have also been found to be such leadership variables conducive to proactivity. Proactive behaviors were also reported to be related to coworker relationships, including coworker support and coworker trust (Parker, Williams, & Turner, 2006).

With respect to consequences, OCB has been initially conceptualized as the type of behaviors that in aggregate form may promote organizational effectiveness. Indeed, meta-analytic evidence has demonstrated that OCB is not only related to individual performance and performance appraisal results but also team and organizational effectiveness (e.g., MacKenzie et al., 2011; N. P. Podsakoff et al., 2009; Podsakoff et al., 1997).

Proactivity, including both proactive personality and proactive behavior, has also been reported to be related to individual job performance and career success (Fuller & Marler, 2009; Thomas, Whitman, & Viswesvaran, 2010). However, this is not always the case—proactivity is not always beneficial to individual employees. Indeed, one study reported that voice had some adverse effect on career progression (Seibert et al., 2001). Proactive personality has also been found to be related to envy from coworkers (Sun, Li, Liden, Li, & Li, under review).

As discussed earlier in the 2 x 2 figure, whenever people are selected, the cells have different frequencies and, therefore, in real work situations, there may be correlations between OCB and proactivity even if the two concepts follow different processes and need to be differentiated conceptually. To provide empirical evidence to demonstrate their relationship, we conducted a meta-analysis. In terms of proactivity, we included proactive personality and three proactive behaviors (i.e., voice, taking charge, and personal initiative). Given that the three proactive behaviors are highly correlated with each other (their corrected correlations ranged from .77 to .78; see Tornau & Frese, 2013), we combined their correlations with helping in our meta-analyses. Our analyses showed a corrected average correlation of .28 (95% confidence interval [CI] = [.11, .45]) between proactive personality and helping (both self- and other-rated) ($n = 443$, $k = 3$). The corrected average correlation between proactive behaviors and helping was .40 (95% CI = [.27, .52]) ($n = 2{,}248$, $k = 8$). This correlation was smaller than the corrected correlation between change-oriented OCB (including taking charge, voice, adaptive performance, personal initiative, creativity, and innovation) and OCB-I (Chiaburu et al., 2011), perhaps because the distinctive conceptualizations and operationalizations of the different constructs. Such findings offer some preliminary support for the linkage between OCB and proactivity.

Conclusion

In this chapter, we discuss the differences and similarities between proactivity and OCB (i.e., helping). We specifically focus on the core defining characteristic of OCB: helping. We contend that proactivity and OCB are related because of their functions to human survival and reproduction from a perspective of evolutionary psychology. We argue that the two constructs may also have differential biological roots as they are related to various forms of hormones. Our meta-analysis showed that they are also somewhat related to each other, given the similar individual difference and organizational contextual variables that may be related to both. We encourage future research to tackle the intersection between proactivity and OCB from a general integrative agency–communion framework.

References

Abele, A. E., Cuddy, A. J., Judd, C. M., & Yzerbyt, V. Y. (2008). Fundamental dimensions of social judgment. *European Journal of Social Psychology, 38*(7), 1063–1065.

Arvey, R. D., Li, W. D., & Wang, N. (2016). Genetics and organizational behavior. *Annual Review of Organizational Psychology and Organizational Behavior*, 3, 167–190.

Arvey, R. D., Wang, N., Song, Z., & Li, W. (2014). The biology of leadership. In D. Day (Ed.), *Oxford handbook of leadership and organizations* (pp. 75–92). New York: Oxford University Press.

Baer, M., & Frese, M. (2003). Innovation is not enough: Climates for initiative and psychological safety, process innovations, and firm performance. *Journal of Organizational Behavior, 24*, 45–68.

Bakan, D. (1966). *The duality of human existence.* Chicago, IL: Rand McNally.

Bandura, A. (2001). Social cognitive theory: An agentic perspective. *Annual Review of Psychology, 52*(1), 1–26.

Barnard, C. I. (1938). *The functions of the executive.* Cambridge, MA: Harvard University Press.

Bateman, T. S., & Crant, J. M. (1993). The proactive component of organizational behavior: A measure and correlates. *Journal of Organizational Behavior, 14*(2), 103–118.

Bateman, T. S., & Organ, D. W. (1983). Job satisfaction and the good soldier: The relationship between affect and employee "citizenship." *Academy of Management Journal, 26*(4), 587–595.

Baumgartner, T., Heinrichs, M., Vonlanthen, A., Fischbacher, U., & Fehr, E. (2008). Oxytocin shapes the neural circuitry of trust and trust adaptation in humans. *Neuron, 58*(4), 639–650.

Benjamin, J., Li, L., Patterson, C., Greenberg, B. D., Murphy, D. L., & Hamer, D. H. (1996). Population and familial association between the D4 dopamine receptor gene and measures of novelty seeking. *Nature Genetics, 12*(1), 81–84.

Bindl, U. K., & Parker, S. K. (2010). Proactive work behavior: Forward-thinking and change-oriented action in organizations. In S. Zedeck (Ed.), *APA handbook of industrial and organizational psychology* (Vol. 2, pp. 567–598). Washington, DC: American Psychological Association.

Bönte, W., Procher, V. D., & Urbig, D. (2016). Biology and selection into entrepreneurship—The relevance of prenatal testosterone exposure. *Entrepreneurship Theory and Practice, 40*(5), 1121–1148.

Booth, A., Shelley, G., Mazur, A., Tharp, G., & Kittok, R. (1989). Testosterone, and winning and losing in human competition. *Hormones and Behavior, 23*(4), 556–571.

Bouissou, M.-F. (1978). Effect of injections of testosterone propionate on dominance relationships in a group of cows. *Hormones and Behavior, 11*(3), 388–400.

Bruch, H., & Ghoshal, S. (2002). Beware the busy manager. *Harvard Business Review* (Feb.), 63–69.

Bruch, H., & Ghoshal, S. (2004). Management is the art of doing and getting done. *Business Strategy Review, 15*(3), 4–13.

Buss, D. M. (2008). *Evolutionary psychology: The new science of the mind.* Boston, MA: Allyn & Bacon.

Cain, D. M., Dana, J., & Newman, G. E. (2014). Giving versus giving in. *The Academy of Management Annals, 8*(1), 505–533.

Carter, C. S. (2014). Oxytocin pathways and the evolution of human behavior. *Annual Review of Psychology, 65*, 17–39.

Chi, W., Li, W. D., Wang, N., & Song, Z. (2016). Can genes play a role in explaining frequent job changes? An examination of gene-environment interaction from human capital theory. *Journal of Applied Psychology*, 101(7), 1030–1044.

Chiaburu, D. S., & Harrison, D. A. (2008). Do peers make the place? Conceptual synthesis and meta-analysis of coworker effects on perceptions, attitudes, OCBs, and performance. *Journal of Applied Psychology, 93*(5), 1082–1103.

Chiaburu, D. S., Oh, I.-S., Berry, C. M., Li, N., & Gardner, R. G. (2011). The five-factor model of personality traits and organizational citizenship behaviors: A meta-analysis. *Journal of Applied Psychology, 96*(6), 1140–1166.

Coates, J. M., Gurnell, M., & Rustichini, A. (2009). Second-to-fourth digit ratio predicts success among high-frequency financial traders. *Proceedings of the National Academy of Sciences, 106*(2), 623–628.

Cummins, D. (2005). Dominance, status, and social hierarchies. In D. M. Buss (Ed.), *The handbook of evolutionary psychology* (pp. 676–697). Hoboken, NJ: John Wiley & Sons.

Dawkins, R. (1976). *The selfish gene.* New York, NY Oxford University Press.

Den Hartog, D. N., & Belschak, F. D. (2012). When does transformational leadership enhance employee proactive behavior? The role of autonomy and role breadth self-efficacy. *Journal of Applied Psychology, 97*(1), 194–202.

Depue, R. A., & Collins, P. F. (1999). Neurobiology of the structure of personality: Dopamine, facilitation of incentive motivation, and extraversion. *Behavioral and Brain Sciences, 22*(3), 491–517.

Digman, J. M. (1997). Higher-order factors of the Big Five. *Journal of Personality and Social Psychology, 73*(6), 1246–1256.

Dolgin, K. G. (1985). An action-theory perspective of the tool-using capacities of chimpanzees and human infants. In M. Frese & J. Sabini (Eds.), *Goal directed behavior: The concept of action in psychology* (pp. 35–47). Hillsdale, NJ: Erlbaum.

Donaldson, Z. R., & Young, L. J. (2008). Oxytocin, vasopressin, and the neurogenetics of sociality. *Science, 322*(5903), 900–904.

Dulebohn, J. H., Bommer, W. H., Liden, R. C., Brouer, R. L., & Ferris, G. R. (2012). A meta-analysis of antecedents and consequences of leader-member exchange integrating the past with an eye toward the future. *Journal of Management, 38*(6), 1715–1759.

Ebstein, R. P., Knafo, A., Mankuta, D., Chew, S. H., & Lai, P. S. (2012). The contributions of oxytocin and vasopressin pathway genes to human behavior. *Hormones and Behavior, 61*(3), 359–379.

Ebstein, R. P., Novick, O., Umansky, R., Priel, B., Osher, Y., Blaine, D., . . . Belmaker, R. H. (1996). Dopamine D4 receptor (D4DR) exon III polymorphism associated with the human personality trait of novelty seeking. *Nature Genetics, 12*(1), 78–80.

Fay, D., & Frese, M. (2001). The concept of personal initiative: An overview of validity studies. *Human Performance, 14*(1), 97–124.

Fay, D., & Sonnentag, S. (2002). Rethinking the effects of stressors: A longitudinal study on personal initiative. *Journal of Occupational Health Psychology, 7*(3), 221–234.

Fehr, E., & Fischbacher, U. (2003). The nature of human altruism. *Nature, 425*(6960), 785–791.

Festinger, L. (1983). *The human legacy*. New York, NY: Columbia University Press.

Frese, M., & Fay, D. (2001). Personal initiative: An active performance concept for work in the 21st century. *Research in Organizational Behavior, 23*, 133–187.

Frese, M., Garst, H., & Fay, D. (2007). Making things happen: Reciprocal relationships between work characteristics and personal initiative in a four-wave longitudinal structural equation model. *Journal of Applied Psychology, 92*(4), 1084–1102.

Frese, M., & Zapf, D. (1994). Action as the core of work psychology: A German approach. In H. C. Triandis, M. D. Dunnette, & L. Hough (Eds.), *Handbook of industrial and organizational psychology* (Vol. 4, pp. 271–340). Palo Alto, CA: Consulting Psychologists Press.

Fuller, B., & Marler, L. E. (2009). Change driven by nature: A meta-analytic review of the proactive personality literature. *Journal of Vocational Behavior, 75*, 329–345.

Garbarino, E., Slonim, R., & Sydnor, J. (2011). Digit ratios (2D: 4D) as predictors of risky decision making for both sexes. *Journal of Risk and Uncertainty, 42*(1), 1–26.

Glaub, M., Frese, M., Fischer, S., & Hoppe, M. (2014). Increasing personal initiative in small business managers/owners leads to entrepreneurial success: A theory-based controlled randomized field intervention for evidence based management. *Academy of Management Learning & Education, 13*, 354–379.

Grant, A. M., & Ashford, S. J. (2008). The dynamics of proactivity at work. *Research in Organizational Behavior, 28*, 3–34.

Grant, A. M., Parker, S., & Collins, C. (2009). Getting credit for proactive behavior: Supervisor reactions depend on what you value and how you feel. *Personnel Psychology, 62*(1), 31–55.

Griffin, M. A., Neal, A., & Parker, S. K. (2007). A new model of work role performance: Positive behavior in uncertain and interdependent contexts. *The Academy of Management Journal, 50*(2), 327–347.

Hamilton, W. D. (1964). The genetical evolution of social behaviour I and II. *Journal of theoretical biology, 7*(1), 1–52.

Helgeson, V. S. (1994). Relation of agency and communion to well-being: Evidence and potential explanations. *Psychological Bulletin, 116*(3), 412–428.

Hogan, R. (1982). A socioanalytic theory of personality. In M. M. Page (Ed.), *Nebraska symposium on motivation: Personality-current theory and research* (pp. 58–89). Lincoln, NE: University of Nebraska Press.

Hogan, R., & Blickle, G. (2013). Socioanalytic theory. In N. Christiansen & R. Tet (Eds.), *Handbook of personality at work* (pp. 53–70). New York, NY: Routledge.

Hönekopp, J. (2011). Relationships between digit ratio 2D: 4D and self-reported aggression and risk taking in an online study. *Personality and Individual Differences, 51*(1), 77–80.

Ilies, R., Nahrgang, J. D., & Morgeson, F. P. (2007). Leader-member exchange and citizenship behaviors: A meta-analysis. *Journal of Applied Psychology, 92*(1), 269–277.

Judd, C. M., James-Hawkins, L., Yzerbyt, V., & Kashima, Y. (2005). Fundamental dimensions of social judgment: Understanding the relations between judgments of competence and warmth. *Journal of Personality and Social Psychology, 89*(6), 899–913.

Katz, D., & Kahn, R. L. (1978). *The social psychology of organizations* (2nd ed.). New York, NY: John Wiley & Sons, Inc.

Kim, E., & Glomb, T. M. (2010). Get smarty pants: Cognitive ability, personality, and victimization. *Journal of Applied Psychology, 95*(5), 889–901.

Kim, E., & Glomb, T. M. (2014). Victimization of high performers: The roles of envy and work group identification. *Journal of Applied Psychology, 99*(4), 619–634.

Kosfeld, M., Heinrichs, M., Zak, P. J., Fischbacher, U., & Fehr, E. (2005). Oxytocin increases trust in humans. *Nature, 435*(7042), 673–676.

Lee, H.-J., Macbeth, A. H., Pagani, J. H., & Young, W. S. (2009). Oxytocin: The great facilitator of life. *Progress in Neurobiology, 88*(2), 127–151.

Li, W. D. (2011). *Proactive personality and work success: Disentangling genetic and environmental influences*. Paper presented at the The 2011 Annual Academy of Management Meeting, San Antonio, Texas.

Li, W. D., Fay, D., Frese, M., Harms, P. D., & Gao, X. (2014). Reciprocal relationships between proactive personality and work characteristics: A latent change score approach. *Journal of Applied Psychology, 99*(5), 948–965.

Li, W. D., Wang, N., Arvey, R., Soong, R., Saw, S. M., & Song, Z. (2015). A mixed blessing? Dual mediating mechanisms in the relationship between dopamine transporter gene DAT1 and leadership role occupancy. *The Leadership Quarterly, 26*(5), 671–686.

Li, W. D., Wang, Y., Taylor, P., Shi, K., & He, D. (2008). The influence of organizational culture on work-related personality requirement ratings: A multilevel analysis. *International Journal of Selection & Assessment, 16*(4), 367–385.

MacKenzie, S. B., Podsakoff, P. M., & Podsakoff, N. P. (2011). Challenge-oriented organizational citizenship behaviors and organizational effectiveness: Do challenge-oriented behaviors really have an impact on the organization's bottomline. *Personnel Psychology, 64*(3), 559–592.

Mazur, A., & Booth, A. (2014). Testosterone is related to deviance in male army veterans, but relationships are not moderated by cortisol. *Biological Psychology, 96*, 72–76.

McAllister, D. J., Kamdar, D., Morrison, E. W., & Turban, D. B. (2007). Disentangling role perceptions: How perceived role breadth, discretion, instrumentality, and efficacy relate to helping and taking charge. *Journal of Applied Psychology, 92*, 1200–1211.

Moon, H., Van Dyne, L., & Wrobel, K. (2005). The circumplex model and the future of organizational citizenship behavior research. In D. L. Turnipseed (Ed.), *Handbook of organizational citizenship behavior* (pp. 3–23). New York, NY: Nova Science.

Morrison, E. W. (1994). Role definitions and organizational citizenship behavior: The importance of the employee's perspective. *Academy of Management Journal, 37*(6), 1543–1567.

Morrison, E. W., & Phelps, C. C. (1999). Taking charge at work: Extrarole efforts to initiate workplace change. *Academy of Management Journal, 42*, 403–419.

Munafò, M. R., Yalcin, B., Willis-Owen, S. A., & Flint, J. (2008). Association of the Dopamine D4 Receptor (DRD4) gene and approach-related personality traits: Meta-analysis and new data. *Biological Psychiatry, 63*(2), 197–206.

Nicolaou, N., Shane, S., Adi, G., Mangino, M., & Harris, J. (2011). A polymorphism associated with entrepreneurship: Evidence from dopamine receptor candidate genes. *Small Business Economics, 36*(2), 151–155.

Organ, D. W. (1988). *Organizational citizenship behavior: The good soldier syndrome.* Lexington, MA: Lexington Books.

Organ, D. W., Podsakoff, P. M., & Podsakoff, N. P. (2011). Expanding the criterion domain to include organizational citizenship behavior: Implications for employee selection. In S. Zedeck (Ed.), *APA handbook of industrial and organizational psychology* (Vol. 2, pp. 281–323). Washington, DC: American Psychological Association.

Parker, S. K., Williams, H. M., & Turner, N. (2006). Modeling the antecedents of proactive behavior at work. *Journal of Applied Psychology, 91*(3), 636–652.

Penner, L. A., Dovidio, J. F., Piliavin, J. A., & Schroeder, D. A. (2005). Prosocial behavior: Multilevel perspectives. *Annual Review of Psychology, 56*, 365–392.

Piccolo, R. F., & Colquitt, J. A. (2006). Transformational leadership and job behaviors: The mediating role of core job characteristics. *Academy of Management Journal, 49*(2), 327–340.

Podsakoff, N. P., Whiting, S. W., Podsakoff, P. M., & Blume, B. D. (2009). Individual-and organizational-level consequences of organizational citizenship behaviors: A meta-analysis. *Journal of Applied Psychology, 94*(1), 122–141.

Podsakoff, P. M., Ahearne, M., & MacKenzie, S. B. (1997). Organizational citizenship behavior and the quantity and quality of work group performance. *Journal of Applied Psychology, 82*(2), 262–270.

Podsakoff, P. M., MacKenzie, S. B., Paine, J. B., & Bachrach, D. G. (2000). Organizational citizenship behaviors: A critical review of the theoretical and empirical literature and suggestions for future research. *Journal of Management, 26*(3), 513–563.

Rodell, J. (2013). Finding meaning through volunteering: Why do employees volunteer and what does it mean for their jobs? *Academy of Management Journal, 56*(5), 1274–1294.

Rodrigues, S. M., Saslow, L. R., Garcia, N., John, O. P., & Keltner, D. (2009). Oxytocin receptor genetic variation relates to empathy and stress reactivity in humans. *Proceedings of the National Academy of Sciences, 106*(50), 21437–21441.

Saphire-Bernstein, S., Way, B. M., Kim, H. S., Sherman, D. K., & Taylor, S. E. (2011). Oxytocin receptor gene (OXTR) is related to psychological resources. *Proceedings of the National Academy of Sciences, 108*(37), 15118–15122.

Schurig, V. (1985). Stages in the development of tool behavior in the chimpanzee (Pan troglodytes). In M. Frese & J. Sabini (Eds.), *Goal directed behavior: The concept of action in psychology* (pp. 20–34). Hillsdale, NJ: Erlbaum.

Seibert, S. E., Kraimer, M. L., & Crant, J. M. (2001). What do proactive people do? A longitudinal model linking proactive personality and career success. *Personnel Psychology, 54*(4), 845–874.

Smith, C. A., Organ, D. W., & Near, J. P. (1983). Organizational citizenship behavior: Its nature and antecedents. *Journal of Applied Psychology, 68*(4), 653–663.

Song, Z., Li, W. D., & Arvey, R. D. (2011). Associations between dopamine and serotonin genes and job satisfaction: Preliminary evidence from the Add Health Study. *Journal of Applied Psychology, 96*(6), 1223–1233.

Speier, C., & Frese, M. (1997). Generalized self efficacy as a mediator and moderator between control and complexity at work and personal initiative: A longitudinal field study in East Germany. *Human Performance, 10*(2), 171–192.

Spitzmuller, M., & Van Dyne, L. (2013). Proactive and reactive helping: Contrasting the positive consequences of different forms of helping. *Journal of Organizational Behavior, 34*(4), 560–580.

Spitzmuller, M., Van Dyne, L., & Ilies, R. (2008). Organizational citizenship behavior: A review and extension of its nomological network. In J. Barling & C. L. Cooper (Eds.), *The SAGE handbook of organizational behavior* (Vol. 1, pp. 106–123). Thousand Oaks, CA: Sage.

Stenstrom, E., Saad, G., Nepomuceno, M. V., & Mendenhall, Z. (2011). Testosterone and domain-specific risk: Digit ratios (2D: 4D and rel2) as predictors of recreational, financial, and social risk-taking behaviors. *Personality and Individual Differences, 51*(4), 412–416.

Suddendorf, T., & Corballis, M. C. (2007). The evolution of foresight: What is mental time travel, and is it unique to humans? *Behavioral and Brain Sciences, 30*(03), 299–313.

Sun, J., Li, W. D., Liden, R., Li, S., & Li, Y. Dark Side of Being Proactive? A Multilevel Investigation Linking Proactive Personality to Being Envied, under review

Thomas, J. P., Whitman, D. S., & Viswesvaran, C. (2010). Employee proactivity in organizations: A comparative meta-analysis of emergent proactive constructs. *Journal of Occupational and Organizational Psychology, 83*(2), 275–300.

Thompson, R., George, K., Walton, J., Orr, S., & Benson, J. (2006). Sex-specific influences of vasopressin on human social communication. *Proceedings of the National Academy of Sciences, 103*(20), 7889–7894.

Tornau, K., & Frese, M. (2013). Construct clean-up in proactivity research: A meta-analysis on the nomological net of work-related proactivity concepts and incremental validity. *Applied Psychology: An International Review, 62*(1), 44–96.

Trivers, R. L. (1971). The evolution of reciprocal altruism. *Quarterly Review of Biology, 46*, 35–57.

Unger, J. M., Rauch, A., Weis, S. E., & Frese, M. (2015). Biology (prenatal testosterone), psychology (achievement need) and entrepreneurial impact. *Journal of Business Venturing Insights, 4*, 1–5.

Van Dyne, L., Cummings, L. L., & McLean Parks, J. (1995). Extra-role behaviors: In pursuit of construct and definitional clarity (a bridge over muddied waters). In L. L. Cummings & B. M. Staw (Eds.), *Research in organizational behavior* (Vol. 17, pp. 215–330). Greenwich, CT: JAI Press.

Van Dyne, L., & Ellis, J. B. (2004). Job creep: A reactance theory perspective on organizational citizenship behavior as over-fulfillment of obligations. In J. A. M. Coyle-Shapiro, L. M. Shore, M. S. Taylor & L. E. Tetrick (Eds.),

The employment relationship: Examining psychological and contextual perspectives (pp. 181–205). Oxford, UK: Oxford University Press.

Van Dyne, L., & LePine, J. A. (1998). Helping and voice extra-role behaviors: Evidence of construct and predictive validity. *Academy of Management Journal, 41*(1), 108–119.

van Vugt, M., Hogan, R., & Kaiser, R. B. (2008). Leadership, followership, and evolution: Some lessons from the past. *American Psychologist, 63*(3), 182–196.

Wang, G., Oh, I.-S., Courtright, S. H., & Colbert, A. E. (2011). Transformational leadership and performance across criteria and levels: A meta-analytic review of 25 years of research. *Group & Organization Management, 36*(2), 223–270.

Wiggins, J. S. (1991). Agency and communion as conceptual coordinates for the understanding and measurement of interpersonal behavior. In W. Grove & D. Ciccetti (Eds.), *Thinking clearly about psychology: Essays in honor of Paul Everett Meehl* (pp. 89–113). Minneapolis, MN: University of Minnesota Press.

Wu, C. H., & Parker, S. K. (2012). The role of attachment styles in shaping proactive behaviour: An intra-individual analysis. *Journal of Occupational and Organizational Psychology, 85*(3), 523–530.

Wu, C. H., Parker, S. K., & De Jong, J. P. (2014). Need for cognition as an antecedent of individual innovation behavior. *Journal of Management, 40*(6), 1511–1534.

Ybarra, O., Chan, E., Park, H., Burnstein, E., Monin, B., & Stanik, C. (2008). Life's recurring challenges and the fundamental dimensions: An integration and its implications for cultural differences and similarities. *European Journal of Social Psychology, 38*(7), 1083–1092.

Zellars, K. L., Tepper, B. J., & Duffy, M. K. (2002). Abusive supervision and subordinates' organizational citizenship behavior. *Journal of Applied Psychology, 87*(6), 1068–1076.

CHAPTER

6

The Other Side of the Coin?: Similarities and Differences Between Organizational Citizenship Behavior and Counterproductive Work Behavior

Reeshad S. Dalal *and* Nichelle C. Carpenter

Abstract

This chapter examines the relationship between two important forms of job performance: organizational citizenship behavior and counterproductive work behavior. There are several reasons (e.g., construct definitions, relationships with antecedents) to suspect that these two constructs are strongly negatively related, perhaps even opposite ends of a single behavioral continuum. However, empirical results demonstrate a relationship that is typically weakly to moderately negative and occasionally even positive. We discuss theory and empirical results (where possible, meta-analytic) at not just the traditional between-person level of analysis but also the within-person and between-unit levels. Our review suggests several important future research opportunities at the traditional between-person level (e.g., a pressing need for more and better theory). Yet, in our view, the most exciting research opportunities exist at the within-person level. Overall, the relationship between citizenship and counterproductive behavior promises to remain a vibrant and influential area of research for the foreseeable future.

Key Words: organizational citizenship behavior, counterproductive work behavior, within-person, between-person, level of analysis, theory

The question of whether people are inherently "good" or "bad" has a venerable history. The philosopher Thomas Hobbes believed that humans are not social animals, that the "state of nature" involves "continual fear, and danger of violent death," and that life is "solitary, poor, nasty, brutish, and short" (Hobbes, 1651/2011, p. 126). The philosopher John Locke, in contrast, held a more optimistic view. Locke believed that humans are social animals, that the state of nature involves people making and keeping obligations to each other, and that life is for the most part communal, peaceful, and more pleasant than Hobbes allowed (Locke, 1689/1982).

With regard to employee behavior in work organizations, one way of examining the question of whether people are good or bad involves, in turn, examining the relationship between the constructs of organizational citizenship behavior and counterproductive work behavior. If people are either good or bad, there should be a strong negative relationship between these two constructs because any given person would score high on organizational citizenship behavior and low on counterproductive work behavior, or vice versa. If, however, a strong negative relationship does not exist, it is overly simplistic to conclude that people are either good or bad.

But, of course, the question can be reformulated in a more nuanced manner. Even if people are not either good or bad per se, are they either good or bad *on a particular occasion*? In other words, is there a strong negative relationship between organizational citizenship behavior and counterproductive work behavior on a particular occasion—such that a person who engages in organizational citizenship behavior does not *simultaneously* (or within a short period of time) engage in counterproductive work behavior, or vice versa?

The current chapter will discuss questions such as these, along with other (related) questions regarding the *theoretical arguments* for and against a strong negative relationship between organizational citizenship behavior and counterproductive work behavior as well as yet other questions about *methodological choices* that appear to strengthen or weaken the relationship between the two constructs. Of late, research in this area has been thriving (for just a few examples, see Dalal, 2005; Dalal, Lam, Weiss, Welch, & Hulin, 2009; Spector, Bauer, & Fox, 2010; Spector & Fox, 2002, 2010a, 2010b). This is fortunate because clarification of the relationship between these two constructs directly addresses a fundamental problem in organizational research: the "criterion problem" or, simply put, the fact that organizational researchers unfortunately know less about the constructs they are trying to predict (i.e., criteria) than they do about the constructs they are using as predictors (Austin & Villanova, 1992; Weitz, 1961).

Overview of Chapter

We begin this chapter by introducing the constructs of organizational citizenship behavior and counterproductive work behavior—and by discussing the meta-analytic relationship between them. We then turn to a discussion of their antecedents, and in that context we discuss both empirical (typically meta-analytic) results and extant theory regarding these constructs at multiple levels of analysis. After that, we discuss several methodological factors that influence the magnitude of the relationship between these constructs. Finally, although we discuss avenues for future research throughout the chapter, in the last major section we provide several suggestions for future theoretical and empirical research.

Construct Definitions and Meta-Analytic Relationships

Organizational citizenship behavior (hereafter, OCB) is employee behavior that improves the functioning of the organization. OCB was, furthermore, originally viewed (e.g., Organ, 1988) as behavior that is intentional but discretionary (i.e., voluntary)—for instance, behavior that is typically not recognized or rewarded by the organization. Of late, however, it has been acknowledged that OCB may be recognized during performance appraisals and may contribute toward rewards such as raises (Organ, 1997; Organ, Podsakoff, & MacKenzie, 2006). Examples of OCB include helping others who have heavy workloads, assisting one's supervisor with his or her work without being asked, taking time to listen to coworkers' problems and worries, being mindful of how one's behavior affects other people's jobs, volunteering for tasks that are not required but that are nonetheless beneficial to the organization, giving advance notice when unable to come to work, and adhering to informal rules designed to maintain order (Podsakoff, MacKenzie, Moorman, & Fetter, 1990; Smith, Organ, & Near, 1983; Williams & Anderson, 1991). OCB is often structured on the basis of the target or recipient of the behavior: other individuals in the organization (OCB-I; e.g., helping others) versus the organization itself (OCB-O; e.g., adhering to rules, Williams & Anderson, 1991).

Counterproductive work behavior (hereafter, CWB), sometimes referred to as workplace deviant behavior (Bennett & Robinson, 2000), is employee behavior that harms the legitimate interests of an organization (Gruys & Sackett, 2003; Sackett & DeVore, 2001). Like OCB, CWB is defined as intentional behavior (Sackett & DeVore, 2001). Thus, for instance, accidental harm to the organization does not count as CWB. Examples of CWB include purposely damaging equipment or property, taking a longer break than allowed, purposely failing to follow instructions, taking money from one's employer without permission, coming to work under the influence of alcohol or drugs, verbally abusing someone at work, and threatening someone at work with violence (Gruys & Sackett, 2003; Spector et al., 2006). Similar to OCB, CWB is often structured on the basis of the target or recipient of the behavior: other individuals in the organization (CWB-I; e.g., verbal abuse) versus the organization itself (CWB-O; e.g., theft of organizational property, Bennett & Robinson, 2000).

The definitions of OCB and CWB are in some senses mirror images of each other (viz., OCB helps and CWB harms the organization). The targets of OCB and CWB are also identical. This provides a basis for questions about the relationship between OCB and CWB (Dalal, 2005). Specifically, are OCB and CWB so strongly negatively related as to be opposite ends of a broader behavioral continuum? Can employees be categorized as either "good citizens" or "deviants?"

Existing research on the relationship between OCB and CWB does not support this contention. Dalal (2005) reported a corrected (for unreliability) meta-analytic OCB–CWB correlation of –0.32. This relationship is certainly negative in direction. However, it is—according to Cohen's (1992) rules of thumb—barely a moderate, let alone a strong, relationship.

Both Dalal (2005) and Berry, Ones, and Sackett (2007) also report more granular meta-analytic relationships at the level of facets of OCB and CWB. The strongest of these relationships reported by Dalal was $\rho = -0.33$ (between OCB-O and CWB-O), and the strongest of these relationships reported by Berry et al. was $\rho = -0.44$ (between CWB-O and overall OCB). Even these relationships, however, fall short of what Cohen (1992) would characterize as a strong relationship—and they fall *considerably* short of a relationship sufficiently strong that researchers would consider the two constructs to be opposites.

But, of course, there is another, albeit more indirect, way of estimating the relationship between OCB and CWB: namely, by comparing these constructs' relationships with a set of presumed antecedents. Such an examination would also shed light on extant theories proposed by researchers to explain the enactment of OCB and CWB. It is therefore to this topic that we turn next.

Antecedents of the OCB–CWB Relationship: Theoretical Formulations and Empirical Findings

OCB and CWB have traditionally been studied at the between-person level of analysis, and theory regarding their enactment has therefore also traditionally been focused at this level. Recently, however, there has been considerable attention devoted to the study of psychological phenomena, including but not limited to OCB and CWB, at the within-person level of analysis. This new focus has been accompanied by a flurry of theory building at the within-person level. The unit (collective) level of analysis has also begun to receive some attention, with accompanying theoretical models. We discuss antecedents—and associated theories—at each of these levels in turn.

The Between-Person Level of Analysis

At this level, OCB and CWB are individual differences in behavior (or job performance). They are associated with broader behavior "types," or perhaps stereotypes, such as "the good citizen" and "the deviant." In this section, we discuss antecedents shared by these two constructs.

The contention that OCB and CWB are opposite ends of the same continuum translates into a twofold prediction regarding OCB's and CWB's relationships with antecedents. First, OCB's and CWB's relationships with external constructs such as antecedents should be opposite in direction (i.e., sign). For instance, if OCB is related positively to a particular antecedent, CWB should be related negatively to that antecedent. Second, if OCB and CWB are opposite ends of the same continuum, they should share similar patterns of magnitudes (sizes) of relationships with antecedents. For instance, if OCB is strongly related to Antecedent A, moderately related to Antecedent B, and weakly related to Antecedent C, then CWB too should exhibit this pattern of relationships (albeit in the opposite direction). We examine empirical results related to antecedent–OCB and antecedent–CWB relationships, and we do so in the context of the theoretical formulations that might explain these antecedent–behavior relationships.

Antecedents of OCB and CWB fall into two broad categories. The first category is dispositional. The idea here is that some people are dispositionally inclined to engage in certain levels of OCB and CWB. In this category, we discuss the personality trait of conscientiousness as well as habitual (trait) patterns of emotionality. The second category is situational. However, rather than pertaining directly to characteristics of situations (e.g., Meyer et al., 2014; Rauthmann et al., 2014), this category of antecedents can more accurately be described as employees' reactions to situations: for instance, appraisals such as perceived organizational justice and attitudes such as job satisfaction and organizational commitment. We discuss these antecedents in turn, along with (where available) relevant theory.

CONSCIENTIOUSNESS

Meta-analyses of the literature (Dalal, 2005; see also Berry et al., 2007) suggest that conscientiousness is related to OCB (positively) and CWB (negatively). In other words, compared to employees who score low on conscientiousness, employees who score high on conscientiousness are more likely to engage in OCB and less likely to engage in CWB. Moreover, in terms of magnitude, conscientiousness–OCB relationships tend to be in the 0.23 to 0.30 range, whereas conscientiousness–CWB relationships tend to be in the –0.26 to –0.42 range (Berry et al., 2007; Dalal, 2005).[1] Conscientiousness–OCB relationships therefore appear to be somewhat weaker than conscientiousness–CWB relationships.

It is noteworthy that there is little in the way of theory to explain these relationships. Rather, the assumption simply seems to be that "people with a particular personality behave in a particular way." Although the lack of theory is unfortunate, it is regrettably the norm in applied personality research. Personality researchers typically conceptualize personality in two ways (Dalal et al., 2015): (1) a descriptor of aggregated past behavior or (2) some sort of causal agent for behavior. The first conceptualization of personality does not readily lend itself to theory about personality–behavior relationships. Rather, personality–behavior relationships under this conceptualization simply reflect the maxim that past behavior predicts present and future behavior. Conscientiousness, therefore, would relate positively to "conscientious behavior" such as OCB and would relate negatively to "unconscientious behavior" such as CWB. The second conceptualization of personality is in principle more promising for theories of personality–behavior relationships, but this promise has not yet been actualized. Specifically, this conceptualization has not yet been adequately fleshed out to identify the mechanisms through which personality predicts behavior (Dalal et al., 2015).

In summary, then, although conscientiousness is indeed related in opposite directions to OCB and CWB, the theoretical basis for these relationships remains unclear.

TRAIT AFFECT

Trait affect refers to habitual or characteristic patterns of emotionality. Trait positive affect refers to the extent to which people characteristically feel enthusiastic, active, and alert, whereas trait negative affect refers to the extent to which people characteristically encounter aversive mood states (Watson, Clark, & Tellegen, 1988). Trait positive and negative affect are related but not identical to the personality traits of extraversion and neuroticism, respectively (Kaplan, Bradley, Luchman, & Haynes, 2009). Meta-analytic findings (Dalal, 2005) suggest that OCB is related positively to PA and negatively to NA, and that CWB is related positively to NA and negatively to PA. Thus, OCB and CWB do exhibit opposite-direction relationships with trait affect. In terms of magnitude, Dalal (2005) reported two somewhat discrepant estimates of the meta-analytic PA–OCB relationship ($\rho = 0.12$ and 0.34) and one estimate of the meta-analytic PA–CWB relationship ($\rho = -0.34$). Dalal moreover reported two highly convergent estimates of the meta-analytic NA–OCB relationship (both ρs = -0.10) and one estimate of the meta-analytic NA–CWB relationship ($\rho = 0.41$). These results suggest that the relative magnitudes of the PA–OCB and PA–CWB relationships are uncertain, but that the NA–OCB relationship is weaker than the NA–CWB relationship.

At this point, we would normally turn to the theoretical rationale for these between-person relationships. Indeed, theory regarding affect–OCB and affect–CWB relationships certainly exists (e.g., Weiss & Cropanzano, 1996). However, extant theory actually pertains to the manner in which within-person fluctuations in affect influence within-person fluctuations in OCB and CWB (Dalal et al., 2009, 2014)—that is, to the relationship between *state* affect and *state* behavior. Although the theory has frequently been applied to the relationship between *trait* affect and *trait* behavior, this application is at best imprecise (requiring additional assumptions of homology across levels of analysis; Chen, Bliese, & Mathieu, 2005). We therefore discuss theory regarding affect–OCB and affect–CWB relationships in a subsequent section of this chapter, in the context of within-person affect-behavior relationships.

SITUATIONAL APPRAISALS: ORGANIZATIONAL JUSTICE, JOB SATISFACTION, AND ORGANIZATIONAL COMMITMENT

Another set of antecedents stems from employees' reactions to their work situations—in particular, appraisals such as perceived organizational justice and attitudes such as job satisfaction and organizational commitment. Meta-analytic results (Dalal, 2005) indicate that these antecedents are related positively to OCB and negatively to CWB. Moreover, these results suggest that justice, satisfaction, and commitment are related more strongly to CWB than to OCB.

The predominant theory employed by both OCB and CWB researchers to explain these results is social exchange theory (Thibaut & Kelley, 1959) or a variant (see Gouldner, 1960; Rousseau, 1989). According to social exchange theory, employees respond to fair workplace processes, outcomes, and interactions and to satisfying working conditions by exhibiting commitment to the organization and by intentionally behaving in ways that benefit the organization and/or other employees (i.e., OCB). Conversely, employees respond to unfair workplace processes, outcomes, and interactions and to dissatisfying working conditions by exhibiting a lack of commitment to the organization and by intentionally behaving in ways that harm the organization and/or other employees (i.e., CWB). Social exchange theory, therefore, explains the opposite-direction relationships exhibited by antecedents with OCB and CWB. On its surface, the theory is also seemingly conducive to the idea that OCB and CWB are opposite ends of the same continuum: Employees, for instance, might react to unfair conditions by engaging in CWB and by refraining from OCB, and they might react to fair conditions by engaging in OCB and by refraining from CWB. However, research on the distinction between positive and negative reciprocity (e.g., Eisenberger, Lynch, Aselage, & Rohdieck, 2004) suggests that employees may react to unfair treatment with negative behavior (CWB) without any implications for positive behavior (OCB)—and vice versa for fair treatment. This latter perspective suggests that OCB and CWB should not be strongly interrelated.

Regardless, the typical assumption underlying social exchange theory has been that work situations—and therefore appraisals of and attitudes toward these work situations—are stable over long periods of time. For example, a particular job might be characterized by a high level of situational constraints, which according to social exchange theory would yield job dissatisfaction and low levels of perceived organizational justice, which in turn would yield high CWB and (perhaps) low OCB. Yet situations are also likely to change over time within a given job (Dalal et al., 2014). We will return to this idea in a subsequent section, where we will discuss the role of volatile situations (such as workplace events) and their impact on OCB and CWB through momentary levels of affect. For the moment, however, we will note simply that although social exchange theory is certainly compatible with momentary, within-person processes, it has not typically been used to describe such processes.

BETWEEN-PERSON THEORY REGARDING ANTECEDENTS: SUMMARY

Meta-analytic results regarding between-person antecedents do suggest that several antecedents are related to OCB and CWB in opposite directions. However, there may well be other antecedents that are related to OCB and CWB in the same direction—a topic we discuss in a subsequent section of this chapter. The meta-analytic results discussed in this section moreover suggest that although antecedent–CWB relationships are generally stronger than antecedent–OCB relationships (consistent with the common finding, in psychology, that "bad is stronger than good"; Baumeister, Bratslavsky, Finkenauer, & Vohs, 2001), the extent of this discrepancy may itself differ across antecedents (Dalal, 2005). In other words, OCB and CWB do not appear to exhibit the same pattern of results with antecedents. Therefore, antecedent relationships at the between-person level do not provide compelling support for the contention that OCB and CWB are opposite ends of the same underlying continuum.

Moreover, a notable theme from the earlier discussion of antecedents is the sorry state of theory regarding the between-person antecedents of OCB and CWB and, in turn, the OCB–CWB relationship. Specifically, at the between-person level, theory is largely absent (in the case of conscientiousness), applied inappropriately (in the case of trait affect), or overly focused on stability at the expense of change (in the case of the situational antecedents). A major area for future research, therefore, involves better theory associated with the antecedents of OCB and CWB at the between-person level. Moreover, even in the best-case scenario, the between-person level of analysis provides an incomplete picture of the drivers of OCB and CWB. For a complete picture, it is necessary to examine theories and empirical findings regarding the antecedents of OCB and CWB at the within-person level of analysis.

The Within-Person Level of Analysis

Existing between-person theories focusing on the impact of the work situation can frequently be reconceptualized as within-person (or multilevel) theories. This can be achieved by focusing on momentary situations (e.g., events, episodes, or tasks) rather than chronic situations. In fact, the within-person approach is the more general one (Dalal et al., 2014): Chronic situations can be thought of as density distributions of momentary situations, with these distributions characterized by means, standard deviations, and so forth of momentary situations.

Take, for instance, social exchange theories. Traditionally, organizational justice has been viewed in such theories as a chronic situational characteristic (or appraisal thereof), such that some workplaces are unjust whereas others are just. A within-person social exchange theory may instead focus on the occurrence of events denoting justice and injustice at work, cognitive appraisals of and affective (mood and emotion) reactions to these justice-related events, and the ultimate consequences of these events in terms of OCB and CWB. An event appraised as unjust is likely to result in momentary (state) negative affect and, ultimately, momentary CWB. In contrast, an event appraised as just is likely to result in momentary positive affect and, ultimately, momentary OCB.

Importantly, such an approach would not preclude the study of between-person (or between-job) differences in reactions to (in)justice. Work situations (e.g., jobs) could be characterized in terms of the mean level of occurrence of unjust events, the variability with which unjust events occur, and so forth. Some jobs are likely to have high mean occurrence levels of unjust events, whereas other jobs are likely to have low mean occurrence levels. Importantly, however, even after controlling statistically for mean occurrence levels, some jobs may simply exhibit more variability across time than others in the occurrence of unjust events. That is, in addition to differences in the *level* (high vs. low) of injustice, jobs may be characterized by differences in the *volatility* (high vs. low) of injustice. A within-person (or multilevel) approach therefore provides the potential for rich theoretical explanations even with regard to between-person research questions (Dalal et al., 2014).

A within-person approach is, moreover, necessary to address the surprising neglect of affect in empirical studies of organizational justice (Dalal & Hulin, 2008). Within-person theories of OCB and CWB—especially those pertaining to the impact of situations on OCB and CWB—implicate affect as a central construct. Indeed, the core of affective events theory (Weiss & Cropanzano, 1996) is the Event → Affect → Behavior chain. The basic idea is fairly simple. Events occur in any workplace. These events can be expected or unexpected, can pertain directly to work or impinge indirectly on work (e.g., a child who falls ill may require a parent to leave early from work), and so forth. The events trigger appraisal and affective processes, which are closely intertwined at the within-person level. These appraisal and affective reactions to events, in turn, trigger behavioral reactions such as OCB and CWB. It may be that there exists a certain symmetry of valence, such that negative events trigger negative affect and, in turn, CWB, whereas positive events trigger positive affect and, in turn, OCB (Spector & Fox, 2002).

Affective events theory therefore suggests a substantial reorientation of research aiming to understand OCB, CWB, and their relationship. Yet affective events theory was intended as a framework or simplifying heuristic, aimed at explicating the importance of within-person Event → Affect → Behavior processes. It was not intended as a comprehensive theory. We therefore provide examples of a few theories that begin to flesh out the within-person process in more detail.

One such theory is Fredrickson's (2003, 2013) broaden and build theory. An important contribution of this theory is the delineation of the time frame associated with the translation of negative affect into CWB versus that of positive affect into OCB (Dalal et al., 2014). Negative affect, according to broaden and build theory, is an evolutionarily derived action tendency to aid in survival when the organism is threatened. The negative emotion of anger is believed to immediately activate the tendency to fight, which frequently results in the behavior of aggression. Similarly, the negative emotion of fear is believed to immediately activate the tendency to flee, which frequently results in the behavior of withdrawal. In the workplace, both aggression and withdrawal are components of CWB (Carpenter & Berry, 2017; Dalal et al., 2009). In contrast, positive affect increases a person's receptivity to new information and enhances the scope of attention. This broadened mindset gradually (over time) builds resources that can be drawn upon to engage in OCB.

Thus, according to broaden and build theory, the time frame between the experience of a negative event and the enactment (via negative affect) of CWB should be much shorter than the time frame between the experience of a positive event and the enactment (via positive affect) of OCB. Certain extensions of broaden and build theory (for instance, tipping-point positivity ratios) have been found to be incorrect, but the core of the theory appears to have received empirical support (Fredrickson, 2013). Researchers should therefore be aware of the likelihood of the discrepancy in Event → Affect → Behavior time frames for positive versus negative events, because this discrepancy increases the complexity of studying the OCB–CWB relationship at the momentary, within-person level.

A second relevant theory requires the assumption that employees (and people more generally) are hedonistic and prefer to experience good moods than bad moods (Dalal et al., 2009). People who are already in good moods wish to remain in good moods, whereas people who are in bad moods wish to improve their moods. People attempt to manage their moods using behavior such as OCB and CWB in accordance with their "folk theories" of mood maintenance and repair. Some of these folk theories may not be accurate. For instance, *contra* Freud, there is little evidence that cathartic displays of aggression (i.e., CWB) help to repair future mood (Bushman, 2002). However, the point is that behavior is driven by strategies that people believe to be effective rather than by strategies that are actually effective (Bushman, Baumeister, & Phillips, 2001).

The aforementioned explanations suggest that OCB and CWB are negatively related (albeit perhaps not very strongly so). Several other affective avenues, however, can result in *positive* relationships between OCB and CWB. We discuss three possibilities suggested in previous research (Bolino, Klotz, Turnley, & Harvey, 2013; Spector & Fox, 2010a, 2010b).

In some cases, OCB and CWB are common outcomes of third variables. For example, understimulation (which can be thought of as the absence of skill-engaging events) can lead to a state of boredom. Boredom, in turn, can lead to novelty seeking, which can then lead to both OCB and CWB.

In other cases, OCB can lead to CWB. For instance, an employee may sometimes feel that he or she is required to engage in OCB due to constraints or due to a coworker's low performance. If the employee attributes the need for OCB to factors within the control of other employees or the organization at large (e.g., if the employee perceives that a coworker's low performance is attributable to the coworker's unwillingness to work hard), the required OCB may lead to anger, which in turn may lead to CWB. Similarly, on occasions when an employee feels that the organization could, but chooses not to, reward (or even acknowledge) his or her OCB, the result may be anger and, in turn, CWB. As another example, an employee who has engaged in OCB may feel that he or she has earned a "moral license" or entitlement to engage in CWB (see also Klotz & Bolino, 2013).

In yet other cases, conversely, CWB can lead to OCB. For instance, on some occasions an employee may enact CWB but may subsequently feel that the CWB was unjustified. The employee is then likely to feel guilty. To alleviate the guilty mood (i.e., to engage in "moral cleansing"), the employee may engage in OCB (see also Ilies, Peng, Savani, & Dimotakis, 2013).

In summary, over the course of just a few years, the burgeoning within-person perspective has provided several very interesting possibilities regarding specific pathways within the broad Event → Affect → Behavior framework suggested by Weiss and Cropanzano's (1996) affective events theory. Both negative and positive within-person OCB–CWB relationships have been theorized under different circumstances. These theories do need to be further fleshed out theoretically, integrated (or contrasted) with each other theoretically (for details, see Dalal et al., 2014), and tested empirically. Yet what is clear is that the state of theory is already far superior at the within-person level than at the traditional between-person level.

The Unit Level of Analysis

Although we have focused on the between-person and within-person levels of analysis, we would be remiss if we did not also briefly mention the unit (i.e., group/team, division, organization, or any other collective) level of analysis. Some research has been conducted on unit-level—or, technically, between-unit-level—OCB and CWB. For instance, Ehrhart (2004) and Podsakoff, Podsakoff, MacKenzie, Maynes, and Spoelma (2014) have suggested that unit-level OCB reflects aggregated employee perceptions of OCB exhibited in the unit as a whole as opposed to aggregated employee reports of their own OCB—that is, through a reference-shift consensus composition model as opposed to a direct consensus composition model (Chan, 1998). Mayer, Kuenzi, Greenbaum, Bardes, and Salvador (2009) defined unit-level CWB as the normative level of CWB enacted within a unit, thereby similarly suggesting the importance of perceptions of CWB throughout the unit.

An important question regarding unit-level OCB and CWB is whether relationships at the individual level of analysis hold at the unit level—that is, whether relationships are homologous across levels (Chen et al., 2005). For example, Ehrhart (2004) suggested that unit-level Leadership → Justice → OCB relationships were similar to the effects at the individual employee level (i.e., the between-person level) and were similarly motivated by a social exchange theory framework. Whitman, Van Rooy, and Viswesvaran (2010) reported unit-level meta-analytic results showing that OCB was related to job satisfaction (.42) and unit performance (.29). The unit-level relationship between OCB and job satisfaction is stronger than the corresponding individual-level relationship (.16; Dalal, 2005), whereas the unit-level relationship between OCB and job performance is similar in size to the corresponding individual-level relationship (.27; Podsakoff et al., 2009).

It is currently unknown whether the relationship between OCB and CWB at the unit level is similar to or different from the relationship at other levels of analysis. At the unit level, the OCB–CWB relationship represents the relationship between the typical *collective* enactment of OCB and CWB in organizational units. In support of the perspective that OCB and CWB are opposite ends of the same continuum, antecedents that may influence employees in teams, departments, or organizations to engage collectively in OCB (e.g., attitudes, fairness perceptions) could also influence CWB in the opposite direction. For example, units containing collectively dissatisfied employees may be the site of lower levels of OCB and higher levels of CWB, contributing to a negative unit-level OCB–CWB relationship. However, we note that possible *positive* OCB–CWB relationships at the individual level have not yet been considered at the unit level.

One promising way to understand the unit-level relationship between OCB and CWB is to consider the norms for OCB or CWB at the unit level (e.g., O'Boyle, Forsyth, & O'Boyle, 2011), including how these norms develop. For instance, Ehrhart and Naumann (2004; see also Naumann & Ehrhart, 2011) have suggested a multilevel theoretical model of the relationship between descriptive and group-prescribed OCB norms (both at the unit level) and individual-level OCB. Raver, Ehrhart, and Chadwick (2012) have emphasized how unit-level norms develop through the compilation of individual-level personality traits, beliefs, and values. Raver et al. also suggest that, at the unit level, it is OCB that leads to OCB norms.

In conjunction, these papers appear to suggest that unit-level OCB (along with unit-level personality, etc.) results in unit-level OCB norms, which in turn result in individual-level OCB. This is an interesting prediction, and it is presumably intended to indicate reciprocal unit-level (i.e., unit-level OCB → unit-level Norms) and cross-level (i.e., unit-level Norms → individual-level OCB) relationships. However, to avoid being circular, this prediction would benefit from a clearer delineation of the time frames (Dalal et al., 2014) across which the unit-level and cross-level relationships operate. Might it, for instance, be the case that unit-level OCB requires long time frames (e.g., months or years) to be codified into unit-level norms, whereas unit-level norms facilitate individual-level OCB more quickly (e.g., minutes, hours, or days; Dalal et al., 2014)? Similar research is necessary with regard to CWB. Of course there is no requirement that time frames for OCB and CWB be similar.

In general, then, the unit level represents an interesting developing area for multilevel research on OCB, CWB, and their relationship. To take just one example, a reason for the absence of a strong negative individual-level OCB–CWB relationship may be the absence of a strong negative unit-level relationship between norms for OCB and norms for CWB. We therefore encourage researchers to pursue theory development and empirical tests involving the individual employee level (i.e., the between-person level) and the unit level simultaneously.

Methodological Factors Relevant to the OCB–CWB Relationship

Efforts to understand the conceptual and empirical relationship between OCB and CWB have been complicated by a number of methodological issues. Examples include the presence versus absence of reverse-scored items in the measure of OCB, the source of the OCB and CWB ratings, and the type of response scale used to measure OCB and CWB. We explore these and other issues next.

Presence Versus Absence of Reverse-Scored Items

OCB scales contain several antithetical items, intended to measure the absence or avoidance of OCB. These antithetical items are subsequently reverse-scored when calculating an overall OCB scale score. Researchers, however, have noticed that these antithetical items seem conceptually to represent not the avoidance of OCB but rather the enactment of CWB (e.g., Carpenter, Son, Harris, Alexander, & Horner, 2016; Dalal, 2005). Moreover, these antithetical OCB items are similar to actual items in CWB scales. The OCB item "takes undeserved breaks" (from Williams & Anderson, 1991), for example, is similar to the CWB item "taken an additional or longer break than is acceptable at your workplace" (from Bennett & Robinson, 2000), and the OCB item "consumes a lot of time complaining about trivial matters" (from Podsakoff et al., 1990) is similar to the CWB item "complains about insignificant things at work" (from Fox & Spector, 1999).

This observation prompted the question of whether the confusion regarding the OCB–CWB empirical relationship was due in part to the presence of antithetical items on OCB scales. Dalal's (2005) meta-analysis found that the OCB–CWB correlation was significantly larger when antithetical items were included in the OCB scale (–.66) than when they were not (–.19). This provided the first demonstration that measurement artifacts were at least partly to blame for the large OCB–CWB correlation.

Spector et al. (2010) extended this work by using an experimental design to simultaneously evaluate the influence of (a) presence of antithetical items, (b) rating source (i.e., self-rater versus supervisor-rater), and (c) response scale (i.e., frequency versus agreement scale) on the OCB–CWB relationship. To manipulate the presence or absence of antithetical items, the authors administered an OCB scale developed without antithetical items (OCB-Checklist ["OCB-C"]; Fox, Spector, Bruursema, Kessler, & Goh, 2007) as well as an existing OCB scale containing antithetical items ("PODS"; Podsakoff et al., 1990). The findings generally demonstrated that the PODS OCB scale was likely to yield more negative OCB–CWB correlations. For self-ratings, CWB correlated –.37 with the PODS scale and .21 with the OCB-C. For supervisor ratings, CWB correlated –.46 with the PODS scale and .01 with the OCB-C.

Spector et al. (2010) also showed that the type of OCB scale influenced OCB's nomological network. For example, self-rated OCB had stronger relationships with job satisfaction when measured using the PODS scale than when using the OCB-C. In addition, the type of OCB scale influenced the *direction* of relationships. For example, the PODS scale exhibited negative relationships with conflict and constraints, whereas for the OCB-C some of these relationships were positive (Spector et al., 2010). Similarly, Fox, Spector, Goh, Bruursema, and Kessler (2012) showed that, when OCB is measured using the OCB-C, OCB and CWB exhibit relationships of similar magnitude and the *same direction* with correlates such as organizational constraints, interpersonal conflict, distributive justice, and negative affect. When OCB is measured using the PODS measure, in contrast, OCB and CWB exhibit opposite-direction relationships with correlates. Thus, the inclusion of antithetical items of OCB scales influences our understanding of not only OCB's empirical relationship with CWB but also its relationships with a broader set of correlates.

Interestingly, antithetical items typically appear only in measures of OCB, not in measures of CWB. This may be because OCB developed as a construct before CWB. OCB scholars may therefore have developed the reverse-worded items to represent the absence of OCB, without realizing that the items would overlap with future operationalizations of CWB and that, as a result, such items would lead not only to more negative relationships with CWB scales but also, more generally, to an altered nomological network for OCB.

Source of Ratings: Observer Versus Self

The understanding of OCB and CWB, in terms of both their bivariate relationship and their nomological networks, is also influenced by how they are measured: via employee self-ratings or via supervisor or coworker "observer ratings." Because OCB and CWB are important forms of work behavior, they are often measured with multiple rater perspectives. Research has focused on how the type of rater influences the OCB–CWB relationship, as well as on the extent to which self-ratings and observer ratings of a given behavior converge. That is, do self-ratings and observer ratings reflect the same behavioral construct?

If the empirical relationship between OCB and CWB is due to same-source bias, we would expect large OCB–CWB correlations when both forms of behavior are rated by the same source. However, reality may be more complicated; the specific source appears to matter as well. Specifically, Dalal's (2005) meta-analysis did show that the OCB–CWB relationship was strong (–.71) when both forms of behavior were rated by the employee's supervisor. However, Dalal's results also showed that the relationship was weak (–.15) when both forms of behavior were self-rated.

These results suggest that supervisor ratings may be influenced by halo error, such that if a supervisor perceives an employee to be engaging in high OCB, and if the supervisor does not have much knowledge about the employee's CWB (which is often the case, because much CWB is likely to be performed covertly; Dalal, 2005), the supervisor assumes that this employee also engages in low CWB. Though self-ratings are expected to be influenced by a desire to present oneself in a socially desirable light (DeNisi & Shaw, 1977), the relatively weak magnitude of the relationship between self-rated OCB and CWB suggests that employees do not simultaneously provide greatly inflated ratings of their OCB and greatly deflated ratings of their CWB. Indeed, the size of the self-rated correlation is more similar to the different-source OCB–CWB correlations reported by Berry, Carpenter, and Barratt (2012): –.19 when correcting for unreliability using Cronbach's alphas and –.23 when correcting for observer-reported CWB using interrater reliability. This suggests that common method variance (including halo error) may be a bigger issue for supervisor ratings than self-ratings.

Next, it is important to consider whether self-ratings and observer (e.g., supervisor) ratings are convergent measures of OCB or CWB. In the CWB domain, this question became increasingly important as researchers called for the use of observer ratings, rather than self-ratings, to measure CWB (e.g., Stewart, Bing, Davison, Woehr, & McIntyre, 2009). Berry et al. (2012) meta-analyzed the relationship between self-ratings and observer ratings of CWB and found the following: (a) the self–observer relationship was modest in magnitude (.38); (b) in general, self-ratings and observer ratings of CWB were similarly related to theorized correlates such as Big 5 personality traits, job attitudes, and organizational perceptions (the only correlate to which observer-rated CWB was more strongly related than self-rated CWB was interactional justice); and (c) mean levels of CWB enactment were actually higher for self-ratings than for observer ratings ($\delta = .35$). These findings provide important evidence supporting the construct validity of self-rated CWB for research purposes, because the extra time and financial cost associated with obtaining observer ratings do not seem to yield appreciable validity gains. Additionally, although researchers' calls for the increased use of observer ratings were motivated by assumptions that self-raters were motivated to hide their CWB, Berry et al.'s findings regarding the mean-level reporting of CWB demonstrated that employees' self-reported level of CWB, although perhaps lower than their actual level of CWB, is higher than the observer-reported level of their CWB.

One could reason that, because CWB reflects negative behavior employees wish to conceal whereas OCB reflects positive behavior employees would be happy to reveal, the self–observer patterns shown for CWB may not compare to those for OCB. Specifically, one could reason that the self–observer relationship should be stronger for OCB than for CWB. However, Carpenter, Berry, and Houston's (2014) meta-analysis of the self–observer relationship for OCB revealed a surprisingly modest self–observer relationship for OCB (.26)—one that was in fact appreciably weaker than the aforementioned meta-analytic self–observer relationship for CWB (.38) reported by Berry et al. (2012).

Carpenter et al. (2014) also evaluated whether the unique information reflected in self-ratings and observer ratings of OCB explained variability in OCB's nomological network. Self-rated OCB contributed more incremental variance than observer-rated OCB to conscientiousness (12.9% versus .4%), interactional justice (8% versus .2%), procedural justice (4.5% versus 0%), job satisfaction (3.2% versus .1%), perceived organizational support (15.4% versus .7%), self-rated CWB (2.9% versus 0%), and self-rated task performance (25% versus 0%), whereas observer-rated OCB contributed more incremental variance only to observer-rated task performance (52% versus 0%) and observer-rated CWB (16% versus 1%). This pattern of findings indicated that self-rated OCB and observer-rated OCB were stronger predictors of correlates rated by the same source. However, the findings strongly refute the blanket preference, among many researchers, for observer-rated OCB over self-rated OCB (see Allen, Barnard, Rush, & Russell, 2000; Organ & Ryan, 1995).

The research described earlier shows that the use of self-ratings versus observer ratings influences not only the relationship between OCB and CWB but also the respective relationships OCB and CWB have with nomological correlates. However, the question of "Which rating source is best?" has not yet been answered definitively because researchers still do not know whether self-ratings or observer ratings are more "accurate"—in other words, more closely reflect actual behavior. That is, to what extent do subjective self-ratings versus subjective observer ratings converge with nonsubjective measures of OCB or CWB? With regard to task performance (as opposed to OCB or CWB), a meta-analysis by Bommer, Johnson, Rich, Podsakoff, and MacKenzie (1995) demonstrated that the correlation between subjective supervisor-rated criteria and more objective measures of criteria (e.g., dollar amount of sales, number of parts assembled) was generally moderate (.39), and in fact was quite strong (.71) in the very few cases where primary studies assessed *precisely* the same task performance criteria both subjectively and objectively. This indicates that supervisor ratings do contain at least a moderate amount of "truth." However, the extent to which this also holds for self-ratings and coworker ratings is thus far unknown. Moreover, examinations that focus specifically on OCB and CWB (as opposed to task performance) are also missing. As a result, it is still not entirely clear whether OCB and CWB should be measured using self-ratings or observer ratings. This represents an important area for future research.

Type of Response Scale: Agreement Versus Frequency

Another methodological factor influencing the understanding of OCB and CWB is the type of response scale for ratings: agreement versus frequency. These types of response scale are important because they reflect different response models and processes that can change the representation of a construct.

Specifically, frequency response scales (e.g., "Indicate how frequently you engaged in the following behavior at work during the past year") are typically matched with the dominance response model (Dalal, 2005). This model assumes a linear relationship between the rater's standing on the underlying latent construct (i.e., theta) and his or her probability of endorsing a response category. The probability of a rater endorsing a particular frequency category (e.g., "Daily") will increase as the rater's theta (e.g., enactment of CWB) increases. For instance, if employee X is asked to rate his or her CWB on a frequency scale, then this employee will be more likely to choose "Daily" if he or she engages in CWB on *at least* a daily basis.

In contrast, agreement response scales (e.g., "Indicate the extent to which you agree with the following statements regarding your behavior at work") are more often matched with ideal point response processes and unfolding response models (Coombs, 1975; Thurstone, 1928). The ideal point model assumes that the relationship between the rater's theta and his or her probability of endorsing a level of agreement is curvilinear because there needs to be a match between the rater's standing on the construct (e.g., amount of enactment of CWB) and the level of the construct indicated in the item (Thurstone, 1928). As a result, if the behavior item is too far below *or above* the respondent's theta, the item will not be endorsed. For example, employee X may disagree with a CWB item such as "I sometimes spend time daydreaming instead of working" both if the employee never daydreams instead of working and if he or she *almost always* daydreams instead of working.

Spector et al. (2010) reasoned that frequency scales may be more difficult for raters because they have to provide a precise estimate of how often they (or, in the case of observer ratings, the target employees) have engaged in a behavior. The authors also noted that agreement ratings may not measure the employee's behavior as much as the employee's attitude toward the behavior (or, in the case of observer ratings, the rater's attitude toward the employee). Moreover, agreement ratings may be more susceptible than frequency ratings to halo errors. This is reflected in Dalal's (2005) meta-analysis, which showed that the OCB–CWB correlation was significantly larger when agreement scales (–.68) versus frequency scales (–.27) were used. Spector et al.'s primary study also showed interesting results. For self-ratings, OCB and CWB were most strongly negatively correlated when the agreement scale (and the OCB PODS scale) was used (–.57, versus –.37 for frequency). OCB and CWB were most strongly positively correlated when the frequency scale (and the OCB-C scale) was used (.21, versus –.00 for agreement). These patterns were mirrored for supervisor reports.

At this point, it is evident that the measurement issues we discuss in this section (e.g., rating source, rating scale) are somewhat intertwined with each other. It is therefore important to consider whether the type of rating scale influences issues of convergence between self-raters and observer raters of either OCB or CWB. Berry et al.'s (2012) meta-analytic examination of self–observer convergence for CWB could not additionally examine the influence of response format due to low variability in how CWB was measured in primary studies. However, Carpenter et al.'s (2014) meta-analytic examination of self–observer convergence for OCB showed that self-raters and observer raters provided relatively similar mean levels of OCB enactment regardless of whether frequency (δ = .29) or agreement (δ = .32) scales were used. However, self–observer OCB correlations were significantly larger for agreement formats (.31) than frequency formats (.18). This suggests that frequency ratings may be more difficult for all raters, thus weakening the convergence between sources. Alternately, it may suggest that, as mentioned previously, agreement ratings may represent not behavior but rather attitudes toward behavior—and that attitudes toward OCB and CWB may be more "consistent" (i.e., negatively correlated) than OCB and CWB themselves (Dalal, 2005).

Thus, the use of frequency or agreement rating scales is likely to influence our understanding of the OCB–CWB relationship. Frequency scales may be more difficult than agreement scales for raters to use (because frequency scales require raters to provide precise estimates of how often they enacted various behaviors over a long period of time, such as the past year), but frequency scales do appear to be less vulnerable than agreement scales to halo error (Spector et al., 2010). Indeed, the use of agreement scales generally produces strong negative correlations, suggesting that an employee who engages in OCB does not engage in CWB and vice versa, whereas frequency scales generally produce moderate positive correlations, suggesting that an employee who engages in high levels of OCB also engages in high levels of CWB and vice versa. However, in closing this section we note that much of the speculation regarding the impact of and comparison between agreement and frequency scales has not yet been examined empirically. We therefore encourage future research that tests these propositions.

Role of Social Desirability

A factor that has the potential to influence the extent to which OCB and CWB are related is socially desirable responding. Socially desirable responding is due to self-enhancement biases (Leary, 2007), such that employees would be expected to present themselves in a positive light by inflating their level of OCB and deflating their level of CWB. This, in turn, could lead to the appearance of an OCB–CWB relationship that appears more negative than it actually is.

Social desirability also influences the current understanding of OCB and CWB by affecting the measurement of OCB and CWB's common correlates. For example, personality traits such as conscientiousness and neuroticism (or trait negative affect) are some of the most important predictors of both CWB (Berry, Ones, & Sackett, 2007; Dalal, 2005) and OCB (e.g., Chiaburu, Oh, Berry, Li, & Gardner, 2011; Dalal, 2005; Organ & Ryan, 1995). However, these are also the personality traits most vulnerable to socially desirable responding (Ones, Viswesvaran, & Reiss, 1996), suggesting that these traits' relationships with OCB and CWB may be distorted by socially desirable responding.

Yet, common ways of minimizing the impact of socially desirable responding are problematic. For instance, researchers could measure respondents' tendency to behave in a socially desirable manner—and could then correct statistically for this tendency while measuring the OCB–CWB relationship. However, previous research in other domains has demonstrated important theoretical and empirical deficiencies with such an approach (Burns & Christiansen, 2006; Ellingson, Sackett, & Hough, 1999). A different and more effective approach would be to *deter* socially desirable responding in the first place by prefacing the measures of OCB and CWB with a warning to respondents that inaccurate responses are detectable and will be penalized (e.g., Tomassetti, Dalal, & Kaplan, 2016). We are not aware of extant research that has examined the impact of such warnings on the OCB–CWB relationship, so this represents a worthwhile avenue for future research.

In fact, there are reasons to suspect that social desirability may not greatly contaminate measures of either OCB or CWB. If substantial contamination did occur, we would expect self-raters to inflate their level of OCB and deflate their level of CWB compared to supervisors and coworkers, who should not be influenced by this reporting bias. However, as mentioned earlier, Berry et al.'s (2012) meta-analysis showed that employees themselves reported levels of CWB that were appreciably larger than the levels reported for them by supervisors (δ = .44) and coworkers (δ = .23). Similarly, Carpenter et al.'s (2014) meta-analysis showed that employees themselves reported levels of OCB that were appreciably larger than the levels reported for them by supervisors (δ = .33) and coworkers (δ = .38). This demonstrates that the influence of social desirability on self-ratings of either CWB or OCB may not be as great as assumed.

Another reason the impact of socially desirable responding on OCB, CWB, and their relationship may be ameliorated is that respondents are almost always assured, ahead of time, that their responses will be kept confidential by the researchers. Socially desirable responding may have a larger impact on self-reports if respondents were instead cautioned that their responses would be shared with management and would contribute to their annual performance appraisals.

Finally, the impact of socially desirable responding may be ameliorated at the within-person level relative to the between-person level. If one assumes that the extent of socially desirable responding is a between-person-level (i.e., trait) factor, then, for a given respondent, socially desirable responding should be as much (or as little) of an issue for each of the many surveys taken by a given respondent in a within-person design. In other words, socially desirable responding would presumably inflate self-reported OCB and/or deflate self-reported CWB to the same extent across each survey in a within-person design. However, unlike a between-person design, which emphasizes comparisons between people, a within-person design emphasizes comparisons between a person and himself or herself on other occasions (surveys). Therefore, fluctuations in the levels of OCB and CWB across occasions—the basis for the within-person OCB–CWB relationship—should still be meaningful even in the presence of a between-person-level tendency to behave in a socially desirable manner.

Construct and Measure Proliferation

Another issue affecting the understanding of OCB, CWB, and their relationship is actually a combination of methodological and theoretical issues. Specifically, both constructs are unfortunately victims of construct and measure proliferation.

OCB has been labeled prosocial behavior (Brief & Motowidlo, 1986), contextual performance (Borman & Motowidlo, 1993), and extra-role behavior (Van Dyne, Cummings, & Parks, 1995), among other labels. Moreover, researchers have measured these constructs via over 30 scales in the extant literature (e.g., Podsakoff et al. 1990; Smith et al., 1983; Williams & Anderson, 1991), many of which are currently commonly used.

This is mirrored for CWB, for which similar labels include workplace deviance (Bennett & Robinson, 2000; Robinson & Bennett, 1995), bullying (e.g., Rayner, 1997), antisocial behavior (Robinson & O'Leary-Kelly, 1998), retaliation (Skarlicki & Folger, 1997), revenge (Aquino, Tripp, & Bies 2001), incivility (e.g., Andersson & Pearson, 1999), and workplace aggression (Neuman & Baron, 1998). Similarly, there exist many operationalizations of these constructs (e.g., Bennett & Robinson, 2000; Cortina, Magley, Williams, & Langhout, 2001; Gruys & Sackett, 2003; Spector et al., 2004).

Within both the OCB and CWB domains, the varied behaviors are conceptualized as having distinctive features, yet the large overlap among these concepts is quite troubling (Hershcovis, 2011). As a result of this *jangle fallacy* (Kelley, 1927), there have been calls for the integration of literatures involving the differently labeled constructs. It has become clear that, due to construct proliferation, researchers in ostensibly different areas have been studying (and restudying) the same relationships (Hershcovis, 2011). Indeed, one of the major consequences of construct proliferation is the stifling of theoretical development because the understanding of OCB and CWB ends up advancing in piecemeal fashion (Aquino & Thau, 2009). This serious issue points to the need for more conceptual and theoretical integration within the OCB domain and within the CWB domain.

Because the proliferation of conceptualizations of OCB and CWB lead to the proliferation of operationalizations of these constructs, researchers have evaluated whether the varied operationalizations nevertheless represent the same construct. For example, Hoffman, Blair, Meriac, and Woehr (2007) and LePine, Erez, and Johnson (2002) both provided meta-analytic support for multiple operationalizations of OCB fitting OCB's generally expected dimensional structure. The extent to which varied CWB scales fit the same underlying dimensional structure, however, appears less clear. Marcus, Taylor, Hastings, Sturm, and Weigelt (2016) conducted a structural meta-analysis of CWB items to determine the best-fitting measurement model and found support for the two-factor model representing interpersonal and organizational targets. However, a notable caveat to this research is that the authors relied only on samples using Spector et al.'s (2004) CWB-C measure. It remains unknown whether CWB's dimensional structure generalizes to other common measures of CWB.

In sum, a clear understanding of the OCB–CWB relationship will be difficult to determine without clarity and parsimony in how OCB and CWB are defined and measured.

Statistical Corrections for Interrater Reliability

It is well known that effect sizes are attenuated when the measures used are unreliable. Statistical corrections for unreliability, conducted with the aim of detecting the "true" effect size, are therefore common in both meta-analyses and primary studies (Schmidt & Hunter, 2015). Most IOOB researchers would therefore argue that it is appropriate to correct the observed OCB–CWB relationship statistically for unreliability in the measures of OCB and CWB.

However, reliability can be estimated in many ways, and the choice of how to estimate reliability can have profound effects. In particular, the use of interrater reliability in statistical corrections has been severely criticized (Murphy & DeShon, 2000) because there is reason to believe that variance in performance ratings attributable to raters is at least in part due to systematic factors rather than random error. For instance, the correlation between ratings from two raters is dependent on the raters' opportunity to observe the ratee (Rothstein, 1990). Therefore, it may not be appropriate to refer to the correlation between two raters' ratings as an index of "reliability" per se.

These conceptual concerns aside, there is an important practical issue involved. Interrater reliability estimates are typically considerably lower than internal consistency reliability estimates (e.g., Cronbach's alpha). Therefore, the extent of statistical "correction" is typically much larger when using interrater reliability than when using internal consistency reliability. The concern is that using interrater reliability in statistical adjustments leads to an overcorrection that yields overly high effect size estimates—in other words, an OCB–CWB relationship that appears larger than it is.

Judge, Thoresen, Bono, and Patton's (2001) meta-analysis of the relationship between job satisfaction and job performance is instructive in this regard. These authors reported the observed/uncorrected effect size (0.18) as well as two effect sizes corrected for unreliability in job performance: one using interrater reliability and the other using internal consistency reliability. Judge et al. concluded that the magnitude of the correction (i.e., the change in the size of the correlation) was 0.12 when using interrater reliability but only 0.07 when using Cronbach's alpha. The difference is likely to be even more pronounced when correcting for unreliability in both components of the effect size (rather than only one, as in Judge et al.).

We therefore caution researchers that OCB–CWB relationships corrected statistically for interrater reliability may yield overestimates of the true OCB–CWB relationship. One option, then, would be for researchers to avoid the use of interrater reliability in statistical corrections. Another option would be for researchers to emulate Judge et al. (2001) and report the uncorrected OCB–CWB correlation as well as *two* corrected OCB–CWB correlations: one using interrater reliability and the other using internal consistency reliability.

Time Frames Across Which OCB and CWB Are Studied

Judging by the response scales employed in typical between-person studies of OCB and CWB (e.g., Spector et al., 2010), these studies ask respondents to indicate their behavior either in general or over an extended time period—for instance, the previous year. Now, nobody would contend that respondents have either the ability or the willingness to accurately recall each and every incident of OCB and CWB they have enacted over an extended time period. Instead, research on recall (e.g., Robinson & Clore, 2002) suggests that respondents are likely to "fill in the gaps" using bias-prone beliefs about their identity (e.g., "I'm a good person; therefore, I enact OCB but not CWB") as well as bias-prone beliefs about how situations affect their behavior (e.g., "I could see myself enacting CWB only when I'm very frustrated, and I think I get very frustrated only about once a month; therefore, I might engage in CWB at most once a month").

There are, in other words, reasons for grave concern regarding the accuracy of between-person measures of OCB and CWB. Importantly, the bias associated with such measures may lead to an artificially strong negative OCB–CWB relationship. In addition, between-person measures by definition cannot answer the question of why a person engages in OCB or CWB *on a particular occasion*. These are additional reasons for studying OCB and CWB—and their relationship—at the within-person level.

Future Research Agenda

At several points in this chapter, we have suggested avenues for future research. Here, we propose several additional avenues.

Integrated Multilevel Model of OCB, CWB, and Their Relationship

In this chapter, we have discussed potential antecedents to OCB and CWB at several levels of analysis: the unit level, the individual employee level (i.e., the between-person level), and the within-person level. However, what we have not attempted to do is to integrate theoretical frameworks across these levels. This would constitute a program of research in its own right.

Here, we merely list some considerations that should inform integrated theoretical frameworks. How should antecedents of OCB and CWB be characterized at the various levels of analysis? For instance, should situations be characterized as chronic situations at the between-person level of analysis but as discrete events or episodes at the within-person level? If within-person (i.e., momentary or state) OCB and CWB—and their relationship—are the ultimate outcomes of interest, then which unit-level and between-person-level antecedents exhibit direct effects and which ones exhibit mediated effects (through within-person antecedents) on the outcomes of interest? Moreover, to what extent do unit-level and between-person-level variables moderate the relationships between within-person antecedents and within-person OCB and CWB? Much theoretical work and many empirical tests will be needed before a well-regarded and well-validated multilevel model of the antecedents of within-person OCB and CWB can be said to exist.

Same-Direction Antecedents of OCB and CWB

Most of the antecedents we have discussed are related to OCB and CWB in opposite directions. The personality trait of conscientiousness, for instance, is related positively to OCB and negatively to CWB. However, given that the OCB–CWB relationship is not, in fact, strongly negative, it would behoove researchers to seek out antecedents that relate in the *same direction* to both OCB and CWB. Personality traits associated with novelty/risk/adventure-seeking may represent such antecedents (see, e.g., Gomà-i-Freixanet, 2001), and so may the momentary state of boredom (Spector & Fox, 2010a). Specifically, for individuals who are dispositionally inclined to seek out adventure, as well as for individuals who are simply bored in the moment (Spector & Fox, 2010a), both OCB and CWB offer avenues of escape from one's work. Many other constructs may similarly yield same-direction relationships with OCB and CWB, and we urge future research to concentrate on identifying such constructs.

How do Employees Learn Norms About OCB and CWB?

Although we understand a great deal about the attitudinal, dispositional, and situational factors that influence the enactment of both OCB and CWB, what is unknown is the extent to which employees develop an understanding of the existing norms regarding both OCB and CWB within their organizations. For example, although employees may possess levels of personality traits (e.g., neuroticism and conscientiousness) that influence whether they will engage in OCB and/or CWB, how do these personality traits combine with socialization practices or with informal peer interactions to influence employees' actual enactment of the behaviors? Researchers have shown that OCB and CWB both exist as collective phenomena (e.g., O'Boyle et al., 2011; Podsakoff, Whiting, Podsakoff, & Blume, 2009; Robinson & O'Leary-Kelly, 1998), which suggests that these behaviors are not enacted in isolation. Rather, employees actively observe others' behavior, receive informal cues about acceptable and unacceptable behavior, and share information about experiences in the organization—all of which can influence each other's behavior. Future research should aim to explicate these processes. For example, qualitative approaches such as interviews or focus groups may reveal how employees' initial weeks in the organization shape their perceptions of the behavior beyond task performance they need to enact to succeed on the job. Such approaches could also illustrate how employees learn about norms regarding minor forms of CWB, such as tardiness, as well as regarding more serious forms of CWB, such as theft: Some organizations may be relatively tolerant of the former, but few are tolerant of the latter.

How Does the Cultural Context Influence Measurement and Theory?

Researchers have demonstrated that OCB's definition and measurement depend on the cultural context. For example, Kwantes, Karam, Kuo, and Towson (2008) showed that the extent to which employees considered OCB to be a part of their required role ("in-role") or separate from their required tasks ("extra-role") was influenced by culturally related variables such as social flexibility, social cynicism, and religiosity. Organ et al. (2006) noted that, compared to supervisors in individualistic cultures, supervisors in collectivistic cultures may expect employees to enact OCB more frequently but that such supervisors may also consider OCB to be "in-role" behavior rather than "extra-role" behavior.

Thus, it is also plausible that the very definition of "citizenship" and/or "counterproductive" behavior is laden with culture-specific meaning. For example, Munene (1995) described "not on seat" behavior as a situation in which managerial employees in Nigeria arrive to work on time but leave shortly thereafter, only to return after several hours. The author considered *not* engaging in this behavior as OCB, but, as we have discussed previously in the context of antithetical OCB items, engaging in "not on seat" behavior actually fits the definition of CWB.

As another example, Rotundo and Xie (2008) examined whether the forms of CWB identified in Western contexts generalized to employees from, or working in, China. This work identified some new behaviors that are not currently considered CWB in Western contexts, for example: "deny responsibility," "boast about one's abilities but fail to demonstrate [them]," and "inconsistency between what employee says and does." Researchers' understanding of the OCB–CWB relationship must therefore account for cultural influences in the conceptualization of OCB and CWB. Both commonalities and differences across cultures should be studied further.

Additional Levels of Analysis Issues

Estimating the OCB–CWB relationship at levels of analysis other than the between-person level requires more attention to the measurement of OCB and CWB at those levels. Consider, for instance, Dalal et al. (2009), who used an experience sampling study to estimate the within-person OCB–CWB relationship. Dalal et al. suggested that existing (between-person-level) OCB and CWB scales were inappropriate because these scales: (a) contained too large a number of items, per se, for an experience sampling study, (b) contained items that could not feasibly occur during the 2- to 3-week duration of an experience sampling study, and (c) used response options involving behavioral frequency over a long period of time (e.g., 1 year), which was obviously inappropriate for an experience sampling study. Dalal et al. instead combined items from multiple extant scales, such that all their items could reasonably be expected to occur during the duration of an experience sampling study. They moreover asked respondents simply to indicate whether ("Yes") or not ("No") the respondents had engaged in each form of OCB and CWB in the last few hours (i.e., since the previous survey).

Dalal et al.'s (2009) choices were reasonable, and indeed many other experience sampling studies assessing OCB and, especially, CWB have made similar choices. However, such choices do leave some intriguing questions unanswered. To take just one example, Dalal et al. intentionally prioritized higher frequency CWBs over lower frequency CWBs. In so doing, however, Dalal et al. probably also prioritized lower severity CWBs over higher severity CWBs. For instance, it is unclear whether the presumably higher frequency and lower severity CWB item "Excluded a coworker from a conversation" relates differently to OCB than the presumably lower frequency and higher severity CWB item "Got into a fistfight with a coworker." Admittedly, it is hard to argue with the contention that including higher severity CWB items in the typical experience sampling survey would result in very little if any variability in scores on these items (Dalal et al., 2009) and therefore in an artifactually low OCB–CWB relationship. It is possible, however, that an experience sampling study could pick up some variability in higher severity CWBs if (1) the study were to ask respondents about their behavior over the course of the previous week (rather than the previous few hours), with surveys then being conducted weekly for about half a year, and (2) the study were deliberately conducted in a high-stress setting so as to maximize the potential for higher severity CWB.[2] The more general issue suggested by this example is the need to conduct scale validation studies for OCB and CWB directly at the within-person level of analysis.

Measurement issues also exist at other levels of analysis. Consider, for instance, the unit level of analysis. Generally, studies examining OCB or CWB at this level (e.g., Ehrhart, 2004) have used existing scales that were validated and meant for use at the individual employee level. Moreover, unit-level studies must concern themselves with issues of aggregation from the individual employee to the unit. Virtually all unit-level studies seem to use a composition model (Chan, 1998) in which the mean score for employees in a particular unit represents the score for the unit as long as employees within the unit demonstrate adequate agreement.[3] In other words, within-unit agreement is treated as a statistical hurdle. Instead, we (like Podsakoff et al., 2014) suggest that it is more interesting psychologically—and more appropriate scientifically—to view within-unit agreement as a variable of interest in its own right, using a dispersion composition model (Chan, 1998). The unit-level mean, the extent of within-unit agreement, and their interaction could, in other words, be modeled simultaneously. Doing so would align the study of unit-level OCB and CWB with the study of unit-level climate—especially the recent focus on "climate strength" (Lee & Dalal, 2016). Extant unit-level research using a dispersion model, however, is virtually nonexistent (Podsakoff et al., 2014), thereby suggesting an important avenue for future research.

In addition to careful thought about the content of items, response options, and (where appropriate) composition models, research conducted at levels of analysis other than the individual employee level (i.e., the between-person level) should be concerned about the structure of OCB and CWB. After all, there is no inherent requirement that factor structures of OCB and CWB should be identical across levels. At the within-person level, researchers could conduct "chain P-technique" (Cattell, 1963; see Dalal et al., 2009, for an example) or dynamic (Nesselroade, McArdle, Aggen, & Meyers, 2002) factor analysis of OCB and CWB items. At the unit level, factor analysis should be conducted on scores that have already been aggregated to the unit level. An alternative is to conduct multilevel factor analysis (Muthén, 1991) in which the factor structure is examined simultaneously at the lower and higher levels (e.g., individual employee level and unit level). Insufficient attention to the structure of OCB and CWB at levels of analysis other than the individual employee level may lead to inaccurate estimates of the OCB–CWB relationship at those levels.

Changes in OCB Definitions Over Time

An interesting line of future inquiry pertains to how the OCB–CWB relationship may be influenced by constructs that have more recently been introduced to the OCB domain space. As one example, OCB is now considered to include, within its construct space, behavior such as challenging the status quo ("taking charge"; Morrison & Phelps, 1999) and offering suggestions for improvement ("voice"; Van Dyne & LePine, 1998). These "challenging" forms of OCBs reflect behavior that supports or helps the organization but that also deviates from established norms or traditional ways of working in a particular organization. Reactions to such behavior may be in the eye of the beholder. For example, supervisors may have varying reactions to proactive or challenging behavior on the part of their employees: Some supervisors may welcome such behavior, whereas others may feel that such behavior challenges their authority (e.g., Grant, Parker, & Collins, 2009). For the latter category of supervisors, the relationship between CWB and "challenging" OCBs may actually be strong and *positive*. Despite this, nomological network correlates may continue to be related to challenging OCB in an opposite direction from CWB. For example, job satisfaction is positively related to "challenging" OCB (.20; Thomas, Whitman, & Viswesvaran, 2010) but negatively related to CWB.

In summary, as exemplified by these "challenging" forms of OCB, definitions of OCB and CWB are likely to continue to change over time. Researchers should account for the possibility that the OCB–CWB relationship, too, will change over time as a result.

The Changing Nature of Work and Technology

The changing nature of work represents another reason for measures of OCB and CWB, and hence the OCB–CWB relationship, to be reevaluated periodically. Perhaps the biggest change in the nature of work recently involves the rise of telework. In 2011, roughly 1 in 7 US employees teleworked at least 1 day per week—and the increase in non-self-employed employees who considered their home as their primary work location increased almost 50% between 2004 and 2011 (Holland, Simpson, Dalal, & Vega, 2016). Holland et al. noted that, if existing CWB scales were applied *in toto* to a telework context, the result would be (1) errors of commission—that is, criterion contamination—due to the use of CWB items inappropriate to a telework context (e.g., "Hit or pushed someone at work"; Spector et al., 2006), and (2) errors of omission—that is, criterion deficiency—due to the failure to include new CWB items particularly relevant to a telework context (e.g., "Faked an illness to justify telecommuting"). Holland et al. therefore developed and validated a telework-specific CWB scale. However, until such time as a comparable effort is made on the OCB side, researchers will not be able to accurately estimate the OCB–CWB relationship in the large and growing segment of the working population that teleworks at least part of the time.

The changing nature of work is, of course, inextricably intertwined with advances in technology. Telework is facilitated by the widespread proliferation of technologies such as broadband Internet and videoconferencing. However, technology has disrupted our understanding of the nature of work in multiple other ways. Consider, for example, the smartphone.

On the one hand, the smartphone permits employees (including those who do not telework in the traditional sense) to respond readily to work-related emails during nights and weekends in ways that even a laptop computer does not. Are employees who are extremely responsive to email at highly irregular hours engaging in OCB? Over time, might work roles expand (or have they already expanded) such that such responsiveness becomes a requirement for most employees?

On the other hand, the smartphone permits employees to engage in nonwork behavior while at work, for instance, playing games, checking social media accounts, or browsing sports headlines. Such behavior would usually be considered to fall within the realm of CWB. But what about, say, checking work-related email while at a work meeting? Deciding whether such behavior is a CWB may require a complex determination of the comparative amount of harm to the organization if such a behavior is versus is not performed.

As these examples suggest, the impact of a single technology on OCB, CWB, and their relationship is far from simple. Technology and the changing nature of work will require researchers to reexamine the construct definitions of OCB and CWB in an attempt to find the core of each construct that generalizes across work arrangements and work-related technologies (Holland et al., 2016).

Conclusion

As we have seen in this chapter, existing research has clearly answered the question of whether OCB and CWB are so strongly related that they form opposite ends of the same broader behavioral continuum. The answer is that they are not so strongly negatively related. In fact, they are relatively independent constructs.

At least in terms of behavior in organizational settings, then, it is an oversimplification to say that people are either good or bad. This conclusion represents a meaningful advance in researchers' understanding of "the criterion problem" (Austin & Villanova, 1992). This conclusion also provides useful information for practitioners. Practitioners who wish to select job applicants with a high propensity to engage in OCB should be aware that they are not simultaneously selecting job applicants with a high propensity to avoid engaging in CWB, and vice versa. Similarly, practitioners who design workplace interventions to facilitate OCB should be aware that these interventions will not simultaneously deter CWB, and vice versa.

Now that the question of whether OCB and CWB are "opposites" has been answered quite definitively, researchers can pay more attention to the more interesting question: *Why* are they not opposites? Or, more precisely, why are they relatively independent? The two constructs, after all, have definitional parallels, a common set of antecedents that relate to them in opposite directions, and so forth. In the current chapter, we have laid out an agenda for future research on this question. Many interesting and important issues remain to be examined at the traditional between-person level of analysis, but we suspect that the most fruitful theoretical and empirical research on the OCB–CWB relationship will be conducted at other levels of analysis—primarily the within-person level. Overall, there are many exciting unstudied aspects to this relationship that should keep researchers busy for a considerable period of time. It is conceivable that the OCB–CWB relationship will be a moribund area of research in a decade from now, when the next iteration of this chapter makes its appearance, but that is certainly nowhere near the case now.

Notes

1. Where possible, in this chapter we report meta-analytic correlations (ρ) corrected for attenuation due to unreliability in measures of both constructs.
2. Employing such a long time frame (1 week) would, however, stretch the definition of an experience sampling study. It would also introduce the types of recall errors that experience sampling researchers appropriately criticize in traditional cross-sectional studies. For this reason, elicitations of CWB (and OCB) in such a study would probably need to be preceded by memory prompts—for example, asking participants to briefly look back at their calendars and thereby attempt to reconstruct their whereabouts, activities, and social interactions during the past week (see, e.g., Kahneman et al., 2004). Moreover, the deliberate choice of a high-stress environment may itself distort the OCB–CWB relationship. In sum, such a study would solve some problems but would create others.
3. Albeit often using a reference-shift consensus composition model (Chan, 1998). Podsakoff et al. (2014) suggest that, for OCB, the majority of extant studies have used a reference-shift consensus model rather than a direct consensus model.

References

Allen, T. D., Barnard, S., Rush, M. C., & Russell, J. E. (2000). Ratings of organizational citizenship behavior: Does the source make a difference? *Human Resource Management Review, 10*, 97–114.

Andersson, L. M., & Pearson, C. M. (1999). Tit for tat? The spiraling effect of incivility in the workplace. *Academy of Management Review, 24*, 452–471.

Aquino, K., & Thau, S. (2009). Workplace victimization: Aggression from the target's perspective. *Annual Review of Psychology, 60*, 717–741.

Aquino, K., Tripp, T. M., & Bies, R. J. (2001). How employees respond to personal offense: The effects of blame attribution, victim status, and offender status on revenge and reconciliation in the workplace. *Journal of Applied Psychology, 86*, 52–59.

Austin, J. T., & Villanova, P. (1992). The criterion problem: 1917–1992. *Journal of Applied Psychology, 77*, 836–874.

Baumeister, R. F., Bratslavsky, E., Finkenauer, C. & Vohs, K. D. (2001). Bad is stronger than good. *Review of General Psychology, 5*, 323–370.

Bennett, R. J., & Robinson, S. L. (2000). Development of a measure of workplace deviance. *Journal of Applied Psychology, 85*, 349–360.

Berry, C. M., Carpenter, N. C., & Barratt, C. L. (2012). Do other-reports of counterproductive work behavior provide an incremental contribution over self-reports? A meta-analytic comparison. *Journal of Applied Psychology, 97*, 613–636.

Berry, C. M., Ones, D. S., & Sackett, P. R. (2007). Interpersonal deviance, organizational deviance, and their common correlates: a review and meta-analysis. *Journal of Applied Psychology, 92*, 410–424.

Bolino, M. C., Klotz, A. C., Turnley, W. H., & Harvey, J. (2013). Exploring the dark side of organizational citizenship behavior. *Journal of Organizational Behavior, 34*, 542–559.

Bommer, W. H., Johnson, J. L., Rich, G. A., Podsakoff, P. M., & MacKenzie, S. B. (1995). On the interchangeability of objective and subjective measures of employee performance: A meta-analysis. *Personnel Psychology, 48*, 587–605.

Borman, W. C., & Motowidlo, S. J. (1993). Expanding the criterion domain to include elements of contextual performance. In N. Schmitt & W. C. Borman (Eds.), *Personnel selection* (pp. 71–98). San Francisco, CA: Jossey-Bass.

Brief, A. P., & Motowidlo, S. J. (1986). Prosocial organizational behaviors. *Academy of Management Review, 11*, 710–725.

Burns, G. N., & Christiansen, N. D. (2006). Sensitive or senseless: On the use of social desirability measures in selection and assessment. In R. L. Griffith & M. H. Peterson (Eds.), *A closer examination of applicant faking behavior* (pp. 113–148). Greenwich, CT: Information Age Publishing.

Bushman, B. J. (2002). Does venting anger feed or extinguish the flame? Catharsis, rumination, distraction, anger, and aggressive responding. *Personality and Social Psychology Bulletin, 28*, 724–731.

Bushman, B. J., Baumeister, R. F., & Phillips, C. M. (2001). Do people aggress to improve their mood? Catharsis beliefs, affect regulation opportunity, and aggressive responding. *Journal of Personality and Social Psychology, 81*, 17–32.

Carpenter, N. C., & Berry, C. M. (2017). Are counterproductive work behavior and withdrawal empirically distinct? A meta-analytic investigation. *Journal of Management, 43*, 834–863.

Carpenter, N. C., Berry, C. M., & Houston, L. (2014). A meta-analytic comparison of self-reported and other-reported organizational citizenship behavior. *Journal of Organizational Behavior, 35*, 547–574.

Carpenter, N. C., Son, J., Harris, T. B., Alexander, A. L., & Horner, M. T. (2016). Don't forget the items: Item-level meta-analytic and substantive validity techniques for reexamining scale validation. *Organizational Research Methods, 19*, 616–650.

Cattell, R. B. (1963). The structuring of change by P-technique and incremental R-technique. In C. W. Harris (Ed.), *Problems in measuring change* (pp. 167–198). Madison, WI: University of Wisconsin Press.

Chan, D. (1998). Functional relations among constructs in the same content domain at different levels of analysis: A typology of composition models. *Journal of Applied Psychology, 83*, 234–246.

Chen, G., Bliese, P. D., & Mathieu, J. E. (2005). Conceptual framework and statistical procedures for delineating and testing multilevel theories of homology. *Organizational Research Methods, 8*, 375–409.

Chiaburu, D. S., Oh, I. S., Berry, C. M., Li, N., & Gardner, R. G. (2011). The five-factor model of personality traits and organizational citizenship behaviors: A meta-analysis. *Journal of Applied Psychology, 96*, 1140–1166.

Cohen, J. (1992). A power primer. *Psychological Bulletin, 112*, 155–159.

Coombs, C. H. (1975). A note on the relation between the vector model and the unfolding model for preferences. *Psychometrika, 40*, 115–116.

Cortina, L. M., Magley, V. J., Williams, J. H., & Langhout, R. D. (2001). Incivility in the workplace: Incidence and impact. *Journal of Occupational Health Psychology, 6*, 64–80.

Dalal, R. S. (2005). A meta-analysis of the relationship between organizational citizenship behavior and counterproductive work behavior. *Journal of Applied Psychology, 90*, 1241–1255.

Dalal, R. S., Bhave, D. P., & Fiset, J. (2014). Within-person variability in job performance: A theoretical review and research agenda. *Journal of Management, 40*, 1396–1436.

Dalal, R. S., & Hulin, C. L. (2008). Motivation for what? The criterion question. In R. Kanfer, G. Chen, & R. Pritchard (Eds.), *Work motivation: Past, present and future* (pp. 63–100). New York, NY: Routledge.

Dalal, R. S., Lam, H., Weiss, H. M., Welch, E. R., & Hulin, C. L. (2009). A within-person approach to work behavior and performance: Concurrent and lagged citizenship-counterproductivity associations, and dynamic relationships with affect and overall job performance. *Academy of Management Journal, 52*, 1051–1066.

Dalal, R. S., Meyer, R. D., Bradshaw, R. P., Green, J. P., Kelly, E. D., & Zhu, M. (2015). Personality strength and situational influences on behavior: A conceptual review and research agenda. *Journal of Management, 41*, 261–287.

DeNisi, A. S., & Shaw, J. B. (1977). Investigation of the uses of self-reports of abilities. *Journal of Applied Psychology, 62*, 641–644.

Ehrhart, M. G. (2004). Leadership and procedural justice climate as antecedents of unit-level organizational citizenship behavior. *Personnel Psychology, 57*, 61–94.

Ehrhart, M. G., & Naumann, S. E. (2004). Organizational citizenship behavior in work groups: A group norms approach. *Journal of Applied Psychology, 89*, 960–974.

Eisenberger, R., Lynch, P., Aselage, J., & Rohdieck, S. (2004). Who takes the most revenge? Individual differences in negative reciprocity norm endorsement. *Personality and Social Psychology Bulletin, 30*, 787–799.

Ellingson, J. E., Sackett, P. R., & Hough, L. M. (1999). Social desirability corrections in personality measurement: Issues of applicant comparison and construct validity. *Journal of Applied Psychology, 84*, 155–166.

Fox, S., & Spector, P. E. (1999). A model of work frustration–aggression. *Journal of Organizational Behavior, 20*, 915–931.

Fox, S., Spector, P. E., Bruursema, K., Kessler, S., & Goh, A. (2007, August). *Necessity is the mother of behavior: Organizational constraints, CWB and OCB.* Paper presented at the meeting of the Academy of Management, Philadelphia, PA.

Fox, S., Spector, P. E., Goh, A., Bruursema, K., & Kessler, S. R. (2012). The deviant citizen: Measuring potential positive relations between counterproductive work behaviour and organizational citizenship behaviour. *Journal of Occupational and Organizational Psychology, 85*, 199–220.

Fredrickson, B. L. (2003). The value of positive emotions: The emerging science of positive psychology is coming to understand why it's good to feel good. *American Scientist, 91*, 330–335.

Fredrickson, B. L. (2013). Updated thinking on positivity ratios. *American Psychologist, 68*, 814–822.

Gomà-i-Freixanet, M. (2001). Prosocial and antisocial aspects of personality in women: A replication study. *Personality and Individual Differences, 30*, 1401–1411.

Gouldner, A. W. (1960). The norm of reciprocity: A preliminary statement. *American Sociological Review, 25*, 161–178.

Grant, A. M., Parker, S., & Collins, C. (2009). Getting credit for proactive behavior: Supervisor reactions depend on what you value and how you feel. *Personnel Psychology, 62*, 31–55.

Gruys, M. L., & Sackett, P. R. (2003). Investigating the dimensionality of counterproductive work behavior. *International Journal of selection and assessment, 11*, 30–42.

Hershcovis, M. S. (2011). "Incivility, social undermining, bullying . . . oh my!": A call to reconcile constructs within workplace aggression research. *Journal of Organizational Behavior, 32*, 499–519.

Hobbes, T. (1651/2011). *Leviathan.* Peterborough, ON, Canada: Broadview.

Hoffman, B. J., Blair, C. A., Meriac, J. P., & Woehr, D. J. (2007). Expanding the criterion domain? A quantitative review of the OCB literature. *Journal of Applied Psychology, 92,* 555–566.

Holland, S., Simpson, K., Dalal, R. S., & Vega, R. (2016). I can't steal from a coworker if I work from home: Conceptual and measurement-related issues associated with studying counterproductive work behavior in a telework setting. *Human Performance, 29,* 172–190.

Ilies, R., Peng, A. C., Savani, K., & Dimotakis, N. (2013). Guilty and helpful: An emotion-based reparatory model of voluntary work behavior. *Journal of Applied Psychology, 98,* 1051–1059.

Judge, T. A., Thoresen, C. J., Bono, J. E., & Patton, G. K. (2001). The job satisfaction–job performance relationship: A qualitative and quantitative review. *Psychological Bulletin, 127,* 376–407.

Kahneman, D., Krueger, A. B., Schkade, D. A., Schwarz, N., & Stone, A. A. (2004). A survey method for characterizing daily life experience: The day reconstruction method. *Science, 306,* 1776–1780.

Kaplan, S., Bradley, J. C., Luchman, J. N., & Haynes, D. (2009). On the role of positive and negative affectivity in job performance: A meta-analytic investigation. *Journal of Applied Psychology, 94,* 162–176.

Kelley, T. L. (1927). *Interpretation of educational measurement.* Yonkers, NY: World Book.

Klotz, A. C., & Bolino, M. C. (2013). Citizenship and counterproductive work behavior: A moral licensing view. *Academy of Management Review, 38,* 292–306.

Kwantes, C. T., Karam, C. M., Kuo, B. C., & Towson, S. (2008). Culture's influence on the perception of OCB as in-role or extra-role. *International Journal of Intercultural Relations, 32,* 229–243.

Leary, M. R. (2007). Motivational and emotional aspects of the self. *Annual Review of Psychology, 58,* 317–344.

Lee, S., & Dalal, R. S. (2016). Climate as situational strength: Safety climate strength as a cross-level moderator of the relationship between conscientiousness and safety behavior. *European Journal of Work and Organizational Psychology, 25,* 120–132.

LePine, J. A., Erez, A., & Johnson, D. E. (2002). The nature and dimensionality of organizational citizenship behavior: A critical review and meta-analysis. *Journal of Applied Psychology, 87,* 52–65.

Locke, J. (1689/1982). *Second treatise of government: An essay concerning the true original, extent and end of civil government.* Wheeling, IL: Harlan Davidson.

Marcus, B., Taylor, O. A., Hastings, S. E., Sturm, A., & Weigelt, O. (2016). The structure of counterproductive work behavior: A review, a structural meta-analysis, and a primary study. *Journal of Management, 42,* 203–233.

Mayer, D. M., Kuenzi, M., Greenbaum, R., Bardes, M., & Salvador, R. B. (2009). How low does ethical leadership flow? Test of a trickle-down model. *Organizational Behavior and Human Decision Processes, 108,* 1–13.

Meyer, R. D., Dalal, R. S., José, I. J., Hermida, R., Chen, T. R., Vega, R. P., Brooks, C. K., & Khare, V. P. (2014). Measuring job-related situational strength and assessing its interactive effects with personality on voluntary work behavior. *Journal of Management, 40,* 1010–1041.

Morrison, E. W., & Phelps, C. C. (1999). Taking charge at work: Extrarole efforts to initiate workplace change. *Academy of Management Journal, 42,* 403–419.

Munene, J. C. (1995). "Not-on-seat": An investigation of some correlates of organisational citizenship behaviour in Nigeria. *Applied Psychology: An International Review, 44,* 111–122.

Murphy, K. R., & DeShon, R. (2000). Interrater correlations do not estimate the reliability of job performance ratings. *Personnel Psychology, 53,* 873–900.

Muthén, B. O. (1991). Multilevel factor analysis of class and student achievement components. *Journal of Educational Measurement, 28,* 338–354.

Naumann, S. E., & Ehrhart, M. G. (2011). Moderators of the relationship between group helping norms and individual helping. *Small Group Research, 42,* 225–248.

Nesselroade, J. R., McArdle, J. J., Aggen, S. H., & Meyers, J. M. (2002). Dynamic factor analysis models for representing process in multivariate time-series. In D. M. Moskowitz & S. L. Hershberger (Eds.), *Modeling intraindividual variability with repeated measures data: Advances and techniques* (pp. 235–265). Mahwah, NJ: Lawrence Erlbaum Associates.

Neuman, J. H., & Baron, R. A. (1998). Workplace violence and workplace aggression: Evidence concerning specific forms, potential causes, and preferred targets. *Journal of Management, 24,* 391–419.

O'Boyle, E. H., Forsyth, D. R., & O'Boyle, A. S. (2011). Bad apples or bad barrels: An examination of group-and organizational-level effects in the study of counterproductive work behavior. *Group & Organization Management, 36,* 39–69.

Ones, D. S., Viswesvaran, C., & Reiss, A. D. (1996). Role of social desirability in personality testing for personnel selection: The red herring. *Journal of Applied Psychology, 81,* 660–679.

Organ, D. W. (1988). *Organizational citizenship behavior: The good soldier syndrome.* Lexington, MA: Lexington Books.

Organ, D. W. (1997). Organizational citizenship behavior: It's construct clean-up time. *Human Performance, 10,* 85–97.

Organ, D. W., Podsakoff, P. M., & MacKenzie, S. B. (2006). *Organizational citizenship behavior: Its nature, antecedents, and consequences.* Thousand Oaks, CA: Sage Publications.

Organ, D. W., & Ryan, K. (1995). A meta-analytic review of attitudinal and dispositional predictors of organizational citizenship behavior. *Personnel Psychology, 48,* 775–802.

Podsakoff, P. M., MacKenzie, S. B., Moorman, R. H., & Fetter, R. (1990). Transformational leader behaviors and their effects on followers' trust in leader, satisfaction, and organizational citizenship behaviors. *Leadership Quarterly, 1,* 107–142.

Podsakoff, N. P., Podsakoff, P. M., MacKenzie, S. B., Maynes, T. D., & Spoelma, T. M. (2014). Consequences of unit-level organizational citizenship behaviors: A review and recommendations for future research. *Journal of Organizational Behavior, 35,* S87–S119.

Podsakoff, N. P., Whiting, S. W., Podsakoff, P. M., & Blume, B. D. (2009). Individual-and organizational-level consequences of organizational citizenship behaviors: A meta-analysis. *Journal of Applied Psychology, 94,* 122–141.

Rauthmann, J. F., Gallardo-Pujol, D., Guillaume, E. M., Todd, E., Nave, C. S., Sherman, R. A., Ziegler, M., Jones, A. B., & Funder, D. C. (2014). The Situational Eight DIAMONDS: A taxonomy of major dimensions of situation characteristics. *Journal of Personality and Social Psychology, 107,* 677–718.

Raver, J. L., Ehrhart, M. G., & Chadwick, I. C. (2012). The emergence of team helping norms: Foundations within members' attributes and behavior. *Journal of Organizational Behavior, 33*, 616–637.

Rayner, C. (1997). The incidence of workplace bullying. *Journal of Community & Applied Social Psychology, 7*, 199–208.

Robinson, S. L., & Bennett, R. J. (1995). A typology of deviant workplace behaviors: A multidimensional scaling study. *Academy of Management Journal, 38*, 555–572.

Robinson, M. D., & Clore, G. L. (2002). Belief and feeling: Evidence for an accessibility model of emotional self-report. *Psychological Bulletin, 128*, 934–960.

Robinson, S. L., & O'Leary-Kelly, A. M. (1998). Monkey see, monkey do: The influence of work groups on the antisocial behavior of employees. *Academy of Management Journal, 41*, 658–672.

Rothstein, H. R. (1990). Interrater reliability of job performance ratings: Growth to asymptote level with increasing opportunity to observe. *Journal of Applied Psychology, 75*, 322–327.

Rotundo, M., & Xie, J. L. (2008). Understanding the domain of counterproductive work behaviour in China. *The International Journal of Human Resource Management, 19*, 856–877.

Rousseau, D. M. (1989). Psychological and implied contracts in organizations. *Employee Responsibilities and Rights Journal, 2*, 121–139.

Sackett, P. R., & DeVore, C. J. (2001). Counterproductive behaviors at work. In N. Anderson, D. Ones, H. Sinangil, & C. Viswesvaran (Eds.), *Handbook of industrial, work, and organizational psychology* (Vol. *1*, pp. 145–164). London, UK: Sage.

Schmidt, F. L., & Hunter, J. E. (2015). *Methods of meta-analysis: Correcting error and bias in research findings* (3rd ed.). Los Angeles, CA: Sage.

Skarlicki, D. P., & Folger, R. (1997). Retaliation in the workplace: The role of distributive, procedural, and interactional justice. *Journal of Applied Psychology, 82*, 434–443.

Smith, C. A., Organ, D. W., & Near, J. P. (1983). Organizational citizenship behavior: Its nature and antecedents. *Journal of Applied Psychology, 68*, 653–663.

Spector, P. E., Bauer, J. A., & Fox, S. (2010). Measurement artifacts in the assessment of counterproductive work behavior and organizational citizenship behavior: Do we know what we think we know? *Journal of Applied Psychology, 95*, 781–790.

Spector, P. E., & Fox, S. (2002). An emotion-centered model of voluntary work behavior: Some parallels between counterproductive work behavior and organizational citizenship behavior. *Human Resource Management Review, 12*, 269–292.

Spector, P. E., & Fox, S. (2010a). Counterproductive work behavior and organisational citizenship behavior: Are they opposite forms of active behavior? *Applied Psychology: An International Review, 59*, 21–39.

Spector, P. E., & Fox, S. (2010b). Theorizing about the deviant citizen: An attributional explanation of the interplay of organizational citizenship and counterproductive work behavior. *Human Resource Management Review, 20*, 132–143.

Spector, P. E., Fox, S., Penney, L. M., Bruursema, K., Goh, A., & Kessler, S. (2004). Development of the counterproductive work behavior checklist (CWB-C). Unpublished paper, University of South Florida, Tampa.

Spector, P. E., Fox, S., Penney, M., Bruursema, K., Goh, A., & Kessler, S. (2006). The dimensionality of counterproductivity: Are all counterproductive behaviors created equal? *Journal of Vocational Behavior, 68*, 446–460.

Stewart, S. M., Bing, M. N., Davison, H. K., Woehr, D. J., & McIntyre, M. D. (2009). In the eyes of the beholder: A non-self-report measure of workplace deviance. *Journal of Applied Psychology, 94*, 207–215.

Thibaut, J., & Kelley, H. (1959). *The social psychology of groups.* New York, NY: Wiley.

Thomas, J. P., Whitman, D. S., & Viswesvaran, C. (2010). Employee proactivity in organizations: A comparative meta-analysis of emergent proactive constructs. *Journal of Occupational and Organizational Psychology, 83*, 275–300.

Thurstone, L. L. (1928). Attitudes can be measured. *American Journal of Sociology, 33*, 529–554.

Tomassetti, A. J., Dalal, R. S., & Kaplan, S. A. (2016). Is policy capturing really more resistant than traditional self-report techniques to socially desirable responding? *Organizational Research Methods, 19*, 255–285.

Van Dyne, L., Cummings, L. L., & Parks, J. M. (1995). Extra-role behaviors: In pursuit of construct and definitional clarity (a bridge over muddied waters). In L. L. Cummings & B. M. Staw (Eds.), *Research in organizational behavior* (vol. *17*, pp. 215–285). Greenwich, CT: JAI.

Van Dyne, L., & LePine, J. A. (1998). Helping and voice extra-role behaviors: Evidence of construct and predictive validity. *Academy of Management Journal, 41*, 108–119.

Watson, D., Clark, L. A., & Tellegen, A. (1988). Development and validation of brief measures of positive and negative affect: The PANAS scales. *Journal of Personality and Social Psychology, 54*, 1063–1070.

Weiss, H. M., & Cropanzano, R. (1996). Affective events theory: A theoretical discussion of the structure, causes and consequences of affective experiences at work. *Research in Organizational Behavior, 19*, 1–74.

Weitz, J, (1961). Criteria for criteria. *American Psychologist, 16*, 228–231.

Whitman, D. S., Van Rooy, D. L., & Viswesvaran, C. (2010). Satisfaction, citizenship behaviors, and performance in work units: A meta-analysis of collective construct relations. *Personnel Psychology, 63*, 41–81.

Williams, L. J., & Anderson, S. E. (1991). Job satisfaction and organizational commitment as predictors of organizational citizenship and in-role behaviors. *Journal of Management, 17*, 601–617.

CHAPTER

7

The Role of a Good Soldier: A Review of Research on Organizational Citizenship Behavior Role Perceptions and Recommendations for the Future Research

Nathan P. Podsakoff, Elizabeth W. Morrison, *and* Tomas M. Martinez

Abstract

Although the original conceptualization of organizational citizenship behavior (OCB) defined these behaviors as discretionary in nature, over two decades of research on how employees view OCBs and their job responsibilities indicates that the boundary between in-role and extra-role behavior is blurry, and that there is substantial variation in employees' OCB role perceptions. In this chapter, we provide a review of over 40 articles that have examined the perceived boundary between required and discretionary citizenship behaviors. These include studies that have examined the predictors of OCB role perceptions, role perceptions as antecedents of OCBs, and role perceptions as mediators and moderators of the relationships between other predictors and OCBs. We conclude with several recommendations regarding future research directions for scholars interested in further understanding how OCBs are perceived by employees and the implications of different role perceptions for understanding employee performance.

Key Words: organizational citizenship behaviors, helping behavior, voice behavior, contextual performance, role theory, role perceptions, role/job breadth, role definitions, role enlargement, role discretion

In their original and seminal conceptualization of organizational citizenship behavior (OCB), Organ and his colleagues (Bateman & Organ, 1983; Organ, 1988; Smith, Organ, & Near, 1983) defined this construct as behaviors beyond the formal requirements of an employee's job (i.e., extra-role). In fact, one reason that OCB attracted such research interest was that, despite being essential to the effective functioning of a work unit, OCB was not something that could be formally specified or required. Over the years, however, researchers have come to recognize that the types of behaviors conceptualized and operationalized as OCBs are often *not* seen as extra-role by employees engaging in those work behaviors. Moreover, there has been recognition that perceptions of whether particular activities are extra-role or in-role (i.e., expected parts of the job) vary across employees in some predictable ways, and that these role perceptions have implications for how likely employees are to engage in these activities.

This recognition has some fundamental implications for how we study and understand OCB. If we accept that employees will be more likely to perform an activity if they believe it to be in-role rather than discretionary, because they perceive less choice, then an important determinant of supervisory ratings of OCB is the breadth with which employees define their job responsibilities. In other words, individuals rated as good citizens by their supervisors may simply be doing what they feel is part of their job rather than purposefully choosing to contribute above and beyond what is expected or required. This notion shifts the focus of research from the question of "Why are some employees motivated to go above and beyond how they see their job?" to the question of "Why do some employees see their jobs more broadly?"

Changing the Way We View Organizational Citizenship Behavior

The original definition of OCB was as follows: "individual behavior that is discretionary, not directly or explicitly recognized by the formal reward system, and that in the aggregate promotes the effective functioning of the organization" (Organ, 1988, p. 3). Organ (1988) went on to explain that by "discretionary," he means that the behavior "is not an enforceable requirement of the role or the job description, that is, the clearly specifiable terms of the person's employment contract with the organization; the behavior is rather a matter of personal choice, such that its omission is not generally understood as punishable" (p. 3).

Organ's early writing and empirical work on OCB gave rise to a large number of studies seeking to understand why it is that employees do or do not display this type of behavior. This research was motivated by a central question: If a behavior is not a part of one's job and is unrewarded, and if failure to display it is not punished, what motivates employees to engage in the behavior? Answers to this question largely revolved around notions of fairness and social exchange (see Organ et al., 2006). Specifically, Organ argued that employees use OCB to reciprocate the organization for fair treatment or withhold it in response to unfair treatment.

However, a 1994 paper by Morrison ignited some rethinking of the core assumptions being made about the motivation behind OCB. Building conceptually from research on role making (Graen, 1976), and consistent with a number of papers that raised questions about how OCB was conceptualized and measured (George & Brief, 1992; McAllister, 1991; Van Dyne, Cummings, & Parks, 1995), Morrison argued that perceptions of whether a particular behavior is perceived as extra-role varies across employees, and between employees and their supervisors. She sampled 317 clerical employees at a hospital and presented them with a list of 20 behaviors taken from existing measures of OCB. For 18 of the 20 behaviors, more employees defined the activity as in-role rather than extra-role. In addition, she found that managers' and employees' classifications of the behaviors were largely uncorrelated, although they converged to a greater extent when the supervisor and employee regularly interacted with one another.

Morrison (1994) introduced the notion of *perceived job breadth* or *OCB role definitions*, reflecting the extent to which behaviors typically assumed to be OCBs are viewed by the employee as part of his or her job. Her study also demonstrated that employees who define their job more broadly display more citizenship behaviors. In other words, employees engaging in these behaviors are not always doing so because they are motivated to go above and beyond their job, but in some cases because they see the behaviors as part of their job. Morrison argued that if researchers wish to truly understand the motivational basis for OCB, they need to understand how employees conceptualize their responsibilities.

In the 20 years since Morrison's (1994) study was published, there has been growing recognition that the defining features of OCB (discretionary, nonrewarded) are slippery constructs. Organ (1997), for example, has noted that "we guarantee construct muddiness if we define OCB as requiring that it be extra-role." (p. 88). In the revised version of his book, he and his colleagues (Organ et al., 2006) also offered a more nuanced definition of "discretionary" (i.e., "not an absolute requirement of the job description") and noted that the degree to which a contribution is rewarded versus nonrewarded is a continuum rather than reflecting a discrete boundary between required job performance and OCB.

However, despite these revisions, the typical measurement of OCB continues to reflect the assumption that the boundary between what is and is not OCB is objective and agreed upon, and the assumption that employees who are rated more highly on an OCB scale are choosing to contribute above and beyond their job. OCB is typically measured by presenting supervisors with a list of behaviors and asking them to rate how frequently each employee engages in those behaviors. Employees who score high are considered to be "good citizens," yet without any evidence that the behaviors being assessed are seen by those employees in a way that corresponds to the definition of OCB.

Even though the measurement of OCB has remained largely unchanged, researchers have increasingly recognized, at least conceptually, that employees can hold very different perceptions about OCB. This idea has generated a number of studies exploring the nature, antecedents, and consequences of perceived job breadth, defined as the extent to which employees view OCBs as in-role versus extra-role. Furthermore, studies have looked at other ways in which perceptions of traditional OCBs vary across individuals, such as the extent to which these behaviors are seen as rewarded, discretionary, or expected. To reflect this breadth, we have selected the term *OCB role perceptions* to refer to the various ways in which employees can perceive citizenship behaviors.

OCB role perceptions represent an active area of inquiry in the citizenship literature, with studies focused on addressing a variety of different research questions. However, a comprehensive review and integration of this literature does not exist, an omission that likely inhibits progress in this literature. Therefore, the primary purpose of this chapter is to provide such a review in an attempt to capture the current state of knowledge in this domain. A second purpose of this chapter is to use the information obtained from this review to make recommendations for potentially fruitful future research directions.

Organizational Citizenship Behavior Role Perceptions

OCB role perceptions refer to how employees define and classify behaviors that customarily have been assumed to be OCBs (McAllister et al., 2007). Several types of role perceptions have been discussed and studied in the literature. As noted earlier, Morrison (1994) was the first to articulate the concept of *perceived job breadth* with respect to citizenship behaviors. In her conceptualization, "broad" job definitions mean that an employee defines many OCBs as part of his or her role and responsibilities, whereas "narrow" job definitions indicate that employees define most OCBs as above and beyond their role or responsibilities. Job breadth is typically assessed by raters indicating whether specific OCBs are in-role or extra-role, using either a binary response format (0 = "You see this as somewhat above and beyond what is expected for your job" versus 1 = "You see this as an expected part of your job") or an interval scale (1 = "definitely part of my job" to 7 = "definitely exceeds my job requirements").

Although perceived job/role breadth is the most popular and often-studied type of OCB role perception, researchers have examined a few other types. In an effort to "disentangle OCB-related role perceptions that were either confounded in past research or studied individually," McAllister et al. (2007, p. 1201) identified and assessed three additional types of OCB role perceptions: (a) *OCB instrumentality*, or the extent to which an individual perceives a relationship between the performance of an OCB and important outcomes (rewards and punishments); (b) *OCB discretion*, or the extent to which an individual believes it is his or her choice to engage in a particular form of OCB; and (c) OCB *role efficacy*, the extent of an individual's belief in his or her competence to perform particular OCBs. The final role perception is similar to Parker's (1998) concept of "role-breadth self-efficacy," which captures employees' perceptions regarding their capability to perform different types of OCB. We have excluded research on this construct from our review because it pertains more to how employees perceive their own competence rather than how they perceive the nature of their job requirements. Finally, Finkelstein and Penner (2004) examined role identity, or the extent to which employees internalize the role of helper (or another form of "good citizen") as part of their self-concept.

Literature Review

Using a variety of computer-assisted and manual searches of the literature, we identified over 40 empirical articles that have examined the nature of OCB role perceptions and/or their relationships with other variables. These articles fall into four general groups: (1) studies examining predictors of OCB role perceptions, (2) examinations of OCB role perceptions as predictors of OCB, (3) studies of role perceptions as mediators of predictor relationships with OCB, and (4) studies of role perceptions as moderators of predictor relationships with OCB. In the following sections, we summarize the research in each of these categories.

Predictors of Organizational Citizenship Behavior Role Perceptions

Through our search of this literature, we found 25 empirical articles that focused on antecedents of OCB role perceptions. These studies examined over two dozen unique predictors. In the discussion that follows, we group these predictors into three categories: individual differences, job attitudes and perceptions, and position in the organization.

INDIVIDUAL DIFFERENCES

A number of personality traits are related to how employees define their roles. For example, in a study of 262 service workers and their managers, Tangirala, Kamdar, Venkataramani, and Parke

(2013) reported that an employee's duty orientation had a positive relationship with the breadth of his or her voice behavior role conceptualizations, whereas employee achievement orientation had a negative association with this perception. In addition, Tangirala et al. reported that the positive relationship between duty orientation and voice behavior role conceptualizations was stronger when voice efficacy was high compared to low; and that the negative relationship between achievement orientation and voice behavior role conceptualizations was stronger when psychological safety was low compared to high. Proactive personality has also been shown to predict role perceptions (Bergeron, Schroeder, & Martinez, 2014). In a study of over 500 faculty members employed by American academic institutions, role definitions with respect to professional service were shown to be broader for individuals who were more proactive. Using a sample of 242 county government employees, Finkelstein and Penner (2004) found that prosocial values were positively related to role identity. In other words, employees with motives to engage in prosocial behavior, such as assisting others or volunteering, were more likely to internalize citizenship as part of their self-concept.

In their study of 219 engineers working in India, Kamdar, McAllister, and Turban (2006) tested relationships between reciprocation wariness, empathic concern, and perspective taking, and role definitions of interpersonal helping and loyal boosterism. They reported that empathic concern and perspective taking were both positively related to role perceptions for interpersonal helping, whereas reciprocation wariness had a negative relationship with role perceptions for loyal boosterism. The authors also found that reciprocation wariness and perspective taking moderated the effect of procedural justice (PJ) on OCB role definitions. PJ had a positive relationship with interpersonal helping role perceptions when perspective taking was low, but no relationship when it was high. Similarly, PJ had a positive relationship with loyal boosterism role perceptions only when reciprocation wariness was low.

Chiaburu and Byrne (2009) examined the relationship between role definitions and exchange ideology, defined as the strength of employees' beliefs that their work effort and concern for the organization should be based on how well they are treated by the organization. These authors collected data from a sample of over 200 employees working in a variety of jobs and reported that employees with a stronger exchange ideology had narrower OCB role definitions. In addition, based on a study of 363 undergraduate students, Kwantes, Karam, Kuo, and Towson (2008) reported that social cynicism and belief in religiosity were related to narrower OCB role definitions, whereas the belief that hard work is rewarded was related to broader role definitions.

Studies have also reported nonsignificant relationships between certain dispositional variables and OCB role definitions. For example, using a mixed sample of Chinese managers and American MBA students, Blakely, Srivastava, and Moorman (2005) reported that although an individual's work locus of control was positively related to OCB role definitions, an individual's work role centrality was not related to this outcome. In addition, Vey and Campbell (2004) found neither employee agreeableness nor conscientiousness to be related to OCB role definitions in a sample of 248 undergraduate students with work experience. It is worth noting that participants in the study were asked to play the role of either a supermarket cashier or cashier shift supervisor when completing their measures. The fact that these individuals were not providing role perceptions for an occupation in which they necessarily had experience may explain the lack of significant relationships in this study.

Demographic variables have also been examined in relation to OCB role definitions. Li and Wan (2007) reported that employee age had a positive relationship with perceived job breadth. In other words, older employees tended to view OCBs as more in-role than extra-role. However, even though tenure and age tend to be highly correlated, Morrison (1994) did not find job tenure to be significantly related to role definitions.

Gender has not been found to have much effect on OCB role perceptions, with two studies (Li & Wan, 2007; Vey & Campbell, 2004) reporting that gender was unrelated to how broadly an employee perceived his or her job. We did, however, find studies that reported a relationship between an employee's gender and the extent to which *other people expected* the employee to engage in OCB (Chiaburu et al., 2014; Farrell & Finkelstein, 2007). For example, using experimental designs and two samples of undergraduate students, Chiaburu et al. (2014, p. 183) concluded that other's "expectations for civic virtue are diminished for women, but only when gender stereotypes and threat are activated."

Although examined in only two studies that we are aware of, it appears that nationality can also have an effect on OCB role definitions. Lam et al. (1999) reported that employees and supervisors from Hong Kong and Japan had broader courtesy role definitions than those from Australia, and had broader sportsmanship role definitions than those from Australia and the United States. However, the other dimensions of OCB role definitions they examined (altruism, conscientiousness, civic virtue) did not display significant differences across countries. In addition, Blakely et al. (2005) reported that Chinese participants in their sample had broader OCB role definitions than did American participants. Although these findings are consistent with cultural differences in individualism-collectivism, it is difficult to determine whether the results are necessarily a function of culture or the fact that the Chinese participants held managerial positions, whereas the American participants were MBA students (albeit with work experience).

PERCEPTIONS AND ATTITUDES

Our review of the literature indicates that employees' job attitudes and various perceptions related to their job and workplace are significant predictors of OCB role perceptions. These attitudes and perceptions include organizational justice, trust, organizational commitment, and relationship quality with one's supervisor (LMX).

The relationship between employee perceptions of organizational justice and their OCB role definitions has been consistently supported in several studies. As hypothesized by Tepper et al. (2001) and Coyle-Shapiro et al. (2004), employee perceptions of procedural justice (PJ) were related to broader OCB role definitions in both of those studies. Similarly, Coyle-Shapiro et al. (2004), Chiaburu (2007), and Ando and Matsuda (2010) all reported that employee perceptions of interactional justice were related to broader OCB role definitions.

Chiaburu and Byrne (2009) found that trust in the organization was related to broader employee role definitions regarding OCBs aimed at organization improvement (OCB-O), and that this relationship was moderated by job satisfaction. Specifically, these authors reported that the positive relationship between OCB-O role definitions and trust in the organization was stronger when employees were more versus less satisfied. In addition, using a sample of 186 American workers, Chiaburu and Marinova (2006) reported that employee perceptions of trust in their *organization* were related to broader role definitions for behaviors directed at the organization (OCB-O), whereas employee perceptions of trust in their *manager* were related to broader role definitions for behaviors directed at other individuals (OCB-I). The relationships between trust in the organization and OCB-I role definitions, and trust in the manager and OCB-O role definitions, were not significant. In sum, although generally positive in nature, the relationships between OCB role definitions and trust seem to be contingent upon an employee's job satisfaction and the target of the citizenship behavior.

In contrast, the relationship between organizational commitment and OCB role definitions does not seem to be contingent upon the type of commitment, and all of the relationships we identified were positive. Both Morrison (1994) and Garcia-Cabrera and Garcia-Soto (2011) reported that affective and normative commitment were related to broader OCB role definitions. Similarly, Chiaburu and Byrne (2009) reported that organizational commitment (which they referred to as psychological attachment) was related to broader OCB role definitions, and that this variable mediated the relationships between exchange ideology and role definitions, and trust and role definitions. Coyle-Shapiro et al. (2004) took an even broader perspective, using a construct they called mutual commitment, defined as the employee's perception that he or she is committed to the organization and the organization is committed to him or her. The authors used a combination of perceived organizational support and organizational concern items to measure this variable. They reported that higher levels of mutual commitment were related to broader OCB role definitions.

Although dozens of studies have examined job satisfaction as a predictor of OCB (Organ & Ryan, 1995), we identified only two empirical studies testing the relationships between job satisfaction and OCB role definitions. Morrison (1994) reported that job satisfaction was related to broader OCB role definitions, whereas Chiaburu and Byrne (2009) reported that there was no relationship between these two variables. Although job satisfaction has received limited attention, researchers in this domain have examined the effect of other affect-laden constructs. For example, using a scenario-based experimental design, Bachrach and Jex (2000) reported that subjects who received a positive mood induction reported broader OCB role definitions than subjects who received a negative mood induction (subjects in the positive and neutral conditions did not differ in their OCB role definitions). As another example, Finkelstein and Penner (2004) found that positive affect and pride toward the organization were positively related to the extent to which employees internalized citizenship into their role identity.

Perceptions about one's relationship with his or her supervisor have also been found to relate to an employee's OCB role definitions. Hofmann and his colleagues (2003) found that employees indicating higher quality LMX had broader role definitions related to safety behavior. Hsiung and Tsai (2009) focused on the relationship between LMX and relative job breadth, or how broadly an employee views his or her job in relation to how broadly his or her supervisor views the job. Based on a study of 184 Taiwanese subordinate–supervisor dyads, these authors reported that LMX had a positive relationship with relative OCB role breadth. In other words, as the quality of the relationship between the supervisor and subordinate increased, subordinates tended to view their jobs more broadly, at least with respect to safety-related behaviors, than did their supervisors.

Lastly, Turner et al. (2005) examined the relationship between perceived control and job demands and role definitions with respect to workplace safety behaviors and perceptions of job-related demands (Hofmann et al., 2003). Based on a sample of 334 rail workers in the United Kingdom, these authors reported that perceptions of greater job demands were related to narrower role definitions with respect to workplace safety behaviors, whereas perceptions of greater job control were related to broader safety-related role definitions.

POSITION IN THE ORGANIZATION

Researchers have argued that hierarchical position within the organization may influence how employees view the boundary between in-role and extra-role behavior for their jobs. Specifically, as one moves up the hierarchy, role definitions become broader. Consistent with this notion, Chiaburu and Byrne (2009) reported that, compared with lower level employees, those with supervisory responsibilities were more likely to view traditional OCBs as part of their roles. In addition, Li and Wan (2007) reported that general managers had broader role definitions than district managers or employees (district managers and employees did not differ in their role definitions). In contrast to these findings, Vey and Campbell (2004) reported that supervisory work experience (a binary variable) did not predict variance in reported role definitions. However, as noted earlier, this study required participants to role-play an occupation for which their supervisory work experience may not have been applicable.

An important contribution of Morrison's (1994) study was that it showed that employees and supervisors often had different views of the same job with respect to the boundary between in-role and extra-role behavior, suggesting another way in which one's position influences the perspective that employees take on the responsibilities for a particular job. In another study comparing these perceptions, Lam et al. (1999) reported that, relative to employees' own role definitions, managers had broader definitions of employees' role responsibilities for each of five dimensions of OCB: altruism, conscientiousness, sportsmanship, courtesy, and civic virtue.

Belogolovsky and Somech (2010) also examined the influence of positional perspective on role definitions. These authors assessed teacher OCB role definitions as perceived by 29 principals, 245 teachers, and 345 parents of children in 30 Israeli elementary schools. These authors found that both teachers and principals had broader role definitions than parents for OCB directed toward the school, yet both groups perceived narrower role definitions than parents for OCB directed toward students. The findings of these various studies suggest that (a) hierarchical position can influence perceptions of what behaviors will likely be considered in-role versus extra-role for a job (Morrison, 1994), and (b) perspectives on OCB role definitions for a target entity, obtained from different sources, are often not highly correlated.

When taken together, it is clear that a major theme in the research literature is identifying antecedents of the degree to which individuals define citizenship behaviors as in-role or extra-role, and that a number of such antecedents have been identified. In addition, a number of articles in this literature have examined the effects of OCB role perceptions on actual citizenship behavior, which we turn to in the following section.

The Relationship Between Organizational Citizenship Behavior Role Perceptions and Ratings of Organizational Citizenship Behavior

A key premise of Morrison's (1994) paper was that if an employee defines a behavior as in-role, then he or she is more likely to perform that behavior than if he or she defines it as extra-role, because the perceived incentives for in-role behavior are generally stronger than for extra-role behavior. In other words, an important factor determining whether OCB is exhibited will be how broadly an employee defines his or her job. Theoretically, this has important implications for how we understand OCB, as it means that employees rated by their supervisor as going above and beyond their job responsibilities may simply be doing what they feel is part of their job rather than engaging in behavior that they perceive to be above and beyond role requirements.

Consistent with Morrison's (1994) arguments and findings, over three dozen studies have examined the association between OCB role definitions and ratings of organizational citizenship behaviors. In an effort to summarize these empirical studies, Jiao, Richards, and Hackett (2013) performed a meta-analysis of 34 independent samples and reported that the average corrected correlation between OCB role breadth and ratings of OCBs was .43. Comparing these findings to those reported in other meta-analyses, Jiao et al. (2013, p. 707) indicate that "role breadth correlates more strongly with OCB than do these other established predictors," referring to dispositional traits, leadership behaviors, and explicit incentives as examples.

Although these meta-analytic estimates were based on bivariate correlations, the relationship between role definitions and OCBs seems to be robust when other variables are also considered in multivariate analyses. For example, Kamdar et al. (2006) reported that role definitions for loyal boosterism and interpersonal helping were significant predictors of their respective OCBs when controlling for perceptions of PJ and other individual differences. Coyle-Shapiro et al. (2004) reported that OCB role definitions explained significant incremental variance in OCB ($\Delta R^2 = 11\%$) beyond that explained by both justice perceptions and mutual commitment. Consistent with these findings, McAllister et al. (2007) reported that perceived role breadth remained a significant predictor of helping and taking-charge behaviors when controlling for PJ. These authors also compared the predictive value of different OCB role perceptions (i.e., perceived role breadth, instrumentality, discretion) and found that perceived role breadth was the most dominant predictor for helping behavior, explaining 33% of the variance in ratings of this type of OCB. Perceived role breadth was also a strong predictor of ratings of taking-charge behavior, accounting for 13% of the variance in this activity.

Our review of the studies reporting a significant correlation between role perceptions and OCB ratings indicates that role perceptions remained significant predictors in over 90% of studies in which they were included in multivariate analyses with other predictors. Thus, we agree with Jiao et al. (2013) that OCB role definitions seem to be among the strongest, and potentially most proximal, predictors of OCB examined in the literature.

The Role Enlargement Effect: Organizational Citizenship Behavior Role Perceptions as a Mediator

In her initial work on OCB role definitions, Morrison (1994) argued that employees who were more satisfied with their jobs and more committed to their organizations would define their job requirements broadly and subsequently perform higher levels of citizenship behavior. In other words, OCB role definitions were hypothesized to serve as mediating mechanisms for the effects of job attitudes on OCBs. This idea was a potentially important one in terms of altering our understanding of the reasons why employees engage in behaviors that have traditionally been seen as extra-role. Specifically, it suggested that positive job attitudes did not necessarily motivate employees to contribute beyond the boundaries of their job, but rather, that they cause employees to see those boundaries in a different way.

Other researchers have likewise argued that role definitions will serve as mediators between OCB and previously identified predictors of OCB, or what Tepper, Lockhart, and Hoobler (2001) refer to as the *role enlargement* effect. In essence, the argument is that certain factors lead employees to enlarge what they consider to be their role in the organization "which, in turn, causes them to perform those activities with greater frequency (because the motivation for inrole behavior is greater than the motivation for extrarole behavior; Katz, 1964)" (Tepper et al., 2001, p. 790).

Over the years, a variety of individual differences, attitudes, and perceptions have been used to test the role enlargement hypothesis, with the hypothesis receiving mixed support. Morrison (1994) reported that perceived job breadth fully mediated the relationship between affective commitment and four different dimensions of OCB (altruism, conscientiousness, involvement, and keeping-up behavior), and it fully mediated the relationship between tenure and keeping-up behavior. Job breadth also partially mediated the relationship between normative commitment and involvement, and the relationships between job satisfaction and both conscientiousness and keeping-up behavior. In total, Morrison reported support for half (8 of 16) of the potential mediating relationships she tested.

Coyle-Shapiro et al. (2004) and Finkelstein and Penner (2004) provided support for the role enlargement hypothesis using attitudinal constructs similar to those employed by Morrison. Specifically, Coyle-Shapiro et al. found that OCB role definitions partially mediated the relationship between mutual commitment and civic virtue behavior, while Finkelstein and Penner found that role identity partially mediated the relationship between organizational concern values and both OCB-O and OCB-I.

Tests of the role enlargement hypothesis using employee justice perceptions as the predictor have not found similar support. Using Baron and Kenny's (1986) criteria for testing mediation, Tepper et al. (2001) failed to find evidence that OCB role definitions mediate the relationship between perceptions of procedural justice and OCB. Chiaburu (2007) tested the role enlargement hypothesis using interactional justice (IJ) as the predictor and OCB-I as the dependent variable, arguing that it was "more likely that individual-directed OCBs are predicted by fair treatment originating from the direct supervisor (interactional justice) rather than by procedural justice" (p. 209). However, he too was unable to find support for a mediating effect of OCB role definitions on the relationship between justice perceptions and OCB.

Generally speaking, studies testing the role enlargement effect using dispositional variables have found more consistent support. For example, Tangirala et al. (2013) reported that voice role conceptualizations fully mediated the relationships between duty and achievement orientation and employee voice behavior. Consistent with their expectations, Bergeron et al. (2014) reported that role breadth fully mediated the relationships between employee proactive personality and both general and professional-service forms of OCB, but it did not mediate the relationship between this trait and task behavior. Similarly, Finkelstein and Penner (2004) examined the mediating effect of role identity on the relationships between prosocial values and OCB-O and OCB-I, finding support for partial mediation of both relationships. Kim, Van Dyne, Kamdar, and Johnson (2013) reported that helping role cognitions mediated the relationship between prosocial values and helping behavior, and the relationship between impression management motives and helping behavior. They also found that voice role cognitions mediated the relationship between organizational concern motives and voice behavior.

Finally, we identified two studies that tested the role enlargement hypothesis using leader-related predictors of OCBs. Jiao, Richards, and Zhang (2011) tested the potential mediating effects of individual OCB instrumentality (the belief that OCB is related to rewards and/or punishments) and perceptions of organizational OCB instrumentality (the belief that OCBs impact workplace functionality and effectiveness) on the relationships between transformational and contingent-reward behaviors and OCB. These authors reported that organizational instrumentality partially mediated the relationship between transformational leadership and OCB and the relationship between contingent-reward and OCB, whereas individual instrumentality had only a marginally significant and partially mediating effect on the relationships between these leader behaviors and OCB. In the second study, Hofmann et al. (2003) reported that safety citizenship role definitions did not mediate the relationship between LMX and safety OCBs.

In summary, the results related to the role enlargement hypothesis have been mixed. This is somewhat surprising because research has shown that (a) OCB role perceptions are predicted by many of the attitudes and dispositions that have been shown to predict OCB ($X \rightarrow M$); (b) OCB role perceptions are a strong predictor of OCB ($M \rightarrow Y$); *but* (c) support has not always been demonstrated for mediation ($X \rightarrow M \rightarrow Y$). This raises questions about the reasons for the inconsistent findings. One possible explanation is methodological in nature. Many of the mediating effects tests reported in this literature used Baron and Kenny's (1986) criteria for testing mediation. Although extremely popular, several experts (Cheung & Lau, 2008; MacKinnon, 2008; MacKinnon, Lockwood, Hoffman, West, & Sheets, 2002) have been critical of the Baron and Kenny approach, because some of their criteria for assessing whether mediation is present are overly restrictive. This means that some studies testing the role enlargement hypothesis using Baron and Kenny's criteria (e.g., Hofmann et al. 2003; Tepper et al. 2001) may have incorrectly concluded the absence of a mediating effect for OCB role definitions, when such an effect did exist. We recommend that future research testing mediating effects in the role definitions literature use the product of coefficients approach and bootstrapped confidence intervals as recommended by MacKinnon et al. (2002).

The second explanation is both methodological and conceptual in nature. Specifically, inconsistent findings with respect to tests of the role enlargement hypothesis may signal the presence of moderators. In other words, there could be individual differences, contextual factors, and/or differences in the designs and methods employed by these studies that would explain when mediation is present and when it is not. This suggests that researchers would benefit from combining tests of mediation with an examination of boundary conditions, in what Muller, Judd, and Yzerbyt (2005) refer to as moderated mediation. These authors indicate that "Moderated mediation happens if the mediating process that is responsible for producing the effect of the treatment on the outcome depends on the value of a moderator variable" (Muller et al., 2005, p. 854). Given the importance of the role enlargement hypothesis to this literature, we encourage researchers to explore potential moderators when they are testing for mediated effects. However, before engaging in such studies, researchers should understand the existing research on how role perceptions interact with other variables in predicting OCBs.

The Role Discretion Effect: Organizational Citizenship Behavior Role Perceptions as Moderators

As an alternative to viewing OCB role perceptions as potential mediating mechanisms, some researchers have hypothesized that these perceptions instead moderate the relationship between various antecedents and OCB. The original argument, by Tepper and colleagues (2001), was that employees who define OCB as more extra-role see fewer situational constraints on their performance of OCB, thus allowing them to modify their OCB based on how they are treated. Specifically, Tepper and colleagues predicted that justice perceptions correlate more strongly with OCBs when employees regard those behaviors as extra-role rather than in-role. They referred to this as the *role discretion* effect. Using a sample of 160 working MBA students and their managers, and a second sample of 110 supervisor–subordinate dyads working in a large automobile manufacturer, these authors examined the interactive effect of role definitions and procedural justice on four types of OCB: interpersonal helping, personal industry, individual initiative, and loyal boosterism.

In the first sample, they found significant interactions between justice and role breadth for personal industry and loyal boosterism. In the second sample, they found significant interactions between justice and role breadth for interpersonal helping and personal industry. In all these cases, consistent with the role discretion hypothesis, the relationship between PJ and OCB was more strongly positive to the extent that employees defined citizenship behaviors as extra-role rather than in-role.

Zellars et al. (2002) similarly reported that the positive relationship between procedural justice and OCB was stronger when citizenship was defined as extra-role compared to in-role. In an effort to extend the generalizability of the phenomenon, Tepper and Taylor (2003) examined the role discretion effect for both subordinate and supervisor forms of OCB. They reported more strongly positive relationships between subordinates' PJ perceptions and subordinates' OCB, and between supervisors' PJ perceptions and supervisors' mentoring behavior, when these respective groups defined citizenship behavior as more extra-role than in-role. Kamdar et al. (2006) also argued for an interaction between fairness perceptions and role breadth. Although they used a different conceptual framework, their results were largely consistent with those of Tepper et al. (2001). In addition, Chiaburu (2007) examined the interactive effect of role definitions and IJ on OCBs. Similar to the results for PJ, they found that the positive relationship between IJ and OCB was stronger when employees define their role narrowly versus broadly.

McAllister et al. (2007) tested the role discretion effect using two different types of behavior (helping and taking charge) and two different types of role perceptions: role breadth and perceived discretion. The latter was defined as the extent to which employees perceived that they had choice regarding the performance of OCBs. Consistent with the logic used by Tepper et al. (2001), they predicted that the effect of procedural justice on OCB would be stronger when discretion was perceived to be high. The findings supported their predictions for helping behavior, but not for taking charge. For role breadth, McAllister and colleagues predicted that the interaction would differ depending on the type of behavior. In the case of helping behavior, they expected results similar to those hypothesized in previous studies (Kamdar et al., 2006; Tepper et al., 2001). However, for taking charge they predicted that the effect would be reversed. In other words, the relationship would be stronger when OCB was seen as *in-role* (i.e., broader OCB role breadth), compared to *extra-role* (i.e., narrower OCB role breadth). McAllister et al. posited that this is a function of the higher levels of risk associated with taking-charge behavior: When employees view taking charge as within the bounds of their roles, or in other words, when role breadth is high, they will perceive that behavior as less risky. As a result, they will be more likely to perform taking charge in exchange for fair treatment (McAllister et al., 2007). The authors reported support for both hypotheses.

We identified two empirical studies examining the role discretion effect for leader-related predictors of OCB. In the first study, Zellars et al. (2002) examined the moderating effect of OCB role definitions on the relationship between abusive supervision and OCB. These authors reported that this relationship was more strongly negative when OCBs were defined as extra-role compared to in-role. Van Dyne, Kamdar, and Joireman (2008) examined LMX as a predictor, assessing both challenge- and affiliation-oriented forms of OCB as dependent variables, and examining both supervisors and the organization as targets for these behaviors. Across two samples of employees, these authors reported consistent support for their expectations. More specifically, they found that (a) the positive relationships between LMX and helping behavior aimed at the supervisor and at the organization were stronger when this behavior was seen as extra-role compared to when it was seen as in-role, and (b) the positive relationships between LMX and voice behavior targeted toward the supervisor and the organization were stronger when this behavior was seen as in-role compared to extra-role. When considered together with the results reported by McAllister et al. (2007), these findings support a revised perspective on the role discretion hypothesis, which requires consideration for the specific type of OCB an employee is defining as in-role or extra-role, and in turn, exhibiting.

Finally, Clark, Zickar, and Jex (2014) examined the role discretion hypothesis for a group-level variable—safety climate. They reported that the positive relationship between safety climate and peer-rated OCBs exists only when OCB role definitions are narrow, whereas this relationship is nonsignificant when OCB role definitions are broad.

When taken together, the research has been generally supportive of the role discretion hypothesis, with the results tending to be more consistent than for the role enlargement hypothesis. Specifically, while there is evidence that role definitions mediate the effects of several OCB antecedents (with two thirds of the hypothesized effects receiving support), there is somewhat stronger evidence for moderation (with four fifths of the hypothesized effects receiving support). It is worth noting, however, that most of the research on the moderating effect of role definitions has focused on justice perceptions, whereas the research on role definitions as a mediator has examined a wider range of attitudes, perceptions, and dispositions.

Importantly, the research on the role discretion effect also suggests that the moderating effect of role definitions varies depending on the type of OCB. McAllister et al. (2007) argued that the traditional role discretion hypothesis is applicable to affiliation-oriented, but not challenge-oriented, forms of OCB. As noted, these authors found that the role discretion effect reversed for taking-charge behavior, such that the effect of PJ was stronger when taking charge was perceived as in-role compared to extra-role. Given that Van Dyne et al. (2008) reported similar findings for voice behavior, it seems important for researchers to reconsider how the role discretion effect may operate for behaviors that are challenging or risky. In particular, we encourage research examining the underlying mechanisms that account for these different moderating relationships.

Future Directions for Research

Our intent in writing this chapter was not only to review the research on OCB role perceptions but also to provide some suggestions for future research. The research on role perceptions has been robust, yet there are some noteworthy gaps, especially related to antecedents of perceived job breadth. In particular, although a number of employee-level antecedents have been identified (e.g., personality traits, job attitudes, etc.), there has been very little research on predictors at other levels of analysis. This is surprising because role theory suggests that a variety of job, group, and organizational variables may affect how employees define their work roles (Sluss, van Dick, & Thompson, 2011). There has also been a lack of systematic research on the role of more macro factors, such as national culture. Therefore, a useful tool for future research would be the development of a model of the predictors of OCB role perceptions that includes variables across multiple levels.

To this end, in Figure 7.1 we present a preliminary model of multilevel antecedents of OCB role perceptions. The variables included are certainly not exhaustive. Moreover, a detailed discussion of each of the relationships presented in this figure is beyond the scope of this chapter. We will, however, try to give a feel for some of the proposed relationships indicted in the figure.

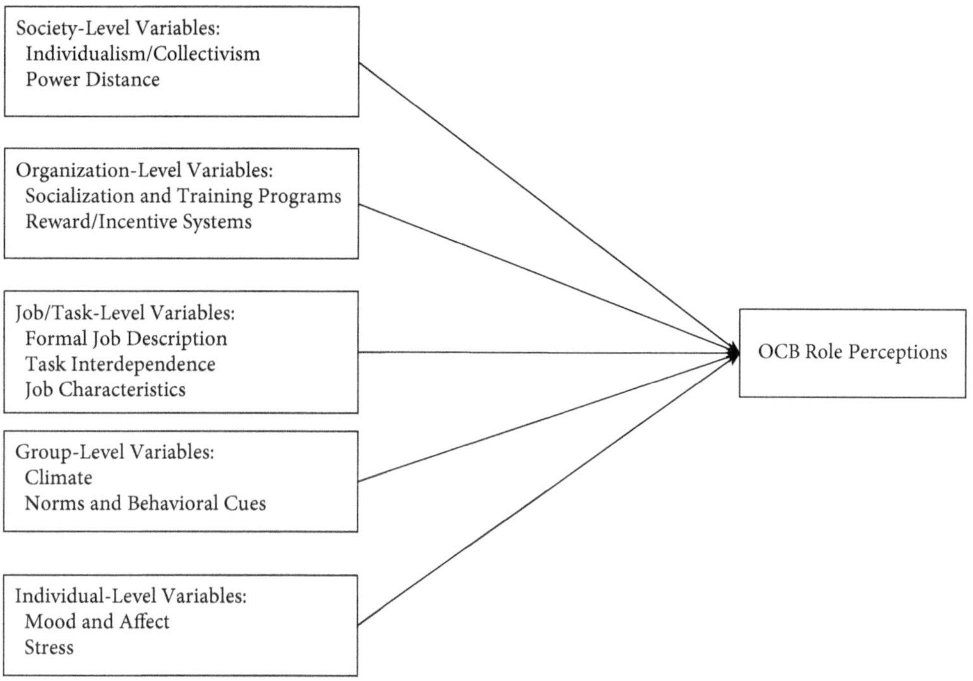

Figure 7.1 Potential predictors of organizational citizenship behavior (OCB) role perceptions at multiple levels.

Starting at the most macro level in the model, there may be several factors at the societal level worth exploring. In our review, we found two primary studies (Blakely et al., 2005; Lam et al., 1999) that reported differences in OCB role perceptions across countries. Consistent with the bulk of cross-cultural research published in the OCB literature (Organ et al., 2006), both of these studies focused on individualistic versus collectivistic cultures. The results suggest that employees in or from countries that are more collectivistic in nature will have broader job/role breadth than those in or from individualistic cultures. Although not definitive evidence, Jiao et al. (2013) reported meta-analytic results indicating that Confucian Asian samples reported significantly broader job definitions in general, and specifically for affiliation-oriented behaviors such as helping, when compared to Anglo-American samples. However, it is important to note at least three things about these results: (1) the range of countries examined in these studies is very limited, (2) the countries that were selected represent fairly extreme differences, and (3) these countries also differ on a variety of other factors. Therefore, we recommend that future research study countries that represent a broader sampling of the individualism/collectivism spectrum (Hofstede & Hofstede, 2005). For example, some Central and South American countries are highly collectivistic (e.g., Costa Rica, Colombia, Venezuela, Panama, and Guatemala), yet differ in many ways from the Asian countries most often used to represent this end of the spectrum. In addition, it might be advantageous for researchers to explore role definitions in countries that occupy the middle of the individualism–collectivism continuum, such as Germany, Spain, Argentina, or Iran. Exploring a broader set of countries would also uncover the potential of other cultural factors that may be important to employee role definitions. For example, it is likely that differences in power distance (Hofstede & Hofstede, 2005) will affect specific types of employees' OCB role definitions. Specifically, employees in or from high power-distance cultures should be more likely to perceive OCBs that challenge authority or the status quo, such as voice behavior or taking charge, as extra-role, compared to employees in lower power-distance countries/cultures.

Organization-level factors can also affect the way employees define their roles, and this is likely to occur in a variety of formal and informal ways (Sluss et al., 2011). For example, organizations use formal socialization and training programs to reinforce the prescribed tasks, duties, and responsibilities associated with the job and with being a member of the organization. Therefore, the content and effectiveness of organizational training and socialization programs may have an effect on participants' OCB role definitions, and they may moderate the effect of other predictors on this outcome. Examining predictors at the organizational level may also provide opportunities to study other forms of OCB role perceptions. For example, it is likely that training and socialization programs will influence not just role breadth but also the OCB role efficacy (McAllister et al., 2007) of participants. In other words, programs that instruct employees on how to perform proactive or change-oriented behaviors, and that reinforce this learning with practice, would likely increase participants' perceptions that they have the competency to perform these OCBs. We also expect that organizational reward and incentive systems would affect OCB instrumentality, or the extent to which an employee perceives a link between exhibited OCB and important outcomes (McAllister et al., 2007). If incentive systems are designed to formally or informally reward employees for being more proactive or prosocial, and managers distribute rewards accordingly, employees should perceive stronger links between these OCBs and valued outcomes. In sum, organizational-level predictors represent a potentially fruitful avenue for researchers interested not only in job breadth but also other dimensions of OCB role perceptions.

Given that this literature focuses on predicting *job* breadth, consideration for *job*-level predictors is particularly important, and yet surprisingly absent in the extant literature. However, several aspects of an employee's job are likely to affect their role definitions. For example, a rigid formal job description should lead to narrower role breadth than a job description that is more open ended. We would also expect employees whose jobs require greater interdependence or teamwork to have broader role definitions with respect to affiliation-oriented OCBs, such as helping behaviors. Interestingly, we could not find any study that examined the effect of formally specified job requirements on employee OCB role perceptions. There is also little research on the role of job characteristics, such as autonomy, complexity, or feedback, either as main or interactive effect predictors of OCB role perceptions. Yet these characteristics are likely to play an important role. For example, employees' perceptions of the extent to which they have the autonomy to decide which tasks they will perform, when they will perform them, and how they will perform them may represent a strong situation that will moderate the relationship between individual differences and OCB role definitions, such that the relationship will be stronger when autonomy is high as compared to low. Thus, attention to this level is important, and full of possibilities for moving our understanding of OCB role definitions forward.

Despite the importance of group-level factors in forming role perceptions (Sluss et al., 2011), our review identified only one study which examined a predictor of OCB role definitions at the group level—the study by Hofmann et al. (2003) on the effect of safety climate. In addition to examining other forms of climate (e.g., justice, affect, engagement), we believe that it would be valuable to consider how social cues, particularly from coworkers and teammates, shape employees' OCB role perceptions. Indeed, conceptual arguments and empirical evidence from the social information processing (Thomas & Griffin, 1983), group norms (Ehrhart & Naumann, 2004), and social proof (Cialdini, 2001) literatures all suggest that cues from coworkers can have a strong effect on individuals' perceptions about what is acceptable, expected, or required with respect to their jobs. Morrison (1994) argued that employees will define their job responsibilities similarly to the extent that they interact with the same set of other employees, and are thus exposed to similar social cues. However, subsequent research has not explored this phenomenon in detail, nor the mechanisms by which information from others shapes an employee's role perceptions. As a starting point, we would offer the hypothesis that employees will tend to have broader role definitions to the extent that a large proportion of the group frequently exhibits behaviors typically considered to be OCBs (Ehrhart & Naumann, 2004).

Although a large number of individual-level predictors have been discussed in the OCB role perceptions literature, we have added a few additional variables to this category in Figure 7.1. For example, it is likely that mood or affect will influence an employee's perceived job breadth. A focus on mood would enable an examination of within-person differences in OCB role perceptions, or in other words, an examination of how they vary daily, weekly, or monthly over time. Although researchers have used diary or experience-sampling methods to demonstrate the relationship between employee mood or affective states and OCB (see the Scott, Matta, & Koopman chapter in this book for a review), none of these studies examine how broadly or narrowly employees perceive their role or job. In addition, the daily stressors or demands employees experience may result in variations in the extent to which they include or exclude certain citizenship behaviors in their role definitions. Days that are particularly stressful, or filled with high levels of demands, may cause employees to narrow their roles in an attempt to better fulfill their core job duties. This intraindividual approach represents an opportunity to examine the "process" by which individuals create, develop, and alter their OCB role perceptions over time—an area of inquiry we believe is much needed in this literature.

Finally, we should note that predictors of job/role breadth could exist at other levels, such as the dyad (supervisor–employee or coworker–employee). Having said that, we believe that the categories and variables reported in Figure 7.1 represent important factors that will contribute to our understanding of the predictors of OCB role perceptions that exist at different levels of analysis.

Conclusion

The purpose of this chapter was to summarize the literature on role perceptions, which has had an impact on our understanding of what organizational citizenship behaviors are and why they occur. Our review identified a variety of individual-level predictors of how broadly employees view their job role, and thus how they perceive the boundary between in-role and extra-role behavior. We also highlighted the strong and consistent relationship between employee role perceptions and the extent to which employees engage in behaviors that are typically assumed to be examples of OCB. In addition, we summarized a number of studies that, together, provide evidence for both mediating and moderating effects of role perceptions. We concluded with a model to help researchers explore the multilevel antecedents of OCB role perceptions. We hope that this model, and the identification of some of the gaps in the current literature, will facilitate future research examining the nature and nomological net of OCB role perceptions.

References

Ando, N., & Matsuda, S. (2010). How employees see their roles: The effect of interactional justice and gender. *Journal of Service Science and Management, 3*, 281–286.

Bachrach, D. G., & Jex, S. M. (2000). Organizational citizenship and mood: An experimental test of perceived job breadth. *Journal of Applied Social Psychology, 30*, 641–663.

Baron, R. M., & Kenny, D. A. (1986). The moderator-mediator variable distinction in social psychological research: Conceptual, strategic, and statistical considerations. *Journal of Personality and Social Psychology, 51*, 1173–1182.

Bateman, T. S., & Organ, D. W. (1983). Job satisfaction and the good soldier: The relationship between affect and employee "citizenship." *Academy of Management Journal, 26*, 587–595.

Belogolovsky, E., & Somech, A. (2010). Teachers' organizational citizenship behavior: Examining the boundary between in-role behavior and extra-role behavior from the perspective of teachers, principals and parents. *Teacher and Teacher Education, 26*, 914–923.

Bergeron, D. M., Schroeder, T. D., & Martinez, H. A. (2014). Proactive personality at work: Seeing more to do and doing more? *Journal of Business and Psychology, 29*, 71–86.

Blakely, G. L., Srivastava, A., & Moorman, R. H. (2005). The effects of nationality, work role centrality, and work locus of control on role definitions. *Journal of Leadership and Organizational Studies, 12*, 103–117.

Cheung, G. W., & Lau, R. S. (2008). Testing mediation and suppression effects of latent variables—Bootstrapping with structural equation models. *Organizational Research Methods, 11*, 296–325.

Chiaburu, D. S. (2007). From interactional justice to citizenship behaviors: Role enlargement or role discretion? *Social Justice Research, 20*, 207–227.

Chiaburu, D. S., & Byrne, Z. S. (2009). Predicting OCB role definitions: Exchanges with the organization and psychological attachment. *Journal of Business and Psychology, 24*, 201–214.

Chiaburu, D. S., & Marinova, S. V. (2006). Employee role enlargement: Interactions of trust and organizational fairness. *Leadership & Organization Development Journal, 27*, 168–182.

Chiaburu, D. S., Sawyer, K., Smith, T. A., Brown, N., & Harris, T. B. (2014). When civic virtue isn't seen as virtuous: The effect of gender stereotyping on civic virtue expectations for women. *Sex Roles, 70*, 183–194.

Cialdini, R. B. (2001). *Influence: Science and practice* (4th ed.). Needham Heights, MA: Allyn and Bacon.

Clark, O. L., Zickar, M. J., & Jex, S. M. (2014). Role definition as moderator of the relationship between safety climate and organizational citizenship behavior among hospital nurses. *Journal of Business and Psychology, 29*, 101–110.

Coyle-Shapiro, J. A-M., Kessler, I., & Purcell, J. (2004). Exploring organizationally directed citizenship behaviour: Reciprocity or "It's my job"? *Journal of Management Studies, 41*, 85–106.

Ehrhart, M. G., & Naumann, S. E. (2004). Organizational citizenship behavior in work groups: A group norms approach. *Journal of Applied Psychology, 89*, 960–974.

Farrell, S. K., & Finkelstein, L. M. (2007). Organizational citizenship behavior and gender: Expectations and attributions for performance. *North American Journal of Psychology, 9*, 81–96.

Finkelstein, M. A., & Penner, L. A. (2004). Predicting organizational citizenship behavior: Integrating the functional and role identity approaches. *Social Behavior and Personality, 32*, 383–398.

García-Cabrera, A. M., & García-Soto, M. G. (2011). MNC commitment, OCB role definition and intent to leave in subsidiary top managers: The moderating effect of uncertainty avoidance values. *International Journal of Intercultural Relations, 35*, 641–657.

George, J. M., & Brief, A. P. (1992). Feeling good-doing good: A conceptual analysis of the mood at work-organizational spontaneity relationship. *Psychological Bulletin, 112*, 310–329.

Graen, G. B. (1976). Role making processes within complex organizations. In M. D. Dunnette (Ed.), *Handbook of industrial and organizational psychology* (pp. 1201–1245). Chicago, IL: Rand-McNally.

Hofmann, D. A., Morgeson, F. P., & Gerras, S. J. (2003). Climate as a moderator of the relationship between leader-member exchange and content specific citizenship: Safety climate as an exemplar. *Journal of Applied Psychology, 88*, 170–178.

Hofstede, G., & Hofstede, G. J. (2005). *Culture and organizations: Software of the mind* (2nd ed.). New York, NY: McGraw-Hill.

Hsiung, H.-H., & Tsai, W.-C. (2009). Job definition discrepancy between supervisors and subordinates: The antecedent role of LMX and outcomes. *Journal of Occupational and Organizational Psychology, 82*, 89–112.

Jiao, C, Richards, D. A., & Hackett, R. D. (2013). Organizational citizenship behavior and role breadth: A meta-analytic and cross-cultural analysis. *Human Resource Management, 52*, 697–714.

Jiao, C., Richards, D. A., & Zhang, K. (2011). Leadership and organizational citizenship behavior: OCB-specific meanings as mediators. *Journal of Business and Psychology, 26*, 11–25.

Kamdar, D., McAllister, D. J., & Turban, D. B. (2006). "All in a day's work": How follower individual differences and justice perceptions predict OCB role definitions and behavior. *Journal of Applied Psychology, 91*, 841–855.

Katz, D. (1964). The motivational basis of organizational behavior. *Behavioral Science, 9*, 131–146.

Kim, Y.-J., Van Dyne, L., Kamdar, D., & Johnson, R. E. (2013). Why and when do motives matter? An integrative model of motives, role cognitions, and social support as predictors of OCB. *Organizational Behavior and Human Decision Processes, 121*, 231–245.

Kwantes, C. T., Karam, C. M., Kuo, B. C. H., & Towson, S. (2008). Culture's influence on the perception of OCB as in-role or extra-role. *International Journal of Intercultural Relations, 32*, 229–243.

Lam, S. S. K., Hui, C., & Law, K. S. (1999). Organizational citizenship behavior: Comparing perspectives of supervisors and subordinates across four interactional samples. *Journal of Applied Psychology, 84*, 594–601.

Li, W., & Wan, W. (2007). A demographic study on citizenship behavior as in-role orientation. *Personality and Individual Differences, 42*, 225–234.

MacKinnon, D. (2008). *Introduction to statistical mediation analysis*. New York, NY: Lawrence Erlbaum Associates.

MacKinnon, D., Lockwood, C., Hoffman, J., West, S., & Sheets, V. (2002). A comparison of methods to test mediation and other intervening variable effects. *Psychological Methods, 7*, 83–104.

McAllister, D. J. (1991). Regrounding organizational citizenship behavior research. Paper presented at the annual meeting of the Academy of Management, Miami Beach, FL.

McAllister, D. J., Kamdar, D., Morrison, E. W., & Turban, D. B. (2007). Disentangling role perceptions: How perceived role breadth, discretion, instrumentality, and efficacy relate to helping and taking charge. *Journal of Applied Psychology, 92*, 1200–1211.

Morrison, E. W. (1994). Role definitions and organizational citizenship behavior: The importance of the employee's perspective. *Academy of Management Journal, 37*, 1543–1567.

Muller, D., Judd. C., & Yzerbyt, V. (2005). When moderation is mediated and mediation is moderated. *Journal of Personality and Social Psychology, 89*, 852–863.

Organ, D. W. (1988). *Organizational citizenship behavior: The good soldier syndrome*. Lexington, MA: Lexington Books.

Organ, D. W. (1997). Organizational citizenship behavior: It's construct clean-up time. *Human Performance, 10*, 85–97.

Organ, D. W., Podsakoff, P. M., & MacKenzie, S. B. (2006). *Organizational citizenship behavior: Its nature, antecedents, and consequences*. Thousand Oaks, CA: Sage.

Organ, D. W., & Ryan, K. (1995). A meta-analytic review of attitudinal and dispositional predictors of organizational citizenship behavior. *Personnel Psychology, 48*, 775–802.

Parker, S. K. (1998). Enhancing role breadth self-efficacy: The roles of job enrichment and other organizational interventions. *Journal of Applied Psychology, 83*, 835–852.

Sluss, D. M., van Dick, R., & Thompson, B. S. (2011). Role theory in organizations: A relational perspective. In S. Zedeck (Ed.), *APA handbook of industrial and organizational psychology, Vol 1: Building and developing the organization. APA Handbooks in Psychology* (pp. 505–534). Washington, DC: American Psychological Association.

Smith, C. A, Organ, D. W., & Near, J. P. (1983). Organizational citizenship behavior: Its nature and antecedents. *Journal of Applied Psychology, 68*, 653–663.

Tangirala, S., Kamdar, D., Venkataramani, V., & Parke, M. R. (2013). Doing right versus getting ahead: The effects of duty and achievement orientations on employees' voice. *Journal of Applied Psychology, 98*, 1040–1050.

Tepper, B. J., Lockhart, D., & Hoobler, J. (2001). Justice, citizenship, and role definition effects. *Journal of Applied Psychology, 86*, 789–796.

Tepper, B. J., & Taylor, E. C. (2003). Relationships among supervisor' and subordinates' procedural justice perceptions and organizational citizenship behaviors. *Academy of Management Journal, 46*, 97–105.

Thomas, J., & Griffin, R. (1983). The social information processing model of task design: A review of the literature. *Academy of Management Review, 8*, 672–682.

Turner, N., Chmiel, N., Walls, M. (2005). Railing for safety: Job demands, job control, and safety citizenship role definition. *Journal of Occupational Health Psychology, 10*, 504–512.

Van Dyne, L., Cummings, L. L., & Parks, J. M. (1995). Extra-role behaviors: In pursuit of construct and definitional clarity (A bridge over muddied waters). In L. L. Cummings & B. M. Staw (Eds), *Research in organizational behavior* (Vol. 17, pp. 215–285). Greenwich, CT: JAI Press.

Van Dyne, L., Kamdar, D., & Joireman, J. (2008). In-role perceptions buffer the negative impact of low LMX on helping and enhance the positive impact of high LMX on voice. *Journal of Applied Psychology, 93*, 1195–1207.

Vey, M. A., & Campbell, J. P. (2004). In-role or extra-role organizational citizenship behavior: Which are we measuring? *Human Performance, 17*, 119–135.

Zellars, K. L., Tepper, B. J., & Duffy, M. K. (2002). Abusive supervision and subordinates' organizational citizenship behavior. *Journal of Applied Psychology, 87*, 1068–1076.

CHAPTER

8

Individual- and Organizational-Level Consequences of Organizational Citizenship Behaviors

Scott B. MacKenzie, Nathan P. Podsakoff, *and* Philip M. Podsakoff

Abstract

Although the effects of organizational citizenship behaviors on individual-level and organizational-level outcomes have been well documented in the literature, far less is known about the theoretical mechanisms that explain these effects, or the boundary conditions that influence their strengths. Thus, for the purposes of this chapter, after providing a brief summary of the effects of OCB on individual- and organizational-level outcomes, we identify the theoretical mechanisms through which OCBs are believed to produce their effects, and the individual, group, supervisor, task, organizational, and cultural/environmental characteristics that moderate these effects. In addition, we also suggest how several prototypical forms of OCB (helping, sportsmanship, and voice) might be related to these mediators and how the relationships between these different forms of OCB and individual- and organizational-level outcomes might be influenced by these moderators.

Key Words: organizational citizenship behavior, individual-level consequences, organizational-level consequences, mediating mechanisms, organizational citizenship behaviors

The previous chapters have focused primarily on the origins and definition of organizational citizenship behavior (OCB) and how it differs from related constructs. However, in this chapter, we are going to turn our attention to the consequences of OCB for both individuals and their organizations. Perhaps the primary reason for the widespread interest in OCB is that in the aggregate, over time, and across people, this behavior is believed to enhance organizational effectiveness (Organ, 1988; Organ, Podsakoff, & MacKenzie, 2006; Podsakoff & MacKenzie, 1994; Podsakoff & MacKenzie, 1997). Therefore, after providing a brief discussion of the nature of OCB, we will begin by reviewing the empirical evidence of the effects of OCB on a variety of organizational-level outcomes. This review will reveal that OCB is positively related to a number of important indicators of organizational effectiveness. Following this, we will examine the consequences of OCB for individuals. This discussion will identify a number of important consequences of OCB for the people exhibiting the behavior, their managers, and coworkers, and summarize the empirical studies examining these relationships. Next, we will identify the proposed theoretical mechanisms through which OCBs are believed to produce their effects and the individual, group, supervisor, task, organizational, and cultural/environmental characteristics that determine the strengths of these effects. Based on this discussion, we will end the chapter by identifying a number of important directions for future research, first at the organizational level and then at the individual level.

On the Nature of Organizational Citizenship Behavior

Nearly 40 different types of OCBs have been identified in the literature over the past 30 years

(Coleman & Borman, 2000; LePine, Erez, & Johnson, 2002; Organ et al., 2006; Podsakoff, Podsakoff, MacKenzie, Maynes, & Spoelma, 2014; Podsakoff, MacKenzie, Paine, & Bachrach, 2000), including altruism, courtesy, helping, cheerleading, peacekeeping, sportsmanship, civic virtue, voice behavior, compliance, taking charge, individual initiative, job dedication, self-development, and organizational support/loyalty. Perhaps, not surprisingly, this proliferation of constructs has led researchers to search for a smaller number of factors underlying these many different types of behavior. Undoubtedly, the two most popular ways of organizing the OCB dimensions have been proposed by Williams and Anderson (1991) and Van Dyne, Cummings, and Parks (1995). Although Williams and Anderson (1991) and Van Dyne and her colleagues (1995) both argue that the various types of OCB can be captured by two higher order dimensions, they disagree about the nature these dimensions. Williams and Anderson (1991) distinguish between forms of OCB on the basis of who benefits from the behavior. According to these authors, OCBI behaviors "immediately benefit specific individuals and indirectly through this means contribute to the organization," whereas OCBO behaviors "benefit the organization in general" (Williams & Anderson (1991, pp. 601–602). In contrast, Van Dyne et al. (1995) distinguish between forms of OCB based on the nature of the behavior itself and whether it maintains or disrupts the status quo. Affiliation-oriented citizenship behaviors (AOCBs) are interpersonal and cooperative in nature and tend to strengthen or maintain relationships with other people, whereas challenge-oriented citizenship behaviors (COCBs) challenge the status quo and may disrupt interpersonal relationships.

Podsakoff et al. (2014) categorized the different forms of organizational citizenship behavior identified in the literature according to these two frameworks and Table 8.1 reproduces their findings. As indicated in the table, some citizenship behaviors (e.g., helping, altruism, courtesy, peacekeeping, cheerleading) are both affiliation oriented and intended to benefit an individual in the organization, whereas other behaviors (e.g., organizational loyalty; sportsmanship; endorsing, defending, and supporting the organization) are both affiliation oriented and intended to benefit the unit/organization as a whole. A third set of behaviors (e.g., voice, making constructive suggestions, and principled dissent) is both challenge oriented and intended to benefit the organization. Interestingly, they found no behaviors that are both challenge oriented and intended to benefit a specific individual in the organization; although they note that some forms of voice behavior (e.g., offering constructive criticism to a coworker) could be both challenge oriented and intended to benefit a specific individual. Finally, there are citizenship behaviors (e.g., conscientiousness, job dedication, and taking charge) that are intended to benefit the organization as a whole, but that are not particularly interpersonal and cooperative in nature, or challenging to the status quo. Because both of these categorization schemes have merit, and have been referred to extensively in the literature, we will use both of these general frameworks in our subsequent review of the literature.

Organizational Citizenship Behaviors as an Organizational/Unit-Level Construct

Many have observed that OCBs are only important to the organization in the aggregate (across individuals) and over time. Indeed, Organ (1988) argued that "most OCB action, taken singly, would not make a dent in the overall performance of the organization . . . But that is the nature of OCB—any single occurrence of it usually is modest or trivial" (p. 8). Thus, although OCBs may be exhibited at the individual level, it is only when these behaviors are aggregated to the unit level that they have a meaningful effect on unit performance. This raises two important issues. The first issue is whether the OCB constructs are isomorphic across levels of analysis—that is, are the constructs the same at both levels? For example, the key distinction between OCBI and OCBO is that the former is defined as directly benefitting an individual and only indirectly benefitting the organization. But what happens when OCBI is conceptualized at the unit level? Recently, Podsakoff et al. (2014, p. S91) suggested that the nature of OCBI may be different at this level of analysis:

> For example, if members of a unit consistently help each other with work-related problems and thereby collectively exhibit a high level of what is regarded as a prototypical OCBI behavior, it is hard to imagine why this would not directly benefit the organization by enhancing the unit's performance. It seems obvious that it would. But according to the OCBI/OCBO framework, if the unit's collective level of helping behavior directly benefits the organization then, at the unit-level of analysis, helping behavior would be an OCBO behavior rather than an OCBI behavior. Indeed, one could argue that at the

Table 8.1 Summary of Types of Organizational Citizenship Behaviors

	Affiliation-Oriented OCB	Challenge-Oriented OCB	Neither
OCB-I	• Helping • Interpersonal helping • Altruism • Altruism toward colleagues • Courtesy • Peacekeeping • Cheerleading • Interpersonal facilitation • Interpersonal harmony		
OCB-O	• Organizational loyalty • Loyal boosterism • Organizational identification • Endorsing, supporting, defending the organization • Spreading goodwill • Promoting company image • Sportsmanship • Compliance • Organizational obedience • Protecting company resources • Following organizational rules and procedures • Civic virtue (attending meetings and other functions that are not required, reading and keeping up with organizational announcements)	• Voice • Making constructive suggestions • Civic virtue (when civic virtue refers to voice) • Principled dissent • Advocacy participation • Organizational participation • Issue selling	• Conscientiousness • Individual initiative • Taking charge • Personal industry • Job dedication • Volunteering to carry out task activities • Self-development • Self-training • Career development • Individual innovation

Source: Podsakoff, N. P., Podsakoff, P. M., MacKenzie, S. B., Maynes, T. D., & Spoelma, T. M. (2014). Consequences of unit-level organizational citizenship behaviors: A review and recommendations for future research. *Journal of Organizational Behavior, 35,* S87–S119. Used with permission.

> unit-level of analysis, helping behavior would more directly benefit the organization, than attending and participating in meetings, defending and supporting the organization, or making constructive suggestions on how to improve the organization, all of which are prototypical OCBO behaviors.

The second issue is whether the mechanisms that account for the effects of OCB at the individual level also explain the effects of OCB at the unit level of analysis. Recently, MacKenzie, Podsakoff, and Podsakoff (2011, pp. 561–562) argued that several of the key theoretical mechanisms underlying the effects of OCB at the individual level should generalize to the unit level for three reasons.

> First, consistent with Bandura's (1977) social learning theory, the modeling of challenge-oriented (and affiliation-oriented) OCBs by individuals in the group could create an environment where other group members are encouraged to imitate these behaviors. Second, when individuals in the group engage in constructive, challenge-oriented (or affiliation-oriented) behaviors, it could create implicit obligations via social exchange processes that others feel they need to reciprocate (Blau, 1964). Third, norms could develop in the group if challenge-oriented (or affiliation-oriented) behaviors are repeated often enough to create a climate that encourages OCBs (Ehrhart & Naumann, 2004).

Consequences of Organizational Citizenship Behavior

Organizational/Unit-Level Consequences

Our review of the literature indicates that a wide variety of organizational/unit-level consequences of OCB have been examined in the research conducted to date. Table 8.2, which is adapted from Podsakoff et al. (2014), groups these outcomes into four categories based roughly on Kaplan and Norton's (1992) balanced scorecard framework. According

Table 8.2 Types of Outcome Variables in Unit-Level Organizational Citizenship Behavior Studies

Unit/Team/Organizational Measures	Improving Business Process Measures
• Subjective overall performance and/or effectiveness of group/team/organization (Aube & Rousseau, 2005; Chen, Lam, Naumann, & Schaubroeck, 2005; Chi, Chung, & Tsai, 2011; Choi & Sy, 2010; Day & Carroll, 2004; De Dreu & Van Vianen, 2001; DeGroot & Brownlee, 2006; Dunlop & Lee, 2004; Ehrhart, Bliese, & Thomas, 2006; Frazier & Bowler, 2015; Hu & Liden, 2011; Hyatt & Ruddy, 1997; Kim & Gong, 2009; Naumann & Bennett, 2002; Nielsen, Bachrach, Sundstrom, & Halfhill, 2012; Pearce & Ensley, 2004; Tanghe, Wisse, & van der Flier, 2010; Varela, Burke, & Landis, 2008; Wang & Howell, 2010) • Subjective "in-role" or "task" performance of group (Frazier & Bowler, 2015; MacKenzie et al., 2011; Walumbwa, Morrison, & Christensen, 2012) • Subjective estimate of project goal achievement (Ferreira, Braun, & Sydow, 2013) • Objective measures of school achievement and/or student academic performance and/or subjective team project grades (Cropanzano, Li, & Benson, 2011; DiPaola & Hoy, 2005; Koh, Steers, & Terborg, 1995; Ng & Van Dyne, 2005) • Total number of tasks completed (Rico, Bachrach, Sanchez-Manzanares, & Collins, 2011; Varela, Burke, & Landis (2008) • Objective measure of quantity produced (Podsakoff, Ahearne & MacKenzie, 1997) • Turnover (George & Bettenhausen, 1990; MacKenzie, Podsakoff, & Podsakoff, 2011; McClean, Burris, & Detert, 2013; Sun, Aryee, & Law, 2007) • Team viability (Hu, 2012) • Perceptions of quality, budget, time, overall success, and relationship quality (Braun, Ferreira, & Sydow, 2013) • Service performance (Lam & Mayer, 2014)	• Speed and accuracy in task completion (Bachrach, Powell, Collins, & Richey, 2006) • Counter service time; drive-through service time; food waste (Dunlop & Lee, 2004) • Product quality (percentage of paper produced that was either rejected by quality control or the customer) (Podsakoff, Ahearne, & MacKenzie, 1997) • Branch efficiency (cost of employees' salaries, overtime pay) (Yen & Niehoff, 2004) • Operating costs (Rego & Cunha, 2008) • Service response times (Hyatt & Ruddy, 1997) • Meeting service delivery benchmarks (Bienstock, DeMoranville, & Smith, 2003) • Corporate innovation, venturing, and strategic renewal (Zhang, Wan, & Jia, 2008) • Innovative solutions to improve the organization (Detert, Burris, Harrison, & Martin, 2013)

Customer Measures	Financial Measures
• Perceived service quality, quality of care received, quality of service, and reputation (Allen, Smith, Mael, O'Shea, & Eby, 2009; Detert, Burris, Harrison, & Martin, 2013; Hyatt & Ruddy, 1997; Messersmith, Patel, Lepak, & Gould-Williams, 2011; Yen & Niehoff, 2004; Yoon, 2009; Yoon & Suh, 2003) • Customer service behavior (Yen & Niehoff, 2004) • Market performance (marketing, sales growth, market share) (Chuang & Liao, 2010 • Customer satisfaction (Chang, Chiang, & Han, 2012; Fisher, McPhail, & Menghetti,2010; Kirkman, Tesluk, & Rosen, 2001; Koys, 2001; Nishii, Lepak, & Schneider, 2008; Schneider, Ehrhart, Mayer, Saltz, & Niles-Jolly, 2005) • Enhanced customer efficiency and innovation (Yoon, 2009)	• Profitability (Chuang & Liao, 2010; Fisher, McPhail, & Menghetti, 2010; Koys, 2001; MacKenzie, Podsakoff, & Podsakoff, 2011; Naumann & Bennett, 2002; Raver & Gelfand, 2005; Rego & Cunha, 2008) • Sales and/or revenue (Ahearne, MacKenzie, Podsakoff, Mathieu, & Lam, 2010; Fisher, McPhail, & Menghetti, 2010; George & Bettenhausen, 1990; Hunter et al., 2013; Kizilos, Cummings, & Cummings, 2013; Lin & Peng, 2010; Liu, Gong, & Liu, 2014; MacKenzie, Podsakoff, & Podsakoff, 2011; Podsakoff & MacKenzie, 1994; Schneider, Ehrhart, Mayer, Saltz, & Niles-Jolly, 2005; Sun, Aryee, & Law, 2007) • Percentage of sales quota achieved by the team (Ahearne, MacKenzie, Podsakoff, Mathieu, & Lam, 2010) • Commission dollars (Chi, Chung, & Tsai, 2011) • Return-on-assets (ROA) (Chun, Shin, Choi, & Kim, 2013; Kim & Gong, 2009) • Tobin's Q (Kim & Gong, 2009)

Source: Adapted from Podsakoff, N. P., Podsakoff, P. M., MacKenzie, S. B., Maynes, T. D., & Spoelma, T. M. (2014). Consequences of unit-level organizational citizenship behaviors: A review and recommendations for future research. *Journal of Organizational Behavior, 35,* S87–S119. Used with permission.

to Kaplan and Norton (1992), effective organizations not only meet or exceed their financial goals but also perform their primary tasks well, satisfy their customers, and continually strive to improve business processes. To begin with, as shown in the upper left quadrant of Table 8.2, there are quite a few studies that have examined the relationship between OCB and unit-level performance (quantity of work produced, quality of work, work goal achievement, and/or turnover). Somewhat surprisingly, given the difficulty of obtaining these types of measures, there are also quite a few studies that have examined the relationships between OCB and unit-level measures of financial performance (e.g., profitability, ROA, sales, revenue, percent of quota, Tobin's Q, operating costs). Beyond this, there is also empirical research examining the relationships between unit-level OCB and business process efficiency measures (e.g., speed and accuracy of task completion, operating cost efficiency, and service response time) and customer measures (e.g., customer satisfaction, sales growth, market share, and perceived service quality).

In addition, a meta-analysis by Podsakoff, Whiting, Podsakoff, and Blume (2009) involving 38 independent samples comprised of 3,611 units indicates that many of these relationships are significant and strong. For example, these authors report that the corrected correlation between unit-level OCB and unit-level performance is .43, between unit-level OCB and unit-level productivity is .37, between unit-level OCB and unit-level cost is –.52, between unit-level OCB and customer satisfaction is .23, and between unit-level OCB and turnover is –.22. Interestingly, they also found that unit-level OCB was generally more strongly related to unit-level performance when the measure of OCB preceded the measure of performance (corrected $r = .56$) than when these constructs were measured concurrently (corrected $r = .37$). This evidence is important because it strengthens the inference that it is OCB that causes these outcomes rather than vice versa. Taken together, the diverse set of outcomes to which unit-level OCB is related, the strong corrected correlations from the meta-analysis, and the fact that the time-lagged effect of OCB on performance is stronger than the cross-sectional effect, provides strong support for Organ's (1988, p. 5) assumption that organizational citizenship behavior "in the aggregate promotes the efficient and effective functioning of the organization" in a variety of different ways.

Individual-Level Consequences

We now turn our attention to the relationships between OCB and its individual-level consequences. Among the individual-level consequences that have been examined in the literature are performance evaluations, reward allocations, and employee withdrawal behaviors. Table 8.3, which is adapted from Podsakoff et al. (2009), summarizes correlations between OCB and these consequences derived from their meta-analysis of 168 independent samples comprised of 51,235 respondents/subjects. As shown in the table, the corrected correlations between OCB and performance evaluations is .60, between OCB and reward recommendations is .77, between OCB and actual rewards is .26, between OCB and turnover intentions is –.22, between OCB and actual turnover is –.14, and between OCB and absenteeism is –.16. Beyond this, these authors also tested the effect of OCB on performance evaluations while controlling for task performance and found that the impact of OCB on performance evaluations was significant and generally accounted for at least as much variance in performance evaluations as did task performance.

There are two points worth noting about the strengths of these relationships reported earlier. First, the magnitudes of the relationships between OCB and performance evaluations are substantially affected by common method bias (MacKenzie & Podsakoff, 2012; Podsakoff, MacKenzie, Lee, & Podsakoff, 2003; Podsakoff, MacKenzie, & Podsakoff, 2012). Podsakoff, Whiting, Welsh, and Mai (2013) separated studies that obtained both OCB and performance evaluations from the same source and compared them with studies where this information was obtained from different sources and found that when the measures are obtained from the same source, the corrected correlation (.62) is significantly greater than when these measures are obtained from different sources (.32). Second, it is interesting to note that the relationship between OCB and reward recommendations is substantially stronger than the relationship between OCB and actual rewards; and that the relationship between OCB and turnover intentions is somewhat stronger than the relationship between OCB and actual turnover. One potential reason for these differences is that there are many things that may affect actual rewards other than the manager's reward recommendation (e.g., amount of managerial discretion in determining raises, HR and/or senior management oversight, budgetary considerations,

Table 8.3 Relationships Between Organizational Citizenship Behaviors and Individual-Level Outcomes

Relationship	*k*	*N*	*r*	90% Confidence Interval		r_c	SDr_c	*Q*
				Lower	Upper			
OCB-job performance ratings	72	21,881	.49	.48	.50	.60	.26	648.36**
Task behavior-job performance ratings	27	8,065	.46	.44	.47	.52	.23	191.42**
OCB-actual rewards	8	2,631	.21	.18	.24	.26	.11	22.28**
OCB-reward recommendations	10	4,330	.58	.56	.60	.77	.00	4.54
OCB-turnover intentions	90	26,510	–.17	–.18	–.16	–.22	.17	513.22**
OCB-turnover	12	3,917	–.13	–.16	–.11	–.14	.08	31.61**
OCB-absenteeism	15	4,037	–.13	–.16	–.11	–.16	.07	28.17**

Note: *k* = number of independent samples; *N* = sample size; *r* = average correlation coefficient; r_c = average correlation coefficient corrected for measurement and sampling error; SDr_c = standard deviation of corrected correlation coefficient; and Q = q statistic.

** $p < .01$.

* $p < .05$.

Source: Podsakoff, N. P., Whiting, S. W., Podsakoff, P. M., & Blume, B. D. (2009). Individual- and organizational-level consequences of organizational citizenship behavior: A meta-analysis. *Journal of Applied Psychology, 94,* 122–141. Used with permission.

etc.), and there are many things that affect actual turnover other than one's intentions (e.g., whether other acceptable jobs are available, employment or noncompete contracts, tenure/seniority protections, family considerations, etc.).

In addition, given that OCB has been found to influence performance appraisals, one would expect that OCB might also be related to other types of appraisals and selection decisions. Podsakoff, Whiting, Podsakoff, and Mishra (2011) tested this hypothesis in a laboratory study involving 480 subjects. They developed videotape interview segments that manipulated candidate responses to interview questions tapping task performance and three types of organizational citizenship behaviors (helping, voice, and loyalty). Subjects were asked to view the interview segments and rate the candidate's perceived competence and the appropriateness of hiring the candidate. Their results indicated that task performance had the strongest significant effect on the perceived competence of the candidate (partial $\eta^2 = .57$), followed by voice (partial $\eta^2 = .13$), helping behavior (partial $\eta^2 = .04$), and organizational loyalty (partial $\eta^2 = .02$). A similar pattern was observed for the overall evaluation of whether the candidate should be hired in that task performance had the strongest effect (partial $\eta^2 = .48$), followed by voice (partial $\eta^2 = .16$), helping behavior (partial $\eta^2 = .05$), and organizational loyalty (partial $\eta^2 = .03$).

Although the findings reported by Podsakoff et al. (2011) represent an important first step in examining the effects of OCB on selection decision-making processes, the study is somewhat limited because it was conducted in an experimental setting with students who have limited experience in selecting employees into real organizational settings. However, the same limitations cannot be levied at the recent study reported by Whiting and Maynes (2016). For the purposes of their study, these authors were interested in examining the effects of college football players' prior task performance, OCB, and counterproductive work behaviors on (a) National Football League (NFL) decision makers' evaluations of college football players in the NFL draft and (b) the performance of the players in their first year in the NFL. Their sample consisted of all of the linebackers (222) and wide receivers (225) that were selected in the NFL drafts from 2006 to 2012. Interestingly, Whiting and Maynes found that, in addition to the performance that players exhibited on the field in college, OCB-like behavior (in the form of helping and conscientiousness) influenced the player's draft order and the amount of money the player received in his first-year contract, as well as his performance on the field in his first year in the NFL.

Although further replication of the findings reported by Podsakoff et al. (2011) and Whiting and Maynes (2016) will obviously need to be provided before the results of these studies can be generalized, the results of these studies suggest that OCB not only enhances evaluations and reward allocations on the job, but it also may help candidates get a job in the first place.

There is also some evidence in the literature that organizational citizenship might influence career success. For example, Shore, Barksdale, and Shore (1995) found that OCB (i.e., altruism) is positively related to ratings of employee promotability. Similarly, Jawahar and Ferris (2011) reported evidence that interpersonal facilitation and job dedication (two aspects of contextual performance) are positively related to judgments of a person's promotability. These effects on promotability ratings are also consistent with Hui, Lam, and Law (2000), who found that employee self-ratings of altruism and compliance behavior, and a supervisor rating of the employees' helping, initiative, and conscientiousness, were positively related to whether or not the employee actually was promoted to the position of teller supervisor in a bank. Beyond this, there is also evidence that OCB may influence the number of promotions a person receives in his or her career with a specific organization. For example, Allen (2006) reports that both OCBO and OCBI are positively related to the number of promotions respondents received in their organizations, even after controlling for a variety of demographic variables (e.g., age, education, marital status, race, and tenure). Similarly, the results of Ng and Feldman's (2010) meta-analytic structural equation modeling of the factors influencing career success in 16 studies involving 8,478 respondents indicates that contextual performance has a significant positive impact on the number of promotions the respondent received within a single organization, even after controlling for the effect of task performance on this criterion variable. Finally, Van Scotter, Motowidlo, and Cross (2000) report that two aspects of contextual performance (interpersonal facilitation and job dedication) are positively related to promotions in rank for military personnel, even after controlling for task performance.

Potential Negative Consequences of Organizational Citizenship Behavior

Although our discussion earlier indicates that there are many functional consequences of OCB for individuals, the literature suggests there is also evidence of negative consequences. For example, Bolino and Turnley (2005, p. 741) argue that because "OCBs are acts that typically go somewhat beyond an employee's formally prescribed job duties," it seems logical that exhibiting OCBs "require(s) additional resources on the part of employees, particularly in terms of their time and energy," which can cause employees to "feel that there are too many responsibilities or activities expected of them in light of the time available, their abilities, and other constraints," and this can subsequently cause job stress and work–family conflict. To test these expectations, these authors examined the relationship between individual initiative (some forms of which are OCB) and role overload, job stress, and work–family conflict in a cross-sectional study and found that all three are significantly and positively influenced by initiative, even after controlling for a variety of demographic variables (e.g., age, gender, marital status, organizational tenure, negative affectivity, etc.). Similar results with respect to the relationship between OCB and work–family conflict have been reported by Halbesleben, Harvey, and Bolino (2009). Consistent with the findings of Bolino and Turnley (2005), these authors reported that OCB is positively related to time-based, strain-based, and behavior-based forms of work–family conflict in three different samples. Beyond this, we are aware of only one other study which explicitly modeled the effect of OCB on job stress. In a cross-sectional study, Tsang, Chen, Wang, and Tai (2012) examined the effect of a composite measure of OCB that included altruism toward colleagues, interpersonal harmony, conscientiousness, identification with the company, and protecting company resources on perceptions of job stress in a nursing context. Interestingly, in contrast to the findings of Bolino and Turnley (2005), Tsang et al. found that OCB had a negative impact on job stress. They reasoned that OCB is negatively related to job stress because it is a surrogate for social support. Thus, the findings of the studies explicitly examining the impact of OCB on job stress and work–family conflict are themselves in conflict. In addition, the fact that Eatough, Chang, Miloslavic, and Johnson's (2011) meta-analysis of 42 empirical studies shows negative relationships between OCB and job stressors like role overload (corrected correlation = –.06) and role conflict (corrected correlation = −.16) muddies the waters even more because one might expect that the sign of the relationship between OCB and job stress would be the same as the relationships between job stressors and OCB. Therefore, it is obvious that additional research—particularly experimental or longitudinal—is needed on this topic.

Another negative consequence of OCB identified in the literature is citizenship fatigue (Bolino, Hsiung, Harvey, & LePine, 2015). According to Bolino et al. (2015, p. 57), citizenship fatigue is defined as a "state in which feeling worn out, tired, or on edge, is attributed to engaging in OCB." They argue that engaging in OCB causes individuals to more feel worn out, tired, or on edge in situations where (a) perceived organizational support is low, (b) team–member exchange relationship quality is low, or (c) pressure to exhibit OCB is high. Consistent with their hypotheses, these authors found that perceived organizational support, team–member exchange relationship quality, and pressure to exhibit OCB all moderated the impact of engaging in OCB on OCB fatigue. In addition, they argued that feeling worn out, tired, or on edge and attributing it to OCB would also decrease future occurrences of OCB. In support of this, Bolino et al. found that OCB fatigue accounted for a statistically significant ($p < .05$ one-tailed) but small percentage of the variance ($R^2 = 1\%$) in future occurrences of OCB. Taken together with Bolino and Turnley (2005) and Halbesleben et al. (2009), this research suggests that OCB can lead to stress and we believe this makes good sense. Indeed, we have no doubt that many readers of this chapter (including the present authors) have felt this stress in their own jobs.

Nevertheless, we believe the results of this research should be interpreted with caution for several reasons. First, although the concept of citizenship fatigue has some appeal, it is important to recognize that *any* behavior performed frequently enough will lead to fatigue and can result in feelings of being tired, worn out, or on edge. For example, when people have task performance fatigue, it is called "burnout." Therefore, the fact that OCB can sometimes lead to fatigue, just like many other behaviors, is not unique to OCB. Second, the findings reported by Bolino et al. (2015) indicate that OCB only influences citizenship fatigue under certain conditions (i.e., there was no main effect), and citizenship fatigue has only a small effect (1%) on subsequent OCB. Finally, the concept of citizenship fatigue captures the extent to which people *attribute* their feelings of being worn out to OCB. Thus, measuring it by means of a self-report requires people to have insight into how much of their feelings of being tired, worn out, or on edge are specifically due to OCB rather than to other aspects of their job, home life, medical condition, lifestyle, and so on. As noted by Nisbett and Wilson (1977, p. 231), this may require people to "tell more than they can know" and in such circumstances, "their reports are [often] based on a priori, implicit causal theories, or judgments about the extent to which a particular stimulus is a plausible cause of a given response." In the case at hand, since the measure of OCB fatigue explicitly identifies OCB as a potential cause of fatigue, this may artificially enhance the salience of OCB as a cause of fatigue in the minds of the respondents. This is potentially problematic, because as noted by Fiske, Kenny, and Taylor (1982, p. 106), there is a great deal of evidence that:

> Salient social stimuli have an impact on causal attribution that is disproportionate to their causal relevance. Numerous studies reveal that when a person's attention is disproportionately directed to particular stimuli in a social situation, those stimuli are assigned a greater causal role. Such stimuli may include another person, the self, or aspects of the environment (McArthur & Post, 1977; Storms, 1973; Taylor & Fiske, 1975; . . . see Taylor & Fiske, 1978, for a review). Not only do salience effects emerge from a wide range of circumstances, over a wide range of stimuli, but salience effects are highly robust and generalizable (Taylor, Crocker, Fiske, Sprinzen, & Winkler, 1979), showing up despite the best efforts to put boundary conditions around them.

Another potential negative consequence of OCB suggested by some researchers (Bergeron, 2007; Bergeron, Shipp, Rosen, & Furst, 2013; Bolino, 1999) is that it decreases task performance. For example, Bolino has argued that when people exhibit OCB in order to manage the impressions of others, rather than for altruistic reasons, it undermines task performance because "when individuals undertake actions based on impression management concerns, they are less able to devote their full attention to the task at hand. Consequently . . . this concern frequently impairs their performance" (Bolino, 1999, p. 90). For different reasons, Bergeron et al. (2013, pp. 964–965) also argue that OCB decreases task performance. They argue that OCB and task performance should be negatively related because "Any change in time allocated to OCB may come at a cost to task performance, and vice versa" and that "the trade-off between OCB and task performance should exist regardless of the type of control system." In support of this, they report that the correlation between OCB and task performance was negative and significant in their sample ($r = -.43$).

However, many more studies have found that OCB and task performance are either unrelated or positively correlated. For example, Organ et al. (2006) report that the average correlation between OCB and task performance is .08 in studies that obtained measures of OCB and task performance from separate sources (Lowery & Krilowicz, 1994; MacKenzie et al., 1991; MacKenzie, Podsakoff, & Paine, 1999; Motowidlo & Van Scotter, 1994; Podsakoff & MacKenzie, 1994; Van Scotter & Motowidlo, 1996), and the average correlation between OCB and task performance is .50 in studies that that obtained both measures from the same source (Allen & Rush, 1998; Bagozzi, Verbeke, & Gavino, 2003; Barksdale & Werner, 2001; Chen, Tsui, & Farh, 2002; Ferris, Witt, & Hochwarter, 2001; Hui, Law, & Chen, 1999; MacKenzie, Podsakoff, & Rich, 2001; MacKenzie, Podsakoff, & Fetter, 1993; Podsakoff, Niehoff, MacKenzie, & Williams, 1993; Randall, Cropanzano, Borman, & Birjulin, 1999; Rupp & Cropanzano, 2002; Settoon, Bennett, & Liden, 1996; Turnley, Bolino, Lester, & Bloodgood, 2003; Van Dyne & LePine, 1998; Williams & Anderson, 1991). In addition, Podsakoff et al.'s (2009) meta-analysis of approximately two dozen studies (some of which are cited earlier) reports that the average corrected correlation between OCB and task performance is strongly positive ($r_c = .47$ for OCBI and $r_c = .54$ for OCBO). Taken together, this pattern of results suggests two things. First, when common method variance is not present, there is a weak positive relationship between OCB and task performance. Second, when common method variance is present, OCB and task performance are much more strongly related, but in exactly the opposite direction from the one predicted by Bolino (1999) and Bergeron (2007; Bergeron et al., 2013). Specifically, these results show that the higher an employee's OCB, the higher his or her task performance.

Perhaps this conflict in the empirical findings can be partially explained by recent research reporting that, under certain conditions, there may be a curvilinear (diminishing returns or inverted-U shaped) relationship between OCB and task performance at both the individual level (Ellington, Dierdorff, & Rubin, 2014; Rapp, Bachrach, & Rapp, 2013; Rubin, Dierdorff, & Bachrach, 2013) and unit level (MacKenzie et al., 2011). For example, Ellington et al. report that the relationship between interpersonal helping OCB and task performance is concave downward when the people exhibiting the citizenship behavior have low interpersonal skills, task interdependence is low, or social density is low. Note, however, that although they found significant curvilinear effects, they did not report statistical tests of whether the relationships between citizenship behavior and task performance merely leveled off (diminishing returns) or actually became negative (inverted-U shape). Similarly, Rubin et al. (2013) report that the relationship between citizenship behavior and task behavior increases at a decreasing rate (diminishing returns) and that this relationship is moderated by accountability and autonomy (but not role ambiguity). More specifically, these authors found that high levels of accountability amplify, and high levels of autonomy attenuate, the diminishing returns of citizenship behavior on task performance. Finally, Rapp et al. (2013) examined the relationship between OCB helping and three measures of task performance (call activity, customer service, and percent of quota) and found that the relationship between OCB helping and call activity and percent of quota (but not customer service) showed diminishing returns; and that the shape of this curve for OCB helping and call activity is moderated by time management skills such that the concave downward relationship existed only for employees with poor time management skills. Thus, although there is considerable evidence that OCB positively influences task performance, there is also evidence that sometimes the nature of the relationship between them depends upon the level of OCB. More specifically, under certain conditions: (a) as OCB increases from low to moderate levels, the evidence suggests that the relationship is generally positive, but (b) as OCB increases from moderate to high levels, the evidence suggests that the relationship can be nonsignificant or negative.

Mediators of the Effects of Organizational Citizenship Behavior on Consequences

Given the vast amount of research that has been done on OCB, one of the things that is most surprising is that there has been relatively little empirical research examining the mediators of the effects of OCB on the various outcome variables that have been studied. This is surprising because there is no shortage of hypotheses in the literature about what the potential mediators might be. Therefore, in the next two sections we will summarize the existing empirical research examining the mediators of the effects of OCB, first at the unit level and then at the individual level. (Note that we will identify the additional ones that have been suggested but not empirically tested in a later section.)

UNIT-LEVEL MEDIATORS

To our knowledge, only six studies have empirically examined the mediators of the effects of OCB on the unit-level outcomes (see Table 8.4 for a summary of these studies). Two studies have examined group task performance as a potential mediator of the relationships between OCBs and measures of unit effectiveness in a service context (Bienstock, DeMoranville, & Smith, 2003; MacKenzie et al., 2011). Bienstock et al. (2003) found that the relationship between unit OCB (measured as a composite of loyalty, obedience, and participation) and customer measures of service quality in a sample of 49 units of a fast-food chain was fully mediated by two measures of unit task performance (a monthly general manager's inspection report of the extent to which the restaurant meets organizational standards for customer service in a variety of areas; and a detailed quarterly inspection report conducted by the general manager). OCB was positively related to both of these mediators, but surprisingly one of these mediators (the monthly report) was negatively related to the service outcome measures, whereas the other (the quarterly report) was positively related to these criteria as expected. These authors conclude that it is unclear why the monthly report measure of task performance was negatively related to unit-level performance and suggest that this finding may have been "an artifact of this particular data set." MacKenzie et al. (2011) reported that the relationships between two forms of OCB (challenge-oriented and affiliation-oriented citizenship behavior) and several measures of unit-level effectiveness (e.g., profitability, sales, and employee retention) in a sample of 150 units of a limited-menu restaurant chain were fully mediated by task performance.

We identified two studies that examined group cohesiveness as a potential mediator of the effects of unit-level OCBs on organizational effectiveness. Using a sample of 47 work groups from a diverse set of organizations, Higgins (2002) found that task cohesiveness mediated the relationships between unit-level altruism and team viability and satisfaction; and group coordination mediated the relationship between unit-level sportsmanship and team viability and satisfaction. In the second study, Lin and Peng (2010) reported that (a) group cohesiveness mediated the positive relationship between OCBI and team performance but not the relationship between OCBO and team performance; and (b) collective efficacy mediated the positive relationship between OCBO and team performance, but not the relationship between OCBI and this outcome.

Finally, Grant, Gino, and Hofmann (2011) found in a lab study that the perceived receptivity of a leader to new ideas/recommendations mediated the interactive effects of leader extroversion and group proactivity (i.e., voice behavior, taking-charge behavior, and upward influence) on group performance. And a study by Schneider, Ehrhart, Mayer, Saltz, and Niles-Jolly (2005) conducted in departments of a supermarket chain found the relationship between unit-level OCBs *directed at customers* and quarterly unit sales was fully mediated by customer satisfaction with the unit.

Our review demonstrates that (a) only a few mediators of the relationships between unit OCBs and unit-level performance have been found; (b) the mediators identified are usually not tested in competitive models that pit multiple mediators against each other in rigorous tests of mediation, and when they are, the results are inconsistent (cf. Higgins, 2002 and Lin & Peng, 2010); and (c) the mediators have not consistently been examined in models using different dimensions of OCBs, and/or different types of outcomes measures. Therefore, although some tests of mediation have been conducted, a coherent pattern fails to emerge from the empirical findings. Thus, one might argue that Organ's conclusion about the state of the research during the 1990s is still valid today: "A few studies have looked at the group or organizational level, but virtually entirely so in a straightforward aggregative and descriptive style. We are left with a 'black box' of 'process'. . . . Although we have some reassuring data in support of the connection between OCB and systematic performance, little if any analysis has dealt with the means by which OCB has these effects" (Organ, 1997, p. 95).

INDIVIDUAL-LEVEL MEDIATORS

Our review of the empirical literature identified eight studies that examined mediators of the impact of various forms of OCB on individual-level outcomes. Key aspects of these studies and their findings are summarized in Table 8.5. The most

Table 8.4 Mediators of the Effects of Unit-Level Organizational Citizenship Behavior on Unit-Level Outcomes

Researcher(s)	Study Setting	Sample	Type(s) of OCB	Outcome(s)	Mediator(s)	Findings
Higgins (2002)	Field study	47 work groups from a diverse set of organizations	Altruism Sportsmanship	Team viability Team satisfaction	Task cohesiveness Group coordination	Task cohesiveness mediated the relationships between unit-level altruism and team viability and satisfaction; and group coordination mediated the relationship between unit-level sportsmanship and team viability and satisfaction.
Bienstock, DeMoranville, & Smith (2003)	Field study	49 fast food restaurants	Composite OCB (loyalty, obedience, and participation)	Customer measures of service quality	Two measures of unit task performance: (a) a monthly general manager's inspection report of the extent to which the restaurant meets organizational standards for customer service in a variety of areas (b) a detailed quarterly inspection report conducted by the general manager	OCB was positively related to both mediators. However, one of these mediators (the monthly report) was negatively related to the service outcome measures, whereas the other (the quarterly report) was positively related to these criteria as expected.
Schneider, Ehrhart, Mayer, Saltz, & Niles-Jolly (2005)	Field study	56 supermarket departments	Customer-focused OCB	Quarterly unit sales	Customer satisfaction	Customer satisfaction fully mediated the relationship between unit-level OCBs directed at customers and quarterly unit sales.
Lin & Peng (2010)	Field study	62 branches of a financial institution in Taiwan	OCBI OCBO	Team performance	Group cohesiveness Collective efficacy	Group cohesion mediated the positive relationship between OCBI and team performance but not the relationship between OCBO and team performance; and collective efficacy mediated the positive relationship between OCBO and team performance, but not the relationship between OCBI and this outcome.
Grant, Gino, & Hofmann (2011)	Lab study	56 groups comprised of undergraduate students	Group proactivity (a composite of voice behavior, taking charge behavior, and upward influence)	Group performance	Perceived receptivity of a leader to new ideas/recommendations	Perceived receptivity of a leader to new ideas/ recommendations mediated the interactive effects of leader extroversion and group proactivity on group performance
MacKenzie, Podsakoff, & Podsakoff (2011)	Field study	150 limited-menu restaurants	Challenge-oriented OCB (COCB) Affiliation-oriented OCB (AOCB)	Unit-level effectiveness (e.g., profitability, sales, and employee retention	Group task performance	Group task performance fully mediated the effects of COCB, AOCB, and their interaction on unit-level effectiveness (e.g., profitability, sales, and employee retention)

Table 8.5 Mediators of the Effects of Individual-Level Organizational Citizenship Behavior on Individual-Level Outcomes

Researcher(s)	Study Setting	Sample	Type(s) of OCB	Outcome(s)	Mediator(s)	Findings
Shore, Barksdale, & Shore (1995)	Field study	Manager ratings of 339 employees in a multinational firm	Altruism Compliance	Promotability Managerial potential Leader reward behavior Manager fulfillment of employee requests	Perceived affective commitment Perceived continuance commitment	Managers' ratings of employee affective commitment mediated the relationships between both altruism and compliance and three outcome variables (ratings of employees' promotability, managerial potential, and leader reward behavior); but it did not mediate the relationships between altruism or compliance and managers' fulfillment of employees' requests. Managers' ratings of employees' continuance commitment did not mediate any of the relationships between altruism and compliance and any of the outcomes.
Allen & Rush (1998)	Field study	Supervisor ratings of 148 employees in a manufacturing firm	Composite measure of OCB	Overall performance evaluation Reward recommendation	Liking Perceived affective commitment Attribution of altruistic motive Attribution of instrumental motive	Liking mediated the relationships between OCB and overall performance evaluations and reward recommendations. Perceived affective commitment mediated the relationship between OCB and overall performance evaluations, but not the relationship between OCB and reward recommendations. Attributions of altruistic motives mediated the relationship between OCB and overall performance evaluations, but not the relationship between OCB and reward recommendations. Attributions of instrumental motives did not mediate the relationships between OCBs and the outcomes.

Allen & Rush (1998)	Lab study	136 students	Videotaped teacher OCB behaviors	Overall performance evaluation Reward recommendation	Liking Perceived affective commitment	Liking mediated the effects of OCB on overall performance evaluations and reward recommendations. Perceived affective commitment mediated the effect of OCB on reward recommendations, but not the effect of OCB on overall performance evaluations.
Johnson, Erez, Kiker, & Motowidlo (2002) Study 2	Lab study	207 students	Manipulated helpfulness	Reward allocation decision	Liking Altruistic motive Instrumental motive	Liking partially mediated the effect of helping on reward allocation decisions. Attributions of altruistic motives partially mediated the effect of helping on reward allocation decisions. Attributions of instrumental motives did not mediate the effect of OCB on reward allocation decisions.
Vilela, Gonzalez, & Ferrin (2008)	Field setting	122 salespeople working in 35 Spanish firms	Composite OCB (altruism, courtesy, cheerleading, peacemaking, civic virtue, sportsmanship)	Overall performance evaluation	Liking	Liking partially mediated the relationship between helping and overall performance evaluations.
Whiting, Maynes, Podsakoff, & Podsakoff (2012) Study 1	Lab study	292 undergraduate students	Characteristics of voice behavior—recommending a solution (no/yes) and timing of voice behavior (late/early)	Overall performance evaluation	Liking Perceived prosocial motive Perceived constructiveness	Liking, prosocial motives, and perceived constructiveness of voice behavior fully mediated the effect of recommended solution on overall performance evaluations. Perceived constructiveness of the voice behavior fully mediated the effect of timing on overall performance evaluations.
Whiting, Maynes, Podsakoff, & Podsakoff (2012) Study 3	Lab study	428 undergraduate students	Characteristics of voice behavior—recommending a solution (no/yes), and timing of voice behavior (late/early)	Overall performance evaluation	Liking Perceived prosocial motive Perceived constructiveness	Liking, prosocial motives, and perceived constructiveness of voice behavior fully mediated the effect of recommended solution on overall performance evaluations. Liking and perceived constructiveness of voice behavior fully mediated the effect of timing on overall performance evaluations.

(continued)

Table 8.5 Continued

Researcher(s)	Study Setting	Sample	Type(s) of OCB	Outcome(s)	Mediator(s)	Findings
Maynes & Podsakoff (2014)	Field study	222 MBA students	Supportive voice Constructive voice Defensive voice Destructive voice	Overall performance evaluation Reliance on voicer's opinion	Organizational concern Perceived positive impact Perceived negative impact	Voicer's perceived concern for the organization and perceived positive impact of the voice behavior fully mediated the relationship between supportive voice behavior and overall performance evaluations and the relationship between supportive voice behavior and reliance on the voicer's opinion. Perceived positive impact of the voice behavior and perceived negative impact of the voice behavior fully mediated the relationship between constructive voice behavior and overall performance evaluations and the relationship between constructive voice behavior and reliance on the voicer's opinion. Perceived positive impact of the voice behavior and perceived negative impact of the voice behavior fully mediated the relationship between defensive voice behavior and overall performance evaluations and the relationship between defensive voice behavior and reliance on the voicer's opinion. Voicer's perceived concern for the organization and perceived negative impact of the voice behavior fully mediated the relationship between destructive voice behavior and overall performance evaluations and the relationship between destructive voice behavior and reliance on the voicer's opinion.

frequently studied mediator of the effects of OCB on the individual-level consequences was the manager's liking for the employee exhibiting the OCB. This mediator was examined in several studies and the findings indicate that liking mediates the impact of various forms of OCB on overall performance evaluations (Allen & Rush, 1998 both field and lab studies; Vilela, Gonzalez, & Ferrin, 2008; Whiting, Maynes, Podsakoff, & Podsakoff, 2012, Study 1 and Study 3) and reward allocations (Allen & Rush, 1998; both field and lab studies; Johnson, Erez, Kiker, & Motowidlo, 2002). Another mediator examined in several studies was the manager's perception of the affective commitment of the employee exhibiting the OCB. Perceived affective commitment was found to mediate the relationships between OCB and overall performance evaluations (Allen & Rush, 1998 field study), reward recommendations (Allen & Rush, 1998 lab study), and ratings of the employee's promotability (Shore et al., 1995). Another mediator of the effect of OCB on important individual outcomes that has been identified in the literature is the motive of the employee exhibiting the OCB—specifically whether the employee's motive is altruistic, prosocial, or demonstrates a concern for the organization. Altruistic/prosocial/concern motives have been found to mediate the impact of OCB on overall performance evaluations (Allen & Rush, 1998, field study; Maynes & Podsakoff, 2014; Whiting et al., 2012, Study 1 and Study 3), reward recommendations (Johnson et al. 2002), and the manager's judgment of how much the employees opinion could be relied upon (Maynes & Podsakoff, 2014). The relationships between certain forms of voice behavior and overall evaluations of performance were found by Whiting et al. (2012, Study1 and Study 2) to be mediated by the rater's perception of the constructiveness of the voice behavior itself; and by Maynes and Podsakoff (2014) to be mediated by the rater's perception of the impact that the OCB exhibited by the employee will have on the team. In addition, Maynes and Podsakoff (2014) also found that perceptions of positive and negative impact mediate the relationship between voice behavior and the rater's willingness to rely on the employee's opinion. Finally, continuance commitment and instrumental motives were examined, but neither was found to mediate the relationships between OCB and individual-level outcomes (Allen & Rush, 1998, field study; Johnson et al. 2002; Shore et al., 1995). Taken together, these finding suggest that affective feelings of the raters for the person exhibiting the OCB or the raters' perceptions that the person feels positively toward the organization seem to be the principal mechanisms through which OCB influences individual-level outcomes.

Moderators of the Effects of Organizational Citizenship Behavior on Unit- and Individual-Level Outcomes

UNIT-LEVEL MODERATORS

Given that nearly 100 studies reported in the literature have examined the relationships between unit-level OCB and some type of unit-level outcomes, it is a little surprising that only 13 studies have tested moderators of these relationships (see Table 8.6 for a summary). This is important because doing so can help to identify the boundary conditions for these relationships and facilitate the assessment of the generalizability of the findings reported in the literature. Therefore, each of these articles will be briefly summarized in the paragraphs to follow.

Turning first to studies examining moderators of the relationship between OCB and group performance, three studies have examined whether task interdependence (TI) moderates this relationship. In a laboratory setting, Bachrach et al. (2006) examined the effect of TI on the nature of the relationship between group helping behavior and group performance, and found that aggregated individual helping behavior is positively related to group performance when TI is high and has an inverted-U shaped relationship when TI is low. Thus, when TI is high, helping behavior is beneficial, but when TI is low, moderate levels of helping behavior may produce the highest level of performance. (Note however, that Bachrach et al.'s scatterplot of the low TI condition suggests that this effect may have been produced by an outlier.) In another lab study, Rico, Bachrach, Sanchez-Manzanares, and Collins (2011) reported that TI, team virtuality, and the TI x virtuality interaction moderated the positive effect of interpersonal OCB (OCBP) on team performance. A plot of their effects revealed that, although the relationship between OCBP and team performance is positive for the high virtuality/high TI and high virtuality/low TI conditions, this relationship is nonsignificant for the low virtuality/high TI condition, and it is negative for the low virtuality/low TI condition. Thus, these findings suggest that OCBP is positively related to team performance when virtuality is high (regardless of the level of TI); and OCBP is negatively associated with team performance when both virtuality and TI are low. In contrast to the previous two laboratory studies,

Table 8.6 Moderators of the Effects of Unit-Level Organizational Citizenship Behavior on Unit-Level Outcomes

Researcher(s)	Study Setting	Sample	Type(s) of OCB	Unit-Level Outcome	Moderator	Findings
Baker (1999)	Field study	35 branches of a financial services company (United States)	OCBI OCBO	Customer perceptions of unit service quality	Organizational deviance behavior (ODB)	ODB did not moderate the relationships between OCBI or OCBO and customer perceptions of service quality.
Sepulveda-Martinez (2001)	Field study	71 bank branches (Mexico)	Composite measure of OCB	Unit-level service quality Customer satisfaction	Customer-oriented behavior (COB)	COB did not moderate the relationship between OCB and service quality or the relationship between OCB and customer satisfaction.
DeGroot & Brownlee (2006)	Field study	78 departments from firms that had employees registered as SHRM members (United States)	Composite OCB (interpersonal, organizational, and job/task dimensions)	Supervisor's ratings of department effectiveness	Department structure (high mechanistic structure vs. low, organic structure)	Department structure did not moderate the relationship between OCB and supervisor's perceptions of department effectiveness.
Bachrach, Powell, Collins, & Richey (2006)	Lab study	62 student groups (United States)	Helping behavior	Combination of speed and accuracy in task completion	Task interdependence	Helping behavior was positively related to group performance in the high task interdependence condition, but had an inverted-U shaped relationship with group performance in the low task interdependence condition.
Mariadoss (2007)	Field study (3-month time lag)	200 pharmaceutical sales teams (international)	Helping behavior Civic virtue Sportsmanship	Percentage of quota	Sales team experience	Sales team experience moderated the relationship between unit sportsmanship and team performance, such that this relationship was positive when sales team experience was low, but negative when experience was high. Sales experience moderated the relationship between unit civic virtue and team performance, such that this relationship was negative when team experience was low, but positive when team experience was high. Team experience did not moderate the relationship between unit helping and team performance.

Sun, Aryee, & Law (2007)	Field study	81 hotel (China)	Service-oriented OCB	Sales per employee Unit-level turnover	Business strategy (service quality vs. low cost strategy) National unemployment rate	Unemployment rate moderated the negative relationship between service-oriented OCBs and turnover such that it was more strongly negative when the unemployment rate was higher compared to when it was lower (business strategy term did not significantly moderate this relationship). Business strategy moderated the positive relationship between service oriented OCBs and sales productivity such that this relationship was more strongly positive when the unit had a service quality business strategy, compared to when it had a low-cost business strategy (unemployment rate did not moderate this relationship).
Grant, Gino, & Hofmann (2011)	Field study (7-week time lag)	57 pizza delivery stores (United States)	Proactive behavior	Profitability	Leader extroversion	The relationship between unit-level OCB (proactivity) and profitability was positive when the leader was low in extroversion and negative when the leader was high in extroversion.
Grant, Gino, & Hofmann (2011)	Lab study	56 student groups (United States)	Proactive behavior	Number of tee shirts folded	Leader extroversion	Proactive groups achieved higher performance when the leader was low in extroversion than when the leader was high in extroversion.
MacKenzie, Podsakoff, & Podsakoff (2011)	Field study (4- month time lag)	150 limited-menu restaurants (United States)	Challenge-oriented OCB (COCB)	Sales; Profit as a % of sales; Employee turnover	Affiliation-oriented OCB (AOCB)	AOCB moderated the inverted-U shaped relationship between COCB and workgroup task performance such that COCBs were more positively related to task performance when AOCBs in the workgroup were high than when AOCBs in the workgroup were low.
Rico, Bachrach, Sanchez-Manzanares, & Collins (2011)	Lab study	64 student teams (Spain)	Person-oriented OCB (OCBP)	Number of correctly completed merit evaluations	Task interdependence Team virtuality	Task interdependence moderated the relationship between OCBP and team performance; virtuality moderated the relationship between OCBP and team performance; and a three-way interaction between virtuality, task interdependence, and OCBP had a significant effect on team performance. A plot of this three-way interaction revealed that although the slopes for the OCBP—team performance relationship were positive for the high virtuality/high task interdependence and high virtuality/low task interdependence conditions, the slope for the low virtuality/high task interdependence condition was nonsignificant, and the slope for the low virtuality/low task interdependence condition was negative.

(*continued*)

Table 8.6 Continued

Researcher(s)	Study Setting	Sample	Type(s) of OCB	Unit-Level Outcome	Moderator	Findings
Nielsen, Bachrach, Sundstrom, & Halfill (2012)	Field study (6-month time lag)	46 intact work groups in six organizations (United States)	Helping behavior Civic virtue Sportsmanship Composite OCB	Subjective rating of group's performance by internal customers	Task interdependence	Task interdependence moderated the relationships between all four OCBs and group performance such that the relationships were positive when task interdependence was higher, but not significant when task interdependence was lower.
Detert, Burris, Harrison, & Martin (2013)	Field study (12-month time lag)	93 branches/ units of nine North American credit unions	Employee voice behavior	Unit performance rating	Target of voice behavior (leader or coworker) Origin of voice behavior (from within unit or from outside of unit)	Although the analysis did not test any interaction effects per se, the findings indicate that the effects of voice behavior on unit performance were positive for voice behavior directed at the leader (regardless of origin) and negative for voice behavior directed at coworkers within the unit.
McClean, Burris, & Detert (2013)	Field study (6-month time lag)	136 restaurants (United States)	Employee voice behavior	Unit-level turnover	Managerial access to organizational resources Manager participation in upper-level decision making Management team change orientation	All three moderators had effects when entered into separate regression equations, such that the relationships between voice and turnover were *negative* when access to resources was higher, unit managers had a higher level of decision making participation, or management teams had higher levels of change orientation; but *positive* when managerial access to resources was lower, unit managers had a lower level of decision making participation, or management teams had lower levels of change orientation. However, when all three potential moderators were entered into a single regression, only the voice x management team change orientation interaction remained significant.

Nielsen, Bachrach, Sundstrom, and Halfhill (2012) examined the potential moderating effect of TI in a field study. These authors found that helping, civic virtue, sportsmanship, and a composite OCB measure are all positively related to group performance ratings (although the effect of civic virtue is only marginally significant); and that TI moderates the relationships between these four types of OCB and group performance in a similar manner. Specifically, the relationships between each type of OCB and perceptions of group performance are positive when TI is higher, but nonsignificant when TI is lower. Taken together, the studies examining the moderating effects of task interdependence have generally found that the relationship between OCB and group performance is stronger when groups have tasks that are more interdependent than when group tasks are less interdependent.

Others have investigated whether leader, team, and/or organizational characteristics may also moderate the relationship between unit-level OCB and group performance. For example, Grant et al. (2011) found that leader extroversion also moderates this relationship. More specifically, these authors found that the relationship between group proactivity and group performance is positive when a leader is low in extroversion but is negative when a leader is high in extroversion. Mariadoss (2007) explored the potential moderating effect of sales team experience on the relationships between three types of OCBs and team performance (measured by percent of quota). Mariadoss found that (a) the relationship between unit sportsmanship and team performance is positive when sales team experience is low, but negative when experience is high; (b) the relationship between unit civic virtue and team performance is negative when team experience is low, but positive when team experience is high; and contrary to expectations (c) the relationship between unit helping and team performance is not significantly influenced by sales experience. Because prior performance was included as a control variable in the analyses, these findings suggest that unit helping has a positive effect on the *change* in team performance, whereas unit civic virtue has a negative effect on the *change* in team performance. Finally, DeGroot and Brownlee (2006) investigated the possibility that department/organizational structure (high mechanistic structure versus low, organic structure) moderates the relationship between unit-level OCB (comprised of interpersonal, organizational, and job/task dimensions) and supervisors' perceptions of department effectiveness, but they found no significant moderating effects.

A study by MacKenzie et al. (2011) examined the moderating effects of one form of OCB on the shape of the relationship between another form of OCB and group performance. More specifically, MacKenzie et al. (2011) reported that (a) unit-level COCBs have an inverted-U shaped relationship with group task performance; (b) this relationship is more positive when unit-level AOCBs are high compared to when they are low; and (c) the relationships between both types of OCB and several other group-level measures of effectiveness (i.e., sales, profits, and turnover) are fully mediated by group task performance.

Another set of studies examined moderators of the impact of OCBs on other important organizational outcomes, including customer perceptions of service quality, customer satisfaction, and employee turnover. For example, Baker (1999) examined the moderating effects of organizational deviance behavior (ODB) on the relationships between two forms of unit-level OCB (OCBO and OCBI) and customer perceptions of several dimensions of service quality. Although Baker reported that the OCBs tended to be positively related to the different aspects of customer service quality, the interactions between ODB and the OCBs were not significant in any of the regressions predicting dimensions of customer service quality. Sepulveda-Martinez (2001) also examined the potential moderating effects of a type of behavior on the relationship between OCB and customer service quality. More specifically, Sepulveda-Martinez investigated whether customer-oriented behavior (COB; e.g., having a friendly, helpful attitude toward customers, handling special requests or problems) moderates the relationships between unit-level OCB (a composite of altruism, courtesy, sportsmanship, conscientiousness, and civic virtue) and unit-level service quality and customer satisfaction. However, contrary to expectations, the results indicated that the interactions between OCB and COB did not significantly predict either outcome. McClean, Burris, and Detert (2013) examined three potential moderators of the relationship between unit-level OCB (i.e., voice behavior) and unit-level turnover: managerial access to organizational resources, manager participation in upper-level decision making, and management team change orientation. They reported that all three interactions with unit-level voice behavior were significant (in separate regressions). More specifically, the relationship between unit-level voice behavior and turnover was negative (positive) when access to resources was higher (lower), unit managers had a higher (lower) level of decision-making participation, or management teams had higher (lower) levels of change orientation. However, when all interactive terms were included in a single regression, only the voice behavior by management team change orientation interaction was significant.

Finally, Sun, Aryee, and Law (2007) hypothesized that municipal unemployment rates would moderate the relationship between aggregated service-oriented OCB and turnover; and that business strategy (service quality versus low-cost strategy) would moderate the relationship between service-oriented OCB and unit productivity (measured as sales per employee). These authors found that (a) service-oriented OCB was negatively related to turnover, and the unemployment rate moderated this relationship such that it was more strongly negative when the municipal unemployment rate was higher compared to when it was lower (the service-oriented OCB by business strategy term had a marginal effect on turnover); and (b) service-oriented OCBs had a positive effect on productivity, and that business strategy moderated this relationship, such that it was more strongly positive when the unit had a service quality strategy, compared to when it had a low-cost business strategy (unemployment rate did not moderate this relationship).

In summary, our knowledge of the boundary conditions constraining the relationships between unit-level OCB and key outcome variables is limited. Only a few significant moderators of the effects of OCB on performance, turnover, and service quality have been identified, and research has yet to identify any moderators of the impact of OCB on a host of other important organizational outcomes like product quality, employee attitudes, absenteeism, market performance, efficiency, innovation, profitability, operating costs, and return on assets. In addition, very few studies have (a) attempted to pit multiple moderators against each other in competitive model tests or (b) examined the effects of one moderator in the context of others that have been previously identified (McClean et al., 2013, is a notable exception).

INDIVIDUAL-LEVEL MODERATORS

As indicated in Table 8.7, the moderating effects of task performance on the relationship between OCB and individual-level outcomes have been examined in 20 laboratory and field studies. An examination of the overall pattern of these significant interaction effects indicates that, generally speaking, higher task performers (high or medium) benefit more from engaging in OCB than lower task performers. This general pattern of findings suggests that individuals must perform at some minimum level before OCBs have an impact on their overall performance evaluations, reward allocations, or promotion recommendations. However, it is important to note that with only one exception (MacKenzie et al., 1993, N = 261 insurance agents), all of the studies in which this pattern was observed were conducted in experimental settings. Although it is not clear why this pattern appeared almost exclusively in laboratory settings, it is possible that the lab studies permitted an artificially wide range of performance levels to be manipulated. Perhaps in field settings, the very lowest performers were either fired or sought employment elsewhere, which naturally censors the distribution of scores on performance from below. This would be consistent with the fact that a significant task performance by OCB interaction effect was not observed in any of the field studies included in Table 8.5, and the majority of the samples used in these studies came from sales settings in which very poor performers are unlikely to survive for long. Thus, we recommend that researchers attempt to replicate these findings in other nonsales field settings in the future.

Three studies have examined the moderating effects of perceptions of prosocial values on the relationship between OCB and individual-level outcomes. Eastman (1994) reported that extra-role behaviors that were attributed to prosocial motives received higher performance evaluations and greater pay raises than extra-role behaviors that were attributed to ingratiation. Similar results were reported by Grant et al. (2009) who found that prosocial values moderated the relationship between proactive behavior and performance evaluations such that the relationship was positive for employees high in prosocial values, but not significant for employees low in prosocial values (study 1); and that prosocial values moderated the relationship between anticipatory helping behavior and performance evaluations such that that the relationship was positive for employees high in prosocial values, but not significant for employees low in prosocial values (study 2).

In addition, Grant et al. (2009) also examined the moderating effects of negative affectivity on the positive relationships between both proactive behavior and anticipatory helping behavior and overall performance evaluations. They reported that negative affectivity moderated (a) the relationship

Table 8.7 Moderators of the Effects of Individual-Level Organizational Citizenship Behavior on Individual-Level Outcomes

Researcher(s)	Study Setting	Sample	Type(s) of OCB	Outcome	Moderator	Findings
Park (1986)	Laboratory study	137 working professionals and managers	Manipulated negative or positive OCB	Overall performance evaluations % raise recommended Promotion recommendation Training recommendation	Manipulated (low, medium, or high) task performance	Task performance moderated the effects of OCB on overall evaluations and promotion recommendations, but not the effects of OCB on salary recommendation or training recommendations. Generally speaking, medium and high task performers who exhibited positive OCBs received higher performance evaluations and higher promotion recommendations than low task performers who exhibited positive OCBs.
MacKenzie, Podsakoff, & Fetter (1991). Based on reanalysis reported in Organ et al. (2006).	Field study	259 Insurance agents	Composite OCB (altruism, civic virtue, conscientiousness, sportsmanship)	Overall performance evaluations	Task performance (objective sales performance)	Task performance did not moderate the relationship between OCB and overall performance evaluations.
MacKenzie, Podsakoff, & Fetter (1991). Based on reanalysis reported in Organ et al. (2006).	Field study	113 Insurance agents	Composite OCB (altruism, civic virtue, conscientiousness, sportsmanship)	Overall performance evaluations	Task performance (objective sales performance)	Task performance did not moderate the relationship between OCB and overall performance evaluations.
MacKenzie, Podsakoff, & Fetter (1993). Based on reanalysis reported in Organ et al. (2006).	Field study	261 Insurance agents	Composite OCB (altruism, civic virtue, conscientiousness, sportsmanship)	Overall performance evaluations	Task performance (objective sales performance)	Task performance moderated the relationship between OCB and overall performance evaluations, such that low and moderate task performers who exhibited high levels of OCB generally received the same evaluations as did high task performers who exhibited high levels of OCB.

(*continued*)

Table 8.7 Continued

Researcher(s)	Study Setting	Sample	Type(s) of OCB	Outcome	Moderator	Findings
MacKenzie, Podsakoff, & Fetter (1993). Based on reanalysis reported in Organ et al. (2006).	Field study	204 petrochemical salespeople	Composite OCB (altruism, civic virtue, conscientiousness, sportsmanship)	Overall performance evaluations	Task performance (objective sales performance)	Task performance did not moderate the relationship between OCB and overall performance evaluations.
MacKenzie, Podsakoff, & Fetter (1993). Based on reanalysis reported in Organ et al. (2006).	Field study	108 pharmaceutical sales managers	Composite OCB (altruism, civic virtue, conscientiousness, sportsmanship)	Overall performance evaluations	Task performance (objective sales performance)	Task performance did not moderate the relationship between OCB and overall performance evaluations.
Podsakoff & MacKenzie (1994). Based on reanalysis reported in Organ et al. (2006).	Field study	987 Insurance agents	Composite OCB (helping, civic virtue, sportsmanship)	Overall performance evaluations	Task performance (objective sales performance)	Task performance did not moderate the relationship between OCB and overall performance evaluations.
Eastman (1994)	Experimental study	91 working EMBA students	Extrarole behaviors	Overall performance evaluations Pay raise recommendations	Attribution of the motive for extra-role behavior to prosocial motives or to ingratiation	Extra-role behaviors that were attributed to prosocial motives received higher performance evaluations and greater pay raises than extrarole behaviors that were attributed to ingratiation.
Werner (1994).	Lab study	116 supervisors working for a university	Manipulated OCBI	Overall performance evaluations	Manipulated task (in-role) performance	Task performance did not moderate the effect of OCB on overall performance evaluations.
Allen & Rush (1998). Based on reanalysis reported in Organ et al. (2006).	Field study	148 employees from multiple organizations	Composite OCB (altruism, civic virtue, conscientiousness, sportsmanship)	Performance evaluations Reward recommendations	Task performance	Task performance did not moderate the relationships between OCB and performance evaluations or reward recommendations.

Allen & Rush (1998). Based on reanalysis reported in Organ et al. (2006).	Lab study	136 business and psychology students	Manipulated OCB by teachers	Performance evaluations Reward recommendations	Task performance	OCB was positively related to performance evaluations and reward recommendations when task performance was high, but not when it was low.
Kiker & Motowidlo (1999)	Lab study	494 undergraduate students	Manipulated interpersonal facilitation	Reward recommendation	Manipulated task performance	Task performance moderated the effect of OCB on reward recommendations, such that moderately high and high task performers exhibiting moderately high or high levels of OCB generally received higher evaluations than did low or moderately low task performers exhibiting moderately high or high levels of OCB.
Lovell et al. (1999)	Field study	109 resident advisers (55 women and 41 men)	Composite OCB measure (altruism, sportsmanship, mediation)	Overall performance evaluations	Gender	Gender did not moderate the relationship between OCB and performance evaluations.
MacKenzie, Podsakoff, & Paine (1999). Based on reanalysis reported in Organ et al. (2006).	Field study	161 Insurance sales managers	Composite OCB (helping, civic virtue, sportsmanship)	Overall performance evaluations	Task performance	Task performance did not moderate the relationship between OCB and overall performance evaluations.
Allen & Rush (2001) Study 2	Lab study	136 undergraduates (75 men, 61 women)	Manipulated extra-role behaviors	Overall performance evaluations Reward recommendations	Gender	No significant OCB x gender effect was found for either performance evaluations or reward recommendations.
Johnson, Erez, Kiker, & Motowidlo (2002)	Lab study	207 students	Manipulated helpfulness	Reward allocation decisions	Reputation of helper	Helpful people with a good reputation received more rewards than helpful people with a bad reputation.

(continued)

Table 8.7 Continued

Researcher(s)	Study Setting	Sample	Type(s) of OCB	Outcome	Moderator	Findings
Rotundo & Sackett (2002)	Policy-capturing experimental study	504 managers, administrators, and supervisors from a variety of organizations	Manipulated OCB	Overall performance evaluations	Manipulated task performance	Task performance moderated the effect of OCB on overall evaluations, such that increases in OCB resulted in a larger increase in ratings of overall performance for high task performers than for low task performers.
Heilman & Chen (2005)	Lab study	135 undergraduate students	Manipulated altruism (performed altruism, did not perform altruism, no information about altruism)	Overall performance evaluations Reward recommendations	Gender	When males perform altruistic behavior, they receive significantly higher performance evaluations and reward recommendations compared to when no information is provided about their altruistic behavior. In contrast, when females perform altruistic behavior they do not receive higher performance evaluations or reward recommendations compared to when no information is provided about their altruistic behavior. When males did not perform altruistic behavior, their performance evaluations and reward recommendations were no lower than when no information was provided about their altruistic behavior. In contrast, when females did not perform altruistic behavior, their performance evaluations and reward recommendations were significantly lower than when no information was provided about their altruistic behavior.
Heilman & Chen (2005)	Lab study	99 MBA and MA students	Manipulated altruism (performed altruism, did not perform altruism, no information about altruism)	Overall performance evaluations Reward recommendations	Gender	When males perform altruistic behavior, they receive significantly higher performance evaluations and reward recommendations compared to when no information is provided about their altruistic behavior. In contrast, when females perform altruistic behavior, they do not receive higher performance evaluations or reward recommendations compared to when no information is provided about their altruistic behavior. When males did not perform altruistic behavior, their performance evaluations and reward recommendations were no lower than when no information was provided about their altruistic behavior. In contrast, when females did not perform altruistic behavior, their performance evaluations and reward recommendations were significantly lower than when no information was provided about their altruistic behavior.

Allen (2006)	Field study	440 employees from a utility company and a women's professional business association (329 women, 109 men)	OCBI OCBO	Salary Promotion rates	Gender OCBI OCBO	The relationship between OCBI and promotion rates and OCBO and promotions was found to be significant for men, and nonsignificant for women. Gender was not found to moderate the relationships between either OCBI or OCBO and salary. OCBI was found to interact with OCBO to influence promotion rates. The combination of high OCBI and OCBO was associated with the highest promotion rates. OCBI and OCBO did not interact to influence salary.
Bommer, Dierdorff, & Rubin (2007)	Field study	736 employees in 100 work group	Altruism Sportsmanship	Performance evaluation	Group level OCB (altruism and sportsmanship)	Group-level OCB moderated the relationship between individual-level OCB and performance evaluations, such that the relationship between individual-level OCB and performance evaluations was stronger when group-level OCB was low, than when it was high.
Yun, Takeuchi, & Liu (2007)	Field study	84 full-time working students	OCBI OCBO	Reward recommendations	Perceived affective commitment	Perceived affective commitment moderated the relationship between OCBI and reward recommendation such that the relationship was stronger for employees perceived to be high on commitment than those low on commitment. Commitment was not found to moderate the relationship between OCBO and reward recommendations.
Whiting, Podsakoff, & Pearce (2008) Study 1	Lab study	137 undergraduate students	Manipulated helping behavior Manipulated voice behavior	Overall performance evaluations	Task performance Other forms of OCB	There was a significant two-way interaction between helping and voice, and a significant three-way interaction between helping, voice, and task behavior. A plot of the three-way interaction indicated that although helping behavior had little effect on the strength of the relationship between voice behaviors and overall performance evaluations when task performance was high, the relationship between voice behavior and performance evaluations was stronger when the ratees exhibited high levels of helping when task performance was low. Neither the task x helping, nor the task x voice two-way interaction was significant.

(*continued*)

Table 8.7 Continued

Researcher(s)	Study Setting	Sample	Type(s) of OCB	Outcome	Moderator	Findings
Whiting, Podsakoff, & Pearce (2008) Study 2	Lab study	147 undergraduate students	Manipulated helping behavior Manipulated loyalty behavior	Overall performance evaluations	Task performance Other forms of OCB	There was a significant two-way interaction between helping and loyalty, and a significant three-way interaction between helping, loyalty, and task behavior. A plot of the three-way interaction indicated that in the case of low task performers the impact of loyalty on evaluations is roughly equivalent for high and low helpers, in that both lines have nearly equal slopes. However, for high task performers, the amount of loyalty exhibited is particularly important to low helpers, in that the slope of the relationship between loyalty and appraisals is somewhat stronger for them than it is for high helpers. Neither the task x helping, nor the task x loyalty two-way interactions was significant.
Grant, Parker, & Collins (2009) Study 1	Field study	103 managers (employees) enrolled in part-time EMBA program and their direct supervisors	Composite proactive behavior (voice, taking charge, and issue selling)	Overall performance evaluations	Prosocial values (employees) Negative affect (employees)	Prosocial values moderated the positive relationship between proactive behavior and performance evaluations such that that the relationship was positive for employees high in prosocial values, but not significant for employees low in prosocial values. Negative affect moderated the positive relationship between proactive behavior and performance evaluations such that that the relationship was stronger for employees with low negative affect than for employees with high negative affect.
Grant, Parker, & Collins (2009) Study 2	Field study	55 firefighters (employees) and their supervisors	Anticipatory helping behavior	Overall performance evaluations	Prosocial values (employees) Negative affect (employees)	Prosocial values moderated the relationship between anticipatory helping behavior and performance evaluations such that that the relationship was positive for employees high in prosocial values, but not significant for employees low in prosocial values. Negative affect moderated the relationship between anticipatory helping behavior and performance evaluation such that that the relationship was positive for employees low in negative affect, but not significant for employees high in negative affect.
Hung, Yeh, & Shih (2012)	Field study	258 hotel employees	Voice behavior	Overall performance evaluations	Political skill of employee	The relationship between voice behavior and performance evaluations was negative for employees low in political skills but not significant for those high in political skills.

between proactive behavior and overall performance evaluations such that the relationship was stronger for employees with low negative affectivity than for employees with high negative affectivity; and (b) the relationship between anticipatory helping behavior and overall performance evaluations such that the relationship was positive for employees with low negative affectivity but not significant for employees with high negative affectivity.

Yun, Takeuchi, and Liu (2007) examined the moderating effects of perceived affective commitment on the relationships between OCBI and OCBO and reward recommendations. They reported that although perceived affective commitment did not moderate the OCBO–reward recommendation relationship, it did moderate the OCBI–reward recommendation relationship such that the relationship was stronger for employees perceived to be high on affective commitment than for employees perceived to be low on affective commitment.

One study (Johnson et al., 2002) examined the potential moderating effects of a person's reputation (good vs. bad) on the relationship between helping behavior and reward allocation decisions. They found the impact of helping behavior on reward allocation decisions was more positive for people with good reputations than for people with bad reputations.

Hung, Yeh, and Shih (2012) examined the potential moderating effects of the political skill of the employee on the relationship between voice behavior and overall performance evaluations, and found that this relationship was negative for employees low in political skills but not significant for employees high in political skills. They hypothesized that voice behavior negatively affects a manager's overall evaluation of employees because it undermines cooperation; is perceived as being critical of the manager; may cause the manager to feel embarrassed, threatened, or incompetent; and can upset the status quo of the relationships in the organization. But support for this hypothesis was found only when the employee exhibiting the voice behavior lacked sincerity, social astuteness, and interpersonal influence skills (three of the four dimensions of the political skill scale).

Taken together, the research on the moderating effects of prosocial motives (Eastman, 1994; Grant et al., 2009), affective organizational commitment (Yun et al., 2007), negative affectivity (Grant et al., 2009), reputation (Johnson et al., 2002), and political skill (Hung et al., 2012) indicates that these variables shape the impact of OCB on individual-level outcomes. More specifically, the results suggest that whether you are perceived by the rater to have good intentions (prosocial motives and positive organizational commitment) and whether you are perceived in a positive or negative light (reputation, political skills, and negative affectivity) determine the impact of OCB on overall evaluations of performance or reward allocation decisions.

Beyond this, three studies examined the moderating effects of one form of OCB on the relationship between another form of OCB and individual-level outcomes. Allen (2006) found that OCBO moderated the relationship between OCBI and career promotion rates such that the relationship became more positive as OCBO increased. However, Allen also found that OCBO did not moderate the relationship between OCBI and salary. Interestingly, research by Whiting, Podsakoff, and Pierce (2008) suggests that the interaction effect of different forms of OCB on overall performance evaluations may depend upon the level of task performance. In their studies, Whiting et al. simultaneously examined the moderating effects of both helping behavior and task performance on the relationship between another form of OCB (either voice or loyalty) and overall performance evaluations in two studies. In their first study, they reported a significant two-way interaction between task performance and voice behavior, and a significant three-way interaction between helping, voice, and task performance behavior. A plot of the three-way interaction indicated that although helping behavior had little effect on the strength of the relationship between voice behaviors and overall performance evaluations when task performance was high, the relationship between voice behavior and overall performance evaluations was stronger when the ratees exhibited high levels of helping when task performance was low. Neither the helping x task, nor the helping x voice two-way interactions were significant. In their second study, Whiting et al. reported a significant two-way interaction between helping and loyalty on overall performance evaluations, and a significant three-way interaction between helping, loyalty, and task behavior on overall performance evaluations. A plot of the three-way interaction indicated that in the case of low task performers the impact of loyalty on evaluations is roughly equivalent for high and low helpers, in that both lines have nearly equal slopes. However, for high task performers, the amount of loyalty exhibited is particularly important to low helpers, in that the slope of the relationship between loyalty and appraisals is somewhat stronger for them than it is for high helpers. Neither the helping x task nor the task x loyalty two-way interaction was significant. Although the interactions between these different forms of OCB were not hypothesized in any of these studies, the fact that significant interactions between different forms of OCB have now been found in several studies at the individual level, and one study at the unit level (MacKenzie et al., 2011), suggests that more attention should be given to this in future research.

In an interesting study, Bommer, Dierdorff, and Rubin (2007) examined the moderating effect that unit-level OCB has on the relationship between individual-level OCB and performance evaluations. Consistent with their hypothesis, they found that the relationship between individual-level OCB and performance evaluations was stronger when unit-level OCB was low than when it was high. These findings suggest that managers take the level of OCB occurring in the work group into account when they are evaluating the performance of specific individuals within the group.

Finally, five studies have examined the moderating effects of gender on the relationship between OCB and individual-level outcomes. Two studies (Allen & Rush, 2001; Lovell et al., 1999) found that gender did *not* moderate the relationship between OCB and overall performance evaluations. In contrast, Heilman and Chen (2005) found that gender did moderate the effects of OCB on overall performance evaluations and reward recommendations such that (a) when males (females) perform altruistic behavior, they receive (did not receive) significantly higher performance evaluations and reward recommendations compared to when no information is provided about their altruistic behavior; and (b) when males (females) did not perform altruistic behavior, their performance evaluations and reward recommendations were not lower (were significantly lower) than when no information was provided about their altruistic behavior. To complicate the situation even more, Allen (2006) reported that the relationships between OCBI and promotion rates and between OCBO and promotion rates were significant for males, but were not significant for females; however she did not find gender to moderate the relationships between OCBI or OCBO and salary. Thus, perhaps the best that can be said is that the results of the tests of the moderating effects of gender are inconsistent.

Future Directions

Up to this point, the primary focus of our chapter has been to identify (a) the mediating mechanisms through which OCBs influence individual- and organizational-level outcomes, and (b) the boundary conditions that determine the strengths of these relationships. Somewhat surprisingly, although many mediators of the effects of OCB on unit-level and individual-level consequences have been suggested, our review of the literature suggests that relatively few of them have been empirically examined. A similar point could be made for the moderators of the relationships between OCB and its unit- and individual-level consequences. Therefore, to facilitate future research in this area, we will organize the many different mediators and moderators that have been suggested in the literature (most of which have not been tested) and highlight how the mediators might be related to different forms of OCB and how the moderators might influence the nature of the relationship between OCBs and their outcomes. Note that as we do this, we will combine the individual- and unit-level mediators and moderators because the theoretical arguments for why they might mediate or moderate are often quite similar across these levels.

Potential Mediating Mechanisms

UNIT-LEVEL MEDIATORS

As discussed in a previous section, a number of different mediators of the relationships between OCB and unit-level outcomes (e.g., group task performance, group cohesiveness, customer satisfaction, etc.) and a number of different mediators of the relationships between OCB and individual-level outcomes (e.g., perceived affective commitment, prosocial and instrumental motives, liking, etc.) have been empirically tested in the research literature. Nevertheless, one of the most surprising things revealed by a comprehensive review of the literature is the abundance of mediators that have been suggested—but never empirically tested. Table 8.8, which is adapted from Podsakoff et al. (2014), summarizes the many mediators that have been identified in the literature. The middle column of this table provides a systematic account of the many reasons why OCBs might influence organizational effectiveness that have been suggested by scholars, and groups these potential mediators into five categories based on the functions that they serve. As indicated in the table, some of these mediators are believed to have their impact by enhancing a group's ability to successfully accomplish its assigned tasks

Table 8.8 Potential Mediators of the Effects of Unit-Level Organizational Citizenship Behaviors on Unit-Level Outcomes

Function of Mediators	Mediators	Expected Effect of Types of OCB on the Mediators		
		Helping	Sportsmanship	Voice
Group Ability—Factors that enhance the group's abilities to successfully accomplish the task to which they are assigned or committed.	• Attracting and retaining talented people (Podsakoff & MacKenzie, 1997; Podsakoff et al., 2000)	+	+	
	• Dissemination of expertise and/or specialized knowledge (Podsakoff et al., 2000)	+		+
	• Knowledge dissemination (e.g., sharing skills, expertise, and tacit knowledge with coworkers) enhances human capital (Bolino et al., 2002; Kizilos, Cummings, & Cummings, in press; Lin & Peng, 2010; Sun, Aryee, & Law, 2007; Yen & Niehoff, 2004)	+		+
	• Learning from others on the team (Lin & Peng, 2010; Morrison & Millikan, 2000; Podsakoff et al., 2000; Van der Vegt & Bunderson, 2005)	+		+
	• Enhances coworker productivity (Bienstock et al., 2003; MacKenzie et al., 2011; Podsakoff & MacKenzie, 1994, 1997; Podsakoff et al., 2000; Varela, Burke, & Landis, 2008; Walz & Niehoff, 2000)	+		+
	• Enhances team's ability to adapt to environmental change; improves organizational flexibility (DeGroot & Brownlee, 2006; Podsakoff & MacKenzie, 1997; Podsakoff et al., 2000)	+		+
	• Overcoming obstacles more quickly (Varela, Burke, & Landis, 2008)	+	+	+
	• Improves problem solving or decision making (Greenslade & Jimmieson, 2011; Koys, 2001; Walumbwa, Morrison, & Christensen, 2012)	+		+
	• Diminishes errors (Koys, 2001)	+		+
	• Realizing beneficial effects of task conflict (MacKenzie et al., 2011)	+		+

(continued)

Table 8.8 Continued

Function of Mediators	Mediators	Expected Effect of Types of OCB on the Mediators		
		Helping	Sportsmanship	Voice
Group Resource Utilization—Factors that enhance or improve the efficiency of the group's task performance.	• Free up resources for more productive purposes (Organ, 1988; Podsakoff & MacKenzie, 1997; Podsakoff et al., 2000)	+		+
	• Efficient allocation of employee capabilities (Podsakoff et al., 2000)	+		+
	• Enhance managerial productivity (Podsakoff & MacKenzie, 1994, 1997; Podsakoff et al., 2000; Walz & Niehoff, 2000)	+	+	+
	• Efficient use of labor (Yen & Niehoff, 2004)	+	+	+
	• Optimizing resource allocation (Chun, Shin, Choi, & Kim, 2013; Mossholder, Richardson, & Settoon, 2011; Podsakoff & MacKenzie, 1997; Podsakoff et al., 2000; Walz & Niehoff, 2000)	+	+	+
	• Improved efficiency of information exchange (Whiting et al., 2008)			+
Group Motivation—Factors that enhance the group's willingness to expend effort to perform the task.	• Team potency (Guzzo, Yost, Campbell, & Shea, 1993)	+		+
	• Collective self-efficacy (Lin & Peng, 2010; Nielsen, Bachrach, Sundstrom, & Halfhill, 2012)	+		+
	• Generalized self-efficacy (Chen & Kanfer, 2006)	+		+
	• Group motivation/effort (Kizilos, Cummings, & Cummings, 2013)	+		
	• Team spirit (Ahearne et al., 2010; Podsakoff et al., 2000)	+	+	
	• Team attachment and/or involvement (Lin & Peng, 2010; Sun et al., 2007; Yen & Niehoff, 2004)	+		
	• Task commitment	+		–/?

Table 8.8 Continued

Function of Mediators	Mediators	Expected Effect of Types of OCB on the Mediators		
		Helping	Sportsmanship	Voice
Group Climate—Factors that enhance the group's shared perceptions of its routines, practices, procedures, rewards, standards, norms, and goals.	• Development of team norms (Ehrhart & Naumann, 2004: Raver, Ehrhart, & Chadwick, 2012)	+		–
	• Supportive/trusting climate (Gong, Chang, & Cheung, 2010); social tone or climate (Varela, Burke, & Landis, 2008)	+		–
	• Learning orientation (Porter, 2005)			+
	• Team shared vision (Pearce & Ensley, 2004)	+/?		
Group Maintenance Functions—Factors that help the group to manage and regulate its social interactions.	• Reduce the need to devote scarce resources to maintenance functions (Organ, 1988; Podsakoff et al., 1997)	+	+	
	• Builds relational social capital (Bolino, Turnley, & Bloodgood, 2002; Kizilos, Cummings, & Cummings, 2013; Lin & Peng, 2010)	+	+	
	• Managing interdependencies between members of a team (Organ, 1988; Podsakoff & MacKenzie, 1994)	+	+	
	• Enhances team cohesiveness (Ahearne et al., 2010; Lin & Peng, 2010; Nielsen, Bachrach, Sundstrom, & Halfhill, 2012)	+	+	
	• Improves team coordination (Ahearne et al., 2010; Karambayya, 1990; Podsakoff & MacKenzie, 1997; Podsakoff et al., 2000); cooperation (Yu & Cable, 2011)	+	+	
	• Reduces relationship conflict and social friction (MacKenzie et al., 2011; Podsakoff & MacKenzie, 1997; Walumbwa, Morrison, & Christensen, 2012)	+	+	– (short run)
	• Increases team member satisfaction (Karambayya, 1990)	+	+	– (short run)

(*continued*)

Table 8.8 Continued

Function of Mediators	Mediators	Expected Effect of Types of OCB on the Mediators		
		Helping	Sportsmanship	Voice
	• Enhances liking for other team members (Lefkowitz, 2000)	+	+	– (short run)
	• Strengthens team positive affective regard (Barsade, 2002; Dovidio, Gaertner, Isen, & Lowrance, 1995; Estrada, Isen, & Young, 1994; Isen, Daubman & Nowicki, 1987; Lyubomirsky, King, & Diener, 2005; Spoor & Kelly, 2004, 2007)	+	+	– (short run)
	• Strengthens team loyalty/commitment (Podsakoff et al., 2000)	+	+	– (short run)
	• Increases trust in fellow workers	+	+	– (short run)
	• Enhances collective team identification (Van der Vegt & Bunderson, 2005)	+	+	– (short run)

Note: + = expected positive effect of OCB on this potential mediator; – = expected negative effect of OCB on this potential mediator; blank = the expected relationship between OCB and this potential mediator is not clear.

Source: Adapted from Podsakoff, N. P., Podsakoff, P. M., MacKenzie, S. B., Maynes, T. D., & Spoelma, T. M. (2014). Consequences of unit-level organizational citizenship behaviors: A review and recommendations for future research. *Journal of Organizational Behavior, 35*, S87–S119. Used with permission.

or ones to which it is committed (Group Ability). For example, researchers have suggested that OCBs enhance group performance because they help attract and retain talented people; facilitate knowledge dissemination and learning from others on the team, thereby enhancing coworker productivity; and enable the group to adapt to environmental changes and overcome obstacles more quickly. Another set of mediators seem to have their primary effect by improving the efficiency of the group's resource utilization and task performance (Group Resource Utilization). For example, it has been suggested that OCBs affect group performance because they optimize resource allocation; free up resources for more productive purposes; enhance information exchange; and improve managerial productivity by enabling the manager to spend more time on essential tasks. The third set of mediators has its effects by enhancing Group Motivation. These factors include team potency, collective self-efficacy, team spirit, and task commitment. The theme underlying the fourth set of mediators is that they enhance the group's shared perceptions of its routines, practices, procedures, rewards, standards, and norms (Group Climate). Examples of this include development of team OCB norms; supportive/trusting climate; learning orientation; and team shared vision. The function served by the final category of mediators is that they all help a group to manage and regulate its social interactions (Group Maintenance). Examples of these mediators include building relational social capital; enhancing team cohesiveness and coordination; reducing relationship conflict and social friction; and strengthening team loyalty, commitment, and collective team identification.

In the last three columns of Table 8.8, we speculate about the impact that three prototypical forms of OCB may have on each of these mediators. We used helping behavior as the prototypical form of affiliative and OCBI behaviors; sportsmanship as the prototypical form of affiliative and OCBO behavior; and voice as the prototypical form of challenge and OCBO behavior, because these are the most widely examined forms of these behaviors in the literature. A "+" ("–") symbol means that we believe that there are reasons to expect that the form of citizenship behavior at the top of the column has a positive (negative) effect on the mediator listed in that row. Blank entries in these columns mean that we are unsure what to expect about the relationship between the form of the OCB and the potential mediator. Of course, it is important for the reader to remember that these propositions are tentative and should be regarded as speculative until a solid theoretical foundation can be articulated based on the literature.

Having said that, the "+" in the helping column of the fifth row of the table indicates that we speculate that helping behavior (and perhaps other affiliative/OCBI behaviors) should indirectly influence unit/organization effectiveness by enhancing coworker productivity. This is consistent with the arguments of Organ et al. (2006, p. 199), who have noted that "experienced employees voluntarily helping new coworkers learn the ropes enable the new workers to become productive employees faster, thus enhancing the efficiency of the work group or unit." It is also consistent with the observation of Podsakoff et al. (2000, p. 544) that "Over time, helping behavior can help to spread 'best practices' throughout the work unit or group." The "+" under the voice column in this row indicates that we expect that voice behavior (and perhaps other challenge/OCBO behaviors) will also have a positive effect on coworker productivity, because suggestions by group members may make the group's task less complex, more efficient, or easier to perform.

As another example, in the seventh row from the bottom of the table, the "+" in the helping and sportsmanship columns indicates that we expect that helping and sportsmanship should "reduce relationship conflict and social friction." This is consistent with Podsakoff et al.'s (2000, p. 544) argument that "Employees who exhibit courtesy (an aspect of helping behavior) toward others reduce intergroup conflict, thereby diminishing the time spent on conflict management activities." Similarly, exhibiting sportsmanship by not making mountains out of molehills and by maintaining a positive attitude when things don't go your way should also reduce relationship conflict. In contrast, the "–" in the voice column of this same row indicates that voice behavior may increase relationship conflict—at least in the short run. This prediction is consistent with Van Dyne and LePine (1998), who argued that because of its challenging nature, voice may upset interpersonal relationships with others; and MacKenzie et al. (2011, p. 560), who noted that voice behaviors are "change-oriented and include the risk that they could damage relationships with others because they criticize the status quo."

As a final example, the "+" in the helping and voice columns of the first row of the Group Resource Utilization category indicates that we expect helping and voice behavior to indirectly influence organizational effectiveness by freeing up resources for more productive purposes. This is consistent with Podsakoff et al. (2000, p. 544), who argued that "To the extent that experienced employees help in the training and orienting of new employees, it reduces the need to devote organizational resources to these activities." A similar argument could be made about voice behavior in the sense that employees who (a) make constructive suggestions about how to address organizational problems or issues should reduce the need to devote scarce resources to continue to deal with these problems; and (b) suggest more efficient ways of performing group tasks conserve organizational resources that can be used for other productive purposes.

INDIVIDUAL-LEVEL MEDIATORS

Table 8.9 summarizes the potential mediators of the effects of individual-level OCB on individual-level outcomes (e.g., performance appraisals, reward allocations, support, etc.). A "+" symbol in the second column means that we believe that there are reasons to expect that the form of citizenship behavior at the top of the column has a positive effect on the mediator listed in that row, and blank entries in these columns mean that we are unsure what to expect about the relationship between the form of the OCB and the potential mediator. Again, it is important to remind the reader that these propositions are tentative and should be regarded as speculative until a solid theoretical foundation can be articulated based on the literature. For example, the + signs in the first row indicate that when an employee helps others with work-related problems, is a good sport and does not complain when things don't go his or her way, and makes recommendations for ways to improve the organization's effectiveness, his or her manager is likely to feel obligated to reciprocate by giving the employee a higher performance evaluation or recommending greater rewards. Similarly, managers may give higher performance evaluations, and greater rewards, to employees who help others in the organization, are good sports, and/or make constructive suggestions, because employees who exhibit these behaviors are likely to improve the manager's personal productivity. Finally, Ozer (2011) has argued that when employees help each

Table 8.9 Potential Mediators of the Effects of Individual-Level Organizational Citizenship Behaviors on Individual-Level Outcomes

Mediators	Expected Effect of Types of OCB on the Mediators		
	Helping	Sportsmanship	Voice
Rater's felt obligation to reciprocate to the ratee (Organ et al., 2006; Podsakoff et al., 2000)	+	+	+
Rater's personal productivity (Podsakoff & MacKenzie, 1997; Podsakoff et al., 2000)	+	+	+
Rater's liking for the ratee (Allen & Rush, 1998; Lefkowitz, 2000; Organ et al., 2006; Sutton, Baldwin, Wood, & Hoffman, 2013)	+	+	+
Rater's affective trust in the ratee (Reiche et al., 2014)	+	+	+
Rater's perception of the ratee's affective commitment to the organization (Allen & Rush, 1998; Shore et al., 1995)	+	+	+
Rater's perception of ratee's altruistic/concern motive (Allen & Rush, 1998; Johnson et al., 2002; Whiting et al., 2012)	+	+	+
TMX relationships with coworkers mediate the impact of OCBI on performance rating by manager (Ozer, 2011)	+		

other, managers evaluate their performance higher, because it enhances team–member exchange (TMX) relationships with coworkers.

Taken together, it is our hope that the examples provided in Tables 8.8 and 8.9 will stimulate additional research examining the potential mechanisms through which OCBs influence organizational effectiveness and individual-level outcomes. This is important because, although many ideas have been advanced about the potential mediators of the effects of OCBs on individual- and organizational-level consequences, very few of them have been empirically tested and, at the present time, little is known about their relative importance.

Potential Moderators of the Effects of Organizational Citizenship Behaviors

UNIT-LEVEL MODERATORS

Our review indicated that few studies have looked at moderators of the OCB–outcome relationships. Therefore, as is the case with mediators, we have attempted to identify a broader set of potential moderators of the impact of OCBs on unit-level outcomes. As indicated in Table 8.10, we have divided these potential moderators into five categories (group, supervisor, task, organizational, and cultural/environmental characteristics), and in the last three columns we speculate about the impact that the moderators have on the relationships between the three prototypical forms of OCB and unit-level outcomes. A "+" (or "–") symbol means that we believe there are reasons to expect that the moderator listed in the row strengthens (or weakens) the impact of the form of citizenship behavior on organizational effectiveness. Blank entries in these columns mean that we are unsure what to expect about the effects of the potential moderator.

As indicated in the table, we expect that some moderators (e.g., task interdependence) strengthen the impact of all three of the prototypical forms of OCB on unit-level outcomes, whereas others (e.g., spatial distance among group members, need for independence, and competitive vs. cooperative compensation systems) generally weaken the impact of OCBs. For example, the proposed moderating effects of task interdependence on the impact of all three OCBs on unit-level outcomes are consistent with Organ (1988), who speculated that "one would expect OCB to have more importance in connection with intensive . . . technologies, because . . . mutual dependencies among members . . . require spontaneous give-and take [and] accommodating gestures among the parties in order to achieve effective coordination of their respective efforts" (p. 109). This proposition has been partially

Table 8.10 Potential Moderators of the Relationships Between Organizational Citizenship Behaviors and Organizational Effectiveness and Some Tentative Hypotheses About Their Effects

Moderator Category	Specific Moderators	Expected Effect of the Moderator on the OCB-Outcome Relationship		
		Helping	Sportsmanship	Voice
Group characteristics	• Ability, experience, training, and knowledge	+		+
	• Need for independence	–	–	–
	• Group cohesiveness	+		+
	• Spatial distance among group members	–	–	–
Supervisor characteristics	• Lacks the authority to change policies and procedures			–
	• Does not have the resources to implement changes recommended by employees			–
	• Has a low tolerance for risk (i.e., are risk averse)			–
	• Feels threatened by employee suggestions			–
	• Does not trust employees making the recommendations			–
	• Has good relationships with their employees			+
	• Has high need for control			–
Task characteristics	• Task interdependence	+	+	+
	• Task variety	+		+
	• Task complexity	+		+
	• Task autonomy	+		+
	• Intragroup task specialization	–		–
	• Intergroup task specialization	+		+
	• Role ambiguity	+		+
Organizational characteristics	• Organizational formalization			–
	• Organizational inflexibility			–
	• Competitive (vs. cooperative) compensation systems	–	–	–
Cultural/ environmental characteristics	• Collectivism	+	+	
	• Power distance			–
	• Environmental uncertainty	+		+

Note: + means that the relationship between unit-level OCBs and organizational effectiveness is strengthened by the moderator; – means that the relationship between unit-level OCBs and organizational effectiveness is weakened by the moderator; blank means it is not clear whether the relationship between unit-level OCBs and organizational effectiveness is strengthened, weakened, or unaffected by the moderator.

Source: Adapted from Podsakoff, N. P., Podsakoff, P. M., MacKenzie, S. B., Maynes, T. D., & Spoelma, T. M. (2014). Consequences of unit-level organizational citizenship behaviors: A review and recommendations for future research. *Journal of Organizational Behavior, 35*, S87–S119. Used with permission.

confirmed by Bachrach et al. (2006) with respect to helping behavior. Similarly, spatial distance is expected to weaken the effects of all three forms of OCB on unit-level outcome variables, because a high level of spatial distance inhibits the communication and interaction among group members that facilitates the impact of these OCBs; a high level of the need for independence among group members weakens the impact of all three forms of OCBs, because helpful behavior is less likely to be accepted from others, constructive suggestions are less likely to be heeded and acted upon, and sportsmanship is less likely to be valued, when group members have a high need for independence; and competitive compensation systems are expected to weaken the impact of all three OCBs, because they decrease the likelihood that group members will help each other, make recommendations for change, and be good sports, thus constraining the variation in these forms of behavior and attenuating their effects on outcome measures.

In addition, there are some moderators that have their primary effect on only one form of OCB. For example, we speculate that the impact of voice on unit-level outcomes will be weaker if (a) the group's leader lacks the authority to change policies and procedures; lacks the resources to implement the recommended changes; has a low tolerance for risk; feels threatened by employees' suggestions, does not trust the employees making the recommendations, or has a high need for control; (b) the group works in an organization that has a highly formalized or inflexible structure; and/or (c) the organization operates within a high power distance national culture. Once again, we would like to caution the reader to remember that the propositions in Table 8.10 are tentative and need a solid theoretical foundation based on the literature.

In addition to the potential moderators identified in Table 8.10, a few studies (MacKenzie et al., 2011; Ng & Van Dyne, 2005) have found support for curvilinear effects of helping behavior, and helping by voice interaction effects on group-level performance. Therefore, we believe that additional attention should be paid to curvilinear relationships between OCBs and unit-level outcome variables. Indeed, curvilinear effects have been of recent interest in OCB studies at the individual level (Le et al., 2011; Rubin, Dierdorff, & Bachrach, 2013; Tangirala & Ramanujam, 2008).

As a final note, we emphasize that, although we have talked about these moderators as if they affected a direct relationship between the OCBs and unit-level outcomes, as previously noted in Table 8.4, we expect these relationships to be mediated by a variety of different factors. This raises the question of where the moderators have their effects. For example, Edwards and Lambert (2007) in their discussion of moderated mediation, have called attention to the effect that moderators may have on the relationship between an exogenous variable and a mediator (stage 1), between a mediator and the ultimate endogenous variable (stage 2), or both. Although it is beyond the scope of this review to attempt to develop hypotheses at this level of detail, we encourage future research in this area to consider these possibilities.

INDIVIDUAL-LEVEL MODERATORS

In Table 8.11 we have attempted to identify potential moderators of the impact of OCBs on individual-level outcomes. As indicated in the table, we have divided these potential moderators into six categories (individual, group, supervisor, task, organizational, and cultural/environmental characteristics), and in the last three columns we speculate about the impact that these moderators might have on the relationships between the three prototypical forms of OCB and unit-level outcomes. For example, we speculate that employee expertise will moderate the relationships between helping and voice behaviors and individual-level outcomes (e.g., performance appraisals, reward allocation decisions, etc.) because these behaviors are likely to be perceived by the rater as being more valuable when they come from someone with high expertise rather than low expertise. Consistent with the arguments provided by Bommer, Dierdorff, and Rubin (2007), we also expect that OCBs will have less effect on individual-level outcomes when everyone else in the group exhibits them as well because they are perceived to be less rare or distinctive under these circumstances. Several researchers (Eastman, 1994; Grant et al., 2009) have suggested that the rater's inferences about the motives or values of the employee exhibiting the OCB influences the impact of OCBs on individual-level outcomes, such that the impact of OCBs is greater when they are perceived to arise from the employees' altruistic/prosocial motives. Finally, we might expect that the impact of voice on individual-level outcomes would be less in cultures with high power distance beliefs than in cultures with low power distance beliefs.

Of course, we do not mean to imply that the moderators identified in Table 8.11 are the only potential moderators of the relationships between

Table 8.11 Potential Moderators of the Relationships Between Organizational Citizenship Behaviors and Individual-Level Outcomes and Some Tentative Hypotheses About Their Effects

Moderator Category	Specific Moderators	Expected Effect of the Moderator on the OCB-Outcome Relationship		
		Helping	Sportsmanship	Voice
Individual characteristics	• Employee's task performance	+		+
	• Expertise	+		+
	• Negative affectivity	–	–	–
	• Positive affectivity	+	+	+
	• Gender	?	?	?
Group characteristics	• Average level of OCB exhibited by the group	–	–	–
Supervisor characteristics	• Has a low tolerance for risk (i.e., is risk averse)			–
	• Feels threatened by employee suggestions			–
	• Has good relationships with employees	+		+
	• Has high need for control			–
Supervisor perceptions/ attributions	• Believes the employee has altruistic/ prosocial motives	+	+	+
	• Believes the employee has impression management or instrumental motives	–		–
	• Believes the employee is affectively committed to the organization	+		+
	• Believes the employee is not trustworthy			–
Task characteristics	• Task interdependence	+	+	
Cultural/ environmental characteristics	• Collectivism	+	+	
	• Power distance			–

Note: + means that the relationship between the OCB and individual-level outcomes is strengthened by the moderator; – means that the relationship between the OCB and individual-level outcomes is weakened by the moderator; blank means it is not clear whether the relationship between the OCB and individual-level outcomes is strengthened, weakened, or unaffected by the moderator.

OCBs and individual-level outcomes. Indeed, we suspect a case can be made that a manager's beliefs about the beneficial effects of unit-level OCBs on unit-level performance identified in the middle column of Table 8.8 might also moderate the impact of individual-level OCBs on individual-level outcomes. For example, a manager may give higher evaluations and rewards to employees who exhibit OCB to the extent that the manager believes that unit-level OCB enhances the team's cohesiveness, collective self-efficacy, potency, knowledge dissemination, coordination, social capital, or reduces the need to devote scarce resources to maintenance functions. Although we are not aware of any research that has tested these potential moderating effects, they seem theoretically plausible. Therefore, we encourage future research examining these possibilities.

Conclusions

Perhaps the primary reason for interest in organizational citizenship behavior has been the effects that it has been shown to have on both individual- and organizational-level outcomes. However, less research has focused on the theoretical mechanisms that explain why OCBs have these effects or on the boundary conditions that influence the strengths of these effects. Therefore, in this chapter we have identified the theoretical mechanisms through which OCBs are believed to produce their effects, and the individual, group, supervisor, task, organizational, and cultural/environmental characteristics that determine the strengths of these effects. In addition, we have also suggested how several prototypical forms of OCB (helping, sportsmanship, and voice) might be related to these mediators and how the effects of these different forms of OCB on individual- and organizational-level outcomes might be influenced by these moderators.

References

Ahearne, M. J., MacKenzie, S. B., Podsakoff, P. M., Mathieu, J. E., & Lam S. K. (2010). The role of consensus in sales team performance. *Journal of Marketing Research, 47*, 458–469.

Allen, T. D. (2006). Rewarding good citizens: The relationship between citizenship behavior, gender, and organizational rewards. *Journal of Applied Social Psychology, 36*, 120–143.

Allen, T. D., & Rush, M. C. (1998). The effects of organizational citizenship behavior on performance judgments: A field study and a laboratory experiment. *Journal of Applied Psychology, 83*, 247–260.

Allen, T. D., & Rush, M. C. (2001). The influence of ratee gender on ratings of organizational citizenship behavior. *Journal of Applied Social Psychology, 31*, 2561–2587.

Allen, T. D., Smith, M. A., Mael, F. A., O'Shea, P. G., & Eby, L. T. (2009). Organizational-level mentoring and organizational performance within substance abuse centers. *Journal of Management, 35*, 1113–1128.

Aube, C., & Rousseau, V. (2005). Team goal commitment and team effectiveness: The role of task interdependence and supportive behaviors. *Group Dynamics: Theory, Research, and Practice, 9*, 189–204.

Bachrach, D. G., Powell, B. C., Collins, B. J., & Richey, R. G. (2006). Effects of task interdependence on the relationship between helping behavior and group performance. *Journal of Applied Psychology, 91*, 1396–1405.

Bagozzi, R. P., Verbeke, W., & Gavino, J. C. (2003). Culture moderates the self-regulation of shame and its effects on performance: The case of salespersons in the Netherlands and the Philippines. *Journal of Applied Psychology, 88*, 219–233.

Baker, R. C. (1999). *Customers' perceptions of the service they receive: The influence of employee extra-role job behaviors.* Unpublished doctoral dissertation, Louisiana State University and Agricultural and Mechanical College.

Bandura, A. (1977). *Social learning theory.* Englewood Cliffs, NJ: Prentice Hall.

Barsade, S. G. (2002). The ripple effect: Emotional contagion and its influence on group behavior. *Administrative Science Quarterly, 47*, 644–675.

Barksdale, K., & Werner, J. M. (2001). Managerial ratings of in-role behaviors, organizational citizenship behaviors, and overall performance: Testing different models of their relationship. *Journal of Business Research, 51*, 145–155.

Bergeron, D. M. (2007). The potential paradox of organizational citizenship behavior: Good citizens at what cost? *Academy of Management Review, 32*, 1078–1095.

Bergeron, D. M., Shipp, A. J., Rosen, B. & Furst, S. A. (2013). Organizational citizenship behavior and career outcomes: the cost of being a good citizen. *Journal of Management, 39*, 958–984.

Bienstock, C. C., DeMoranville, C. W., & Smith, R. K. (2003). Organizational citizenship behavior and service quality. *Journal of Services Marketing, 17*, 357–378.

Blau, G. (1964). *Exchange and power in social life.* New York, NY: Wiley.

Bolino, M. C. (1999). Citizenship and impression management: Good soldiers or good actors? *Academy of Management Review, 24*, 82–98.

Bolino, M. C., Hsiung, H-H., Harvey, J. & LePine, J. A. (2015). "Well, I'm tired of tryin!" Organizational citizenship behavior and citizenship fatigue. *Journal of Applied Psychology, 100*, 56–74.

Bolino, M. C., & Turnley, W. H. (2005). The personal costs of citizenship behavior: The relationship between individual initiative and role overload, job stress, and work–family conflict. *Journal of Applied Psychology, 90*, 740–748.

Bolino, M. C., Turnley, W. H., & Bloodgood, J. M. (2002). Citizenship behavior and the creation of social capital in organizations. *Academy of Management Review, 27*(4), 505–522.

Bommer, W. H., Dierdorff, E. C., & Rubin, R. S. (2007). Does prevalence mitigate relevance? The moderating effect of group-level OCB on employee performance. *Academy of Management Journal, 50*, 1481–1494.

Braun, T., Ferreira, A. I., & Sydow, J. (2013). Citizenship behavior and effectiveness in temporary organizations. *International Journal of Project Management, 31*, 862–876.

Chang, A., Chiang, H-H., & Han, T-S. (2012). A multilevel investigation of relationships among brand-centered HRM, brand psychological ownership, brand citizenship behaviors, and customers satisfaction. *European Journal of Marketing, 46*, 626–662.

Chen, G., & Kanfer, R. (2006). Toward a systems theory of motivated behavior in work teams. *Research in Organizational Behavior, 27*, 223–267.

Chen, X.-P., Lam, S. K., Naumann, S. E., & Schaubroeck, J. (2005). Group citizenship behavior: Conceptualization and preliminary tests of its antecedents and consequences. *Management and Organization Review, 1*, 273–300.

Chen, Z. X., Tsui, A. S., & Farh, J. L. (2002). Loyalty to supervisor vs. organizational commitment: Relationships to employee performance in China. *Journal of Occupational and Organizational Psychology, 75*, 339–356.

Chi, N-W., Chung, Y-Y., & Tsai, W-C. (2011). How do happy leaders enhance team success? The mediating roles of transformational leadership, group affective tone, and team processes. *Journal of Applied Social Psychology, 41*, 1421–1454.

Choi, J. M., & Sy, T. (2010). Group-level organizational citizenship behavior: Effects of demographic faultlines and conflict

in small work groups. *Journal of Organizational Behavior, 31,* 1032–1054.
Chuang, C-H., & Liao, H. (2010). Strategic human resource management in service context: Taking care of business by taking care of employees and customers. *Personnel Psychology, 63,* 153–196.
Chun, J. S., Shin, Y., Choi, J. N., & Kim, M. S. (2013). How does corporate ethics contribute to firm financial performance? The mediating role of collective organizational commitment and organizational citizenship behavior. *Journal of Management, 39,* 853–877.
Coleman, V. I., & Borman, W. C. (2000). Investigating the underlying structure of the citizenship performance domain. *Human Resource Management Review, 10,* 25–44.
Cropanzano, R., Li, A., & Benson, L. (2011). Peer justice and teamwork process. *Group & Organization Management, 36,* 567–596.
Day, A. L., & Carroll, S. A. (2004). Using an ability-based measure of emotional intelligence to predict individual performance, group performance, and group citizenship behaviours. *Personality and Individual Differences, 36,* 1443–1458.
De Dreu, C. K. W., & Van Vianen, A. E. M. (2001). Managing relationship conflict and the effectiveness of organizational teams. *Journal of Organizational Behavior, 22,* 309–328.
DeGroot, T., & Brownlee, A. L. (2006). Effect of department structure on the organizational citizenship behavior-department effectiveness relationship. *Journal of Business Research, 59,* 1116–1123.
Detert, J. R., Burris, E. R., Harrison, D. A., & Martin, S. R. (2013). Voice flows to and from leaders: Understanding when units are helped or hurt by employee voice. *Administrative Science Quarterly, 58,* 624–668.
DiPaola, M. F., & Hoy, W. K. (2005). Organizational citizenship of faculty and achievement of high school students. *The High School Journal, 88,* 35–44.
Dovidio, J. F., Gaertner, S. L., Isen, A. M., & Lowrance, R. (1995). Group representations and intergroup bias: Positive affect, similarity, and group size. *Personality and Social Psychology Bulletin, 21,* 856–865.
Dunlop, P. D., & Lee, K. (2004). Workplace deviance, organizational citizenship behavior, and business unit performance: The bad apples do spoil the whole barrel. *Journal of Organizational Behavior, 25,* 67–80.
Eastman, K. W. (1994). In the eyes of the beholder: An attributional approach to ingratiation and organizational citizenship behavior. *Academy of Management Journal,* 37, 1379–1391.
Eatough, E. M., Chang, C-H., Miloslavic, S. A., & Johnson, R. E. (2011). Relationships of role stressors with organizational citizenship behavior: A meta-analysis. *Journal of Applied Psychology, 96,* 619–632.
Edwards, J. R., & Lambert, L. S. (2007). Methods for integrating moderation and mediation: A general analytical framework using moderated path analysis. *Psychological Methods, 12,* 1–22.
Ehrhart, M. G., Bliese, P. D., & Thomas, J. L. (2006). Unit-level OCB and unit effectiveness: Examining the incremental effect of helping behavior. *Human Performance, 19,* 159–173.
Ehrhart M. G., & Naumann, S. E. (2004). Organizational citizenship behavior in work groups: A group norms approach. *Journal of Applied Psychology, 89,* 960–974.
Ellington, J. K., Dierdorff, E. C., & Rubin, R. S. (2014). Decelerating the diminishing returns of citizenship on task performance: The role of social context and interpersonal skill. *Journal of Applied Psychology, 99,* 748–758.
Estrada, C. A., Isen, A. M., & Young, M. J. (1994). Positive affect facilitates integration of information and decreases anchoring in reasoning among physicians. *Organizational Behavior and Human Decision Processing, 72,* 117–135.
Ferreira, A. I., Braun, T., & Sydow, J. (2013). Citizenship behavior in project-based organizing: Comparing German and Portuguese project managers. *The International Journal of Human Resource Management, 24,* 3772–3793.
Ferris, G. R., Witt. L. A., & Hochwarter, W. A. (2001). Interaction of social skill and general mental ability on job performance and salary. *Journal of Applied Psychology, 86,* 1075–1082.
Fisher, R., McPhail, R., & Menghetti, G. (2010). Linking employee attitudes and behaviors with business performance: A comparative analysis of hotels in Mexico and China. *International Journal of Hospitality Management, 29,* 397–404.
Fiske, S. T., Kenny, D. A., & Taylor, S. E. (1982). Structural models for the mediation of salience effects on attribution. *Journal of Experimental Social Psychology, 18,* 105–127.
Frazier, M. L., & Bowler, W. M. (2015). Voice climate, supervisor undermining, and work outcomes: A group-level examination. *Journal of Management, 41,* 841–863.
George, J. M., & Bettenhausen, K. (1990). Understanding prosocial behavior, sales performance, and turnover: A group-level analysis in a service context. *Journal of Applied Psychology, 75,* 698–709.
Gong, Y., Chang, S., & Cheung, S-Y. (2010). High performance work system and collective OCB: A collective social exchange perspective. *Human Resource Management Journal, 20,* 119–137.
Grant, A. M., Gino, F., & Hofmann, D. A. (2011). Reversing the extraverted leadership advantage: The role of employee proactivity. *Academy of Management Journal, 54,* 528–550.
Grant, A. M., Parker, S., & Collins, C. (2009). Getting credit for proactive behavior: Supervisor reactions depend on what you value and how you feel. *Personnel Psychology, 62,* 31–55.
Greenslade, J. H., & Jimmieson, N. L. (2011). Organizational factors impacting on patient satisfaction: A cross sectional examination of service climate and linkages to nurses' effort and performance. *International Journal of Nursing Studies, 48,* 1188–1198.
Guzzo, R. A., Yost, P. R., Campbell, R. J., & Shea, G. P. (1993). Potency in groups: Articulating a construct. *British Journal of Social Psychology, 32,* 87–106.
Heilman, M. E., & Chen, J. J. (2005). Same behavior, different consequences: Reactions to men's and women's altruistic citizenship behavior. *Journal of Applied Psychology, 90,* 431–441.
Higgins, K. D. (2002). *How organizational citizenship behavior influences group effectiveness.* Unpublished doctoral dissertation, Northern Illinois University.
Halbesleben, J. R. B., Harvey, J., & Bolino, M. C. (2009). Too engaged? A conservation of resources view of the relationship between work engagement and work interference with family. *Journal of Applied Psychology, 94,* 1452–1465.
Hu, J. (2012). *A team-level social exchange model: The antecedents and consequences of leader-member exchange.* Unpublished doctoral dissertation, University of Illinois at Chicago.
Hu, J., & Liden, R. C. (2011). Antecedents of team potency and team effectiveness: An examination of goal and process

clarity and servant leadership. *Journal of Applied Psychology, 96*, 851–862.
Hui, C., Lam, S. S. K., & Law, K. K. S. (2000). Instrumental values of organizational citizenship behavior for promotion: A field quasiexperiment. *Journal of Applied Psychology, 85*, 822–828.
Hui, C. Law, K. S., & Chen, Z. X. (1999). A structural equation model of the effects of negative affectivity, leader-member exchange, and perceived job mobility on in-role and extra-role performance: A Chinese case. *Organizational Behavior and Human Decision Processes, 77*, 3–21.
Hung, H-K., Yeh, R-S., & Shih, H-Y. (2012). Voice behavior and performance ratings: The role of political skill. *International Journal of Hospitality Management, 31*, 442–450.
Hunter, E. M., Neubert, M. J., Perry, S. J., Witt, L. A., Penney, L. M., & Weinberger, E. (2013). Servant leaders inspire servant followers: Antecedents and outcomes for employees and the organization. *Leadership Quarterly, 24*, 316–331.
Hyatt, D. E., & Ruddy, T. M. (1997). An examination of the relationship between work group characteristics and performance: Once more into the breach. *Personnel Psychology, 50*, 553–585.
Isen, A. M., Daubman, K. A., & Nowicki, G. P. (1987). Positive affect facilitates creative problem-solving. *Journal of Personality and Social Psychology, 52*, 1112–1131.
Jawahar, I. M., & Ferris, G. R. (2011). A longitudinal investigation of task and contextual performance influences on promotability judgements. *Human Performance, 24*, 251–269.
Johnson, D. E., Erez, A., Kiker, D. S., & Motowidlo, S. J. (2002). Liking and attributions of motives as mediators of the relationships between individuals' reputations, helpful behaviors, and raters' reward decisions. *Journal of Applied Psychology, 87*(4), 808–815.
Kaplan, R. S., & Norton, D. P. (1992). The balanced scorecard—Measures that drive performance. *Harvard Business Review, 70*, 71–79.
Karambayya, R. (1990). *Contexts for organizational citizenship behavior: Do high performing and satisfying units have better "citizens."* Working paper. York University.
Kiker, D. S., & Motowidlo, S. J. (1999). Main and interaction effects of task and contextual performance on supervisory reward decisions. *Journal of Applied Psychology, 84*(4), 602–609.
Kim, H., & Gong, Y. (2009). The roles of tacit knowledge and OCB in the relationship between group-based pay and firm performance. *Human Resource Management Journal, 19*, 120–139.
Kirkman, B. L., Tesluk, P. E., & Rosen, B. (2001). Assessing the incremental validity of team consensus ratings over aggregation of individual-level data in predicting team effectiveness. *Personnel Psychology, 54*, 645–667.
Kizilos, M. A., Cummings, C., & Cummings, T. G. (2013). How high involvement work processes increase organizational performance: The role of organizational citizenship behavior. *Journal of Applied Behavioral Science, 49*, 413–436.
Koh, W. L., Steers, R. M., & Terborg, J. R. (1995). The effects of transformational leadership on teacher attitudes and student performance in Singapore. *Journal of Organizational Behavior, 16*, 319–333.
Koys, D. J. (2001). The effects of employee satisfaction, organizational citizenship behavior, and turnover on organizational effectiveness: A unit-level, longitudinal study. *Personnel Psychology, 54*, 101–114.
Lam, C. F., & Mayer, D. M. (2014). When do employees speak up for their customers? A model of voice in a customer service context. *Personnel Psychology, 67*, 637–666.
Le, H., Oh, I-S., Robbins, S. B., Ilies, R., Holland, E., & Westrick, P. (2011). Too much of a good thing: Curvilinear relationships between personality traits and job performance. *Journal of Applied Psychology, 96*, 113–133.
Lefkowitz, J. (2000). The role of interpersonal affective regard in supervisory performance ratings: A literature review and proposed causal model. *Journal of Occupational and Organizational Psychology, 7*, 67–85.
LePine, J. A., Erez, A., & Johnson, D. E. (2002). The nature and dimensionality of organizational citizenship behavior: A critical review and meta-analysis. *Journal of Applied Psychology, 87*, 52–65.
Lin, C-C., & Peng, T. K. (2010). From organizational citizenship behaviour to team performance: The mediation of group cohesion and collective efficacy. *Management and Organization Review, 6*, 55–75.
Liu, W., Gong, Y., & Liu, J. (2014). When do business units benefit more from collective citizenship behavior of management teams? An upper echelons perspective. *Journal of Applied Psychology, 99*, 523–534.
Lovell, S. E., Kahn, A. S., Anton, J., Davidson, A., Dowling, E., Post, D., & Mason, C. (1999). Does gender affect the link between organizational citizenship behavior and performance evaluations? *Sex Roles, 41*, 469–478.
Lowery, C. M., & Krilowicz, T. J. (1994). Relationships among nontask behaviors, rated performance, and objective performance measures. *Psychological Reports, 74*, 571–578.
Lyubomirsky, S., King, L., & Diener, E. (2005). The benefits of frequent positive affect: Does happiness lead to success? *Psychological Bulletin, 131*, 803–855.
MacKenzie, S. B., & Podsakoff, P. M. (2012). Common method bias in marketing: Causes, mechanisms, and procedural remedies. *Journal of Retailing, 88*, 556–562.
MacKenzie, S. B., Podsakoff, P. M., & Fetter, R. (1991). Organizational citizenship behavior and objective productivity as determinants of managerial evaluations of salespersons' performance. *Organizational Behavior and Human Decision Processes, 50*(1), 123–150.
MacKenzie, S. B., Podsakoff, P. M., & Fetter, R. (1993). The impact of organizational citizenship behavior on evaluations of salesperson performance. *Journal of Marketing, 57*(1), 70–80.
MacKenzie, S. B., Podsakoff, P. M., & Paine, J. E. (1999). Do citizenship behaviors matter more for managers than for salespeople? *Journal of the Academy of Marketing Science, 27*, 396–410.
MacKenzie, S. B., Podsakoff, P. M., & Podsakoff, N. P. (2011). Challenge-oriented organizational citizenship behaviors and organizational effectiveness: Do challenge-oriented behaviors really have an impact on the organization's bottom line? *Personnel Psychology, 64*, 559–592.
MacKenzie, S. B., Podsakoff, P. M., & Rich, G. (2001). Transformational and transactional leadership and salesperson performance. *Journal of the Academy of Marketing Sciences, 29*, 115–134.
Mariadoss, B. J. L. (2007). *Two essays on team perspectives in sales.* Unpublished doctoral dissertation, University of Houston.
McArthur, L. Z., & Post, D. L. (1977). Figural emphasis and person perception. *Journal of Experimental Social Psychology, 13*, 520–535.

Maynes, T. D., & Podsakoff, P. M. (2014). Speaking more broadly: An examination of the nature, antecedents, and consequences of an expanded set of employee voice behaviors. *Journal of Applied Psychology, 99*, 87–112.

McClean, E. J., Burris, E. R., & Detert, J. R. (2013). When does voice lead to exit? It depends on leadership. *Academy of Management Journal, 56*, 525–548.

Messersmith, J. G., Patel, P. C., Lepak, D. P., & Gould-Williams, J. S. (2011). Unlocking the black box: Exploring the link between high-performance work systems and performance. *Journal of Applied Psychology, 96*, 1105–1118.

Morrison, E. W., & Milliken, F. J. (2000). Organizational silence: a barrier to change and development in a pluralistic world. *Academy of Management Review, 25*, 706–725.

Mossholder, K. W., Richardson, H. A., & Settoon, R. P. (2011). Human resource systems and helping in organizations: A relational perspective. *Academy of Management Review, 36*, 33–52.

Motowidlo, S. J., & Van Scotter, J. R. (1994). Evidence that task-performance should be distinguished from contextual performance. *Journal of Applied Psychology, 79*, 475–480.

Naumann, S. E., & Bennett, N. (2002). The effects of procedural justice climate on work group performance. *Small Group Research, 33*, 361–377.

Ng, T. W. H., & Feldman, D. C. (2010). Human capital and objective indicators of career success: The mediating effects of cognitive ability and conscientiousness. *Journal of Occupational and Organizational Psychology, 83*, 207–235.

Ng, K. Y., & Van Dyne, L. (2005). Antecedents and performance consequences of helping behavior in work groups: A multilevel analysis. *Group & Organization Management, 30*, 514–540.

Nielsen, T. M., Bachrach, D. G., Sundstrom, E., & Halfhill, T. (2012). Utility of OCB: Organizational citizenship behavior and group performance in a resource allocation framework. *Journal of Management, 38*, 668–694.

Nisbett, R. E., & Wilson, T. D. (1977). Telling more than we can know—Verbal reports on mental processes. *Psychological Review, 84*, 231–259.

Nishii, L. H., Lepak, D. P., & Schneider, B. (2008). Employee attributions of the "why" of HR practices: Their effects on employee attitudes and behaviors, and customer satisfaction. *Personnel Psychology, 61*, 503–545.

Organ, D. W. (1988). *Organizational citizenship behavior: The good soldier syndrome*. Lexington, MA: Lexington Books.

Organ, D. W. (1997). Organizational citizenships behavior: It's construct cleanup time. *Human Performance, 10*, 85–97.

Organ, D. W., Podsakoff, P. M., & MacKenzie, S. B. (2006). *Organizational citizenship behavior: Its nature, antecedents, and consequences*. Thousand Oaks, CA: Sage Publications.

Ozer, M. (2011). A moderated mediation model of the relationship between organizational citizenship behaviors and job performance. *Journal of Applied Psychology, 96*, 1328–1336.

Park, O. S. (1986). *Beyond cognition in leadership: Prosocial behavior and affect in managerial judgment*. Unpublished doctoral dissertation, Pennsylvania State University, State College.

Pearce, C. L., & Ensley, M. D. (2004). A reciprocal and longitudinal investigation of the innovation process: The central role of shared vision in product and process innovation teams (PPITs). *Journal of Organizational Behavior, 25*, 259–278.

Podsakoff, N. P., Whiting, S. W., Podsakoff, P. M., & Blume, B. D. (2009). Individual- and organizational-level consequences of organizational citizenship behaviors: A meta-analysis. *Journal of Applied Psychology, 94*, 122–141.

Podsakoff, N. P., Whiting, S. W., Podsakoff, P. M., & Mishra, P. (2011). Effects of organizational citizenship behaviors on selection decisions in employment interviews. *Journal of Applied Psychology, 96*, 310–326.

Podsakoff, N. P., Whiting, S. W., Welsh, D. T., & Mai, K. M. (2013). Surveying for "artifacts": The susceptibility of the OCB-performance evaluation relationship to common rater, item, and measurement context effects. *Journal of Applied Psychology, 98*, 863–874.

Podsakoff, N. P., Podsakoff, P. M., MacKenzie, S. B., Maynes, T. D., & Spoelma, T. (2014). Consequences of unit-level organizational citizenship behaviors: A review and recommendations for future research. *Journal of Organizational Behavior, 35*, S87–S119.

Podsakoff, P. M., Ahearne, M., & MacKenzie, S. B. (1997). Organizational citizenship behavior and the quantity and quality of work group performance. *Journal of Applied Psychology, 82*, 262–270.

Podsakoff, P. M., & MacKenzie, S. B. (1994). Organizational citizenship behaviors and sales unit effectiveness. *Journal of Marketing Research, 31*, 351–363.

Podsakoff, P. M., & MacKenzie, S. B. (1997). Impact of organizational citizenship behavior on organizational performance: A review and suggestions for future research. *Human Performance, 10*, 133–151.

Podsakoff, P. M., MacKenzie, S. B., Lee, J. Y., & Podsakoff, N. P. (2003). Common method biases in behavioral research: A critical review of the literature and recommended remedies. *Journal of Applied Psychology, 88*, 879–903.

Podsakoff, P. M., MacKenzie, S. B., Paine, J. B., & Bachrach, D. G. (2000). Organizational citizenship behaviors: A critical review of the theoretical and empirical literature and suggestions for future research. *Journal of Management, 26*(3), 513–563.

Podsakoff, P. M., MacKenzie, S. B., & Podsakoff, N. P. (2012). Sources of method bias in social science research and recommendations on how to control it. *Annual Review of Psychology, 63*, 539–569.

Podsakoff, P. M., Niehoff, B. P., MacKenzie, S. B., & Williams, M. L. (1993). Do substitutes for leadership really substitute for leadership? An empirical examination of Kerr and Jermier's situational leadership model. *Organizational Behavior and Human Decision Processes, 54*, 1–44.

Porter, C. O. L. H. (2005). Goal orientation: Effects of backing up behavior, performance, efficacy, and commitment in teams. *Journal of Applied Psychology, 90*, 811–818.

Randall, M. L., Cropanzano, R., Borman, C. A., & Birjulin, A. (1999). Organizational politics and organizational support as predictors of work attitudes, job performance, and organizational citizenship behavior. *Journal of Organizational Behavior, 20*, 159–174.

Rapp, A. A., Bachrach, D. G., & Rapp, T. L. (2013). The influence of time management skill on the curvilinear relationship between organizational citizenship behavior and task performance. *Journal of Applied Psychology, 98*, 668–677.

Raver, J. L., Ehrhart, M. G., & Chadwick, I. C. (2012). The emergence of team helping norms: Foundations within members' attributes and behavior. *Journal of Organizational Behavior, 33*, 616–637.

Raver, J. L., & Gelfand, M. J. (2005). Beyond the individual victim: Linking sexual harassment, team processes, and team performance. *Academy of Management Journal, 48*, 387–400.

Rego, A., & Cunha, M. P. E. (2008). Organisational citizenship behaviours and effectiveness: An empirical study in two small insurance companies. *Services Industry Journal, 28*, 541–554.

Reiche, S. B., Cardona, P., Lee, Y-T., Canela, M. A., Akinnukawe, E., Briscoe, J. P., . . . Wilkinson, H. (2014). Why do managers engage in trustworthy behavior? A multilevel cross-cultural study in 18 countries. *Personnel Psychology, 67*, 61–98.

Rico, R., Bachrach, D. G., Sanchez-Manzanares, M., & Collins, B. J. (2011). The interactive effects of person-focused citizenship behavior, task interdependence, and virtuality on team performance. *European Journal of Work and Organizational Psychology, 50*, 700–726.

Rotundo, M., & Sackett, P. R. (2002). The relative importance of task, citizenship, and counterproductive performance to global ratings of job performance: A policy-capturing approach. *Journal of Applied Psychology, 87*, 66–80.

Rubin, R. S., Dierdorff, E. C., & Bachrach, D. G. (2013). Boundaries of citizenship behavior: Curvilinearity and context in citizenship and performance relationship. *Personnel Psychology, 66*, 377–406.

Rupp, D. E., & Cropanzano, R. (2002). The mediating effects of social exchange relationships in predicting workplace outcomes from multifoci organizational justice. *Organizational Behavior and Human Decision Processes, 89*, 925–946.

Schneider, B., Ehrhart, M. G., Mayer, D. M., Saltz, J. L., & Niles-Jolly, K. (2005). Understanding organization-customer links in service settings. *Academy of Management Journal, 48*, 1017–1032.

Sepulveda-Martinez, C. J. (2001). *Relationship of organizational citizenship behaviors and customer orientation to service quality and customer satisfaction.* Unpublished doctoral dissertation, Tulane University.

Settoon, R. P., Bennett, N. & Liden, R. C. (1996). Social exchange in organizations: Perceived organizational support, leader-member exchange, and employee reciprocity. *Journal of Applied Psychology, 81*, 219–227.

Shore, L. M., Barksdale, K., & Shore, T. H. (1995). Managerial perceptions of employee commitment to the organization. *Academy of Management Journal, 38*(6), 1593–1615.

Spoor, J. R., & Kelly, J. R. (2004). The evolutionary significance of affect in groups: Communication and group bonding. *Group Processes & Intergroup Relations, 7*, 398–412.

Spoor, J. R., & Kelly, J. R. (2007). Naive theories about the effects of mood in groups: A preliminary investigation. *Group Processes & Intergroup Relations, 10*, 203–222.

Storms, M. D. (1973). Videotape and attribution process—Reversing actors and observers points of view. *Journal of Personality and Social Psychology, 27*, 165–175.

Sun, L.-Y., Aryee, S., & Law, K. S. (2007). High-performance human resource practices, citizenship behavior, and organizational performance: A relational perspective. *Academy of Management Journal, 50*, 558–577.

Sutton, A. W., Baldwin, S. P., Wood, L., & Hoffman, B. J. (2013). A meta-analysis of the relationship between rater liking and performance ratings. *Human Performance, 26*, 409–429.

Tanghe, J., Wisse, B., & van der Flier, H. (2010). The formation of group affect and team effectiveness: The moderating role of identification. *British Journal of Management, 21*, 340–358.

Tangirala, S., & Ramanujam, R. (2008). Exploring nonlinearity in employee voice: The effects of personal control and organizational identification. *Academy of Management Journal, 51*, 1189–1203.

Taylor, S. E., Crocker, J., Fiske, S. T. Sprinzen, M., & Winkler, J. D. (1979). Generalizability of salience effects. *Journal of Personality and Social Psychology, 37*, 357–368.

Taylor, S. E., & Fiske, S. T. (1975). Point of view and perceptions of causality. *Journal of Personality and Social Psychology, 32*, 439–445.

Taylor, S. E., & Fiske, S. T. (1978). Salience, attention, and attributions: Top of the head phenomena. In L. Berkowitz (Ed.). *Advances in experimental social psychology, Vol. 11* (pp. 249–288). New York, NY: Academic Press.

Tsang, S. S., Chen, T-Y., Wang, S. F., & Tai, H-L. (2012). Nursing work stress: The impacts of social network structure and organizational citizenship behavior. *Journal of Nursing Research, 20*, 9–18.

Turnley, W. H., Bolino, M. C., Lester, S. W., & Bloodgood, J. M. (2003). The impact of psychological contract fulfillment on the performance of in-role and organizational citizenship behaviors. *Journal of Management, 29*, 187–206.

Van der Vegt, G. S., & Bunderson, J. S. (2005). Learning and performance in multidisciplinary teams: The importance of collective team identification. *Academy of Management Journal, 48*, 532–547.

Van Dyne, L., Cummings, L. L., & Parks, J. M. (1995). Extra-role behaviors: In pursuit of construct and definitional clarity. *Research in Organization Behavior, 17*, 215–285.

Van Dyne, L., & LePine, J. A. (1998). Helping and voice extra-role behaviors: Evidence of construct and predictive validity. *Academy of Management Journal, 41*, 108–119.

Van Scotter, J. R., & Motowidlo, S. J. (1996). Interpersonal facilitation and job dedication as separate facets of contextual performance. *Journal of Applied Psychology, 81*, 525–531.

Van Scotter, J. R., Motowidlo, S. J., & Cross, T. C. (2000). Effects of task performance and contextual performance on systemic rewards. *Journal of Applied Psychology, 85*, 526–535.

Varela, O. E., Burke, M. J., & Landis, R. S. (2008). A model of emergence and dysfunctional effects of emotional conflict in groups. *Group Dynamics: Theory, Research, and Practice, 12*, 112–126.

Vilela, B. B., Gonzalez, J. A. V. & Ferrin, P. F. (2008). Person-organization fit, OCB and performance appraisal: Evidence from matched supervisor-salesperson data set in a Spanish context. *Industrial Marketing Management, 37*, 1005–1019.

Walumbwa, F. O., Morrison, E. W., & Christensen, A. L. (2012). Ethical leadership and group in-role performance: The mediating effect of group conscientiousness and group voice. *Leadership Quarterly, 23*, 953–964.

Walz, S. M., & Niehoff, B. P. (2000). Organizational citizenship behaviors: Their relationship to organizational effectiveness. *Journal of Hospitality & Tourism Research, 24*, 301–319.

Wang, X-H., & Howell, J. M. (2010). Exploring the dual-level effects of transformational leadership on followers. *Journal of Applied Psychology, 95*, 1134–1144.

Werner, J. M. (1994). Dimensions that make a difference: Examining the impact of in-role and extra-role behaviors on supervisory ratings. *Journal of Applied Psychology, 79*, 98–107.

Whiting, S. W., & Maynes, T. D. (2016). Selecting team players: Considering the impact of contextual performance and workplace deviance on selection decisions in the National Football League. *Journal of Applied Psychology, 101*, 484–497.

Whiting, S. W., Maynes, T. D., Podsakoff, N. P., & Podsakoff, P. M. (2012). Effects of message, source, and context on evaluations of employee voice behavior. *Journal of Applied Psychology*, *97*, 159–182.

Whiting, S. W., Podsakoff, P. M., & Pierce, J. R. (2008). Effects of task performance, helping, voice, and organizational loyalty on performance appraisal ratings. *Journal of Applied Psychology*, *93*, 125–139.

Williams, L. J., & Anderson, S. E. (1991). Job satisfaction and organizational commitment as predictors of organizational citizenship and in-role behaviors. *Journal of Management*, *17*, 601–617.

Yen, H. R., & Niehoff, B. P. (2004). Organizational citizenship behaviors and organizational effectiveness: Examining relationships in Taiwanese banks. *Journal of Applied Social Psychology*, *34*, 1617–1637.

Yoon, C. (2009). The effects of organizational citizenship behaviors on ERP system success. *Computers in Human Behavior*, *25*, 421–428.

Yoon, M. H., & Suh, J. (2003). Organizational citizenship behaviors and service quality as external effectiveness of contact employees. *Journal of Business Research*, *56*, 597–611.

Yu, K. Y. T., & Cable, D. M. (2011). Unpacking cooperation in diverse teams: Incorporating long-term orientation and civic virtue in the study of informational diversity. *Team Performance Management*, *17*, 63–82.

Yun, S., Takeuchi, R. & Liu, W. (2007). Employee self-enhancement motives and job performance behaviors: Investigating the moderating effects of employee role ambiguity and managerial perceptions of employee commitment. *Journal of Applied Psychology*, *92*, 745–756.

Zhang, Z., Wan, D., & Jia, M. (2008). Do high-performance human resource practices help corporate entrepreneurship? The mediating role of organizational citizenship behavior. *Journal of High Technology Management Research*, *19*, 128–138.

CHAPTER

9 Citizenship Behavior and Objective Career Outcomes: A Review and Agenda for Future Work

Diane M. Bergeron, Chantal van Esch, *and* Phillip S. Thompson

Abstract

A small but growing body of research on organizational citizenship behavior (OCB) and objective career outcomes highlights the need for more consistency across studies. This chapter critically examines extant literature and highlights key issues in current research. More specifically, we identify three main issues in the current literature. First, many OCB studies do not include a corollary measure of task behavior. Second, there seems to be an assumption that performance evaluations are positively related to objective career outcomes. Third, it is important to acknowledge that studying reward recommendations is not the same as studying actual rewards. Following discussion of these three issues, we then review the studies on OCB and various objective career outcomes (i.e., productivity, salary and financial rewards, other rewards, promotion and career advancement); point out patterns and trends across the studies; and make recommendations for how the field can move forward in terms of future research directions.

Key Words: organizational citizenship behavior, in-role behavior, rewards, career outcomes, resource allocation, task behavior

No good deed ever goes unpunished.

—*variously ascribed (e.g., Clare Boothe Luce, George Greeves, Oscar Wilde)*

Although a vast amount of research shows a positive relationship between organizational citizenship behavior and subjective performance evaluations (see meta-analysis by N. P. Podsakoff, Whiting, Podsakoff, & Blume, 2009), there has been less focus on the relationship between citizenship behavior and objective career outcomes such as compensation, promotion, and career advancement. Extant literature shows strong positive relationships between citizenship behavior and organizational and group-level outcomes such as productivity, efficiency, and customer satisfaction (e.g., N. P. Podsakoff et al., 2009). As such, these behaviors yield great benefits at the organizational level. Because engaging in citizenship behavior goes above and beyond one's job, it is important to understand if spending time on these behaviors benefits individuals' career success as well as organizational success.

The domain of individual job performance is comprised of task behavior (also known as in-role behavior) and organizational citizenship behavior (J. P. Campbell, 1990; Organ, 1988). In-role, or task, behavior refers to the set of core job behaviors that are an expected part of one's job (Borman & Motowidlo, 1993). They tend to be job-specific and can often be found in traditional job descriptions (Williams & Anderson, 1991). In contrast, organizational citizenship behavior (OCB) is the set of behaviors that "support the social and psychological environment in which task performance takes place" (Organ, 1997, p. 95). These behaviors tend to be similar across jobs and, because they are not easily enforceable, performing them is usually at the discretion of the individual (Borman & Motowidlo, 1993; Organ, 1997). Examples of such behaviors include helping others, improving morale, volunteering for extra work, complying with rules and regulations, and facilitating cooperation (Organ, 1990; Organ, Podsakoff, & MacKenzie, 2005).

Although much research has focused on the positive aspects of OCB, some researchers have argued that there may be costs to individuals who engage in too much OCB (e.g., Bergeron, 2007; Bolino, Turnley, & Niehoff, 2004; Bolino, Klotz, Turnley, & Harvey, 2013). While research shows that both task behavior and OCB are positively related to performance evaluations (N. P. Podsakoff et al., 2009) and rewards or reward recommendations (e.g., Allen & Rush, 2001; Kiker & Motowidlo, 1999), these results may or may not translate to other types of objective career outcomes. The purpose of this chapter is to summarize and review the existing literature on OCB and objective career outcomes. In the first section of this chapter, we highlight three key problems in existing OCB research related to career outcomes: (1) many studies do not include measures of task, or in-role, behavior; (2) there exists the assumption that performance evaluations are positively related to objective career outcomes; and (3) reward recommendations are not the same thing as actual rewards. In the second section, we review the current studies on the relationship between OCB and objective career outcomes (e.g., productivity, compensation, career advancement) and discuss each set of studies categorized by outcome. We also review the two main types of control systems used in organizations and highlight the results of studies conducted within each type of system. We identify patterns and trends across the set of studies and point out some issues that need to be resolved with additional research. In the third section of the chapter, we show how using a resource allocation framework and different measurements of OCB is likely to lead to different results. Finally, we present seven recommendations for future research that we feel are most pressing and will make the largest contributions to the field.

Three Key Problems in Existing Organizational Citizenship Behavior Research

Before reviewing the relevant studies regarding OCB and objective career outcomes, we identify and briefly discuss three main problems in existing research: the lack of inclusion of a measure of task or in-role behavior when studying OCB and outcomes; the field's focus on performance evaluations as an outcome variable; and the difference between recommendations and actual rewards as outcome variables. We highlight these three issues now so that the findings of the reviewed studies can be interpreted in light of these issues.

Inclusion (or Not) of Task/In-Role Behavior Measures

A main issue in much research on OCB is the lack of inclusion of a measure of task or in-role behavior. Due to shared variance between OCB and task behavior measures (Stone-Romero, Alvarez, & Thompson, 2009; Vey & Campbell, 2004), studies that only include OCB may inadvertently measure aspects of task behavior (Vey & Campbell, 2004). Thus, an alternative explanation for the significant findings in OCB studies may be that they actually reflect task behavior rather than OCB. Indeed, the average meta-analytic correlation between OCB and task behavior ranges from .49 to .60 (Hoffman, Blair, Meriac, & Woehr, 2007), thus underscoring the importance of including both measures. These findings have led some researchers to comment that there may be some difficulty of interpretation with past empirical work on OCB (Organ & Konovsky, 1989; Scholl, Cooper, & McKenna, 1987). Recommendations have been made to assess task or in-role behavior in all OCB studies, yet not all researchers follow this recommendation. As evidence, a meta-analysis (N. P. Podsakoff et al., 2009) analyzing relationships among OCB, task behavior, and performance evaluations listed 72 samples using OCB, but only 27 samples including a measure of task behavior. When OCB and task behavior ratings are from different sources, meta-analytic results show that task behavior has the stronger impact on performance ratings (N. P. Podsakoff et al., 2009). Without including task behavior, it is difficult to know the true relationship between OCB and outcomes.

The Assumption That Performance Evaluations Are Linked to Other Career Outcomes

The field's focus on performance evaluations as the most oft-studied outcome variable is likely fueled by ease of data collection and predicated on the assumption that good performance evaluations lead to other types of positive career outcomes. There are a few problems with this. First, there is little support for this assumption in extant literature. After examining the papers cited as providing evidence that performance evaluations are linked to other types of career outcomes, our conclusion is that these papers lack empirical support for such a claim. These fall into seven (nonexclusive) categories: (1) the cited studies are conceptual and merely postulate a connection between evaluations and other career outcomes although the actual paper contains no empirical evidence (e.g., Cocanougher, Ivancevich & Sharma, 1978; Muczyk & Gable, 1987); (2) it is an empirical paper studying some aspect of performance evaluation (e.g., different ratings systems) but does not specifically study the relationship between performance evaluations and objective career outcomes (e.g., Churchill Jr., Ford, & Walker Jr., 1976; Clausen, Jones, & Rich, 2008; Dubinsky & Barry, 1982; Patton III & King, 1992; Stewart & Gudykunst, 1982); (3) it is a paper in which career outcomes are based completely on objective criteria (Chonko, Howell, & Bellenger, 1986; Kerber & Campbell, 1987) rather than on subjective ratings of performance; (4) the study does not use actual performance evaluations from the organization (for example, some studies asked supervisors to complete a research measure of performance developed by academics [e.g., Greenhaus, Parasuraman, & Wormley, 1990; Siegel, 1993]; yet another asked for ratings of technical competence [Rosen, Billings, & Turney, 1976;]); (5) the outcomes were current rankings of promotability rather than actual career outcomes (e.g., Greenhaus et al., 1990; Igbaria & Baroudi, 1995; Igbaria & Wormley, 1992; Siegel, 1993); (6) the study used a Monte Carlo simulation instead of real-world data (e.g., Schwab & Olson, 1990); or (7) it was a simulated scenario with little background or consequence (e.g., London & Stumpf, 1983; Patton III & King, 1992; Taylor, 1975) or a lab study generally using students and asking them to use performance ratings to assign career outcomes such as promotions (e.g., DeNisi & Stevens, 1981; Stumpf & London, 1981). Such studies are notoriously lacking in real-world issues such as resource constraints, politics, or personal consequences (e.g., R. Griffin & Kacmar, 1991). Additional research into the link between performance evaluations and tangible career outcomes yields little. We identified only a few studies including both variables (e.g., Bergeron, Shipp, Rosen, & Furst, 2013; Lyness & Heilman, 2006; Scandura & Schriesheim, 1994) and no studies in which this relationship was the primary research focus. Lyness and Heilman found a mere .16 ($p < .01$) correlation between performance rating composites and promotion, while Scandura and Schriesheim found a similar correlation of .15 (*ns*) between performance evaluations and promotion, and a slightly higher correlation of .23 ($p < .01$) between performance evaluations and salary. Clearly, more research is needed to ascertain the relationship between performance evaluations and objective career outcomes.

Second, research in the gender and diversity arena suggests that bias plays out differently depending on the type of outcome studied. For instance, Castilla (2008, p. 1479) notes a "performance-reward bias" against females and minorities, with White males receiving larger rewards than women and minorities performing at the same level (Castilla, 2012). Indeed, a recent meta-analysis (Joshi, Son, & Roh, 2015) found no significant differences between men and women's performance evaluations but found a significant difference in career rewards (pay and promotion, $d = .56$) that was 14 times larger than that found in performance evaluations ($d = .04$). Thus, it is critical to examine a range of objective career outcomes beyond performance evaluations (Baron & Pfeffer, 1994; Reskin, 2003).

Finally, while the vast majority of studies show a positive relationship between OCB and performance evaluations (e.g., N. P. Podsakoff et al., 2009), this relationship may not hold for all types of career outcomes. That is, while there is a positive relationship between OCB and performance evaluations, this does not guarantee a positive relationship between OCB and objective types of career outcomes. Generally, performance evaluations happen either once or a few times per year. As such, they can be considered a short-term outcome and may even be used as a low-cost reward to recognize a job well done (Suazo, Martínez, & Sandoval, 2009). This immediate acknowledgment is in contrast to an outcome such as promotion, which may happen only once every few years. Promotions are generally viewed as costly because they are usually associated with a pay increase (Baker, Jensen, &

Murphy, 1988; D. Campbell, 2008). As such, there may be a different relationship between OCB and more lagged (and organizationally costly) career outcomes. Research has shown these performance-over-time measures to be more reliable indicators of performance (Meyer, 1987). To be clear, we are not arguing that performance evaluations are unimportant. Rather, what we are arguing is that there needs to be a wider range of outcomes under study.

Reward "Recommendations" Are Not the Same Thing as Actual Rewards

Another main issue in much research on OCB and rewards is that participants are generally asked to make a reward *recommendation* (e.g., Allen & Rush, 1998; Yun, Takeuchi, & Liu, 2007) or to make a decision in a lab study without real-world consequences (Kiker & Motowidlo, 1999; Orr, Sackett, & Mercer, 1989). Thus, participants are saying what they *intend* to do. Meta-analytic results show a corrected correlation between OCB and reward recommendations of .77. However, the corrected correlation between OCB and *actual* rewards is only .26 (N. P. Podsakoff et al., 2009). The authors commented that recommendations do not always translate into actual rewards. Indeed, research on intentions shows there is a significant gap between what individuals intend to do and their actual behavior. Intentions account for roughly 28% of the variance in behavior (see meta-analysis by Sheeran, 2002), suggesting that while intentions may be important, they are not the same thing as actual behavior. As such, intentions to reward an employee may not lead to actual rewards for the individual. Thus, there is a difference in the strength of the relationship between OCB and a subjective recommendation compared to OCB and an objective outcome.

Citizenship Behavior and Objective Career Outcomes

The relationship between organizational citizenship behavior and objective career outcomes has received relatively less attention than other individual outcomes of citizenship behavior. By objective career outcomes (e.g., Judge, Cable, Boudreau, & Bretz, 1995), we refer to such outcomes as productivity, salary, promotions, and the like. Table 9.1 summarizes studies conducted on such career outcomes. The authors of each study are listed in the first column. The study design (field or lab, i.e., experimental) is in the second column. The third column contains the sample used in each study. The fourth column, labeled "OCB response scale," lists how OCB was measured (e.g., as a rating of frequency [how often one engages in OCB], as effectiveness [in terms of the value of the OCB], etc.). The fifth column indicates whether a measure of task or in-role behavior was included in the study. The sixth column gives the type of control system (discussed later, i.e., the organizational reward system). Finally, the relevant results of each study are presented in the last column, indicating the type of relationship between OCB and the outcome variable. Where possible, we have included the type of OCB investigated in each study. The majority of studies, however, seemed to use a global measure of OCB, often combining items from different dimensions to form a composite scale. The 17 published papers (containing 19 studies) are organized by outcome variable (e.g., rewards, promotion) and type of control system. As such, studies that included more than one outcome variable appear in Table 9.1 more than once. Control systems are an important factor because they may moderate the relationships between OCB and career outcomes (Bergeron, 2007; Bergeron et al., 2013).

The two dominant types of organizational control systems are *behavior-based* control systems and *outcome-based* control systems (Ouchi, 1980). Control systems are used to ensure that an individual's goals are aligned with an organization's goals. Such systems monitor and reward individuals so they pursue the collective interest (Eisenhardt, 1985). Organizations using behavior-based systems focus on monitoring inputs (i.e., employee behaviors), rather than on monitoring results (Oliver & Anderson, 1994). Common examples of behavior-based reward systems include customer service, patient care, marketing or human resources, and administrative roles. The evaluation processes in behavior-based reward systems are more subjective and complex based on what employees know (e.g., knowledge, aptitude) and what employees do (i.e., behaviors), and require high levels of management direction. Managers generally rate employees on a number of behaviors, which may be used to create a composite performance evaluation. In contrast, outcome-based control systems focus on monitoring outputs and rely heavily on objective results (Oliver & Anderson, 1994). Common contexts with this type of reward system include sales, professional service firms, and research universities. In such systems, there is a focus on objective results rather than on behaviors, often with less managerial direction and relatively less monitoring of employee behaviors (Oliver & Anderson,

Table 9.1 **Summary of Empirical Studies on Organizational Citizenship Behavior and Objective Career Outcomes**

Author	Study Design	Sample	OCB Response Scale	Task or In-Role Behavior	Control (i.e., Reward) System[1]	Relationships Between IRB, OCB, and Outcomes[2]
Productivity						
Marshall, Moncrief, Lassk, & Shepherd (2012)	Field study	Salespeople (n = 207)	Effectiveness	No	Largely behavior-based	OCB Number of Sales Calls ($\beta = .30^{*}$) % of Sales Quota Reached, *ns*
Piercy, Cravens, Lane, & Vorhies (2006)	Field study	Salespeople (n = 214)	Effectiveness	Yes	Largely behavior-based	Overall Productivity[a] OCB-altruism ($\beta = .16^{*}$) OCB-team building ($\beta = .14^{*}$) OCB-civic virtue ($\beta = .16^{**}$) OCB-sportsmanship ($\beta = .16^{*}$) In-role behavior (IRB) ($\beta = .54^{*}$)
Bergeron, Ostroff, Schroeder, & Block (2014)[b]	Field study	Faculty members in research universities (n = 614)	Frequency	Yes	Outcome-based	Short-Term Productivity OCB ($\beta = -.14^{**}$) IRB ($\beta = .28^{**}$) Long-Term Productivity OCB ($\beta = -.13^{**}$) IRB ($\beta = .19^{**}$)
Lowery & Krilowicz (1994)[c]	Field study	Sewing machine operators (n = 73)	Effectiveness	No	Outcome-based	*Performance Evaluation* ($r = .82^{**}$) Earnings ($r = .31^{*}$)
MacKenzie, Podsakoff, & Paine (1999)[c]	Field study	Insurance agents (n = 987) Managers (n = 161)	Effectiveness	No	Outcome-based	*Performance Evaluation*[d] OCB-helping ($\beta = .48^{**}/.07$) OCB-civic virtue ($\beta = .14^{**}/.16^{**}$) OCB-sportsmanship ($\beta = .11^{**}/.04$) Policies Sold, *ns* for all dimensions Sales Commissions OCB-helping ($r = .12^{*}$) OCB-civic virtue ($r = .02$, *ns*) OCB-sportsmanship ($r = .07^{*}$) *Performance Evaluation*[d] OCB-helping ($\beta = .25^{**}/.34^{*}$) OCB-civic virtue ($\beta = .39^{**}/.48^{**}$) OCB-sportsmanship ($\beta = .16/.30$) Manager Sales Commissions OCB-helping ($r = -.19^{*}$) OCB-civic virtue ($r = -.25^{**}$) OCB-sportsmanship ($r = -.11$, *ns*)

(continued)

Table 9.1 Continued

Author	Study Design	Sample	OCB Response Scale	Task or In-Role Behavior	Control (i.e., Reward) System[1]	Relationships Between IRB, OCB, and Outcomes[2]
Puffer (1987)[c]	Field study	Salespeople (n = 141)	Frequency	No	Outcome-based	Sales Performance OCB (β = –.03, *ns*)
Salary and Financial Rewards						
Allen (2006)	Field study	Utility company employees & members of women's profess. association (n = 440)	Unclear (Williams & Anderson, 1991)	No	Mixed	Salary OCBI (β = –.03, *ns*) OCBO (β = –.01 *ns*)
Marshall, Moncrief, Lassk, & Shepherd (2012)	Field study	Salespeople (N = 207)	Effectiveness	No	Largely behavior-based	Compensation OCB (β = –.18*)
Orr, Sackett, & Mercer (1989)	Policy capturing study	Medical supply managers (n = 17)	Effectiveness	Yes	Behavior-based	Dollar Value of Performance OCB (13% of variance)[e] TB (63%–68% of variance)
Seibert, Kraimer, & Crant, 2001	Field study	Employees (n = 180) and supervisors	Effectiveness	No	Mixed	Salary Increase OCB-voice (β = –.31**)
Bergeron, Shipp, Rosen, & Furst (2013)	Field study	Consultants in a professional services firm (n = 3,680)	Time spent	Yes	Outcome-based	Salary Increase OCB (β = –.05**) IRB (β = .32**)
Other Rewards						
Allen & Rush (1998)[f]	Field study Lab study	Managers in a mfg. firm (n = 148) Undergraduates (n = 136)	Agreement Manipulated	Yes Yes	Mixed Behavior-based	*Performance Evaluation* OCB (β = .31**) IRB (β = .43**) Reward Recommendations OCB (β = .39**) IRB (β = .51**) *Performance Evaluation* OCB (β = .30**) IRB (β = .58**) Reward Recommendations OCB (β = .41**) IRB (β = .62**)

Heilman & Chen (2005)[g]	Lab study Lab study	Undergraduates (n = 135) MA-level students working full-time (n = 99)	Manipulated Manipulated	No No	Behavior-based Behavior-based	*Performance Evaluation* OCB-altruism (M = 5.41) Reward Recommendations OCB-altruism (M = 5.51) *Performance Evaluation* OCB-altruism (M = 5.61) Reward Recommendations OCB-altruism (M = 5.17)
Johnson, Erez, Kiker, & Motowidlo (2002)	Lab study	Undergraduates (n = 106)	N/A	No	Behavior-based	Reward Recommendations OCB-helping ($\beta = .63^{**}$)[h]
Kiker & Motowidlo (1999)	Lab study	Undergraduates (n = 494)	N/A	Yes	Behavior-based	Reward Recommendations OCB ($\eta^2 = .14^{*}$) IRB ($\eta^2 = .31^{*}$)
Van Scotter, Motowidlo, & Cross (2000)[i]	Field study	Sample 1: Air Force mechanics (n = 422) Sample 2: Air Force mechanics (n = 991)	Likelihood	Yes	Behavior-based	Medals OCB ($\Delta R^2 = .04^{**}$) IRB ($\Delta R^2 = .02^{*}$) Rewards OCB ($\Delta R^2 = .08^{**}$) IRB ($\Delta R^2 = .03^{**}$) Medals OCB ($\Delta R^2 = .02^{**}$ IRB ($\Delta R^2 = .04^{**}$) Rewards OCB ($\Delta R^2 = .08^{**}$) IRB ($\Delta R^2 = .04^{**}$)
Yun, Takeuchi, & Liu (2007)	Field study	Managers rated employees (n = 84)	Unclear (Williams & Anderson, 1991)	Yes	Mixed	Reward Recommendations OCBI ($\beta = .36^{**}$) OCBO ($\beta = .21^{*}$) IRB (β = .16, *ns*)
Promotion and Advancement Speed						
Allen (2006)	Field study	Utility company employees & members of women's profess. association (n = 440)	Unclear (Williams & Anderson, 1991)	No	Mixed	Promotion OCBI ($\beta = .25^{**}$) OCBO ($\beta = .32^{**}$)
Hui, Lam, & Law (2000)	Field study	Bank tellers (n = 359) and their supervisors (n = 90)	Effectiveness	No	Hybrid system	Promotion OCB ($\beta = .18^{**}$)

(*continued*)

Table 9.1 Continued

Author	Study Design	Sample	OCB Response Scale	Task or In-Role Behavior	Control (i.e., Reward) System[1]	Relationships Between IRB, OCB, and Outcomes[2]
Seibert, Kraimer, & Crant, 2001	Field study	Employees (n = 180) and supervisors	Effectiveness	No	Mixed	Promotion OCB-voice ($\beta = -.31^{**}$)
Van Scotter, Motowidlo, & Cross (2000)[i]	Field study	Sample 1: Air Force mechanics (n = 422) Sample 2: Air Force mechanics (n = 991)	Likelihood	Yes	Behavior-based	*Promotability Rating* OCB ($\Delta R^2 = .16^{**}$) IRB ($\Delta R^2 = .06^{**}$) Promotion (one year later) OCB ($\Delta R^2 = .00$, *ns*) IRB ($\Delta R^2 = .02^{*}$) Promotion (two years later) OCB ($\Delta R^2 = .00$, *ns*) IRB ($\Delta R^2 = .02^{*}$) *Promotability Rating* OCB ($\Delta R^2 = .12^{**}$) IRB ($\Delta R^2 = .10^{**}$) Promotion (one year later) OCB ($\Delta R^2 = .03^{**}$) IRB ($\Delta R^2 = .03^{**}$) Promotion (two years later) OCB ($\Delta R^2 = .03^{**}$) IRB ($\Delta R^2 = .01^{**}$)
Bergeron, Ostroff, Schroeder, & Block (2014)[b]	Field study	Faculty members in research universities (n = 614)	Frequency	Yes	Outcome-based	Promotion OCB ($\beta = -.07$, *ns*) IRB ($\beta = .49^{**}$) Advancement Speed OCB ($\beta = -.10^{*}$) IRB ($\beta = .11^{*}$)

Bergeron, Shipp, Rosen, & Furst (2013)	Field study	Consultants in a professional services firm (n = 3,680)	Time spent	Yes	Outcome-based	*Performance Evaluation* OCB (β = .04*) IRB (β = .21**) Promotion OCB (β = –.02, *ns*) IRB (β = .02**) Advancement Speed OCB (β = –.06**) IRB (β = .18**)

* $p < .05$;
** $p < .01$.
[1] This variable was coded according to information provided within each paper. "Hybrid" reward systems are those that use a blend of both behavior and outcomes in determining rewards. For instance, Hui et al. (2000) note that "promotion . . . was based on both objective performance indicators and managers' evaluations of the teller's performance" (p. 825). Two of the studies with hybrid systems, however, noted a heavy emphasis on behaviors; that is, Marshall et al. (2012) state the "performance management system and related compensation plan reflect a bias toward behavioral based control . . . a heavy base [salary] plus commission/bonus orientation" (pp. 493–494), comprised of 67% salary and 33% commission. Similarly, Piercy et al. (2006) state that the reward system is heavily weighted toward behaviors with only 15% of total compensation based on incentive pay. Hence, these two studies are coded as "Largely Behavior-Based." "Mixed" reward systems are those that likely contain participants from both types of pure reward systems (outcome- and behavior-based) as well as hybrid systems. For instance, the samples of both Seibert et al. (2001) and Yun et al. (2007) represent various organizations and industries (e.g., accounting, engineering, manufacturing, finance, professional services, nursing); thus, it is likely that some participants (e.g., those in professional services, sales) were in outcome-based systems, some were in behavior-based systems (e.g., nursing, marketing), and others may have been in hybrid systems (e.g., finance) with differential weightings of behaviors and objective performance measures. Descriptions of outcome-based and behavior-based control systems are in the text.
[2] Unless otherwise noted, OCB was measured using a global OCB measure, often consisting of items taken from two or more OCB dimensions.
[a] Composite outcome measure consisting of a combination of percentage of sales target achieved, contribution to sales unit revenue, and meeting annual sales targets.
[b] Professional service OCB was not included in the table as it is a categorically different type of OCB.
[c] Because this organization's compensation system is based on productivity, sales commission is essentially more a measure of productivity than of salary or financial rewards.
[d] The first set of numbers is not controlling for common method variance; the second set of numbers is controlling for common method variance.
[e] Only 10 of the 17 supervisors took OCB into account; all 17 took IRB or task behavior into account.
[f] Allen and Rush (2001) also examined the relationship between OCB and reward recommendations but only reported interactions effects with gender. They did not report main effects of OCB; therefore, this study was not included in the review.
[g] Means across gender for helping conditions were used.
[h] Results were taken from study 2, Table 5.
[i] Results were taken from step 2 in Tables 3 and 4.
IRB, in-role behavior; *ns*, nonsignificant; OCB = organizational citizenship behavior; OCBI = OCB directed toward an individual; OCBO OCB directed toward the organization.

1995). Instead, employees are held responsible for their results, which are generally assessed by some type of objective measure (e.g., sales, billable hours, publications), against which employees are evaluated and rewarded. Of the nineteen studies, nine took place in behavior-based or largely behavior-based control systems, five were in outcome-based control systems, four reflected mixed systems (i.e., participants were likely from both types of systems or hybrid systems), and one was categorized as a hybrid system (i.e., including both behavior and outcome-based components). For each outcome variable (e.g., productivity), studies are reviewed according to the type of system in which they were categorized.

Productivity

The findings with regard to OCB and productivity are discrepant—both across the six studies and even within studies. For example, in the studies conducted in behavior-based systems, one study found no relationship between the OCB of salespeople and their productivity (Piercy, Cravens, Lane, & Vorhies, 2006) while another found mixed results (Marshall, Moncrief, Lassk, & Shepherd, 2012). In the latter study, Marshall et al. found a positive relationship between salespersons' OCB and the number of sales calls made, but no relationship between OCB and the percentage of sales quota reached. In the former study, Piercy et al. found that task behavior fully mediated the relationship between four OCB dimensions and productivity, such that OCB had no significant direct relationships to productivity when task behavior was included in the model.

Studies in outcome-based systems followed a similar pattern but included a wider range of results. In a field study of sewing machine operators (Lowery & Krilowicz, 1994), there was a positive relationship between OCB and earnings (which was essentially a measure of productivity as this was a piece-work incentive system). Puffer (1987) found no relationship between the frequency of OCB and sales performance in a sample of retail furniture salespeople. She suggests OCB may help the organization but may not provide tangible benefits to the individual. A study by MacKenzie, Podsakoff, and Paine (1999) had two samples, each showing different results for three OCB dimensions. In the sample of insurance agents, none of the three types of OCB had any relationship to the number of policies sold. With regard to sales commissions, both helping and sportsmanship had positive relationships while civic virtue was not significantly related. The second sample was the insurance agents' managers. In this sample, all three OCB dimensions had a negative relationship to the managers' sales commissions, although they were positively related to performance evaluations and had a positive relationship to unit-level productivity. This study is interesting because it shows that OCB may have different effects at different levels of an organization's hierarchy. Although OCB hindered the managers' personal productivity, it enhanced the productivity of the unit as a whole, which is the manager's main responsibility. Finally, in a sample of faculty members in research universities, frequency of OCB was associated with lower research productivity (Bergeron, Ostroff, Schroeder, & Block, 2014). In this study, OCB was negatively related to both short-term publications (over the previous 3 years) and long-term publications (over the course of the career). In this set of studies on productivity, there are two notable occurrences. The first is that two studies included a measure of task behavior (Bergeron et al., 2014; Piercy et al., 2006) and both showed a positive relationship between task behavior and productivity. In these same studies, OCB either had a negative or nonsignificant relationship to productivity (after considering the effect of in-role behavior), suggesting the importance of including a measure of task or in-role behavior. The second notable finding is that the negative relationships between OCB and productivity only occurred in outcome-based systems. We comment more on these two issues further in the chapter.

Salary and Financial Rewards

With regard to salary and financial rewards, this small set of studies ($n = 5$) seems to suggest that OCB either has no impact or even a negative impact on financial outcomes, regardless of the type of control system. In a mixed sample (utility company employees, members of a women's professional association), Allen (2006) found that two OCB dimensions, OCB directed at specific individuals (OCBI) and at an organization (OCBO; Williams & Anderson, 1991), were not related to salary. In a study designed to understand how managers use information when valuing performance (Orr et al., 1989), 17 managers in a large medical supply company rated the profiles of 50 hypothetical programmer analysts. Each profile had ratings on 10 dimensions of task or in-role behavior and 3 dimensions of OCB. The results showed that all 17 managers took task behavior into account when evaluating performance, but only 10 managers took OCB into account. Task behavior accounted for 63%–68% of the variance in dollar value performance while OCB accounted for an additional 13% of the variance. In a field study of salespeople, results showed that both civic virtue and helping behavior were negatively related to compensation (Marshall et al., 2012). Because this was largely a behavior-based system (compensation was 67% salary), the authors expected that salespeople would be financially rewarded for engaging in helpful behaviors. Their explanation for the negative results was that OCB was only one of a number of factors which influence compensation (e.g., past sales, favoritism, tenure). In a sample of employees and supervisors, results showed that OCB (in the form of voice) was negatively related to salary increase (Seibert, Kraimer, & Crant, 2001). These authors were also expecting a positive relationship and suggested that this form of OCB is challenging and can be perceived as critical, which may cause friction in interpersonal relationships (Van Dyne & LePine, 1998). Finally, in a sample of consultants in a professional services firm, results showed that OCB was negatively related to salary increase (Bergeron et al., 2013). In this instance, it was an outcome-based control system and OCB was measured as time spent on this category of behaviors. Thus, it seems that time spent on OCB took time away from focusing on results (i.e., billable hours). In this same study, task behavior was strongly and positively related to salary increase ($\beta = .32, p < .01$).

Other Rewards

With regard to rewards, all eight studies (nine samples) found a positive relationship between OCB and rewards or reward recommendations. For example, Allen and Rush (1998) found a positive relationship between OCB, task behavior, and overall reward recommendations (e.g., a composite of several items, including a fast track development program, pay increase, promotion, etc.) in both a lab study of undergraduates and a mixed field sample of managers from many organizations. Task behavior, however, seemed to have a stronger relationship to reward recommendations than did OCB. A positive relationship between OCB and reward recommendations was also found in three other laboratory studies with student samples (two in Heilman & Chen, 2005; one in D. E. Johnson, Erez, Kiker, & Motowidlo, 2002). A study by Kiker and Motowidlo (1999), including both task behavior and OCB, found main effects for both variables but showed that task behavior had more than double the impact of OCB on reward decisions. The authors also found a significant interaction such that the benefit of task behavior increased with higher OCB, and the benefit of OCB increased with higher task behavior. Their explanation is that "raters discount the value of effectiveness in one dimension when they notice ineffective performance on another important dimension" (p. 607). In a field study of participants from a variety of companies (Yun et al., 2007), both OCBI and OCBO were positively related to reward recommendations. Interestingly, in this same study, task behavior had no significant relationship to reward recommendations. It may be that the variety of jobs in this mixed sample (e.g., nurse, software engineer, management consulting, mortgage broker) represented different types of control systems in which OCB relationships may differ, or it may be because the outcome measure was a composite of different rewards which may have muddied the results.

The only study to examine actual rewards (as opposed to reward recommendations) was a field study using two samples of Air Force mechanics (Van Scotter, Motowidlo, & Cross, 2000). In this study, both awards (i.e., medals) and rewards were included as outcome variables. Rewards included such items as a recommendation for a new position or additional training, a nomination for an award, a letter of appreciation, or being put in charge of a special project. The results showed that OCB was positively related to both medals and rewards in both samples. Interestingly, task behavior showed a positive relationship to medals in both samples but not to rewards. It seems that these types of informal rewards may be a key way in which supervisors can informally recognize a subordinate's OCB performance. The authors contend that if OCB has value, supervisors will find ways, either formal or informal, to acknowledge it.

Promotion and Advancement Speed

Of the six studies examining promotion, two had mixed samples, one had a hybrid system, one was in a behavior-based control system, and two were in outcome-based control systems. All six used field samples. Within the behavior-based, mixed and hybrid samples, the results for the relationship between OCB and promotion were varied. In the mixed samples, Allen (2006) found no relationship between OCBI and promotion but found a positive relationship between OCBO and promotion (although the results were stronger for males than females). Similar to their results for salary, Seibert et al. (2001) found a negative relationship between OCB (voice) and promotion. The authors point out that organizations want employees to speak up and create change but may actually punish employees who do so. In the hybrid system, a study of bank tellers and their supervisors showed a positive relationship between promotion and both supervisor and self-ratings of OCB (Hui, Lam, & Law, 2000). The final study, a behavior-based field study, included two samples of Air Force mechanics (Van Scotter et al., 2000). This study also included promotability ratings. In the first sample, OCB was positively related to the promotability ratings but had no relationship to promotion (i.e., rank) either 1 or 2 years later. Task behavior was positively related to promotability rating as well as to promotion both 1 and 2 years later. In the second sample, OCB and task behavior were both positively related to promotability ratings and to rank 1 and 2 years later.

The last two studies were in outcome-based control systems and both included measures of task behavior. In examining the relationship between OCB and promotion, the researchers also included a measure of career advancement speed (Bergeron et al., 2013, 2014). Both studies found that task behavior was positively related to promotion and advancement speed; and both found that OCB was not significantly related to promotion but was negatively related to advancement speed. In the sample of academics (Bergeron et al., 2014), in which OCB was assessed as how often individuals engaged in OCB, results showed that faculty members who engaged in OCB more frequently either plateaued at the associate rank or took longer to advance to full professor. In the sample of consultants (Bergeron et al., 2013), in which OCB was assessed as time spent on OCB, those who spent more time on OCB took longer to be promoted to the next rank. It is noteworthy that in the latter sample OCB had a positive relationship to performance evaluation. Post hoc analyses in this study showed that performance evaluation was a strong predictor of promotion but had no relationship to career advancement speed.[1]. Furthermore, after controlling for performance evaluation, OCB continued to be negatively related to advancement speed (as well as salary) and task behavior continued to be positively related to salary and advancement speed. The authors point out that if promotion had been the only career outcome examined, they would have concluded that OCB is important because it contributes to performance evaluations which are a key determinant of promotion. Instead, they state that promotion:

> is essentially a "tournament" (Turner, 1960). That is, a competition among a number of employees for the same position where the most deserving person wins. High performance evaluations are the cost of entry to get into the tournament. However, once you are in the game, task performance determines who wins the fastest. Thus, performance evaluations may be a "necessary but not sufficient" condition for advancement in outcome-based control systems. (p. 977)

Summary

It is important to acknowledge that there are many differences across the set of studies (e.g., type of control system, lack of task or in-role behavior measure, OCB operationalization) which limit the conclusions that can be drawn. Second, due to the small number of studies, it is imperative that more research be conducted that holds a greater number of variables constant across studies. To summarize the studies, OCB seems to have a mixed relationship with productivity, showing positive, negative, and nonsignificant relationships. Some of the results may depend on the type of control system and some may be due to the lack of inclusion of a measure of task behavior. For salary and financial rewards, OCB seems to have a negative or nonsignificant relationship, regardless of the type of system. OCB does, however, have a positive relationship with rewards and reward recommendations. With regard to promotion, most of the studies indicated that the relationship between OCB and promotion was either minimal or not significant. Two of the studies that did show a positive relationship (Allen, 2006; Hui et al., 2000) did not include measures of task behavior, which makes it difficult to know the true relationship between OCB and promotion. With regard to career advancement (at least in outcome-based systems), the available research shows that OCB is not related to promotion and that it results in slower career advancement speed. For most outcomes, the overall trend is that task behavior is more important than OCB in determining these outcomes. Of the 19 studies only 9 included measures of both OCB and task behavior. Seven studies showed that task behavior was much more important than OCB in terms of objective career outcomes. Although OCB did have a negative relationship to outcomes in some of the studies, in no case did task behavior ever have a negative relationship to any of the outcomes (in contrast, OCB was negative 11 times). It may be that task behavior is much more important in determining lagged outcomes because "doing your job" is what is most important and closest to the organization's mission (Borman & Motowidlo, 1993), whereas OCB (although informally rewarded and acknowledged in performance evaluations) may not be as strongly coupled to such outcomes.

A Resource Allocation Framework

The aforementioned patterns beg the question of where employee time is better spent—on OCB or task behavior. Past theoretical frameworks examining OCB have used a social exchange perspective (Konovsky & Pugh, 1994; Van Dyne & Ang, 1998) or an impression management perspective (e.g., Bolino, 1999). Employing a resource allocation framework, Bergeron (2007) proposed that there may be a career cost to good citizens, that is, those who perform high levels of OCB (Bateman & Organ, 1983). Resource allocation is the process by which limited resources (i.e., time, energy) are allocated among different activities (Becker, 1965; Robert & Hockey, 1997). In the context of job performance, employees must make decisions as to what behaviors and activities they will allocate their limited time. Because it can be difficult to engage in two types of behavior at the same time (Schmidt & Dolis, 2009), it becomes a zero-sum choice such that individuals are forced to choose one activity (e.g., OCB) at the expense of another (e.g., task behavior). In this way, behaviors may not be independent of each other.

Bergeron proposed that time allocated to OCB may come at a cost to task behavior and vice versa, such that there is a tradeoff between the two types of job behaviors. Extant research including both task behavior and OCB (e.g., Allen & Rush, 1998; Avila, Fern, & Mann, 1988; Turnley, Bolino, Lester, & Bloodgood, 2003; Yun et al., 2007), however, would seem to dispute this. Such research tends to show a positive and moderately strong correlation between the two types of job performance. In fact, the results of two meta-analyses show that the average correlation between task behavior and OCB ranges between .47 and .60 (Hoffman et al., 2007; N. P. Podsakoff et al., 2009).

To explain this, Bergeron et al. (2013) suggested that one reason for this positive relationship is due to the manner in which OCB is measured. Most work on OCB has investigated its effectiveness in terms of supervisory ratings (J. W. Johnson, 2001; Rotundo & Sackett, 2002) or self-reports using Likert-type response formats, as evidenced in Table 9.1 (column 4). This is in contrast to alternative measurements of OCB such as its frequency (e.g., Bergeron et al., 2013; Puffer, 1987) or how much time is spent on such behaviors (Bergeron et al., 2013; Borman, Dorsey, & Ackerman, 1992). From a resource allocation perspective, such measures may be more important than measures of effectiveness. It is quite easy to imagine an employee who spends little time on OCB but is rated as quite effective while another spends a lot of time on OCB but it goes unnoticed. Regardless, the latter individual still subsumes the "time cost" (Bergeron, 2007, p. 1090) of engaging in OCB, and this time may be at the cost of task behavior and subsequent productivity.

Several studies show the tradeoff between OCB and other activities. Bergeron et al. (2013) showed that time spent on OCB was negatively related to time spent on task performance ($\beta = -.40$, $p < .01$), and it was subsequently negatively related to important career outcomes. In another study, when participants were given a difficult goal, they chose not to spend time helping others in order to increase their task performance (Wright, George, Farnsworth, & McMahan, 1993). In yet another study, employees who were perceived as performing too many unreciprocated favors had lower productivity (Flynn, 2003). Results of a study at the team level showed that time-consuming types of OCB had negative relationships with performance in certain groups (Nielsen, Bachrach, Sundstrom, & Halfhill, 2012).

When task behavior is more important than OCB in determining certain career outcomes, individuals who spend too much time on OCB may have less career success, particularly over time (e.g., Bergeron, 2007; Bergeron et al., 2013, 2014). This is because the impact of OCB is longer term in that such behaviors cumulate (Merton, 1973; Organ, 1988). Some research suggests that levels of OCB remain somewhat consistent over time showing fairly high correlations between measures of OCB using self-reported, co-worker-rated and supervisor-rated measures of OCB. For instance, over a 6-month period of time, these significant correlations ranged from .37 to .71 with an average correlation of .60 (Donaldson, Ensher, & Grant-Vallone, 2000; Hui et al., 2000; Vigoda-Gadot & Angert, 2007). Over a 1-year period, the average correlation across four OCB dimensions was .72 (Blakely, Andrews, & Fuller, 2003). Finally, over a period of 5 years, two different OCB dimensions were correlated .49 and .72, respectively (Bergeron, Schroeder, Martinez, Amdurer, & van Esch, 2012). Thus, there seems to be some empirical support for the consistency of OCB over time, suggesting that the effect can be cumulative.

Most research has been conducted in behavior-based control systems where a wide variety of behaviors are evaluated and rewarded. In such systems, it is possible to compensate for low task behavior by engaging in OCB (M. A. Griffin, Neal, & Neale, 2000). Therefore, it is not surprising that OCB tends to exhibit positive relationships with individual outcomes (e.g., N. P. Podsakoff et al., 2009). In outcome-based systems, however, there is less variance and flexibility with regard to what is rewarded. As such, the tradeoff between OCB and task behavior is exacerbated in such systems for at least two reasons. First, task behavior tends to be much more important than OCB in such systems (Piercy et al., 2006). Second, because results are what count and tend to be measured objectively (Oliver & Anderson, 1994), it is unlikely that high levels of OCB can compensate for poor task behavior. Given that productivity is what is rewarded in this type of system, engaging in OCB takes time away from results and therefore is negatively related to certain objective career outcomes (Bergeron et al., 2013, 2014).

It is clear that much more research is needed in determining the relationship between OCB and career outcomes. Beyond addressing the issues already mentioned (i.e., including a measure of task behavior in all OCB research; measuring actual rewards vs. recommendations), it is critical that we conduct more studies that go beyond performance evaluations and also include objective career outcomes (compensation, actual rewards, promotion, advancement speed). Future research should also replicate any findings from laboratory samples with managerial samples. Lab studies lack the realism and constraints of real-world settings. Allen and Rush (1998) noted that there are no consequences for students who assign rewards or make recommendations in a lab setting. In contrast, managers face direct personal consequences. Not only do managers confront budgetary constraints in determining salaries, but they also face a limited number of open positions for promotion and have certain political realities to consider. Thus, the results of lab studies cannot be generalized to field settings when such important outcomes are under investigation.

A Future Research Agenda: Unresolved Questions and Recommendations

Organ (1988) noted that "what one does to enhance OCB may well militate against the attainment of . . . other valued commodities" (p. 109). Thus, spending too much time on OCB may come at a cost to productivity, career progression, or other important outcomes. Our review shows that OCB can have a positive relationship to performance evaluations but no relationship (or even a negative relationship) to other, arguably more important, career outcomes. Thus, the relationship between OCB and objective career outcomes may be different than the relationship between OCB and performance evaluations. Given this, the simplistic conclusion would be that time is better spent on task behavior than on OCB. This thinking would be faulty for two reasons. First, it assumes the relationship between task behavior and outcomes is linear. It is more likely that the impact of task behavior on career outcomes levels off at a certain point (at least in behavior-based control systems). Second, it eschews the possibility of OCB having positive indirect relationships that may have a powerful impact on objective career outcomes. We discuss this and other future research directions next.

Explore Indirect Positive Relationships Between Organizational Citizenship Behavior and Outcomes

Past research shows that other variables have indirect relationships to OCB which may influence career outcomes. For example, Allen and Rush (1998) found that liking and attribution of motive are mediators of the relationships between OCB and reward recommendations. Similarly, OCB has positive relationships to both supervisor liking (Bolino, Varela, Bande, & Turnley, 2006) and leader–member exchange (Ilies, Nahrgang, & Morgeson, 2007). Based on social exchange theory, exchanges tend to be ongoing transactions that are mutually beneficial (Blau, 1964) and are often reciprocated (Gouldner, 1960). These exchange relationships may take multiple forms. First, OCB may come back to individuals indirectly in the form of information, resources, or support, all of which have been shown to be positively related to higher salaries and more promotions (Seibert, Kraimer, & Liden, 2001). Second, OCB is a way to build social capital (Bolino, Turnley, & Bloodgood, 2002). This increased social capital may result in better relationships with high-status others and lead to better social network positions (e.g., Podolny & Baron, 1997) which are related to higher career success (Burt, 1992; Seibert et al., 2001). Third, OCB may be rewarded indirectly in the form of mentoring (Lapierre, Bonaccio, & Allen, 2009). Mentoring has been shown to have a significant positive impact on a number of career outcomes, including compensation, number of promotions, salary growth, and career satisfaction (see meta-analysis by Allen, Eby, Poteet, Lentz, & Lima, 2004). Finally, according to signaling theory (Spence, 1973), engaging in OCB can be a way to indicate one's competence and build one's reputation (Salamon & Deutsch, 2006), which is positively related to reward decisions (D. E. Johnson et al., 2002). In sum, OCB may have strong indirect positive relationships to other important variables related to career success such that there is a net gain over time in terms of career outcomes (Bergeron et al., 2013).

Investigate the Target of Organizational Citizenship Behavior as a Moderator

It also seems likely that the target of OCB will moderate the relationship between OCB and objective career outcomes. Investing in OCB toward an individual is more likely to result in a reciprocal social exchange than investing in OCB toward a group or organization because OCB is likely to be more visible to an individual and because individuals are guided by the norm of reciprocity (Gouldner, 1960). Engaging in OCB toward a group however, in which there are multiple beneficiaries, may be less likely to result in an exchange because no one individual feels the need to reciprocate. Similarly, targeting OCB toward high-status individuals is likely to pay off more than targeting OCB toward low-status individuals. Indeed, Bolino (1999) proposed that the target of OCB (i.e., supervisor or coworker) may be a critical factor in managing impressions. Furthermore, higher-status individuals are likely to have more resources and power with which to reciprocate than lower-status individuals (Berger, Rosenholtz, & Zelditch, 1980; Ragins, 1997). The target of OCB is likely to be more important for women than for men because, based on social roles, women are considered to be lower status (Connell, 1987; Lips, 1991), are generally found in lower organizational positions (Eagly & Steffen, 1984; Reskin & Ross, 1992), and are less likely to be central in social networks (Ibarra, 1992; Mehra, Kilduff, & Brass, 1998). Because men's networks tend to be made up primarily of other men (Burt, 1992; Gersick, Dutton, & Bartunek, 2000; Ibarra, 1992), women are more often excluded from informal networks (Lyness & Thompson, 2000), which can make it more difficult to develop informal mentoring relationships (Ragins & Cotton, 1991) and to access the career-enhancing benefits provided by social networks (e.g., Podolny & Baron, 1997). In sum, from a social exchange perspective, targeting OCB toward higher-status individuals seems to represent the best OCB investment. Empirical research in this realm is warranted.

Differentiate the Impact of Various Organizational Citizenship Behavior Dimensions

A third direction for future research is to investigate how different types of OCB are related to career outcomes. As evidenced in Table 9.1, OCB has varying relationships to different types of career outcomes. Part of the issue may be that many of the studies used an overall global measure of OCB rather than specific dimensions. These global measures differ in terms of their content (e.g., Marshall et al. [2012] used civic virtue and helping items while Lowery and Krilowicz [1994] used items reflective of civic virtue, sportsmanship, helping, and conscientiousness), thus likely muddying results. At least 30 forms of OCB have been proposed or researched (Organ et al., 2005). They vary in terms of how challenging or affiliative they are (Van Dyne, Cummings, & Parks, 1995), how time-consuming and costly they are (Bergeron, 2007; Nielsen et al., 2012), how visible they are, and their likelihood of being noticed or rewarded (Bergeron, 2007). As such, it is likely they have different payoffs in terms of their value. Time-consuming types of OCB are likely to have a more negative impact on career outcomes than less time-consuming types of OCB because they can detract from task behavior (Bergeron, 2007; Nielsen et al., 2012). In contrast, engaging in types of OCB that require a certain level of skill are likely to have more value than engaging in types of OCB which anyone can offer. For instance, staying late to help a coworker put together binders for a big meeting requires much less skill than working to unite two warring factions of a work team facing a tight customer deadline. We suggest that future research studies examine the impact of specific OCB dimensions on outcomes rather than an overall measure of OCB.

Examine How Time "Substitutes" Act as a Moderator

Because personal resources such as time and energy are finite (e.g., Becker, 1965) and because engaging in OCB consumes resources, having abundant resources in other areas may shift the relationship between OCB and career outcomes. Viewed through a temporal lens, job demands can be seen as proxies for time in that it takes time to fulfill the demands of one's job. For example, going on a sales call, teaching a class, or engaging in OCB all require a certain amount of time. Work resources, however, can function as time "substitutes" (Bergeron, 2010). Although it is physically impossible to add more time to a given interval (i.e., more hours cannot be added to a 24-hour day) (Becker, 1965), work resources can, in a sense, "buy time." This can happen by having extra funds, additional staff, or time-saving technology or equipment (Hobfoll, 1989).

Therefore, resources may moderate the relationship between OCB and objective career outcomes. An additional benefit is resources may make individuals more desirable as social exchange partners, possibly resulting in a higher return on social exchanges.

Tease Out the Dynamic Processes of the Citizenship Behavior–Outcomes-Citizenship Behavior Relationships

Similar to Bergeron (2007), it is our contention that the relationship between OCB and career outcomes is an ongoing dynamic process and yet it is generally studied as a one-time static process. More longitudinal work (both theoretical and empirical) on OCB is needed that begins to tease out the dynamics involved in this process (cf. Methot, Lepak, Shipp, & Boswell, 2017). For instance, although a resource allocation framework proposes that time spent on OCB is time taken away from task behavior, what happens to employees who are less competent at expected job behaviors? It may be that they step up (or are asked to step up) in terms of citizenship behaviors as a way to compensate for lower task behavior, most likely as a way to fairly distribute work within a group or department. In this way, it is not always the case that OCB is the exogenous factor with regard to career outcomes. Although a fundamental assumption in OCB research is that OCB "causes" the outcome (P. M. Podsakoff & MacKenzie, 1994, 1997), it can also be the case that OCB is the outcome (Bergeron, 2007). When OCB results as a compensatory mechanism for poor job performance, different work spiral patterns are established. That is, poor performers may be expected to engage in more OCB over time as part of their job. As such, it may become less rewarded than if it were viewed as something "extra" (Van Dyne et al., 1995). This may result in fewer opportunities (and time) to devote to task behavior which may further negatively impact career outcomes. In contrast, employees who are high task performers likely attract mentors and opportunities which lead to a positive upward trajectory in terms of career outcomes. Because of these dynamic processes, it is questionable to assume that OCB is always the antecedent. Related to this topic, it is likely that both task behavior and OCB have a point of diminishing returns in terms of career outcomes (Bergeron et al., 2014). This may only be seen, however, when viewed from a "time spent" perspective. It is important to understand if returns are, in fact, linear. Others have noted that otherwise positive attributes, when taken to the extreme, can have a negative effect on performance (Minbashian, Bright, & Bird, 2009) such that nonlinear relationships exist (Grant & Schwartz, 2011).

Assess the Impact That Organizational Variables Have on the Organizational Citizenship Behavior–Objective Career Outcomes Relationship

Research is needed to investigate how organizations can buffer against any negative individual impact of performing OCB. Although engaging in OCB consumes time, it can also require emotional resources (Cropanzano, Rupp, & Byrne, 2003), thus depleting resources needed to meet job demands (Hobfoll, 1989, 2001). If employees perceive that the organization values their contributions and cares for their well-being (Eisenberger, Huntington, Hutchison, & Sowa, 1986), provides a psychologically safe environment in which to work (Edmondson, 1999), and fulfills implicit promises (Rousseau, 1990), these positive organizational actions may serve as "a solid resource reservoir" (Hobfoll, 2001, p. 349) to replace the resource deficit created by performing high levels of OCB. More empirical research is needed to assess whether perceived organizational variables mitigate the loss of resources associated with performing OCB.

Consider Important Subjective Career Outcomes

Finally, the focus on objective career outcomes is predicated on economic assumptions. An economic way of thinking favors self-interest, rationality, and efficiency (Miller, 1999; Wang, Malhotra, & Murnighan, 2011). Clearly, objective career outcomes have instrumental and economic value and, in modern organizations, management practices encourage an economic evaluation of time use (see Pfeffer & DeVoe, 2009, for a review). However, as Miller (1999) and others have noted, "the power accorded self-interest . . . promotes a misleading and impoverished view of the human agent" (p. 1053). Individuals engage in work and, more importantly, in OCB for reasons beyond pure economic goals. Meta-analytic research shows the importance of subjective career outcomes, in addition to objective ones, for individuals (Judge et al., 1995; Ng, Eby, Sorensen, & Feldman, 2005). There are a variety of subjective outcomes that are important to individuals at work, such as job and career satisfaction (Judge, Kammeyer-Mueller, & Bretz, 2004), doing meaningful work (e.g., Wrzesniewski, McCauley, Rozin, & Schwartz, 1997), wanting to make a prosocial difference (Grant, 2007), growth and development

(Fletcher, 1998), and maintaining a state of well-being (Diener, Suh, Lucas, & Smith, 1999). Do the personal connections developed from OCB allow individuals to feel more fulfilled, have higher job satisfaction, or have less work–life conflict? Can performing OCB lead to a more grateful attitude, which positively impacts emotions toward work and life? It is likely OCB has a positive relationship to a wide variety of outcomes related to work, many of which may be more meaningful than promotion or compensation. These questions will be important going forward if the nonutilitarian benefits of OCB can compensate for some of its potential costs.

In closing, it is important for individuals to know what behaviors are rewarded and to be strategic about the behaviors in which they choose to engage. Certain aspects of any job are likely to be resource consumptive but may not result in an equivalent payoff for the time invested. It is clear that supervisors will find ways to reward OCB (perhaps informally in terms of award nominations or new opportunities), although the core part of the job (i.e., what one is hired to do) still seems to matter most in key career decisions.

Note

1. It should be noted that this study was in an outcome-based control system in which performance evaluations are strongly influenced by objective results (i.e., billable hours).

References

Allen, T. D. (2006). Rewarding good citizens: The relationship between citizenship behavior, gender, and organizational rewards. *Journal of Applied Social Psychology*, *36*(1), 120–143.

Allen, T. D., Eby, L. T., Poteet, M. L., Lentz, E., & Lima, L. (2004). Career benefits associated with mentoring for proteges: A meta-analysis. *Journal of Applied Psychology*, *89*(1), 127–136.

Allen, T. D., & Rush, M. C. (1998). The effects of organizational citizenship behavior on performance judgments: A field study and a laboratory experiment. *Journal of Applied Psychology*, *83*(2), 247–260.

Allen, T. D., & Rush, M. C. (2001). The influence of ratee gender on ratings of organizational citizenship behavior. *Journal of Applied Social Psychology*, *31*(12), 2561–2587.

Avila, R. A., Fern, E. F., & Mann, O. K. (1988). Unravelling criteria for assessing the performance of salespeople: A causal analysis. *Journal of Personal Selling & Sales Management*, *8*(1), 45–54.

Baker, G. P., Jensen, M. C., & Murphy, K. J. (1988). Compensation and incentives: Practice vs. theory. *Journal of Finance*, *43*(3), 593–616.

Baron, J. N., & Pfeffer, J. (1994). The social psychology of organizations and inequality. *Social Psychology Quarterly*, *57*, 190–209.

Bateman, T. S., & Organ, D. W. (1983). Job satisfaction and the good soldier: The relationship between affect and employee citizenship. *Academy of Management Journal*, *26*(4), 587–595.

Becker, G. S. (1965). A theory of the allocation of time. *Economic Journal*, *75*(299), 493–517.

Berger, J., Rosenholtz, S. J., & Zelditch, M. (1980). Status organizing processes. *Annual Review of Sociology*, *6*, 479–508.

Bergeron, D. M. (2007). The potential paradox of organizational citizenship behavior: Good citizens at what cost? *Academy of Management Review*, *32*(4), 1078–1095.

Bergeron, D. M. (2010, August). The role of time in resource models: Relationships between job characteristics and performance. Paper presented at the annual meeting of the Academy of Management, Toronto, Canada.

Bergeron, D. M., Ostroff, C., Schroeder, T., & Block, C. (2014). The dual effects of organizational citizenship behavior: Relationships to research productivity and career outcomes in academe. *Human Performance*, *27*(2), 99–128.

Bergeron, D. M., Schroeder, T. D., Martinez, H. M., Amdurer, E. E., & van Esch, C. (2012, August). The stability of organizational citizenship behavior over time: Women as good citizens. Paper presented at the annual meeting of the Academy of Management, Boston.

Bergeron, D. M., Shipp, A. J., Rosen, B., & Furst, S. A. (2013). Organizational citizenship behavior and career outcomes: The cost of being a good citizen. *Journal of Management*, *39*(4), 958–984.

Blakely, G. L., Andrews, M. C., & Fuller, J. (2003). Are chameleons good citizens? A longitudinal study of the relationship between self- monitoring and organizational citizenship behavior. *Journal of Business & Psychology*, *18*(2), 131–144.

Blau, P. M. (1964). *Exchange and power in social life*. New Brunswick, NJ: Transaction Publishers.

Bolino, M. C. (1999). Citizenship and impression management: Good soldiers or good actors? *Academy of Management Review*, *24*(1), 82–98.

Bolino, M. C., Klotz, A. C., Turnley, W. H., & Harvey, J. (2013). Exploring the dark side of organizational citizenship behavior. *Journal of Organizational Behavior*, *34*(4), 542–559.

Bolino, M. C., Turnley, W. H., & Bloodgood, J. M. (2002). Citizenship behavior and the creation of social capital in organizations. *Academy of Management Review*, *27*(4), 505–522.

Bolino, M. C., Turnley, W. H., & Niehoff, B. P. (2004). The other side of the story: Reexamining prevailing assumptions about organizational citizenship behavior. *Human Resource Management Review*, *14*(2), 229–246.

Bolino, M. C., Varela, J. A., Bande, B., & Turnley, W. H. (2006). The impact of impression-management tactics on supervisor ratings of organizational citizenship behavior. *Journal of Organizational Behavior*, *27*(3), 281–297.

Borman, W. C., Dorsey, D., & Ackerman, L. (1992). Time-spent responses as time allocation strategies: Relations with sales performance in a stockbroker sample. *Personnel Psychology*, *45*(4), 763–777.

Borman, W. C., & Motowidlo, S. (1993). Expanding the criterion domain to include elements of contextual performance. In N. Schmitt, & W. C. Borman (Eds.), *Personnel selection in organizations* (pp. 71–98). San Francisco, CA: Jossey-Bass.

Burt, R. S. (1992). *Structural holes: The social structure of competition*. Cambridge, MA: Harvard University Press.

Campbell, J. P. (1990). An overview of the army selection and classification project (Project A). *Personnel Psychology*, *43*(2), 231–239.

Campbell, D. (2008). Nonfinancial performance measures and promotion-based incentives. *Journal of Accounting Research*, *46*(2), 297–332.

Castilla, E. J. (2008). Gender, race, and meritocracy in organizational careers. *American Journal of Sociology, 113*(6), 1479–1526.

Castilla, E. J. (2012). Gender, race, and the new (merit-based) employment relationship. *Industrial Relations, 51*, 528–562.

Chonko, L. B., Howell, R. D., & Bellenger, D. N. (1986). Congruence in sales force evaluations: Relation to sales force perceptions of conflict and ambiguity. *Journal of Personal Selling & Sales Management, 6*(1), 35–48.

Churchill, G. A. Jr., Ford, N. M., & Walker, O. C. Jr. (1976). Organizational climate and job satisfaction in the salesforce. *Journal of Marketing Research, 13*(4), 323–332.

Clausen, T. S., Jones, K. T., & Rich, J. S. (2008). Appraising employee performance evaluation systems. *CPA Journal, 78*(2), 64–67.

Cocanougher, A. B., Ivancevich, J. M., & Sharma, S. (1978). "Bars" performance rating for sales force personnel. *The Journal of Marketing, 42*(3), 87–95.

Connell, R. W. (1987). *Gender and power: Society, the person and sexual politics*. Palo Alto, CA: Stanford University Press.

Cropanzano, R., Rupp, D. E., & Byrne, Z. S. (2003). The relationship of emotional exhaustion to work attitudes, job performance, and organizational citizenship behaviors. *Journal of Applied Psychology, 88*(1), 160–169.

DeNisi, A. S., & Stevens, G. E. (1981). Profiles of performance, performance evaluations, and personnel decisions. *Academy of Management Journal, 24*(3), 592–602.

Diener, E., Suh, E. M., Lucas, R. E., & Smith, H. L. (1999). Subjective well-being: Three decades of progress. *Psychological Bulletin, 125*(2), 276–302.

Donaldson, S., Ensher, E., & Grant-Vallone, E. (2000). Longitudinal examination of mentoring relationships on organizational commitment and citizenship behavior. *Journal of Career Development, 26*(4), 233–249.

Dubinsky, A. J., & Barry, T. E. (1982). A survey of sales management practices. *Industrial Marketing Management, 11*(2), 133–141.

Eagly, A. H., & Steffen, V. J. (1984). Gender stereotypes stem from the distribution of women and men into social roles. *Journal of Personality and Social Psychology, 46*(4), 735–754.

Edmondson, A. (1999). Psychological safety and learning behavior in work teams. *Administrative Science Quarterly, 44*(2), 350–383.

Eisenberger, R., Huntington, R., Hutchison, S., & Sowa, D. (1986). Perceived organizational support. *Journal of Applied Psychology, 71*(3), 500–507.

Eisenhardt, K. M. (1985). Control: Organizational and economic approaches. *Management Science, 31*(2), 134–149.

Fletcher, J. K. (1998). Relational practice: A feminist reconstruction of work. *Journal of Management Inquiry, 7*(2), 163–186.

Flynn, F. J. (2003). How much should I give and how often? The effects of generosity and frequency of favor exchange on social status and productivity. *Academy of Management Journal, 46*(5), 539–553.

Gersick, C. J. G., Dutton, J. E., & Bartunek, J. M. (2000). Learning from academia: The importance of relationships in professional life. *Academy of Management Journal, 43*(6), 1026–1044.

Gouldner, A. W. (1960). The norm of reciprocity: A preliminary statement. *American Sociological Review, 25*(2), 161–178.

Grant, A. M. (2007). Relational job design and the motivation to make a prosocial difference. *Academy of Management Review, 32*(2), 393–417.

Grant, A. M., & Schwartz, B. (2011). Too much of a good thing: The challenge and opportunity of the inverted U. *Perspectives on Psychological Science, 6*(1), 61–76.

Greenhaus, J. H., Parasuraman, S., & Wormley, W. M. (1990). Effects of race on organizational experience, job performance evaluations, and career outcomes. *Academy of Management Journal, 33*(1), 64–86.

Griffin, R., & Kacmar, M. (1991). Laboratory research in management: Misconceptions and missed opportunities. *Journal of Organizational Behavior, 12*(4), 301–311.

Griffin, M. A., Neal, A., & Neale, M. (2000). The contribution of task performance and contextual performance to effectiveness: Investigating the role of situational constraints. *Applied Psychology: An International Review, 49*(3), 517–533.

Heilman, M. E., & Chen, J. J. (2005). Same behavior, different consequences: Reactions to men's and women's altruistic citizenship behavior. *Journal of Applied Psychology, 90*(3), 431–441.

Hobfoll, S. E. (1989). Conservation of resources: A new attempt at conceptualizing stress. *American Psychologist, 44*(3), 513–524.

Hobfoll, S. E. (2001). The influence of culture, community, and the nested-self in the stress process: Advancing conservation of resources theory. *Applied Psychology, 50*(3), 337–421.

Hoffman, B. J., Blair, C. A., Meriac, J. P., & Woehr, D. J. (2007). Expanding the criterion domain? A quantitative review of the OCB literature. *Journal of Applied Psychology, 92*(2), 555–566.

Hui, C., Lam, S. S. K., & Law, K. K. S. (2000). Instrumental values of organizational citizenship behavior for promotion: A field quasi-experiment. *Journal of Applied Psychology, 85*(5), 822–828.

Ibarra, H. (1992). Homophily and differential returns: Sex differences in network structure and access in an advertising firm. *Administrative Science Quarterly, 37*(3), 422–447.

Igbaria, M., & Baroudi, J. J. (1995). The impact of job performance evaluations on career advancement prospects: An examination of gender differences in the IS workplace. *MIS Quarterly, 19*(1), 107–123.

Igbaria, M., & Wormley, W. M. (1992). Organizational experiences and career success of MIS professionals and managers: An examination of race differences. *MIS Quarterly, 16*(4), 507–529.

Ilies, R., Nahrgang, J. D., & Morgeson, F. P. (2007). Leader-member exchange and citizenship behaviors: A meta-analysis. *Journal of Applied Psychology, 92*(1), 269–277.

Johnson, J. W. (2001). The relative importance of task and contextual performance dimensions to supervisor judgments of overall performance. *Journal of Applied Psychology, 86*(5), 984–996.

Johnson, D. E., Erez, A., Kiker, D. S., & Motowidlo, S. J. (2002). Liking and attributions of motives as mediators of the relationships between individuals' reputations, helpful behaviors, and raters' reward decisions. *Journal of Applied Psychology, 87*(4), 808–815.

Joshi, A., Son, J., and Roh, H. (2015). When can women close the gap? A meta-analytic test of sex differences in performance and rewards. *Academy of Management Journal, 58*, 1516–1545.

Judge, T. A., Cable, D. M., Boudreau, J. W., & Bretz, R., D. Jr. (1995). An empirical investigation of the predictors of executive career success. *Personnel Psychology, 48*(3), 485–519.

Judge, T. A., Kammeyer-Mueller, J., & Bretz, R. D. (2004). A longitudinal model of sponsorship and career success. *Personnel Psychology*, *57*(2), 271–303.

Kerber, K. W., & Campbell, J. P. (1987). Correlates of objective performance among computer salespeople: Tenure, work activities, and turnover. *Journal of Personal Selling & Sales Management*, *7*(3), 39–50.

Kiker, D. S., & Motowidlo, S. J. (1999). Main and interaction effects of task and contextual performance on supervisory reward decisions. *Journal of Applied Psychology*, *84*(4), 602–609.

Konovsky, M. A., & Pugh, S. D. (1994). Citizenship behavior and social exchange. *Academy of Management Journal*, *37*(3), 656–669.

Lapierre, L. M., Bonaccio, S., & Allen, T. D. (2009). The separate, relative, and joint effects of employee job performance domains on supervisors' willingness to mentor. *Journal of Vocational Behavior*, *74*(2), 135–144.

Lips, H. M. (1991). *Women, men, and power*. Mountain View, CA: Mayfield.

London, M., & Stumpf, S. A. (1983). Effects of candidate characteristics on management promotion decisions: An experimental study. *Personnel Psychology*, *36*(2), 241–259.

Lowery, C. M., & Krilowicz, T. J. (1994). Relationships among nontask behaviors, rated performance, and objective performance measures. *Psychological Reports*, *74*(2), 571–578.

Lyness, K. S., & Heilman, M. E. (2006). When fit is fundamental: Performance evaluations and promotions of upper-level female and male managers. *Journal of Applied Psychology*, *91*(4), 777–785.

Lyness, K. S., & Thompson, D. E. (2000). Climbing the corporate ladder: Do female and male executives follow the same route? *Journal of Applied Psychology*, *85*(1), 86–101.

MacKenzie, S. B., Podsakoff, P. M., & Paine, J. B. (1999). Do citizenship behaviors matter more for managers than for salespeople? *Journal of the Academy of Marketing Science*, *27*(4), 396–410.

Marshall, G. W., Moncrief, W. C., Lassk, F. G., & Shepherd, C. D. (2012). Linking performance outcomes to salesperson organizational citizenship behavior in an industrial sales setting. *Journal of Personal Selling & Sales Management*, *32*(4), 491–502.

Mehra, A., Kilduff, M., & Brass, D. J. (1998). At the margins: A distinctiveness approach to the social identity and social networks of underrepresented groups. *Academy of Management Journal*, *41*(4), 441–452.

Merton, R. K. (1973). *The sociology of science: Theoretical and empirical investigations*. Chicago, IL: University of Chicago Press.

Methot, J., Lepak, D., Shipp, A. & Boswell, W. (2017). Good citizen interrupted: Calibrating a temporal theory of citizenship behavior. *Academy of Management Review*, *42*(1), 10–31.

Meyer, H. H. (1987). Predicting supervisory ratings versus promotional progress in test validation studies. *Journal of Applied Psychology*, *72*(4), 696–697.

Miller, D. T. (1999). The norm of self-interest. *American Psychologist*, *54*(12), 1053–1060.

Minbashian, A., Bright, J. E. H., & Bird, K. D. (2009). Complexity in the relationships among the subdimensions of extraversion and job performance in managerial occupations. *Journal of Occupational & Organizational Psychology*, *82*(3), 537–549.

Muczyk, J. P., & Gable, M. (1987). Managing sales performance through a comprehensive performance appraisal system. *Journal of Personal Selling & Sales Management*, *7*(1), 41–52.

Ng, T. W. H., Eby, L. T., Sorensen, K. L., & Feldman, D. C. (2005). Predictors of objective and subjective career success. A meta-analysis. *Personnel Psychology*, *58*(2), 367–408.

Nielsen, T. M., Bachrach, D. G., Sundstrom, E., & Halfhill, T. R. (2012). Utility of OCB: Organizational citizenship behavior and group performance in a resource allocation framework. *Journal of Management*, *38*(2), 668–694.

Oliver, R. L., & Anderson, E. (1994). An empirical test of the consequences of behavior-and outcome-based sales control systems. *Journal of Marketing*, *58*(4), 53–67.

Oliver, R. L., & Anderson, E. (1995). Behavior- and outcome-based sales control systems: Evidence and consequences of pure-form and hybrid governance. *Journal of Personal Selling & Sales Management*, *15*(4), 1–15.

Organ, D. W. (1988). *Organizational citizenship behavior: The good soldier syndrome*. Lexington, MA: Lexington Books.

Organ, D. W. (1990). The motivational basis of organizational citizenship behavior. *Research in Organizational Behavior*, *12*, 43–72.

Organ, D. W. (1997). Organizational citizenship behavior: It's construct clean-up time. *Human Performance*, *10*(2), 85–97.

Organ, D. W., Podsakoff, P. M., & MacKenzie, S. B. (2005). *Organizational citizenship behavior: Its nature, antecedents, and consequences*. Thousand Oaks, CA: Sage Publications.

Organ, D. W. & Konovsky, M. (1989). Cognitive versus affective determinants of organizational citizenship behavior. *Journal of Applied Psychology*, *74*(1), 157–164.

Orr, J. M., Sackett, P. R., & Mercer, M. (1989). The role of prescribed and nonprescribed behaviors in estimating the dollar value of performance. *Journal of Applied Psychology*, *74*(1), 34–40.

Ouchi, W. G. (1980). Markets, bureaucracies, and clans. *Administrative Science Quarterly*, *25*(1), 129–141.

Patton, W. E. III, & King, R. H. (1992). The use of human judgement models in sales force selection decisions. *Journal of Personal Selling & Sales Management*, *12*(2), 1–14.

Pfeffer, J., & DeVoe, S. E. (2009). Economic evaluation: The effect of money and economics on attitudes about volunteering. *Journal of Economic Psychology*, *30*(3), 500–508.

Piercy, N. F., Cravens, D. W., Lane, N., & Vorhies, D. W. (2006). Driving organizational citizenship behaviors and salesperson in-role behavior performance: The role of management control and perceived organizational support. *Journal of the Academy of Marketing Science*, *34*(2), 244–262.

Podolny, J. M., & Baron, J. N. (1997). Resources and relationships: Social networks and mobility in the workplace. *American Sociological Review*, *62*(5), 673–693.

Podsakoff, P. M., & MacKenzie, S. B. (1994). Organizational citizenship behaviors and sales unit effectiveness. *Journal of Marketing Research*, *31*(3), 351–363.

Podsakoff, P. M., & MacKenzie, S. B. (1997). Impact of organizational citizenship behavior on organizational performance: A review and suggestions for future research. *Human Performance*, *10*(2), 133–151.

Podsakoff, N. P., Whiting, S. W., Podsakoff, P. M., & Blume, B. D. (2009). Individual- and organizational-level consequences of organizational citizenship behaviors: A meta-analysis. *Journal of Applied Psychology*, *94*(1), 122–141.

Puffer, S. M. (1987). Prosocial behavior, noncompliant behavior, and work performance among commission salespeople. *Journal of Applied Psychology, 72*(4), 615–621.

Ragins, B. R. (1997). Diversified mentoring relationships in organizations: A power perspective. *Academy of Management Review, 22*(2), 482–521.

Ragins, B. R., & Cotton, J. L. (1991). Easier said than done: Gender differences in perceived barriers to gaining a mentor. *Academy of Management Journal, 34*(4), 939–951.

Reskin, B. F. (2003). Including mechanisms of ascriptive inequality. *American Sociological Review, 68*, 1–21.

Reskin, B. F., & Ross, C. E. (1992). Jobs, authority, and earnings among managers: The continuing significance of sex. *Work and Occupations, 19*(4), 342–365.

Robert, G., & Hockey, J. (1997). Compensatory control in the regulation of human performance under stress and high workload: A cognitive-energetical framework. *Biological Psychology, 45*(1), 73–93.

Rosen, N., Billings, R., & Turney, J. (1976). The emergence and allocation of leadership resources over time in a technical organization. *Academy of Management Journal, 19*(2), 165–183.

Rotundo, M., & Sackett, P. R. (2002). The relative importance of task, citizenship, and counterproductive performance to global ratings of job performance: A policy-capturing approach. *Journal of Applied Psychology, 87*(1), 66–80.

Rousseau, D. M. (1990). New hire perceptions of their own and their employer's obligations: A study of psychological contracts. *Journal of Organizational Behavior, 11*(5), 389–400.

Salamon, S. D., & Deutsch, Y. (2006). OCB as a handicap: An evolutionary psychological perspective. *Journal of Organizational Behavior, 27*(2), 185–199.

Scandura, T. A., & Schriesheim, C. A. (1994). Leader-member exchange and supervisor career mentoring as complementary constructs in leadership research. *Academy of Management Journal, 37*, 1588–1602.

Schmidt, A. M., & Dolis, C. M. (2009). Something's got to give: The effects of dual-goal difficulty, goal progress, and expectancies on resource allocation. *Journal of Applied Psychology, 94*(3), 678–691.

Scholl, R. W., Cooper, E. A., & McKenna, J. F. (1987). Referent selection in determining equity perceptions: Differential effects on behavioral and attitudinal outcomes. *Personnel Psychology, 40*(1), 113–124.

Schwab, D. P., & Olson, C. A. (1990). Merit pay practices: Implications for pay-performance relationships. *Industrial & Labor Relations Review, 43*(3), 237-S–255-S.

Seibert, S. E., Kraimer, M. L., & Crant, J. M. (2001). What do proactive people do? A longitudinal model linking proactive personality and career success. *Personnel Psychology, 54*(4), 845–874.

Seibert, S. E., Kraimer, M. L., & Liden, R. C. (2001). A social capital theory of career success. *Academy of Management Journal, 44*(2), 219–237.

Sheeran, P. (2002). Intention—behavior relations: A conceptual and empirical review. *European Review of Social Psychology, 12*(1), 1–36.

Siegel, S. R. (1993). Relationships between current performance and likelihood of promotion for old versus young workers. *Human Resource Development Quarterly, 4*(1), 39–50.

Spence, M. (1973). Job market signaling. *Quarterly Journal of Economics, 87*(3), 355–374.

Stewart, L. P., & Gudykunst, W. B. (1982). Differential factors influencing the hierarchical level and number of promotions of males and females within an organization. *Academy of Management Journal, 25*(3), 586–597.

Stone-Romero, E., Alvarez, K., & Thompson, L. F. (2009). The construct validity of conceptual and operational definitions of contextual performance and related constructs. *Human Resource Management Review, 19*(2), 104–116.

Stumpf, S. A., & London, M. (1981). Capturing rater policies in evaluating candidates for promotion. *Academy of Management Journal, 24*(4), 752–766.

Suazo, M. M., Martínez, P. G., & Sandoval, R. (2009). Creating psychological and legal contracts through human resource practices: A signaling theory perspective. *Human Resource Management Review, 19*(2), 154–166.

Taylor, R. N. (1975). Age and experience as determinants of managerial information processing and decision making performance. *Academy of Management Journal, 18*(1), 74–81.

Turner, R. H. (1960). Sponsored and contest mobility and the school system. *American Sociological Review, 25*(6), 855–867.

Turnley, W. H., Bolino, M. C., Lester, S. W., & Bloodgood, J. M. (2003). The impact of psychological contract fulfillment on the performance of in-role and organizational citizenship behaviors. *Journal of Management, 29*(2), 187–206.

Van Dyne, L., & Ang, S. (1998). Organizational citizenship behavior of contingent workers in Singapore. *Academy of Management Journal, 41*(6), 692–703.

Van Dyne, L., Cummings, L. L., & Parks, J. M. (1995). Extra-role behaviors: In pursuit of construct and definitional clarity (A bridge over muddied waters). *Research in Organizational Behavior, 17*, 215–285.

Van Dyne, L., & LePine, J. A. (1998). Helping and voice extra-role behaviors: Evidence of construct and predictive validity. *Academy of Management Journal, 41*(1), 108–119.

Van Scotter, J., Motowidlo, S. J., & Cross, T. C. (2000). Effects of task performance and contextual performance on systemic rewards. *Journal of Applied Psychology, 85*(4), 526–535.

Vey, M. A., & Campbell, J. P. (2004). In-role or extra-role organizational citizenship behavior: Which are we measuring? *Human Performance, 17*(1), 119–135.

Vigoda-Gadot, E., & Angert, L. (2007). Goal setting theory, job feedback, and OCB: Lessons from a longitudinal study. *Basic & Applied Social Psychology, 29*(2), 119–128.

Wang, L., Malhotra, D., & Murnighan, J. K. (2011). Economics education and greed. *Academy of Management Learning & Education, 10*(4), 643–660.

Williams, L. J., & Anderson, S. E. (1991). Job satisfaction and organizational commitment as predictors of organizational citizenship and in-role behaviors. *Journal of Management, 17*(3), 601–617.

Wright, P. M., George, J. M., Farnsworth, S. R., & McMahan, G. C. (1993). Productivity and extra-role behavior: The effects of goals and incentives on spontaneous helping. *Journal of Applied Psychology, 78*(3), 374–381.

Wrzesniewski, A., McCauley, C., Rozin, P., & Schwartz, B. (1997). Jobs, careers, and callings: People's relations to their work. *Journal of Research in Personality, 31*(1), 21–33.

Yun, S., Takeuchi, R., & Liu, W. (2007). Employee self-enhancement motives and job performance behaviors: Investigating the moderating effects of employee role ambiguity and managerial perceptions of employee commitment. *Journal of Applied Psychology, 92*(3), 745–756.

CHAPTER

10 Helping That Hurts Intended Beneficiaries: A New Perspective on the Dark Side of Helping Organizational Citizenship Behavior

Anna C. Lennard *and* Linn Van Dyne

Abstract

Organizational citizenship behavior (OCB) is essential for organizations to gain and maintain competitive advantage in environments with constantly evolving demands. Although most of the literature implicitly assumes that OCB predicts positive work attitudes, affective states, cognitions, and behavior for employees and organizations, some work raises the question of when OCB fails to produce positive consequences, and scholars have called for a more balanced perspective that acknowledges possible negative consequences of OCB. In this chapter, we focus on the unintended negative outcomes of helping OCB to recipients. More specifically, we consider factors that paradoxically cause positively intended helping to backfire and have negative effects on recipients. To date, most research on outcomes of OCB has focused on performance outcomes. In contrast, we focus on nonperformance outcomes for recipients of helping because nonperformance outcomes are more proximal and can shed light on processes that influence more distal outcomes, such as performance.

Key Words: organizational citizenship behavior, helping, empathy, self-esteem, nonperformance outcomes

Organizational citizenship behavior (OCB) is essential for organizations to maintain their competitive edge in environments with constantly evolving demands (Organ, 1988). OCB is defined as discretionary behavior that employees perform with positive intentions to contribute to the goals, functioning, and social or psychological environment of the organization (Organ, 1988; Organ, Podsakoff, & MacKenzie, 2006). These behaviors go beyond formal job requirements and include helping peers, working extra hours, assuming additional responsibilities, and speaking up with constructive suggestions for change.

Most of the literature implicitly assumes that OCB predicts positive work attitudes, affective states, cognitions, and behavior for employees and organizations (Organ, 1988; Organ et al., 2006). A smaller amount of work, however, raises the question of when OCB fails to produce positive consequences, and scholars have called for a more balanced perspective that acknowledges possible negative consequences of OCB (Van Dyne & Ellis, 2004). For example, Bolino, Turnley, and Niehoff (2004) challenged the implicit assumption that OCB has positive outcomes, and Bolino, Klotz, Turnley, and Harvey (2013) enumerated a variety of personal and professional costs of OCB. Bergeron (2007) theorized that OCB can detract from task performance in some types of jobs. Initial empirical results are consistent with these arguments and have demonstrated that OCB is positively related to stress and work–family conflict (Bolino & Turnley, 2005; Halbesleben, Harvey, & Bolino, 2009) and can be negatively related to job satisfaction, performance, and career progression (Bergeron, Shipp, Rosen, & Furst, 2013; Munyon, Hochwarter, Perrewé, & Ferris, 2010).

Organizational Citizenship Behavior as a Multidimensional Construct

It is important to note that OCB is a multidimensional construct, and there are distinct nomological networks for affiliative and change-oriented OCB (Van Dyne, Cummings, & McLean Parks, 1995). Affiliative OCB is promotive and positively intended. It aims to reinforce relationships and includes helping coworkers and showing high levels of courtesy to others. Change-oriented OCB is also promotive and positively intended. It is, however, challenging and aims to change the status quo in ways that should enhance performance (Van Dyne & LePine, 1998). Change-oriented OCB includes voice and taking charge.

In this chapter, we focus on the unintended negative outcomes of helping OCB to recipients. More specifically we consider factors that cause positively intended helping to backfire and have negative consequences for recipients of helping. In contrast to the research that has focused on performance outcomes of OCB (Detert, Burris, Harrison, & Martin, 2013; MacKenzie, P. Podsakoff, & N. Podsakoff, 2011; Maynes & P. Podsakoff, 2014; Van Dyne & LePine, 1998; Whiting, Maynes, N. Podsakoff, & P. Podsakoff, 2012; Whiting, P. Podsakoff, & Pierce, 2008), we focus on nonperformance outcomes for recipients of helping because nonperformance outcomes are more proximal and can shed light on processes that influence more distal outcomes, such as performance. Although it would also be interesting to consider unexpected negative outcomes of voice OCB, we focus on outcomes of helping OCB because the field has placed more emphasis on the paradoxical nature of voice (although positively intended, voice is not always viewed positively by others), and the literature implicitly emphasizes the overall value of helping OCB to organizations and recipients.

We note that a number of other terms are sometimes used synonymously with helping OCB. These include extra-role behavior, contextual performance, prosocial behavior, and altruism. We define each of these constructs briefly and note differences and similarities compared to helping OCB. We draw on previous research on these similar constructs in developing our model and arguments but also note important differences in the nomological networks of these constructs.

As previously indicated, OCB is "individual behavior that is discretionary, not directly or explicitly recognized by the formal reward system, and that in the aggregate promotes the effective functioning of the organization" (Organ, 1988, p. 4). OCB is therefore a form of extra-role behavior (ERB). "Extra-role behavior is defined as behavior which benefits the organization and/or is intended to benefit the organization, which is discretionary and which goes beyond existing role expectations" (Van Dyne et al., 1995, p. 218). Although OCB and ERB are similar, extra-role behavior is a broader construct. One of the key differences between OCB and ERB is that ERB need not be positively intended. Instead, it is defined as actions that fall outside formal role expectations. Thus, ERB can be positively or negatively intended. For example, OCB and counterproductive behavior are both discretionary and nonrequired extra-role behaviors. Their nomological networks, however, are significantly different.

Contextual performance (Borman & Motowidlo, 1997) is another construct that is related to OCB. Contextual performance is defined as behavior that doesn't contribute to the organization's technical core but aims to contribute to overall organizational effectiveness "in ways that shape the organization, social, and psychological context that serves as the catalyst for task activities and processes" (p. 100). Contextual performance, like OCB, includes a range of behaviors—such as cooperating and helping others complete tasks, performing behaviors not specifically required by the job, and complying with organizational procedures and rules. Accordingly, contextual performance and OCB are similar in that they are positively intended. The key difference between OCB and contextual performance is that contextual performance "does not require that the behavior be extra-role nor that it be nonrewarded" (Organ, 1997, p. 90). Instead, contextual performance is "nontask" because it contributes to the "maintenance and/or enhancement of the context of work" (Organ, 1997, p. 90).

Prosocial behavior is another set of positively intended behaviors. Penner, Dovidio, Piliavin, and Schroeder (2005) conceptualized prosocial behavior as "a broad category of acts that are defined by some segment of society and/or one's social group as generally beneficial to others." Importantly, however, prosocial behavior can be directed at strangers and does not necessarily aim to benefit an organization. Thus, some OCB could be considered a form of prosocial behavior that occurs in organizations, but other forms of prosocial behavior do not occur in organizational contexts.

Finally, altruism is also similar to some forms of OCB. Altruism is defined as "helping in the absence of external rewards" (Batson, Bolen, Cross, & Neuringer-Benefiel, 1986, p. 220). Altruism, however, typically emphasizes self-less behavior where the act is driven by the needs of another person. Although helping OCB aims to benefit others, it does not emphasize self-sacrifice. Early work on OCB initially used the term *altruism* (Smith, Organ, & Near, 1983), but more recent research uses the term *helping* because it is more descriptive and avoids the philosophical debate about the extent to which any behavior can be self-less. Thus, some helping OCB may overlap with altruism, but other types of OCB, such as change-oriented OCB, are less likely to be driven by altruism.

To summarize, we have noted constructs that are similar to helping OCB. As we proceed with our literature review and theory building on the unexpected negative consequences of helping OCB to recipients of helping, we draw on this broader literature, but with a special focus on factors that paradoxically cause positively intended helping to have negative effects on recipients.

Building a Conceptual Framework for the Negative Consequences of Helping

Despite growing research that identifies potential negative consequences of helping OCB, most research to date has focused on negative outcomes to helpers (those who engage in helping). In contrast, little research has considered the negative consequences of helping to the intended beneficiaries. This is an important omission because it limits our understanding of the nomological network of helping. It is also intriguing because helping OCB, by definition, is positively intended (Organ, 1988), and so it is important to develop theory that offers systematic reasons for why some instances of helping hurt recipients, instead of benefiting them. In sum, the goal of this chapter is to shed light on boundary conditions that cause unintended negative consequences to intended beneficiaries of helping OCB.

Our approach differs from prior research on the dark side of helping OCB in two distinct ways. First, consistent with Organ's (1988) conceptualization of OCB, we assume that the behavior is performed with positive, empathic intentions, and not for impression management or manipulative purposes. Thus, we do not consider outcomes of behaviors that look like helping OCB but are driven by self-interest, such as impression management (Bolino, 1999; Eastman, 1994). Second, we shift attention away from outcomes of helping to helpers and instead focus on outcomes of helping to recipients. Examples of possible negative outcomes to recipients include negative attitudes and feelings such as threat to self-esteem (Barnes et al., 2008; Fisher & Nadler, 1974; Marigold, Cavallo, Holmes, & Wood, 2014), low self-worth, weak group identity (Halabi, Nadler, & Dovidio, 2011), sense of inferiority (Fisher, Nadler, & Whitcher-Alagna, 1982), negative mood (Bolger & Amarel, 2007), stress (Bolger, Zuckerman, & Kessler, 2000), sense of inadequacy (Barnes et al., 2008), anger, low motivation (Halabi et al., 2011), uncomfortable interdependencies between helpers and recipients (Bamberger, 2009), and conflict (Fisher et al., 1982).

Although a small amount of research has considered boundary conditions that start to shed light on when helping OCB has negative versus positive consequences (e.g., Nadler & Chernyak-Hai, 2014; Nadler, Harpaz-Gorodeisky, & Ben-David, 2009), the field lacks a conceptual framework for organizing moderators that explain the inconsistent outcomes of helping OCB for recipients. This is problematic because lack of a framework makes it difficult to integrate and summarize research findings. In this chapter, we draw on attribution theory (Weiner, 1985) to provide a systematic conceptual framework for thinking about and guiding future research on boundary conditions that cause positively intended helping OCB to backfire and produce negative outcomes for recipients.

Attribution theory posits that people consider characteristics of others, characteristics of themselves, and characteristics of the situation when they try to understand why an event occurred. Applied to helping, we propose that recipients of helping make judgments about the helper, themselves, and the situation when they make causal inferences about why the helping occurred. Was the helping triggered by the needs and capabilities of the helper, their own needs and capabilities, or by the demands of the situation? We posit that these causal attributions made by recipients determine the extent to which they react positively or negatively to being helped. Thus, attributions function as moderators that influence the relationship between helping and recipient reactions.

We aim to make three key contributions in this chapter. First, we provide an integrated, critical review of the literature on the dark side of helping OCB. Second, we develop a theoretical model of how boundary conditions can cause positively intended helping to result in negative outcomes to recipients. Third, we draw on attribution theory to advance an organizing framework for thinking systematically about factors that cause positively intended helping to backfire and have negative consequences for recipients.

Outcomes of Helping Organizational Citizenship Behavior

Previous research on helping OCB has focused primarily on the ways that OCB facilitates performance and helps firms to function more efficiently. This includes positive effects on employee work experiences, coworker relationships, work performance, and work environments (Organ, 1988; N. Podsakoff, Whiting, P. Podsakoff, & Blume, 2009; Podsakoff, Podsakoff, MacKenzie, Maynes, & Spoelma, 2013). This research is important because it provides evidence that helping OCB can benefit individuals and organizations. Nevertheless, some research has also demonstrated negative effects and suggests a more complex and nuanced set of relationships. We briefly describe the positive and negative outcomes of helping OCB and organize these consequences into three categories: consequences for helpers, consequences for recipients, and consequences for organizations. To be consistent with the main focus of this chapter, we emphasize the under-researched negative consequences. This is important because Bolino, Valcea, and Harvey (2010) observed that little research has systematically examined the negative effects that helping OCB can have on firms, helpers, and recipients. Noting the existence of positive and negative consequences, we then focus on moderators that trigger negative consequences of helping OCB.

Research has used two different approaches for considering negative outcomes of helping. The first focuses on negative motivations for engaging in helping, and the second focuses on negative outcomes of positively intended OCB. For example, Bolino (1999) theorized that some types of helping are driven by relatively self-oriented motives, such as impression management or dissatisfaction with one's personal life (see also Bolino et al., 2004). In contrast, other incidents of helping could be driven by positive intentions to benefit others but produce negative outcomes because, for example, the helping might be low quality (Bolino et al., 2004) or because it detracts from in-role task responsibilities (Bergeron, 2007). We focus on this second approach because we limit our review and theory building to positively intended helping OCB that backfires and has negative consequences for recipients.

Helper Outcomes

Research on the positive outcomes of helping OCB for helpers far exceeds that which acknowledges or demonstrates negative effects on helpers. We briefly note conceptual explanations for positive effects and examples of positive effects. Spitzmuller and Van Dyne (2013) elucidated five reasons why helping OCB should have positive consequences for helpers. First, helping others creates reputational benefits which should trigger reciprocal helping where helpers receive help from their peers. It also creates idiosyncratic credits such that others give helpers the benefit of the doubt if they make an error or are late. Second, helping enhances well-being. It enhances positive affect, life satisfaction, and sense of personal control and reduces negative affect. Third, helping increases self-evaluations. For example, helping can increase self-esteem and determination. Fourth, helping contributes to need satisfaction. This includes autonomy, relatedness, and competence. Fifth, helping contributes to self-development. For example, helping reinforces positive habits and enhances quality of life. It also allows expression of personal values.

Consistent with these conceptual arguments, a large number of studies have demonstrated positive relationships between helping OCB and performance evaluations of helpers (e.g., Allen & Rush, 1998; MacKenzie, Podsakoff, & Fetter, 1991, 1993; Whiting et al., 2008). Research also reports that helping OCB predicts reward decisions (Johnson, Erez, Kiker, & Motowidlo, 2002), ratings of competence, and salary recommendations (N. Podsakoff, Whiting, P. Podsakoff, & Mishra, 2011), as well as satisfaction (Bateman & Organ, 1983; Park, Van Dyne, & Ilgen, 2013). Additionally, results demonstrate positive relationships between helping and well-being (Brown, Nesse, Vinokur, & Smith, 2003; Glomb, Bhave, Miner, & Wall, 2011; Penner et al., 2005; Piliavin, 1981).

Switching our focus to negative outcomes of helping OCB for helpers, we note that most research on the dark side of helping OCB addresses the idea that although OCB is by definition discretionary and extra-role, expectations from others can pressure individuals to engage in helping, such that the behavior becomes expected, or in-role. This pressure can be triggered by organizational goals to make the most of the workforce, employee concerns about downsizing (Van Dyne & Ellis, 2004), supervisor expectations that employees should do whatever they can to help the organization (Vigoda-Gadot, 2006), and coworker expectations of normative behavior (Ehrhart & Naumann, 2004). In each of these cases, the discretionary or extra-role nature of helping as OCB is compromised because employees feel pressured to keep up appearances or protect their jobs (Bolino & Turnley, 2003).

Researchers have referred to this transformation of extra-role behavior into an in-role expectation as job creep, citizenship pressure, and compulsory citizenship behavior. Job creep occurs when an individual feels pressure over time to continue performing more than his or her explicit job requirements (Van Dyne & Ellis, 2004). Citizenship pressure occurs when an individual feels pressure to perform OCB (Bolino et al., 2010). Compulsory citizenship behavior (CCB) occurs when a manager or supervisor explicitly expects employees to perform behaviors that are not a part of their formal job requirements (Vigoda-Gadot, 2006). Although the constructs of job creep, citizenship pressure, and compulsory citizenship offer somewhat different perspectives on how extra-role behaviors can become in-role, they all have negative implications for those who engage in helping.

To date, Bolino and colleagues have offered the most conceptual insights into reasons why helping OCB might have negative effects on helpers. For instance, Bolino and colleagues (2004) theorized that some helping that looks like OCB is not prosocial and instead might be based on dissatisfaction with personal life; some helping could be an attempt to compensate for poor performance; and some helping causes role ambiguity, role overload, job stress, and work–family conflict. Bergeron (2007) posited that helping OCB detracts from task performance, especially in jobs that emphasize individual contributions. More recently, Bolino and colleagues' (2013) systematic review of the literature differentiated personal and professional costs to helpers of engaging in OCB.

Although there is not a large amount of empirical work showing negative outcomes of helping OCB for helpers, Barnes and colleagues (2008) demonstrated a negative effect of helping OCB on task performance. Bergeron and colleagues (2013) showed a negative relationship with pay raises and professional advancement. Munyon and colleagues (2010) reported a negative link with job satisfaction, and Dalal (2005) showed a positive relationship with counterproductive behavior. Additionally, helping can deplete regulatory resources (Baumeister, Bratslavsky, Muraven, & Tice, 1998) and can have negative implications for creative behavior (Mueller & Kamdar, 2011). Finally, Halbesleben and colleagues (2009) demonstrated a positive relationship between helping OCB and work–family conflict. Taking a somewhat different approach, Bolino & Turnley (2009) demonstrated that citizenship pressure (feeling expected to engage in OCB) predicted job stress, intentions to turnover, and work–family conflict. Thus, negative outcomes to helpers can occur at work and at home. In sum, research on the dark side of helping OCB has enhanced our understanding of ways that the behavior can detract from well-being and performance.

Organizational Outcomes

Definitionally, Organ (1988) conceptualized helping OCB as beneficial to the organization when aggregated across individuals. Most of the literature on the organizational benefits of helping cites the work of Katz and Kahn (1966), who argued that discretionary behavior is critical for ongoing successful firm performance.

Consistent with these arguments, research has considered helping OCB a valuable resource for organizations because it contributes to efficiency and effectiveness (Podsakoff, Ahearne, & MacKenzie, 1997, p. 263; Smith et al., 1983, p. 654). Podsakoff and colleagues (1997) described three key reasons why helping OCB should predict unit effectiveness. These include more efficient transfer of knowledge from experienced to inexperienced employees, less supervisory time required from managers which allows them to work on more strategic issues, and positive effects on group cohesion and retention. Extending these ideas, Bolino, Turnley, and Bloodgood (2002) theorized that helping OCB creates relational social capital.

Although most helping OCB research examines outcomes at the individual level, a considerable number of studies consider effects on unit or organizational outcomes (e.g., Ehrhart, Bliese, & Thomas, 2006; Koys, 2001; MacKenzie et al., 2011; Naumann & Bennett, 2002; Nishii, Lepak, & Schneider, 2008; Podsakoff, MacKenzie, & Bommer, 1996; Raver, Ehrhart, & Chadwick, 2012; Walz & Niehoff, 2000). Additionally, most studies examining organizational or unit outcomes of helping OCB have demonstrated positive effects. For example, Ehrhart and colleagues (2006) demonstrated that unit-level helping behavior positively predicted unit effectiveness and explained additional variance above and beyond other group process variables. Walz and Niehoff (2000) demonstrated positive relationships with objective measures of restaurant performance, including revenue and operation efficiency. MacKenzie and colleagues (1991) reported positive effects on percent of team sales quota. Podsakoff and colleagues (1996) demonstrated positive effects of aggregated helping on objective quality and quantity of manufacturing performance, 4 months later. Koys (2001) reported a positive relationship between helping OCB and unit performance, and George and Bettenhausen (1990) showed a positive relationship with store sales.

In contrast, study two of Podsakoff and MacKenzie's (1994) paper on insurance sales agents demonstrated a negative relationship between aggregated helping and an objective measure of unit performance. In discussing this unexpected relationship, they suggested that helping others can detract from performance when jobs are highly individualistic. Helping may also backfire when turnover is high and those receiving help do not stay long enough for the help they received to influence their performance. Research also demonstrates that helping OCB is negatively related to unit performance when task interdependence is low (Bachrach, Powell, Collins, & Richey, 2006; Nielsen, Bachrach, Sundstrom, & Halfhill, 2012). Finally, in some jobs, helping may have a negative effect in the short run, but positive effects in the long run.

Thus far, we have described positive and negative consequences of helping OCB for helpers and for organizations. We now shift our attention to the consequences of helping for recipients. Again, we briefly discuss positive consequences and then focus on negative consequences.

Recipient Outcomes

A fundamental assumption of the OCB literature is that the behavior aims to benefit recipients. Interestingly, although a growing amount of research has examined consequences of helping OCB for helpers, groups, and organizations, much less research has focused on the effects of helping on recipients. Perhaps this is due to the strength of generally held assumptions about reciprocal altruism—which emphasize the positive reciprocal effects of prosocial behavior, altruism, and helping (Penner et al., 2005; Trivers, 1971) based on the norm of reciprocity (Gouldner, 1960). For example, Korsgaard, Meglino, Lester, and Jeong (2010) argued that help recipients generally have a sense of obligation to reciprocate because they have internalized the norm of reciprocity (Kelman, 2006). In general, researchers draw on social exchange theory (Blau, 1964) to describe a positive self-reinforcing cycle where helpers benefit recipients, who reciprocate by helping in return.

Consistent with these arguments, Smith and colleagues (1983) posited that OCB has positive outcomes because it "lubricates the social machinery of the organization" (p. 654). Building on and extending this notion, Bolino and colleagues (2002) theorized that helping citizenship creates relational social capital, with benefits to coworkers. This is because helping OCB strengthens the quality of interpersonal relationships, such that they are characterized by trust, intimacy, and liking. As a result, cooperation among peers becomes more likely. Using a different set of arguments, communal exchange theory (Clark & Mills, 1979) posited that family members and those in close communal relationships go out of their way to benefit recipients without regard for future reciprocity. Likewise, Meglino and Korsgaard (2004) theorized that those with the trait of high other orientation help and continue to help, even in the absence of reciprocity.

Some empirical research provides indirect support for these arguments. For example, Bowler and Brass (2006) and Lyons and Scott (2012) used social network analysis and demonstrated reciprocal benefits of helping between coworkers. More specifically, Lyons and Scott (2012) demonstrated that "the extent to which a focal employee engaged in help and harm toward a given coworker was a strong and significant predictor of the amount of help and harm received from that coworker, respectively" (p. 76). Mills and Clark (1982) showed benefits of helping to recipients in communal exchange relationships. Weinstein and Ryan (2010) showed positive effects of discretionary helping on the well-being of both recipients and helpers through need satisfaction. Additionally, Roberts and colleagues (1999) showed improvements in social adjustment for helping recipients, especially when groups were characterized by high integration. Overall, however, there is a dearth of research on positive outcomes of helping to recipients, even though this is a fundamental assumption in most research on helping. Thus, even though our primary focus is on the negative outcomes of helping OCB to recipients, our model also provides guidelines for when helping should have positive outcomes to recipients.

Some research acknowledges that helping can have negative effects on recipients. One of the most influential perspectives on the negative consequences of helping to recipients is the threat to self-esteem model of Fisher and colleagues (1982).

The core premise of this model is that recipient reactions to receiving help are a function of the extent to which the event (receiving help) triggers a sense of personal threat. Research supports this assertion and demonstrates that helping can cause recipients to feel incompetent, dependent, or low in status (Lee, 1997; Nadler & Chernyak-Hai, 2014). Being a recipient of helping can be a negative experience because those who feel dependent often suffer from low self-esteem (Wells, Glickauf-Hughes, & Jones, 1999), low confidence, and experience a loss of selfhood (Lindley, Giordano, & Hammer, 1999). These attributions not only have negative effects on mood and self-concept, but research also demonstrates that receiving helping can decrease motivation in recipients and result in lower and less challenging goals, further reducing the likelihood of improvement (Bolino, Turnley, Gilstrap, & Suazo, 2010; Ilies & Judge, 2005).

Given that these results are paradoxically at odds with the presumed positive intent of helping OCB, we next describe attribution theory as a promising lens for thinking about why recipients of helping might react negatively. Previous research has applied attribution theory to the OCB literature to explain the behavior of helpers as well as reasons why recipients need help (Reisenzein, 1986), and research has demonstrated that supervisor attributions influence their responses to employee extra-role behavior (Eastman, 1994). Similarly, research demonstrates that a coworker's decision to offer help is affected by his or her causal attributions and empathy for the target (Bettencourt, 1990). Going beyond this prior research, we propose that attribution theory can also be used to make sense of recipient reactions to help.

Attribution Theory

The fundamental idea advanced by attribution theory is that individuals are motivated to understand behavior and events when they are unique, unexpected, negative, or important to them (Weiner, 1985, 1986). We want to "understand the environment, to penetrate ourselves and our surroundings" (Weiner, 1985, p. 548). Making attributions allows individuals to make sense of the world around them, determine how best to react to their environment, and learn how to exert control in their lives (Martinko, Harvey, & Dasborough, 2011). Attribution theory portrays individuals as active agents and not merely passive observers of behaviors and events that occur around them.

Two perspectives have dominated most work on attribution theory: Kelley (1967) and Weiner et al. (1971). Although both approaches emphasize the processes individuals use to make attributions, the focus of the two approaches differs. Kelley was primarily concerned with attributions based on consensus, consistency, and distinctiveness and proposed that individuals make judgments about the covariations between an observed behavior and its many possible causes. Weiner, on the other hand, was more concerned with how people judge the successes and failures of themselves and others and argued that attributions influence people's expectations, emotions, and future behaviors.

Although both approaches offer important perspectives on how individuals interpret and make sense of behavior, we draw on Weiner's approach for two reasons. First, we are primarily concerned with attributions about why helping occurred, and this is directly relevant to Weiner's emphasis on "success" and "failure." Second, Kelley's theory has been criticized for failing to adequately distinguish between behaviors that are intentional versus unintentional, and this is an important distinction with implications for recipient reactions to helping (Malle, 1999).

Weiner (1985, 1986) proposed that when people try to understand a behavior (regardless of whether it happened to the self or to another person), they make attributions based on three factors, (a) locus of causality, (b) controllability, and (c) stability. Locus of causality refers to whether the behavior can be attributed to the external environment or whether it is due to the actor's internal characteristics. Controllability refers to whether the behavior occurred because the individual did not put forth enough effort or did not have the right abilities. Stability refers to whether the behavior happens frequently or infrequently.

Attributions have important implications for actors and observers in work organizations. Some research on helping and OCB has examined the role of attribution theory in explaining when and why people need help (Reisenzein, 1986). Martinko and colleagues (2011) concluded that attribution theory has "been underutilized in the organizational sciences" (p. 144). Given the emphasis attribution theory places on causal explanations, we suggest that this theory is particularly relevant for understanding the actions of helpers and the reactions of recipients.

One example of previous research on attributions and helping is the theorizing of LePine and

Van Dyne (2001), who argued that people consider external and internal causes of events when deciding whether to offer help to peers, and what type of help to offer. When the need for help is attributed as being outside of the recipient's control, the observer may take pity on the recipient and offer help. On the other hand, when the need for help is attributed to causes that are seen as controllable, the observer may feel justified in not offering help and may even engage in punishment (Nadler & Chernyak-Hai, 2014). Therefore, if a helper makes a negative attribution about a coworker who seems unable to complete a task or handle a situation, the helper may conclude that the person is low status or chronically dependent on others. "Because of the low performance expectations associated with low status persons, their need for help implies chronic dependency and is expected to be attributed to the uncontrollable, internal, and stable causes of lack of ability and characteristic low motivation to cope" (Nadler & Chernyak-Hai, 2014, p. 59). Taggar and Neubert (2004) demonstrated that attributions helped to explain how observers reacted to the poor performance of other team members. They also showed that attributions influenced emotions and behavioral consequences. In one of the few laboratory experiments on attributions and helping, Eastman (1994) demonstrated that supervisor attributions that employee behavior was ingratiation instead of helping influenced their responses to the behavior. Research also demonstrates that when behaviors are attributed internally to an actor, they are often viewed as general tendencies and are generalized beyond a single event (Greenberg & Frisch, 1972).

Employees want to understand the actions of others, and they also need to understand the causes of their own actions. Thus, they need to make sense of the helper's behavior, their own behavior, and the situation as a whole. They reflect on their own perspective (Why did I need help?), on the perspective of the helper (Why did he or she help me? Am I viewed as incompetent?), and on the situation (Were there particularly difficult and challenging demands?). In sum, recipients use attributions to decide if they should feel grateful or threatened by the helping event. If recipients make negative internal attributions about themselves, this could cause them to blame another person or the situation, or they might engage in impression management (Mehlman & Snyder, 1985). The attributions employees make about receiving help can also trigger changes in the self (Eberly, Holley, Johnson, & Mitchell, 2011).

Theoretical Development

Even though helping is generally valued by recipients and generally benefits recipients, our lack of understanding of when and why helping sometimes leads to negative consequences creates an interesting paradox that warrants deeper thinking about underlying mechanisms that can shed light on reasons why some instances of helping backfire and have negative consequences for recipients. We organize moderators of the relationship between positively intended helping OCB and recipient reactions into three broad categories: characteristics of the helper, characteristics of the recipient, and characteristics of the situation. Figure 10.1 highlights attributions as moderators that determine when positively intended helping OCB triggers threats to self-esteem and negative outcomes for the attitudes, feelings, and behaviors of recipients in contrast to the typically expected and assumed positive consequences of helping for recipients. For our propositions, we conceptualize helping as a continuous variable because the level of helping can range from low to high.

We focus on three general categories of moderators (characteristics of the helper, recipient, and situation) because they are aligned with Weiner's attribution theory and reflect the three key attributions. Recipient attributions about characteristics of the helper include empathy, motives, and behavior of the helper. These characteristics correspond with the locus of causality dimension of attribution theory because, for example, high helper empathy attributions suggest the help was based on the helper's need to provide help (not the recipient's need for help). In other words, recipients make external attributions for why they were helped (low threat). Recipient attributions about their own characteristics include self-perceptions as well as their attributions for the helper's judgments of their adequacy. These characteristics correspond with the controllability dimension of attribution theory because judgments of high adequacy indicate that the need for help was not based on personal inadequacy such as incompetence, laziness, or stupidity (low threat). Recipient attributions about characteristics of the situation include demands of the task, time constraints, and the cooperative/competitive nature of rewards and relationships. These characteristics correspond with the stability dimension of attribution theory because judgments about the task environment indicate the extent to which the situation is atypical, suggesting that the need for help was based on unusual demands (low threat). In the next three sections, we develop propositions about moderators (in each of the three categories) that influence the relationship between positively intended helping OCB and recipient reactions. This allows us to describe prior research and also highlight areas where more research is needed.

Characteristics of the Helper

Our first moderator is recipient attributions about characteristics of the helper. According to attribution theory, people use their judgments about other people when they try to make sense of behaviors and events (Weiner, 1985, 1986). Therefore, judgments about the helper have implications for how recipients interpret helping. As illustrated in Figure 10.1, we posit that recipient attributions about the helper's empathy are a critical boundary condition that determines the direction of the relationship between helping and recipient reactions to being helped. Three recipient judgments predict attributions that the helper had low empathy: judgments that the helper is not a friend, has little shared experience relative to the helping situation, and is not similar. These three judgments share a similar underlying characteristic because they all signal that the helper is low in empathy toward the recipient. Empathy is defined as an individual's sensitivity to the emotional experiences of others and the ability to put oneself in another person's shoes (Lazarus, 1991). When helping recipients conclude that their helper is low in empathy toward them, this should be threatening to their sense of self-esteem. Thus, empathy attributions function as a boundary condition that qualifies the relationship between positively intended helping and recipient reactions. Consistent with Fisher and Nadler's (1974) work on threat to self-esteem, we propose that the relationship between helping and threat to self-esteem is positive when empathy attributions are low and negative when empathy attributions are high. This is because positively intended helping combined with recipient attributions of helper empathy characterize typical assumptions about the beneficial implications of helping, suggesting a negative relationship between helping and threat to self-esteem. In contrast, when recipients attribute helping to low helper empathy, even when helper intentions are positive, the relationship between helping and recipient threat to self-esteem is positive. In other words, recipient attributions are proximal and powerful factors that override the positive intentions of helpers. Figure 10.2 illustrates this crossed interaction—with the paradoxical positive and negative effects of positively intended helping on the recipient's threat to self-esteem, depending on recipient attributions.

Empirical research provides indirect support for this proposition. First, Fisher and colleagues (1982) demonstrated that help is less threatening to recipients when it is provided by a friend. Receiving help from a close other alleviates the need for immediate reciprocity because the ongoing relationship allows ample opportunities to help in the future, and this makes the help less of a burdensome obligation (Nadler, Fisher, & Streufert, 1976). Second, people generally believe that "one's own prior experience with a need facilitates, if not creates, empathy for others experiencing that need" (Batson et al., 1996, p. 474). Consistent with this logic, Hodges, Kiel, Kramer, Veach, and Villanueva (2009) argued that when recipients believe the helper has shared experiences, recipients are more likely to feel that the helper empathizes with them and they are more likely to view the help positively. Third, research has demonstrated that perceived donor-recipient similarity predicts positive recipient reactions to being helped (Nadler et al., 1976). When people view helpers as similar, they have more favorable beliefs about the person's intentions and ability to help them (e.g., similarity attraction; see Byrne, 1971). Accordingly, we posit that

> *P1: Recipient judgments that the helper (P1a) is not a friend, (P1b) does not have similar experiences (regarding needing help), or (P1c) is not similar to them predict recipient attributions about helper empathy, which, in turn, determines whether the relationship between helping and threat to self-esteem is positive (low empathy attributions) or negative (high empathy attributions).*

Characteristics of the Recipient

Our second moderator is recipient attributions about how they are viewed by the helper. Attribution theory posits that individuals use judgments about themselves and how they are viewed by others as cues for making sense of specific behaviors (Weiner, 1985, 1986). As depicted in Figure 10.1, we posit that recipient attributions about the helper's views of his or her adequacy are a key factor that influences the relationship between helping and recipient reactions. Three recipient judgments predict attributions that the helper views them

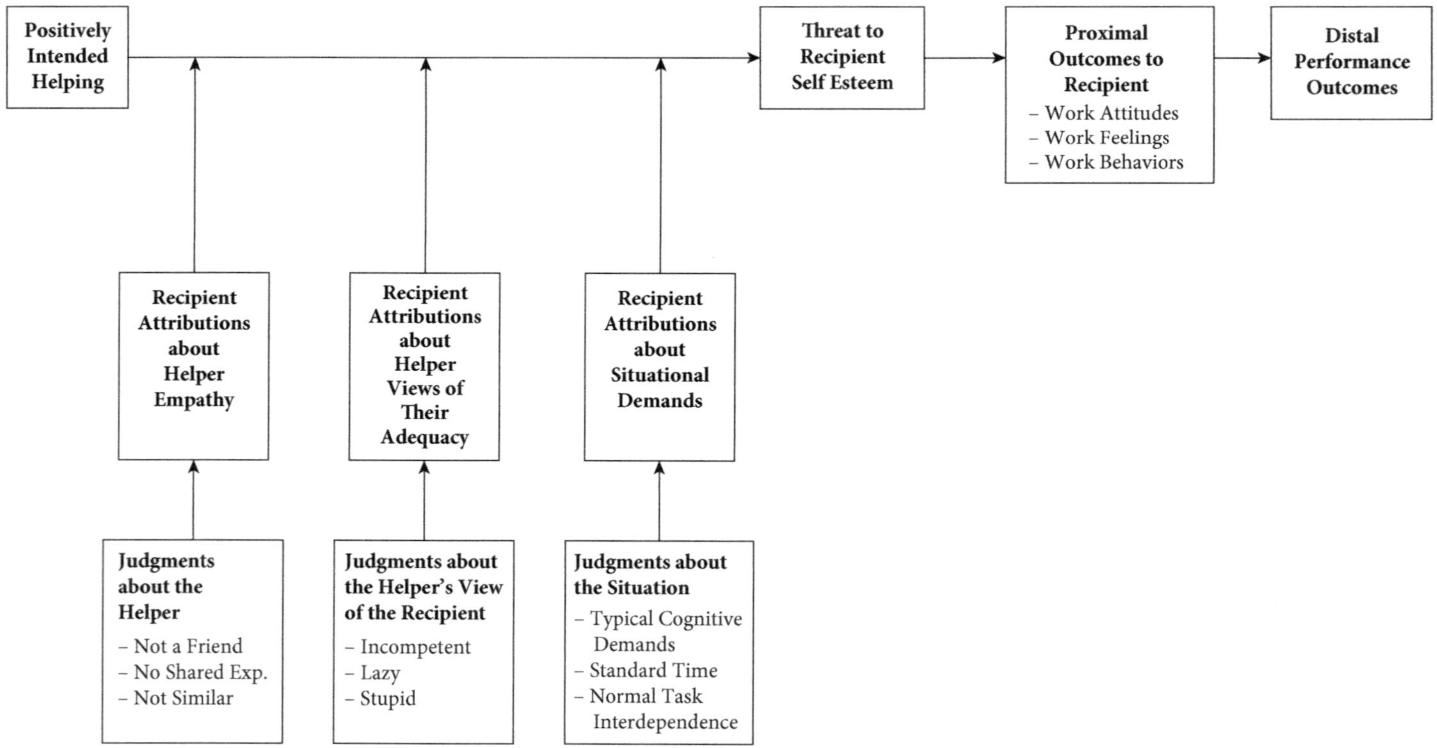

Figure 10.1 Theoretical model.

as inadequate: judgments that they are viewed as incompetent, lazy, or stupid. These three judgments are similar because they all signal that the helper has concluded the recipient is fundamentally inadequate. This sort of attribution suggests uncontrollability because the helper seems to be emphasizing uncontrollable recipient character flaws and has negative views of the recipient's capabilities. Adequacy is defined as the ability to "successfully execute the behavior required to produce the outcomes" (Bandura, 1977, p. 193). When a recipient of helping concludes that the person who provided help views him or her as fundamentally inadequate, this negative judgment triggers a positive relationship between helping and threat to self-esteem. In contrast, when a recipient concludes that the helper views him or her as adequate, the helping should be viewed positively and negatively predict threat to self-esteem. Thus, as illustrated in Figure 10.2, we predict a crossed interaction.

Research provides indirect support for this proposition. Ilies and Judge (2005) demonstrated a negative relationship between help that is viewed as based on personal inadequacy and sense of self-worth. If recipients conclude that they received help because the helper views them as incompetent, lazy, or stupid (Lee, 1997; Nadler & Chernyak-Hai, 2014), the implication is that they are lacking in ability and/or motivation, and this should cause them to feel uncomfortable and indebted to the helper (Greenberg & Shapiro, 1971). This attribution—that they are at fault and personally responsible for needing the help—is threatening. Thus, we posit

P2: Recipient judgments that the helper views the recipent as (P2a) incompetent, (P2b) lazy, or (P2c) stupid predict recipient attributions about how the helper views his or her adequacy, which, in turn, determines whether the relationship between helping and threat to self-esteem is positive (low adequacy attributions) or negative (high adequacy attributions).

Characteristics of the Situation

Our third moderator is recipient attributions about the nature of the situation. According to attribution theory, individuals use cues from the environment to make sense of behaviors and events around them (Weiner, 1985, 1986). Therefore, judgments about the situation are important in influencing recipient interpretations of helping. As illustrated in Figure 10.1, we posit that recipient attributions about situational demands determine the nature of the relationship between helping and recipient reactions. Three recipient judgments predict attributions that the situation does not include unusual demands: judgments that the cognitive demands of the task are typical, the time requirements are standard, and the situation involves normal task interdependence. These three judgments share similarities because they all suggest that the situation is stable and contains no extenuating circumstances that might justify the need for help. "Demands of the situation" is defined as the amount of cognitive, social, self-regulatory, physical, and motor coordination that is required in a given situation (Shoda, Mischel, & Wright, 1993). When helping recipients conclude that the situation is not unusual, they think they should have been able to avoid the need for help and this is a personally threatening experience. In contrast, receiving help in unusually demanding situations is more acceptable and less threatening. In sum, viewing the situation as typical should cause a positive relationship between helping and threat to self-esteem, whereas viewing the situation as unusually demanding should result in a negative relationship between helping and threat to self-esteem, as illustrated in Figure 10.2.

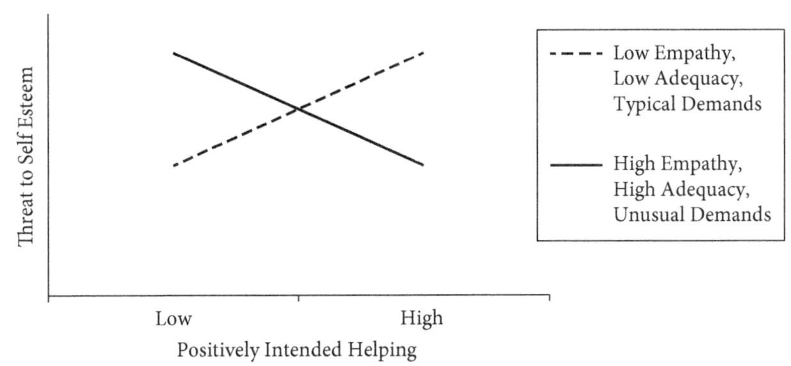

Figure 10.2 Graph of interaction.

Research provides indirect support for this proposition. According to Nadler and colleagues (1976), "Both practitioners' reports and experimental studies have found that aid may have either favorable or unfavorable effects on the recipient's self-perceptions, depending on associated situational conditions" (p. 392). Research, for example, demonstrates that task difficulty influences reactions to being helped. When a task is considered to be easy, it has low cognitive demands, standard time constraints, and normal task interdependence. In this type of situation, receiving help triggers negative reactions (Halabi et al., 2011). Nadler (1991) emphasized the importance of typical demands and work routines, such as the extent to which others need help. Therefore, when helping recipients conclude that the situational demands are not unusual, they should react negatively, and this should cause a positive relationship between helping and threat to self-esteem. In contrast, when recipients conclude that the situation is unusually demanding, positively intended helping should be viewed positively and the relationship between helping and threat to self-esteem is negative.

P3: Recipient attributions that the situation is characterized by (P3a) routine cognitive demands, (P3b) standard time constraints, or (P3c) normal task interdependence predict recipient attributions that the situational demands are typical, which, in turn, determines whether the relationship between helping and threat to self-esteem is positive (typical demands) or negative (unusual demands).

Proximal and Distal Outcomes

Considering these three moderators and their effect on the relationship between positively intended helping and threat to self-esteem is important because helping and threat to self-esteem have implications for other outcomes. We focus first on proximal outcomes such as recipient work attitudes, work feelings, and work behaviors and then later acknowledge that these proximal outcomes influence more distal outcomes, such as work performance.

Research shows that receiving help can suggest low status and dependence on others (Lee, 1997). Therefore, receiving help triggers social comparison processes and causes recipients to conclude that they are "viewed as relatively weak and incompetent" (Nadler & Chernyak-Hai, 2014, p. 58). Receiving help can trigger negative judgments about the self, including low self-confidence (Lindley et al., 1999), self-worth (Fisher et al., 1982), and self-esteem (Wells et al., 1999). For example, "receiving help can undermine a person's feeling of worth, undermining their confidence and motivation to succeed" as well as trigger "resistance and rejection on the part of the recipient" (Halabi et al., 2011, p. 2793). Additionally, receiving help creates obligations to reciprocate and repay the debt, and this makes many people uncomfortable (Greenberg & Shapiro, 1971) because the norm of reciprocity dictates that "people should help those who have helped them" (Gouldner, 1960, p. 171). Accordingly, feeling indebted implies that "they have surrendered some of their freedom in future dealings with the donor. This loss of freedom incurred by their indebtedness may be a major source of distress to recipients" (Greenberg & Westcott, 1983, p. 87).

When helping occurs in a work context and recipients make negative attributions that threaten their sense of self-esteem, this has negative implications for work attitudes, work feelings, and work behaviors. This could include negative attitudes toward helpers, negative attitudes toward coworkers who have not received help, low identification with the work group, negative affect about work in general, negative affect directed at helpers, or negative behaviors such as reduced effort, shirking, withdrawal, absenteeism, and counterproductive work behaviors. Thus, we posit first-stage moderated mediation. Positively intended helping has negative mediated effects on proximal recipient work outcomes via threat to self-esteem when recipients make negative attributions for why they received help (low helper empathy, personal inadequacy, or typical situational demands).

P4: Negative recipient attributions (low helper empathy, being viewed as inadequate, and seeing the situation as typical) interact with positively intended helping to negatively predict proximal outcomes to the recipient, including (P4a) work attitudes, (P4b) work feelings, and (P4c) work behaviors, via threat to self-esteem.

For our last proposition, we acknowledge that negative attributions not only influence the relationship between positively intended helping and proximal work attitudes, feelings, and behaviors, via threat to self-esteem, but also have implications for more distal outcomes, such as work performance. Thus, even though this chapter focuses on nonperformance outcomes of helping, we think it is important to acknowledge effects on more distal performance outcomes. If helping recipients make negative attributions for why they received help (low helper empathy, personal inadequacy, or typical situational demands), threat to self-esteem has mediated effects on work performance via the more proximal negative effects on work attitudes, cognitions, and behaviors. In sum, threat to self-esteem causes employees to conclude that they do not have the skills or motivation to do the job, and so they reduce their effort and fail to learn new skills (Bolino et al., 2010), set less challenging goals, reduce learning, and avoid personal development (Ilies & Judge, 2005). All of these reactions have negative performance implications. In sum, negative attributions about receiving help ultimately have negative implications for work performance.

P5: Negative recipient attributions (low helper empathy, being viewed as inadequate, and seeing the situation as typical) interact with positively intended helping to negatively effect threat to self-esteem, which has negative implications for work performance, via more proximal work attitudes, cognitions, and behaviors

Conclusion

The goal of this chapter was to answer calls for a more balanced perspective on the consequences of helping OCB. "Both practitioner's reports and experimental studies have found that aid may have either favorable or unfavorable effects" on recipients, depending on "associated situational conditions" (Nadler et al., 1976, p. 392). Receiving help has both costs and rewards, and so helping is "a mixed blessing at best" (Fisher & Nadler, 1974, p. 231). Receiving help can provide an opportunity to build skills and provide opportunities for growth, but many recipients also find it humiliating to receive help because it can imply inferiority, dependence, helplessness, and incompetence.

In sum, we have advanced a novel conceptual model of nonperformance outcomes to recipients of positively intended helping. Based on attribution theory, we have developed the argument that positively intended helping can backfire and cause negative recipient reactions when they make attributions that the helper has low empathy, views the recipient as inadequate, or the situation is typical. In contrast, our crossed interaction propositions also acknowledge the generally positive reactions to helping when it does not trigger threat to self-esteem. We hope the chapter highlights "factors which determine whether aid will be a positive or a self-threatening experience" (Fisher & Nadler, 1974, p. 231) and that our model facilitates more nuanced research on outcomes of helping.

References

Allen, T. D., & Rush, M. C. (1998). The effects of organizational citizenship behavior on performance judgments: A field study and a laboratory experiment. *Journal of Applied Psychology, 83*(2), 247–260.

Bachrach, D. G., Powell, B. C., Collins, B. J., & Richey, R. G. (2006). Effects of task interdependence on the relationship between helping behavior and group performance. *Journal of Applied Psychology, 91*(6), 1396–1405.

Bamberger, P. (2009). Employee help-seeking: Antecedents, consequences and new insights for future research. *Advances in Library Administration and Organization, 28*, 49–98.

Bandura, A. (1977). Self-efficacy: Toward a unifying theory of behavioral change. *Psychological Review, 84*(2), 191–215.

Barnes, C. M., Hollenbeck, J. R., Wagner, D. T., DeRue, D. S., Nahrgang, J. D., & Schwind, K. M. (2008). Harmful help: The costs of backing-up behavior in teams. *Journal of Applied Psychology, 93*(3), 529–539.

Bateman, T. S., & Organ, D. W. (1983). Job satisfaction and the good soldier: The relationship between affect and employee "citizenship." *Academy of Management Journal, 26*(4), 587–595.

Batson, C. D., Bolen, M. H., Cross, J. A., & Neuringer-Benefiel, H. E. (1986). Where is the altruism in the altruistic personality? *Journal of Personality and Social Psychology, 50*(1), 212–220.

Batson, C. D., Sympson, S. C., Hindman, J. L., Decruz, P., Todd, R. M., & Weeks, J. L. (1996). "I've been there, too": Effect on empathy of prior experience with a need. *Personality and Social Psychology Bulletin, 22*, 474–482.

Baumeister, R. F., Bratslavsky, E., Muraven, M., & Tice, D. M. (1998). Ego depletion: Is the active self a limited resource? *Journal of Personality and Social Psychology, 74*, 1252–1265.

Bergeron, D. M. (2007). The potential paradox of organizational citizenship behavior: Good citizens at what cost? *Academy of Management Review, 32*(4), 1078–1095.

Bergeron, D. M., Shipp, A. J., Rosen, B., & Furst, S. A. (2013). Organizational citizenship behavior and career outcomes: The cost of being a good citizen. *Journal of Management, 39*, 958–984.

Bettencourt, H. (1990). An attribution-empathy model of helping behavior: Behavioral intentions and judgments of help-giving. *Personality and Social Psychology Bulletin, 16*(3), 573–591.

Blau, P. M. (1964). *Exchange and power in social life*. New York, NY: Wiley.

Bolino, M. C. (1999). Citizenship and impression management: Good soldiers or good actors? *Academy of Management Review, 24*(1), 82–98.

Bolino, M. C., Klotz, A. C., Turnley, W. H., & Harvey, J. (2013). Exploring the dark side of organizational citizenship behavior. *Journal of Organizational Behavior, 34*, 542–559.

Bolino, M. C., & Turnley, W. H. (2003). Going the extra mile: Cultivating and managing employee citizenship behavior. *Academy of Management Executive, 17*(3), 60–71.

Bolino, M. C., & Turnley, W. H. (2005). The personal costs of citizenship behavior: The relationship between individual initiative and role overload, job stress, and work-family conflict. *Journal of Applied Psychology, 90*(4), 740–748.

Bolino, M. C., & Turnley, W. H. (2009). Relative deprivation among employees in lower-quality leader-member exchange relationships. *Leadership Quarterly, 20*(3), 276–286.

Bolino, M. C., Turnley, W. H., & Bloodgood, J. M. (2002). Citizenship behavior and the creation of social capital in

organizations. *Academy of Management Review, 27*(4), 505–522.
Bolino, M. C., Turnley, W. H., Gilstrap, J. B., & Suazo, M. M. (2010). Citizenship under pressure: What's a "good soldier" to do?" *Journal of Organizational Behavior, 31*, 835–855.
Bolino, M. C., Turnley, W. H., & Niehoff, B. P. (2004). The other side of the story: Reexamining prevailing assumptions about organizational citizenship behavior. *Human Resource Management Review, 14*, 229–246.
Bolino, M., Valcea, S., & Harvey, J. (2010). Employee, manage thyself: The potentially negative implications of expecting employees to behave proactively. *Journal of Occupational and Organizational Psychology, 83*, 325–345.
Bolger, N., & Amarel, D. (2007). Effects of social support visibility on adjustment to stress: Experimental evidence. *Journal of Personality and Social Psychology, 92*, 458–475.
Bolger, N., Zuckerman, A., & Kessler, R. C. (2000). Invisible support and adjustment to stress. *Journal of Personality and Social Psychology, 79*, 953–961.
Borman, W. C., & Motowidlo, S. J. (1997). Task performance and contextual performance: The meaning for personnel selection research. *Human Performance, 10*(2), 99–109.
Bowler, W. M., & Brass, D. J. (2006). Relational correlates of interpersonal citizenship behavior: A social network perspective. *Journal of Applied Psychology, 91*(1), 70.
Brown, S. L., Nesse, R. M., Vinokur, A. D., & Smith, D. M. (2003). Providing social support may be more beneficial than receiving it: Results from a prospective study of mortality. *Psychological Science, 14*(4), 320–327.
Byrne, D. (1971). *The attraction paradigm*. New York, NY: Academic Press.
Clark, M. S., & Mills, J. (1979). Interpersonal attraction in exchange and communal relationships. *Journal of Personality and Social Psychology, 37*(1), 12–24.
Dalal, R. S. (2005). A meta-analysis of the relationship between organizational citizenship behavior and counterproductive work behavior. *Journal of Applied Psychology, 90*(6), 1241–1255.
Detert, J. R., Burris, E. R., Harrison, D. A., & Martin, S. R. (2013). Voice flows to and around leaders: Understanding when units are helped or hurt by employee voice. *Administrative Science Quarterly, 58*(4), 624–668.
Eastman, K. K. (1994). In the eyes of the beholder: An attributional approach to ingratiation and organizational citizenship behavior. *Academy of Management Journal, 37*(5), 1379–1391.
Eberly, M. B., Holley, E. C., Johnson, M. D., & Mitchell, T. R. (2011). Beyond internal and external: A dyadic theory of relational attributions. *Academy of Management Journal, 36*(4), 731–753.
Ehrhart, M. G., Bliese, P. D., & Thomas, J. L. (2006). Unit-level OCB and unit effectiveness: Examining the incremental effect of helping behavior. *Human Performance, 19*(2), 159–173.
Ehrhart, M. G., & Naumann, S. E. (2004). Organizational citizenship behavior in work groups: A group norms approach. *Journal of Applied Psychology, 89*, 960–974.
Fisher, J. D., & Nadler, A. (1974). The effect of similarity between donor and recipient on recipient's reactions to aid. *Journal of Applied Social Psychology, 4*(3), 230–243.
Fisher, J. D., Nadler, A., & Whitcher-Alagna, S. (1982). Recipient reactions to aid. *Psychological Bulletin, 91*(1), 27–54.
George, J. M., & Bettenhausen, K. (1990). Understanding prosocial behavior, sales performance, and turnover: A group-level analysis in a service context. *Journal of Applied Psychology, 75*(6), 698–709.
Glomb, T. M., Bhave, D. P., Miner, A. G., & Wall, M. (2011). Doing good, feeling good: Examining the role of organizational citizenship behaviors in changing mood. *Personnel Psychology, 64*(1), 191–223.
Gouldner, A. W. (1960). The norm of reciprocity: A preliminary statement. *American Sociological Review, 25*, 161–178.
Greenberg, M. S., & Frisch, D. M. (1972). Effect of intentionality on willingness to reciprocate a favor. *Journal of Experimental Social Psychology, 5*, 99–111.
Greenberg, M. S., & Shapiro, S. P. (1971). Indebtedness: An adverse aspect of asking for and receiving help. *Sociometry, 34*(2), 290–301.
Greenberg, M. S., & Westcott, D. R. (1983). Indebtedness as a mediator of reactions to aid. In J. D. Fisher, A. Nadler, & B. M. DePaulo (Eds.), *New directions in helping (Vol 1) Recipient reactions to aid*. New York, NY: Academic Press.
Halabi, S., Nadler, A., & Dovidio, J. F. (2011). Reactions to receiving assumptive help: The moderating effects of group membership and perceived need for help. *Journal of Applied Social Psychology, 41*(12), 2793–2815.
Halbesleben, J. R., Harvey, J., & Bolino, M. C. (2009). Too engaged? A conservation of resources view of the relationship between work engagement and work interference with family. *Journal of Applied Psychology, 94*(6), 1452–1465.
Hodges, S. D., Kiel, K. J., Kramer, A. D. I., Veach, D., & Villanueva, B. R. (2009). Giving birth to empathy: The effects of similar experience on empathic accuracy, empathic concern, and perceived empathy. *Personality and Social Psychology Bulletin, 36*, 398–409.
Ilies, R., & Judge, T. A. (2005). Goal regulation across time: The effects of feedback and affect. *Journal of Applied Psychology, 90*, 453–467.
Johnson, D. E., Erez, A., Kiker, D. S., & Motowidlo, S. J. (2002). Liking and attributions of motives as mediators of the relationships between individuals' reputations, helpful behaviors and raters' reward decisions. *Journal of Applied Psychology, 87*(4), 808–815.
Katz, D., & Kahn, R. L. (1966). *The social psychology of organizations*. New York, NY: Wiley.
Kelley, H. H. (1967). Attribution theory in social psychology. *Nebraska Symposium on Motivation, 15*, 192–240.
Kelman, H. C. (2006). Interests, relationships, identities: Three central issues for individuals and groups in negotiating their social environment. *Annual Review of Psychology, 57*, 1–16.
Korsgaard, M. A., Meglino, B. M., Lester, S. W., & Jeong, S. S. (2010). Paying you back or paying me forward: Understanding rewarded and unrewarded organizational citizenship behavior. *Journal of Applied Psychology, 95*(2), 277–290.
Koys, D. J. (2001). The effects of employee satisfaction, organizational citizenship behavior, and turnover on organizational effectiveness: A unit-level, longitudinal study. *Personnel Psychology, 54*(1), 101–114.
Lazarus, R. S. (1991). *Emotion and adaptation*. New York, NY: Oxford University Press.
Lee, F. (1997). When the going gets tough, do the tough ask for help? Help seeking and power motivation in organizations. *Organizational Behavior and Human Decision Processes, 72*(3), 336–363.

LePine, J. A., & Van Dyne, L. (2001). Peer responses to low performers: An attributional model of helping in the context of groups. *Academy of Management Review, 26*(1), 67–84.
Lindley, N. R., Giordano, P. J., & Hammer, E. D. (1999). Codependency: Predictors and psychometric issues. *Journal of Clinical Psychology, 55*, 59–64.
Lyons, B. J., & Scott, B. A. (2012). Integrating social exchange and affective explanations for the receipt of help and harm: A social network approach. *Organizational Behavior and Human Decision Processes, 117*(1), 66–79.
MacKenzie, S. B., Podsakoff, P. M., & Fetter, R. (1991). Organizational citizenship behavior and objective productivity as determinants of managerial evaluations of salespersons' performance. *Organizational Behavior and Human Decision Processes, 50*(1), 123–150.
MacKenzie, S. B., Podsakoff, P. M., & Fetter, R. (1993). The impact of organizational citizenship behavior on evaluations of salesperson performance. *Journal of Marketing, 57*(1), 70–80.
MacKenzie, S. B., Podsakoff, P. M., & Podsakoff, N. P. (2011). Challenge-oriented organizational citizenship behaviors and organizational effectiveness: Do challenge-oriented behaviors really have an impact on the organization's bottom line? *Personnel Psychology, 64*, 559–592.
Malle, B. F. (1999). How people explain behavior: A new theoretical framework. *Personality and Social Psychology Review, 3*(1), 23–48.
Marigold, D. C., Cavallo, J. V, Holmes, J. G., & Wood, J. V. (2014). You can't always give what you want: The challenge of providing social support to low self-esteem individuals. *Journal of Personality and Social Psychology, 107*(1), 56–80.
Martinko, M. J., Harvey, P., & Dasborough, M. T. (2011). Attribution theory in the organizational sciences: A case of unrealized potential. *Journal of Organizational Behavior, 32*, 144–149.
Maynes, T. D., & Podsakoff, P. M. (2014). Speaking more broadly: An examination of the nature, antecedents, and consequences of an expanded set of employee voice behaviors. *Journal of Applied Psychology, 99*(1), 87–112.
Meglino, B. M., & Korsgaard, A. (2004). Considering rational self-interest as a disposition: Organizational implications of other orientation. *Journal of Applied Psychology, 89*(6), 946–959.
Mehlman, R. C., & Snyder, C. R. (1985). Excuse theory: A test of the self-protective role of attributions. *Journal of Personality and Social Psychology, 49*(4), 994–1001.
Mills, J., & Clark, M. S. (1982). Exchange and communal relationships. *Review of Personality and Social Psychology, 3*, 121–144.
Mueller, J. S., & Kamdar, D. (2011). Why seeking help from teammates is a blessing and a curse: A theory of help seeking and individual creativity in team contexts. *Journal of Applied Psychology, 96*, 263–276.
Munyon, T. P., Hochwarter, W. A., Perrewé, P. L., & Ferris, G. R. (2010). Optimism and the nonlinear citizenship behavior–job satisfaction relationship in three studies. *Journal of Management, 36*, 1505–1528.
Nadler, A. (1991). Help-seeking behaviors: Psychological costs and instrumental benefits. *Prosocial Behavior, 12*, 290–311.
Nadler, A., & Chernyak-Hai, L. (2014). Helping them stay where they are: Status effects on dependency/autonomy-oriented helping. *Journal of Personality and Social Psychology, 106*(1), 58–72.
Nadler, A., Fisher, J. D., & Streufert, S. (1976). When helping hurts: Effects of donor-recipient similarity and recipient self-esteem on reactions to aid. *Journal of Personality, 44*(3), 392–409.
Nadler, A., Harpaz-Gorodeisky, G., & Ben-David, Y. (2009). Defensive helping: Threat to group identity, ingroup identification, status stability, and common group identity as determinants of intergroup help-giving. *Journal of Personality and Social Psychology, 97*(5), 823–834.
Naumann, S. E., & Bennett, N. (2002). The effects of procedural justice climate on work group performance. *Small Group Research, 33*(3), 361–377.
Nielsen, T. M., Bachrach, D. G., Sundstrom, E., & Halfhill, T. R. (2012). Utility of OCB organizational citizenship behavior and group performance in a resource allocation framework. *Journal of Management, 38*(2), 668–694.
Nishii, L. H., Lepak, D. P., & Schneider, B. (2008). Employee attributions of the "why" of HR practices: Their effects on employee attitudes and behaviors, and customer satisfaction. *Personnel Psychology, 61*(3), 503–545.
Organ, D. W. (1988). *Organizational citizenship behavior: The good soldier syndrome*. Lexington, MA: Lexington Books.
Organ, D. W. (1997). Organizational citizenship behavior: It's construct clean-up time. *Human Performance, 10*(2), 85–97.
Organ, D. W., Podsakoff, P. M., & MacKenzie, S. B. (2006). *Organizational citizenship behavior: Its nature, antecedents, and consequences*. Thousand Oaks, CA: Sage.
Park, G., Van Dyne, L., & Ilgen, D. (2013). Satisfaction pursuing approach and avoidance goals: Effects of regulatory fit and individual temperaments. *Motivation and Emotion, 37*, 424–432.
Penner, L. A., Dovidio, J. F., Piliavin, J. A., & Schroeder, D. A. (2005). Prosocial behavior: Multilevel perspectives. *Annual Review of Psychology, 56*, 365–392.
Piliavin, J. A. (1981). Methods, findings, and history in attitude-behavior research: A rejoinder to Hanson. *Psychology: A Journal of Human Behavior, 18*(4), 1.
Podsakoff, P. M., Ahearne, M., & MacKenzie, S. B. (1997). Organizational citizenship behavior and the quantity and quality of work group performance. *Journal of Applied Psychology, 82*(2), 262–270.
Podsakoff, P. M., & MacKenzie, S. B. (1994). An examination of the psychometric properties and nomological validity of some revised and reduced substitutes for leadership scales. *Journal of Applied Psychology, 79*(5), 702–713.
Podsakoff, P. M., MacKenzie, S. B., & Bommer, W. H. (1996). Transformational leader behaviors and substitutes for leadership as determinants of employee satisfaction, commitment, trust, and organizational citizenship behaviors. *Journal of Management, 22*(2), 259–298.
Podsakoff, N. P., Podsakoff, P. M., Mackenzie, S. B., Maynes, T. D., & Spoelma, T. M. (2013). Consequences of unit-level organizational citizenship behaviors: A review and recommendations for future research. *Journal of Organizational Behavior, 35*(1), 87–119.
Podsakoff, N. P., Whiting, S. W., Podsakoff, P. M., & Blume, B. D. (2009). Individual-and organizational-level consequences of organizational citizenship behaviors: A meta-analysis. *Journal of Applied Psychology, 94*(1), 122–141.
Podsakoff, N. P., Whiting, S. W., Podsakoff, P. M., & Mishra, P. (2011). Effects of organizational citizenship behaviors on selection decisions in employment interviews. *Journal of Applied Psychology, 96*(2), 310–326.

Raver, J. L., Ehrhart, M. G., & Chadwick, I. C. (2012). The emergence of team helping norms: Foundations within members' attributes and behavior. *Journal of Organizational Behavior, 33*(5), 616–637.

Reisenzein, R. (1986). A structural equation analysis of Weiner's attribution-affect model of helping behavior. *Journal of Personality and Social Psychology, 50*(6), 1123–1133.

Roberts, L. J., Salem, D., Rappaport, J., Toro, P. A., Luke, D. A., & Seidman, E. (1999). Giving and receiving help: Interpersonal transactions in mutual-help meetings and psychosocial adjustment of members. *American Journal of Community Psychology, 27*(6), 841–868.

Shoda, Y., Mischel, W., & Wright, J. C. (1993). The role of situational demands and cognitive competencies in behavior organization and personality coherence. *Journal of Personality and Social Psychology, 65*(5), 1023–1035.

Smith, C. A., Organ, D. W., & Near, J. P. (1983). Organizational citizenship behavior: Its nature and antecedents. *Journal of Applied Psychology, 68*, 655–663.

Spitzmuller, M., & Van Dyne, L. (2013). Proactive and reactive helping: Contrasting the positive consequences of different forms of helping. *Journal of Organizational Behavior, 34*, 560–580.

Taggar, S., & Neubert, M. (2004). The impact of poor performers on team outcomes: An empirical examination of attribution theory. *Personnel Psychology, 57*, 935–968.

Trivers, R. L. (1971). The evolution of reciprocal altruism. *Quarterly Review of Biology, 46*(1), 35–57.

Van Dyne, L., Cummings, L. L., & McLean Parks, J. (1995). Extra-role behaviors: In pursuit of construct and definitional clarity. *Research in Organizational Behavior, 17*, 215–285.

Van Dyne, L., & Ellis, J. B. (2004). Job creep: A reactance theory perspective on organizational citizenship behavior as overfulfillment of obligations. In J. A. M. Coyle-Shapiro, L. M. Shore, M. S. Taylor, & L. E. Tetrick (Eds.), *The employment relationship: Examining psychological and contextual perspectives* (pp. 181–205). Oxford, UK: Oxford University Press.

Van Dyne, L. & LePine, J. A. (1998). Helping and voice extra-role behaviors: Evidence of construct and predictive validity. *Academy of Management Journal, 41*(1), 108–119.

Vigoda-Gadot, E. (2006). Compulsory citizenship behavior: Theorizing some dark sides of the good soldier syndrome in organizations. *Journal for the Theory of Social Behavior, 36*(1), 77–93.

Walz, S. M., & Niehoff, B. P. (2000). Organizational citizenship behaviors: Their relationship to organizational effectiveness. *Journal of Hospitality and Tourism Research, 24*, 301–319.

Weiner, B. (1985). An attributional theory of achievement motivation and emotion. *Psychological Review, 92*(4), 548–573.

Weiner, B. (1986). *An attributional theory of motivation and emotion.* New York, NY: Springer-Verlag.

Weiner, B., Frieze, I., Kukla, A., Reed, L., Rest, S., & Rosenbaum, R. M. (1971). *Perceiving the causes of success and failure.* Morristown, NJ: General Learning Publishing Group.

Weinstein, N., & Ryan, R. M. (2010). When helping helps: Autonomous motivation for prosocial behavior and its influence on well-being for the helper and recipient. *Journal of Personality and Social Psychology, 98*(2), 222–244.

Wells, M., Glickauf-Hughes, C., & Jones, R. (1999). Codependency: A grass roots construct's relationship to shame-proneness, low self-esteem, and childhood parentification. *American Journal of Family Therapy, 27*(1), 63–71.

Whiting, S. W., Maynes, T. D., Podsakoff, N. P., & Podsakoff, P. M. (2012). Effects of message, source, and context on evaluations of employee voice behavior. *Journal of Applied Psychology, 97*(1), 159–182.

Whiting, S. W., Podsakoff, P. M., & Pierce, J. R. (2008). Effects of task performance, helping, voice, and organizational loyalty on performance appraisal ratings. *Journal of Applied Psychology, 93*(1), 125–139.

CHAPTER

11

The Unintended Consequences of Organizational Citizenship Behaviors for Employees, Teams, and Organizations

Mark C. Bolino, Anthony C. Klotz, *and* William H. Turnley

Abstract

Researchers have identified a number of reasons why organizational citizenship behavior (OCB) should contribute to the effective functioning of workgroups and organizations, and many studies have found that OCB is indeed positively related to both workgroup-level and organizational-level indicators of effectiveness. Nevertheless, there is mounting evidence that OCBs can sometimes have negative consequences for employees, teams, and organizations. In this chapter, we review research that has focused on these unintended consequences and explain how these negative effects could potentially undermine the positive outcomes that are typically associated with OCB. We conclude our chapter by identifying directions for future research and discussing methodological considerations for investigations of OCB's unintended consequences. Some practical implications about managing citizenship in the workplace are addressed as well.

Key Words: citizenship behavior, prosocial behavior, helping, voice, individual initiative, citizenship pressure, dark side, group performance, organizational effectiveness

There are downsides to everything; there are unintended consequences to everything.

—*Steve Jobs, former cofounder, chairman, and CEO of Apple, Inc. (Goodell, 2003)*

As organizations transitioned into the 21st century, management researchers identified a number of changes in the business environment. In particular, organizations are increasingly affected by the forces of globalization, intense competition, uncertainty, and rapid technological change (Cascio, 1995; Cascio & Aguinis, 2008). To survive in this dynamic environment, firms have embraced new approaches to organizing that allow them to adapt to changes in the market more rapidly than ever. For example, contemporary organizations are now characterized by more decentralized management structures that empower employees and offer them opportunities to take more initiative at work (Lawler, Mohrman, & Benson, 2001; Seibert, Wang, & Courtright, 2011). To be more innovative and flexible, organizations have also placed a greater emphasis on cooperation, coordination, and collaboration (Khazanchi, Lewis, & Boyer, 2007; Nahapiet & Ghoshal, 1998). Finally, in this era of constrained resources, companies have sought to do more with less, and therefore have become more reliant on employees who are willing to go beyond their formal job duties to support their teammates and the organization more broadly (Organ, 1988; Organ, Podsakoff, & MacKenzie, 2006). That is, one way organizations gain a competitive advantage in today's marketplace is by developing a workforce of individuals who not only perform their in-role responsibilities effectively but who also engage in extra-role behaviors (Bolino & Turnley, 2003).

These extra-role behaviors have most commonly been investigated under the label of organizational citizenship behavior (OCB) (Bateman & Organ, 1983; Organ et al., 2006). OCB is employee behavior that is relatively discretionary, less likely to be formally rewarded (in comparison to in-role job behavior), and contributes to the effective functioning of an organization by supporting its social and psychological context (Organ, 1997; Organ et al., 2006). Researchers have identified a number of OCBs, including behaviors that are interpersonal and affiliative, such as helping others (Organ, 1988; Van Dyne, Cummings, & McLean Parks, 1995); behavior that goes beyond the call of duty, such as putting in extra hours, taking on additional responsibilities, and attending work-related functions on one's personal time (Bolino & Turnley, 2005); and behaviors that involve challenging the status quo and speaking up with suggestions on how to make the organization more effective, like voice (LePine & Van Dyne, 1998; Van Dyne et al., 1995). Given its potential value to organizations, it is understandable that early research on OCB focused on identifying its antecedents (see Organ & Ryan [1995] and Podsakoff, MacKenzie, Paine, & Bachrach [2000] for reviews of this work); further, a number of studies have also shown that OCB is positively related to both individual (e.g., performance evaluation ratings, rewards) and organizational (e.g., efficiency, customer satisfaction, turnover) outcomes (see Podsakoff, Whiting, Podsakoff, & Blume [2009] and Podsakoff, Podsakoff, MacKenzie, Maynes, & Spoelma [2014] for reviews of this work).

Although research has generally found that OCB has positive implications for employees and organizations, an emerging line of research has also started to explore the "dark side" of OCB (Bolino, Klotz, Turnley, & Harvey, 2013; Bolino, Turnley, & Niehoff, 2004). For instance, researchers have argued that OCB may be driven by political motives or the desire to impress one's boss or coworkers (Bolino, 1999; Bolino & Turnley, 2012). Likewise, because going beyond the call of duty can consume resources, OCB might be associated with role overload, job stress, and work–family conflict (Bolino & Turnley, 2005). Similarly, employees may sometimes engage in OCBs at the expense of their in-role responsibilities, which can undermine their job performance and career prospects (Bergeron, 2007; Bergeron, Shipp, Rosen, & Furst, 2011). With regard to the effective functioning of teams and organizations, there is also evidence that OCBs can actually undermine the effectiveness of teams and organizations in some circumstances (Bachrach, Powell, Collins, & Richey, 2006; MacKenzie, Podsakoff, & Podsakoff, 2011; Nielsen, Bachrach, Sundstrom, & Halfhill, 2012). Thus, while OCB generally has positive implications, the purpose of this chapter is to examine some of the unintended consequences of OCB for employees, teams, and organizations.

To do so, we organize our review of this literature by focusing on the different ways that OCBs are thought to contribute to organizational effectiveness (Organ et al., 2006; Podsakoff, Ahearne, & MacKenzie, 1997). Specifically, it has been argued that OCBs are beneficial because they: (1) reduce the need for organizations and managers to devote scarce resources to purely maintenance functions; (2) free up resources for more productive purposes; (3) enhance coworker productivity; (4) create social capital and serve as an effective means of coordinating activities between team members and across workgroups; and (5) enhance the organization's ability to attract and retain the best people by making it a more attractive place to work (Organ et al., 2006). In the following sections, we describe how unintended consequences may attenuate the positive effects of OCB in each of these areas; Table 11.1 summarizes these arguments by explaining how OCBs are thought to enhance organizational effectiveness and then highlighting the unintended consequences of such behavior. We conclude our chapter by identifying avenues for future research, highlighting methodological and measurement issues that need to be considered, and discussing some practical implications associated with the work reviewed here.

Do Organizational Citizenship Behaviors Reduce the Need for Group Maintenance Resources?

Within organizations, much of managers' time and energy is spent fostering a climate among workgroup members that is cohesive, psychologically safe, and free from interpersonal conflict (Hackman & Wageman, 2007). As such, a core component of

Table 11.1 How Organizational Citizenship Behaviors (OCBs) Can Have Unintended Negative Effects on Organizational Effectiveness

Positive Effects of OCBs on Organizations	Unintended Negative Consequences of OCBs
OCBs reduce the need for group maintenance resources, such as conflict-management activities.	OCB may license subsequent deviant behavior, thereby damaging group cohesiveness and increasing the need to dedicate resources to purely maintenance functions (Klotz & Bolino, 2013; Ormiston & Wong, 2013; Yam et al., 2017).
	OCB may deplete employees' self-control resources (e.g., Bolino & Turnley, 2005), leaving them more likely to engage in unethical behavior that could harm team functioning and require management intervention (e.g., Yam et al., 2016; Welsh & Ordonez, 2014).
OCBs conserve managerial and administrative resources by reducing the need for support for activities such as training, coaching, and feedback.	OCBs can cause role overload, stress, and work–family conflict in employees, the negative effects of which may require additional administrative resources to combat (Bolino & Turnley, 2005; Halbesleben et al., 2009).
	OCB may lead to emotional exhaustion and reduced job satisfaction and commitment, in part by lowering employees' perceptions of work goal progress (Koopman et al., 2016; Munyon et al., 2010). To offset these negative consequences of OCB, more managerial involvement may be necessary.
	Citizenship fatigue may result when organizations fail to invest resources in employees, and this fatigue results in lowered effort toward future acts of citizenship. In this way, managers must expend resources in order to keep employees engaging in OCBs (Bolino et al., 2015).
OCBs enhance coworker and managerial productivity by spreading best practices more quickly, providing useful feedback on new ideas, helping one another learn faster, and so forth.	OCBs may harm coworker productivity when job creep occurs, and acts of citizenship become in-role expectations for employees, thereby creating feelings of guilt and resentment in and among peers (Van Dyne & Ellis, 2004).
	When OCBs become compulsory (CCB), they may harm others' productivity through higher levels of job stress, perceptions of politics, intentions to quit, and burnout, and lower levels of job satisfaction, in-role performance, and innovation (Vigoda-Gadot, 2006, 2007).
	Increased levels of work–family conflict, work–leisure conflict, job stress, and intent to quit result when employees feel pressured to engage in behaviors that are considered to be voluntary by other organizational members (i.e., citizenship pressure; Bolino et al., 2010); the management of these negative outcomes of OCBs may also hamper managerial and coworker productivity.

(continued)

Table 11.1 Continued

Positive Effects of OCBs on Organizations	Unintended Negative Consequences of OCBs
OCBs create social capital and serve as an effective means of coordinating activities between team members and across work groups.	Helping may harm group coordination when the helper's lost productivity is not offset by gains in the recipient's performance, when advice is offered by a nonexpert, or when offers of help are resented by the receiver (Podsakoff et al., 1997).
	OCBs that require a relatively large time investment negatively influence group performance when task interdependence is low (Nielsen et al., 2012).
	OCBs may drive unhealthy competition among coworkers when compensation is based on individual performance (Podsakoff & MacKenzie, 1994).
OCBs make organizations more attractive places to work for both potential employees and those already working at the organization.	Engagement in OCBs may reduce in-role performance, thereby limiting employees' career success, increasing turnover, and making the organization a less appealing place to work (Bergeron, 2007; Bergeron et al., 2013).
	The careers of employees who struggle with time management, or who lack political skill, may be particularly harmed by performing acts of citizenship, thereby making organizations that encourage the performance of OCBs especially unattractive places to work for these types of individuals (Ellington et al., 2014; Rapp et al., 2013).
	In jobs with low autonomy or high accountability, OCBs may be especially likely to derail one's career; in these fields, then, companies that expect OCBs will be relatively less attractive to job seekers and incumbents than less citizenship-centric firms (Ellington et al., 2014; Rubin et al., 2013).

some foundational theories of leadership involves the maintenance of positive interpersonal relations among team members and between employees and their managers (e.g., House, 1971; Fiedler, 1978). When employees are willing to engage in OCBs, though, the need for managers and other individuals to expend resources on the maintenance of the workgroup's climate may be reduced. For example, when employees help one another perform their jobs, then workgroup cohesion should be high (Lin, 2010). Similarly, conflict among employees tends to be less common within teams in which OCBs are performed more often (Kacmar, Bachrach, Harris, & Noble, 2012). Taken together, empirical evidence seems to support the idea that when employees help one another and are especially courteous to their peers, the overall climate of their workgroup will be positive, thereby reducing the need for managers to spend time dealing with interpersonal problems and making sure that everyone feels comfortable in the workgroup.

However, two recent streams of work in psychology suggest that engaging in good deeds, like OCBs, may have the unintentional consequence of making employees *more* likely to engage in deviant behavior when opportunities to do so arise. In this way, the extent to which "good soldiers" reduce the need for managers and colleagues to engage in group maintenance functions may be offset to some degree by the subsequent counterproductive behavior caused by their acts of citizenship. Next, we describe two paths through which OCBs may engender subsequent employee deviance—moral licensing and resource depletion—thereby explaining how acts of citizenship may cause harm to the functioning of workgroups and increase, rather than decrease, the need for workgroup maintenance.

Moral Licensing

A growing body of both theoretical and empirical work has provided support for the phenomenon known as moral licensing (also referred to as psychological licensing; Effron & Miller, 2010). In particular, prior research has proposed, and demonstrated, that when individuals engage in morally laudable behavior, or call to mind their prior good deeds, they grant themselves a license to engage in some degree of morally dubious behavior in the future (Miller & Effron, 2010; Monin & Miller, 2001; Nisan, 1990, 1991). The moral licensing effect has been observed across a wide variety of settings, both in lab and field studies. For example, Mazar and Zhong (2010) found that after shoppers opted to purchase environmentally friendly products, they were more likely to cheat and steal than those who purchased conventional versions of the same products. In addition, when people call to mind a time in which they helped someone, they become less likely to act prosocially later in the day. In a field experiment, Tiefenbeck, Staake, Roth, and Sachs (2013) showed that when homeowners were given positive feedback for reducing their water consumption, they tended to subsequently behave less environmentally friendly by increasing their electricity consumption. Finally, at the firm level, the results of Ormiston and Wong (2013) suggest that corporate leaders who engage in high levels of corporate social responsibility are particularly likely to later behave unethically toward their shareholders.

Klotz and Bolino (2013) focused on the effects of moral licensing as they relate to the performance of OCBs. Specifically, they argued that when employees engage in OCB that is morally praiseworthy (i.e., it benefits others or the organization, engenders greater personal costs than rewards, is proactive, and exceeds formal and informal work requirements), employees will feel licensed to engage in subsequent counterproductive behavior. Furthermore, Klotz and Bolino (2013) predicted that a moral license may provide employees with moral credentials that enable them to engage in a certain degree of deviance without harming their own image of themselves or their reputation with others. Recent empirical work has revealed that moral licensing may also occur when employees feel compelled to engage in OCBs by external sources, such as managerial pressure. Specifically, the findings of Yam, Klotz, He, and Reynolds (2017) suggest that when employees engage in OCB because they feel like they have to, they are more likely to feel entitled to engage in deviant behavior when the opportunity presents itself.

Further work indicates that OCBs may also license the bad behavior of other workgroup members. Indeed, Kouchaki (2011) showed that the good behavior of members of one's in-group is enough to license subsequent counterproductive behavior by individuals. This suggests that in cohesive workgroups, employees may "borrow" a moral license from a coworker who has engaged in citizenship behaviors in order to license their own deviant acts. Moreover, recent work demonstrating that people proactively create moral credentials when they anticipate an upcoming need to act badly suggests that employees may engage in OCBs in order to offset planned future acts of deviance (Merritt, Effron, & Monin, 2010). For instance, if an employee knows that she is going to call in sick on Friday, she may work especially hard on helping her coworkers during the week in order to earn the license necessary to skip work on Friday with impunity. Finally, moral credentials may also be created by recalling instances in which the temptation to engage in deviance was resisted (Effron, Miller, & Monin, 2012), suggesting that OCBs that involve the avoidance of bad behavior, such as acts of sportsmanship, can elicit licensing effects as well.

Taken together, the moral licensing literature suggests that the extent to which OCBs alleviate the need for managers to engage in maintenance activities for the workgroup will be reduced if counterproductivity follows acts of citizenship. That is, while OCBs like helping, sportsmanship, and courtesy should enhance the climate of the workgroup and reduce the likelihood of interpersonal conflict, these gains will not be sustained if they are followed by acts of unethical behavior by the same employees who performed the good deeds in the first place.

Resource Depletion

A second stream of research that has linked ostensibly good deeds (like OCBs) to bad behavior involves the depletion of employees' self-control resources (Baumeister, Bratslavsky, Muraven, & Tice, 1998). According to this perspective, individuals have a limited amount of self-control resources. When these reserves are depleted, people are unable to use self-control to face challenging situations or avoid temptation (Muraven, Tice, & Baumeister, 1998). As such, after people engage in resource-depleting OCBs, they should be more likely to engage in unethical behavior than those who are not depleted. In support of this argument, a number of recent studies have shown that when employees' self-control resources are depleted (i.e., ego depletion), they become more likely to engage in unethical behavior (e.g., Gino, Schweitzer, Mead, & Ariely, 2011; Lanaj, Johnson, & Barnes, 2014; Welsh & Ordonez, 2014; Yam, Chen, & Reynolds, 2014); likewise, when managers are depleted, they are more likely to abuse their subordinates (Yam, Fehr, Keng-Highberger, Klotz, & Reynolds, 2016).

Prior empirical work has investigated the effects of OCBs on self-control resources, and the results suggest that good citizens can become drained as a result of their engagement in such behavior (Gabriel, Koopman, Rosen, & Johnson, 2018; Lanaj, Johnson, & Wang, 2016). Beyond this evidence, it stands to reason that many OCBs require high levels of self-control and therefore may result in ego depletion. For example, staying late at work, refraining from complaining about certain aspects of the job, attending optional meetings, and challenging the status quo all involve overriding the impulses to get home on time, vent frustrations to coworkers, attend only required company events, and keep quiet rather than speak up at work, respectively. As such, it is likely that many OCBs contribute to the depletion of employees' self-control resources, thereby increasing the likelihood that they will behave unethically when the opportunity to do so presents itself.

Thus, the contribution of citizenship behaviors to organizational functioning will be reduced when they cause resource depletion among employees. Indeed, when this happens, managers and employees may need to expend additional resources looking after the interpersonal climate of the workgroup due to the unethical behaviors that can result from the depletion of self-control resources.

Do Organizational Citizenship Behaviors Free Up Resources for More Productive Purposes?

OCBs are also thought to facilitate organizational effectiveness because such behaviors free up resources for more productive purposes. For instance, when employees are willing to help each other or engage in self-development, it may reduce the need for costly formal training programs (Organ et al., 2006); likewise, the willingness of employees to share creative ideas and suggestions can free up financial resources that the organization might otherwise spend on outside consultants or research and development efforts. When employees are conscientious and manage themselves, there should be less need for monitoring and control systems, and when employees keep abreast of organizational changes and developments, it conserves resources that the organization might otherwise have to explicitly devote to such purposes. Thus, one way that OCB contributes to effectiveness is by freeing up resources that can then be allocated to more productive endeavors (Organ et al., 2006). At the same time, OCB may also create the need for other maintenance functions related to employee well-being.

It has been estimated that workplace stress costs companies around the world billions of dollars annually due to increased absenteeism, turnover, health care costs, and ineffective job performance; in response, many companies have started offering programs designed to reduce employee stress and improve employee health and well-being (O'Boyle & Harter, 2013; Weber & Shellenbarger, 2013). Researchers have spent years investigating how occupational and job demands (e.g., time pressure, workload, work environment, shift work) can contribute to employee stress. More recent work, though, suggests that discretionary behaviors like OCB may have negative implications for employee stress and well-being.

Organ and Ryan (1995) first noted that employees who engage in OCB might feel overloaded. Nevertheless, the notion that going beyond the call of duty could contribute to employee stress and overload remained unexamined for a number of years. In an attempt to address this oversight, Bolino and Turnley (2005) explored the possibility that OCB in the form of individual initiative may have personal costs. Individual initiative is a broad type of OCB that involves employees working on their days off, attending work-related functions on their personal time, traveling whenever asked by their organization, volunteering for special projects, participating in community activities that benefit the organization, and so forth. Prior work has shown that behaviors like these are associated with a number of positive outcomes for employees (e.g., higher performance appraisal ratings; Podsakoff et al., 2009). However, in a sample of professional employees, Bolino and Turnley (2005) found that individual initiative was also associated with increased levels of role overload and job stress. Moreover, they found that individual initiative was positively related to work–family conflict (and that this relationship was stronger among female employees). Thus, their findings indicate that engaging in some forms of OCB can undermine key indicators of employee well-being.

Likewise, Halbesleben, Harvey, and Bolino (2009) provided evidence that engaged employees were more likely to perform affiliative OCBs and that these OCBs, in turn, were positively related to work–family conflict. Their study extends the work of Bolino and Turnley (2005) in some notable ways. In particular, the employees in the Halbesleben et al. (2009) study were more diverse both demographically and with regard to their occupations; furthermore, whereas Bolino and Turnley (2005) focused on individual initiative (a type of OCB that is more organizationally focused), Halbesleben et al. (2009) examined OCBs that were more interpersonal in nature. Furthermore, Halbesleben et al. (2009) also discovered that the relationship between OCB and work–family conflict was more pronounced among less conscientious employees, which suggests that employees who are more conscientious may be better able to manage the demands associated with performing extra-role behaviors.

Most recently, Koopman, Lanaj, and Scott (2016) sought to examine both the benefits and the costs of engaging in OCB. First, they developed a conceptual model which proposes that OCB can concurrently generate resources through enhanced positive affect and consume resources by impeding work-goal progress; the generation and consumption of resources, in turn, influences emotional exhaustion, job satisfaction, and affective commitment (i.e., indicators of employee well-being). Using an experience sampling methodology, Koopman and colleagues examined these relationships for 10 workdays in a sample of 82 employees and found that OCB increased positive affect, which in turn resulted in higher levels of job satisfaction and commitment. However, they also found that engaging in OCB resulted in reduced perceptions of work-goal progress, which in turn resulted in higher levels of emotional exhaustion and lower levels of job satisfaction and commitment. The idea that engaging in OCB could actually undermine job satisfaction is intriguing, given that job satisfaction is typically considered a key antecedent of OCB. This aspect of Koopman and colleagues' findings complement those of Munyon, Hochwarter, Perrewé, and Ferris (2010), who found a curvilinear relationship between OCB and job satisfaction among employees who were low in optimism.

In another recent study, Bolino, Hsiung, Harvey, and LePine (2015) looked at an additional outcome of engaging in OCB that may also be harmful—namely, *citizenship fatigue*. Bolino et al. (2015, p. 57) define citizenship fatigue "as a state in which employees feel worn out, tired, or on edge attributed to engaging in OCB." They argue that employees who engage in OCB are volunteering to invest cognitive, emotional, and physical resources in order to go beyond the call of duty. Using data collected at three points in time, they found that OCBs (especially helping and individual initiative) were more likely to lead to citizenship fatigue when employees did not feel like their organization supported them, and that OCB was less likely to lead to citizenship fatigue when employees had high-quality exchange relationships with their teammates and did not feel pressured to engage in OCB. Furthermore, as expected, they found that employees who reported high levels of citizenship fatigue were less likely to engage in OCBs (especially helping and voice) 4 months later.

As noted earlier, OCBs are generally thought to free up organizational resources (Organ et al., 2006). At the same time, emerging work suggests that engaging in OCB can contribute to higher levels of stress, overload, work–family conflict, and citizenship fatigue. Likewise, employees who engage in OCB may worry that they are not getting their work done, which can adversely affect their job attitudes and well-being. These effects appear to occur most often when employees lack certain individual traits (e.g., optimism, conscientiousness) or in certain contexts (e.g., when the pressure to perform OCB is high, when the organization is not supportive). Nevertheless, when OCB harms employee well-being, it is likely that organizations will have to devote additional resources to assist employees in managing these unintended consequences associated with going the extra mile. When this occurs, OCBs are less likely to free up resources and increase organizational productivity.

Do Organizational Citizenship Behaviors Enhance Coworker or Managerial Productivity?

OCBs may also facilitate the performance of coworkers. For instance, colleagues who receive help from their teammates may be more productive. Likewise, when employees voice concerns about current procedures and come up with new ways of doing things, it is likely to improve the productivity of those around them. Using a resource allocation framework, Nielsen et al. (2012) argued that when workgroups are interdependent, OCBs on the part of some team members can enable other team members and team supervisors to focus on more productive tasks. At the same time, there is evidence that the performance of OCB can also contribute to dysfunctional dynamics among colleagues. When this occurs, rather than enhancing coworker or managerial productivity, OCB can have the opposite effect.

Ehrhart and Naumann (2004) developed a theory describing the development of citizenship norms in workgroups. They argue that when employees in an organizational unit engage in OCB, especially those who are prototypical or high-status members, this behavior becomes normative and sends cues to other employees that such behavior is acceptable or expected. These social cues increase the likelihood that other members of the group, especially those who are attentive to social cues and want to be a part of the group, will conform to citizenship norms and engage in OCB. Managers may also encourage the development of citizenship norms by touting the importance of OCB and engaging in acts of citizenship themselves. In these ways, expectations for employees to go beyond the call of duty may develop, and OCB may subsequently become more commonplace.

However, Van Dyne and Ellis (2004) note that when individuals continually exceed their in-role requirements by engaging in OCBs, it is increasingly likely that coworkers and supervisors will expect OCBs from all employees in the future. Furthermore, they argue that this will result in *job creep*, which they describe as "the gradual and informal expansion of role responsibilities where discretionary contributions (such as OCB) become viewed as in-role obligations by supervisors and peers" (Van Dyne & Ellis, 2004, p. 184). They propose that while employees may initially react positively to job creep because they feel good about taking on additional duties and going beyond the call of duty, the felt obligation to engage in OCB will eventually begin to undermine their sense of freedom. They go on to argue that peers may feel that their personal freedom is restricted when other employees engage in OCBs and will develop feelings of resentment and guilt that could lead to decreased satisfaction and increased turnover. Furthermore, job creep may contribute to discord among group members as certain employees may seek to regulate how frequently their colleagues engage in OCB by ostracizing, isolating, or directly confronting those who are seen as doing too much. When OCB in the workplace contributes to job creep, then, it is more likely to undermine, rather than to enhance, the productivity of coworkers and managers.

Vigoda-Gadot (2006) also questioned the idea that OCB is always voluntary and argued that such behaviors can be coerced by managers and powerful coworkers; when this occurs, OCB becomes compulsory citizenship behavior (CCB) that is enacted against employees' free will. In an empirical study of 206 Israeli school teachers, Vigoda-Gadot (2007) found that 75% felt that their managers and peers forced or pressured them to help others, work extra hours, and show additional effort against their will and without any formal rewards. Moreover, CCB was associated with a variety of negative outcomes—including higher levels of job stress, perceptions of politics, intentions to quit, and burnout, and lower levels of job satisfaction, in-role performance, and innovation.

More recently, Bolino, Turnley, Gilstrap, and Suazo (2010, p. 836) further enhanced our understanding of the effect of OCBs on employee well-being by identifying *citizenship pressure*, which they defined as "a specific job demand in which an employee feels pressured to engage in OCBs." Citizenship pressure is somewhat different from CCB and job creep. In particular, job creep suggests that OCBs, over time, may become considered part of employees' in-role responsibilities; likewise, as the name suggests, CCB involves employees being forced or coerced into performing acts of citizenship. In contrast, citizenship pressure conceptualizes OCB as discretionary behavior, but it addresses situations in which employees nonetheless feel pressured to engage in such actions. Consistent with their hypotheses, Bolino et al. (2010) found that citizenship pressure was associated with higher levels of OCB, but that it was also associated with increased levels of work–family conflict, work–leisure conflict, job stress, and intent to quit—even after controlling for other job demands (e.g., hours worked, role overload).

Clearly, when employees engage in OCB, it can help increase the productivity of those around them. At the same time, when employees perform OCBs, it can also contribute to the expectation that other employees should engage in similar behaviors. When OCB starts to become seen as in-role behavior or starts to feel coerced, it may disrupt the relationships among coworkers and lead to conflict and perceptions of politics (Van Dyne & Ellis, 2004; Vigoda-Gadot, 2006, 2007). Likewise, if employees feel pressured to engage in OCBs, the adverse effects of citizenship pressure may result in coworkers and managers devoting additional time and energy to assisting peers who are dealing with stress and conflict and questioning their interest in remaining with their employer.

Do Organizational Citizenship Behaviors Enhance the Coordination of Activities and Improve Group Functioning?

Prior research suggests that OCBs generally increase the social capital between organizational members (Bolino, Turnley, & Bloodgood, 2002) and serve as an effective means of coordinating activities within workgroups (Karambayya, 1989; Smith, Organ, & Near, 1983). For instance, OCBs can help to increase the extent to which a mutual understanding develops among team members, increasing cognitive social capital (Bolino et al., 2002). When this occurs, employees are able to more effectively transfer ideas, share knowledge, and offer assistance to one another (Nahapiet & Ghoshal, 1998). Likewise, OCBs may allow veteran employees to show their less experienced colleagues better and more efficient ways of performing tasks and may allow the more senior employees to teach their junior colleagues various "tricks of the trade" (Podsakoff et al., 1997). Additionally, OCBs may allow for greater coordination of activities within workgroups and may provide a mechanism for constructive suggestions that enhance group or organizational performance (Nielsen et al., 2012). On the whole, then, OCBs are generally thought to enhance group and organizational performance by allowing team members to coordinate their activities and work together more effectively.

Nevertheless, there is mounting evidence that OCBs sometimes reduce the effectiveness with which team members interact with one another. As such, there are times that acts of citizenship impede, rather than enhance, group performance. Indeed, prior research has found that the relationship between OCB and team or unit performance varies dramatically and that sometimes the effect of OCB on team performance is negative (e.g., Bachrach et al., 2006; Naumann & Bennett, 2002; Nielson et al., 2012; Podsakoff & MacKenzie, 1994).

Previous studies also indicate that certain types of OCB may be especially likely to have a harmful effect on the coordination of activities within workgroups. Somewhat surprisingly, at least three studies have suggested that helping behavior may be particularly likely to reduce the effectiveness of workgroups (Bachrach et al., 2006; Nielsen et al., 2012; Podsakoff & MacKenzie, 1994). According to this line of research, there are several reasons that helping may have a harmful effect on workgroup performance (Bachrach et al., 2006; Nielsen et al., 2012).

First, helping is generally considered to be a relatively time-intensive form of citizenship (Nielsen et al., 2012). As such, resource allocation theory (Bergeron, 2007) indicates that providing assistance to another employee may detract from the helper's ability to accomplish his or her own work and may, by extension, hurt the group's ability to accomplish its tasks. In this regard, Podsakoff et al. (1997) posit that helping will only increase work unit performance when the assistance provided to the recipient more than makes up for the lost productivity of the person providing the help. Second, there are many times when behavior that is intended to be beneficial is not actually helpful (Podsakoff et al., 1997). Perhaps the person offering assistance is not as much of an expert as he or she believes or perhaps he or she does not have all the information needed to offer useful advice in a particular situation. Regardless of the specific reason, many offers of assistance end up not being particularly helpful, while others end up actually being harmful. Third, there are times when the advice and help that are offered is resented by the recipient. Control theory (Liden, Wayne, & Bradway, 1997) suggests that some helping behavior is resented because it is viewed as an indication that the recipient is not trusted. When this occurs, the offers of assistance can be a form of demotivating feedback that creates resentment, reduces the recipient's willingness to engage with his or her colleague, and impinges upon the individual's ability to do his or her job as he or she sees fit (Nielsen et al., 2012). In all of these cases, then, helping is likely to hinder rather than help the functioning of work teams, which makes it more likely that OCBs will be negatively related to workgroup performance.

Prior research further indicates that other types of OCB may not enhance group performance either. For instance, in a study of work teams in a paper mill, Podsakoff et al. (1997) found that sportsmanship was not related to the quality of workgroup performance and that civic virtue was not related to either the quality or quantity of workgroup performance. Similarly, Nielsen et al. (2012) found that civic virtue was unrelated to group performance in some situations and negatively related to group performance in others. Thus, there is growing evidence that other forms of citizenship do not always generate the positive effects on group performance that are expected, which signals that there may be broader instances in which OCBs lead to reduced coordination and less effective collaboration among colleagues.

In addition to the type of citizenship behavior that is being performed, there are several other factors that influence the extent to which OCB is likely to harm group functioning. Most notably, significant attention has been paid to the role that task interdependence plays in determining whether citizenship behavior is harmful rather than helpful (e.g., Bachrach et al., 2006). On the whole, this line of research indicates that OCBs tend to have a positive effect on group performance when tasks are relatively interdependent (Nielsen et al., 2012). In such situations, OCBs do help to improve the coordination of activities among group members. In contrast, Nielsen et al. (2012) found that OCBs that required a high investment of time (e.g., helping and civic virtue) actually had a negative influence on group performance when task interdependence was low (i.e., when individuals in a work unit perform their tasks relatively independently). In addition, when group members working on relatively independent tasks feel pressured to reach consensus or adopt similar work approaches, as sometimes happens when citizenship behaviors are commonplace (Bolino & Turnley, 2003), then individuals may experience a decrease in perceptions of empowerment and autonomy (Bachrach et al., 2006; Manz & Angle, 1986). This may reduce both individual motivation and the extent to which team members work effectively together (Bachrach et al., 2006). Thus, task interdependence appears to be one of the key situational characteristics that influences whether citizenship behavior has a positive or negative effect on group performance (Podsakoff et al., 2000).

In addition to task interdependence, several other situational factors are likely to influence the extent to which OCBs facilitate or detract from the effective coordination of activities within the workgroup. For example, the type of reward system being utilized may help to determine the extent to which OCBs improve group functioning (Podsakoff et al., 1997). When compensation systems focus on rewarding all team members for the performance of the group, then the motivation to engage in citizenship behaviors that enhance the coordination of activities within the group is likely to be strong. As a result, OCBs may result in enhanced group functioning and performance. In contrast, when compensation systems focus on individual rewards, then employees may be less motivated to ensure that their citizenship behaviors actually enhance the performance of their colleagues (Podsakoff & MacKenzie, 1994). Additionally, on rare occasions, individuals who feel that they are in competition with other employees might even intentionally provide unhelpful suggestions or assistance to their colleagues, which could obviously reduce overall unit performance (Podsakoff et al., 1997).

Employee experience is also likely to play a role in determining the extent to which citizenship behaviors help or harm organizational functioning and performance. Naturally, many organizations depend on more experienced employees to help socialize less experienced employees on how best to perform their jobs. However, the OCBs performed by relatively inexperienced employees may do more harm than good either because the quality of the behavior is low or because of the resentment that such actions provoke among more senior colleagues (Podsakoff et al., 1997). When more experienced workers resent the OCBs of their junior colleagues, such behaviors may reduce the extent to which the more experienced employees are willing to work with their less experienced counterparts.

Lastly, when turnover rates within an organization or work unit are high, it is less likely that OCBs will enhance workgroup functioning. In particular, when turnover is high, then the costs of time-intensive forms of citizenship may outweigh the benefits of such actions (Podsakoff et al., 1997). For instance, Podsakoff and MacKenzie (1994) note that high turnover rates may be one of the reasons that the relationship between helping and work unit performance was negative in their study. In situations where turnover is rampant, the time that more experienced employees spend getting relatively new employees up to speed ends up being wasted because the less experienced employees leave the organization before the benefits of the assistance that they have received have a chance to fully materialize (Podsakoff et al., 1997).

Does Organizational Citizenship Behavior Make Organizations More Attractive Places to Work?

Podsakoff and MacKenzie (1997) proposed that engagement in OCBs will make companies more attractive to job seekers and will enhance organizations' ability to retain their best employees. In other words, to the extent that a workforce collectively engages in OCBs, recruitment outcomes should be more positive and voluntary turnover should be lower. The boost to organizational attraction caused by OCBs should occur through direct means, such as when employees promote the company to outsiders, and through more indirect means, such as increased affective commitment to the organization as a result of having coworkers that help one another and do not complain about trivial problems (Organ et al., 2006). Simply put, although employee OCBs impact coworker attitudes in different ways, they all have the potential to contribute to an overall organizational climate that is pleasant for insiders and attractive to outsiders.

Empirical support for the role of OCBs in enhancing employees' perceptions of organizational attractiveness comes primarily from studies of the attitudes of those who have been the recipients of coworker acts of citizenship. For example, OCBs tend to elevate the job satisfaction and affective commitment of coworkers exposed to them (as long as abusive supervision is not present; Tepper, Duffy, Hoobler, & Ensley, 2004). In addition, Regts and Molleman (2013) found that nurses who received high levels of helping from their peers had significantly lower turnover intentions that those who were helped less frequently. Taken together, these findings support the notion that employees bond more strongly with their organization when OCBs are commonplace, leading to lower turnover across the firm (Podsakoff et al., 2009, 2014).

Although it makes intuitive sense that job seekers should find organizations with high levels of OCB more attractive than those with low levels of such behavior, research has yet to link employee OCB to perceptions of organizational attractiveness among job seekers. However, prior work has shown that job seekers are drawn to organizations that perform good deeds in general (Turban & Greening, 1997). Moreover, positive word of mouth about companies also drives positive recruitment outcomes (Turban, 2001; Van Hoye & Lievens, 2007). Because employee OCBs should lead to more positive word of mouth, it stands to reason that they should indirectly yield higher levels of attraction among job seekers. More directly, OCBs in the form of promoting the organization to outsiders (i.e., organizational loyalty), should also enhance job seeker attraction to hiring firms.

The Negative Impact of Organizational Citizenship Behavior on Career Success

Despite the evidence suggesting that OCBs positively influence coworker attitudes and reduce turnover, recent research indicates that OCBs also have the potential to harm employee career success and increase turnover by negatively impacting their in-role (i.e., task) performance. Most notably, Bergeron (2007) argued that when workers have a fixed amount of time in which to complete their work, performing OCBs will be particularly likely to come at the expense of in-role performance, thereby harming one's career. She went on to propose that employees' careers will suffer as a result of engagement in OCBs when organizational reward systems are focused on outcomes rather than behaviors, when job roles are unambiguous, and when OCBs are relatively low in visibility. In support of the idea that OCBs can lead to lower career outcomes, Bergeron et al. (2011) found that when employees prioritized citizenship performance over in-role performance, they tended to have lower performance evaluations, reduced salary, slower advancement, and fewer promotions than their peers who dedicated relatively more time to the core elements of their jobs.

Additional work has unearthed other boundary conditions related to the positive effect of OCBs on individual outcomes. The findings identified in these studies shed light on when OCBs may actually reduce career success. For instance, in jobs with low autonomy and high accountability, it appears particularly likely that high levels of employee citizenship will cause task performance to suffer (Rubin, Dierdorff, & Bachrach, 2013). Furthermore, individuals with poor time management skills seem especially prone to the negative effects that OCBs can have on task performance (Rapp, Bachrach, & Rapp, 2013). Relatedly, the findings of Ellington, Dierdorff, and Rubin (2014) provide additional support for Bergeron's (2007) claim that OCBs may come at the expense of task performance, and go on to indicate that these effects can be mitigated by interpersonal skill, or by workplaces characterized by interdependent work or close working conditions.

Collectively, the results of recent investigations cast some doubt on the notion that organizations typified by high levels of OCBs will be more satisfactory places to work. Although some employees may appreciate working alongside good citizens, those performing the acts of citizenship may not appreciate the harm that can result to their own careers, leading them to turn over at higher rates than others when their performance evaluations suffer or their careers do not advance as they hope. Clearly, if job seekers became aware that those who go above and beyond the call of duty often see their careers suffer because of it, then such information is likely to negatively impact their perceptions of the organizational as a good place to work as well (Van Hoye & Lievens, 2007).

Organizational Citizenship Behavior May Harm Organizational Reputation and Performance

Higher performing organizations should be more appealing to job seekers than firms with lower performance (Turban & Cable, 2003). As such, to the extent that OCBs have a negative impact on firm-level performance, the company will be somewhat less attractive to recruits. Although limited, there is some prior work indicating that OCBs sometimes reduce unit-level and organization-level performance. Indeed, Podsakoff and MacKenzie (1994) found that helping behavior negatively related to unit performance in a sample of sales agents. The authors speculated that this negative relationship could have been caused by several different situational factors, such as because misguided helping can sometimes be harmful, because helping by high performers can reduce their high output, or because the receivers of help often quit their jobs before the positive benefits of helping are realized. Regardless of the cause, the decrements in unit performance caused by helping have the potential to also lower the attractiveness of those units to potential employees.

More recent work has focused on how an abundance of challenge-oriented citizenship behaviors (e.g., voice; Van Dyne & LePine, 1998) may result in lower levels of organizational performance. Indeed, MacKenzie et al. (2011) found that the more that employees in a given store engaged in challenge-oriented OCBs above the organizational average, the worse their workgroup performed, which led to lower sales, profit, and turnover for that store (although the damage done to workgroup performance by high levels of challenge-oriented OCBs was mitigated when employees also engaged in affiliative OCBs). As such, the findings of this study suggest that organizations may be less attractive to current and prospective employees when they are saturated with behaviors that challenge the status quo (particularly when affiliative OCBs, such as helping, are absent).

As Podsakoff and MacKenzie (1997) proposed, in general, OCBs should contribute to organizational effectiveness by making the organization a more appealing place to work from the perspective of both insiders and outsiders. Research over the past two decades has not proven otherwise; however, as we have discussed, a growing line of inquiry has identified a collection of boundary conditions which, when present, may diminish the positive effect of OCBs on how current and potential future workers view the organization.

Discussion

As evident from the other chapters in this volume and an abundance of research findings, OCBs typically have positive implications for employees who engage in them and for organizations where employees are willing to go beyond the call of duty (Podsakoff et al., 2009, 2014). Indeed, there is research supporting the notion that OCBs can reduce the need for organizations and managers to devote scarce resources to purely maintenance functions, free up resources for more productive purposes, enhance coworker productivity, facilitate the development of social capital and act as a coordinating mechanism, and enhance organizations' ability to attract and retain the best people by making it a more attractive place to work (Organ et al., 2006). At the same time, researchers have more recently explored the possibility that the effects of OCB are not inevitably positive (Bolino et al., 2013). Here, then, we have highlighted some of the unintended consequences associated with OCB. In light of the findings described in this chapter, we briefly outline some avenues for future research that would further our understanding of the positive and negative consequences of OCB. In addition, we identify some measurement issues in studying the unintended consequences of OCB.

Directions for Future Research

First, we organized our review around the different mechanisms that are thought to explain why OCBs might enhance the effectiveness of organizations and workgroups. Although there is evidence that OCB does indeed facilitate organizational success, the theoretical mechanisms that are thought to account for this relationship have yet to be examined directly (Podsakoff et al., 2014); this is unfortunate and somewhat surprising, given that most of these mechanisms have been discussed in the OCB literature for a number of years. To truly understand how OCB can contribute to the effective functioning of organizations, empirical investigations of these mechanisms are necessary. It would also be helpful to discern which mechanisms are most relevant and which might be less relevant, or irrelevant, in affecting organizational effectiveness. Furthermore, it is likely that certain mechanisms may be more relevant for organizations competing in certain industries, using certain strategies, relying on certain types of human resource management practices, and so forth. Thus, while these ideas provide a general sense of how OCBs should make organizations more successful, it is important to develop and test more sophisticated theoretical models that account for contingencies and context.

Second, although recent research has revealed a number of ways that OCB can have unintended consequences that may undermine the otherwise positive effects of such behavior, these unintended consequences have not been organized into any larger theoretical framework. We hope that our systematic review of this literature will provide a starting point for organizing the various unintended consequences and enable researchers to see some of the potential pitfalls associated with OCB. For instance, in looking across the various studies discussed in this review, it seems clear that OCBs are more likely to have harmful effects when they result in resource depletion and undermine employee well-being. Likewise, our review of this literature suggests that OCBs should be less likely to facilitate organizational effectiveness when employees feel compelled or pressured to engage in such behaviors or when such behaviors become an expected part of the job. Again, though, it is not clear how these mechanisms fit together in explaining the unintended consequences of OCB and how they might undermine the otherwise positive effects of OCB. The models that result from this process should also address different issues regarding the negative effects of OCB. For instance, is it the pressure to perform OCBs that is most harmful, or are OCBs most harmful when enacted at very high levels, regardless of the reason they are performed? Furthermore, are the unintended consequences something that build up and worsen over time, or is this something that ebbs and flows over time? For instance, if employees who experience citizenship fatigue reduce their levels of OCB at a later date, do they eventually start performing OCBs again once they have had some time to recover? Answering these questions would provide the foundation for a more comprehensive conceptual model that might explain when, why, and how OCBs can have unintended consequences that can harm organizational effectiveness over time.

Finally, once we have a better understanding of the ways in which OCB can both facilitate and undermine the effective functioning of organizations and workgroups, it would be useful to develop a megatheory of OCB and organizational effectiveness that simultaneously addresses the relevant mechanisms that are involved. Clearly, such a theory is likely to be very complex and must incorporate multiple mediators and moderators, and delineate relationships that are curvilinear. Indeed, given that prior research has increasingly found that OCB can have curvilinear effects on important outcomes (e.g., MacKenzie et al., 2011; Munyon et al., 2010; Rapp et al., 2013; Rubin et al., 2013), Bolino et al. (2013) called for more work that examines the negative effects associated with OCB using the too-much-of-a-good-thing perspective (Grant & Schwartz, 2011; Pierce & Aguinis, 2013). Thus, it is necessary to adopt conceptualizations and models that go beyond simple linear relationships and effects. Furthermore, as Koopman et al. (2016) recently demonstrated, it is possible to develop and test theoretical models that simultaneously consider both the positive and negative effects of OCB on individuals, and we encourage researchers to test similar models when examining the effects of citizenship behavior on organizational outcomes.

Measurement Issues in Studying the Unintended Consequences of Organizational Citizenship Behavior

Previous research has highlighted the fact that there are unique methodological and measurement issues that come into play when examining the outcomes of OCB (Podsakoff et al., 2014). Naturally, many concerns that arise in this regard apply whether one is examining the positive or negative consequences of such behavior. However, there are some methodological and measurement issues that are particularly important when examining the unintended consequences of OCB.

First, as previously discussed, there may be certain types of OCB that are especially likely to lead to unintended consequences, and there are many different types of harmful outcomes that can occur. In this regard, Bergeron (2007) noted that there were over 30 types of OCB, each of which may lead to different outcomes. However, many studies examine the influence of a very narrow set of OCBs on a limited set of outcomes. For instance, Podsakoff et al. (2014) indicate that over 75% of studies examine affiliative forms of citizenship behavior (e.g., helping, altruism). Likewise, many studies utilize a composite or general measure of OCB, even though such measures can hide the negative effects that specific forms of citizenship have on certain outcomes (Nielsen et al., 2012). Thus, to develop a more accurate understanding of the ways in which OCBs may have harmful consequences, it is important for future research to measure a broader array of OCBs and a wider set of outcomes.

Second, questions commonly arise regarding who represents the best source of information for evaluating citizenship behaviors (e.g., whether OCB should be rated by supervisors or peers or by utilizing self-evaluations). The source of the data may be especially important when examining the unintended consequences of citizenship behavior. For instance, if an individual engages in a high degree of helping, he or she may be seen as an exceptional employee by a supervisor who does not realize that the employee's colleagues see him or her as overly controlling. Moreover, certain types of citizenship may have both positive and negative consequences, depending upon one's perspective. A high level of individual initiative may make one a more productive employee, generating a positive assessment from one's supervisor, but such behavior may also result in heightened work–family conflict, resulting in harmful outcomes for one's spouse (Bolino & Turnley, 2005). Thus, to truly understand both the positive and negative ramifications of citizenship behavior, data may need to be collected from multiple sources.

Third, it is important to consider when citizenship is measured in relation to the assessment of various outcomes. Some types of OCB may influence outcomes in the short term, whereas the effects of other forms of OCB may only show up over time. In particular, the time lag between various forms of OCB and the consequences of those actions are unlikely to be the same (Podsakoff et al., 1997). For example, too much helping may lead to short-term resentment from colleagues, but, if the behavior does not occur regularly, those feelings may abate over time. In contrast, OCBs like conscientiousness and individual initiative may have few negative consequences in the short term, but in the longer term they may be associated with higher levels of stress, work–family conflict, and turnover (Bolino & Turnley, 2005).

Fourth, it is important to note that assessments of OCB may be biased by group performance (Bachrach, Bendoly, & Podsakoff, 2001), perhaps masking some of the harmful effects of such behavior. In particular, when group performance is perceived to be good, evaluators tend to rate OCB as high as well, even when the performance information is not accurate. Thus, given that most supervisors and team members know how well or poorly the work unit is performing, it is likely that such knowledge influences their judgments of the level of OCB performed by group members. To the extent that this is the case, it makes it more difficult to find instances where OCBs harm group performance, suggesting that such occurrences may happen more frequently than has been documented.

Finally, it is also critical to measure OCBs at the correct level of analysis. Specifically, whether the respondent is asked to focus on the behaviors of an individual or the behaviors of the work group is an important consideration, and research focused on the group level of analysis presents unique measurement and analytical requirements. Data aggregation issues are of particular concern when OCB ratings are obtained from multiple members, as are questions regarding the need for homogeneity among raters (Podsakoff et al., 2014). Additionally, the presumed advantages associated with particular sources of information may differ depending on whether OCB is being measured at the individual or group level of analysis.

Implications for Practice

Prior research demonstrates that OCBs commonly enhance organizational functioning and effectiveness (Podsakoff et al., 2000). However, as this chapter points out, research just as clearly indicates that OCBs sometimes have unintended consequences for employees, teams, and the organization as a whole. One important concern for organizations is that the potentially harmful consequences of citizenship behavior are often overlooked (Bolino et al., 2013). Thus, at a practical level, managers need to make certain that they create a work climate in which the positive consequences of OCBs are retained, and the harmful effects of going beyond the call of duty are mitigated (Bolino et al., 2004).

The main lesson of this chapter for practicing managers is that OCBs are not without cost. Clearly, managers should do what they can to motivate their employees to be good organizational citizens. However, when managers successfully create a culture in which their employees are regularly engaging in OCBs, they must also then attend to the unintended consequences caused by such actions. For example, since the performance of OCB depletes employees' resources, managers should proactively find ways for their good citizens to recharge. Prior research has shown that self-affirmation interventions can restore depleted self-control resources (Schmeichel & Vohs, 2009). As such, managers seeking to minimize the toll that engaging in OCB sometimes takes should look for opportunities to bolster employees' sense of selves by giving them positive feedback, providing them with opportunities to see their best selves, and allowing them to express their core values at work (Sherman & Cohen, 2006). Moreover, given that positive affect can counteract the effects of ego depletion (Tice, Baumeister, Shmueli, & Muraven, 2007), to the extent that managers can keep their employees happy, the harmful effects of resource depletion should be less severe.

In addition, organizational leaders should pay more attention to the extent to which their employees feel compelled to engage in citizenship behavior. Indeed, managers would be wise to have frank conversations with their employees regarding the extent to which their subordinates feel pressured to engage in supposedly voluntary behaviors. When a high level of citizenship behavior is regularly required from employees, it is more likely that those employees will eventually feel overwhelmed and experience stress and work–family conflict. In these cases, managers can change their own behavior to reduce the amount of citizenship pressure their employees feel. Likewise, it is also important for supervisors to pay close attention to the consequences of specific types of citizenship. A supervisor who is inattentive may miss the fact that colleagues resent the supposedly "helpful" actions of a particular teammate or the fact that some of those contributing the most in terms of citizenship are contributing less in terms of their in-role performance.

Given the evidence that OCBs can sometimes detract from group performance, team leaders should be careful not to overemphasize interpersonal acts of citizenship, especially in teams characterized by low interdependence. Clearly, teamwork, in general, is a good thing, but teamwork that comes at the expense of the team's task performance is not ideal. Furthermore, when a team needs to innovate, managers may be better off fostering a climate in which employees feel comfortable challenging one another's ideas than developing one in which employees are overly compliant and courteous to one another (Bradley, Postlethwaite, Klotz, Hamdani, & Brown, 2012).

Finally, managers should keep in mind that OCBs are more relevant and helpful in some organizational roles and jobs than in others. Thus, managers should learn to coach, provide guidance, and offer feedback to their employees regarding the appropriate level, type, timing, and focus of their citizenship behavior. Likewise, managers may find it useful to set expectations regarding the appropriate balance of task performance and OCB associated with certain organizational roles. In addition, knowing the potentially negative career implications that can sometimes result from over-engaging in OCBs, managers should intervene when employees' good citizenship appears to be coming at the expense of their in-role performance. Ultimately, then, managers need to consider more thoughtfully both the positives and negatives associated with citizenship in order for these behaviors to contribute to, rather than detract from, organizational effectiveness.

References

Bachrach, D. G., Bendoly, E., & Podsakoff, P. M. (2001). Attributions of the "causes" of group performance as an alternative explanation of the relationship between organizational citizenship behavior and organizational performance. *Journal of Applied Psychology, 86*(6), 1285–1293.

Bachrach, D. G., Powell, B. C., Collins, B. J., & Richey, R. G. (2006). Effects of task interdependence on the relationship between helping behavior and group performance. *Journal of Applied Psychology, 91*(6), 1396–1405.

Bateman, T. S., & Organ, D. W. (1983). Job satisfaction and the good soldier: The relationship between affect and employee "citizenship." *Academy of Management Journal, 26*(4), 587–595.

Baumeister, R. F., Bratslavsky, E., Muraven, M., & Tice, D. M. (1998). Ego depletion: Is the active self a limited resource? *Journal of Personality and Social Psychology, 74*(5), 1252–1265.

Bergeron, D. M. (2007). The potential paradox of organizational citizenship behavior: Good citizens at what cost? *Academy of Management Review, 32*(4), 1078–1095.

Bergeron, D. M., Shipp, A. J., Rosen, B., & Furst, S. A. (2011). Organizational citizenship behavior and career outcomes: The cost of being a good citizen. *Journal of Management, 39*(4), 958–984.

Bolino, M. C. (1999). Citizenship and impression management: Good soldiers or good actors?" *Academy of Management Review, 24*(1), 82–98.

Bolino, M. C., Hsiung, H. H., Harvey, J., & LePine, J. A. (2015). "Well, I'm tired of tryin!" Organizational citizenship behavior and citizenship fatigue. *Journal of Applied Psychology, 100*(1), 56–74.

Bolino, M. C., & Klotz, A. C. (2015). The paradox of the unethical organizational citizen: The link between organizational citizenship behavior and unethical behavior at work. *Current Opinion in Psychology, 6*, 45–49.

Bolino, M. C., Klotz, A. C., Turnley, W. H., & Harvey, J. (2013). Exploring the dark side of organizational citizenship behavior. *Journal of Organizational Behavior, 34*(4), 542–559.

Bolino, M. C., & Turnley, W. H. (2003). Going the extra mile: Cultivating and managing employee citizenship behavior. *Academy of Management Executive, 17*(3), 60–71.

Bolino, M. C., & Turnley, W. H. (2005). The personal costs of citizenship behavior: The relationship between individual initiative and role overload, job stress, and work-family conflict. *Journal of Applied Psychology, 90*(4), 740–748.

Bolino, M. C., & Turnley, W. H. (2012). Organizational citizenship behavior: A review of the political perspective. In G. R. Ferris & D. C. Treadway (Eds.), *Politics in organizations: Theory and research considerations* (pp. 161–190). New York, NY: Routledge.

Bolino, M. C., Turnley, W. H., & Bloodgood, J. M. (2002). Citizenship behavior and the creation of social capital in organizations. *Academy of Management Review, 27*(4), 505–522.

Bolino, M. C., Turnley, W. H., & Niehoff, B. P. (2004). The other side of the story: Reexamining prevailing assumptions about organizational citizenship behavior. *Human Resource Management Review, 14*(2), 229–246.

Bolino, M. C., Turnley, W. H., Gilstrap, J. B., & Suazo, M. M. (2010). Citizenship under pressure: What's a "good soldier" to do? *Journal of Organizational Behavior, 31*(6), 835–855.

Bradley, B. H., Postlethwaite, B. E., Klotz, A. C., Hamdani, M. R., & Brown, K. G. (2012). Reaping the benefits of task conflict in teams: The critical role of team psychological safety climate. *Journal of Applied Psychology, 97*(1), 151–158.

Cascio, W. F. (1995). Whither industrial and organizational psychology in a changing world of work? *American Psychologist, 50*(11), 928–939.

Cascio, W. F., & Aguinis, H. (2008). Research in industrial and organizational psychology from 1963 to 2007: Changes, choices, and trends. *Journal of Applied Psychology, 93*(5), 1062–1081.

Effron, D. A., Miller, D. T., & Monin, B. (2012). Inventing racist roads not taken: The licensing effect of immoral counterfactual behaviors. *Journal of Personality and Social Psychology, 103*(6), 916–932.

Effron, D. A., & Monin, B. (2010). Letting people off the hook: When do good deeds excuse transgressions? *Personality and Social Psychology Bulletin, 36*(12), 1618–1634.

Ehrhart, M. G., & Naumann, S. E. (2004). Organizational citizenship behavior in work groups: A group norms approach. *Journal of Applied Psychology, 89*(6), 960–974.

Ellington, J. K., Dierdorff, E. C., & Rubin, R. S. (2014). Decelerating the diminishing returns of citizenship on task performance: The role of social context and interpersonal skill. *Journal of Applied Psychology, 99*(4), 748–758.

Fiedler, F. E. (1978). The contingency model and the dynamics of the leadership process. *Advances in Experimental Social Psychology, 11*, 59–112.

Gabriel, A. S., Koopman, J., Rosen, C. C., & Johnson, R. E. (2018). Helping others or helping oneself? An episodic examination of the behavioral consequences of helping at work. *Personnel Psychology*, 71(1), 85–107. doi:10.1111/peps.12229

Gino, F., Schweitzer, M. E., Mead, N. L., & Ariely, D. (2011). Unable to resist temptation: How self-control depletion promotes unethical behavior. *Organizational Behavior and Human Decision Processes, 115*(2), 191–203.

Goodell, S. (2003, December 3). Steve Jobs: The Rolling Stone interview. *Rolling Stone.*

Grant, A. M., & Schwartz, B. (2011). Too much of a good thing: The challenge and opportunity of the inverted U. *Perspectives on Psychological Science, 6*(1), 61–76.

Hackman, J. R., & Wageman, R. (2007). Asking the right questions about leadership: Discussion and conclusions. *American Psychologist, 62*(1), 43–47.

Halbesleben, J. R., Harvey, J., & Bolino, M. C. (2009). Too engaged? A conservation of resources view of the relationship between work engagement and work interference with family. *Journal of Applied Psychology, 94*(6), 1452–1465.

House, R. J. (1971). A path goal theory of leader effectiveness. *Administrative Science Quarterly, 16*(3), 321–339.

Kacmar, K. M., Bachrach, D. G., Harris, K. J., & Noble, D. (2012). Exploring the role of supervisor trust in the associations between multiple sources of relationship conflict and organizational citizenship behavior. *The Leadership Quarterly, 23*(1), 43–54.

Karambayya, R. (1989). *Contexts for organizational citizenship behavior: Do high performing and satisfying units have better "citizens."* York University Working Paper, North York, Ontario, Canada.

Khazanchi, S., Lewis, M. W., & Boyer, K. K. (2007). Innovation-supportive culture: The impact of organizational values on process innovation. *Journal of Operations Management, 25*(4), 871–884.

Klotz, A. C., & Bolino, M. C. (2013). Citizenship and counterproductive work behavior: A moral licensing view. *Academy of Management Review, 38*(2), 292–306.

Koopman, J., Lanaj, K., & Scott, B. (2016). Integrating the bright and dark sides of OCB: A daily investigation of the benefits and costs of helping others. *Academy of Management Journal.* Advance online publication, *59*(2), 414–435.

Kouchaki, M. (2011). Vicarious moral licensing: The influence of others' past moral actions on moral behavior. *Journal of Personality and Social Psychology, 101*(4), 702–715.

Lanaj, K., Johnson, R. E., & Barnes, C. M. (2014). Beginning the workday yet already depleted? Consequences of late-night smartphone use and sleep. *Organizational Behavior and Human Decision Processes, 124*(1), 11–23.

Lanaj, K., Johnson, R. E., & Wang, M. (2016). When lending a hand depletes the will: The daily costs and benefits of helping. *Journal of Applied Psychology*, 101(8), 1097–1110. doi: 10.1037/apl0000118

Lawler, E. E., Mohrman, S. A., & Benson, G. (2001). *Organizing for high performance: Employee involvement, TQM, reengineering, and knowledge management in the Fortune 1000.* San Francisco, CA: Jossey-Bass.

LePine, J. A., & Van Dyne, L. (1998). Predicting voice behavior in work groups. *Journal of Applied Psychology, 83*(6), 853–868.

Liden, R. C., Wayne, S. J., & Bradway, L. K. (1997). Task interdependence as a moderator of the relation between group control and performance. *Human Relations, 50*(2), 169–181.

Lin, C. P. (2010). Learning task effectiveness and social interdependence through the mediating mechanisms of sharing and helping: A survey of online knowledge workers. *Group & Organization Management, 35*(3), 299–328.

MacKenzie, S. B., Podsakoff, P. M., & Podsakoff, N. P. (2011). Challenge-oriented organizational citizenship behaviors and organizational effectiveness: Do challenge-oriented behaviors really have an impact on the organization's bottom line? *Personnel Psychology, 64*(3), 559–592.

Manz, C. C., & Angle, H. (1986). Can group self-management mean a loss of personal control: Triangulating a paradox. *Group and Organizational Studies, 11*(4), 309–334.

Mazar, N., & Zhong, C. B. (2010). Do green products make us better people? *Psychological Science, 21*(4), 494–498.

Merritt, A. C., Effron, D. A., & Monin, B. (2010). Moral self-licensing: When being good frees us to be bad. *Social and Personality Psychology Compass, 4*(5), 344–357.

Miller, D. T., & Effron, D. A. (2010). Psychological license: When it is needed and how it functions. *Advances in Experimental Social Psychology, 43*, 115–155.

Monin, B., & Miller, D. T. (2001). Moral credentials and the expression of prejudice. *Journal of Personality and Social Psychology, 81*(1), 33–43.

Munyon, T. P., Hochwarter, W. A., Perrewé, P. L., & Ferris, G. R. (2010). Optimism and the nonlinear citizenship behavior—Job satisfaction relationship in three studies. *Journal of Management, 36*(6), 1505–1528.

Muraven, M., Tice, D. M., & Baumeister, R. F. (1998). Self-control as a limited resource: Regulatory depletion patterns. *Journal of Personality and Social Psychology, 74*(3), 774–789.

Nahapiet, J., & Ghoshal, S. (1998). Social capital, intellectual capital, and the organizational advantage. *Academy of Management Review, 23*(2), 242–266.

Naumann, S. E., & Bennett, N. (2002). The effects of procedural justice climate on work group performance. *Small Group Research, 33*(3), 361–377.

Nielsen, T. M., Bachrach, D. G., Sundstrom, E., & Halfhill, T. R. (2012). Utility of OCB: Organizational citizenship behavior and group performance in a resource allocation framework. *Journal of Management, 38*(2), 668–694.

Nisan, M. (1990). Moral balance: A model of how people arrive at moral decisions. In T. E. Wren (Ed.), *The moral domain* (pp. 283–314). Cambridge, MA: MIT Press.

Nisan, M. (1991). The moral balance model: Theory and research extending our understanding of moral choice and deviation. In W. M. Kurtines & J. L. Gewirtz (Eds.), *Handbook of moral behavior and development* (Vol. *3*, pp. 213–249). Hillsdale, NJ: Lawrence Erlbaum Associates.

O'Boyle, E., & Hartner, J. (2013). *State of the global workplace: Employee engagement insights for business leaders worldwide.* Washington, DC: Gallup Poll.

Organ, D. W. (1988). *Organizational citizenship behavior: The good soldier syndrome.* Lexington, MA: Lexington Books.

Organ, D. W. (1997). Organizational citizenship behavior: It's construct clean-up time. *Human Performance, 10*(2), 85–97.

Organ, D. W., Podsakoff, P. M., & MacKenzie, S. B. (2006). *Organizational citizenship behavior: Its nature, antecedents, and consequences.* Thousand Oaks, CA: Sage Publications.

Organ, D. W., & Ryan, K. (1995). A meta-analytic review of attitudinal and dispositional predictors of organizational citizenship behavior. *Personnel Psychology, 48*(4), 775–802.

Ormiston, M. E., & Wong, E. M. (2013). License to ill: The effects of corporate social responsibility and CEO moral identity on corporate social irresponsibility. *Personnel Psychology, 66*(4), 861–893.

Pierce, J. R., & Aguinis, H. (2013). The too-much-of-a-good-thing effect in management. *Journal of Management, 39*(2), 313–338.

Podsakoff, P. M., Ahearne, M., & MacKenzie, S. B. (1997). Organizational citizenship behavior and the quantity and quality of work group performance. *Journal of Applied Psychology, 82*(2), 262–270.

Podsakoff, P. M., & MacKenzie, S. B. (1994). An examination of the psychometric properties and nomological validity of some revised and reduced substitutes for leadership scales. *Journal of Applied Psychology, 79*(5), 702–713.

Podsakoff, P. M., & MacKenzie, S. B. (1997). The impact of organizational citizenship behaviors on organizational performance: A review and suggestions for future research. *Human Performance, 10*(2), 133–151.

Podsakoff, P. M., MacKenzie, S. B., Paine, J. B., & Bachrach, D. G. (2000). Organizational citizenship behaviors: A critical review of the theoretical and empirical literature and suggestions for future research. *Journal of Management, 26*(3), 513–563.

Podsakoff, N. P., Podsakoff, P. M., MacKenzie, S. B., Maynes, T. D., & Spoelma, T. M. (2014). Consequences of unit-level organizational citizenship behaviors: A review and recommendations for future research. *Journal of Organizational Behavior, 35*(S1), 87–119.

Podsakoff, N. P., Whiting, S. W., Podsakoff, P. M., & Blume, B. D. (2009). Individual and organizational-level consequences of organizational citizenship behaviors: A meta-analysis. *Journal of Applied Psychology, 94*(1), 122–141.

Rapp, A. A., Bachrach, D. G., & Rapp, T. L. (2013). The influence of time management skill on the curvilinear relationship between organizational citizenship behavior and task performance. *Journal of Applied Psychology, 98*(4), 668–677.

Regts, G., & Molleman, E. (2013). To leave or not to leave: When receiving interpersonal citizenship behavior influences an employee's turnover intention. *Human Relations, 66*(2), 193–218.

Rubin, R. S., Dierdorff, E. C., & Bachrach, D. G. (2013). Boundaries of citizenship behavior: Curvilinearity and context in the citizenship and task performance relationship. *Personnel Psychology, 66*(2), 377–406.

Schmeichel, B. J., & Vohs, K. (2009). Self-affirmation and self-control: Affirming core values counteracts ego depletion. *Journal of Personality and Social Psychology, 96*(4), 770–782.

Seibert, S. E., Wang, G., & Courtright, S. H. (2011). Antecedents and consequences of psychological and team empowerment in organizations: A meta-analytic review. *Journal of Applied Psychology, 96*(5), 981–1003.

Sherman, D. K., & Cohen, G. L. (2006). The psychology of self-defense: Self-affirmation theory. In M. P. Zanna (Ed.), *Advances in experimental social psychology* (Vol. *38*, pp. 183–242). San Diego, CA: Academic Press.

Smith, C. A., Organ, D. W. & Near, J. P. (1983). Organizational citizenship behavior: Its nature and antecedents. *Journal of Applied Psychology, 68*(4), 655–663.

Tepper, B. J., Duffy, M. K., Hoobler, J., & Ensley, M. D. (2004). Moderators of the relationships between coworkers' organizational citizenship behavior and fellow employees' attitudes. *Journal of Applied Psychology, 89*(3), 455–465.

Tice, D. M., Baumeister, R. F., Shmueli, D., & Muraven, M. 2007. Restoring the self: Positive affect helps improve self-regulation following ego depletion. *Journal of Experimental Social Psychology, 43*(3), 379–384.

Tiefenbeck, V., Staake, T., Roth, K., & Sachs, O. (2013). For better or for worse? Empirical evidence of moral licensing in a behavioral energy conservation campaign. *Energy Policy, 57*, 160–171.

Turban, D. B. (2001). Organizational attractiveness as an employer on college campuses: An examination of the applicant population. *Journal of Vocational Behavior, 58*(2), 293–312.

Turban, D. B., & Cable, D. M. (2003). Firm reputation and applicant pool characteristics. *Journal of Organizational Behavior, 24*(6), 733–751.

Turban, D. B., & Greening, D. W. (1997). Corporate social performance and organizational attractiveness to prospective employees. *Academy of Management Journal, 40*(3), 658–672.

Van Dyne, L., Cummings, L. L., & McLean Parks, J. (1995). Extra-role behaviors: In pursuit of construct and definitional clarity (a bridge over muddied waters). In B. M. Staw & L. L.

Cummings (Eds.), *Research in organizational behavior* (Vol. *17*, pp. 215–285). Greenwich, CT: JAI Press.
Van Dyne, L., & Ellis, J. B. (2004). Job creep: A reactance theory perspective on organizational citizenship behavior as overfulfillment of obligations. In J. A. M. Coyle-Shapiro, L. M. Shore, M. S. Taylor, & L. E. Tetrick (Eds.), *The employment relationship: Examining psychological and contextual perspectives* (pp. 181–205). Oxford, UK: Oxford University Press.
Van Dyne, L., & LePine, J. A. (1998). Helping and voice extra-role behaviors: Evidence of construct and predictive validity. *Academy of Management Journal, 41*(1), 108–119.
Van Hoye, G., & Lievens, F. (2007). Social influences on organizational attractiveness: Investigating if and when word of mouth matters. *Journal of Applied Social Psychology, 37*(9), 2024–2047.
Vigoda-Gadot, E. R. A. N. (2006). Compulsory citizenship behavior: Theorizing some dark sides of the good soldier syndrome in organizations. *Journal for the Theory of Social Behaviour, 36*(1), 77–93.
Vigoda-Gadot, E. (2007). Leadership style, organizational politics, and employees' performance: An empirical examination of two competing models. *Personnel Review, 36*(5), 661–683.
Weber, L., & Shellenbarger, S. (2013). Office stress: His vs. hers. *The Wall Street Journal.* Retrieved from http://online.wsj.com/article/SB10001424127887324678604578340332290414820.html
Welsh, D. T., & Ordóñez, L. D. (2014). Conscience without cognition: The effects of subconscious priming on ethical behavior. *Academy of Management Journal, 57*(3), 723–742.
Yam, K. C., Chen, X. P., & Reynolds, S. J. (2014). Ego depletion and its paradoxical effects on ethical decision making. *Organizational Behavior and Human Decision Processes, 124*(2), 204–214.
Yam, K. C., Fehr, R., Keng-Highberger, F. T., Klotz, A. C., & Reynolds, S. J. (2016). Out of control: A self-control perspective on the link between surface acting and abusive supervision. *Journal of Applied Psychology, 101*(2), 292–301.
Yam, K. C., Klotz, A., He, W., & Reynolds, S. J. (2017). From good soldiers to psychologically entitled: Examining when and why citizenship behavior leads to deviance. *Academy of Management Journal, 60*(1), 373–396.

CHAPTER

12

Five-Factor Model of Personality Traits and Organizational Citizenship Behavior: Current Research and Future Directions

Dan S. Chiaburu, In-Sue Oh, *and* Sophia V. Marinova

Abstract

For over a quarter of a century, organizational scholars have sought to understand the ways in which employees contribute to organizational success through their organizational citizenship behavior (OCB). Concurrently, personality traits have provided an important lens for illuminating what motivates such discretionary efforts. Our first purpose is to provide a state-of-the art, theoretically grounded review of the literature linking five-factor model (FFM) of personality traits to OCB. Second, we strive to clarify both our criterion construct (OCB) and our predictor space in order to facilitate the integration of past research and pave the way for future research. For our criterion space, we focus on three prominent types of OCB: directed toward individuals (OCB-I), toward the organization (OCB-O), and toward change (OCB-CH). For our predictor space, we examine FFM personality traits and FFM-based dark-side personality traits. Third, we offer new fruitful directions for future research. We conclude with three key themes for future research.

Key Words: five-factor model, general mental ability, organizational citizenship behavior, dark side, maladaptive personality, task performance

Individual differences have been considered important predictors of organizational citizenship behavior (OCB) since the introduction of the construct (Organ, 1988, 1994; Organ & Lingl, 1995). Arguments for individual differences as predictors of OCB have relied directly on the construct definition of OCB as "individual behavior that is discretionary, not directly or explicitly recognized by the formal reward system, and in the aggregate promotes the efficient and effective functioning of the organization" (Organ, 1988, p. 4; see also Organ, Podsakoff, & MacKenzie, 2006, p. 3; Podsakoff, MacKenzie, Paine, & Bachrach, 2000). If citizenship behaviors are defined as discretionary, individual differences such as altruistic personality should serve as valuable predictors of these behaviors. Even when contextual pressures may compel employees to engage in helping others via interpersonally directed OCB (Bolino, Turnley, Gilstrap, & Suazo, 2010), individuals still retain—according to the original construct definition—some of their discretion. Likewise, even if contextual pressures such as individualistic performance incentives discourage OCB, employees' altruistic personality may prompt them to help others. Important in this definition is that individuals can use OCB as a means of expressing their *personal identity*. As Hogan and Holland's (2003) socioanalytic framework suggests, individuals with altruistic personality (an indicator of agreeableness) may help others to express and validate their sense of self-worth and identity as prosocial people. And an individual with dutiful personality (an indicator of conscientiousness) may complete his or her tasks beyond expectations to manifest and validate a sense of identity as a competent person.

Given the importance of personality in predicting OCB, here we review the literature examining the relationship between individual differences and OCB primarily in terms of the five-factor model (FFM) of personality traits and major dimensions of OCB (as well as global OCB). For completeness, we evaluate some prominent propositions from the staffing literature (e.g., Borman & Motowidlo, 1993; Motowidlo, Borman, & Schmit, 1997), suggesting that due to its discretionary nature OCB is mainly predicted by personality constructs, whereas task performance is predicted by general mental ability (GMA). We do this by contrasting OCB (or contextual performance) with task performance, as predicted by GMA and by the FFM personality traits, as reviewed in relevant meta-analytic studies. We follow our meta-analytic review with a discussion of fruitful avenues for research by offering novel takes on personality and individual differences relevant to multidimensional OCBs.

To review the existing empirical literature, we rely on meta-analyses, with occasional forays into primary studies when meta-analytic evidence is not available or when individual studies present more nuanced insights. So far, the connection between FFM personality traits and OCBs has been examined in multiple meta-analyses in the past two decades (Hurtz & Donovan, 2000; Ilies, Fulmer, Spitzmuller, & Johnson, 2009; Judge, Rodell, Klinger, Simon, & Crawford, 2013; LePine, Erez, & Johnson, 2002; Organ & Ryan, 1995). Here, we mostly draw on the most up-to-date meta-analysis (Chiaburu, Oh, Berry, Li, & Gardner, 2011), where FFM personality traits were connected to three forms of OCB: individual-directed (OCB-I), organization-directed (OCB-O), and change-oriented OCB (OCB-CH). When comparisons are necessary, we also employ the most recent meta-analyses relating (1) FFM traits with task performance (Hurtz & Donovan, 2000); (2) GMA with OCB and task performance (Gonzalez-Mulé, Mount, & Oh, 2014a); (3) FFM traits with task performance, contextual performance (similar to OCB-I and OCB-O), and proactive performance (similar to OCB-CH) (Li et al., 2014); and (4) FFM personality traits and facets with contextual performance (Judge et al., 2013). A number of narrative reviews focusing on the relationships between FFM personality traits and OCB have been published recently as well (Borman & Conway, 2013; Borman, Penner, Allen, & Motowidlo, 2001; Hanson & Borman, 2006; Hoffman & Dilchert, 2012; Sackett & Walmsley, 2014). We hope that our chapter provides some useful complementary ideas by taking stock of our current knowledge and identifying roads less traveled in research on personality and OCB.

Five-Factor Model Personality Traits and Organizational Citizenship Behavior: Some Past and Current Findings

The predictor side of the FFM personality traits–OCB relationship is relatively straightforward. The FFM traits are finite in number, clearly defined, distinct from one another (Costa & McCrae, 1988), cross-culturally stable (Church, 2001; McCrae et al., 2005), and genetically anchored (Yamagata et al., 2006). The criterion space of OCB is somewhat ambiguous in terms of construct definition (an issue to which we return) and content (with variations capturing individual-directed, organization-directed, and change-directed, among others). To remain within the boundaries of available meta-analytic evidence, we consider global OCB (e.g., contextual performance) and two traditional (prosocial) forms of OCB (i.e., OCB-I and OCB-O; Organ et al., 2006; Williams & Anderson, 1991) supplemented with the more recent (proactive) form of OCB (i.e., OCB-CH; Bindl & Parker, 2010; Chiaburu et al., 2011; Choi, 2007; Li et al., 2014).

Five-Factor Model Personality Traits and Organizational Citizenship Behavior

Day and Schleicher (2006) argued that, "in understanding how and why personality variables are relevant to (i.e., demonstrate predictive validity in) work settings, what is first needed is an articulation of the criterion space" (p. 687, parentheses original). This criterion-oriented approach is also consistent with arguments by Hogan and Holland (2003), who noted that when personality traits are aligned with relevant behavioral criteria either theoretically (e.g., socioanalytic theory) or via job analysis, predictive validity by personality traits is enhanced. Accordingly, we briefly define and discuss the OCB criterion domain first before discussing its relationships with the FFM personality traits.

In comparison to task performance, defined as job-specific behaviors that contribute to the organization by enhancing its technical core functioning through the transformation of organizational resources into goods or services, OCB has been defined as voluntary behaviors that contribute to the organization by improving its effective psychosocial functioning (Coleman & Borman, 2000). Organ and Ryan (1995) defined OCB as "individual contributions in the workplace that go beyond role requirements and contractually rewarded job achievements" (p. 775). OCB, then—also sometimes called contextual performance—might not contribute directly to the main function of a job, but instead supports the context surrounding job-relevant tasks (Borman & Motowidlo, 1993; Organ et al., 2006).

An early approach for categorizing OCB was based on five related yet distinct clusters of behaviors (altruism, courtesy, conscientiousness, sportsmanship, and civic virtue; Organ, 1988; Podsakoff, MacKenzie, Moorman, & Fetter, 1990). LePine et al. (2002; see also Hoffman, Blair, Meriac, & Woehr, 2007) contended that OCB should be conceptualized as a global, latent construct with the five clusters being its indicators. Williams and Anderson (1991) took a middle-range approach by specifying OCB as having two target-based facets depending on whether the behavior is directed at other individuals (OCB-I) or at the organization as a whole (OCB-O). Examples of OCB-I include altruism, helping people who are absent, taking interest in a new employee, and showing courtesy or cooperation. OCB-O, on the other hand, consists of exemplary work ethic, compliance with organizational rules and polices, providing advance notice when missing work, and promoting the organizational image.

Williams and Anderson's (1991) framework was popularized by the target-similarity model or multifocal social exchange theory. Rupp and Cropanzano (2002) argued that, "individuals in social exchange relationships tend to more strongly identify with the person or entity with which they are engaged" (pp. 926–927). Dalal (2005) and Ilies et al. (2009) also echoed these arguments with evidence that the two dimensions of OCB are related but have their differential nomological networks with other constructs (including some FFM traits). From a conceptual standpoint, research has separated the dimensions of OCB (Ilies et al., 2009) into "interpersonal" (OCB-I) and "impersonal" behaviors (OCB-O). Other recent research on the dimensionality of OCB adds an additional classification scheme of stability (e.g., compliance types of OCB-O) and adaptability (change-oriented types of OCB or OCB-CH) (Choi, 2007; Marinova, Moon, & Van Dyne, 2010). Based on this additional classification, OCB-CH emerges as an important OCB focused on organizational adaptability.

Several meta-analyses conducted before Chiaburu et al.'s meta-analysis (2011) consistently found that conscientiousness and, to a lesser extent, agreeableness—among the FFM traits—are two of the best predictors of OCB (e.g., Borman et al., 2001; Hurtz & Donovan, 2000). Further, when two distinct yet related facets of OCB (OCB-I and OCB-O) were considered, it was found that (although the difference was often rather small) agreeableness was the better predictor of OCB-I and conscientiousness was the better predictor of OCB-O (e.g., Borman et al., 2001; Hurtz & Donovan, 2000; Ilies et al., 2009), thereby supporting the target-based view of OCB. Emotional stability showed a meaningful relationship with task performance and with OCB-I and OCB-O in Hurtz and Donovan (2000), but it received little attention in subsequent personality–OCB meta-analyses. Extraversion and openness did not show noticeable relationships with any form of OCB and were often excluded. For example, Ilies et al. (2009) included only conscientiousness and agreeableness in their meta-analysis (see Chiaburu et al., 2011, p. 1159, for a review of existing FFM–OCB meta-analyses). In sum, until recently, it was expected that conscientiousness, given its job- or organization-oriented and impersonal attributes, would be more predictive of OCB-O and that agreeableness, given its relationship-oriented and interpersonal attributes, would predict OCB-I.

Unlike prior meta-analyses, the most up-to-date and comprehensive meta-analysis by Chiaburu et al. (2011) has expanded and reorganized the criterion space of OCB into OCB-I, OCB-O, and OCB-CH (a proactive, improvement-oriented form of OCB; Allen & Rush, 2001; Choi, 2007; Organ et al., 2006; Van Dyne, Cummings, & McLean-Parks, 1995). In particular, OCB-O and OCB-I contribute to the organization by "maintaining" organizational functioning in prosocial and pro-organizational ways (without disruptions), whereas OCB-CH contributes to the organization by "enhancing," changing organizational functioning in proactive, future-oriented ways (albeit with possible disruptions to existing routines). Examples of OCB-CH include voice by suggesting new ideas and challenging the current work process, taking charge, innovative work behaviors, and personal initiative (Chiaburu, Lorinkova, & Van Dyne, 2013; Choi, 2007).

From a predictive standpoint, conscientiousness, agreeableness, and emotional stability have been linked to both OCB-O and OCB-I (e.g., Chiaburu et al., 2011) and thus all contribute to a more positive work environment. From a theoretical standpoint, these FFM traits can be interpreted as an individual's inclination to be prosocial (and pro-organizational), communal (e.g., Digman, 1997), and to "get along" (Hogan & Holland, 2003). The remaining two FFM traits, extraversion and openness, although often neglected in OCB research, as noted earlier, are interpreted as an individual's desire to be agentic (Digman, 1997) and proactive (to demonstrate "positively valued dynamic qualities and individual ascendancy"; Saucier & Goldberg, 2003, p. 8). Therefore, extraversion and openness are relevant to OCB-CH. With the aforementioned theoretical rationale, Chiaburu et al. (2011) have meta-analytically related all FFM traits to three forms of OCB—that is, OCB-O, OCB-I, and OCB-CH (only rated by supervisors or peers, excluding self-reports of OCB) based on the largest database available at the time (87 statistically independent samples from 77 studies).

Several important findings have emerged from the meta-analysis of Chiaburu and coauthors (2011). First, contrary to conventional wisdom, their findings indicate that although conscientiousness is the best FFM predictor of overall OCB aggregated across OCB forms ($\bar{\rho}$ = .22), it is followed closely by both agreeableness and openness/intellect ($\bar{\rho}$ = .17 for both). Of course, this finding is due in part to the expanded criterion space by the inclusion of OCB-CH. Indeed, the best FFM predictor of OCB-CH is openness/intellect ($\bar{\rho}$ = .17) followed by extraversion ($\bar{\rho}$ = .15) and by conscientiousness ($\bar{\rho}$ = .12). However, it is also notable that conscientiousness ($\bar{\rho}$ = .20), openness/intellect ($\bar{\rho}$= .20), and agreeableness ($\bar{\rho}$ = .19) all have virtually the same relationships with OCB-O (see Table 2 of Chiaburu et al., 2011). For OCB-I, the best FFM predictor is conscientiousness ($\bar{\rho}$ = .25) followed by openness/intellect and agreeableness ($\bar{\rho}$ = .20 for both). One noteworthy finding in Chiaburu et al. (2011) is that openness/intellect has emerged as the best or second best predictor across all OCB forms.

Second, findings in Chiaburu et al. (2011) do not lend strong support for differential nomological networks of OCB-O and OCB-I, which is contrary to findings in Ilies et al.'s (2009) where self-reports of OCB were included and not all FFM traits were considered. Specifically, the FFM traits were related to OCB-I and OCB-O to a similar degree and in a similar pattern. Although this finding is only limited to the FFM traits (the focus of Chiaburu et al.'s 2011 meta-analysis), it suggests the possibility for a framework of OCB based on the distinction between prosocial or "maintenance-oriented" OCB (including both OCB-O and OCB-1) and proactive or "enhancement-oriented" OCB (OCB-CH), rather than based on the distinction between targets- OCB-I and OCB-O (in which OCB-CH is sometimes included).

Third, by comparing their meta-analytic findings on the FFM–OCB relationship with Hurtz and Donovan's (2000) findings on the FFM–task performance relationship, Chiaburu et al. (2011) have shown that Borman and Motowidlo's (1993) proposition that personality traits should predict OCB more strongly than they would predict task performance is supported only for agreeableness and openness/intellect, but not for the other FFM traits. Conscientiousness and emotional stability are equally predictive of OCB and task performance.

Another issue in the OCB literature that we turn to next is whether OCB is more predicted by FFM traits or GMA. Although we take stock of existing research, we do not present novel theoretical frameworks connecting FFM-based traits and GMA to OCB and performance; such theoretical approaches have been addressed elsewhere (e.g., Barrick, Mount, & Li, 2013; Li, Barrick, Zimmerman, & Chiaburu, 2014). In the next section, we turn to meta-analytic evidence about the relationships between FFM traits and GMA with task performance and OCB.

Is Organizational Citizenship Behavior Predicted by Five-Factor Model Traits Versus General Mental Ability? New Meta-Analytic Evidence

Debates over whether differential predictions of OCB and task performance can be made based on FFM personality traits and GMA, respectively, have emerged periodically based on the conceptual model of Borman and Motowidlo (1993; see Motowidlo et al., 1997). These authors proposed that, due to its discretionary nature, OCB should be predicted primarily by FFM personality traits, whereas task performance should be predominantly predicted by GMA.

Much of the discussions examining support of this differential prediction relied on primary studies (Hanson & Borman, 2006, pp. 155–156; Hoffman & Dilchert, 2012, p. 553; and Borman & Conway, 2013, pp. 593–594), which are less generalizable due to the biasing effects of statistical artifacts and to sampling error. Cumulating primary studies in a meta-analysis, Gonzalez-Mulé et al. (2014a) connected GMA to all major OCB dimensions and task performance. Consistent with the prediction of Borman and Motowidlo (1993), task performance was indeed more strongly predicted by GMA than by the FFM traits in combination (89% vs. 11% relative weight [RW]).[1] Inconsistent with Borman and Motowidlo (1993), however, overall OCB was similarly predicted by the combined FFM traits and GMA (47% vs. 53% RW).

Gonzalez-Mulé and coauthors (2014a) further showed that GMA is more strongly related to OCB-CH ($\bar{\rho}$ = .24) than to OCB-O ($\bar{\rho}$ = .18) and OCB-I ($\bar{\rho}$ = .16). Recent research suggests that employees perceive OCB-CH behaviors (e.g., taking charge) as relatively more rewarded and in-role compared to other forms of OCB (Marinova et al., 2010). This may be one possible reason for the stronger relationship of GMA with OCB-CH than with other OCB dimensions. However, Chiaburu et al. (2011) have shown that OCB-CH is still more likely extra-role because it is more strongly related to OCB-O ($\bar{\rho}$ = .49) and OCB-I ($\bar{\rho}$ = .57) than to task performance ($\bar{\rho}$ = .29). Thus, another possibility is that GMA predicts OCB-CH (e.g., problem solving, coming up with new or creative ideas) more strongly because OCB-CH is more cognitively loaded. Yet more primary studies are needed to elucidate the underlying mechanism through which GMA influences OCB-CH. Figure 12.1 summarizes the true-score correlations of the FFM traits and GMA with the three forms of OCB discussed herein and with task performance.

Summary of the Current Findings

The aforementioned review suggests that each of the FFM personality traits is a useful predictor

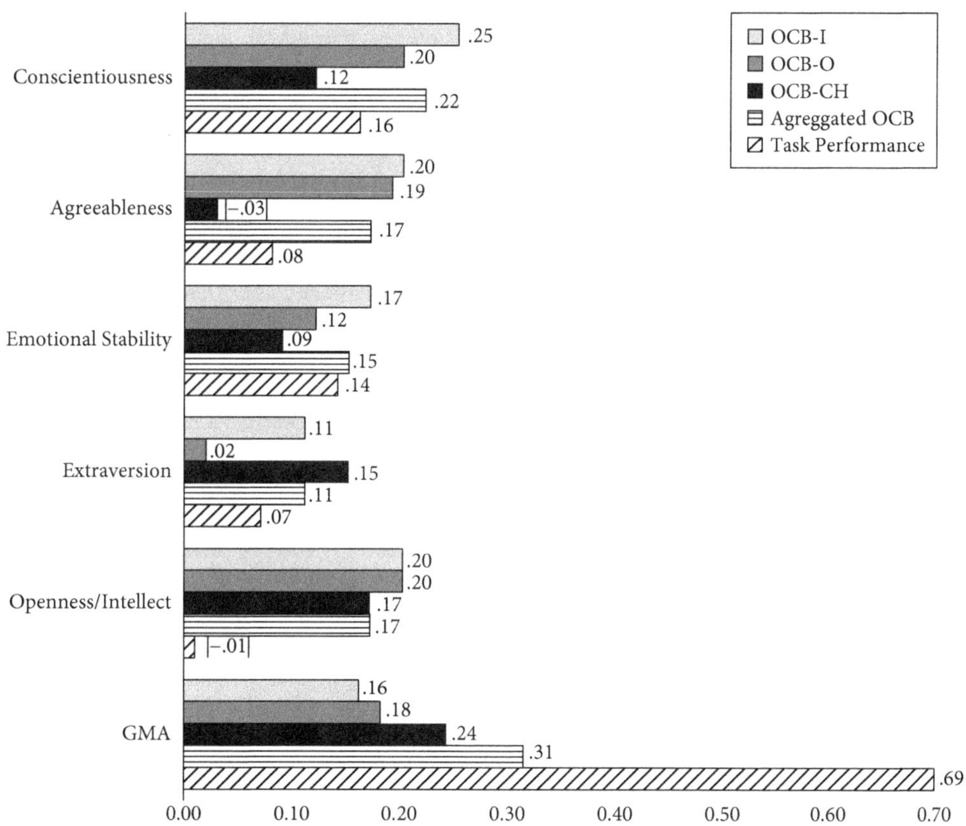

Figure 12.1 The true-score correlations of the five-factor model (FFM) traits and general mental ability (GMA) to organizational citizenship behavior (OCB) and task performance. Results for the FFM traits are based on Chiaburu et al. (2011 for OCB) and Hurtz and Donovan (2000 for task performance) and those for GMA are based on Gonzalez-Mulé et al. (2014a). True-score correlations are corrected for range restriction and measurement error using internal consistency reliability in the personality and GMA measures and measurement error using interrater reliability in the OCB and task performance measures. For symmetry, negative numbers are presented as absolute values.

to some extent. In particular, conscientiousness, openness/intellect, and agreeableness are useful in predicting prosocial/maintenance-oriented OCB, whereas openness, extraversion, and conscientiousness are useful in predicting proactive/enhancement-oriented OCB. The FFM traits as a whole are as useful as GMA in predicting OCB (Chiaburu et al., 2011; Gonzalez-Mulé et al., 2014a). However, there is still much room for improvement in prediction, particularly on the FFM personality traits side. For example, Judge and coauthors' (2013) meta-analysis has shown that narrow personality traits (e.g., FFM facets or aspects) predict OCB better than do broad personality traits (e.g., FFM factors). In addition, an examination of dark-side personality traits or personality disorders based on FFM has recently emerged as a promising way to further understand how personality and OCB relate to one another and to increase the predictive power of personality for job performance (and possibly OCB). Finally, recent research (Huang & Ryan, 2011) has shown that momentary personality (personality states) may be a better predictor of momentary job performance (and possibly OCB) or performance change compared to mean-level personality across time (personality traits). We elaborate on these issues in the next section.

Five-Factor Model Personality Traits as Predictors: New Directions

We present three possible new directions, including (a) the possibility of "zooming in" (Judge et al., 2013) and making predictions based on "dark-side" dimensions built on the FFM (e.g., antagonism, conceptualized as extreme lack of agreeableness; Krueger, Derringer, Markon, Watson, & Skodol, 2012); (b) the possibility to "zoom out" and use broad predictors based on the FFM connected with broad criteria (Li et al., 2014); and (c) the introduction of research designs that account for personality states (Fleeson, 2007; Huang & Ryan, 2011).

Zooming In and the Dark Side

THE ADVANTAGE OF ZOOMING IN (FACET-BASED PREDICTIONS)

Some researchers have argued for increased prediction accuracy of personality when the focus is at the facet level instead of the broad FFM trait level. This has been supported in primary studies (Moon, Hollenbeck, Marinova, & Humphrey, 2008) and in meta-analyses (Dudley, Orvis, Lebiecki, & Cortina, 2006, for conscientiousness; Judge et al., 2013, for all FFM traits). For example, achievement-striving and duty (two of the core facets of conscientiousness) have differential relationships with OCB. Moon, Kamdar, Mayer, and Takeuchi (2008) demonstrated that duty has a positive relationship with taking charge (OCB-CH), whereas achievement-striving has a negative relationship with taking charge. Furthermore, Marinova, Moon, and Kamdar (2013) showed that duty was positively related to helping behavior (a type of OCB-I), whereas achievement-striving was positively related to helping only when the behavior is perceived as in-role and rewarded. Moon et al. (2008) demonstrated that some facets of extraversion (e.g., positive emotions) were positively associated with global OCB, whereas others were unrelated or even negatively related (e.g., surgency) to OCB. These primary studies are informative, but meta-analyses provide more credible information regarding generalizable relationships, to which we turn next.

Judge and coauthors (2013) have recently conducted a meta-analysis on the relationships between the FFM traits (both factors and facets) and major performance dimensions, including OCB. Judge et al.'s (2013) study is based on the aggregation of global OCB (OCB-O and OCB-I combined, with no separate results reported). Their results show that although the best FFM predictor of OCB is conscientiousness, the second predictor is extraversion, with neither agreeableness nor openness being predictive. Openness was not highly related to OCB in this study, most likely because OCB-CH was not included in their criterion. Importantly, Judge and colleagues (2013) further show that FFM facets (a) predict OCB better than their corresponding global FFM factors and (b) provide incremental validity over their corresponding global FFM factors. For example, the corrected multiple correlations by all six facets of extraversion (activity, assertiveness, excitement seeking, gregariousness, positive emptions, and warmth) in predicting OCB is .491, compared with a corrected correlation by global extraversion of only .218 (Judge et al., 2013). The six facets of the FFM outperformed corresponding global traits in predicting the overall OCB criterion across four FFM traits (i.e., agreeableness, neuroticism, openness, and extraversion). Conscientiousness was the only trait that remained somewhat equally predictive of the OCB criterion at both the facet and the global factor levels (see Judge et al.'s [2013] Table 7, p. 890).

Despite the insights gleaned from the aforementioned primary studies and meta-analyses examining the predictive validity of both facets and broad traits to OCB (Judge et al., 2013), such studies have employed only "bright-side" personality traits, restricting the FFM to positive facets or dimensions (e.g., DeYoung, Quilty, & Peterson, 2007) and excluding dark-side personality traits or the negative aspects of the FFM. As we propose next, a more accurate picture may emerge providing new insights through a focus on (FFM-based) negative aspects either at a facet level (Krueger et al., 2012; Lynam et al., 2011; Widiger, Costa, & McCrae, 2013) or at both the facet and broad levels (Markon, Krueger, & Watson, 2005; see our Table 12.1).

FACETS AND THE DARK SIDE

Discussions related to the connections between the FFM-based narrow personality traits and personality disorders have been ongoing for at least two decades (Costa & Widiger, 1994, 2001; Widiger & Costa, 2013).[2] More recently, the *Diagnostic and Statistical Manual of Mental Disorders* (*DSM-5*; APA, 2013) has recognized the utility of a FFM trait-based approach in conceptualizing and assessing personality disorders. According to the current view, personality disorders can be assessed by measuring maladaptive traits based on the FFM (Krueger et al., 2012; Lynam et al., 2011; see Table 12.1, panels A and B). In one of the FFM-based theories of personality disorder, Lynam and coauthors (2011, see Table 12.1, panel A) have proposed that extremely low extraversion, for example, consists of coldness, dominance, and thrill seeking. Similar facets are offered for the other dark-side FFM traits, except openness. From another direction, Krueger and coauthors (2012; see Table 12.1, panel B) propose a dark-side view of FFM personality traits that would include a focus on negative affect (neuroticism), detachment (low extraversion), antagonism (low agreeableness), disinhibition (low conscientiousness), and psychoticism (high openness).

We note that the "dark-side" conceptualizations based on the FFM (panels A through D in Table 12.1) are not necessarily consistent with one another. Yet they can provide a starting point for researchers interested to go beyond a view based exclusively on the "bright side" of the FFM.

In addition to the Krueger at al. (2012) and Lynam et al. (2011) models (presented in Table 12.1, panels A and B), a more precise and comprehensive model is presented by Widiger and coauthors (2013), who recognize both (a) the need to include all FFM model traits thus extending the Lynam et al. (2011) conceptualization, where openness was not included and (b) the need to explicate the bipolarity of FFM personality traits, noting that a specific FFM trait may be maladaptive at both very low and very high levels. This contrasts with the Lynam et al. (2011) and Krueger et al. (2012) models, where the focus is primarily on low dimensions of a specific trait (e.g., low agreeableness, in the form of aggression). Agreeableness for example, as noted by Widiger and coauthors (2013), can be maladaptive *both* at low levels, as aggression (in the form of arrogance, attention seeking, grandiosity, and manipulativeness) and at high levels (in the form of meekness, subservience, and gullibility). Likewise, conscientiousness can be maladaptive at low levels in the form of irresponsibility and lack of persistence, but it could also be maladaptive at high levels in the form of perfectionism and ruminative deliberation (see Table 12.1, panel C).

The idea of dark-side personality traits is not new in the management, organizational behavior, and applied psychology literatures. For example, O'Boyle, Forsyth, Banks, Story and White (2015) meta-analytically demonstrate a robust connection between the FFM traits and their constituent facets and the dark triad of Machiavellianism, narcissism, and psychopathy. In two conceptual papers, Judge and coauthors (Judge & LePine, 2007; Judge, Piccolo, & Kosalka, 2009) presented cogent arguments suggesting that "bright" personality traits, such as conscientiousness, could have a dark side. When selecting for conscientiousness, for example, to what extent are selected employees not only dutiful and cautious but also obsessive-compulsive or perfectionistic? The former narrow traits are in general desirable, but the latter narrow traits that are desirable in moderation become less desirable in excess and can impede OCB. As another example, whereas high levels of agreeableness may increase both OCB-O and OCB-I, the subservient and self-denigrating nature of some highly agreeable individuals may lead them to exhibit less OCB-CH (e.g., taking charge, voice). Conversely, extremely low levels of agreeableness—represented by aggressiveness and suspicion—should decrease OCB-I and OCB-O, while possibly increasing the extent to which an individual challenges the status quo through OCB-CH.

Meta-analytic evidence shows that conscientiousness is positively correlated with obsessive-compulsive personality disorders (Samuel & Widiger, 2008; Saulsman & Page, 2004). Being conscientious includes tendencies "to follow norms and rules" (Roberts, Jackson, Fayard, Edmonds, & Meints, 2009, p. 369), which is a possible liability

Table 12.1 Models of Personality Disorder Based on the Five-Factor Model (FFM) of Personality

A. Elemental Psychopathy Assessment (EPA)

Agreeableness	Conscientiousness	Extraversion	Neuroticism
Distrust Manipulation Self-centeredness Opposition Callousness Arrogance	Disobligation Impersistence Rashness	Coldness Dominance Thrill seeking	Unconcern Anger Self-contempt Self-assurance Urgency Invulnerability

B. Personality Inventory for *Diagnostic and Statistical Manual of Mental Disorders* (5th ed.) (PID-5)

Agreeableness (Antagonism)	Conscientiousness (Disinhibition)	Extraversion (Detachment)	Neuroticism (Negative affect)	Openness (Psychoticism)
Manipulativeness Deceitfulness Grandiosity Attention seeking Callousness	Irresponsibility Impulsivity Rigid perfectionism Distractibility Risk taking	Withdrawal Anhedonia Depressivity Intimacy avoidance Suspiciousness	Emotional lability Anxiousness Restricted affectivity Separation insecurity Hostility Preservation Submissiveness	Unusual beliefs Eccentricity Perceptual dysregulation

C. Maladaptive Traits for High and Low FFM Personality Traits

Agreeableness	Conscientiousness	Extraversion	Neuroticism	Openness
High Subservient Meek Selfless Self-denigrating Gullible	*High* Perfectionism Orderliness Ruminative deliberation Acclaim seeking Workaholism	*High* Excessive attachment Flirtatious Authoritarian Attention seeking Reckless sensation seeking	*High* Anxiousness Depressiveness Emotional instability Angry hostility Self pathology Helplessness	*High* Odd and eccentric Aberrant perceptions Aberrant ideas Dissociative tendencies Romanticizes
Low Aggressive Callous Suspicious Arrogant Manipulative Self-centered	*Low* Irresponsible Impersistent Rash decision making Ineptitude	*Low* Social withdrawal Social anhedonia Physical anhedonia Detached coldness	*Low* Glib, shameless charm Fearless	*Low* Alexithymic Closed-minded Inflexible

D. Structural Model of Normal and Abnormal Personality

Alpha Factor			Beta Factor	
Negative emotionality	*Disinhibition*		*Positive emotionality*	
Negative emotionality	Disagreeable disinhibition	Unconscientious disinhibition	Positive emotionality	
Neuroticism	Agreeableness	Conscientiousness	Extraversion	Openness

Notes. EPA based on Lynam et al. (2011) shows low and maladaptive levels of FFM traits. Panel B: PID-5 is based on Krueger et al. (2012). Panel C: Maladaptive traits for high and low FFM personality traits based on Widiger et al. (2013). Panel D: Structure of normal and abnormal personality based on Markon et al. (2005).

for proactive forms of citizenship such as OCB-CH. Furthermore, perfectionistic employees may even impede aspects of the psychosocial work context by behaving in overly rigid and inflexible manner (e.g., by excessively sticking to rules or enforcing them too strictly and thus not allowing for any creative or innovative ideas) or by being too harsh with others and thereby negatively impacting various dimensions of OCB. If conscientiousness in combination with less desirable traits is less predictive of OCB, then basing our theory and predictions *exclusively* on broad-level conscientiousness becomes problematic. The issue, then, is how to consider conscientiousness *minus* the potential undesirable traits associated with it (e.g., conventionality, formalness, perfectionism, Roberts et al., 2009; disinhibition, Lynam et al., 2011, Markon et al., 2005; ruminative deliberation, workaholism, Widiger et al., 2013). Theory building and empirical testing are thus needed to establish which traits diminish (or enhance) the effectiveness of conscientiousness (and other FFM traits).

Notwithstanding the possible limitations of the dark-side views presented earlier (Piedmont, Sherman, & Sherman, 2012; Piedmont, Sherman, Sherman, Dy-Liacco, & Williams, 2009; Widiger et al., 2013), the approach looks promising. It can allow researchers to formalize some propositions about how negative aspects of personality may predict the three types of OCB. Given the lack of primary findings on the topic, we recommend that empirical research looks specifically at all facets at the extremely high and extremely low end of the FFM model alongside normal levels of each of the FFM traits in order to formulate a more informative research idea. Ideally, research should also include both bright- and dark-side personality traits and a multiplicity of the primary OCB types (OCB-O, OCB-I, and OCB-CH) and their constituent behaviors to capture the complexity of both phenomena using linear and nonlinear functions, and joint effects (interactions).

Zooming Out and the "Dark Side

THE ADVANTAGES OF ZOOMING OUT (BROAD TRAITS)

One approach to increase validities based on FFM predictors, as discussed earlier, is to compare prediction by broad factors versus prediction by facets (Dudley et al., 2006; Judge et al., 2013), with results seeming to favor facets as predictors. Zooming out and taking a broad view provides an alternative view. Researchers have proposed and demonstrated that broad FFM personality traits predict broad performance criteria (Li et al., 2014). Li and coauthors (2014) conducted a meta-analysis to examine the relationships of the FFM traits (only at the factor level) and work performance at the dimensional level as well as at the latent factor level. Specifically, Li and colleagues (2014) combined task performance, contextual performance (similar to OCB-I and OCB-O), and proactive performance (similar to OCB-CH) to represent the *latent factor* of employee *work performance*. Li et al. (2014) found that the relationship (corrected correlation) between the FFM traits and work performance at the latent level is higher (10% to 120%) than the relationships between the FFM traits and specific dimensions of work performance (based on Barrick, Mount, & Judge, 2001).[3] Therefore, when prediction of overall work performance is targeted, broad FFM personality traits perform quite well. However, Li et al. (2014) cautioned that "this does not mean that narrow personality traits do not have utility; we agree with the consensus, that to predict specific criteria, one must rely on narrower traits than the FFM. Nevertheless, when talking about very broad indicators of success at work, the FFM predict better than we have recognized" (p. 377). In a more general vein, profiles of the FFM are rarely explored. Investigating combinations of FFM traits (i.e., profiles) would be an interesting addition to the zooming-out literature.

ZOOMING OUT AND THE DARK SIDE

Despite the apparent gain, the predictor set used by Li and coauthors (2014) included only positive aspects of the FFM traits, without examining the influence of negative ones, in the form of personality disorders. In what follows we propose yet another direction, whereby the focus is on the dark side of either the personality traits themselves or their combinations. In addition, although most researchers agree that the Big Five personality dimensions enjoy robust empirical support in terms of convergent and discriminant validity (Costa & McCrae, 1988), the lack of an underlying theoretical structure weakens arguments connecting FFM personality traits with OCB. To address this issue, researchers draw on broader models attempting to group the FFM traits into a lower number of factors reflecting "getting along" and "getting ahead" motives (Oh & Berry, 2009; based on Digman, 1997) or use other groupings based on five or six factors (Ashton & Lee, 2001; DeYoung et al., 2007).

An alternative way of highlighting and capturing the dark side is to capitalize on the hierarchical approach demonstrated via meta-analysis by Markon and coauthors (2005; see panel D in our Table 12.1). Digman (1997) provided a higher level framework for the FFM, which resulted in identifying two higher level latent factors capturing the FFM-alpha similar to the communal motive to get along (represented by agreeableness, conscientiousness, and emotional stability) and FFM-beta consistent with the motive to get ahead (represented by openness and extraversion). Building on Digman's work, Markon and coauthors presented a hierarchical structure attempting to include *both* normal and abnormal personality dimensions. Their basic line of reasoning focused on the idea that normal and abnormal personality dimensions "can be treated within a single unified structural framework" (Markon et al., 2005, p. 139). Their structure starts at item level and continues to the five-factor level (where one encounters the FFM). At a four-factor level, extraversion and openness are subsumed by positive emotionality, while the remaining factors are under one factor each: neuroticism under negative emotionality, agreeableness under disagreeable disinhibition, and conscientiousness under unconscientious disinhibition. The three-factor model further collapses disinhibition, before reaching Digman's (1997) two-factor structure based on alpha (the low end of "getting along" capturing negative emotionality and disinhibition) and beta corresponding to positive emotionality.

One promising line of investigation, then, is to relate higher order structures with a respectively broad work effectiveness criterion (Harrison, Newman, & Roth, 2006; Hough & Oswald, 2005), including task performance in addition to traditional (OCB-I and -O) and more recent (OCB-CH) forms of citizenship. Such empirical tests can address both the issue of *breadth*—with a higher order structure model being broader than a five-factor model, and of *valence*—provided that Markon and coauthors' (2005) arrived at this structure by analyzing a meta-analytic matrix of both normal and abnormal personality constructs.

Outside the Five-Factor Model Straightjacket?

The aforementioned solutions, of increasing validity by including FFM-based dark-side constructs at broad or facet levels, attempt to optimize the prediction while remaining within the boundaries of the FFM. Yet fitting the square pegs of the FFM personality traits into the round hole of theories focused on broader constructs such as agency and communion (e.g., Digman, 1997) begs the questions of whether constructs based on dimensions other than the FFM should be explored. For the prediction of OCB, one possible research direction is to measure communion and agency or related communal constructs such as other-oriented empathy and helpfulness (Penner, Fritzsche, Craiger, & Freifeld, 1995) and agentic constructs such as proactive personality (Hoffman & Dilchert, 2012; Marinova, Peng, Lorinkova, Van Dyne & Chiaburu, 2015). For example, Marinova and coauthors (2015) approached meta-analytically the comparison of the prediction of OCB-CH achieved by proactive personality against two agentic FFM personality traits (extraversion and openness) and two communal FFM personality traits (agreeableness and conscientiousness) to directly compare their usefulness in the prediction of change-oriented citizenship. Their theory and findings reveal that proactive personality is a better predictor of OCB-CH. Such findings suggest that even though the FFM has generalizable appeal, other individual traits may be equally or more relevant in the prediction of the different kinds of OCB.

Likewise, to increase validities for OCB-I, Penner and coauthors proposed constructs such as other-oriented empathy and helpfulness (Penner et al., 1995). Because OCB-I involves helpfulness and courteousness to others (Marinova et al., 2010), it may be especially well predicted by individual differences that address its interpersonal core and the sensitivity to others' needs. Rioux and Penner (2001) demonstrate that prosocial value motives (a construct similar to empathy and helpfulness) predict OCB-I. By comparison, some traditional examples of OCB-O include exemplary compliance (Marinova et al., 2010) and may be predicted well by the individual's orientation to authority or concern for their organization (Rioux & Penner, 2001). From another direction, Oh and colleagues (2014) have found that honesty-humility defined as a propensity to avoid exploitation, opportunism, and greediness and to be genuine and fair with others is positively related to global OCB after controlling for the FFM traits. The same study finds no incremental validity of honesty-humility for task performance, highlighting the possibility for unique motivational forces driving OCB versus task performance.

A comprehensive meta-analysis by Parks-Leduc, Feldman, and Bardi (2015) further provides evidence that researchers should consider personal values ("rather stable broad life goals that are important to people in their lives and guide their perceptions, judgments, and behavior," p. 3) in addition to personality traits. As their results show, although values are related to traits, they exhibit significant unique variability. When applied to the OCB domain, *benevolence* (promoting the welfare of all people and nature) may be critical in eliciting OCB-I; *conformity, tradition*, and *security* may increase general OCB-O (e.g., compliance) but could decrease OCB-CH, while *stimulation* could predict OCB-CH (e.g., taking initiative, taking charge). Overall, given the importance of person–organization fit to organizational and individual performance and well-being, a more in-depth understanding of values can provide insights not only to organizations regarding individuals that would fit their cultural values but also to individuals who can use their values to select into contexts more likely to favor the types of citizenship that they would be suited for. Therefore, there are still many bright-side *individual differences* outside of the FFM straightjacket that are theoretically relevant and should be incorporated into the study of traits and OCB.

From another direction, O'Boyle, Forsyth, Banks, and McDaniel (2012) meta-analytically examined the relationships between the "dark triad" (Machiavellianism, narcissism, and psychopathy) and job performance (without reporting separate results for OCB, given a paucity of relevant primary studies). The dark triad can be useful in predicting OCB as well. Narcissists have a strong desire to attract and obtain others' attention and recognition and are likely to help others (OCB-I) and provide ideas and suggestions (OCB-CH) particularly in public settings. But it is possible that they may falsify their travel reports in private settings (or when they believe they have been unfairly treated) because they believe that they deserve special treatment (high self-entitlement). In addition, trait cynicism may be positively related to OCB-CH. Cynics may engage in OCB-CH (e.g., pointing out problems in the current work process) given their tendencies to view the world through a critical lens (Thundiyil, Chiaburu, Oh, Banks, & Peng, 2015); however, they may do this without providing alternatives.

Because of their incremental nature (i.e., add a specific construct to increase predictive validity), the ideas mentioned earlier may loosen but not completely remove the FFM "straightjacket." For the prediction of OCB—but also for more general predictions in organizational behavior—we need frame-breaking personality theories that are, at the same time, theoretically grounded. The lack of an underlying theoretical structure to explain the FFM personality traits remains frustrating. Of more concern, existing theoretical models (Ashton & Lee, 2001; DeYoung et al., 2007; Digman, 1997) lack complexity. The development of empirically based (but not necessarily factor analytic-based) theories of personality requires addressing some complex issues (Lenzenweger & Clarkin, 2005; Westen, 1995). One relevant direction for our discussion includes both the *continuity* of functional and dysfunctional personality traits and the state-trait (or *stability*) issue (see Lenzenweger & Clarkin, 2005). We now turn to the latter idea—personality states.

Trait Salience Through Personality States and Trait Activation

So far, our discussion has focused on personality traits as predictors, sidestepping the issue of their potential variation at a within-person level. Recently, Huang and Ryan (2011) proposed and demonstrated that there is variance in how personality traits manifest at the within-individual level as *personality states*. Huang and Ryan's refocus from personality traits to personality states builds on the work of Fleeson (e.g., Fleeson & Gallagher, 2009; Fleeson, 2012), who describe a state as an individual's personality at a given moment. A perspective focused on states has advantages, including being able to capture within-person level variations. State extraversion, for example, is variable, with the distribution of states for high extraverts and high introverts overlapping (Fleeson & Gallagher, 2009). If both extraverts and introverts *can* engage in OCBs at a given moment, the predictive task shifts from determining the optimal profile (e.g., high extraverts, or ambiverts, depending on the outcome) to assessing (a) within-individual variation and (b) what situational cues reliably increase extraversion (or other traits). Researchers have found, for example, that state extraversion was increased by situational contingencies characterized by friendliness (Fleeson, 2007; Huang & Ryan, 2011). Momentary predictions are informative for OCB constructs, especially the ones involving proactivity, when actions such as initiative, taking charge, or voice are important to pursue at a specific time (e.g., in organizational change). Likewise, contextual "pressure points" can accentuate the emergence of some dark personality traits. Sudden, substantial, changes in organizations or units could influence (personality) states such as anxiousness, separation insecurity, and even hostility.

A different way to increase the validities of the FFM predictors is to match the trait with the job context and to provide the employees with more opportunities to express traits that represent, for them, preferred ways to perceive, think, and act. Meta-analytic evidence in this direction is presented by Judge and Zapata (2015), who show that validities increase up to two (and for some traits close to three times) in the "right" situations, described as weak situations where the trait is theoretically relevant (Judge & Zapata, 2015). Extraversion was particularly predictive of performance in contexts requiring social skills, while openness was more strongly related to performance in situations that favored innovation. Whereas the results reported by Judge and Zapata pertain to task performance and to overall performance (their dependent constructs), their theory is relevant for OCBs. As noted at the offset of the chapter, when citizenship is seen as discretionary, "right situations" for trait expression could strengthen the connection between the personality trait and OCB outcomes.

Unresolved Issues and Additional Research Directions

Organizational Citizenship Behavior and Its Measurement

Two important qualifiers in the original definition of OCB were its discretionary and unrewarded nature. Once removed, organizational citizenship may be as well assimilated with broader constructs in social psychology, such as altruism or helping (Batson, 2011) or incorporated into general task performance. If the differentiating elements of being (a) discretionary and (b) not explicitly rewarded are to be maintained in the definition, they need to be also explicitly measured in the operationalization of the citizenship. Specifically, because role breadth or definition is in the eye of the beholder (Chiaburu & Byrne, 2009; Marinova et al., 2010; Morrison, 1994), questions asking respondents about OCB should also explicitly assess the extent to which managers and employers see the behavior as discretionary and not formally rewarded (Stone-Romero, Alvarez, & Thompson, 2009).

Much literature has now acknowledged that OCBs have clear utility for organizational outcomes and are often viewed as somewhat expected and as contributing to performance ratings. A meta-analysis by Podsakoff, Whiting, Podsakoff, and Blume (2009) demonstrates generalizable relationships between OCB and performance ratings and reward decisions as well as between OCB and organizational effectiveness. Recent models also portray a nuanced picture of how different OCBs are viewed by employees. Marinova and colleagues (2010) show that employees perceive systematic differences in how rewarded and in-role OCBs are. Taking charge, one type of OCB-CH, is perceived by employees as especially salient for rewards and expected of them. At the other extreme, employees perceive sportsmanship, a type of interpersonal OCB (OCB-I), as least likely to receive formal recognition and rewards. Therefore, individual differences related to reward sensitivity may better predict OCB-CH, whereas individual differences reflective altruistic personality may be more predictive of OCB-I. Furthermore, whether OCB is seen as in-role versus extra-role OCB can change the strength of the situation and modify the relationship between personality factors and different types of OCB.

Unique construct validity issues are present for change-oriented OCB. In one integrative study, the construct includes "taking charge; personal initiative; adaptive, creative, and innovative performance; and voice" (Chiaburu et al., 2011, p. 1144). Evidence from meta-analytic (Tornau & Frese, 2013) and primary studies (Parker & Collins, 2010) in the proactivity domain suggests that some of these constructs "hang together." Chiaburu and coauthors (2013) offered some construct validity evidence via expert ratings' percentage of substantive agreement (Anderson & Gerbing, 1991), confirming that expert raters (N = 14) see creative performance (1.00), taking charge (.93), personal initiative (.93), proactive performance (.93), adaptive performance (.86), and voice (.62) as change-oriented forms of OCB. Yet problems remain. Among them is the extent to which expert ratings are representative and whether other behaviors should be included. That creativity is seen as more central to change-oriented OCB than voice warrants further investigation. Additionally, the notion that supervisors may react to voice positively or negatively has been long recognized in the whistle-blowing literature, but it has only recently started to receive attention in the mainstream OCB literature (Burris, 2012). Given our interest in dark traits, we believe that when OCB-CH comes from someone who scores high on some of the dark traits, OCB-CH may be viewed more negatively. Interestingly, as with the traditional OCB construct (Organ, 1988; Organ et al., 2006), the "extra-role" qualifier features prominently in the definition of OCB-CH constructs, without receiving corresponding coverage in the underlying measure (e.g., taking charge; Morrison & Phelps, 1999).

To better establish the contrast between OCB and task performance, researchers may have to look at multidimensional frameworks of OCB and account for a more contextualized view of their similarities and differences. At its core, OCB is probably still more discretionary than typical forms of job or task performance. However, context matters. In some academic environments research productivity (task performance) is weighed more heavily in the performance evaluation of a typical research professor when compared with service (a type of OCB). However, in other academic environments, or depending on the rank of a professor, service (a type of OCB) may be weighed equally or as more important to overall employee effectiveness. In sum, we recommend that future research adopt a more contextualized approach to some of the underlying OCB definitional and operationalization level issues, including its in-role versus extra-role distinction.

Mediators and Moderators

Although we have advanced research on personality and OCB over the years, there are some important yet unresolved issues presented as follows. First, more research should be conducted in testing the causal relationships linking distal individual differences such as the FFM traits and GMA, proximal mediators such as task and contextual knowledge/skill and habit, and distal job performance dimensions such as task performance and OCB (proposed by Motowidlo et al., 1997). A practical test of this model (e.g., missing the link between personality and contextual knowledge/skills) has been reported in two primary studies (Bergman, Donovan, Drasgow, Overton, & Henning, 2008; Borman, Brantley, & Henson, 2014), but a full test is yet to be conducted. As lamented by Gonzalez-Mulé and coauthors (2014a), we particularly need more research on the relationships between distal individual differences (i.e., personality) and proximal mediators (e.g., contextual knowledge). In addition, although recent research has made good progress on the boundary conditions of the personality–job performance relationship, empirical tests of the boundary conditions of the FFM traits and OCB are needed, while focusing on the personality side (e.g., personality strength; see Dalal, Meyer, Bradshaw, Green, Kelly, & Zhu, 2015), the OCB side (e.g., OCB types; see Chiaburu et al., 2011), and the situation side (e.g., situational strength and trait-relevant cues; see Judge & Zapata, 2015).

Nonlinear Relationships

Second, the linear relationship between personality and OCB has been challenged in several primary studies. Le and coauthors (2011) have shown that the relationship between emotional stability and OCB can be curvilinear and further moderated by the level of job complexity. Specifically, the relationship between emotional stability and OCB is more positive at high levels of job complexity. In contrast, when job complexity is low, emotional stability displays an inverted-U shape to OCB. Initially emotional stability is positively related to OCB, but after the midpoint, an increase in emotional stability decreases OCB in simple jobs.

Relatedly, Grant (2013) has recently found that ambiverts, individuals who score in the middle of the extraversion scale, are more effective in sales performance than both extreme introverts and extraverts. As discussed in Converse and Oswald (2014), we need a better understanding of what middle (or extreme) scores on the FFM traits represent conceptually. It could be that the employee who is in the middle on some FFM traits is more balanced and enjoys the benefits employing both approaches to a moderate extent (Grant, 2013; Grant & Schwartz, 2011).

Although predictive, scores that are elevated, depressed, or moderate (Grant, 2013; Le et al., 2011) provide little information on the *why* of the relationship; theoretical clarity can be nevertheless gained through delineating personality subdimensions, an issue discussed earlier, by focusing on FFM-based personality disorders. Such nonlinearity may become particularly relevant to some maladaptive traits at the high level of FFM because, realistically, the presence of some of these facets (e.g., selflessness, perfectionism, workaholism) in *some* degree is both normal and desirable. However, it is likely that at extreme levels, these traits become detrimental not only to the individual's well-being, but to OCB and to overall employee effectiveness as well.

Rating Sources and Other Measurement Issues

Finally, meta-analytic work has also demonstrated that sources of personality ratings matter (Connelly & Ones, 2010; Oh, Wang, & Mount, 2011). It has been found that observer ratings of personality are more valid than corresponding self-reports of personality in predicting aggregated job performance across task performance, OCB, and overall job performance. Although separate findings are not available for OCB, it is likely that observer ratings of personality as an indicator of one's reputation better predict OCB than self-reports of personality. Relatedly, Shaffer and Postlethwaite (2012) meta-analysis confirms that work-specific self-reported personality (e.g. Conscientiousness at work) is a better predictor of aggregated job performance than general self-reported personality by providing a clearer frame of reference in responding to personality items.

The relationship between personality and OCB is also influenced by the rating source of OCB and other measurement issues in the OCB variable (see Podsakoff, Whiting, Welsh, & Mai, 2013). Additional work needs to be done on how to enhance the magnitude of the personality–OCB relationship in terms of OCB measurement. One possible way to increase the degree of the relationship is to collect OCB ratings from multiple raters and sources so that the OCB measure is less criterion deficient. Supervisors are more motivated (better suited) to observe the target's OCB-O and OCB-CH given their primary interest in task completion, whereas subordinates and peers are more motivated to observe the target's OCB-I, given their interest in relationship building (Kammeyer-Mueller, Steel, & Rubenstein, 2010; Oh & Berry, 2009).

Practical Implications

One open question is how organizations and managers can fully incorporate personality trait assessment into their work processes (Organ, Podsakoff, & Podsakoff, 2010). Although personality has gained momentum as a valuable approach to helping organizations select employees who would fit the nature of the tasks and organizational needs, issues concerning the validation of more complex relationships will emerge. For example, extremely high or low levels of FFM traits may add to the prediction of employee effectiveness. Likewise, examining other relevant traits or values can also increase predictive validity of personality. And, when we turn our attention to dark traits, we are facing additional dilemmas. Dark traits could be associated with mental disorders (Duggan et al., 2003). On one hand, from a legal and perhaps even moral standpoint, organizations should attempt to provide reasonable accommodation to individuals with disabilities, which may include mental disorders. On the other hand, if specific dark traits predict OCB and other in-role and extra-role performance outcomes negatively, there may be valid reasons to use selection testing based on these negative extreme traits. Importantly, such information may be used by managers to better understand their employees' training and development needs. At the same time, given the legal ramifications, organizations may be caught in a vicious circle of not properly addressing their organizational needs or their employees' needs (Christiansen, Quirk, Robie, & Oswald, 2014). Although we recommend that organizations approach these issues with great caution and we acknowledge that there is no silver bullet for this complex situation, we believe that there is utility for organizations to find ways to ethically incorporate such assessment into their work processes. One advantage of using variants of the FFM is that FFM is geared toward normal personality and thus less likely to directly tap into protected categories of disorders. Yet some of the terms used in the maladaptive FFM traits such as "depressivity" and "depressiveness" may have to be deliberately avoided due to their potential for discrimination. Another promising direction would be to use situational judgment tests (SJTs) for assessing personality because they may provide a valid yet less invasive method for predicting the applicant's behavior.

As noted earlier, although typologies of OCBs traditionally tried to demarcate in-role and extra-role performance, OCBs are often relevant performance dimensions (e.g., Stone-Romero et al., 2009). Organizations recognize this reality through complex multidimensional work performance taxonomies: good team player (OCB-I), conscientious employee (OCB-O), and good change agent who provides constructive ideas for change (OCB-CH). Therefore, organizations may be well advised to develop predictive validity studies for their own performance needs, tapping relevant traits and tapping relevant OCB dimensions.

Multilevel Implications

Personality has traditionally been considered as inherent to the individual level of analysis. However, a number of researchers have argued for a multilevel view to incorporate other levels such as the team level (Gonzalez-Mulé, DeGeest, McCormick, Seong, & Brown, 2014b; LePine, Buckman, Crawford, & Methot, 2011) and the organizational level (Oh, Kim, & Van Iddekinge, 2015). Such multilevel areas of studying personality are burgeoning, with some studies examining the effect of the FFM traits on helping norms and helping in teams (e.g., Gonzalez-Mulé et al., 2014b). For example, research by Gonzales-Mulé and colleagues (2014b) demonstrates that both average level of agreeableness and extraversion *and* the variance of agreeableness and extraversion (e.g., presence of highly agreeable and highly disagreeable individuals) in teams predict helping norms in teams and, in turn, helping behaviors.

Other studies take this relationship to a higher level by showing a link of the personality of a CEO and the top management team with organizational performance outcomes (Colbert, Barrick, & Bradley, 2014); and between some of the managerial FFM traits (based on their mean and variance as well as their interactive effects) and labor productivity and profitability (Oh et al., 2015).

Departing from past research, future research utilizing multilevel theory and frameworks can relate not only the FFM traits but also non-FFM traits and dark-side traits to complex multidimensional frameworks of OCB across levels of analysis. Moreover, applying facet approaches and dark-trait approaches should bring additional insight into the team dynamics of personality and OCB. For instance, does the concentration or variance in dark traits matter to team OCB and to performance outcomes? Similarly, CEO's dark traits may predict organizational outcomes, including organizational survival versus organizational bankruptcy, and may trickle down to influence employee engagement in OCB versus deviance. A recent meta-analysis by Wang, Holmes, Oh, and Zhu (2016) offers useful insights into these issues by reporting a relationship between CEO characteristics and firm strategic actions and performance.

Conclusion

In this chapter, we reviewed and integrated the literature pertaining to personality and OCB in an attempt to answer the question: Who is the good organizational citizen? We followed our initial review with multidirectional and multilevel agendas for future research, which we hope will stimulate a discussion of neglected and relatively underinvestigated areas of research.

Notes

1. Relative weights reflect the magnitude of each predictor (or set of predictors) as a percentage of the overall explained variance in the criterion of interest. The sum of relative weights adds up to 100%.
2. To remain consistent with the current (mostly clinical psychology) literature, we are using the term "personality disorders" to describe these traits and their facets. Yet, especially when assessed in workplace settings where their severity may be reduced, the terms "personality styles" or "personality patterns" seem more appropriate.
3. Li et al. (2014, Table 12.1, p. 374) report increases of 10% for agreeableness, 17% for extraversion, 22% for conscientiousness, 25% for emotional stability, and 120% for openness in terms of corrected correlation (validity).

References

Allen, T. D., & Rush, M. C. (2001). The influence of ratee gender on ratings of organizational citizenship behavior. *Journal of Applied Social Psychology, 31*, 2561–2587.

American Psychiatric Association (2013). *Diagnostic and statistical manual of mental disorders* (5th ed.). Washington, DC: American Psychiatric Association.

Anderson, J. C., & Gerbing, D. W. (1991). Predicting the performance of measures in a confirmatory factor analysis with a pretest assessment of their substantive validities. *Journal of Applied Psychology, 76*(5), 732–740.

Ashton, M. C., & Lee, K. (2001). A theoretical basis for the major dimensions of personality. *European Journal of Personality, 15*(5), 327–353.

Barrick, M. R., Mount, M. K., & Judge, T. A. (2001). Personality and performance at the beginning of the new millennium: What do we know and where do we go next? *International Journal of Selection and Assessment, 9*, 9–30.

Barrick, M. R., Mount, M. K., & Li, N. (2013). The theory of purposeful work behavior: The role of personality, higher-order goals, and job characteristics. *Academy of Management Review, 38*, 132–153.

Batson, C. D. (2011). *Altruism in humans.* New York, NY: Oxford University Press.

Bergman, M. E., Donovan, M. A., Drasgow, F., Overton, R. C., & Henning, J. B. (2008). Test of Motowidlo et al.'s (1997) theory of individual differences in task and contextual performance. *Human Performance, 21*, 227–253.

Bindl, U. K., & Parker, S. K. (2010). Proactive work behavior: Forward-thinking and change-oriented action in organizations. In S. Zedeck (Ed.), *APA handbook of industrial and organizational psychology* (Vol. 2, pp. 567–598). Washington, DC: American Psychological Association.

Bolino, M. C., Turnley, W., H., Gilstrap, J. B., & Suazo, M. M. (2010). Citizenship under pressure: What's a "good soldier" to do? *Journal of Organizational Behavior, 31*, 835–855.

Borman, W. C., Brantley, L. B., & Hanson, M. A. (2014). Progress toward understanding the structure and determinants of job performance: A focus on task and citizenship performance. *International Journal of Selection and Assessment, 22*(4), 422–431.

Borman, W. C., & Conway, J. S. (2013). Validity of personality for predicting citizenship performance. In N. Christiansen & R. P. Tett (Eds.), *Handbook of personality at work* (pp. 591–605). Philadelphia, PA: Taylor & Francis.

Borman, W. C., & Motowidlo, S. J. (1993). Expanding the criterion domain to include elements of contextual performance. In N. Schmitt & W. C. Borman (Eds.), *Personnel selection in organizations* (pp. 71–98). San Francisco, CA: Jossey-Bass.

Borman, W. C., Penner, L. A., Allen, T. D., & Motowidlo, S. J. (2001). Personality predictors of citizenship performance *International Journal of Selection and Assessment, 9*, 52–69.

Burris, E. R. (2012). The risks and rewards of speaking up: Managerial responses to employee voice. *Academy of Management Journal, 55*, 851–875.

Chiaburu, D. S., & Byrne, Z. S. (2009). Predicting OCB role definitions: Exchanges with the organization and psychological attachment. *Journal of Business and Psychology, 24,* 201–214.

Chiaburu, D. S., Lorinkova, N. M., & Van Dyne, L. (2013). Employees' social context and change-oriented citizenship: A meta-analysis of leader, coworker, and organizational influences. *Group & Organization Management, 38,* 291–333.

Chiaburu, D. S., Oh, I.-S., Berry, C. M., Li, N., & Gardner, R. G. (2011). The five-factor model of personality traits and organizational citizenship behaviors: A meta-analysis. *Journal of Applied Psychology, 96,* 1140–1166.

Choi, J. N. (2007). Change-oriented organizational citizenship behavior: Effects of work environment characteristics and intervening psychological processes. *Journal of Organizational Behavior, 28,* 467–484.

Christiansen, N. D., Quirk, S. W., Robie, C. & Oswald, F. L. (2014). Light already defines the darkness: Understanding normal and maladaptive personality in the workplace. *Industrial and Organizational Psychology, 7*(1), 138–143.

Church, T. A. (2001). Personality measurement in cross-cultural perspective. *Journal of Personality, 69,* 979–1006.

Colbert, A. E., Barrick, M. R., & Bradley, B. H. (2014). Personality and leadership composition in top management teams: Implications for organizational effectiveness. *Personnel Psychology, 67,* 351–387.

Coleman, V. I., & Borman, W. C. (2000). Investigating the underlying structure of the citizenship performance domain. *Human Resource Management Review, 10*(1), 25–44.

Connelly, B. S., & Ones, D. S. (2010). An other perspective on personality: Meta-analytic integration of observers' accuracy and predictive validity. *Psychological Bulletin, 136*(6), 1092–1122.

Converse, P. D., & Oswald, F. L. (2014). Thinking ahead: Assuming linear versus nonlinear personality-criterion relationships in personnel selection. *Human Performance, 27*(1), 61–79.

Costa, P. T., & McCrae, R. R. (1988). Personality in adulthood: A six-year longitudinal self-reports and spouse ratings on the NEO Personality Inventory. *Journal of Personality and Social Psychology, 54,* 853–863.

Costa, P. T., & Widiger, T. A. (Eds.). (1994). Personality disorders and the five-factor model of personality (1st ed.). Washington, DC: American Psychological Association.

Costa, P. T., & Widiger, T. A. (Eds.) (2001). *Personality disorders and the five-factor model of personality* (2nd ed.). Washington, DC: American Psychological Association.

Dalal, R. S. (2005). A meta-analysis of the relationship between organizational citizenship behavior and counterproductive work behavior. *Journal of Applied Psychology, 90*(6), 1241–1255.

Dalal, R. S., Meyer, R. D., Bradshaw, R. P., Green, J. P., Kelly, E. D., Zhu, M. (2015). Personality strength and situational influences on behavior: A conceptual review and research agenda. *Journal of Management, 41*(1), 261–287.

Day, D. V., & Schleicher, D. J. (2006). Self-monitoring at work: A motive-based perspective. *Journal of Personality, 74*(3), 685–713.

DeYoung, C. G., Quilty, L. C., & Peterson, J. B. (2007). Between facets and domains: 10 aspects of the Big Five. *Journal of Personality and Social Psychology, 93*(5), 880–896.

Digman, J. M. (1997). Higher-order factors of the Big Five. *Journal of Personality and Social Psychology, 73,* 1246–1256.

Dudley, N. M., Orvis, K. A., Lebiecki, J. E., & Cortina, J. M. (2006). A meta-analytic investigation of conscientiousness in the prediction of job performance: Examining the intercorrelations and the incremental validity of narrow traits. *Journal of Applied Psychology, 91,* 40–57.

Duggan, C., Milton, C., Egan, V., McCarthy, L., Palmer, B., & Lee, A. (2003). Theories of general personality and mental disorder. *British Journal of Psychiatry, 182*(44), s19–s23.

Fleeson, W. (2007). Situation-based contingencies underlying trait-content manifestation in behavior. *Journal of Personality, 75,* 825–862.

Fleeson, W. (2012). Perspectives on the person: Rapid growth and opportunities for integration. In K. Deaux & M. Snyder (Eds.), *The Oxford handbook of personality and social psychology* (pp. 33–63). New York, NY: Oxford University Press.

Fleeson, W., & Gallagher, P. (2009). The implications of Big Five standing for the distribution of trait manifestation in behavior: Fifteen experience-sampling studies and a meta-analysis. *Journal of Personality and Social Psychology, 6,* 1097–1114.

Gonzalez-Mulé, E., Mount, M. K., & Oh, I.-S. (2014a). A meta-analysis of the relationship between general mental ability and non-task performance. *Journal of Applied Psychology, 99*(6), 1222–1243.

Gonzalez-Mulé, E., DeGeest, D. S., McCormick, B. W., Seong, J. Y., & Brown, K. G. (2014b). Can we get some cooperation around here? The mediating roles of group norms in the relationship between team personality and individual helping behaviors. *Journal of Applied Psychology, 99*(5), 988–999.

Grant, A. M. (2013). Rethinking the extraverted sales ideal: The ambivert advantage. *Psychological Science, 24,* 1024–1030.

Grant, A. M., & Schwartz, B. (2011). Too much of a good thing: The challenge and opportunity of the inverted-U. *Perspectives on Psychological Science, 6,* 61–76.

Hanson, M. A., & Borman, W. C. (2006). Citizenship performance: An integrative review and motivational analysis. In W. Bennett, D. J. Woehr, & C. E. Lance (Eds.), *Performance measurement: Current perspectives and future challenges* (pp. 141–173). Mahwah, NJ: Lawrence Erlbaum Associates.

Harrison, D. A., Newman, D. A., & Roth, P. L. (2006). How important are job attitudes? Meta-analytic comparisons of integrative behavioral outcomes and time sequences. *Academy of Management Journal, 49,* 305–325.

Hoffman, B. J., Blair, C. A., Meriac, J. P., & Woehr, D. J. (2007). Expanding the criterion domain? A quantitative review of the OCB literature. *Journal of Applied Psychology, 92*(2), 555–566.

Hoffman, B. J., & Dilchert, S. (2012). A review of citizenship and counterproductive behavior in organizational decision-making. In N. Schmitt (Ed.), *The Oxford handbook of personnel assessment and selection* (pp. 543–569). Oxford, UK: Oxford University Press.

Hogan, J., & Holland, B. (2003). Using theory to evaluate personality and job-performance relations: A socioanalytic perspective. *Journal of Applied Psychology, 88*(1), 100–112.

Hough, L. M., & Oswald, F. L. (2005). They're right, well . . . mostly right: Research evidence and an agenda to rescue personality testing from 1960s insights. *Human Performance, 18,* 373–387.

Huang, J. L., & Ryan, A. M. (2011). Beyond personality traits: A study of personality states and situational contingencies in customer service jobs. *Personnel Psychology, 64*(2), 451–488.

Hurtz, G. M., & Donovan, J. J. (2000). Personality and job performance: The Big Five revisited. *Journal of Applied Psychology, 85*, 869–879.

Ilies, R., Fulmer, I. S., Spitzmuller, M., & Johnson, M. D. (2009). Personality and citizenship behavior: The mediating role of job satisfaction. *Journal of Applied Psychology, 94*(4), 945–959.

Judge, T. A., & LePine, J. A. (2007). The bright and dark sides of personality: Implications for personnel selection and team configuration. In J. Langan-Fox, C. Cooper, & R. Klimoski (Eds.), *Research companion to the dysfunctional workplace: Management challenges and symptoms* (pp. 332–355). Cheltenham, UK: Edward Elgar Publishing.

Judge, T. A., Piccolo, R. F., & Kosalka, T. (2009). The bright and dark sides of leader traits: A review and theoretical extension of the leader trait paradigm. *Leadership Quarterly, 20*, 855–875.

Judge, T. A., Rodell, J. B., Klinger, R. L., Simon, L. S., & Crawford, E. R. (2013). Hierarchical representations of the five-factor model of personality in predicting job performance: Integrating three organizing frameworks with two theoretical perspectives. *Journal of Applied Psychology, 98*(6), 875–925.

Judge, T. A., & Zapata, C. P. (2015). The person-situation debate revisited: Effect of situation strength and trait activation on the validity of the Big Five personality traits predicting job performance. *Academy of Management Journal, 58*(4), 1149–1179.

Kammeyer-Mueller, J., Steel, P. D. G., & Rubenstein, A. (2010). The other side of method bias: The perils of distinct source research designs. *Multivariate Behavioral Research, 45*(2), 294–321.

Krueger, R. F., Derringer, J., Markon, K. E., Watson, D., & Skodol, A. E. (2012). Constructing a personality inventory for DSM-5. *Psychological Medicine, 42*, 1878–1890.

Le, H., Oh, I.-S., Robbins, S. B., Ilies, R., Holland, E., & Westrick, P. (2011). Too much of a good thing: Curvilinear relationships between personality traits and job performance. *Journal of Applied Psychology, 96*, 113–133.

Lenzenweger, M. F., & Clarkin, J. F. (Eds.). (2005). *Major theories of personality disorder* (2nd ed.). New York, NY: Guilford Press.

LePine, J. A., Buckman, B. R., Crawford, E. R., & Methot, J. R. (2011). A review of research on personality in teams: Accounting for pathways spanning levels of theory and analysis. *Human Resource Management Review, 21*, 311–330.

LePine, J. A., Erez, A., & Johnson, D. E. (2002). The nature and dimensionality of organizational citizenship behavior: A critical review and meta-analysis. *Journal of Applied Psychology, 87*, 52–65.

Li, N., Barrick, M. R., Zimmerman, R. D., & Chiaburu, D. S. (2014). Retaining the productive employee: The role of personality. *Academy of Management Annals, 8*, 347–395.

Lynam, D. R., Gaughan, E. T., Miller, J. D., Miller, D. J., Mullins-Sweatt, S., & Widiger, T. A. (2011). Assessing the basic traits associated with psychopathy: Development and validation of the Elemental Psychopathy Assessment. *Psychological Assessment, 23*(1), 108–124.

Marinova, S. V., Moon, H., & Kamdar, D. (2013). Getting ahead or getting along? The two-facet conceptualization of conscientiousness and leadership emergence. *Organization Science, 24*(4), 1257–1276.

Marinova, S. V., Moon, H., & Van Dyne, L. (2010). Are all good soldier behaviors the same? Supporting multidimensionality of organizational citizenship behaviors based on rewards and roles. *Human Relations, 63*(10), 1463–1485.

Marinova, S. V., Peng, C., Lorinkova, N., Van Dyne, L. & Chiaburu, D. S. (2015). Change-oriented behavior: A meta-analysis of individual and job design predictors. *Journal of Vocational Behavior, 88*, 104–120.

Markon, K. E., Krueger, R. F., & Watson, D. (2005). Delineating the structure of normal and abnormal personality: An integrative hierarchical approach. *Journal of Personality and Social Psychology, 88*(1), 139–157.

McCrae, R. R., Terracciano, A., & Members of the Personality Profiles of Culture Project (2005). Universal features of personality traits from the observer's perspective: Data from 50 cultures. *Journal of Personality and Social Psychology, 88*(3), 547–561.

Moon, H., Hollenbeck, J. R., Marinova, S., & Humphrey, S. E. (2008). Beneath the surface: Uncovering the relationship between extraversion and organizational citizenship behavior through a facet approach. *International Journal of Selection and Assessment, 16*, 143–154.

Moon, H., Kamdar, D., Mayer, D. & Takeuchi, R. (2008). Me or we? The role of personality and justice as other-centered antecedents to innovative citizenship behaviors within organizations. *Journal of Applied Psychology, 93*(1), 84–94.

Morrison, E. W. (1994). Role definitions and organizational citizenship behavior: The importance of the employee's perspective *Academy of Management Journal, 37*, 1543–1567.

Morrison, E. W., & Phelps, C. (1999). Taking charge at work: Extrarole efforts to initiate workplace change. *Academy of Management Journal, 42*(4), 403–419.

Motowidlo, S. J., Borman, W. C., & Schmit, M. J. (1997). A theory of individual differences in task and contextual performance. *Human Performance, 10*, 71–83.

O'Boyle, E. H., Forsyth, D. R., Banks, G. C., & McDaniel, M. A. (2012). A meta-analysis of the Dark Triad and work behavior: A social exchange perspective. *Journal of Applied Psychology, 97*, 557–579.

O'Boyle, E. H., Forsyth, D. R., Banks, G. C., Story, P. A., & White, C. D. (2015). A meta-analytic test of redundancy and relative importance of the dark triad and five-factor model of personality. *Journal of Personality, 83*(6), 644–664.

Oh, I.-S., & Berry, C. M. (2009). The five-factor model of personality and managerial performance: Validity gains through the use of 360 degree performance ratings. *Journal of Applied Psychology, 94*, 1498–1513.

Oh, I.-S., Kim, S., & Van Iddekinge, C. H. (2015). Take it to another level: Do personality-based human capital resources matter to firm performance? *Journal of Applied Psychology, 100*(2), 935–947.

Oh, I.-S., Le, H., Whitman, D., Kim, K., Yoo, T.-Y., Hwang, J.-O., & Kim, C.-S. (2014). The incremental validity of Honesty-Humility over cognitive ability and the Big Five personality traits. *Human Performance, 27*(3), 206–224.

Oh, I.-S., Wang, G., & Mount, M. K. (2011). Validity of observer ratings of the five-factor model of personality traits: A meta-analysis. *Journal of Applied Psychology, 96*, 762–773.

Organ, D. W. (1988). *Organizational citizenship behavior: The good soldier syndrome*. Lexington, MA: Lexington Books.

Organ, D. W. (1994). Personality and organizational citizenship behavior. *Journal of Management, 20*(2), 465–478.

Organ, D. W., & Lingl, A. (1995). Personality, satisfaction, and organizational citizenship behavior. *Journal of Social Psychology, 135,* 339–350.

Organ, D. W., Podsakoff, P. M., & MacKenzie, S. B. (2006). *Organizational citizenship behavior: Its nature, antecedents, and consequences.* Thousand Oaks, CA: Sage Publications.

Organ, D. W., Podsakoff, P. M., & Podsakoff, N. P. (2010). Expanding the criterion domain to include organizational citizenship behavior (OCB): Implications for employee selection. In S. Zedeck (Ed.), *APA handbook of industrial and organizational psychology* (Vol. 2, pp. 281–323). Washington, DC: APA.

Organ, D. W., & Ryan, K. (1995). A meta-analytic review of attitudinal and dispositional predictors of organizational citizenship behavior *Personnel Psychology, 48,* 775–802.

Parker, S. K., & Collins, C. G. (2010). Taking stock: Integrating and differentiating multiple proactive behaviors. *Journal of Management, 36,* 633–662.

Parks-Leduc, L., Feldman, G., & Bardi, A. (2015). Personality traits and personal values: A meta-analysis. *Personality and Social Psychology Review, 19*(1), 3–29.

Penner, L. A., Fritzsche, B. A., Craiger, J. P., & Freifeld, T. S. (1995). Measuring the prosocial personality. In J. N. Butcher & C. D. Spielberger (Eds.), *Advances in personality assessment,* Vol. 10 (pp. 147–163). Hillsdale, NJ: Erlbaum.

Piedmont, R. L., Sherman, M. F., & Sherman, N. C. (2012). Maladaptively high and low openness: The case for experiential permeability. *Journal of Personality, 80*(6), 1641–1668.

Piedmont, R. L., Sherman, M. F., Sherman, N. C., Dy-Liacco, G. S., & Williams, J. E. G. (2009). Using the five-factor model to identify a new personality disorder domain: the case for experiential permeability. *Journal of Personality and Social Psychology, 96*(6), 1245–1258.

Podsakoff, P. M., MacKenzie, S. B., Paine, J. B., & Bachrach, D. G. (2000). Organizational citizenship behaviors: A critical review of the theoretical and empirical literature and suggestions for future research. *Journal of Management, 26,* 513–563.

Podsakoff, N. P., Whiting, S. W., Welsh, D. T., & Mai, K. M. (2013). Surveying for "artifacts": The susceptibility of the OCB–performance evaluation relationship to common rater, item, and measurement context effects. *Journal of Applied Psychology, 98*(5), 863–874.

Podsakoff, P. M., MacKenzie, S. B., Moorman, R. H., & Fetter, R. (1990). Transformational leader behaviors and their effects on followers' trust in leader, satisfaction and organizational citizenship behaviors. *Leadership Quarterly, 1*(2), 107–142.

Podsakoff, N. P., Whiting, S. W., Podsakoff, P. M., & Blume, B. D. (2009). Individual- and organizational-level consequences of organizational citizenship behaviors: A meta-analysis. *Journal of Applied Psychology, 94,* 122–141.

Rioux, S. M., & Penner, L. A. (2001). The causes of organizational citizenship behavior: A motivational analysis. *Journal of Applied Psychology, 86*(6), 1306–1314.

Roberts, B. W., Jackson, J. J., Fayard, J. V., Edmonds, G., & Meints, J. (2009). Conscientiousness. In Leary, M. R., & Hoyle, R. H. (Eds). *Handbook of individual differences in social behavior* (pp. 369–381). New York, NY: The Guilford Press.

Rupp, D. E., & Cropanzano, R. (2002). The mediating effects of social exchange relationships in predicting workplace outcomes from multifoci organizational justice. *Organizational Behavior and Human Decision Processes, 89,* 925–946.

Sackett, P. R., & Walmsley, P. T. (2014). Which personality attributes are most important in the workplace? *Perspectives on Psychological Science, 9*(5), 538–551.

Samuel, D. B., & Widiger, T. A. (2008). A meta-analytic review of the relationships between the five-factor model and DSM-IV-TR personality disorders: A facet level analysis. *Clinical Psychology Review, 28*(8), *1326–1342.*

Saucier, G., & Goldberg, L. R. (2003). The structure of personality attributes. In M. Barrick & A. M. Ryan (Eds.), *Personality and work* (pp. 1–29). San Francisco, CA: Jossey-Bass-Pfeiffer.

Saulsman, L. M., & Page, A. C. (2004). The five-factor model and personality disorder empirical literature: A meta-analytic review. *Clinical Psychology Review, 23*(8), 1055–1085.

Shaffer, J. A. & Postlethwaite, B. E. (2012). A matter of context: A meta-analytic investigation of the relative validity of contextualized and noncontextualized personality measures. *Personnel Psychology, 65,* 445–494.

Stone-Romero, E. F., Alvarez, K., & Thompson, L. F. (2009). The construct validity of conceptual and operational definitions of contextual performance and related constructs. *Human Resource Management Review, 19*(2), 104–116.

Thundiyil, T. G, Chiaburu, D. S., Oh, I.-S., Banks, G., & Peng, A. C. (2015). Cynical about change? A preliminary meta-analysis of organizational change cynicism correlates. *Journal of Applied Behavioral Science, 51,* 429–450.

Tornau, K., & Frese, M. (2013). Construct clean-up in proactivity research: A meta-analysis on the nomological net of work-related proactivity concepts and their incremental validities. *Applied Psychology: An International Review, 62*(1), 44–96.

Van Dyne, L., Cummings, L. L., & McLean Parks, J. (1995). Extra-role behaviors: In pursuit of construct and definitional clarity (a bridge over muddy waters). *Research in Organizational Behavior, 17,* 215–285.

Wang, G., Holmes, M., Oh, I.-S., & & Zhu, W. (2016). Do CEOs matter to firm strategic actions and firm performance? A meta-analytic investigation based on upper echelons theory. *Personnel Psychology, 69,* 775–862.

Westen, D. (1995). A clinical-empirical model of personality: Life after the Mischelian ice age and the NEO-lithic era. *Journal of Personality, 63,* 495–524.

Widiger, T. A., & Costa, P. T. (2013). *Personality disorders and the five-factor model of personality* (3rd ed.). Washington, DC: American Psychological Association.

Widiger, T. A., Costa, J. P. T., & McCrae, R. R. (2013). Diagnosis of personality disorder using the five-factor model and the proposed DSM–5 five-factor model personality disorder research. In T. A. Widiger & P. T. Costa (Eds.), *Personality disorders and the five-factor model of personality* (3rd ed.). Washington, DC: American Psychological Association.

Williams, L. J., & Anderson, S. E. (1991). Job satisfaction and organizational commitment as predictors of organizational citizenship and in-role behaviors. *Journal of Management, 17,* 601–617.

Yamagata, S., Suzuki, A., Ando, J., Ono, Y., Kijima, N., Yoshimura, K., & Jang, K. L. (2006). Is the genetic structure of human personality universal? A cross-cultural twin study from North America, Europe, and Asia. *Journal of Personality and Social Psychology, 90*(6), 987–998.

CHAPTER

13 Gender and Organizational Citizenship Behavior

Tammy D. Allen *and* Seulki "Rachel" Jang

Abstract

The current chapter reviews theory and findings with regard to relationships between gender and organizational citizenship behavior (OCB). Based on self-report OCB studies, female employees tend to report that they perform more communal OCB (e.g., altruism) than do male employees, whereas male employees tend to report that they perform more agentic OCB (e.g., sportsmanship) than do female employees. However, supervisors do not appear to rate male and female employees differently on OCB performance. Our review also suggests that even with the same amount of OCB performance, female employees tend to be disadvantaged with regard to career-related outcomes (e.g., promotion) relative to male employees. For future research, we encourage researchers to distinguish between actual and perceived OCB performance and examine associated gender differences. Measurement invariance of OCB across gender, different career success outcomes between males and females, and the effects of gender egalitarianism in cultures also need further investigation.

Key Words: organizational citizenship behaviors, gender role beliefs, gender role differences, communal behaviors, agentic behaviors, gender egalitarianism, career-related outcomes

The study of organizational citizenship behavior (OCB) has flourished over the past several decades (e.g., Organ, Podsakoff, & Podsakoff, 2011; Podsakoff, MacKenzie, & Organ, 2006). Much of the existing OCB research has focused on antecedents such as dispositional variables and job attitudes (e.g., Chiaburu, Oh, Berry, Li, & Gardner, 2011; Ilies, Fulmer, Spitzmuller, & Johnson, 2009). In addition, a considerable body of research has demonstrated that OCB predicts a wide variety of individual outcomes (Podsakoff, Whiting, Podsakoff, & Blume, 2009) that include evaluations of overall performance (e.g., Allen & Rush, 1998; Motowidlo & Van Scotter, 1994; Whiting, Podsakoff, & Pierce, 2008) and organizational rewards (e.g., Allen, 2006; Allen & Rush, 1998; Hui, Lam, & Law, 2000; Jawahar & Ferris, 2011; Van Scotter, Motowidlo, & Cross, 2000). Pertinent to this chapter, a small body of research has focused on OCB and gender. Specifically, researchers have examined if ratings of, and the outcomes associated with, OCB differ across gender (e.g., Allen, 2006; Allen & Rush, 2001; Farrell & Finkelstein, 2007; Kidder & Parks, 2001).

An in-depth review of the existing literature that links OCB and gender at this juncture is important for several reasons. There is a long history of research investigating gender differences in task performance evaluations (e.g., Joshi, Son, & Roh, 2015). We know that men and women are often evaluated differently for their task performance. For example, recent research indicates that the competence signals that enable both men and women job applicants to be hired (e.g., educational attainment) can result in a drop in the subsequent performance evaluations of women. Specifically, Inesi and Cable (2015) found that women with stronger competence signals were given worse performance evaluations than were women with weaker competence signals. Given that OCB is related to a variety of organizational rewards, a similar body of research examining OCB ratings is needed. If men and women are consistently evaluated differently with regard to OCB, there are implications for workplace fairness and career advancement. By taking stock of the small body of existing research, we provide researchers with a roadmap for conducting future research in this area.

The purpose of the current chapter is to review the literature that links OCB and gender. First, we begin the chapter with a review of theoretical perspectives that provide explanations as to why gender should be taken into account when considering the performance of OCB. Second, we review research findings from both the organizational behavior and the social psychology literatures that concern the direct relationship between OCB and gender. Third, we examine gender as a moderator of predictor–OCB relationships followed by gender as a moderator of OCB–outcome relationships. Fourth, we review the small number of studies that have examined gender of the supervisor as a variable of interest associated with OCB. Finally, we conclude the chapter with a discussion of implications and future research.

Theoretical Background

Gender Role Beliefs

Gender is often described as the most recognized and earliest learned social dichotomy (Fausto-Sterling, 1985; Fiske & Taylor, 1991). Gender differentiation begins at birth (e.g., blue is for boys and pink is for girls) and continues throughout the adult life span (e.g., women should take care of the children and men should take care of the lawn). Gender roles refer to the shared beliefs that apply to members of society based on their socially identified sex (Eagly, 1987). Societal views with regard to the idea that there are careers, activities, and emotions that are better suited for one sex over the other sex are pervasive and persistent across time. Such perspectives lead to stereotyped views of men and women. Descriptive stereotypes refer to beliefs with regard to what men and women are assumed to be like, whereas prescriptive stereotypes refer to the ways in which men and women ought to behave (Eagly, 1987; Heilman, 2001). Women are presumed to possess high levels of communal attributes such as friendliness, unselfishness, and concern for others, whereas men are thought to possess agentic attributes such as confidence, independence, and assertiveness (e.g., Bakan, 1966; Eagly, 2009). The traits ascribed to each gender become the basis for judgments concerning the suitable ways in which women and men should and should not behave at home and at work. For example, women should be family caretakers, whereas men should be financial providers. As described by Eagly (2009), gender role beliefs are embedded in the expectations of others and therefore can act as a social norm. Moreover, others often punish those who commit norm violations (Cialdini & Trost, 1998).

Gender role beliefs imply different prosocial behaviors across men and women (Eagly, 2009). As noted by Eagly, prosocial behaviors are more common to women to the extent that the behavior has a communal focus and more common to men to the extent that the behavior has an agentic focus. Also, Spence and Helmreich (1980) argued that feminine behaviors or expressive behaviors (e.g., empathy) are considered other-oriented behaviors, whereas masculine or instrumental behaviors (e.g., competitiveness) are considered self-oriented behaviors. Based on their arguments, Kidder and Parks (2001) indicated that other-oriented behaviors (e.g., OCB-I, altruism, courtesy) are consistent with female communal characteristics, and self-oriented behaviors (e.g., OCB-O, civic virtue, conscientiousness, sportsmanship) are consistent with male agentic characteristics.

Several studies have investigated expectations to perform OCB, providing some evidence that OCB is indeed a sex-stereotyped behavior. However, support for dimension-specific ties has been mixed. Allen and Rush (2001) examined rater expectations for men and women to engage in OCB. Overall, they found that there were greater expectations for women than for men to perform OCB. Allen and Rush did not examine dimensional differences, asserting that in general women would be more expected to engage in OCB than would men. Consistent with the theorizing of Kidder and Parks (2001), Ehrhart and Godfrey (2003) found that helping behaviors (OCB-I) were more consistent with participants' schema for women, whereas civic virtue behaviors (OCB-O) were more consistent with participants' schema for men. Farrell and Finkelstein (2007) examined sex differences at the dimensional level and found that there were greater expectations for women than for men to perform altruism across three studies. However, only one of the three studies provided evidence to support the notion that men would be expected to engage in civic virtue behaviors more so than would women. Across two studies, Chiaburu, Sawyer, Smith, Brown, and Harris (2014) found that by activating gender stereotypes, participants expected more civic virtue from male employees than from female employees. Chiaburu, Harris, and Smith (2014) focused on expectations concerning sportsmanship citizenship behaviors, finding no gender differences in sportsmanship citizenship behaviors performance.

Shifting Standards

The basic premise that underlies the shifting standards model is that stereotypes activate within-category standards (Biernat, 2003, 2012). For example, assuming a stereotype that women are more suitable preschool teachers than are men, one is likely to judge the preschool teaching performance of a particular man relative to standards for men and the preschool teaching performance of a particular woman relative to standards of performance for women. The result is that strong performance by a woman does not mean the same as does strong performance by a man. In essence, raters do not make ratings based on the average performance of preschool teachers, but rather they shift their rating to sex-specific standards for rating men and women.

These types of shifts in judgments are theorized to be possible due to the subjectivity of language (Biernat, 1993, 2003). Specifically, routinely used adjectival evaluations (e.g., "she is strong"; "he is emotional") rely on language open to interpretation, thus enabling individuals to receive similar labels that may actually differ on the construct in question. For example, a "big" domestic housecat is not the same size as a "big" tiger. Within-category scales such as Likert-type scales permit shifts in judgment to occur in that their rated points can be differentially defined and adjusted according to the individual rater. In contrast, common-rule or objective scales rely on units of measurement that have constant meaning across contexts. That is, they are tied to units of measurement that are not easily differentially adjusted (e.g., standardized test scores; inches; dollars earned; percentages).

The shifting standards model predicts that ratings based on common-rule formats are more likely to reveal assimilative stereotyping effects, whereas ratings based on within-category formats may mask the influence of stereotypes or suggest a contrast effect. For example, because we have different behavioral expectations about men versus women, an "aggressive" man may have engaged in different behaviors than an "aggressive" women but be rated similarly on scales based on subjective rating units (i.e., Likert-type scales) (Biernat, 2012). Evidence for the existence of shifting rating standards has been found in a variety of domains that pertain to gender, including height estimates, athleticism, and leadership competence (e.g., Biernat, Crandall, Young, Kobrynowicz, & Halpin, 1998; Biernat & Kobrynowicz, 1997; Biernat, Manis, & Nelson, 1991). Moreover, meta-analytic research shows that when judging targets on dimensions that favor high-status group members (e.g., the hireability of men and women for masculine jobs), stereotypical judgments (e.g., men judged more favorably than women in this case) were significantly stronger when based on common-rule response scales (d = .47) than when based on subjective response scales (d = .19) (Manning et al., 2011). Applied to ratings of OCB, consistent with shifting standards, Wilkinson and Allen (2006) found that women were rated as performing more OCB than were men and that the rating difference was larger when the response format was based on a common metric than when the response format was based on a Likert-type scale.

Gender as a Predictor of Organizational Citizenship Behavior/Prosocial Behavior

One issue of interest is the relationship between gender and OCB. That is, do differences exist with regard to the extent men and women engage in OCB? In this section, we review literature drawn from industrial-organizational psychology/organizational behavior (IO/OB) and from social psychology that concerns the relationship between gender and OCB/prosocial behavior. We review the IO/OB literature first, followed by the social psychology literature.

Industrial-Organizational Psychology/ Organizational Behavior

The literature concerning OCB and gender varies in several ways. One is the source of data concerning OCB. In some studies, self-reports are provided, and in other studies, supervisors provide reports. A second variation is the way in which OCB is operationalized. For example, researchers may operationalize OCB as a unidimensional construct or may consider multiple facets of OCB. Accordingly, we organize our review as follows: (1) self-ratings of unidimensional OCB, (2) self-ratings of multidimensional OCB, and (3) supervisor ratings of employee unidimensional and multidimensional OCB. Table 13.1 provides a summary of

Table 13.1 Summary of Studies Examining Gender as a Predictor of Organizational Citizenship Behavior (OCB)/ Prosocial Behavior

Study	Sample	Type of OCB	Significant Gender Differences?
Studies Examining Self-Ratings of Unidimensional OCBs			
Ang, Van Dyne, and Begley (2003)	466 Chinese technical employees (253 local employees and 213 foreign workers) working in Singapore (28% female local employees; 14% female foreign workers)	Helping behavior	No
Beauregard (2012)	223 British from local government council and a college (62.3% female)	Composite OCB (interpersonal helping, loyal boosterism, CV, compliance/obedience)	No
Lambert, Hogan, Dial, Altheimer, and Barton-Bellessa (2012)	160 staff at a Midwest correctional facility (41% female)	Composite OCB (altruism and compliance)	No
Lev and Koslowsky (2012)	153 Israeli high school teachers (76.5% female)	Helping behavior	No
Lovell et al. (1999)	96 US resident advisers at East Coast university (57.3% female)	Composite OCB (altruism, CV, conscientiousness, courtesy, and sportsmanship)	No
Watty-Benjamin and Udechukwu (2014)	185 US employees (80% female)	Composite OCB	Female < male
Studies Examining Self-ratings of Multi-dimensional OCBs			
Allen (2006)	440 US employees (162 from utility company; 278 from women's professional business association) (74.8% female)	OCB-I and OCB-O	No
Cheung and Cheung (2013)	242 Chinese full-time school teachers (68.9% female)	OCB-I and OCB-O	No
Farh, Earley, and Lin (1997)	206 Taiwanese employees from eight companies in electronics industry (44.4% female)	Chinese five-dimension OCBs (altruism, conscientiousness, identification with company, interpersonal harmony, and protecting company resources)	No
Kidder (2002)	251 nurses from Midwest state nurses' association; 195 engineers from northeastern university engineering school alumni (86.9% female nurses; 27.7% female engineers)	Altruism, CV	Altruism: female > male CV: male > female

Table 13.1 Continued

Study	Sample	Type of OCB	Significant Gender Differences?
Lin (2008)	314 Taiwanese evening college students (58.6% female)	Altruism, CV, conscientiousness, courtesy, sportsmanship	Altruism: female > male Sportsmanship: male > female Nonsignificant: CV, conscientiousness, and courtesy
Morin, Morizot, Boudrias, and Madore (2011)	560 Canadians from three service organizations (270 insurance company, 170 pharmaceutical company, 120 communications company) (65.6% female)	OCB–Customers, OCB–Group, OCB–Organization, OCB–Supervisor, OCB–Tasks	OCB–Customers: male > female OCB–Group: male > female OCB–Organization: male > female OCB–Supervisor: male > female Nonsignificant: OCB–Tasks
Piercy, Cravens, and Lane (2003)	267 British sales managers (23.6% female)	CV, conscientiousness, courtesy, helping behaviors, sportsmanship	CV: male > female Conscientiousness: female > male Nonsignificant: courtesy, helping behaviors, and sportsmanship
Ryan (2001)	116 US accounting and consulting firm employees (46% female)	CV, helping, sportsmanship	Sportsmanship: male > female Nonsignificant: CV and helping
Schusterschitz, Stummer, and Geser (2012)	132 Austrians attending professional development course (43% female)	Altruism, CV, conscientiousness, loyalty, sportsmanship	Loyalty: female > male Nonsignificant: altruism, CV, conscientiousness, sportsmanship
Zhang (2014)	1110 Chinese in variety of jobs and occupations (43% female)	Altruism, CV, conscientiousness, courtesy, sportsmanship	Altruism: female > male CV: female > male Nonsignificant: conscientiousness, courtesy, sportsmanship
Studies Examining Supervisor-Ratings of Employee Unidimensional and Multidimensional OCBs			
Aquino and Bommer (2003)	418 US manufacturers from five locations (66% female)	Composite OCB (altruism courtesy, sportsmanship)	No
Carter, Mossholder, Feild, and Armenakis (2014)	230 pairs of US supervisors and subordinates working in various industries (36% female subordinates; 33% female supervisors)	Composite OCB (altruism, CV, conscientiousness, courtesy, sportsmanship)	No
Cropanzano, Rupp, and Byrne (2003)—Study 1	204 US subordinates and 150 supervisors working in a large hospital (81.9% female subordinates)	OCB-I and OCB-S (toward a supervisor)	No
Cropanzano, Rupp, and Byrne (2003)—Study 2	232 pairs of US supervisors and subordinates working in various industries (76% female)	OCB-O and OCB-S (toward a supervisor)	OCB-O: female > male Nonsignificant: OCB-S

(continued)

Table 13.1 Continued

Study	Sample	Type of OCB	Significant Gender Differences?
Diefendorff, Brown, Kamin, and Lord (2002)	130 US employed college students (66.9% female)	Altruism, CV, conscientiousness, courtesy, and sportsmanship	No
Kacmar, Bachrach, Harris, and Zivnuska (2011)	288 US full-time state government employees (54% female)	Person-focused OCB and task-focused OCB	No
Loi and Ngo (2009)	256 pairs of Chinese supervisors and subordinates in a foreign-investment enterprise (46.6% female subordinates; 48.1% female supervisors)	OCB-I and OCB-O	No
Wilkinson and Allen (2006)	195 US employees from multiple companies (51.3% female); 220 supervisor raters (34.5% female)	OCB-I and OCB-O	Common-metric rating of OCB-I: female > male Likert-type ratings of OCB-I: female > male Nonsignificant: common-metric rating of OCB-O, Likert-type ratings of OCB-O

CV, civic virtue.

findings organized by each of the three categories noted earlier.

Self-Ratings of Unidimensional Organizational Citizenship Behavior

Several studies are based on employee self-reported measures of overall OCB. There is little evidence to show that self-reports of OCB are associated with gender (e.g., Ang, Van Dyne, & Begley, 2003; Beauregard, 2012; Lambert, Hogan, Dial, Altheimer, & Barton-Bellessa, 2012; Lev & Koslowsky, 2012; Lovell et al., 1999). In other words, women and men do not differ in their own reports of performance of OCB. This finding also appears to be robust across occupations and countries. It is worth noting that all of these studies have been based on Likert-type agreement scales.

In a departure from the nonsignificant effects reported earlier, Watty-Benjamin and Udechukwu (2014) found gender was significantly associated with self-ratings of overall OCB, such that women reported higher scores than did men. The sample was drawn from the three main branches of government in the United States.

Self-Ratings of Multidimensional Organizational Citizenship Behavior

Multiple studies have investigated gender differences and self-reports of various OCB dimensions. Different dimensional structures have been employed. Some studies are based on Organ's (1988) five dimensions: OCB–altruism (helping), OCB–civic virtue, OCB–conscientiousness, OCB–loyalty (courtesy), and OCB–sportsmanship (e.g., Kidder, 2002; Lin, 2008; Piercy, Cravens, & Lane, 2003; Ryan, 2001; Schusterschitz, Stummer, & Geser, 2012; Zhang, 2014). Other studies used two dimensions: OCB-I and OCB-O (e.g., Allen, 2006; Cheung & Cheung, 2013). Finally, there are some studies based on unique facets (e.g., Farh, Earley, & Lin, 1997; Morin, Morizot, Boudrias, & Madore, 2011).

We first summarize results based on Organ's (1988) five dimensions. Lin (2008) showed women reported higher OCB–altruism scores than did men and men reported higher OCB–sportsmanship scores than did women. No gender differences were found on self-reported OCB–civic virtue, OCB–conscientiousness, or OCB–courtesy. Zhang (2014) also used Organ's five facets. Results revealed that women self-reported greater OCB–altruism and greater OCB–civic virtue than did men; however, no gender differences were found in self-ratings of OCB–conscientiousness, OCB–courtesy, or OCB–sportsmanship.

In another study based on Organ's five facets, Schusterschitz et al. (2012) found women self-reported greater loyalty (i.e., courtesy) than did men. No other significant gender differences were detected. However, results of this study should be viewed with caution given that the alpha values of all OCB facets were low (ranging from .54 to .72). Piercy et al. (2003) found male managers reported more OCB–civic virtue behaviors than did female managers and female managers reported more OCB–conscientiousness than did male managers. However, no gender differences were found on OCB–courtesy, OCB–helping behaviors, or OCB–sportsmanship. Ryan (2001) used three of Organ's dimensions and sampled professionals in the United States. Male employees reported that they were more likely to engage in OCB–sportsmanship than did female employees. No gender differences were detected with regard to OCB–civic virtue or OCB–helping.

Kidder (2002) focused on two facets: OCB–altruism and OCB–civic virtue. Results showed males reported greater OCB–civic virtue than did females and females reported greater OCB–altruism than did males. Kidder (2002) also assessed the subjective gender orientation of employees. Masculine orientation was related to OCB–civic virtue and to OCB–altruism. Feminine orientation was related to OCB–altruism, but not to OCB–civic virtue.

Several studies have been based on the OCB-I and OCB-O distinction. Results showed that gender was not significantly related to self-ratings of OCB-I or to self-ratings of OCB-O (Allen, 2006; Cheung & Cheung, 2013).

A few studies have been conducted using other ways of dimensionalizing OCB. Morin et al. (2011) included OCB–customer, OCB–group, OCB–organization, OCB–supervisor, and OCB–tasks. Results indicated gender was significantly associated with self-ratings of OCB–customer, OCB–group, OCB–organization, and OCB–supervisor such that men reported higher OCB than did women. No significant difference was found for OCB–tasks. Farh et al. (1997) used the Chinese OCB scale, which includes five facets: altruism toward colleagues, conscientiousness, identification with company, interpersonal harmony, and protecting company resources. Results showed no gender differences across self-reports of any of the facets.

Supervisor Ratings of Unidimensional and Multidimensional Organizational Citizenship Behavior

Employee self-ratings of OCB measures are prevalent in the current literature due to the relative ease of the data collection process. However, to avoid common source bias, OCB is often measured based on data from other sources such as supervisors. This section summarizes studies that examined employee gender differences based on supervisor ratings of global OCB and of OCB facets (e.g., Aquino & Bommer, 2003; Carter, Mossholder, Feild, & Armenakis, 2014; Cropanzano, Rupp, & Byrne, 2003; Diefendorff, Brown, Kamin, & Lord, 2002; Kacmar, Bachrach, Harris, & Zivnuska, 2011; Loi & Ngo, 2009; Wilkinson & Allen, 2006). Specific findings are detailed next.

Based on an overall assessment of OCB, Aquino and Bommer (2003) found no significant target gender differences, nor did Carter et al. (2014). Kacmar et al. (2011) measured supervisor ratings of task-focused OCB and person-focused OCB. No gender differences were revealed for task-focused OCB or for person-focused OCB.

Cropanzano et al. (2003) conducted two studies. In both studies, supervisors reported their subordinates' OCB directed toward the organization (OCB-O) and OCB directed toward one's supervisor (OCB-S). In Study 1, employee gender was not significantly related to OCB-O or to OCB-S. In Study 2, employee gender was significantly related to OCB-O such that women were rated as providing more OCB-O than were men. No differences were found with regard to OCB-S.

Wilkinson and Allen (2006) examined OCB-I and OCB-O based on measures that employed a Likert-type "strongly disagree" to "strongly agree" scale and found that supervisors reported that women engaged in more OCB-I than did men. No significant difference in OCB-O was detected. In a test of shifting standards theory, they also used a rating scale based on a common metric. Results were similar in that supervisors reported that women were more likely to engage in OCB-I than were men, but no significant difference in OCB-O was detected. Loi and Ngo (2009) conducted a similar study examining supervisor ratings of OCB-I and OCB-O and found no significant employee gender differences.

Diefendorff et al. (2002) obtained supervisor ratings of five OCB facets: OCB–altruism, OCB–civic virtue, OCB–conscientiousness, OCB–courtesy, and OCB–sportsmanship. No gender differences were detected for across any of the dimensions.

SUMMARY

Overall several patterns emerge from our review of the relationship between OCB and gender. First, gender differences are more likely to be detected with self-reports rather than with supervisor reports of OCB. Second, gender differences are more likely to emerge when multidimensional rather than global measures of OCB are used. Third, of the various dimensions, gender differences are most likely to emerge with regard to altruism such that women are reported to engage in more of this behavior than are men. Related, differences in OCB–sportsmanship were reported in several studies. In those cases, men reported greater engagement than did women. These dimensional differences are consistent with the gender-role perspective. We did not detect any patterns that indicated gender differences were more likely to emerge based on contextual factors (e.g., occupation, nation), but the number of studies overall may be too small at this juncture to identify such differences.

Social Psychology

Social psychologists have long been interested in examining the predictors of prosocial behavior. Dispositions and gender role expectations are thought to shape the prosocial behaviors of women and men (Wood & Eagly, 2010). As noted previously, women are described as communal, whereas men are described as agentic (Eagly, 2009).

Research on dispositional differences indicates that women are more oriented toward helping and caring for others than are men in that in the aggregate women report greater altruism, agreeableness, and warmth relative to men (Costa, Terracciano, & McCrae, 2001; Schmitt, Realo, Voracek, & Allik, 2008). In addition, consistent with the notion that women are driven by a communal desire to help others is research indicating that women have higher rates of charitable giving than do men (e.g., Leslie, Snyder, & Glomb, 2013; Simmons & Emanuele, 2007). Research also shows that women are more likely to provide social support, a form of helping others, than are men (e.g., Griffith, 1985; Neff & Karney, 2005). Studies concerning cooperation suggest that women are more likely to engage in the cooperative types of behaviors that are most consistent with OCB and OCB-I in particular (Eagly, 2009; Eagly & Crowley, 1986). However, these findings may also depend on the situation. In a meta-analytic study, Balliet, Li, Macfarlan, and Van Vugt (2011) found that the overall average effect size for gender and cooperation was not statistically different from zero. They reported that women are more cooperative than men in mixed-sex interactions. Men are more cooperative than women in same-sex groups and become more cooperative over repeated iterations of a dilemma with the same partner. Meta-analytic research also indicates that men are more likely to engage in chivalrous or heroic acts of helping that require physical strength than are women (Eagly, 2009; Eagly & Crowley, 1986). In sum, studies from social psychology linking gender and prosocial behavior have some consistency with those from the IO/OB literature in that they suggest that women are more likely to engage in altruistic behaviors than are men.

Gender as a Moderator

Some studies investigate gender as a moderator (1) in a relationship between a predictor and OCB or (2) in a relationship between OCB and an outcome. The following sections illustrate the specific studies examining the moderating effects of gender on the relationships. Findings are summarized in Table 13.2.

Predictors–Organizational Citizenship Behavior Relationship

A variety of predictors of OCB have been investigated. Leader-related predictors (ethical leadership, leader–member exchange) have been examined in several studies with no gender moderating effects found (Kacmar et al., 2011; Lo, Ramayah, & Hui, 2006). Two studies have investigated gender as a moderator of the relationship between work–family conflict and OCB. Beham (2011) investigated two directions of work–family conflict and three dimensions of OCB. The two directions are work interference with family (WIF) and family interference with work (FIW), and the three dimensions of OCB are OCB directed toward the organization (OCB-O), OCB directed toward individuals (OCB-I), and task-oriented OCB (OCB-T). Results revealed greater WIF was associated with lower OCB-O for men, but not for women. A different pattern emerged for FIW. Greater FIW was associated with less OCB-I and less OCB-T for women, but not for men. Similarly, Cloninger, Selvarajan, Singh, and Huang (2015) found greater FIW was negatively

Table 13.2 Summary of Studies Examining Gender as a Moderator

Study	Sample	Type of OCB	Findings
Predictor–OCB Relationship			
Beauregard (2012)	223 British employees from local government council and a college (62.3% female)	Composite OCB (interpersonal helping, loyal boosterism, CV, compliance/obedience)	Self-efficacy ⇒ OCB: males > females
Beham (2011)	286 Spanish employees (59.1% female)	OCB-I, OCB-O, OCB-T (toward tasks)	WIF ⇒OCB-O: males > females FIW ⇒OCB-I: females > males FIW ⇒OCB-T: females > males
Cloninger, Selvarajan, Singh, and Huang (2015)	435 US full-time employees working at various organizations (59% female)	Composite OCB	FIW ⇒ OCB: females (negatively) > males (positively)
Farh, Earley, and Lin (1997)	206 Taiwanese employees from eight companies in electronics industry (44.4% female)	Chinese five-dimension OCBs (altruism, conscientiousness, identification with company, interpersonal harmony, protecting company resources)	DJ, IJ, participation ⇒ identification with company: males > females DJ, IJ, appeal mechanism ⇒ altruism: males > females DJ, IJ ⇒ conscientiousness: males > females DJ, IJ, participation ⇒ interpersonal harmony: males > females IJ, participation ⇒ protecting company resources: males > females Not significant: Appeal mechanism ⇒ identification with company Participation ⇒ altruism toward colleagues Participation, appeal mechanism ⇒ conscientiousness Appeal mechanism ⇒ interpersonal harmony Appeal mechanism ⇒ protecting company resources
van Emmerik and Jawahar (2005)	178 Dutch from three organizations (95 bank, 35 city council, 48 university) (43.3% female)	Composite OCB	Altruism ⇒ OCB: females > males Nonsignificant: Work hours ⇒ OCB

(continued)

Table 13.2 Continued

Study	Sample	Type of OCB	Findings
Kacmar, Bachrach, Harris, and Zivnuska (2011)	288 US full-time state government employees (54% female)	Person-focused OCB and task-focused OCB	Nonsignificant: Perceptions of politics ⇒ Task-focused OCB, Person-focused OCB Ethical leadership ⇒ Task-focused OCB, Person-focused OCB
Lev and Koslowsky (2012)	153 Israeli high school teachers (76.5% female)	Helping behaviour	On-the-job embeddedness ⇒ OCB: females > males
Lo, Ramayah, and Hui (2006)	94 pairs of Malaysian supervisors–subordinates in manufacturing companies (38% female subordinates; 31% female supervisors)	Altruism, CV, conscientiousness, and courtesy	Nonsignificant: Contribution respect ⇒ altruism, CV, conscientiousness, courtesy Affect loyalty ⇒ altruism, CV, conscientiousness, courtesy
Schusterschitz, Stummer, and Geser (2012)	132 Austrians attending professional development course (43% female)	Altruism, CV, conscientiousness, loyalty, and sportsmanship	Anxiety attachment ⇒ conscientiousness: females > males Avoidance attachment ⇒ CV: females > males Nonsignificant: Anxiety attachment ⇒ altruism, CV, loyalty, sportsmanship Avoidance attachment ⇒ altruism, conscientiousness, loyalty, sportsmanship
Zhang (2014)	1110 Chinese employees at a variety of jobs and occupations (43% female)	Altruism, CV, conscientiousness, courtesy, and sportsmanship	Job involvement ⇒ altruism, courtesy, sportsmanship: males > females Nonsignificant: Job involvement ⇒ CV, conscientiousness
OCB–Outcome Relationship			
Allen (2006)	440 US employees (165 utility company, 278 from women's professional business association) (74.8% female)	OCB-I and OCB-O	Significant: OCB-O, OCB-I ⇒ promotion: males > females Nonsignificant: OCB-O, OCB-I ⇒ salary
Aquino and Bommer (2003)	418 US manufacturers from the five locations (66% female)	Composite OCB (altruism courtesy, sportsmanship)	Nonsignificant: OCB ⇒ perceived victimization

Table 13.2 Continued

Study	Sample	Type of OCB	Findings
Heilman and Chen (2005)—Study 1	135 US undergraduate students (about 66% female)	Altruistic citizenship (provided an altruistic citizenship behavior episode report)	Altruistic citizenship ⇒performance evaluation: males > females Altruistic citizenship ⇒reward recommendations: males > females Nonsignificant: Altruistic citizenship ⇒competence, interpersonal civility
Heilman and Chen (2005)—Study 2	99 US MBA and MA students (41% female)	Altruistic citizenship (provided an altruistic citizenship behavior episode report)	Altruistic citizenship ⇒ performance evaluation: males > females Nonsignificant: Altruistic citizenship ⇒ reward recommendations, competence, interpersonal civility
Khalid et al. (2009)	577 pairs of Malaysian supervisors and subordinates hotel workers (45% female subordinates)	CV, conscientiousness, helping, patience, sportsmanship	Helping ⇒ turnover intent: females > males Nonsignificant: CV, conscientiousness, patience, sportsmanship ⇒ turnover intent
Lin (2008)	314 Taiwanese students at an evening college (58.6% female)	Altruism, CV, conscientiousness, courtesy, and sportsmanship	Altruism ⇒ knowledge sharing: females > males Courtesy ⇒ knowledge sharing: males > females Sportsmanship ⇒ knowledge sharing: males > females Nonsignificant: CV, conscientiousness, knowledge sharing
Lovell et al. (1999)	109 US resident advisers of East Coast university (57.3% female)	Composite OCB (altruism, CV, conscientiousness, courtesy, sportsmanship)	Nonsignificant: OCB ⇒ performance evaluation
NicDomhnaill (2007)	266 US full-time and part-time workers (58.9% female)	OCB-I and OCB-O	Overall OCB ⇒ performance appraisal: females > males OCB-O ⇒ performance appraisal: females > males Nonsignificant: OCB ⇒ compensation, promotion, burnout OCB-O ⇒ compensation, promotion, burnout

(*continued*)

Table 13.2 Continued

Study	Sample	Type of OCB	Findings
Wilkinson and Allen (2006)	195 US full-time employees from multiple companies (51.3% female); 220 supervisor raters (34.5% female)	OCB-I and OCB-O	Supervisor ratings OCB-I ⇒ salary: males >females Supervisor ratings OCB-O ⇒ salary: positive for males but negative for females Nonsignificant: Supervisor ratings OCB-I, OCB-O ⇒ promotion

CV, civic virtue; DJ, distributive justice; FIW, family interference with work; IJ, interactional justice; OCB, organizational citizenship behavior; WIF, work interference with family.

associated with OCB for women, but weakly positively associated with OCB for men. They did not test for an interaction involving WIF. The pattern of findings is consistent with gender role theory, which would suggest that women may be particularly sensitive to interferences that occur in the family domain and thus reduce their OCB input to help preserve resources.

Individual difference variables have been the target of investigation. Beauregard (2012) found that the positive relationship between self-efficacy and OCB was stronger among males than among females. Van Emmerik and Jawahar (2005) reported that the positive relationship between altruism and OCB was stronger among females than among males. Schusterschitz et al. (2012) examined attachment orientation (anxiety and avoidance) and OCB (OCB–civic virtue, OCB–sportsmanship, OCB–altruism, OCB–conscientiousness, and OCB–loyalty). Two significant effects were detected. Specifically, there was a positive relationship between anxious attachment and OCB–conscientiousness for women, but not for men. Similarly, there was a positive relationship between avoidant attachment and OCB–civic virtue for women, but not for men.

Job attitudes studies have produced mixed results. Lev and Koslowsky (2012) found that gender moderated the relationship between on-the-job embeddedness and OCB among teachers, such that on-the-job embeddedness was a stronger predictor of OCB among females than among males. Zhang (2014) investigated job involvement and OCB (OCB–altruism, OCB–sportsmanship, OCB–courtesy, OCB–civic virtue, and OCB–conscientiousness). Results indicated job involvement was a more significant predictor of OCB–altruism, OCB–courtesy, and OCB–sportsmanship among males than among females. Farh et al. (1997) tested whether gender moderates the relationship between different forms of organizational justice and different dimensions of OCBs. Generally, the pattern of results indicated that the positive relationship between justice and OCB was stronger for men than for women.

SUMMARY

Among the studies that have examined gender as a moderator, there is considerable evidence that gender makes a difference with regard to the strength of the relationship between OCB predictors and OCB. Given the relatively small number of studies overall with few multiple studies of the same predictor, specific conclusions would be premature. However, based on the findings to date, we can tentatively speculate that the work environment itself may spark greater OCB among men than among women while dispositional factors may play a greater role for women.

Organizational Citizenship Behavior–Outcome Relationship

Gender has also been investigated as a moderator of the relationship between OCB and a variety of outcome variables. Two studies have examined overall job performance evaluation as an outcome of OCB and revealed different results. NicDomhnaill (2007) found that the positive relationship between OCB and performance evaluations was stronger among females than among males. In contrast, Lovell et al. (1999) did not find a moderating effect of gender on the relationship between OCB and an overall job performance evaluation. There are several possible explanations for the inconsistent results. NicDomhnaill (2007) collected self-reported job performance evaluation information based on a single item ("Please indicate your most recent performance appraisal rating"). Lovell et al. (1999) gathered overall job performance evaluations from a director. In addition, Lovell et al. (1999) included a small number of participants, and power might not have been sufficient to detect moderation. In an experimental study based on vignettes, Heilman and Chen (2005) examined how women and men were evaluated when they did or did not perform helping behavior (against a no-helping information condition). When a man did not help, there was no effect on performance evaluation. In contrast, when a woman did not help, her performance was rated significantly lower than when no information with regard to helping was provided. When men and women were depicted as helping, there was a positive effect on performance evaluations for men, but not for women relative to the no-helping information condition.

Gender has also been examined as a moderator of the relationship between OCB and objective career success (e.g., promotion rates, salary attainment, and compensation). Allen (2006) found that both self-reported OCB-I and OCB-O were positively related to promotion rates for males, but not for females. However, performing OCB-I or OCB-O was not associated with higher salary attainment for either males or females. Wilkinson and Allen (2006) found that the relationship between supervisor ratings of OCB and salary was moderated by sex, revealing that men were more highly rewarded for OCB than were women. They did not find a moderation effect for promotions as an outcome. NicDomhnaill (2007) also examined promotion and compensation as objective career success associated with OCB. In contrast to the findings in Allen (2006), OCB was not significantly linked to higher promotion rates for males or for females. In addition, no significant moderating effect of gender was found on the relationship between OCB and compensation. In their experimental study, Heilman and Chen (2005) also examined reward recommendations as an outcome variable. The findings in Study 1 were similar to those described previously for performance evaluations. Women were given more negative reward recommendations for not helping, whereas there was no difference for men. Men were given more positive reward recommendations for helping, whereas women were not.

Strain indicators have been measured as outcomes of OCB. Khalid and colleagues (2009) revealed OCB–helping behavior was negatively related to turnover intent, and this relationship was stronger for women than for men. However, gender was not a significant moderator with regard to other OCB facets (e.g., OCB–civic virtue, OCB–conscientiousness, OCB–patience, and OCB–sportsmanship). NicDomhnaill (2007) reported that gender did not moderate the relationship between OCB and burnout. Aquino and Bommer (2003) found no significant moderating effect of gender on the relationship between OCB and perceived victimization.

Finally, knowledge sharing, a dyadic interaction outcome, has also been examined in relation to OCB and gender. Lin (2008) reported that greater OCB–altruism was more strongly associated with knowledge sharing for women than for men. In contrast, OCB–courtesy and OCB–sportsmanship were more strongly related to knowledge sharing for men than for women. No significant moderating effects of gender were detected for OCB–civic virtue and OCB–conscientiousness.

SUMMARY

In conclusion, results of studies examining gender as a moderator of OCB and OCB-related outcomes are inconsistent. However, OCB facets seem to be more responsible for significant moderating effects than overall OCB. Moreover, when gender does moderate the relationship between OCB and career-related outcomes, women are consistently disadvantaged relative to men.

Supervisor Gender

A small body of research has investigated if the gender of the supervisor and/or supervisor and subordinate gender similarity relates to ratings of OCB (e.g., Carter et al., 2014; Loi & Ngo, 2009). These studies provide evidence that female supervisors generally give their subordinates higher OCB ratings than do male supervisors. However, results with regard to gender similarity on ratings of OCB are mixed. Based on an overall measure of OCB from a business school alumni sample, Carter et al. (2014) found gender similarity between supervisors and subordinates did not significantly relate to OCB ratings. Loi and Ngo (2009) also examined gender similarity and found that supervisors gave higher ratings of OCB-O to same-gender subordinates than to different-gender subordinates. However, no significant difference was found with regard to OCB-I between same-gender subordinates and different gender subordinates.

In addition, there is some evidence that female supervisors induce more OCB among team members than do male supervisors (Piercy, Lane, &

Cravens, 2002). Piercy et al. (2002) investigated whether manager gender predicted OCB as reported by the manager's team members. They hypothesized that female managers would encourage more OCB from team members than would male managers. Results supported the hypothesis: Sales team members who had a female manager reported significantly higher sportsmanship, civic virtue, altruism, courtesy, peacemaking, cheerleading, and overall OCB than did sales team members who had a male manager. No significant difference was found for OCB–conscientiousness.

SUMMARY

Given the small number of studies, it is premature to draw conclusions, but the results concerning supervisor gender are intriguing. Female supervisors appear to report greater OCBs when rating subordinates than do their male counterparts. Moreover, subordinates working for female supervisors may engage in more OCB than subordinates working for male managers. Additional research investigating different dyadic combinations (gender similarity and gender dissimilarity) would be useful to the literature.

Future Research on Organizational Citizenship Behavior and Gender

A small but growing body of research has focused on the intersection of gender and OCB. Given the interesting findings to date, this is a topic that clearly merits additional research as much remains to be learned. Next we describe several topics we believe are particularly important to the advancement of knowledge concerning when and how gender matters with regard to OCB.

Perceived Versus Actual Gender Differences

One important question that remains unanswered is whether one gender objectively engages in OCB more frequently than the other gender. Although accuracy in performance ratings has long been a subject of interest within the performance evaluation literature (Murphy, 2008), little of the work within the OCB literature has focused on issues such as rating accuracy. In fact, to our knowledge only one study has focused on rater accuracy. In Allen and Rush (2001), participants were asked to view videotaped instructor lectures in which the level of OCB had been manipulated and then to provide ratings of citizenship behavior based on a behavioral observation rating scale. The researchers found males were rated most accurately under the high OCB performance condition, whereas females were rated most accurately under the low OCB performance condition. Such findings have important implications for field studies in which supervisors are the rating source, particularly in light of research that demonstrates differential reactions to helping versus not helping (e.g., Heilman & Chen, 2005). A line of research that incorporates different scale types guided by shifting standards theory is also needed to better understand the accuracy of OCB rating reports (Biernat, 2012). For example, to examine gender differences in OCB rating reports, actual OCB information could be obtained by evaluating scenarios or by behavioral monitoring. Male and female supervisors could be asked to report OCB performance of the employee on both frequency (e.g., "How many times does this employee help a coworker?") and agreement scales (e.g., "Do you think this employee is helpful to a coworker?"). With comparisons between the actual OCB performance and the reported OCB performance in frequency and agreement scales, researchers may be able to disentangle when gender differences are more or less likely to emerge.

Measurement

One factor that may mask a complete understanding of sex differences is a lack of information about the extent that measures of OCB are invariant across sex. Measurement invariance (MI) refers to the consistency of measurements across comparison groups of interest (e.g., gender) (Teo, 2010). The OCB construct has been subjected to considerable psychometric scrutiny, including tests for measurement invariance across OCB rating sources. In general, the measurement invariance of OCB across rating sources appears to hold (e.g., Blair, Hoffman, & Helland, 2008; Netemeyer & Maxham, 2007; Scullen, Mount, & Judge, 2003). However, tests of measurement invariance across sex have yet to be conducted. Conducting such tests is important because a lack of equivalence can result in flawed between-group comparisons. Because an unambiguous understanding of mean differences is dependent on the between-group equivalence of the underlying measurement model of a psychological construct, comparing OCB without establishing measurement invariance across sex may result in erroneous interpretations (Vandenberg & Lance, 2000). Thus, we currently cannot assume that OCB has the same meaning across gender.

Career Success

The small body of research that has investigated gender as a moderator of OCB and career outcomes has potentially important implications and is ripe for further investigation. Disparities in career outcomes between men and women continue despite legislative and social changes (Catalyst, 2014; Hegewisch, Williams, & Harbin, 2012). One potential reason for this disparity is that men and women are not rewarded equally for their OCB. As indicated in our review, several studies revealed that OCB positively relates to organizational rewards for men, but not for women. These findings are intriguing in that they could help explain why the objective career outcomes of women continue to lag behind those of men.

To further the line of work that examines differential outcomes for men versus women as related to OCB, future studies are needed that include more fine-grained measures of OCB that capture office "housework." In their series of articles for *The New York Times* on women and work, Sandberg and Grant (2015) noted that women tend to help more at the office but benefit less from it. Specifically, they suggested that women take on more of the office "housework"—the tasks that help keep an office running (taking meeting notes; planning office parties)—but that do not pay off. Engaging in altruistic behavior such as those that could be considered office housework is less optional for women than for men (Heilman & Chen, 2005). A consideration of office housework as part of OCB could help better reveal gender differences with regard to the types of OCB men versus women engage in as well as differences in outcomes associated with OCB as moderated by gender.

Cross-Cultural Perspectives

Given the inconsistent results found across this literature, it is also important to identify the conditions under which moderating gender effects are most likely to emerge. Cross-cultural values such as gender egalitarianism may be one factor. Because people's underlying beliefs and values are influenced by cultural characteristics (Hofstede, 1980), cultural characteristics also influence the gender role beliefs of individuals in the workplace. For example, according to House, Hanges, Javidan, Dorfman, and Gupta (2004), some countries value and practice gender egalitarianism more so than other countries. If a society respects gender egalitarianism and is less likely to subscribe to gender-specific roles, people in that society might not have different gender expectations with regard to OCB. However, if a society has strong gender role beliefs, people in that society might have strong gender expectations with regard to OCB. Investigating the effects of cultural characteristics on OCB expectations could strengthen theoretical explanations as to how gender role beliefs are shaped and influence the gender-specific expectations of OCB performance.

Conclusion

Our review illustrated theoretical reasons as to why gender would relate to OCB, summarized relevant empirical studies, and concluded that gender demonstrates both main effects and moderating effects in association with OCB. Future research that incorporates rating accuracy assessments as well as tests of measurement invariance across OCB and gender are needed to provide a more comprehensive and nuanced understanding of the topic. We believe that investigating gender and OCB not only expands our understanding of OCB in general but also has the potential to better our understanding of the differential workplace experiences of men and women that can impact their quality of worklife and career outcomes. As such, we hope this review spurs researchers to continue investigation of this worthwhile topic.

References

Allen, T. D. (2006). Rewarding good citizens: The relationship between citizenship behavior, gender and organizational rewards. *Journal of Applied Social Psychology*, *36*(1), 120–143.

Allen, T. D., & Rush, M. C. (1998). The effects of organizational citizenship behavior on performance judgments: A field study and a laboratory experiment. *Journal of Applied Psychology*, *83*(2), 247–260.

Allen, T. D., & Rush, M. C. (2001). The influence of ratee gender on ratings of organizational citizenship behavior. *Journal of Applied Social Psychology*, *31*(12), 2561–2587.

Ang, S., Van Dyne, L., & Begley, T. M. (2003). The employment relationships of foreign workers versus local employees: A field study of organizational justice, job satisfaction, performance, and OCB. *Journal of Organizational Behavior*, *24*(5), 561–583.

Aquino, K., & Bommer, W. H. (2003). Preferential mistreatment: How victim status moderates the relationship between organizational citizenship behavior and workplace victimization. *Organization Science*, *14*(4), 374–385.

Bakan, D. (1966). *The duality of human existence: An essay on psychology and religion*. Chicago, IL: Rand McNally.

Balliet, D., Li, N. P., Macfarlan, S. J., & Van Vugt, M. (2011). Sex differences in cooperation: A meta-analytic review of social dilemmas. *Psychological Bulletin*, *137*(6), 881–909.

Beauregard, T. A. (2012). Perfectionism, self-efficacy and OCB: The moderating role of gender. *Personnel Review*, *41*(5), 590–608.

Beham, B. (2011). Work–family conflict and organizational citizenship behavior: Empirical evidence from Spanish employees. *Community, Work & Family, 14*(1), 63–80.
Biernat, M. (1993). Gender and height: Developmental patterns in knowledge and use of an accurate stereotype. *Sex Roles, 29*(9–10), 691–713.
Biernat, M. (2003). Toward a broader view of social stereotyping. *American Psychologist, 58*(12), 1019–1027.
Biernat, M. (2012). *Standards and expectancies: Contrast and assimilation in judgments of self and others*. New York, NY: Psychology Press.
Biernat, M., & Kobrynowicz, D. (1997). Gender-and race-based standards of competence: Lower minimum standards but higher ability standards for devalued groups. *Journal of Personality and Social Psychology, 72*(3), 544–557.
Biernat, M., Crandall, C. S., Young, L. V., Kobrynowicz, D., & Halpin, S. M. (1998). All that you can be: Stereotyping of self and others in a military context. *Journal of Personality and Social Psychology, 75(2), 301–317.*
Biernat, M., Manis, M., & Nelson, T. E. (1991). Stereotypes and standards of judgment. *Journal of Personality and Social Psychology, 60*(4), 485–499.
Blair, C. A., Hoffman, B. J., & Helland, K. R. (2008). Narcissism in organizations: A multisource appraisal reflects different perspectives. *Human Performance, 21*(3), 254–276.
Carter, M. Z., Mossholder, K. W., Feild, H., & Armenakis, A. A. (2014). Transformational leadership, interactional justice, and organizational citizenship behavior: The effects of supervisor-subordinate racial and gender dissimilarity. *Group & Organization Management, 39*(6), 691–719.
Catalyst (2014). *Statistical overview of women in the workplace*. Retrieved from http://www.catalyst.org/knowledge/statistical-overview-women-workplace
Cheung, F. Y. L., & Cheung, R. Y. H. (2013). Effect of emotional dissonance on organizational citizenship behavior: Testing the stressor-strain-outcome model. *The Journal of Psychology, 147*(1), 89–103.
Chiaburu, D. S., Harris, T. B., & Smith, T. A. (2014). Ideology and gender: Observers' system justification and targets' gender as interactive predictors of citizenship expectations. *The Journal of Social Psychology, 154*(4), 283–298.
Chiaburu, D. S., Oh, I. S., Berry, C. M., Li, N., & Gardner, R. G. (2011). The five-factor model of personality traits and organizational citizenship behaviors: A meta-analysis. *Journal of Applied Psychology, 96*(6), 1140–1166.
Chiaburu, D. S., Sawyer, K., Smith, T. A., Brown, N., & Harris, T. B. (2014). When civic virtue isn't seen as virtuous: The effect of gender stereotyping on civic virtue expectations for women. *Sex Roles, 70*(5), 183–194.
Cialdini, R. B., & Trost, M. R. (1998). Social influence: Social norms, conformity, and compliance. In D. T. Gilbert, S. T. Fiske, & G. Lindzey (Eds.), *The handbook of social psychology* (pp. 151–192). Boston, MA: McGraw-Hill.
Cloninger, P. A., Selvarajan, T. T., Singh, B., & Huang, S. (2015). The mediating influence of work–family conflict and the moderating influence of gender on employee outcomes. *The International Journal of Human Resource Management, 26*(18), 2269–2287.
Costa, P. Jr, Terracciano, A., & McCrae, R. R. (2001). Gender differences in personality traits across cultures: Robust and surprising findings. *Journal of Personality and Social Psychology, 81*(2), 322–331.
Cropanzano, R., Rupp, D. E., & Byrne, Z. S. (2003). The relationship of emotional exhaustion to work attitudes, job performance, and organizational citizenship behaviors. *Journal of Applied Psychology, 88*(1), 160–169.
Diefendorff, J. M., Brown, D. J., Kamin, A. M., & Lord, R. G. (2002). Examining the roles of job involvement and work centrality in predicting organizational citizenship behaviors and job performance. *Journal of Organizational Behavior, 23*(1), 93–108.
Eagly, A. H., & Crowley, M. (1986). Gender and helping behavior: A meta-analytic review of the social psychological literature. *Psychological Bulletin, 100*(3), 283–308.
Eagly, A. H. (1987). Reporting sex differences. *American Psychologist, 42*, 756–757.
Eagly, A. H. (2009). The his and hers of prosocial behavior: An examination of the social psychology of gender. *American Psychologist, 64*, 644–658.
Ehrhart, M. G., & Godfrey, E. G. (2003). *The role of schemas in gender and organizational citizenship research*. Paper presented at the 18th Annual Conference for the Society of Industrial and Organizational Psychology, Orlando, FL.
Farh, J. L., Earley, P. C., & Lin, S. C. (1997). Impetus for action: A cultural analysis of justice and organizational citizenship behavior in Chinese society. *Administrative Science Quarterly, 42*(3), 421–444.
Farrell, S. K., & Finkelstein, L. M. (2007). Organizational citizenship behavior and gender: Expectations and attributions for performance. *North American Journal of Psychology, 9*(1), 81–96.
Fausto-Sterling, A. (1985). *Myth of gender: Biological theories about women and men*. New York, NY: Basic Books.
Fiske, S. T., & Taylor, S. E. (1991). *Social cognition* (2nd ed.). New York, NY: McGraw-Hill.
Griffith, D. C. (1985). Women, remittances, and reproduction. *American Ethnologist, 12*(4), 676–690.
Hegewisch, A., Williams, C., & Harbin, V. (2012). *The gender wage gap by occupation*. Retrieved from the Institute for Women's Policy Research: http://www.iwpr.org/publications/pubs/the-gender-wage-gap-by-occupation-1/
Heilman, M. E. (2001). Description and prescription: How gender stereotypes prevent women's ascent up the organizational ladder. *Journal of Social Issues, 57*(4), 657–674.
Heilman, M. E., & Chen, J. J. (2005). Same behavior, different consequences: Reactions to men's and women's altruistic citizenship behavior. *Journal of Applied Psychology, 90*(3), 431–441.
Hofstede, G. (1980). *Culture's consequences: International differences in work-related values*. Beverly Hills, CA: Sage.
House, R. J., Hanges, P. J., Javidan, M., Dorfman, P. W., & Gupta, V. (Eds.). (2004). *Culture, leadership, and organizations: The GLOBE study of 62 societies*. Thousand Oaks, CA: Sage.
Hui, C., Lam, S. S., & Law, K. K. (2000). Instrumental values of organizational citizenship behavior for promotion: A field quasi-experiment. *Journal of Applied Psychology, 85*(5), 822–828.
Ilies, R., Fulmer, I. S., Spitzmuller, M., & Johnson, M. D. (2009). Personality and citizenship behavior: The mediating role of job satisfaction. *Journal of Applied Psychology, 94*(4), 945–959.
Inesi, M. E., & Cable, D. M. (2015). When accomplishments come back to haunt you: The negative effect of competence

signals on women's performance evaluations. *Personnel Psychology, 68*, 615–657.
Jawahar, I. M., & Ferris, G. R. (2011). A longitudinal investigation of task and contextual performance influences on promotability judgments. *Human Performance, 24*(3), 251–269.
Joshi, A., Son, J., & Roh, H. (2015). When can women close the gap? A meta-analytic test of sex differences in performance and rewards. *Academy of Management Journal, 58*(5), 1516–1545.
Kacmar, K. M., Bachrach, D. G., Harris, K. J., & Zivnuska, S. (2011). Fostering good citizenship through ethical leadership: Exploring the moderating role of gender and organizational politics. *Journal of Applied Psychology, 96*(3), 633–642.
Khalid, S. A., Jusoff, H. K., Ali, H., Ismail, M., Kassim, K. M., & Rahman, N. A. (2009). Gender as a moderator of the relationship between OCB and turnover intention. *Asian Social Science, 5*(6), 108–117.
Kidder, D. L. (2002). The influence of gender on the performance of organizational citizenship behaviors. *Journal of Management, 28*(5), 629–648.
Kidder, D. L., & Parks, J. M. (2001). The good soldier: Who is s(he)? *Journal of Organizational Behavior, 22*(8), 939–959.
Lambert, E. G., Hogan, N. L., Dial, K. C., Altheimer, I., & Barton-Bellessa, S. M. (2012). Examining the effects of stressors on organizational citizenship behaviors among private correctional staff: A preliminary study. *Security Journal, 25*(2), 152–172.
Leslie, L. M., Snyder, M., & Glomb, T. M. (2013). Who gives? Multilevel effects of gender and ethnicity on workplace charitable giving. *Journal of Applied Psychology, 98*(1), 49–62.
Lev, S., & Koslowsky, M. (2012). Teacher gender as a moderator of the on-the-job embeddedness–OCB relationship. *Journal of Applied Social Psychology, 42*(1), 81–99.
Lin, C. P. (2008). Clarifying the relationship between organizational citizenship behaviors, gender, and knowledge sharing in workplace organizations in Taiwan. *Journal of Business and Psychology, 22*(3), 241–250.
Lo, M. C., Ramayah, T., & Hui, J. K. S. (2006). An investigation of leader member exchange effects on organizational citizenship behavior in Malaysia. *Journal of Business and Management, 12*(1), 5–23.
Loi, R., & Ngo, H. Y. (2009). Work outcomes of relational demography in Chinese vertical dyads. *The International Journal of Human Resource Management, 20*(8), 1704–1719.
Lovell, S. E., Kahn, A. S., Anton, J., Davidson, A., Dowling, E., Post, D., & Mason, C. (1999). Does gender affect the link between organizational citizenship behavior and performance evaluation? *Sex Roles, 41*(5–6), 469–478.
Manning, M., Molix, L., Eidelman, S., Schlegel, R., Biernat, M., & Bettencourt, B. A. (2011, January). Meta-analytic tests of norm and expectancy violations: Implications for gender evaluations. Paper presented at the annual meeting of the Society for Personality and Social Psychology, San Antonio, TX.
Morin, A. J., Morizot, J., Boudrias, J. S., & Madore, I. (2011). A multifoci person-centered perspective on workplace affective commitment: A latent profile/factor mixture analysis. *Organizational Research Methods, 14*(1) 58–90.
Motowidlo, S. J., & Van Scotter, J. R. (1994). Evidence that task performance should be distinguished from contextual performance. *Journal of Applied Psychology, 79*(4), 475–480.
Murphy, K. R. (2008). Explaining the weak relationship between job performance and ratings of job performance. *Industrial and Organizational Psychology, 1*(2), 148–160.
Neff, L. A., & Karney, B. R. (2005). Gender differences in social support: A question of skill or responsiveness? *Journal of Personality and Social Psychology, 88*(1), 79–90.
Netemeyer, R. G., & Maxham, J. G. (2007). Employee versus supervisor ratings of performance in the retail customer service sector: Differences in predictive validity for customer outcomes. *Journal of Retailing, 83*(1), 131–145.
Nicdomhnaill, O. M. (2007). Understanding gender inequality in employment: The impact of sex and gender identity on organizational citizenship behaviors and its proposed impact on compensation, promotion, and burnout. *Dissertation Abstracts International Section B: The Sciences and Engineering, 67*(10-B), 6104.
Organ, D. W. (1988). A restatement of the satisfaction-performance hypothesis. *Journal of Management, 14*(4), 547–557.
Organ, D. W., Podsakoff, P. M., & Podsakoff, N. P. (2011). Expanding the criterion domain to include organizational citizenship behavior (OCB): Implications for employee selection. In S. Zedeck (Ed.), *APA handbook of industrial and organizational psychology* (Vol. 2, pp. 281–323). Washington, DC: APA.
Piercy, N. F., Cravens, D. W., & Lane, N. (2003). Sales manager behavior control strategy and its consequences: The impact of manager gender differences. *Journal of Personal Selling & Sales Management, 23*(3), 221–237.
Piercy, N. F., Lane, N., & Cravens, D. W. (2002). A gender perspective on salesperson organizational citizenship behaviour, sales manager control strategy and sales unit effectiveness. *Women in Management Review, 17*(8), 373–391.
Podsakoff, N. P., Whiting, S. W., Podsakoff, P. M., & Blume, B. D. (2009). Individual-and organizational-level consequences of organizational citizenship behaviors: A meta-analysis. *Journal of Applied Psychology, 94*(1), 122–141.
Podsakoff, P. M., MacKenzie, S. B., & Organ, D. W. (2006). *Organizational citizenship behavior: Its nature, antecedents, and consequences*. Beverly Hills, CA: Sage.
Ryan, J. J. (2001). Moral reasoning as a determinant of organizational citizenship behaviors: A study in the public accounting profession. *Journal of Business Ethics, 33*(3), 233–244.
Sandberg, S., & Grant, A. (2015, February 6). Madam C.E.O., Get Me a Coffee. *The New York Times*. Retrieved from http://www.nytimes.com/2015/02/08/opinion/sunday/sheryl-sandberg-and-adam-grant-on-women-doing-office-housework.html
Schmitt, D. P., Realo, A., Voracek, M., & Allik, J. (2008). Why can't a man be more like a woman? Sex differences in Big Five personality traits across 55 cultures. *Journal of Personality and Social Psychology, 94*(1), 168–182.
Schusterschitz, C., Stummer, H., & Geser, W. (2012). Going the extra-mile: A question of attachment orientations and gender? *International Journal of Organizational Analysis, 22*(3), 356–371.
Scullen, S. E., Mount, M. K., & Judge, T. A. (2003). Evidence of the construct validity of developmental ratings of managerial performance. *Journal of Applied Psychology, 88*(1), 50–66.
Simmons, W. O., & Emanuele, R. (2007). Male–female giving differentials: Are women more altruistic? *Journal of Economic Studies, 34*, 534–550.
Spence, J. T., & Helmreich, R. L. (1980). Masculine instrumentality and feminine expressiveness: Their relationships

with sex role attitudes and behaviors. *Psychology of Women Quarterly, 5*(2), 147–163.
Teo, T. (2010). Gender differences in the intention to use technology: A measurement invariance analysis. *British Journal of Educational Technology, 41*(6), E120–E123.
van Emmerik, H. I. J., & Jawahar, I. M. (2005). Lending a helping hand: Provision of helping behaviors beyond professional career responsibilities. *Career Development International, 10*(5), 347–358.
Van Scotter, J., Motowidlo, S. J., & Cross, T. C. (2000). Effects of task performance and contextual performance on systemic rewards. *Journal of Applied Psychology, 85*(4), 526–535.
Vandenberg, R. J., & Lance, C. E. (2000). A review and synthesis of the measurement invariance literature: Suggestions, practices, and recommendations for organizational research. *Organizational Research Methods, 3*(1), 4–70.
Watty-Benjamin, W., & Udechukwu, I. (2014). The relationship between HRM practices and turnover intentions: A study of government and employee organizational citizenship behavior in the Virgin Islands. *Public Personnel Management, 43*(1), 58–82.
Whiting, S. W., Podsakoff, P. M., & Pierce, J. R. (2008). Effects of task performance, helping, voice, and organizational loyalty on performance appraisal ratings. *Journal of Applied Psychology, 93*(1), 125–139.
Wilkinson, L., & Allen, T. D. (2006, May). The influence of gender stereotypes of citizenship performance on organizational rewards. In T. D. Allen (Chair), *Gender and culture: Emerging directions for organizational citizenship research*. Paper presented at the 21st Annual Conference of the Society for Industrial and Organizational Psychology, Dallas, TX.
Wood, W., & Eagly, A. H. (2010). Gender. In S. T. Fiske, D. T. Gilbert, & G. Lindzey (Eds.), *Handbook of social psychology* (Vol. 1, 5th ed., pp. 629–667). New York, NY: Wiley.
Zhang, S. (2014). Impact of job involvement on organizational citizenship behaviors in China. *Journal of Business Ethics, 120*(2), 165–174.

CHAPTER

14 What Are the Motives for Employees to Exhibit Citizenship Behavior?: A Review of Prosocial and Instrumental Predictors of Organizational Citizenship Behavior

Tom Bellairs *and* Jonathon Halbesleben

Abstract

In this chapter, we review the literature concerning motives for engaging in organizational citizenship behavior (OCB) and frame this review within the broader literature on the functional, goal-driven approach to behavior. We extend this approach by viewing OCB in a context of one's future work self—aspirations based on one's salient view of his or her future in a work context—and how individuals can accomplish many goals through a single behavior (i.e., multifinality) or substitute various means (i.e., equifinality) in order to best satisfy goal-driven approaches to connect individuals to their ideal future work selves. In essence, we argue that people are motivated to select behaviors that give them the best opportunity to achieve their future goals with respect to work, which often manifests as OCBs.

Key Words: OCB, future work selves, multifinality, equifinality, goal-driven approach

Organizational citizenship behaviors (OCBs) are important to both employee and organizational performance (Bergeron, 2007; Podsakoff & MacKenzie, 1997). For individuals, OCBs are characterized as discretionary behaviors that do not have embedded rewards (or punishments for not doing them), and they are assumed to promote organizational effectiveness and performance (Organ, 1988). Research supports this notion that OCBs are connected to performance (Allen & Rush, 1998; MacKenzie, Podsakoff, & Paine, 1999; Motowidlo & Van Scotter, 1994), rewards (Allen & Rush, 2001; Van Scotter, Motowidlo, & Cross, 2000), and career progress (Kiker & Motowidlo, 1999). In addition, previous research indicates that managers use information about OCB when making performance decisions about subordinates (Halbesleben, Bowler, Bolino, & Turnley, 2010; Podsakoff & MacKenzie, 1994; Van Scotter & Motowidlo, 1996). Employee OCB influences how managers allocate rewards and promotions (Allen & Rush, 1998). Though OCB was treated historically as behavior that was outside of the job role and not directly rewarded (Organ, 1988), there appears to be clear rewards for engaging in OCB. Indeed, managers either expect OCB or assume employees should engage in behaviors (whether in a formal job description or not) they see fit to promote organizational effectiveness (Podsakoff, MacKenzie, Paine, & Bachrach, 2000). From an organizational perspective, OCBs indicate quantity and quality of output (Podsakoff, Ahearne, & MacKenzie, 1997) and contribute to effectiveness; higher performance; efficiency; customer satisfaction; and employee, manager, and work group productivity (Borman & Motowidlo, 1993; Ehrhart & Naumann, 2004; MacKenzie, Podsakoff, & Fetter, 1991; Podsakoff & MacKenzie, 1994; Walz & Niehoff, 1996).

In light of the many positive benefits of OCBs, employees may be motivated to engage in OCBs, and managers may be interested in encouraging such behavior. To do so, managers need to understand the underlying motives of OCB. Understanding why people engage in OCB has become increasingly important for scholars and organizations (Borman & Penner, 2001; Hanson & Borman, 2006; Organ, 1990). To understand why people engage in OCB, researchers have focused on the conscious and subconscious decision processes that guide workplace behaviors (Grant & Mayer, 2009; Kruglanski, 1996; Penner, Midili, & Kegelmeyer, 1997). As a result, a variety of different motives for OCBs has been described in the literature. For example, individuals may choose to engage in OCB because they are concerned with the welfare of others and the organization (Bolino & Turnley, 2005; Grant, 2007), because they can identify strategic ways to engage in OCB at times that bolster their reputations (Deutsch-Salamon & Deutsch, 2006), or some combination of both (Bolino, 1999; Grant & Mayer, 2009). Along those lines, Rioux and Penner (2001) proposed that OCB can be driven by prosocial values, organizational concern, and impression management (see also Bolino, 1999; Grant & Mayer, 2009).

In addition to understanding the variety of motives that lead to OCBs, researchers have examined the conditions under which certain motives emerge (Kim, Van Dyne, Kamdar, & Johnson, 2013; Penner & Orom, 2010). Motives based on dispositional factors have a distal effect on OCB (Kim et al., 2013). In contrast, individual perceptions of the situational context explain when OCBs may occur, and role cognitions (Morrison, 1994) help link dispositional motives with OCBs based on the situation (Kim et al., 2013). Morrison (1994) found that differences in employees' perceptions of in-role and extra-role behavior (i.e., differences in "role cognitions") led to OCB. For example, when employees characterized a behavior as in-role, they were more likely to exhibit OCB than if they perceived the same behavior as extra-role (Morrison, 1994). Individual perceptions, based on the situation, are often context dependent and can motivate individuals to select behaviors that give them the best opportunity to achieve their future goals with respect to work. Thus, OCB is a function of how individuals view not only their present responsibilities (Morrison, 1994) but also how they view their future job opportunities. Other researchers linked employee motives, social support, and role cognitions to OCB to explain why and when dispositional motives predicted OCB (Kim et al., 2013). Kim and colleagues demonstrated that role cognitions (Morrison, 1994) were a proximal motivational factor for engaging in OCB. Overall, they found that motives have distal effects on OCB and role cognitions are context specific with proximal effects.

Building on this, research explored the relationship between task performance and OCB in a given situation. Employees may be unaware of differences between task performance and OCB (particularly the consequences of performing each) and may not be conscious of the trade-offs between task performance and OCB (Bergeron, 2007; Deutsch-Salamon & Deutsch, 2006). For example, even when individuals expect that task performance is more valuable than OCB, they may not allocate their time in a rational and deliberate manner; in fact, many decisions are habitual and can be primed subconsciously (Bargh & Barndollar, 1996; Bergeron, 2007; Goode, 1960; Kruglanski, 1996).

The purpose of this chapter is to review the literature concerning motives for OCB. To that end, we start by reviewing the literature concerning motives for engaging in OCB (e.g., prosocial motives, organizational concern, impression management). We build on the research that incorporated the role of an employee and situation into OCB motives (Bourdage, Lee, Lee, & Shin, 2012; Kim et al., 2013; Snyder, 1987). This lays a foundation for why individuals choose certain OCBs because it accounts for situated identity (Farmer & Van Dyne, 2010) and a proximal-distal effect of one's disposition on such behaviors.

From the review, we elucidate several gaps in the literature concerning OCB motives, most notably related to the relationship between future outcomes and motives to engage in OCB in the present. For example, employees may engage in OCBs with the hope of obtaining a better position in the future (Allen, Lentz, & Day, 2006). However, when employees view OCBs as instrumental to career success, OCBs decrease after promotions (Hui, Lam, & Law, 2000). Another example is that helping others may have positive short-term effects but could be detrimental in the long term (Bergeron, 2007; Deutsch-Salamon & Deutsch, 2006; Schnake, 1991). Such deleterious effects may include role overload, stress, work–family conflict, and unreciprocated help that lowers productivity (Bergeron, Ostroff, Schroeder, & Block, 2014; Bolino, & Turnley, 2005; Flynn, 2003). Furthermore, too much OCB focused on one's organization (i.e., internal OCB) was negatively related to productivity (e.g., billable hours), increased salary, and promotions in a services firm over time (Bergeron, Shipp, Rosen, & Furst, 2013). Impression management motives may make others perceive that politics rule the organization (Ferris, Harrell-Cook, & Dulebohn, 2000), which leads to other negative outcomes (Randall, Cropanzano, Bormann, & Birjulin, 1999).

To help address those gaps, we provide a framework for how OCBs surface and how individuals navigate the decision processes behind such behaviors. We incorporate research on goal-driven behavior because goals are flexible and context dependent; goals explain how OCB motives emerge and change based on situational framing (Kosic, Kruglanski, Pierro, & Mannetti, 2004; Köpetz, Faber, Fishbach, & Kruglanski, 2011; Köpetz, Kruglanski, Arens, Etkin, & Johnson, 2012). To better understand how motives link to OCBs, we incorporate the view of one's future work self as an antecedent to OCB (cf. Strobel, Tumasjan, Spörrle, & Welpe, 2013). One's future work self (FWS)—aspirations based on one's salient view of his or her future in a work context (Strauss, Griffin, & Parker, 2012)—bridges a gap in the literature concerning the extent to which OCBs have a future-related component (Strobel et al., 2013); FWS helps detail how and why one engages in OCB. As noted, disposition and role cognitions interact to produce distal and proximal effects on OCB, but they do not account for decision-making processes. To better understand how these psychological processes unfold, research shows that, as individuals have a more salient view of their future in a work context (i.e., a clear FWS), they tend to pick work activities (i.e., OCBs) that serve multiple objectives. For example, holding both prosocial and impression management motives may encourage employees to engage in visible, recognizable forms of citizenship for instrumental purposes (e.g., Deutsch-Salamon & Deutsch, 2006), increasing the likelihood that observers will be aware of their citizenship (Grant & Mayer, 2009).

We enhance this view by drawing on the functional, goal-driven approach to behavior from which much of the OCB motives literature emerged (e.g., Kruglanski, 1996). By taking a multifinal approach (i.e., satisfying more than one objective via a single action) to goal attainment (Kruglanski, 1996), individuals may be incorporating an unconscious decision-making process that combines selfless and selfish motives. In addition, an equifinal approach (i.e., attaining the same outcome via separate behaviors) denotes how individuals engage in different OCBs to attain the same goal (Kruglanski, 1996). Thus, we incorporate one's FWS and explain how it leads to OCBs through a lens of multifinality and equifinality. We integrate multifinality and equifinality to help explain why people engage in OCB and help explain the mechanism of how this behavior surfaces in the workplace across time.

Motives for Organizational Citizenship Behavior

Organizational Citizenship Behavior

OCB is discretionary behavior that is not formally required, does not have embedded rewards (or punishments for not engaging in it), and that is assumed to promote organizational effectiveness and performance (Katz, 1964; Organ, 1988). Early work organized OCB into five areas: altruism, courtesy, conscientiousness, civic virtue, and sportsmanship (Organ, 1988; Podsakoff, MacKenzie, Moorman, & Fetter, 1990; Podsakoff et al., 2000). Altruism involves one person helping another on work tasks. Courtesy is aimed at preventing problems at work, especially with coworkers. Conscientiousness indicates that a person is concerned with following rules, being punctual, and going beyond minimum organizational requirements. Civic virtue refers to behaviors that show concern for and commitment to the organization. Sportsmanship occurs when an employee is willing to tolerate less than ideal circumstances, inconveniences, or other problems at work while maintaining a positive outlook and not complaining.

Some studies have classified OCB into two categories: affiliative and challenging (Chiaburu & Baker, 2006; Grant & Mayer, 2009; Van Dyne, Cummings, & McLean Parks, 1995; Van Dyne, Graham, & Dienesch, 1994). Affiliative citizenship behaviors support existing processes to maintain present work circumstances and include helping coworkers, courtesy, and working extra (Van Dyne et al., 1995). Challenging citizenship behaviors are directed at changing current circumstances at work by voicing problems, taking the initiative to make changes, or improve existing processes or relationships (Van Dyne et al., 1995). Other studies organized OCBs into two broad categories. OCB-O encompasses behaviors targeted at benefiting the organization, and OCB-I focuses on behaviors that benefit individuals (Bergeron, 2007; Halbesleben & Bowler, 2007; Halbesleben & Wheeler, 2011; Williams & Anderson, 1991). In sum, there have been many conceptualizations of OCB and, as a result, to understand motives one needs to understand the different ways that OCB can be conceptualized. Incorporating these concepts has become important to understanding the antecedents of OCB, particularly the motives to engage in OCB.

Organizational Citizenship Behavior Motives

Expanding on these conceptualizations of OCB, organizational scholars began researching the motivational perspectives of OCB, because, to understand how OCB emerges, one must first consider the reasons or psychological processes that prompt one to engage in such behaviors (Organ, 1990; Penner et al., 1997). Early work in this area suggested that individuals were motivated to engage in OCB because of personality and dispositional variables, rather than situational cues such as incentives (Borman & Motowidlo, 1993; Motowidlo, Borman, & Schmit, 1997; Organ, 1988; Organ & Ryan, 1995; Podsakoff et al., 2000). However, Organ and Ryan's (1995) meta-analysis found a relatively small direct relationship in the literature between personality and OCB.

Three predominant motives (i.e., prosocial motives, organizational concern, and impression management) emerged as reasons why individuals engage in OCB (Rioux & Penner, 2001). Prosocial values indicate a desire to help others while being courteous to them and concerned about them. Individuals show organizational concern by caring about the company and being committed to its long-term success. Impression management is an attempt to influence how one is perceived by others; in the OCB context, impression management is a process by which employees engage in OCBs with the goal of obtaining rewards or other positive outcomes for themselves (Bolino, 1999; Rosenfeld, Giacalone, & Riordan, 1995). None of these three motives is necessarily the sole cause for one to engage in OCB. In fact, it is likely that individuals have a variety of motives that lead to OCB; they choose among various actions (i.e., OCBs) that best accomplish more distal goals. This represents equifinality in goal accomplishment. However, behaviors are situation or context dependent; there is no assumption that because two people engage in the same behavior, they have the same motives. Furthermore, we do not assume that behaviors serve only one motive. Instead, we incorporate equifinality and multifinality to explain how individuals choose actions to fulfill many different goals. For example, any number of actions (e.g., extended work hours, more communication with the boss, helping coworkers, excellent in-role performance) could result in a person obtaining rewards at work but does not uncover the reasons why or motives behind these actions. Equifinality suggests that individuals choose the most salient or viable options and the range of substitutability (how likely these behaviors can be substituted and how many behaviors are viable) of those options (Kruglanski et al., 2002). As such, we seek to develop a better understanding of the motives behind these actions.

The aforementioned motives tended to be strongly related to personality such that they reflect a stable dispositional tendency with distal effects on OCBs in a variety of settings; that is, personality is linked to motives, which drive OCBs in situations that favor the expression of specific traits (Kim et al., 2013; Rioux & Penner, 2001). Prosocial motives predict OCBs targeted at helping others, and organizational concern has a strong relationship with OCBs geared toward organizational improvement (Grant & Mayer, 2009; Rioux & Penner, 2001). Impression management was found to have mixed ties to OCB (Finkelstein, 2006; Rioux & Penner, 2001; Yun, Takeuchi, & Liu, 2007) until it was incorporated as an interactive term with coworker support based on the situation (Kim et al., 2013). Coworker support is a proximal indicator of the type of help one receives in the social context of daily work. As such, coworker support greatly influences how employees experience their jobs (Chiaburu & Harrison, 2008).

When coworkers are less helpful, research indicates an individual's disposition and future focus are more likely to motivate engagement in OCB (Kim et al., 2013; Strobel et al., 2013). This is because low coworker support provides a context by which individuals rely on their own role cognitions and what they expect of themselves as they progress toward their FWS. When coworker support is high, individuals feel obligated to engage OCBs by reciprocating support to colleagues, which may not align with their FWS and career path plans. Findings show that one's predisposition to helping others and building positive relationships with others (i.e., prosocial values) or managing one's image (i.e., impression management) is more likely to motivate individuals to help others (i.e., OCB) when coworker support is low (Kim et al., 2013). This interesting finding, especially in the case of prosocial values motivating OCBs even when coworkers are less helpful, indicates that individuals do choose when, where, and to what extent to engage in OCB based on how they view a given situation in concert with their vision of their career paths. In essence, the social context matters, as does the outcome of the OCB.

By definition, individuals engage in OCB to increase organizational effectiveness (Organ, 1988) and to make the workplace better (Dewett & Denisi, 2007), which means OCB is inherently future focused. Collectively, these ideas (i.e., social context, OCB outcomes, future goals) are consistent with multifinality, which incorporates the strength of cognitive associations between means and future goals (Kruglanski et al., 2002). Individual perceptions of the situational context explain when and to what extent OCBs may occur, and role cognitions (Morrison, 1994) help link one's dispositional motives with OCBs based on an individual's perception of a given situation (Kim et al., 2013). In other words, the way individuals perceive the context of a situation in concert with their future goals (i.e., FWS) helps explain individuals' behaviors, choices, and preferences combining cognitive and motivational principles (Köpetz et al., 2012). An understanding of how individuals connect their actions to future goals helps bridge a gap in the literature concerning the relationship between why individuals engage in OCB now and how those behaviors are tied to future goals at work.

To aid in that understanding, we look more closely at how goals emerge. In doing so, we start by identifying various antecedents of OCB. A meta-analysis reported four major types of OCB antecedents: (1) individual (e.g., employee attitudes, dispositions), (2) task (e.g., task feedback, routinization, intrinsic satisfaction), (3) organizational (e.g., formalization, flexibility), and (4) leadership characteristics (Podsakoff et al., 2000). Indeed, personality traits (dispositions) have been identified as antecedents to OCB (Kamdar & Van Dyne, 2007; Kim et al., 2013; Organ & Ryan, 1995; Podsakoff et al., 2000) as have person-based differences (Penner et al., 1997; Rioux & Penner, 2001). Research indicates that motives, based on personality traits, are distal antecedents to engage in OCB because dispositions are consistent across situations (Penner et al., 1997; Rioux & Penner, 2001); one's disposition can influence how one perceives a situation, which drives the nature of OCBs that follow. As noted, the way individuals view their roles (i.e., role cognitions) or interpret the specific context of a situation has been identified as a more proximal antecedent of OCB (Kim et al., 2013).

The pursuit of multifinality helps explain how focal and distal goals emerge because individuals try to maximize the value of the actions (e.g., OCBs) they take (Köpetz et al., 2012). Goal pursuit is resource dependent such that individuals must chose which actions to take given the availability of resources. Equifinality determines the number of choices that are available. As individuals decide which course of actions is best, they (consciously and unconsciously) weigh the options against the results they expect (Kruglanski, 1996). The presence of many goals or competing goals may draw a person's resources away from his or her focal (i.e., proximal) goal. Recall, with high coworker support, individuals felt obligated to reciprocate, regardless of how the behavior fit into their own future goals. This situation indicates that coworkers, or expected organizational characteristics (including culture and norms), may be influencing an individual's choice in behavior in a specific context (Morrison, 1994). With low coworker support, an individual is more likely to act on his or her individual characteristics when deciding if and to what extent to engage in OCB. Although individuals can develop ways to offset or avoid such pulls on their resources, doing so may have unforeseen consequences. For example, if an individual does not reciprocate helping behaviors when coworker support is high, he or she may not get needed support in the future when pursuing a more distal goal. Because of these uncertainties, with many concurrent goals, individuals may detest choosing which goals to pursue (Köpetz et al., 2012). Instead, individuals may seek actions that are better suited to handling situations when they feel their resources are pulled in multiple directions. Because multiple goals can be active at a given time, individuals may explore solutions to satisfy multiple goals concurrently.

Multifinality represents the choice of behaviors that is perceived to be instrumental to all active goals in the pursuit of simultaneous accomplishment (Köpetz et al., 2012). This process can happen consciously or unconsciously (i.e., explicitly or implicitly) because people may or may not be aware of all of the goals that are affecting their choices in behaviors. This helps explain how one's disposition influences behavior as a distal antecedent of OCB. In addition, past experiences may influence future choices because results from earlier situations may strengthen a person's association between active goals and corresponding means (Köpetz et al., 2012). As goals become more salient, they activate an individual's choice in means to accomplish these goals in a multifinal sense; that is, individuals learn which previous behaviors satisfy multiple goals most efficiently.

Because individuals pursue many concurrent goals, they can simultaneously consider multiple underlying objectives and outcomes. For example, those with impression management motives may choose opportune times to engage in OCBs that they perceive are tied to promotions and other rewards (Halbesleben, Bowler, Bolino, & Turnley, 2010). Overlapping objectives in this case could be the desire to help others, to look good while doing so, and to plan those actions for when they are most noticeable. Other research showed that individuals with a lower status in the organization are more likely to help those with a higher status, but those with a higher status are unlikely to help those with less organizational influence (Bowler & Brass, 2006). Again, this suggests that multiple, underlying motives drive behavior and that individuals must make choices in their actions to satisfy many goals concurrently.

More recent work has developed the three-motive taxonomy further and extended it to understand variants on the three motives. Many of these ideas are rooted in the growing body of research that questions the extent to which OCBs are positive and promote effective organizational functioning (Bolino, Klotz, Turnley, & Harvey, 2013; Bolino, Turnley, & Niehoff, 2004; Fineman, 2006). These studies build on the notion that OCB may be self-serving (e.g., impression management) and not purely altruistic or prosocial. In addition, employees may be looking for other opportunities at work, even if these opportunities fall outside the scope of the formal job description. Moreover, outside forces (e.g., family, personal dissatisfaction, transgressions) may motivate OCBs in ways that are counterproductive for the organization (Bolino et al., 2004; Klotz & Bolino, 2013). Other times, it may not be clear that OCBs benefit the organization. This is especially true if the OCB is performed at the expense of in-role tasks. If employees see coworkers reaping benefits from engaging in OCBs, they may feel obligated to exhibit the same types of behaviors (Bolino & Turnley, 2003). This "escalating citizenship" makes OCBs seem required, makes it hard for workers to get away from work or separate in-role and extra-role behaviors, and may not be as beneficial if the behaviors feel required (Bergeron, 2007; Bolino & Turnley, 2003). Thus, sometimes workers feel required to do more (sometimes called "job creep"), and other times managers expect workers to do more than is listed in formal job requirements (known as compulsory citizenship behaviors or CCBs) (Van Dyne & Ellis, 2004; Vigoda-Gadot, 2006). This overarching "citizenship pressure" makes employees feel obligated to increase OCBs and has been associated with job stress, counterproductive behaviors, job dissatisfaction; turnover intentions, and work–family conflict (Bolino, Turnley, Gilstrap, & Suazo, 2010; Munyon, Hochwarter, Perrewé, & Ferris, 2010; Vigoda-Gadot, 2007). In essence, OCBs may have reached a saturation point such that there can be "too much of a good thing" and may indicate that there are context-specific inflection points upon which OCBs go from positive to negative (Grant & Schwartz, 2011; Pierce & Aguinis, 2013).

Understanding Motives

Researchers have started to seek a deeper understanding of these motives by recognizing different mechanisms that link motives to OCBs, particularly the choice of a specific form of OCB to engage in. For example, those with prosocial motives focus outward and seek ways to help others and their organizations (Meglino & Korsgaard, 2004). They find ways to improve the welfare of others and are concerned with the organization, which increases the likelihood they feel committed to the organization (Grant, 2007, 2008; Ilies, Scott, & Judge, 2006). Furthermore, someone with prosocial values is likely to display civic virtue and altruism when helping coworkers with work-related behaviors, which should increase productivity in the workgroup (Podsakoff et al., 2000). Individuals who often engage in OCBs tend to have increased social status among their peers (Flynn, 2003). Because those with impression management motives may select opportune times to engage in OCB, their actions may be more visible, target image enhancement, or appear status seeking (Bowler & Brass, 2006; Finkelstein, 2006; Yun et al., 2007).

The choice to engage in different OCBs due to varying motives is important, in part, because different OCBs have relationships with specific outcomes (Podsakoff et al., 2000; Rioux & Penner, 2001). For example, across many studies (Podsakoff et al., 1997; Podsakoff & MacKenzie, 1994; Walz & Niehoff, 1996) helping behaviors seem predictive of nearly all outcomes variables (e.g., product quality, customer satisfaction, performance quality, operating efficiency, revenue), whereas civic virtue and sportsmanship are often unrelated to many dependent variables. In fact, civic virtue and sportsmanship were negatively related to customer complaints, but helping behavior was unrelated (Podsakoff et al., 2000; Walz & Niehoff, 1996). Furthermore, some personality traits may influence the manner in which OCBs impact an outcome; for example, Halbesleben, Harvey, and Bolino (2009) found that employees higher in conscientiousness were less likely to experience higher levels of work interference with family when engaging in higher levels of OCB at work.

Because of mixed connections among motives, behaviors, and outcomes, it is important to incorporate a long-term perspective that incorporates one's processes to accomplishing goals in OCB research. A short-term focus on OCB outcomes is myopic because short-run benefits may lead to undesirable long-term consequences (Randall et al., 1999). One may engage in work-related behaviors that are individually beneficial (or that result in positive short-term rewards) but could harm the organization over time or be perceived negatively by coworkers or superiors (Halbesleben et al., 2010; Hui et al., 2000). For example, impression management behavior was found to have dysfunctional effects over time, even when it seemed to be beneficial in the short run (Schnake, 1991). Furthermore, prosocial motives can be beneficial when they inspire one to speak favorably about the organization he or she is committed to but can be detrimental if an individual spends time helping colleagues that have fallen behind in their work or volunteering for unassigned tasks that detract from in-role productivity (Schnake, 1991).

As researchers further understood motives, they began to examine how others perceive OCB, how they perceive others' motives for OCB, and the consequences of perceiving different motives (Halbesleben et al., 2010; Podsakoff et al., 2000; Podsakoff & MacKenzie, 1997). Indeed, research indicates that managers consider OCB in performance evaluations (Organ, Podsakoff, & MacKenzie, 2006; Podsakoff et al., 2000; Podsakoff, MacKenzie, & Hui, 1993), but the impact on the performance evaluation depends on the nature of the motive that the observer attributes to the OCB. For example, under certain circumstances, citizenship can be labeled ingratiation and result in fewer rewards (Eastman, 1994). Other studies show that altruistic helping leads to more rewards than helping for personal or selfish reasons (Allen & Rush, 1998; Johnson, Erez, Kiker, & Motowidlo, 2002). Essentially, supervisors consider not only the behavior but also the motives behind why a person engaged in the behavior. With this in mind, to expand our understanding of the different types of motives (i.e., self-serving motives with potentially detrimental consequences and altruistic helping motives that target promoting the organization or others), we propose that the path forward should include a more explicit understanding of cognitive processes individuals employ when pursuing goals in the workplace.

Extending the Functional Approach to Organizational Citizenship Behavior Motives

The previous discussion underscores that to understand why a behavior was performed, one must identify the purpose behind actions and the potential consequences that the individual perceived before engaging in the behavior (Rioux & Penner, 2001; Snyder, 1993). The functional approach (i.e., purpose served by a behavior) to behavior (Snyder, 1993) indicates that behavior is motivated by personal goals and desires, and the same behavior may result from the same or different motives. For example, if the boss asks all of his or her subordinates for a ride to the airport for a business trip, he or she is likely to engender more volunteers than if it was one of the subordinates asking the other subordinates for a ride. Although taking the boss to the airport is important to the organization and may have short-term positive effects (e.g., facetime with the boss, a chance to converse with the boss), it may be detrimental in the long term, especially if this request morphs into a requirement. If a person offers to give the boss a ride to the airport, this may be due to prosocial, impression management, or a combination of both types of motives. Furthermore, behaviors can serve one or multiple motives, and the consequences of behaviors may vary based on the behavior, situation, or both (Kim et al., 2013; Rioux & Penner, 2001). In this example, the consequences of taking the boss to the airport can vary and be hidden. This is because it is likely that the individual receives praise from the boss for this OCB (i.e., short-term benefits), but his or her coworkers may perceive this as ingratiation. Long-term consequences could stem from lost productivity that outweighs the cost of alternate transportation (e.g., ride-share or taxi). Although helping behaviors clearly have short-term benefits, it is much harder to quantify and compare the long-term impacts. Furthermore, the time an individual spends driving to and from the airport could be better spent completing in-role tasks. The time away from work could put pressure on the work unit to meet goals, which highlights potentially negative consequences in engaging in OCB, regardless of the motive. If the person driving the boss falls behind on task performance, other workers may need to pick up any slack or work later that they expected to ensure the work is completed. If coworkers perceive that OCBs are linked to impression management and attribute this to politics in the organization, research indicates this is linked to many negative outcomes such as job dissatisfaction and turnover (Randall et al., 1999).

Thus, the functional approach to behavior helps identify why the behavior occurred (Snyder, 1993). Understanding motives for OCB allows one to explain not only why the behavior occurred but also what makes it more likely to occur in the future. By focusing on individuals' goals and needs, researchers began understanding how this process unfolds by connecting present actions with future work plans (Rioux & Penner, 2001; Strauss et al., 2012; Strobel et al., 2013). Scholars built on the work in goal theories as they noted motives, actions, and results can vary widely among individuals (Kruglanski, 1996; Rioux & Penner, 2001).

To achieve goals, one must act. In a work context, these actions can manifest as task performance and/or OCB and often have a cognitive and motivational property (Kruglanski, 1996). That is, people are motivated by what we have described earlier (i.e., disposition and OCB motives) and also go through a mental process to decide which behavior is best suited for a given context or situation. In addition, goals can reside in one's subconscious and can be subliminally primed; unconscious goals can impact conscious choices (Bargh & Barndollar, 1996). Furthermore, goals are distinguishable between present, near-term, "focal" goals and long-term, distal "background" goals. Overall, goals indicate that individuals have a malleable and dynamic, cognitive and motivational desire to act in order to achieve success as defined by positive outcomes associated with reaching a preferred end (i.e., goal attainment). Put differently, people constantly seek ways (means) to attain goals in the most efficient manner as they perceive opportunities and outcomes based on situations they face. Accordingly, to extend the functional approach to OCBs and their motives, one must explore two key areas: goal selection choices and temporal framing of goals.

Goal Choice

When it comes to goals, the correspondence between goal, action, and expected outcome is rarely one to one. Equifinality refers to situations where several means (i.e., behaviors or OCBs) can be linked to one goal; equifinality represents a choice of paths that can be interchanged (substituted) to satisfy one goal (Chun, Kruglanski, Friedman, & Sleeth-Keppler, 2011; Heider, 1958; Kruglanski, 1996). Multifinality suggests that one means can satisfy several goals; a multifinal means can serve focal and distal goals concurrently (Köpetz et al., 2011; Kruglanski, 1996). Multifinality and equifinality explicate a cognitive approach to motivation based on goal systems theory (Kruglanski et al., 2002). Goal systems theory is built on earlier scholars' depiction of goal-related phenomena and human behavior (James, 1890; Lewin, 1935; Skinner, 1953; Tolman, 1925). Although scholars depicted cognition and motivation (i.e., a separated and static view) as a way to explain levels of performance and satisfaction (Kruglanski, 1996), they did not account for motivation being malleable and dynamic (Kruglanski et al., 2002). Indeed, recent work indicates that goals are flexible and context dependent because their shape and form can change based on situational framing (Köpetz et al., 2011, 2012; Kosic et al., 2004).

For example, consider a work unit that has 10 employees and there is one new manager positon opening for which all 10 are prospective candidates. In this case, the employees know that they want their actions to result in the promotion. It seems clear that the opportunity for promotion operates as a distal goal that can be a conscious or unconscious motivating factor for employees to engage in OCB. Because of this distal but salient motive (i.e., the promotion), it is likely that these employees, especially those with the most salient picture of their future as a manager, will engage in more OCBs. Indeed, organizations that value future-oriented cognition promote OCB, and workers seeking promotions tend to increase OCB (Hui et al., 2000; Jelinek & Ahearne, 2006). Incorporating multifinality and equifinality is an important step in explaining the decision processes of OCB. Individuals adept in managing impressions may be able to select favorable times to engage in OCBs. For example, they may work late to impress the boss when the boss is also at work late, or they may be more proactive in helping others in order to bolster their own reputations and be recognized with higher levels of social status from coworkers (Deutsch-Salamon & Deutsch, 2006; Flynn, 2003). All of these behaviors act as separate means to accomplishing the goal of being promoted; they are equifinal in this regard and can be interchanged to best suit the objective (i.e., earning a promotion) based on an individual's perception of what creates the most favorable images in the eyes of others (Bolino, 1999; Kruglanski, 1996).

With respect to OCB, individuals may identify multifinal means to satisfy a set of active goals to promote their concurrent attainment (Köpetz et al., 2011). For example, although the primary or focal goal is getting the promotion, other objectives, or background goals (e.g., helping others, increasing customer satisfaction, smooth performance, workplace safety), are also prevalent (Köpetz et al., 2011). Because goals can influence people subconsciously (Ferguson, Hassin, & Bargh, 2008; Fishbach & Ferguson, 2007; Kruglanski & Köpetz, 2009a, 2009b), the means available to be substituted (using equifinality) are narrowed based on background goals that individuals may not know are influencing them (Köpetz et al., 2011). This indicates that being able to incorporate multifinality could be subconsciously constrained because there are fewer available options that can serve a focal and distal goal. To address these concerns, it is important to gain a deeper understanding of how conflicting goals are managed given one's cognitive resources.

Because choices may be driven by unconscious motives, multifinality in goal attainment implies that one may choose an action (means) that not only satisfies a focal goal but also satisfies a background goal without being consciously aware of the distal goal. Indeed, choice of means, based on the perceived value of available options, often affects people's decisions outside of conscious choice or voluntary control (Köpetz et al., 2012). For example, hungry participants preferred food that was typical to eat based on the time of day when they took part in a study (i.e., individuals preferred breakfast foods in the morning and dinner foods in the evening) (Markman, Brendl, & Kim, 2007). In addition, goals can be automatically activated based on almost anything one encounters (e.g., other people, objects, emails, strangers etc.). For example, if a coworker begins to eat his or her lunch in the office, the smell may stimulate multiple responses from others. One such response may be that others now want to eat lunch. Now, the goal of eating lunch has become activated by the environment. In doing so, other goals (often subconsciously) become activated; individuals may want a quick, low-cost meal that provides health benefits. The set of choices for lunch, or the equifinality of choice, is limited so individuals must decide (i.e., seeking multifinal means) which option(s) leads to multiple goal attainment (i.e., satisfying competing goals of quickness, low cost, and healthiness). To attain multiple goals, individuals will choose an option that satisfies a focal goal (e.g., satisfying hunger) and a background, likely subconscious, goal such as maintain one's self-image by eating healthy or saving money.

In a work context, one may assume he or she is merely having a casual conversation with the boss (focal goal) but could also be serving a distal goal (e.g., getting promoted or receiving excellent performance ratings) by highlighting recent accomplishments (i.e., incorporating impression management). Here, some goals are activated consciously and pursued (e.g., going to talk to the boss), whereas other goals can be activated automatically (e.g., mentioning recent accomplishments) based on the context of the situation (Kruglanski et al., 2002). Serving multiple goals via one means should lead to more efficient outcomes but can also lead to goal conflict. Multiple goals may compete for one's available cognitive resources (Baumeister, Bratslavsky, Muraven, & Tice, 1998; Shah, 2005) and pursuing one goal may be perceived as sacrificing another (Crocker & Park, 2004; Dhar, 1997; Ferraro, Shiv, & Bettman, 2005; Kuhl, 1984; Kuhl & Weiss, 1994; Van Hook & Higgins, 1988; Ward & Mann, 2000; Wertenbroch, 1998).

For example, a worker may have mixed feelings about staying late at work to impress the boss (i.e., an impression management motive), going home to interact with his or her family, or working late from home but still engaging in OCBs (e.g., sending emails to the boss on completed tasks or forwarding important information to coworkers). If one has many concurrent active goals, finding a multifinal means would not only be more valuable but also more difficult to attain. Equifinality, then, can be useful in a multifinal approach because the presence of many goals should constrain the equifinal choice in means to satisfy a given focal goal (Kruglanski et al., 2002). In this example, one may have the occasional option to work from home instead of going into the office each day. Equifinality indicates that, because more than one means (e.g., working from home vs. driving to work) is connected to the same goal (e.g., future career employability), the substitutability of the means in this example can become multifinal and allow one to attain goals that have higher perceived value. By working from home, this one means satisfies both a focal (i.e., family is happy) and distal goal (i.e., future career success) and is multifinal.

Multifinality and equifinality enhance our understanding of OCB because we can investigate the choices people make between means (i.e., job tasks, OCBs) that satisfy one or more goals. For decades, job design implied that managers knew what was best for workers and could direct their tasks, provide employees the means to accomplish the tasks, and set goals for employees to attain (Hackman & Oldham, 1975, 1976, 1980; Oldham & Hackman, 2010). This approach may have constrained workers and limited opportunities for OCB, but scholars noted that future research should include ways to incorporate structural changes to the job to account for the interdependent dynamics of groups (Hackman & Oldham, 1976). Building on this, research explained that individuals internalize expectations of their behaviors with respect to their roles at work and do so based on motives that link present behaviors with planned futures at work (Markus & Nurius, 1986; Strauss et al., 2012; Strobel et al., 2013). Employees may alter their approach to work based on their felt need to helps others (Kim et al., 2013) in order to derive personal meaning from their work (Berg, Dutton, & Wrzesniewski, 2013; Berg, Wrzesniewski, & Dutton, 2010; Wrzesniewski & Dutton, 2001). Such an approach (identified as job crafting) suggests employees use their latitude to decide which behaviors are most important to them given the context of the current situation at work (Wrzesniewski & Dutton, 2001). Because OCB is discretionary by definition, individuals have control over if, when, and to what extent they engage in OCB (Halbesleben et al., 2010). This provides a basis for why individuals choose certain OCBs because it accounts for situated identity (Farmer & Van Dyne, 2010) and a proximal-distal effect of one's disposition on behaviors that result in goal accomplishment. Assuming that workers are motivated and employ requisite levels of autonomy to change work tasks or engage in OCB, they can select among equifinal means and substitute those which offer the best perceived value in satisfying multifinal goals.

Temporal Considerations in Organizational Citizenship Behavior Motives

Recently, researchers have investigated goals in the context of one's career trajectory and how one's envisioned FWS is realized by altering the boundaries of present tasks at work (Strobel et al., 2013; Wrzesniewski & Dutton, 2001). One's FWS represents who he or she wants to become in relation to work. FWS expresses one's career aspirations based on one's perceived trajectory at work (Markus & Nurius, 1986; Strauss et al., 2012). One's FWS is an incentive to engage in workplace behaviors (e.g., OCB) today that link one's current self-concept to becoming one's future self at work (Markus & Nurius, 1986; Wrzesniewski & Dutton, 2001). The salience of the FWS construct as a distal goal—how clearly and effortlessly individuals can think of their future selves—plays a key role in how individuals alter job tasks and engage in OCB at work today to become their FWS.

In connection with goal systems theory, understanding which choices individuals make and why should shed light on our understanding of how one envisions (i.e., cognitive) and plans (i.e., motivational) to achieve his or her FWS. This point of departure enhances our understanding of why individuals choose certain in-role tasks or OCBs and how they may go about making those choices. Including a future view (i.e., one's FWS) and a present focus (i.e., current OCBs) facilitates our understanding of how this process may unfold over time because we gain insight into how goals are expressed and accomplished. For example, individuals that identify a promotion as integral to achieving their FWS are likely to engage in behaviors that satisfy current work needs and make themselves more attractive for the promotion (i.e., multifinal in choice). As noted, OCBs decrease after a promotion if individuals view OCBs as instrumental to promotions (Hui et al., 2000), and goals explain how OCB motives emerge and change based on situation framing. When individuals earn promotions and accomplish their goal of becoming their FWS, OCBs tend to decrease going forward (Hui et al., 2000; Kim et al., 2013). If one is relying on or expecting OCB to increase his or her chances of earning a promotion, then, once the promotion is obtained, the individual may not need or want to engage in OCBs as much as before. Similarly, if individuals achieve their FWS, they may not feel as compelled to engage in OCB, especially if they perceive OCB is more compulsory than discretionary. From this perspective, if individuals are in their ideal positions, they may be more selective in how often and to what extent they help others or otherwise engage in OCB. This highlights potential context-specific inflection points for OCB. To some degree individuals will help others regardless of the consequences (i.e., true OCBs by definition), but the context of work (e.g., promotions, time constraints, helping the helpless, reciprocity) indicates

OCB may occur in a fashion tied more to perceived rewards and benefits than originally assumed.

Thus, these changes in OCB could negatively impact performance, which has been positively associated with OCB (Allen & Rush, 1998; MacKenzie et al., 1999; Motowidlo & Van Scotter, 1994). It is quite possible that OCBs appear in a cyclical manner. That is, everyone has a starting level or predisposed level of OCBs (i.e., a baseline level) he or she would engage in that is truly discretionary. The organization's culture likely further influences the extent to which individuals display citizenship. However, promotional considerations, citizenship pressure, and how one perceives OCB is valued will likely affect the trajectory and amount of OCB. A longitudinal study that extended the findings in Hui et al. (2000) would be useful to understand the full cycle of OCB. As noted, individuals tend to ramp up OCB when promotions draw near and decrease OCB once promoted (Hui et al., 2000). However, it is likely that individuals continue assessing their new roles, the organizational culture surrounding OCB, and perceived rewards others receive from engaging in OCB. Once they understand which behaviors are most valued in their new roles, it is likely that OCBs ramp up in conjunction with the next round of promotions. This cycle is likely to continue until one reaches his or her FWS or is reasonably confident he or she will not be promoted further. Here, OCBs will likely drop off to levels closer to initial baselines.

To address the cyclical nature of OCB, we suggest that by understanding a future view of one's career goals, managers could more accurately predict changes in behaviors, such as OCBs, over time. In particular, this could be useful in understanding employment, turnover, promotion, and other human capital decisions. By investigating what type of future an individual wants at work, connecting this with dispositional tendencies, and coupling this with a better understanding of workplace motives, one should be able to predict which types and when OCBs will occur and in what context.

Implications for Research and Practice

We illuminate a pathway for scholars to investigate OCB in a more modern work environment. By focusing on worker disposition, motives (i.e., prosocial values, organizational concern, impression management), and why (e.g., FWS, career aspirations), scholars can better understand which situational cues will trigger OCB among different workers. We incorporate the literature on multifinality and equifinality, which stem from goal systems theory, to better articulate the cognitive processes inspiring individual behaviors. In doing so, we highlight the fact that goals can be conscious or reside in one's subconscious. This is an important addition to the OCB literature because it provides a deeper understanding of how OCBs manifest. Because individuals have a malleable and dynamic desire to alter means and goals in order to achieve success, they incorporate equifinality to substitute means (i.e., behaviors) in order to achieve a single goal (e.g., getting promoted) most effectively. Because equifinal means may be constrained by various factors (e.g., time, cost, situation), individuals incorporate multifinality to select the most efficient behaviors among means that can satisfy both a near-term, focal goal (e.g., helping a coworker) and a long-term, distal goals (e.g., promotions or status). In particular, we explain how distal FWS goals impact proximal goals and impact not only direct choices regarding OCB, but structural changes to the job (such as job crafting) that impact OCBs. This point of departure may be a fruitful avenue for future research on OCBs over time and how these activities may be planned with the future in mind.

Recommendations for Future Research

As noted earlier, numerous studies have shown empirical support for multifinality and equifinality (cf. Chun & Kruglanski, 2005; Köpetz et al., 2011, for reviews). Empirical research indicated that people's choices, given an explicit focal goal, reflect a need to fulfill implicit background goals. The implications of these findings are that both explicit and implicit goals affect the individual behavior selected but when both goals are simultaneously present, individuals choose means that serve a multifinal purpose (Chun et al., 2011). When studying goal-related phenomena, these findings support the idea that people can carry out assessments of which means are most likely to result in goal attainment. In combination with one's FWS, this point of departure for OCB research can account for how multiple goals are valued and prioritized. Further implications denote that there are considerable powers of unconscious information processing that collectively manifest with the "motivation as cognition" approach outlined by goal systems theory (Dijksterhuis, 2004; Kruglanski et al., 2002). These studies offer alternative ways to understand goal-priming effects; individuals can be given certain focal goals but may choose means (consciously or subconsciously) that also serve distal goals (Bargh, 2002).

Researchers must continue to examine how actual motives influence behavior and how others interpret this behavior and make attributions based on these perceptions. In addition, it is important to understand how accurate these attributions are. This is especially true for impression management; coworkers and managers may attribute behavior to an individual being helpful and caring about the organization, but the individual may be more concerned with getting a promotion or enhancing his or her reputation. Managers and organizations may benefit by creating a future-focused culture at work that couples employees' dispositions with OCB motives and encourages future focus as a cognitive process to enhance task performance.

Future research is needed regarding the psychological process of incorporating proximal and distal goals when choosing actions. As Grant and Mayer (2009) noted, it is plausible that impression management may not only be self-serving; in fact, impression management may have a prosocial component. Thus, individuals may incorporate equifinality to substitute between means to accomplish a goal at work. Understanding the malleable and dynamic nature of the tradeoff among means can be a beneficial avenue to pursue for future researchers. Furthermore, understanding how one's conscious and unconscious choices may culminate in one action that serves more than one goal (i.e., multifinal means) may give scholars and practitioners alike an edge in predicting if, when, how, and to what extent employees engage in OCB.

Implications for Practice

If a manager knows that a newly hired employee has a prosocial motivation, the manager will want to monitor how much helping this new employee is doing. The manager will want to make sure that these OCBs are not cannibalizing in-role, required duties. However, the manager can be cognizant of this individual's predisposition to help others without self-regard. For example, if the organization was sponsoring a charity basketball tournament, the manager could encourage the employee to be in charge of the event. By doing so, the manager harmonizes organizational goals (i.e., activities the organization values) and activities the individual values. This gives the individual a chance to engage in prosocial behaviors while doing so in a controlled (or at least approved) manner within the organization. Furthermore, the manager could highlight (or the employee could recognize) potential career-bolstering opportunities from this activity. For example, this task could highlight the employee's attention to detail, ability to manage others, or fundraising capabilities. These qualities could make the employee more attractive for future promotions, thereby bringing him or her closer to achieving his or her FWS. The same example can also be attractive to those with impression management motives. By leading this event, an employee may have unprecedented exposure to corporate executives and other higher level managers. This exposure could generate rewards or allow the individual to acquire other social rewards (Halbesleben et al., 2010).

This example highlights the value of knowing what motivates employees, understanding their FWS and career aspirations, and realizing how a manager can connect these items to better promote organizational effectiveness. This combinatory effect (i.e., FWS, OCBs, and manager oversight) can help resolve differences between the more recently defined "dark side" motives (or potentially negative implications of OCB) and the original OCB definition of discretionary behaviors that promote organizational functioning (Bolino et al., 2013; Organ, 1988). Our review also helps managers correctly attribute motives of employees engaging in OCB. Because the manager has knowledge of employees, their motives, and potential extra-role opportunities, the manager can increase organizational effectiveness by highlighting options that fit individual career paths.

By connecting individuals and opportunities, the manager can increase the possibility of goal accomplishment. In doing so, both the employees and managers are incorporating multifinality and equifinality. In our example, the manager incorporates multifinality by satisfying at least two goals. He or she satisfies a near-term, proximal goal by finding an employee to be in charge of the charity basketball tournament. A distal goal can be satisfied by encouraging an employee that may benefit from the opportunity to lead others. In this context, a manager can see how well the employee manages a project that is not vital to the organization. This will help the manager gauge the long-term success an employee may have if promoted to a role that includes managing others. From the employee's perspective, organizing an event serves multiples goals as well. By engaging in a prosocial activity, the employee satisfies a focal goal of helping others. The distal goal for the employee may be salient and tied to his or her FWS; if the employee can show that he or she works hard and can manage this event, he or she could manage other issues at work in the current role or be more attractive for a promotion. In addition, because motives can be primed subconsciously, the employee may be unconsciously choosing tasks that fulfill his or her career aspirations and the likelihood of becoming his or her FWS.

Conclusion

The goal of this chapter was to review the literature on OCB motives. We explained how different motives (i.e., prosocial motives, organizational concern, impression management) could influence individuals to engage in varying types of OCBs, and much of this is based on the situation or context. We also detailed some of the OCB motives that may have detrimental consequences and how OCBs can shape the attributions of others. We incorporated research on goal-driven behavior because goals are flexible and context dependent; goals explain how OCB motives emerge and change based on situation framing. Multifinality and equifinality are rooted in goal systems theory. Going back further, these constructs stem from work on one's cognition and motivation. Multifinality and equifinality combine this approach such that "motivation as cognition" represents how choices among means can best serve multiple goals. Understanding these concepts can help researchers gather evidence on cognitive processes explaining how or why OCBs occur, especially when OCBs may have negative consequences or take the place of expected in-role behaviors. Combining recent work on one's FWS, scholars can dig deeper into the progress individuals make in their careers based on these psychological mechanisms. Going forward, goal priming, in a work context, can give researchers a better understanding of which types of goals (explicit or implicit) drive individuals to alter job tasks at work today to become their FWS. Taken together, this chapter suggests that FWS is a valuable cognitive resource for motivating not only in-role task performance but also OCBs. Properly harnessed, future thinking in organizations can foster employees' OCBs and promote workplace behaviors that result in positive long-term organizational success.

References

Allen, T. D., Lentz, E., & Day, R. (2006). Career success outcomes associated with mentoring others: A comparison of mentors and nonmentors. *Journal of Career Development, 32*(3), 272–285.

Allen, T. D., & Rush, M. C. (1998). The effects of organizational citizenship behavior on performance judgments: A field study and a laboratory experiment. *Journal of Applied Psychology, 83*(2), 247–260.

Allen, T. D., & Rush, M. C. (2001). The influence of ratee gender on ratings of organizational citizenship behavior. *Journal of Applied Social Psychology, 31*(12), 2561–2587.

Bargh, J. A. (2002). Losing consciousness: Automatic influences on consumer judgment, behavior, and motivation. *Journal of Consumer Research, 29*(2), 280–285.

Bargh, J. A., & Barndollar, K. (1996). Automaticity in action: The unconscious as repository of chronic goals and motives. In P. M. Gollwitzer & J. A. Bargh (Eds.), *The psychology of action* (pp. 457–481). New York, NY: Guilford.

Baumeister, R. F., Bratslavsky, E., Muraven, M., & Tice, D. M. (1998). Ego-depletion: Is the active self a limited resource? *Journal of Personality and Social Psychology, 74*(5), 1252–1265.

Berg, J. M., Dutton, J. E., & Wrzesniewski, A. (2013). Job crafting and meaningful work. In B. J. Dik, Z. S. Byrne, & M. F. Steger (Eds.), *Purpose and meaning in the workplace* (pp. 81–104). Washington, DC: American Psychological Association.

Berg, J. M., Wrzesniewski, A., & Dutton, J. E. (2010). Perceiving and responding to challenges in job crafting at different ranks: When proactivity requires adaptivity. *Journal of Organizational Behavior, 31*(23), 158–186.

Bergeron, D. M. (2007). The potential paradox of organizational citizenship behavior: Good citizens at what cost? *Academy of Management Review, 32*(4), 1078–1095.

Bergeron, D. M., Ostroff, C., Schroeder, T., & Block, C. (2014). The dual effects of organizational citizenship behavior: Relationships to research productivity and career outcomes in academe. *Human Performance, 27*(2), 99–128.

Bergeron, D. M., Shipp, A. J., Rosen, B. & Furst, S. A. (2013). Organizational citizenship behavior and career outcomes: The cost of being a good citizen. *Journal of Management, 39*(4), 958–984.

Bolino, M. C. (1999). Citizenship and impression management: Good soldiers or good actors? *Academy of Management Review, 24*(1), 82–98.

Bolino, M. C., Klotz, A. C., Turnley, W. H., & Harvey, J. (2013). Exploring the dark side of organizational citizenship behavior. *Journal of Organizational Behavior, 34*(4), 542–559.

Bolino, M. C., & Turnley, W. H. (2003). Going the extra mile: Cultivating and managing employee citizenship behavior. *The Academy of Management Executive, 17*(3), 60–71.

Bolino, M. C., & Turnley, W. H. (2005). The personal costs of citizenship behavior: The relationship between individual initiative and role overload, job stress, and work–family conflict. *Journal of Applied Psychology, 90*(4), 740–748.

Bolino, M. C., Turnley, W. H., Gilstrap, J. B., & Suazo, M. M. (2010). Citizenship under pressure: What's a "good soldier" to do? *Journal of Organizational Behavior, 31*(6), 835–855.

Bolino, M. C., Turnley, W. H., & Niehoff, B. P. (2004). The other side of the story: Reexamining prevailing assumptions about organizational citizenship behavior. *Human Resource Management Review, 14*(2), 229–246.

Borman, W. C., & Motowidlo, S. M. (1993). Expanding the criterion domain to include elements of contextual performance. In N. Schmitt & W. C. Borman (Eds.), *Personnel selection in organizations* (pp. 71–98). San Francisco, CA: Jossey-Bass.

Borman, W. C., & Penner, L. A. (2001). Citizenship performance: Its nature, antecedents, and motives. In B. W. Roberts & R. Hogan (Eds.), *Personality psychology in the workplace* (pp. 45–61). Washington, DC: American Psychological Association.

Bourdage, J. S., Lee, K., Lee, J. H., & Shin, K. H. (2012). Motives for organizational citizenship behavior: Personality correlates and coworker ratings of OCB. *Human Performance, 25*(3), 179–200.
Bowler, W. M., & Brass, D. J. (2006). Relational correlates of interpersonal citizenship behavior: A social network perspective. *Journal of Applied Psychology, 91*(1), 70–82.
Chiaburu, D. S., & Baker, V. L. (2006). Extra-role behaviors challenging the status-quo: Validity and antecedents of taking charge behaviors. *Journal of Managerial Psychology, 21*(7), 620–637.
Chiaburu, D. S., & Harrison, D. A. (2008). Do peers make the place? Conceptual synthesis and meta-analysis of coworker effects on perceptions, attitudes, OCBs, and performance. *Journal of Applied Psychology, 93*, 1082–1103.
Chun, W. Y., & Kruglanski, A. W. (2005). Consumption as a multiple-goal pursuit without awareness. In F. R. Kardes, P. M. Herr, & J. Nantel (Eds.), *Applying social cognition to consumer-focused strategy* (pp. 201–217). Mahwah, NJ: Erlbaum.
Chun, W. Y., Kruglanski, A. W., Friedman, R., & Sleeth-Keppler, D. (2011). Multifinality in implicit choice. *Journal of Personality and Social Psychology, 101*(5), 1124–1137.
Crocker, J., & Park, L. E. (2004). The costly pursuit of self-esteem. *Psychological Bulletin, 130*(3), 392–414.
Deutsch-Salamon, S. D., & Deutsch, Y. (2006). OCB as a handicap: An evolutionary psychological perspective. *Journal of Organizational Behavior, 27*(2), 185–199.
Dewett, T., & Denisi, A. S. (2007). What motivates organizational citizenship behaviours? Exploring the role of regulatory focus theory. *European Journal of Work and Organizational Psychology, 16*(3), 241–260.
Dhar, R. (1997). Consumer preference for a no-choice option. *Journal of Consumer Research, 24*(2), 215–231.
Dijksterhuis, A. (2004). Think different: The merits of unconscious thought in preference development and decision making. *Journal of Personality and Social Psychology, 87*(5), 586–598.
Eastman, K. K. (1994). In the eyes of the beholder: An attributional approach to ingratiation and organizational citizenship behavior. *Academy of Management Journal, 37*(5), 1379–1391.
Ehrhart, M. G., & Naumann, S. E. (2004). Organizational citizenship behavior in work groups: A group norms approach. *Journal of Applied Psychology, 89*(6), 960–974.
Farmer, S. M., & Van Dyne, L. (2010). The idealized self and the situated self as predictors of employee work behaviors. *Journal of Applied Psychology, 95*(3), 503–516.
Ferguson, M. J., Hassin, R., & Bargh, J. A. (2008). Implicit motivation: Past, present, and future. In J. Y. Shah & W. Gardner (Eds.), *Handbook of motivation science* (pp. 150–166). New York, NY: Guilford Press.
Ferraro, R., Shiv, B., & Bettman, J. R. (2005). Let us eat and drink, for tomorrow we shall die: Effects of mortality salience and self-esteem on self-regulation in consumer choice. *Journal of Consumer Research, 32*(1), 65–75.
Ferris, G. R., Harrell-Cook, G., & Dulebohn, J. H. (2000). Organizational politics: The nature of the relationship between politics perceptions and political behavior. In S. B. Bacharach & E. J. Lawler (Eds.), *Research in the sociology of organizations* (Vol. *17*, pp. 89–130). Stamford, CT: JAI Press.
Fineman, S. (2006). On being positive: Concerns and counterpoints. *Academy of Management Review, 31*(2), 270–291.
Finkelstein, M. A. (2006). Dispositional predictors of organizational citizenship behavior: Motives, motive fulfillment, and role identity. *Social Behavior and Personality, 34*(6), 603–616.
Fishbach, A., & Ferguson, M. J. (2007). The goal construct in social psychology. In A. W. Kruglanski & E. T. Higgins (Eds.), *Social psychology: Handbook of basic principles* (pp. 490–515). New York, NY: Guilford Press.
Flynn, F. J. (2003). How much should I give and how often? The effects of generosity and frequency of favor exchange on social status and productivity. *Academy of Management Journal, 46*(5), 539–553.
Goode, W. J. (1960). A theory of role strain. *American Sociological Review, 25*(4), 483–496.
Grant, A. M. (2007). Relational job design and the motivation to make a prosocial difference. *Academy of Management Review, 32*(2), 393–417.
Grant, A. M. (2008). Does intrinsic motivation fuel the prosocial fire? Motivational synergy in predicting persistence, performance, and productivity. *Journal of Applied Psychology, 93*(1), 48–58.
Grant, A. M., & Mayer, D. M. (2009). Good soldiers and good actors: Prosocial and impression management motives as interactive predictors of affiliative citizenship behaviors. *Journal of Applied Psychology, 94*(4), 900–912.
Grant, A. M., & Schwartz, B. (2011). Too much of a good thing the challenge and opportunity of the inverted U. *Perspectives on Psychological Science, 6*(1), 61–76.
Hackman, J. R., & Oldham, G. R. (1975). Development of the job diagnostic survey. *Journal of Applied Psychology, 60*(2), 159–170.
Hackman, J. R., & Oldham, G. R. (1976). Motivation through the design of work: Test of a theory. *Organizational Behavior and Human Performance, 16*(2), 250–279.
Hackman, J. R., & Oldham, G. R. (1980). Work redesign. Reading, MA: Addison-Wesley.
Halbesleben, J. R., & Bowler, W. M. (2007). Emotional exhaustion and job performance: The mediating role of motivation. *Journal of Applied Psychology, 92*(1), 93–106.
Halbesleben, J. R., Bowler, W. M., Bolino, M. C., & Turnley, W. H. (2010). Organizational concern, prosocial values, or impression management? How supervisors attribute motives to organizational citizenship behavior. *Journal of Applied Social Psychology, 40*(6), 1450–1489.
Halbesleben, J. R., Harvey, J., & Bolino, M. C. (2009). Too engaged? A conservation of resources view of the relationship between work engagement and work interference with family. *Journal of Applied Psychology, 94*(6), 1452–1465.
Halbesleben, J. R., & Wheeler, A. R. (2011). I owe you one: Coworker reciprocity as a moderator of the day-level exhaustion–performance relationship. *Journal of Organizational Behavior, 32*(4), 608–626.
Hanson, M. A., & Borman, W. C. (2006). Citizenship performance: An integrative review and motivational analysis. In W. Bennett Jr., C. E. Lance, & D. J. Woehr (Eds.), *Performance measurement: Current perspectives and future challenges* (pp. 141–173). Mahwah, NJ: Erlbaum.
Heider, F. (1958). *The psychology of interpersonal relations.* New York, NY: Wiley.
Hui, C., Lam, S., & Law, K. (2000). Instrumental values of organizational citizenship behavior for promotion: A field quasi-experiment. *Journal of Applied Psychology, 85*(5), 822–828.
Ilies, R., Scott, B. A., & Judge, T. A. (2006). The interactive effects of personal traits and experienced states on

intraindividual patterns of citizenship behavior. *Academy of Management Journal, 49*(3), 561–575.

James, W. (1890). *The principles of psychology*. New York, NY: Holt.

Jelinek, R., & Ahearne, M. (2006). The enemy within: Examining salesperson deviance and its determinants. *Journal of Personal Selling & Sales Management, 26*(4), 327–344.

Johnson, D. E., Erez, A., Kiker, D. S., & Motowidlo, S. J. (2002). Liking and attributions of motives as mediators of the relationships between individuals' reputations, helping behaviors, and raters' reward decisions. *Journal of Applied Psychology, 87*, 808–815.

Kamdar, D., & Van Dyne, L. (2007). The joint effects of personality and workplace social exchange relationships in predicting task performance and citizenship performance. *Journal of Applied Psychology, 92*, 1286–1289.

Katz, D. (1964). The motivational basis of organizational behavior. *Behavioral Science, 9*, 131–146.

Kiker, D. S., & Motowidlo, S. J. (1999). Main and interaction effects of task and contextual performance on supervisory reward decisions. *Journal of Applied Psychology, 84*(4), 602–609.

Kim, Y. J., Van Dyne, L., Kamdar, D., & Johnson, R. E. (2013). Why and when do motives matter? An integrative model of motives, role cognitions, and social support as predictors of OCB. *Organizational Behavior and Human Decision Processes, 121*(2), 231–245.

Klotz, A. C., & Bolino, M. C. (2013). Citizenship and counterproductive work behavior: A moral licensing view. *Academy of Management Review, 38*(2), 292–306.

Köpetz, C., Faber, T., Fishbach, A., & Kruglanski, A. W. (2011). The multifinality constraints effect: How goal multiplicity narrows the means set to a focal end. *Journal of Personality and Social Psychology, 100*(5), 810–826.

Köpetz, C. E., Kruglanski, A. W., Arens, Z. G., Etkin, J., & Johnson, H. M. (2012). The dynamics of consumer behavior: A goal systemic perspective. *Journal of Consumer Psychology, 22*(2), 208–223.

Kosic, A., Kruglanski, A. W., Pierro, A., & Mannetti, L. (2004). The social cognition of immigrants' acculturation: Effects of the need for closure and the reference group at entry. *Journal of Personality and Social Psychology, 86*(6), 796–813.

Kruglanski, A. W. (1996). Goals as knowledge structures. In P. M. Gollwitzer & J. A. Bargh (Eds.), *The psychology of action*. New York, NY: Guilford Press.

Kruglanski, A. W., & Köpetz, C. (2009a). The role of goal systems in self-regulation. In E. Morsella, J. A. Bargh, & P. M. Gollwitzer (Eds.), *Oxford handbook of human action* (pp. 350–367). New York, NY: Oxford University Press.

Kruglanski, A. W., & Köpetz, C. (2009b). What is so special (and nonspecial) about goals? A view from the cognitive perspective. In G. B. Moskowitz & H. Grant (Eds.), *The psychology of goals* (pp. 27–55). New York, NY: Guilford Press.

Kruglanski, A. W., Shah, J. Y., Fishbach, A., Friedman, R., Chun, W. Y., & Sleeth-Keppler, D. (2002). A theory of goal systems. *Advances in Experimental Social Psychology, 34*, 331–378.

Kuhl, J. (1984). Volitional aspects of achievement motivation and learned helplessness: Toward a comprehensive theory of action control. In B. A. Maher & W. A. Maher (Eds.), *Progress in experimental personality research* (pp. 99–171). New York, NY: Academic Press.

Kuhl, J., & Weiss, M. (1994). Performance deficits following uncontrollable failure: Impaired action control or generalized expectancy deficits? In J. Kuhl & J. Beckmann (Eds.), *Volition and personality: Action versus state orientation* (pp. 317–328). Gottingen, Germany: Hogrefe.

Lewin, K. (1935). *A dynamic theory of personality: Selected papers*. New York, NY: McGraw Hill.

MacKenzie, S. B., Podsakoff, P. M., & Fetter, R. (1991). Organizational citizenship behavior and objective productivity as determinants of managerial evaluations of salespersons' performance. *Organizational Behavior and Human Decision Processes, 50*(1), 123–150.

MacKenzie, S. B., Podsakoff, P. M., & Paine, J. B. (1999). Do citizenship behaviors matter more for managers than for salespeople? *Journal of the Academy of Marketing Science, 27*(4), 396–410.

Markman, A. B., Brendl, C. M., & Kim, K. (2007). Preference and the specificity of goals. *Emotion, 7*(3), 680–684.

Markus, H., & Nurius, P. (1986). Possible selves. *American Psychologist, 41*(9), 954–969.

Meglino, B. M., & Korsgaard, A. (2004). Considering rational self-interest as a disposition: Organizational implications of other orientation. *Journal of Applied Psychology, 89*(6), 946–959.

Morrison, E. W. (1994). Role definitions and organizational citizenship behavior: The importance of the employee's perspective. *Academy of Management Journal, 37*(6), 1543–1567.

Motowidlo, S. J., Borman, W. C., & Schmit, M. J. (1997). A theory of individual differences in task and contextual performance. *Human Performance, 10*(2), 71–83.

Motowidlo, S. J., & Van Scotter, J. R. (1994). Evidence that task performance should be distinguished from contextual performance. *Journal of Applied Psychology, 79*(4), 475–480.

Munyon, T. P., Hochwarter, W. A., Perrewé, P. L., & Ferris, G. R. (2010). Optimism and the nonlinear citizenship behavior—Job satisfaction relationship in three studies. *Journal of Management, 36*(6), 1505–1528.

Oldham, G. R., & Hackman, J. R. (2010). Not what it was and not what it will be: The future of job design research. *Journal of Organizational Behavior, 31*(23), 463–479.

Organ, D. W. (1988). *Organizational citizenship behavior: The good soldier syndrome*. Lexington, MA: Lexington Books.

Organ, D. W. (1990). The motivational basis of organizational citizenship behavior. In B. M. Staw & L. L. Cummings (Eds.), *Research in organizational behavior* (Vol. *12*, pp. 43–72). Greenwich, CT: JAI Press.

Organ, D. W., Podsakoff, P. M., & MacKenzie, S. B. (2006). *Organizational citizenship behavior: Its nature, antecedents, and consequences*. Thousand Oaks, CA: Sage.

Organ, D. W., & Ryan, K. (1995). A meta-analytic review of attitudinal and dispositional predictors of organizational citizenship behavior. *Personnel Psychology, 48*(4), 775–802.

Penner, L. A., Midili, A. R., & Kegelmeyer, J. (1997). Beyond job attitudes: A personality and social psychology perspective on the causes of organizational citizenship behavior. *Human Performance, 10*(2), 111–132.

Penner, L. A., & Orom, H. (2010). Enduring goodness: A person-by-situation perspective on prosocial behavior. In M. Mikulincer & P. R. Shaver (Eds.), *Prosocial motives, emotions, and behavior: The better angels of our nature* (pp. 55–72). Washington, DC: American Psychological Association.

Pierce, J. R., & Aguinis, H. (2013). The too-much-of-a-good-thing effect in management. *Journal of Management, 39*(2), 313–338.

Podsakoff, P. M., Ahearne, M., & MacKenzie, S. B. (1997). Organizational citizenship behavior and the quantity and quality of work group performance. *Journal of Applied Psychology, 82*(2), 262–270.

Podsakoff, P. M., & MacKenzie, S. B. (1994). Organizational citizenship behaviors and sales unit effectiveness. *Journal of Marketing Research, 31*(3), 351–363.

Podsakoff, P. M., & MacKenzie, S. B. (1997). Impact of organizational citizenship behavior on organizational performance: A review and suggestion for future research. *Human Performance, 10*(2), 133–151.

Podsakoff, P. M., MacKenzie, S. B., & Hui, C. (1993). Organizational citizenship behaviors and managerial evaluations of employee performance: A review and suggestions for future research. In G. R. Ferris (Ed.), *Research in personnel and human resources management* (Vol. *11*, pp. 1–40). Greenwich, CT: JAI Press.

Podsakoff, P. M., MacKenzie, S. B., Moorman, R. H., & Fetter, R. (1990). Transformational leader behaviors and their effects on followers' trust in leader, satisfaction, and organizational citizenship behaviors. *Leadership Quarterly, 1*(2), 107–142.

Podsakoff, P. M., MacKenzie, S. B., Paine, J. B., & Bachrach, D. G. (2000). Organizational citizenship behaviors: A critical review of the theoretical and empirical literature and suggestions for future research. *Journal of Management, 26*(3), 513–563.

Randall, M. L., Cropanzano, R., Bormann, C. A., & Birjulin, A. (1999). Organizational politics and organizational support as predictors of work attitudes, job performance, and organizational citizenship behavior. *Journal of Organizational Behavior, 20*(2), 159–174.

Rioux, S. M., & Penner, L. A. (2001). The causes of organizational citizenship behavior: A motivational analysis. *Journal of Applied Psychology, 86*(6), 1306–1314.

Rosenfeld, P., Giacalone, R. A., & Riordan, C. A. (1995). *Impression management in organizations: Theory, measurement, practice.* New York, NY: Routledge.

Schnake, M. (1991). Organizational citizenship: A review, proposed model, and research agenda. *Human Relations, 44*(7), 735–759.

Shah, J. Y. (2005). The automatic pursuit and management of goals. *Current Directions in Psychological Science, 14*(1), 10–13.

Skinner, B. F. (1953). Some contributions of an experimental analysis of behavior to psychology as a whole. *The American Psychologist, 8*(2), 69–78.

Snyder, M. (1987). *Public appearances, private realities: The psychology of self-monitoring.* New York, NY: Freeman.

Snyder, M. (1993). Basic research and practical problems: The promise of a "functional" personality and social psychology. *Personality and Social Psychology Bulletin, 19*(3), 251–264.

Strauss, K., Griffin, M. A., & Parker, S. K. (2012). Future work selves: How salient hoped-for identities motivate proactive career behaviors. *Journal of Applied Psychology, 97*(3), 580–598.

Strobel, M., Tumasjan, A., Spörrle, M., & Welpe, I. M. (2013). The future starts today, not tomorrow: How future focus promotes organizational citizenship behaviors. *Human Relations, 66*(6), 829–856.

Tolman, E. C. (1925). Purpose and cognition: The determiners of animal learning. *Psychological Review, 32*(4), 285–297.

Van Dyne, L., Cummings, L. L., & McLean Parks, J. (1995). Extra-role behaviors: In pursuit of construct and definitional clarity. In L. L. Cummings & B. M. Staw (Eds.), *Research in organizational behavior* (Vol. *17*, pp. 215–285). Greenwich, CT: JAI Press.

Van Dyne, L., & Ellis, J. B. (2004). Job creep: A reactance theory perspective on organizational citizenship behavior as overfulfillment of obligations. In J. A. M. Coyle-Shapiro, L. M. Shore, M. S. Taylor, & L. E. Tetrick (Eds.), *The employment relationship: Examining psychological and contextual perspectives* (pp. 181–205). Oxford, UK: Oxford University Press.

Van Dyne, L., Graham, J. W., & Dienesch, R. M. (1994). Organizational citizenship behavior: Construct redefinition, measurement, and validation. *Academy of Management Journal, 37*(4), 765–802.

Van Hook, E., & Higgins, E. T. (1988). Self-related problems beyond the self-concept: Motivational consequences of discrepant self-guides. *Journal of Personality and Social Psychology, 55*(4), 625–633.

Van Scotter, J. R., & Motowidlo, S. J. (1996). Interpersonal facilitation and job dedication as separate facets of contextual performance. *Journal of Applied Psychology, 81*(5), 525–531.

Van Scotter, J. R., Motowidlo, S. J., & Cross, T. C. (2000). Effects of task performance and contextual performance on systemic rewards. *Journal of Applied Psychology, 85*(4), 526–535.

Vigoda-Gadot, E. (2006). Compulsory citizenship behavior: Theorizing some dark sides of the good soldier syndrome in organizations. *Journal for the Theory of Social Behaviour, 36*(1), 77–93.

Vigoda-Gadot, E. (2007). Leadership style, organizational politics, and employees' performance: An empirical examination of two competing models. *Personnel Review, 36*(5), 661–683.

Walz, S. M., & Niehoff, B. P. (1996). Organizational citizenship behaviors and their effect on organizational effectiveness in limited-menu restaurants. In J. B. Keys & L. N. Dosier (Eds.), *Academy of Management Best Papers Proceedings* (pp. 307–311). Briarcliff Manor, NY: Academy of Management.

Ward, A., & Mann, T. (2000). Don't mind if I do: Disinhibited eating under cognitive load. *Journal of Personality and Social Psychology, 78*, 753–763.

Wertenbroch, K. (1998). Consumption self-control by rationing: Purchase quantities of virtue and vice. *Marketing Science, 17*(4), 317–337.

Williams, L. J., & Anderson, S. E. (1991). Job satisfaction and organizational commitment as predictors of organizational citizenship and in-role behaviors. *Journal of Management, 17*(3), 601–617.

Wrzesniewski, A., & Dutton, J. E. (2001). Crafting a job: Revisioning employees as active crafters of their work. *Academy of Management Review, 26*(2), 179–201.

Yun, S., Takeuchi, R., & Liu, W. (2007). Employee self-enhancement motives and job performance behaviors: Investigating the moderating effects of employee role ambiguity and managerial perceptions of employee commitment. *Journal of Applied Psychology, 92*(3), 745–756.

CHAPTER

15 Organizational Justice and Organizational Citizenship

Russell Cropanzano, Deborah E. Rupp, Meghan A. Thornton-Lugo, *and* Ruodan Shao

Abstract

In this chapter, we provide a detailed examination of the relationship between employee justice perceptions and organizational citizenship behavior OCB. Beginning with the earliest research on OCB, we articulate how these two topics within organizational sciences developed alongside one another as researchers attempted to articulate not only what kinds of justice would influence extra-role behaviors but also how those effects emerge. We also discuss modern trends in the study of justice and OCB, examining new theoretical perspectives and multifoci, third-party, and multilevel approaches to assessing this phenomenon. Our aim is to provide a comprehensive discussion of not only where research has been but also where it will go as scholars continue to develop new insights into justice and citizenship behaviors in the workplace.

Key Words: organizational citizenship behavior OCB, organizational sciences, extra-role behaviors, justice, citizenship behaviors

In a way, organizational justice and organizational citizenship behavior (OCB) can be said to have grown up together. Although both topics have older antecedent roots, much of their contemporary formulation was articulated in the mid-1980s (e.g., Bateman & Organ, 1983; Bies & Moag, 1986; Folger & Greenberg, 1985; Lind & Tyler, 1988; Smith, Organ, & Near, 1983). Very early in the history of OCB, justice was posited (Organ, 1988) and found (Organ & Konovsky, 1989; Scholl, Cooper, & McKenna, 1987) to be a predictor of citizenship behaviors. Though ensuing research has expanded and elaborated on their relationship, the fundamental point has not changed: When individuals believe that they are being treated fairly, other things being equal, they are more likely to perform OCB (e.g., Cohen-Charash & Spector, 2001; Rupp, Shao, Jones, & Liao, 2014).

Understanding why this is so, as well as the many applications and variants of this basic insight, is a major undertaking. Toward that end, we seek to provide a thorough review of the justice–OCB relationship. Following a brief overview of organizational justice, we will discuss the early history of this research area. This historical introduction will provide a foundation for understanding the roots of contemporary inquiry. We will then consider more recent investigations of the relationship between justice and OCB. To further foreshadow our review, we present an illustrative figure (Figure 15.1) to assist the reader as we traverse through these occasionally convoluted literatures. We will refer back to it as we review the literature, and at the end of this chapter, where we will make a number of summary interpretations and offer recommendations for future research.

Organizational Justice: A Brief Overview

The study of organizational justice concerns judgments of moral propriety and ethical treatment (Cropanzano, Byrne, Bobocel, & Rupp, 2001). To decide whether an action or event is

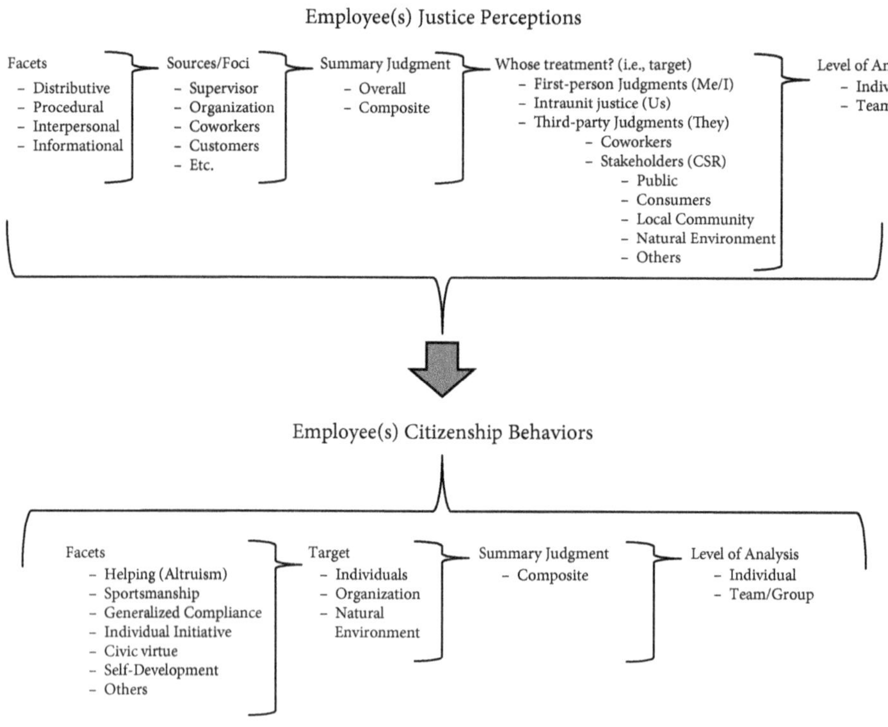

Figure 15.1 Approaches to studying justice and organizational citizenship behaviors.

fair, individuals compare what actually transpired to a set of standards or criteria (Rupp & Paddock, 2010). These standards are called *justice rules* (e.g., by Colquitt & Rodell, 2015; Leventhal, 1980). If the event, outcome, or incident is aligned with these rules, then the occurrence may be judged as fair (Brockner & Wiesenfeld, 1996). However, if the occurrence did not transpire in accordance with the justice rules, and especially if harm has been done (Brockner, 2002), the event/outcome is said to be unfair. The process is admittedly more complex than this (Cropanzano, Fortin, & Kirk, 2015; Scott, Colquitt, & Paddock, 2009). Fairness judgments are often made through the use of heuristics, rather than by deliberate and effortful consideration (Proudfoot & Lind, 2015). For example, people are more likely to evaluate something as fair when they are in a good mood as opposed to when they are not (Sinclair & Mark, 1991, 1992). Likewise, individuals display a tendency, sometimes marked, to judge an event or outcome as fair to the extent that it benefits their self-interest (Cropanzano & Moliner, 2013; Moliner, Martínez-Tur, Peiró, Ramos, & Cropanzano, 2013). Nevertheless, the general process appears to hold, across a variety of contexts and across multiple levels of analysis (cf. Cropanzano, Stein, & Nadisic, 2011).

Dimensions of Justice

Justice rules have been categorized through the decades in a number of ways. The "Big Three" justice dimensions (i.e., those most widely used in research) are distributive justice, procedural justice, and interactional justice. Distributive justice pertains to the fairness of outcomes (Törnblom & Kazemi, 2015). According to Deutsch (1975, 1985) and Frohlich (2007), the most widely studied outcome distribution rules are equity (outcomes in accordance with contributions), equality (equivalent outcomes for all), and need (outcomes based on necessity or individual requirements). Procedural justice pertains to the fairness of decision-making processes (Bobocel & Gosse, 2015). The best-known rules for procedural justice come from the pioneering work of Leventhal (1976, 1980; Leventhal, Karuza, & Fry, 1980). Just procedures provide consistent treatment, suppression of biases, accuracy, correctability, representative of relevant views (this includes the allowance of voice), and ethicality. Growing out of procedural justice but now generally regarded as distinct (Bies, 2005; Bobocel & Holmvall, 2001), interactional justice pertains to the interpersonal treatment received (Bies, 2001, 2015).

As can be seen from this brief presentation, different facets of justice came to the attention of organizational scientists at different times. Distributive justice is the oldest (e.g., Adams, 1965; Deutsch, 1975) and would have been widely available as early models of citizenship behavior were being formulated (e.g., by Bateman & Organ, 1983; Smith et al., 1983). Procedural justice was applied to organizations a few years later (Folger & Greenberg, 1985; Lind & Tyler, 1988). Interactional justice appeared at about the same time (e.g., Bies, 1987; Bies & Moag, 1986). Still, it would take longer before interactional justice was recognized as distinct from procedural justice (Bobocel & Holmvall, 2001), and this may have delayed its application to the study of OCB (by Bies, Martin, & Brockner, 1993, which is discussed later). For this reason, early OCB research was limited by the conceptual tools that were accessible at the time. Early work emphasized distributive justice (e.g., Organ, 1988; 1990), whereas later work would more fully incorporate procedural and interactional justice (Rupp et al., 2014).

Justice and Organizational Citizenship Behavior: Historical Roots and Conceptual Foundations

In this section we provide a historical review of the justice–OCB literatures. As we shall see, the concept of extra-role behavior—beneficial actions by employees that are not always formalized into work roles—is an old one, having been raised by Barnard (1938), as well Katz (1964; see also, Katz & Kahn, 1978). During the early 1980s, these ideas were expanded and empirically investigated by Organ and his colleagues (e.g., Bateman & Organ, 1983; Organ, 1988; Organ & Konovsky, 1989; Smith et al., 1983). This slightly predates early discussions of procedural justice (Folger & Greenberg, 1985; Lind & Tyler, 1988) and interactional justice (Bies, 1987; Bies & Moag, 1986). As might be imagined, OCB researchers began to make use of these ideas as they became available (e.g., Moorman, 1991).

The Early Years: 1983–1993

In some recognizable form or other, the concept of OCB has circulated for a number of decades. As long ago as the 1930s, Chester Barnard (1938, p. 84) argued that organizations were "cooperative systems" and that business success required workers to show a "willingness to contribute" that went beyond formal job duties. About 25 years later, Katz (1964) listed a number of extra-role behaviors, which can contribute to business effectiveness. His list included such things as volunteering ideas, self-development, and defending the organization's reputation. Katz and Kahn (1978) further developed these themes in their classic book, *The Social Psychology of Organizations.* Although this pioneering work was important, much modern thinking on OCB was inspired by two important articles: Smith et al. (1983) and Bateman and Organ (1983).

HISTORIC INVESTIGATIONS, PART I: SMITH ET AL. (1983) AND BATEMAN AND ORGAN (1983)

To our knowledge, the first empirical investigation of OCB was published by Smith et al. (1983), which appeared a few weeks before Bateman and Organ's (1983) article. Smith and her colleagues provided an influential conceptual definition of citizenship behaviors. OCB was "a category of performance" that went "beyond formal role requirements" (pp. 653–654). OCB was explicitly contrasted with "contractual, enforceable role prescriptions" (p. 654). Following from this definition, Smith and her colleague identified two dimensions of citizenship behavior that would soon become well known to researchers (e.g., Farh, Podsakoff, & Organ, 1990; Organ & Konovsky, 1989). *Altruism* involved "helping a specific person in face-to-face situations" (Smith et al., p. 657). *Generalized compliance,* sometimes simply called "conscientiousness" (e.g., by Rioux & Penner, 2001, p. 1316), involved "a more impersonal form . . . that does not provide immediate aid to any specific person, but rather is indirectly helpful to others involved in the system" (Smith et al., p. 657). Employees were believed to have more discretion when performing either type of OCB, in comparison to formal job tasks. For this reason, citizenship behaviors were expected and found to be more strongly related to job satisfaction and other attitudinal predictors than was in-role job performance (this basic argument had been laid out beforehand by Organ, 1977).

Bateman and Organ's (1983) study placed even more emphasis on the putatively weak relationship between job satisfaction and job performance than did that of Smith and her colleagues (1983). Although research would eventually find evidence that satisfaction is a useful predictor of performance, this would not come to light until much later (Judge, Thoresen, Bono, & Patton, 2001). In the early 1980s, the field was still coming to grips with Vroom's (1964) well-known review, which reported a mean r = .14 (uncorrected) for the job satisfaction–performance relationship. To account for this low correlation, Bateman and Organ posited the existence of discretionary, "supra-role" behaviors

(p. 588). Given that employees have greater leeway to relax or increase supra-role behaviors, and less leeway for adjusting their required performance, the authors maintained that the job satisfaction–OCB relationship would exceed the .14 found by Vroom (again consistent with Organ, 1977, and Smith et al., 1983). Perhaps owing to the newness of justice research, Bateman and Organ did not focus on fairness per se. However, they did mention "supportive or considerate" supervisory behavior as a potential cause of OCB, perhaps with eye to the aforementioned work of Smith and her colleagues.

For all their prescience, justice was mostly conspicuous by its absence in these two seminal articles. Smith et al. (1983) did not formally include justice in their model, though they did refer to the importance of equity (a distributive justice rule). Bateman and Organ (1983) cited Adams's (1965) work on equity but only as an example of social exchange theory. Consequently, distributive justice made a small cameo appearance, but it did not play a major role. This was about to change.

HISTORIC INVESTIGATIONS, PART 2: SCHOLL, COOPER, AND MCKENNA (1987)

Four years after the appearance of Smith et al. (1983) and Bateman and Organ (1983), Scholl and his coauthors (1987) published an empirical investigation of equity theory. As predictors, Scholl and his colleagues used seven different referents—people doing the same job (job equity), people employed by the same organization (company equity), people in different organizations (occupational equity), people with the same education (educational equity), people who had reached the same age (age equity), different expectations from the system (system equity), and self-evaluation of worth (self-equity). These seven referents were used to predict three different criterion variables. The first two were job satisfaction and intent to remain, which are not a major focus of this chapter. However, the third, "extra-role behavior" (Scholl et al., pp. 118–119), was an early measure of OCB. Respondents rated themselves along the following dimensions: "suggestions for improvement, helping others with problems, self-training, taking on extra responsibility, work involvement, meeting deadlines, high personal standards, initiative, dedication, and continuing education" (p. 118).

Scholl et al.'s (1987) findings were unremarkable. When extra-role behavior was regressed onto the seven referents, only job equity—comparisons against other employees who did the same type of work—was shown to be a significant predictor ($\beta = .42$, $p < .01$). Nevertheless, the study is something of a landmark for two reasons. First, Scholl and his coinvestigators appear to have formulated their measure separately from the work of Smith et al. (1983) and Bateman and Organ (1983). Instead, they devised their measure of extra-role behavior based on the work of Katz and Kahn (1978). Second, Scholl et al. formally assessed distributive justice, or at least equity, as a predictor of OCB. The success of their study, even if somewhat limited, would set the stage for later investigations.

A Necessary Digression: Cognition Versus Affect

During the 1980s, the principal rival to social exchange was workplace affect. Early investigators had a great deal of interest in workplace affect as a possible predictor of OCB. As alluded to earlier, these initial studies tended to compare the predictive power of job cognitions to feeling states. Justice became involved in this research—as it was often viewed as a cognitive appraisal—in addition to other cognitions. Feeling states, on the other hand, were sometimes operationalized as job satisfaction (e.g., Bateman & Organ, 1983; Kemery, Bedeian, & Zacur, 1996; Smith et al., 1983). Despite limitations of operationalizing affect as satisfaction, this operational treatment continued sporadically into the 1990s, a time during which some of this work produced intriguing results. For example, McNeely and Meglino (1994) compared cognitions—operationalized as equity and recognition—to job satisfaction as predictors of (a) prosocial behavior intended to benefit the organization and (b) prosocial behaviors intended to benefit the specific individuals. Equity and recognition (i.e., cognitions) predicted beyond satisfaction (i.e., affect), but only when the criterion was prosocial behaviors intended to benefit the organization. Job satisfaction predicted beyond equity/recognition, but only when the criterion was prosocial behavior intended to benefit individuals.

Treating job satisfaction as an operational measure of affect, though common at the time, was later found to pose a rather serious conceptual problem. As Organ and Near (1985, p. 241) observed, "evidence suggests that these [job satisfaction] measures reflect primarily cognitive evaluation rather than affective state or hedonic tone" (see also George, 1991; Williams & Anderson, 1991). As a result of this conceptual issue, researchers began employing direct measures of affect, rather than treating job satisfaction as a proxy.

EARLY STUDIES USING MEASURES OF AFFECT

George (1991) contrasted the predictive power of justice to that of a scale assessing positive feelings at work. She found that mood at work predicted prosocial behaviors directed at customers beyond the effects of justice. These conclusions regarding the predictive power of affect over cognitions, however, were not always shared by other researchers. Organ and Konovsky (1989) assessed a variety of cognitions about jobs and pay, contrasting these against positive and negative affect. These researchers found that the cognitions, and not affect, were better predictors of OCB. Organ and Konovsky argued that their results attested to the importance of fairness cognitions (see also Organ & Moorman, 1993). Lee and Allen (2002) also reported that cognitions, including but not limited to organizational justice, were more closely related to OCBI (defined as citizenship behaviors benefiting individuals—e.g., coworkers, supervisor—in the organization), whereas affect was more closely related to OCBO (defined as citizenship behaviors benefiting the organization). Lee and Allen's conclusions, of course, closely paralleled the aforementioned findings of McNeely and Meglino (1994). Williams and Anderson's (1991) results also attested to the importance of cognitions (as opposed to affect) as predictors of OCB, though this study did not explicitly measure justice.

As the distinction between perceptions of allocations and processes became better known, researchers began to explore the independent effects of procedural and distributive justice. In this regard, Bies et al. (1993) examined employees' responses to an imminent downsizing. Bies and his colleagues found that distributive justice, procedural justice, and affect were each positively related to OCB. However, only procedural justice added incremental variance beyond the other two.

SUMMARY BEFORE MOVING ON

With the exception of a single study by George (1991), research comparing cognitions—including justice—to affect demonstrated that the former predicted OCB at least as well (and possibly better) than the latter. Although this is good news for students of organizational justice, this line of research also had its limitations, particularly with the manner in which the justice–affect relationship was conceptualized. These early studies tended to compare justice to affect, as if they were independent causes. However, the two are closely related (Fortin, Blader, Wiesenfeld, & Wheeler-Smith, 2015), with each capable of causing the other (Cropanzano et al., 2011). Consequently, a stronger approach might have been to build conceptual models that included both justice and affect together, working in a complementary fashion to predict OCB. To date, work that takes this approach remains limited. Yi and Gong (2008) proposed that distributive, procedural, and interactional justice all boost positive affect. Positive affect thereby causes increased OCB. As such, positive feelings mediate the benefits of justice. Yi and Gong tested their model, and the results were generally supportive. These findings suggest that justice and affect need not be considered as competing explanations.

Beyond Distributive Justice: 1991–1999

Explorations of distributive justice and OCB continued into and well past the 1990s. McNeely and Meglino (1994) found that equity perceptions predicted OCB and generally similar results were obtained by Netemeyer, Boles, McKee, and McMurrian (1997) and Schanke, Cochran, and Dumler (1995). Despite the positive results found in studies of distributive justice, it was evident that this single dimension did not exhaust the utility of workplace fairness as a predictor of OCB (Aquino, 1995). Given this recognition, researchers began to broaden their conceptualization of justice, doing so in two distinct ways. The first, and perhaps most obvious, was to directly measure procedural and/or interactional justice in research investigations of OCB. To illustrate this point, we have already reviewed the work of Bies et al. (1993), observing that interactional justice is a potentially important predictor of OCB. In a like fashion, Folger (1993) discussed two unpublished previous studies, each of which demonstrated that procedural justice could predict incremental variance in OCB beyond the effect of distributive justice. The second approach, which was more subtle, was to employ a measure that assessed justice as a single dimension. This single dimension, which was not limited to outcome allocations, could include processes and interactions as well. The instrument might be a composite (aggregating the different types of justice together) or an overall measure (using broad or general items). We will discuss each of these responses in turn.

RESPONSE #1: DIRECT MEASUREMENT OF PROCEDURAL AND/OR INTERACTIONAL JUSTICE

Some studies using this approach have directly assessed just one facet of justice. Chattopadhyay (1999) examined interactional justice, reporting that it was associated with altruism, whereas Deckop, Mangel, and Cirka (1999) noted a relationship between procedural justice and an overall measure of OCB. Others have considered multiple facets at once. For example, Ball, Treviño, and Sims (1994) investigated subordinate responses to workplace punishment, finding that the distributive component of punishment (its harshness) predicted later in-role performance and the procedural component of punishment (worker control) predicted OCB. Similar findings were exhibited when justice was manipulated. In two interventions, Skarlicki and Latham (1996, 1997) trained union leaders in procedural and interpersonal justice. Afterward, members reported greater leader fairness. Moreover, they also performed more citizenship behaviors directed toward the organization (the union, in this case) and toward individuals.

Similarly, Farh, Earley, and Lin (1997) examined all three dimensions of justice—distributive, procedural, and interactional—among a sample of Chinese respondents. These researchers found that distributive and procedural justice predicted OCB, though these effects were moderated by cultural values and gender. To be sure, not every study was equally supportive of the relationship between justice and OCB. Less promising outcomes were obtained by Schappe (1998) and Pond, Nacoste, Mohr, and Rodriguez (1997), both of whom found that neither procedural nor interactional justice related to OCB. In a recent study of hospitality workers in North Cyprus, Nadiri and Tanova (2010) found that distributive justice was a better predictor of OCB than were the other two facets, at least for their sample. Nevertheless, the weight of evidence supported the proposition that justice, including procedural and interactional justice, was associated with OCB.

RESPONSE #2: COMPOSITE AND OVERALL JUSTICE

Other researchers have approached the study of justice and OCB using a composite scale to measure justice (see Figure 15.1). Items on composite scales query the respondent regarding multiple justice dimensions (i.e., distributive justice, procedural, and so forth). However, these dimensions are not considered separately; rather, they are aggregated into a single measure (Li, Cropanzano, & Bagger, 2013). Lee and Allen (2002, see earlier) took an approach akin to that of a composite measure. Similarly, Farh and his colleagues (1990) used a composite measure of leader fairness. Testing their model among 195 Taiwanese employees, they found that leader fairness accounted for unique variance in altruism but not in compliance. Likewise, Bettencourt and Brown (1997) found that composite justice predicted both extra-role customer service behaviors and also cooperativeness with coworkers.[1]

An overall justice measure is a bit different, in that it eschews dimensional items and instead queries the respondent regarding justice "as a whole" or "in general" (Ambrose & Schminke, 2009; Ambrose, Wo, & Griffith, 2015). Overall measures do not examine the justice dimensions separately. Tansky (1993) took this strategy, measuring overall fairness with three items: "management in my organization treats me honestly and ethically," "overall my organization is fair," and "the programs and policies in my organization are fair." Tansky found that an index formed by these items predicted subordinate altruistic behavior (for a reanalysis of these data, see Podsakoff & MacKenzie, 1993). In two later studies, Deluga (1994, 1995) found that an overall measure of leader fairness predicted the OCB dimensions of conscientiousness, sportsmanship, courtesy, and altruism.

TWO THEORETICAL POSITIONS: SOCIAL EXCHANGE THEORY AND THE GROUP-VALUE MODEL

By the middle of the 1990s, it was clear that distributive, procedural, and interactional justice should all be investigated as potential predictors of OCB. However, the large majority of this research had not yet articulated explanatory mechanisms for these effects. Two possibilities received the most attention. These were social exchange theory, which was drawn from OCB research (e.g., Bateman & Organ, 1983), and the group-value model, which was drawn from justice research (Lind & Tyler, 1988; Tyler, Degoey, & Smith, 1996). Both of these models continue to be influential in both justice and OCB research today.

Social Exchange Theory. In a series of publications, Organ and his colleagues (Bateman & Organ, 1983; Organ, 1988, 1990; Organ & Konovsky, 1989; Smith et al., 1983) had pointed toward social exchange theory as a means of explaining the relationship between organizational justice and OCB. Specifically, just transactions were believed to cultivate social exchange relationships (Konovsky

& Pugh, 1994), which are based on trust and commitment (Cropanzano & Mitchell, 2005). Subsequently, the relationships were expected to boost OCB (Organ & Moorman, 1993). As previously discussed, early work emphasized the fair exchange of allocated outcomes (e.g., a distributively just payment for one's time and effort), arguing that this should produce a social exchange relationship and this, in turn, should promote OCB (cf. Bateman & Organ, 1983). Although this all sounds fine, insofar as it goes, we have already seen that it does not go far enough. At least two other dimensions of justice—procedural and interactional—exist. These also have the potential to promote social exchange relationships (Cropanzano, Rupp, Mohler, & Schminke, 2001; Lavelle, Rupp, & Brockner, 2007) and, by extension, increase OCB (Bies et al., 1993; Folger, 1993).

Social exchange theory: Adding procedural and interactional justice. Using social exchange as a theoretical framework, researchers have tested this possibility. Moorman (1991) measured three types of justice—distributive, procedural, and interactional. Using Podsakoff and MacKenzie's (1989) scale, they also assessed five dimensions of OCB—altruism, civic virtue, conscientiousness, courtesy, and sportsmanship. Overall, interactional justice was the only predictor of OCB, showing relationships with every dimension except for civic virtue. In a later investigation, Williams, Pitre, and Zainuba (2002) would report similar findings. Williams and his colleagues observed that interactional justice predicted OCB better than did distributive or procedural justice. However, procedural justice would fare a bit better in various other studies of social exchange theory. For example, Niehoff and Moorman (1993) again found that procedural justice predicted conscientiousness and courtesy, while interactional justice predicted sportsmanship. In Niehoff et al.'s study both of these justice facets were better predictors than was distributive justice. Furthermore, Moorman and Blakely (1995) also reported significant zero-order correlations between procedural justice and four types of OCB—interpersonal helping, individual initiative, personal industry, and loyal boosterism. Likewise, Lee (1995) found that an indicator of procedural justice, the fairness of the skills certification process, predicted extra-role behavior.

Social exchange theory: The mediating role of social exchange relationships. The work we have reviewed thus far used social exchange theory, at least in part, as their interpretative conceptual framework. However, none of these studies tested social exchange relationships as an operational mediator. To address this limitation, Konovsky and Pugh (1994) examined the impact of procedural and distributive justice on supervisor trust. Trust, in addition to perceived support and commitment (Cropanzano & Mitchell, 2005), has been used as an indicator of social exchange relationships. For this reason, it was expected that trust would mediate the impact of justice on OCB. Although Konovsky and Pugh's results were generally supportive, only procedural justice (and not distributive justice) was related to trust. Very similar results regarding justice and leader trust were also obtained by Pillai, Schriesheim, and Williams (1999) and Aryee, Budhwar, and Chen (2002).

These findings would later be updated, but they have never been overturned. Menguc (2000) reported that procedural justice was related to three dimensions of OCB (helping, sportsmanship, and civic virtue). This effect was partially mediated by trust in supervisor (for additional evidence, see also Connell, Ferres, & Travaglione, 2003; Ertürk, 2007; Wong, Wong, & Ngo, 2002). Extending these conclusions, Yang, Mossholder, and Peng (2009) found that supervisory procedural justice actually predicted two types of trust—cognitive trust and affective trust. However, only affective trust was related to interpersonal helping behavior. Thus, Yang et al. argued that the effect of supervisory procedural justice on OCB was specifically mediated by affective trust (and not cognitive trust) in one's supervisor.

Konovsky and Pugh (1994) and Pillai et al. (1999) both treated the supervisor as the source or focus of justice. As an alternative, Moorman, Blakely, and Niehoff (1998) argued that the organization as a whole could also treat an employee more or less fairly. Consequently, a worker could form a social exchange relationship with his or her employing organization. In their study of hospital employees, Moorman and his colleagues found that procedural justice predicted organizational support—another indicator of social exchange relationships. Perceived organizational support then engendered four dimensions of OCB—loyal boosterism, individual initiative, interpersonal helping, and personal industry. In a later study of union members, Aryee and Chay (2001) found that procedural and distributive justice caused perceptions of union supportiveness. This union support, in turn, increased OCBI and OCBO.

Social exchange theory: Hints of a multifoci model. As has been shown, the use of social exchange theory as an explanatory model for explaining the relationship between justice and OCB was originally worked out by Organ (1988, 1990) and later adopted by justice researchers (Cropanzano & Rupp, 2008). By the end of the 1990s and into the early 2000s, a number of studies had been conducted that were seen as consistent with the social exchange approach. Namely, the possibility that social exchange relationships mediated the effects of justice had been successfully examined by Aryee and Chay (2001), Konovsky and Pugh (1994), Moorman et al. (1998), and Pillai et al. (1999). Nevertheless, these three studies raised a new question. Konovsky and Pugh, along with Pillai and her colleagues, argued that supervisor trust was the critical mediator of the effect of justice on OCB. Moorman and his coworkers, however, took a different approach by considering support from the organization overall.

If the conclusions reached by these studies were valid, then they would suggest that individuals form relationships with multiple social entities, including the supervisor and the organization. Though a test of this possibility was not yet available, it was suggested by Moorman (1991, p. 853) with the observation that "interactional fairness was important because the employee was deciding to exhibit behaviors that would benefit the supervisor. . . . Employees were treated fairly by their supervisors and therefore performed more citizenship behaviors that would benefit the supervisors. . . . Therefore, the causes of citizenship behavior could be defined by the target of the citizenship behaviors." In short, justice can build relationships with supervisors, but it can also build relationships with other sources, including the organization as a whole. This critical insight would eventually become important for understanding multifoci justice (e.g., Lavelle et al., 2007; Lavelle, Rupp, Manegold, & Thornton, 2015), and we shall return to this possibility presently.

The Group-Value Model. As we have seen, social exchange theory was imported from the OCB literature and into the justice literature (e.g., by Moorman, 1991; Organ & Konovsky, 1989). Other scholars worked with existing theories of justice, of which perhaps the most notable was the group-value model (e.g., Graham & Organ, 1993). The group-value model was an early example of the relational models of justice (Blader & Tyler, 2015). A later version, the group engagement model (Tyler & Blader, 2000, 2001, 2003), will be discussed when we review contemporary justice–OCB research (e.g., Blader & Tyler, 2009; De Cremer, Brockner, Fishman, van Dijke, van Olffen, & Mayer, 2010). For the moment, it is worth recognizing that all relational models of justice share a common emphasis on human social life, arguing that people care about justice—and especially procedural justice—"because of the relational message conveyed" (Blader & Tyler, 2015, p. 351). In the particular case of the group-value model, procedural justice is said to indicate that a recipient is valued by fellow members. Injustice is hurtful because it indicates a lack of status within the group (Tyler, 1997).

The group-value model has received extensive empirical support (Tyler, 1989; 1994; Tyler et al., 1996), though only a few studies have explicitly studied OCB. In an investigation of 420 cable television employees, Moorman, Niehoff, and Organ (1993) found that procedural justice predicted the OCB dimensions of altruism, conscientiousness, courtesy, and sportsmanship, though not civic virtue. Moreover, procedural justice continued to be related to citizenship behavior, even when organizational commitment and job satisfaction were statistically controlled. Moorman et al. interpreted their findings as consistent with the group-value model. Subsequently, Aquino (1995) investigated three types of fairness—pay equity (distributive), procedural, and interpersonal; they also investigated two dimensions of OCB—altruism and compliance. Although Aquino's predictions for pay equity were derived from equity theory (Adams, 1965) and supported by the work of Scholl et al. (1987), which, as previously noted, found an effect for job equity on extra-role behavior, his predictions for procedural and interpersonal justice were explicitly grounded in the group-value model. Aquino found that both procedural and interpersonal justice were correlated with altruism, whereas all three types of justice showed significant zero-order correlations with compliance. However, when the predictive value of these justice dimensions were considered simultaneously, the effect of procedural justice on altruism was only marginally significant, whereas both equity and interpersonal justice showed similar relationships to compliance. Finally, a third test of the group-value model also found that procedural justice predicted extra-role behavior (Kim & Mauborgne, 1996). Though these three studies support the use of the group-value model as an explanatory mechanism for the justice–OCB relationship, none of them directly tested the explanatory mechanisms outlined by the theory. We therefore caution against making any definitive conclusions regarding its role in the justice–OCB relationship. We also caution that the group-value model has since been updated. As we shall see, modern researchers tend to make use of its more recent heir, the group engagement model, in order to explain the effect of justice on OCB (Tyler & Blader, 2002).

The Early Years Concluded

In the middle of the 1990s, Organ and Ryan (1995) published an initial meta-analysis of the available OCB research. Though the number of studies was not yet large (k = 20), fairness showed a significant and moderately sized relationship to OCB (ρ = .238). Organ's (1988, 1990) and Scholl et al.'s (1987) early arguments about the importance of justice seemed to hold up. Apart from these general conclusions, scholars were beginning to move beyond outcome distributions, obtaining evidence that interactional justice (Bies et al., 1993; Chattopadhyay, 1999; Farh et al., 1997) and procedural justice (Aquino, 1995; Folger, 1993) were predictive of OCB. It was time to begin the new century.

Individual-Level Approaches to Justice and Organizational Citizenship Behavior

Research on justice and OCB has continued apace. Although some studies have not found relationships between justice and OCB (e.g., Ang, Van Dyne, & Begley, 2003; Asgari, Silong, Ahmad, & Samah, 2008; Janseen, Lam, & Huang, 2009), most work has been at least partially supportive (e.g., Burton et al., 2008; Byrne, 2005; Chegini, 2009; Chiaburu & Lim, 2008; Cohen & Kol, 2004; Devonish & Greenidge, 2010; Klammer, Skarlicki, & Barclay, 2002; Lo & Aryee, 2003; Williams, Pitre, & Zainuba, 2002). For example, Burney, Henle, and Widener (2009), Coyle-Shapiro (2002), and Lin, Hung, and Chiu (2008) each reported significant effects for distributive and procedural justice on OCB. Likewise, Rosen, Chang, Johnson, and Levy (2009) reported that procedural justice was associated with both OCBI and OCBO (for similar findings pertaining to procedural justice, see Andrews, Kacmar, & Harris, 2009; Begley, Lee, Fang, & Li, 2002; Bowler & Brass, 2006; Dineen, Lewicki, & Tomlinson, 2006; Kim, Ok, & Lee, 2009; Kirkman, Chen, Farh, Chen, & Lowe, 2009; van Prooijen et al., 2008).

Other research successfully applied justice to specific workplace decisions and policies. For example, Findley, Giles, and Mossholder (2000) and Heslin and VandeWalle (2011) found that the fairness of performance appraisals affected employee citizenship behaviors. Little, Magner, and Welker (2002) found similar results when they explored the fairness of budgetary procedures, and Kickul, Lester, and Finkl (2002) investigated psychological contract breaches during times of organizational change. In a study that harkened back to the pioneering work of Bies et al. (1983), Brennan and Skarlicki (2004) reported that layoff survivors were more likely to engage in generalized compliance (a dimension of OCB) if they felt the downsizing had been handled with interactional justice. Interestingly, this effect was strongest for those employees who were *low* in self-discipline. Those who were high in self-discipline continued to comply even when interactional justice was low.

The ability of justice facets to predict OCB was further confirmed in a meta-analysis by Cohen-Charash and Spector (2001). These authors summarized the quantitative relationships among distributive justice, procedural justice, interactional justice, and OCB. Reflecting the existing literature, OCB was operationalized in a number of different ways. Furthermore, each type of justice was not necessarily available for every type of OCB. However, the results, though incomplete, were supportive. For distributive justice, the mean weighted r was .25 for overall OCB, .16 for altruism, and .20 for conscientiousness. Similarly, for procedural justice, the mean weighted r was .23 for overall OCB, .11 for altruism, and .20 for conscientiousness, as well as .22 for OCBO. Finally, the mean weighted r for interactional justice was .18 for altruism and .23 for conscientiousness. (There were insufficient data to report the relationship between overall OCB and interactional justice.) In their Table 5, Cohen-Charash and Spector report 10 mean weighted r's. These reflect the relationships among the three justice dimensions (distributive, procedural, and interactional) and five operationalizations of OCB (overall, altruism, conscientiousness, OCBO, and OCBI). Of these 10 relationships only a single one fell within a 95% confidence interval that contains zero. Specifically, the weighted mean correlation between procedural justice and OCBI was a modest .03. The 95% confidence interval was between –.03 and .10.

A later meta-analysis by Fassina, Jones, and Uggerslev (2008a) also examined the relationships among three dimensions of justice (procedural, interactional, and distributive) and five dimensions of OCB (altruism, conscientiousness, courtesy, civic virtue, and sportsmanship). The findings of Fassina et al. were even stronger than those of Cohen-Charash and Spector (2001). The corrected correlations between each type of justice and each dimension of OCB always fell within 95% confidence intervals that did not include zero.

Issues of Structure

As we have seen, most research on justice and OCB has used the three-factor model of justice. This structure includes distributive, procedural, and interactional justice. Although the three-factor model continues to be widely used, and it certainly characterizes much of the work on justice and OCB, it is not the only structural approach to justice. The first alternative, which possesses an additional dimension, breaks interactional justice into two component parts: interpersonal and informational (Colquitt & Rodell, 2015). The second alternative, which has only a single dimension, considers the role of overall justice (Ambrose et al., 2015). Following, we review the evidence for each as it pertains to citizenship behaviors.

THE FOUR-FACTOR STRUCTURE OF JUSTICE

An alternative to the three-factor model was proposed by Colquitt (2001; for a more recent review, see Colquitt & Rodell, 2015). Colquitt retained the distributive and procedural justice facets but took a closer look at interactional justice. He observed that previous research described interactional justice as having two broad aspects. The first of these, which Colquitt (2001) called *interpersonal justice*, involved such features as politeness and respectfulness (e.g., Bies, 2001, 2005). The second, *informational justice,* involved the provision and sharing of information (Bies, 1987, 2015), including providing explanations and offering social accounts (e.g., Bies, 1989; Sitkin & Bies, 1993). Given such considerations, Colquitt divided interactional justice into two more specific subdimensions, creating four types of justice in all—distributive, procedural, interpersonal, and informational. These four facets are listed in Figure 15.1. In validating his four-factor model, Colquitt (2001) reported that procedural justice perceptions were related to the OCB dimension of rule compliance, whereas interpersonal justice perceptions were related to helping behavior. Likewise, a meta-analysis by Colquitt, Conlon, Wesson, Porter, and Ng (2001) further indicated that these four dimensions of justice were useful predictors of OCB.

Other evidence supports the use of the four-factor model for predicting OCB (e.g., Jiang & Cheng, 2008; Streicher et al., 2008). Using a four-factor structure very similar to the one suggested by Colquitt (2001), Asgari, Nojabee, and Arjmand (2011) found that procedural and informational justice were each related to citizenship behaviors, whereas the distributive and interpersonal justice (Asgari and his colleagues used the term "interactional," p. 141) were not. Similarly, Piccolo, Bardes, Mayer, and Judge (2008) found that OCB was correlated with procedural and interpersonal justice, while Moliner, Martínez-Tur, Ramos, Peiro, and Cropanzano (2008) reported that OCB was predicted by distributive, procedural, and informational justice.

REVISITING OVERALL JUSTICE

Earlier, we discussed evidence suggesting that both composite justice (Bettencourt & Brown, 1997; Farh et al., 1990; Tansky, 1993) and overall justice (Deluga, 1994, 1995) were associated with OCB. This single-factor structure of justice, though interesting, stood in contrast to multidimensional approaches that had predominated the field of organizational justice literature, and for some time lacked a theoretical foundation. However, this conceptual issue was eventually addressed by Ambrose and her colleagues (for reviews, see Ambrose et al., 2015; Ambrose & Arnaud, 2005).

Event Attitudes and Entity Attitudes. Ambrose, Hess, and Ganesan (2007) began by distinguishing "events" from "entities" (Cropanzano et al., 2001). An event can be defined "as a segment of time at a given location that is known by an observer to have a beginning and an end," whereas a social entity "is an object or unit that persists over time and across situations" (Hollensbe, Khazanchi, & Masterson, 2008, p. 1099). Individuals can form attitudes about both events and entities. Ambrose et al. suggested that the four-factor model of justice affords useful criteria when evaluating the justice of events and that the attitudes toward these events may in turn impact overall ratings of entities.

In their study, Ambrose and her colleagues (2007) found that the four justice dimensions influenced the satisfaction of customers with the manner in which their complaints were handled (event attitude). Satisfaction with complaint handling subsequently impacted customers' overall rating of the service provider (entity attitude). Notice that in this model, event justice was divided into a number of facets, whereas entity attitudes were treated as a single dimension (overall satisfaction, in this case). Ambrose et al. were not the only scholars to reach this conclusion. Holtz and Harold (2009) and Jones and Martens (2009) presented similar models, in which the various specific dimensions of justice were found to cause overall fairness perceptions of entities. Overall fairness, in turn, impacted various work outcomes. Though neither Holtz and Harold nor Jones and Martens measured OCB, their findings were quite suggestive.

Extending these ideas, Ambrose and Schminke (2009) conducted two studies examining overall justice as a possible entity attitude. In these studies Ambrose and Schminke found that three dimensions of event justice (distributive, procedural, and interactional) predicted overall fairness. Overall fairness was conceptualized as "a global assessment of an entity" (p. 493), and it mediated the effect of the justice facets on various outcomes, including OCB (see their Study 2). It is important to note that though overall justice accounts for the effects of justice facets, it does not represent the mere summation of all facet-based or event-based experiences of justice. Rather, it is a distinct cognition about how one has been treated in his or her organization overall (Jones & Martens, 2009).

Other evidence has also been supportive. Johnson, Truxillo, Erdogan, Bauer, and Hammer (2009) found that the overall fairness of a department impacted both OCBI and OCBO. However, its effects on OCBO were moderated by the quality of the leader–member exchange (LMX) relationship. When LMX was high, OCBO remained generally high, regardless of overall justice. When LMX was low, however, OCBO varied with the level of overall justice.

Theoretically, it would seem that a direct measure of overall fairness, as opposed to a composite of the event justice facets, would be the most appropriate measure for predicting OCB. That said, a composite may allow for a useful approximation, and at least some evidence supports the ability of composite justice to predict OCB (Rosen et al., 2009). For example, Maxham, Netemeyer, and Lichtenstein (2008) found that a composite of distributive, procedural, and interactional justice predicted extra-role behaviors within the organization and also extra-role behaviors toward customers. Likewise, Gurbuz (2009) found that a composite of procedural and distributive justice predicted OCB among a group of Turkish soldiers.

Moderating Effects of Overall Justice. In addition to these main effects, overall justice also appears to qualify the impact of event attitudes. Similar to Ambrose et al. (2007), Choi (2008) operationalized event justice perceptions with four dimensions—distributive, procedural, interpersonal, and informational justice. These four dimensions were posited to cause both organization-directed responses (organizational commitment and organization-directed OCB) and supervisor-directed responses (supervisor commitment and supervisor-directed OCB). Importantly, these effects were anticipated to be moderated by other justice experiences. The effects of event justice on organization-directed responses would be moderated by overall organization-focused justice, while the effects of event justice on supervisor-directed responses would be moderated by overall supervisor-focused justice. There was some support for these predictions. In particular, the effects of event interpersonal justice on organization-directed OCB were moderated by overall organization-focused justice. Also, the effects of informational event justice on supervisor-directed OCB were moderated by overall supervisor-focused justice.

Social Exchange Theory

Social exchange theory has continued to be the most commonly used conceptual model for explaining the relationship between justice and OCB (Moorman & Byrne, 2005). Research guided by this framework has generally been supportive (e.g., Bettencourt, Brown, & MacKenzie, 2005; Chen, Cheng-Chen, Tung, & Ko, 2008). For example, Lehmann-Willenbrock, Grohmann, and Kauffeld (2013) found that procedural justice predicted OCBI and OCBO, whereas Zoghbi-Manrique-de-Lara (2008) obtained similar results for interactional justice. Cohen and Keren (2008) and Zhang and Agarwal (2009) reported significant OCB effects for all three of the major justice dimensions.

TWO MECHANISMS FOR SOCIAL EXCHANGE THEORY: ROLE MAINTENANCE AND ROLE ENLARGEMENT

Some attention has also been focused on the underlying mechanisms posited by social exchange theory. Through the successful and mutually beneficial exchange of goods via reciprocity, individuals are posited to form social exchange relationships (Gouldner, 1960; Mitchell, Cropanzano, & Quisenberry, 2012). These relationships, as indicated by such things as greater trust (Konovsky & Pugh, 1994; Pillai et al., 1999) and organizational support (Moorman et al., 1998), are theorized to heighten the sense of obligation to engage in OCB. Taylor and Tepper (1999) referred to this as a *role maintenance effect* (see also Coyle-Shapiro, Kessler, & Purcell, 2004). Consistent with this position, individuals who do not endorse reciprocity norms are less likely to repay the treatment they receive from others. For example, people with a positive exchange ideology are more likely to reciprocate procedurally just treatment (Witt, 1992; Witt & Broach, 1993), whereas people with a negative exchange ideology are more likely to return unjust treatment (Mitchell & Ambrose, 2007). Likewise, Blakely, Andrews, and Moorman (2005) found that equity sensitivity (i.e., the extent to which individuals are sensitive to disparity; Huseman, Hatfield, & Miles, 1987) moderated the relationship between a composite measure of justice and OCB. These findings are consistent with Organ's (1988) conceptual thinking—when the norm of reciprocity is weak (i.e., when equity sensitivity is low), then justice is less apt to produce OCB.

The Role Enlargement Effect. Although role maintenance effects appear to be important, they do not tell the entire story. In an insightful article, Morrison (1994) challenged earlier conceptualizations of OCB, which treated it as discretionary, "extra-role" behavior rather than as required, "in-role" behavior (e.g., Katz, 1964; Katz & Kahn, 1978; Organ, 1988; Smith et al., 1983). Contrary to this earlier definition, Morrison asserted that OCB involved, in effect, a bundle of these tasks. Which of these tasks were extra-role and which were in-role was likely to vary among employees. In a study of about 500 hospital workers, Morrison found evidence that many workers defined so-called discretionary behaviors as part of their job. Similar results were later obtained by Pond et al. (1997).

If Morrison's (1994) only claim had been that OCB is not always viewed by workers as optional, interest in her study may have stopped there. However, she made two other claims, both of which received support. First, Morrison argued that workers with better attitudes (e.g., higher commitment) were most prone to psychologically expanding their job duties, thereby defining OCB as an expected part of their employment. Second, Morrison further maintained that those workers who treated citizenship behaviors as in-role were *more* likely to perform OCB, while those workers who treated citizenship behaviors as extra-role were *less* likely to perform OCB. This tendency has been termed the *role enlargement effect* (Tepper, Lockhart, & Hoobler, 2001), and it was supported in Morrison's study. Consistent results were also obtained by Coyle-Shapiro et al. (2004) and Kamdar, McAllister, and Turban (2006), in that procedural justice led to more expansive definitions of one's job duties, though Kamdar and his colleagues also discovered that this effect was moderated by various individual differences.

The Role Discretion Effect. Tepper et al. (2001) raised a third possibility, *the role discretion effect.* If, as Coyle-Shapiro et al. (2004) asserted, the role maintenance effect had some validity, then at least some individuals should reciprocate just treatment only some of the time. Tepper and his colleagues argued that procedural justice was most likely to predict OCB among employees who saw citizenship behaviors as optional or discretionary. In two independent samples of workers, these authors found support for these ideas.

Supporting these contentions, Zellars, Tepper, and Duffy (2002) examined the relationship of procedural justice and OCB among a sample of National Guard soldiers. Zellars and her colleagues found that procedural justice was, as might be expected, significantly correlated with citizenship behavior (r = .41). However, this effect was moderated by role definitions. Among guard members who defined OCB as part of their work role, the procedural justice–OCB relationship was relatively weaker. Among those who defined OCB as extra-role, the procedural justice–OCB relationship was relatively stronger. Kamdar et al. (2006) found a similar interaction—when role definitions were high (i.e., OCB was treated as part of the job), procedural justice was a weaker predictor, but when role definitions were low (i.e., OCB was not treated as part of the job), procedural justice was a stronger predictor of OCB.

Notice that, at first glance, the Tepper et al. (2001), Zellars et al. (2002), and Kamdar et al. (2006) studies would appear to contradict the research of both Morrison (1994) and Coyle-Shapiro et al. (2001). However, as Tepper and his colleagues observe, this is not the case. In their investigations of the role enlargement effect, on the one hand, Morrison and Coyle-Shapiro et al. posited and found a main effect—just treatment caused employees to view so-called extra-role behaviors as nonoptional. Once they became required (i.e., in-role), then they were more likely to be performed. On the other hand, Tepper et al. posited and found an interaction between justice and role definitions. When OCB was defined as in-role, justice had a limited impact. However, when OCB was defined as extra-role, then justice was a more important predictor. Tepper and his coauthors are arguing that justice affects OCB though two mechanisms—the role enlargement (main) effect that was suggested by Morrison and the role discretion (interactive) effect that was found in other studies.

TRICKLE-DOWN MODELS

A second area that has been influenced by social exchange theory involves the existence of trickle-down effects. These models posit a sequence whereby the initially (un)fair behavior causes an intermediate actor to behave toward others in a similar fashion. Ultimately, justice from supervisors could benefit individuals beyond the immediate party. In an early investigation of this possibility, Bettencourt and Brown (1997) examined these kinds of relationships in the context of customer service. They found that workplace fairness affected customer contact employees. When treated well, these workers were more likely to be cooperative with one another and also to perform extra-role customer service. This, in turn, impacted the quality of the customers' experiences. In a similar investigation, Masterson (2001) explored trickle-down effects in the context of college teaching. She found that instructors' perceptions of distributive and procedural justice, as well as the interaction between them, affected teacher commitment. Commitment, in turn, was associated with increased instructor effort and prosocial behavior, which was associated with students' perceptions of their teachers.

Applied to the justice–OCB relationship, the trickle-down effect suggests that fair treatment toward others might not only result in the target performing OCB but also that the target would then extend similarly fair treatment toward others that would also in turn produce OCB. Supporting this argument, Aryee, Chen, Sun, and Debrah (2007) found that when supervisors felt that their boss had treated them with interactional justice, they were less likely to behave abusively toward their own subordinates. Diminished abusiveness, in turn, was associated with subordinate perceptions of interactional justice. In the final step of the model, fair supervision was associated with subordinate OCBI and OCBO.

MULTIFOCI JUSTICE AND THE TARGET SIMILARITY MODEL

As interpreted by OCB researchers, a series of successful reciprocal transactions can produce social exchange relationships that are characterized by such things as trust (e.g., Konovsky & Pugh, 1994; Menguc, 2000; Pillai et al., 1999; Yang et al., 2009) and support (Aryee & Chay, 2001; Moorman et al., 1998). Other exchange constructs, which are indicative of healthy relationships, include LMX (Burton, Sablynski, & Sekiguchi, 2008) and commitment (Cohen & Keren, 2008; Lin et al., 2008; Zoghbi-Manrique-de-Lara, 2008) and also similarly vary according to source. OCB follows as a result of these social exchange relationships that might vary in quality.

An interesting consequence of social exchange theory, therefore, is that employees will not target their citizenship behaviors evenly across all potential social entities (Cropanzano & Byrne, 2000). Rather, they will direct their OCB toward those individuals or groups that have treated them fairly and, by extension, with whom they have social exchange relationships (Cropanzano et al., 2001). This multifoci view of justice argues that OCB is strategically targeted—citizenship behaviors are directed specifically at fair entities (Cropanzano & Rupp, 2008). The most common entities examined by multifoci researchers are the supervisor, the organization as a whole, peers, and customers (for a thorough review, see Lavelle et al., 2015). This is a large literature, which goes well beyond OCB research (Lavelle et al., 2007). So that our present review does not go too far afield, we will limit ourselves to multifoci work relevant to citizenship behavior.

The first phase: Interactional and procedural justice. Moorman (1991) suggested that individuals target their OCB to help the entity that was fair to them. For instance, if interactional justice comes from the supervisor, then it is repaid by OCB directed to benefit the supervisor. In an important article, Masterson and her colleagues (2000) further addressed this issue by proposing a multifoci model of procedural and interactional justice. According to their framework, there are at least two paths for the effect of justice. A given worker might experience either, both, or neither:

- Procedural justice perceptions are generally derived from the actions of organizations. When they exist, employees feel a sense of organizational support (paralleling Moorman et al., 1998). As a result of this support, these workers direct their OCB toward their employer.

• Interactional justice perceptions are generally derived from the actions of supervisors. When they exist, employees feel a sense of high-quality LMX (similar to Burton et al., 2008). As a result of this high-quality LMX, these workers direct their OCB toward their supervisor.

Masterson and her colleagues conducted an empirical test of this model, and the results were supportive. In the ensuing years, a number of multifoci studies were conducted. Though these were generally consistent with Masterson et al.'s framework, they did not always test the full model (e.g., Burton et al., 2008; Camerman, Cropanzano, & Vandenberghe, 2007; Cropanzano, Prehar, & Chen, 2002; Lehmann-Willenbrock et al., 2013; Wayne, Shore, Bommer, & Tetrick, 2002).

In summarizing the multifoci justice literature to that time, a meta-analysis by Colquitt and his colleagues (2001) found only limited support for, what they termed, the "agent-system" model (p. 388; in this terminology, the "agent" is the supervisor, while the "system" is the organization as a whole). However, a later meta-analysis that was conducted by Fassina, Jones, and Uggerslev (2008b), which added additional studies that had since become available, found support for the agent-system model. This was good news, though by that time the model was already being revised.

The second phase: Disentangling type of justice with source of fairness. As we have seen, original work equated the *type* of justice (interactional vs. procedural) with the *source* of justice (supervisors vs. organizations, respectively). However, based on Wayne et al.'s (2002) study, it was likely that each entity could provide multiple types of justice. For instance, supervisors might institute formal policies (procedural justice) as well as informal communication (interactional justice). These ideas were incorporated into the multifoci model, which was later renamed the *target similarity model* (see Lavelle et al., 2007, 2015). The theoretical basis for this perspective is social exchange. It is argued that consideration of the source of justice is highly relevant, because it is through the social exchange engendered by fair treatment (which is specific to a party, such as supervisors or coworkers) that work-related attitudes and behaviors are formed. And it is not just attitudes and behaviors in general that are focused on here—but attitudes and behaviors *specifically* targeting the original source of fairness. This perspective calls for precision in aligning the focus of fairness and social exchange with the target of attitudes and behaviors (hence the term "target similarity").

As an initial test of this model, Rupp and Cropanzano (2002) assessed four justice variables—supervisory procedural justice, supervisory interactional justice, organizational procedural justice, and organizational interactional justice. They found that the former two—supervisory procedural and interactional justice—predicted supervisory social exchange. This, in turn, predicted OCB directed toward the supervisor. The latter two—organizational procedural and interactional justice—predicted organizational social exchange, which in turn predicted OCB directed toward the organization. These were promising findings. Consistent results were also obtained in subsequent studies by Karriker and Williams (2009); Lavelle, Brockner, and their colleagues (2009); Lavelle, McMahan, and Harris (2009); and Liden, Wayne, Kraimer, and Sparrowe (2003).

An extensive meta-analysis by Rupp and colleagues (2014) found evidence in support of the multifoci justice–target similarity model. Based upon the source of fairness, individuals tend to form social exchange relationships with various entities in their work environment, which then leads to OCB targeting those same entities (Lavelle et al., 2015). Whereas the target similarity model does provide the most robust predictions for source-target matched effects, it also acknowledges the possibility of cross-source effects (cf. Karriker & Williams, 2009). For instance, both Masterson et al. (2000) and Wayne et al. (2002) found that organizational support was positively related to LMX. Rupp and Cropanzano (2002) reported that supervisor social exchange predicted OCBO somewhat better than did organizational social exchange. These cross-source relationships are important, as they suggest an important avenue for future inquiry.

The Group Engagement Model

The group engagement model builds on the early insights from the group-value model (Blader & Tyler, 2015). According to the group engagement model, individuals try to build their social identities as members of important collectives (Tyler & Blader, 2001). Once a strong identity is formed, the group becomes part of the person's self-concept. As a result of this "self–other merging" (De Cremer, Tyler, & den Ouden, 2005,

p. 393), individuals are willing to exert extra effort on behalf of the group, including OCB because there is no longer a strong separation between the person and the collective (Tyler & Blader, 2003). Indeed, when an individual's social identity includes a group, then she or he is concerned about the collective's well-being and is intrinsically motivated to provide assistance (Tyler & Blader, 2000).

ORGANIZATIONAL CITIZENSHIP BEHAVIOR–RELEVANT EVIDENCE SUPPORTING GROUP ENGAGEMENT THEORY

De Cremer and his colleagues (2005) provided two tests of the self–other merging effect. In an initial experimental study, De Cremer et al. found that, if allowed voice, participants indicated themselves and their supervisor as overlapping circles. When not allowed voice, they represented themselves and their supervisor with less overlap. A later field study replicated this effect, where employees of a Dutch company who had merged identities were more likely to exhibit OCB (De Cremer et al., 2005).

Further evidence for the group engagement model was provided by Blader and Tyler (2009), who tested the framework in two field studies. According to these authors, social identity has three parts—identification (the cognitive "sense of 'oneness,'" p. 448), pride ("evaluations of the standing of one's group," p. 448), and respect (evaluations of members' own "standing and acceptance with their group," p. 448). In both of their studies, procedural justice and economic outcomes were found to boost social identity. Social identity, in turn, mediated the effects of procedural justice on extra-role behaviors (for an additionally supportive study, see Begley, Lee, & Hui, 2006).

An intriguing attribute of group engagement theory is that it can generalize to various types of groups. Blader and Tyler (2009) found that their model held for both work teams (Study 1) and employing organizations (Study 2). These findings suggest that the group engagement model might offer something to the study of multifoci justice–target similarity. In a manner reminiscent of Masterson et al. (2000), Olkkonen and Lipponen (2006) tested this possibility directly. Olkkonen and Lipponen reported that distributive justice and procedural justice predicted organizational identification, which in turn predicted extra-role behaviors beneficial to the firm. Interactional justice predicted identification with the work group, which in turn predicted extra-role behaviors beneficial to the team. These findings suggest that there are source or target similarity effects, which can be predicted and demonstrated using the group engagement model.

GROUP STANDING

Social identity formation involves a risk. Individuals will not wish to commit to a group that does not hold them in good standing (Blader & Tyler, 2015). Justice is important, as we have seen, because it signals that the group holds the person to be of value (Tyler & Blader, 2000). De Cremer and his colleagues (2010) provided direct support for this contention. They observed that, in general, procedural justice matters most when outcome fairness is low. One way to summarize this two-way interaction is to argue that fair process (or fair outcomes) can compensate for unfair outcomes (or unfair processes). Although this effect has been well documented (e.g., Brockner, 2002), the group engagement model provides a caveat. If justice matters because it provides evidence of group standing, then the process by outcome interaction should be strongest when standing is uncertain. Four studies by De Cremer et al. demonstrate such an effect. Most relevant here was the authors' Study 3, which found that the predicted three-way interaction (process by outcome by uncertainty) predicted OCB in the expected manner.

Koivisto and Koponen (2015) looked at this same issue but from a different perspective. They argued that if individuals are concerned about their standing in valued groups, then leader justice should have the greatest impact on perceived respect from the group when two conditions are met: (a) the employee identifies with the group and (b) the leader exhibits high in-group prototypicality. Respect, in turn, should affect OCB. Koivisto and Lipponen found support for these predictions. The two-way interaction of identification and prototypicality was related to respect. In particular, respect was lowest when a prototypical leader showed low procedural justice while the employee identified with the group in question. Respect was subsequently related to extra-role behavior, thereby mediating the effect of procedural justice.

CONCLUSIONS

Even though the group-value/group engagement model has yet to receive the same amount of attention as social exchange theory (by both justice and OCB scholars), it has proven to be extremely valuable in understanding employees' experience of and reactions to workplace events. In particular, it has yielded some intriguing predictions that have been strongly supported. We look forward to future research stemming from this theoretical perspective, perhaps that connects in an integrative way with other perspectives.

Third-Party Justice

Another subliterature within the organizational justice domain takes a third-person perspective. That is, rather than asking employees about how fairly they themselves have been treated, researchers inquire about employees' observations pertaining to the treatment of *others*.

These are often referred to as "third-party" justice perceptions (Ellard & Skarlicki, 2002; Skarlicki, O'Reilly, & Kulik, 2015). This is depicted in the fourth panel of Figure 15.1. This research has offered two primary reasons why the treatment of others influences an observing employee's attitudes and behaviors (Skarlicki & Kulik, 2005). The first is self-interest. That is, seeing how a party (e.g., management) treats those around you might be a good signal of their regard for the workforce overall. This line of reasoning is consistent with instrumental perspectives on organizational justice (see Cropanzano, Rupp, et al., 2001). Consequently, employees might interpret the treatment of others as a sign of what they may soon be facing themselves. The second is more morality based; that is, based on the deontic perspective on justice (Folger, 2001). According to this view, people often feel that they and others have a moral duty to behave justly. Justice is seen as being good for its own sake (Folger & Glerum, 2015).

Perceptions of How Fairly Coworkers Are Treated

Porath and Erez (2009, Study 1) conducted a laboratory experiment where participants worked in teams and either did or did not witness a teammate being treated in an interpersonally unfair manner by either the experimenter or a peer. Then, they had the opportunity to engage in citizenship behaviors targeting the experimenter. Results revealed that those not witnessing unfairness were three times as likely to engage in citizenship behaviors benefiting the experimenter, showing a clear link between third-party justice and OCB. In a later experiment, Christian, Christian, Garza, and Ellis (2012) were able to measure the actual withdrawal of supervisor-directed citizenship in response to supervisor injustice targeting either the focal participant (first-person injustice) or another member of the participant's team (third-party injustice). Whereas reactions to injustice were stronger for victims than observers, a marked third-party justice effect was indeed detected—and this was found both at the individual and team levels of analysis.

De Cremer and Van Hiel (2006) carried out two lab experiments and a field study that considered the effects of procedural injustice coming from a supervisor and targeting a teammate, on observers' cooperation and citizenship toward the supervisor. Across all three studies, the authors found that third-party procedural injustice impacted participants' willingness to engage in citizenship behaviors toward the supervisor, but only when the team member who has been mistreated had in the past shown citizenship *toward the observer*. Here is another example of the many directions justice can come from and citizenship may be directed, over time and across situations. It seems if a to-be victim of injustice has withheld citizenship from a to-be observer in the past, that observer may be less likely to provide help and support, or withdraw supervisor-targeted citizenship as a way of punishing the supervisor transgressor.

Corporate Social Responsibility

As we previewed at the start of this section, observing injustice committed to others is not limited to proximal parties, such as coworkers or individual customers. Furthermore, the deliverers of unfairness are not limited to individuals such as supervisors. That is, employees are also often privy to actions taken by the organization as a whole toward external stakeholders such as local communities, consumers (as a broad group), and the natural environment. They might also judge the organization's general commitment to the workforce (as a group, as opposed to individual employees or groups of employees). This takes us into the realm of corporate social responsibility (CSR)—where an organization's citizenship toward its various constituents is judged and reacted to by employees. As such, CSR perceptions have been couched as a special form of third-party justice perceptions (Rupp, Williams, & Aguilera, 2011).

Research has begun to accumulate that suggests (as would be expected based on all we have already reviewed) a relationship between employee perceptions of CSR and their subsequent OCB.

For example, in a sample of 700 employees in China, Zhang, Di Fan, and Zhu (2014) detected a relationship between employee perceptions of corporate social performance (a term often used synonymously with CSR, although which is sometimes a bit broader in scope) and self-reported OCB. Evans, Goodman, and Davis (2010) found a similar relationship between corporate citizenship and OCB as broad constructs; however, they also considered the effects of corporate citizenship facets (economic, legal, ethical, and discretionary citizenship; see Maignan & Ferrell, 2000) separately. These authors found that only economic citizenship (i.e., fiscal responsibility) predicted OCB. Abdullah and Rashid (2012) considered the relationship of CSR (directed toward the government, employees, society, environment, and customers) to OCB among employees in Malaysia. They found employee-, environment-, and customer-directed CSR to predict OCB, but not the other dimensions.

Bozkurt and Bal (2012) also found support for a global relationship between corporate citizenship and OCB, but additionally considered all the possible relationships between Carroll's (1991) four components of corporate citizenship (economic, ethical, legal, and philanthropic) and Organ's (1988) five dimensions of OCB (altruism, conscientiousness, courtesy, sportsmanship, and civic virtue) in a sample of employees working in Turkey. Results indicated that the composite corporate citizenship measure was significantly correlated with each OCB dimension with the exception of conscientiousness (which was also unrelated to any of the CSR dimensions). Composite OCB was significantly correlated with all the CSR dimensions with the exception of ethicality, which was also unrelated to any of the OCB dimensions. Lin, Lyau, Tsai, Chen, and Chiu (2010) looked at the extent to which all of the dimensions of corporate citizenship related to all of the dimensions of OCB. Data from a sample of employees in China indicated that whereas most corporate citizenship dimensions were associated with most OCB dimensions, perceived discretionary citizenship was negatively associated with altruism and courtesy, and it was unrelated to conscientiousness, sportsmanship, and courtesy. Jacinto and Carvalho (2009) considered similar relationships using a sample of employees working in Portugal. They considered three components of CSR (internal, social, and environmental) and two components of OCB (OCBO and OCBI). Perceptions of socially oriented CSR were found to predict OCBI, whereas perceptions of ecologically oriented CSR were found to predict OCBO.

Newman, Nielsen, and Miao (2015) presented one of the few studies to date to consider the CSR–OCB relationship using supervisor-reported OCB. Using data from a sample of employees working in China, they showed that employee perceptions of CSR toward social and nonsocial stakeholders (i.e., the natural environment, future generations, nongovernmental associations, local communities) had a strong relationship to supervisor-rated OCB. Perceptions of CSR efforts focused on employees, customers, and the government were unrelated to OCB, however. Shen and Benson (2014) reported on one of the few multilevel studies exploring the CSR–OCB relationship. Using a sample of 35 manufacturing firms in China, they provided evidence that organizational-level CSR predicted individual-level OCB (as rated by the focal employees' peers). Erdogan, Bauer, and Taylor (2015) considered how employee CSR perceptions (more specifically in this case, their perceptions of their employer's commitment to the ecological environment) were linked not only to their OCBO but also their citizenship directed back to the ecological environment (OCBE). This is analogous to our discussion earlier about citizenship toward potential victims of injustice, except both externally focused and focused on natural resources rather than fellow humans. Using a sample of survey respondents working in Turkey, they showed that their ecological CSR variable predicted OCBO. It was not, however, shown to predict OCBE. Interestingly, Paille, Boiral, and Chen (2013) also explored the relationship between environmentally focused management practice and OCBEs, and they also were unable to detect a relationship. Perhaps the effect of third-party justice and OCB is fundamentally more about the interrelations of people with each other than "treatment" (e.g., of the natural environment) more generally. Or perhaps individuals' ability to engage in OCBEs is more constrained.

MEDIATORS

A number of mediators have been tested to shed light on the CSR–OCB relationship. Both the Shen and Benson (2014) and Jacinto and Carvalo (2009) studies mentioned earlier detected a mediating effect of organizational identification in the relationship between CSR and OCB.

Fu, Ye, and Law (2014), using a sample of hotel employees in China, showed the effect of CSR perceptions on OCB to be serially mediated by organizational identification and organizational commitment. Hansen, Dunford, Boss, Boss, and Angermeier (2011) considered the relationship between a composite measure of CSR perceptions that considered community outreach and charitable giving, diversity and family benefits, employee relations, and the natural environment, with the civic virtue dimension of OCB. They found this relationship to be partially mediated by trust in the organization. Lamm, Tosti-Kharas, and King (2015) explored the relationship between perceived organizational support of the natural environment and employee citizenship behaviors toward the environment (OCBE) in a sample of Chinese employees. They detected a significant relationship between these constructs and further found the relationship to be partially mediated by psychological empowerment.

MODERATORS

Boundary conditions on the CSR–OCB relationship have also been explored. For instance, Shen and Benson (2014) found the relationship to be moderated by perceived organizational support. Jones (2010) studied employees' attitudes toward a corporate volunteerism program in which they could participate during work hours. He considered how these attitudes influenced OCB in the form of loyalty, as well as citizenship behaviors directed at both the organization and coworkers. Whereas these specific CSR perceptions were only found to predict loyalty, Jones detected a moderating effect of exchange ideology. When exchange ideology was high, attitudes toward the program significantly predicted all three forms of OCB.

SUMMARY

Research considering employee CSR perceptions is still in its infancy. A lot of data are being collected all around the world that take into account how employees respond to the more prosocially oriented activities of their employing organizations. As we have shown, the literature remains a bit scattershot, inconsistent findings abound, and there is no unifying theory that integrates this body of research. As theory begins to evolve in this area, we hope a clearer picture will emerge regarding these various relationships (see Aguinis, 2011; Jones & Rupp, in press; and Rupp & Mallory, 2015, for examples of the ways in which the literature to date has been reviewed and synthesized).

Justice and Organizational Citizenship Behavior at the Unit Level

Thus far, our consideration of organizational justice and OCB has been directed at the individual level of analysis, considering how individuals experience and react to justice in terms of their citizenship behaviors. This focus is largely mirrored in the extant body of work on organizational justice at large (see Colquitt, Zapata-Phelan, & Roberson, 2005; Li & Cropanzano, 2009). Although the study of individual experiences of justice is important, groups, teams, and units also have unique experiences of justice that also affect the ways in which groups function within organizations (Li, Cropanzano, & Molina, 2015; Rupp, Bashshur, & Liao, 2007). In this present section, therefore, we move up a level of analysis and consider justice as a unit-level construct. When exploring justice at the unit level, researchers have taken two approaches. Justice climate pertains to collective perceptions of the fairness with which the group as a whole is treated. Peer justice refers to collective perceptions of how team members treat each other (Li et al., 2015). We depict this in Figure 15.1.

Justice Climate Emergence and Organizational Citizenship Behavior

Coworkers often form shared perceptions of how they are treated by authority figures. When the reference of these judgments is the collective as a unit, rather than each worker as an individual, then this is referred to as justice climate (Mossholder, Bennett, & Martin, 1998; Naumann & Bennett, 2000; 2002; Roberson, 2006a). These collective appraisals of fairness are especially likely to emerge when members work interdependently, occupy similar roles, and interact frequently and intensely (Roberson, 2006b). Those units in which members are diverse, dispersed, and differentially treated by leaders, however, are less likely to converge on a similar perception of fairness due to limited information sharing and dissimilar experiences (Roberson & Colquitt, 2005). A growing body of empirical work suggests that justice climate has a significant effect on both individual- and group-level citizenship behaviors. The majority of this research has taken a facet-based approach, focusing on specific types of justice climate, with the lion's share of this literature focusing on procedural justice climate.

PROCEDURAL JUSTICE CLIMATE

Naumann and Bennett (2000), who provided the foundation for current conceptualizations of justice climate, found that procedural justice climate (PJC) was positively related to organizational commitment and (more relevant here) helping behaviors (for similar findings, see Chen, Lam, Naumann, & Schaubroeck, 2005; Li, Liang, & Crant, 2010). In a subsequent study, Naumann and Bennett (2002) expanded these findings, reporting that PJC boosted helping behaviors. These increased helping behaviors, in turn, improved work group performance. Similar findings were also obtained by Yang, Mossholder, and Peng (2007), who found that PJC was associated with increased organizationally focused OCB. This result held primarily among lower teams that reported low power distance and less so among teams that reported high power distance.

Liao and Rupp (2005) took a multifoci approach to studying justice climate. With regard to PJC, they showed that organization-focused PJC was related to organization-focused commitment and citizenship, whereas supervisor-focused PJC predicted supervisor-directed commitment and satisfaction, though not supervisory-directed citizenship behaviors. Though these findings are not fully supportive, they suggest that the target similarity model could apply to justice climate, as it does to individual-level fairness perceptions (cf., Lavelle et al., 2007).

PROCEDURAL JUSTICE CLIMATE AND LEADERSHIP STYLE

A number of studies have found that various leadership styles engender PJC, which in turn facilitates OCB. For example, Ehrhart (2004) found that unit-level perceptions of servant leadership were positively associated with procedural justice climate. PJC, in turn, was associated with unit-level OCB. In other words, PJC mediated the relationship between servant leadership and unit-level OCB. Similarly, Cho and Dansereau (2010) showed that the effect of transformational leadership on group-directed OCB was mediated by PJC. Moreover, Shin, Sung, Choi, and Kim (2015) showed that both PJC and ethical climate mediated the effect of top management ethical leadership on firm-level OCB. These findings suggest that authority figures may "set the tone" for justice. By creating a procedurally just climate, they may inspire citizenship behavior that benefits both workers and the organization.

BEYOND PROCEDURAL JUSTICE CLIMATE: OTHER JUSTICE CLIMATES

Although the prevalent focus in justice climate research has been on PJC (Li & Cropanzano, 2009), there are a few studies that give insight into the relationship between other facet-specific justice climates and OCB. Simons and Roberson (2003) observed that interpersonal justice climate was related to discretionary service behaviors. Similarly, Liao and Rupp (2005) showed that organization-focused informational justice climate predicted citizenship (for related findings, see Ambrose, Schminke, & Mayer, 2013). Whitman, Caleo, Carpenter, Horner, and Bernerth (2012) meta-analyzed findings pertaining to unit-level justice climate facets and composite criterion variables associated with effectiveness (e.g., productivity, customer satisfaction) and processes (e.g., cohesion, OCB). Their findings suggested that whereas all three justice climate variables predicted unit-level effectiveness, distributive justice climate was most highly associated with unit-level performance, whereas interactional justice climate was most highly associated with unit-level processes (including OCB).

In a departure from the use of facet measures of justice, Tang and Tang (2012) examined overall justice climate. Based on the tenets of social exchange and information processing theory, they argued that high-performance human resource practices would influence service-oriented citizenship behavior via both justice and service climate. Using data collected from over 1,000 customer service representatives and over 100 Human Resources managers in over 100 hotels in Taiwan, evidence for the proposed model was provided.

Peer Justice

Recently, Li and colleagues (e.g., Cropanzano, Li, & Benson, 2011; Cropanzano, Li, & James, 2007; Li & Cropanzano, 2009; Li et al., 2013) have articulated arguments for the presence of peer justice or intraunit justice climate. To date, very little research exists on peer justice climate, especially on its influence on OCB. Branscombe, Spears, Ellemers, and Doosje (2002) reported that respect from other team members has a positive effect on pro-group or beneficial group-directed behaviors (Branscombe, Spears, Ellemers, & Doosje, 2002). Other work has found that peer justice climate has a positive effect on cooperative team processes and an indirect effect via cooperative team processes on team satisfaction (Li, Cropanzano, & Bagger, 2013). Cropanzano, Li, and Benson (2011) found that both peer interpersonal and procedural justice climate promoted team citizenship behaviors—specifically, helping and loyalty.

Putting the Pieces Together

Our review attests to the importance of justice as a predictor of OCB. Distributive, procedural, and interactional justice emerged as consistent predictors. Less evidence is available for interpersonal and informational justice, though these dimensions have promise (Colquitt et al., 2001). Research exploring justice and OCB has grown considerably from its early days, and along with this growth has come considerable complexity. For example, Scholl and his colleagues (1987) considered only a single type of justice (equity) and a single dimension of OCB, both of which were measured at the individual level of analysis. Bateman and Organ (1983) also limited themselves to a single dimension of OCB and no direct measures of justice. These days, such simple studies appear almost quaint. With this in mind, it is worth underscoring some of the theoretical distinctions that have been made over the past four decades, as doing so will highlight the research that still needs to be conducted.

First, it is important to distinguish between two seemingly similar, but actually very different ideas. Justice can be assessed with different *referents* (e.g., organization, supervisor, peers) or at different *levels* (e.g., individual, unit; cf. Fulmer & Gelfand, 2012). On the one hand, the multifoci approach suggests that individuals (as opposed to group or teams) match their responses toward particular targets (Lavelle et al., 2007). On the other hand, research on justice climate (Colquitt et al., 2005) and peer justice (Li et al., 2015) suggests that individuals can form collective perceptions of fairness. These two paradigms are not the same, but they overlap. For instance, justice climate and peer justice could be viewed as unit-level justice regarding different referents or targets. It is worth considering that different *referents* can be fully crossed with different *levels*. That is, there could be individual and group assessments of peers, of supervisors, and of the organization as a whole. Research investigations of this possibility are limited (see Liao & Rupp, 2005, for an exception), though this has considerable promise.

Second, it might be worthwhile for justice and OCB researchers to devote more attention to structural issues. Among justice researchers, four models are currently popular—one-factor (overall justice; Ambrose et al., 2015), three-factor (distributive, procedural, and interactional), four-factor (distributive, procedural, interpersonal, and informational; Colquitt, 2001), and multifoci justice (Lavelle et al., 2007, 2015). The relationship among these three approaches could use additional clarification. Notably, they might not be competing. Another possibility could be more substantive. Ambrose and Schminke (2009) suggested that the multifaceted families of justice rules cause overall evaluations of fairness. By this view, the three- or four-factor models could be antecedent to the one-factor framework. Rupp and colleagues have argued how details pertaining to outcomes, procedures, and the like are relevant to assessing the fairness of events, but that these events are classified and encoded into memory according to the party seen as responsible for the event. Over time, events are aggregated within sources, leading to overall perceptions of multifoci justice, which can be further aggregated (by the perceiver, not the researcher) into overall perceptions of justice (see Guo, Rupp, Weiss, & Trougakos, 2011; Rupp et al., 2011; Rupp & Paddock, 2010; Rupp et al., 2014).

Third, since the very early days of justice and OCB research, it has been more or less assumed that the former causes the latter (e.g., Bateman & Organ, 1983; Smith et al., 1983). Although this is no doubt true some of the time (e.g., Skarlicki & Latham, 1996, 1997), it strikes us that the alternative needs to be put to a direct test. It could be that individuals who perform high levels of OCB engender better treatment from their peers and supervisors (cf., Bolino, Turnley, & Niehoff, 2004). Investigations of this possibility could begin with the work on OCB and impression management (Bolino, 1999; Bolino, Kacmar, Turnley, & Gilstrap, 2008), which suggests that individuals are motivated to engage in citizenship, at least in part, from a sense of strategic self-interest (Bolino, Varela, Bande, & Turnley, 2006; Halbesleben, Bowler, Bolino, & Turnley, 2010). For this reason, OCB may not always be advantageous to organizational functioning (Bolino, Turnley, & Niehoff, 2004).

Fourth, to date, much of the research on justice and OCB has been guided by social exchange theory (Cropanzano & Mitchell, 2005) and the relational model of justice (Blader & Tyler, 2015). Although these perspectives have proven valuable, few of these studies actually test the full breadth of relationships implied by these theories (for an exception, see Blader & Tyler, 2009). As a consequence, we still have much to learn about the psychological processes by which just behavior produces OCB.

Conclusion

Without gainsaying these unanswered questions, we would like to conclude this chapter on a positive note. Over 40 years ago, researchers began their investigations of justice and OCB. As this chapter documents, scholarship has been active and much has been learned. Notably, these constructs are predictably related (Rupp et al., 2014), and justice seems to encourage organizational citizenship (Skarlicki & Latham, 1996, 1997). Although much work remains to be done, we have progressed much since the early 1980s. We hope that this review will encourage scholars to further explore this exciting and important area of study.

Note

1. Bettencourt and Brown (1997) use slightly different terminology than that employed here. They refer to their measure of justice as "overall" and not as "composite" (see, for example, their p. 50). However, their operational approach meets the criteria for composite justice, as we have discussed here. Specifically, "overall fairness is modeled as a second-order construct with five indicators represented by the five fairness subscales" (p. 47).

References

Abdullah, M. H., & Rashid, N. R. N. A. (2012). The implementation of corporate social responsibility (CSR) programs and its impact on employee organizational citizenship behavior. *International Journal of Business and Commerce, 2*, 67–75.

Adams, J. S. (1965). Inequity in social exchange. In L. Berkowitz (Ed.), *Advances in experimental social psychology* (Vol. *2*, pp. 267–299). New York: Academic Press.

Aguinis, H., (2011). Organizational responsibility: Doing good and doing well. In S. Zedeck (Ed.), *APA handbook of industrial and organizational psychology, Vol. 3: Maintaining, expanding, and contracting the organization,* pp. 855–879. Washington, DC: American Psychological Association.

Ambrose, M. L., & Arnaud, A. (2005). Distributive and procedural justice: Construct distinctiveness, construct interdependence, and overall justice. In J. Greenberg & J. A. Colquitt (Eds.), *The handbook of organizational justice* (pp. 59–84). Mahwah, NJ: Erlbaum.

Ambrose, M., Hess, R. L., & Ganesan, S. (2007). The relationship between justice and attitudes: An examination of justice effects on event and system-related attitudes. *Organizational Behavior and Human Decision Processes, 103*, 21–36.

Ambrose, M. L., & Schminke, M. (2009). The role of overall justice judgments in organizational justice research: A test of mediation. *Journal of Applied Psychology, 94*, 491–500.

Ambrose, M. L., Schminke, M., & Mayer, D. M. (2013). Trickle-down effects of supervisor perceptions of interactional justice: A moderated mediation approach. *Journal of Applied Psychology, 98*, 678–689.

Ambrose, M. L., Wo, D. X. H., & Griffith, M. D. (2015). Overall justice: Looking back and looking forward. In R. Cropanzano & M. L. Ambrose (Eds.), *Oxford handbook of justice in work organizations* (pp. 109–135). Oxford, UK: Oxford University Press.

Andrews, M. C., Kacmar, K. M., & Harris, K. J. (2009). Got political skill? The impact of justice on the importance of political skill for job performance. *Journal of Applied Psychology, 94*, 1427–1437.

Ang, S., Van Dyne, L., & Begley, T. M. (2003). The employment relationships of foreign workers versus local employees: A field study of organizational justice, job satisfaction, performance, and OCB. *Journal of Organizational Behavior, 24*, 561–583.

Aryee, S., Budhwar, P. S., & Chen, Z. X. (2002). Trust as a mediator of the relationship between organizational justice and work outcomes: Test of a social exchange model. *Journal of Organizational Behavior, 23*, 267–285.

Aryee, S., & Chay, Y. W. (2001). Workplace justice, citizenship behavior, and turnover intentions in a union context: Examining the mediating role of perceived union support and union instrumentality. *Journal of Applied Psychology, 86*, 154–160.

Aryee, S., Chen, Z. X., Sun, L-Y., & Debrah, Y. A. (2007). Antecedents and outcomes of abusive supervision: Test of a trickle-down model. *Journal of Applied Psychology, 92*, 191–201.

Asgari, A., Silong, A. D., Ahmad, A., & Samah, B. A. (2008). The relationship between transformational leadership behaviors, organizational justice, leader-member exchange, perceived organizational support, trust in management and organizational citizenship behaviors. *European Journal of Scientific Research, 23*, 227–242.

Asgari, M. H., Nojabee, S. S., & Arjmand, F. (2011). The relationship between organizational justice and organizational citizenship behavior of the employees. *Middle-East Journal of Scientific Research, 10*, 141–148.

Aquino, K. (1995). Relationships among pay inequity, perceptions of procedural justice, and organizational citizenship. *Employee Responsibilities and Rights Journal, 8*, 21–33.

Ball, G. A., Treviño, L. K., & Sims, H. P., Jr. (1994). Just and unjust punishment: Influences on subordinate performance and citizenship. *Academy of Management Journal, 37*, 299–322.

Barnard, C. I. (1938). *The functions of the executive.* Cambridge, MA: Harvard University Press.

Bateman, T. S., & Organ, D. W. (1983). Job satisfaction and the good soldier: The relationship between affect and employee "citizenship." *Academy of Management Journal, 26*, 587–595.

Begley, T. M., Lee, C., Fang, Y., & Li, J. (2002). Power distance as a moderator of the relationship between justice and employee outcomes in a sample of Chinese employees. *Journal of Managerial Psychology, 17*, 692–711.

Begley, T. M., Lee, C., & Hui, C. (2006). Organizational level as a moderator of the relationship between justice perceptions and work-related reactions. *Journal of Organizational Behavior, 27*, 705–721.

Bies, R. J. (1987). The predicament of injustice: The management of moral outrage. In L. L. Cummings & B. M. Staw (Eds), *Research in organizational behavior* (Vol. *9*, pp. 289–319). Greenwich, CT: JAI Press.

Bies, R. J. (2015). Interactional justice: Looking backward and looking forward. In R. Cropanzano & M. L. Ambrose (Eds.), *Oxford handbook of justice in work organizations* (pp. 89–107). Oxford, UK: Oxford University Press.

Bies, R. J., Martin, C. L., & Brockner, J. L. (1993). Just laid off, but still a "good citizen?" Only if the process is fair. *Employee Responsibility and Rights Journal, 6*(3), 227–238.

Bies, R. J. & Moag, J. S. (1986). Interactional justice: Communication criteria of fairness. In R. J. Lewicki, B. H. Sheppard, & M. Bazerman (Eds.), *Research on negotiation in organizations* (Vol. *1,* pp. 43–55). Greenwich, CT: JAI Press.

Bettencourt, L. A., & Brown, S. W. (1997). Contact employees: Relationships among workplace fairness, job satisfaction and prosocial service behaviors. *Journal of Retailing, 73,* 39–61.

Bettencourt, L. A., Brown, S. W., & MacKenzie, S. B. (2005). Customer-oriented boundary-spanning behaviors: Test of a social exchange model of antecedents. *Journal of Retailing, 81,* 141–157.

Bies, R. J. (1989). Managing conflict before it happens: The role of accounts. In M. A. Rahim (Ed.), *Managing conflict: An interdisciplinary approach* (pp. 83–91). New York, NY: Praeger.

Bies, R. J. (2001). Interactional (in)justice: The sacred and the profane. In J. Greenberg & R. Cropanzano (Eds.), *Advances in organizational justice* (pp. 89–118). Stanford, CA: Stanford University Press.

Bies, R. J. (2005). Are procedural justice and interactional justice conceptually distinct? In J. Greenberg & J. A. Colquitt (Eds.), *Handbook of organizational justice* (pp. 85–112). Mahwah, NJ: Erlbaum.

Blader, S. L., & Tyler, T. R. (2009). Testing and extending the group engagement model: Linkages between social identity, procedural justice, economic outcomes, and extrarole behavior. *Journal of Applied Psychology, 94,* 445–464.

Blader, S. L., & Tyler, T. R. (2015). Relational models of procedural justice. In R. Cropanzano & M. L. Ambrose (Eds.), *Oxford handbook of justice in work organizations* (pp. 351–369). Oxford, UK: Oxford University Press.

Blakely, G. L., Andrews, M. C., & Moorman, R. H. (2005). The moderating effects of equity sensitivity on the relationship between organizational justice and organizational citizenship behaviors. *Journal of Business and Psychology, 20,* 259–273.

Bobocel, D. R., & Gosse, L. (2015). Procedural Justice: A Historical Review and Critical Analysis. *The Oxford Handbook of Justice in the Workplace,* 51.

Bobocel, D. R., & Holmvall, C. M. (2001). Are interactional justice and procedural justice different? Framing the debate. In S. Gilliland, D. Steiner, & D. Skarlicki (Eds.), *Research in social issues in management: Theoretical and cultural perspectives on organizational justice* (Vol. *1,* pp. 85–108). Greenwich, CT: Information Age Publishing.

Bolino, M. C. (1999). Citizenship and impression management: Good soldiers or good actors? *Academy of Management Review, 24,* 82–98.

Bolino, M. C., Kacmar, K. M., Turnley, W. H., & Gilstrap, J. B. (2008). A multi-level review of impression management motives and behaviors. *Journal of Management, 34,* 1080–1109.

Bolino, M. C., Turnley, W. H., Niehoff, B. P. (2004). The other side of the story: Reexamining prevailing assumptions about organizational citizenship behaviors. *Human Resource Management Review, 14,* 229–246.

Bolino, M. C., Varela, J. A., Bande, B., & Turnley, W. H. (2006). The impact of impression-management tactics on supervisor ratings of organizational citizenship behavior. *Journal of Organizational Behavior, 27,* 281–297.

Bowler, W. M., & Brass, D. J. (2006). Relational correlates of interpersonal citizenship behavior: A social network perspective. *Journal of Applied Psychology, 91,* 70–82.

Bozkurt, S., & Bal, Y. (2012). Investigation of the relationship between corporate social responsibility and organizational citizenship behavior: A research. *International Journal of Innovations in Business, 1,* 40–59.

Branscombe, N. R., Spears, R., Ellemers, N., & Doosje, B. (2002). Intragroup and intergroup evaluation effects on group behavior. *Personality and Social Psychology Bulletin, 28,* 744–753.

Brennan, A., & Skarlicki, D. P. (2004). Personality and perceived justice as predictors of survivors' reactions following downsizing. *Journal of Applied Social Psychology, 34,* 1306–1328.

Brockner, J. (2002). Making sense of procedural fairness: How high procedural fairness can reduce or heighten the influence of outcome favorability. *Academy of Management Review, 27,* 58–76.

Brockner, J., & Wiesenfeld, B. M. (1996). An integrative framework for explaining reactions to decisions: Interactive effects of outcomes and procedures. *Psychological Bulletin, 120,* 189–208.

Burney, L. L., Henle, C. A., & Widener, S. K. (2009). A path model examining the relations among strategic performance measurement system characteristics, organizational justice, and extra- and in-role performance. *Accounting, Organizations and Society, 34,* 305–321.

Burton, J. P., Sablynski, C. J., & Sekiguchi, T. (2008). Linking justice, performance, and citizenship via leader-member exchange. *Journal of Business and Psychology, 23,* 51–61.

Byrne, Z. S. (2005). Fairness reduces the negative effects of organizational politics on turnover intentions, citizenship behaviors and job performance. *Journal of Business and Psychology, 20,* 175–200.

Camerman, J., Cropanzano, R., & Vandenberghe, C. (2007). The benefits of justice for temporary workers. *Group and Organization Management, 32,* 176–207.

Carroll, A. B. (1991). The pyramid of corporate social responsibility: Toward the moral management of organizational stakeholders. *Business Horizons, 34,* 39–48.

Chattopadhyay, P. (1999). Beyond direct and symmetrical effects: The influence of demographic dissimilarity on organizational citizenship behavior. *Academy of Management Journal, 42,* 273–287.

Chegini, M. G. (2009). The relationship between organizational justice and organizational citizenship behaviour. *American Journal of Economics and Business Administration, 1,* 171–174.

Chen, X.-P., Lam, S. S. K., Naumann, S. E., & Schaubroeck, J. (2005). Group citizenship behavior: Conceptualization and preliminary tests of its antecedents and consequences. *Management and Organization Review, 1,* 273–300.

Chen, Y-J., Cheng-Chen, L., Tung, Y-C., & Ko, T-T. (2008). Associations of organizational justice and ingratiation with organizational citizenship behavior: The beneficiary perspective. *Social Behavior and Personality, 36,* 289–302.

Chiaburu, D. S., & Lim, A. S. (2008). Manager trustworthiness or interactional justice? Predicting organizational citizenship behaviors. *Journal of Business Ethics, 83*, 453–467.
Cho, J., & Dansereau, F. (2010). Are transformational leaders fair? A multi-level study of transformational leadership, justice perceptions, and organizational citizenship behaviors. *Leadership Quarterly, 21*, 409–421.
Choi, J. (2008). Event justice perceptions and employees' reactions: Perceptions of social entity justice as a moderator. *Journal of Applied Psychology, 93*, 513–528.
Christian, J., Christian, M. S., Garza, A. S., & Ellis, A. P. (2012). Examining retaliatory responses to justice violations and recovery attempts in teams. *Journal of Applied Psychology, 97*, 1218–1232.
Cohen, A., & Keren, D. (2008). Individual values and social exchange variables: Examining their relationship to and mutual effect on in-role performance and organizational citizenship behavior. *Group and Organization Management, 33*, 425–452.
Cohen, A., & Kol, Y. (2004). Professionalism and organizational citizenship behavior: An empirical examination among Israeli nurses. *Journal of Managerial Psychology, 19*, 386–406.
Cohen-Charash, Y., & Spector, P. E. (2001). The role of justice in organizations: A meta-analysis. *Organizational Behavior and Human Decision Processes, 86*, 278–321.
Colquitt, J. A. (2001). On the dimensionality of organizational justice: A construct validation of a measure. *Journal of Applied Psychology, 86*, 386–400.
Colquitt, J. A., Conlon, D. E., Wesson, M. J., Porter, C. O. L. H., & Ng, K. Y. (2001). Justice at the millennium: A meta-analytic review of 25 years of organizational justice research. *Journal of Applied Psychology, 86*, 425–445.
Colquitt, J. A., & Rodell, J. B. (2015). Measuring justice and fairness. In R. Cropanzano & M. L. Ambrose (Eds.), *Oxford handbook of justice in work organizations* (pp. 187–202). Oxford, UK: Oxford University Press.
Colquitt, J. A., Zapata-Phelan, C. P., & Roberson, Q. M. (2005). Justice in teams: A review of fairness effects in collective contexts. In J. J. Martocchio (Ed.), *Research in personnel and human resources management* (Vol. *24*, pp. 53–94). Oxford, UK: Elsevier.
Connell, J., Ferres, N., & Travaglione, T. (2003). Engendering trust in manager-subordinate relationships. *Personnel Review, 32*, 569–587.
Coyle-Shapiro, J. A-M. (2002). A psychological contract perspective on organizational citizenship behavior. *Journal of Organizational Behavior, 23*, 927–946.
Coyle-Shapiro, J. A-M., Kessler, I., & Purcell, J. (2004). Exploring organizationally directed citizenship behavior: Reciprocity or "it's my job"? *Journal of Managerial Studies, 41*, 85–106.
Cropanzano, R., & Byrne, Z. S. (2000). Workplace justice and the dilemma of organizational citizenship. In M. VanVugt, T. Tyler, & A. Biel (Eds.), *Collective problems in modern society: Dilemmas and solutions* (pp. 142–161). London: Routledge.
Cropanzano, R., Byrne, Z. S., Bobocel, D. R., & Rupp, D. E. (2001). Moral virtues, fairness heuristics, social entities, and other denizens of organizational justice. *Journal of Vocational Behavior, 58*, 164–209.
Cropanzano, R., Fortin, M., & Kirk, J. F. (2015). How do we know when we are treated fairly? Justice rules and fairness judgments. In M. R. Buckley, A. R. Wheeler, & J. R. B. Halbesleben (Eds.), *Research in personnel and human resources management* (Vol. *33*, pp. 279–350). Cambridge, UK: Emerald Publishing.
Cropanzano, R., Li, A., & Benson, L. (2011). Peer justice and teamwork process. *Group and Organization Management, 36*, 567–596.
Cropanzano, R., Li, A., & James, K. (2007). *Intraunit justice and interunit justice and the people who experience them.* In F. Dansereau & F. J. Yammarino (Eds.), *Research in Multi-Level Issues* (Vol. *6*, pp. 415–437). Oxford, UK: Elsevier.
Cropanzano, R., & Mitchell, M. S. (2005). Social exchange theory: An interdisciplinary review. *Journal of Management, 31*, 874–900.
Cropanzano, R., & Moliner, C. (2013). Hazards of justice: Egocentric bias, moral judgments, and revenge-seeking. In S. M. Elias (Ed.), *Deviant and criminal behavior in the workplace* (pp. 155–177). New York, NY: New York University Press.
Cropanzano, R., Prehar, C. A., & Chen, P. Y. (2002). Using social exchange theory to distinguish procedural from interactional justice. *Group and Organizational Management, 27*, 324–351.
Cropanzano, R., & Rupp, D. E. (2008). Social exchange theory and organizational justice: Job performance, citizenship behaviors, multiple foci, and a historical integration of two literatures. In S. W. Gilliland, D. P. Skarlicki, & D. D. Steiner (Eds.), *Research in social issues in management: Justice, morality, and social responsibility* (pp. 63–99). Greenwich, CT: Information Age Publishing.
Cropanzano, R., Rupp, D. E., Mohler, C. J., & Schminke, M. (2001). Three roads to organizational justice. In J. Ferris (Ed.), *Research in personnel and human resources management* (Vol. *20*, pp. 1–113). Greenwich, CT: JAI Press.
Cropanzano, R., Stein, J. H., & Nadisic, T. (2011). *Social justice and the experience of human emotion.* New York, NY: Taylor and Francis.
De Cremer, D., Brockner, J., Fishman, A., van Dijke, M., van Olffen, W., & Mayer, D. M. (2010). When do procedural fairness and outcome fairness interact to influence employees' work attitudes and behaviors? The moderating effect of uncertainty. *Journal of Applied Psychology, 95*, 291–304.
De Cremer, D., Tyler, T. R., & den Ouden, N. (2005). Managing cooperation via procedural fairness: The mediating influence of self-other merging. *Journal of Economic Psychology, 26*, 393–406.
De Cremer, D., & Van Hiel, A. (2006). Effects of another person's fair treatment on one's own emotions and behaviors: The moderating role of how much the other cares for you. *Organizational Behavior and Human Decision Processes, 100*, 231–249.
Deckop, J. R., Mangel, R., & Cirka, C. C. (1999). Getting more than you pay for: Organizational citizenship and pay-for-performance plans. *Academy of Management Journal, 42*, 420–428.
Deluga, M. R. J. (1994). Supervisor trust building, leader-member exchange and organizational citizenship behaviour. *Journal of Occupational and Organizational Psychology, 76*, 315–326.
Deluga, R. J. (1995). The relation between trust in the supervisor and subordinate organizational citizenship behavior. *Military Psychology, 7*, 1–6.

Deutsch, M. (1975). Equity, equality, and need: What determines which value will be used as the basis of distributive justice? *Journal of Social Issues, 31*, 137–149.

Deutsch, M. (1985). *Distributive justice*. New Haven, CT: Yale University Press.

Devonish, D., & Greenidge, D. (2010). The effect of organizational justice on contextual performance, counterproductive work behaviors, and task performance: Investigating the moderating role of ability-based emotional intelligence. *International Journal of Selection and Assessment, 18*, 75–86.

Dineen, B. R., Lewicki, R. J., & Tomlinson, E. C. (2006). Supervisory guidance and behavioral integrity: Relationships with employee citizenship and deviant behavior. *Journal of Applied Psychology, 91*, 622–635.

Ehrhart, M. G. (2004). Leadership and procedural justice climate as antecedents of unit-level organizational citizenship behavior. *Personnel Psychology, 57*, 61–94.

Ellard, J. H., & Skarlicki, D. P. (2002). A third-party observers' reactions to employee mistreatment: Motivational and cognitive processes in deservingness assessments. In S. W. Gilliland, D. D. Steiner, & D. P. Skarlicki (Eds.), *Research in social issues in management* (pp. 133–158). Greenwich, CT: Information Age Publishing.

Erdogan, B., Bauer, T. N., & Taylor, S. (2015). Management commitment to the ecological environment and employees: Implications for employee attitudes and citizenship behaviors. *Human Relations, 68*, 1669–1691.

Ertürk, A. (2007). Increasing organizational citizenship behaviors of Turkish academics: Mediating role of trust in supervisor on the relationship between organizational justice and citizenship behaviors. *Journal of Managerial Psychology, 22*, 257–270.

Evans, W. R., Goodman, J. M., & Davis, W. D. (2010). The impact of perceived corporate citizenship on organizational cynicism, OCB, and employee deviance. *Human Performance, 24*, 79–97.

Farh, J-L., Earley, P. C., & Lin, S-C. (1997). Impetus for action: A cultural analysis of justice and organizational citizenship behavior in Chinese society. *Administrative Science Quarterly, 42*, 421–444.

Farh, J., Podsakoff, P. M., & Organ, D. W. (1990). Accounting for organizational citizenship behavior: Leader fairness and task scope versus satisfaction. *Journal of Management, 16*, 705–721.

Fassina, N. E., Jones, D. A., & Uggerslev, K. L. (2008a). Relationship clean-up time: Using meta-analysis and path analysis to clarify relationships among job satisfaction, perceived fairness, and citizenship behaviors. *Journal of Management, 34*, 161–188.

Fassina, N. E., Jones, D. A., & Uggerslev, K. L. (2008b). Meta-analytic tests of relationships between organizational justice and citizenship behavior: Testing agent-system and shared-variance models. *Journal of Organizational Behavior, 29*, 804–828.

Findley, H. M., Giles, W. F., & Mossholder, K. W. (2000). Performance appraisal process and systems facets: Relationships with contextual performance. *Journal of Applied Psychology, 85*, 634–640.

Folger, R. (1993). Justice, motivation, and performance beyond role requirements. *Employee Responsibilities and Rights Journal, 6*, 239–248.

Folger, R. (2001). Fairness as deonance. In S. W. Gilliland, D. D. Steiner, & D. P. Skarlicki (Eds.), *Theoretical and cultural perspectives on organizational justice* (pp. 3–33). Greenwich, CT: Information Age.

Folger, R., & Glerum, D. R. (2015). Justice and deonance: "You ought to be fair." In R. S. Cropanzano & M. A. Ambrose (Eds.), *Oxford handbook of justice in work organizations* (pp. 331–350). Oxford, UK: Oxford University Press.

Folger, R., & Greenberg, J. (1985). Procedural justice: An interpretive analysis of personnel systems. In K. M. Rowland & G. R. Ferris (Eds.), *Research in personnel and human resources management* (Vol. *3*, pp. 141–183). Greenwich, CT: JAI Press.

Fortin, M., Blader, S. L., Wiesenfeld, B. M., & Wheeler-Smith, S. L. (2015). Justice and affect: A dimensional approach. In R. Cropanzano & M. L. Ambrose (Eds.), *Oxford handbook of justice in work organizations* (pp. 419–439). Oxford, UK: Oxford University Press.

Frohlich, N. (2007). A very short history of distributive justice. *Social Justice Research, 20*, 250–262.

Fu, H., Ye, B. H., & Law, R. (2014). You do well and I do well? The behavioral consequences of corporate social responsibility. *International Journal of Hospitality Management, 40*, 62–70.

Fulmer, C. A., & Gelfand, M. J. (2012). At what level (and in whom) we trust: Trust across multiple organizational levels. *Journal of Management, 38*, 1167–1230.

George, J. M. (1991). State or trait: Effects of positive mood on prosocial behaviors at work. *Journal of Applied Psychology, 76*, 299–307.

Gouldner, A. W. (1960). The norm of reciprocity: A preliminary statement. *American Sociological Review, 25*, 161–178.

Graham, J. W., & Organ, D. W. (1993). Commitment and the covenantal organization. *Journal of Managerial Issues, 5*, 483–502.

Guo, J., Rupp, D. R., Weiss, H., & Trougakos, J. (2011). Justice in organizations: A person-centric approach. In S. Gilliland, D. Steiner, & D. Skarlicki (Eds.), *Emerging Perspectives on Organizational Justice and Ethics* (Research in Social Issues in Management, Vol. 7, pp. 3–32). Information Age Publishing.

Gurbuz, S. (2009). Some possible antecedents of military personnel organizational citizenship behavior. *Military Psychology, 21*, 200–215.

Halbesleben, J. R. B., Bowler, W. M., Bolino, M. C., & Turnley, W. H. (2010). Organizational concern, prosocial values, or impression management? How supervisors attribute motives to organizational citizenship behavior. *Journal of Applied Social Psychology, 40*, 1450–1489.

Hansen, S. D., Dunford, B. B., Boss, A. D., Boss, R. W., & Angermeier, I. (2011). Corporate social responsibility and the benefits of employee trust: A cross-disciplinary perspective. *Journal of Business Ethics, 102*, 29–45.

Heslin, P. A., & VandeWalle, D. (2011). Performance appraisal procedural justice: The role of a manager's implicit personality theory. *Journal of Management, 37*, 1694–1718.

Hollensbe, E. C., Khazanchi, S., & Masterson, S. S. (2008). How do I assess if my supervisor and organization are fair? Identifying the rules underlying entity-based justice perceptions. *Academy of Management Journal, 51*, 1099–1116.

Holtz, B. C., & Harold, C. M. (2009). Fair today, fair tomorrow? A longitudinal investigation of overall justice perceptions. *Journal of Applied Psychology, 94*, 1185–1199. doi:10.1037/a0015900

Huseman, R. C., Hatfield, J. D., & Miles, E. W. (1987). A new perspective on equity theory: The equity sensitivityconstruct. *Academy of Management Review, 12*, 222–234.

Jacinto, A., & Carvalho, I. S. (2009). Corporate social responsibility: The influence of organizational practices perceptions in employee's performance and organizational identification. In E. Morin, N. Ramalho, J. Neves, & A. Savoie, *New research trends in effectiveness, health, and work: A Criteos scientific and professional account* (pp. 175–204). Montreal: Criteos/HEC-Montreal.

Janseen, O., Lam, C. K., & Huang, X. (2009). Emotional exhaustion and job performance: The moderating roles of distributive justice and positive affect. *Journal of Organizational Behavior, 31*, 787–809.

Jiang, D-Y., & Cheng, B-S. (2008). Affect- and role-based loyalty to supervisors in Chinese organizations. *Asian Journal of Social Psychology, 11*, 214–221.

Johnson, J., Truxillo, D. M., Erdogan, B., Bauer, T. N., & Hammer, L. (2009). Perceptions of overall fairness: Are effects on job performance moderated by leader-member exchange? *Human Performance, 22*, 432–449.

Jones, D. A. (2010). Does serving the community also serve the company? Using organizational identification and social exchange theories to understand employee responses to a volunteerism programme. *Journal of Occupational and Organizational Psychology, 83*, 857–878.

Jones, D. A., & Martens, M. L. (2009). The mediating role of overall fairness and the moderating role of trust certainty in justice-criteria relationships: The formation and use of fairness heuristics in the workplace. *Journal of Organizational Behavior, 30*, 1025–1051.

Jones, D. A. & Rupp, D. E. (in press). Social responsibility IN and OF organizations: The psychology of corporate social responsibility among organizational members. In Anderson, N., Ones, D. S., Sinangil, H. K., & Viswesvaran, C. (Eds.), *Handbook of industrial, work, and organizational psychology* (2nd ed.). Thousand Oaks, CA: Sage.

Judge, T. A., Thoresen, C. J., Bono, J. E., & Patton, G. K. (2001). The job satisfaction—performance relationship: A qualitative and quantitative review. *Psychological Bulletin, 127*, 376–407.

Kamdar, D., McAllister, D. J., & Turban, D. B. (2006). "All in a day's work": How follower individual differences and justice perceptions predict OCB role definitions and behavior. *Journal of Applied Psychology, 91*, 841–855.

Karriker, J. H., & Williams, M. L. (2009). Organizational justice and organizational citizenship behavior: A mediated multifoci model. *Journal of Management, 35*, 112–135.

Katz, D. (1964). The motivational basis of organizational behavior. *Behavioral Science, 9*, 131–133.

Katz, D., & Kahn, R. L. (1978). *The social psychology of organizations* (2nd ed.). New York, Wiley.

Kemery, E. R., Bedeian, A. G., & Zacur, S. R. (1996). Expectancy-based job cognitions and job affect as predictors of organizational citizenship behaviors. *Journal of Applied Social Psychology, 26*, 635–651.

Kickul, J., Lester, S. W., & Finkl, J. (2002). Promise breaking during radical organizational change: Do justice interventions make a difference? *Journal of Organizational Behavior, 23*, 469–488.

Kim, W., Ok, C., & Lee, M. J. (2009). Antecedents of service employees' organizational citizenship behaviors in full-service restaurants in Korea. *Cornell Hospitality Quarterly, 50*, 180–197.

Kim, W. C., & Mauborgne, R. A. (1996). Procedural justice and managers' in-role and extra-role behavior: The case of the multinational. *Management Science, 42*, 499–515.

Kirkman, B. L., Chen, G., Farh, J-H., Chen, Z. X., & Lowe, K. B. (2009). Individual power orientation and follower reactions to transformational leaders: A cross-level, cross-cultural analysis. *Academy of Management Journal, 52*, 744–764.

Klammer, J., Skarlicki, D. P., & Barclay, L. (2002). Speaking up in the Canadian military: The roles of voice, being heard, and generation in predicting civic virtue. *Canadian Journal of Behavioural Science, 34*, 122–130.

Koivisto, S., & Koponen, J. (2015). A leader's procedural justice, respect and extra-role behaviour: The roles of leader in-group prototypicality and identification. *Social Justice Research, 28*, 187–206.

Konovsky, M. A., & Pugh, S. D. (1994). Citizenship behavior and social exchange. *Academy of Management Journal, 37*, 656–669.

Lamm, E., Tosti-Kharas, J., & King, C. E. (2015). Empowering employee sustainability: Perceived organizational support toward the environment. *Journal of Business Ethics, 128*, 207–220.

Lavelle, J. J., Brockner, J., Konovsky, M. A., Price, K., Henley, A., Taneja, A., & Vinekar, V. (2009). Commitment, procedural fairness, and organizational citizenship behavior: A multifoci analysis. *Journal of Organizational Behavior, 30*, 337–357.

Lavelle, J. J., Rupp, D. E., & Brockner, J. (2007). Taking a multifoci approach to the study of justice, social exchange, and citizenship behavior: The target similarity model. *Journal of Management, 3*, 841–866.

Lavelle, J. J., Rupp, D. E., Manegold, J., & Thornton, M. A. (2015). Multifoci justice and target similarity: Emerging research and extensions. In R. Cropanzano & M. L. Ambrose (Eds.), *Oxford handbook of justice in work organizations* (pp. 165–186). Oxford, UK: Oxford University Press.

Lavelle, J. J., McMahan, G. C., & Harris, C. M. (2009). Fairness in human resource management, social exchange relationships, and citizenship behavior: Testing linkages of the target similarity model among nurses in the United States. *International Journal of Human Resources Management, 20*, 2419–2434.

Lee, C. (1995). Prosocial organizational behaviors: The roles of workplace justice, achievement striving, and pay satisfaction. *Journal of Business and Psychology, 10*, 197–206.

Lee, K., & Allen, N. J. (2002). Organizational citizenship behavior and workplace deviance: The role of affect and cognition. *Journal of Applied Psychology, 87*, 131–142.

Lehmann-Willenbrock, N., Grohmann, A., & Kauffeld, S. (2013). Promoting multifoci citizenship behavior: Time-lagged effects of procedural justice, trust, and commitment. *Applied Psychology: An International Review, 62*, 454–485.

Leventhal, G. S. (1976). Fairness in social relationships. In J. W. Thibaut, J. T. Spence, & R. C. Carson (Eds.), *Contemporary topics in social psychology* (pp. 211–240). Morristown, NJ: General Learning Press.

Leventhal, G. S. (1980). What should be done with equity theory? New approaches to the study of fairness in social relationships. In K. J. Gergen, M. S. Greenberg, & R. H. Willis (Eds.), *Social exchange: Advances in theory and practice* (pp. 27–55). New York, NY: Plenum Press.

Leventhal, G. S., Karuza, J., & Fry, W. R. (1980). Beyond fairness: A theory of allocation preferences. In G. Mikula (Ed.),

Justice and social interaction (pp. 167–218). New York, NY: Springer-Verlag.
Li, A., & Cropanzano, R. (2009). Fairness at the group level: Justice climate and intraunit justice climate. *Journal of Management, 35*, 564–599.
Li, A., Cropanzano, R., & Bagger, J. (2013). Justice climate and peer justice climate. *Small Groups Research, 44*, 563–592.
Li, A., Cropanzano, R., & Molina, A. (2015). Fairness at the unit level: Justice climate, justice strength, and peer justice. In R. Cropanzano & M. L. Ambrose (Eds.), *Oxford handbook of justice in work organizations* (pp. 137–164). Oxford, UK: Oxford University Press.
Li, N., Liang, J., & Crant, J. M. (2010). The role of proactive personality in job satisfaction and organizational citizenship behavior: A relational perspective. *Journal of Applied Psychology, 95*, 395–404.
Liao, H., & Rupp, D. (2005). The impact of justice climate and justice orientation on work outcomes: A cross-level multifoci framework. *Journal of Applied Psychology, 90*, 242–256.
Liden, R. C., Wayne, S. J., Kraimer, M. L., & Sparrowe, R. T. (2003). The dual commitments of contingent workers: An examination of contingents' commitment to the agency and the organization. *Journal of Organization Behavior, 24*, 609–625.
Lin, C-P., Hung, W-T., & Chiu, C-K. (2008). Being good citizens: Understanding a mediating mechanism of organizational commitment and social network ties in OCBs. *Journal of Business Ethics, 81*, 561–578.
Lin, C. P., Lyau, N. M., Tsai, Y. H., Chen, W. Y., & Chiu, C. K. (2010). Modeling corporate citizenship and its relationship with organizational citizenship behaviors. *Journal of Business Ethics, 95*, 357–372.
Lind, E. A., & Tyler, T. R. (1988). *The social psychology of procedural justice*. New York: Plenum Press.
Little, H. T., Magner, N. R., & Welker, R. B. (2002). The fairness of formal budgetary procedures and their enactment: Relationships with managers' behavior. *Group and Organization Management, 27*, 209–225.
Lo, S., & Aryee, S. (2003). Psychological contract breach in a Chinese context: An integrative approach. *Journal of Management Studies, 40*, 1005–1020.
Maignan, I., & Ferrell, O. C. (2000). Measuring corporate citizenship in two countries: The case of the United States and France. *Journal of Business Ethics, 23*, 283–297.
Masterson, S. S. (2001). A trickle-down model of organizational justice: Relating employees' and customers' perceptions of and reactions to fairness. *Journal of Applied Psychology, 86*, 594–604.
Masterson, S. S., Lewis, K., Goldman, B. M., & Taylor, M. S. (2000). Integrating justice and social exchange: The differing effects of fair procedures and treatment on work relationships. *Academy of Management Journal, 43*, 738–748.
Maxham, J. G., III., Netemeyer, R. G., & Lichtenstein, D. R. (2008). The retail value chain: Linking employee perceptions to employee performance, customer evaluations, and store performance. *Marketing Science, 27*, 147–167.
McNeely, B. L., & Meglino, B. M. (1994). The role of dispositional and situational antecedents in prosocial organizational citizenship behavior: An examination of the intended beneficiaries of prosocial behavior. *Journal of Applied Psychology, 79*, 836–844.
Menguc, B. (2000). An empirical investigation of a social exchange model of organizational citizenship behaviors across two sales situations: A Turkish case. *Journal of Personal Selling and Sales Management, XX*, 205–214.
Mitchell, M. S., & Ambrose, M. L. (2007). Abusive supervision and workplace deviance and the moderating effects of negative reciprocity beliefs. *Journal of Applied Psychology, 92*, 1159–1168.
Mitchell, M. S., Cropanzano, R., & Quisenberry, D. (2012). Social exchange theory, exchange resources and interpersonal relationships: A modest resolution of theoretical difficulties. In K. Tornblom & A. Kazemi (Eds.), *Handbook of social resource theory: Theoretical extensions, empirical insights, and social applications* (pp. 99–118). New York, NY: Springer.
Moliner, C., Martínez-Tur, V., Ramos, J., Peiro, J. M., & Cropanzano, R. (2008). Organizational justice and extra-role customer service: The mediating role of well-being at work. *European Journal of Work and Organizational Psychology, 17*, 327–348.
Moliner, C., Martínez-Tur, V., Peiró, J. M., Ramos, J., & Cropanzano, R. (2013). Perceived reciprocity and well-being at work: Fairness or self-interest? *Stress and Health, 29*, 31–39.
Moorman, R. H. (1991). Relationship between organizational justice and organizational citizenship behaviors: Do fairness perceptions influence employee citizenship? *Journal of Applied Psychology, 76*, 845–855.
Moorman, R. H., & Blakely, G. L. (1995). Individualism-collectivism as an individual difference predictor of organizational citizenship behavior. *Journal of Organizational Behavior, 16*, 127–142.
Moorman, R. H., Blakely, G. L., & Niehoff, B. P. (1998). Does perceived organizational support mediate the relationship between procedural justice and organizational citizenship behavior? *Academy of Management Journal, 41*, 351–357.
Moorman, R. H., & Byrne, Z. S. (2005). How does justice affect organizational citizenship behavior? In J. Greenberg & J. A. Colquitt (Eds.), *Handbook of organizational justice* (pp. 355–380). Mahwah, NJ: Erlbuam.
Moorman, R. H., Niehoff, B. P., & Organ, D. W. (1993). Treating employees fairly and organizational citizenship behavior: Sorting the effects of job satisfaction, organizational commitment, and procedural justice. *Employee Responsibilities and Rights Journal, 6*, 209–225.
Morrison, E. W. (1994). Role definition and organizational citizenship behaviors: The importance of the employee's perspective. *Academy of Management Journal, 37*, 1543–1567.
Mossholder, K. W., Bennett, N., & Martin, C. L. (1998). A multilevel analysis of procedural justice context. *Journal of Organizational Behavior, 19*, 131–141.
Nadiri, H., & Tanova, C. (2010). An investigation of the role of justice in turnover intentions, job satisfaction, and organizational citizenship behavior in hospitality industry. *International Journal of Hospitality Management, 29*, 33–41.
Naumann, S. E., & Bennett, N. (2000). A case for procedural justice climate: Development and test of a multilevel model. *Academy of Management Journal, 43*, 881–889.
Naumann, S. E., & Bennett, N. (2002). The effects of procedural justice climate on work group performance. *Small Group Research, 33*, 361–377.
Netemeyer, R. G., Boles, J. S., McKee, D. O., & McMurrian, R. (1997). An investigation into the antecedents of organizational citizenship behaviors in a personal selling context. *Journal of Marketing, 61*, 85–98.

Newman, A., Nielsen, N., & Miao, Q. (2015). The impact of employee perceptions of organizational corporate social responsibility practices on job performance and organizational citizenship behavior: Evidence from the Chinese private sector. *The International Journal of Human Resource Management, 26*, 1226–1242.

Niehoff, B. P. & Moorman, R. H. (1993). Justice as a mediator of the relationship between methods of monitoring and organizational citizenship behavior. *Academy of Management Journal, 36*, 527–556.

Olkkonen, M., & Lipponen, J. (2006). Relationships between organizational justice, identification with organization and work-unit, and group related outcomes. *Organizational Behavior and Human Decision Processes, 100*, 202–215.

Organ, D. W. (1977). A reappraisal and reinterpretation of the satisfaction-causes-performance hypothesis. *Academy of Management Review, 2*, 46–53.

Organ, D. W. (1988). *Organizational citizenship behavior: The good soldier syndrome*. Lexington, MA: Lexington Books.

Organ, D. W. (1990). The motivational basis of organizational citizenship behavior. In B. M. Staw & L. L. Cummings (Eds.), *Research in organizational behavior* (Vol. *12*, pp. 43–72). Greenwich, CT: JAI Press.

Organ, D. W., & Konovsky, M. A. (1989). Cognitive versus affective determinants of organizational citizenship behavior. *Journal of Applied Psychology, 74*, 157–164.

Organ, D. W., & Moorman, R. H. (1993). Fairness and organizational citizenship behavior: What are the connections? *Social Justice Research, 6*, 5–18.

Organ, D. W., & Near, J. P. (1985). Cognition vs. affect in measures of job satisfaction. *International Journal of Psychology, 20*, 85–97.

Organ, D. W., & Ryan, K. (1995). A meta-analytic review of attitudinal and dispositional predictors of organizational citizenship behavior. *Personnel Psychology, 48*, 775–802.

Paillé, P., Boiral, O., & Chen, Y. (2013). Linking environmental management practices and organizational citizenship behaviour for the environment: A social exchange perspective. *The International Journal of Human Resource Management, 24*, 3552–3575.

Piccolo, R. F., Bardes, M., Mayer, D. M., & Judge, T. A. (2008). Does high quality leader-member exchange accentuate the effects of organizational justice? *European Journal of Work and Organizational Psychology, 17*, 273–298.

Pillai, R., Schriesheim, C. A., & Williams, E. S. (1999). Fairness perceptions and trust as mediators of transformational and transactional leadership. *Journal of Management, 25*, 897–933.

Podsakoff, P. M., & MacKenzie, S. B. (1989). *A second generation measure of organizational citizenship behavior.* Unpublished Manuscript. Indiana University.

Podsakoff, P. M., & MacKenzie, S. B. (1993). Citizenship behavior and fairness in organizations: Issues and directions for future research. *Employee Responsibilities and Rights Journal, 6*(3), 257–269.

Pond, S. B., III., Nacoste, R. W., Mohr, M. F., & Rodriguez, C. M. (1997). The measurement of organizational citizenship behavior: Are we assuming too much? *Journal of Social Psychology, 27*, 1527–1544.

Porath, C. L., & Erez, A. (2009). Overlooked but not untouched: How rudeness reduces onlookers' performance on routine and creative tasks. *Organizational Behavior and Human Decision Processes, 109*, 29–44.

Proudfoot, D., & Lind, E. A. (2015). Fairness heuristic theory, the uncertainty management model, and fairness at work. In R. Cropanzano & M. L. Ambrose (Eds.), *Oxford handbook of justice in work organizations* (pp. 371–402). Oxford, UK: Oxford University Press.

Rioux, S. M., & Penner, L. A. (2001). The causes of organizational citizenship behavior: A motivational analysis. *Journal of Applied Psychology, 86*, 1306–1314.

Roberson, Q. M. (2006a). Justice in teams: The activation and role of sensemaking in the emergence of justice climates. *Organizational Behavior and Human Decision Processes, 100*, 177–192.

Roberson, Q. M. (2006b). Justice in teams: The effects of interdependence and identification on referent choice and justice climate strength. *Social Justice Research, 19*, 323–344.

Roberson, Q. M., & Colquitt, J. A. (2005). Shared and configural justice: A social network model of justice in teams. *Academy of Management Review, 30*, 595–607.

Rosen, C. C., Chang, C. H., Johnson, R. E., & Levy, P. E. (2009). Perceptions of the organizational context and psychological contract breach: Assessing competing perspectives. *Organizational Behavior and Human Decision Processes, 108*, 202–217.

Rupp, D. E., Bashshur, M., & Liao, H. (2007). Justice climate past, present, and future: Models of structure and emergence. In F. Dansereau & F. J. Yammarino (Eds.), *Multi-level issues in organizations and time* (Vol. *6*, pp. 357–396). Oxford, UK: Elsevier.

Rupp, D. E., & Cropanzano, R. (2002). The mediating effects of social exchange relationships in predicting workplace outcomes from multifoci organizational justice. *Organizational Behavior and Human Decision Processes, 89*, 925–946.

Rupp, D. E. & Mallory, D. B. (2015). Corporate social responsibility: Psychological, person-centric, and progressing. *Annual Review of Organizational Psychology and Organizational Behavior, 2*, 211–236.

Rupp, D. E., & Paddock, E. L. (2010). From justice events to justice climate: A multilevel temporal model of information aggregation and judgment. *Research on Managing Groups and Teams, 13*, 239–267.

Rupp, D. E., Shao, R., Jones, K. S., & Liao, H. (2014). The utility of a multifoci approach to the study of organizational justice: A meta-analytic investigation into the consideration of normative rules, moral accountability, bandwidth-fidelity, and social exchange. *Organizational Behavior and Human Decision Processes, 123*, 159–185.

Rupp, D. E., Williams, C., Aguilera, R. (2011). Increasing corporate social responsibility through stakeholder value internalization (and the catalyzing effect of new governance): An application of organizational justice, self-determination, and social influence theories, In M. Schminke (Ed.). *Managerial ethics: Managing the psychology of morality* (pp. 71–90). New York, NY: Routledge/Psychology Press.

Schanke, M., Cochran, D., & Dumler, M. (1995). Encouraging organizational citizenship: The effects of job satisfaction, perceived equity, and leadership. *Journal of Managerial Issues, VII*, 209–221.

Schappe, S. P. (1998). The influence of job satisfaction, organizational commitment, and fairness perceptions on organizational citizenship behavior. *The Journal of Psychology, 132*, 277–290.

Scholl, R. W., Cooper, E. A., & McKenna, J. F. (1987). Referent selection in determining equity perceptions: Differential effects on behaviors and attitudinal outcomes. *Personnel Psychology, 40*, 113–124.

Scott, B. A., Colquitt, J. A., & Paddock, E. L. (2009). An actor-focused model of justice rule adherence and violation: The role of managerial motives and discretion. *Journal of Applied Psychology, 94*, 756–769.

Shen, J., & Benson, J. (2014). When CSR is a social norm: How socially responsible human resource management affects employee work behavior. *Journal of Management, 20*, 1–24.

Shin, Y., Sung, S. Y., Choi, J. N., & Kim, M. S. (2015). Top management ethical leadership and firm performance: Mediating role of ethical and procedural justice climate. *Journal of Business Ethics, 129*, 43–57.

Simons, T., & Roberson, Q. (2003). Why managers should care about fairness: The effects of aggregate justice perceptions on organizational outcomes. *Journal of Applied Psychology, 88*, 432–443.

Sinclair, R. C., & Mark, M. M. (1991). Mood and the endorsement of egalitarian macrojustice principles versus equity-based microjustice principles. *Personality and Social Psychology Bulletin, 17*, 369–375.

Sinclair, R. C., & Mark, M. M. (1992). The influence of mood state on judgment and action: Effects on persuasion, categorization, social justice, person perception, and judgmental accuracy. In L. L. Martin & A. Tesser (Eds.), *The construction of social judgments* (pp. 165–193). Hillsdale, NJ: Erlbaum.

Sitkin, S. B., & Bies, R. J. (1993). Social accounts in conflict situations: Using explanations to management conflict. *Human Relations, 46*, 349–370.

Skarlicki, D. P., & Kulik, C. (2005). Third party reactions to employee mistreatment: A justice perspective. In B. Staw & R. Kramer (Eds.), *Research in organizational behavior* (Vol. *26*, pp. 183–230). Greenwich, CT: JAI Press.

Skarlicki, D. P., & Latham, G. P. (1996). Increasing citizenship behavior within a labor union: A test of organizational justice theory. *Journal of Applied Psychology, 81*, 161–169.

Skarlicki, D. P., & Latham, G. P. (1997). Leadership training in organizational justice to increase citizenship behavior within a labor union. *Personnel Psychology, 50*, 617–633.

Skarlicki, D. P., O'Reilly, J., & Kulik, C. T. (2015). The third-party perspective of (in)justice. In R. Cropanzano & M. A. Ambrose (Eds.), *Oxford handbook of justice in work organizations* (pp. 257–271). Oxford, UK: Oxford University Press.

Smith, C. A., Organ, D. W., & Near, J. P. (1983). Organizational citizenship behavior: Its nature and antecedents. *Journal of Applied Psychology, 68*, 653–666.

Streicher, B., Jonas, E., Maier, G. W., Frey, D. Woschée, R., & Waßmer, B. (2008). Test of the construct and criteria validity of a German measure of organizational justice. *European Journal of Psychological Assessment, 24*, 131–139.

Tang, T.-W., & Tang, Y.-Y. (2012). Promoting service-oriented organizational citizenship behaviors in hotels: The role of high-performance human resource practices and organizational social climates. *International Journal of Hospitality Management, 31*, 885–895.

Tansky, J. W. (1993). Justice and organizational citizenship behavior: What is the relationship? *Employee Responsibilities and Rights Journal, 6*, 195–207.

Taylor, E. C., & Tepper, B. J. (1999, August). Mediating and moderating effects of role definitions on relationships between organizational justice and organizational citizenship behavior. Paper presented at the Annual Meeting of the Academy of Management. Chicago, IL.

Tepper, B. J., Lockhart, D., & Hoobler, J. (2001). Justice, citizenship, and role definition effects. *Journal of Applied Psychology, 86*, 789–796.

Törnblom, K., & Kazemi, A. (2015). Distributive justice: Revising past statements and reflecting on future prospects. In R. Cropanzano & M. L. Ambrose (Eds.), *Oxford handbook of justice in work organizations* (pp. 15–50). Oxford, UK: Oxford University Press.

Tyler, T. R. (1989). The psychology of procedural justice: A test of the group-value model. *Journal of Personality and Social Psychology, 57*, 830–838.

Tyler, T. R. (1994). Psychological models of the justice motive: Antecedents of distributive and procedural justice. *Journal of Personality and Social Psychology, 67*, 850–863.

Tyler, T. R. (1997). The psychology of legitimacy: A relational perspective on voluntary deference to authorities. *Personality and Social Psychology Review, 1*, 323–345.

Tyler, T. R., & Blader, S. (2000). *Cooperation in groups: Procedural justice, social identity, and behavioral engagement*. Philadelphia, PA: Psychology Press.

Tyler, T. R., & Blader, S. L. (2001). Identity and cooperative behavior in groups. *Group Processes and Intergroup Relations, 4*, 207–226.

Tyler, T. R., & Blader, S. L. (2002). Autonomous vs. comparative status: Must we be better than others to feel good about ourselves? *Organizational Behavior & Human Decision Processes, 89*, 813–838.

Tyler, T. R., & Blader, S. L. (2003). Procedural justice, social identity and cooperative behavior. *Personality and Social Psychology Review, 7*, 349–361.

Tyler, T. R., Degoey, P., & Smith, H. (1996). Understanding why the justice of group procedures matters: A test of the psychological dynamics of the group-value model. *Journal of Personality and Social Psychology, 70*, 913–930.

Van Prooijen, J-W., De Cremer, D., van Beest, I., Stahl, T., van Dijke, M., & Van Lange, P. A. M. (2008). The egocentric nature of procedural justice: Social value orientation as moderator of reactions to decision-making procedures. *Journal of Experimental Social Psychology, 44*, 1303–1315.

Vroom, V. H. (1964). *Work and motivation*. New York, NY: Wiley.

Wayne, S. J., Shore, L. M., Bommer, W. H., & Tetrick, L. E. (2002). The role of fair treatment and rewards in perceptions of organizational support and leader-member exchange. *Journal of Applied Psychology, 87*, 590–598.

Whitman, D. S., Caleo, S., Carpenter, N. C., Horner, M. T., & Bernerth, J. B. (2012). Fairness at the collective level: A meta-analytic examination of the consequences and boundary of organizational justice climate. *Journal of Applied Psychology, 97*, 776–791.

Williams, L. J., & Anderson, S. E. (1991). Job satisfaction and organizational commitment as predictors of organizational citizenship and in-role behaviors. *Journal of Management, 17*, 601–617.

Williams, S., Pitre, R., & Zainuba, M. (2002). Justice and organizational citizenship behavior intentions: Fair treatment vs. fair rewards. *Journal of Social Psychology, 143*, 33–44.

Witt, L. A. (1992). Exchange ideology as a moderator of the relationships between importance of participation in decision making and job attitudes. *Human Relations, 45*, 73–85.

Witt, L. A., & Broach, D. (1993). Exchange ideology as a moderator of the procedural justice-satisfaction relationship. *Journal of Social Psychology, 133*, 97–103.

Wong, Y-T., Wong, C-S., & Ngo H-Y. (2002). Loyalty to supervisor and trust in supervisor of workers in Chinese joint ventures: A test of two competing models. *International Journal of Human Resource Management, 13,* 883–900.

Yang, J., Mossholder, K. W., & Peng, T. K. (2007). Procedural justice climate and group power distance: An examination of cross-level interaction effects. *Journal of Applied Psychology, 92,* 681–692.

Yang, J., Mossholder, K. W., & Peng, T. K. (2009). Supervisory procedural justice effects: The mediating roles of cognitive and affective trust. *Leadership Quarterly, 20,* 143–154.

Yi, Y., & Gong, T. (2008). The effects of justice perception and affect on customer citizenship behavior and customer dysfunctional behavior. *Industrial Marketing Management, 37,* 767–783.

Zellars, K. L., Tepper, B. J., & Duffy, M. L. (2002). Abusive supervision and subordinates' organizational citizenship behavior. *Journal of Applied Psychology, 87,* 1068–1076.

Zhang, H., & Agarwal, N. C. (2009). The mediating roles of organizational justice on the relationships between HR practices and workplace outcomes: An investigation in China. *International Journal of Human Resources Management, 20,* 676–693.

Zhang, M., Di Fan, D., & Zhu, C. J. (2014). High-performance work systems, corporate social performance and employee outcomes: Exploring the missing links. *Journal of Business Ethics, 120,* 423–435.

Zoghbi-Manrique-de-Lara, P. (2008). Fairness, teachers' non-task behavior and alumni satisfaction: The influence of group commitment. *Journal of Educational Administration, 46,* 514–538.

CHAPTER

16

Organizational Citizenship Behavior and Trust: The Double Reinforcing Spiral

Robert Moorman, Holly Brower, *and* Steven Grover

Abstract

Research on trust and organizational citizenship behavior (OCB) has focused mostly on how OCB performance may be a consequence of trusting relationships. However, recent studies of trust have sought to both broaden and deepen our understanding of trust and develop our appreciation of the complexity of the construct. This chapter examines how contemporary treatments of trust enhance our understanding of how trust and OCB performance interrelate. We argue that the relationship between trust and OCB is best modeled as reciprocal, taking the form of a double reinforcing spiral. We further discuss how this model informs our understanding of felt trust, trust violation, and trust recovery.

Key Words: OCB, organizational citizenship behavior, trust, felt trust, reinforcing spiral, trust violation

Ironically, trust begets trust—when we give it away, it returns to us tenfold.

—*Anderson (2015)*

The visible practice of distinctive forms of OCB by top managers communicates the message that participants can trust each other and join in the process.

—*Organ (1988), p. 95*

As he has described many times, Organ (1988, 1997) proposed organizational citizenship behavior (OCB) as a form of job performance because it could address a conflict between rigorous research and common sense. The question that first prompted his development of the construct was whether workers holding positive job attitudes could be expected to perform better in their jobs, or, asked colloquially, are happy workers more productive? What was most interesting to Organ was that research designed to test this relationship had found relatively weak relationships between positive attitudes and work performance. However, instead of concluding that common sense was flawed, Organ (1977) asked whether researchers had properly operationalized job performance. Embracing Katz and Kahn's (1978) performance typology, Organ suggested that the reason why job attitudes were only weakly related to performance could be a result of narrow definitions of performance. Instead, he considered how job attitudes might be more highly related to "spontaneous and innovative behaviors" as well as extreme provisions of their "joining and staying" and "dependable activity" behaviors in Katz and Kahn's (1978) performance typology. Organ (1988) coined the term "organizational citizenship behavior" (OCB) to describe affiliative, cooperative behaviors that support the work of others (such as helping behavior and courtesy) and promotive behaviors to help improve group functioning (such as civic virtue behaviors and personal industry) (Moorman, 1991; Moorman & Blakely, 1995; Van Dyne, Cummings, & Parks, 1995).

Important to this present chapter is Organ's determination that OCBs are more discretionary than traditional aspects of job performance and could become the avenue through which workers manifest positive job attitudes. In the intervening years, a great deal of research has explored the relationships between various job attitudes and psychological states with OCB performance and has found that many are at least as predictive of OCB as they are of other forms of performance (Hoffman, Blair, Meriac, & Woehr, 2007). One of these, trust, is defined as "a psychological state comprising the intention to accept vulnerability based upon positive expectations of the intentions or behavior of another" (Rousseau, Sitkin, Burt, & Camerer, 1998, p. 395). Weber, Malhotra, and Murnighan (2005) argue that trust is an essential element of effective relationships in organizations because it increases both the efficiency and effectiveness of interpersonal exchanges. When present in a relationship, trust increases cooperation without waiting on time and resource-consuming efforts to define every act and outcome needed (Dirks & Ferrin, 2001, 2002; Lewicki, Tomlinson, & Gillespie, 2006; Mayer, Davis, & Schoorman, 1995; McEvily, 2011; Schoorman, Mayer, & Davis, 2007; Sitkin & Roth, 1993). As noted by Solomon and Flores (2001), "[w]ithout trust the corporation becomes not a community but a brutish state of nature, a war of all against all in which employment tends to be nasty, brutish, and short" (p. 5). Instead, trust facilitates cooperation because it prevents one party's vulnerability from restricting their behavior (Möllering, Bachman, & Lee, 2004). In the relationship, parties can bypass the need for inefficient safeguards against negative outcomes, relying instead on promises of benefits and expectations of success (Burke, Sims, Lazzara, & Salas, 2007; Butler, 1991; Dirks, 2000; Mayer & Davis, 1999; Mayer & Gavin, 2005; Rousseau et al., 1998).

Given that both trust and OCB are useful in understanding how the nature of relationships in organizations can affect work performance, our purpose is to extend our understanding of how trust and OCB interrelate. Although the relationship between trust and OCB has been studied extensively (e.g., Deluga, 1995; Kacmar, Bachrach, Harris, & Noble, 2012; Korsgaard, Whitener, & Brodt, 2002; MacKenzie, Podsakoff, & Rich, 2001; Pearce, 1993, Pillai, Schriesheim, & Williams, 1999; Wagner & Rush, 2000), most studies only consider OCB a consequence of trust. However, research and theory on the nature of trust and the rich ways in which trust develops suggest that the two constructs may relate in a more complex fashion. Our intent is to show that the relationship between trust and OCB is better thought of as reciprocal and that the relation between them is best described as a reinforcing spiral.

In this chapter, we first review research on how trust affects OCB performance and then use this as a starting point to describe how trust and OCB may affect the incremental development of the other. We propose a double-spiral model to describe this process and identify how recent research on felt trust and trust violation and repair illustrates how the spiral model is sustained and made stable. We conclude by describing how new research on the development of multilevel trust illustrates how new directions in OCB research may be informed by advances in our understanding of trust.

The Simple Relationship Between Trust and Organizational Citizenship Behavior

We begin our exploration of the relationship between trust and OCB by reviewing the straightforward relationship that has been tested in an expansive literature. Most research on the trust and OCB relationship examines trust as antecedent to OCB performance. For example, Podsakoff, MacKenzie, Moorman, and Fetter (1990) argue that trust mediates the relationship between transformational leader behaviors and OCB because (a) individualized consideration offered by transformational leaders and the ways that leaders signal their competence bolsters trust; and (b) OCB represents the type of job performance offered by subordinates who trust their leaders. Similarly, Konovsky and Pugh (1994) position trust as a mediator to explain why justice perceptions would affect OCB because trust indicates that the relationship between parties is one of social exchange and OCB may emerge as a likely way to reciprocate benefits received. Since these two studies, other articles have reported robust support for the relationship between trust and OCB (Deluga, 1995; Korsgaard, Brower, & Lester, 2015; Korsgaard et al., 2002; MacKenzie et al., 2001; Pearce, 1993, Pillai et al., 1999; Wagner & Rush, 2000) and between trust and broader measures of job performance (Aryee, Budhwar, & Chen, 2002; Colquitt, Scott, & LePine, 2007; Deluga, 1995; Earley, 1986; Farh, Tsui, Xin, & Chang, 1998; Pettit, Goris, & Vaught,

1997; Podsakoff, MacKenzie, & Bommer, 1996; Rich, 1997).

Colquitt, LePine, Piccolo, Zapata, and Rich (2012) offer two primary explanations for why trust leads to OCB. The first is that social exchange theory suggests that trust motivates OCB performance because it transforms relationships from economic exchange relationships to social exchange relationships. Economic exchange refers to the contractual relationship concerning performance expectations and compensation, focusing on performing the formal duties of the job. However, depending on the quality of the relationships employees and employers foster, employees may consider themselves in a social exchange relationship where the exact parameters of the job and its compensation are more loosely defined. Blau (1964) suggests this relationship "involves favors that create diffuse future obligations, not precisely specified ones, and the nature of the return cannot be bargained about, but must be left to the discretion of the one who makes it" (p. 93).

Social exchange relationships are the likely setting for OCB performance because, unlike economic exchange relationships where all elements are strictly determined, social exchange relationships rely on diffuse obligations satisfied in a variety of ways. As Konovsky and Pugh (1994) suggest, trust may affect OCB performance because "trust provides the basis for social exchange relationships and serves as the key element in the emergence and deepening of such relationships" (cited in Colquitt et al., 2012, p. 4). They proposed that trust is related to OCB because it is a necessary condition for relationships to evolve from an economic exchange relationship to a social exchange relationship. Trust becomes the precondition that must be present for exchange partners to move away from contractual parameters toward the more diffuse contributions and obligations that define social exchange. Furthermore, with this trust-inspired evolution, OCB now becomes a viable way to reciprocate the psychological benefits of a trusting relationship (Konovsky & Pugh, 1994).

A second mechanism that explains why trust motivates OCB performance is that trust reduces uncertainty that may constrain performance in its many forms (Colquitt & Zipay, 2015). Colquitt et al. (2012) use fairness heuristic theory and uncertainty management theory to identify trust as "an uncertainty-reducer," suggesting that trust may help by reducing extraneous concerns that may drag on performance. Fairness heuristic theory recognizes a "fundamental social dilemma" where employees benefit from cooperating with authority figures, yet doing so increases the chances for exploitation. However, "[t]rustworthiness becomes relevant to the fundamental social dilemma because the risks of exploitation seem lower if authorities are trustworthy" (Colquitt & Zipay, 2015, p. 79). Therefore, trust may increase OCB by removing or reducing questions about whether such cooperation is beneficial.

Using similar logic, Mayer and Gavin (2005) use an information-processing approach to study how trust increases performance by increasing a person's ability to focus on the most important tasks at hand. They cite information-processing theory (Kanfer & Ackerman, 1989) to suggest that limits on cognitive resources reduce task performance. Trust may serve to remove concerns that "divert one's focus of attention" such as an unwillingness to accept influence, a search for hidden agendas, and the establishment of self-protection mechanisms. Similarly, the lack of trust diminishes information-processing efficiency. Sitkin and Roth (1993), for example, note that organizations use legalistic remedies to provide ways for two parties to cooperate in the absence of trust. However, they warn that "the adoption of legalistic 'remedies' (i.e., institutionalized mechanisms that mimic legal forms and exceed legal/regulatory requirements) impose[s] a psychological and/or an interactional barrier between the two parties that stimulates an escalating spiral of formality and distance (Granovetter, 1985; Homans, 1974; Larson, 1992; Zucker, 1986) and leads to a need for more rules (Fox, 1974; Peachey & Lerner, 1981; Shapiro, 1987)" (p. 369). The result of increased formality is that, even though cooperation remains possible, the efficiency of the cooperation is significantly compromised as the parties seek to both cooperate and comply with the rules. Much like its role in reducing uncertainty and increasing focus, trust affects performance because it increases the efficient action of cooperative relationships toward work goals. McEvily (2011) extends these information-processing concepts to determine hybrid forms of trust in which people use the automatic heuristic of high trust to reduce information processing, whereas less automatic levels of trust require the most extensive arrangements to mitigate risk.

In sum, trust has been studied extensively as an antecedent to job performance and OCB. Two main mechanisms have emerged to explain this relationship. Social exchange mechanisms focus on trust's role in creating social exchange relationships where OCB may be commonly used as a means to reciprocate benefits received. Uncertainty-reducing mechanisms focus instead on how trust reduces the uncertainty present in cooperative relationships. When uncertainty is reduced, those who trust may be more likely to offer OCB to support the relationship because doing so is not a risky alternative to prescribed in-role performance.

Increasing the Complexity of the Relationship: Trust and Organizational Citizenship Behavior as a Reinforcing Spiral

Even though research on trust and OCB has mostly supported the unidirectional, simple relationship where increases in trust prompt increases in OCB performance, models of trust depict more complex relationships where both parties may converge on mutual levels of trust or may hold asymmetric perceptions of the trustworthiness of their partner (Korsgaard et al., 2015). We believe there is value in thinking about how trust and OCB mutually influence one another, creating a reinforcing spiral. Trust promotes OCB; OCB performance promotes trust; and the occurrence of each reinforces the continued and growing occurrence of the other. This is a virtuous spiral when it occurs in the positive direction and more like a death spiral when it occurs in the negative direction.

The trust–OCB relationship can be considered as a reinforcing spiral because (a) the relationship between trust and OCB is reciprocal—trust promotes OCB performance and OCB performance also promotes trust; and (b) trust and OCB develop iteratively over time and repeated occurrences, such that the intensity of the behavior or perception may also grow (or reduce) over time. We are not the first to describe a spiraling process to explain the development of mutual trust (for example, see Ferrin, Bligh, & Kohles, 2008). However, we extend the reinforcing spiral concept in the following section by first offering arguments describing why we can consider OCB as an antecedent to trust and then discussing why the development of both OCB and trust fit the reinforcing spiral model.

An Organizational Citizenship Behavior to Trust Relationship?

The robust influence of the relationship between trust and OCB was reviewed earlier where trust is considered antecedent to OCB performance. However, a reinforcing spiral requires that the relationship between trust and OCB be reciprocal. Empirical research has yet to examine OCB as an antecedent to trust, but trust development theory supports such a causal role for OCB performance.

Models of trust development suggest that those who trust may be informed by judgments of the other's character and motives (Mayer at al., 1995; Whitener, Brodt, Korsgaard, & Werner, 1998), because trust rests on "[an] assessment of others' intentions, sincerity, motivations, character, reliability, and integrity" (Burke et al., 2007, p. 610). Luhmann (1979) states the issue in more esoteric terms, suggesting that "[t]rust rests on illusion. In actuality, there is less information available than would be required to give assurance of success" (p. 32). What prompts the trustor to act in the face of a threat of exploitation is the belief that trust is justified by information about the trustee that reduces the risk. Luhmann (1979) further argues that trusting relationships do not follow from previous prescriptions of expected performance, but follow from surplus performance—or OCB—because this performance indicates a greater investment in the concern for and support of the other.

Thus, models of trust antecedents argue that a trustor's decision to trust another likely results from assessments of the trustee's character to the extent that making oneself vulnerable is a reasonably safe choice that is unlikely to result in opportunistic abuse. Mayer et al. (1995) underscore this concept as they describe how a decision to trust another results from judgments about the characteristics of the trustee—his or her trustworthiness. Although Mayer et al. (1995) review a long list of potential antecedents, the three cited most frequently were ability, integrity, and benevolence. Although it may be possible to argue indirectly that OCB performance could affect judgments of ability and integrity, the most direct way in which OCB performance affects trust is through judgments of benevolence. Mayer et al. (1995) define benevolence as "the extent to which a trustee is believed to want to do good to the trustor, aside from an egocentric profit motive" (p. 718). To illustrate, they offer the example of a mentor and a protégé, where "the mentor wants to help the protégé, even though the mentor is not required to be helpful, and there is no extrinsic reward for the mentor" (p. 719). We note that Organ (1988, 1990) originally defined OCB as behavior that is discretionary (not required) and is not directly related to the formal organizational reward system (not extrinsically rewarded). Thus, Mayer et al.'s (1995) mentorship and helping behavior examples are really illustrations of how OCB performance can increase trust.

In their spiral reinforcement model, Ferrin et al. (2008) similarly identified cooperative behavior as a signal to an actor about whether the partner was trustworthy. They explicitly assert that OCB is a form of cooperative behavior that informs perceptions of the actor's ability, benevolence, and integrity (trustworthiness). Finally, Whitener et al. (1998) also argue that trust "is derived from the trustor's perceptions, beliefs, and attributions about the trustee, based on his or her observations of the trustee's behavior" (p. 513). In particular, Whitener et al. (1998) suggest that judgments of benevolence built on such typical OCBs as showing consideration and sensitivity, acting in a way that protects others' interests, and refraining from exploiting others for the benefit of one's own interests can signal loyalty and benevolence.

In sum, models of the antecedents of trust suggest that actions by the trustee affect how the trustor develops perceptions of trust because these actions signal information about the trustee's character and motives. OCB can affect trust perceptions because they signal that the trustee is benevolent, helpful, and of caring character. These impressions increase trust because they reduce the risk associated with making oneself vulnerable to another.

Spiral Development of Organizational Citizenship Behavior and Trust

The present chapter proposes a spiral model to capture the iterative development processes of OCB and trust. Much like the development process of trust, OCB performance may begin with small gestures but increases in strength and frequency. Because there is a risk that performing OCB may divert performance from prescribed, in-role behaviors (Bolino, 1999; Bolino, Klotz, Turnley, & Harvey, 2013), Organ (1988, 1990) argues that OCB performance develops over time as the employee experiences continued reasons for its appropriateness. OCB can be appropriate as long as the relationship continues to be defined as social exchange (Blau, 1964). However, if conditions change such that OCB is no longer viewed as warranted, an employee will see reasons to reign in his or her extra-role performance.

Zand (1972) and Ferrin et al. (2008) describe a similarly iterative trust development process. Zand (1972) presents a reinforcement model of trust development in which groups who expected trustworthy behavior responded with higher trust and more risk-taking behaviors as opposed to groups who anticipated less trustworthiness. At the first point in a relationship where parties do not know each other, their levels of trust are based upon a relatively stable psychological predisposition of trust propensity (Mayer et al., 1995; Rotter, 1967, 1980; Yakovleva, Reilly, & Werko, 2010). However, like OCB, trust develops through a social exchange process (Balliet & Van Lange, 2013; Jones & George, 1998) where previous experience with the actor leads the partner to more or less trust, followed by a corresponding level of sharing information, control, and influence (risky behavior).

Ferrin et al. (2008) present one of the very few works that includes the full development of trust involving direct and reflective perceptions of both the leader and the subordinate and how this development involves the spiraling effects of trust outcomes feeding back to further perceptions of trustworthiness and then more or less trust. They specifically propose a double-spiral model where trust leads to cooperation and then back to trust such that the two parties in the relationship ultimately form mutual trust levels through the iterative patterns of trust and cooperation. In empirical tests of their model, they found that the spiraling development of perceived trustworthiness in actors and partners was mediated by cooperation. Specifically, they found that actors and partners simultaneously observe each other's cooperative behavior, make assertions about the other's trustworthiness, and then reciprocate accordingly.

Butler (1983) presents a similar process by which trust develops iteratively over time as a result of a series of interactions between parties. Butler found that one party signals to the other trustworthiness through positive attitudes and expectations, who, in turn, reciprocates those positive attitudes. This process is consistent with a robust literature demonstrating how the norm of reciprocity helps determine the nature of dyadic relationships (e.g., Blau, 1964; Gouldner, 1960; Konovsky & Pugh, 1994; Moorman, 1991; Organ, Podsakoff, & MacKenzie, 2005).

Finally, Mayer et al. (1995) include a feedback loop from trustworthiness to perceptions of trust to risk-taking behavior and other outcomes. The resultant outcomes, in turn, lead to further perceptions about trustworthiness, and so on in an iterative fashion.

The Double Reinforcing Spiral

Empirical examinations of how trust affects other outcomes typically consider the relationships as existing on a single plane. They examine relationships of trustworthiness to trust and to all sorts of resulting behaviors, including performance, commitment, delegation, and OCB. Yet they rarely consider the idea that one variable may affect the occurrence of the other, and, more important, effect change in its magnitude. Modeling the relationship between trust and OCB as a reinforcing spiral suggests that trust and OCB performance mutually influence one another, *and* they also affect the positive or negative growth of the other. Said differently, increasing trust affects OCB performance and the future growth of OCB. Increasing OCB affects trust perceptions and their future growth as well. Conversely, decreasing trust and OCB diminishes both trust perceptions and OCB performance, while hastening their future reduction.

High-quality relationships encourage trust and OCB, and these relationships build over time and depend on the individual preferences of each of the two parties. Rarely can we extract this time zero raw relationship where no impression of the other party has been formed; therefore, whether trust or OCB acts first to move the level of trust upward or downward is less important than the point that these constructs develop across time and depend on the mutual perceptions of each party. The spiraling process progresses as the two parties interact such that OCB performance of one Actor signals trustworthiness to the Partner. The Partner is more likely, then, to trust the Actor and behaves accordingly engaging in OCB risk-taking behavior (i.e., information sharing, delegation, participative decision making). That behavior signals to the Actor a reciprocal trust and the Actor feels trusted. As a result of that felt trust, the Actor engages in more OCB behavior and the spiral reinforces in a positive direction.

The model is complicated by the fact that two individuals each form perceptions about the other and behave according to those perceptions. Thus, it is not a simple spiraling process, but a double-spiral development where the trustworthiness perceptions of the Actor ultimately lead to the Partner's OCB (Figure 16.1). At the same time, the Actor's risk-taking behavior signals the Partner about the Actor's trust in the Partner. These signals lead to the development of the Partner's perceptions about the Actor's trustworthiness, thus leading to the Actor's OCB.

Having related mutual trust and OCB development to a reinforcing double spiral, the remainder of this chapter explores that spiral in the context of current research on trust and trust development. Acknowledging that trust has emerged as a very complicated construct, we chose to focus on two advances in trust research to illustrate how our

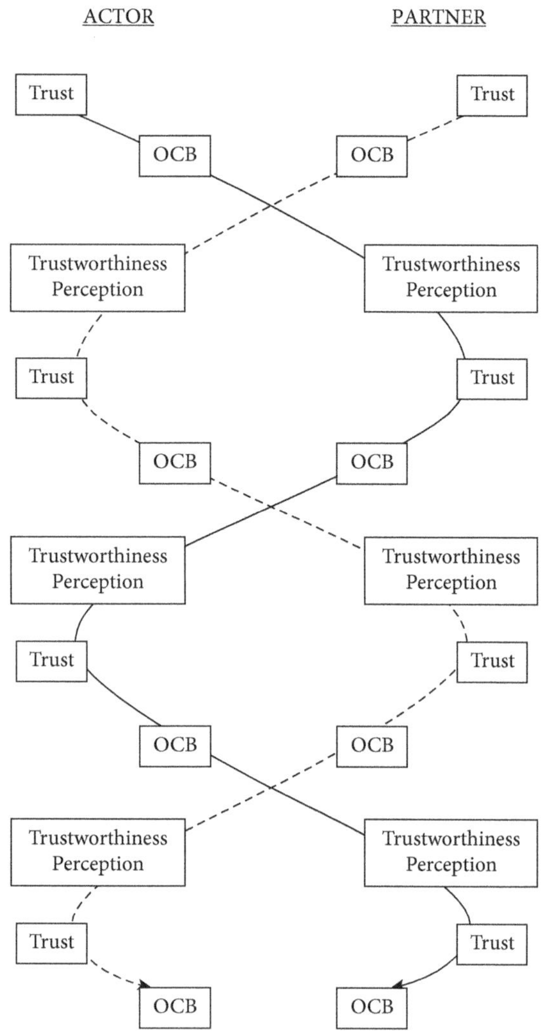

Figure 16.1 Reinforcing spiral process of trust development through organizational citizenship behavior (OCB) performance.

understanding of trust helps us develop a more sophisticated model of how trust and OCB interrelate. In the following section we examine how the concepts of felt trust and trust violations and recovery may affect the double reinforcing spiral model.

Felt Trust

Felt trust is integral to the double-spiral model as it links the trust formation process in the two parties. Felt trust is a novel operationalization of trust and its relationship with OCB involves not only active perceptions of the other party but also reflective impressions of each party. Lester and Brower (2003) defined felt trustworthiness as the "extent to which one party (the Actor) perceives that their Partner in the relationship evaluates him/her to be trustworthy" (p. 18). To the degree that the Actor has a positive perception, the Actor *feels* trusted. Thus, *felt trust* is distinguishable from *trust* in that the focal person of the trust is oneself. The evaluation is about whether one feels trusted by the other party. In organizational relationships, trust in the manager is considered "upward trust," and trust in the subordinate is referred to as "downward trust." The vast majority of published research investigates the influence of upward trust on subordinate outcomes. However, felt trust is one measure of downward trust (from the perspective of the subordinate) in that the level of downward trust is taken from the perspective of the subordinate. In other words, to what degree does the subordinate feel trusted by her supervisor?

The experience of feeling trusted has an impact on OCB. For example, Brower, Lester, Korsgaard, and Dineen (2008) found that a manager's trust in the subordinate (downward trust) actually had a stronger effect on subordinates' OCB performance than upward trust had. Thus, where most previous studies of the relationship between trust and OCB have suggested that OCB performance resulted from trust in one's supervisor, this study was possibly the first to show that a supervisor's trust for the subordinate predicted OCB performance. Furthermore, when measured as felt trust, it has stronger predictive ability on OCB performance than upward trust (Lester & Brower, 2003). Taken together, these results suggest that felt trust contributes to the relationship between trust and OCB by linking the extra-role behavior of the Actor and the Partner's trust in the actor as long as that the Actor feels trusted by the Partner.

One reason for felt trust increasing OCB is that feeling trust builds one's self-esteem (Lau, Lam, & Wen, 2014). The increase in self-esteem is likely, in turn, to build one's confidence and self-efficacy. As a result of those positive self-perceptions, we can expect OCB performance to increase as people perform above and beyond requirements. In fact, Lau and her colleagues (2014) found that self-esteem mediates the relationship between feeling trusted and OCB. Other related research also found that feeling trusted led to team-level OCB (Lam & Lau, 2008). Furthermore, Salamon and Robinson (2008) demonstrated that employees who collectively felt trusted by management performed better. Therefore, there is evidence that feeling trust positively impacts outcomes like performance and OCB.

Felt trust is important to the reinforcing spiral model because it demonstrates the reciprocal nature of perceptions between parties. Trust builds over time and is shared between parties as they build the relationships. As managers gain trust in subordinates and behave in a way to signal their trust, for example, the subordinates experience felt trust and have the confidence to engage in OCB. Thus, whereas an Actor's trust in a Partner precipitates OCB performance in the Actor, this model suggests that the Actor's OCB performance also may be predicated on the felt trust the Actor feels from the Partner.

Trust Violation and Recovery

The spiral model also suggests that trust and OCB mutually accumulate over time, and the behavioral components of this process are those behaviors that contribute to or detract from trust and OCB. The trust literature casts these as trust violations and trust recovery behaviors. Trust violations influence the reinforcing spiral of trust and OCB performance. In addition to the positive direction that this paper has discussed, the spiral can move in a negative trust direction over time. This section examines trust violation as the negative incarnation of the spiral.

Trust violations underscore the reciprocal nature of OCB and trust in that just as trust builds cooperation and OCB in a spiral fashion, violations diminish trust and OCB. From a social exchange perspective, trust violations are events or circumstances that fail to meet expectations, thereby reducing trust. Then, new, lower, or nonexistent trust expectation levels are set. This cycle of violations, responses, and renewed or reduced trust relates to OCB in a spiral fashion due to the link with cooperation. We cooperate with people for whom we have heuristic expectations of benevolence by engaging in OCB and likely reducing OCB performance as trust diminishes. Trust violations may completely undermine trust and therefore have a similar effect on OCB, or in some cases, trust can be recovered by apologizing or taking action to restore trust. To explore the trust violation-recovery components of the reinforcing spiral, it is informative to consider (a) different types of trust violations; (b) the reasons behind trust violations and how they affect perceptions; and (c) trust recovery efforts and their effectiveness.

Violation Types

Trust violations are actions or inactions taken by an Actor that affect a Partner and subsequently reduce perceptions of trustworthiness about the Actor. Mayer and colleagues' (1995) conceptualization of trustworthiness as ability, benevolence, and integrity is useful for considering different kinds of violations, because violations may influence each of the three dimensions. Trust violations involve a wide range of behavior, from behaviors purposely intended to undermine people's abilities to do their jobs to more mundane actions such as providing incorrect information (Grover, Hasel, Manville, & Serrano Archimi, 2014).

People respond to trust violations and recovery attempts based on whether the offenses are violations of competence or of integrity (Kim, Cooper, Dirks, & Ferrin, 2013; Kim, Dirks, Cooper, & Ferrin, 2006; Kim, Ferrin, Cooper, & Dirks, 2004). Trust can be restored more readily following competence violations because people view competence violations (i.e., mistakes) as correctable and transient, whereas they view integrity errors as failures of indelible characteristics (Kim, Dirks, & Cooper, 2009), and violations attributed to outright deception are viewed more negatively (Boles, Croson, & Murnighan, 2000). Kim and colleagues show that trust recovers more readily when people apologize for their violations of competence and that subsequent trust rarely returns when the violations were based on integrity. Their paradigm asks participants to imagine that they are hiring an accountant who made a mistake on a tax return either as an error (competence violation) or on purpose to the benefit of the client (integrity violation).

Subsequent trust recovery research on the leader–follower relationship follows a similar pattern to Kim and colleagues: Followers willingly forgive and attempt to reengage with supervisors who make a host of recoverable violations that are largely based on failures of competence. Yet followers are unwilling to continue a meaningful, trusting relationship with leaders who intentionally and harmfully violate followers' trust (Andiappan & Treviño, 2010; Grover et al., 2014). The value of apologies and substantive repair lies with assessments about the character of the offender, the one who violated trust, and therefore are moderated by beliefs about whether people can change (Haselhuhn, Schweitzer, & Wood, 2010). These assessments of character are informed by the type of violation, its severity, and importantly the motivation behind the violation, which hinges on intent and severity of the offense (Fehr, Gelfand, & Nag, 2010; Lewicki & Bunker, 1996; Tomlinson, Dineen, & Lewicki, 2004). Therefore, the effort to repair or the likelihood of accepting repair hinges on whether the harmed party believes that the cause of the violation can be addressed or is simply endemic to the person, or perhaps institution, from which it emanates (Grover, Manville, Abid-Dupont, & Hasel, 2015). Trust violations therefore reduce trust and subsequent OCB in the reinforcing spiral model. Thus, we expect that violations that are perceived to be related to an Actor's character (benevolence or integrity) lead to a downward spiral as the Partner perceives the Actor to have low trustworthiness. As a result, the Partner may refrain from OCB opportunities, which may signal to the Actor a lack of trust. When the Actor experiences lower felt trust, there may be similar withdrawal behaviors; thus, the relationship is likely to spiral downward without some intervention by one or both of the members or some outside agent.

Trust Recovery Efforts

Trust recovery depends on the amount of trust prior to a breach of trust, and recovery is more likely in a trusting relationship compared to one in which trust was lower prior to the violation. Breaches of trust that occur near the beginning of a relationship have greater impact compared to those that occur later in the relationship (Lount, Zhong, Sivanathan, & Murnighan, 2008). In this way, the consequences of trust violations may be mitigated by whether a history of OCB performance by a violator has enhanced trust over time. However, if OCB performance diminishes significantly and signals that trust was not as warranted, a trust violation has a more profound impact.

Trust violations harm trust but do not destroy it in many circumstances. A variety of actions can help to return trust (Elangovan, Werner, & Erna, 2015). Apologies, for example, may help to acknowledge that wrongs have been done and thus psychologically help to move a relationship in a positive direction (Schweitzer, Hershey, & Bradlow, 2006). Apologies, however, can be conceptualized as "cheap talk" and taking substantive action should be more likely to return trust (Nakayachi & Watabe, 2005). Schweitzer and colleagues found that substantive action, such as accepting a temporary loss in repeated round bargaining, was more effective in returning vanquished trust compared to simply apologizing (Schweitzer et al., 2006). Interestingly, Dirks, Kim, Ferrin, and Cooper (2011) find both apologies and substantive action work to restore trust to the extent that they signal repentance from the offender, thereby encouraging the other party back into the positive trust spiral.

Particularly relevant to OCB and the workplace is the finding that followers prefer making plans for the future that clarify perceptions of trust violation in the past (Grover et al., 2014).

The reinforcing spiral model works in the negative direction as described by the trust violation literature. Trust erodes slowly with most violations and, on the downward spiral, commensurate OCB is withdrawn. For most events that process may be fairly slow and can be remedied with repair actions. These actions depend largely on other character-related features of the other party (Grover & Hasel, 2015), which reinforces the mutual relationship development component of the reinforcing spiral model.

In summary, trust violation and recovery are part of normal daily interactions in organizations that interrelate with OCB. The likelihood of regaining lost trust depends largely on assessments of offenders' character and can be helped by making efforts toward reconciliation.

Future Extensions

One advantage of viewing the relationship between trust and OCB as dynamic and self-reinforcing is that it increases the potential ways that trust and OCB may affect each other. For example, while most work on trust and OCB suggests that the relationship is dyadic, focusing on the individual person, trust researchers have recently considered trust as a multilevel phenomenon that could affect the spiral model (Gillespie & Dietz, 2009; Korsgaard et al., 2015; Schilke & Cook, 2013). In fact, both OCB and trust are multilevel phenomena to the extent that they are subject to interpersonal-, group-, and organization-level influences (Bommer, Dierdorff, & Rubin, 2007). People have trust in the organizations that employ them to the extent that they invest in the organization's benefit with the belief that the organization as an entity will take care of them. This perception has a particularly strong effect on OCB, because OCB results from satisfaction with the organization. Similarly, whereas research on organizational-level trust is still slim, people presumably vary in the degree to which they willingly make themselves vulnerable to the organization, with the expectation that the organization attends to their interests. Gillespie and Dietz (2009) theorize that individual employees make attributions about the trustworthiness of the employing organization, suggesting that the attribution is multidimensional and comes from the leadership, culture, strategy, and structures, as well as external governance and public reputation. Distrust can be generated by these same characteristics, or rather, violations of trust may be derived from these characteristics, and therefore trust repair at the organizational level depends on the degree to which these issues are addressed.

Gillespie and Dietz's robust theory still has little empirical support with the exception of Gillespie, Dietz, and Lockey (2014), which examines how an organization returns trust after a fraud and data manipulation scandal. Part of trust rebuilding in that case was the organization itself showing penance through apologies but also a changing of the guard, which is a substantive action to indicate the make-up of the organization has changed.

The group within which people work is also an important level of analysis. Group performance is enhanced as group-level trust increases (Dirks, 1999). The group engagement model (Tyler & Blader, 2003) suggests that people invest in groups to the extent that their social identity is invested in the group and both the group trusts them and they trust the group. In particular, people invest in the group to the extent that they feel valued by the group (Ellemers, Sleebos, Stam, & de Gilder, 2013; Sleebos, Ellemers, & De Gilder, 2007). These are commensurate with OCB performance, albeit measured in a slightly different manner, and it is only a small theoretical step to suggest that this dynamic extends to OCB. OCB performance occurs at the group level and interacts with individual-level OCB. Group-level OCB corresponds with unit-level performance (Nielsen, Hrivnak, & Shaw, 2009; Podsakoff, Podsakoff, MacKenzie, Maynes, & Spoelma, 2014; Podsakoff, Whiting, Podsakoff, & Blume, 2009). As OCB level increases at the group level, it seems relevant that it should encourage OCB development (MacKenzie, Podsakoff, & Podsakoff, 2011). In sum, the spiral model of trust and OCB may extend to or be influenced by multilevel effects.

Concluding Remarks

This chapter has explored the relationship between OCB and trust with the express purpose of examining the complexities of the relationship through the lens of contemporary thinking about trust. Although research has clearly supported the idea that trust perceptions affect OCB performance, we propose that OCB performance also enhances trust perceptions. This reciprocal relationship supports the view that trust and OCB build in a reinforcing spiral, supporting both their positive occurrence and growth or their reduction and diminished growth. Enhancing and sustaining the reinforcing spiral relationship are the effects of felt trust and trust violation and recovery. This model challenges the traditional representation of OCB performance that depends on trust in a relationship and offers that both are in continuous development and mutually dependent. Both trust and OCB are strongly influenced by the actions of both parties in the relationship, the perceptions about and responses to those actions.

References

Anderson, K. (2015). 5 ways to build trust. *Results Coaching Global*. http://resultscoachingglobal.com/5-ways-to-build-trust/.

Andiappan, M., & Treviño, L. K. (2010). Beyond righting the wrong: Supervisor-subordinate reconciliation after an injustice. *Human Relations, 64*, 359–386.

Aryee, S., Budhwar, P. S., & Chen, Z. X. (2002). Trust as a mediator of the relationship between organizational justice and work outcomes: Test of a social exchange model. *Journal of Organizational Behavior, 23*, 267–285.

Balliet, D., & Van Lange, P. A. M. (2013). Trust, conflict, and cooperation: A meta-analysis. *Psychological Bulletin, 139*, 1090–1112.

Blau, P. M. (1964). *Exchange and power in social life*. New York, NY: Wiley.

Boles, T. L., Croson, R. T., & Murnighan, J. K. (2000). Deception and retribution in repeated ultimatum bargaining. *Organizational Behavior and Human Decision Processes, 83*, 235–259.

Bolino, M. C. (1999). Citizenship and impression management: Good soldiers or good actors? *Academy of Management Review, 24*, 82–98.

Bolino, M. C., Klotz, A. C., Turnley, W. H., & Harvey, J. (2013). Exploring the dark side of organizational citizenship behavior. *Journal of Organizational Behavior, 34*, 542–559.

Bommer, W. H., Dierdorff, E. C., & Rubin, R. S. (2007). Does prevalence mitigate relevance? The moderating effect of group-level OCB on employee performance. *Academy of Management Journal, 50*, 1481–1494.

Brower, H. H., Lester, S. W., Korsgaard, M. A., & Dineen, B. R. (2008). A closer look at trust between managers and subordinates: Understanding the effects of both trusting and being trusted on subordinate outcomes. *Journal of Management, 35*, 327–347.

Burke, C. S., Sims, D. E., Lazzara, E. H., & Salas, E. (2007). Trust in leadership: A multi-level review and integration. *The Leadership Quarterly, 18*, 606–632.

Butler, J. K. (1991). Toward understanding and measuring conditions of trust: Evolution of the conditions of trust inventory. *Journal of Management, 17*, 643–663.

Butler, J. K. (1983). Reciprocity of trust between professionals and their secretaries. *Psychological Reports, 53*, 411–416.

Colquitt, J. A., LePine, J. A., Piccolo, R. F., Zapata, C. P., & Rich, B. L. (2012). Explaining the justice–performance relationship: Trust as exchange deepener or trust as uncertainty reducer? *Journal of Applied Psychology, 97*, 101–123.

Colquitt, J. A., Scott, B. A., & LePine, J. A. (2007). Trust, trustworthiness, and trust propensity: A meta-analytic test of their unique relationships with risk taking and job performance. *Journal of Applied Psychology, 92*, 909–927.

Colquitt, J. A., & Zipay, K. P. (2015). Justice, fairness, and employee reactions. *Annual Review of Organizational Psychology and Organizational Behavior, 2*, 75–99.

Deluga, R. J. (1995). The relation between trust in the supervisor and subordinate organizational citizenship behavior. *Military Psychology, 7*, 1–16.

Dirks, K. T. (1999). The effects of interpersonal trust on work group performance. *Journal of Applied Psychology, 84*, 445–455

Dirks, K. T. (2000). Trust in leadership and team performance: Evidence from NCAA basketball. *Journal of Applied Psychology, 85*, 1004–1012.

Dirks, K. T., & Ferrin, D. L. (2001). The role of trust in organizational settings. *Organization Science, 12*, 450–467.

Dirks, K. T., & Ferrin, D. L. (2002). Trust in leadership: Meta-analytic findings and implications for research and practice. *Journal of Applied Psychology, 87*, 611–628.

Dirks, K. T., Kim, P. H., Ferrin, D. L., & Cooper, C. D. (2011). Understanding the effects of substantive responses on trust following a transgression. *Organizational Behavior and Human Decision Processes, 114*, 87–103.

Earley, P. C. (1986). Trust, perceived importance of praise and criticism, and work performance: An examination of feedback in the United States and England. *Journal of Management, 12*, 457–473.

Elangovan, A. R., Werner, A.-R., & Erna, S. (2015). It's the act that counts: minimizing post-violation erosion of trust. *Leadership & Organization Development Journal, 36*, 81–96.

Ellemers, N., Sleebos, E., Stam, D., & de Gilder, D. (2013). Feeling included and valued: How perceived respect affects positive team identity and willingness to invest in the team. *British Journal of Management, 24*, 21–37.

Farh, J. L., Tsui, A. S., Xin, K., & Cheng, B. S. (1998). The influence of relational demography and guanxi: The Chinese case. *Organization Science, 9*, 471–488.

Fehr, R., Gelfand, M. J., & Nag, M. (2010). The road to forgiveness: A meta-analytic synthesis of its situational and dispositional correlates. *Psychological Bulletin, 136*, 894–914.

Ferrin, D. L., Bligh, M. C., & Kohles, J. C. (2008). It takes two to tango: An interdependence analysis of the spiraling of perceived trustworthiness and cooperation in interpersonal and intergroup relationships. *Organizational Behavior and Human Decision Processes, 107*, 161–178.

Fox, A. (1974). *Beyond contract: Work, power and trust relations*. London: Faber & Faber.

Gillespie, N., & Dietz, G. (2009). Trust repair after an organization-level failure. *Academy of Management Review, 34*, 127–145.

Gillespie, N., Dietz, G., & Lockey, S. (2014). Organizational reintegration and trust repair after an integrity violation: A case study. *Business Ethics Quarterly, 24*, 374–410.

Gouldner, A. W. (1960). The norm of reciprocity: A preliminary statement. *American Sociological Review, 25*, 161–178.

Granovetter, M. (1985). Economic action and social structure: The problem of embeddedness. *American Journal of Sociology, 91*, 481–510.

Grover, S. L., & Hasel, M. C. (2015). How leaders recover (or not) from publicized sex scandals. *Journal of Business Ethics, 129*, 177–194.

Grover, S. L., Hasel, M. C., Manville, C., & Serrano Archimi, C. (2014). Follower reactions to leader trust violations: A grounded theory of violation types, likelihood of recovery, and recovery process. *European Management Journal, 32*, 689–702.
Grover, S. L., Manville, C., Abid-Dupont, M.-A., & Hasel, M. C. (2015). *Trust recovery between leaders and followers: The importance of character attributions.* Paper presented at the annual meetings of the Academy of Management, Vancouver.
Haselhuhn, M. P., Schweitzer, M. E., & Wood, A. M. (2010). How implicit beliefs influence trust recovery. *Psychological Science, 21*, 645–648.
Hoffman, B. J., Blair, C. A., Meriac, J. P., & Woehr, D. J. (2007). Expanding the criterion domain? A quantitative review of the OCB literature. *Journal of Applied Psychology, 92*, 555.
Homans, G. C. (1974). *Social behavior: Its elementary forms* (Revised ed.). New York, NY: Harcourt Brace.
Jones, G. R., & George, J. M. (1998). The experience and evolution of trust: Implications for cooperation and teamwork. *Academy of Management Review, 23*, 531–546.
Kacmar, K. M., Bachrach, D. G., Harris, K. J., & Noble, D. (2012). Exploring the role of supervisor trust in the associations between multiple sources of relationship conflict and organizational citizenship behavior. *The Leadership Quarterly, 23*, 43–54.
Kanfer, R., & Ackerman, P. L. (1989). Motivation and cognitive abilities: An integrative/aptitude-treatment interaction approach to skill acquisition. *Journal of Applied Psychology, 74*, 659–690.
Katz, D., & Kahn, R. L. (1978). *The social psychology of organizations.* New York, NY: Wiley.
Kim, P. H., Cooper, C. D., Dirks, K. T., & Ferrin, D. L. (2013). Repairing trust with individuals vs. groups. *Organizational Behavior and Human Decision Processes, 120*, 1–14.
Kim, P. H., Dirks, K. T., & Cooper, C. D. (2009). The repair of trust: A dynamic bilateral perspective and multilevel conceptualization. *Academy of Management Review, 34*, 401–422.
Kim, P. H., Dirks, K. T., Cooper, C. D., & Ferrin, D. L. (2006). When more blame is better than less: The implications of internal vs. external attributions for the repair of trust after a competence- vs. integrity- based trust violation. *Organizational Behavior and Human Decision Processes, 34*, 401–422.
Kim, P. H., Ferrin, D. L., Cooper, C. D., & Dirks, K. T. (2004). Removing the shadow of suspicion: The effects of apology versus denial for repairing competence- versus integrity-based trust violations. *Journal of Applied Psychology, 89*, 104–118.
Konovsky, M. A. & Pugh, S. D. (1994). Citizenship behavior and social exchange. *Academy of Management Journal, 37*, 656–669.
Korsgaard, M. A., Brower, H. H., & Lester, S. W. (2015). It isn't always mutual: A critical review of dyadic trust. *Journal of Management, 41*, 47–70.
Korsgaard, M. A., Whitener, E. M., & Brodt, S. E. (2002). Trust in the face of conflict: The role of managerial trustworthy behavior and organizational context. *Journal of Applied Psychology, 87*, 312–319.
Lam, L. W., & Lau, D. C. (2008). Work climate and customer satisfaction: The role of trust in the retail context. *Journal of Management & Organization, 14*, 141–154.
Larson, A. (1992). Network dyads in entrepreneurial settings: A study of the governance of exchange relationships. *Administrative Science Quarterly, 37*, 76–104.
Lau, D. C., Lam, L. W., & Wen, S. S. (2014). Examining the effects of feeling trusted by supervisors in the workplace: A self-evaluative perspective. *Journal of Organizational Behavior, 35*, 112–127.
Lester, S. W., & Brower, H. H. (2003). In the eyes of the beholder: The relationship between subordinates' felt trustworthiness and their work attitudes and behaviors. *Journal of Leadership & Organizational Studies, 10*, 17–33.
Lewicki, R. J., & Bunker, B. B. (1996). Developing and maintaining trust in work relationships. In R. M. Kramer & T. R. Tyler (Eds.), *Trust in organizations: Frontiers of theory and research* (pp. 114–139). Thousand Oaks, CA: Sage.
Lewicki, R. J., Tomlinson, E. C., & Gillespie, N. (2006). Models of interpersonal trust development: Theoretical approaches, empirical evidence, and future directions. *Journal of Management, 32*, 991–1022.
Lount, R. B., Jr., Zhong, C. B., Sivanathan, N., & Murnighan, J. K. (2008). Getting off on the wrong foot: The timing of a breach and the restoration of trust. *Personality and Social Psychology Bulletin, 34*, 1601–1612.
Luhmann, N. (1979). *Trust and power.* New York, NY: John Willey & Sons.
MacKenzie, S. B., & Podsakoff, P. M., & Podsakoff, N. P. (2011). Effects of challenge-oriented and affiliation-oriented OCBs on organizational effectiveness: Do challenge-oriented behaviors really have an impact on the organization's bottom-line? *Personnel Psychology, 64*, 559–592.
MacKenzie, S. B., Podsakoff, P. M., & Rich, G. A. (2001). Transformational and transactional leadership and salesperson performance. *Journal of the Academy of Marketing Science, 29*, 115–134.
Mayer, R. C. & Davis, J. H. (1999). The effect of the performance appraisal system on trust for management: A field quasi-experiment. *Journal of Applied Psychology, 84*, 123.
Mayer, R. C., Davis, J. H., & Schoorman, F. D. (1995). An integrative model of organizational trust. *Academy of Management Review, 20*, 709–734.
Mayer, R. C., & Gavin, M. B. (2005). Trust in management and performance: Who minds the shop while the employees watch the boss? *Academy of Management Journal, 48*, 874–888.
McEvily, B. (2011). Reorganizing the boundaries of trust: From discrete alternatives to hybrid forms. *Organization Science, 22*, 1266–1276.
Möllering, G., Bachmann, R., & Lee, S. H. (2004). Introduction: Understanding organizational trust-foundations, constellations, and issues of operationalization. *Journal of Managerial Psychology, 19*, 556–570.
Moorman, R. H. (1991). Relationship between organizational justice and organizational citizenship behaviors: Do fairness perceptions influence employee citizenship? *Journal of Applied Psychology, 76*, 845–855.
Moorman, R. H., & Blakely, G. L. (1995). Individualism-collectivism as an individual difference predictor of organizational citizenship behavior. *Journal of Organizational Behavior, 16*, 127–142.
Nakayachi, K., & Watabe, M. (2005). Restoring trustworthiness after adverse events: The signaling effects of voluntary "hostage posting" on trust. *Organizational Behavior and Human Decision Processes, 97*, 1–17.
Nielsen, T. M., Hrivnak, G. A., & Shaw, M. (2009). Organizational citizenship behavior and performance: A meta-analysis of group-level research. *Small Group Research, 40*, 555–577.

Organ, D. W. (1977). A reappraisal and reinterpretation of the satisfaction-causes-performance hypothesis. *Academy of Management Review, 2,* 46–53.

Organ, D. W. (1988). *Organizational citizenship behavior: The good soldier syndrome.* Lexington, MA: Lexington Books.

Organ, D. W. (1990). The motivational basis of organizational citizenship behavior. In B. M. Staw & L. L. Cummings (Eds.), *Research in organizational behavior* (Vol. 12, pp. 43–72). Greenwich, CT: JAI Press.

Organ, D. W. (1997). Organizational citizenship behavior: It's construct clean-up time. *Human Performance, 10,* 85–97.

Organ, D. W., Podsakoff, P. M., & MacKenzie, S. B. (2005). *Organizational citizenship behavior: Its nature, antecedents, and consequences.* Thousand Oaks, CA: Sage Publications.

Peachey, D. E., & Lerner, M. J. (1981). Law as a social trap. In M. J. Lerner & S. C. Lerner (Eds.), *The justice motive in social behavior* (pp. 439–461). New York, NY: Springer.

Pearce, J. L. (1993). Toward an organizational behavior of contract laborers: Their psychological involvement and effects on employee co-workers. *Academy of Management Journal, 36,* 1082–1096.

Pettit, J. D., Goris, J. R., & Vaught, B. C. (1997). An examination of organizational communication as a moderator of the relationship between job performance and job satisfaction. *Journal of Business Communication, 34,* 81–98.

Pillai, R., Schriesheim, C. A., & Williams, E. S. (1999). Fairness perceptions and trust as mediators for transformational and transactional leadership: A two-sample study. *Journal of Management, 25,* 897–933.

Podsakoff, N. P., Podsakoff, P. M., MacKenzie, S. B., Maynes, T. D., & Spoelma, T. M. (2014). Consequences of unit-level organizational citizenship behaviors: A review and recommendations for future research. *Journal of Organizational Behavior, 35,* S87–S119.

Podsakoff, N. P., Whiting, S. W., Podsakoff, P. M., & Blume, B. D. (2009). Individual- and organizational-level consequences of organizational citizenship behaviors: A meta-analysis. *Journal of Applied Psychology, 94,* 122–141.

Podsakoff, P. M., MacKenzie, S. B., & Bommer, W. H. (1996). Transformational leader behaviors and substitutes for leadership as determinants of employee satisfaction, commitment, trust, and organizational citizenship behaviors. *Journal of Management, 22,* 259–298.

Podsakoff, P. M., MacKenzie, S. B., Moorman, R. H., & Fetter, R. (1990). Transformational leader behaviors and their effects on followers' trust in leader, satisfaction, and organizational citizenship behaviors. *The Leadership Quarterly, 1,* 107–142.

Rich, G. A. (1997). The sales manager as a role model: Effects on trust, job satisfaction, and performance of salespeople. *Journal of the Academy of Marketing Science, 25,* 319–328.

Rotter, J. (1967). A new scale for the measurement of interpersonal trust. *Journal of Personality, 35,* 651–65.

Rotter, J. B. (1980). Interpersonal trust, trustworthiness, and gullibility. *American Psychologist, 35,* 1.

Rousseau, D. M., Sitkin, S. B., Burt, R. S., & Camerer, C. (1998). Not so different after all: A cross-discipline view of trust. *Academy of Management Review, 23,* 393–404.

Salamon, S. D., & Robinson, S. L. (2008). Trust that binds: The impact of collective felt trust on organizational performance. *Journal of Applied Psychology, 93,* 593.

Schilke, O., & Cook, K. S. (2013). A cross-level process theory of trust development in interorganizational relationships. *Strategic Organization, 11,* 281–303.

Schweitzer, M. E., Hershey, J. C., & Bradlow, E. T. (2006). Promises and lies: Restoring violated trust. *Organizational Behavior and Human Decision Processes, 101,* 1–19.

Schoorman, F. D., Mayer, R. C., & Davis, J. H. (2007). An integrative model of organizational trust: Past, present, and future. *Academy of Management Review, 32,* 344–354.

Shapiro, S. P. (1987). The social control of impersonal trust. *American Journal of Sociology, 93,* 623–658.

Sitkin, S. B., & Roth, N. L. (1993). Explaining the limited effectiveness of legalistic "remedies" for trust/distrust. *Organization Science, 4,* 367–392.

Sleebos, E., Ellemers, N., & de Gilder, D. (2007). Explaining the motivational forces of (dis) respect: How self-focused and group-focused concerns can result in the display of group-serving efforts. *Group Dynamics and Organizational Consulting, 38,* 327–342.

Solomon, R. C., & Flores, F. (2001). *Building trust: In business, politics, relationships, and life.* New York, NY: Oxford University Press.

Tomlinson, E. C., Dineen, B. R., & Lewicki, R. J. (2004). The road to reconciliation: Antecedents of victim willingness to reconcile following a broken promise. *Journal of Management, 30,* 165–187.

Tyler, T. R., & Blader, S. L. (2003). The group engagement model: Procedural justice, social identity, and cooperative behavior. *Personality and Social Psychology Review, 7,* 349–361.

Van Dyne, L., Cummings, L. L., & Parks, J. M. (1995). Extra-role behaviors—In pursuit of construct and definitional clarity (a bridge over muddied waters). *Research in Organizational Behavior, 17,* 215–285.

Wagner, S. L., & Rush, M. C. (2000). Altruistic organizational citizenship behavior: Context, disposition, and age. *The Journal of Social Psychology, 140,* 379–391.

Weber, J. M., Malhotra, D., & Murnighan, J. K. (2005). Normal acts of irrational trust: Motivated attributions and the trust development process. *Research in Organizational Behavior, 26,* 75–101.

Whitener, E. M., Brodt, S. E., Korsgaard, M. A., & Werner, J. M. (1998). Managers as initiators of trust: An exchange relationship framework for understanding managerial trustworthy behavior. *Academy of Management Review, 23,* 513–530.

Yakovleva, M., Reilly, R. R., & Werko, R. (2010). Why do we trust? Moving beyond individual to dyadic perceptions. *Journal of Applied Psychology, 95,* 79–91.

Zand, D. E. (1972). Trust and managerial problem solving. *Administrative Science Quarterly, 17,* 229–239.

Zucker, L. G. (1986). Production of trust: Institutional sources of economic structure, 1840–1920. *Research in Organizational Behavior, 8,* 53–111.

CHAPTER

17 Leadership [Is] Organizational Citizenship Behavior: Review of a Self-Evident Link

Ronald F. Piccolo, Claudia Buengeler, *and* Timothy A. Judge

Abstract

In this chapter, we focus on the theoretical and empirical relationship between leadership and organizational citizenship behavior (OCB), arguing that leadership, at its conceptual core, is extra-role behavior (i.e., leadership [is] OCB). Updating and extending Organ, Podsakoff, and MacKenzie's (2006) chapter, we review both traditional (e.g., transformational leadership, transactional leadership, initiating structure, and consideration behaviors) and contemporary models of leader behavior (e.g., ethical, authentic, and servant leadership behaviors). In doing so, we report meta-analytic results comparing leadership models and the activities that underlie those models. We close by discussing three potential avenues for continued research in this domain.

Key Word: leadership, OCB, review, meta-analysis, extra-role behavior

In both modern and classical models of effective leadership, a link between leadership and followers' willingness to exhibit contextual, prosocial or extra-role behavior is largely self-evident. Effective leadership is often defined in terms of outcomes that reflect fundamental citizenship among followers, and leadership, in some respects, is revealed when followers do more than they would otherwise, or more than that required by a particular job (i.e., contextual performance). Persuasive leaders find ways to move followers beyond the "zone of indifference" (Barnard, 1938), or that troublesome state realized when individuals complacently and unconsciously accept orders and limits without active pursuit of anything more.

Several of the most popular scales used to measure modern concepts in leadership include items that assess a follower's willingness to go beyond formal requirements of the job (e.g., leader–member exchange [LMX], "I am willing to apply extra efforts, beyond those normally required, to help my supervisor"; Liden & Maslyn, 1998). In this way, leadership is defined by an employee's willingness to go above and beyond (i.e., to exhibit organizational citizenship behavior [OCB]). If effective management is revealed by one's ability to encourage employee efficiency in completing assignments (Kotter, 1990), leadership may be defined, at least in part, by one's ability to encourage OCB.

A number of recent studies have summarized effects of leadership on variants of OCB (e.g., Chiaburu, Lorinkova, & Van Dyne, 2013; Ilies, Nahrgang, & Morgeson, 2007; Judge & Piccolo, 2004, Podsakoff, Bommer, Podsakoff, & MacKenzie, 2006). In general, primary studies and literature reviews report robust influence of various leadership styles with facets of OCB, and they explain those effects, to the extent possible, through both cognitive (*job perceptions*; Piccolo & Colquitt, 2006) and affective mechanisms (*trust*; Podsakoff, MacKenzie, & Bommer, 1996a; Podsakoff, MacKenzie, Moorman, & Fetter, 1990). These summaries provide insight on the classic and neo-classical models of leadership such as LMX (Ilies et al., 2007), transformational leadership (Judge

& Piccolo, 2004), and substitutes for leadership (Podsakoff, MacKenzie, & Bommer, 1996b).

In this chapter, we seek to extend Organ, Podsakoff, and MacKenzie's (2006) review of the literature linking leadership and OCB by introducing studies of "new" models of leadership (servant, ethical, and authentic leadership) with the various manifestations of organizational citizenship (e.g., altruism, sportsmanship, etc.). In doing so, we follow the structure and organization of their chapter. First, we describe how leadership is often defined and measured in terms of the citizenship behavior exhibited by followers. Second, we summarize several recently published meta-analyses that clarify links between various models of leadership and OCB. Third, we review a sample of primary studies published since 2006 that highlight a leader's role in providing the motivation and opportunity (Organ et al., 2006) for followers to engage in OCB. In doing so, we highlight the various theoretical mechanisms that specify the role of leader behaviors in the encouragement of follower OCBs. Finally, we report results of a meta-analysis based on a sample of studies of servant, ethical, and authentic leadership. Results reveal similarities and differences in the extent to which these leadership models affect aggregate OCB.

Leadership [Is] Organizational Citizenship Behavior

In an influential treatment of the difference between management and leadership, Kotter (1990) described the essential activities of managers as dealing with complexity in organizations by structuring processes to ensure consistency and order. According to Kotter, especially effective managers deal with complexity by developing specific plans and budgets that guide decision making, crafting control systems that distinguish between which activities are rewarded and which are punished, and clarifying role expectations that delineate position-specific responsibilities and authority. In essence, managers use organizational controls to direct employee behavior toward task-oriented aspects of performance.

As a contrast, Kotter (1990) described the essential activities of leaders as dealing with change (rather than complexity). By articulating vision and broad direction (rather than a specific plan) and by tapping basic human needs, leaders, according to Kotter, inspire followers to overcome obstacles and enthusiastically adapt to organizational changes. These particular employee adaptations are akin to the sportsmanship dimension (Organ, 1988) of organizational citizenship. Kotter also noted that leaders equip their followers to solve problems on their own and advance the organization's mission. These actions reflect the conscientiousness and civic virtue aspects of OCB. According to this characterization, leaders are different from managers because leadership is ultimately realized in the extra effort of those being led.

In the wide array of models, theories, and philosophies of leadership, several concepts are directly reflective of Kotter's description of essential management activities. Initiating Structure, for example, is a fundamental set of behaviors from the Ohio State studies of leadership that focus on task accomplishment and goal attainment. Leaders who "initiate structure" seek to establish specific patterns of communication with followers, encourage the use of uniform procedures, and ask group members to follow standard rules and regulations (Stogdill, 1963). Initiating Structure is the degree to which leaders define and organize their role and the roles of their followers making special effort to maintain standards for the manner in which work is to be accomplished (Fleishman, 1973). As such, the Initiating Structure concept includes many of the management activities described by Kotter but also touches on conscientiousness (e.g., adherence to the rules, regulations, and procedures of the organization), a fundamental manifestation of OCB. Initiating Structure is positively associated with a host of important organizational outcomes, including motivation, task performance, and job satisfaction (Judge, Piccolo, & Ilies, 2004).

Contingent reward is the most active of three components of transactional leadership in Avolio and Bass's (1991) Full Range of Leadership model, a continuum of leader behaviors ranging from passive and ineffective (laissez-faire), to active, inspirational, and productive (transformational; Avolio, 2011). The Full Range model consolidates and characterizes distinctive leader behaviors, ascribing varied levels of effectiveness to different leadership styles. According to the model, contingent reward is less active, impactful, and effective than transformational leadership, but more so than laissez-faire.

Those who utilize "contingent reward" leadership clarify expectations for performance and behavior, and specify rewards for meeting those expectations. Similar to Initiating Structure and Kotter's description of managerial attempts to effect control, leaders use contingent reward to discuss in specific terms the share of responsibility among team members and what employees can expect when goals are achieved (Bass & Avolio, 1995). A persistent assertion in the Full Range model is an augmentation effect, in which transformational leadership adds to, and *augments*, the effect of transactional leadership. Bass (1985) described this effect as the degree to which "transformational leadership styles build on the transactional base in contributing to the extra effort and performance of followers" (p. 5). Thus, in terms of encouraging OCBs, transformational leadership would presumably yield higher overall effects.

However, the contingent reward dimension of transactional leadership goes well beyond short-term economic exchange. This particular dimension in the Full Range model engenders a long-term social exchange relationship between leaders and followers, especially regarding praise and recognition, which are often internalized as indicators of approval, status, and success. Further, by specifying the outcomes associated with specific levels of task accomplishment, contingent reward fosters a direct link between performance and rewards, strengthening the motivational impact of incentives and enhancing the expectancy that effort will be rewarded (Vroom, 1964). Consequently, contrary to Bass and Avolio's (1995) declaration of the transformational leadership's superiority, contingent reward is as strongly associated with indicators of leadership effectiveness (follower job satisfaction, motivation, leader performance) as transformational leadership (Judge & Piccolo, 2004).

In recognition that Avolio and Bass's (1991) Full Range model of leadership did not include task and strategic-facilitation functions of managers, Antonakis and House (2002) extended the Path-Goal (House, 1971) model of leadership by identifying a set of *instrumental leadership* activities such as environmental monitoring, strategy formulation and implementation, goal facilitation, and outcome monitoring. These particular activities are familiar to any practicing executive who knows that the success of an enterprise can depend only sparingly on the motivation, inspiration, or psychological arousal of its members. Instrumental leader behaviors reflect the realities of operating an organization in a competitive context. When the rubber meets the road, leaders must understand the context in which an organization lives, identify competitive strategies, and remove obstacles to goal attainment.

We highlight these three concepts in managerial behavior to demonstrate how Kotter's (1990) "manager vs. leader" description is realized in popular models and theories of leadership. We also provide a contrast between supervisory behaviors that foster control, conformity, and consistency with those that encourage deviations from standards and strict boundaries. When evaluated in relation to broader leadership models, supervisory activities emphasizing control, conformity, and consistency tend to yield lower overall validities (Judge & Piccolo, 2004; Piccolo et al., 2012) with OCB. Our own meta-analysis reported at the end of this chapter draws on Yukl, Gordon, and Taber's (2002) hierarchical taxonomy of leader behaviors to estimate effects associated with particular leader behaviors (e.g., task oriented), rather than isolated theories. Doing so identifies the utility of specific leader behaviors, independent of model origin. This contrast highlights differences between managerial behaviors that specify roles, responsibilities, and rewards for employees to meet expectations, and leader behaviors that encourage employees to go above and beyond. In doing so, we seek to make a case for one possible answer to the question, What is leadership? It is the ability to get others to go above and beyond.

Defining Leadership as Organizational Citizenship Behavior

In the following paragraphs, we seek to illustrate that the link between leadership and OCB is self-evident in two distinct ways. First, leadership is often defined and measured by the extra-role behaviors of followers, such that a follower's willingness to engage in OCBs is an explicit indicator of a leader's effectiveness. As such, leadership is ultimately realized when followers do more than expected. One could argue, for example, when followers go above and beyond, leadership has occurred.

Second, many models of leadership define the concept by highlighting how leaders themselves go beyond the basic instrumental tasks of supervision. That is, leadership, at its core, is extra-role behavior, especially when the role is managing others or an organization. As distinct from managers, for example, leaders engage in actions, emotions, and relationship-building activities that are beyond that required by traditional day-to-day operations. It is for this reason that Bass and Avolio (1993) suggested that transformational leadership, comprised of enhanced activities such as intellectual stimulation, would augment basic management functions such as specifying task demands and related rewards (transactional leadership).

As described earlier, leadership is often defined and measured in terms of the extra-role, prosocial and citizenship behavior of followers. In Liden and Maslyn's (1998) measure of LMX, for example, employees are asked to indicate the extent to which they work or provide support for their supervisors that *goes beyond what is specified in their job descriptions*, along with their willingness to *apply extra efforts, beyond those normally required*, to help their supervisors. In other words, the quality of a leader's relationship with subordinates (i.e., LMX) is defined in part by the employee's willingness to exhibit OCB.

Additional examples of this phenomenon can be found in measures of servant, transformational, and charismatic leadership. To assess servant leadership, followers indicate the extent to which managers encourage them to "volunteer in the community" (Barbuto & Wheeler, 2006), a concept that reflects the civic virtue dimension of OCB. To assess transformational leadership (Podsakoff et al., 1990), followers report whether managers encourage them to collaborate with work group members, be "team players," and demonstrate team attitude and spirit. These items reflect the altruism and sportsmanship aspects of OCB. Lastly, Conger and Kanungo (1998) measured charismatic leadership in part by asking followers about their loyalty to the organization (civic virtue) and willingness to express ideas and opinions (voice).

Table 17.1 provides a sample of items from popular scales used to measure various leadership concepts. As these measures suggest, it is common to define and equate leadership behavior (and implicitly, its effectiveness) with the OCBs of followers. To paraphrase United States Supreme Court Justice

Table 17.1 Sample of Leadership Scale Items That Refer to Concepts in Organizational Citizenship

Leadership Construct	Item Examples	OCB Dimension
Servant Leadership Barbuto & Wheeler (2006)	*My leader . . .* - Encourages me to have a community spirit in the workplace. - Goes above and beyond the call of duty to meet my needs. - Encourages me to volunteer in the community.	 Civic virtue Extra-role Civic virtue
Servant Leadership Liden et al. (2008)	- Cares about my personal well-being. - Takes time to talk to me on a personal level.	OBC-I [a] Courtesy
Transformational Leadership Podsakoff et al. (1990)	- Fosters collaboration among work groups. - Encourages employees to be "team players." - Develops a team attitude and spirit among employees.	Altruism Sportsmanship Sportsmanship
Leader–Member Exchange Liden and Maslyn (1998)	- Does work that goes beyond what is specified in the job description. - Is willing to apply extra efforts, beyond those normally required, to help others.	Extra-role Extra-role
Ethical Leadership Brown et al. (2005)	- Listens to what employees have to say.	Voice
Consideration Schriesheim and Stogdill (1975)	- Does little things to make it pleasant to be a member of the group. - Looks out for the personal welfare of group members.	Altruism OCB-O[a] Prosocial[b]
Initiating Structure Schriesheim and Stogdill (1975)	- Encourages the use of uniform procedures. - Asks that group members follow standard rules and regulations.	Civic virtue Conscientiousness

[a] Williams and Anderson (1991).

[b] Brief and Motowidlo (1986).

Potter Stewart's famous threshold evaluation of obscenity ("I'll know it when I see it"), how might we know leadership? According to many of the most popular academic measures, we know it when we see followers engage in OCBs. Van Knippenberg and Sitkin (2013) explicitly critiqued the pervasiveness of this phenomenon, noting that in much of modern leadership research, especially the transformational and charismatic paradigm, "conceptualization and operationalization confounds [leadership] with its effects" (p. 1).

In addition, the very concept of "leadership" itself is often realized by the demonstration of extra-role behavior by the leader (i.e., leadership *is* organizational citizenship). Indeed, popular descriptions of exceptional leaders highlight the extent to which leaders interact with followers in ways that go above and beyond the basic functions of instrumental supervision. The *Leadership Practices Inventory* (Kouzes & Posner, 1987), for example, seeks to assess the degree to which supervisors actively listen to diverse points of view (voice), treat people with dignity and respect (courtesy), and show others how their interests can be realized (courtesy). Barbuto and Wheeler's (2006) measure of servant leaders asks followers to indicate the extent to which leaders "[go] above and beyond the call of duty" to meet follower needs. And given that leaders, both formal and informal, are typically expected to demonstrate loyalty and pride for the organization, take action to protect the organization from harm, express concern for the well-being of group members, and take personal interest in others—all common expressions of organizational citizenship—one can clearly see how common descriptions of "leadership" treat a link with OCB as self-evident.

Empirical Summaries Linking Leadership With Organizational Citizenship Behavior

In the last three decades, the link between leadership and OCBs has been examined in hundreds of primary studies and summarized in several empirical reviews. In the following paragraphs, we highlight the reviews published since the publication of Organ's et al. (2006) book on OCB that link different models of leadership with OCB. In particular, there has been an ongoing interest in linking the effects of traditional leadership constructs, such as LMX and the Full Range of Leadership model with some form of OCB, as evidenced in most of the published empirical reviews. We then summarize a sample of primary studies of relatively new concepts: servant, ethical, and authentic leadership.

Traditional Leadership Constructs

LMX theory is based on the social exchange relationships that form between leaders and followers. On the basis of 9,324 employees clustered in 50 independent samples that were surveyed before or during 2005, Ilies et al. (2007) performed a meta-analysis of the relationship between LMX and employee OCB. The overall correlation between LMX and OCB was positive (ρ = .37), suggesting very clearly that followers who have a high-quality relationship with their supervisors are more likely to exert extra effort. Effect sizes were higher for citizenship behaviors directed to individuals (e.g., altruism, helping, courtesy, interpersonal facilitation) as compared to behaviors directed to the organization (e.g., demonstrating loyalty to the organization, offering ideas to improve organizational functioning). The estimated population correlation reported in the Ilies et al. study suggests that the benefits arising from LMX exceed the realm of in-role performance. Similar results were reported by Dulebohn et al. (2012), who summarized results from 247 studies to report a positive association between LMX and OCB (ρ = .39). These findings support the idea that followers tend to reciprocate positive treatment from leaders by engaging in extra-role behavior.

The studies by Ilies et al. (2007) and Dulebohn et al. (2012) confirm a robust link between relationship quality (e.g., LMX) and followers' willingness to engage in OCB (See also, Vidyarthi et al., 2010). These effects can be attributed to a felt obligation among followers who are often compelled to reciprocate the good favor they have received by acting in ways that are beneficial for the supervisor, colleagues, and the organization as a whole. Because of this sense of obligation, followers in high-quality relationships feel as though they *ought* to go above and beyond the call of duty. Thus, the relationship between LMX and OCB is typically explained as a function of social exchange and a shared obligation.

LMX is strongly associated with OCB in its various forms, but these effects may vary based on contextual factors such as national culture. In a meta-analysis based on 282 independent samples (N = 68,587) derived from 23 countries, Rockstuhl, Dulebohn, Ang, and Shore (2012) showed that the positive relationship of LMX with OCB was stronger in national cultures with a horizontal-individualistic orientation than with a vertical-collectivistic orientation. Horizontal individualism is a way of seeing the self as fully autonomous, believing that equality between individuals is an ideal (Triandis & Gelfand, 1998). Vertical collectivism is a way of seeing the self as a part of a collective and being willing to accept hierarchy and inequality within that collective. Thus, although employees' engagement in extra-role behaviors appears to be sensitive to a leader's treatment in both cultural configurations, the smaller effect size in countries with a vertical-collectivistic orientation suggests that other factors such as role-based loyalty and the interests of the collective may be influential in this setting as well. This finding highlights limits on the ability of exchange-based dyadic relationships to stimulate extra-role behavior in certain cultural settings. Interestingly, national culture did not moderate the LMX–in-role performance relationship.

Chiaburu et al. (2013) used meta-analysis to compare the effects of three forms of leadership (transformational leadership, contingent reward, and LMX) on employee proactive versus prosocial examples of contextual performance. Based on 42 independent samples containing responses from 8,882 employees, the authors found that all three types of leadership are positively related to OCB. Unexpectedly, change-oriented (transformational) leadership was not more effective than the other two forms of leadership in stimulating contextual performance.

On the basis of 117 independent samples, Wang, Oh, Courtright, and Colbert (2011) sought to meta-analytically disentangle the effects of transformational as compared with contingent reward leadership on other-rated contextual and task performance at various levels of analysis. Transformational leadership was more strongly and positively associated with supervisor-rated OCB and other extra-role behavior than with task performance at the individual level. Transformational leadership explained more variance in contextual performance, whereas contingent reward was found to explain more variance in task performance. For individual-level contextual performance, transformational leadership augmented the positive effect of contingent reward, whereas contingent reward did not explain additional variance beyond transformational leadership.

Jackson, Rossi, Rickamer Hoover, and Johnson (2012) performed structural equation modeling using meta-analytic estimates of the associations between leader reward behavior and employee outcomes in the form of OCB, task performance, and turnover intention, and the intervening mechanisms of employee fairness perceptions and work morale. Although the authors could not establish a direct relationship between a leader's contingent reward behavior and OCB, there was an indirect relationship between contingent reward and OCB. Specifically, contingent reward positively related to employee justice perceptions and OCB, a link that was fully mediated by employee morale. By contrast, there was a direct link between contingent reward and task performance. These results suggest that contingent reward as such may not instigate extra-role behavior directly, but through shaping perceptions related to commitment, satisfaction, and justice.

Podsakoff, Bommer, Podsakoff, and MacKenzie (2006) collected new and published primary data to meta-analytically estimate the link between contingent and noncontingent leader reward and punishment behavior and follower outcomes, including extra effort and the dimensions of OCB, namely altruism, courtesy, conscientiousness, civic virtue, and sportsmanship. The strength and direction of the established relationships between reward and punishment behavior with OCB were comparable with those found with task performance (except for civic virtue). With respect to employee extra effort, contingent reward and noncontingent punishment had the strongest impact (β = .65 and β = –.13, respectively). Examining the unique effects of each of the studied leader behavior on OCB (controlling for the effects of the respective other leader behaviors) revealed that contingent reward had a markedly stronger effect on extra effort (β = .83) than noncontingent punishment behavior (β = –.33). By contrast, the effects of both contingent reward and noncontingent punishment on employee in-role performance were similarly strong (but diametrically opposed: average β = .15 and –.15, respectively), and they were stronger than those of noncontingent reward behavior (β = .06) and contingent punishment (β = .02). For the dimensions of OCB, the authors hypothesized that contingent reward was a stronger predictor than noncontingent reward, which was confirmed in their meta-analysis.

Modern Leadership Constructs

Using 35 independent samples, Simons, Leroy, Collewaert, and Masschelein (2015) examined the relationship between a leader's integrity, a fundamental component of ethical and authentic leadership, and follower outcomes, including OCB. Results of the meta-analysis revealed a positive relationship between leader behavioral integrity, defined as the alignment between words and deeds, and follower OCB. Seeking to disentangle different aspects of leader integrity, the authors showed that effects of leader integrity on OCB were larger for behavioral integrity than for moral integrity and psychological contract breach by comparing effect sizes obtained from prior meta-analyses. Subsequent meta-analytic structural equation modeling revealed that behavioral integrity impacts performance (in-role performance and OCB) both directly and indirectly through trust and commitment. According to the authors, the partial mediation suggests the existence of other mechanisms through which behavioral integrity affects in-role and extra-role performance such as communication clarity.

In their meta-analysis based on 57 studies, Schyns and Schilling (2013) illuminated the effects of the dark side of leadership (e.g., abusive supervision, coercive power, social undermining, despotic leadership, and unsupportive managerial behaviors) on both positive (OCB, individual performance) and negative outcomes. Overall, abusive supervision (k = 7) and other forms of destructive leadership (k = 5) had a significant negative effect on a composite measure of in-role and extra-role performance, including OCB, performance, and work effort (r = –.18 and –.22, respectively). However, effects of destructive leadership on attitudinal outcomes related to the leader (e.g., satisfaction with the leader) or the job (e.g., job satisfaction) were more strongly negative than those on performance.

Theoretical Explanations for the Relationship Between Leadership and Organizational Citizenship Behavior

Organ et al. (2006) argued that an employee's willingness and motivation to engage in citizenship behavior is "determined by how much the employee *wants* to engage in the behavior and/or how much the employee feels that he or she *ought* to engage" (p. 93). Citizenship behavior is also a function of an employee's *ability* to engage, in an environment where such behavior is encouraged and supported (i.e., employees have an *opportunity* to engage). Thus, OCBs, like most other common behaviors, are shaped by an individual's ability, motivation, obligation, and opportunity. Leaders play a critical role in fostering each of these determinants of citizenship.

In the following paragraphs, we describe recently developed models of leadership, highlight primary studies that have linked leadership with various aspects of organizational citizenship, and summarize the proposed theoretical mechanisms that underlie observed effects. We specifically focus on "new" models of leadership, including servant, ethical, and authentic leadership. Organ et al.'s (2006) summary included extended reviews of instrumental and supportive leadership behaviors, leader rewards and punishment behaviors, transformational leadership, LMX, and leadership empowerment. Consequently, we focus on leadership styles that emerged in the last decade and styles that suggest additional ways in which leaders encourage OCB. In doing so, we highlight how leaders affect employees' ability, motivation, obligation, and opportunity to exhibit OCBs, and we conclude with an empirical summary of the links between servant, ethical, and authentic leadership with aggregate OCB using meta-analysis on a sample of the studies examining these concepts.

Servant Leadership

The "servant" approach to leadership is characterized by a leader's personal integrity, a specific and persistent focus on the needs of followers, a community spirit, and genuine desire to "serve" others first (Greenleaf, 1977; Liden, Wayne, Zhao, & Henderson, 2008). Liden et al. described servant leadership as composed of seven distinct leader behaviors: (1) behaving ethically, (2) providing emotional support, (3) putting subordinates first, (4) helping subordinates grow and succeed, (5) empowering others, (6) creating value for the community, and (7) possessing conceptual skills. Several studies have revealed the positive influence of servant leadership on both individual- and team-level OCBs (e.g., Hu & Liden, 2011). Servant leaders attend to the needs of followers (Mayer, Bardes, & Piccolo, 2008), create a trusting environment (Sturm, 2009), and treat others fairly (Chung, Jung, Kyle, & Petrick, 2010). As such, followers of servant leadership are motivated to exert extra effort for their leaders, and they are supported for doing so.

Conceptualizing servant leadership and OCB at the team level of analysis, Hu and Liden (2011) studied 71 teams of banking professionals. Servant leadership was positively associated with collaboration and helping behavior among team members (i.e., team-level OCB), an effect that was realized, in part, through team potency (a shared belief about a team's collective capability). Hu and Liden (2011) explained these effects as a function of social exchange (Blau, 1964) and the norms of reciprocity (Gouldner, 1960). Having been treated fairly, team members developed an obligation to the servant leader to "reciprocate the benefits they have received by exerting effort, including OCBs that are directed toward team performance" (Hu & Liden, 2011, p. 853). In essence, employees felt as though they *ought* to support teammates because of the treatment they themselves had received.

Ehrhart (2004) examined servant leadership and OCB by aggregating these concepts to the unit level of analysis (e.g., 249 grocery store departments). Results revealed that servant leadership predicted unit-level OCB as aggregated from employee perceptions, and that procedural justice climate in the unit partially mediated this effect (results for manager ratings of unit-level OCB were inconsistent). According to the author, servant leaders fostered a climate of fairness and justice, which created an *opportunity* for employees to help each other with work-related problems (helping) and attend faithfully to expectations (conscientiousness). Further, by being helpful and conscientious themselves, servant leaders act as influential role models of the extra-role behavior they aim to nurture in followers. Thus, as reasoned by Ehrhart (2004), servant leaders foster the conditions that encourage OCBs among followers, who learn to emulate similar behaviors exhibited by ethical and attentive leaders.

From a sample of 815 employees clustered in 123 work groups from seven multinational firms in Kenya, Walumbwa, Hartnell, and Oke (2010) found that group-level service climate in conjunction with group-level procedural justice climate as well as individual-level commitment to the supervisor and self-efficacy acted as partial mediators of the link between group-level servant leadership and follower OCB. These results show that servant leaders facilitate followers' opportunity to engage in OCB as well as nurture their *ability* to do so, as visible in followers' increased self-efficacy.

Similarly, Hunter and colleagues (2013) drew from social learning theory to argue that collective-level servant leadership stimulates follower helping toward coworkers. Followers are likely to display the same helping behavior toward their coworkers that they witness from their servant leader. The authors argued that servant leaders create a service climate in the units they lead, emphasizing personal and organizational growth and helping. Hence, through social learning, servant leaders should be able to increase followers' *ability* and *motivation* to engage in OCB. In a study of 224 stores of a retail organization, store-level servant leadership predicted store-level task-focused helping behavior as rated by followers and store-level person-focused helping behavior as rated by the leaders. Service climate acted as partial mediator of the relationship between store-level servant leadership and follower ratings of task-focused helping behavior; no partial mediation effect was observed for OCB as rated by the leaders.

The following study further underlines that servant leadership can promote follower OCB through *motivation*. Studying 250 employees, Neubert, Kacmar, Carlson, Chonko, and Roberts (2008) contrasted the effects of servant leadership and initiating structure on employee behavioral outcomes through the regulatory focus promoted by these leadership behaviors. As their results revealed, whereas initiating structure engendered prevention focus in employees which predicted in-role behavior, servant leadership instilled a promotion focus in followers, with positive effects on their extra-role behavior, including helping. The effect of servant leadership on helping was shown to be partially mediated through promotion focus, an inclination to exert extra effort toward goal accomplishment and attributing failure to a lack of effort rather than lack of ability (Higgins, 1997).

Ebener and O'Connell (2010) conducted a comprehensive study of three successful Catholic parishes to illuminate how servant leadership inspires OCB in the communities they serve. From their case analysis, the authors derived both direct and indirect means of eliciting OCB in followers, as revealed in helping, initiating, participating, and self-developing. Invitation, inspiration, and affection serve as direct means of influence, whereas servant leadership's promotion of a culture of service and structural mechanisms sustaining this culture and creating opportunities to engage in citizenship behavior in the organization act as indirect means to stimulate OCB. As shown in the research presented earlier as well, creating *opportunities* and *motivation* are thus fundamental mechanisms through which servant leadership exerts its influence on follower OCB.

Aside from uncovering important mediating mechanisms linking servant leadership and OCB, research has also examined moderators of this relationship. Focusing on enhancers of the effectiveness of servant leadership in engendering OCB, Vondey (2010) illuminated person–organization fit and organizational identification as moderators of the relationship between several dimensions of servant leadership as well as OCB. The author argued that high-value congruence with the organization also increases the willingness to engage in OCB; this receptivity should strengthen the positive effect of servant leadership. Likewise, employees should be more receptive to servant leaders' role modeling when experiencing high organization identification given that individuals with high identification are more likely to act in congruence with their identity, and thus the welfare of the organization (social identity theory; Ashforth & Mael, 1989).

In a sample of 114 employees working across industries, Vondey (2010) found partial support for two moderation hypotheses. High person–organization fit strengthened the relationships of the servant leadership dimensions of helping subordinates grow, behaving ethically, and agapao love (genuine care and compassion for employees) with the OCB dimension of individual initiative, but not with the other OCB dimensions, including helping others and promoting the organization. Organizational identification positively moderated the relationship between the servant leadership dimensions of helping subordinates grow and creating value for the community with interpersonal helping, initiative, and loyal boosterism (promoting the firm's image to others), and between agapao love and interpersonal helping as well as initiative.

In sum, servant leadership encourages individual- and team-level OCBs by fostering a supportive work environment (e.g., procedural justice climate, Ehrhart, 2004; Walumbwa et al., 2010), encouraging an obligation on the part of followers (e.g., social exchange, norm of reciprocity, Hu & Liden, 2011), motivating an interest in others (e.g., Vondey, 2010), engendering approach motivation in employees (Neubert et al., 2008), and nurturing organizational- and team-level mechanisms to enable OCB (Ebener & O'Connell, 2010; Hu & Liden, 2011). Servant leaders, therefore, foster motivation and obligation among followers, and they create the opportunity for OCBs, especially in contexts that allow for high organizational identification and person–organization fit.

Ethical Leadership

The ethical nature of a leader is typically reflected in employee perceptions that are inferred from the leader's behavior. According to Brown, Trevino, and Harrison (2005), ethical leadership is "the demonstration of normatively appropriate conduct through personal actions and interpersonal relationships, and the promotion of such conduct to followers through two-way communication, reinforcement, and decision making" (p. 120). To act in a normatively appropriate way means to behave consistently with general expectations about how leaders should behave at work. Ethical leaders are perceived as honest, trustworthy, willing to take responsibility for their own actions, and holding others accountable not only for outcomes but for the manner in which those outcomes were achieved.

A number of studies have focused on explaining and empirically examining the relationship between ethical leadership and OCB. For instance, Brown et al. (2005) confirmed the validity of ethical leadership for predicting extra effort in a sample of 183 work groups. Conceptualizing ethical leadership from a social learning perspective, the authors argue that ethical leaders induce followers to engage in positive behaviors beyond the call of duty through the mechanism of social learning. Ethical leaders listen to their employees and act in ways that are considerate of others. In many ways, models of servant and ethical leadership are similar (van Dierendonck, 2011). Both rely on social learning and norms of reciprocity to encourage behaviors that are favorable for multiple stakeholders.

Also arguing on the grounds of social learning mechanisms, Mayer, Kuenzi, Greenbaum, Bardes, and Salvador (2009) examine how ethical leadership "trickles down" an organization's hierarchy by studying 904 employees clustered in 195 departments from 160 organizations. The authors showed that the ethical behavior of the organization's top leaders was related to department-level OCB through ethical leadership of the department's supervisor.

Shin (2012) examined the idea that CEO ethical leadership could elicit firm-level interpersonally directed OCB through engendering an ethical climate. The author collected self-reported ethical leadership ratings from 223 CEOs, and OCB and ethical climate information from 6,021 employees in South Korea. Results confirmed that CEO ethical leadership indeed related to an ethical climate, which in turn predicted OCB, but only if the climate was strong rather than weak (and organizational members thus agreed on the climate). According to Shin, the effect of CEO ethical leadership on ethical climate and OCB can be explained through role modeling in the context of social learning theory (Bandura, 1977, 1986) and processes of attraction-selection-attrition (ASA; Schneider, Goldstein, & Smith, 1995).

According to Resick, Hargis, Shao, and Dust (2013), ethical cognition in the form of moral equity judgments could play an important role in explaining the relationship between ethical leadership and OCB. Adopting a social cognitive lens, supervisors are an important source providing proximal information regarding what is normatively appropriate behavior. Ethical leaders act in ethical ways that guide decisions, set ethical standards, and treat others in just ways. Through social learning and sense making as a social construction process (Berger & Luckmann, 1966; Maitlis, 2005; Weick, 1995), followers can thus be stimulated to make positive moral equity judgments of OCB and subsequently show OCB. In a study using 190 supervisor–subordinate dyads, the authors found a direct effect of ethical leadership on OCB as well as an indirect one via positive moral equity judgments of OCB.

Research has also focused on trust as a mechanism underlying the link between ethical leadership and OCB. Lu (2014) argued that ethical leadership engenders a social exchange relationship characterized by cognitive and affective trust; follower OCB serves as a resource for exchange. In a sample of 104 supervisor–subordinate dyads in the public sector in China, the author found that *affective* trust mediated the effect of ethical leadership on interpersonal- and organization-focused OCB. *Cognitive* trust, however, did not emerge as a viable mediating mechanism.

In a study on 894 employees and their supervisors in a financial institution, Walumbwa and Schaubroeck (2009) established group psychological safety as a partial mediator of the link between group-level ethical leadership and supervisor-rated voice behavior. By engendering trust and a work climate of respect, and by acting truthfully and honestly, ethical leaders promote psychological safety, which in turn facilitates constructive voice in followers. This study provides further evidence that ethical leaders create the climate, opportunity, and conditions for employees to actively engage in behaviors that go above and beyond typical responsibilities.

Piccolo, Greenbaum, Den Hartog, and Folger (2010) adopted a motivation-through-work design lens to explain the effects of ethical leadership on task and citizenship aspects of performance, including aggregate OCB. Using a sample of 181 pairs of coworkers, the authors argued and showed that ethical leadership altered employee perceptions of their jobs in terms of task significance and autonomy, which in turn provided the motivation to do the little things that enhance performance in the eyes of supervisors and coworkers.

A number of studies also emphasized boundary conditions of the effects of ethical leadership on some form of OCB. Studying boundary conditions helps to understand the context in which leadership is particularly (in)effective, and thus to shed light on potential mechanisms with which leadership influences outcomes (Nishii & Mayer, 2009).

Focusing on characteristics of the leader, for example, Kacmar, Carlson, and Harris (2013) investigated the interactive effects of ethical leadership and leader influence tactics on helping behavior in a governmental setting. Leaders' use of supplication as an influence tactic was negatively related to helping behavior when perceived ethical leadership was low, and it was unrelated to helping behavior when perceived ethical leadership was high. Supplication is often treated as a form of prayer, wherein one humbly pleads or begs for favor from another. The authors explained this effect using social exchange theory. Leaders who make use of supplication reveal themselves as dependent on help, increasing perceptions of obligations in followers. When ethicality perceptions of leaders are high, this request for help is credible and increases trust in future reciprocation of favors, whereas when leaders are not perceived as ethical, followers will be less willing to engage in the requested helping behavior.

Avey, Palanski, and Walumbwa (2011) hypothesized and confirmed the attenuating effect of employee self-esteem on the relationship between ethical leadership and employee OCB. Arguing on the grounds of behavioral plasticity, the authors suggested that ethical leadership, as contextual cue, should be more salient for individuals with lower (compared with higher) self-esteem because of these individuals' higher dependence on cues from the leader regarding desirable behavior. As ethical leadership provides cues regarding the desirability of extra-role behavior, the link between ethical leadership and OCB should be strengthened for followers lower in self-esteem.

In a sample of 147 leader–follower dyads in the Netherlands, Kalshoven, Den Hartog, and de Hoogh (2013a) found job autonomy to moderate the mediated relationship between ethical leadership and follower helping and initiative via followers' demonstrated responsibility. This relationship was positive when levels of job autonomy were high, but neutral when job autonomy was low. As the authors argue, high job autonomy allows followers to show the responsibility at work that ethical leadership instigates, which in turn translates into actual helping behavior and more initiative.

The same authors showed in a study on 256 employees in the Netherlands that a climate of moral awareness and empathic concerns in workgroups acts as an important boundary condition to ethical leadership's potential to elicit employee helping and courtesy. Using substitutes-for-leadership theory and social learning theory as underlying rationales, Kalshoven, Den Hartog, and de Hoogh (2013b) argue that both moral awareness and empathic concerns substitute for the impact of ethical leadership on followers' extra-role behavior. Ethical leadership at the individual and group levels of analysis related more positively to both employee behaviors under the condition of low moral awareness, and less positively in the case of higher moral awareness. Against predictions, high empathic concern strengthened the relationship between ethical leadership and courtesy. For helping behavior as an outcome, there was no interaction effect between ethical leadership and empathic concern.

Kacmar, Bachrach, Harris, and Zivnuska (2011) examined both follower-related and organizational moderators of the ethical leadership–OCB relationship in a sample of 288 supervisor–subordinate dyads. Arguing via social role theory, this relationship should vary according to follower gender and politics perceptions. Results revealed that perceived organizational politics—the perception that peers' behavior is motivated by self-interest—and follower gender moderated the ethical leadership–OCB relationship such that for female employees, lower levels of perceived politics strengthened this relationship, whereas for male subordinates, high levels of perceived politics weakened this relationship.

Authentic Leadership

Definitions of authentic leadership vary in scope and theoretical origin, but a common core is its concern with the extent to which a leader is genuine, real, and true to one's own personality and spirit (Gardner, Cogliser, Davis, & Dickens, 2011). Kernis and Goldman (2006) conceptualized authenticity as a construct composed of four aspects: namely awareness; unbiased processing; behavior aligned with one's values, needs, and inclinations; and relational orientation, which served as a basis for several theories on authentic leadership (e.g., Gardner, Avolio, Luthans, May, & Walumbwa, 2005; Ilies, Morgeson, & Nahrgang, 2005; Walumbwa, Avolio, Gardner, Wernsing, & Peterson, 2008). Authentic leaders foster loyalty and trust among followers, who express their enthusiastic support by enhancing their own performance and that of the organization.

Empirical research has sought to understand authentic leadership effects, including those on followers' citizenship behavior. In their validation of a measure of authentic leadership, Walumbwa, Avolio, Gardner, Wernsing, and Peterson (2008) established the relationship between authentic leadership and outcomes such as OCB while controlling for the effect of transformational leadership and ethical leadership, respectively. In two independent samples of university students, path analysis confirmed a causal link between authentic leadership and OCB. The authors explain this effect with reference to hedonic and eudemonic well-being (Ryan & Deci, 2001). According to the authors, "when organizational leaders know and act upon their true values, beliefs, and strengths, while helping others to do the same, higher levels of employees' well-being will accrue, which in turn have been shown to positively impact follower performance" (p. 91). In this way, authentic leaders enhance the *ability* and *motivation* of followers to offer their best effort.

In a sample of 220 employees in Spain, Valsania, Leon, Alonso, and Cantisano (2012) undertook a more fine-grained analysis of the relationships between the components of authentic leadership and the dimensions of OCB. Employing multiple regression analyses, the authors found that only two of the four dimensions of authentic leadership—moral perspective and relational transparency—had significant relationships with OCB directed toward the organization. Only the authentic leadership dimension of relational transparency significantly affected OCB directed toward others in the organization. The effect of authentic leadership was stronger on OCB directed toward the organization than for OCB toward others in the organization.

Hsiung (2012) explained authentic leadership's relationship with employee voice behavior via social contagion, social exchange, and organizational learning. Consistently, the author theorized and found in a sample of 70 teams working in a real estate agent firm that the relationship between team-level authentic leadership and employee voice behavior was mediated by the positive mood of followers and the relationship quality as perceived by followers.

Wong, Spence Laschinger, and Cummings (2010) focused on personal identification with the manager, social identification with the work group, trust in the manager, and work engagement to explain how authentic leadership translates into beneficial follower voice, which in turn should translate into higher quality performance of the group. Testing their hypotheses using structural equation modeling on a sample of 280 nurses in acute care hospitals in western Canada, results showed that authentic leadership translated into trust, which in turn translated into work engagement, which then affected voice positively. The indirect effect of authentic leadership on voice was significant and positive.

Peus, Wesche, Streicher, Braun, and Frey (2012) examined followers' extra effort as a result of authentic leadership. Arguing in line with prior research, authentic leadership should instill extra effort in followers through engendering trust. In particular, the authors focus on predictability of the leader as a facet of trust related to his or her honesty, integrity, reliability, and predictability and show in a sample of 157 employees in Germany that predictability of the leader partially mediates the relationship between authentic leadership and follower outcomes, including extra effort, in a broader path model.

In sum, like servant and ethical leadership, authentic leaders encourage followers to help each other on work-related tasks (courtesy), focus on what's right about being part of an organization (sportsmanship), and feel comfortable to being true to their authentic selves. As revealed in recent primary studies, authentic leaders encourage OCBs by promoting trust in the leader (e.g., Peus et al., 2012; Wong et al., 2010), developing genuine relationships with followers and stimulating positive affect (Hsiung, 2012), and helping followers derive meaning in work (Walumbwa et al., 2008). More research is needed to show whether authentic leadership uses all described pathways—motivation, ability, opportunity, and structure—to elicit OCB in followers.

Meta-Analysis of Servant, Ethical, and Authentic Leadership with Aggregate Organizational Citizenship Behavior

In the previous sections, we briefly reviewed recently published meta-analyses on the relationships between traditional models of leadership (e.g., transformational leadership, LMX) and OCB. We then described primary studies that represent the general character of relationships between modern leadership conceptions (servant, ethical, and authentic leadership) and follower OCBs, with explanations for how leaders affect the motivation, ability, and opportunity for followers to exhibit citizenship. We now present results of a small meta-analysis on a sample of those primary studies (Table 17.2). Such an analysis allows us to summarize effects of leadership on OCB, and to estimate effects of modern models relative to traditional models.

To identify studies for this analysis, we searched the PsycINFO database (1887–2016) for studies that referenced "servant," "ethical," or "authentic" leadership, as well as included terms reflective of organizational citizenship, such as "voice," "altruism," "compliance," "initiative," "helping," "courtesy," "sportsmanship," "civic virtue," and so on. Studies that measured and contained a measure

Table 17.2 Overall Validities of Leadership Concepts With Aggregated Organizational Citizenship Behavior

Leadership Concept	k	N	r	ρ	80% CV Lower	80% CV Upper	90% CI Lower	90% CI Upper
Servant Leadership	43	12,460	.24	.29	.11	.47	.25	.33
Ethical Leadership	41	21,479	.21	.25	.11	.39	.21	.29
Authentic Leadership	25	6,804	.26	.31	.15	.48	.26	.37
Leader–Member Exchange[a]	50	9,324	.32	.37	.22	.51	.33	.41
Contingent Reward[b]	5	1,184	.15	.17	.06	.27	.08	.26
Transformational Leadership[b]	21	4.399	.21	.24	.12	.36	.19	.29

Notes: k = number of correlations; N = combined sample size; ρ = estimated true score correlation; CV = credibility interval; CI = confidence interval.

[a] Ilies et al. (2007).

[b] Chiaburu et al. (2013).

of association among the variables of interest were selected for inclusion in the final dataset.

We used the meta-analytic method recommended by Hunter and Schmidt (1990) to estimate the average validities reported in Table 17.2, and then corrected each primary correlation for attenuation due to unreliability in the predictor and the criterion. We computed sample-weighted means of corrected correlations. When reliabilities for the leadership or OCB scales were not reported in the primary studies, we averaged the reliabilities reported in the studies that did provide such estimates, and we used these mean reliability values to correct the primary correlations. The average coefficient alpha reliabilities of servant, ethical, and authentic leadership were .90, .89, and .83, respectively, and the average reliability of OCB measures, including measures of all its subfacets, was .83. In addition to reporting point estimates for corrected correlations, we report 80% credibility intervals and 90% confidence intervals around the estimated population correlations. To compare current results with existing empirical summaries, we include in Table 17.2 summary correlations between OCB and contingent reward, transformational leadership (Chiaburu et al., 2013), and LMX (Ilies et al., 2007). Additional details about this analysis were presented by Piccolo, Buengeler, and Judge (2016).

The philosophical roots and core aspects of the servant, ethical, and authentic models of leadership are similar in terms of the descriptions of what constitutes effective and admirable leadership. It is therefore no surprise that the average population validities for these three models with OCB are similar (servant, ρ = .29, ethical, ρ = .25, authentic, ρ = .31), and consistent with traditional predictors (e.g., LMX, transformational leadership). To estimate these effects, we examined studies that reported correlations between the respective models of leadership and OCB in various forms, including OCB-O and OCB-I (Lee & Allen, 2002), voice behavior (Van Dyne & LePine, 1998), and courtesy (MacKenzie et al., 1991).

In this exploratory analysis, we sought to estimate overall effects of the leadership models. Therefore, similar to Ilies et al. (2007) and Chiaburu et al. (2013), we collapsed all subdimensions of OCB into a single criterion. As these results suggest, the "new" models of leadership are similar to each other in their associations with OCB, and similar to the most popular predictors, leadership predictors (LMX, transformational leadership). With the exception of contingent reward and LMX, all 95% confidence intervals around population correlations overlap. This indicates similarity in the predictive utility of the various leadership models. The one exception: a leadership style that emphasizes trust and high-quality relationship development (i.e., LMX) is a better predictor of extra effort than a leadership style that relies on articulating a clear link between effort and reward (i.e., contingent reward).

Given the results presented in Table 17.2, we sought to examine variations in the link between leadership and OCB at the behavioral, rather than theoretical, level of abstraction. In a secondary analysis, we considered broad behavioral categories (task-oriented, relationship-oriented, or change-oriented) that cut across the most popular models and theories of leadership, rather than examinations of individual theories (e.g., LMX, servant leadership). To do so, we used Yukl et al.'s (2002) taxonomy of leadership activity.

In recognition of a lack of theoretical and conceptual integration in leadership research, Yukl et al. (2002) reviewed a broad array of leadership models and measures, and proposed three meta-categories of activity: task, relationship, and/or change oriented. According to the authors, the primary concern for leaders using task-oriented behavior is "high efficiency in the use of resources and personnel, and high reliability of operations, products, and services" (p. 17). Drawing on concepts such as Initiating Structure and contingent reward, task-oriented behaviors include developing specific plans for short-term activities, clarifying task objectives and role expectations, and monitoring performance.

Leaders who use relationship-oriented behaviors are especially concerned with fostering a strong commitment among team members to the organization and its mission. These leaders seek to develop a high level of mutual trust and cooperation among members. With reference to concepts such as Consideration (Fleishman, 1973) and the individualized consideration aspect of Transformational Leadership (Podsakoff et al., 1990), relationship-oriented leaders provide encouragement and support to followers, empower team members to take initiative, and help develop their skills and confidence in handling complex tasks (Yukl et al., 2002).

Lastly, Yukl et al. (2002) suggest that change-oriented leaders are interested in making "major innovative improvements (in processes, products, or services), and adaptation to external changes" (p. 17). Drawing on the concepts in instrumental leadership (Antonakis & House, 2002), as well as the intellectual stimulation aspect of transformational leadership,

Table 17.3 Validities of Leader Behavioral Clusters With Aggregated Organizational Citizenship Behavior

Leadership Concept	k	N	*r*	*ρ*	80% CV Lower	80% CV Upper	90% CI Lower	90% CI Upper
Task-oriented	43	29,745	–.13	–.16	–.49	.18	–.23	–.08
Relationship-oriented	58	41,553	.29	.34	.23	.45	.32	.36
Change-oriented	159	72,358	.20	.23	.08	.47	.21	.25

Notes: k = number of correlations; N = combined sample size; ρ = estimated true score correlation; CV = credibility interval; CI = confidence interval.

change-oriented leaders monitor the external environment, encourage innovative thinking, and take risks to improve an organization's operations.

We followed Yukl et al.'s (2002) hierarchical taxonomy of leader behaviors and categorized studies in our meta-analytic database as reflective of task-, relationship-, or change-oriented leadership. Results are presented in Table 17.3 and shed light on which leader activities are most strongly associated with extra-role behaviors among followers. Consistent with the aforementioned distinction between management and leadership, the correlation between task-oriented activities, such as Initiating Structure, Contingent Reward, and directive leadership (Peterson, 1997) and aggregated OCB was negative ($\rho = -.16$, $p < .05$) and significantly different from relationship-oriented styles (e.g., servant leadership, Consideration, LMX; $\rho = .34$, $p < .05$). Confidence intervals for these point estimates (task: –.23, –.08; relationship: .32, .36) did not overlap. Leaders who clarify role expectations with a clear focus on efficiency in goal accomplishment seem to discourage extra-role behaviors that may not have a short-term or direct influence on individual or group performance.

In that confidence intervals around point estimates do not overlap, both task- and relationship-oriented leadership were significantly different from change-oriented leadership (e.g., idealized influence, Charismatic Leadership; $\rho = .23$, $p < .05$). As the mechanisms that underlie the effects of task-, relationship-, and change-oriented behaviors surely differ, these results not only reveal the extent to which different leader activities foster OCBs among followers, but also clarify the mechanisms that explain, in part, how individuals react and evaluate different leadership styles.

An Emerging Trend and Ideas for Future Research

Organ et al. (2006) suggested several opportunities for additional research on the relationship between leadership and OCB, including the identification of key mediating mechanisms, the possibility that followers' extra-role behavior and group interaction (i.e., group process) might indeed be the cause (rather than the consequence) of leadership, and how boundary conditions, such as national or organizational culture, might accentuate or attenuate a leader's influence. Organ et al. identified trust, a sense of obligation, perceptions of fairness, and liking of the supervisor as the most likely and most prominent explanations of the leadership–OCB link. Fortunately, in the last decade, a number of studies have confirmed and extended these explanations to include need satisfaction (Mayer et al., 2008), a sense of self-worth (Spears & Lawrence, 2002), and overall well-being (Walumbwa et al., 2010). Despite the important progress that has occurred in the last decade, additional opportunities for future research exist.

Comprehensive Examination of Relative Predictive Validity of Various Models

In this chapter, we have presented an early summary of the "new" models of leadership, including a meta-analysis meant to estimate overall effects of three leadership styles with OCB. However, there remains a great opportunity to extend this analysis and estimate relative effects of various leadership theories (both "old" and "new"), and distinguish those effects on the variants of individual- (voice, sportsmanship, courtesy) and group/organization-focused OCB (e.g., boosterism, innovation). Further, important insights can be gained by examining effects at the behavioral, rather than theoretical, level of abstraction. Future research should seek to identify the specific leader behaviors, rather than the broad models and theories, which encourage extra effort. At its core, each model of leadership represents a particular view of the leader–follower relationship. Thus, it is reasonable to consider whether collectivistic, relationship-oriented theories (e.g., LMX, servant leadership) offer different predictions of particular OCB subdimensions (e.g., altruism) than leadership models that focus on the behavior of a leader (ethical, authentic leadership).

Lastly, similar to that presented here, future studies should examine the relative effects of multiple leadership theories in the same study. For one, it will be interesting to discover whether different leadership conceptions vary in their prediction of OCB facets (e.g., voice, altruism, sportsmanship, etc.). Such an effort would also answer calls for more thorough integration of the leadership literature (e.g., Avolio et al, 2009; DeRue et al., 2011; Piccolo et al., 2012).

Leader Organizational Citizenship Behavior

Earlier in this chapter, we made a case that leadership is, in fact, the demonstration of behaviors that encourage employee and group development, demonstrate loyalty to the organization, and constitute the little things that make work pleasant. In other words, we argue that leadership is realized when one does more than required by the perfunctory tasks of basic management and supervision. From our point of view, a link between leadership and OCB is self-evident: Leadership is OCB.

However, we recognize that this perspective is not shared by all leadership scholars. Drawing on tenets of social learning and social facilitation, Yaffe and Kark (2011), for example, recently tested a moderated mediation model of the effects of "leader OCB" on group OCB. In this study, the authors specifically examined, measured, and tested the extent to which "group managers engaged in OCB directed toward the organization" (p. 812) utilizing a common measure of OCB (Moorman & Blakely, 1995), which assessed the initiative, loyalty, and pride of the leader. Suggesting a "leading-by-example" effect, Yaffe and Kark show links—both direct and indirect—of OCB on the part of the leader with OCB on the part of intact groups. The authors have clearly attempted to separate OCBs from common behavioral manifestations in most leadership models. Future research on the topic should systematically delineate behaviors that are expected of leaders, and those that truly go above and beyond.

Differentiated Leadership

A third promising area for future research is on the effects of team leadership in general, and differentiated leadership in particular. Differentiation occurs when leaders treat members of the same team differently, in terms of their trust, encouragement, or support. A number of recent studies have challenged a long-standing and central suggestion in LMX theory: Leaders should differentiate between high-performing (in-group) and low-performing (out-group) employees in order to maximize the effectiveness of the leader's time and effort (e.g., Harris et al., 2014). However, the effects of differentiation on group productivity and employee behavior in teams are mixed, especially in terms of extra effort and courtesy (e.g., individual OCB). Initial evidence clearly suggests that not all differentiation is the same.

Within this nascent stream of research, many studies have examined the effects of varying relationship qualities between a leader and his or her team members (e.g., LMX differentiation; Henderson et al., 2008), given that LMX by definition is a dyadic leadership construct. Other studies have examined the implications of differential levels of transformational or empowering leadership (Nielsen & Daniels, 2012) on various outcomes, including OCB. We briefly summarize these studies later, with specific emphasis on how differentiation by the leader affects followers' willingness to engage in OCBs.

In a sample of 223 followers and their leaders that worked in 60 teams, Harris et al. (2014) showed that the effects of a high-quality LMX relationship between employee and supervisor on OCB are weakened when there is higher variability in relationship qualities in the team (i.e., high differentiation), or when the employee's LMX relationship deviates more from the relationship qualities of other members of the group. That is, high-quality LMX was most strongly related to OCB when relationship quality was consistent across members of the same team, or when a follower's standing, in terms of the relationship quality with the leader, resembled that of the rest of the group. The Harris et al. study highlights the importance of an interaction between the mean level of a construct (e.g., LMX) and its variance (i.e., LMX differentiation).

Sampling 287 employees in 31 teams in the manufacturing industry, Henderson et al. (2008) employed a multilevel analysis to show that an assessment of relationship quality relative to a group of close peers (i.e., relative LMX) was significantly associated with two examples of OCB: sportsmanship and helping behavior. The authors argue that members of a work group are keenly aware of the strength, nature, and quality of relationships that group leaders form with all members. One's own judgment of relationship quality, relative to immediate team members, shaped the extent to which he or she was willing to actively assist other group members. In sum, LMX differentiation had an effect on followers' willingness to engage in OCB.

Using information from 276 employees nested in 25 retail stores in Turkey, Erdogan and Bauer (2010) examined the effects of LMX differentiation on employees' helping behaviors targeting coworkers as dependent on the justice climate in the team. When a team's distributive justice climate was high (low), LMX differentiation was positively (neutrally) linked to individual employees' helping behavior targeting coworkers. Procedural justice climate did not moderate this relationship. This reveals that LMX differentiation can contribute to OCB if favorable perceptions are present in a team.

Based on time-lagged data collected from 579 employees clustered in 74 work groups and their managers, Herdman et al. (2014) studied whether the effect of LMX differentiation on team effectiveness via helping, communication, and cooperation in the team was moderated by upward leader–leader exchange (LLX; the team leader's relationship quality with his or her superior). When LLX was low, high LMX differentiation positively affected teamwork-related extra-role behaviors, which in turn benefitted team effectiveness. The authors argue that when leaders have low LLX relations with their superiors, and thus a low standing and lack of resources themselves, team members accept differential treatment through (and thus differential resources from) their leader more because they can justify differential treatment, without feeling deprived. This allows the benefits of differentiation in terms of coordination efficiencies to emerge.

Chen et al. (2014) focus on the main and moderating effects of differentiation from an indigenous perspective. In particular, the authors examine differentiation in the Chinese leader member *guanxi* (LMG), which refers to the quality of the personal relationship between a leader and his or her followers, which comprises elements such as affective attachment, deference, and inclusion. Whereas LMG differentiation negatively impacted individual attitudes and behavior, it positively impacted the relationship between LMG and coworker helping, along with other favorable outcomes in a sample of 228 employees clustered in 60 teams in China. This reveals that employees with a high LMG relationship tend to help coworkers more when their "insider" status is clearly visible in their group.

Using a multisource dataset with more than 16,000 employees from 157 firms, Kunze et al. (2013) propose and test a path model which links organization-level differentiated individual-focused leadership—defined as differentiation in the two individual-focused facets of transformational leadership (intellectual stimulation and individualized consideration) and organizational-level OCB climate via affective organizational commitment climate. Whereas collective-focused transformational leadership serves to enhance organizational effectiveness via commitment and OCB, differentiated individual-focused leadership among leaders throughout the firm was detrimentally related to effectiveness via these two mechanisms.

In conclusion, research on leadership and team-level OCB suggests the importance of accounting for the effects of leadership in teams and organizations (e.g., differentiated leadership) and the effects of leadership on teams to increase understanding of how OCB can be nurtured. These expansions enrich our understanding of the interrelations of leadership and OCB, and cater to possibly changing demands in the environment of leadership over time. Clearly, however, more research is needed that accounts for the increased role of teams in modern organizations and specific leadership challenges arising from this team focus (i.e., effectively catering to individual followers in a team).

Follower Organizational Citizenship Behavior as a Cause of Leader Behavior

A typical assumption in studies of leadership is that it is a cause (proximal or distal) of outcomes at individual or organization levels, rather than the effect. Most studies expect that leadership causes follower behavior (e.g., OCBs), not the other way around. However, several recent studies have tested this notion, finding evidence that ratings of leadership may in fact be the consequence of employee action, rather than the cause. This phenomenon represents a great opportunity for scholars of leadership or citizenship behavior, especially in terms of identifying whether leaders—despite their formal authority—modify their behaviors based on the frequency and nature of employee OCBs.

Smith and Kirkman (2012), for example, suggested that a follower's personality shaped the ability of a leader (transformational, transactional, and LMX) to encourage proactive OCBs. According to the authors, variations in the nature and magnitude of observed effects were caused by a leader's willingness to engage in each style.

Similarly, Howell and Shamir (2005) offered a theoretical model to suggest that the type of charismatic leadership—personalized or socialized—exhibited by a leader depended, in part, on a follower's self concepts. These two examples highlight the role of the follower in shaping the leader's behavior and effectiveness. Despite Organ et al.'s (2006) call for extended research on this possibility, especially in regard to OCB, little has been done in the last decade. Certainly, this creates an opportunity to challenge many assumptions in prevailing leadership theories by testing the reciprocal relationship between leaders and followers. Generally, we assume that variance in followers' behavior is explained by the leader. The reverse is surely worth exploring.

References

Antonakis, J., & House, R. J. (2002). The full-range leadership theory: The way forward. In B. J. Avolio & F. J. Yammarino (Eds), *Transformational and charismatic leadership: The road ahead* (pp. 3–33). Amsterdam, the Netherlands: JAI Press.

Ashforth, B. E., & Mael, F. (1989). Social identity theory and the organization. *Academy of Management Review, 14*, 20–39.

Avey, J. B., Palanski, M. E., & Walumbwa, F. O. (2011). When leadership goes unnoticed: The moderating role of follower self-esteem on the relationship between ethical leadership and follower behavior. *Journal of Business Ethics, 98*, 573–582.

Avolio, B. J. (2011). *Full range leadership development* (2nd ed.). Thousand Oaks, CA: Sage.

Avolio, B. J., & Bass, B. M. (1991). *The full range leadership development programs: Basic and advanced manuals*. Binghamton, NY: Bass, Avolio & Associates.

Avolio, B. J., Walumbwa, F. O., & Weber, T. J. (2009). Leadership: Current theories, research, and future directions. *Annual Review of Psychology, 60*, 421–449.

Bandura, A. (1977). Self-efficacy: Toward a unifying theory of behavioral change. *Psychological Review, 84*, 191–215.

Bandura, A. (1986). *Social foundations of thought and action: A social cognitive theory*. Englewood Cliffs, NJ: Prentice-Hall.

Barbuto, J. E., & Wheeler, D. W. (2006). Scale development and construct clarification of servant leadership. *Group & Organization Management, 31*, 300–326.

Barnard, C. I. (1938). *The function of the executive*. Cambridge, MA: Harvard University Press.

Bass, B. M. (1985). *Leadership and performance beyond expectations*. New York: Free Press.

Bass, B. M., & Avolio, B. J. (1995). *MLQ Multifactor Leadership Questionnaire*. Redwood City, CA: Mind Garden.

Berger, P., & Luckmann, T. (1966). *The social construction of knowledge: A treatise in the sociology of knowledge*. New York, NY: Doubleday.

Blau, P. M. (1964). *Exchange and power in social life*. New York, NY: Wiley.

Brief, A. P., & Motowidlo, S. J. (1986). Prosocial organizational behaviors. *Academy of Management Review, 11*, 710–725.

Brown, M. E., Trevino, L. K., & Harrison, D. A. (2005). Ethical leadership: A social learning perspective for construct development and testing. *Organizational Behavior and Human Decision Processes, 97*, 117–134.

Chen, Y., Yu, E., & Son, J. (2014). Beyond leader–member exchange (LMX) differentiation: An indigenous approach to leader–member relationship differentiation. *The Leadership Quarterly, 25*, 611–627.

Chiaburu, D. S., Lorinkova, N. M., & Van Dyne, L. (2013). Employees' social context and change-oriented citizenship: A meta-analysis of leader, coworker, and organizational influences. *Group & Organization Management, 38*, 291–333.

Chung, J. Y., Jung, C. S., Kyle, G. T., & Petrick, J. F. (2010). Servant leadership and procedural justice in the US national park service: The antecedents of job satisfaction. *Journal of Park and Recreation Administration, 28*, 1–15.

Conger, J. A., & Kanungo, R. N. (1998). *Charismatic leadership in organizations*. Thousand Oaks, CA: Sage.

Derue, D. S., Nahrgang, J. D., Wellman, N. E. D., & Humphrey, S. E. (2011). Trait and behavioral theories of leadership: An integration and meta-analytic test of their relative validity. *Personnel Psychology, 64*, 7–52.

Dulebohn, J. H., Bommer, W. H., Liden, R. C., Brouer, R. L., & Ferris, G. R. (2012). A meta-analysis of antecedents and consequences of leader-member exchange integrating the past with an eye toward the future. *Journal of Management, 38*, 1715–1759.

Ebener, D. R., & O'Connell, D. J. (2010). How might servant leadership work? *Nonprofit Management and Leadership, 20*, 315–335.

Ehrhart, M. G. (2004). Leadership and procedural justice climate as antecedents of unit-level organizational citizenship behavior. *Personnel Psychology, 57*, 61–94.

Erdogan, B., & Bauer, T. N. (2010). Differentiated leader-member exchanges: The buffering role of justice climate. *Journal of Applied Psychology, 95*, 1104–1120.

Fleishman, E. A. (1973). Patterns of leadership behavior related to employee grievances and turnover. *Personnel Psychology, 15*, 43–56.

Gardner, W. L., Avolio, B. J., Luthans, F., May, D. R., & Walumbwa, F. (2005). "Can you see the real me?" A self-based model of authentic leader and follower development. *The Leadership Quarterly, 16*, 343–372.

Gardner, W. L., Cogliser, C. C., Davis, K. M., & Dickens, M. P. (2011). Authentic leadership: A review of the literature and research agenda. *The Leadership Quarterly, 22*, 1120–1145.

Gouldner, A. (1960). The norm of reciprocity, a preliminary statement. *American Sociological Review, 25*, 161–170.

Greenleaf, R. K. (1977). *Servant leadership*. New York, NY: Paulist Press.

Harris, T. B., Li, N., & Kirkman, B. L. (2014). Leader–member exchange (LMX) in context: How LMX differentiation and LMX relational separation attenuate LMX's influence on OCB and turnover intention. *The Leadership Quarterly, 25*, 314–328.

Henderson, D. J., Wayne, S. J., Shore, L. M., Bommer, W. H., & Tetrick, L. E. (2008). Leader–member exchange, differentiation, and psychological contract fulfillment: A multilevel examination. *Journal of Applied Psychology, 93*, 1208–1219.

Herdman, A. O., Yang, J., & Arthur, J. B. (2014, January). Does LMX differentiation affect work group effectiveness? The role of leader-leader exchange. In *Academy of Management Proceedings* (Vol. 2014, No. 1, p. 13843). Boston, MA: Academy of Management.

Higgins, E. (1997). Beyond pleasure and pain. *American Psychologist, 52,* 1280–1300.
House, R. J. (1971). Path-goal theory of leadership effectiveness. *Administrative Science Quarterly, 16,* 321–339.
Howell, J. M., & Shamir, B. (2005). The role of followers in the charismatic leadership process: Relationships and their consequences. *Academy of Management Review, 30,* 96–112.
Hsiung, H. H. (2012). Authentic leadership and employee voice behavior: A multi-level psychological process. *Journal of Business Ethics, 107,* 349–361.
Hu, J., & Liden, R. C. (2011). Antecedents of team potency and team effectiveness: An examination of goal and process clarity and servant leadership. *Journal of Applied Psychology, 96,* 851–862.
Hunter, E. M., Neubert, M. J., Perry, S. J., Witt, L. A., Penney, L. M., & Weinberger, E. (2013). Servant leaders inspire servant followers: Antecedents and outcomes for employees and the organization. *The Leadership Quarterly, 24,* 316–331.
Hunter, J. E., & Schmidt, F. L. (1990). *Methods of meta-analysis.* Newbury Park, CA: Sage.
Ilies, R., Morgeson, F. P., & Nahrgang, J. D. (2005). Authentic leadership and eudaemonic well-being: Understanding leader–follower outcomes. *The Leadership Quarterly, 16,* 373–394.
Ilies, R., Nahrgang, J. D., & Morgeson, F. P. (2007). Leader–member exchange and citizenship behaviors: A meta-analysis. *Journal of Applied Psychology, 92,* 269–277.
Jackson, E. M., Rossi, M. E., Rickamer Hoover, E., & Johnson, R. E. (2012). Relationships of leader reward behavior with employee behavior: Fairness and morale as key mediators. *Leadership & Organization Development Journal, 33,* 646–661.
Judge, T. A., & Piccolo, R. F. (2004). Transformational and transactional leadership: A meta-analytic test of their relative validity. *Journal of Applied Psychology, 89,* 755–768.
Judge, T. A., Piccolo, R. F., & Ilies, R. (2004). The forgotten ones? The validity of Consideration and Initiating Structure in leadership research. *Journal of Applied Psychology, 89,* 36–51.
Kacmar, K. M., Bachrach, D. G., Harris, K. J., & Zivnuska, S. (2011). Fostering good citizenship through ethical leadership: Exploring the moderating role of gender and organizational politics. *Journal of Applied Psychology, 96,* 633–642.
Kacmar, K. M., Carlson, D. S., & Harris, K. J. (2013). Interactive effect of leaders' influence tactics and ethical leadership on work effort and helping behavior. *Journal of Social Psychology, 153,* 577–597.
Kalshoven, K., Den Hartog, D. N., & de Hoogh, A. H. B. (2013a). Ethical leadership and followers' helping and initiative: The role of demonstrated responsibility and job autonomy. *European Journal of Work and Organizational Psychology, 22,* 165–181.
Kalshoven, K., Den Hartog, D. N., & De Hoogh, A. H. B. (2013b). Ethical leadership and follower helping and courtesy: Moral awareness and empathic concern as moderators. *Applied Psychology-an International Review-Psychologie Appliquee-Revue Internationale, 62,* 211–235.
Kernis, M. H., & Goldman, B. M. (2006). A multicomponent conceptualization of authenticity: Theory and research. *Advances in Experimental Social Psychology, 38,* 283–357.
Kotter, J. P. (1990). *How leadership differs from management.* New York, NY: Free Press.
Kouzes, J. M. & Posner, B. Z. (1987). *The leadership challenge: How to get extraordinary things done in organizations.* San Francisco, CA: Jossey-Bass.
Kunze, F., de Jong, S. B., & Bruch, H. (2013). Consequences of collective-focused leadership and differentiated individual-focused leadership: Development and testing of an organizational-level model. *Journal of Management, 42,* 886–914.
Lee, K., & Allen, N. J. (2002). Organizational citizenship behavior and workplace deviance: The role of affect and cognitions. *Journal of Applied Psychology, 87,* 131–142.
Liden, R. C., & Maslyn, J. M. (1998). Multidimensionality of leader-member exchange: An empirical assessment through scale development. *Journal of Management, 24,* 43–72.
Liden, R. C., Wayne, S. J., Zhao, H., & Henderson, D. (2008). Servant leadership: Development of a multidimensional measure and multi-level assessment. *The Leadership Quarterly, 19,* 161–177.
Lu, X. J. (2014). Ethical leadership and organizational citizenship behavior: the mediating roles of cognitive and affective trust. *Social Behavior and Personality, 42,* 379–389.
MacKenzie, S. B., Podsakoff, P. M., & Fetter, R. (1991). Organizational citizenship behavior and objective productivity as determinants of managerial evaluations of salespersons' performance. *Organizational Behavior and Human Decision Processes, 50,* 123–150.
Maitlis, S. (2005). The social processes of organizational sensemaking. *Academy of Management Journal, 48,* 21–49.
Mayer, D. M., Bardes, M., & Piccolo, R. F. (2008). Do servant-leaders help satisfy follower needs? An organizational justice perspective. *European Journal of Work and Organizational Psychology, 17,* 180–197.
Mayer, D. M., Kuenzi, M., Greenbaum, R., Bardes, M., & Salvador, R. (2009). How low does ethical leadership flow? Test of a trickle-down model. *Organizational Behavior and Human Decision Processes, 108,* 1–13.
Moorman, R. H., & Blakely, G. L. (1995). Individualism–collectivism as an individual difference predictor of organizational citizenship behavior. *Journal of Organizational Behavior, 16,* 127–142.
Neubert, M. J., Kacmar, K. M., Carlson, D. S., Chonko, L. B., & Roberts, J. A. (2008). Regulatory focus as a mediator of the influence of initiating structure and servant leadership on employee behavior. *Journal of Applied Psychology, 93,* 1220–1233.
Nielsen, K., & Daniels, K. (2012). Does shared and differentiated transformational leadership predict followers' working conditions and well-being? *Leadership Quarterly, 23,* 383–397.
Nishii, L. H., & Mayer, D. M. (2009). Do inclusive leaders help to reduce turnover in diverse groups? The moderating role of Leader-Member Exchange in the diversity to turnover relationship. *Journal of Applied Psychology, 94,* 1412–1426.
Organ, D. W. (1988). *Organizational citizenship behavior: The good soldier syndrome.* Lexington, MA: Lexington Books.
Organ, D. W., Podsakoff, P. M., & MacKenzie, S. B. (2006). *Organizational citizenship behavior.* Thousand Oaks, CA: Sage.
Peterson, R. S. (1997). A directive leadership style in group decision making can be both virtue and vice: Evidence from elite and experimental groups. *Journal of Personality and Social Psychology, 72,* 1107–1121.
Peus, C., Wesche, J. S., Streicher, B., Braun, S., & Frey, D. (2012). Authentic leadership: An empirical test of its antecedents, consequences, and mediating mechanisms. *Journal of Business Ethics, 107,* 331–348.

Piccolo, R. F., Bono, J. E., Heinitz, K., Rowold, J., Duehr, E., & Judge, T. A. (2012). The relative impact of complementary leader behaviors: Which matter most? *The Leadership Quarterly, 23*, 567–581.
Piccolo, R. F., Buengeler, C., & Judge, T. A. (2016). Leadership and OCB: Going above and beyond. In N. P. Podsakoff & T. M. Martinez (Chairs), *Traditional predictors of OCB: Reviews and recommendations for future research.* Paper presented at the annual meeting of the Academy of Management, Anaheim, CA.
Piccolo, R. F., & Colquitt, J. A. (2006). Transformational leadership and job behaviors: The mediating role of core job characteristics. *Academy of Management Journal, 49*, 327–340.
Piccolo, R. F., Greenbaum, R., Den Hartog, D. N., & Folger, R. (2010). The relationship between ethical leadership and core job characteristics. *Journal of Organizational Behavior, 31*, 259–278.
Podsakoff, P. M., Bommer, W. H., Podsakoff, N. P., & MacKenzie, S. B. (2006). Relationships between leader reward and punishment behavior and subordinate attitudes, perceptions, and behaviors: A meta-analytic review of existing and new research. *Organizational Behavior and Human Decision Processes, 99*, 113–142.
Podsakoff, P. M., MacKenzie, S. B., & Bommer, W. H. (1996a). Transformational leader behaviors and substitutes for leadership as determinants of employee satisfaction, commitment, trust, and organizational citizenship behaviors. *Journal of Management, 22*, 259–298.
Podsakoff, P., MacKenzie, S. B., & Bommer, W. H. (1996b). Meta-analysis of the relationships between Kerr and Jermier's substitutes for leadership and employee job attitudes, role perceptions, and performance. *Journal of Applied Psychology, 81*, 380–399.
Podsakoff, P. M., MacKenzie, S. B., Moorman, R. H., & Fetter, R. (1990). Transformational leader behaviors and their effects on followers' trust in leader, satisfaction, and organizational citizenship behaviors. *The Leadership Quarterly, 1*, 107–142.
Resick, C. J., Hargis, M. B., Shao, P., & Dust, S. B. (2013). Ethical leadership, moral equity judgments, and discretionary workplace behavior. *Human Relations, 66*, 951–972.
Rockstuhl, T., Dulebohn, J. H., Ang, S., & Shore, L. M. (2012). Leader-member exchange (LMX) and culture: A meta-analysis of correlates of LMX across 23 countries. *Journal of Applied Psychology, 97*, 1097–1130.
Ryan, R. M., & Deci, E. L. (2001). On happiness and human potentials: A review of research on hedonic and eudaimonic well-being. *Annual Review of Psychology, 52*, 141–166.
Schneider, B., Goldstein, H. W., & Smith, D. B. (1995). The ASA framework: An update. *Personnel Psychology, 48*, 747–773.
Schriesheim, C. A., & Stogdill, R. M. (1975). Differences in factor structure across three version of the Ohio State leadership scales. *Personnel Psychology, 28*, 189–206.
Schyns, B., & Schilling, J. (2013). How bad are the effects of bad leaders? A meta-analysis of destructive leadership and its outcomes. *The Leadership Quarterly, 24*, 138–158.
Shin, Y. (2012). CEO Ethical leadership, ethical climate, climate strength, and collective organizational citizenship behavior. *Journal of Business Ethics, 108*, 299–312.
Simons, T., Leroy, H., Collewaert, V., & Masschelein, S. (2015). How leader alignment of words and deeds affects followers: A meta-analysis of behavioral integrity research. *Journal of Business Ethics, 132*, 831–844.
Smith, T., & Kirkman, B. (2012). Understanding leadership: The followers' influence on leader effectiveness. In *Academy of Management Proceedings* (No. 1, pp. 1–1). Boston, MA: Academy of Management.
Spears, L. C., & Lawrence, M. (Eds.). (2002). *Focus on leadership: Servant-leadership for the twenty-first century.* New York, NY: John Wiley & Sons.
Stogdill, R. M. (1963). *Manual for the Leader Behavior Description Questionnaire-Form XII: An experimental revision.* Bureau of Business Research, College of Commerce and Administration, Ohio State University.
Sturm, S. (2009). Negotiating workplace equality: A systemic approach. *Negotiation and Conflict Management Research, 2*, 92–106.
Triandis, H. C. & Gelfand, M. J. (1998). Converging measurement of horizontal and vertical individualism and collectivism. *Journal of Personality and Social Psychology, 74*, 118–128.
Valsania, S. E., Leon, J. A. M., Alonso, F. M., & Cantisano, G. T. (2012). Authentic leadership and its effect on employees' organizational citizenship behaviours. *Psicothema, 24*, 561–566.
Van Dierendonck, D. (2011). Servant leadership: A review and synthesis. *Journal of Management, 37*, 1228–1261.
Van Dyne, L., & LePine, J. A. (1998). Helping and voice extra-role behaviors: Evidence of construct and predictive validity. *Academy of Management Journal, 41*, 108–119.
Van Knippenberg, D. & Sitkin, S. B. (2013) A critical assessment of Charismatic—Transformational leadership research: Back to the drawing board? *The Academy of Management Annals, 7*, 1–60.
Vidyarthi, P. R., Liden, R. C., Anand, S., Erdogan, B., & Ghosh, S. (2010). Where do I stand? Examining the effects of leader-member exchange social comparison on employee work behaviors. *Journal of Applied Psychology, 95*, 849–861.
Vondey, M. (2010). The relationships among servant leadership, organizational citizenship behavior, person-organization fit, and organizational identification. *International Journal of Leadership Studies, 6*, 3–27.
Vroom, V. H. (1964). *Work and motivation.* San Francisco, CA: Jossey-Bass.
Walumbwa, F. O., Avolio, B. J., Gardner, W. L., Wernsing, T. S., & Peterson, S. J. (2008). Authentic leadership: Development and validation of a theory-based measure. *Journal of Management, 34*, 89–126.
Walumbwa, F. O., Hartnell, C. A., & Oke, A. (2010). Servant leadership, procedural justice climate, service climate, employee attitudes, and organizational citizenship behavior: A cross-level investigation. *Journal of Applied Psychology, 9*, 517–529.
Walumbwa, F. O., & Schaubroeck, J. (2009). Leader personality traits and employee voice behavior: mediating roles of ethical leadership and work group psychological safety. *Journal of Applied Psychology, 94*, 1275.
Wang, G., Oh, I. S., Courtright, S. H., & Colbert, A. E. (2011). Transformational leadership and performance across criteria and levels: A meta-analytic review of 25 years of research. *Group & Organization Management, 36*, 223–270.
Weick, K. E. (1995). What theory is not, theorizing is. *Administrative Science Quarterly, 40*, 385–390.
Williams, L. J., & Anderson, S. E. (1991). Job satisfaction and organizational commitment as predictors of organizational

citizenship and in-role behaviors. *Journal of Management, 17*, 601–617.
Wong, C. A., Spence Laschinger, H. K., & Cummings, G. G. (2010). Authentic leadership and nurses' voice behaviour and perceptions of care quality. *Journal of Nursing Management, 18*, 889–900.
Yaffe, T., & Kark, R. (2011). Leading by example: the case of leader OCB. *Journal of Applied Psychology, 96*, 806–826.
Yukl, G., Gordon, A., & Taber, T. (2002). A hierarchical taxonomy of leadership behavior: Integrating a half century of behavior research. *Journal of Leadership & Organizational Studies, 9*, 15–32.

CHAPTER

18

A Social Network Perspective on Organizational Citizenship Behavior

Daniel J. Brass

Abstract

This chapter provides a brief general primer on social network theory and how it might be applied to organizational citizenship behavior (OCB) as an alternative perspective to the undersocialized (isolated individual) and oversocialized (norm and culture) views of behavior in organizations. I identify social network relationships that are likely to affect the performance and receipt of OCBs and propose a model of the diffusion of OCBs through an organization, noting differences between organizational networks such as cliques and core-periphery structures. In the process, I attempt to identify research questions that may be of interest to both academics and managers. The overarching goal is to provide readers with enough information to apply a social network perspective to OCB.

Key Words: social networks, network analysis, tie formation, closed networks, structural holes and bridges, network centrality, organizational citizenship behavior, helping behavior, voice behavior

Few organizational topics have received more research attention over the past 30 years than organizational citizenship behavior (OCB). Indeed, a quick review of this literature is anything but quick. At the risk of being repetitive, some basics are common across the multitude of research studies. OCB is typically defined as intentional, discretionary behavior that exceeds minimum requirements of the job (Organ, 1997). Following Katz's (1964) suggestion that organizations must depend on more than job requirements to be successful, and spurred on by the absence of a strong correlation between employee satisfaction and performance, extra-role OCB joined in-role job performance as the dependent variable of organizational interest to researchers and managers. Research focused on such behaviors as "helping co-workers with a job related problem; accepting orders without a fuss; tolerating temporary impositions without complaint; helping to keep the work area clean and uncluttered; making timely and constructive statements about the work unit or its head to outsiders; promoting a work climate that is tolerable and minimizes the distractions created by interpersonal conflict; and protecting and conserving organizational resources" (Bateman & Organ, 1983, p. 588). As research progressed, the topic included prosocial behavior (Brief & Motowidlo, 1986), extra-role behavior (Van Dyne, Cummings, & Parks, 1995), altruism (Moorman, 1993), voice behavior (LePine & Van Dyne, 1998), and contextual performance (Borman & Motowidlo, 1993). Although some recent research has suggested a downside to OCB (Bolino, Turnley, & Niehoff, 2004), most studies included the notion that OCB provides a positive lubricant that reinforces the social and psychological work environment. Following Williams and Anderson (1991), I categorize OCBs in relation to their target: OCBI is directed toward individuals, such as interpersonal helping behavior; OCBO is directed toward the organization, such as endorsing/defending organizational objectives (Borman & Motowidlo, 1997). Although directed toward the organization, I treat voice behavior (LePine &

Van Dyne, 1998) separately because it may involve policy change rather than loyalty or defense.

As originally suggested by Bateman and Organ (1983), theoretical explanations for predicting the antecedents of OCB have focused on variations of (1) social exchange theory and (2) positive affect theory. Social exchange theory (Adams, 1965; Blau, 1964; Cropanzano & Mitchell, 2005) predicts that norms of reciprocity will motivate employees to reciprocate positive treatment from their organizations (or organizational representatives) by engaging in OCB. Positive affective theory (Clark & Isen, 1982; Spector & Fox, 2002) suggests that when employees experience a generalized positive mood state, they are more likely to exhibit more of the prosocial, citizenship behaviors. General positive affect tends to generalize to a host of positive behaviors, regardless of what caused it (Rosenhan et al. 1974). Thus, attitudinal variables such as job satisfaction, organizational commitment, and procedural justice have been linked to OCB (Podsakoff et al., 2000). Whereas some studies have focused on more macro contextual factors such a norms and culture/climate, most research has adopted a micro, psychological perspective, with recent studies suggesting a within-individual process (Bolino et al., 2012; Dalal, Bhave, & Fiset, 2014). Although debates have centered on definitions and measures, after hundreds of studies and a multitude of empirical findings, OCB can only be described as an extremely well-developed line of research.

Consequentially, one has to wonder why it might be important, or even feasible, to offer a different approach, that of social network analysis, to the study of OCB. With a few exceptions (Bowler & Brass, 2006; Bolino, Turnley, & Bloodgood, 2002; Lyons & Scott, 2012; Settoon & Mossholder, 2002; Venkataramani & Dalal, 2007), the study of OCB has progressed quite well without the benefits of a social network perspective. Yet the importance of the social network perspective hinges on the basic assumption that actors, whether they are individuals, groups, or organizations, do not exist in isolation. Rather, individuals are embedded in networks of relationships that likely affect important outcomes. For example, attitudes and norms are not formed in isolation but are subject to social influence. Equity considerations and subsequent reciprocations (to individuals as well as the organization) are not made in isolation but in comparison to others' inputs and outcomes. The spread of OCBs in organizations may be facilitated or hindered by the social relationships that exist. The social network perspective represents a midpoint between the "undersocialized" approach of focusing on the psychological attributes of individuals, such as personality traits and individual attitudes, and the "oversocialized" approach of sociological norms and culture in which everyone is identically responsive to normative/cultural constraints (Granovetter, 1985). Although seemingly different, the two conceptualizations both assume that attitudes and behavior are independent of ongoing social relationships. I propose a social network perspective on OCB, not as an alternative, but as a complement to current approaches; as a way of bridging the undersocalized and oversocializeded approaches to organizational research. It is these social relationships that provide opportunities and constraints and are as much the causal forces behind behaviors such as OCBs as within-individual attributes or cultural norms. Yet relatively few studies of social networks and OCB exist.

To possibly remedy this situation, my goal in this chapter is (1) to provide a brief general primer on social networks (for elaborations, see Borgatti & Foster, 2003; Brass, 2012; Brass, Galaskiewicz, Greve, & Tsai, 2004; Kilduff & Brass, 2010); (2) to identify social network relationships that are likely to affect the performance and receipt of OCBs; (3) to propose a model of the diffusion of OCBs through an organization; and, in the process (4) to identify research questions that may be of interest to both academics and managers. The overarching goal is to provide readers enough information to apply a social network perspective to OCB.

A Primer on Social Networks

The social network perspective begins with the assumption that actors are embedded within a network of interrelationships with other actors. The emphasis is on the structure or arrangement of relationships as a complement to the attributes of the actors and the context within which the network exists. It is the intersection of relationships that defines an individual's position in the network. Although network measures such as centrality can be assigned to individual actors, they are a function of the entire network and can change as other actors form or dissolve relationships. In addition to actors' positions in the network, we can also focus on the overall arrangement of ties to identify groups (e.g., cliques) or describe the structure of the entire network (e. g., dense, centralized, core-periphery structure). The networks of relationships provide the opportunities and constraints that may be as much, or more, the causal forces of OCBs as the psychological attributes of the actors or the norms/culture of the organization.

I define a social network as a set of actors and the set of ties representing some relationship or absence of relationship between the actors. Actors can be connected in a variety of ways: physical proximity, membership in the same group, similar attributes such as gender or kinship, affective relations such as friendship, interactions such as communicating with or giving/receiving advice, or flows of resources such as information or money (Borgatti et al. 2009). In organizational research, the ties typically involve some form of interaction, such as communication or advice and the flow of information, or represent expressions of affect such as friendship or negative affect. Ties may be actual or perceived depending on the research question. They may be measured as binary (present or absent) or valued (e. g., frequency of communication or degree of positive affect), and some ties may be asymmetric (Dan helps Phil but Phil does not help Dan) or directional (Phil goes to Dan for advice). Networks may be composed of actors' responses to questions about dyadic relationships (a typical method in organizational research) or based on observations or archival data (e.g., coauthor networks or interorganizational alliances).

As differentiated from human capital (an individual's skills, ability, intelligence, personality, etc.) or financial capital (money), the popularized concept of social capital refers to outcomes (typically considered beneficial) derived from relationships with others (see Adler & Kwon, 2002, for a discussion of the history of usage of the term). Organizational network research has generally focused on two general outcomes: (1) how actors are different, as the network or positions in the network provide differential advantages to actors (cf., Burt, 1992); and (2) how actors are the same, as the network or positon in the network results in similar attitudes and behaviors such as adoption of innovations in diffusion/contagion studies (cf. Valente, 1995). Podolny (2001) coined the term "pipes" to refer to the "flow" aspect of networks but also noted that networks can serve as "prisms," conveying mental images of status, for example, to observers. The focal actor in a network is referred to as "ego"; the other actors with whom ego has direct relationships are called "alters." The commonly used designation "social network analysis" (SNA) likely reflects the multitude of mathematical measures developed and the alternative statistical methods necessitated when abandoning the typical statistical assumption that actors are independent (Borgatti, Brass, & Halgin, 2014).

Although any number of actors and relationships (even no relationships) can technically define a network, networks are commonly conceived of as including at least three actors and more than one tie (Brass, 2012). The distinctive value of the network perspective is that it goes beyond the dyad and provides a way of considering the structural arrangement of many actors. Networks are not simply separate dyads with separate alters. Rather, the focus is on the relationships among the dyadic relationships, allowing for such notions as indirect links and paths (e.g., "six degrees of separation" and the common expression, "It's a small world"; see Watts, 2003).

The social network perspective also suggests a different methodological approach to organizational research. While organizational friendship and advice networks are typically studied, the challenge for OCB researchers is to capture a "citizenship network." In addition to collecting traditional attribute data that can be assigned to individuals (such as supervisor ratings of OCB), a network methodology allows for independent reports of who helps whom as in the case of OCBIs (cf. Bowler & Brass, 2006). This involves collecting relational data that are entered in matrix format with cells representing the binary presence or absence of a relationship, or the value/frequency/salience/intensity of relationships captured via interval scales. Network software, such as UCINET (Borgatti, Everett, & Freeman, 2002), is used to calculate measures (see Borgatti, Everett, & Johnson, 2013, for detailed discussion of methods and analysis).

Organizational Citizenship Behavior and Tie Formation

I begin with basic tie formation because it is inherently linked to consideration of others and the performance of helping behavior, or OCBI. Previous social network research has identified a number of correlates of tie formation (Brass, 2012), such as the "law of propinquity" (Krackhardt, 1994). Despite the advent of email and "working from home," the probability of two people forming a relationship is inversely proportional to the distance between them. Although help can easily be provided via email, some relationship must exist that allows for communication or provides some degree of interdependency such that help can be provided and received. Although dependencies can create conflict as well, it seems likely that OCBI in the form of helping behavior will be dependent on spatial and temporal proximity—being in the same place at the same time. In organizations, workflow and hierarchy locate employees in physical and temporal space and may be predictive of OCBIs.

Of those proximate, interdependent others, homophily, a preference for interacting with similar others, may be a major factor in tie formation. Research has shown homophily on such salient attributes as race, gender, age, religion, attitudes, and a host of other attributes, including status homophily (see McPherson, Smith-Lovin, & Cook, 2001, for a cogent review of "birds of a feather flock together"). Similarity is thought to ease communication and foster the predictability of trust and reciprocity and, consequently, homophily may be a powerful predictor of OCBIs. Homophily can be extended to "social foci" (Feld, 1981): activities and settings around which actors with similar demographics, attitudes, and behaviors will meet, interact with each other, and reinforce their similarity of interests. Similarity is a relational concept and organizational design may provide both opportunities and constraints (minorities may have fewer choices for forming relationships on the basis of similarity; Mehra, Kilduff, & Brass, 1998).

All interactions have an affective component, and we tend to form ties with those whom we like and avoid further interaction with those we dislike. Although strong positive affect will reinforce the relationship, strong negative affect will shorten the life of, or destabilize, the tie when interdependence is low. Affect will likely be related to "tie strength," a frequently researched topic in social networks. Granovetter (1973) famously noted that tie strength was a function of time, emotional intensity, intimacy, and reciprocal services. Frequency of interaction may not always relate to positive affect in organizations where certain interactions are required, but frequency will surely be related to proximity. Close friends and family are often synonymous with strong ties, while weak ties may be thought of as acquaintances. Whereas weak ties may be the source of novel, creative information as they often provide connections across social circles, strong ties may be the sources of reliable, trustworthy information and reciprocity. Strong ties are often thought to be more influential, more motivated to provide information, and of easier access than weak ties. Strong-tie friends may also be perceived as open to requests for help; we are more likely to seek assistance from friends than strangers or acquaintances. For example, Krackhardt (1992) showed that strong ties were influential in determining the outcome of a union election. Whereas weak ties might be more useful in searching out helpful information, strong ties are more useful for the effective transfer of helpful information, or OCBIs (Hansen, 1999). Uzzi (1997) found that strong "embedded ties" were characterized by higher levels of trust and greater problem-solving capabilities when compared to weak "arm's-length" ties. On the downside, strong ties require more time and energy to maintain and come with stronger obligations to reciprocate.

The expected effects of tie strength have been confirmed at the dyadic level. Bowler and Brass (2006) found that OCBIs (helping behavior as reported by the recipients) were correlated with friendship even when controlling for job satisfaction, commitment, procedural justice, hierarchical level, demographic similarity, and job similarity. Likewise, Venkataramani and Dalal (2007) and Lyons and Scott (2012) found a positive relationship between positive affective relationships and helping behavior. We would expect negative ties (dislike) to be inversely related to tie formation and helping behavior. Emotions may outweigh norms of reciprocity (Lyons & Scott, 2012), especially negative feelings toward others. Indeed, research on negative ties suggests that negative relationships may be more powerful predictors of outcomes than positive relationships (Baumeister, Bratslavsky, Finkenauer, & Vohs 2001; Labianca & Brass, 2006). For example, Labianca, Brass, and Gray (1998) found that positive relationships (friends in the other groups) were not related to perception of intergroup conflict, but negative relationships were (disliking someone in the other group). Venkataramani and Dalal (2007) found that positive affective relationships were not significantly inversely related to harmful behavior, but negative relationships were positively related to harm.

Closely related to the notion of strong ties are multiplex ties: when two actors are connected in multiple ways. For example, two employees may be connected in the workflow, advice, and friendship networks. Multiple connections create durable ties and the possibility that one type of tie may be appropriated for another. As in the case of Girl Scout cookies, one type of tie (friend, neighbor) might be appropriated for a different use (sale of cookies). As in the case of strong affective ties, we would expect OCBIs to be performed and reciprocated between employees with multiplex relationships. The failure to provide help may jeopardize existing relationships. However, multiplexity also creates the possibility for "not in-kind" reciprocation (e.g., helping behavior may be reciprocated via friendship).

In sum, a brief review of some of the antecedents of tie formation suggests that OCBIs will be related to characteristics of dyadic relationships, as opposed to, or in combination with, OCBIs directed toward others in general (Venkataramani & Dalal, 2007). Even within-individual characteristics such as positive affectivity may be selectively demonstrated on the basis of dyadic relationships. It is likely that tie formation and OCBIs may be reciprocally related. For example, Bolino and colleagues (Bolino, Turnley, & Bloodgood, 2002) provide a theoretical model of how Van Dyne, Graham, and Dienesch's (1994) five OCB dimensions can foster relationships characterized by liking, trust, and identification, and can promote shared narratives and language. Thus, it is likely that interpersonal helping behavior leads to positive affect and tie formation, as well as vice versa. Rather than argue "the chicken and the egg," researchers should recognize that tie formation and OCBIs are inextricably linked.

Organizational OCBs (OCBOs) may also be a function of dyadic relational characteristics such as proximity, homophily, and affect. Breiger (1988) pointed out "the duality of persons and groups." Each interpersonal interaction not only represents an exchange between two people but an exchange between the groups that they represent. Because supervisors are sometimes the only faces of larger "faceless" organizations, interactions with supervisors and other representatives of the organization should affect OCBOs (Masterson, Lewis, Goldman, & Taylor, 2000; Wang, Law, Hackett, Wang, & Chen, 2005). Other than supervisors, it remains to be seen whether characteristics of interpersonal, dyadic relationships moderate the relationship between OCBI and OCBO.

Beyond the Dyad

Third Parties and Balance

Although proximity, homophily, and affect as measured by tie strength are typical social network variables of interest, they represent attributes of dyadic relationships and, while important, fail to take full advantage of the "beyond the dyad" network perspective. Rather than treating dyadic relationships in isolation, the network perspective combines dyads to create networks of relationships. As regards tie formation, Granovetter's notion of embedded ties suggests that actors are embedded within a network to the extent that they show a preference for repeat transactions with network members and to the extent that social ties are forged, renewed, and even extended through existing ties rather than through actors outside one's "neighborhood" (Kilduff & Brass, 2010). This suggests that new tie formation is more likely to occur with third parties—those people tied to ego's immediate alters.

The notion of embeddedness is illustrated in cognitive balance theory (Heider, 1958). A friend of a friend is a friend; a fiend of an enemy is an enemy, and an enemy of an enemy is a friend. Extending the previous hypothesis, an employee is likely to provide helping behavior to a friend of the employee's friend. This hypothesis was supported by Bowler and Brass (2006); in this case, the employee was a third party, linked to the recipient only via a mutual friend. In a slight extension of this notion, Krackhardt (1998) coined the term "Simmelian ties" to refer to super-strong ties in which both parties have strong ties to a third party (a triad of strong, positive ties). Such ties are not only strong but "sticky." They tend to be long lasting and difficult to break. Balance is not a perfect predictor, but extending balance via social network analysis, we could identify cliques of reciprocated strong ties within which OCBIs occur on a frequent, regular basis. However, closed cliques can become constraining and prevent OCBIs from occurring across different cliques. As in-group/out-group biases develop (Linville & Jones, 1980), OCBIs across cliques may be particularly difficult. This hypothesis remains to be tested.

Closed Networks

Some overlap exists between the technical social network definition of a clique (all actors connected to each other) and Coleman's (1990) focus on the social capital of the collective and how groups of actors build relationships that provide benefits to the group. Coleman (1990) focuses on social capital as norms of reciprocity, trust, and mutual obligations, as well as monitoring and sanctioning of inappropriate behavior, that result from "closed" networks (a high number of interconnections between members of a group; ego's alters are connected to each other). Closed networks allow for the development of shared norms, social support, and a sense of identity. Information circulates easily within closed networks, and the potential damage to one's reputation discourages inappropriate behavior and, consequentially, fosters generalized trust among members of the network (Brass, Butterfield, & Skaggs, 1998). Third parties in closed networks have incentives to mediate conflicts and preserve the trust and social support of a tightly knit group. Thus, we would predict that employees within closed networks would be more cooperative, more likely to focus on mutual interests, provide help, and, in general, perform OCBIs (at least within the group) rather than exhibit inappropriate, opportunistic behavior, or counterproductive work behavior (Lyons & Scott, 2012).

Structural Holes and Bridges

Connecting to others who are themselves connected results in closure in the network and the social capital associated with trust, norms, and group sanctions. However, one can be "trapped in your own net" as closed networks can constrain action (Gargiulo & Benassi, 2000). In the case of OCBs, this constraint promotes good outcomes within the group (trust, norms of reciprocity, monitoring and sanctioning of inappropriate behavior), but it can result in bad outcomes (circulating redundant information, a lack of novel ideas). Employees may attempt to balance their networks by maintaining a group of densely tied close friends while, at the same time, developing "structural holes" by extending their external networks in search of helpful, diverse information (Reagans, Zuckerman, & McEvily, 2004).

A structural hole exists when ego is connected to two alters who are not themselves connected (Burt, 1992). The ties to ego provide the "bridge" between the two alters. The absence of a relationship between the two alters creates opportunities for ego to control the flow of resources and possibly play one off against the other. A substantial number of studies have related structural holes to a variety of performance outcomes (Brass, 2012), but OCBs have not been tested. As an alternative to having a closed network, we might expect a negative correlation between OCBIs and structural holes in an employee's network. However, as a power position (Brass, 1984), we can hypothesize that employees with many structural holes in their networks will be the recipients of OCBIs as actors attempt to ingratiate themselves with powerful others (also see the later discussion on centrality).

Being the recipient of OCBIs may partially explain the significant positive effect of structural holes on in-role performance. However, the theoretically more important advantage of structural holes is that alters who are not themselves connected tend to provide diverse, nonredundant information. Alters who are connected share the same information and are often part of the same social circles. Alters who are not connected often represent different closed social circles and are sources of different, nonredundant information—information that may prove useful in providing different perspectives that lead to creative problem solving. Because information circulates easily in closed networks, connecting to two alters in the same closed social circle provides ego with redundant information. Diverse, nonredundant information obtained via structural holes may be a source of creativity and change. Thus, we can predict that structural holes will be positively related to voice: expressing opinions and ideas for change.

Network Centrality

Actors can be differentiated on the basis of their centrality within a network. Various social network measures of centrality exist: number of ties (degree centrality); number of in-coming ties (in-degree centrality); the number of path links it takes to reach everyone in the network (closeness centrality); the extent to which the actor falls on the shortest path between any pair of other actors (betweenness), and many other related measures (see Borgatti, Everett, & Johnson for additional measures). Regardless of the measure, the concept of centrality implies that central actors are more likely to be the recipients of whatever is flowing through the network. One might therefore expect that central actors are more likely to be both the providers and recipients of OCBIs. Settoon and Mossholder (2002) found that in-degree centrality related to supervisors' ratings of person- and task-focused interpersonal citizenship behavior. However, using a closeness centrality measure, Venkataramani and Dalal (2007) found that while central actors were more likely to be the recipients of helping behavior, they were not more likely to provide helping behavior than peripheral actors. Although this result may change if measuring centrality in the advice network, it is consistent with Bowler and Brass's (2006) finding that supervisors, and third-party friends of supervisors, were the recipients of OCBIs.

These results suggest that power/status is an important predictor of OCBIs. Network centrality has been related to power in a number of studies (Brass, 1984; Brass & Burkhardt, 1993; Burkhardt & Brass, 1990). Central positions provide both access and control of resources, such as information. It is likely that actors provide help to central, powerful others in exchange for valuable resources, or in hope of future reciprocation. This explanation is consistent with Bolino's (1999) notion that some OCBs are the result of self-serving, impression management tactics—good actors rather than good soldiers. However, relationships often hinge on the cognitive interpretations of actions by the parties involved. For example, we are not likely to form relationships or reciprocate OCBIs with people whose motives are perceived as self-serving (Kleinbaum, Jordan, & Audia, 2015). Calculated self-interest, if perceived, is self-defeating. This may provide a partial explanation for why powerful others are recipients rather than providers of OCBIs, and it suggests that perceived motives may be an important moderator of outcomes associated with OCBs. Alternatively, powerful others may not see benefit in reciprocating helping behavior to less powerful others, or they may feel that their position does not necessitate reciprocation.

Actors in central positions in the network also may have better knowledge of networks outside their own particular connections and a better idea of "who knows what" and knowing whom to ask for help than peripheral actors. Krackhardt (1990) has shown that accurate perceptions of the entire network are associated with power.

The power associated with central positions in the network is also the theoretical basis for Venkataramani and Tangirala's (2010) finding that actor centrality in the workflow network was related to voice—"the expression of challenging but constructive opinions, concerns, or ideas on work related issues" (p. 582). They argue that central actors develop a better understanding of work-related issues by virtue of their connections, and, because of this, their opinions are more influential. Central actors are more likely to be able to sway others and affect group decisions. As a result, their personal influence motivates them to express concerns and suggest changes out of a sense of duty to the group or organization and/or a belief that such efforts will be successful. Whereas peripheral actors may be hesitant to express contrary opinions or suggest changes for fear of negative reactions by coworkers, powerful central actors are more comfortable and willing to constructively challenge the status quo (Venkataramani & Tangirala, 2010). On the other hand, those in power may be motivated to maintain the status quo (Brass & Krackhardt, 2012).

Ties to Powerful Alters

Lin (1999) has argued that tie strength and the structural holes among alters are less important than whether the alters possess resources useful to ego. Although a more complete focus might address the complementarity of ego and alters' resources, this approach has primarily relied on status indicators. For example, Brass (1984) found that links to the dominant coalition of executives in a company were related to power and promotions for nonmanagerial employees. Following our theme of powerful others being the recipients of OCBIs, we might expect those actors who are connected to powerful alters to be providers of OCBIs targeted toward the powerful alters. Connections to powerful alters may also provide insightful information that fosters voice and the confidence to express suggestions for change. The perception of being connected to powerful others, the prism effect of network connections, carriers a "spillover" effect such that employees connected to powerful alters are also perceived as powerful, high performers (Kilduff & Krackhardt, 1994). You are known by the company you keep. Bowler and Brass (2006) found that friends of supervisors were recipients of OCBIs. Thus, the direction of the targeted OCBs may provide a useful avenue for research. Our analysis suggests that when ego is connected to a powerful alter, ego will direct OCBIs toward the powerful alter, but will also be the recipient of OCBIs from other less powerful alters.

Passing It Forward: The Diffusion of Organizational Citizenship Behavior

Research has consistently shown that OCB is positively related to attitudes such as job satisfaction, organizational commitment, and perceptions of procedural justice (Podsakoff et al., 2000). Attitudinal studies typically have treated such attitudes as independent, and recent studies of within-individual predictors of OCB have reinforced this approach (Bolino, Harvey, & Bachrach, 2012). Yet many attitudes and behaviors are not formed or exhibited in isolation but are the result of social influence. Erickson (1988) argues that people are not born with their attitudes and provides the theory and research concerning the "relational basis of attitudes." Attitude formation and change occurs primarily through social interaction. As people attempt to make sense of reality, they compare their own perceptions with those of others, in particular, similar others. They look to their proximate environment, most often their coworkers, for cues concerning which attitudes (such as OCBs) are appropriately expressed and reinforced. Differences in comparison to the attitudes of dissimilar others have little effect. Disagreements can be attributed to the dissimilarity, and they may even be used to reinforce one's own attitudes. Rice and Aydin (1991) found support for Erickson's approach, and additional network studies have found evidence for attitude similarity based on the frequency of interaction and structural equivalence (occupying similar positions in the network) (see Brass, 1995a, for review). Structural equivalence does not hinge on direct interaction. Instead, actors cognitively compare their own attitudes and behaviors with those of others occupying similar roles, rather than being influenced by direct communications from others in dissimilar roles. This is an observation and imitation form of diffusion. Although network studies of attitudes can predict similarity, they cannot predict whether the attitude will be positive or negative. However, they do confirm the notion that attitudes and behaviors can be contagious, similar to diffusion of innovation studies that follow the networks of adopters of innovations.

Diffusion refers to the spread of ideas, opinions, products, and so on through society, and it may be affected by many factors. Contagion occurs via interpersonal influence. It refers to a specific process of diffusion involving actors being influenced by other actors (through simple contact as in contagious diseases, through observation and imitation, and through persuasion by others in decision making). Social networks can help us understand where new ideas come from, identify opinion leaders, trace paths, estimate how quickly things spread, and so on. Of particular interest to OCB researchers may be emotional contagion (Brasade, 2002): the transfer and diffusion of moods, emotions, and OCBs within an organization. We thus combine the social influence and network perspectives to consider the diffusion of OCBs in organizations.

Clique Network Structure

Diffusion may begin with ego providing help to an alter (the performance of an OCBI). The seed behavior may be the result of a within-individual characteristic, high job satisfaction, or any other of the established antecedents of OCBIs. Diffusion will occur more quickly if ego is central to the network. The target, or recipient of the OCBI, will be based on proximity, homophily, or affect, as hypothesized earlier. As suggested by social exchange theory, the alter is likely to reciprocate the OCBI to ego, but reciprocation may also depend on proximity, homophily, and affect. However, reciprocation does not promote diffusion unless it is directed to other alters in a generalized fashion. Diffusion only occurs when the alter "passes it forward." Balance theory provides a theoretical explanation for localized diffusion: a friend of a friend is a friend. Thus, diffusion may occur, as hypothesized, through third-party friends or Simmilean ties, resulting in cliques, or clusters of individuals who reciprocate OCBIs and develop norms endorsing helping behavior.

The result is an OCBI network approximating the clique or "small world" structure shown in Figure 18.1. It is characterized by clusters of relatively tight-knit actors that result from tendencies toward forming ties on the basis of proximity, embeddedness, homophily, and balance. Ties are maintained by within-group reinforcement of values, reduction of uncertainty, and trust and emotional support. It's nice to be surrounded by a group

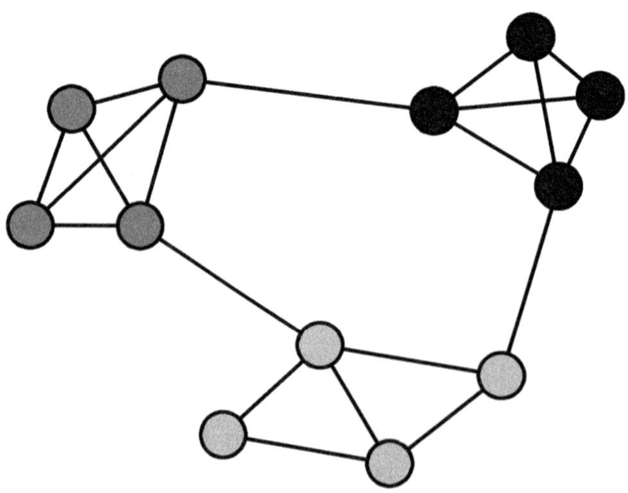

Figure 18.1 Clique network structure.

of trusting, loyal friends. Such cliques of densely connected actors can be a primary source of identity development. For example, the normative performance of OCBs can establish the "good citizen" social identity (Methot, Lepak, Shipp, & Boswell, in press). In-group, out-group biases (Linville & Jones, 1980) prevent larger, more inclusive clusters from forming, resulting in within-group homogeneity and across-group diversity.

Diffusion across groups can be difficult and only accomplished by actors with structural holes in their networks: ties to alters who are otherwise disconnected. These bridging, structural hole ties can connect different cliques and result in a "small world." Relatively few such bridging ties are necessary to create short paths to otherwise disconnected groups and result in "six degrees of separation" (see Watts, 2003, for elaboration of the "small world" phenomenon). Thus, diffusion through a clique/small-world network is dependent on bridging ties across cliques.

Such a network structure may result from OCBIs or may follow existing network structures such as the friendship or advice networks. As noted, tie formation and OCBIs may be reciprocal processes, each building on the other. Such structures are reinforced by proximity and workflow requirements accompanying functional departments in organizations. The common description of "silos" in organizations is synonymous with a clique structure and emphasizes the difficulty of diffusion across functional groups. Thus, organizations often promote cross-functional teams to provide opportunities for formation of homophilous, affective ties that bridge structural holes.

In the case of the diffusion of OCBOs, no individual is targeted and reciprocation is not directed to other individuals. However, as with OCBIs, the behavior is likely observed by others and the possibility of diffusion exists. Although the helping behavior associated with OCBIs is generally viewed positively by most employees, attitudes toward the organization and subsequent OCBOs may show considerably more variance. This raises the possibility of résistance toward exhibited OCBs by coworkers. Unlike contagious diseases where a single, simple contact is all that is required for diffusion, the diffusion of attitudes and behavior may require more. Based on Asch's (1951) conformity experiments, at least one positive response to an initial OCBO is necessary for the diffusion to continue. Employees retain their beliefs if they achieve initial support, or abandon them if they are surrounded by people who disagree with them. Likewise, a single observation of an OCBO may not be sufficient for an alter to follow suit. Centola (2010) refers to attitudinal and behavioral change as complex contagion (as differentiated from simple, disease contagion), and his experiments suggest that targets are more susceptible to persuasion when approached by different advocates at different times, each reinforcing the particular attitude or behavior. Thus, alters are more likely to imitate OCBOs when exposed to multiple others exhibiting the behavior.

The possibility of attitudinal or behavioral variance in OBCOs, or résistance, does not necessarily result in a different network structure than the clique structure described for OCBIs. Indeed, it may foster such a clique structure as employees seek out other employees with similar attitudes and behaviors (value homophily) and form cliques that reinforce those values. Thus, in instances of high variance in OCBOs or attitudes toward the organization, the cliques represent groups with differing, often conflicting attitudes. These differences reinforce in-group/out-group biases and make diffusion across groups more difficult. At the same time, they may solidify within-group helping behavior (OCBIs). Thus, we may find instances of negative relationships between OCBI and OCBO in groups that coalesce around negative attitudes and behavior toward the organization.

Core-Periphery Network Structure

An alternative network structure, a core-periphery structure as shown in Figure 18.2, may result when OCBIs are targeted toward powerful alters (rather than friends), or OCBOs are exhibited by powerful others. The core-periphery structure is characterized by a core of densely connected actors, surrounded by peripheral actors who are rarely connected to each other. This sort of network structure results from status homophily and status aspiration, or preferential attachment. Core-periphery structures in organizations are reinforced by the organizational hierarchy. Powerful actors form a core, and less powerful actors target OCBIs toward them (rather than other less powerful or equally powerful actors) in hopes of reciprocation and eventual inclusion in the core. Likewise, peripheral actors may perform OCBOs in hopes of impressing the powerful core. In this case, reciprocation of OCBs is less likely from powerful others (as noted earlier). In a core-periphery structure, central, core actors are key to the diffusion of

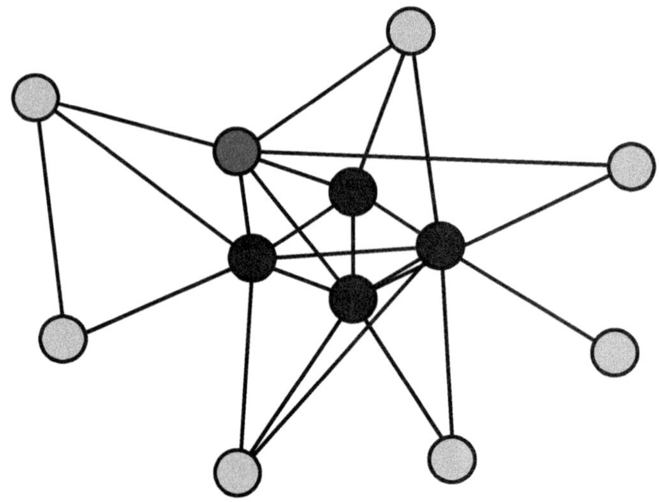

Figure 18.2 Core-periphery network structure.

OCBIs and the initiation of OCBOs. Diffusion of OCBs occurs only when the central actors in the core "pass it forward."

In reality, both clique and core-periphery structures exist, and in combination, they look a lot like organizational charts with an elite, central core of high-level managers and the peripheral actors grouped together in functional, clique-like departments with few connections across departments. Given this combined structure, diffusion of OCBs is dependent on a combination of actors who bridge structural holes between departments and central actors in the core.

Voice

Although the expression of challenging, constructive ideas may be contagious in the same manner as other forms of OCB, I consider it separately because it typically suggests change, and the spread of voice behavior may be contingent on whether others adopt the expressed change. I begin with the assumption that employees will be hesitant to express voice if challenges and suggested changes are ignored, suppressed by resistance to change, or fail to be successfully adopted and implemented. Nothing suppresses the motivation to express voice more than the feeling that "it makes no difference—nothing will happen." Successful change in organizations involves dissatisfaction with the status quo, the clear expression of the benefits of a constructive alternative, and skillfully managing the process of implementation. Clearly superior ideas will be easily implemented, clearly inferior ideas will be quickly abandoned, but it is the challenging, often controversial ideas that will likely succeed or fail based on social influence.

I begin with the assumption that constructive organizational change begins with a creative idea. Because recombination of diverse information often leads to creative ideas (Burt, 2004), people with diverse networks that span across differentiated clusters of knowledge will be the sources of good ideas. Thus, weak ties and structural holes (connections to disconnected sources of nonredundant information) will be instrumental in generating ideas and voice (Brass, 1995b; Perry-Smith, 2006; Zhou et al., 2009). The challenge for those expressing voice is to build a coalition of support for their ideas.

The first task of employees with ideas for change is to find someone who likes their ideas. Initial support is essential because employees will abandon or suppress their ideas if they are surrounded by people who disagree with them. As demonstrated in the Ash (1951) experiments, subjects will resist conforming to the majority if they have one confederate expressing support. Knowledge of the network may be particularly important. Employees may seek out others close to them in the network for feedback on the value of their ideas, and closed cliques of friends often provide social support. However, extensive bridging ties can extend this search beyond local connections and may provide a less biased reaction to an idea. Although recurring interactions based on affect, advice, or workflow may provide a probable template for building support, networks often form around issues. Employees with extensive weak-tie, bridging networks will likely have an advantage in knowing how possible partners stand on particular issues (Murnighan & Brass, 1991).

Avoiding negative opinions, especially from powerful others, may be particularly important. Because central, powerful alters may be motivated to maintain the status quo, this may mean approaching peripheral actors who are more likely to be open to change. Central actors who disagree with the proposed idea may be able to use their power or extensive network to mobilize resistance and effectively block the diffusion process. However, central actors who agree, or are the source of challenging ideas, may facilitate the diffusion. As noted earlier, Venkataramani and Tangirala (2010) found that workflow centrality was related to voice. By approaching like-minded alters, and avoiding others, those expressing voice can build the number of advocates who can, in turn, extend the diffusion process until it reaches the "tipping point." Employees are more susceptible to persuasion when approached by different advocates at different times, each reinforcing the change (Centola, 2010).

Consistent with this approach, Krackhardt's (1997) network computer simulation of organizational change suggests that employees with good ideas focus on local clusters on the periphery of the organization and avoid central core positions until requisite numbers are achieved. When the idea is controversial, nonadvocates are as likely to convert advocates to remain with the status quo as vice versa; ties across clusters tend to give the advantage to the status quo. Thus, employees first need to establish cohesive clusters of support so that nonadvocates are not mobilized. This also involves avoiding minority advocates in majority nonadvocate cliques, as the majority will quickly convert the minority advocate. Once a base is established, advocates can carefully move to adjacent clusters with sufficient numbers to convert more adopters before attempting to convert the central core or the entire organization. Krackhardt (1997) refers to this as the "principle of optimal viscosity." Organizational change is accomplished when actors in subunits are minimally connected and "the seed for change is planted at the periphery, not the center, of the network" (McGrath & Krackhardt, 2003, 328). The alternative is to be strongly connected to a central, powerful actor who is a willing advocate. As in the case of the core-periphery structure, central core actors can extend or halt the spread of ideas.

Relationships play an important role in the formation of ties, the performance of reciprocation, and possible diffusion of OCBs. Even when accounting for within- individual characteristics (Dalal, Bhave, & Fiset, 2014), OCB overload, fatigue, mood, and stress, relationships and social networks that extend beyond dyadic relationships play an important role in the diffusion of OCBs. Passing it forward reduces fatigue and encourages the establishment of normative benefits of OCB. Diffusion focuses on the longer term variation in OCB.

Conclusions

Overall, I have attempted to illustrate how a social network perspective might contribute to our understanding of OCB. The social network perspective represents an approach that falls between the undersocialized notion of within-individual differences and independent actors, and the oversocialized notion that actors readily conform to norms. I have argued that the performance and receipt of OCBs will be contingent on the network of interpersonal relationships and that the organization is not the only exchange partner. I have tried to fill in the process of going from individual characteristics and attitudes to organizational norms by focusing on the diffusion of OCBs and how the process may be affected by the network structure of the organization. In the process, I have tried to note opportunities for future research.

It has become popular to apply network thinking to various established lines of research, much as I have done in this chapter. Equally profitable would be a reverse process of applying findings from traditional research to social network analysis. What can social network researchers learn from OCB research? Existing research suggests that the study of OCB and the study of social networks represent two well-established cliques with few connecting bridges. Hopefully, this chapter will foster such bridges by energizing collaborative research.

Acknowledgments

I am indebted to Matt Bowler, Steve Borgatti, Dan Halgin, Joe Labianca, Ajay Mehra, Jessica Methot, and the other faculty and PhD students at the Links Center for Social Network Analysis for the many interesting and insightful discussions that form the basis for chapters such as this.

References

Adams, J. A. (1965). Inequity in social exchange. In L. Berkowitz (Ed.), *Advances in experimental social psychology* (Vol. 2, pp. 267–299). New York, NY: Academic Press.

Adler, P. S., & Kwon, S. (2002). Social capital: Prospects for a new concept. *Academy of Management Review, 27*, 17–40.

Asch, S. E. (1951). Effects of group pressure upon the modification and distortion of judgments. In H. Guetzkow (Ed.), *Groups, leadership, and men* (pp. 151–162). Pittsburgh, PA: Carnegie Press.

Bateman, T. S., & Organ, D. W. (1983). Job satisfaction and the good soldier: The relationship between affect and employee "citizenship." *Academy of Management Journal, 26*, 587–595.

Baumeister, R. F., Bratslavsky, E., Finkenauer, C. & Vohs, K. D. (2001). Bad is stronger than good. *Review of General Psychology, 5*, 323–370.

Blau, P. (1964). *Exchange and power in social life*. New York, NY: Wiley.

Bolino, M. C. (1999). Citizenship and impression management: Good soldiers or good actors? *Academy of Management Review, 24*, 82–98.

Bolino, M. C., Harvey, J., & Bachrach, D. G. (2012). A self-regulation approach to understanding citizenship behavior in organizations. *Organizational Behavior and Human Decision Processes, 119*, 126–139.

Bolino, M. C., Turnley, W. H., & Bloodgood, J. M. (2002). Citizenship behavior and the creation of social capital in organizations. *Academy of Management Review, 27*, 505–522.

Bolino, M. C., Turnley, W. H., & Niehoff, B. P. (2004). The other side of the story: Reexamining prevailing assumptions about organizational citizenship behavior. *Human Resource Management Review, 14*, 229–246.

Borgatti, S., Brass, D. J., & Halgin, D. S. (2014). Social network research: Confusions, criticisms, and controversies. In D. J. Brass, G. Labianca, A. Mehra, D. S. Halgin, & S. Borgatti (Eds.), *Research in the sociology of organizations* (pp. 1–33). Bradford, UK: Emerald.

Borgatti, S. P., Everett, M. G., & Freeman. (2002). *UCINET for Windows: Software for social network analysis*. Cambridge, MA: Analytic Technologies.

Borgatti, S. P., Everett, M. G., & Johnson, J. C. (2013). *Analyzing social networks*. London, UK: Sage.

Borgatti, S. P., & Foster, P. C. (2003). The network paradigm in organizational research: A review and typology. *Journal of Management, 29*, 991–1013.

Borgatti, S. P., Mehra, A., Brass, D. J., & Labianca, G. (2009). Network analysis in the social sciences. *Science, 323*, 892–895.

Borman, W. C., & Motowidlo, S. J. (1993). Expanding the criterion domain to include elements of contextual performance. In N. Schmitt & W. C. Borman (Eds.), *Personnel selection* (pp. 71–98). San Francisco, CA: Jossey-Bass.

Borman, W. C., & Motowidlo, S. J. (1997). Task performance and contextual performance: The meaning for personnel selection research. *Human Performance, 10*, 99–109.

Bowler, M., & Brass, D. J. (2006). Relational correlates of interpersonal citizenship behavior: A social network perspective. *Journal of Applied Psychology, 91*, 70–82.

Brasade, S. G. (2002). The ripple effect: Emotional contagion and its influence on group behavior. *Administrative Science Quarterly, 47*, 644–692.

Brass, D. J. (1984). Being in the right place: A structural analysis of individual influence in an organization. *Administrative Science Quarterly, 29*, 518–539.

Brass, D. J. (1995a). A social network perspective on human resources management. In G. Ferris (Ed.), *Research in personnel and human resources management* (Vol. 13, pp. 39–79). Greenwich, CT: JAI Press.

Brass, D. J. (1995b). Creativity: It's all in your social network. In C. M. Ford & D. A. Gioia (Eds.), *Creative actions in organizations* (pp. 94–99). London, UK: Sage.

Brass, D. J. (2012). A social network perspective on organizational psychology. In S. W. J. Kozlowski (Ed.), *The Oxford handbook of organizational psychology*, (pp. 667–695). New York: Oxford University Press.

Brass, D. J., & Burkhardt, M. E. (1993). Potential power and power use: An investigation of structure and behavior. *Academy of Management Journal, 36*, 441–470.

Brass, D. J., Butterfield, K. D., & Skaggs, B. C. (1998). Relationships and unethical behavior: A social network perspective. *Academy of Management Review, 23*, 14–31.

Brass, D. J., Galaskiewicz, J., Greve, H. R., & Tsai, W. (2004). Taking stock of networks and organizations: A multilevel perspective. *Academy of Management Journal, 47*, 795–819.

Brass, D. J., & Krackhardt, D. (2012). Power, politics, and social networks in organizations. In G. R. Ferris & D. C. Treadway (Eds.), *Politics in organizations: Theory and research considerations* (pp. 355–375). New York, NY: Routledge.

Breiger, R. L. (1988). The duality of persons and groups. In Barry Wellman and S. D. Berkowitz (Eds.), *Social structures: A network approach* (pp. 83–98). Cambridge, UK: Cambridge University Press.

Brief, A. P., & Motowidlo, S. J. (1986). Prosocial organizational behaviors. *Academy of Management Review, 11*, 710–725.

Burkhardt, M. E., & Brass, D. J. (1990). Changing patterns or patterns of change: The effects of a change in technology on social network structure and power. *Administrative Science Quarterly, 35*, 104–124.

Burt, R. S. (1992). *Structural holes—The social structure of competition*. Cambridge, MA: Harvard University Press.

Burt, R. S. (2004). Structural holes and good ideas. *American Journal of Sociology, 110*, 349–399.

Centola, D. (2010). The spread of behavior in an online social network experiment. *Science, 329*, 1194–1197.

Clark, M. S., & Isen, A. M. (1982). Toward understanding the relationship between feelings, tastes and social behavior. In A. H. Hastorf & A. M. Isen (Eds.), *Cognitive social psychology* (pp. 73–108). New York, NY: Elsevier.

Coleman, J. S. (1990). *Foundations of social theory*. Cambridge, MA: Harvard University Press.

Cropanzano, C., & Mitchell, M. S. (2005). Social exchange theory: An interdisciplinary review. *Journal of Management, 31*, 874–900.

Dalal, R., Bhave, D., & Fiset, J. (2014). Within-person variability in job performance: A theoretical review and research agenda. *Journal of Management, 40*, 1396–1436.

Erickson, B. H. (1988). The relational basis of attitudes. In Barry Wellman and S. D. Berkowitz (eds.), *Social structures: A network approach* (pp. 99–121). Cambridge, UK: Cambridge University Press.

Feld, S. (1981). The focused organization of social ties. *American Journal of Sociology, 86*, 1015–1035.

Gargiulo, M., & Benassi, M. (2000). Trapped in your own net: Cohesion, structural holes and the adaptation of social capital. *Organization Science, 11*, 183–196.

Granovetter, M. S. (1973). The strength of weak ties. *American Journal of Sociology, 6*, 1360–1380.

Granovetter, M. (1985). Economic action and social structure: The problem of embeddedness. *American Journal of Sociology, 91*, 481–510.

Hansen, M. T. (1999). The search-transfer problem: The role of weak ties in sharing knowledge across organization subunits. *Administrative Science Quarterly, 44*, 82–111.

Heider, R. (1958). *The psychology of interpersonal relations*. New York, NY: Wiley.

Katz, D. (1964). Motivational basis of organizational behavior. *Behavioral Science, 9*, 31–146.

Kilduff, M., & Brass, D. J. (2010). Organizational social network research: Core ideas and key debates. In J. P. Walsh & A. P. Brief (Eds.), *Academy of Management Annuals* (Vol. 4, pp. 317–357). London, UK: Routledge.

Kilduff, M., & Krackhardt, D. (1994). Bringing the individual back in: A structural analysis of the internal market for reputation in organizations. *Academy of Management Journal, 37*, 87–108.

Kleinbaum, A. M., Jordan, A. H., & Audia, P. G. (2015). An alternative perspective on the origins of brokerage in social networks: How perceived empathy moderates the self-monitoring effect. *Organization Science*, 1–17.

Krackhardt, D. (1990). Assessing the political landscape: Structure, cognition, and power in organizations. *Administrative Science Quarterly, 35*, 342–369.

Krackhardt. D. (1992). The strength of strong ties: The importance of Philos. In N. Nohria & R. Eccles (Eds.), *Networks and organizations: Structure, form, and action* (pp. 216–239). Boston, MA: Harvard Business School Press.

Krackhardt, D. (1994). Constraints on the interactive organization as an ideal type. In C. Hecksher & A. Donnellon (Eds.), *The post-bureaucratic organization: New perspectives on organizational change*, (pp. 211–222). Thousand Oaks, CA: Sage.

Krackhardt, D. (1997). Organizational viscosity and the diffusion of controversial innovations. *Journal of Mathematical Sociology, 22*, 177–199.

Krackhardt, D. (1998). Simmelian ties: Super strong and sticky. In R. M. Kramer & M. Neale (eds.), *Power and influence in organizations* (pp. 21–38). Thousand Oaks, CA: Sage.

Labianca, G., & Brass, D. J. (2006). Exploring the social ledger: Negative relationships and negative asymmetry in social networks in organizations. *Academy of Management Review, 31*, 596–614.

Labianca, G., Brass, D. J., & Gray, B. (1998). Social networks and perceptions of intergroup conflict: The role of negative relationships and third parties. *Academy of Management Journal, 41*, 55–67.

LePine, J. A., & Van Dyne, L. (1998). Predicting voice behavior in work groups. *Journal of Applied Psychology, 83*, 853–868.

Lin, N. (1999). Social networks and status attainment. *Annual Review of Sociology, 25*, 467–487.

Linville, P. W., & Jones, E. E. (1980). Polarized appraisals of ingroup members. *Journal of Personality and Social Psychology, 38*, 689–703.

Lyons, B. J., & Scott, B. A. (2012). Integrating social exchange and affective explanations for the receipt of help and harm: A social network approach. *Organizational Behavior and Human Decision Processes, 117*, 66–79.

Masterson, S. S., Lewis, K., Goldman, B. M., & Taylor, M. S. (2000). Integrating justice and social exchange: The differing effects of fair procedures and treatment on work relationships. *Academy of Management Journal, 43*, 738–748.

McGrath, C., & Krackhardt, D. (2003). Network conditions for organizational change. *The Journal of Applied Behavioral Science, 39*, 324–336.

McPherson, J. M., Smith-Lovin, L., & Cook, J. M. (2001). Birds of a feather: Homophily in social networks. *Annual Review of Sociology, 27*, 415–444.

Mehra, A., Kilduff, M., & Brass, D. J. (1998). At the margins: A distinctiveness approach to the social identity and social networks of underrepresented groups. *Academy of Management Journal, 41*, 441–452.

Methot, J. R., Lepak, D. P., Shipp, A. J., & Boswell, W. (in press). Good citizen interrupted: Calibrating a temporal theory of citizenship behavior. *Academy of Management Review.*

Moorman, R. H. (1993). The influence of cognitive and affective based job satisfaction measures on the relationship between satisfaction and organizational citizenship behavior. *Human Relations, 46*, 759–776.

Murnighan, J. K., & Brass, D. J. (1991). Intraorganizational coalitions. In M. Bazerman, B. Sheppard, & R. Lewicki (Eds.), *Research on negotiations in organizations* (Vol. 3, pp. 283–307). Greenwich, CT: JAI Press.

Organ, D. W. (1997). Organizational citizenships behavior: It's construct cleanup time. *Human Performance, 10*, 85–97.

Perry-Smith, J. E. (2006). Social yet creative: The role of social relationships in facilitating creativity. *Academy of Management Journal, 49*, 85–101.

Podolny, J. M. (2001). Networks as the pipes and prisms of the market. *American Journal of Sociology, 107*, 33–60.

Podsakoff, P. M., MacKenzie, S. B., Paine, J. B., & Bachrach, D. G. (2000). Organizational citizenship behaviors: A critical review of the theoretical and empirical literature and suggestions for future research. *Journal of Management, 26*, 513–563.

Reagans, R., Zuckerman, E., and McEvily, B. (2004). How to make the team: Social networks vs. demography as criteria for designing effective teams. *Administrative Science Quarterly, 49*, 101–133.

Rice, R. E., & Aydin, C. (1991). Attitudes toward new organizational technology: Network proximity as a mechanism for social information processing. *Administrative Science Quarterly, 36*, 219–244.

Rosenhan, D. L., Underwood B., & Moore, B. (1974). Affect moderates self-gratification and altruism. *Journal of Personality and Social Psychology, 30*, 546–552.

Settoon, R. P., & Mossholder, K. W. (2002). Relationship quality and relationship context as antecedents of person- and task-focused interpersonal citizenship behavior. *Journal of Applied Psychology, 87*, 255–267.

Spector, P. E., & Fox, S. (2002). An emotion-centered model of voluntary work behavior: Some parallels between counterproductive behavior and organizational citizenship behavior. *Human Resource Management Review, 12*, 269–292.

Uzzi, B. (1997). Social structure and competition in interfirm networks: The paradox of embeddedness. *Administrative Science Quarterly, 42*, 35–67.

Valente, T. W. (1995). *Network models of the diffusion of innovations*. Kreskill, NJ: Hampton Press.

Van Dyne, L., Cummings, L. L., & Parks, J. M. (1995). Extra-role behaviors: In pursuit of construct and definitional clarity (A bridge over muddied waters). In L. L. Cummings & B. M. Staw (Eds.), *Research in organizational behavior* (Vol. 17, pp. 215–285). Greenwich, CT: JAI Press.

Van Dyne, L., Graham, J. W., & Dienesch, R. M. (1994). Organizational citizenship behavior: Construct redefinition, measurement, and validation. *Academy of Management Journal, 37*, 765–802.

Venkataramani, V., & Dalal, R. S. (2007). Who helps and harms whom? Relational antecedents of interpersonal helping and harming in organizations. *Journal of Applied Psychology, 92*, 952–966.

Venkataramani, V., & Tangirala, S. (2010). When and why do central employees speak up? An examination of mediating and moderating variables. *Journal of Applied Psychology, 93*, 582–591.

Wang, H., Law, K. S., Hackett, R. D., Wang, D., & Chen, Z. X. (2005). Leader-member exchange as a mediator of the relationship between transformational leadership and followers' performance and organizational citizenship behavior. *Academy of Management Journal, 48*, 420–432.

Watts, D. J. (2003). *Six degrees: The science of a connected age*. New York, NY: WW Norton.

Williams, L. J., & Anderson, S. E. (1991). Job satisfaction and organizational commitment as predictors of organizational citizenship and in-role behaviors. *Journal of Management, 17*, 601–617.

Zhou, J., Shin, S. J., Brass, D. J., Choi, J., & Zhang, Z. (2009). Weak ties, conformity, and creativity. *Journal of Applied Psychology, 94*, 1544–1552.

CHAPTER

19 The Employee–Organization Relationship and Organizational Citizenship Behavior

Jacqueline A-M. Coyle-Shapiro, Marjo-Riitta Diehl, *and* Chiachi Chang

Abstract

Drawing upon social exchange theory and the norm of reciprocity, we review the employee–organization relationship (EOR). A number of EOR frameworks share common theoretical ground yet have developed independently: psychological contracts, perceived organizational support, employment relationship, social and economic exchange, and idiosyncratic deals. We examine the empirical evidence linking each of the frameworks to employees' organizational citizenship behavior (OCB). Relationships based on minimal investment (quasi-spot contracts and transactional psychological contracts) and psychological contract breach are negatively related to OCB. Economic exchange is unrelated to OCB. Relationships that demonstrate investment, support, fulfillment of obligations, and granting of idiosyncratic deals are positively related to OCB because they signal a trusting and benefit conferring relationship. We outline challenges and future research directions that address the "value addedness" of the EOR frameworks.

Key Words: employee–organization relationship, psychological contracts, perceived organizational support, idiosyncratic deals, social and economic exchange, inducement-contribution model, social exchange theory, reciprocity, organizational citizenship behavior

Give as much as you take, all shall be very well.

—*Mauss (1950, p. 71)*

This opening quote aptly illustrates the norm of reciprocity underpinning social exchange relationships and serves as a basis for this review of the employee–organization relationship (EOR) and organizational citizenship behavior (OCB). The EOR is "an overarching term to describe the relationship between the employee and organization" (Shore et al., 2004, p. 292). It encompasses a number of frameworks to include psychological contracts (Rousseau, 1989), perceived organizational support (POS) (Eisenberger, Huntington, Hutchison, & Sowa, 1986), and employment relationship (Tsui, Pearce, Porter, & Tripoli, 1997) alongside more recent frameworks such as social and economic exchange (Shore, Tetrick, Lynch, & Barksdale, 2006) and idiosyncratic deals (i-deals) (Rousseau, 2005; Rousseau, Ho, & Greenberg, 2006). Although these frameworks developed independently and are distinct, they share common ground in capturing the relationship (or some element of it) that employees develop with their organization or the relationship the organization develops with a group of employees. They also share their theoretical foundation in social exchange theory (Blau, 1964) and the inducement-contribution model (March & Simon, 1958).

Social exchange theory is one of the most influential conceptual frameworks for understanding behavior in organizations (Cropanzano & Mitchell, 2005); it is a prominent micro theory in the *Academy of Management Journal* (Colquitt & Zapata-Phelan, 2007) and one of the most often evoked theories in the *Journal of Applied Psychology* (Colquitt, Baer, Long, & Halvorsen-Ganepola, 2014). Its versatility is illustrated by the number of phenomena it explains, which include workplace exclusion (Scott, Restubog, & Zagenczyk, 2013), negative employee behaviors (Bordia, Restubog, & Tang, 2008; Parzefall & Salin, 2010), customer satisfaction (Zablah, Carlson, Donavan, Maxham, & Brown, 2016), corporate social responsibility (Slack, Corlett, & Morris, 2014), and employee health (Heaphy & Dutton, 2008). Our focus here is to examine how the EOR frameworks that draw upon social exchange theory help explain organizational citizenship behavior (OCB). Although the origins of OCB can be traced back to Barnard (1938) and Katz (1964), it was Organ and his colleagues who first used the term to capture "individual behavior that is discretionary, not directly or explicitly recognized by the formal reward system, and that in the aggregate promotes the effective functioning of the organization" (Organ, 1988, p. 4). Organ's (1988) conceptualization of OCB included five dimensions: altruism, conscientiousness, sportsmanship, courtesy, and civic virtue and has received the greatest amount of empirical attention (LePine, Erez, & Johnson, 2002). That said, there are a number of different taxonomies of OCB (Borman & Motowidlo, 1993; Morrison, 1994; Van Dyne, Graham, & Dienesch, 1994) and Podsakoff, MacKenzie, Paine, and Bachrach's (2000) comprehensive review identify almost 30 potentially different forms of OCB that they organize into seven themes: helping behavior, sportsmanship, organizational loyalty, organizational compliance, individual initiative, civic virtue, and self-development. Williams and Anderson (1991) subgroup citizenship behaviors dependent upon the target beneficiary such that altruism and courtesy are behaviors directed toward individuals (OCBI) and sportsmanship, civic virtue, and conscientiousness are behaviors directed toward the organization (OCBO). This subgrouping is germane to this review as we examine whether there is a differential impact of the EOR on OCBO and OCBI.

Our review is organized as follows. First, we present the theoretical foundation of the EOR frameworks by reviewing the tenets of social exchange theory and the norm of reciprocity. We then review each of the frameworks prior to examining the empirical evidence linking the EOR to employees' OCB. Finally, we present some reflections on the EOR–OCB relationship and close with some challenges and future research directions.

Employee–Organization Relationship Frameworks

Understanding the EOR from an exchange perspective has captured the attention of researchers as reflected in the number of frameworks that purport to capture some element of this relationship. Three of the frameworks, psychological contracts, idiosyncratic deals, and employment relationship, capture the resources and contributions in the exchange relationship—the former two from the perspective of the employee and the latter from the perspective of the organization. POS and social and economic exchange capture relationship quality; the amount of support provided (or perceived to be provided) is the key element of POS, whereas social and economic exchange capture high and low relationship quality though some consideration is given to the resources exchanged (socioemotional and economic).

Our inclusion/exclusion decision in terms of EOR frameworks was guided by the criteria of a relational focus, capturing some element of the exchange between the employee and organization (and vice versa) and drawing upon social exchange theory as a theoretical basis. With this in mind, we excluded constructs that draw upon social exchange theory to capture the relationship that develops between an employee and his or her supervisor such as leader–member exchange (Graen & Uhl-Bien, 1995) and perceived supervisor support (Rhoades, Eisenberger, & Armeli, 2001). We also exclude organizational justice because it does not capture the relationship per se that develops between employees and their organization, although we do recognize that justice facilitates the development of social exchange relationships (Colquitt et al., 2013).

Underpinning Theories in the Employee–Organization Relationship

The EOR literature primarily draws upon two theoretical frameworks: social exchange theory (Blau, 1964; Gouldner, 1960) and the inducements-contribution model (March & Simon, 1958). The inducements-contribution model (March & Simon, 1958) has its roots in Barnard's (1938) notion of "exchange of utilities" and explicitly focuses on the resources exchanged as part of the employee–organization relationship. A key element of this model is the idea that organizations need to provide inducements that are greater in value vis-à-vis the contribution employees are required to make—it is these contributions that enable the organization to continue to provide future inducements. The organization can only succeed (and survive) as long as the contributions from employees are sufficient to elicit the inducements from the organization, which must be "large enough" to elicit those contributions—reflecting a contingent interplay between inducements provided and contributions required.

Although March and Simon (1958) did not explicitly discuss reciprocity, it is implicit in their theorizing. Gouldner (1960) was the first to define reciprocity and outline its functioning. He suggests that the norm of reciprocity is universal and makes two demands of individuals: "(1) people should help those who have helped them, and (2) people should not injure those who have helped them" (Gouldner, 1960 p. 171). The obligation to reciprocate is contingent upon the value of the benefit received such that the "debt is in proportion to and varies with—among other things—the intensity of the recipient's need at the time the benefit was bestowed ('a friend in need . . . '), the resources of the donor ('he gave although he could ill afford it'), the motives imputed to the donor ('without thought of gain'), and the nature of the constraints which are perceived to exist or be absent ('he gave of his own free will')" (Gouldner, 1960, p. 171). According to Gouldner (1960), when one party gives a benefit, an obligation is created and the recipient is indebted to the donor until such point as he or she repays the benefit.

Blau (1964) is credited with distinguishing social from economic exchange (for a detailed review of the historical development of social exchange theory, see Coyle-Shapiro & Diehl, 2018). Social exchange and economic exchange differ along the following dimensions: specificity of the exchange, trust, and duration of the relationship. Economic exchange captures a specified exchange where the formal agreement assures that each party fulfils its obligations to the other (Blau, 1964). Blau (1964) defines social exchange as involving unspecified obligations—"favors that create diffuse future obligations, not precisely specified ones, and the nature of the return cannot be bargained about but must be left to the discretion of the one who makes it" (p. 93). Social exchange takes time to develop, starting with small exchanges. As trust develops, so too does the nature of the resources exchanged. As Blau (1964) notes, "doing a favour demonstrates trust in another; the other's reciprocation validates this trust as justified" (p. 107). According to Blau (1964), the timing of reciprocation is important—"posthaste reciprocation of favors, which implies a refusal to stay indebted for a while and hence an insistence on a more businesslike relationship is condemned as improper" (p. 99) because this would demonstrate ingratitude. This would hinder the development of trust. Finally, economic and social exchange differ in terms of duration of the relationship—economic exchange is time limited, whereas social exchange is indefinite and ongoing with a longer term orientation. The long-term orientation facilitates the development of trust and enables a predictability to develop between the exchange partners in terms of bestowing a benefit, creating an obligation to reciprocate, and discharging that obligation.

In sum, social exchange theory posits that social exchange relationships develop slowly as the value of the resources exchanged increases and trust develops through the adherence to the norm of reciprocity. The latter demonstrates each party's trustworthiness to reciprocate prior benefits received and indebtedness to the other party for a period of time, which facilitates the development of trust. Having reviewed the theoretical underpinnings of the EOR frameworks, we now examine each in more detail.

Psychological Contracts

Rousseau (1989, p. 123) defines psychological contracts as "an individual's beliefs regarding the terms and conditions of a reciprocal exchange agreement between the focal person and another party." Psychological contract captures an employee's subjective evaluation of the reciprocal exchange with the organization in terms of what both parties promise to each other. Although psychological contracts can take a variety of forms (Rousseau, 1995; Rousseau & Wade-Benzoni, 1994; Thompson & Bunderson, 2003), the primary emphasis of empirical investigations has been on transactional and relational contracts. Transactional contracts capture short-term economic relationships where mutual obligations are clearly specified. Relational contracts are characterized by the long-term exchange of socioemotional resources (Rousseau, 1995).

In comparison to the content of the psychological contract, an individual's evaluation of his o her psychological contract (fulfilment, breach, and violation) has garnered a significant body of empirical evidence. Psychological contract fulfilment is defined as "the extent to which one party to the contract deems the other has met its obligations" (Lee, Liu, Rousseau, Hui, & Chen, 2011, p. 204). In contrast, psychological contract breach is defined as "the cognition that one's organization has failed to meet one or more obligations within one's psychological contract in a manner commensurate with one's contributions" (Morrison & Robinson, 1997), whereas violation captures the emotional and affective reaction arising from the experience of psychological contract breach (Morrison & Robinson, 1997) and is described as "an intense reaction of outrage, shock, resentment, and anger" (Rousseau, 1989, p. 129). These evaluations or experiences of the psychological contract are conceptually and empirically distinct. Psychological contract fulfilment and breach capture an individual's cognitive judgement and evaluation, whereas violation captures the emotional reaction. Moreover, fulfilment potentially shapes the relationship positively, whereas both breach and violation could signal the disruption of the relationship and induce negative change (Shore, Coyle-Shapiro, & Chang, in press). Therefore, we would expect a positive association between relational contracts, contract fulfilment, and OCB and a negative association between contract breach/violation and OCB.

Perceived Organizational Support

Perceived organizational support (POS) captures an individual's perception concerning the degree to which an organization values his or her contributions and cares about his or her well-being (Eisenberger et al., 1986). Organizational support theory posits that employees make attributions concerning the organization's intentions behind their receipt of favorable or unfavorable treatment and that favorable discretionary treatment and treatment that fulfils the needs of employees should enhance POS (Kurtessis et al., in press). Such discretionary treatment signals that the donor genuinely values and respects the recipient and hence POS is thought to fulfil socioemotional needs. On the basis of the norm of reciprocity, POS evokes a felt obligation to care about the welfare of the organization and help the organization achieve its objectives (Rhoades & Eisenberger, 2002).

The development of organizational support is influenced by the discretionary nature of the favorable treatment received, and two meta-analyses support the importance of organizational justice in positively affecting employees' perceptions of organizational support (Kurtessis et al., in press; Rhoades & Eisenberger, 2002). Additional antecedents include supervisor support and human resource practices that signal investment in and a positive valuation of employees. Thus, positive treatment of employees creates perceptions of organizational support that, in turn, creates an obligation to reciprocate; one way of discharging this obligation is for employees to engage in OCB.

Employment Relationships

Tsui et al. (1997) define the employment relationship as "the employer's expectations about specific contributions that it desires from employees and the inducements that it uses to effect the desired contributions" (p. 1091). Drawing upon the inducement-contribution model and exchange theory (Blau, 1964; March & Simon, 1958), Tsui et al. (1997) outline four approaches based on relative balance between contributions/inducements and whether the content of the inducements/contributions is economic or social. The quasi-spot contract represents a balanced economic exchange that is highly specific, in which the employer offers short-term purely economic inducements in return for highly specified outcomes. The second type of balanced relationship is termed "mutual investment," which presents a balanced social exchange that arises when both the employee and employer have an open-ended, long-term investment that is broad in scope. The two unbalanced relationships are underinvestment and overinvestment. The underinvestment approach favors the employer: They expect broad and open-ended obligations from employees in return for short-term economic inducements without committing to a long-term relationship. The overinvestment approach favors the employee: The employer offers long-term investment and open-ended rewards in return for highly specified employee outcomes. An important distinguishing feature of this framework is that it captures the *employer's* perspective—how managers view the exchange of inducements and contributions for employees in particular jobs within the organization. Although Tsui et al. (1997) recognize that employees' expectations are important, they argue that it is the employer who defines the bulk of employment contracts with employees.

These four types of employment relationships are likely to have a differential effect on the extent to which employers expect employees to engage in OCB. In the quasi-spot contract, given the highly specific nature of employee contributions in terms of their core job, engagement in OCB is likely to be low because these types of behaviors are not expected by the organization. Citizenship-type behaviors are also likely to be low under the overinvestment approach as those behaviors are unlikely to be expected by the organization. However, how employees respond to overinvestment by the organization may elicit OCB as a way of alleviating feelings of indebtedness. Tsui et al. (1997) argue that in the underinvestment approach where the organization expects employees to engage in behaviors that help the organization yet at the same time, these employees can be laid off at short notice, OCB is likely to be low. Although organizations expect it, employees may not engage in OCB as a way of "rebalancing" the imbalance favoring the employer in that relationship. Finally, in the mutual investment approach, employees receive high investments from the organization in terms of job security and career development and, in return, there is an expectation that employees will have the organization's broad interests and needs in mind and consequently engage in cooperative behaviors that protect and enhance the interests of the organization. Unlike the other EOR frameworks that adopt the perspective of the employee and his or her willingness to engage in OCB based on employer treatment, the attention here is on whether the employer can expect employees to engage in OCB as part of their contributions.

Social and Economic Exchange

Shore and colleagues (2006) developed a process model based on Blau's (1964) differentiation between social and economic exchange to focus on the nature of the relationship employees develop with their organization. Drawing on Blau's (1964) theorizing, the authors differentiated social from economic exchange along the following criteria: trust, investment, time orientation (long term versus short term), and socioemotional versus financial focus of exchange. *Trust* is needed for building a social exchange relationship because risk is taken by the donor regarding if, when, and how beneficial treatment will be reciprocated. In economic exchange, trust is not needed because there is specification of what is reciprocated as part of the exchange. Social exchange requires *investment* because it begins with small gestures and develops gradually with exchanges of increasing value that facilitate the development of trust and the continuation of the relationship. Given the specificity of economic exchange and the lack of trust required, investment is not an element of economic exchange. Social exchange has a *long-term orientation* because the timing of returns for beneficial treatment is unspecified and diffuse, whereas the relationship is time bound for economic exchange. The nature of resources differs—social exchange emphasizes *socioemotional* elements (e.g., trust, commitment, support), whereas economic exchange emphasizes *financial and tangible* elements (e.g., pay and benefits). In view of these differences, one would anticipate a positive relationship between social exchange and OCB. Economic exchange and OCB should be unrelated because impersonal inducements do not signal that employees are valued by the organization (Shore et al., 2006). Hence, the basis of reciprocation is absent.

Shore et al. (2006) developed and validated measures of social (e.g., there is a lot of give and take in my relationship with my organization) and economic (e.g., the most accurate way to describe my work situation is to say that I give a fair day's work for a fair day's pay) exchange, which were found to be distinct yet negatively correlated (–.35 to –.52). The authors found differential relations to both antecedents and outcomes supporting the distinctiveness of the two exchanges.

Idiosyncratic Deals

The idiosyncratic deals (i-deals) framework describes an employment relationship wherein its terms are individually agreed. According to Rousseau and colleagues (2006, p. 978), i-deals can be defined as "voluntary, personalized agreements of a nonstandard nature negotiated between individual employees and their employers regarding terms that benefit each party." Although i-deals have long existed for star performers, increased labor market pressures and workers' heightened expectations toward their work and employer have made such arrangement more common (cf. Liao, Wayne, & Rousseau, 2016). The majority of empirical studies capture i-deals relating to flexibility and personal/professional development (Conway & Coyle-Shapiro, 2015). By individualizing employment conditions according to employee needs, employers provide special conditions that employees eventually reciprocate (Anand, Vidyarthi, Liden, & Rousseau, 2010; Hornung, Rousseau, & Glaser, 2008; Liu, Lee, Hui, Kwan, & Wu, 2013; Ng & Feldman, 2015).

I-deals can be characterized by the following four features (Rousseau, 2005; Rousseau et al., 2006). First, i-deals are individually initiated by either the employer or the employee, although it is more common for an employee to negotiate such an arrangement. Second, the terms of i-deals are heterogeneous, creating differing conditions for employees working in similar positions in the same workplace. For example, some i-deals may be more driven by developmental needs and career aspirations, whereas others are geared toward flexibility in working times or specific tasks (Hornung, Rousseau, Glaser, Angerer, & Weigl, 2010). Third, i-deals mutually benefit the employee and the employer, so that both parties have their interests served. Whereaes employers' interest in i-deals is typically driven by a motivation and need to recruit, retain, and reward valued performers, for employees i-deals serve as an indicator of their value (Rosen, Slater, Chang, & Johnson, 2013; Rousseau, 2005; Rousseau et al., 2006) and allow for preferred working conditions and flexibility (Liao et al., 2016). Fourth, the scope of i-deals varies so that the relative proportion of the idiosyncratic to standardized conditions varies (Rousseau, 2005; Rousseau et al., 2006). The degree to which such customization is beneficial to the parties involved is presently not known (Liao et al., 2016). I-deals can provide a reason for employees to reciprocate, for example, through OCB, especially when an i-deal is construed as a form of organizational support by the recipient (Anand et al., 2010; Rousseau et al., 2006).

Another important aspect of i-deals concerns the coworkers of employees who have negotiated i-deals. As Rousseau and colleagues (2006) observe, i-deals can in fact be considered as an exchange between three parties as the special treatment of one person can create costs for others, especially when resources are constrained. By definition, i-deals create differences among coworkers in conditions of the EOR and will need to be carefully managed to avoid exacerbation of injustice and eradication of trust (Lai, Rousseau, & Chang, 2009). As a result, coworkers may need to adjust their performance in order to fill the gaps created by the nonstandard arrangements granted to i-dealers. For example, coworkers may need to cover up some tasks of a colleague who has negotiated a workload reduction. In such situations, coworker behaviors may be expected or explicitly agreed and therefore not discretionary; they may at times also involve OCB where the target is either the organization or i-dealer or another colleague affected by the i-deal (Rousseau et al., 2006). Furthermore, coworkers who go an extra mile to compensate for an i-dealer may in return expect reciprocation from the i-dealer, which may take the form of OCB.

The underlying premise of the EOR frameworks covered here is that POS, social exchange, psychological contract fulfilment, i-deals, and two types of ER—mutual investment and overinvestment—should be positively associated with citizenship behavior. In contrast, quasi-spot contract, psychological contract breach, and violation are negatively associated with OCB, whereas economic exchange is unrelated. We now turn to the empirical evidence.

Empirical Evidence: Psychological Contracts

Psychological contract breach has received the greatest empirical attention in terms of its consequences (Conway & Briner, 2009) and, not surprising, psychological contract breach has been found to be negatively associated with OCB (Chen, Tsui, & Zhong, 2008; Lo & Aryee, 2003; Robinson, 1996), supporting the idea that employees reciprocate detrimental treatment with a withdrawal of OCB. Conversely, psychological contract fulfilment is positively related to OCB (Coyle-Shapiro & Kessler, 2000) and Shih and Lin (2012) found that felt obligations mediated the relationship between psychological contract fulfilment and OCB in a Taiwanese sample. Turning to psychological contract content, Zagenczyk, Restubog, Kiewitz, Kiazad, and Tang (2014) provide convergent support, based on four studies in the Philippines, that a transactional psychological contract is negatively associated with OCB, consistent with the findings of two studies in China (Hui, Lee, & Rousseau, 2004; Si, Wei, & Li, 2008). In addition, transactional psychological contract was found to be the mediator between employee Machiavellianism and OCB (Zagenczyk et al., 2014). Do these relationships hold true for OCBO and OCBI?

As psychological contracts capture an employee's relationship with his or her organization, it stands to reason that it should have a greater impact on OCBO than OCBI (Robinson & Morrison, 1995). Current empirical evidence is, however, mixed. Turnley, Bolino, Lester, and Bloodgood (2003) found that fulfilment is more strongly associated with OCBO than OCBI, and this pattern is replicated with breach in another study (Rosen, Chang, Johnson, & Levy, 2009). In their longitudinal study, Conway, Kiefer, Hartley, and Briner (2014) empirically established a negative relationship between breach and OCBO, but the relationship between breach and OCBI was not significant. The evidence questioning the differential effect of psychological contracts on OCBO and OCBI is contradictory—with breach significantly associated with both OCBO and OCBI and no difference in term of the strength of associations (Chen et al., 2008; Restubog, Bordia, & Tang, 2007; Suazo & Stone-Romero, 2011). One potential explanation for these mixed findings is culture. All the studies supporting a differential effect were conducted in the United States and the United Kingdom, suggesting that target-specific reciprocation may be more prominent in individualistic cultures. Evidence of a differential effect has not yet been demonstrated with an Asian sample (Chen et al., 2008; Restubog et al., 2007; Suazo & Stone-Romero, 2011).

A prominent explanation for the relationship between psychological contract breach/fulfilment, although rarely tested empirically, is the norm of reciprocity. Recent empirical studies (Bordia et al., 2008; Restubog, Zagenczyk, Bordia, Bordia, & Chapman, 2015) have explicitly tested the motivational intent underlying employees' responses to contract breach and find support for the negative norm of reciprocity as revenge cognitions mediate the relationship between breach and employee deviance. However, for the most part, the relationship between contract fulfilment and positive employee responses is assumed to occur as a result of the positive norm of reciprocity. Coyle-Shapiro (2002) found that employees engage in reactive and proactive reciprocation to explain the relationship between perceived employer obligations and perceived delivered inducements on OCB—employees reciprocate inducements received but also engage in OCB to ensure that employer obligations materialize into inducements in the future.

Aside from reciprocity, other explanations have been identified. Robinson and Morrison (1995) found that psychological contract breach negatively predicted trust in the employer 1 year later, and trust fully mediated the relationship between breach and employees' civic virtue behavior. The same mediational effect of trust was demonstrated in two other studies (Lo & Aryee, 2003; Robinson, 1996). Drawing on expectancy theory (Vroom, 1964), Hui et al. (2004) argue that the instrumentality of OCB, which refers to the degree to which the employees believe their supervisors value OCB, will mediate the relationship between psychological contract content and OCB. Their findings suggest that relational and balanced contracts enhance the instrumentality of OCB because these relationships are long term and open ended, implicitly signaling that OCB is valued. This, in turn, increases OCB. However, Shih and Chen (2011) failed to find the same mediational effect of instrumentality in the relationship between relational, balanced psychological contract fulfilment and OCB.

Psychological contract breach is likely to undermine employees' feelings of oneness with the organization, and it may lead to a negative reevaluation of the organization's attraction to the employee (Wei & Si, 2013; Zagenczyk et al., 2013; Zagenczyk, Gibney, Few, & Scott, 2011). Topa, Francisco, Morales, and Moriano (2009) found that organizational identification mediates the negative relationship between breach and OCB, supporting the idea that when employees psychologically detach from a relationship, their behavior follows suit. Restubog, Hornsey, Bordia, and Esposo (2008) integrate trust and organizational identification to explain how contract breach leads to a reduction in OCB. The authors argue that the strength of organizational identification depends on an expectation toward the future, which is epitomized by trust in the organization. Empirically, they demonstrate that trust mediates the effect of breach on organizational identification that, in turn, mediates the effect of trust on OCB.

A meta-analysis conducted by Zhao, Wayne, Glibkowski, and Bravo (2007) finds that psychological contract breach will initially provoke an affective reaction, which leads to cognitive reaction and then a behavioral consequence. Based on affective-events theory (Weiss & Cropanzano, 1996), Zhao et al., (2007) found that breach strongly predicts cognitive responses such as commitment, and this relationship is mediated by affective responses such as mistrust. The meta-analysis found that the cognitive response mediated the effect of affective responses on OCB.

A number of studies have examined individual and cultural moderators in the relationship between breach and OCB. Agreeableness, conscientiousness, empathy, equity sensitivity, and exchange ideology have been found to moderate the relationship between breach and OCB. Employees high in agreeableness or conscientiousness tend to have lower tolerance for negative relational events such as breach, or regard breach as an achievement failure leading to great disappointment. As a result, the effect of breach on OCB is amplified for highly agreeable or conscientious employees (Shih & Chuang, 2013). Employees who possess high levels of empathy are better able to view psychological contract breach from the organization's viewpoint, which mitigates the negative relationship between breach and citizenship behavior (Shih & Chen, 2011). Equity sensitivity refers to the preferences of outcome/input ratios, with individuals high in equity sensitivity preferring overrewarded situations (Huseman, Hatfield, & Miles, 1987). It is argued that employees with higher equity sensitivity tend to be more vigilant in monitoring the exchange relationship and are more likely to get even by reducing OCB when they experience breach. Restubog et al. (2007) found that equity sensitivity amplified the negative effect of breach on OCB. Finally, there is a paucity of studies examining how culture impacts employee responses to psychological contracts. Traditionality, which includes values of authority, fatalism, sense of powerlessness, and obedience, has been shown to weaken the negative relationship between breach and OCB in China (Chen et al., 2008).

Empirical Evidence: Perceived Organizational Support

Empirical evidence supporting a relationship between POS and OCB is positive and consistent across studies. A number of studies have found a positive relationship between POS and OCB (Eisenberger, Fasolo, & Davis-LaMastro, 1990; Shore & Wayne, 1993; Wayne, Shore, & Liden, 1997) and Moorman, Blakely, and Niehoff (1998) found that POS mediated the relationship between procedural justice and three dimensions of OCB: interpersonal helping, personal industry, and loyal boosterism but not individual initiative. This finding is consistent with a recent meta-analysis (Colquitt et al., 2013) revealing that the effects of organizational justice on OCB are mediated through social exchange quality (trust, organizational commitment, POS, and LMX). Masterson, Lewis, Goldman, and Taylor (2000) found that POS was positively related to OCBO (and partially mediated the effects of procedural justice), and LMX fully mediated the effects of interactional justice on supervisor-directed OCB. Lavelle, McMahan, and Harris (2009) found support for the target similarity model, which proposes target-specific links between justice, social exchange, and citizenship behavior. Their findings reveal that organizational procedural justice was uniquely associated with POS; supervisor procedural justice explained unique variance in perceived supervisor support while workgroup interactional justice explained unique variance in perceived workgroup support. These different sources of support were differentially related to forms of citizenship behavior such that POS was uniquely related to OCBO; perceived supervisor support related to OCBI directed to supervisors, and workgroup support was related to OCBI toward the workgroup. The authors argue that "employees selectively direct their citizenship behavior toward certain beneficiaries depending upon the level of perceived support from these parties" (p. 2430).

Three meta-analytic studies provide consistent support for the relationship between POS and OCB. Riggle, Edmondson, and Hansen (2009) found a weak positive relationship between POS and contextual performance ($r = .26$, $p < .001$) but did not differentiate between the target beneficiary of such behaviors. Rhoades and Eisenberger (2002) found in their meta-analysis of 70 studies that the relationship between POS and OCBI was positive and small, whereas the relationship between POS and OCBO was positive and moderate. In a recent meta-analysis of 558 studies, Kurtessis et al. (2017) found that POS was more strongly related to OCBO than OCBI, supporting a multifoci perspective on social exchange (Lavelle, Rupp, & Brockner, 2007). The empirical evidence suggests that employees reciprocate organizational supportiveness by engaging in OCB and the idea that beneficial treatment should create a felt obligation to care about and aid the organization was explicitly examined by Eisenberger, Armeli, Rexwinkel, Lynch, and Rhoades (2001). The authors found that felt obligation mediated the relationship between POS and organizational spontaneity rated by supervisors. This finding supports the central tenet of social exchange theory—the conferring of a benefit creates an obligation to reciprocate.

To determine the direction of influence between POS and OCB, Chen, Eisenberger, Johnson, Sucharski, and Aselage (2009) conducted a longitudinal study measuring POS and extra-role performance at two points 3 years apart. They found that POS was positively related to temporal change in extra-role performance but that extra-role performance was not related to temporal change in POS. These findings support the view that POS leads to extra-role performance and as such is consistent with the tenets of social exchange theory. This study did not differentiate between OCBO and OCBI.

Given that the evidence thus far suggests that POS conforms to the predictions of social exchange theory, we now turn our attention to potential boundary conditions and in particular the role of exchange-related dispositions and cultural moderators. Because social exchange assumes that the reciprocation of valued benefits initiates and facilitates the development of social exchange relationships, individuals may view the receipt of valuable resources with a degree of suspicion stemming from a generalized fear of mistreatment and the vulnerability of being taken advantage of. Eisenberger, Cotterell, and Marvel (1987) identified reciprocation wariness as a generalized cautiousness in reciprocating aid due to a fear of exploitation, and this can apply not only to interpersonal relationships but also the employee–organization relationship (Lynch, Eisenberger, & Armeli, 1999). Wary individuals are hesitant to provide aid or return aid as they fear that others will use the norm of reciprocity to exploit them if they respond generously to favorable treatment (Lynch et al., 1999). Lynch et al. (1999) conclude "in deciding whether to work beyond the minimum required in standard job activities and engage in extra-role actions that aid the organization, reciprocation-wary employees consider the extent to which the organization values their contributions and cares about their well-being" (p. 477). The authors found that when POS was low, reciprocation wariness was negatively related to extra-role performance because employees' fear of exploitation reduced their willingness to go "the extra mile." However, when POS was high, reciprocation wariness was positively related to extra-role performance, suggesting that unexpected favorable treatment may reduce anxiety and fear of exploitation among wary employees. Exchange ideology captures the extent to which individuals base their concern for the welfare of the organization and their work effort on the favorability of their treatment by the organization (Eisenberger et al., 2001) such that an individual with a strong exchange ideology would base what he or she does for the organization on how favorably the organization treats him or her. Eisenberger et al. (2001) found that the relationship between POS and felt obligation was greater for employees with a strong exchange ideology.

To what extent do these findings hold true in different cultural contexts? Farh, Hackett, and Liang (2007) examined power distance and traditionality in the relationship between POS and OCB—altruism (OCBI), voice, and conscientiousness (OCBO). They found that power distance moderated the relationship between POS and all three dimensions of OCB such that the relationship was stronger for individuals who were low rather than high on power distance. Traditionality captures "the extent to which an individual endorses the traditional hierarchical role relationships prescribed by Confucian social ethics" (Farh et al., 2007, p. 717), and the findings support the moderating role of traditionality in the relationship between POS and OCB such that the relationship is stronger for individuals who are low on traditionality. Knippenberg, Prooijen, and Sleebos (2015) examined the moderating role of collectivism in the relationship between POS and OCB in the Netherlands. The authors argue that collectivists will be less likely to evaluate their relationship with the organization in terms of the exchange of benefits and hence less based on reciprocity. Their findings suggest that POS is positively related to OCB rated by supervisors for employees with less collectivistic values, whereas POS was unrelated to OCB for employees with more collectivistic values.

A recent meta-analysis (Rockstuhl, Ang, Shore, & Mesdaghinia, 2015) of POS–OCB relationship across 42 countries demonstrated that POS was more strongly related to OCB in vertical collectivist than horizontal-individualist cultures, controlling for national differences in regulatory control, political democracy, capital availability, and market liquidity. The authors explain this based on the greater interdependence of the self with social institutions; hence, organizations are an important source of affiliative need fulfilment, and felt obligation to help the organization would have a more influential role in employee behavior.

Overall, the weight of the evidence suggests a positive relationship between POS and OCB and, in particular, citizenship behavior directed toward the organization. Developing perceptions of organizational support creates an obligation to reciprocate which employees discharge by engaging in OCB, which is consistent with social exchange theory. Although the thrust of the empirical evidence suggests that this relationship is universal (Rockstuhl et al., 2015), there are exchange and cultural moderators that strengthen (e.g., low wariness, low power distance, low traditionality, and low collectivism) this relationship.

Empirical Evidence: Employment Relationships

A starting point to note when reviewing the empirical evidence between the ER and OCB is the relative absence (in comparison to the other EOR frameworks) of empirical studies. Tsui et al. (1997) found that the mutual investment approach was associated with higher ratings of OCBO than the quasi-spot contract or underinvestment approaches but was not significantly higher than the overinvestment approach. These findings suggest that from an organization's perspective, offering open-ended inducements and a high level of social exchange pays off in terms of employee engagement in OCB. This occurs when the exchange is balanced (mutual investment) or skewed in the employee's favor (overinvestment), demonstrating the organization's investment in the relationship. One could speculate that organizational investment in employees creates an obligation on their part to reciprocate (independent from employer expectations), and this may explain why both the investment approaches are associated with OCB.

Hom et al. (2009) found that mutual investment increased social exchange relative to underinvestment ERs and quasi-spot contracts. Whereas overinvestment was also positively related to social exchange, mutual investment was more strongly related. This finding was replicated in an 18-month lagged study demonstrating that mutual investment and, to a lesser extent, overinvestment were positively related to perceptions of social exchange. In a sample of middle managers in China, Song, Tsui, and Law (2009) found that the mutual investment approach (as reported by top managers) was positively related to OCB of middle managers (altruism, conscientiousness, and civic virtue), whereas quasi-spot contract (as reported by top managers) was negatively related to middle managers' OCB. The authors hypothesize that the mutual investment approach is likely to be interpreted by employees as a social exchange relationship because it signals trust and investment, which employees reciprocate by engaging in OCB. Conversely, a quasi-spot contract will signal a short-term calculative economic exchange and employees will not contribute beyond their assigned tasks. The study findings did not support the mediating role of social exchange in the relationship between mutual investment and OCB. However, economic exchange mediated the relationship between quasi-spot contract and OCB.

In another study of Chinese telcom employees, Wang, Zhou, and Wen (2014) examined the relationship between two employment modes (mutual investment and quasi-spot contract) and OCB rated by supervisors and found that job security partially mediated this relationship. The authors argue that a mutual investment mode leads to perceptions of job security that, in turn, prompt OCB, and the converse would hold true for quasi-spot contracts. This finding suggests that benefits (signaling investment by the organization) given to employees provide the basis for reciprocation in the form of OCB. Although OCBO and OCBI were measured, the analysis was done on OCB overall.

The empirical work that exists suggests that mutual investment ER yields better explanatory power in explaining OCB than the other ER modes. Although it would be premature to make any definitive conclusions on the role of social exchange in explaining how ER modes are related to OCB due to the paucity of empirical investigations, a few tentative observations can be made. First, the empirical evidence suggests that quasi-spot contracts do not reflect a level of organizational investment required to prompt employee reciprocation in the form of OCB. Second, it seems that while it is possible that a mutual investment approach can facilitate the development of social exchange relationships, prompting employees to go beyond the call of duty, other mechanisms need to be explored, such as job embeddedness (Hom et al., 2009).

Empirical Evidence: Social and Economic Exchange

In their development and validation study of social and economic exchange, Shore et al. (2006) found that employee perceptions of their social exchange relationship (with their organization) were positively associated with manager ratings of altruism citizenship behavior, whereas economic exchange was not found to be related to OCB. High levels of POS were related to social exchange, and low levels of POS contributed to economic exchange. The study found that social exchange mediated the relationship between POS and OCB. The findings support the idea that social exchange encourages behavior that contributes to organizational goals.

A number of empirical studies have examined the mediating roles of social and economic exchange. Kim, Aryee, Loi, and Kim (2013) found that employees' perceptions of their social exchange relationship with their organization mediated the relationship between person–organization fit and OCBO rated by the supervisor in a South Korean organization. This suggests that organizations can facilitate the development of a social exchange relationship through careful attention to selection processes. Redmond (2013), using a sample of Norwegian employees, found that social exchange positively mediated the relationship between employees' perception of their organization's competency model and OCBO, whereas economic exchange fully mediated the negative relationship between competency model perceptions and OCBO. Jiang and Law (2013) found that social exchange mediated the relationship between procedural justice and OCBI (altruism and courtesy), but social exchange did not mediate the relationship between procedural justice and OCBO (civic virtue, conscientiousness, and sportsmanship). Kuvaas and Dysvik (2009) found that social exchange perceptions of temporary workers mediated the relationship between perceived investment in permanent employee development and OCBI. The authors explain this by arguing that temporary workers' perceptions of how permanent employees are treated reflects a climate of trust, cooperation, and long-term orientation that influences temporary workers' OCB. Additional support for the positive relationship between social exchange and OCB is provided by Elstad, Christophersen, and Turmo (2011) in a sample of Norwegian teachers, and this study found no relationship between economic exchange and OCB.

No empirical investigation has explored cultural moderators in the relationship between social exchange and OCB, and the one study that examined reciprocation wariness did not find that it moderated the relationship between social exchange and supervisor-directed altruism in a sample of Korean employees. Rather, social exchange was positively related to altruism directed toward the supervisor. The authors speculate that the absence of a moderating role for reciprocation wariness may be because wary employees may carefully manage their altruistic behavior toward their supervisor as this relationship is critical for a successful career.

Overall, the limited evidence paints a consistent picture of the positive relationship between perceptions of social exchange and OCB. However, there is less consistency in terms of a differential relationship between social exchange and OCBO/OCBI.

Empirical Evidence: Idiosyncratic Deals

Researchers typically use social exchange theory to explain the effects of i-deals on employee attitudes and behavior such that i-deals are a benefit and hence create obligations to reciprocate the supervisor, the organization, or the coworkers who enable such idiosyncrasy (Anand et al., 2010; Liu et al., 2013; Ng & Feldman, 2012). As OCB captures discretionary behaviors and i-deals imply a low degree of standardization in the employment relationship, OCB is an especially central outcome variable to consider in research on i-deals. Ng and Lucianetti (2016) argue that i-dealers are likely to reciprocate their special arrangements by engaging in extra-role behaviors, especially toward their supervisor who agreed to the i-deal. As mentioned earlier, these special arrangements can trigger OCB from the coworkers of i-dealers (Rousseau et al., 2006). However, studies that have examined the impact of i-deals on the helping behaviors of i-dealers are few and empirical evidence concerning the theorized impact of i-deals on coworkers' engagement in OCB is even more limited. Nonetheless, the existing evidence is aligned with the theoretical assertions made in the literature (e.g., Anand et al., 2010; Huo, Luo, & Tam, 2014).

The studies also identify some mechanisms and boundary conditions to the positive relationship between i-deals and OCB. For example, Anand and collegues (2010) found that leader–member exchange (LMX) and team member exchange (TMX) affect the impact of i-deals on OCB in such a way that the lower the LMX or TMX quality, the stronger the positive effect of i-deals on OCB. Whereas LMX influenced both OCBO and OCBI, TMX moderated the relationship between i-deals and OCBO only. In explaining their findings, the authors argue that i-deals can offset poor relationship quality. In other words, although OCB is likely to be common in high LMX and TMX relations even without the presence of ideals, i-deals can be especially powerful in inducing employee reciprocity in low-quality relationships.

Studying i-deals in a Chinese context, Huo and colleagues (2014) found that i-dealers were likely to engage in OCBI and that this relationship was strongest with high perceived visibility and low traditionality. In the same sample, coworkers' beliefs in obtaining future i-deals predicted their engagement in OCBI and were strongest for individuals with high perceptions of others' individualized arrangements and low traditionality. Ng and Lucianetti (2016), in turn, established that employees' perceptions of their own i-deals positively predicted different performance indicators, including OCB-I and voice. Furthermore, their study found that witnessing coworkers receiving i-deals was positively related to employees' perceptions of their own deals and that i-deals moderated the direct and the interactive effects of personality characteristics on performance indicators. This, along of the findings of Huo and colleagues (2014), confirms that in the context of i-deals, employees pick up social cues from their environment that guide their work-related attitudes and behavior.

In terms of explanatory mechanisms in the relationship between i-deals and OCB, Ng and Feldman (2015) found that i-deals relating to flexibility fostered trust, which in turn positively influenced employee willingness to engage in voice. In other words, i-deals appear to foster high-quality exchange relationships characterized by trust, which in turn trigger employees to engage in helping behaviors, operationalized as voice in this particular study. In a series of three studies, Ho and Kong (2015) showed that task-related i-deals have a positive impact on OCB through competence need satisfaction. Diverting from the dominant social exchange theory framework in i-deals research, the authors explain this finding through signaling and self-determination theories. Specifically, the authors argue that i-deals indicate employees' value at the workplace, thereby enhancing their sense of competence, which in turn positively contributes to OCB.

Overall, the albeit limited evidence so far shows that i-deals positively influence OCB for both i-dealers and their coworkers. Additional empirical evidence is needed to assess the underpinning mechanisms and boundary conditions to the relationship between i-deals and OCB from the perspective of both the i-dealer and third parties.

Reflections on the EOR–OCB Relationship

What can be gleaned from the empirical evidence thus far? It seems that the EOR does matter in eliciting OCB and, more so, the type of relationship is important. Relationships based on minimal investment (quasi-spot contracts and transactional psychological contracts) are negatively related to OCB or have no relationship with OCB (economic exchange). Events such as broken promises also trigger a reduction in OCB. Relationships that demonstrate investment, support and the fulfilment of obligations and granting of i-deals are positively related to OCB because they signal a trusting and benefit-conferring relationship.

Reciprocity is a dominant although not exclusive explanation for the relationship between EOR and OCB. This is particularly evident for the effects of POS and social exchange and to a lesser degree for mutual investment ER. Empirical evidence in psychological contracts and i-deals has demonstrated additional mechanisms, beyond reciprocity, to explain why employees engage in OCB such as organizational identification and competence need satisfaction.

The picture is less clear cut when it comes to the target beneficiary of citizenship-type behavior. The weight of the evidence suggests that POS is more strongly related to OCBO than OCBI, which makes sense given that the donor of support is the organization. The emerging evidence from i-deals suggests that it is more strongly related to OCB toward the supervisor, yet the receipt of an i-deal for a focal employee may trigger OCBI from coworkers. As i-deals need to be negotiated with an authority figure (generally supervisors), it is clear to the employee who has granted the i-deal and hence not surprising that OCB is directed toward that specific individual. The implication for coworkers may be pressure to engage in OCBI or OCBO to pick up slack as a result of an i-deal granted to a focal employee. Research on mutual investment has not differentiated between OCBO and OCBI and, therefore, no tentative conclusions can be made. The empirical evidence from the psychological contract suggests that it can affect both OCBO and OCBI. Although culture may play a role in explaining the absence of a differential effect on OCBO/OCBI, another explanation might be the cloudiness of who is responsible for fulfilling certain obligations. If one looks at the range of employer obligations covered, it is clear that specific obligations pertaining to work (autonomy, training, performance feedback, etc.) fall within the domain of the supervisor and hence may explain why psychological contract fulfilment affects both OCBO and OCBI.

Challenges and Future Research Directions

In reviewing the empirical evidence, it is clear that the EOR serves as a basis to understanding OCB, yet there are a number of challenges and future research directions and we focus on a few: (a) "value addedness" of the EOR constructs; (b) OCB as discretionary reciprocation or part of the EOR; (c) temporality and OCB; and (d) expanding a social exchange explanation for OCB.

Value Addedness?

To what extent do the EOR constructs add value to understanding OCB? To begin to address this issue, we examine empirical studies that have concurrently included two EOR frameworks. A developing strand of research has raised a question of whether social exchange relationships buffer or intensify the effects of negative events (i.e., psychological contract breach) on employees' engagement in OCB. Two competing views are empirically supported. First, a support perspective postulates that high-quality exchange relationships will have a protective effect and buffer the effects of psychological contract breach on OCB (Dulac, Coyle-Shapiro, Henderson, & Wayne, 2008) such that high-quality relationships engender positive cognitive biases (Tekleab, Takeuchi, & Taylor, 2005), and it provides the frame of reference through which an individual interprets events consistent with prior beliefs (Dulac et al., 2008).

In contrast, a betrayal perspective posits that higher quality relationships will elicit a positive frame of reference for employees, and when employees' experience contract breach, they will reduce their OCB because of the inconsistency between the event experienced and the relationship itself (Bal, Chiaburu, & Jansen, 2010; Robinson & Rousseau, 1994). For example, Bal et al. (2010) found that POS moderated the relationship between contract breach and OCB in an intensifying manner such that when POS was high, employees responded to contract breach by reducing their OCBO. The same effect was found for social exchange and LMX, such that the negative relationship between contract breach and OCBO was intensified when employees perceive a high social exchange relationship with their organization (Bal et al., 2010), and breach had a stronger negative relationship with OCB under conditions of high LMX (Restubog, Bordia, Tang, & Krebs 2010). What is clear is that the quality of employees' relationship with their organization (as operationalized through POS or social exchange) provides the relational context in which employees to a greater or lesser degree reciprocate employer treatment by engaging in OCB. Anand et al.'s (2010) findings suggest that i-deals can act as a substitute for poor-quality relationships such that individuals in low-LMX relationships engage in as much OCBO when they are the recipient of an i-deal as those in high-LMX relationships. As noted by the authors, "i-deals offer a potential remedy for relational challenges" (p. 982). This is an avenue ripe for future research—under what conditions do relationships buffer or intensify the effects of a lack of resources on employees' OCB? Can resources substitute for poor relationships or can they, like an "anchoring event" (resources at a critical point in time when needed) (Ballinger & Rockmann, 2010) fundamentally alter the nature of the relationship and its consequences for employee engagement in OCB?

In attempting to disentangle the effects of multiple EOR frameworks on OCB, a simple response is "it's complicated!" (see Figure 19.1). If the frameworks are broadly classified into those that focus on the resources exchanged (mutual investment, i-deals, PC breach, and fulfilment), the empirical evidence suggests that resources lead to the development of the relationship (social exchange and POS) that, in turn, prompts reciprocation in the form of OCB. Proceeding from left to right in Figure 19.1 is consistent with how relationships *develop* from a social exchange perspective. However, in ongoing relationships, the relationship itself provides the lens (positive or negative) through which employees evaluate the inducements offered (or not) with potential consequences for OCB. In addition, the relationship itself can moderate the relationship between resources and OCB, as discussed earlier. Resources can have a direct effect on OCB, as evidenced by the empirical studies on psychological contracts and i-deals. Finally, OCB can be conceptualized as employees' contribution to the relationship (reciprocation for past inducements or relationship quality) that becomes a subsequent benefit to the organization that creates an obligation for the organization to discharge and so on as

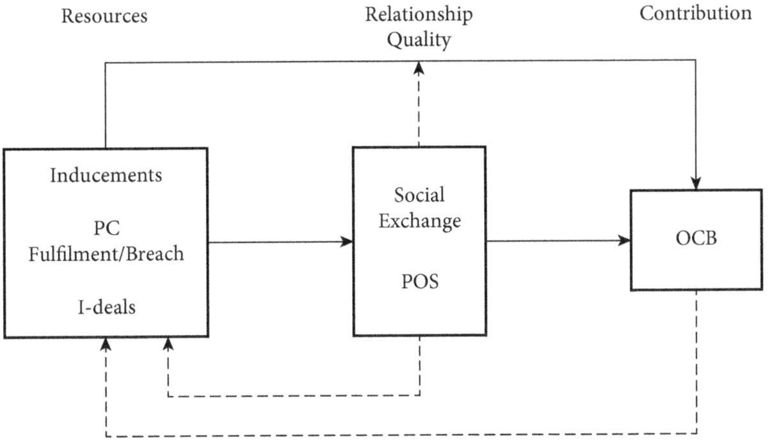

Figure 19.1 Employee–organization relationship frameworks and organizational citizenship behavior. OCB, organizational citizenship behavior; PC, psychological contract; POS, perceived organizational support.

the cycle continues. This explains the feedback loop from OCB to the resources provided to employees. If employees perceive that the organization is not reciprocating their OCB, this may begin to negatively alter employees' view of the resources provided and undermine the quality of the relationship. Bolino, Hsiung, Harvey, and LePine (2015) introduce the term "citizenship fatigue," which they define as "a state in which employees feel worn out, tired, or on edge attributed to engaging in OCB" (p. 57). Using conservation of resources theory, the authors find support for the argument that engagement in OCB is associated with greater citizenship fatigue when POS is low compared to when POS is high. This suggests that organizational support buffers the effects of OCB on citizenship fatigue (which is negatively related to subsequent OCB) such that employees consistently engage in OCB in supportive relationships. Future research could integrate social exchange theory and conservation of resources theory to examine the consequences of OCB for future engagement in OCB—to what extent do employees become unable (the draining effect) or unwilling (the "nonreciprocation" effect) to sustain their OCB over time?

"It's complicated" also reflects that research downplays temporality, as aptly noted by Cropanzano and Mitchell (2005) who state that "usual tests of SET focus on relatively discrete sets of contingent transactions . . . the possibility exists that the transaction series has gone on for some time and/or could continue into the future" (p. 889). To elicit OCB as a form of reciprocation, there need to be a basis: resources, the relationship, or both. However, employees not only engage in reactive reciprocation where they reciprocate inducements received, but they may also engage in proactive reciprocation whereby they engage in OCB, for example, to ensure continuity or future delivery of inducements (Coyle-Shapiro, 2002). Korsgaard, Meglino, Lester, and Jeong (2010) find empirical support through experiments of the dual social exchange mechanisms that underlie prosocial behavior: (a) expected reciprocity, which is based on the expectation of future benefits; and (b) obligation to reciprocate, which is based on the receipt of past benefits. Therefore, employee engagement in OCB, which is the outcome of the EOR at a point in time, becomes an input into the next cycle of transactions. Almost exclusively, empirical research treats OCB as an outcome, yet as an employee contribution to the organization, it becomes an input into what is potentially an ongoing series of "giving and taking"—whether OCB is an output or input depends on the temporal perspective taken.

Organizational Citizenship Behavior as Discretionary Reciprocation or Part of the Employee–Organization Relationship?

Organ (1990) views OCB as a contribution employees can use to "rebalance" the treatment from the organization—lowering or raising it contingent upon fair treatment. As such, it is within the discretion of the employee to decide whether to engage or withhold OCB. Research has challenged the discretionary nature of OCB, and Morrison (1994) argued that employees vary in terms of how broadly or narrowly they define their job responsibilities and found that employees were more likely to engage in citizenship-type behaviors if they defined those behaviors as in-role. To what extent is OCB an integral part of the employee–organization relationship such that organizations expect employees to engage in OCB as part of their contributions? Jia, Shaw, Tsui, and Park's (2013) measure of a mutual investment ER captures elements of OCB (initiative to make constructive suggestions, adopt new ideas and methods actively to improve work, continuously improve work procedures and methods, and take initiative to carry out new or challenging assignments), suggesting that in social exchange relationships, citizenship-type behaviors may be part of the "deal." In the POS literature, the reciprocity norm would trigger employees' felt obligation to care about the organization and, as Eisenberger et al. (2001) note, "meeting obligations helps employees maintain the positive self-image of those who repay debts, avoid the social stigma associated with the reciprocity norm's violation" (p. 42). In psychological contract research, employee obligations to their employer may include citizenship-type behaviors such as volunteering to do tasks that fall outside their job description (Tekleab & Taylor, 2003), make personal sacrifices for their organization, take their organization's concerns personally (Rousseau, 2000), assist their colleagues in their work, work extra hours to get the job done, and take personal initiative to attend additional training courses (De Vos, Buyens, & Schalk, 2003). Citizenship-type behaviors, therefore, may be expected from employers as part of a mutual investment approach or employees may view those behaviors as their part of the reciprocal obligations that exist between them and their employer. As Mauss (1950) noted in his seminal work that provided the foundation for subsequent development of social exchange theory, there is no such thing as a free gift—"a gift is received with a burden attached" (p. 41).

Recent empirical work on OCB has highlighted the role of *citizenship pressure* as a specific job demand that can arise from internal or external forces (Bolino, Turnley, Gilstrap, & Suazo, 2010). Empirically, Bolino et al. (2010) find support for the positive association between citizenship pressure and OCB and highlight the need for additional work to uncover potential antecedents of citizenship pressure. From an EOR vantage point, the source of citizenship pressure may emanate from the exchange relationship that develops between an employee and employer as employees are motivated to meet employer expectations or fulfil their obligations to their employer. In this respect, the citizenship pressure may be nothing more than employees striving to keep their side of the deal. One would anticipate that citizenship pressure would be stronger for mutual investment approaches and relational psychological contracts and less (at best) for quasi-spot contracts and economic exchange, all things equal. Likewise, in established ongoing and stable social exchange relationships, employees may consistently engage in OCB to the point that it is habitual (Bolino, Harvey, & Bachrach, 2012). The extent to which long-term social exchange relationships drive habitual OCB from employees deserves future research attention. One might anticipate that employees' habitual OCB that is unreciprocated by the organization may trigger employees to view their relationship as unbalanced (in favor of the organization), thereby changing the relationship itself to one that is potentially exploitative.

Temporality and Organizational Citizenship Behavior

Empirical research on the EOR and employee contributions (i.e., OCB) has not paid adequate attention to the temporal element in social exchange relationships. Timing is important; according to Blau (1964), "posthaste reciprocation of favors, which implies a refusal to stay indebted for a while and hence an insistence on a more businesslike relationship is condemned as improper" (p. 99) because this would signal ingratitude. This has implications for the timing of OCB. Furthermore, Gouldner (1960) argued that the obligation to reciprocate is contingent upon the value of the benefit received such that the felt indebtedness experienced by the recipient is greater when the recipient is in need, the donor has limited resources but gave freely and unselfishly. From a social exchange theory stance, one would expect a time lag between employer treatment and employees' OCB and perhaps the magnitude of OCB would vary contingent upon employees' need at the time of the employer's treatment. If employees are reciprocating employer treatment, one would anticipate that the nature and intensity of OCB would ebb and flow over time.

Although the EOR literature has remained quite silent on temporality, it is gaining traction in OCB research. In their recent theoretical work, Bolino and colleagues (2012, p. 127) argue that OCB is an "ongoing, dynamic, and time-dependent outcome of an active process of feedback-driven goal pursuit" and call researchers to systematically examine how OCB changes over time. In addition to the dynamic nature of OCB, researchers have noted that OCB consumes time and may thus have consequences for task performance.

Indeed, time represents a crucial resource when performing OCB (Mueller & Kamdar, 2011). Given the limited resources employees have available, there is a need to manage the tension between task performance and OCB engagement. Rapp, Bachrach, and Rapp (2013) found that an inverted U-shaped relationship between OCB and task performance varies depending on time management skills. Specifically, they (2013, p. 670) found that managers more skilled in time management were "more efficient in demonstrating OCB and more effective in 'cashing in' their OCB with coworkers." Consequently, they create more value from OCB than less skilled time managers because they are more effective in managing their OCB contributions as well as the further reciprocal exchanges initiated by these behaviors. Joireman, Daniels, George-Falvy, and Kamdar (2006) argue that engagement in OCB presents a social dilemma for employees as it promises costs in the short run and benefits only in the long run. Consistent with this argument, they found that the likelihood of engaging in OCB was higher among those high in empathy and concern with future consequences; and less likely among those instructed to imagine they would leave their company in 3 months.

Turning to fluctuations in OCB, explaining OCB through affective events theory draws attention to daily events as triggers for helping behaviors. Weiss and Cropanzano (1996) argue that emotions are a proximal predictor of behavior because emotions have the ability to preoccupy individuals and guide behavior into new directions, thereby creating a tendency to behave in untypical ways. Consistent with their predictions made in line with affective events theory, Spence, Brown, Keeping, and Lian (2014) found that momentary feelings of gratitude predict daily fluctuations in OCB. The author (2014, p. 730) conclude that "meaningful within-person variation in the construct [OCB] exists" and that their study "provides additional impetus for researchers to devote greater attention to *when* individuals will and will not engage in OCB" (emphasis added). Drawing on conservation of resources theory, researchers have argued that OCB can be exhausting for employees and consume their resources (Bolino et al., 2015). For example, coworkers filling in the gaps for i-dealers may well reduce their OCB over time as their resources get depleted. Furthermore, repeated failure by the organization to reciprocate employee OCB may over time begin to negatively alter employees' view of the resources provided and undermine the quality of the relationship, ultimately leading to reductions in OCB (Bolino et al., 2015).

Future research in the EOR could more fully incorporate temporality to empirical investigations of its effect on OCB. Specifically, how does time facilitate or hinder the demonstration of gratitude for a benefit received and hence reciprocation through OCB? Is time important to the occurrence of OCB? Do organizations value OCB that occurs when it is needed or is it stability that is important? Does timing matter to the beneficiary?

Expanding a Social Exchange Explanation for Organizational Citizenship Behavior

Social exchange theory provides strong theoretical and empirical arguments for examining and explaining various employee attitudes and behaviors (Cropanzano & Mitchell, 2005). As this chapter demonstrates, the EOR frameworks convincingly explain the occurrence of OCB as employee reciprocation for treatment received. However, existing research points to alternative explanations for employee engagement in OCB that can independently or in interaction with social exchange theory provide a more comprehensive understanding of OCB.

Rioux and Penner (2001) present three motives for engaging in OCB. These include *prosocial values*, referring to a desire to be helpful and to build positive relationships with others; *organizational concern*, capturing the wish for the company to do well; and *impression management* (IM), concerning the attempt to appear in a positive light to colleagues and to obtain rewards. The first two reflect the "good soldier" motives captured in the original spirit of OCB (Organ, 1988). The third captures a more instrumental "good actor" motive to be helpful to the organization. Empirical evidence indicates that these three motives play a role in predicting employee engagement in OCB and each counts for unique variance in OCB (Bolino, Varela, Bande, & Turnley, 2006; Finkelstein, 2006; Grant & Mayer, 2009; Rioux & Penner, 2001). Although an expectation for *employer* reciprocity is bound to be integral to the extrinsic IM motivation, the expectation of "payback" plays less of a role when OCB is driven by prosocial values and a good actor motive. For example, personality (e.g., proactive personality, conscientiousness, emotional stability), values, and moral identity may explain employee motivations to be a good actor and the resulting engagement in OCB (Bolino et al., 2006; Chiaburu, Oh, Berry, Li, & Gardner, 2011; Grant & Mayer, 2009).

Another alternative explanation for engagement in OCB stems from affect and emotions, highlighting the importance of positive and negative events at work in line with affective events theory (Weiss & Cropanzano, 1996). Spector and Fox (2002) propose that positive and negative situations at work elicit corresponding positive and negative emotional reactions and that positive emotions are associated with OCBs, and negative emotions are associated with CWBs. Dalal, Lam, Weiss, Welch, and Hulin (2009) showed that OCBs (and CWBs) are triggered by affect-generating events that employees experience at work such that positive events result in positive affect and consequent acts of citizenship, whereas negative events induce negative affect and eventually lead to CWBs. Spector and Fox (2010a, 2010b) have also argued that employees may engage in OCBs because they feel guilty about having behaved in ways that harm or hurt the organization or other employees. In other words, feelings of guilt resulting from CWBs may motivate employees to perform OCBs. Furthermore, conceptualizing gratitude as a positive emotion, Spence and colleagues (2014) found that gratitude is a significant, positive predictor of OCB, especially targeting supervisors and coworkers (versus the organization). This finding is aligned with Lee and Allen's (2002) study that shows that OCB-O is driven more by cognition, whereas OCBI is driven more by affect. According to Lee and Allen (2002, p. 133), OCBI is more likely to be an "expression of employees' affect at work," and it is less likely to reflect an employee's deliberate attempt to restore balance in social exchange. Consequently, affect and emotions present opportunities to expand the social exchange theory–based reasoning for employees engaging in OCB. Social learning theory can also be used as a framework to explain OCB as a group-level phenomenon. For example, Mayer and colleagues (2009) stressed the role of social learning theory to complement social exchange theory in order to explain the relationship between ethical leadership and OCBs. In line with social learning theory, they found that leaders serve as role models for subordinates. Specifically, ethical leaders set an example for the appropriate way to behave for employees—including OCB—who imitate the behavior of their leaders. In an earlier study, Ehrhart and Naumann (2004) suggested that the establishment and maintenance of OCB norms in work units rely on a cyclical relationship between different level processes, namely individual and group level, and ultimately offer an explanation for how OCB norms are established and maintained in work groups.

Finally, complementing the studies stemming from social exchange theory, recent research has pointed to the importance of mutual understanding and balance in the exchange relationship. A recent study by Matta, Scott, Koopman, and Conlon (2015) showed that employees were more likely to engage in higher levels of OCB-O and OCB-I, when they and their respective leader agreed on the quality of their LMX relationship, and less so when their perceptions diverged, irrespective of whether LMX was low or high. Drawing on Heider's balance theory (1958), the authors explain that perceived asymmetry in evaluations of the relationship creates tension, uncertainty, and discomfort, thereby supporting the assertions of social exchange theory regarding the drive toward equilibrium (Blau 1964).

Conclusions

Social exchange theory provides an important theoretical basis to understanding OCB in the workplace, and this is supported by the empirical evidence reviewed here. Although the norm of reciprocity is a dominant explanation for why employees engage in OCB as they reciprocate the resources received or the quality of the relationship they have with their organization, it is by no means the only explanation. Despite the expanding number of empirical studies linking the EOR to OCB, there are a number of challenges to advancing understanding of these linkages: the complexity of the interrelationships between the EOR frameworks and OCB and the role of time; the extent to which OCB is expected as part of the employee–organization exchange relationship; greater integration between social exchange theory and other theories to more fully comprehend when, why, and for how long employees engage in OCB.

References

Anand, S., Vidyarthi, P. R., Liden, R. C., & Rousseau, D. M. (2010). Good citizens in poor-quality relationships: Idiosyncratic deals as a substitute for relationship quality. *Academy of Management Journal, 53*(5), 970–988. http://doi.org/10.5465/AMJ.2010.54533176

Bal, P. M., Chiaburu, D. S., & Jansen, P. G. W. (2010). Psychological contract breach and work performance: Is social exchange a buffer or an intensifier? *Journal of Managerial Psychology, 25*(3–4), 252–273. http://doi.org/10.1108/02683941011023730

Ballinger, G. A., & Rockmann, K. W. (2010). Chutes versus ladders: Anchoring events and a punctuated-equilibrium perspective on social exchange relationships. *Academy of Management Review, 35*(3), 373–391.

Barnard, C. I. (1938). *The functions of the executive.* Cambridge, MA: Harvard University Press.

Blau, P. M. (1964). *Exchange and power in social life.* New Brunswick, New Jersey: Transaction Publishers.

Bolino, M. C., Harvey, J., & Bachrach, D. G. (2012). A self-regulation approach to understanding citizenship behavior in organizations. *Organizational Behavior and Human Decision Processes, 119*(1), 126–139. http://doi.org/10.1016/j.obhdp.2012.05.006

Bolino, M. C., Hsiung, H.-H., Harvey, J., & LePine, J. A. (2015). "Well, I'm tired of tryin'!" Organizational citizenship behavior and citizenship fatigue. *Journal of Applied Psychology, 100*(1), 56–74. http://doi.org/10.1037/a0037583

Bolino, M. C., Turnley, W. H., Gilstrap, J. B., & Suazo, M. M. (2010). Citizenship under pressure: What's a "good soldier" to do? *Journal of Organizational Behavior, 31*(6), 835–855. http://doi.org/10.1002/job.635

Bolino, M. C., Varela, J. A., Bande, B., & Turnley, W. H. (2006). The impact of impression-management tactics on supervisor ratings of organizational citizenship behavior. *Journal of Organizational Behavior, 27*(3), 281–297. http://doi.org/10.1002/job.379

Bordia, P., Restubog, S. L. D., & Tang, R. L. (2008). When employees strike back: Investigating mediating mechanisms between psychological contract breach and workplace deviance. *Journal of Applied Psychology, 93*(5), 1104–1117. http://doi.org/10.1037/0021-9010.93.5.1104

Borman, W., & Motowidlo, S. (1993). Expanding the criterion domain to include elements of contextual performance. In *Personnel selection in organizations* (pp. 71–98). San Francisco, CA: Jossey-Bass.

Chen, Z., Eisenberger, R., Johnson, K. M., Sucharski, I. L., & Aselage, J. (2009). Perceived organizational support and extra-role performance: Which leads to which? *The Journal of Social Psychology, 149*(1), 119–124. http://doi.org/10.3200/SOCP.149.1.119-124

Chen, Z. X., Tsui, A. S., & Zhong, L. (2008). Reactions to psychological contract breach: A dual perspective. *Journal of Organizational Behavior, 29*(5), 527–548. http://doi.org/10.1002/job.481

Chiaburu, D. S., Oh, I.-S., Berry, C. M., Li, N., & Gardner, R. G. (2011). The five-factor model of personality traits and organizational citizenship behaviors: A meta-analysis. *Journal of Applied Psychology, 96*(6), 1140–1166. http://doi.org/10.1037/a0024004

Colquitt, J. A., Baer, M. D., Long, D. M., & Halvorsen-Ganepola, M. D. (2014). Scale indicators of social exchange relationships: A comparison of relative content validity. *Journal of Applied Psychology, 99*(4), 599–618. http://doi.org/10.1037/a0036374

Colquitt, J. A., Scott, B. A., Rodell, J. B., Long, D. M., Zapata, C. P., Conlon, D. E., & Wesson, M. J. (2013). Justice at the millennium, a decade later: A meta-analytic test of social exchange and affect-based perspectives. *Journal of Applied Psychology, 98*(2), 199–236. http://doi.org/10.1037/a0031757

Colquitt, J. A., & Zapata-Phelan, C. P. (2007). Trends in theory building and theory testing: A five-decade study of the *Academy of Management Journal. Academy of Management Journal, 50*(6), 1281–1303. http://doi.org/10.5465/AMJ.2007.28165855

Conway, N., & Briner, R. B. (2009). Fifty years of psychological contract research: what do we know and what are the main challenges? In G. P. Hodgkinson & J. K. Ford (Eds.), *International review of industrial and organizational psychology 2009, Vol 24* (Vol. 24, pp. 71–130). Chichester, UK: John Wiley & Sons.

Conway, N., & Coyle-Shapiro, J. (2015). Not so I-deal: A critical review of idiosyncratic-deals theory and research. In P. M. Bal & D. M. Rousseau (Eds.), *Idiosyncratic deals between employees and organizations: Conceptual issues, applications, and the role of coworkers* (pp. 36–64). New York, NY: Psychology Press.

Conway, N., Kiefer, T., Hartley, J., & Briner, R. B. (2014). Doing more with less? Employee reactions to psychological contract breach via target similarity or spillover during public sector organizational change. *British Journal of Management, 25*(4), 737–754. http://doi.org/10.1111/1467-8551.12041

Coyle-Shapiro, J. A-M. (2002). A psychological contract perspective on organizational citizenship behavior. *Journal of Organizational Behavior, 23*(8), 927–946. http://doi.org/10.1002/job.173

Coyle-Shapiro, J. A-M., & Diehl, M.-R. (2018). *Social exchange theory—Where is trust?* In R. Searle, A. M. Nienaber, & S. Sitkin (Eds.), *Routledge companion to trust.* New York, NY: Routledge.

Coyle-Shapiro, J. A-M., & Kessler, I. (2000). Consequences of the psychological contract for the employment relationship: A large scale survey. *Journal of Management Studies, 37*(7), 903–930. http://doi.org/10.1111/1467-6486.00210

Cropanzano, R., & Mitchell, M. (2005). Social exchange theory: An interdisciplinary review. *Journal of Management, 31*(6), 874–900. http://doi.org/10.1177/0149206305279602

Dalal, R. S., Lam, H., Weiss, H. M., Welch, E. R., & Hulin, C. L. (2009). A within-person approach to work behavior and performance: Concurrent and lagged citizenship-counterproductivity associations, and dynamic relationships with affect and overall job performance. *Academy of Management Journal, 52*(5), 1051–1066. http://doi.org/10.5465/AMJ.2009.44636148

De Vos, A., Buyens, D., & Schalk, R. (2003). Psychological contract development during organizational socialization: Adaptation to reality and the role of reciprocity. *Journal of Organizational Behavior, 24*(5), 537–559. http://doi.org/10.1002/job.205

Dulac, T., Coyle-Shapiro, J. A-M., Henderson, D. J., & Wayne, S. J. (2008). Not all responses to breach are the same: The interconnection of social exchange and psychological contract processes in organizations. *Academy of Management Journal, 51*(6), 1079–1098.

Ehrhart, M. G., & Naumann, S. E. (2004). Organizational citizenship behavior in work groups: A group norms approach. *The Journal of Applied Psychology, 89*(6), 960–974. http://doi.org/10.1037/0021-9010.89.6.960

Eisenberger, R., Armeli, S., Rexwinkel, B., Lynch, P. D., & Rhoades, L. (2001). Reciprocation of perceived organizational support. *The Journal of Applied Psychology, 86*(1), 42–51.

Eisenberger, R., Cotterell, N., & Marvel, J. (1987). Reciprocation ideology. *Journal of Personality and Social Psychology, 53*(4), 743–750. http://doi.org/10.1037/0022-3514.53.4.743

Eisenberger, R., Fasolo, P., & Davis-LaMastro, V. (1990). Perceived organizational support and employee diligence, commitment, and innovation. *Journal of Applied Psychology, 75*(1), 51–59. http://doi.org/10.1037/0021-9010.75.1.51

Eisenberger, R., Huntington, R., Hutchison, S., & Sowa, D. (1986). Perceived organizational support. *Journal of Applied Psychology, 71*(3), 500–507. http://doi.org/10.1037/0021-9010.71.3.500

Elstad, E., Christophersen, K. A., & Turmo, A. (2011). Social exchange theory as an explanation of organizational citizenship behaviour among teachers. *International Journal of Leadership in Education, 14*(4), 405–421. http://doi.org/10.1080/13603124.2010.524250

Farh, J.-L., Hackett, R. D., & Liang, J. (2007). Individual-level cultural values as moderators of perceived organizational support–employee outcome relationships in china: Comparing the effects of power distance and traditionality. *Academy of Management Journal, 50*(3), 715–729. http://doi.org/10.5465/AMJ.2007.25530866

Finkelstein, M. A. (2006). Dispositional predictors of organizational citizenship behavior: Motives, motive fulfillment, and role identity. *Social Behavior and Personality: An International Journal, 34*(6), 603–616. http://doi.org/10.2224/sbp.2006.34.6.603

Gouldner, A. W. (1960). The norm of reciprocity: A preliminary statement. *American Sociological Review, 25*(2), 161. http://doi.org/10.2307/2092623

Graen, G. B., & Uhl-Bien, M. (1995). Relationship-based approach to leadership: Development of leader-member exchange (LMX) theory of leadership over 25 years: Applying a multi-level multi-domain perspective. *The Leadership Quarterly, 6*(2), 219–247. http://doi.org/10.1016/1048-9843(95)90036-5

Grant, A. M., & Mayer, D. M. (2009). Good soldiers and good actors: Prosocial and impression management motives as interactive predictors of affiliative citizenship behaviors. *Journal of Applied Psychology, 94*(4), 900–912. http://doi.org/10.1037/a0013770

Heaphy, E. D., & Dutton, J. E. (2008). Positive social interactions and the human body at work: Linking organizations and physiology. *Academy of Management Review, 33*(1), 137–162. http://doi.org/10.5465/AMR.2008.27749365

Heider, F. (1958). *The psychology of interpersonal relations.* New York, NY: Psychology Press.

Hom, P. W., Tsui, A. S., Wu, J. B., Lee, T. W., Zhang, A. Y., Fu, P. P., & Li, L. (2009). Explaining employment relationships with social exchange and job embeddedness. *Journal of*

Applied Psychology, 94(2), 277–297. http://doi.org/10.1037/a0013453

Hornung, S., Rousseau, D. M., & Glaser, J. (2008). Creating flexible work arrangements through idiosyncratic deals. *Journal of Applied Psychology, 93*(3), 655–664. http://doi.org/10.1037/0021-9010.93.3.655

Hornung, S., Rousseau, D. M., Glaser, J., Angerer, P., & Weigl, M. (2010). Beyond top-down and bottom-up work redesign: Customizing job content through idiosyncratic deals. *Journal of Organizational Behavior, 31*(2–3), 187–215. http://doi.org/10.1002/job.625

Ho, V. T., & Kong, D. T. (2015). Exploring the signaling function of idiosyncratic deals and their interaction. *Organizational Behavior and Human Decision Processes, 131*, 149–161. http://doi.org/10.1016/j.obhdp.2015.08.002

Hui, C., Lee, C., & Rousseau, D. M. (2004). Psychological contract and organizational citizenship behavior in China: Investigating generalizability and instrumentality. *Journal of Applied Psychology, 89*(2), 311–321. http://doi.org/10.1037/0021-9010.89.2.311

Huo, W., Luo, J., & Tam, K. L. (2014). Idiosyncratic deals and good citizens in China: The role of traditionality for recipients and their coworkers. *The International Journal of Human Resource Management, 25*(22), 3157–3177. http://doi.org/10.1080/09585192.2014.919949

Huseman, R. C., Hatfield, J. D., & Miles, E. W. (1987). A new perspective on equity theory: The equity sensitivity construct. *Academy of Management Review, 12*(2), 222–234. http://doi.org/10.5465/AMR.1987.4307799

Jia, L., Shaw, J., Tsui, A., & Park, T.-Y. (2013). A social-structural perspective on employee-organization relationships and team creativity. *Academy of Management Journal, 57*(3), 869–891. http://doi.org/10.5465/amj.2011.0147

Jiang, J. Y., & Law, K. S. (2013). Two parallel mechanisms of the relationship between justice perceptions and employees' citizenship behaviour: A comparison of the organizational identification and social exchange perspective. *European Journal of Work and Organizational Psychology, 22*(4), 423–435. http://doi.org/10.1080/1359432X.2012.658157

Joireman, J., Daniels, D., George-Falvy, J., & Kamdar, D. (2006). Organizational citizenship behaviors as a function of empathy, consideration of future consequences, and employee time horizon: an initial exploration using an in-basket simulation of OCBs. *Journal of Applied Social Psychology, 36*(9), 2266–2292. http://doi.org/10.1111/j.0021-9029.2006.00103.x

Katz, D. (1964). The motivational basis of organizational behavior. *Behavioral Science, 9*(2), 131–146. http://doi.org/10.1002/bs.3830090206

Kim, T.-Y., Aryee, S., Loi, R., & Kim, S.-P. (2013). Person-organization fit and employee outcomes: Test of a social exchange model. *International Journal of Human Resource Management, 24*(19), 3719–3737. http://doi.org/10.1080/09585192.2013.781522

Knippenberg, D. van, Prooijen, J.-W. van, & Sleebos, E. (2015). Beyond social exchange: Collectivism's moderating role in the relationship between perceived organizational support and organizational citizenship behaviour. *European Journal of Work and Organizational Psychology, 24*(1), 152–160. http://doi.org/10.1080/1359432X.2013.858699

Korsgaard, M. A., Meglino, B. M., Lester, S. W., & Jeong, S. S. (2010). Paying you back or paying me forward: Understanding rewarded and unrewarded organizational citizenship behavior. *The Journal of Applied Psychology, 95*(2), 277–290. http://doi.org/10.1037/a0018137

Kurtessis, J. N., Eisenberger, R., Ford, M. T., Buffardi, L. C., Stewart, K. A., & Adis, C. S. (2017). Perceived organizational support: A meta-analytic evaluation of organizational support theory. *Journal of Management, 63*(6), 1854–1884. http://doi.org/10.1177/0149206315575554

Kuvaas, B., & Dysvik, A. (2009). Perceived investment in permanent employee development and social and economic exchange perceptions among temporary employees. *Journal of Applied Social Psychology, 39*(10), 2499–2524.

Lai, L., Rousseau, D. M., & Chang, K. T. T. (2009). Idiosyncratic deals: Coworkers as interested third parties. *Journal of Applied Psychology, 94*(2), 547–556. http://doi.org/10.1037/a0013506

Lavelle, J. J., McMahan, G. C., & Harris, C. M. (2009). Fairness in human resource management, social exchange relationships, and citizenship behavior: Testing linkages of the target similarity model among nurses in the United States. *International Journal of Human Resource Management, 20*(12), 2419–2434. http://doi.org/10.1080/09585190903363748

Lavelle, J. J., Rupp, D. E., & Brockner, J. (2007). Taking a multifoci approach to the study of justice, social exchange, and citizenship behavior: The target similarity model. *Journal of Management, 33*(6), 841–866. http://doi.org/10.1177/0149206307307635

Lee, C., Liu, J., Rousseau, D. M., Hui, C., & Chen, Z. X. (2011). Inducement, contributions, and fulfillment in new employee psychological contracts. *Human Resource Management, 50*(2), 201–226. http://doi.org/10.1002/hrm.20415

Lee, K., & Allen, N. J. (2002). Organizational citizenship behavior and workplace deviance: The role of affect and cognitions. *Journal of Applied Psychology, 87*(1), 131–142. http://doi.org/10.1037/0021-9010.87.1.131

LePine, J. A., Erez, A., & Johnson, D. E. (2002). The nature and dimensionality of organizational citizenship behavior: A critical review and meta-analysis. *Journal of Applied Psychology, 87*(1), 52–65. http://doi.org/10.1037//0021-9010.87.1.52

Liao, C., Wayne, S. J., & Rousseau, D. M. (2016). Idiosyncratic deals in contemporary organizations: A qualitative and meta-analytical review. *Journal of Organizational Behavior, 37*, S9–S29. http://doi.org/10.1002/job.1959

Liu, J., Lee, C., Hui, C., Kwan, H. K., & Wu, L.-Z. (2013). Idiosyncratic deals and employee outcomes: The mediating roles of social exchange and self-enhancement and the moderating role of individualism. *Journal of Applied Psychology, 98*(5), 832–840. http://doi.org/10.1037/a0032571

Lo, S., & Aryee, S. (2003). Psychological contract breach in a Chinese context: An integrative approach. *Journal of Management Studies, 40*(4), 1005–1020. http://doi.org/10.1111/1467-6486.00368

Lynch, P. D., Eisenberger, R., & Armeli, S. (1999). Perceived organizational support: Inferior versus superior performance by wary employees. *Journal of Applied Psychology, 84*(4), 467–483. http://doi.org/10.1037/0021-9010.84.4.467

March, J. G., & Simon, H. A. (1958). *Organizations* (SSRN Scholarly Paper No. ID 1496194). Rochester, NY: Social Science Research Network. Retrieved from http://papers.ssrn.com/abstract=1496194

Masterson, S. S., Lewis, K., Goldman, B. M., & Taylor, M. S. (2000). Integrating justice and social exchange: the differing effects of fair procedures and treatment on work relationships. *Academy of Management Journal, 43*(4), 738–748. http://doi.org/10.2307/1556364

Matta, F. K., Scott, B. A., Koopman, J., & Conlon, D. E. (2015). Does seeing "eye to eye" affect work engagement and organizational citizenship behavior? A role theory perspective on LMX agreement. *Academy of Management Journal, 58*(6), 1686–1708. http://doi.org/10.5465/amj.2014.0106

Mauss, M. (1950). *The gift: The form and reason for exchange in archaic societies.* New York, NY: Norton. (Republished New York, Norton, 1990). Translation of Mauss (1950) by W. D. Halls.

Mayer, D. M., Kuenzi, M., Greenbaum, R., Bardes, M., & Salvador, R. (Bombie). (2009). How low does ethical leadership flow? Test of a trickle-down model. *Organizational Behavior and Human Decision Processes, 108*(1), 1–13. http://doi.org/10.1016/j.obhdp.2008.04.002

Moorman, R. H., Blakely, G. L., & Niehoff, B. P. (1998). Does perceived organizational support mediate the relationship between procedural justice and organizational citizenship behavior? *Academy of Management Journal, 41*(3), 351–357. http://doi.org/10.2307/256913

Morrison, E. W. (1994). Role definitions and organizational citizenship behavior: the importance of the employee's perspective. *Academy of Management Journal, 37*(6), 1543–1567. http://doi.org/10.2307/256798

Morrison, E. W., & Robinson, S. L. (1997). When employees feel betrayed: A model of how psychological contract violation develops. *The Academy of Management Review, 22*(1), 226. http://doi.org/10.2307/259230

Mueller, J. S., & Kamdar, D. (2011). Why seeking help from teammates is a blessing and a curse: A theory of help seeking and individual creativity in team contexts. *The Journal of Applied Psychology, 96*(2), 263–276. http://doi.org/10.1037/a0021574

Ng, T. W. H., & Feldman, D. C. (2012). Employee voice behavior: A meta-analytic test of the conservation of resources framework. *Journal of Organizational Behavior, 33*(2), 216–234. http://doi.org/10.1002/job.754

Ng, T. W. H., & Feldman, D. C. (2015). Idiosyncratic deals and voice behavior. *Journal of Management, 41*(3), 893–928. http://doi.org/10.1177/0149206312457824

Ng, T. W. H., & Lucianetti, L. (2016). Goal striving, idiosyncratic deals, and job behavior. *Journal of Organizational Behavior, 37*(1), 41–60. http://doi.org/10.1002/job.2023

Organ, D. W. (1988). *Organizational citizenship behavior: The good soldier syndrome* (Vol. *xiii*). Lexington, MA: Lexington Books.

Organ, D. W. (1990). The motivational basis of organizational citizenship behavior. In B. M. Staw & L. L. Cummings (Eds.), *Research in organizational behavior* (Vol. 12, pp. 43–72). Greenwich, CT: JAI.

Parzefall, M.-R., & Salin, D. M. (2010). Perceptions of and reactions to workplace bullying: A social exchange perspective. *Human Relations, 63*(6), 761–780. http://doi.org/10.1177/0018726709345043

Podsakoff, P. M., MacKenzie, S. B., Paine, J. B., & Bachrach, D. G. (2000). Organizational citizenship behaviors: A critical review of the theoretical and empirical literature and suggestions for future research. *Journal of Management, 26*(3), 513–563. http://doi.org/10.1177/014920630002600307

Rapp, A. A., Bachrach, D. G., & Rapp, T. L. (2013). The influence of time management skill on the curvilinear relationship between organizational citizenship behavior and task performance. *Journal of Applied Psychology, 98*(4), 668–677. http://doi.org/10.1037/a0031733

Redmond, E. (2013). Competency models at work: The value of perceived relevance and fair rewards for employee outcomes. *Human Resource Management, 52*(5), 771–792. http://doi.org/10.1002/hrm.21560

Restubog, S. L. D., Bordia, P., & Tang, R. L. (2007). Behavioural outcomes of psychological contract breach in a non-western culture: The moderating role of equity sensitivity. *British Journal of Management, 18*(4), 376–386. http://doi.org/10.1111/j.1467-8551.2007.00531.x

Restubog, S. L. D., Bordia, P., Tang, R. L., & Krebs, S. A. (2010). Investigating the moderating effects of leader-member exchange in the psychological contract breach-employee performance relationship: A test of two competing perspectives. *British Journal of Management, 21*(2), 422–437. http://doi.org/10.1111/j.1467-8551.2009.00673.x

Restubog, S. L. D., Hornsey, M. J., Bordia, P., & Esposo, S. R. (2008). Effects of psychological contract breach on organizational citizenship behaviour: Insights from the group value model. *Journal of Management Studies, 45*(8), 1377–1400. http://doi.org/10.1111/j.1467-6486.2008.00792.x

Restubog, S. L. D., Zagenczyk, T. J., Bordia, P., Bordia, S., & Chapman, G. J. (2015). If you wrong us, shall we not revenge? Moderating roles of self-control and perceived aggressive work culture in predicting responses to psychological contract breach. *Journal of Management, 41*(4), 1132–1154. http://doi.org/10.1177/0149206312443557

Rhoades, L., & Eisenberger, R. (2002). Perceived organizational support: A review of the literature. *Journal of Applied Psychology, 87*(4), 698–714. http://doi.org/10.1037/0021-9010.87.4.698

Rhoades, L., Eisenberger, R., & Armeli, S. (2001). Affective commitment to the organization: The contribution of perceived organizational support. *Journal of Applied Psychology, 86*(5), 825–836. http://doi.org/10.1037//0021-9010.86.5.825

Riggle, R. J., Edmondson, D. R., & Hansen, J. D. (2009). A meta-analysis of the relationship between perceived organizational support and job outcomes: 20 years of research. *Journal of Business Research, 62*(10), 1027–1030. http://doi.org/10.1016/j.jbusres.2008.05.003

Rioux, S. M., & Penner, L. A. (2001). The causes of organizational citizenship behavior: A motivational analysis. *Journal of Applied Psychology, 86*(6), 1306–1314. http://doi.org/10.1037/0021-9010.86.6.1306

Robinson, S. L. (1996). Trust and breach of the psychological contract. *Administrative Science Quarterly, 41*(4), 574. http://doi.org/10.2307/2393868

Robinson, S. L., & Morrison, E. W. (1995). Psychological contracts and OCB: The effect of unfulfilled obligations on civic virtue behavior. *Journal of Organizational Behavior, 16*(3), 289–298. http://doi.org/10.1002/job.4030160309

Robinson, S. L., & Rousseau, D. M. (1994). Violating the psychological contract: Not the exception but the norm. *Journal of Organizational Behavior, 15*(3), 245–259. http://doi.org/10.1002/job.4030150306

Rockstuhl, T., Ang, S., Shore, L. M., & Mesdaghinia, S. (2015). *POS and culture: A meta-analysis of correlates across 43 countries.* In symposium (Eisenberger, Chair) titled "Perceived Organizational Support: Culture, Emotion, Well-being, and Practical Application," Annual Meeting of the Academy of Management, Vancouver, Canada.

Rosen, C. C., Chang, C.-H., Johnson, R. E., & Levy, P. E. (2009). Perceptions of the organizational context and psychological contract breach: Assessing competing perspectives. *Organizational Behavior and Human Decision Processes, 108*(2), 202–217. http://doi.org/10.1016/j.obhdp.2008.07.003

Rosen, C. C., Slater, D. J., Chang, C.-H. (Daisy), & Johnson, R. E. (2013). Let's make a deal development and validation of the ex post I-Deals Scale. *Journal of Management, 39*(3), 709–742. http://doi.org/10.1177/0149206310394865

Rousseau, D. M. (1989). Psychological and implied contracts in organizations. *Employee Responsibilities and Rights Journal, 2*(2), 121–139. http://doi.org/10.1007/BF01384942

Rousseau, D. M. (1995). *Psychological contracts in organizations: Understanding written and unwritten agreements.* Thousand Oaks, CA: Sage.

Rousseau, D. M. (2000) *Psychological contract inventory: Technical report (Tech. Rep No. 2).* Pittsburgh, PA: Carnegie Mellon University.

Rousseau, D. M. (2005). *I-deals, idiosyncratic deals employees bargain for themselves.* Armonk, NY: M.E. Sharpe.

Rousseau, D. M., Ho, V. T., & Greenberg, J. (2006). I-Deals: Idiosyncratic terms in employment relationships. *Academy of Management Review, 31*(4), 977–994. http://doi.org/10.5465/AMR.2006.22527470

Rousseau, D. M., & Wade-Benzoni, K. A. (1994). Linking strategy and human resource practices: How employee and customer contracts are created. *Human Resource Management, 33*(3), 463–489. http://doi.org/10.1002/hrm.3930330312

Scott, K. L., Restubog, S. L. D., & Zagenczyk, T. J. (2013). A social exchange-based model of the antecedents of workplace exclusion. *Journal of Applied Psychology, 98*(1), 37–48. http://doi.org/10.1037/a0030135

Shih, C.-T., & Chen, S. (2011). The social dilemma perspective on psychological contract fulfilment and organizational citizenship behaviour. *Management and Organization Review, 7*(1), 125–151. http://doi.org/10.1111/j.1740-8784.2010.00202.x

Shih, C.-T., & Chuang, C.-H. (2013). Individual differences, psychological contract breach, and organizational citizenship behavior: A moderated mediation study. *Asia Pacific Journal of Management, 30*(1), 191–210. http://doi.org/10.1007/s10490-012-9294-8

Shih, C.-T., & Lin, C.-C. T. (2012). From good friends to good soldiers: A psychological contract perspective. *Asia Pacific Journal of Management, 31*(1), 309–326. http://doi.org/10.1007/s10490-012-9333-5

Shore, L. M., Coyle-Shapiro, J. A-M., & Chang, C. (in press). Exchange in the employee-organization relationship. In N. Anderson, C. Viswesvaran, H. K. Sinangil, and D. Ones (Eds.), *Handbook of industrial work and organizational psychology* (2nd ed.).

Shore, L. M., Tetrick, L. E., Lynch, P., & Barksdale, K. (2006). Social and economic exchange: Construct development and validation. *Journal of Applied Social Psychology, 36*(4), 837–867. http://doi.org/10.1111/j.0021-9029.2006.00046.x

Shore, L. M., Tetrick, L. E., Taylor, M. S., Coyle-Shapiro, J., Liden, R., McLean Parks, J., . . . Van Dyne, L. (2004). The employee-organization relationship: A timely concept in a period of transition. In J. Martocchio (Ed.), *Research in personnel and human resources management* (vol. 23, pp. 291–370). Greenwich, CT: JAI Press.

Shore, L. M., & Wayne, S. J. (1993). Commitment and employee behavior: Comparison of affective commitment and continuance commitment with perceived organizational support. *Journal of Applied Psychology, 78*(5), 774–780. http://doi.org/10.1037/0021-9010.78.5.774

Si, S. X., Wei, F., & Li, Y. (2008). The effect of organizational psychological contract violation on managers' exit, voice, loyalty and neglect in the Chinese context. *International Journal of Human Resource Management, 19*(5), 932–944. http://doi.org/10.1080/09585190801995849

Slack, R. E., Corlett, S., & Morris, R. (2014). Exploring employee engagement with (corporate) social responsibility: A social exchange perspective on organisational participation. *Journal of Business Ethics, 127*(3), 537–548. http://doi.org/10.1007/s10551-014-2057-3

Song, L. J., Tsui, A. S., & Law, K. S. (2009). Unpacking employee responses to organizational exchange mechanisms: The role of social and economic exchange perceptions. *Journal of Management, 35*(1), 56–93. http://doi.org/10.1177/0149206308321544

Spector, P. E., & Fox, S. (2002). An emotion-centered model of voluntary work behavior: Some parallels between counterproductive work behavior and organizational citizenship behavior. *Human Resource Management Review, 12*(2), 269–292. http://doi.org/10.1016/S1053-4822(02)00049-9

Spector, P. E., & Fox, S. (2010a). Counterproductive work behavior and organisational citizenship behavior: Are they opposite forms of active behavior? *Applied Psychology, 59*(1), 21–39. http://doi.org/10.1111/j.1464-0597.2009.00414.x

Spector, P. E., & Fox, S. (2010b). Theorizing about the deviant citizen: An attributional explanation of the interplay of organizational citizenship and counterproductive work behavior. *Human Resource Management Review, 20*(2), 132–143. http://doi.org/10.1016/j.hrmr.2009.06.002

Spence, J. R., Brown, D. J., Keeping, L. M., & Lian, H. (2014). Helpful today, but not tomorrow? Feeling grateful as a predictor of daily organizational citizenship behaviors. *Personnel Psychology, 67*(3), 705–738. http://doi.org/10.1111/peps.12051

Suazo, M. M., & Stone-Romero, E. F. (2011). Implications of psychological contract breach: A perceived organizational support perspective. *Journal of Managerial Psychology, 26*(5), 366–382. http://doi.org/10.1108/02683941111138994

Tekleab, A. G., Takeuchi, R., & Taylor, M. S. (2005). Extending the chain of relationships among organizational justice, social exchange, and employee reactions: The role of contract violations. *Academy of Management Journal, 48*(1), 146–157. http://doi.org/10.5465/AMJ.2005.15993162

Tekleab, A. G., & Taylor, M. S. (2003). Aren't there two parties in an employment relationship? Antecedents and consequences of organization–employee agreement on contract obligations and violations. *Journal of Organizational Behavior, 24*(5), 585–608. http://doi.org/10.1002/job.204

Thompson, J. A., & Bunderson, J. S. (2003). Violations of principle: Ideological currency in the psychological contract. *Academy of Management Review, 28*(4), 571–586. http://doi.org/10.5465/AMR.2003.10899381

Topa, G., Francisco Morales, J., & Moriano, J.-A. (2009). Psychological contract breach and social identity: Their influences on Spanish soldiers' job satisfaction and organizational citizenship behaviour. *Estudios De Psicologia, 30*(3), 303–315.

Tsui, A. S., Pearce, J. L., Porter, L. W., & Tripoli, A. M. (1997). Alternative approaches to the employee-organization relationship: Does investment in employees pay off? *Academy of Management Journal, 40*(5), 1089–1121. http://doi.org/10.2307/256928

Turnley, W., Bolino, M., Lester, S., & Bloodgood, J. (2003). The impact of psychological contract fulfillment on the performance of in-role and organizational citizenship behaviors. *Journal of Management, 29*(2), 187–206. http://doi.org/10.1177/014920630302900204

Van Dyne, L., Graham, J. W., & Dienesch, R. M. (1994). Organizational citizenship behavior: construct redefinition, measurement, and validation. *Academy of Management Journal, 37*(4), 765–802. http://doi.org/10.2307/256600

Vroom, V. H. (1964). *Work and motivation.* Oxford, England: Wiley.

Wang, S., Zhou, H., & Wen, P. (2014). Employment modes, charismatic leadership and organizational citizenship behavior: Explanations from perceived job security. *Pakistan Journal of Statistics, 30*(5), 827–836.

Wayne, S. J., Shore, L. M., & Liden, R. C. (1997). Perceived organizational support and leader-member exchange: A social exchange perspective. *Academy of Management Journal, 40*(1), 82–111. http://doi.org/10.2307/257021

Wei, F., & Si, S. (2013). Psychological contract breach, negative reciprocity, and abusive supervision: the mediated effect of organizational identification. *Management and Organization Review, 9*(3), 541–561. http://doi.org/10.1111/more.12029

Weiss, H. M., & Cropanzano, R. (1996). Affective events theory: A theoretical discussion of the structure, causes and consequences of affective experiences at work. In B. M. Staw & L. L. Cummings (Eds.), *Research in organizational behavior: An annual series of analytical essays and critical reviews* (Vol. 18, pp. 1–74). New York, NY: Elsevier Science/JAI Press.

Williams, L. J., & Anderson, S. E. (1991). Job satisfaction and organizational commitment as predictors of organizational citizenship and in-role behaviors. *Journal of Management, 17*(3), 601–617. http://doi.org/10.1177/014920639101700305

Zablah, A. R., Carlson, B. D., Donavan, D. T., Maxham, J. G., & Brown, T. J. (2016). A cross-lagged test of the association between customer satisfaction and employee job satisfaction in a relational context. *The Journal of Applied Psychology, 101*(5), 743–755. http://doi.org/10.1037/apl0000079

Zagenczyk, T. J., Cruz, K. S., Woodard, A. M., Walker, J. C., Few, W. T., Kiazad, K., & Raja, M. (2013). The moderating effect of Machiavellianism on the psychological contract breach-organizational identification/disidentification relationships. *Journal of Business and Psychology, 28*(3), 287–299. http://doi.org/10.1007/s10869-012-9278-1

Zagenczyk, T. J., Gibney, R., Few, W. T., & Scott, K. L. (2011). Psychological contracts and organizational identification: the mediating effect of perceived organizational support. *Journal of Labor Research, 32*(3), 254–281. http://doi.org/10.1007/s12122-011-9111-z

Zagenczyk, T. J., Restubog, S. L. D., Kiewitz, C., Kiazad, K., & Tang, R. L. (2014). Psychological contracts as a mediator between Machiavellianism and employee citizenship and deviant behaviors. *Journal of Management, 40*(4), 1098–1122. http://doi.org/10.1177/0149206311415420

Zhao, H., Wayne, S. J., Glibkowski, B. C., & Bravo, J. (2007). The impact of psychological contract breach on work-related outcomes: A meta-analysis. *Personnel Psychology, 60*(3), 647–680. http://doi.org/10.1111/j.1744-6570.2007.00087.x

CHAPTER

20 Fitting In and Doing Good: A Review of Person–Environment Fit and Organizational Citizenship Behavior Research

Amy L. Kristof-Brown, Christina S. Li, *and* Benjamin Schneider

Abstract

This chapter presents a comprehensive review of the relationships between different types of person–environment (PE) fit—namely person–organization, person–group, person–supervisor, and person–job—and organizational citizenship behaviors (OCBs). Relying on both affinity and exchange explanations, we demonstrate that individuals who experience good fit are more likely to engage in OCBs. However, the strength of the relationship is contingent on many factors, especially with regard to the operationalization of fit (the kind of fit measure used), the characteristics on which fit is assessed (e.g., values, goals, personality), the types of OCBs studied (overall OCBs, OCBs focused toward the organization, and OCBs focused toward individuals), the source of the ratings of OCBs (self-report versus others' reports), and the level of analysis (individual vs. unit). Mediators and moderators of the PE fit–OCB relationship are also reviewed. We conclude with recommendations for future research to better understand the PE fit–OCB relationship.

Key Words: person–environment fit, organizational citizenship behaviors, person–organization fit, person–group fit, person–supervisor fit, person–job fit

Person–environment (PE) fit is one of the most venerable lines of scholarship in applied psychology and management. The fundamental idea is that individuals are better suited for certain work environments than for others. It rests on Kurt Lewin's maxim that B = f (P, E), with outcomes being dependent on both the person and the environment. Finding an environment in which the person's characteristics are compatible with those of others', and with the conditions of the job and organization, is the crucible of good fit. Fit has many positive consequences for individuals, including less stress and more satisfaction, commitment, trust, and team cohesion (Arthur, Bell, Villado, & Doverspike, 2006; Kristof-Brown, Zimmerman, & Johnson, 2005; Oh, Guay, Kim, Harold, Lee, Heo & Shin., 2014). Organizations also benefit, with fit being related to reduced employee withdrawal, turnover, deviance, and cynicism (Mulki, Jaramillo, & Locander, 2006; Naus, Van Iterson, & Roe, 2007). Fit has also been found to relate to performance, with contextual performance, including organizational citizenship behaviors (OCBs), as a more predictable outcome than task performance (Kristof-Brown et al., 2005; Oh et al., 2014). The purpose of this chapter is to review the existing empirical research connecting PE fit and OCBs, draw conclusions about the current state of knowledge, and promote a research agenda for the expansion of existing data and theory.

Person–Environment Fit Types and Operationalizations

The PE fit literature includes many different types of fit, and understanding those types provides an important base from which to build a comprehensive model of OCBs and fit. PE fit is the conceptual umbrella for fit with various aspects of the environment, including the organization (person–organization or PO fit), the job (person–job or PJ fit), the work group (person–group or PG fit) and the supervisor (person–supervisor or PS fit). Within each type of fit, there are certain personal and environmental characteristics on which fit is typically assessed. For example, the match between individual abilities and job demands or between individual needs and job supplies is often the focus of PJ fit studies. Alternatively, PO fit studies emphasize the similarity between individual and organizational values. For the types of fit based on interpersonal compatibility (PG and PS fit), studies have typically focused on personality, goal, and work style similarity, or the match between individual skills and needs of the group (Kristof, 1996). Many studies have not always described these studies in terms of "fit" —in some cases constructs such as value congruence or values internalization were used. Conceptually, these fall under the rubric of fit, so in what follows we review the relationships between each of these constructs and OCBs.

In addition to different types of fit, fit has also been operationalized in a wide variety of ways, making the measurement of fit a key factor to consider when reviewing the literature. The three primary types of fit measurement have been as follows: direct measures of perceived fit, indirect measures of subjective fit, and indirect measures of objective fit. Direct measures of perceived fit ask respondents to report their overall perception of how they fit with a particular part of their work environment (i.e., "My values are a good match with those of my company" or "My skills are a good match to my job demands"). This type of measure requires the participant to consider his or her personal characteristics as well as the environment's characteristics, and then to compare them to form an overall judgment of perceived fit. Indirect measures of subjective fit ask respondents to first assess their personal characteristics and then to separately assess the environment's characteristics. A calculation, such as a difference score or a profile similarity index, is then done by the researcher to produce the measure of subjective fit. For the example of fit on values, this would require the individual to first respond to a question, "How much do you value X?" and then secondly to respond to the question "To what extent does your organization value X?" A difference score or profile similarity score (if multiple values were assessed) would then be calculated on these two responses to create the measure of subjective fit, with smaller scores indicating a better fit. Finally, objective approaches calculate the similarity of a person's self-reported attributes to measures of environmental attributes as reported by others. Continuing the values example, the individual would still be asked to respond to the question, "How much do you value X?" However, the question "To what extent does your organization value X?" would be asked of others expected to have a good grasp of company culture, such as an HR manager, top management team members, or other incumbents. Objective fit would be calculated by computing a difference score between these two values, with smaller differences indicating better fit. If multiple values were assessed simultaneously, a profile similarity index could be used to assess the fit between individual and organizational value profiles.

Research has demonstrated that these three fit measures often differ, sometimes dramatically, in how they relate to each other and how they relate to outcome variables, even when fit of the same type (e.g., PO, PJ, PS, PG) is calculated (Edwards, Cable, Williamson, Lambert, & Shipp, 2006). As we will show, direct perceived measures of fit have the strongest relationships with most outcomes, particularly with various job attitudes, turnover intentions, and attraction to jobs and organizations (Kristof-Brown et al., 2005). In what follows, we thus not only review how different types of fit (PO, PG, PJ) relate to OCBs but, where available, we present evidence on the relationship between different operationalizations of fit and their relationship with OCBs.

In addition to these three measurement strategies, fit is sometimes inferred rather than assessed, through polynomial regression analysis (PRA). Edwards (1994, 1995; Edwards & Parry, 1993) advocated for the use of polynomial regression and surface plot analysis instead of profile comparisons or the difference score methods commonly used to calculate subjective and objective fit. Although difference scores can be useful to capture a degree of similarity, they suffer from reduced reliability, ambiguous interpretation, confounded level and dispersion effects, untested statistical constraints, and the reduction of three-dimensional relationships into two-dimensions ones (Edwards, 2002). Therefore, Edwards and colleagues demonstrated how polynomial regression and three-dimensional surface plot analysis could be used to depict more precise relationships between P, E, and outcome variables when testing indirect subjective and objective operationalizations of fit.

So, according to the polynomial regression argument, the usefulness of fit research is to show that P and E alone as predictors of an outcome can be enhanced by inclusion of the interaction term and their higher order quadratic terms (P^2 and E^2). In other words, if the higher order P and E terms are significant, then fit above and beyond simply the P and E effects is inferred. Thus, polynomial regression studies do not allow a specific effect size to be reported for fit. Instead, they focus on whether the addition of the interaction and quadratic terms held explain additional variance in the outcome. Three-dimensional surface plot analysis is then used to portray in precise terms what type of relationship exists between P and E and the outcome of interest—for this chapter, OCBs.

Organizational Citizenship Behavior Types and Operationalizations

In addition to types and operationalization of PE fit, we will also demonstrate that the types and operationalization of OCBs influences the strength of the reported relationships between fit and OCBs. Although most research on fit and OCBs has examined what we label "overall OCBs" or "OCBs without distinctions," there are also a considerable number of studies that examine particular types of OCBs. Williams and Anderson (1991) suggested that OCBs directed toward individuals (OCBI) are distinct from OCBs directed toward the organization (OCBO). Some examples of OCBI behaviors include helping and altruism, whereas OCBO behaviors include conscientiousness, sportsmanship, and civic virtue. Because the various types of PE fit emphasize different parts of the environment, such as the organization or the team, we will examine where possible, whether particular types of fit are more strongly related to OCBIs or OCBOs. For example, it makes sense that OCBs directed toward the organization may be more influenced by PO fit than OCBs directed toward particular individuals, whereas OCBs directed toward individuals may be more impacted by PG or PS fit. However, whether these hypothesized relationships are valid is an empirical question.

Finally, we consider whether the operationalization, specifically the source of measurement for OCBs, influences the strength of the relationships with PE fit. In some studies the OCBs are self-reports, while in other studies the ratings of OCBs come from others. These others predominantly include supervisors, sometimes peers, and sometimes an average or compilation of multiple sources. If individuals self-report their personal fit and OCBs, consistency bias likely upwardly biases the strength of their reported relationships. Thus, we anticipated that the relationship between self-reported OCBs with all types and measures of PE fit will be stronger than the relationships with other-reported OCBs. Again, this is an empirical question, which we will address when the data are available to do so.

Overview of the Chapter

Meta-analyses of the fit literature (Arthur et al., 2006; Hoffman & Woehr, 2006; Kristof-Brown et al., 2005) report a positive moderate relationship between all types of PE fit and OCBs. When compared with task or overall performance, the relationship of fit with contextual performance (conceptually similar to OCBs) is stronger (Kristof-Brown et al., 2005), making OCBs a topic of interest for PE fit scholars. In the following section, we review the studies included in that meta-analysis, as well as recent studies of each type of fit with OCBs, to gain a better understanding of the nuances of these relationships.

Our review highlights that fit has most often been studied as a direct predictor of OCBs. Yet we uncovered a few studies that also considered mediating processes (to be explicitly noted later), which helped explain the relationship between fit and OCBs. These mediators most often included job attitudes, but there was little consistency on the types of attitudes that were considered. Moreover, we found very few studies that examined boundary conditions or moderators of the fit–OCB relationship. In our review we add fit and OCB type, as well as operationalizations of each, to the list of possible moderators of these relationships. By doing so, we seek to clarify where the strongest relationships exist, as well as potential reasons why their strength varies.

The chapter unfolds as follows. First we consider the conceptual/theoretical underpinnings of the hypothesized relationship between fit and OCBs. Then we take each type of fit in turn (PO, PG, PS, and PJ) and review the research that has been done on it with OCBs. Within each of these sections we note contingencies on the general relationships across studies, especially with regard to the operationalization of fit (the kind of fit measure used), the types of OCBs studied (overall OCBs, individually focused OCBs, and organizationally focused OCBs), and the source of the ratings of OCBs (self-report versus others' reports). The final two substantive issues we address concern the few studies of mediators and moderators of the PE fit–OCB relationship. We conclude with a summary with implications for future research on this relationship.

Why Should Person–Environment Fit Matter for Organizational Citizenship Behaviors?

There are several theories that would suggest why PE fit would relate to OCBs. First is the similarity–attraction paradigm (Byrne, 1971), which predicts that individuals who perceive similarity to others will be attracted to those others, resulting in more frequent communication, greater social integration, stronger desire to maintain group affiliation, and more cohesive work relations (Lincoln & Miller, 1979; Wharton & Baron, 1987). The more similar a person is to others in the work environment, the more he or she will like and want to support that environment. Because OCBs are directly aimed toward helping others, whether it is individuals, groups, or organizations, they are more likely to be engaged by people who feel similarity-induced liking toward their colleagues. This theory would seem to be particularly appropriate as a framework for understanding the relationships between interpersonal types of fit, such as PG and PS fit, with OCBs.

A second theory that would suggest a fit–OCB relationship is social exchange theory (Blau, 1964). This theory purports that people engage in subjective cost-benefit analysis to determine whether they will provide something to another entity in exchange for what they are provided. In one type of fit (PJ fit: needs-supplies), people's needs are met by aspects of their environment, making it likely they will feel a sense of reciprocity to continue the exchange. Of course, this logic applies equally well to PG, PS, and PO fit in which relationships with others are beneficial and thus deserving of reciprocity. Because OCBs can generate positive gains for the entity toward which they are directed, engaging in OCBs would be viewed as a way to reciprocate for the supplies received, perhaps attributed to the group, the supervisor, or the organization itself.

Finally, when PJ fit is assessed as demands-abilities fit, a person's abilities match the demands of the environment. When a match occurs, the person is capable of performing the task-related functions of the job and may therefore have discretionary time to perform additional citizenship behaviors. We are less compelled by this explanation, however, because most research has demonstrated that contextual performance (nee OCBs) is more related to a person's self-initiated behaviors regardless of circumstances than to capability in terms of time (Borman & Motowidlo, 1993, 1997; Motowidlo & Van Scotter, 1994; Van Scotter & Motowidlo, 1996). In our estimation, the affinity and social exchange explanations, because they focus on initiative rather than capability, are more likely to explain why people who perceive or objectively have superior fit would also be better citizens.

In summary, there are compelling conceptual reasons for why individuals will be motivated to engage in higher levels of OCBs when they fit with their work environments. In particular, reciprocity norms should stimulate OCBs directed toward the particular aspects of the environment where fit, either perceived or objective, is the greatest. We begin the in-depth qualitative review of OCB correlates with studies of PO fit, move on to PG and PS fit, and we conclude with PJ fit within each section, noting how fit was assessed, the kind of OCBs studied as outcome, and how the OCBs were assessed (self vs. other). We summarize the research graphically in a series of tables, one for each type of PE fit: the characteristics on which fit is assessed, the measures used to assess fit, the type of OCBs studied, who provided the ratings of OCBs, and the level of analysis at which the study was conducted (individual vs. unit).

Person–Organization Fit and Organizational Citizenship Behaviors

PO fit has been studied more extensively than other forms of PE fit. PO fit research addresses the compatibility between the individual and organization (Kristof, 1996). Research on PO fit has typically emphasized similarity between individuals and their organization on underlying characteristics, including values, goals, and personality, with operationalizations that include direct perceived, indirect subjective, and indirect actual measures. Because of the extensive list of studies investigating PO fit and OCBs, we will review them based on the criterion first (i.e., the type of OCB being predicted), and then based on fit operationalization (Table 20.1).

Overall Organizational Citizenship Behaviors

When OCBs are categorized broadly, positive moderate-sized relationships with perceived PO fit have consistently been reported. Many of these studies have operationalized PO fit as direct perceptions of value congruence or values internalization

Table 20.1 Person-Organization Fit and Organizational Citizenship Behavior Studies

Study	Fit Measure	Fit Characteristics	OCB Types	OCB Measure	Level of Analysis
Becker (1992)	Direct perceived	Values Internalization	Overall OCB OCBO OCBI	Average of self, peer, and supervisor	Individual
Cable & DeRue (2002)	Direct perceived	Values	Overall OCB	Supervisor	Individual
Cha, Chang, & Kim (2014)	Indirect perceived; polynomial regression analyses	Values	OCBO OCBI	Self	Individual
Chandrakumara (2007)	Indirect actual	Needs-supplies	Overall OCB	Supervisor	Individual
Goodman & Svyantek (1999)	Indirect perceived; polynomial regression analyses	Values	Overall OCB OCBO OCBI	Supervisor	Individual
Lauver & Kristof-Brown (2001)	Direct perceived	Values	Overall OCB	Peer	Individual
Lemmon & Wayne (2015)	Direct perceived	Values	OCBO	Supervisor	Individual
Netemeyer, Boles, McKee, & McMurrian (1997)	Direct perceived	Values	Overall OCB	Self	Individual
O'Reilly & Chatman (1986)	Direct perceived	Values Internalization	Overall OCB	Self	Individual
Rich, Lepine, & Crawford (2010)	Direct perceived	Values	Overall OCB	Supervisor	Individual
Tsai, Chen, & Chen (2012)	Indirect actual	Values	Overall OCB	Self	Individual
Vigoda (2000)	Indirect perceived	Demands Abilities Needs-supplies Values Personality	OCBO OCBI	Supervisor	Individual
Vogel & Feldman (2009)	Direct perceived	Values Goals	OCBI	Supervisor	Individual
Wei (2012)	Direct perceived	General compatibility	OCBO OCBI	Supervisor	Individual

OCB, organizational citizenship behavior; OCBI, OCB directed toward the individual; OCBO, OCB directed toward the organization.

(which Kristof-Brown et al. [2005] coded as values congruence due to the similarity in question items for the two concepts). Assessing PO fit as perceived value congruence, Lauver and Kristof-Brown (2001) report a correlation of .28 with employees' contextual performance (which we will consider as overall OCBs in this chapter) as reported by peers. Their contextual performance scale included a measure of persisting with extra effort, volunteering to carry out extra activities, helping/cooperating with others, and endorsing organizational objectives. Expanding the taxonomy of overall OCBs to include supervisors' ratings of helping, voice, sportsmanship, civic virtue, and conscientiousness, Cable and DeRue (2002) reported a similar moderate sized relationship with perceived value congruence (r = .22). Becker (1992) reported a direct correlation of .20 between perceived values internalization and overall OCBs, calculated as an average of self, peer, and supervisor ratings. Rich, Lepine, and Crawford (2010) reported a slightly stronger direct correlation (r = .29) between perceived value congruence and supervisor-reported overall OCBs, but added that this relationship was mediated by engagement.

Slightly stronger relationships were reported in studies that used self-reported overall OCBs and perceived PO fit. Using self-reports, Netemeyer, Boles, McKee, and McMurrian (1997) reported overall OCBs with perceived value congruence (r = .29–41), and O'Reilly and Chatman (1986) reported a range of relationships between perceived values internalization with self-reported extra-role behaviors (r = .17–.36). Because of the common reporting source for the predictor and criterion in these studies, the stronger relationships are not surprising. We discuss the impact of OCB measurement at the conclusion of our review of the PO fit–OCB studies.

Two additional studies assessed the relationship with overall OCBs using indirect measures of PO fit. Chandrakumara (2007) demonstrated that when employees' preferences for HRM practices were better aligned with actual HRM practices (as reported by HR managers and CEOs), their OCBs as reported by their supervisors were higher (r = .16–.22) than when there was misalignment between preferences and actual HRM practices. Thus, even using an objective, rather than perceived, measure of PO fit, this study suggests a moderately strong positive relationship between PO fit with overall OCBs. Similarly, Tsai, Chen, and Chen (2012) assessed objective value congruence by comparing individuals' self-reported values with organizational values reported by five senior managers. Their results showed that the direct relationship between objective value congruence and self-reported OCB was r = .22. Additionally, they report that objective fit accounted for a significant 2% variance increase in explaining overall OCBs, after controlling for the impact of individual differences.

A final study (Goodman & Svyantek, 1999) used polynomial regression analysis to determine whether the interaction between individuals' preferred values and perceived organizational values predicted OCBs. In this study they found that both individual values and perceived organizational values had significant main effects on supervisor-reported OCBs, but that the interaction between them was not significant for any of the 16 values they examined. However, because this study did not include the quadratic terms (P^2 and O^2) that would normally be included in a polynomial regression analysis, the results did not fully test a congruence relationship (i.e., fit occurs when P and O values are congruent). With the exception of Goodman and Svyantek (1999), these studies present consistent evidence that the relationship between both perceived and objective PO fit with overall OCBs is positive and of moderate strength.

OCBOs and OCBIs

When OCB is separated out into subdimensions of OCBO and OCBI, we find the relationships with PO fit to be weaker and less consistent. We located six studies that split OCBs into clear subdimensions. The OCBO behaviors included were conscientiousness, sportsmanship, and civic virtue. Three studies reported significant direct correlations of perceived PO fit with OCBOs that ranged from .10 to .22 (Becker, 1992; r = .10 for conscientiousness, r = .18 for nonidleness; Lemmon & Wayne, 2015; r = .22; Wei, 2012; r = .19). Each of these studies used self-reported perceptions of fit and supervisor ratings of OCBs or, in the case of Becker (1992), the average of supervisor, peer, and self-ratings of OCBs. A study by Vigoda (2000) used a difference score to calculate the similarity between a broad range of individual and perceived organizational characteristics, including values, personality, needs/supplies, and abilities/demands. This indirect subjective measure of PO fit correlated .11 with supervisor-rated OCBOs, but was not statistically significant.

Two additional studies used a polynomial regression approach to investigate the precise nature of the relationship between personal and perceived organizational characteristics with OCBOs. Cha, Chang, and Kim (2014) investigated the relationship between people's self-reported prosocial identities and the prosocial identities they perceive in their organizations. Their results showed that although both individual and perceived organizational identities had main effects on self-reported OCBOs, the interaction between them did not. There appeared to be an additive effect in which the highest levels of OCBOs emerged when both individuals and perceived organizations had high levels of prosocial identity, but no significant additional variance was explained in OCBOs when their interaction was considered. Similarly, Goodman and Svyantek (1999) found support for main effects of personal and perceived organizational culture on supervisor-rated OCBOs, but no significant interaction between the two. In light of the polynomial regression results, we conclude that OCBOs are modestly related to perceived PO fit, but that the relationship does not seem to be based on strict similarity between individual and perceived organizational characteristics. Overall, these results portray a relatively small effect size for the OCBO and perceived PO fit relationship, with very little evidence for a congruence relationship between P and O being associated with higher OCBOs.

Within the category of OCBIs, which includes behaviors such as helping others and altruism, there were similarly equivocal results. Three studies reported weak to moderate, but statistically significant relationships, between supervisor-rated OCBIs and direct measures of perceived PO fit (Becker, 1992; $r = .16$ for altruism; Vogel & Feldman, 2009; $r = .05$; Wei, 2012; $r = .21$). Vigoda (2000), using the indirect measure of similarity between a broad range of personal and perceived organizational characteristics, which we described earlier, reported no direct relationship of similarity and supervisor-rated OCBIs ($r = .01$).

As in the research on OCBOs, the set of polynomial regression studies showed strong main effects of person and organizational values, but little evidence for exact congruence between P and O influencing self-rated (Cha, Chang, & Kim, 2014) or supervisor-rated (Goodman & Svyantek, 1999) OCBIs. The only statistically significant interaction between personal and perceived organization values (in this case, prosocial identity) reported in Cha et al. (2014) was that when P and O prosocial values were incongruent; OCBI was generally higher than when they were congruent! This was true with the one exception of the high P–high O combination, which resulted in the highest level of OCBIs. In most of the other cases, as long as the person *or* the organization was seen as having a high prosocial identity, high OCBIs were reported.

Taken as a whole, the relationships of perceived PO fit with OCBIs were somewhat smaller (.01–.21) than those reported for OCBOs ($r = .10–.22$). This is not surprising, as the focus of OCBOs is on the broader organization, versus OCBIs which focus on behaviors toward specific individuals. In almost every case, however, the relationships of PO fit with the more comprehensive and broader measures of overall OCBs were greater ($r = .16–.41$) than with either of OCBs' subdimensions. This held true regardless of whether PO fit was measured directly as fit perceptions or indirectly as similarity with the subjective or objective environment. Thus, unless there are strong theoretical reasons for dividing OCBs into more precise subdimensions, we would recommend that PO fit researchers utilize the overall OCB construct and measures, rather than focusing on more specific subdimensions.

Studies of PO fit and OCBs present a convincing picture that the two are positively associated, with the strongest support for a relationship between overall OCBs and PO fit, followed by OCBOs, and then OCBIs. Yet, given the variety of ways that OCBs and PO fit have been operationalized, it is useful to consider whether differences in effect sizes might be due to the operationalization of either or both constructs. We first deal with the measurement of OCBs and next with the measurement of fit.

Measurement of Organizational Citizenship Behaviors

More closely examining the range of effect sizes between PO fit and overall OCBs reveals that when OCBs are rated by a peer or supervisor, the effect sizes are somewhat smaller ($r = .16–.29$) than when OCBs are self-reported ($r = .17–.41$). This is most noticeable on the high end of the range. Regardless of the OCB rating source, a weak to moderate positive relationship appears to exist with PO fit. Although the relationship with others' ratings of OCBs is slightly lower, these are more compelling because they are uncontaminated by consistency bias. Looking at the studies of OCBOs and OCBIs, the majority used supervisors' or peers' ratings. Thus, some of the weaker relationships of OCBOs and OCBIs with PO fit reported earlier may be due to the fact that these studies almost exclusively used the less biased others' reports of OCBs. A more equivalent comparison, then, is to compare only the other-rated studies for overall OCBs, OCBIs, and OCBOs. Doing this, the effect sizes for other-rated overall OCBs are reduced, but still remain higher (.16–.29) than those for other-rated OCBOs (r = .10–.22) and OCBIs (.01–.21). Thus, when holding measurement of OCBs equal and to the highest standard, there still appears to be an advantage to assessing overall OCBs versus its subdimensions when studying PO fit as a predictor.

Measurement of Person–Organization Fit

In addition to the measurement of OCBs, we consider whether the approach used to assess PO fit may have influenced the strength of reported relationships. Research has demonstrated that different measures of fit are not interchangeable (Edwards et al., 2006) and may yield dramatically different effect sizes for behavioral outcomes like OCBs. Direct measures of fit are often more strongly correlated with behavioral outcomes than indirect measures of fit (Arthur et al., 2006; Kristof-Brown et al., 2005). Given past findings, we expect that direct measures of fit will be more strongly correlated with all types of OCBs.

To best assess the impact of the measurement of PO fit, it is optimal to hold the measurement of OCBs constant. Therefore, we compare different ways of assessing PO fit with considering only the non-self-report ratings of OCBs; that is, those that were provided by supervisors or peers, uncontaminated by self-report bias. Doing this, we find that the unweighted average effect sizes for PO fit assessed using direct perceived measures were slightly higher (r = .27) than when indirect measures of fit were used (r = .19) for overall OCBs. This difference was similar for the average relationship for OCBOs (r = .17 direct, .11 indirect). For OCBIs, however, the difference was more than two times greater (r = .14 direct, .01 indirect). These results suggest that the measurement strategy used to assess fit impacts the strength of the relationship that is likely to be found between PO fit and OCBs. Indirect measures of PO fit produce slightly weaker relationship for overall OCBs and OCBOs, and dramatically weaker relationships with OCBIs. This story is told perhaps even more clearly when it is noted that the studies that did not support a direct link between PO fit (or the interaction of P and O) with OCBOs or OCBIs (e.g., Cha et al., 2014; Goodman & Svyantek, 1999; Vigoda, 2000) all used indirect ways of assessing or inferring fit using polynomial regression. Conversely, studies that reported a statistically significant relationship between these constructs (e.g., Becker, 1992; Lemmon & Wayne, 2015; Vogel & Feldman, 2009; Wei, 2012) all used direct measures of perceived PO fit.

Summary

The accumulation of results with regard to OCBs and PO fit leads us to conclude that the relationship between OCBs and PO fit is highly contingent on the type of OCB being predicted as well as the operationalization of OCBs and PO fit. Our review suggests that overall OCBs have the strongest relationship with PO fit, particularly when fit is measured as direct perceptions. This is followed by OCBOs, measured by direct and then indirect perceptions. In all of these cases, however, the measurement of fit only slightly weakens the reported relationship with overall OCBs or OCBOs. Where the measurement of PO fit seems to make the most difference is when predicting OCBIs. In those cases only when fit is measured as a direct perception is there any relationship at all reported with OCBIs. Finally, the relationships are consistently stronger when OCBs are self-reported but, especially for overall OCBs, they remain of moderate size.

Our conclusion that PO fit is a better predictor of overall OCBs, compared to OCBOs and OCBIs, is somewhat surprising given that others have reported that the different conceptualizations of OCBs generally have no meaningful differences when considered with different predictors (LePine, Erez, & Johnson, 2002). However, our analysis reveals a more nuanced story for the case of PO fit: The overall OCBs appear to be best predicted by PO fit regardless of how fit is operationalized and how the OCBs are measured. Perhaps the PO fit construct, addressing fit to the entire organization, provides for a more inclusive social exchange motivation directed at both general organizational extra-role behavior and helpfulness and cooperation with individuals. By including a more comprehensive set of OCBs, as in the measurement of overall OCBs, the strongest relationship between PO fit and OCBs is obtained. Of course, there may be occasions when separating OCBs into its subdimensions may be driven by alternative research questions, such as addressing different outcomes of OCBs or psychological mechanisms (Podsakoff, Podsakoff, MacKenzie, Maynes, & Spoelma, 2014). As future research continues to explore the relationship between PO fit and OCBs, it is important that studies consider what form of OCBs are most relevant and what measurement strategy for PO fit is consistent with the research question and theory. Using others' reports (not self-reports) of overall OCBs, as predicted by perceived or subjective ratings of PO fit, seems likely to yield the most compelling validity results.

Person–Group Fit and Organizational Citizenship Behaviors

PG fit focuses on the compatibility between the individual and the work group (Jansen & Kristof-Brown, 2005; Kristof, 1996). Although there has been increasing research and interest in PG fit, it has been understudied compared to other types of fit. To our knowledge, there are under a handful of studies that examined PG fit with OCBs. Of this small number, however, all existing studies found a positive and moderate-sized relationship between the two. Because of the small number of studies, we review each study and then discuss how the different conceptualizations of OCB (overall, OCBO, and OCBI) relate to PG fit (Table 20.2).

Becker (1992) examined the effect of PG fit, assessed as perceived work group values internalization, on overall prosocial behavior (which we will consider as overall OCBs in this chapter) and on different prosocial subdimensions, including altruism (OCBI), conscientiousness (OCBO), and nonidleness (OCBO). Prosocial behaviors were measured by averaging self, peer, and supervisor ratings of OCBs. For overall prosocial behavior, the direct correlation with perceived group values' internalization was a modest $r = .16$. Relationships with the subdimensions were in the low to modest range (conscientiousness $r = .15$), with the OCBI criterion of altruism ($r = .18$) being the highest and nonidleness being somewhat of an outlier at a low ($r = .02$). Overall, the results indicated evidence that PG fit operationalized as perceived work group values internalization was a modest correlate of prosocial OCBs, particularly for an OCBI behavior.

In a polynomial regression study, Jansen and Kristof-Brown (2005) examined how the fit between individual and aggregate group work styles impacted helping behavior, a measure of OCBs that included items for helping work group members with heavy workloads (OCBI) and volunteering for doing things that are not required (OCBO). Therefore, we classify this scale as assessing overall OCB, but note that most of the items emphasized helping immediate work group members. Results indicated 8% of the total variance (comparable to an effect size of .28) in individuals' helping behavior rated by supervisors was explained by P (individual), G the objective average of all other members' work pace preferences), and the relationship between them. In this case the main effects of P and G were not significant, but the P x G interaction was, suggesting the possibility of a fit or congruence relationship. The shape of the three-dimensional surface graph indicated that individuals' helping behavior was highest when individual and group preferred work styles were aligned. When either the group exceeded the preferred work pace of the individual, or the individual exceeded the preferred pace of the group, helping behaviors dropped steeply. These polynomial regression results demonstrate a moderately sized relationship between objective fit (i.e., congruence) and overall OCBs. Individuals were more likely to engage in OCBs when they had

Table 20.2 Person–Group Fit and Organizational Citizenship Behavior Studies

Study	Fit Measure	Fit Characteristics	OCB Types	OCB Measure	Level of Analysis
Becker (1992)	Direct perceived	Values Internalization	Overall OCB OCBO OCBI	Average of self, peer, and supervisor	Individual
Salvaggio (2003)	Direct perceived	Demands Abilities Values Personality General compatibility	Unit Overall OCB	Supervisor	Unit
Jansen & Kristof-Brown (2005)	Indirect actual; polynomial regression analyses	Work pace	Overall OCB	Supervisor	Individual

OCB, organizational citizenship behavior; OCBI, OCB directed toward the individual; OCBO, OCB directed toward the organization.

similar preferences for working styles with the other members of their work groups.

Working at a different level of analysis, Salvaggio (2003) examined whether aggregate PG fit, the average of individuals' perceptions of PG fit in a group, had a significant relationship with unit-level OCBs. Unit-level OCBs were reported by supervisors as their perceptions of the units' overall level of helping and conscientious behaviors. As hypothesized, a significant moderate-sized correlation (r = .38) was found between aggregate PG fit (the average level of PG fit of people in the unit) and unit-level OCBs. The larger effect size from this study is consistent with previous studies (e.g., Ostroff & Rothausen, 1997; Vancouver, Millsap, & Peters, 1994) that demonstrate that fit–outcome relationships are stronger when they are assessed at higher levels of analysis, such as a work group, department, or school.

Summary

Because of the focus on work group members, we expected that OCBs directed toward individuals (OCBIs) would be more strongly related to PG fit than those directed toward the organization (OCBOs). This conclusion received some support, with Becker (1992) reporting the highest unweighted average effect size for OCBI (r = .18) versus OCBOs (r = .09). However, comparable relationships were found between PG fit and broader measures of overall OCBs (Becker, 1992; Jansen & Kristof-Brown, 2005). These results provide preliminary support for the idea that OCBOs are weakly associated with PG fit, whereas a modest-sized relationship exists between PG fit and overall OCBs and OCBIs. It is noteworthy that all of these studies used non-self-report ratings of OCBs, which is a strong test of the relationships. Using others' reports of overall OCBs or OCBIs, as predicted by either perceived or objective ratings of PG fit, seems likely to generate compelling validity results. The small number of studies and emerging pattern of results suggest that more research in this area is badly needed.

Examining the polynomial regression results in more detail, Jansen and Kristof-Brown (2005) present a strong case for objective PG fit relating to non-self-reported overall OCBs. Because objective fit (i.e., perfect congruence) is often *not* supported with polynomial regression analysis, their results should spark interest in additional investigation of objective similarity between individuals and work group members as a determinant of OCBs. Finally, Salvaggio's (2003) results suggest that a fit–OCB relationship may hold even more strongly at higher levels of analysis, making this area ripe for continued research. These results along with recent studies investigating collective PG (a unit-level predictor) highlight the importance of group-level fit perceptions for predicting group-level outcomes (Kristof-Brown, Seong, DeGeest, Park, & Hong, 2014; Seong, Kristof-Brown, Park, Hong, & Shin, 2015). Thus, although only a handful of studies currently investigate the relationship of PG fit and OCBs, we have every reason to expect that this will become a promising area of research.

Person–Supervisor Fit and Organizational Citizenship Behaviors

The third category of studies that we review is person–supervisor (PS) fit, which focuses on the dyadic relationships between individuals and their immediate supervisors (Kristof-Brown et al., 2005). We begin by reviewing the studies that used direct perceived measures of PS fit and move on to those using polynomial regression to examine the more precise relationship of P and S characteristics on OCBs (Table 20.3).

Assessing PS fit as perceived supervisor-focused values internalization, Becker (1992) reported a significant positive correlation of .21 with overall OCBs, reported as the average of self, peer, and supervisor ratings. This suggests that individuals who report that they have internalized and share values with their supervisor are also more likely to be reported as having higher levels of overall OCBs. With supervisor-reported OCBIs, the relationship was consistent (r = .19 with altruism), whereas the relationships with OCBOs were slightly lower (r = .16 with conscientiousness, r = .11 with non-idleness). Alternatively, Tomlinson, Lewicki, and Ash (2014) reported a significant positive correlation (r = .33–.34) for the relationship of perceived PS fit with self-reported OCBOs, but only a weak relationship (r = .06, ns) with self-reported OCBIs. Because both fit and OCBs were self-rated in this study, the strong relationship with OCBOs and the low relationship with OCBIs suggest that subordinates differentiated strongly between the types of OCBs they see themselves as engaging in at work.

Using a polynomial regression approach to assess the similarity of individuals' and supervisors' self-reported values, Shin, Kim, Choi, Kim, and Oh (2014) found significant support for an objective PS fit relationship with both self-reported OCBIs

Table 20.3 Person–Supervisor Fit and Organizational Citizenship Behavior Studies

Study	Fit Measure	Fit Characteristics	OCB Types	OCB Measure	Level of Analysis
Becker (1992)	Direct perceived	Values Internalization	Overall OCB OCBI OCBO	Average of self, peer, and supervisor	Individual
Lambert, Tepper, Carr, Holt, & Barelka (2012)	Indirect perceived; polynomial regression analyses	Needs-supplies	OCBI OCBO	Supervisor	Individual
Shin, Kim, Choi, Kim, & Oh (2014)	Indirect actual; polynomial regression analyses	Values	OCB change OCBI maintenance OCBO maintenance	Self	Individual
Tomlinson, Lewicki, & Ash (2014)	Direct perceived	Values	OCBI OCBO	Self	Individual
Cole, Carter, & Zhang (2013)	Indirect actual; polynomial regression analyses	Values	Overall team OCB	Supervisor	Unit

OCB, organizational citizenship behavior; OCBI, OCB directed toward the individual; OCBO, OCB directed toward the organization.

and OCBOs. The polynomial regression analyses indicated main effects for individuals and supervisors' prevention values (i.e., the value they placed on job security and avoiding failures at work), as well as a significant P x S interaction. The three-dimensional surface plot showed that individuals' OCBIs and OCBOs were highest when individuals and their supervisors reported the same level of the prevention value. OCBOs, and particularly OCBIs, saw a decline when the P or S values deviated from each other. It did not matter whether the supervisor had stronger or weaker prevention values than the individual; any case of deviation from similarity led to a decrement in the self-reported OCBs. The amount of variance explained was not included in their tables, so although their graphs indicate a stronger decrement to OCBIs than OCBOs in cases of misfit, we are unable to determine whether there were differences in the magnitude of the effect.

Shin et al.'s (2014) results were different when they assessed the relationship of individuals' and supervisors' promotion values (i.e., the value attached to growth and accomplishment at work) with change-oriented OCBs, defined as behaviors directed toward improving the current organizational situation (Dewett & Denisi, 2007). The polynomial regression results indicated that change-oriented OCBs were predicted only by individuals' own promotion values (i.e., a significant main effect), regardless of the level of their leader's values. Taken as a whole, Shin et al. (2014) found partial support for an objective fit relationship between individuals' and supervisors' values for both OCBI and OCBO, but not for change-oriented OCBs. Thus, we again see evidence that the type of OCB, and in this case also the specific values, being assessed matter when describing a fit–OCB relationship.

In another polynomial regression study, Lambert, Tepper, Carr, Holt, and Barelka (2012) tested the relationship between needs–supplies PS fit and OCBs as rated by the supervisors. PS fit was assessed on the amount of leader consideration and initiating structure (two common leadership styles; Stogdill, 1963) subordinates reported needing and receiving (providing indirect subjective measurement of fit). They demonstrated a significant P x S interaction for initiating structure, such that when subordinates reported receiving a level of initiating structure from their supervisors that matched what they wanted, they engaged in higher levels of OCBIs (R^2 = .03 for the full set of P and S variables) and OCBOs (R^2 = .09 for the full set of P and S variables). However, in the case of the amount of consideration wanted and received, individuals engaged in higher levels of OCBIs and OCBOs when they received a level of consideration from their leader that was equal to or higher than what they wanted. This suggests that some supervisory behaviors (i.e., those geared toward making the subordinate feel valued) can be provided in excess of what is needed, with little to no detriment to subordinate attitudes or OCBs. Taken as a whole, Lambert et al.'s (2012) results suggest that only sometimes does the fit between what is needed and received from a leader relate to OCBIs and OCBOs. For some behaviors, such as consideration, the main effect of the leaders' perceived behavior is most influential. As we will discuss later, Lambert et al. (2012) provide additional evidence that these effects (both fit effects and main effects) work through the intermediary mechanism of trust in the leader.

One study examined PS fit effects at a higher level of analysis. Cole, Carter, and Zhang (2013) examined the relationship between PS fit, operationalized as the congruence between leaders' and their teams' average power distance values, with supervisor-rated team OCBs.[1] Cole et al. (2013) concluded that supervisor-subordinate similarity on power distance values has a positive indirect effect on overall team OCBs, working through the mechanism of procedural justice climate. However, analyzing their three-dimensional surface plot in more detail, we find that the effect is dominated by a main and quadratic effect of the average subordinate values, rather than by the type of interaction between supervisor and subordinate values that would be indicative of fit. Thus, we conclude that a PS fit–OCB effect is not supported in this study at the unit level.

Summary

Studies of PS fit and OCBs provide preliminary evidence that small- to modest-sized relationships exist for fit on some characteristics, but not on others. When fit is assessed as perceived or objectively assessed shared values, there is some evidence that PS fit is positively related to OCBs, but there may be some differences in the magnitude of these relationships depending on the OCB measures. Specifically, when supervisors' reports of OCBs are used, OCBIs tended to have a stronger correlation with perceived PS fit than did OCBOs. Alternatively, for self-reports the PS fit–OCBO relationship was stronger, and there was no relationship with change-oriented OCBs. Whether these differences are meaningful has yet to be established, as they are based on a handful of studies.

For needs–supplies PS fit and OCBs the evidence was also mixed. As in the case of PS value congruence, supervisor-rated OCBOs again had a stronger relationship with PS fit than did OCBIs. However, fit (assessed as congruence between what P needs and what S is perceived as supplying) only occurred for some needs and not others. Initiating structure was a supply that appeared to be most beneficial to OCBs when provided at an equal level to what the employee reported needing. Alternatively, supervisors could provide more consideration than was needed, with little detriment to OCBs. Taken as a whole, these results suggest that the specific dimension on which PS fit is assessed matters. They also suggest that the impact of PS fit is most noticeable by supervisors on employees' OCBOs. Individuals who perceive a fit with their supervisor may see themselves as contributing more OCBIs, but the supervisors' ratings do not reflect this relationship to the same degree.

Person–Job Fit and Organizational Citizenship Behaviors

The final type of fit we consider is PJ fit, defined as the relationship between a person's characteristics and those of the job that is performed by the person at work (Kristof, 1996). PJ fit is often conceptualized as demands–abilities fit (an individual's abilities match the requirements of the job) and needs–supplies fit (an individual's needs are met by characteristics of the job; Edwards, 1991). As mentioned earlier, we are not convinced by the notion that PJ fit conceptualized as demands–abilities fit encourages OCBs. That is, since OCBs are discretionary behaviors not immediately related to the performance by individuals of their own immediate jobs, demands–abilities fit would not be expected to result in such behaviors. Conversely, given that discretionary behaviors, being discretionary by definition, require the motivation to engage in them, we expect needs–supplies based PJ fit to be a more important determinant of OCBs. Invoking our earlier notion of exchange theory, it seems reasonable to expect that when a job offers things that people want, the fit–OCB relationship will be stronger than when abilities meet job demands, due to the obligation to reciprocate (Table 20.4).

Consistent with these expectations, three out of the four studies that tested OCB and PJ fit found little to no evidence for a relationship, particularly for demands–abilities based fit. Cable and DeRue (2002) conceptualized overall OCB as a combination of helping and voice behaviors rated by supervisors. They reported evidence for a weak relationship of self-reported perceived needs–supplies

Table 20.4 Person–Job Fit and Organizational Citizenship Behavior Studies

Study	Fit Measure	Fit Characteristics	OCB Types	OCB Measure	Level of Analysis
Cable & DeRue (2002)	Direct perceived	Demands Abilities Needs-supplies	Overall OCB	Supervisor	Individual
Lauver & Kristof-Brown (2001)	Direct perceived	Demands Abilities	Overall OCB	Peer	Individual
Li & Hung (2010)	Direct perceived	Demands Abilities Needs-supplies	OCBI OCBO	Self	Individual
Vogel & Feldman (2009)	Direct perceived	Demands Abilities Needs-supplies	OCBI	Supervisor	Individual

OCB, organizational citizenship behavior; OCBI, OCB directed toward the individual; OCBO, OCB directed toward the organization.

fit (r = .16, ns) with supervisor-rated OCBs, and zero relationship with perceived demands–abilities fit (r = .01, ns). Vogel and Feldman (2009) reported a correlation of .19 for perceived needs–supplies PJ fit and .14 for demands–abilities PJ fit. They concluded that despite the raw correlation, there was no substantial evidence that PJ fit and OCBs are related. An even smaller effect size was reported by Lauver and Kristof-Brown (2001), who reported a –.01 correlation between employees' perceived PJ demands–abilities fit and contextual performance as reported by supervisors.

All three of these studies found little to no statistical evidence for a relationship of perceived PJ fit and other-reported OCBs. The outlier in this case is a study by Li and Hung (2010), who report a significant positive large effect for PJ fit and OCBI (r = .62) and OCBO (r = .59). This was the only study in which both fit and OCBs were self-reported, and thus the large effect size may well represent upwardly biased relationships. As mentioned earlier, self-rated OCBs tend to produce larger effect sizes. Additionally, given that self-reported OCBs assessed with self-reported fit is likely inducing a strong consistency bias, based on the preponderance of the evidence, we conclude that there is a fairly small relationship between perceived needs–supplies PJ fit and other-reported OCBs, and no relationship between perceived demands–abilities fit and other-reported OCBs.

Mediators of Fit and Organizational Citizenship Behaviors

Mediators of the PO Fit–OCBs Relationship

Fit has most often been studied as a direct predictor of OCBs. However, we did uncover a few studies that considered job attitudes as mediators between PO fit and PS fit with OCBs. In a study of PO fit, Netemeyer et al. (1997) investigated antecedents of OCB in a selling context, proposing job satisfaction as a direct predictor of OCBs and perceived PO fit as an indirect predictor through its effects on job satisfaction. They tested their proposed model in two different selling contexts: cell phone salesmen and real estate brokers. For both contexts, they found a direct significant relationship from PO fit to job satisfaction. However, in the cell phone context, when they added a direct path from PO fit to OCB, the relationship between job satisfaction and OCB became nonsignificant. This study suggests that job satisfaction is a potential mediator between PO fit and OCB, but that PO fit alone accounts for much of that relationship in certain contexts.

Vigoda (2000) examined employees' perceptions of organizational politics as a mediator between PO fit and OCBs. Both direct and indirect models of fit were examined for the effects of PO fit and organizational politics for OCBIs and OCBOs as rated by supervisors. Results indicated better support for the indirect model. Specifically, perceived PO fit was negatively related to individuals' reports of organizational politics, which in turn, had a negative relationship with both OCBIs and OCBOs. Thus, superior levels of PO fit may stimulate OCBs in part because people who perceive higher levels of fit also perceive their organizations as less political, making them more likely to contribute OCBs.

Rich et al. (2010) studied several potential mediators between PO fit operationalized as perceived value congruence and supervisor-rated OCBs of firefighters. They proposed that job engagement would mediate PO fit and OCBs, and that other affective-motivational variables (job involvement, job satisfaction, and intrinsic motivation) would not exceed engagement in explaining the relationship between fit and OCBs. Results supported their hypothesis, finding only job engagement, but not the other motivational variables (job involvement, job satisfaction, and intrinsic motivation), as a significant mediator of the perceived PO fit–OCB relationship.

Finally, Lemmon and Wayne (2015) investigated a commonly known motive of OCBs, altruistic concern (Batson & Shaw, 1991), as a mediator between perceived PO fit and OCBs as rated by supervisors. The authors found that altruistic concern fully mediated the relationship between PO fit and citizenship behaviors toward the organization (OCBO), but not for citizenship behaviors towards supervisors (OCBI).

Mediators of the PS Fit–OCBs Relationship

In studies considering mediating processes between PS fit and OCBs, mediators that involve employees' attitudes toward their supervisors have received the strongest support. Lambert et al. (2012) reported that trust in the supervisor mediated the PS fit–OCB relationship, when both supervisor-rated OCBIs and OCBOs were considered. Trust in the supervisor fully mediated the relationship between congruence on desired and received initiating structure leadership behaviors and OCBIs, and partially mediated the relationship with OCBOs. In another study, Cole et al. (2013) found that perceived team procedural justice was a mediator between leaders' and teams' average power distance values and supervisors' ratings of average OCBs in the team. Taken as a whole, these findings suggest that a fit between perceived individual and supervisor characteristics may prompt individuals to form certain positive attitudes toward their supervisors or work units, and therefore engage in more OCBs.

Summary

Although there are only a handful of studies that consider mediating processes, the evidence suggests attitudes function as mediating mechanisms to partially or even fully explain the positive relationships between fit and OCBs. These include job satisfaction, organizational politics, job engagement, altruistic concern, trust in supervisors, and perceived procedural justice. Job involvement and intrinsic motivation have been considered as possible mediators of PO fit and OCBs, but they did not receive support when they were considered with engagement. Other types of fit (PG and PJ) have not yet considered mediators that could help explain the psychological mechanism that translates perceived fit into helping behaviors. Future research should consider multiple mediating processes between these types of fit and OCBs, perhaps verifying some of the same mechanisms (such as engagement and trust), but also exploring additional concepts such as cohesion (for PG fit) and job involvement (for PJ fit). In particular, we encourage investigations to explore the affinity and exchange explanations described earlier in the chapter. Currently, the results regarding attitudes toward the environment (i.e., trust in supervisor, satisfaction toward the job) provide support for an affinity explanation of the fit–OCB link. Studies are needed to explore additional exchange-based mechanisms.

Moderators of Fit and Organizational Citizenship Behaviors

When considering the relationship between various types of fit and OCB, there are certain contingencies that might influence the strength of the relationship. Although there aren't many, we did locate a few studies that have considered moderators of the fit and OCB relationship.

Wei (2012) examined the moderating effect of time evaluation on PO fit and OCBs. They proposed that individuals with a present orientation time perspective will be more concerned with present consequences and focus on tasks with more predictable feedback. Since it takes time to transform citizenship behaviors to rewards, present time perspective will reduce the relationship between perceived PO fit and OCBs. They investigated this relationship with Taiwanese financial specialists and found support for their hypothesis that the relationship between PO fit and OCBs as measured by supervisors was weaker when employees have a higher present orientation time perspective.

Meta-analytic results and our qualitative review of the literature demonstrate that different ways of operationalizing fit can also influence the strength of the relationship between fit and OCBs. Although it is difficult to compare the effect sizes for direct measures of perceived fit with other indirect assessments, our review indicates that the strongest relationships are reported between direct measures of perceived fit with overall OCBs (particularly self-reported OCBs, although the relationship remains consistent and significant for other-rated OCBs as well). In most cases the indirect measures, such as difference scores or profile similarity indices, showed consistent but somewhat weaker results. These results in combination suggest that greater similarity between individuals and the environment (either subjective or objective) is linked to higher levels of OCBs. We note, however, that the polynomial regression analyses give pause to a straightforward interpretation of difference score measures. In less than half of the polynomial regression cases were there significant interactions that represented a strict congruence-based fit relationship with OCBs. More often, one of the main effects (either person or environment) explained the greatest, and only statistically significant, portion of the variance in OCBs. Finally, a meta-analysis by Hoffman and Woehr (2006) considered PO fit operationalized as perceived value congruence against other forms of PO fit. They report that perceived value congruence (ρ = .25) has a slightly stronger relationship with OCBs than other operationalizations of PO fit (ρ = .17).

A final consideration for moderators comes from the various types of PE fit, and the possible interactions that they may have with each other. Vogel and Feldman (2009) looked at a comprehensive model of different types of self-reported PE fit and supervisor-rated OCBs. They found that PG fit was a significant moderator of the relationship between PJ fit and OCBs. Specifically, a negative interaction between the two types of fit indicated that the presence of high levels of PG fit resulted in a weaker relationship between PJ fit and OCBs than did a low level of PG fit. Supervisor-reported OCBs were lowest when both PJ and PG were perceived to be low and next lowest when both types of fit were perceived to be high. The highest level of supervisor-reported OCBs occurred when individuals perceived high levels of PG fit combined with low levels of PJ fit. These results suggest that when both PJ and PG fit are high, individuals may be torn between doing their job well and performing citizenship-focused behaviors. More studies that examine multiple types of fit in the same study would allow for this type of potential conflict between types of fit to be explored.

Summary

There are only a few studies that have considered moderating variables of fit and OCB. However, given the collection of results that demonstrates that fit measurement strategy is an important moderator of most fit–outcome relationships, and also our analysis, which suggest that the measurement of both fit and OCBs may modify the strength of the relationship, it is apparent that there are contingencies to the fit–OCB relationship. Additional boundary conditions for fit and OCB relationships warrant research attention, lest the simplistic direct relationships be misguided.

Summary and Suggestions for Future Person–Environement Fit Research With Organizational Citizenship Behaviors

Tables 20.1–20.4 reveal the great variety of approaches that have been taken for exploring the seemingly simple question of how PE fit links to OCBs. The tables show that there are different definitions of the "E" ranging from the organization (PO fit) to the job (PJ fit), different operationalizations of how fit will be indexed (direct perceptions, indirect subjective and indirect objective calculations, or three-dimensional representations generated by polynomial regression analysis), with different ways of assessing OCBs (self vs. other observations) and a focus on overall OCBs compared to OCBs focusing on individuals (OCBIs) or the organization more broadly (OCBOs). Notably, there are also a few studies that have been conducted at the unit level of analysis (PG and PS fit) with supportive results.

Several conclusions have emerged as we reviewed each of the approaches to studying the PE fit links to OCBs. Perhaps the major conclusions emerged from the area in which there have been the most studies, PO fit (see Table 20.1), and they were confirmed in results obtained from other types of fit as well:

- Perceived fit correlates most consistently (moderately) with overall OCBs, but indirect subjective and indirect objective PO fit also correlates significantly across studies with overall OCBs.
- Segmenting OCBs into OCBOs and OCBIs yields weaker relationships with fit, with OCBOs more likely than OCBIs to be significantly related to PO fit, and vice versa for PG fit.
- The weak results for demands–abilities PJ fit leads us to infer that the social exchange and reciprocity explanations for a fit–OCBs relationship are more germane than is the discretionary time justification. People are choosing to engage in OCBs because of a sense of wanting to give back to their environment, not because they have extra time on their hands.
- The operationalization of fit via the response surface methodology reveals less consistent findings for fit as an important correlate of OCBs. That is, the fact that P and E significantly correlate with OCBs alone compared to finding significant effects for the interaction of P and E has implications for

future research on PE fit and OCBs, which we explore in some detail next.

The studies we reviewed on the response surface methodology approach seemed to be split approximately 50–50 as to whether a significant interaction of P and E emerged. This finding gave us some pause, and we wondered why in the indirect subjective and indirect objective approaches to indexing fit, more work has not been done on looking at P and E separately as correlates of OCBs. So, it would seem to follow from the response surface studies that P and E alone can frequently explain "fit" effects, so it is incumbent on researchers using the calculated fit (whether subjective or objective) to explore whether the fit indicator is necessary at all.

This leads further to the question as to whether it is P and E data that also explain some of the effects of the direct perception findings. That is, direct perceptions of fit—the approach that yields the most consistent findings—are perhaps a function of the "P" and/or the "E" unmeasured variance. For example, suppose we hypothesized that particular kinds of people are more likely to report they fit a place. Based on the Big Five model of personality, we might propose that people who are higher on Agreeableness are more likely to say they have higher levels of fit. In this case it would be the "P" that is significant. Or suppose the "Es" in which people work in a company vary in the degree to which they are supportive. In this case, for a study of PG fit done in a single company against rated OCBs, it would be the "E" that would be the significant factor, not fit. Our point here is that even when the direct method of fit is used, it might be wise to collect data on P and E characteristics to ensure it is fit and not the P and/or the E that is determinant of the relationship between fit and OCBs.

This line of thinking about attributes of the setting being important in PE fit research vis-à-vis OCBs led us to be surprised in our review of the PE fit and OCBs literature that there were not more studies including fit with other possible correlates of OCBs. So, except for the few mediators (where there were consistent attitudinal effects) and moderator studies we reviewed, we found no studies on comparing or integrating fit with leadership or pay practices or climate and culture as a way to explore the relative impact of these issues on OCBs. We believe that more research on integrating across the possible correlates of OCBs, including fit, would be useful going forward.

Another surprise to us was the few studies of PE fit and OCBs that have been done at other than the individual level of analysis. As the studies we cited did find significant effects, it suggests that future research on PE fit and OCBs, as in much of the OCB world now (Podsakoff et al., 2014), might also be best accomplished at the group or unit levels of analysis—or perhaps even be multilevel in nature.

Last but not least, we want to encourage researchers to have ratings of the OCBs by other than the self. Fortunately, as noted earlier, the research on OCBs seems to be supportive of the PE fit and OCBs link even when others are doing the ratings. But if this line of work—and work on any correlates of OCBs—is to be influential with management, it needs to be based on ratings of OCBs by others.

Conclusion

The title of this chapter poses the question whether people who experience a better fit in their environment are better citizens. After examining the preponderance of the evidence, the answer appears to be a resounding "Yes, . . . but." As with most other relationships, the link between fit and OCBs appears to be highly specific to the type of fit (and even the specific characteristics on which fit is assessed), as well as the types of OCBs in question. The affinity and exchange explanations we offered to explain the relationship suggest that when people feel or experience fit on certain characteristics, positive attitudes toward that part of the environment are induced. These attitudes, in turn, may result in OCBs directed toward that or some additional aspect of the work environment. In the end, when people experience a better fit with their environment, they appear motivated to give back by engaging in OCBs.

Note

1. Although they describe this relationship as indicative of PG fit, because it reflects the similarity of supervisors with their subordinates and predicted average ratings of individual subordinates' OCBs, we categorized the type of fit as PS.

References

Arthur, W., Jr., Bell, S. T., Villado, A. J., & Doverspike, D. (2006). The use of person-organization fit in employment decision making: An assessment of its criterion-related validity. *Journal of Applied Psychology, 91*(4), 786–801.

Batson, C. D., & Shaw, L. L. (1991). Evidence for altruism: Toward a pluralism of prosocial motives. *Psychological Inquiry, 2*(2), 107–122.

Becker, T. E. (1992). Foci and bases of commitment: Are they distinctions worth making? *Academy of Management Journal, 35*(1), 232–244.

Blau, P. M. (1964). *Exchange and power in social life*. New York, NY: Wiley.
Borman, W. C., & Motowidlo, S. J. (1997). Task performance and contextual performance: The meaning for personnel selection research. *Human Performance, 10*(2), 99–109.
Borman, W. C., & Motowidlo, S. M. (1993). Expanding the criterion domain to include elements of contextual performance. In *Personnel selection in organizations* (pp. 71–98). San Francisco, CA: Jossey-Bass.
Byrne D. (1971). *The attraction paradigm*. New York, NY: Academic Press.
Cable, D. M., & DeRue, D. S. (2002). The convergent and discriminant validity of subjective fit perceptions. *Journal of Applied Psychology, 87*(5), 875–884.
Cha, J., Chang, Y. K., & Kim, T. Y. (2014). Person–organization fit on prosocial identity: Implications on employee outcomes. *Journal of Business Ethics, 123*(1), 57–69.
Chandrakumara, A. (2007). Does HRM fit really matter to citizenship and task performance? Sri Lankan manufacturing sector experience. *Employee Relations, 29*(6), 611–639.
Cole, M. S., Carter, M. Z., & Zhang, Z. (2013). Leader–team congruence in power distance values and team effectiveness: The mediating role of procedural justice climate. *Journal of Applied Psychology, 98*(6), 962–973.
Dewett, T., & Denisi, A. S. (2007). What motivates organizational citizenship behaviours? Exploring the role of regulatory focus theory. *European Journal of Work and Organizational Psychology, 16*(3), 241–260.
Edwards, J. R. (1991). Person-job fit: A conceptual integration, literature review. And methodological critique. In C. L. R. I. T. Cooper (Ed.), *International review of Industrial and organizational psychology* (Vol. 6, pp. 283–357). Chichester, UK: Wiley.
Edwards, J. R. (1994). Alternatives to difference scores as dependent variables in the study of congruence in organizational research. *Organizational Behavior and Human Decision Processes, 64*, 307–324.
Edwards, J. R. (1995). Alternatives to difference scores as dependent variables in the study of congruence in organizational research. *Organizational Behavior and Human Decision Processes, 64*(3), 307–324.
Edwards, J. R. (2002). Alternatives to difference scores: Polynomial regression and response surface methodology. In F. Drasgow & N. W. Schmitt (Eds.), *Advances in Measurement and Data Analysis* (pp. 350–400). San Francisco: Jossey-Bass.
Edwards, J. R., & Parry, M. E. (1993). On the use of polynomial regression equations as an alternative to difference scores in organizational research. *Academy of Management Journal, 36*(6), 1577–1613.
Edwards, J. R., Cable, D. M., Williamson, I. O., Lambert, L. S., & Shipp, A. J. (2006). The phenomenology of fit: Linking the person and environment to the subjective experience of person-environment fit. *Journal of Applied Psychology, 91*(4), 802–827.
Goodman, S. A., & Svyantek, D. J. (1999). Person–organization fit and contextual performance: Do shared values matter? *Journal of Vocational Behavior, 55*(2), 254–275.
Hoffman, B. J., & Woehr, D. J. (2006). A quantitative review of the relationship between person–organization fit and behavioral outcomes. *Journal of Vocational Behavior, 68*(3), 389–399.
Jansen, K. J., & Kristof-Brown, A. L. (2005). Marching to the beat of a different drummer: Examining the impact of pacing congruence. *Organizational Behavior and Human Decision Processes, 97*(2), 93–105.
Kristof, A. L. (1996). Person-organization fit: An integrative review of its conceptualizations, measurement, and implications. *Personnel Psychology, 49*(1), 1–49.
Kristof-Brown, A. L., Seong, J. Y., DeGeest, D. S., Park, W., & Hong, D. (2014). Collective fit perceptions: A multilevel investigation of person-group fit with individual and group-level outcomes. *Journal of Organizational Behavior. 35*, 969–989.
Kristof-Brown, A. L., Zimmerman, R. D., & Johnson, E. C. (2005). Consequences of individuals' fit at work: A meta-analysis of person–job, person–organization, person–group, and person–supervisor fit. *Personnel Psychology, 58*(2), 281–342.
Lambert, L. S., Tepper, B. J., Carr, J. C., Holt, D. T., & Barelka, A. J. (2012). Forgotten but not gone: An examination of fit between leader consideration and initiating structure needed and received. *Journal of Applied Psychology, 97*(5), 913–930.
Lauver, K. J., & Kristof-Brown, A. (2001). Distinguishing between employees' perceptions of person–job and person–organization fit. *Journal of Vocational Behavior, 59*(3), 454–470.
Lemmon, G., & Wayne, S. J. (2015). Underlying motives of organizational citizenship behavior comparing egoistic and altruistic motivations. *Journal of Leadership & Organizational Studies, 22*(2), 129–148.
LePine, J. A., Erez, A., & Johnson, D. E. (2002). The nature and dimensionality of organizational citizenship behavior: A critical review and meta-analysis. *Journal of Applied Psychology, 87*(1), 52–65.
Li, C. K., & Hung, C. H. (2010). An examination of the mediating role of person-job fit in relations between information literacy and work outcomes. *Journal of Workplace Learning, 22*(5), 306–318.
Lincoln, J. R., & Miller, J. (1979). Work and friendship ties in organizations: A comparative analysis of relation networks. *Administrative Science Quarterly, 24*(2), 181–199.
Motowidlo, S. J., & Van Scotter, J. R. (1994). Evidence that task performance should be distinguished from contextual performance. *Journal of Applied Psychology, 79*(4), 475–480.
Mulki, J. P., Jaramillo, F., & Locander, W. B. (2006). Emotional exhaustion and organizational deviance: Can the right job and a leader's style make a difference? *Journal of Business Research, 59*(12), 1222–1230.
Naus, F., Van Iterson, A., & Roe, R. (2007). Organizational cynicism: Extending the exit, voice, loyalty, and neglect model of employees' responses to adverse conditions in the workplace. *Human Relations, 60*(5), 683–718.
Netemeyer, R. G., Boles, J. S., McKee, D. O., & McMurrian, R. (1997). An investigation into the antecedents of organizational citizenship behaviors in a personal selling context. *The Journal of Marketing, 61*(3), 85–98.
Oh, I. S., Guay, R. P., Kim, K., Harold, C. M., Lee, J. H., Heo, C. G., & Shin, K. H. (2014). Fit happens globally: A meta-analytic comparison of the relationships of person–environment fit dimensions with work attitudes and performance across East Asia, Europe, and North America. *Personnel Psychology, 67*(1), 99–152.
O'Reilly, C. A., & Chatman, J. (1986). Organizational commitment and psychological attachment: The effects of compliance, identification, and internalization on prosocial behavior. *Journal of Applied Psychology, 71*(3), 492–499.

Ostroff, C., & Rothausen, T. J. (1997). The moderating effect of tenure in person-environment fit: A field study in educational organizations. *Journal of Occupational and Organizational Psychology, 70*, 173–188.

Podsakoff, N. P., Podsakoff, P. M., MacKenzie, S. B., Maynes, T. D., & Spoelma, T. M. (2014). Consequences of unit-level organizational citizenship behaviors: A review and recommendations for future research. *Journal of Organizational Behavior, 35*(S1), S87–S119.

Rich, B. L., Lepine, J. A., & Crawford, E. R. (2010). Job engagement: Antecedents and effects on job performance. *Academy of Management Journal, 53*(3), 617–635.

Salvaggio, A. N. (2003). *To help or to leave: Person-group fit as a correlate of aggregate organizational citizenship behavior and turnover* (Unpublished doctoral dissertation). University of Maryland, College Park.

Seong, J. Y., Kristof-Brown, A. L., Park, W., Hong, D., & Shin, Y. (2015). Person-group fit: Diversity antecedents, proximal outcomes and performance at the group-level. *Journal of Management, 41*(4), 1184–1213.

Shin, Y., Kim, M. S., Choi, J. N., Kim, M., & Oh, W. K. (2014). Does leader-follower regulatory fit matter? The role of regulatory fit in followers' organizational citizenship behavior. *Journal of Management*, 0149206314546867.

Stogdill, R. M. (1963). *Manual for the Leader Behavior Description Questionnaire–Form XII*. Columbus: Bureau of Business Research, Ohio State University.

Tomlinson, E. C., Lewicki, R. J., & Ash, S. R. (2014). Disentangling the moral integrity construct values congruence as a moderator of the behavioral integrity–citizenship relationship. *Group & Organization Management*, 39(6), 720–743.

Tsai, W. C., Chen, H. Y., & Chen, C. C. (2012). Incremental validity of person-organization fit over the big five personality measures. *The Journal of Psychology, 146*(5), 485–509.

Van Scotter, J. R., & Motowidlo, S. J. (1996). Interpersonal facilitation and job dedication as separate facets of contextual performance. *Journal of Applied Psychology, 81*(5), 525–531.

Vancouver, J. B., Millsap, R. E., & Peters, P. A. (1994). Multilevel analysis of organizational goal congruence. *Journal of Applied Psychology, 79*(5), 666–679.

Vigoda, E. (2000). Internal politics in public administration systems an empirical examination of its relationship with job congruence, organizational citizenship behavior, and in-role performance. *Public Personnel Management, 29*(2), 185–210.

Vogel, R. M., & Feldman, D. C. (2009). Integrating the levels of person-environment fit: The roles of vocational fit and group fit. *Journal of Vocational Behavior, 75*(1), 68–81.

Wei, Y. C. (2012). Person-organization fit and organizational citizenship behavior: Time perspective. *Journal of Management & Organization, 18*(6), 833–844.

Wharton, A. S., & Baron, J. N. (1987). So happy together? The impact of gender segregation on men at work. *American Sociological Review, 52*(5), 574–587.

Williams, L. J., & Anderson, S. E. (1991). Job satisfaction and organizational commitment as predictors of organizational citizenship and in-role behaviors. *Journal of Management, 17*(3), 601–617.

CHAPTER

21 Exploring the Relationship Between Job Embeddedness and Organizational Citizenship Behavior

Brooks C. Holtom *and* Tomoki Sekiguchi

Abstract

As we developed the concept of job embeddedness, we were determined to create a construct that explained as comprehensively as possible the reasons why people stay in organizations. Later, scholars theorized and found that on-the-job embeddedness also increased the probability of organizational citizenship behaviors (OCBs) and better job performance. More recently, Kiazad and colleagues (2015) have argued that conservation of resources theory offers a parsimonious explanation for the growing nomological network around job embeddedness. Building on this work, we explore promising directions that may contribute to the theoretical enrichment of the job embeddedness–OCB relationship including the different motives of OCBs as mediators, the relationship between job embeddedness and different types of OCBs, a closer look at the causality between job embeddedness and OCBs, theoretical integration with the social network perspective, and factors interacting with job embeddedness in influencing OCBs.

Key Words: organizational citizenship behavior, measurement, modeling, review, OCB

The purpose of this chapter is to explore the evolution of job embeddedness theory to better understanding its relationship with organizational citizenship behaviors (OCBs) and to identify promising directions for future research. To do so, we will first provide a historical perspective on the development of the job embeddedness construct. We will next review the research that links job embeddedness and OCBs. Finally, we will examine a wide range of approaches and constructs that might be profitably combined with job embeddedness and OCBs to produce informative new research.

Historical Perspective on Job Embeddedness

Initial Construct Development

In March and Simon's (1958) seminal book *Organizations*, they assert that the individual is essentially faced with two decisions with respect to his or her contributions to organizations, each reflecting different considerations. The first is the decision to participate, and the second is the decision to produce. The decision to participate is based on the concept of organization equilibrium, which refers to the benefits provided to members in exchange for their continued participation in the organization. The decision to produce is a function of the perceived consequences of performance and their relationship to the individual's goals and values. The decision to produce also incorporates information about external alternatives.

As we developed the concept of job embeddedness (Mitchell, Holtom, Lee, Sablynski, & Erez, 2001) at the University of Washington starting in the fall of 1994, these two seemingly different decisions loomed in the background of our conversations. We decided to create a construct that was primarily about the decision to participate. In other

Table 21.1 Subdimensions of Job Embeddedness

Subdimension	Definition
Fit–Organization	Employee's perceived compatibility with an organization
Links–Organization	Discernable connections people have on the job
Sacrifice–Organization	The perceived cost of material or psychological benefits that may be forfeited by leaving one's job
Fit–Community	Employee's perceived compatibility with a community
Links–Community	Discernable connections people have off the job
Sacrifice–Organization	The perceived cost of material or psychological benefits that may be forfeited by leaving one's community

words, we sought to explain as comprehensively as possible the reasons why people stay in organizations. As we were developing a general theory of staying, we conducted extensive focus groups and individual interviews. These interactions with real people in real organizations affirmed to us that there are many reasons why people choose to continue to participate in different firms. Some of those reasons are primarily "organizational" factors. However, many of those reasons were outside of the organization. We integrated these outside factors into what we ultimately called the "community" dimension. This thinking guided our initial test of the job embeddedness model.

In the 2001 articulation of job embeddedness theory (Mitchell et al., 2001). we conceptualized it as the combination of a broad set of factors that influence retention. The overall construct is broken down into three dimensions: fit, links, and sacrifice. Each dimension has two subdimensions: on the job (sometimes called "organizational embeddedness") and off-the-job (sometimes called "community embeddedness"). Job embeddedness is measured as the aggregate of these six subdimensions (see Table 21.1). Each of the subdimensions contributes unique understanding and predictive power to the overall job embeddedness concept (see Figure 21.1).

Fit refers to an employee's perceived compatibility with an organization and the community. This sense of compatibility may contain both affective reactions and nonaffective judgments. Fit in the organization relates to alignment with the job itself, personal values, career goals, and future plans. Fit in the community includes one's compatibility with the local weather, culture of the community, entertainment, and political and religious activities. The better the fit, the more likely people will feel professionally and personally tied to their organization and community.

Links refer to the connections people have both on and off the job. These connections can be to people (e.g., mentors) or to institutions (e.g., nonprofit board of directors). The number and importance of links contribute to a general sense of embeddedness. The higher the number of links between the person

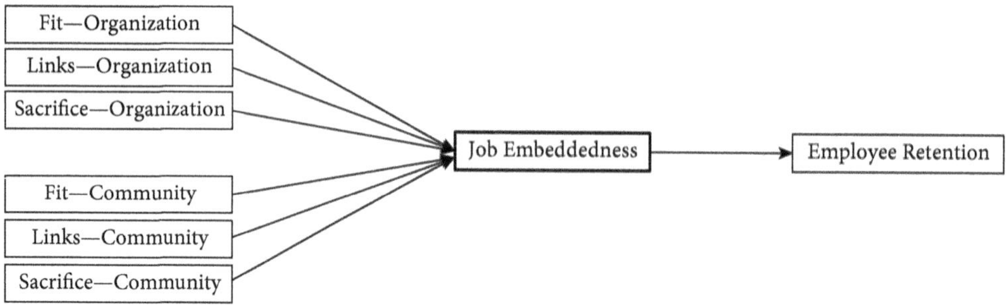

Figure 21.1 First-generation job embeddedness theory. Key findings: after controlling for job satisfaction, organizational commitment, job search behavior, and perceived job alternatives, job embeddedness predicts voluntary turnover (Mitchell, Holtom, Lee, Sablynski, & Erez, 2001).

and the web in which she is embedded, the more she is bound to the job, organization, and community.

Sacrifice is the perceived cost of material or psychological benefits that may be forfeited by leaving a job. For example, leaving a job likely entails leaving colleagues, perks, and projects. Additionally, many switching costs may also factor into the decision (e.g., new health care or pension plans, stock options) as well as opportunities for job stability or advancement. Community sacrifices are mostly an issue when people consider relocating. Leaving a safe, comfortable community where one has family and friends can be very difficult. But even changing organizations within the same region may entail sacrifices such as an easy commute, carpool arrangements, or flextime agreements. In sum, the more one has to give up, the more difficult it is to break from the current job.

Additionally, it is important to note that the measurement of job embeddedness (at least in its original formative operationalization by Mitchell et al., 2001) is largely nonaffective. Whereas affective commitment (Allen & Meyer, 1990) reflects one's liking for a job and emotional attachment of an organization, job embeddedness was developed with little affective content. For example, the measurement of links is primarily about things that can be counted (e.g., how many work teams a person is on, how many colleagues he or she regularly interacts with, how long he or she has been employed by the organization). It is similarly important to note that the fit-in-the-organization component as operationalized follows Cable and Parsons's notion that it "represents a cognitive belief rather than an emotional response" (1999, p. 24).

In 2007, Crossley, Bennett, Jex, and Burnfield published an article that developed and tested a global, reflective measure of job embeddedness. The reflective measure was more like traditional psychological constructs such as job satisfaction and organizational commitment. Its purpose was, they argued, to "overcome important limitations and serves as a companion to the original composite measure" (p. 1031). As Crossley et al. (2007) note:

> [A] global measure of embeddedness would assume that the whole is greater than the sum of its parts and assess overall impressions of attachment by asking general questions. This approach suggests that some sort of mental processing occurs and simply asks for the end product. During this process, respondents subjectively weigh various facets and may even incorporate additional relevant information that might have been omitted from facet-level scales. (p. 1032)

Thus was born a seven-item global reflective measure. The measure proved reliable and predictive of withdrawal behaviors, including intention to search, intention to quit, and actual voluntary turnover. Moreover, the global measure predicted turnover after controlling for job satisfaction, perceived alternatives, and intentions to search. Over time, researchers have used the original formative measure (Mitchell et al., 2001), a revised, shortened formative measure (Holtom, Tidd, Mitchell, & Lee, 2013), and the global reflective measure (Crossley et al., 2007) to produce a generally similar pattern of results, which are discussed later (c.f., Jiang, Liu, McKay, Lee, & Mitchell, 2012). All items for these measures are provided in the Appendix.

Organizational Outcomes Predicted by Job Embeddedness

In the past decade many studies have examined job embeddedness as an antecedent to a variety of consequences, including voluntary and involuntary turnover, as well as absenteeism, all reflecting the decision to participate. However, more recently, attention has been directed to in-role and extra-role performance. Put differently, scholars have expanded the scope of job embeddedness to address also March and Simon's (1958) "decision to produce." In the following section, we review key findings that help us better understand the nomological network surrounding job embeddedness and OCB (Holtom, Mitchell, Lee, & Eberly, 2008).

Empirical Relationship Between Job Embeddedness and Related Constructs

In their meta-analysis, Jiang and colleagues (2012) reported the following mean sample size, weighted, corrected correlations between organizational embeddedness and community embeddedness (r_c = .31), actual turnover (r_c = –.19), turnover intentions (r_c = –.48), job performance (r_c = .18), affective commitment (r_c = .61), and job satisfaction (r_c = .64). In general and not surprisingly, the correlations between community embeddedness and the same constructs were smaller: actual turnover (r_c = –.12), turnover intentions (r_c = –.22), job performance (r_c = .10), affective commitment (r_c = .16), and job satisfaction (r_c = .22). It is worth noting as well that the same meta-analysis reports the following pattern for affective commitment: actual turnover (r_c = –.22), turnover intentions (r_c = -.44), job performance (r_c = .18), and job satisfaction (r_c = .68). Job satisfaction also demonstrated significant correlations with these key variables as follows: actual turnover (r_c = –.16), turnover intentions (r_c = –.52), and job performance (r_c = .19). Thus, it is clear that job embeddedness correlates with important organizational outcomes such as voluntary turnover and in-role performance at approximately the same level as affective commitment and job satisfaction. However, while there were insufficient studies for them to calculate the meta-analytic correlations between job embeddedness and organizational citizenship behaviors, the summary of studies identified reveal that the correlations between organizational embeddedness and OCB were r = .19 and the correlations between community embeddedness and OCB ranged from r = .10 to r = .11. Interestingly, these correlations are higher than those reported in the same studies for the relationship between OCB and job satisfaction (r = .07) and organizational commitment (r = .06). In sum, job embeddedness appears to explain unique variance and, thus, may be useful to OCB researchers.

Job Embeddedness and Prosocial Behaviors

Hulin and associates enlarged scholars' conceptualization of withdrawal. They advocated for and empirically demonstrated the validity of a general withdrawal construct (Hanish & Hulin, 1991). They theorized that withdrawal included multiple work behaviors occurring sequentially over time, such as reduced organizational citizenship behavior, decreased job performance, increased absences, and finally leaving. Hulin (1998, p. 11) noted that the withdrawing person demonstrates "a progression of withdrawal from the very mild and easy to the difficult and decisive." These ideas suggest that the decisions to participate and to produce are related, with the decision to participate preceding the decision to produce.

Building on this insight, Lee, Mitchell, Sablynski, Burton, and Holtom (2004) theorized and found that off-the-job embeddedness decreased the probability of turnover and absenteeism, whereas on-the-job embeddedness increased the probability of OCBs and better job performance (see Figure 21.2). Subsequent research extended those findings, demonstrating that on-the-job embeddedness is correlated with workplace attitudes (turnover intentions, job satisfaction, affective commitment) and behaviors (job search, performance) more strongly than off-the-job embeddedness (Allen, 2006; Holtom, Mitchell, & Lee, 2006; Ng & Feldman, 2014; Wheeler, Harris, & Sablynski, 2012).

Furthermore, Burton, Holtom, Sablynski, Mitchell, and Lee (2010) examined the impact of negative shocks and observed that job-embedded employees do not react with worse performance or lower organizational citizenship behaviors when experiencing job shocks such as poor performance reviews or low pay raises. In sum, an emerging body of evidence demonstrates the utility of the construct and how it complements existing concepts that are adjacent in the nomological network.

Theorists explain that one reason why individuals invest resources like effort and time (Halbesleben, Neveu, Paustian-Underdahl, & Westman, 2014) into extra-role behaviors (e.g., socializing newcomers, attending outside-work functions, helping colleagues) is to accumulate more resources and in the process become more embedded (Halbesleben & Wheeler, 2015; Ng & Feldman, 2012a; Podsakoff, Whiting, Podsakoff, & Blume, 2009). Thus, one might act altruistically toward superiors or colleagues to build goodwill and reciprocity to repay such kindness (earning them higher performance

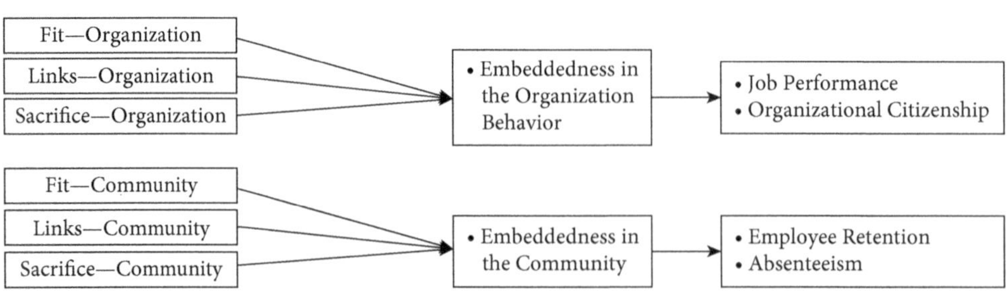

Figure 21.2 Second-generation job embeddedness theory. Key findings: after controlling for job satisfaction and organizational commitment, (1) embeddedness in the organization predicts job performance and organizational citizenship behavior, and (2) embeddedness in the community predicts voluntary turnover and absenteeism (Lee, Mitchell, Sablynski, Burton, & Holtom, 2004).

reviews, including favorable 360-degree feedback) with the ultimate effect being deeper job embeddedness.

As regards task performance, high-performing employees can expect greater extrinsic (e.g., favorable reviews, pay raises, promotions) and intrinsic (e.g., feeling valuable and competent) benefits (Lanaj, Chang, & Johnson, 2012; Rotondo & Sackett, 2002; Salamin & Hom, 2005). Thus, it is reasonable to expect that people embedded in occupations, organizations, and jobs should thus be motivated to invest time and effort toward superior task performance to meet professional goals. Also, because job-embedded incumbents have the requisite demands–abilities job fit (Kristof, 1996) and links (social capital from high-density colleague networks; Sparrowe, Liden, Wayne, & Kraimer, 2001) to reach high performance standards, on-the-job embeddedness should most promote high job performance. Finally, because counterproductive work behaviors (e.g., Internet surfing, abusing colleagues) can lead to termination, lost opportunities for advancement, or a tarnished reputation (Feldman, Ng, & Vogel, 2012; Lee et al., 2004; Rotundo & Sackett, 2002), it is not surprising that people who are highly embedded in their organizations are less likely to engage in such behaviors.

Like Lee et al. (2004), Wijayanto and Kimono (2004) were interested in examining the relationship between job embeddedness and OCBs. They predicted that "sense of responsibility" would mediate the relationship. To test their ideas, they surveyed a sample of 300 nurses who reported their levels of job embeddedness and sense of responsibility, paired with their 41 direct supervisors who rated the nurses' OCB. The researchers found that job embeddedness in the organization correlated with three dimensions of OCB (altruism: $r = 0.23$; conscientiousness: $r = 0.17$; and loyalty: $r = 0.18$). However, embeddedness in the community was not correlated with OCB (altruism: $r = 0.09$, n.s.; conscientiousness: $r = 0.12$, n.s; and loyalty: $r = 0.10$, n.s). Furthermore, they found no evidence that the effects of job embeddedness on OCBs were mediated through sense of responsibility.

Sekiguchi, Burton, and Sablynski (2008) examined the role of job embeddedness as a moderator of relationships among leader–member exchange (LMX), organization-based self-esteem (OBSE), and OCBs. They posited that because highly embedded employees have many connections to other employees or projects (i.e., links), they will be able to obtain resources such as technical and contextual knowledge and information through the social web within the organization, which will help perform their tasks better and engage in OCBs in a timely and appropriate manner. Additionally, such employees can apply their knowledge and skills better when there is sufficient supervisory support or reciprocal obligation because they fit well with their current job or organization (i.e., fit). Therefore, when the quality of LMX is high, highly embedded employees would make the most of the advantages of being embedded or situated in the social web of the organization.

Sekiguchi et al. (2008) were also the first to allude to a dark side of job embeddedness and its potential to keep individuals in unfavorable situations. In the case of low-quality LMX but high embeddedness employees, their links, fit, and sacrifice would make them reluctant to leave their current job or organization. So, even while job embeddedness offers potential advantages in helping individuals perform their tasks and engage in OCBs, the low-quality LMX, including poor supervisory support and less reciprocal obligation, would prevent them from making use of such advantages. Rather, they may have a strong feeling of inconsistency between their high job embeddedness and their poor-quality LMX, which could cause stress and negative reactions such as reducing task performance and OCBs. The results of two studies involving 367 employees and 41 supervisors (in a telecommunications company and a manufacturing company) demonstrated job embeddedness acts as a moderator of the relationship between LMX and OCBs as well as OBSE and OCBs in the manufacturing sample. Furthermore, they hypothesized a three-way interaction involving job embeddedness, LMX, and OBSE on task performance and found support in the sample of manufacturing employees but found no such effects for OCBs. Thus, there was some limited evidence of a "dark side" of job embeddedness, though it did not obtain in the case of OCBs.

Kim, Lee, and Choi (2012) sought to see if there was any mediating effect of OCB between job embeddedness and turnover intention in hospital nurses. To test their ideas, data were collected from 241 nurses in three tertiary hospitals and two secondary hospitals in Korea. They observed negative relationships between job embeddedness and turnover intention ($r = -.53$, $p < .01$) and organizational citizenship behavior and turnover intention ($r = -.39$, $p < .01$) but a positive relationship between job embeddedness and organizational citizenship behavior ($r = .39$, $p < .01$). Although they found direct effects of job embeddedness on turnover intentions, based on structural equations modeling, they concluded that organizational citizenship behavior also partially mediates the relationship between job embeddedness and turnover intention in hospital nurses.

Job Embeddedness and Social Effects

In 2013, Ng and Feldman reported the results of a study examining how perceived supervisor embeddedness relates to employees' own affect toward, attachment to, and behavior within the firm. An important contribution of this work is the development of a theoretical explanation for how and why employees respond to social cues about embeddedness as they do. Much of the literature in this area has focused on the fact that employees pick up social cues from their environments (e.g., Felps et al., 2009), but less attention has been paid to how employees react to those social cues. In this study, Ng and Feldman (2013) theorized that supervisor embeddedness would affect employees' own embeddedness through the mediating role of organizational trust. This would encourage employees with greater organizational trust to be more willing to sink deeper roots in their present organizations. Conversely, perceived decreases in supervisor embeddedness would signal to employees that current levels of supervisory support may disappear or that working conditions may start declining. So, employees would be more likely to search for external job opportunities. Interestingly, they asserted that unlike turnover behavior, which might be constrained by many other factors beyond the employee's control, constructive voice behavior is largely discretionary in nature (Takeuchi, Chen, & Cheung, 2012). As such, employees can control how much voice behavior they engage in as their levels of embeddedness increase or decrease over time. Thus, by studying voice as the behavioral dependent variable in this study, Ng and Feldman were able to illustrate how the subtle processes of observing and making sense of social cues ultimately influence individuals' concrete contributions to team and organizational performance.

Three key findings came out of this research. First, they found that the level of supervisor embeddedness as perceived by the employees changes over time. Some employees experienced increases in perceived supervisor embeddedness and others experienced decreases in it. Second, these changes in perceived supervisor embeddedness were both directly and indirectly related to employees' own embeddedness over time. Third, perceived supervisor embeddedness was also related to constructive voice through the mediating effects of organizational trust and employee embeddedness. Although previous research has focused on how embeddedness can decrease counterproductive work behavior in the organization (such as turnover), this study suggests that embeddedness can have a positive impact on pro-organizational activities, too.

In a 2014 publication, Ng and Feldman drew on conservation of resources (COR) theory (Hobfoll, 1989) to reconceptualize the relationship between community embeddedness and organizational embeddedness. In a clever study using latent growth modeling, they demonstrated that changes in organizational embeddedness mediate the relationships of changes in community embeddedness with changes in job motivation, social networking behavior (measured as doing favors for supervisors, internal networking, and external networking), and organizational identification. So, while they did not measure OCBs explicitly, they did find evidence of the impact of community and organizational embeddedness on related behaviors such as doing favors for supervisors.

Building on insights from COR, Ng and Feldman (2014) note that while much of the previous research in this area has examined how job and family demands create conflicts across work and nonwork domains (e.g., Allen, Herst, Bruck, & Sutton, 2000), this research suggests that embeddedness can generate resource surpluses that create positive cross-domain outcomes. We believe that future research identifying the specific types of resource surpluses that lead to the positive outcomes found in their work would be valuable. At the same time, we think that research looking at potentially negative outcomes that result from high levels of community or organizational embeddedness should also be pursued.

Job Embeddedness and Innovation

In a study reported in 2010, Ng and Feldman proposed that job embeddedness strengthens employees' motivation to generate, spread, and implement innovative ideas in organizations. In a longitudinal study with a diverse sample, they found that job embeddedness was positively and significantly related to innovation-related behaviors, even after controlling for demographic variables, job attitudes, and job perceptions that are frequently associated with job embeddedness. Specifically, they found that the relationship between job embeddedness and implementing innovative ideas was stronger for individuals in the mid- and late stages of their careers than for those in the early stage of their careers. Although implementing innovative ideas is not considered to be OCB strictly speaking, in general such behavior positively affects organizational functioning and certainly is in the spirit of extra-role contributions.

Conceptual Refinements

In 2012(b), Ng and Feldman proposed to reconceptualize the community dimension of job embeddedness. They renamed it "off-the-job embeddedness" (OTJE) as a separate and distinct (though related) construct from job embeddedness. They recommend OTJE encompass the "totality of outside-work forces which keep an individual bound to his/her current geographical area." They argue that this expansion will accommodate a number of important factors not considered in the original job embeddedness formulation (Mitchell et al., 2001).

They further argued that OTJE would lead to a reduction of deviant behavior (such as theft). This would occur because employees would be unlikely to engage in behaviors that would end in their termination from their present employer or poison their reputations with other firms in the local economy. However, they argued that OTJE will lead to less OCBs. Citing research that finds high levels of job embeddedness lead to emotional exhaustion (Bolino & Turnley, 2005), they expected employees to have less time and energy to invest in OCBs on the job.

In addition to these direct effects, they argued that OTJE will indirectly affect work outcomes by moderating the relationship between embeddedness and outcomes such as task performance or OCBs. Building on social identity theory and the prioritization of different social system identities, they explain how individuals confront conflicting role demands. When employees are embedded in the work domain but not outside of work, they will potentially feel less compelled to demonstrate high levels of in-role and extra-role performance because they sense less urgency to remain in the location. In contrast, when on- and off-the-job embeddedness are both strong, employees will experience urgency to remain employed in the location and, thus, expend more effort to perform at a higher level.

More recently, Kiazad, Holtom, Newman, and Hom (2015) published a theoretical extension of job embeddedness theory based on conservation of resources (COR) theory (Hobfoll, 1989) (see Figure 21.3). In the following pages, we review key insights

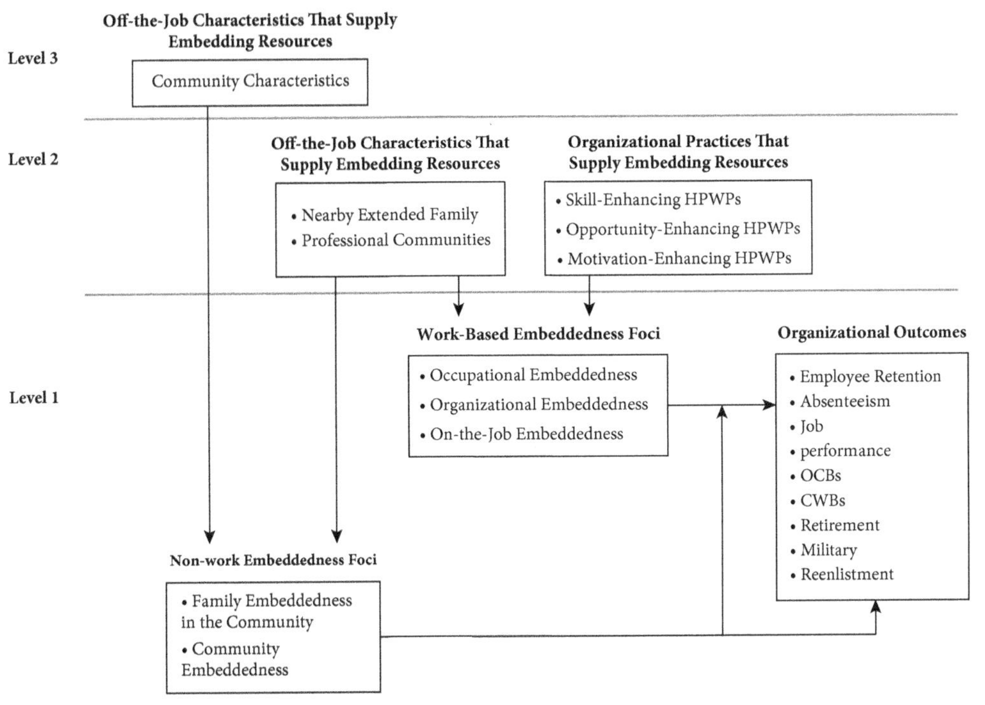

Figure 21.3 Third-generation job embeddedness theory (Kiazad, Holtom, Newman, & Hom, 2015). CWBs, counterproductive work behaviors; HPWPs, high performance work practices; OCBs, organizational citizenship behaviors.

from this extension as a preview of future research opportunities at the intersection with OCBs.

On-the-Job and Organizational Embeddedness

In 2007, Ng and Feldman first distinguished between on-the-job and organizational embeddedness. Whereas Mitchell et al. (2001) assumed that people embedded in jobs are also embedded in organizations, Ng and Feldman (2007) reasoned that incumbents can be embedded in one but not necessarily the other. They noted that an employee may fit job demands, have multiple ties to colleagues in local work environs, and sacrifice a corner office upon leaving a job. However, these employees may lack fit with corporate values, have few links to employees outside work units, and possess few organizational perks (e.g., pension) that would be forfeited by leaving. So, they may be embedded in a particular job but not the organization. Because jobs are nested within firms, on-the-job embeddedness often translates into higher workplace retention. Job-embedded incumbents may nonetheless quit if their employer reassigns (or promotes) them to a different job that they find less fulfilling or perform less proficiently (Ng & Feldman, 2007). Despite how on-the-job and organizational embeddedness can differ, job embeddedness researchers have largely treated them synonymously. It is likely that following the recommendation of Ng and Feldman (2007) to separate these two embedding foci will likely advance understanding as they may differentially affect work outcomes.

Occupational Embeddedness

In 2007, Feldman and Ng also introduced "occupational embeddedness"—or "the totality of forces that keep people in their present occupations" (p. 353)—to clarify why incumbents remain in occupational fields and may even leave companies to hone or practice their professional skills elsewhere. In contrast to the original job embeddedness construct, this form of embeddedness may not promote staying in an organization. Feldman and Ng (2007) further conceptualize that people are embedded in occupations via links. In an initial test, Ng and Feldman (2009) found that occupational embeddedness explains unique variance in task performance, counterproductive work behaviors, and creativity after controlling for organizational embeddedness.

Family Embeddedness in the Community

A number of researchers have sought to advance a reconceptualization of outside-work forces keeping individuals bound to their current locale (Feldman et al., 2012; Ramesh & Gelfand, 2010). Defining off-the-job embeddedness "as the cumulative forces of an individual's family, community, and nonwork activities which bind an individual to his/her current location" (p. 215), Feldman and associates (2012) differentiate what personally embeds an individual in the community (e.g., recreational pursuits) from that which embeds an individual indirectly through his or her family (e.g., domestic partner and other relatives living in the household). As an example, an employee's family may be embedded in a geographic area (e.g., spouse owns a local business, teenagers attend magnet schools), thereby embedding the employee. However, such "embeddedness by proxy" (or "family embeddedness in community") should not be confused with community attachment. Similarly, Hom, Mitchell, Lee, and Griffeth (2012) also theorize that felt extrinsic constraints (i.e., family pressure) can emanate from family embeddedness and drive different withdrawal states that are distinct from other embedding forces.

Finally, Ramesh and Gelfand (2010) also promulgated the concept of "family embeddedness." This is defined as families becoming embedded within workplaces. This occurs when family members favorably appraise firms, befriend other employees, and personally partake of job benefits. Hence, employees may feel compelled to stay in a job or community they misfit because their families prefer that they stay or receive benefits from their employment (e.g., health insurance, family status). In support, Ramesh and Gelfand (2010) demonstrated that family embeddedness in the organization explains additional variance in turnover beyond that of on-the-job and community embeddedness.

Toward Theoretical Enrichment of the Job Embeddedness–Organizational Citizenship Behavior Relationship

Kiazad and colleagues (2015) have argued that COR theory offers a parsimonious explanation for the growing nomological network relating job embeddedness to its many antecedents and consequences. Building on their recent review, we focus specifically on the relationship between job embeddedness and OCBs to explore theoretical and empirical issues that could be investigated in future research. In the following pages, we discuss several promising directions that may contribute to the theoretical enrichment of the job embeddedness–OCB relationship: the different motives of OCBs as mediators, the relationship between job embeddedness and different types of OCBs, a closer look at the causality between job embeddedness and OCBs, theoretical integration with the social network perspective, and factors interacting with job embeddedness in influencing OCBs.

Different Motives for Organizational Citizenship Behaviors as Mediators

Employees may engage in OCBs because of different motives. For example, Rioux and Penner (2001) identified three major motives for engaging in OCBs: prosocial motives, organizational concern motives, and impression management motives. Employees who are motivated by prosocial values tend to be more relationally oriented and to engage in OCBs directed toward other individuals (OCBI). Employees who are motivated by organizational concern tend to have a collective self-concept and to focus more on OCBs directed toward the organization (OCBO) (Bolino, Harvey, & Bachrach, 2012; Takeuchi, Bolino, & Lin, 2015). These two motives are both other-oriented motives, and they focus on others' well-being (i.e., employee are motivated to help others). On the other hand, employees engaging in OCBs motivated by impression management motives represent "good actors" as opposed to "good citizens" (Takeuchi et al., 2015). That is, employees who engage in OCBs by impression management motives have desires to be seen positively and to avoid being seen negatively.

The research on job embeddedness and OCBs has not systematically theorized and empirically tested how job embeddedness may affect the activation of different motives, which, in turn, promote OCBs. As we have seen in this review, the majority of researchers who examined the relationship between job embeddedness and OCBs have used social exchange theory and COR theory to explain why highly embedded employees tend to engage in OCBs. One interesting question might be how these theoretical frameworks, or other ones, explain the relationship between job embeddedness and different motives for OCBs. Do the different foci of job embeddedness (e.g., organizational embeddedness or occupational embeddedness) or the different dimensions of job embeddedness (e.g., links, fit and sacrifice) activate different motives for OCBs? If so, what theories are the most appropriate to explain the relationships? For example, it is likely that individuals with high levels of organizational embeddedness and low levels of occupational embeddedness engage in more OCBOs than those with low levels of organizational embeddedness and high levels of occupational embeddedness. Similarly, it is plausible that individuals with high levels of organizational links would exhibit more OCBIs than those with few links. Additionally, there may be situational and/or individual difference factors that moderate the relationship between job embeddedness and the motives for OCBs. To investigate these issues, future empirical research could measure the different motives for OCBs and examine the mediating role of these motives in the relationship between job embeddedness and OCBs.

Relationship Between Job Embeddedness and Different Types of Organizational Citizenship Behaviors

Related to the aforementioned issue is that OCBs have several different dimensions or types. However, past studies on the job embeddedness–OCB relationship have not paid much attention to these differences. The majority of theoretical and empirical work that examined the relationship between job embeddedness and OCBs tended to treat the broad OCB construct. As we know, OCB researchers have identified different dimensions or types of OCBs. For example, based on the OCB literature, Podsakoff, MacKenzie, Paine, and Bachrach (2000) identified numerous potentially different forms of OCBs and organized them into seven common themes. The dimensions include helping, sportsmanship, organizational loyalty, organizational compliance, individual initiative, civic virtue, and self-development. One of the most parsimonious and most frequently studied classifications of OCBs is Williams and Anderson's (1991) distinction between OCBI and OCBO. This classification is based on the idea that OCBs can be differentiated based on the beneficiary or target. OCBI are the behaviors that immediately benefit specific individuals and indirectly contribute to the organization through this means. OCBO are the behaviors that benefit the organization in general.

Understanding the relationship between job embeddedness and different motives for OCBs, as raised in the previous point, may contribute to the theorizing of the relationship between job embeddedness and different types of OCBs such as OCBI and OCBO. For example, prosocial motives would be more related to OCBI, and organizational concern motives would be more related to OCBO (Takeuchi et al., 2015). Thus, considering the motives for OCBs as mediators could also enable us to theorize the relationship between different foci or dimensions of job embeddedness and different types of OCBs (Podsakoff et al., 2000).

A relatively new framework that might aid researchers in developing ideas to test along these lines is the proximal withdrawal states perspective advanced by Hom and colleagues (Hom et al., 2012). They argue that some employees leave organizations reluctantly while others leave enthusiastically. Similarly, some employees will stay reluctantly while others will stay enthusiastically. Although OCB scholars will not be particularly interested in the leavers, this framework may be very helpful for understanding the extra-role behaviors of the two types of stayers. For example, Hom et al. (2012) posit that enthusiastic stayers are characterized by "staying mindsets" based both on their strength of desire to stay (affective forces) and extrinsic constraints on leaving. Thus, it is expected that enthusiastic stayers are likely to exhibit a wide range of prosocial actions. In contrast, reluctant stayers (also known as psychological quits or dissatisfied stayers) who may be blocked from leaving will likely be absent or tardy or prone to counterproductive work behaviors (CWBs), such as unionization or sabotage. They may perform unsatisfactorily and engage in fewer discretionary behaviors on behalf of firms or suggest fewer workplace improvements. Some scholars characterize this phenomenon as "dysfunctional retention" (Hom et al., 2012). This may be especially important to understand in the context of a recession when their ranks in the workforce can swell.

Closer Look at the Causality Between Job Embeddedness and Organizational Citizenship Behaviors

Most studies on job embeddedness and OCBs have theorized that job embeddedness is an antecedent of OCBs, or that job embeddedness moderates the relationship between some antecedent variables (e.g., LMX) and OCBs. However, there are several reasons to theorize that OCBs could also be the antecedent of job embeddedness, especially on-the-job embeddedness or organizational embeddedness. Put differently, on-the-job embeddedness or organizational embeddedness and OCBs might be mutually reinforcing such that an employee's job embeddedness promotes his or her OCBs, and the OCBs in turn enhance on-the-job embeddedness or organizational embeddedness.

Bolino, Turnley, and Bloodgood (2002) argue that OCBs contribute to the development of social capital in the organization. Social capital refers to a resource that is derived from the relationship among individuals, organizations, and communities. The social capital has its structural, relational, and cognitive dimensions (Nahapiet & Ghoshal, 1998). Structural social capital refers to the network ties, network configuration, and network appropriability. Relational social capital is characterized by high levels of trust, shared norms, and perceived obligations, and a sense of mutual identifications. Cognitive social capital refers to the extent to which employees within a social network share a common perspective or understanding (Bolino et al., 2002). According to Bolino et al.'s (2001) framework, OCBs enhance structural social capital through the formation of network ties, an improvement in the overall configuration of ties, and greater network appropriability. OCBs also enhance relational social capital through the development of liking, trust, and identification among employees. Moreover, OCBs contribute to the cognitive social capital through shared language and shared narratives.

Similar arguments can be made in the relationship between OCBs and on-the-job embeddedness or organizational embeddedness. That is, OCBs would contribute to the on-the-job embeddedness or organizational embeddedness through the formation of network ties that corresponds to the links dimension, the development of liking and trust that contributes to the fit dimension, and the enhancement of appropriability of network ties that leads to the sacrifice dimension of on-the-job embeddedness or organizational embeddedness.

In the future, conducting longitudinal studies measuring job embeddedness and OCBs at multiple times would enable the researchers to examine causality in the relationship between job embeddedness and OCBs. The longitudinal research design would also enable researchers to take a closer look at the temporal dynamics of job embeddedness and OCBs to observe how quickly changes on one variable manifest in the other.

Theoretical Integration With Social Network Perspective

The construct of job embeddedness was originally developed based on idea of social networks as a constraint or "stuckness" (Mitchell el al., 2001) and reflects the idea of employees being situated or connected in a social web. Therefore, not surprisingly, researchers in sociology and social network theory have also developed a similar construct using the term "embeddedness" (e.g., Granovetter, 1985; Uzzi, 1996). In the sociological and social network literature, the construct of embeddedness has been used to explain the process by which social relations influence and constrain economic action. Social network researchers usually differentiate between structural embeddedness and relational embeddedness. Structural embeddedness represents the configuration of one's network such as the presence or absence of ties between actors. Variables related to structural embeddedness include closure, density, connectivity, and hierarchy (Wasserman & Faust, 1994). Relational embeddedness refers to the quality of dyadic exchanges such as the levels of trust, shared norms and perceived obligations, and a sense of mutual identifications (Simsek, Lubatkin, & Floyd, 2003).

The embeddedness construct in the sociological and social network literature has been used in many organization-level analyses (e.g., Simsek et al., 2003; Uzzi, 1996), while other studies use the embeddedness construct in interpersonal relationships such as the personal network of managers within the organizations (e.g., Moran, 2005). The conceptual similarity suggests the possibility of the theoretical integration of social network theory and job embeddedness. Indeed, several researchers have examined the relationship between social network and OCBs (Bowler & Brass, 2006; Tsang, Chen, Wang, & Tai, 2012). For example, Bowler and Brass (2006) showed that social network ties are related to both performance and receipt of OCBI. Tsang et al. (2012) showed that work network centrality and friendship network centrality among nurses predict their OCBs. By introducing the construct of job embeddedness to this line of research, it might be possible to theorize and empirically test the argument that job embeddedness as a psychological variable mediates the relationship between the characteristics of a social network and OCBs. Specifically, it would be interesting to investigate how the characteristics of social network (e.g., centrality, density) are related to the links, fit, and sacrifice dimensions of job embeddedness, which in turn may enhance OCBs.

Recent work by Ballinger, Cross, and Holtom (in press) amplifies our understanding of job embeddedness links by demonstrating how network position (i.e., reputation via eigenvector centrality) and structure (i.e., brokerage opportunities via structural holes) influence turnover. Put differently, they show that all links are not equal. The structure of those links matters. For instance, because of increased access to information through their unique network position, some individuals will be in a position to perform especially valuable OCBs. To the degree these individuals are highly embedded and thus more likely to demonstrate prosocial behavior, the benefit to organizations will be enhanced. To the degree that individuals with high power are not embedded, the organization may be at heightened risk of damaging CWBs or at the very least the beneficiary of fewer high-impact OCBs. In sum, research empirically examining how structural and relational embeddedness (measured as social network variables) are related to OCBs through job embeddedness (measured as a psychological variable) may be valuable.

Factors Interacting With Job Embeddedness in Influencing Organizational Citizenship Behavior

Finally, researchers should examine a broad spectrum of situational and individual difference factors that strengthen or weaken the relationship between job embeddedness and OCBs. Examples of situational factors include organizational structure, organizational culture and climate, human resource practices, and the characteristics of work teams. Examples of individual difference factors include abilities, personality traits, and values. Introducing these moderating factors should be grounded on the theories explaining why they alter the underlying mechanisms connecting job embeddedness and OCBs.

In this regard, one of the promising directions for future research is to introduce international and cross-cultural variables into the theoretical framework. With respect to turnover as an outcome variable, Jiang et al. (2012) showed through their meta-analysis that the degree in which job embeddedness predicts employee retention is stronger for collectivistic countries than individualistic countries. Jiang et al. (2012) argued that employees from collectivistic countries devote a great deal of personal time and effort to establishing and maintaining harmonious relationships with coworkers and others and that they respond actively to job embeddedness cues. On the other hand, job embeddedness may be less meaningful to employees in individualistic countries because they tend to place a high premium on their personal achievements and to be less influenced by embeddedness in general. Hence, it might be argued that the degree to which job embeddedness predicts OCBs is stronger for collectivistic countries than individualistic countries.

Conclusion

In this chapter we have sought to review the development of job embeddedness and the research examining its effects on other critical outcomes for organizations. One of the most interesting areas of past research and promising areas for future research is the relationship between job embeddedness and OCBs. We sincerely hope that the provocative questions raised in the latter part of this chapter will motivate future research.

References

Allen, T., Herst, D. E., Bruck, C. S., & Sutton, M. (2000). Consequences associated with work-to-family conflict: A review and agenda for future research. *Journal of Occupational Health Psychology, 5*, 278–308.

Allen, D. (2006). Do organizational socialization tactics influence newcomer embeddedness and turnover? *Journal of Management, 32*, 237–256.

Allen, N., & Meyer, J. (1990). The measurement and antecedents of affective, continuance, and normative commitment to the organization. *Journal of Occupational Psychology, 63*, 1–18.

Ballinger, G., Cross, R., & Holtom, B. (in press). The right friends in the right places: Understanding network structure as a predictor of voluntary turnover. *Journal of Applied Psychology*.

Bolino, M. C., & Turnley, W. H. (2005). The personal costs of citizenship behavior: the relationship between individual initiative and role overload, job stress, and work-family conflict. *Journal of Applied Psychology, 90*, 740–748.

Bolino, M. C., Harvey, J., & Bachrach, D. G. (2012). A self-regulation approach to understanding citizenship behavior in organizations. *Organizational Behavior and Human Decision Processes, 119*, 126–139.

Bolino, M. C., Turnley, W. H., & Bloodgood, J. M. (2002). Citizenship behavior and the creation of social capital in organizations. *Academy of Management Review, 27*, 505–522.

Bowler, W. M., & Brass, D. J. (2006). Relational correlates of interpersonal citizenship behavior: a social network perspective. *Journal of Applied Psychology, 91*, 70–82.

Burton, J., Holtom, B., Sablynski, C., Mitchell, T., & Lee, T. (2010). The buffering effects of job embeddedness on negative shocks. *Journal of Vocational Behavior, 76*, 42–51.

Cable, D., & Parsons, C. (1999). Establishing person-organization fit during organizational entry. Paper presented at the Annual Meetings of the Academy of Management, Chicago, IL.

Crossley, C., Bennett, R., Jex, S., & Burnfield, J. (2007). Development of a global measure of job embeddedness and integration into a traditional model of voluntary turnover. *Journal of Applied Psychology, 92*, 1031–1042.

Feldman, D. C., & Ng, T. W. (2007). Careers: Mobility, embeddedness, and success. *Journal of Management, 33*, 350–377.

Feldman, D. C., Ng, T. W., & Vogel, R. M. (2012). Off-the-job embeddedness: A reconceptualization and agenda for future research. *Research in Personnel and Human Resources Management, 31*, 209–251.

Felps, W., Mitchell, T., Hekman, D., Lee, T., Harman, W., & Holtom, B. (2009). Turnover contagion: How coworkers job embeddedness and coworkers job search behaviors influence quitting. *Academy of Management Journal, 52*, 545–561.

Granovetter, M. (1985). Economic action and social structure: The problem of embeddedness. *American Journal of Sociology, 91*, 481–510.

Halbesleben, J. R., & Wheeler, A. (2015). To invest or not? The role of coworker support and trust in daily reciprocal gain spirals of helping behavior. *Journal of Management, 41*, 1628–1650.

Halbesleben, J. R., Neveu, J. P., Paustian-Underdahl, S. C., & Westman, M. (2014). Getting to the "COR": Understanding the role of resources in conservation of resources theory. *Journal of Management, 40*, 1334–1364.

Hanisch, K., & Hulin, C. (1991). General attitudes and organizational withdrawal: An evaluation of a causal model. *Journal of Vocational Behavior, 39*, 110–128.

Hobfoll, S. E. (1989). Conservation of resources: A new attempt at conceptualizing stress. *American Psychologist, 44*, 513–524.

Holtom, B., Mitchell, T., & Lee, T. (2006). Increasing human and social capital by applying job embeddedness theory. *Organizational Dynamics, 35*, 316–331.

Holtom, B., Mitchell, T., Lee, T., & Eberly, M. (2008). Turnover and retention research: A glance at the past, a closer review of the present, and a venture into the future. *Academy of Management Annals, 2*, 231–274.

Holtom, B., Tidd, S., Mitchell, T., & Lee, T. (2013). Temporal dependency in the prediction of newcomer turnover. *Human Relations, 66*, 1337–1352.

Hom, P., Mitchell, T., Lee, T., & Griffeth, R. (2012). Reviewing employee turnover: Focusing on proximal withdrawal states and an expanded criterion. *Psychological Bulletin, 138*, 831–858.

Hulin, C. L. 1998. *Behaviors, constructs and time: Potholes on the road well-traveled.* Invited address, annual meeting of the Society for Industrial and Organizational Psychology, Dallas, TX.

Jiang, K., Liu, D., McKay, P., Lee, T., & Mitchell, T. (2012). When and how is job embeddedness predictive of turnover? A meta-analytic investigation. *Journal of Applied Psychology, 97*, 1077–1096.

Kiazad, K., Holtom, B., Newman, A., & Hom, H. (2015). Job embeddedness: An integrative review and research agenda. *Journal of Applied Psychology, 100*, 641–659.

Kim, E. H., Lee, E., & Choi, H. J. (2012). Mediation effect of organizational citizenship behavior between job embeddedness and turnover intention in hospital nurses. *Journal of Korean Academy of Nursing Administration, 18*, 394–401.

Kristof, A. (1996). Person-organization fit: An integrative review of its conceptualizations, measurement, and implications. *Personnel Psychology, 49*, 1–49.

Lanaj, K., Chang, C., & Johnson, R. (2012). Regulatory focus and work-related outcomes: A meta-analysis. *Psychological Bulletin, 138*, 998–1034.

Lee, T., Mitchell, T., Sablynski, C., Burton, J., & Holtom, B. (2004). The effects of job embeddedness on organizational citizenship, job performance, volitional absences, and voluntary turnover. *Academy of Management Journal, 47*, 711–722.

March, J. G., & Simon, H. A. (1958). *Organizations*. Oxford, UK: Wiley.

Mitchell, T., Holtom, B., Lee, T., Sablynski, C., & Erez, M. (2001). Why people stay: Using job embeddedness to predict voluntary turnover. *Academy of Management Journal, 44*, 1102–1121.

Moran, P. (2005). Structural vs. relational embeddedness: Social capital and managerial performance. *Strategic Management Journal, 26*, 1129–1151.
Nahapiet, J., & Ghoshal, S. (1998). Social capital, intellectual capital, and the organizational advantage. *Academy of Management Review, 23*, 242–266.
Ng, T., & Feldman, D. (2007). Organizational embeddedness and occupational embeddedness across career stages. *Journal of Vocational Behavior, 65*, 336–351.
Ng, T., & Feldman, D. (2009). Occupational embeddedness and job performance. *Journal of Organizational Behavior, 30*, 863–891.
Ng, T., & Feldman, D. (2010). The impact of job embeddedness on innovation-related behaviors. *Human Resource Management, 49*, 1067–1087.
Ng, T., & Feldman, D. (2012a). Employee voice behavior: A meta-analytic test of the conservation of resources framework. *Journal of Organizational Behavior, 33*, 216–234.
Ng, T., & Feldman, D. (2012b). The effects of organizational and community embeddedness on work-to-family and family-to-work conflict. *Journal of Applied Psychology, 97*, 1233–1251.
Ng, T., & Feldman, D. (2013). Changes in perceived supervisor embeddedness: Effects on employees' embeddedness, organizational trust, and voice behavior. *Personnel Psychology, 66*, 645–685.
Ng, T., & Feldman, D. (2014). Community embeddedness and work outcomes: The mediating role of organizational embeddedness. *Human Relations, 67*, 71–103.
Podsakoff, N., Whiting, S., Podsakoff, P., & Blume, B. (2009). Individual- and organizational-level consequences of organizational citizenship behaviors: A meta-analysis. *Journal of Applied Psychology, 94*, 122–141.
Podsakoff, P. M., MacKenzie, S. B., Paine, J. B., & Bachrach, D. G. (2000). Organizational citizenship behaviors: A critical review of the theoretical and empirical literature and suggestions for future research. *Journal of Management, 26*, 513–563.
Ramesh, A. & Gelfand, M. (2010). Will they stay or will they go? The role of job embeddedness in predicting turnover in individualistic and collectivistic cultures. *Journal of Applied Psychology, 95*, 807–823.
Rioux, S. M., & Penner, L. A. (2001). The causes of organizational citizenship behavior: A motivational analysis. *Journal of Applied Psychology, 86*, 1306–1314.
Rotundo, M., & Sackett, P. (2002). The relative importance of task, citizenship, and counterproductive performance to global ratings of job performance: A policy capturing approach. *Journal of Applied Psychology, 87*, 66–80.
Salamin, A., & Hom, P. (2005). In search of the elusive u-shaped performance–turnover relationship: Are high performing Swiss bankers more liable to quit? *Journal of Applied Psychology, 90*, 1204–1216.
Sekiguchi, T., Burton, J. P., & Sablynski, C. J. (2008). The role of job embeddedness on employee performance: The interactive effects with leader-member exchange and organization-based self-esteem. *Personnel Psychology, 61*, 761–792.
Simsek, Z., Lubatkin, M. H., & Floyd, S. W. (2003). Inter-firm networks and entrepreneurial behavior: A structural embeddedness perspective. *Journal of Management, 29*, 427–442.
Sparrowe, R., Liden, R., Wayne, S., & Kraimer, M. (2001). Social networks and the performance of individuals and groups. *Academy of Management Journal, 44*, 316–325.
Takeuchi, R., Bolino, M. C., & Lin, C. C. (2015). Too many motives? The interactive effects of multiple motives on organizational citizenship behavior. *Journal of Applied Psychology, 100*, 1239–1248.
Takeuchi, R., Chen, Z., & Cheung, S. Y. (2012). Applying uncertainty management theory to employee voice behavior: An integrative investigation. *Personnel Psychology, 65*, 283–323.
Tsang, S. S., Chen, T. Y., Wang, S. F., & Tai, H. L. (2012). Nursing work stress: The impacts of social network structure and organizational citizenship behavior. *Journal of Nursing Research, 20*, 9–18.
Uzzi, B. (1996). The sources and consequences of embeddedness for the economic performance of organizations: The network effect. *American Sociological Review, 61*, 674–698.
Wasserman, S., & Faust, K. (1994). *Social network analysis: Methods and applications.* Cambridge, UK: Cambridge University Press.
Wheeler, A., Harris, K., & Sablynski, C. (2012). How do employees invest abundant resources? The mediating role of work effort in the job-embeddedness/job-performance relationship. *Journal of Applied Social Psychology, 42*, 244–266.
Wijayanto, B. R., & Kismono, G. (2004). The effect of job embeddedness on organizational citizenship behavior: The mediating role of sense of responsibility. *Gadjah Mada International Journal of Business, 6*, 335–354.
Williams, L. J., & Anderson, S. E. (1991). Job satisfaction and organizational commitment as predictors of organizational citizenship and in-role behaviors. *Journal of Management, 17*, 601–617.

Appendix Measures of Job Embeddedness

Original [Formative] Model of Job Embeddedness (Mitchell, Holtom, Lee, Sablynski, & Erez, 2001)

Fit–Community

1. I really love the place where I live.
2. The weather where I live is suitable for me.
3. This community is a good match for me.
4. I think of the community where I live as home.
5. The area where I live offers the leisure activities that I like.

Fit–Organization

6. I like the members of my work group.
7. My coworkers are similar to me.
8. My job utilizes my skills and talents well.
9. I feel like I am a good match for this company.
10. I fit with the company's culture.
11. I like the authority and responsibility I have at this company.

*Additional items in hospital sample noted below.

12. My values are compatible with the organization's values.

13. I can reach my professional goals working for this organization.

14. I feel good about my professional growth and development.

Links–Community

15. Are you currently married?

16. If you are married, does your spouse work outside the home?

17. Do you own the home you live in?

*Additional items in hospital sample noted below.

18. My family roots are in this community.

19. How many family members live nearby?

20. How many of your close friends live nearby?

Links–Organization

21. How long have you been in your present position?

22. How long have you worked for this company?

23. How long have you worked in the grocery industry?

24. How many coworkers do you interact with regularly?

25. How many coworkers are highly dependent on you?

26. How many work teams are you on?

27. How many work committees are you on?

Sacrifice–Community

28. Leaving this community would be very hard.

29. People respect me a lot in my community.

30. My neighborhood is safe.

Sacrifice–Organization

31. I have a lot of freedom on this job to decide how to pursue my goals.

32. The perks on this job are outstanding.

33. I feel that people at work respect me a great deal.

34. I would sacrifice a lot if I left this job.

35. My promotional opportunities are excellent here.

36. I am well compensated for my level of performance.

37. The benefits are good on this job.

38. The health-care benefits provided by this organization are excellent.

39. The retirement benefits provided by this organization are excellent.

40. The prospects for continuing employment with this company are excellent.

Revised [Formative] Job Embeddedness Measure (Holtom, Tidd, Mitchell, & Lee, 2013)

Fit–Community

1. I really love the place where I live.

2. The place where I live is a good match for me.

3. The area where I live offers the leisure activities that I like (sports, outdoor activities, cultural events and arts).

Fit–Organization

4. My job utilizes my skills and talents well.

5. I feel like I am a good match for my organization.

6. If I stay with my organization, I will be able to achieve most of my goals.

Links–Community

7. My family roots are in this community.

8. I am active in one or more community organizations (e.g., churches, sports teams, schools, etc.).

9. I participate in cultural and recreational activities in my local area.

Links–Organization

10. I am a member of an effective work group.

11. I work closely with my coworkers.

12. On the job, I interact frequently with my work group members.

Sacrifice–Community

13. Leaving the community where I live would be very hard.

14. If I were to leave the community, I would miss my nonwork friends.

15. If I were to leave the area where I live, I would miss my neighborhood.

Sacrifice–Organization

16. I have a lot of freedom on this job to pursue my goals.

17. I would sacrifice a lot if I left this job.

18. I believe the prospects for continuing employment with my organization are excellent.

Global [Reflective] Measure of Job Embeddedness (Crossley, Bennett, Jex, & Burnfield, 2007)

1. I feel attached to this organization.
2. It would be difficult for me to leave this organization.
3. I'm too caught up in this organization to leave.
4. I feel tied to this organization.
5. I simply could not leave the organization that I work for.
6. It would be easy for me to leave this organization.
7. I am tightly connected to this organization.

CHAPTER

22 A Cultural Perspective on Organizational Citizenship Behavior

P. Christopher Earley *and* Goran Calic

Abstract

In this chapter, we discuss research related to the organizational citizenship behavior (OCB) construct from a cross-cultural perspective and propose a framework to aid in understanding how cultural frames influence the engagement and display of OCB. The terms "intercultural" and "cross-cultural," as defined in this chapter, are not limited by geographic boundaries and can be used to depict differences in individual values regardless of nationality. In creating such a synthesis, we aim to stimulate a conversation about potential directions for future work at the intersection of these two literatures. Here we explore how the contextual impact of culture and its relation to motivational, metacognitive/cognitive, and behavioral processes in individuals helps us better understand OCB using facets of justice (interactional, procedural, and distributive) as a linking mechanism.

Key Words: cross-cultural perspective, organizational citizenship behavior, cultural intelligence, CQ, intercultural

The construct of organizational citizenship behavior (OCB) has received a great deal of research attention in the past several decades, including its origins in seminal work by Organ (1988) and Podsakoff and with their colleagues (P. M. Podsakoff, MacKenzie, Moorman, & Fetter, 1990). There are a number of studies that have pushed the boundaries of OCB by looking at it from a cultural perspective. One example is Farh, Earley, and Lin's (1997) work in which an intranational, but cross-cultural, study was conducted looking at cultural value orientations, such as traditionality/modernity and individualism/collectivism.

On the basis of preliminary observations, Paine and Organ (2000) concluded that "the challenge lies not so much in debating whether OCB exists around the world but in understanding and defining what constitutes OCB in various cultures and countries" (p. 58). Several studies have proposed results in understanding how context affects OCB. Lai, Lam, and Lam (2013) scrutinize the team relationships of work groups from a cultural perspective. Their findings indicate that team culture affects which types of OCB are more influential on team performance. OCB targeting individuals improved rated performance in high collectivist teams only, whereas only OCB targeting the organization produced a significant improvement in performance ratings of highly individualistic teams. In a meta-analytic study of 34 independent samples, Jiao, Richards, and Hackett (2013) find that Confucian Asians consider OCB as part of their job to a greater extent than do their North American counterparts and that affiliate kinds of OCB (e.g., helping conscientiousness, and courtesy) are more likely to be considered a part of one's job than change-oriented OCB (e.g., voice, taking charge, and initiative). Others have investigated the validity of OCB measurements in non-US contexts. Paillé (2009) makes an effort to understand which salient forms of OCB apply to French employees using Podsakoff et al.'s scales (P. M. Podsakoff & MacKenzie, 1997; P.

M. Podsakoff et al., 1990). Results indicate that in the French context, Podsakoff et al.'s measurements provide a model with four components (altruism, helping behavior, civic virtue, and sportsmanship). These studies highlight the importance of context to OCB.

OCB continues to be of great interest to cross-cultural scholars because the construct taps at orientations around justice perceptions, altruism, and voluntary engagement, just to name a few, and these orientations have their roots in a society's underpinnings. Likewise, a cross-cultural perspective provides important insight for OCB scholars. Culture plays a crucial role in shaping the social and psychological environment within which OCB takes place. An understanding of OCB would be incomplete without taking into account the environment within which organizational members find themselves.

But most existing research focusing on OCB and culture has looked to value orientations, values and norms identified through an individual's country of origin. The Farh et al. paper was an early exception in that the study compared cultural groupings within a single country following the tradition of cultural anthropologists. More recently, Lai et al. (2013) explore the social and psychological environment of group culture. In this chapter, we take a somewhat different approach through leveraging work conducted by Earley and Ang (2003) as well as Thomas and Inkson (2004), who identified and described the concept of cultural intelligence (CQ).

In this chapter, we review these research streams and propose a new framework for understanding OCB antecedents, behavior and outcomes drawing from a general model of cultural intelligence. Cultural orientations are integrated into a discussion of OCB through the CQ mechanisms. From this general model, we provide a number of specific illustrations of moderating and reciprocal effects of CQ and OCB, connecting these to a number of cultural examples.

We take this CQ framework and explore the antecedents, behavior, and outcomes approach utilized in many conceptualizations of OCB. In some instances, we will identify aspects of CQ operating as moderating influences (e.g., through cultural values on the link of justice to altruism or courtesy as an example), whereas others will have a reciprocal effect (e.g., impact of metacognitive processing on how outcomes from one cultural interaction might impact subsequent concepts of justice, traditionality/modernity, and core identity).

Cultural Intelligence

Cultural Intelligence, or CQ, refers to an individual's capability to adapt and explore alternative cultural environments, drawing from three general facets—metacognition/cognition, motivation, and behavior (Earley & Ang, 2003; Thomas & Inkson, 2004). The metacognitive/cognitive facet refers to information processing aspects of intelligence, and it is conceptualized using self-concept theory. In self-concept theory, the "self" is a dynamic interpretive structure that mediates most significant intrapersonal and interpersonal processes. The metacognitive/cognitive facet of CQ can be viewed as the total knowledge and experience of an individual stored in memory concerning cultural adaptation. Knowing yourself is not sufficient for high CQ—awareness does not guarantee flexibility; adaptability of self-concept and ease of integrating new facets into it are, however, associated with high CQ, since understanding new cultures may require abandoning pre-existing conceptualizations of how and why people function as they do.

CQ metacognition refers to higher level cognitive processes as part of a person's processing of information, or "thinking about thinking." Thus, metacognition can be broken down into two complementary elements, including metacognitive knowledge (what and how to deal with knowledge gained under a variety of circumstances) and metacognitive experience (what and how to incorporate relevant experiences as a general guide for future interactions). For example, the demands placed on learning about a new culture that shares little in common with that of an expatriate manager are great, and the individual is likely to realize that a great deal of attention and persistence is required. The final aspect of metacognitive knowledge refers to strategy variables, or the procedures used to achieve some desired goal.

Metacognition experience is a critical aspect of CQ because much of what is required in a new culture is putting together patterns into a coherent picture, even if one does not know what this coherent picture might look like. To do so requires a higher level of strategy about people, places, and events. It is for this reason that many cultural training programs fail because they overemphasize the specific example at the expense of a more general metalearning process. Many companies train their global managers by providing country-specific information. This approach is not only limited by a person's involvement in the training method, but it does not prepare a manager adequately for understanding and mastering novel situations that the training did not specifically cover. A high-CQ person must inductively create a proper mapping of the social situation to function effectively. This requires a general but broad foundation of knowledge about cultures and societies similar to the training recommended by an anthropological view covering topics such as economic systems, religious and political institutions, social relationships, and so on.

The second facet of CQ refers to its motivational aspect. It is insufficient to have information about how a group of people may deal with the world. You must be able (and motivated) to use this knowledge to produce a culturally appropriate response. Cultural intelligence reflects self-concept and directs and motivates adaptation to new cultural surroundings. A central aspect of motivation is an individual's self-efficacy, or engagement and perseverance (Bandura, 1986; Bandura & Schunk, 1981). Self-efficacy plays an important role in CQ because successful intercultural interaction is based on a person's sense of efficacy for social discourse in a novel cultural setting. A person who does not believe in personal capability to understand people from novel cultures is likely to disengage after experiencing early failures. If the motivational facet of cultural intelligence is weak, adaptation does not occur.

Efficacy alone is not a full description of the motivational facet of CQ and an important, and related, addition is goal setting (Earley & Lituchy, 1991; Locke & Latham, 1990). In an intercultural encounter, a challenge is to determine the goals of others coming from a different cultural and personal background. The interactive importance of goal setting and efficacy expectations is illustrated in work by many scholars (see Bandura, 1997, for a review). The process of evaluating the significance of knowledge about what is happening with our personal well-being generates emotions. Only through the recognition that we have something to gain or to lose, that is, that the outcome of a transaction is relevant to goals and well-being, do we generate an emotional reaction. Thus, goal appraisal is necessary not only for activating a response toward goal attainment but also for generating emotions that are necessary for energizing action. That is, our goals may act as cognitive anchors, thereby guiding subsequent actions (Locke & Latham, 1990).

A person's norms and values are related to CQ, and they are an important aspect of the self as they guide what features of the social environment that a person attends to and what she values (Hofstede, 1991; Schwartz, 1994). Values and norms guide our choice of activities as well as help define our evaluation of them (Triandis, 1972). Values are standards that lead individuals to take positions over issues, predispose individuals to favor particular ideologies, guide self-presentations, evaluate and judge ourselves and others, act as a basis for morality and competence comparisons with others, direct individuals concerning what ideas of others should be challenged, and tell individuals how to rationalize beliefs and actions that would otherwise be unacceptable so as to preserve self-image (Rokeach, 1973, p. 13). Values serve to motivate instrumentally by providing enticement through desired end states as well as terminally by representing superordinate goals and reinforcing a sense of self. For example, a person having strong group-based values is likely to avoid situations requiring personal actions. Furthermore, such a person is likely to evaluate individual, idiosyncratic behavior negatively. Thus, cultural adjustment may be impaired by one's cultural values and norms if they are held extremely strongly and inflexibly.

The third facet of cultural intelligence refers to a person's behavior. Behavioral CQ reflects a person's capability to acquire or adapt behaviors appropriate for a new culture. The behavioral element of CQ suggests that adaptation is not only knowing what and how to do (cognitive), and having the wherewithal to persevere and exert effort (motivational); it requires an individual to engage in appropriate actions. Lacking these specific behaviors, a person must have the capability to acquire such behaviors.

A person may know and wish to enact a culturally appropriate behavior but cannot do so because of some deep-set reservation. For example, imagine a manager who is thrust into an uncomfortable social situation and is not able to control his nonverbal communication cues. This type of response (or lack of it) can be thought of in behavioral terms. Even if a person is able to provide a desired response in a cultural encounter, it remains problematic because the host may detect hesitation and react negatively. Persistence is necessary for the acquisition of new skills, and so is a person's aptitude to acquire these new skills. That is, it is not enough to be willing to try and learn new behaviors—a high-CQ person has an aptitude to determine where new behaviors are needed and how to execute them effectively.

Self-presentation is particularly important in *social* behaviors because behaviors enacted in the process of social interaction are motivated primarily by the need for impression management and self-presentation (Goffman, 1959, 1967). For example, a person may eat at a local restaurant in a host country. His primary goal is to satisfy hunger while his concerns about self-presentation may be of secondary concern. Even so, he is likely to follow eating etiquette to avoid offending others in that culture. By adapting his eating behavior and etiquette, he satisfies both his hunger as well as a desire to maintain a positive self-image.

Organizational Citizenship Behavior

Dennis Organ (1988) original defined OCB as "individual behavior that is discretionary, not directly or explicitly recognized by the formal reward system, and that in the aggregate promotes the effective functioning of the organization" (p. 4). In 1997, Organ redefined OCB as "performance that supports the social and psychological environment in which task performance takes place" (Organ, 1997, p. 95). This revision borrows liberally from Borman and Motowidlo's (1993) definition of contextual performance, which is "behaviors [that] do not support the technical core itself so much as they support the broader organizational, social, and psychological environment in which the technical core must function" (p. 73). This new definition offers several important advantages over the old definition that are relevant to the relationship between CQ and OCB; specifically it highlights the importance of context (N. P. Podsakoff, Whiting, Podsakoff, & Blume, 2009). Extant literature in OCB can be broken down into research on the antecedents of OCB, the dimensionality and measurement of OCB, and outcomes of OCB.

Two popular conceptualizations of OCB have been developed by Organ (1988) and Williams and Anderson (1991). Organ originally developed a model that described OCB using five dimensions: altruism, courtesy, conscientiousness, civic virtue, and sportsmanship. He later expanded this model to include peacekeeping and cheerleading (Organ, 1990). Williams and Anderson conceptualize OCB on the basis of the target or direction of the behavior. They call behavior directed toward the benefit of other individuals as OCB-I and behavior directed at the benefit of the organization OCB-O. All of Organ's dimensions can be captured in Williams and Anderson's conceptual scheme. Organ's altruism, courtesy, peacekeeping, and cheerleading dimensions can be included in Williams and Anderson's OCBI category (N. P. Podsakoff et al., 2009). Conscientiousness, civic virtue, and sportsmanship are exemplary of OCB-O (Coleman & Borman, 2000; Hoffman, Blair, Meriac, & Woehr, 2007; LePine, Erez, & Johnson, 2002).

Organizational Citizenship Behavior Antecedents

Research on OCB antecedents has focused on four major categories: individual (or employee) characteristics, task characteristics, organizational characteristics, and leadership behaviors.

Employee characteristics are probably the most frequently explored antecedents of OCB. Early employee antecedents of OCB can be split into two factors (Organ & Ryan, 1995): the affective "moral" factor and dispositional factor. The moral factor includes employee satisfaction, organizational commitment, perceptions of fairness, and perceptions of leader supportiveness. Those variables composing of employee moral have all been found to have a positive relationship with OCB and appear to be important determinates of citizenship behavior (P. M. Podsakoff, MacKenzie, Paine, & Bachrach, 2000). The various dispositional factors include agreeableness, conscientiousness, positive affectivity, and negative affectivity. Rather than directly affecting OCB, these orientations are seen as predisposing individuals to citizenship behavior. An examination of these factors indicates that conscientiousness, agreeableness, and positive affectivity have the strongest effects.

Employee role perceptions have been found to have a statistically significant relationship with OCB, although the magnitude of this relationship is small (P. M. Podsakoff et al., 2000). Indifference to rewards was also found to have a consistently positive relationship with citizenship behavior. Task characteristics have a consistent relationship with OCB. All task variables included in the Podsakoff, MacKenzie, Paine, and Bachrach (2000) review (task feedback, task routinization, and intrinsically satisfying tasks) were significantly related to OCBI and OCBO. Employees that received feedback and those that found their task intrinsically satisfying were more likely to engage in citizenship behavior, while those who found their tasks routine were less likely to do so.

Turning to organizational characteristics the evidence suggests that group cohesiveness, perceived organizational support, and organizational justice were positively associated with OCB. Rewards outside the leaders control were negatively related to citizenship behavior. Leadership characteristics were strongly associated with acts of citizenship behavior. Of the leadership characteristics, transformation leadership behaviors, supportive leader behavior, leader role clarification, and leader–member exchange were positively related to OCB. Noncontingent punishment behavior was found to be negatively related to citizenship behavior.

A cross-cultural perspective may provide a new perspective on understanding the relationship between OCB and its antecedents. Culture may affect which antecedents are observed at work, the frequency with which they occur, the strength of their relationship with OCB, and the mechanisms through which they affect citizenship behavior. For instance, culture can affect how justice affects OCB. The relationship between OCB antecedents and cultural context is covered in more detail in a later section of this chapter.

Organizational Citizenship Behavior Outcomes

We now turn our attention to the relationship between OCB and individual and organizational outcomes. Citizenship behavior is positively related with a variety of individual-level outcomes (N. P. Podsakoff et al., 2009). Because citizenship behavior is likely to make the supervisor's job easier (Blau, 1964) and because citizenship behavior may serve as a signal of the employee's commitment to the success of the organization (Shore, Barksdale, & Shore, 1995), the supervisor will include it as part of the individual's job performance evaluation. Meta-analytic evidence suggests that the relationship between OCB and job performance ratings was at least as strong as the relationship between task performance and job ratings (N. P. Podsakoff et al., 2009). Managers like employees who exhibit OCB and are more likely to recommend these employees for reward allocation. However, this relationship did not always translate to higher rewards. Overall, several studies suggest that OCB is negatively related with turnover intentions and actual turnover (X. P. Chen, 2005; X. P. Chen, Hui, & Sego, 1998).

Generally, OCB is positively related to overall organizational performance measures. Citizenship behavior can positively influence organizational performance through increased organizational effectiveness, higher customer satisfaction, and lower group- or unit-level turnover. Several explanations exist for the positive relationship between OCB and organizational effectiveness. Experienced employees may exhibit OCB by showing less experienced employees how to be more effective at work; employees may provide managers with useful suggestions on how to improve effectiveness or reduce costs; and OCB may enhance work spirit, morale, or cohesiveness and sense of belonging among employees (N. P. Podsakoff et al., 2009). Evidence also supports the relationship between OCB and customer satisfaction (Yen & Niehoff, 2004). Organizational units that have more employees who exhibit citizenship behavior are also likely to have more satisfied customers than units whose employees exhibit lower levels of OCB. More specifically, employees who exhibit altruism or courtesy are more likely to encourage the cooperation that is necessary to deliver goods and services effectively.

Insights from a cross-cultural perspective can also help explain some of the mechanisms through which OCB affects organizational and individual outcomes. Job performance ratings are a function of the supervisor's ability to assess the task and non-task performance of their employee. Higher CQ supervisors are more likely to read signals accurately that employees are committed to organizational success and therefore be more likely to award higher job performance ratings. This, in turn, will increase an employee's trust in the supervisor as well as her perception of organizational fairness, both of which are antecedents of citizenship behavior. In this simplified example, we can highlight the virtuous cycle of cultural intelligence to the antecedents and consequences of citizenship behavior.

Linking Organizational Citizenship Behavior to Culture

The literature on citizenship behavior has focused on a wide variety of determinants of citizenship behavior and its relationship to variables in a broad network of constructs. Despite the voluminous and fruitful literature stemming from Organ's (1988) seminal work in this area and early work on construct and measurement development (P. M. Podsakoff et al., 1990; e.g., Van Dyne, Graham, & Dienesch, 1994), we are still learning about citizenship behavior in a global context. We begin to provide an understanding of citizenship behavior and its relevant correlates for people who vary in their cultural values by exploring whether citizenship behavior has a universal meaning in cultures in which expectations for employees vary drastically. We do this by looking at several key cultural characteristics relevant to OCB, namely, justice, hierarchy, and core identity. By "justice," we refer to cultural expectations concerning distributive, procedural, and interactional forms of relationships. Hierarchy and core identity are captured by the cultural norms of traditionality versus modernity.

The OCB literature has focused on the fairness of outcomes received by an employee (e.g., pay, benefits) and the procedures used to determine those outcomes (Moorman, 1991). Findings suggest that if both job satisfaction and organizational justice are used to predict citizenship behavior, justice typically shows a stronger relationship to citizenship behavior than does satisfaction. Although it is not known exactly how justice affects citizenship behavior, trust appears to be an important mediating variable (Konovsky & Pugh, 1994). Organizational justice enhances employee trust, which in turn stimulates the display of citizenship behavior. Van Dyne, Graham, and Dienesch (1994) argued that a number of individual and contextual factors influence citizenship behavior through the mediating role of a covenantal relationship—a personal relationship resulting in action being performed without expectations of reciprocity. Over time, the vitality of the relationship itself becomes an important focus for those who have covenantal ties, and citizenship behavior is a way the relationship is maintained and strengthened (also see Fiske, 1991; Foa & Foa, 1976). A number of authors have suggested that this form of relationship is characteristic of people who have a common family structure, shared history, closely linked outcomes, or closely shared cultural perspectives (Farh et al., 1997; Fiske, 1991).

Organizational justice has proven to be an important antecedent of OCB; this relationship may differ as a function of individual and contextual attributes. Justice is a critical feature of human functioning and one of the universal constructs underpinning cultural interactions (Fiske, 1991; Wilson, 1993), and concepts of justice are known to vary according to people's cultural backgrounds. For instance, Leung and Bond (1984) examined the distributive aspects of reward allocation in Chinese, Japanese, American, and Korean samples. They found that people from collectivistic cultures used different norms of equity and equality than people in individualistic cultures. Norms of distributive justice appear to differ as a function of cultural background. Similar concerns over the etic nature of procedural justice effects have been raised as well (Lind & Tyler, 1988).

In some cultures, there is an emphasis on contractual relationships (Fiske, 1991) and interpersonal dynamics (Triandis, 1990). These relationships are often tied to the hierarchy in a society, related to what Hofstede (1991) called power distance. The structure of transactions and expectations of exchanges are universal and not tied to role occupants in these transactions. Thus, in a hierarchical society, treatment of one another is prescribed largely by expected standards of conduct. People having power are expected (and able) to use their power to influence others who are less powerful and this is expected and accepted. But this treatment must be reflective of an overall fairness of outcome, lest it be perceived as an abuse of power. For a given relationship between an employer and employee, for example, the employer must show appropriate respect for the employee for a strong relationship to exist. Over time, assuming consistent and fair treatment, this relationship may shift from an instrumental to a relational agreement based on trust and good faith, such as that found in a social exchange or covenantal relationship (Graham & Organ, 1993). We posit that the transition point of a relationship from a legitimate to a more personal level of trust becomes critical for the display of OCB in a hierarchical society. Procedural justice influences citizenship behavior similarly, in that it enhances a person's trust in his or her supervisor and organization, which in turn leads to OCB.

These two facets, justice and power, enhance the display of citizenship behavior by creating an environment conducive to a covenantal relationship between an employee and his or her organization. If employees believe that procedures used in allocating organizational outcomes are fair and just, they will be satisfied and more likely to engage in citizenship behavior (Brockner & Adsit, 1986; Konovsky & Pugh, 1994). Indeed, related work on interactional justice (Bies, 2015) focuses on universals, including truth and human dignity whereby actions and consequences that reaffirm membership within a community. OCB becomes a natural offshoot of individuals, demonstrating their commitment to their communities through engaging in prosocial behavior.

Different predictions can be generated if alternative assumptions are made concerning what constitutes contractual relationships in a society. In societies emphasizing expressive, or covenantal, ties among people, exchange is not always based on a universalistic principle of an equitable distribution of outcomes; rather, it is often based on a particularistic principle of need or social status distribution (Fiske, 1991; Foa & Foa, 1976). For example, the behavior of Chinese holding traditional values (traditionality) is determined situationally, and whether they feel they have been treated fairly does not strongly affect their behavior. In a traditional Chinese context, the particularistic conditions of a given relationship govern expectations of exchange and behavior. Thus, social structure provides role relationships (e.g., father to son) that are comparable to a covenantal relationship. Whereas market forces may govern an instrumental relationship, an expressive one is regulated through personal integrity and devotion to the good of the relationship, as in a covenantal relationship. In cultures focusing on role-based relationships, trust and faith in one's superiors are built into the social structure of organizations, and we would not expect any relationship between justice and citizenship behavior, because employees' actions would not need to be motivated by enhanced trust. Of course, such an idyllic society is no more likely to exist than a purely instrumental society; rather, societies differ according to the relative balance of these various forms of contracts. Thus, current thinking about justice and citizenship behavior may be limited to a cultural context emphasizing justice as a means of enhancing trust in forming relational contracts.

For the sake of illustration looking at power distance and OCB, we provide an example from a culture syndrome referred to as traditionality versus modernity (Farh et al., 1997; Inkeles & Smith, 1974; Yang, 1993). In a culture characterized by traditionality, there is an emphasis on expressive ties among people and values such as respect for authority, filial piety, fatalism, and a general sense of powerlessness (Yang, 1993). For instance, in traditional Chinese culture, there are five fundamental relationships among people referred to as *wu-lun*, including emperor–subject, father–son, husband–wife, elder–younger, and friend–friend. These relationships indicate how people should relate to one another in dyadic relationships. Thus, the *wu-lun* reflects the relation of people to one another within their social system. For each dyadic *wu-lun* relationship, role prescriptions specify what should and should not be done by the actors. The five cardinal relations (*wu-lun*), even those between friends, are constructed in hierarchical patterns. In each case, the senior member is accorded a wide range of prerogatives and authority with respect to the junior. Yang (1993) has also pointed out that prescriptions for these relations are asymmetric, in that the behavior expectations of the role with less power (e.g., the subject, the son, and the wife) is specified in much more detail than those of the role with greater power. Much more stringent requirements and restrictions are imposed on the less powerful role, and as a result, people in those roles are greatly underprivileged. Moreover, the hierarchical orientation in *wu-lun* has been generalized and extended to wider social contexts (Yang, 1993, p. 40).

This description illustrates a key point about culture, behavior, and OCB—that concepts of power relationships and rules guide what is enacted within a culture as in-role or extra-role behavior, including OCB. Employees engage in citizenship behavior not merely because they perceive the work environment as just; they do so in satisfying their self-derived obligations to their companies (Farh et al., 1997; Jiao et al., 2013).

In contrast to a traditional society, some cultures have gone through industrialization and modernization; that is, they went through revolutionary changes in institutional patterns as well as in people's values and attitudes. This social shift represents an alternative to traditional values and has been referred to as individual modernity (Inkeles & Smith, 1974). Modernity describes a society in terms of egalitarianism and open-mindedness, optimism and assertiveness, affective hedonism, sexual equality, and self-reliance (Yang, 1993). We focused on egalitarianism and open-mindedness here in our use of this construct. Western society is strongly dominated by modernity, as reflected by its emphasis on a principle that everyone has certain basic human rights (Erez & Earley, 1993; Triandis, 1989), and everyone has an equal right to receive rewards based on his or her individual contributions. In a modern society, there is an emphasis on instrumental exchange based on underlying rules of equity.

Traditionality and modernity are not opposite ends of a unidimensional construct. Traditionality reflects the hierarchical nature of a society based on the principles of structured relationships, while modernity reflects an orientation toward egalitarianism, self-reliance, and openness. It is possible for a culture to be both traditional and modern in this usage. Thai society is characterized by a strong respect for hierarchy (i.e., traditional) while emphasizing individuality and self-reliance (i.e., modernity). Other things being equal, there tends to be an acceptance of OCB as in-role activity (a paradox of sorts) in more traditional cultures, whereas OCB reflects extra-role and prosocial behavior in modern cultures.

So there exists an important interplay between cultural modes, cultural intelligence, and OCB. In the next section, we will describe a potential interplay among these constructs.

Conceptual Framework

Organ's 1997 definition of OCB highlights the relevance of culture to citizenship behavior. Specifically relevant to cross-cultural approaches of OCB, the new definition places context at the center of attention. The definition highlights the importance of CQ to both the antecedents and consequences of OCB as well as the citizenship behavior itself. The relationship between culture, cultural intelligence, and OCB is presented in Figure 22.1. The broken line represents the antecedents, behavior, and outcomes of OCB as taking place within a complex cultural milieu with potential interactions, temporal changes, and intra- and interindividual differences. The arrows originating from the cultural intelligence element of the figure signify that high levels of managerial and employee CQ are required to comprehend the links between OCB antecedents, behavior, and outcomes. Finally, lines connecting antecedents, behavior, and outcomes indicate that these factors are reciprocal and interdependent.

We posit that, in general, culturally intelligent employees will be better skilled at enhancing their own outcomes and the outcomes of their organization by behaving in ways appropriate to the context in which they find themselves. For instance, the knowledge of role perceptions, such as those illustrated in the previous section, may result in greater group- or unit-level cohesiveness and thus lead to outcomes that increase profitability, such as superior customer satisfaction. This insight is graphically represented (Figure 22.2) in a simplified version of the relationships introduced in Figure 22.1.

Additionally, more culturally intelligent managers will be more successful architects of an *environment* (i.e., antecedents and outcomes) conducive to citizenship behavior. For example, a manager familiar with a host country's concepts of justice is less liable to exercise noncontingent punishment and reward, which can be detrimental to subordinate citizenship behavior and thus organizational performance. Figure 22.3 illustrates the interdependence between antecedents and outcomes, with cultural intelligence as an important element of understanding and managing complex cultural environments characterized by reciprocal feedback loops.

The preceding illustrations also underline how a person's capacity to adapt effectively to a new cultural context can result in a virtuous cycle between antecedents, behaviors, and consequences. A culturally intelligent employee's skill at exercising correct citizenship behaviors is more likely to result in positive job performance. Because she is culturally intelligent, she is also less likely to misinterpret positive job performance evaluations, which can lead her to

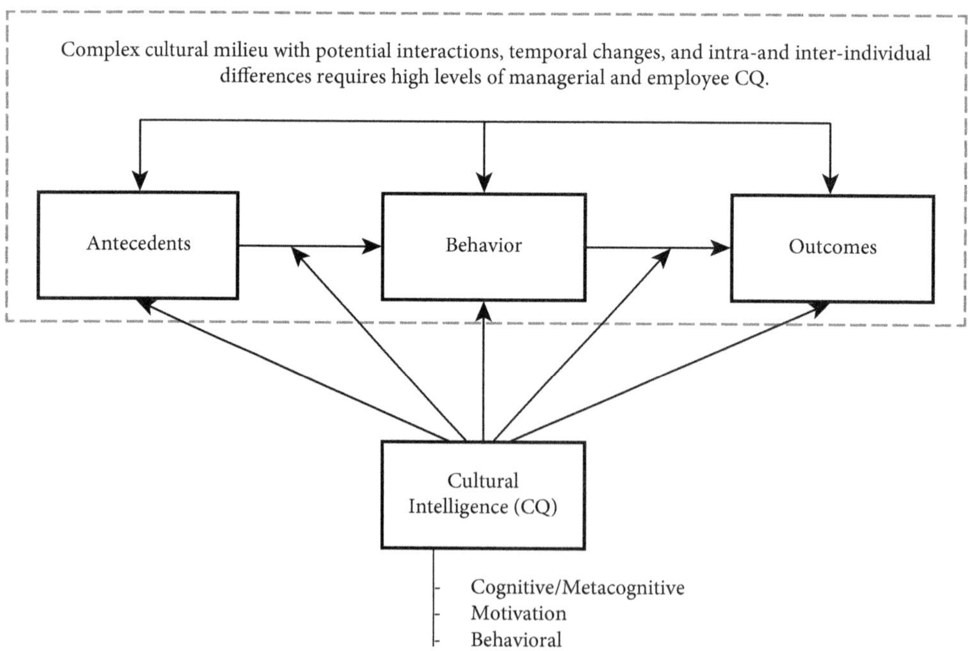

Figure 22.1 The role of cultural intelligence in managing and understanding organizational citizenship behavior in different cultural (intra- and intercultural) environments.

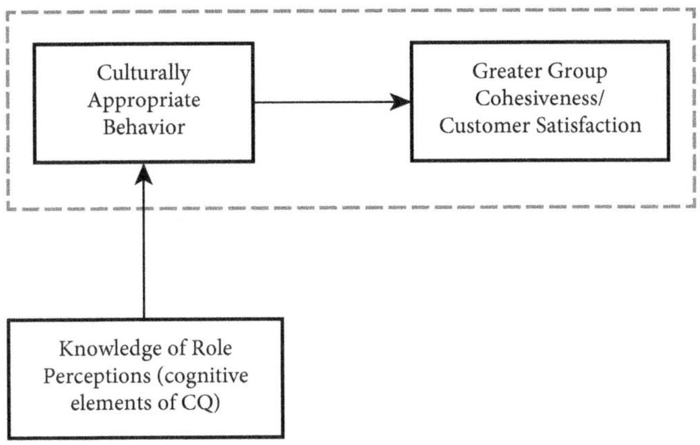

Figure 22.2 The role of cognition in understanding culture and managing behavior for positive organizational and individual outcomes.

exhibit further citizenship behaviors, such as offering the manager useful suggestions that improve unit effectiveness, reduce costs, or free up the manager to spend time on more productive tasks.

Before turning to specific facets of CQ in relation to citizenship behavior, it is important to consider the general context as we described earlier. Within all societies there exist norms and instantiations of justice and traditionality/modernity. But how might these cultural norms relate to the cultural backgrounds and experiences of individuals, and what role does CQ play in understanding this relationship?

As described earlier, the first facet of CQ that can aid in understanding the antecedents and consequences of OCB is cognition. Cognition can be understood as the individual's stock of and ability to process culturally relevant knowledge. The stock of cultural information can explain variation in effects of OCB antecedent on citizenship behavior. While working in mainland China, a North American worker's justice perceptions are unlikely to be affected if he is familiar with cultures characterized by traditionality, high-power distance, and so on. Conversely, a worker who has limited first-hand knowledge and experience of the dyadic role prescriptions in traditional, high-power distance societies may feel he is being treated unjustly. The difference is that under the same circumstance one person is more likely to exhibit OCBs than is the other. Cognitive CQ thus provides one mechanism through which OCBs arise and influence other

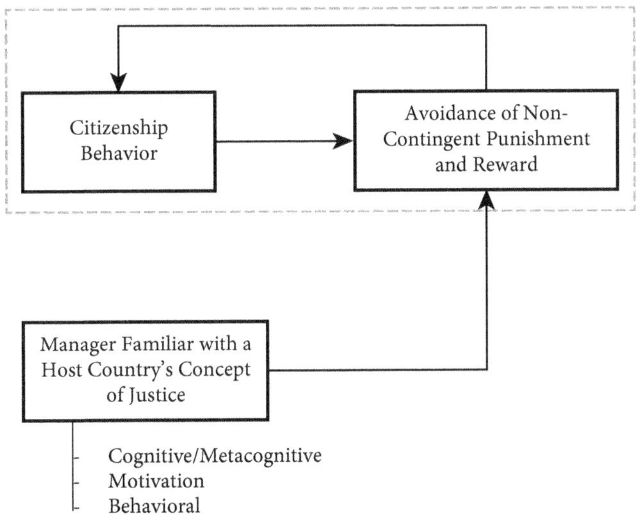

Figure 22.3 Interplay of culture and reward/punishment.

variables. In the following paragraphs, we would like to note an important gap in the OCB/culture literature that cuts several research areas, including creativity, innovation, and brainstorming.

Just as important as CQ's effects on knowledge content, CQ will affect knowledge processing. Evidence suggests that individuals differ in the way they process information, and that at least some of these differences can be accounted for by state factors—such as culture (Earley & Ang, 2003). The effect of culture on information processing is especially relevant for groups attempting to solve open-ended problems requiring high levels of creative problem solving. Creative problem-solving research suggests that diversity, both background (ethnic, religious, etc.) and task (functional, divisional, unit, etc.) diversity, should increase the generation of creative ideas (Bechtoldt, De Dreu, Nijstad, & Choi, 2010; Gielnik, Frese, Graf, & Kampschulte, 2012; Hoever, van Knippenberg, van Ginkel, & Barkema, 2012). Diversity will increase the total pool of ideas and stimulate individuals to make associations they would not have made were they working alone. However, extant literature has reported mixed results of task-relevant diversity and generally negative results of background diversity on group creative problem solving (Hülsheger, Anderson, & Salgado, 2009). How is group creativity related to OCB and culture, and how can CQ help account for these inconsistent findings?

First, as we stated earlier, our focus is not solely on national cultural differences, but cultural differences of all kinds. These include intraorganizational and intranational cultural differences, such as cultural differences found between business or functional units within a single organization. Moreover, creativity, because its outcome cannot, by definition, be made explicit or defined by the organizational reward system, is discretionary (Berry, 2014). Additionally, because creative ideas promote the effective functioning of the organization, they fit the definition of OCB.

Second, group creativity literature has shed light on why groups, particularly diverse groups, are less likely to produce creative outcomes, even when compared to individuals working alone (nominal groups) (Paulus, Dugosh, Dzindolet, Coskun, & Putman, 2002). Individuals in groups are concerned with the evaluative perceptions of other group members and may avoid vocalization. Several studies have shown that "evaluative apprehension" has a strong and negative effect on group creative performance. CQ may play an important role in mitigating, completely eliminating, or in some cases, reversing this effect. Given the importance of creativity and innovation coupled with the broad use of groups to solve problems, such gains would have substantial benefits for individuals, teams, organizations, and society. Indeed, early empirical evidence suggests a complete reversal of this effect is possible. In a study of creative problem solving in mixed-sex groups, imposing (making explicit) political correctness norms reduced uncertainty and boosted creativity (Goncalo, Chatman, Duguid, & Kennedy, 2015). This research is novel because it demonstrates that adding political correctness, which is conventionally thought of as a constraint, actually increased creativity. It is also relevant for our discussion because it demonstrates that knowledge of social norms, values, and beliefs, an indicator of high CQ, can explain inconsistent findings regarding OCB, in this case creativity.

Metacognition provides us with a way of predicting how individuals may engage in OCB. Differences in metacognitive ability are most likely to be reflected in novel cultural situations, such as those of culture shock or in cultural settings with which the individual is unfamiliar. High-CQ individuals will be more skilled at dealing with these situations because they are more capable at incorporating past experiences to these interactions. Metacognition is a mechanism that can account for some variance in OCB outcomes. For instance, a North American manager already familiar with the fundamental relationship structure of *wu-lun* may be as well versed in the fair evaluation of job performance as his Chinese counterpart, but unable to adapt those concepts in a context that is both modern and traditional. Likewise, despite his knowledge of just interactions in a role with more power (with his employees), that same manager may feel lost when he finds himself in a role with less power (interacting with his own superiors).

Cognition alone may not explain the mechanisms through which OCB arises. An individual must be motivated to use the knowledge and experience to produce a culturally appropriate response. A challenge of intercultural encounters is the ability to engage with someone from a different culture and persevere despite the difficulty of the interaction. We suggest that justice perceptions interact with motivational CQ through several means. First, cultural value congruity enhances individual motivation. Conflicts in values orientation may give rise to experiences of injustice, thus eroding OCB. Second, motivational CQ reflects an individual's efficacy and goal orientation. Again, perceptions of justice are key in encouraging a person's participation and commitment to his or her social situation, so lacking such a perception, a person is likely to disengage and lack confidence to engage.

A worker familiar with cultures characterized by modernity and traditionality (as an example) is likely to adapt behaviors to optimize positive consequences for himself or herself. However, in a "just" context, those behaviors will extend out to provide positive consequences for referent for other individuals in a team or group setting, community, or even society. The significant aspect of behavioral CQ is understanding the type of behaviors or actions that will provide benefits to others. Whereas in one culture a gesture of physical contact might provide reassurance or friendship, it might be threatening or off-putting in another culture (e.g., low- versus high-contact cultures). Engaging in reassuring behaviors or ones that demonstrate local understanding (showing that you know how to communicate appropriately) will key a sense of interactional justice and so we enhance the likelihood of OCB.

Summary

Our hope with this discussion is to provide a more general framework for individuals to use in exploring the implications of cultural variables on OCB. Rather than focusing on specific and general predictions of the type "in culture X, we will see OCB more than in culture Y" or "in culture X, OCB will look like A, B, and C," we've sought to provide a linking mechanism, justice (organizational, procedural, and interactional), as a way of understanding what general trigger will increase the display of OCB. We introduced as well the concept of cultural intelligence as a means of helping understand and predict why the link of justice to OCB display across cultural boundaries might or might not be manifested. That is, why might the same justice context in a culture lead one manager to engage in OCB (and to encourage OCB in his/her coworkers) but not for another? We have posited that understanding of that culture through facets of CQ provides such a differentiation.

So as scholars move forward to understand the nature of OCB across cultural boundaries, we argue that it's critical for us to look at a person's capability to understand cultural situations and to engage them proactively and effectively.

References

Bandura, A. (1986). *Social foundations of thought and action: A social cognitive theory*. Englewood Cliffs, NJ: Prentice-Hall.

Bandura, A. (1997). *Self efficacy: The exercise of control*. Englewood Cliffs, NJ: Prentice Hall.

Bandura, A., & Schunk, D. H. (1981). Cultivating competence, self-efficacy, and intrinsic interest through proximal self-motivation. *Journal of Personality and Social Psychology, 41*(3), 586–598.

Bechtoldt, M. N., De Dreu, C. K. W., Nijstad, B. A., & Choi, H.-S. (2010). Motivated information processing, social tuning, and group creativity. *Journal of Personality and Social Psychology, 99*(4), 622.

Berry, J. (2014). If creative ideas have value, why do we give them away? In *Flipping the script: Creativity as an antecedent*. Paper Presented at the Academy of Management, Philadelphia, PA.

Bies, R. J. (2015). Interactional justice: Looking backward, looking forward. In Russell S. Cropanzano and Maureen L. Ambrose (Eds.), *The Oxford handbook of justice in the workplace*. London, England: Oxford University Press.

Blau, P. M. (1964). *Exchange and power in social life*. New Brunswick, NJ: Transaction Publishers.

Borman, W. C., & Motowidlo, S. M. (1993). Expanding the criterion domain to include elements of contextual performance. In *Personnel selection in organizations* (p. 71). San Francisco, CA: Jossey-Bass.

Brockner, J., & Adsit, L. (1986). The moderating impact of sex on the equity–satisfaction relationship: A field study. *Journal of Applied Psychology, 71*(4), 585.

Chen, X. P. (2005). Organizational citizenship behavior: A predictor of employee voluntary turnover. In *Handbook of organizational citizenship behavior* (pp. 435–454). Hauppagge, NY: Nova Science Publishers.

Chen, X.-P., Hui, C., & Sego, D. J. (1998). The role of organizational citizenship behavior in turnover: Conceptualization and preliminary tests of key hypotheses. *Journal of Applied Psychology, 83*(6), 922.

Coleman, V. I., & Borman, W. C. (2000). Investigating the underlying structure of the citizenship performance domain. *Human Resource Management Review, 10*(1), 25–44.

Earley, P. C., & Ang, S. (2003). *Cultural intelligence: Individual interactions across cultures*. Stanford, CA: Stanford Business Books.

Earley, P. C., & Lituchy, T. R. (1991). Delineating goal and efficacy effects: A test of three models. *Journal of Applied Psychology, 76*(1), 81–98.

Erez, M., & Earley, P. C. (1993). *Culture, self-identity, and work*. New York, NY: Oxford University Press.

Farh, J.-L., Earley, P. C., & Lin, S.-C. (1997). Impetus for action: A cultural analysis of justice and organizational citizenship behavior in Chinese society. *Administrative Science Quarterly, 42*(3), 421–444.

Fiske, A. P. (1991). *Structures of social life: The four elementary forms of human relations: Communal sharing, authority ranking, equality matching, market pricing*. New York, NY: Free Press.

Foa, E. B., & Foa, U. G. (1976). Resource theory of social exchange. In J. W. Thibaut, J. T. Spence, and R. C. Carson (Eds.), *Contemporary topics in social psychology* (pp. 53–92). Morristown, NJ: General Learning Press.

Gielnik, M. M., Frese, M., Graf, J. M., & Kampschulte, A. (2012). Creativity in the opportunity identification process

and the moderating effect of diversity of information. *Journal of Business Venturing, 27*(5), 559.
Goffman, E. (1959). *The presentation of self in everyday life.* Garden City, NY: Doubleday Anchor.
Goffman, E. (1967). *Interaction ritual—Essays on face-to-face behavior* (1st ed.). New York, NY: Anchor Books.
Goncalo, J. A., Chatman, J. A., Duguid, M. M., & Kennedy, J. A. (2015). Creativity from constraint? How the political correctness norm influences creativity in mixed-sex work groups. *Administrative Science Quarterly, 60*(1), 1–30. http://doi.org/10.1177/0001839214563975
Graham, J. W., & Organ, D. W. (1993). Commitment and the covenantal organization. *Journal of Managerial Issues, 5*, 483–502.
Hoever, I. J., van Knippenberg, D., van Ginkel, W. P., & Barkema, H. G. (2012). Fostering team creativity: Perspective taking as key to unlocking diversity's potential. *Journal of Applied Psychology, 97*(5), 982–996.
Hoffman, B. J., Blair, C. A., Meriac, J. P., & Woehr, D. J. (2007). Expanding the criterion domain? A quantitative review of the OCB literature. *Journal of Applied Psychology, 92*(2), 555–566.
Hofstede, G. (1991). *Cultures and organizations.* New York, NY: McGraw-Hill.
Hülsheger, U. R., Anderson, N., & Salgado, J. F. (2009). Team-level predictors of innovation at work: A comprehensive meta-analysis spanning three decades of research. *Journal of Applied Psychology, 94*(5), 1128.
Inkeles, A., & Smith, D. H. (1974). *Becoming modern: Individual change in six developing countries.* Cambridge, MA: Harvard University Press.
Jiao, C., Richards, D. A., & Hackett, R. D. (2013). Organizational citizenship behavior and role breadth: A meta-analytic and cross-cultural analysis. *Human Resource Management, 52*(5), 697–714.
Konovsky, M. A., & Pugh, S. D. (1994). Citizenship behavior and social exchange. *Academy of Management Journal, 37*(3), 656–669.
Lai, J. Y. M., Lam, L. W., & Lam, S. S. K. (2013). Organizational citizenship behavior in work groups: A team cultural perspective. *Journal of Organizational Behavior, 34*(7), 1039–1056.
LePine, J. A., Erez, A., & Johnson, D. E. (2002). The nature and dimensionality of organizational citizenship behavior: A critical review and meta-analysis. *Journal of Applied Psychology, 87*(1), 52–65.
Leung, K., & Bond, M. H. (1984). The impact of cultural collectivism on reward allocation. *Journal of Personality and Social Psychology, 47*(4), 793–804.
Lind, E. A., & Tyler, T. R. (1988). *The social psychology of procedural justice.* New York, NY: Plenum.
Locke, E. A., & Latham, G. P. (1990). *A theory of goal setting & task performance* (Vol. *xviii*). Englewood Cliffs, NJ: Prentice-Hall, Inc.
Moorman, R. H. (1991). Relationship between organizational justice and organizational citizenship behaviors: Do fairness perceptions influence employee citizenship? *Journal of Applied Psychology, 76*(6), 845.
Organ, D. W. (1988). *Organizational citizenship behavior: The good soldier syndrome.* Lexington, MA: Lexington Books.
Organ, D. W. (1990). The motivational basis of organizational citizenship behavior. *Research in Organizational Behavior, 12*(1), 43–72.
Organ, D. W. (1997). Organizational citizenship behavior: It's construct clean-up time. *Human Performance, 10*(2), 85–97.
Organ, D. W., & Ryan, K. (1995). A meta-analytic review of attitudinal and dispositional predictors of organizational citizenship behavior. *Personnel Psychology, 48*(4), 775–802.
Paillé, P. (2009). Assessing organizational citizenship behavior in the French context: Evidence for the four-dimensional model. *The Journal of Psychology, 143*(2), 133–146.
Paine, J. B., & Organ, D. W. (2000). The cultural matrix of organizational citizenship behavior: Some preliminary conceptual and empirical observations. *Human Resource Management Review, 10*(1), 45–59.
Paulus, P. B., Dugosh, K. L., Dzindolet, M. T., Coskun, H., & Putman. (2002). Social and cognitive influences in group brainstorming: Predicting production gains and losses. *European Review of Social Psychology, 12*(1), 299–325. http://doi.org/10.1080/14792772143000094
Podsakoff, N. P., Whiting, S. W., Podsakoff, P. M., & Blume, B. D. (2009). Individual-and organizational-level consequences of organizational citizenship behaviors: A meta-analysis. *Journal of Applied Psychology, 94*(1), 122.
Podsakoff, P. M., & MacKenzie, S. B. (1997). Impact of organizational citizenship behavior on organizational performance: A review and suggestion for future research. *Human Performance, 10*(2), 133–151.
Podsakoff, P. M., MacKenzie, S. B., Moorman, R. H., & Fetter, R. (1990). Transformational leader behaviors and their effects on followers' trust in leader, satisfaction, and organizational citizenship behaviors. *The Leadership Quarterly, 1*(2), 107–142.
Podsakoff, P. M., MacKenzie, S. B., Paine, J. B., & Bachrach, D. G. (2000). Organizational citizenship behaviors: A critical review of the theoretical and empirical literature and suggestions for future research. *Journal of Management, 26*(3), 513–563.
Rokeach, M. (1973). *The nature of human values* (Vol. *438*). New York, NY: The Free Press.
Schwartz, S. H. (1994). *Beyond individualism/collectivism: New cultural dimensions of values.* Thousand Oaks, CA: Sage Publications, Inc.
Shore, L. M., Barksdale, K., & Shore, T. H. (1995). Managerial perceptions of employee commitment to the organization. *Academy of Management Journal, 38*(6), 1593–1615.
Thomas, D. C., & Inkson, K. (2004). *Cultural intelligence: People skills for global business.* San Francisco, CA: Berrett-Koehler.
Triandis, H. C. (1972). *The analysis of subjective culture.* New York, NY: Wiley.
Triandis, H. C. (1989). The self and social behavior in differing cultural contexts. *Psychological Review, 96*(3), 506.
Triandis, H. C. (1990). Cross-cultural studies of individualism and collectivism. In J. Berman (Ed.), *Nebraska symposium on motivation* (pp. 41–133). Lincoln, NE: University of Nebraska Press.
Van Dyne, L., Graham, J. W., & Dienesch, R. M. (1994). Organizational citizenship behavior: Construct redefinition, measurement, and validation. *Academy of Management Journal, 37*(4), 765–802.
Williams, L. J., & Anderson, S. E. (1991). Job satisfaction and organizational commitment as predictors of organizational citizenship and in-role behaviors. *Journal of Management, 17*(3), 601–617.

Wilson, J. Q. (1993). The moral sense. *American Political Science Review, 87*(01), 1–11.

Yang, K.-S. (1993). Chinese social orientation: An integrative analysis. In L. Y. Cheng, F. M. C. Cheung, & Char-Nie Chen (Eds.), *Psychotherapy for the Chinese: Selected papers from the First International Conference* (pp. 19–56). Hong Kong: Chinese University of Hong Kong.

Yen, H. R., & Niehoff, B. P. (2004). Organizational citizenship behaviors and organizational effectiveness: Examining relationships in Taiwanese banks. *Journal of Applied Social Psychology, 34*(8), 1617–1637.

CHAPTER

23 Review and Recommended Best Practices for Measuring and Modeling Organizational Citizenship Behavior

Christopher C. Rosen, Eric J. Yochum, Liana G. Passantino, Russell E. Johnson, *and* Chu-Hsiang (Daisy) Chang

Abstract

Organizational citizenship behaviors (OCBs) have been assessed in a variety of ways. We conducted a thorough review of this literature, and we provide a comprehensive discussion of how OCBs have been measured and modeled, with a focus on identifying trends and providing guidelines for future researchers. Our review, which included all empirical studies published in eight top-tier management journals over the past 30 years, is organized around four themes: (1) operational inconsistencies, which include utilizing different levels of specificity, sets of dimensions and facets, and response scales when assessing OCBs across studies; (2) rating source effects, in terms of the appropriateness of self versus nonself (i.e., supervisors and coworkers) sources of OCB ratings; (3) differences in how the higher order multidimensional OCB construct has been modeled across studies; and (4) emerging methodological and measurement issues, including nonindependence, multilevel treatments of OCB, and the utilization of control variables in OCB research.

Key Words: organizational citizenship behavior, measurement, modeling, review, OCB

In this chapter we present a measurement- and methodological-focused review of the organizational citizenship behavior (OCB) literature. In doing so, we set for ourselves two primary aims. The first aim is descriptive in nature, which involves recapping the common practices that are used to measure and model the OCB construct. Our review is based on empirical studies published in eight top-tier management and applied psychology journals (*Administrative Science Quarterly, Academy of Management Journal, Journal of Applied Psychology, Journal of Management, Journal of Organizational Behavior, Organization Science, Organizational Behavior and Human Decision Processes*, and *Personnel Psychology*) over the past 30 years. Given the frequent rate with which OCB appears in published articles, it is perhaps not surprising that the construct has been operationalized via a diverse array of measures (e.g., Podsakoff, MacKenzie, Moorman, & Fetter, 1990; Smith, Organ, & Near, 1983; Williams & Anderson, 1991) and rating sources (e.g., Carpenter, Berry, & Houston, 2014; Vandenberg, Lance, & Taylor, 2005). Despite the various approaches though, certain trends regarding how OCB is measured and modeled have emerged. Whether or not these trends are appropriate is, however, a different issue. Thus, the second aim of our review is prescriptive in nature, which involves evaluating the available evidence to make recommendations and identify best practices for measuring and modeling OCB.

Our descriptive and prescriptive review is organized into four sections. The first section concerns the variations in how OCB is operationalized, which includes different levels of specificity (e.g., overall OCB vs. specific behaviors), sets of dimensions and facets (e.g., helping, sportsmanship, voice, etc.), and response scales (e.g., agreement vs. frequency). The second section focuses on the different sources used to rate OCB, paying particular attention to self versus nonself (e.g., supervisors, coworkers) sources. The third section examines differences in how the higher order multidimensional OCB construct is modeled (e.g., as a superordinate vs. aggregate construct) and the different assumptions that underlie each approach. Finally, the fourth section covers additional methodological and measurement issues that range from issues of nonindependence and multilevel treatments of OCB to the control variables that are commonly used when OCB is examined.

Variations in the Operationalization of Organizational Citizenship Behaviors

A great deal of work has been devoted to mapping out the multidimensional criterion space of job performance, which includes both required in-role activities as well as discretionary extra-role ones (e.g., Borman & Motowidlo, 1993; Campbell, 1990; Katz & Kahn, 1978). OCB belongs to the latter extra-role category, and it has been conceptualized in a variety of ways. According to one taxonomy, for example, OCB is believed to comprise altruism, conscientiousness, sportsmanship, courtesy, and civic virtue (Organ, 1988), whereas other taxonomies include facilitating peer and team performance and demonstrating effort (Campbell, 1990); helping coworkers, spreading goodwill, and making constructive suggestions (George & Brief, 1992); or affiliative and challenging promotive and prohibitive behaviors (Van Dyne, Cummings, & Parks, 1995; see Podsakoff, MacKenzie, Paine, & Bacharach, 2000, for a review). As Rotundo and Sackett (2002) concluded, this plethora of conceptualizations has muddled the meaning of OCB, and in some cases, there is minimal overlap across different OCB taxonomies.

Given its numerous conceptualizations, it is not surprising that numerous operationalizations of OCB also exist. Of the 351 articles included in our literature review, six scales in particular stood out as being the most commonly used. Forty-nine articles (or 14%) used Williams and Anderson's (1991) scale; 44 articles (or 13%) used Van Dyne and LePine's (1998) scale; 42 articles (or 12%) used Podsakoff et al.'s (1990) scale; 35 articles (or 10%) used Lee and Allen's (2002) scale; 20 articles (or 6%) used Smith et al.'s (1983) scale; and 14 articles (or 4%) used Moorman and Blakely's (1995) scale.

All six of these scales specify OCB as having at least two dimensions, one of which typically reflects a form of interpersonal helping, but that is where the similarities end.[1] Two scales (Lee & Allen, 2002; Williams & Anderson, 1991) assess broadly defined OCBs directed at specific individuals (OCBI; e.g., helping a coworker) and directed at the organization (OCBO; e.g., defend the company from criticism). The other four scales capture what can be considered lower order facets of OCBI (e.g., altruism from Smith et al., 1983; altruism and courtesy from Podsakoff et al., 1990; interpersonal helping from Moorman & Blakely, 1995; and helping from Van Dyne & LePine, 1998) and OCBO (general compliance from Smith et al., 1983; conscientiousness, sportsmanship, and civic virtue from Podsakoff et al., 1990; personal industry and loyal boosterism from Moorman & Blakely, 1995; and voice from Van Dyne & LePine, 1998).

As hinted at earlier, one way the scales differ is according to the specific level of OCB that they target. OCB can be represented hierarchically with overall OCB at the top, OCBI and OCBO dimensions in the middle, and behavioral facets (e.g., helping, civic virtue) at the bottom. Two scales (Lee & Allen, 2002; Williams & Anderson, 1991) directly assess the middle dimensions, whereas the remaining scales (Moorman & Blakely, 1995; Podsakoff et al., 1990; Smith et al., 1983; Van Dyne & LePine, 1998) directly assess lower order facets (it is, however, possible to operationalize OCB at higher levels by averaging across multiple facets or dimensions). As Podsakoff, Whiting, Podsakoff, and Blume (2009) pointed out, operationalizing OCB as broad dimensions (OCBI and OCBO) subsumes the lower order facets. However, an advantage of scales that assess behavioral facets at the bottom level is their flexibility. Scores can always be aggregated up to higher levels in the hierarchy, whereas moving down to lower levels is less feasible when overall OCB or its broad dimensions are directly assessed.

The OCB scales also differ according to how clearly defined their boundaries are vis-à-vis other job performance constructs. In particular, many OCB scales include items that overlap with in-role task performance, which may artificially inflate relationships of OCB with performance (Dalal, 2005; Spector, Bauer, & Fox, 2010; Spector & Che, 2014). For example, several items from Smith et al.'s (1983) general compliance subscale (e.g., "Coasts toward the end of the day"), Podsakoff et al.'s (1990) conscientiousness subscale (e.g.,

"Attendance at work is above the norm"), Williams and Anderson's (1991) OCBO subscale (e.g., "Gives advance notice when unable to come to work"), and Moorman and Blakely's (1995) personal industry subscale (e.g., "Performs his/her duties with unusually few errors") are arguably more aligned with in-role task behaviors and obligations than OCB. Organ (1988, p. 9) acknowledged potential overlap between dimensions of OCB and task performance and suggested that OCBs are behaviors that go "well beyond accepted or required levels" (e.g., showing up to work despite extreme weather conditions, engaging in spontaneous acts aimed at improving the work environment, or helping others). As such, the distinction between overlapping aspects of task performance and conscientiousness seems to be based more on differences in degree, as opposed to differences in the kinds of behavior enacted.

Likewise, many OCB scales include items that are also antithetical to counterproductive work behavior (CWB). For example, as noted by Spector et al. (2010), reverse-scored items such as "Consumes a lot of time complaining about trivial matters" (Podsakoff et al., 1990), "Takes undeserved breaks (Smith et al., 1983), "Conducts personal business on company time" (Farh, Earley, & Lin, 1997), and "Takes undeserved work breaks" (Williams & Anderson, 1991) align with items from CWB scales, including "Taken an additional or longer break than is acceptable in your work place" (Bennett & Robinson, 2000), "Taken a longer break than you were allowed to" (Spector et al., 2006), "Complained about insignificant things at work" (Fox & Spector, 1999), and "I used working time for private affairs" (Marcus, Schuler, Quell, & Hümpfner, 2002). Items like these are problematic because they obscure the discriminant validity of OCB with other job behaviors. For example, Spector et al. (2010) found that the average correlation of OCB with CWB was $r = -.56$ when antithetical items were included on OCB scales versus $r = -.13$ when they were excluded, a finding that is consistent with previous meta-analytic research (i.e., Dalal, 2005) which demonstrated that the inclusion of antithetical items resulted in larger average correlations between CWB and OCB ($r = -.54$) compared to when such items were excluded ($r = -.16$).

Looking beyond characteristics of specific scales (e.g., whether they measure broad dimensions vs. narrow behaviors, the inclusion vs. exclusion of antithetical items), our review of the literature also unveiled inconsistencies with how the various OCB scales are used by researchers. One issue involves the type of response options used. In the majority of studies (84%), participants rated the focal person's OCB using agreement–disagreement (or characteristic–uncharacteristic) response options. In the remaining 16% of studies, participants rated the frequency of specific OCBs. Although not often used, frequency ratings are desirable because they require respondents to systematically recall and calculate how often the focal person exhibits the behavior, which centers attention on specific instances of a behavior (Schwarz & Oyserman, 2001). In contrast, agreement scales may not capture behavior at all; rather, they appear to reflect attitudes or intentions toward the behavior or attitudes toward the actor (Dalal, 2005). By drawing attention away from specific instances of behavior, agreement scales result in more biased responding due to, for example, the halo effect and implicit person theories (e.g., Leia is a warm person; thus, she is likely to exhibit all types of OCB; Spector et al., 2010). In support of this claim, it has been found that using agreement scales inflates the positive correlations among OCB facets and the negative correlation between OCB and CWB (Dalal, 2005; Spector et al., 2010). Daily assessments of the frequency of OCB similarly produce weaker facet–facet and OCB–CWB correlations (Dalal, Lam, Weiss, Welch, & Hulin, 2009).

A second issue pertains to operationalizing OCB using only a subset of dimensions or behavioral facets (this was observed in 23% of the coded articles). In some instances, OCB was measured using only two (e.g., altruism and sportsmanship; Bommer, Dierdorff, & Rubin, 2007), three (e.g., altruism, conscientiousness, and sportsmanship; Chen, Hui, & Sego, 1998), or four (e.g., altruism, courtesy, conscientiousness, and sportsmanship; Maslyn & Fedor, 1998) subscales as opposed to all five of Podsakoff et al.'s (1990) subscales. In other instances, OCB was operationalized using only a single subscale, such as altruism or helping (e.g., Ang, Van Dyne, & Begley, 2003; George, Chattopadhyay, & Zhang, 2012; Wayne, Shore, & Liden, 1997). Despite the inconsistent renderings of the construct space across these examples, the focal variable was nonetheless labeled "OCB" in the text. We view this practice as potentially problematic because it ignores the presumed multidimensional nature of OCB by equating the higher order OCB construct with an incomplete set of lower order indicators (and, in some cases, only a single indicator).

Of course, the extent to which this practice is actually problematic hinges on whether or not the nature and nomological network of OCB changes as a function of how many and what dimensions or facets are included as indicators. One possibility is that the exclusion of specific dimensions or facets does not matter because they may reflect interchangeable behaviors that are equally likely to be exhibited by employees who are good citizens. For example, the findings of LePine, Erez, and Johnson's (2002) meta-analytic review suggest that the five facets of Organ's (1988) OCB taxonomy (altruism, courtesy, civic virtue, conscientiousness, and sportsmanship) are equivalent indicators of a higher order OCB factor (e.g., the average corrected correlations among the indicators was $r_c = .67$). Using a limited set of predictors (i.e., satisfaction, organizational commitment, fairness, leader support, and conscientiousness), the authors also found that the five OCB facets had comparable relations with each predictor. Along similar lines, Podsakoff et al. (2009) reported that OCBI and OCBO had, for the most part, comparable relations with individual-level outcomes (e.g., performance ratings, reward recommendations, absenteeism).

Although the aforementioned findings suggest that operationalizing OCB via a subset of indicators (or even just one indicator) may be sufficient, this conclusion is tempered for two reasons. First, the ways in which the OCB facets and dimensions are typically measured may account for some inflation in the correlations between them. As mentioned earlier, the use of agreement scales opens the door for biases that can inflate relationships (Dalal, 2005; Spector et al., 2010). In addition, OCB data are typically provided by a single source and at one point in time, creating conditions that are ripe for common method variance (CMV; Podsakoff, MacKenzie, Lee, & Podsakoff, 2003). CMV is a problem for multidimensional constructs because it can bias relationships among the lower level indicators and the loadings of those indicators on the higher order construct (Johnson, Rosen, & Chang, 2011; Johnson, Rosen, Chang, Djurdjevic, & Taing, 2012).

Our review indicated that steps are often taken to minimize the presence and influence of CMV when examining relations of OCB with its antecedents and consequences. In particular, of the 351 studies that we reviewed, 217 (62%) utilized a procedural technique (e.g., by collecting data from different sources and/or at different times) to control for CMV, 26 (7%) utilized a statistical technique (e.g., confirmatory factor analysis or controlling for social desirability), and 52 (15%) used a combination of statistical and procedural techniques to address threats to validity presented by CMV. Unfortunately, however, a similar approach has not been applied to investigations of the lower order OCB facets and dimensions and the relations among them. There are a variety of method artifacts that might inflate the shared variance among the dimensions/facets (e.g., transient factors like rater mood and stable factors like rater biases [e.g., halo error] and implicit performance theories), thereby blurring the boundaries between the dimensions and facets. Unfortunately, no studies to date have explicitly examined what impact CMV has on higher order multidimensional models of OCB. However, empirical results from other domains (e.g., multidimensional personality variables) clearly indicate that controlling for CMV can significantly alter relations among lower order indicators and the nature of higher order constructs, even to the extent that an indicator may no longer load on the higher order construct (Johnson, Rosen, Chang, & Lin, 2015; Johnson, Rosen, & Djurdjevic, 2011).

A second reason to question the conclusion that the OCB indicators are interchangeable is that the evidence to date is based on limited number of dimensions/facets and correlates of OCB. For example, the LePine et al. (2002) review focused specifically on Organ's (1988) five-facet taxonomy of OCB (altruism, conscientiousness, sportsmanship, courtesy, and civic virtue). Any facets (e.g., generalized compliance and voice) or scales (e.g., Smith et al., 1983; Van Dyne & LePine, 1998) that did not cleanly map onto this taxonomy were excluded. However, as noted earlier, there are several commonly used OCB taxonomies and scales that deviate from Organ's five facets. Thus, excluding them overlooks a large proportion of the OCB literature. Moreover, there is empirical evidence for the distinctiveness among these other OCB dimensions and facets, including OCBI and OCBO (e.g., Dust, Resick, & Mawritz, 2014; Lee & Allen, 2002; Reiche et al., 2014) and helping, loyalty, and voice (e.g., Lin & Johnson, 2015; Van Dyne & LePine, 1998; Whiting, Podsakoff, & Pierce, 2008). Looking beyond the OCB facets and dimensions, the set of OCB correlates that have been considered is similarly limited. Based on the available data at the time of their study, LePine et al. (2002) were only able to consider relations of Organ's (1988) facets with five correlates: satisfaction, organizational commitment, fairness, leader support, and the personality trait of conscientiousness. OCB has, of course, other correlates, several of which show differential relations across dimensions/facets (e.g., prosocial value and organizational concern motives; e.g., Kim, Van Dyne, Kamdar, & Johnson, 2013; Takeuchi, Bolino, & Lin, 2015).

Interestingly, several correlates that LePine et al. (2002) considered are themselves multidimensional (e.g., satisfaction is comprised of task satisfaction, pay satisfaction, coworker satisfaction, etc.; fairness is comprised of distributive, procedural, and interactional fairness; organizational commitment includes affective, normative, and continuance commitment), which has implications for OCB–correlate relations. From a broadband–fidelity perspective, while the OCB facets may not show unique relations with the higher order construct (e.g., overall satisfaction), there may be differential prediction at the facet level (e.g., coworker satisfaction may correlate more strongly with courtesy than civic virtue). These differences are unfortunately obfuscated when relationships are aggregated to the higher level. In line with this idea, OCB facet–fairness relationships appear similar when aggregated across fairness types, as LePine et al. (2002) demonstrate. However, it is commonly found that procedural fairness has stronger relations with OCB facets that target the company (OCBO) and interactional fairness has stronger relations with facets that target individuals (OCBI; e.g., Aryee & Chay, 2001; Johnson, Selenta, & Lord, 2006; Masterson, Lewis, Goldman, & Taylor, 2000). If OCB–correlate relationships are not aggregated across the lower order facets of the correlates (e.g., across procedural and interactional justice, or across coworker and pay satisfaction), then the OCB dimensions/facets may show differential relations. Based on the current evidence, it is premature to conclude that the OCB dimensions/facets are interchangeable and that it is therefore appropriate to operationalize OCB via just one or a subset of indicators.

Another related issue concerning how OCB scales are used is the practice of modifying existing scales (e.g., rewording or removing items) without clearly reporting what changes were made. In about 20% of the studies we coded, the number of OCB items from established scales was cut (sometimes by half or more), yet researchers neglected to report what the final set of items was (e.g., Chun, Shin, Choi, & Kim, 2013; Johnson, Lanaj, & Barnes, 2014; Johnson et al., 2006; Konovsky & Organ, 1996). In a similar vein, a smaller proportion of studies (around 11%) created "Franken-scale" measures of OCB by culling together items from multiple existing scales (e.g., Binnewies, Sonnentag, & Mojza, 2009; Bolino, Turnley, Gilstrap, & Suazo, 2010; Lynch, Eisenberger, & Armeli, 1999). The problem in many of these cases is that it is not clear what items (or subscales) were included versus excluded, making it difficult to judge what exactly the aggregate OCB construct represents (e.g., overall OCB vs. a dimension of OCB [e.g., OCBO] vs. a single facet [e.g., sportsmanship]). If the OCB dimensions/facets are not interchangeable, then the observed results in these studies may have meaningfully differed if different combinations of items and/or subscales been included.

A final issue, albeit a less prevalent one (around 1% of studies coded), is the practice of using a single item to assess either overall OCB (e.g., Bledow & Frese, 2009; Leavitt, Fong, & Greenwald, 2011) or one of its dimensions (e.g., civic virtue; Koys, 2001). Besides the usual concerns with single-item measures (see Nunnally & Bernstein, 1994), doing so is especially problematic for multidimensional constructs. Single-item measures should be used only when the construct of interest is unidimensional and narrow, and when the single item fully captures the intended construct space and is not be subject to interpretations by respondents (Sackett & Larson, 1990). In the case of multidimensional constructs, longer, not shorter, scales are needed in order to measure each dimension reliably and validly (Smith, Fischer, & Fister, 2003).

Based on the preceding discussion, we offer five recommendations for improving OCB measurement. First, it is good practice to *measure OCB at the facet level using multiple items for each facet* (e.g., helping, civic virtue, sportsmanship, making constructive suggestions). Doing so enables researchers to explore whether observed findings are similar across the facets, yet still offers the flexibility to aggregate up to broader dimensions (e.g., OCBI and OCBO) or overall OCB when appropriate to do so (e.g., when there is a lack of differential effects across the facets). Second, as a way of focusing attention on specific instances of behavior and limiting bias owing to attitudes, intentions, and implicit theories, *OCB facets ought to be rated using frequency scales and not agreement scales.* Third, *the full set of items should be reported whenever an existing OCB scale is modified (e.g., items are rewritten or excluded) or items from multiple scales are combined into one scale.* Doing so not only promotes better understanding of the behavior under investigation but also facilitates future research aimed at replicating and extending findings. Fourth, to minimize overlap with other dimensions of job performance, *items that represent low levels of counterproductive (e.g., "Does not abuse the rights of others") and withdrawal (e.g., "Does not take undeserved work breaks") behaviors, and items that represent high levels of required in-role task behaviors (e.g., "Adheres to formal rules devised to maintain order") should be omitted from operationalizations of OCB.* Lastly, to promote more accurate interpretations of findings, *the labels used in text, tables, and figures should correspond to the specific facet that was measured (e.g., "altruism" or "spreading goodwill"); the broad "OCB" label should only be used when an overall score was formed via a comprehensive set of OCB facets.*

Use of Different Sources to Rate Organizational Citizenship Behaviors

OCBs are frequently measured using either self-reports or ratings from other sources, including ratings from supervisors and work peers. In our review of OCB studies, we found that researchers have shown a preference for other ratings of OCB over self-reports. Specifically, a total of 208 studies (59%) utilized either peer (21 studies), supervisor (182 studies), or coworker reports (5 studies), with most studies (i.e., 52%) focusing explicitly on supervisor ratings of OCB. Interestingly, a small portion of the studies that we reviewed (26 out of 351) included ratings of OCB from multiple sources (e.g., self and supervisor ratings, peer and supervisor ratings, peer and self-ratings) and we were able to locate a single study that relied on ratings derived from archival records (i.e., Bergeron, Shipp, Rosen, & Furst, 2013).

Unfortunately, to date, there is no consensus regarding the best source, or combination of sources, of OCB ratings. In addition, over the past three decades, questions have arisen about the appropriateness of different rating sources for assessing OCBs, and researchers have expressed concerns about the construct equivalence of OCB across sources (e.g., Morrison, 1994; Organ, 1990). In particular, proponents of self-reports argue that, as with other work behaviors (e.g., counterproductive work behavior), individual employees possess the greatest knowledge of their own behaviors and, therefore, self-ratings of OCBs are likely to be the most accurate among the various sources considered in prior research (Allen, Barnard, Rush, & Russell, 2000). Moreover, different ratings sources are likely to observe different forms of OCB (i.e., supervisors are likely to observe voice behavior, whereas coworkers are more likely to observe altruistic behaviors aimed at helping other employees). Thus, a single source other than the self is unlikely to be able to accurately report on the total amount of OCB enacted by a particular individual. Ratings from sources other than the self may also be problematic because they are subject to the halo effect, which is an appraisal error that occurs when a rater generalizes from one performance domain to another (e.g., a supervisor assumes that an employee who is above average in task performance is also above average in terms of helping behaviors directed towards coworkers), and rater's implicit theories might also serve to inflate observed correlations among behavioral reports (Bolino, Varela, Bande, & Turnley, 2006; Dalal, 2005; Spector & Che, 2014; Turnipseed & Rassuli, 2005).

Self-ratings of OCBs are, however, not without their own problems. For example, Organ and Ryan (1995) advised against the use of self-report ratings of OCB because such ratings are inherently subjective and, based on their meta-analytic findings, appear to provide unstable assessments of OCB relative to measures taken from other sources. Consistent with this perspective, self-ratings are often viewed as problematic because social desirability biases and self-enhancement motives have the potential to lead individuals to overreport behaviors that are viewed favorably by others (Allen et al., 2000; Ashford, 1989; Carpenter et al., 2014; Chan, 2009; Podsakoff, MacKenzie, & Podsakoff, 2012). In addition, because OCBs are often examined in relation to other self-reported attitudes (e.g., job satisfaction, organizational commitment) and behaviors (e.g., task performance, CWB), self-ratings of OCB may be impacted by common rater effects (i.e., those effects that result from implicit theories, consistency motifs, acquiescence/disacqueiscence biases, and/or mood states of a particular rater), which have the potential to inflate the magnitude of observed correlations between OCBs and other self-reported constructs (Podsakoff, Whiting, Welsh, & Mai, 2013).

Given the purported benefits and limitations associated with different OCB rating sources, there is little agreement regarding which source is most appropriate for assessing OCBs. Fortunately, however, several recent studies have attempted to assess the validity of the aforementioned rating source concerns, and their findings can be used to inform our discussion of why and when different sources are most appropriate. We discuss this research next and, in light of recent findings in this literature, consider the extent to which rating sources matter in terms of the conclusions that can be drawn from OCB research.

Vandenberg et al., (2005) used a latent variable approach to assess the equivalence of different OCB rating sources (i.e., self, supervisor, and subordinate raters). Consistent with prior research (e.g., Morrison, 1994), and the authors' expectation that rating sources might not be equivalent, Vandenberg et al.'s (2005) results yielded weak (i.e., < .30) cross-source correlations among the four OCB dimensions that were considered. In addition, results indicated that the factor loadings of the four dimensions on a latent OCB construct were not equivalent across rating sources, suggesting that OCB items were calibrated in different ways to their respective true scores by self, supervisor, and subordinate raters (Vandenberg et al., 2005). In supplemental analyses, Vandenberg et al. (2005) also found that the factor structure underlying manager and subordinate responses was simpler than that of self-ratings, such that self-raters discriminated among the four dimensions of OCB, whereas managers' and subordinates' responses were best characterized by three factors. These findings are consistent with what would be expected if a halo effect were operating, wherein observers tend to evaluate behavior in more global ways (Organ, 1988; Vandenberg et al., 2005).

Carpenter et al. (2014) conducted a meta-analysis that assessed three lines of evidence that could be used to determine whether self- and other-ratings are interchangeable measures of OCB. The first line of evidence considered the extent to which inflation by self-raters presents a significant problem for OCB measurement, which Carpenter et al. (2014) assessed by applying Cohen's (1992) benchmarks (i.e., small: d = .20; medium: d = .50; large: d = 1.0) for interpreting effect sizes of standardized mean differences. Results indicated that self-raters reported higher levels of OCB relative to other raters, but the magnitude of this difference was relatively small (i.e., < .40), a finding that is consistent with previous research that has investigated rater effects (e.g., Allen et al., 2000). Carpenter et al. (2014) also observed that self-raters reported levels of OCBO (OCBI) similar to supervisor (coworker) raters, suggesting that inflated ratings may not be due to social desirability, but rather may exist because employees have more complete knowledge of their own OCBs relative to others. Next, Carpenter et al. (2014) considered the relationship between self- and other-rated OCBs and found a modest self–other relationship (ρ = .26). Therefore, Carpenter et al. (2014) considered a third line of evidence, which pertained to whether self- and other-rated OCBs have similar relationships with common correlates. Results indicated that self- and other-ratings have similar relationships with variables within OCBs nomological network, though some important exceptions were observed (i.e., the correlations between other ratings of OCB and other ratings of task performance and CWB were substantially larger than the correlations between self-ratings of OCB and self-ratings of task performance and CWB). The latter finding indicates that rater biases, such as halo error, may play a large role in the rating of behavioral correlates, a finding that is consistent with prior research (i.e., Spector et al., 2010; Dalal, 2005), which has considered how rating sources affect relationships between OCB and CWB. Based on these three lines of evidence, Carpenter et al. (2014) concluded that inferences from OCB research are unlikely to be influenced by the source that is used to rate OCBs in a particular study, though they do suggest that future studies utilize different sources to address threats to validity that may be presented by halo error in studies that examine performance correlates.

A recent study by Podsakoff et al. (2013) further addresses common source issues in this literature. In this study, the authors considered the extent to which common method variance has the potential to bias OCB research by performing a mixed-effects meta-analysis that allowed for the investigation of independent effects of three sources of CMV (i.e., common raters, shared item characteristics, and measurement context) on the relationship between OCB and performance evaluations. With regard to rating source effects, results demonstrated that common rating sources bias correlations between OCB and performance evaluations, indicating that studies with a common rater reported correlations that were .22 higher than studies that utilized different rating sources for OCB and performance evaluations. Results also indicated that in studies using a common rater, correlations were .16 higher in studies that utilized the same number of scale anchor points when compared to common rater studies in which a different number of anchor points were used across measures. Overall, therefore, Podsakoff et al.'s (2013) findings provide convincing evidence that utilizing common raters has the potential to bias observed relationships between OCB and other performance behaviors. In addition, a critical takeaway point from this study is that if researchers must rely on the same source ratings, then it would behoove them to vary the number of scale anchor points to attenuate the influence of common rater effects.

Taken together, this set of studies substantiates previously identified concerns (i.e., that ratings may not be equivalent across sources [Organ, 1990], that ratings from sources other than the self may be influenced by halo effects [Werner, 1994], and that common method variance may influence observed relationships between OCB and other constructs that are rated by the same sources [Organ & Ryan, 1995]) about OCB rating sources. Moreover, these studies provide useful insight that can be used to guide future research on OCB. In particular, given that self-raters are the only source that accurately discriminates between different dimensions of OCB and performance (Vandenberg et al., 2005), self-ratings of OCB may be the most accurate in terms of capturing the criterion space (i.e., behaviors "that support the social and psychological environment in which task performance takes place" Organ, 1997, p. 31). Interestingly, however, it does not appear that rating source alone makes a difference, as Carpenter et al.'s (2014) findings suggest that conclusions from research would likely be the same regardless of whether the self or another member of the organization is rating OCB. At the same time, however, there is strong evidence that common source effects pose a significant threat to the validity of research findings in OCB research (Podsakoff et al., 2013). Thus, it is not so much the source of OCB ratings that matters in terms of the inferences that can be drawn from a particular study, but rather the extent to which researchers rely on the same source for ratings of different constructs. This issue is particularly problematic in research that considers relationships between OCB and other performance-related job behaviors, such as task performance and counterproductive work behaviors (Carpenter et al., 2014; Podsakoff et al., 2013).

Based on the preceding discussion, we offer several recommendations. First, self-ratings of OCBs are not inherently problematic or inaccurate and may, in fact, prove to be the most comprehensive measure of OCB (Vandenberg et al., 2005). However, given the threats to validity posed by common source effects, *researchers should carefully design OCB studies so that, when possible, different raters assess OCBs and other focal constructs*. This will serve to minimize the extent to which common method variance poses an alternative explanation for the results of a given study.

Second, if acquiring ratings from multiple sources is not possible (e.g., access to different raters is limited by the organization in which data is being collected) or appropriate (e.g., when a researcher is interested in investigating the relationship between a personality trait or personally held attitude and OCB), then *steps should be taken to reduce the validity threats presented by common source effects*. In this regard, we recommend against using statistical remedies for CMV (e.g., partialing out social desirability from responses or modeling an unmeasured latent method construct), as such techniques are relatively ineffective at reducing the influence of CMV on observed relationships (Johnson, Rosen, & Djurdjevic, 2011). Rather, we recommend that researchers incorporate a priori procedural and design-related remedies that are aimed at either removing different common source influences (e.g., temporal separation via the measurement of different constructs at different points in time) or increasing respondents' motivation to exert cognitive effort to process information presented in scale items (e.g., minimizing the repetitiveness of scales by varying the number of anchor points used for the focal constructs in a study; Podsakoff et al., 2013).

Finally, to ensure the ecological validity of ratings, *when raters other than the self are used to assess OCB, there should be a match between the type of OCB being rated and the source of the ratings*, given that certain rating sources will be better positioned to observe some types of OCB relative to others. For example, supervisors should provide ratings of OCBO (e.g., voice), because they are in the best position to observe these behaviors, whereas subordinates or work peers are in the best position to observe OCBI (e.g., altruistic actions directed toward coworkers). Moreover, an important implication of our review is that when sources other than the self provide OCB ratings, multiple rating sources (e.g., supervisor and coworker) are likely needed to provide a comprehensive measure of the OCBs enacted by an individual, as reliance on a single source (e.g., supervisor) will only be useful for capturing the specific aspect of the OCB domain that a particular rater has the opportunity to observe (e.g., OCBO).

Nature of the Higher Order Organizational Citizenship Behavior Construct

One measurement and modeling question that looms large is "What is the exact nature of the higher order multidimensional OCB construct?" Although it is clear that OCB is a multidimensional construct comprised of several dimensions and facets (as we reviewed in the first section), what is less clear is how these dimensions and facets combine together and what sort of relations they have with the higher order OCB construct (Law, Wong, & Mobley, 1998). There are at least two possibilities. One possibility is that causality flows from the higher order OCB construct to the lower order dimensions and facets, such that the lower order variables (labeled "effects indicators") are manifestations of the higher order construct (labeled a "superordinate construct"). A common example of a superordinate construct is general cognitive ability, which is thought to drive people's performance on various ability measures, such as quantitative, verbal, and reasoning abilities. Another possibility is that causality flows up from the lower order dimensions and facets (labeled "causal indicators") to the higher order OCB construct (labeled an "aggregate construct"). According to this view, OCB can be thought of as a label that encompasses a set of behaviors that share a common definition (e.g., discretionary actions that contribute to the social and psychological context at work; Motowidlo, 2000). An example of an aggregate construct is overall job performance, which is a combination of various desirable (e.g., in-role task completion and cooperative behaviors) and undesirable (e.g., counterproductive and withdrawal behaviors) work behaviors.

Correctly specifying the nature of the higher order OCB construct is important for both theoretical and statistical reasons. In terms of the former, whether OCB is a superordinate or aggregate construct has implications for the nomological network of the lower order dimensions and facets, including the extent to which they are interrelated and the uniqueness of their antecedents and consequences (Johnson et al., 2012; Law et al., 1998). Thus, construct validity hinges in part on correctly specifying the nature of OCB (LePine et al., 2002). Whether OCB is a superordinate or aggregate construct also has statistical implications for how observed scores are calculated, modeled, and evaluated. Failure to accurately specify the nature of the higher order construct can result in biased parameter estimates and increased Type II error rates (Edwards, 2001; MacKenzie, Podsakoff, & Jarvis, 2005). Next we review some key theoretical and statistical considerations of specifying OCB as a superordinate or aggregate construct.

If OCB is a superordinate construct, then it is modeled such that the paths point from higher order OCB to its lower level dimension/facets, and the latent OCB construct is represented solely by the shared variance among the indicators. Conceptually, these effects indicators should be interchangeable, given that the higher order construct is the primary cause of them. Thus, a statistical requirement is that a large proportion of overlapping variance exists among the lower order dimensions and facets, which translates into high intercorrelations and high levels of internal consistency reliability among the indicators (MacKenzie et al., 2005). This requirement can be tested using factor analysis to demonstrate that indicators have sufficiently high loadings (e.g., $\lambda > .70$) on higher order OCB. Composite reliability (i.e., the internal consistency of the higher order construct) and average variance extracted (i.e., the proportion of variance explained by the latent construct relative to the amount of variance owing to measurement error) are also useful for assessing the viability of superordinate models (Johnson et al., 2012). Composite reliability is deemed adequate when it is greater than .70, and construct validity is supported when average variance extracted is greater than .50 (Fornell & Larcker, 1981). In addition to factor loading cutoffs, composite reliability, and average variance extracted, indices of model fit (e.g., root mean square error of approximation, comparative fit index, and standardized root mean square residual) can be used to evaluate superordinate models.

If OCB is an aggregate construct, then the paths point from the lower order dimensions/facets to the higher order construct. In this case, the latent OCB construct is comprised of not only the shared variance among the indictors but also the variance that is unique to each dimension/facet. Conceptually, the indicators are not interchangeable with one another and the presence of high intercorrelations among them is, in fact, not necessary or even desirable. Rather, it is preferable that each dimension/facet taps into nonredundant aspects of the aggregate OCB construct (Diamantopoulos & Siguaw, 2006). Instead of high intercorrelations, a more appropriate benchmark to evaluate an aggregate construct is to verify that it captures the majority of variance in its set of indicators, which can be estimated via the adequacy coefficient (Edwards, 2001). This statistic, which is used for canonical correlation analysis, indicates the proportion of variance extracted by a canonical variate from the set of original variables (Thompson, 1984). For example, an adequacy coefficient of .70 signifies that at least 70% of the variance in the dimensions/facets was extracted by the aggregate OCB construct. In addition to the adequacy coefficient, aggregate models can also be evaluated via model fit indices.

The aforementioned discussion of superordinate and aggregate constructs naturally begs the question: "What type of higher order construct is OCB?" Unfortunately, answers to this question are lacking because no primary studies have directly examined this issue to date. Although LePine et al.'s (2002) meta-analysis explored the extent to which the OCB facets are interchangeable (which is a criterion of superordinate constructs), their review involved a limited set of facets and correlates, and the primary studies that were included were not intended to test the nature of the higher order OCB construct. That is, the authors of the primary studies did not compare the relative fit of superordinate and aggregate OCB models nor did they take steps to control for common method variance among the OCB dimensions and facets, making it difficult to reach any definitive conclusions about the nature of OCB on the basis of their findings. Reaching conclusions about the nature of OCB is also made more difficult by the numerous ways OCB is operationalized and modeled, as we reviewed in the first section. Although multidimensional constructs ought to be modeled as latent constructs to avoid confounding the unique and error variances for each indicator (Edwards, 2001; MacKenzie et al., 2005), the majority of studies included in our review (83%) represented OCB via summed scale scores. This practice of summing scale scores prohibits any test of the nature of the higher order OCB construct. In 17% of studies where OCB is modeled as a latent construct, it is almost always specified as a superordinate construct with effects indicators yet without providing support for such a conceptualization.

An obvious conclusion of this review is that a glaring omission exists in the OCB measurement literature when it comes to the nature of the higher order OCB construct. There is a need for direct tests to verify whether OCB is more appropriately modeled as a superordinate or aggregate construct. Interestingly, the answer might turn out to be both, depending on the focal level in the OCB hierarchy. As discussed earlier, OCB can be represented hierarchically with overall OCB at the top, OCBI and OCBO dimensions in the middle, and behavioral facets (e.g., helping, voice) at the bottom. It is possible that at the higher levels, the OCB variables (overall OCB, OCBI, and OCBO) are aggregate constructs that function as labels for related yet distinct types of behaviors. Consistent with this view, the dimensions that comprise overall OCB and the facets that comprise OCBI and OCBO tend to be empirically separate (e.g., Lee & Allen, 2002; Lin & Johnson, 2015; Van Dyne & LePine, 1998). However, at lower levels, the facets (e.g., helping) may be superordinate constructs that reflect manifestations of interchangeable behaviors (e.g., helping others who have heavy workloads, who have been absent, who are new to the company, etc.). Whether or not OCB operates as a superordinate or aggregate construct may be influenced by other factors as well. For example, rating source can affect the extent to which OCB dimensions and facets are distinguishable, such that ratings by nonself sources (e.g., supervisors, coworkers) may blur the lines between different dimensions and facets owing to biases (e.g., halo) and implicit performance theories.

We therefore call for research *that directly assesses the nature of OCB across different hierarchical levels (overall vs. dimensions vs. facets) and across different sources (self vs. nonself and subjective vs. objective).* To this end, we offer four recommendations. First, given its status as a multidimensional construct, OCB ought to be modeled as a latent construct rather than operationalized as a summed scale score. The latter approach (summed scale score) fails to distinguish between the shared, unique, and error variance components underlying OCB. Second, specify in advance the empirical criteria that will be used to evaluate the superordinate construct (e.g., cutoff values for factor loadings, composite reliabilities, average variance extracted, etc.) and the aggregate construct (e.g., cutoff values for interindicator correlations, adequacy coefficients, etc.). There are several useful resources that detail the assumptions and criteria of superordinate and aggregate constructs (e.g., Edwards, 2001; Johnson et al., 2012; Law et al., 1998; MacCallum & Browne, 1993; MacKenzie et al., 2005). Third, treat the presumed nature of latent OCB constructs as an explicit hypothesis and empirically test it by evaluating the relative fit of a superordinate construct vis-à-vis an aggregate construct. Lastly, when investigating the nature of multidimensional constructs, it is necessary to rule out alternative explanations for the emergence of the higher order construct (Johnson et al., 2012). Given that data on the OCB dimensions and facets are typically provided by a single source at one point in time, one explanation may be CMV (Podsakoff et al., 2003). Thus, techniques should be employed that reduce or control for the presence of CMV among OCB dimensions and facets. There are several options for how to do so (e.g.,

Podsakoff et al., 2003; Richardson, Simmering, & Sturman, 2009; Williams, Hartman, & Cavazotte, 2010), but the preferred techniques are procedural ones that target causes of CMV rather than statistical ones that target consequences of CMV (Johnson, Rosen, & Djurdjevic, 2011; Podsakoff et al., 2012).

Emerging Methodological and Measurement Issues

During the course of our review, we identified a number of emerging methodological issues that are relevant to OCBs. These issues pertain to nonindependence, levels of analysis, and the use of control variables in OCB research. Each of these issues has the potential to influence the inferences that are drawn from OCB research and, thus, have important implications for how OCBs are measured and modeled.

In applied research, when a source other than the self provides ratings of a focal employee's behavior, it is not uncommon for that source to provide ratings for multiple participants within the same study (e.g., supervisors are often asked to rate the OCBs of multiple members of their work group). As a result, the data are structured so that employees are nested within supervisors and the observations are no longer independent. In this scenario, nonindependence of ratings is a concern because rater effects may be responsible for observed differences between participants, particularly those who have different supervisors. From a statistical perspective, nonindependence can bias standard error estimates if it is ignored and, thus, can lead to erroneous conclusions (i.e., Type 1 errors) about how various constructs relate to one another (Bliese, 2002). It is, therefore, important for researchers to acknowledge violations of the independence assumption when it is present and to take steps to control for these issues in their data (Kenny & Judd, 1986). Fortunately, there are a number of ways to address nonindependence. For example, ANOVA can be used to determine the extent to which violations of the nonindependence assumption represents a problem, in terms of the extent to which variance exists within versus between participants rated by different supervisors. In addition, techniques (e.g., multilevel random coefficient models) have been developed for analyzing data when nonindependence is a problem (i.e., when there is greater variance between versus within raters).

To determine the extent to which nonindependence is an issue in the OCB literature, we considered the extent to which authors reported data where nonindependence might be an issue. In 212 out of 351 (60.4%) of the studies that we reviewed, nonindependence of observations was a concern (i.e., observations were nested within raters). Of the 212 studies that violated the assumption of independence, less than half (i.e., 101; 48%) acknowledged this issue or took steps to address it. This has important implications for the conclusions that can be drawn from this body of research, particularly the meta-analyses that have utilized these studies to summarize and test key aspects of this literature. Therefore, we recommend that OCB researchers (a) *explicitly acknowledge when raters have provided multiple ratings of participants within a study*, (b) *take steps to assess whether violating the independence assumption is problematic* (e.g., ANOVA; Kenny, 2014), and (c) *utilize multilevel modeling techniques to reduce the probability of Type 1 errors when OCB ratings for individuals are not independent* (Bliese, 2000; Kenny, Mannetti, Peirro, Livi, & Kashy, 2002).

A related issue pertains to the level of analysis at which OCBs are being studied. Traditionally, researchers have focused on OCBs of individual employees and examined factors that explain between-person differences in OCBs. However, with the growing popularity of experience sampling methodology (ESM), researchers have started to consider the processes that explain within-person variation OCBs. For example, Dalal et al. (2009) demonstrated that OCBs vary considerably within individuals and that this within-person variation is explained by affect. Unfortunately, because they involve repeated measures of behaviors that may not frequently occur, ESM studies typically place constraints on the length of scales that are used and the types of questions that can be asked. As such, the majority of ESM studies that we identified (e.g., Dalal et al., 2009; Spence, Brown, Keeping, & Lian, 2014; Spence, Ferris, Brown, & Heller, 2011) used global measures of OCB that represented abridged measures of existing scales or new measures that had not been previously validated.

Thus, while these studies have yielded interesting findings, and certainly allow researchers to investigate a novel phenomenon (i.e., within-person variation in OCB), the measures used have some of the same operational issues that we discussed in the first section of our chapter. Moreover, the abridged scales used in ESM studies have, by and large, not been developed and validated following the same procedures used for the scales from which they were derived. Therefore, we recommend that ESM researchers take steps to ensure that the measures of OCB that they use are appropriate for examining the phenomenon, as a potential criticism of this research is that because the ESM measures are different from the scales used in more traditional studies of OCB, then they may not be assessing the same construct. Therefore, as with more traditional studies, it is important for ESM researchers to provide a full description of their scales. If they are abridged versions of previously developed scales, then authors need to report which items were dropped and why. For new and abridged scales, *authors ought to provide evidence supporting the validity of the measures that they use* in order to ensure that what they are measuring does, in fact, represent OCB.

Researchers have also started to look at OCBs as a group-level phenomenon (e.g., Bommer et al., 2007; Ehrhart & Naumann, 2004; Nielsen, Hrivnak, & Shaw, 2009; Podsakoff, Ahearne, & MacKenzie, 1997). As with any study, it is important for the measures of constructs in group-level studies to be consistent with the theory, such that researchers can have confidence that the group-level constructs that they are examining exist at the hypothesized level of analysis. To date, studies have typically either aggregated supervisor ratings of OCB to create a group-level OCB construct derived from ratings of members' OCBs or utilized expert raters (i.e., a supervisor once-removed) to provide ratings of group OCBs utilizing a modified scale wherein items from an existing scale are changed to reference a group rather than an individual (Bommer et al., 2007). One issue with the former approach is that rater effects (e.g., the tendency of individual supervisors to systematically inflate or deflate ratings) may explain observed group-level effects. Thus, having an expert (e.g., supervisors once-removed) provide ratings of group OCBs may represent a more appropriate means of assessing OCB as a group-level construct.

Alternatively, individuals within groups could provide assessments of their work group and this information could be aggregated to develop a measure of unit-level OCB that could be linked to other unit-level phenomena (e.g., Ehrhart, Bliese, & Thomas, 2006; Podsakoff et al., 1997), assuming that greater variance of OCBs exists between, rather than within, the work units. Likewise, researchers could ask individuals within groups to report their own OCBs, or those of individual group members (i.e., individuals, and not the work group, serve as the referent), and this information could be aggregated to the group level to develop a measure of the group context. Interestingly, recent research (Podsakoff, Maynes, Whiting, & Podsakoff, 2015) has demonstrated that the referent used (i.e., the group itself versus individual group members) plays an important role in determining the type of information (i.e., frequency of voice events versus the proportion of group members exhibiting voice) that raters use when assessing voice behavior in collectives. Given that a number of important empirical and theoretical questions are yet to be addressed in this domain, *we recommend that researchers focus on developing measures that are consistent with their theory*, in terms of the level of analysis, and that appropriate rating sources (e.g., self, supervisor, expert rater) and referents (i.e., the self, individual members of the collective, or the group) are used (and justification is provided for the use of specific sources and referents) so that measures of OCBs in multilevel studies are appropriate for addressing the research questions being examined in this emerging stream of research.

Finally, our review indicated that a number of different control variables have been included in OCB research and, consistent with other topics in the organizational sciences (Becker, 2005), the inclusion and treatment of control variables has been inconsistent in the OCB literature. In particular, 229 out of the 351 (65%) studies that we reviewed included at least one control variable, with the average number of control variables used per study being 2.73. Of the studies that reported using control variables, 48 out of the 229 studies that included control variables (21%) reported that the results changed as a result of adding or removing the control variables, 28 out of these 229 studies (12%) reported no change in results as a result of adding or removing control variables, and a majority of these studies (i.e., 153 out of 229; 67%) did not report whether adding or removing control variables had an influence on the results. Demographic characteristics were the most popular control variables in the studies that we used, with 163 studies controlling for gender (46%), 150 controlling for age (43%), 141 controlling for tenure (40%), 57 controlling for education (16%), and 14 controlling for ethnicity (4%). In addition, several studies also controlled for other theoretically relevant constructs, with justice (17, 5%), negative affect (15, 4%), and leader–member exchange (9, 3%) being the most common in this category.

It is unclear to what extent control variables (either their inclusion or exclusion) have influenced the results of prior OCB research. Nonetheless, the aforementioned study statistics provide evidence,

Table 23.1 Recommendations for Measuring and Modeling Organizational Citizenship Behaviors (OCBs)

1. Measure OCB at the facet level, using multiple items for each facet
2. Utilize frequency, not agreement, scales for rating OCB facets
3. Report the full set of items when an existing OCB scale is modified
4. Omit items that overlap with other dimensions of job performance when operationalizing OCB
5. Use labels that correspond with the individual facets measured when a comprehensive set of OCB facets are not used to create an overall score
6. Design studies so that different raters assess OCBs and other focal constructs
7. Incorporate procedural and design-related remedies to limit the influence of common source effects when different rating sources are not available
8. Ensure an appropriate match between the type of OCB being rated and the source of ratings
9. Directly assess the nature of OCB across different hierarchical levels and sources
10. Explicitly acknowledge, assess, and control for nonindependence in OCB ratings
11. Provide a full description of validity evidence to support the use of abridged scales
12. Ensure that measures and measurement sources align with theory
13. Report when, how, and why control variables were included in research

limited albeit, that control variables have the potential to influence results reported in the OCB literature. Owing to the cumulative nature of findings in the organizational sciences, this represents an important problem because it makes it difficult for researchers to make cross-study comparisons (i.e., researchers may be comparing apples to oranges if they are comparing results from a study that included several control variables to a study that included no control variables). Therefore, following from Becker (2005), *we recommend that OCB researchers be more explicit with regard to when, how, and why control variables are used in their studies.* In order to do so, researchers will need to (a) provide a clear rationale for including specific control variables, (b) conduct theoretically appropriate tests of control variables (e.g., if the rationale for controlling for gender is that the OCBs of men are more influenced by role stressors relative to women, then instead of partiallng out the main effects of gender, a researcher should control for the moderating effects of this control variable), and (c) report results in a more systematic way, such that if researchers find out that their results are not influenced by the inclusion of control variables, then they should note this (i.e., that results were not influenced by the inclusion/exclusion of control variables) and report the more parsimonious set of results that does not include control variables; when control variables have an influence on results, researchers should report both sets of findings and discuss the differing sets of results (Becker, 2005).

Conclusion

We sought to identify and evaluate measurement and modeling trends in the OCB literature. To this end, we conducted a 30-year review of OCB research published in top-tier management and psychology journals. This review indicated that (a) there is a great deal of variation in terms of how OCBs are operationalized, (b) OCBs are frequently measured using different sources (e.g., the self, supervisors, peers), (c) the higher order nature of the OCB construct is not well understood, and (d) there are a number of contemporary methodological issues (e.g., nonindependence of ratings, within-person and multilevel assessments, inclusion and reporting of control variables) that should be considered when conducting OCB research. Based on our review, we provide a set of prescriptive recommendations (see Table 23.1) for measuring and modeling OCB going forward. Following these steps will serve to develop a more coherent body of OCB research that serves to better inform our understanding of this important organizational phenomenon.

Note

1. The items included on Lee and Allen's (2002) scale were developed based in part on existing scales (e.g., Moorman & Blakely, 1995; Williams & Anderson, 1991).

References

Allen, T. D., Barnard, S., Rush, M. C., & Russell, J. E. (2000). Ratings of organizational citizenship behavior: Does the source make a difference? *Human Resource Management Review, 10*, 97–114.

Ang, S., Van Dyne, L., & Begley, T. (2003). The employment relationships of foreign workers versus local employees: A field study of organizational justice, job satisfaction, performance, and OCB. *Journal of Organizational Behavior, 24*, 561–583.

Aryee, S., & Chay, Y. W. (2001). Workplace justice, citizenship behavior, and turnover intentions in a union context: Examining the mediating role of perceived union support and union instrumentality. *Journal of Applied Psychology, 86,* 154–160.

Ashford, S. J. (1989). Self-assessments in organizations: A literature review and integrative model. *Research in Organizational Behavior, 11,* 133–174.

Becker, T. E. (2005). Potential problems in the statistical control of variables in organizational research: A qualitative analysis with recommendations. *Organizational Research Methods, 8*(3), 274–289.

Bennett, R. J., & Robinson, S. L. (2000). Development of a measure of workplace deviance. *Journal of Applied Psychology, 85*(3), 349–360.

Bergeron, D. M., Shipp, A. J., Rosen, B., & Furst, S. A. (2013). Organizational citizenship behavior and career outcomes: The cost of being a good citizen. *Journal of Management,* 39, 958–984.

Binnewies, C., Sonnentag, S., & Mojza, E. (2009). Daily performance at work: Feeling recovered in the morning as a predictor of day-level job performance. *Journal of Organizational Behavior, 30,* 67–93.

Bledow, R., & Frese, M. (2009). A situational judgment test of personal initiative and its relationship to performance. *Personnel Psychology, 62,* 229–258.

Bliese, P. D. (2000). Within-group agreement, non-independence, and reliability: Implications for data aggregation and analysis. In K. J. Klein & S. W. Kozlowski (Eds.), *Multilevel theory, research, and methods in organizations: Foundations, extensions and new directions* (pp. 349–381). San Francisco, CA: Jossey-Bass.

Bliese, P. D. (2002). Multilevel random coefficient modeling in organizational research. In F. Drasgow & N. Schmitt (Eds.), *Measuring and analyzing behavior in organizations* (pp. 401–445). San Francisco, CA: Jossey-Bass.

Bolino, M. C., Turnley, W. H., Gilstrap, J. B., & Suazo, M. M. (2010). Citizenship under pressure: What's a "good soldier" to do? *Journal of Organizational Behavior, 31,* 835–855.

Bolino, M. C., Varela, J. A., Bande, B., & Turnley, W. H. (2006). The impact of impression-management tactics on supervisor ratings of organizational citizenship behavior. *Journal of Organizational Behavior, 27,* 281–297.

Bommer, W. H., Dierdorff, E. C., & Rubin, R. S. (2007). Does prevalence mitigate relevance? The moderating effect of group-level OCB on employee performance. *Academy of Management Journal, 50,* 1481–1494.

Borman, W. C., & Motowidlo, S. M. (1993). Expanding the criterion domain to include elements of contextual performance. In N. Schmitt & W. C. Borman (Eds.), *Personnel selection in organizations* (pp. 71–98). San Francisco, CA: Jossey-Bass.

Campbell, J. P. (1990). Modeling the performance prediction problem in industrial and organizational psychology. In M. D. Dunnette & L. M. Hough (Eds.), *Handbook of industrial and organizational psychology* (Vol. 1, 2nd ed., pp. 687–732). Palo Alto, CA: Consulting Psychologists Press.

Carpenter, N. C., Berry, C. M., & Houston, L. (2014). A meta-analytic comparison of self-reported and other-reported organizational citizenship behavior. *Journal of Organizational Behavior, 35,* 547–574.

Chan, D. (2009). So why ask me? Are self-report data really that bad? In C. E. Lance & R. J. Vandenberg (Eds.), *Statistical and methodological myths and urban legends: Doctrine, verity, and fable in the organizational and social sciences* (pp. 311–338). New York, NY: Routledge.

Chen, X. P., Hui, C., & Sego, D. J. (1998). The role of organizational citizenship behavior in turnover: Conceptualization and preliminary tests of key hypotheses. *Journal of Applied Psychology, 83,* 922–931.

Chun, J. S., Shin, Y., Choi, J. N., & Kim, M. S. (2013). How does corporate ethics contribute to firm financial performance? The mediating role of collective organizational commitment and organizational citizenship behavior. *Journal of Management, 39,* 853–877.

Cohen, J. (1992). A power primer. *American Psychologist, 112,* 155–159.

Dalal, R. S. (2005). A meta-analysis of the relationship between organizational citizenship behavior and counterproductive work behavior. *Journal of Applied Psychology, 90,* 1241–1255.

Dalal, R. S., Lam, H., Weiss, H. M., Welch, E. R., & Hulin, C. L. (2009). A within-person approach to work behavior and performance: Concurrent and lagged citizenship–counterproductivity associations, and dynamic relationships with affect and overall job performance. *Academy of Management Journal, 52,* 1051–1066.

Diamantopoulos, A., & Siguaw, J. A. (2006). Formative versus reflective indicators in organizational measure development: A comparison and empirical illustration. *British Journal of Management, 17,* 263–282.

Dust, S. B., Resick, C. J., & Mawritz, M. B. (2014). Transformational leadership, psychological empowerment, and the moderating role of mechanistic–organic contexts. *Journal of Organizational Behavior, 35,* 413–433.

Edwards, J. R. (2001). Multidimensional constructs in organizational behavior research: An integrative analytical framework. *Organizational Research Methods, 4,* 144–192.

Ehrhart, M. G., Bliese, P. D., & Thomas, J. L. (2006). Unit-level OCB and unit effectiveness: Examining the incremental effect of helping behavior. *Human Performance, 19*(2), 159–173.

Ehrhart, M. G., & Naumann, S. E. (2004). Organizational citizenship behavior in work groups: a group norms approach. *Journal of Applied Psychology, 89*(6), 960–974.

Farh, J. L., Earley, P. C., & Lin, S. C. (1997). Impetus for action: A cultural analysis of justice and organizational citizenship behavior in Chinese society. *Administrative Science Quarterly, 42*(3), 421–444.

Fornell, C., & Larcker, D. F. (1981). Evaluating structural equation models with unobservable variables and measurement error. *Journal of Marketing Research, 18,* 39–50.

Fox, S., & Spector, P. E. (1999). A model of work frustration–aggression. *Journal of Organizational Behavior, 20*(6), 915–931.

George, J. M., & Brief, A. P. (1992). Feeling good-doing good: A conceptual analysis of the mood at work–organizational spontaneity relationship. *Psychological Bulletin, 112,* 310–329.

George, E., Chattopadhyay, P., & Zhang, L. L. (2012). Helping hand or competition? The moderating influence of perceived upward mobility on the relationship between blended work-groups and employee attitudes and behaviors. *Organization Science, 23,* 355–372.

Johnson, R. E., Lanaj, K., & Barnes, C. M. (2014). The good and bad of being fair: Effects of procedural and interactional justice behaviors on actors' regulatory resources. *Journal of Applied Psychology, 99,* 635–650.

Johnson, R. E., Rosen, C. C., & Chang, C.-H. (2011). To aggregate or not to aggregate: Steps for developing and validating higher-order multidimensional constructs. *Journal of Business and Psychology, 26,* 241–248.

Johnson, R. E., Rosen, C. C., Chang, C.-H., Djurdjevic, E., & Taing, M. U. (2012). Recommendations for improving the construct clarity of higher-order multidimensional constructs. *Human Resource Management Review, 22,* 62–72.

Johnson, R. E., Rosen, C. C., Chang, C.-H., & Lin, S.-H. (2015). Getting to the core of locus of control: Is it a core evaluation of the self or the environment? *Journal of Applied Psychology, 100,* 1568–1578.

Johnson, R. E., Rosen, C. C., & Djurdjevic, E. (2011). Assessing the impact of common method variance on higher-order multidimensional constructs. *Journal of Applied Psychology, 96,* 744–761.

Johnson, R. E., Selenta, C., & Lord, R. G. (2006). When organizational justice and the self-concept meet: Consequences for the organization and its members. *Organizational Behavior and Human Decision Processes, 99,* 175–201.

Katz, D., & Kahn, R. L. (1978). *The social psychology of organizations.* New York, NY: Wiley.

Kenny, D. A. (2014). Dyadic analysis. Retrieved from: http://davidakenny.net/dyad.htm

Kenny, D. A., & Judd, C. M. (1986). Consequences of violating the independence assumption in analysis of variance. *Psychological Bulletin, 99,* 422–431.

Kenny, D. A., Mannetti, L., Pierro, A., Livi, S., & Kashy, D. A. (2002). The statistical analysis of data from small groups. *Journal of Personality and Social Psychology, 83*(1), 126–137.

Kim, Y. J., Van Dyne, L., Kamdar, D., & Johnson, R. E. (2013). Why and when do motives matter? An integrative model of motives, role cognitions, and social support as predictors of OCB. *Organizational Behavior and Human Decision Processes, 121,* 231–245.

Konovsky, M. A., & Organ, D. W. (1996). Dispositional and contextual determinants of organizational citizenship behavior. *Journal of Organizational Behavior, 17,* 253–266.

Koys, D. J. (2001). The effects of employee satisfaction, organizational citizenship behavior, and turnover on organizational effectiveness: A unit-level, longitudinal study. *Personnel Psychology, 54,* 101–114.

Law, K. S., Wong, C. S., & Mobley, W. H. (1998). Toward a taxonomy of multidimensional constructs. *Academy of Management Review, 23,* 741–755.

Leavitt, K., Fong, C. T., & Greenwald, A. G. (2011). Asking about well-being gets you half an answer: Intra-individual processes of implicit and explicit job attitudes. *Journal of Organizational Behavior, 32,* 672–687.

Lee, K., & Allen, N. J. (2002). Organizational citizenship behavior and workplace deviance: The role of affect and cognitions. *Journal of Applied Psychology, 87,* 131–142.

LePine, J. A., Erez, A., & Johnson, D. E. (2002). The nature and dimensionality of organizational citizenship behavior: A critical review and meta-analysis. *Journal of Applied Psychology, 87,* 52–65.

Lin, S.-H., & Johnson, R. E. (2015). A suggestion to improve a day keeps your depletion away: Examining promotive and prohibitive voice behaviors within a regulatory focus and ego depletion framework. *Journal of Applied Psychology, 100,* 1381–1397.

Lynch, P. D., Eisenberger, R., & Armeli, S. (1999). Perceived organizational support: Inferior versus superior performance by wary employees. *Journal of Applied Psychology, 84,* 467–483.

MacCallum, R. C., & Browne, M. W. (1993). The use of causal indicators in covariance structure models: Some practical issues. *Psychological Bulletin, 114,* 533–541.

MacKenzie, S. B., Podsakoff, P. M., & Jarvis, C. B. (2005). The problem of measurement model misspecification in behavioral and organizational research and some recommended solutions. *Journal of Applied Psychology, 90,* 710–730.

Maslyn, J. M., & Fedor, D. B. (1998). Perceptions of politics: Does measuring different foci matter? *Journal of Applied Psychology, 84,* 645–653.

Marcus, B., Schuler, H., Quell, P., & Hümpfner, G. (2002). Measuring counterproductivity: Development and initial validation of a German self-report questionnaire. *International Journal of Selection and Assessment,* 10(1–2), 18–35.

Masterson, S. S., Lewis, K., Goldman, B. M., & Taylor, M. S. (2000). Integrating justice and social exchange: The differing effects of fair procedures and treatment on work relationships. *Academy of Management Journal, 43,* 738–748.

Moorman, R. H., & Blakely, G. L. (1995). Individualism–collectivism as an individual difference predictor of organizational citizenship behavior. *Journal of Organizational Behavior, 16,* 127–142.

Morrison, E. W. (1994). Role definitions and organizational citizenship behavior: The importance of the employee's perspective. *Academy of Management Journal, 37,* 1543–1567.

Motowidlo, S. J. (2000). Some basic issues related to contextual performance and organizational citizenship behavior in human resource management. *Human Resource Management Review, 10,* 115–126.

Nielsen, T. M., Hrivnak, G. A., & Shaw, M. (2009). Organizational citizenship behavior and performance: A meta-analysis of group-level research. *Small Group Research, 40,* 555–577.

Nunnally, J. C., & Bernstein, I. H. (1994). *Psychometric theory* (3rd ed.). New York, NY: McGraw-Hill.

Organ, D. W. (1988). *Organizational citizenship behavior: The good soldier syndrome.* Lexington, MA: Lexington Books.

Organ, D. W. (1990). The motivational basis of organizational citizenship behavior. *Research in Organizational Behavior, 12,* 43–72.

Organ, D. W. (1997). Organizational citizenship behavior: It's construct clean-up time. *Human Performance, 10,* 85–97.

Organ, D. W., & Ryan, K. (1995). A meta-analytic review of attitudinal and dispositional predictors of organizational citizenship behavior. *Personnel Psychology, 48,* 775–802.

Podsakoff, P. M., Ahearne, M., & MacKenzie, S. B. (1997). Organizational citizenship behavior and the quantity and quality of work group performance. *Journal of Applied Psychology, 82*(2), 262–270.

Podsakoff, P. M., MacKenzie, S. B., Lee, J. Y., & Podsakoff, N. P. (2003). Common method biases in behavioral research: A critical review of the literature and recommended remedies. *Journal of Applied Psychology, 88,* 879–903.

Podsakoff, P. M., MacKenzie, S. B., Moorman, R. H., & Fetter, R. (1990). Transformational leader behaviors and their effects on followers' trust in leader, satisfaction, and organizational citizenship behaviors. *Leadership Quarterly, 1,* 107–142.

Podsakoff, P. M., MacKenzie, S. B., Paine, J. B., & Bacharach, D. G. (2000). Organizational citizenship behaviors: A critical review of the theoretical and empirical literature and

suggestions for future research. *Journal of Management, 26*, 513–563.
Podsakoff, P. M., MacKenzie, S. B., & Podsakoff, N. P. (2012). Sources of method bias in social science research and recommendations on how to control it. *Annual Review of Psychology, 63*, 539–569.
Podsakoff, N. P., Maynes, T. D., Whiting, S. W., & Podsakoff, P. M. (2015). One (rating) from many (observations): Factors affecting the individual assessment of voice behavior in groups. *Journal of Applied Psychology, 100*(4), 1189–1202.
Podsakoff, N. P., Whiting, S. W., Podsakoff, P. M., & Blume, B. D. (2009). Individual- and organizational-level consequences of organizational citizenship behaviors: A meta-analysis. *Journal of Applied Psychology, 94*, 122–141.
Podsakoff, N. P., Whiting, S. W., Welsh, D. T., & Mai, K. M. (2013). Surveying for "artifacts": The susceptibility of the OCB–performance evaluation relationship to common rater, item, and measurement context effects. *Journal of Applied Psychology, 98*, 863–874.
Reiche, B. S., Cardona, P., Lee, Y.-T., Canela, M. Á., Akinnukawe, E., Briscoe, J. P., . . . Wilkinson, H. (2014). Why do managers engage in trustworthy behavior? A multilevel cross-cultural study in 18 countries. *Personnel Psychology, 67*, 61–98.
Richardson, H. A., Simmering, M. J., & Sturman, M. C. (2009). A tale of three perspectives: Examining post hoc statistical techniques for detection and correction of common method variance. *Organizational Research Methods, 12*, 762–800.
Rotundo, M., & Sackett, P. R. (2002). The relative importance of task, citizenship, and counterproductive performance to global ratings of job performance: A policy-capturing approach. *Journal of Applied Psychology, 87*, 66–80.
Sackett, P. R., & Larson, J. R., Jr. (1990). Research strategies and tactics in industrial and organizational psychology. In M. D. Dunnette & L. M. Hough (Eds.), *Handbook of industrial and organizational psychology* (2nd ed., Vol. 1, pp. 419–489). Palo Alto, CA: Consulting Psychologists Press.
Schwarz, N., & Oyserman, D. (2001). Asking questions about behavior: Cognition, communication, and questionnaire construction. *American Journal of Evaluation*, 22, 127–160.
Smith, G. T., Fischer, S., & Fister, S. M. (2003). Incremental validity principles in test construction. *Psychological Assessment*, 15, 467–477.
Smith, C. A., Organ, D. W., & Near, J. P. (1983). Organizational citizenship behavior: Its nature and antecedents. *Journal of Applied Psychology, 68*, 655–663.
Spector, P. E., Bauer, J. A., & Fox, S. (2010). Measurement artifacts in the assessment of counterproductive work behavior and organizational citizenship behavior: Do we know what we think we know? *Journal of Applied Psychology, 95*, 781–790.
Spector, P. E., & Che, X. X. (2014). Re-examining citizenship: How the control of measurement artifacts effects observed relationships of organizational citizenship behavior and organizational variables. *Human Performance, 27*, 165–182.
Spence, J. R., Brown, D. J., Keeping, L. M., & Lian, H. (2014). Helpful today, but not tomorrow? Feeling grateful as a predictor of daily organizational citizenship behaviors. *Personnel Psychology, 67*, 705–738.
Spector, P. E., Fox, S., Penney, L. M., Bruursema, K., Goh, A., & Kessler, S. (2006). The dimensionality of counterproductivity: Are all counterproductive behaviors created equal? *Journal of Vocational Behavior, 68*(3), 446–460.
Spence, J. R., Ferris, D. L., Brown, D. J., & Heller, D. (2011). Understanding daily citizenship behaviors: A social comparison perspective. *Journal of Organizational Behavior, 32*, 547–571.
Takeuchi, R., Bolino, M. C., & Lin, C.-C. (2015). Too many motives? The interactive effects of multiple motives on organizational citizenship behavior. *Journal of Applied Psychology, 100*, 1239–1248.
Thompson, B. (Ed.). (1984). *Canonical correlation analysis: Uses and interpretation*. Thousand Oaks, CA: Sage.
Turnipseed, D. L., & Rassuli, A. (2005). Performance perceptions of organizational citizenship behaviours at work: A bi-level study among managers and employees. *British Journal of Management, 16*, 231–244.
Vandenberg, R. J., Lance, C. E., & Taylor, S. C. (2005). A latent variable approach to rating source equivalence: Who should provide ratings on organizational citizenship behavior dimensions? In D. L. Turnipseed (Ed.), *Handbook of organizational citizenship behavior* (pp. 109–141). Hauppauge, NY: Nova Science.
Van Dyne, L., Cummings, L. L., & Parks, J. M. (1995). Extra-role behaviors: In pursuit of construct and definitional clarity (A bridge over muddied waters). In L. L. Cummings & B. M. Staw (Eds.), *Research in organizational behavior* (Vol. 17, pp. 215–285). Greenwich, CT: JAI Press.
Van Dyne, L., & LePine, J. A. (1998). Helping and voice extra-role behaviors: Evidence of construct and predictive validity. *Academy of Management Journal, 41*, 108–119.
Wayne, S. J., Shore, L. M., & Liden, R. C. (1997). Perceived organizational support and leader-member exchange: A social exchange perspective. *Academy of Management Journal, 40*, 82–111.
Werner, J. M. (1994). Dimensions that make a difference: Examining the impact of in-role and extra-role behaviors on supervisory ratings. *Journal of Applied Psychology, 79*, 98–107.
Whiting, S. W., Podsakoff, P. M., & Pierce, J. R. (2008). Effects of task performance, helping, voice, and organizational loyalty on performance appraisal ratings. *Journal of Applied Psychology, 93*, 125–139.
Williams, L. J., & Anderson, S. E. (1991). Job satisfaction and organizational commitment as predictors of organizational citizenship and in-role behaviors. *Journal of Management*, 17, 601–617.
Williams, L., Hartman, N., & Cavazotte, F. (2010). Method variance and marker variables: A review and comprehensive approach using structural equation methods. *Organizational Research Methods, 13*, 477–514.

CHAPTER

24 Within-Person Approaches to the Study of Organizational Citizenship Behaviors: Antecedents, Consequences, and Boundary Conditions

Brent A. Scott, Fadel K. Matta, *and* Joel Koopman

Abstract

This chapter provides a review of the nascent (but growing) literature on organizational citizenship behavior (OCB) at the within-person level of analysis. We organize our review of the existing literature chronologically, discussing antecedents and consequences of within-person fluctuations in OCB. After providing a narrative review of the literature, we provide a quantitative summary of the literature via meta-analysis, summarizing the within-person relationships between OCB and its most common within-person correlates (i.e., positive affect, negative affect, job satisfaction, stressors, strain, and task performance). Looking to the future of OCB at the within-person level of analysis, we suggest that researchers can contribute to the domain by tailoring the measurement of OCB to the within-person level of analysis, better illuminating the causal direction between OCB and affect, clarifying the relationship between OCB and counterproductive work behavior at the within-person level, expanding the "dark side" of within-person OCB, exploring between-person differences in within-person OCB variability, and incorporating new theories.

Key Words: organizational citizenship behavior, meta-analysis, within-person, experience sampling, positive affect, negative affect, job satisfaction, stressors, strain, performance

Since its introduction to the organizational behavior literature, the vast majority of research on organizational citizenship behavior (OCB; Organ, 1988; Smith, Organ, & Near, 1983) and related constructs, including prosocial behavior (George, 1991), organizational spontaneity (George & Brief, 1992), extrarole behavior (Van Dyne & LePine, 1998), proactive behavior (Crant, 2000; Morrison & Phelps, 1999), and contextual performance (Motowidlo & Van Scotter, 1994), has focused on identifying why some employees engage in higher levels of OCB than others (e.g., Organ & Ryan, 1995) and the consequences of their behavioral tendencies for outcomes at both the individual and organizational levels (e.g., Podsakoff, Whiting, Podsakoff, & Blume, 2009). Though research at this *between-person* level of analysis has been critical for understanding OCB, even the best employees sometimes do not engage in OCB; similarly, even the worst employees sometimes do engage in OCB. In other words, there are substantial and systematic fluctuations in employees' episodic, or momentary levels, of OCB. This is an important departure from traditional cross-sectional research, which typically would view such fluctuations as transient error.

The purpose of this chapter is to examine the emerging literature on OCB conducted at the *within-person* level of analysis. We first review the research that has been conducted to date at this level of analysis, focusing on the antecedents and consequences of momentary engagement in OCB. We then provide a quantitative summary of this literature via meta-analysis in order to provide a snapshot of what we know as well as to lay the groundwork for where we might go to move this emerging stream of research forward. In so doing, we draw comparisons to the broader stream of research examining between-person differences in OCB. Finally, and perhaps most important, we discuss the future of research in this area. Issues that we tackle include the measurement of OCB at the within-person level of analysis, the potential "dark side" of engaging in momentary OCB, between-person variability in OCB, and theoretical frameworks that can guide research on OCB at the within-person level.

Within-Person Research on Organizational Citizenship Behavior

The incorporation of experience-sampling methodology (ESM; Larson & Csikszentmihalyi, 1983) has proven to be an invaluable tool for illuminating the dynamic, within-person nature of OCB. Typically, ESM studies (sometimes referred to as diary studies) use systematic or random prompts to obtain observations of focal variables from individuals daily, or perhaps multiple times per day. Initially, ESM was used by researchers to capture moods and emotions (e.g., Alliger & Williams, 1993), which by their nature are fleeting states and thus best examined in situ. It is perhaps not surprising then that the bulk of within-person research on OCB has linked the construct to positive and negative affective states (where *affect* is an umbrella term that encompasses both moods and emotions). Although scholars argued during the early 1990s that OCB and mood should be associated with each other (e.g., George & Brief, 1992), the initial research that followed using ESM captured affective states at the within-person level but assessed OCB at the between-person level (e.g., Fisher, 2003), and therefore the relationship between affect and OCB was still assessed at the between-person level.

This changed with Sonnentag's (2003) publication. In an ESM study of 147 employees from public service organizations who completed daily surveys for a 5-day period, she found that 46% of the variance in proactive behavior (operationalized as personal initiative) was within-persons. Feelings of recovery in the morning were positively associated with reports of proactive behavior at the end of the day, and work engagement mediated this relationship.

Two years later, Miner, Glomb, and Hulin (2005) examined within-person OCB more directly. Drawing from affective events theory (AET; Weiss & Cropanzano, 1996), the authors argued that OCB at the momentary level represents what AET refers to as an "affect-driven behavior" (as opposed to a "cognition-driven behavior," which would be influenced more by job attitudes). Their ESM study consisted of 41 manufacturing employees who completed surveys each day over a 2- to 3-week period. Following a morning survey that assessed initial mood, participants were signaled at four, stratified random times throughout the workday. Mood, or "hedonic tone," was assessed with both positively (e.g., happy, pleased) and negatively valenced (e.g., blue, sad) items. Self-reported OCB was assessed with two items that captured both OCB directed toward the organization (OCBO) and OCB directed toward coworkers (OCBI) (e.g., Williams & Anderson, 1991), with respondents indicating in a *yes/no* format whether they were engaging in these behaviors at the time they were signaled. Participants completed 59% of the daily surveys, and 56% of the variance in hedonic tone was within persons (the percentage of within-person variance in OCB was not reported, though participants did report spending approximately 23% of their time helping coworkers). Although their prediction of a relationship between hedonic tone and OCB was not supported, their investigation laid the groundwork for future research treating OCB as an outcome of affect. It is also noteworthy that Miner et al. (2005) controlled for hedonic tone in the morning, which permitted an examination of whether a change in hedonic tone was associated with OCB—a point to which we return later.

Following the publication of Miner et al. (2005), Ilies, Scott, and Judge (2006) conducted a 3-week ESM study with 62 participants from a variety of occupations. Toward the end of each workday, participants completed measures of positive affect from the Positive and Negative Affect Schedule (PANAS; Watson, Clark, & Tellegen, 1988), job satisfaction, and OCB, with 89% of all daily surveys completed. To assess OCB, the authors utilized 11 items from the widely used OCBI and OCBO scales developed by Lee and Allen (2002), eliminating items that "would be less likely to vary daily" (567). Twenty-nine percent of the variance in OCB was within persons, and both positive affect and job satisfaction were positively associated with daily engagement in OCB. Although the authors did not distinguish between OCBI and OCBO in their main analysis, a supplemental analysis revealed that OCBO was associated with both job satisfaction and positive affect, while OCBI was associated with positive affect only, suggesting that OCBI may be more affect driven. Perhaps most interesting, in an analysis linking within- and between-levels of analysis, trait agreeableness (but not conscientiousness) moderated the within-person relationship between positive affect and OCB, such that the relationship was more positive for those low in agreeableness. In contrast, those high in agreeableness engaged in OCB regardless of their momentary mood. In all, the Ilies et al. (2006) study is important because it reveals the complex ways in which stable, individual traits can interact with experienced states to predict momentary OCB (see also Mischel & Shoda, 1995).

In a rather unique study of 44 flight attendants who completed surveys over three consecutive trips, with three surveys per trip, Xanthopoulou, Heuven, Demerouti, Baker, and Schaufeli (2008) examined the effects of state self-efficacy and colleague support on extra-role (as well as in-role) performance. Extra-role performance was assessed with two items that referenced doing more work than was required and helping colleagues. Participants completed 63% of the diary surveys, and 60% of the variance in extra-role performance was within persons. The results of their model, which was inspired by the job demands–resources model (Demerouti, Bakker, Nachreiner, & Schaufeli, 2001), showed that state self-efficacy, but not colleague support, was positively associated with extra-role performance. Moreover, state work engagement mediated this effect. Overall, their study provides some insight into the motivational processes underlying momentary engagement in OCB, as opposed to purely affective processes.

Several papers examining OCB within persons were published in 2009. In what has proven to be an influential study on the relationship between OCB and counterproductive work behavior (CWB), Dalal, Lam, Weiss, Welch, and Hulin (2009) surveyed 48 employees from a software company (Study 1) and 67 employees from a variety of occupations (Study 2) over a 3-week period (i.e., 15 workdays). In Study 1, the employees completed four surveys each day. OCB was measured with six items adapted from existing sources. Similar to Ilies et al. (2006), the authors omitted items that "were likely to occur rarely, if at all" (Dalal et al., 2009, p. 1056). Similar to Miner et al. (2005), employees indicated whether they had engaged in each behavior (as opposed to the extent to which they had engaged in each behavior), and affect pleasantness was assessed in a bipolar fashion such that negatively valenced items were reverse-coded. However, in contrast to results of Miner et al. (2005), affect pleasantness (at the current time point, but not the previous time point) was positively associated with OCB. OCB and CWB were not related. In Study 2, the employees completed two surveys each day. OCB was assessed more comprehensively, with six items referencing coworkers, six items referencing the supervisor, and six items referencing the organization. The percentage of variance in OCB within individuals was similar for each referent (44.2%, 50%, and 52%, respectively). Importantly, positive and negative affect were kept separate in the analyses (as opposed to the bipolar operationalization utilized in Study 1). Positive affect was positively associated with all three forms of OCB, while negative affect was not. Moreover, neither positive nor negative affect at the previous time point was associated with OCB. Again, the relationship between OCB and CWB was generally weak. Overall, given that lagged predictors were controlled in the regression equation, the results of the studies by Dalal et al. reveal that an increase in affect (specifically, positive affect) was associated with an increase in OCB. Their results also suggest the intriguing notion that, even at the momentary, within-person level of analysis, OCB and CWB are independent, distinct constructs, which parallels findings at the between-person level of analysis (Dalal, 2005).

Binnewies, Sonnentag, and Mojza (2009) drew from conservation of resources theory (Hobfoll, 1989) to explain the relationship between the state of being recovered in the morning and engagement in OCB during that day. Ninety-nine public service employees completed surveys on pocket computers in the morning, immediately after work, and in the evening for four consecutive workdays, with 91% of all surveys completed. OCBI was measured with five items adapted from existing scales, and 50% of the variance was within persons. The results revealed that the state of being recovered was positively associated with OCBI. Moreover, there was a cross-level interaction between individuals' stable levels of job control and recovery, such that the within-person relationship between the state of being recovered and OCB was positive for those with high job control but not significant for those with low job control. Overall, the Binnewies et al. study suggests that resources are important for daily engagement in OCB, and job control is needed in order for employees to capitalize on days when their resource pool has been replenished.

Integrating affective events theory with the transactional model of stress (Lazarus & Folkman, 1984), Rodell and Judge (2009) investigated the within-person relationships among challenge and hindrance stressors, emotions, and both OCB and CWB. Challenge stressors are job demands that create potential for personal growth, whereas hindrance stressors are job demands that present obstacles to personal growth (Cavanaugh, Boswell, Roehling, & Boudreau, 2000). One hundred participants from a variety of organizations were given 3 weeks to complete 10 daily surveys toward the end of their workday. OCB was assessed with 11 items from Lee and Allen's (2002) measure, and 38% of the variance in OCB was within persons. Challenge stressors had a positive, indirect relationship with OCB through the affective state of attentiveness. In addition, both challenge and hindrance stressors had a negative, indirect relationship with OCB through the affective state of anxiety. No differences were observed when OCB was broken down into OCBI and OCBO. As an aside, the authors also assessed CWB, and the within-individual correlation between OCB and CWB was negative and significant. The upshot of the Rodell and Judge (2009) study is that not all stressors are equal when it comes to daily engagement in OCB. Although hindrance stressors appear to be unequivocally "bad," the relationship between challenge stressors and OCB is more complex, with offsetting effects on OCB via a relationship with an affective state that is "good" for OCB (i.e., attentiveness) and an affective state that is "bad" for OCB (i.e., anxiety).

Examining antecedents of daily proactive behavior, Fritz and Sonnentag (2009) had 172 civil service employees complete morning and afternoon surveys for a 3-day period. Proactive behavior was operationalized as taking charge (Morrison & Phelps, 1999). The percentage of variance in proactive behavior that was within persons was not reported. Positive mood was associated with proactive behavior on the same and the following workday. Interestingly, stressors in the form of time pressure and situational constraints were also positively associated with proactive behavior, suggesting that individuals "took charge" in an effort to alleviate their undesirable situation.

Last but not least in 2009, Conway, Rogelberg, and Pitts had 80 participants from a variety of organizations use palm computers to complete five surveys each day for 5 workdays, with 87% of surveys completed. Helping (OCBI) was assessed with a single item ("since the last signal, did you voluntarily help someone else [in a way that was not an assigned duty]?") (p. 328). In contrast to the previously reviewed studies, only 13% of the variance in OCBI was within persons. Positive affect (assessed with four items) in the previous time period was not associated with OCBI. However, trait altruism (but not trait empathy) moderated the within-person relationship between positive affect and OCBI, such that individuals high in altruism engaged in OCBI regardless of their positive affect, while individuals low in altruism engaged in OCBI as their positive affect increased. This result is similar to the finding of Ilies et al. (2006) that agreeableness (of which altruism is a facet) moderated the within-person relationship between positive affect and OCBI. In a supplemental analysis with positive affect as an outcome instead of a predictor, OCBI was not associated with a change in positive affect. Overall, the lack of significant within-person results may have been due, in part, to the restricted amount of within-person variance in OCBI.

Departing methodologically from prior research, Binnewies, Sonnentag, and Mojza (2010) examined weekly relationships involving OCB and recovery. Similar to daily designs, 47.5% of the variance in OCB was within persons. Results indicated that the state of being recovered (assessed on Monday) was positively associated with engagement in OCB that week, suggesting that OCB is more likely for individuals who take time to replenish their resources over the weekend.

Ohly and Fritz (2010) had engineers from an automotive manufacturer rate their daily engagement in proactive behavior (operationalized as personal initiative) for a 3-day period. A total of 43.1% of the variance in proactive behavior was within persons. Similar to the findings of Fritz and Sonnentag (2009), the authors found that challenging characteristics of work (i.e., time pressure and job control) were positively associated with proactive behavior, and these relationships were partially mediated by challenge appraisals.

Miner and Glomb (2010) had 67 call-center employees complete one morning and four or five randomly scheduled surveys throughout the workday for 3 weeks, with 84% of surveys completed. OCB was measured with two items that captured behavior directed toward the organization (OCBO) and behavior directed toward others (i.e., helping; OCBI). The amount of within-person variance in OCB was not reported. Affect ("hedonic tone") was assessed in the morning and during the workday with both positively and negatively valenced items, with negatively valenced items reverse-coded (cf. Miner et al., 2005). Engaging in OCB was not associated with a change in hedonic tone, and "metamood," which captures a person's general tendency to attend to and regulate his or her emotions (Salovey, Mayer, Goldman, Turvey, & Palfai, 1995) did not moderate this within-person relationship. Although the authors found significant results with other predictors (e.g., work withdrawal), the lack of findings for OCB could have been due to the measurement of affect, which utilized a bipolar operationalization as opposed to keeping positive and negative affect separate (cf. Dalal et al., 2009).

Glomb, Bhave, Miner, and Wall (2011) did separate positive and negative affect in their ESM study of 68 managerial and professional employees. In an intriguing departure from prior work, Glomb et al. proposed that individuals engage in OCB in order to repair a negative mood, thereby positioning affect as an outcome rather than an antecedent of OCB. The employees in their sample completed randomly signaled surveys (a morning survey used to capture baseline affect and four surveys throughout the workday) on palmtop computers for 3 weeks. Approximately 53% of the surveys were completed. The altruism and courtesy dimensions of OCB were assessed with multiple items, and similar to previous research, the authors eliminated items less likely to occur on a daily basis. Seventy percent and 87% of the variance in altruism and courtesy, respectively, was within persons. The results of their ESM study showed that negative affect at the previous time period was associated with an increase in altruism but not courtesy. Positive affect at the previous time period was not associated with a change in either form of OCB. Subsequently, engaging in both forms of OCB was associated with an increase in positive affect. However, courtesy was also associated with an increase in negative affect. Finally, there was a cross-level interaction with extraversion such that extraverts' positive affect increased more following their altruistic behavior. What is interesting and important about the Glomb et al. (2011) study is that it departs from the focus on OCB as solely an outcome in within-individual studies. That is, not only might individuals engage in OCB in an attempt to repair their negative mood but also engaging in OCB may have downstream consequences.

In two ESM studies, Halbesleben and Wheeler (2011) drew from conservation of resources theory to understand the relationship between feelings of exhaustion and OCB. In Study 1, 199 participants from a variety of organizations took part in a weeklong study, completing an online survey each day for five workdays. OCBI was assessed using Williams and Anderson's (1991) scale, and 31% of the variance in OCBI was within persons. Counterintuitively, exhaustion was positively associated with OCBI. This association was more positive in relationships where the focal employee received more than she or he contributed (i.e., in relationships characterized by positive reciprocity). In Study 2, 155 participants from a variety of organizations took part in a weeklong ESM study, similar in design to Study 1. Both OCBI and OCBO were assessed using the Williams and Anderson (1991) scale, and 35% of the variance in OCBI, and 22% of the variance in OCBO, was within persons. Again, exhaustion was positively associated with OCBI, and this relationship was stronger in relationships characterized by positive reciprocity. However, exhaustion was negatively associated with OCBO, and this relationship was also stronger in relationships characterized by positive reciprocity. The authors explained the rather counterintuitive finding between exhaustion and OCBI by suggesting that when experiencing a state of exhaustion, employees choose more wisely where to invest their limited resources, and OCBI is more lucrative in this regard compared to OCBO.

Drawing from social comparison theory (Festinger, 1954) and AET (Weiss & Cropanzano, 1996), Spence, Ferris, Brown, and Heller (2011) had 99 participants from a variety of occupations complete an online survey each day for a 2-week period, with 78% of surveys completed. OCB was measured with 14 items from the Lee and Allen (2002) OCBI and OCBO scales. Forty-three percent of the variance in OCB was within persons. Downward social comparisons (where the focal employee perceives that she or he is better off than others) were associated with higher levels of OCB, but upward social comparisons (where the focal employee perceives that she or he is worse off than others) were not associated with OCB. Both forms of social comparisons had an indirect effect on OCB through positive affect. In addition, both of these within-person relationships were moderated by employees' characteristic beliefs in a just world, such that those who believe in a just world were more likely to engage in OCB when they made downward social comparisons but less likely to engage in OCB when they made upward social comparisons. Overall, the Spence et al. (2011) study raises the interesting notion that how employees see themselves in relation to a target influences whether they engage in OCB toward that target.

Fay and Sonnentag (2012), using palmtop computers, had 52 German employees from a variety of organizations participate in a week-long ESM study with three surveys per day. Employees completed 91% of the daily surveys, and 88% of the variance in OCB (operationalized by time spent on proactive behavior) was within persons. Positive affect was associated with an increase in time spent engaging in OCB. In contrast, high levels of momentary experienced competence were associated with more time spent on core task activities and less time spent on OCB. The authors argued (but did not test directly) that low feelings of competence motivate individuals to repair the negative state, and OCB is one way to accomplish this.

Examining forms of support as predictors of OCB, Schreurs, Van Emmerik, Gunter, and Germeys (2012) had 56 Dutch employees complete a weekly survey for 3 weeks, achieving a 95% response rate for the weekly surveys. OCB (extra-role performance) was assessed with seven items developed by Goodman and Svyantek (1999), and 60% of the variance in OCB was within persons. In terms of predictors, although supervisor support was positively associated with OCB, neither colleague support nor job security was associated with OCB.

Wu and Parker (2012) had 58 undergraduates report on their proactive behavior (measured by adapting a scale of proactive personality [Bateman & Crant, 1993) on a monthly basis for 4 months. A total of 40.8% of the variance in proactive behavior was within persons. The states of curiosity, core self-evaluations, and future orientation were all associated with higher levels of proactive behavior at that time. In addition, there were cross-level interactions, such that the within-person relationship between core self-evaluations and proactive behavior was weaker, while the within-person relationship between future orientation and proactive behavior was stronger, for individuals with high levels of relationship anxiety. The authors concluded that people who worry about their social relationships are hesitant to engage in proactive behavior as a result of having a positive self-concept at that time.

Barnes, Ghumman, and Scott (2013) examined the relationship between sleep quantity and daily engagement in OCB. Eighty-five employed university students were surveyed twice daily over the course of 5 workdays, and they completed 78% of the surveys. A preshift survey assessed sleep quantity, and a postshift survey assessed job satisfaction and OCB over the course of the workday. OCB was measured using the 16-item Lee and Allen (2002) measure, and 30% of the variance in OCBI, and 20% of the variance in OCBO, was within persons. Sleep quantity was positively associated with engagement in both OCBI and OCBO, and job satisfaction mediated these relationships.

Three studies on OCB at the within-person level were published in 2014, and they extend the aforementioned research in several ways. First, in a unique focus on managers and their engagement in justice-relevant actions, Johnson, Lanaj, and Barnes (2014) drew from theory on regulatory resources (e.g., Baumeister, Bratslavsky, Muraven, & Tice, 1998) to understand the consequences of engaging in procedural and interpersonal justice for managers themselves. Seventy-nine managers were surveyed in the morning and afternoon for 10 workdays (2 weeks), and they completed 69% of the daily surveys. Managers' engagement in OCBI (helping others) was measured with four items from Fox, Spector, Goh, Bruursema, and Kessler (2012), and 34% of variance in OCBI was within persons. Engaging in procedural justice was associated with an increase in feeling depleted the next day, whereas engaging in interpersonal justice was associated with a decrease in feeling depleted the next day. Moreover, depletion mediated the effects of justice behaviors on OCBI. In a supplemental analysis demonstrating support for the authors' proposed causal direction, OCBI was not associated with either justice or depletion the next day. Finally, the positive, indirect effect of interpersonal justice on OCB via depletion was stronger for managers low in extraversion and for managers high in neuroticism. The findings for depletion, in which feelings of depletion were associated with lower levels of OCB, are somewhat in contrast to the findings of Halbesleben and Wheeler (2011), who found that exhaustion was positively associated with engagement in OCBI.

In an intriguing analysis of within-person variation in personality traits, which historically have been thought to be stable, Judge, Simon, Hurst, and Kelley (2014) collected data from 122 participants from a variety of occupations who took part in a 2-week ESM study. Participants completed 86% of the daily surveys. OCB was measured with 12 items tapping both OCBI and OCBO from the Lee and Allen (2002) scale, and 48% of the variance in OCB was within persons. Engagement in OCB was positively associated with next-day extraversion, agreeableness, and openness to experience. Thus, the more individuals engaged in OCB, the more they reported behaving in an extraverted, agreeable, and open manner the following day. In contrast, the effects of personality states on next-day OCB were not significant. These results suggest that the approach-oriented nature of OCB triggers corresponding, approach-oriented personality states in individuals. As such, they are yet another example of how within-person research can differ dramatically from between-person research, which historically has treated personality as a stable antecedent of OCB (e.g., Organ & Ryan, 1995).

Departing from previous research that has focused on positive and negative affect as broad states, Spence, Brown, Keeping, and Lian (2014) examined the discrete emotion of state gratitude and its relationship with OCB at the within-person level. The authors conducted two ESM studies. The first consisted of 67 participants from various occupations who completed a morning and afternoon survey each day for 5 workdays, with 80% of the surveys completed. OCB was assessed with 14 items from the Lee and Allen (2002) scale, and 38% of the variance in OCB was within persons. State gratitude was positively associated with engagement in OCB. In Study 2, 104 participants from an array of occupations completed an afternoon survey each day for 10 workdays, with 63% of the surveys completed. Dalal et al.'s (2009) 18-item scale was used to assess OCB. In terms of variance, 33%, 41%, and 34% of the variance in OCB directed toward the supervisor, coworkers, and organization, respectively, was within persons. Over and above positive affect, state gratitude was positively associated with OCB directed toward one's supervisor and coworkers, but not toward one's organization. Overall, their study demonstrates the utility of a discrete emotion approach, and it is one of the few studies that have taken such an approach.

In an interesting analysis of the effects of pain on discretionary behavior, Christian, Eisenkraft, and Kapadia (2015) conducted two ESM studies examining promotive, extra-role behaviors within persons. In the first, 85 employees experiencing chronic pain took part in a 3-week study whereby they completed morning and afternoon measures. Participants completed approximately 78% of those surveys, and 49% of the variance in extra-role behavior was within persons. Daily pain was indirectly associated with less extra-role behavior via lower work engagement, but there was not a significant, indirect effect through resource depletion. In the second study, the authors investigated intentions to engage in extra-role behaviors (66% of the variance was within persons). Results of that study, which utilized archival data from 650 participants who provided 6,820 observations over the course of a week, were similar to the results of the first study, except that the indirect effect of pain on extra-role behavior through resource depletion was significant. Overall, their studies demonstrate the important of human energy for momentary engagement in OCB, even over and above moods and emotions.

Gordon, Demerouti, Bipp, and Le Blanc (2015) also examined work engagement in concert with OCB (contextual performance). Their 5-day ESM study of 49 nurses achieved a 60% daily response rate, and 60% of the variance in OCB was within persons. Intuitive decision making was positively associated with OCB, particularly for nurses with high levels of work engagement.

Sonnentag and Starzyk (2015), in a 2-week ESM study of 153 employees who completed two surveys per day, examined a dual, affective pathway model to engagement in proactive behavior (operationalized as issue identification and issue implementation). Roughly half of the variance in these forms of proactive behavior was within persons. In support of their dual-pathway approach, perceptions of prosocial impact were associated with an increase in positive affect later that day, which in turn was associated with greater issue implementation (but not identification). In contrast, perceptions of situational constraints were positively associated with an increase in negative affect later that day, which in turn was associated with greater issue identification (but not implementation). Overall, their findings suggest that different aspects of OCB may be triggered by both positive and negative affect. Moreover, their findings appear to be consistent with research on emotion showing that negative affect causes people to reflect and plan (e.g., Izard & Ackerman, 2000), while positive affect causes people to engage and execute (e.g., Fredrickson, 2001).

In an illustration of the infancy of research on within-individual OCB, Trougakos, Beal, Cheng, Hideg, and Zweig (2015) proposed a model that contradicts the previously discussed manuscript by Halbesleben and Wheeler (2011). Drawing on ego depletion theory, Trougakos et al. (2015) hypothesized that daily surface acting increases emotional exhaustion and decreases engagement in OCBI. Using three items from Williams and Anderson's (1991) OCBI subscale (the percentage of variance that was within individuals was not reported), these authors found support for their model. Note that the direction of the relationship proposed between emotional exhaustion and OCBI is opposite to that proposed and found by Halbesleben and Wheeler (2011). This contradiction is interesting due to several notable differences between the studies. First, although both used items from Williams and Anderson (1991), Trougakos and colleagues used only three items, whereas Halbesleben and Wheeler (2011) used all seven. Could there be differences in the omitted items that influence the relationship that substantially? A more likely culprit is that OCBI was measured from different sources between the studies. Specifically, Halbesleben and Wheeler (2011) relied upon self-reports, as is common in within-individual studies of OCB. Trougakos and colleagues instead obtained a daily report from one of the focal employee's coworkers. We return to some of the implications of this decision in a subsequent section.

Finally, two recent studies illustrate the evolution of ESM research on OCB sparked by Glomb et al. (2011) by focusing not on antecedents, but instead on downstream outcomes. In a follow-up to their 2011 study described earlier, Halbesleben and Wheeler (2015) investigated a mechanism by which OCBI may serve as a resource investment in others. These authors adopted a dyadic ESM method in which 177 pairs of employees completed daily surveys for a 1-week period. Instead of the Lee and Allen (2002) measure, OCBI was assessed using the seven-item OCBI subscale from Williams and Anderson (1991) (the percentage of OCB variance that was within persons was not reported). In support of their hypotheses, Halbesleben and Wheeler showed that on days when a given employee engaged in higher levels of OCBI, his or her coworker perceived higher levels of resources available through that relationship (operationalized as social support). This higher level of support was associated with higher levels of trust that day and increased reciprocation of OCBI the following day. Finally, in support of the notion of resource gain spirals proposed by conservation of resources theory (Halbesleben, Neveu, Paustian-Underdahl, & Westman, 2014; Hobfoll, 1989), these authors showed that levels of support, trust, and OCBI increased over the course of the study.

Koopman, Lanaj, and Scott (2016) similarly focused on the outcomes of OCB to actors, but these authors departed from extant within-individual research on OCB in an important way. In the aforementioned studies, OCB has generally been conceptualized as a positive behavior (e.g., associated with positive affect, a means of investing resources, a mechanism for mood repair). However, OCB research at the between-individual level of analysis has identified a potential "dark side" to these behaviors (for a review, see Bolino, Klotz, Turnley, & Harvey, 2013). Koopman et al. (2016) developed a similar theory at the within-individual level and tested a model illustrating the "bright" and "dark" sides of daily engagement in OCB. In their ESM study, 82 employees from a variety of occupations completed three online surveys each day for a period of 2 weeks (10 workdays), with a 91% day-level response rate. OCBI was assessed with six items reported in Dalal et al. (2009), and 54% of its variance was within persons. On the "bright side," OCBI was associated with an increase in positive affect, and positive affect mediated the relationship between OCBI and both affective commitment and job satisfaction, but not emotional exhaustion. On the "dark side," OCBI was associated with feelings of reduced goal progress, and goal progress mediated the relationship between OCBI and the three well-being outcomes (i.e., affective commitment, job satisfaction, and emotional exhaustion). Interestingly, these opposing relationships were moderated by individuals' trait regulatory focus (Higgins, 1997), such that the positive relationship between OCBI and positive affect was stronger for those with a high promotion focus, while the negative relationship between OCBI and perceptions of work goal progress was stronger for those with a high prevention focus. Combining these analyses, evidence for moderated mediation of the first stage of the indirect effect was found. Overall, the results of the Koopman et al. study suggest that momentary engagement in OCB has both benefits and drawbacks. Although it boosts positive affect, it also interferes with goal progress on core work tasks because engagement in OCB must necessarily come at the expense of task performance at a given moment in time. Thus, when it comes to answering the question as to whether engaging in OCB is "good" or "bad" for a given employee, it appears that the question should be changed to "for whom is OCB good or bad, and why" (Koopman et al., 2016, p. 28)—a point to which we return later.

A "Mini" Meta-Analysis on Within-Person Organizational Citizenship Behavior Research

Having described the existing research on within-person antecedents and consequences of OCB, we wanted, to the extent possible, to provide a quantitative summary of that research. Therefore, we meta-analyzed those within-person relationships involving OCB that have been examined most frequently.

Before we get to those relationships, we wanted to get an idea of the amount of variance in OCB that is within persons. As reviewed earlier, the percentage of variance in OCB that is within persons varies quite a bit from study to study. In fact, the range was approximately 25% to 88%. The average amount of within-person variance was 45.5% (SD = .15). For OCBI, it was slightly higher, at 48.2% (SD = 15.7%). For OCBO, it was slightly lower, at 36.0% (SD = 12.0%). In considering these differences, it could be the case that OCBI varies more within persons because acts such as helping others may depend on interaction opportunities with specific coworkers (or with one's supervisor). Similarly, within-person variance in OCBI may be higher because of greater fluctuations in coworkers' (or one's supervisor's) need for help on a given day. In contrast, OCBO may vary more between persons because one's relationship with the organization is more stable over short periods of time, thus reflecting a general tendency to be a "good citizen." Caution, however, should be taken with respect to the differences between OCBI and OCBO because the results for OCBO were based on only six studies.

How do the variance results for OCB compare to within-person variance in other constructs that have been frequently studied at the within-person level? Quite well, as it turns out. In the studies on OCB that we reviewed earlier and included in our meta-analysis, state-positive (M = 51.4%, SD = 16.5%) and state-negative (M = 57.2%, SD = 10.1%) affect exhibited similar amounts of within-person variance. Because one would expect affective states, which are often fleeting and ephemeral, to exhibit a substantial amount of within-person variance, the similar amount of within-person variance for OCB is noteworthy. For the sake of further comparison, the within-person variance in other constructs included in our review was as follows: job satisfaction (M = 29.4%, SD = .05), task performance (M = 43.8%, SD = 20.4%), stressors (M = 43.0%, SD = 14.1%), and strain (M = 61.5%, SD = 17.7%). Overall, these results demonstrate the importance of examining OCB within persons over time. After all, if scholars only concentrated on between-person variance in OCB, which was the case only a decade ago, they would be missing half of the story.

Turning now to within-individual relationships involving OCB, we conducted our meta-analysis following Hunter and Schmidt's (2004) guidelines. Our results include the sample-size-weighted point estimate of the study correlations (r), a 95% confidence interval around that point estimate, the number of studies (k), and the cumulative sample size (N). In addition, we report the correlation after correcting for unreliability in both the predictor and the criterion (r_c), with corrections performed at the independent sample level (i.e., prior to meta-analyzing the correlations). For studies that did not include reliability information, we substituted the weighted average from the studies that did report that information. Finally, we report both the standard deviation of the corrected meta-analytic correlation (SDr_c), the 80% credibility interval (which provides an estimate of the variability in individual correlations across the studies), and the percentage of variance in the correlations explained by artifacts. Together, these latter three estimates can be used to suggest the presence of moderators.

Table 24.1 presents the results of our "mini" meta-analysis ("mini" simply because there are not a large number of studies on OCB at the within-person level, though that number is increasing). Unfortunately, there were not enough studies that measured OCBO to breakdown our meta-analytic results by referent (i.e., OCBO versus OCBI). For the sake of comparison, in discussing our results, we also present correlations from prior meta-analyses at the between-person level. As shown in Table 24.1, OCB is positively correlated with positive affect (r = .18; r_c = .22), and the 95% confidence interval for this relationship excluded zero. OCB is also positively (albeit weakly) correlated with negative affect (r = .07; r_c = .08), as the 95% confidence interval excluded zero. Shockley, Ispas, Rossi, and Levine (2012) reported a between-person correlation of r_c = .32 for state-positive affect and r_c = –.02 for state-negative affect. Interestingly, the positive correlation between OCB and negative affect supports the view that OCB is used on a momentary basis as a form of mood repair (Glomb et al., 2011). The stronger results for positive affect compared to negative affect also support the view that positive and negative affect should be separated when examining their relationships with OCB (as opposed to

Table 24.1 Meta-Analytic Results of Within-Person Correlates of Organizational Citizenship Behavior

	Organizational Citizenship Behavior	
Correlate	r (95% CI) k (N)	r_c (80% CV) SDr_c ($\%V_{art}$)
Positive affect	.18 (.11, .24) 9 (7,476)	.22 (.04, .39) .14 (8.86)
Negative affect	.07 (.01, .12) 6 (5,606)	.08 (–.01, .17) .08 (26.21)
Job satisfaction	.27 (.14, .41) 3 (2,154)	.33 (.15, .50) .15 (8.08)
Stressors	.24 (.12, .35) 6 (3,003)	.32 (.10, .53) .18 (10.23)
Strain	.02 (–.15, .19) 5 (3,650)	.02 (–.27, .30) .23 (3.98)
Task performance	.23 (.11, .35) 5 (2,432)	.32 (.12, .52) .17 (12.93)

CI, confidence interval around uncorrected population correlation; CV, credibility interval around weighted corrected mean correlation; *k*, number of studies; *N*, cumulative sample size; %Vart, percentage of variance in r_c explained by study artifacts; *r*, uncorrected population correlation; r_c, corrected population correlation.

combining positive and negative affect items into a single "hedonic tone" measure).

OCB is also positively correlated with job satisfaction (r = .27; r_c = .33). Putting these results together with the results for positive affect supports the notion from affective events theory that OCB, if considered an outcome of affective events, is likely both an affect-driven behavior and a cognition-driven behavior (see Weiss & Cropanzano, 1996). Similarly, LePine, Erez, and Johnson (2002) reported a between-person correlation of r_c = .24.

Table 24.1 also shows that OCB is positively associated with stressors (r = .24; r_c = .32), as the 95% confidence interval for this correlation does not include zero. Here, stressors represent a variety of factors, including workload, job insecurity, and job demands, that both challenge and hinder. Between-person research, focused on stressors such as role ambiguity, role conflict, and role overload, have reported corrected correlations ranging from r_c = –.06 to r_c = –.15 (Eatough, Chang, Miloslavic, & Johnson, 2011). With the exception of challenge stressors, between-person research has generally deemed the stressors included in the within-person research we reviewed to be bad for employee well-being. On the one hand, the positive, within-person relationship between OCB and stressors suggests that on days when individuals are faced with a greater than usual level of stressors (and hence feel stressed), they invest their remaining resources into OCB, perhaps with the hope that such behaviors will be reciprocated (cf. Halbesleben & Wheeler, 2011). On the other hand, OCB is not significantly associated with strain (r = .02; r_c = .02). This differs from between-person meta-analytic estimates, which have reported a negative correlation (r_c = –.16) between OCB and strain (specifically, emotional strain) (Chang, Johnson, & Yang, 2007). It should be noted that the relationship between OCB and strain has the lowest percentage of variance explained by study artifacts (at 3.98%), which suggests the presence of moderators. In all, future research is needed to better understand how momentary levels of stressors, stress, and strain relate to engagement in OCB.

Finally, OCB is positively correlated with task performance (r = .23; r_c = .32), which, similar to findings at the between-person level of analysis (r_c = .37 for OCB; r_c = .39 for OCBO; Podsakoff et al., 2009), supports the view that these two dimensions of job performance are distinct.

Issues and Future Directions for Within-Person Research on Organizational Citizenship Behavior

Having reviewed what we know about OCB at the within-person level of analysis, we now discuss issues in the study of OCB at this level of analysis, as well as potential directions for future research in this area, in order to lay the groundwork for where we might go.

Measurement of Organizational Citizenship Behavior Within Persons Over Time

The first issue deals with the measurement of OCB at the within-person level of analysis, and there are several subissues within this larger issue. First, as noted in our review, the majority of within-person investigations of OCB have relied on the OCBI and OCBO scales developed by Lee and Allen (2002). Sometimes OCBI and OCBO are kept separate, and other times they are combined into an overall OCB scale. Although we do not take exception with examining overall OCB, the potentially bigger issue in our mind is that studies differ in the items that they take from these scales. To be fair, most of the within-person studies to date have used the majority of items from the Lee and Allen (2002) scales, but when items are eliminated, it is difficult to make comparisons across studies because the full scale is not provided. Thus, we encourage researchers using existing scales to be clear about which items are included and which items are excluded. Alternatively, future research may benefit from using the scales reported in Dalal et al. (2009), who developed scales of OCB suitable for within-person research by drawing from different sources and provided the items in an Appendix. The use of these scales, which were tailored for a within-person focus, could better allow for "apples to apples" comparisons across studies. That said, a potential downside is that the entire measure consists of 18 items (with OCB toward coworkers, the supervisor, and the organization), and therefore the development of a shorter, overall OCB scale would be welcomed given the practical limitations of ESM.

Second, when items are excluded from existing scales such as Lee and Allen (2002), authors have done so based on the notion that some forms of OCB are unlikely to vary on a daily basis. Such exclusions are reasonable given that these scales were developed to capture differences in OCB between persons. For example, it probably is unlikely that one would observe variation over a short period of time for a behavior such as "adjust your work schedule to accommodate other employees' requests for time off" or "attend functions that are not required but that help the organizational image" (Lee & Allen, 2002). That being said, this is ultimately an empirical question that research has yet (but needs) to answer. Moreover, once items are eliminated, the question is whether this creates deficiency in the measure of OCB. One argument is that it does create deficiency because the full scale is not being used, yet those items are representative of the construct of OCB. However, an alternative argument is that the elimination of items that vary little over short periods of time does not create deficiency because the construct of OCB differs slightly across level of analysis. In other words, over short periods of time, such as hours or days, some of the behaviors thought to represent OCB are so rare as to be virtually irrelevant. Thus, it may be that OCB is not completely isomorphic across levels of analysis, with the degree of isomorphism between "within-person" OCB and "between-person" OCB increasing as the period of time in between measurements of within-person OCB increases.

We noted earlier that shorter scales may be necessary at times given the demanding nature of ESM studies. To get around this issue, some researchers (e.g., Dalal et al., 2009) keep a common core of items on each momentary survey yet cycle other items in. On the one hand, there are several benefits to this technique: a larger aspect of the construct space is captured, reducing potential deficiency that would be created if items were eliminated, and it may reduce priming effects because participants are faced with a slightly different set of items each time (Hulin & Judge, 2003; Miner et al., 2005). On the other hand, the slight differences across scales make it difficult to know whether a relationship at a given moment in time (e.g., an employee reports high levels of both positive affect and OCB on Monday; on Tuesday that same employees reports high positive affect but low OCB) is being accurately captured or is due to differences in item content (the specific types of OCB that this employee engages in were on Monday's scale but not Tuesday's).

A final issue with regard to the measurement of OCB deals with self-report. In between-individual research, it is not overly difficult to have independent raters (e.g., supervisors or coworkers) assess the OCB of a focal employee. Indeed, the inclusion of self-reported OCB in between-persons research is sometimes viewed as a major limitation. However, in within-persons research, particularly in intense ESM studies over short periods of time, independent assessments are unrealistic and infeasible to obtain. Moreover, it may be the case that focal employees are the best sources for information about momentary OCB because independent raters such as supervisors may have limited observational opportunities. Fortunately, some causes of same-source bias can be ruled out by within-person designs, by individually mean-centering the data, which removes causes of same-source bias such response tendencies and trait affect (Podsakoff, MacKenzie, Lee, & Podsakoff, 2003). Nevertheless, within-person investigations of OCB would benefit by incorporating other data besides self-report. Unobtrusive measures may be one promising area, particularly in laboratory settings.

An alternative to unobtrusive measures would be to seek daily ratings from coworkers as we discussed earlier. Though difficult in an ESM study, such designs are not impossible (e.g., Halbesleben & Wheeler, 2015; Trougakos et al., 2015). Moreover, far from being simply a methodological point, such investigations may be necessary to establish the theoretical domain of the daily OCB construct. As noted earlier, OCB may differ somewhat at the within-individual level (compared to the between-individual level). Given the contradiction in the Halbesleben and Wheeler (2015) and Trougakos et al. (2015) papers discussed earlier, perhaps measurement from different sources exacerbates such differences further. That is, at the aggregate, between-individual level perhaps employees can "spread" their OCB around so that the particular coworker providing a measurement is unimportant. Contrast this with the daily level where an employee may engage in a high level of OCB (and would thus self-report this), but the particular coworker providing the measurement was not the recipient of that OCB and therefore reports that the focal employee engaged in little OCB. Future research is necessary to determine how such situations might influence within-person OCB relationships and whether other reports of OCB are even appropriate in ESM studies.

Causal Direction of Affect–Organizational Citizenship Behavior Relationships

Much of the research on affective states and OCB was predicated on affective events theory (Weiss & Cropanzano, 1996). AET positions affective reactions to events as antecedents of behavior; thus, it is perhaps not surprising that studies using AET as a theoretical framework to understand within-person OCB have treated OCB as an outcome of affect. For example, Dalal et al. (2009, p. 1053) noted that "state affect is the primary antecedent of [OCB and CWB]." Spector and Fox's (2002) model of voluntary work behavior also positions affect as an antecedent of OCB and CWB. Yet it is also reasonable (and recent studies have shown) that affect may be a consequence of engaging in OCB (e.g., Glomb et al., 2011; Koopman et al., 2016). Thus, although OCB may indeed be a consequence of affective events, OCB may also constitute an affective event in and of itself that elicits emotion (most likely, positive affect). Given that ESM studies are now often collecting multiple surveys per day, lagged analyses and the examination of change scores are possible, allowing researchers to better illuminate the causal direction between OCB and other constructs.

The Relationship Between Organizational Citizenship Behavior and Counterproductive Work Behavior at the Within-Person Level

Not included in our meta-analysis due to an insufficient number of studies, the within-person relationship between OCB and CWB is important to examine. Dalal (2005), in a meta-analysis at the between-person level of analysis, found that OCB and CWB were only moderately and negatively correlated, and the two constructs exhibit differential patterns of relationships with other variables. Thus, one might conclude at the between-person level of analysis that these two concepts are distinct, such that a person who engages in high levels of OCB may (or may not) engage in high levels of CWB. The independence of OCB and CWB was also the conclusion of Dalal et al. (2009), who found that the two constructs were unrelated at the within-person level. In contrast, Rodell and Judge (2009) reported a negative (albeit small) correlation between OCB and CWB at the within-person level. Although these findings appear to mirror research at the between-person level, we wonder whether they are the result of being unable to capture engagement in OCB and CWB in the same moment in time. That is, by asking about engagement in OCB and CWB over the course of the day (Rodell & Judge, 2009) or since the previous survey (Dalal et al., 2009) and thereby providing participants with a range of time, we allow for the possibility that an employee's OCB and CWB are unrelated. For example, over the course of a day, an employee would have time to engage in both OCB and CWB, high levels of one but not the other, or neither behavior at all. If, however, we dug down to the actual moment of behavioral execution, would we still find OCB and CWB to be independent? We suspect not. Instead, we expect that OCB and CWB (and task performance, if one wants to capture the domain of job performance) to display strong, negative correlations with each other, perhaps to the point of being opposite ends of the same continuum. This is because the more fine-grained the time frame becomes, the more one behavior must be performed at the expense of the other. Thus, it seems highly unlikely that both behaviors can be performed simultaneously. In sum, to provide a more definitive answer to the question as to "whether a person who engages in OCB on a particular occasion must also refrain from CWB on that occasion" (Dalal et al., 2009, p. 1052), it may be that qualitative data or direct observation is needed to capture the precise behaviors that individuals are engaging in at a given point in time.

Expanding the "Dark Side" of Within-Person Organizational Citizenship Behavior

As discussed earlier, the Koopman et al. (2016) paper differed from the other manuscripts that have investigated OCB at the within-individual level by drawing attention to the potential "dark side" of these behaviors. That OCB may have a dark side is already well known, however, theoretical and empirical investigations here have focused on issues such as how OCB conflicts with aggregate task performance or long-run career trajectories (e.g., Bergeron, 2007; Bergeron, Shipp, Rosen, & Furst, 2013; Rubin, Dierdorff, & Bachrach, 2013). Koopman and colleagues illustrated that engaging in OCBs entails tradeoffs at the daily level, too.

This highlights a number of potentially interesting opportunities for future research. Glomb et al. (2011) noted that managers should view engaging in OCB as a means to promote well-being among employees. Is this recommendation contradicted by the findings of Koopman et al. (2016)? It would seem so, given that these authors linked OCB to reduced well-being due to a lack of progress toward daily work goals. However, these authors also noted an increase in well-being through positive affect that was comparatively larger than the reduction in well-being through a lack of work-goal progress, particularly for promotion-focused employees. Should the take-home message then be that, in spite of some downsides, engaging in OCB has a net benefit for employees, particularly in light of the potential social benefits (e.g., Halbesleben & Wheeler, 2011, 2015)? This position has some merit; however, if employees consistently fall short of their work goals, then in the long run they may experience the career-related consequences of OCB noted by others (e.g., Bergeron, 2007). Future research that blends an individual's daily experiences of OCB with the longer run implications of this behavior is needed in order to provide recommendations to both managers and employees.

There is another aspect to the dark side of OCB that has been almost entirely overlooked in research at both the within- and between-individual level: Who is on the receiving end of this helping behavior? This shift in focus is important because there are reasons to think that OCB could have a "double dark side"—that is, not only might it have negative implications to the actor, but it might also be detrimental to the receiver. For example, Deelstra and colleagues (2003) showed that recipients of helping behavior imposed upon them had negative reactions in terms of both reduced self-esteem as well as increased heart rate. Thus, not only might helping behavior be bad for the actor, but it might also be bad for the receiver. Of note here is that the helping behavior was "imposed" upon recipients, and so future research should examine these effects more closely.

One final opportunity for future research on the dark side of OCB that we wish to discuss maintains the dual focus on actor and receiver but also highlights potential negative consequences to the organization as well. Research in other domains has identified that some employees may be considered "core" or "more tightly linked to the overall performance of the team" (Humphrey, Morgeson, & Mannor, 2009, p. 49). Consider then several possible scenarios. Perhaps a "non-core" employee engages in OCB toward a "core employee" on a given day. Although there may be a reduction in performance to the actor (e.g., Barnes, Hollenbeck, Wagner, DeRue, Nahrgang, & Schwind, 2008; Koopman et al., 2016), the overall contribution to team or organizational performance might be a net positive if the help facilitates the work of the core employee that day. However, consider the reverse situation, where a core employee engages in OCB toward a non-core employee. This situation might result in an overall net loss in productivity on that day. Thus, future research on OCB at the within-individual level could attempt to identify *who* is doing the helping, and how this might impact the individuals involved in the behavior as well as the organization.

Using Experience-Sampling Methodology to Study Between-Person Differences in Within-Person Variability

In addition to complementing research on between-individual differences in average levels of OCB with the study of within-individual fluctuations in OCB over time, researchers should also utilize ESM methods to merge these two streams of research by exploring between-individual differences in the stability of OCB over time. This type of approach has furthered our understanding of numerous organizational phenomenon including self-esteem (e.g., Kernis, Cornell, Sun, Berry, & Harlow, 1993), personality (Fleeson, 2001), interpersonal trust (Fleeson & Leicht, 2006), and emotional labor (Scott, Barnes, & Wagner, 2012). Variability in organizational phenomenon has been associated with both beneficial (e.g., Kernis et al., 1993) and detrimental outcomes (e.g., Scott et al., 2012), and it is unclear whether OCB variability will be beneficial or detrimental for employees. On the one hand, OCB variability may be beneficial for an employee because it may lessen the likelihood of job creep (which occurs when others expect employees to engage in OCB as an ongoing part of their role expectations; Van Dyne & Ellis, 2004) and escalating citizenship (which occurs when engaging in OCBs becomes so normative that employees feel obligated to continually increase OCBs to be seen as going the extra mile; Bolino & Turnley, 2003). For example, when OCB is performed consistently (as opposed to variably), it is more likely to be expected and considered the norm. On the other hand, OCB variability may be detrimental for an employee if third parties (e.g., coworkers and supervisors) view these behaviors as impression management. For example, an employee who only performs OCB in the presence of his supervisor may not be viewed as favorably as an employee who performs OCB more consistently and regardless of the situation. Overall, we see between-person differences in within-person OCB variability as a particularly fruitful area for future research.

Incorporating Other Theories to Understand Within-Person Organizational Citizenship Behavior

To date, scholars investigating OCB at the within-individual level have tended to rely on affective events theory or conservation of resources theory as their overarching theoretical frameworks. However, given the relative nascence of research in this area, we feel that scholars may gain interesting insights into OCB at this level of analysis by drawing upon alternative theoretical frameworks. Thus, we conclude our chapter with a brief discussion of how several such theories might be leveraged to increase our understanding of daily OCB.

As reviewed earlier, Trougakos et al. (2015) recently applied ego depletion theory to their investigation of surface acting as an antecedent of OCBI. One challenge to within-individual OCB research is that conservation of resources theory and ego depletion theory are often applied in very similar ways (e.g., that purposeful acts can reduce available resources). However, these theories are not identical. Conservation of resources theory, for example, specifies that certain events may be resource generating as well as being resource consuming. Ego depletion theory does not clearly articulate this generation mechanism; however, it may possibly be more suited to theorizing at the momentary level of analysis where the depletion of available self-regulatory resources might be the proximal cause of either action or inaction. Future research could therefore attempt to parse the mechanisms associated with these two theories to better understand how OCB influences an individual's resources.

Moving beyond these theories, however, we think that there are opportunities to apply a number of other theoretical lenses to within-individual OCB to better understand both why employees engage in OCB, as well as the consequences of this behavior to actors and recipients. One option is moral licensing theory (Merritt, Effron, & Monin, 2010). Briefly, application of this theory suggests that a positive relationship would be found between OCB and CWB as a result of the accumulation or reduction of moral credits. Klotz and Bolino (2013) recently applied this theory to OCB at the between-individual level of analysis, but would similar effects be found at the within-individual level as well? As our discussion of OCB and CWB earlier suggests, it is unlikely that a positive association would be found in concurrent measurement of these constructs. However, if a positive relationship were found over the course of a day or perhaps even from one day to the next, then perhaps a moral licensing framework could be applied to explain this relationship.

Building on the findings of Koopman et al. (2016) and a meta-analysis by Lanaj, Chang, and Johnson (2012), regulatory focus theory could potentially be applied to understanding daily OCB. Lanaj et al. (2012) found that people with high trait promotion focus engage in more OCB, in general, and Koopman et al. (2016) found that high trait promotion focus amplified the positive affective outcomes of OCB. Combining these two findings, perhaps individuals primed with a high *state* promotion focus would be more likely to see OCB as a means of enhancing social relationships (e.g., Halbesleben & Wheeler, 2015) and thus engage in more OCB compared to individuals primed with a high *state* prevention focus, as such individuals might be more attuned to the implications of taking time away from assigned tasks to engage in OCB.

Continuing the theme introduced earlier regarding looking at the recipients of OCB on a daily basis, researchers could draw upon theory on self-esteem threat (Fisher, Nadler, & Whitcher-Alagna, 1982) as one explanatory framework. Deelstra et al. (2003) drew upon this theory to explain why recipients of help reacted negatively, and such an explanation could be similarly incorporated at the within-individual level. However, according to Fisher et al. (1982), help need not always be interpreted as a threat; instead, helping can be seen as supportive as well (for example, see: Halbesleben & Wheeler, 2015). Thus, self-esteem threat could be used to model both the "bright" and "dark" sides of receiving help as well and explain when, why, and for whom receiving help threatens one's self-esteem, and when it does not.

Each of the earlier discussions focuses on those who receive help in the workplace. What about those who do not receive help? Here, theory on social comparisons (Wood, 1996) may be relevant. For example, do employees make social comparisons with their coworkers about the amount of help they receive? Research on LMX social comparisons suggests that employees do make social comparisons with their workgroup peers about the resources they receive from others (e.g., Vidyarthi, Liden, Anand, Erdogan, & Ghosh, 2010). Moreover, social comparison theory has already been a useful lens for understanding within-individual fluctuations in OCB (e.g., Spence et al., 2011). As such, research could explore the influence of daily social comparisons about the amount of help employees receive from others as well as when upward OCB social comparisons result in contrastive (aversive) or assimilative (comforting) social comparison reactions (Greenberg, Ashton-James, & Ashkanasy, 2007).

Finally, considering the important influence that role theory has played on between-person OCB research, it could also be applied to extend our understanding of within-person fluctuations in OCB. At the between-person level, scholars have typically drawn upon role theory to explain why some employees often perceive citizenship as part of their required behavior at work (e.g., Morrison, 1994). Related to our previous discussion about using ESM to study between-person differences in within-person variability in OCB, role theory is likely to be a useful theoretical perspective. Specifically, because role theory suggests that role conceptualizations provide action templates for employees (Katz & Kahn, 1978), role theory would suggest that an employee is likely to consistently strive to engage in OCB on a daily basis when she sees OCB as part of her work role (i.e., her daily action template includes OCB). Alternatively, when an employee sees OCB as extra-role (i.e., her daily action template does not include OCB), role theory would suggest that daily OCB is likely to fluctuate in accordance with the amount of daily resources available for behaviors that are viewed as "not my job" (Morrison, 1994, p. 1563).

Conclusion

Although OCB research has typically focused on identifying antecedents and consequences of between-person differences in levels of OCB, our review documents that research on within-person fluctuations in OCB is beginning to burgeon. Considering the relatively nascent state of the field, we view this domain as one that is ripe for further inquiry. Our review highlights several promising future research opportunities, and we hope it helps stimulate new and novel research on the topic.

References

Alliger, G. M., & Williams, K. J. (1993). Using signal-contingent experience sampling methodology to study work in the field: A discussion and illustration examining task perceptions and mood. *Personnel Psychology, 46,* 525–549.

Barnes, C. M., Ghumman, S., & Scott, B. A. (2013). Sleep and organizational citizenship behavior: The mediating role of job satisfaction. *Journal of Occupational Health Psychology, 18,* 16–26.

Barnes, C. M., Hollenbeck, J. R., Wagner, D. T., Derue, D. S., Nahrgang, J. D., & Schwind, K. M. (2008). Harmful help: The costs of backing-up behavior in teams. *Journal of Applied Psychology, 93,* 529–539. doi:10.1037/0021-9010.93.3.529

Bateman, T. S., & Crant, J. M. (1993). The proactive component of organizational behavior: A measure and correlates. *Journal of Organizational Behavior, 14,* 103–118.

Baumeister, R. F., Bratslavsky, E., Muraven, M., & Tice, D. M. (1998). Ego depletion: Is the active self a limited resource? *Journal of Personality and Social Psychology, 74,* 1252–1265.

Bergeron, D. M. (2007). The potential paradox of organizational citizenship behavior: Good citizens at what cost? *Academy of Management Review, 32,* 1078–1095.

Bergeron, D. M., Shipp, A. J., Rosen, B., & Furst, S. A. (2013). Organizational citizenship behavior and career outcomes: The cost of being a good citizen. *Journal of Management, 39,* 958–984.

Binnewies, C., Sonnentag, S., & Mojza, E. J. (2009). Daily performance at work: Feeling recovered in the morning as a predictor of day-level job performance. *Journal of Organizational Behavior, 30,* 67–93.

Binnewies, C., Sonnentag, S., & Mojza, E. J. (2010). Recovery during the weekend and fluctuations in weekly job performance: A week-level study examining intra-individual relationships. *Journal of Occupational and Organizational Psychology, 83,* 419–441.

Bolino, M. C., Klotz, A. C., Turnley, W. H., & Harvey, J. (2013). Exploring the dark side of organizational citizenship behavior. *Journal of Organizational Behavior, 34,* 542–559. doi:10.1002/job.1847

Bolino, M. C., & Turnley, W. H. (2003). Going the extra mile: Cultivating and managing employee citizenship behavior. *The Academy of Management Executive, 17,* 60–71.

Cavanaugh, M. A., Boswell, W. R., Roehling, M. V., & Boudreau, J. W. (2000). An empirical examination of self-reported work stress among U.S. managers. *Journal of Applied Psychology, 85,* 65–74.

Chang, C., Johnson, R. E., & Yang, L. (2007). Emotional strain and organizational citizenship behaviours: A meta-analysis and review. *Work & Stress, 21,* 312–332.

Christian, M. S., Eisenkraft, N., & Kapadia, C. (2015). Dynamic associations between somatic complaints, human energy, and discretionary behaviors: Experiences with pain fluctuations at work. *Administrative Science Quarterly, 60*, 66–102.

Conway, J. M., Rogelberg, S. G., & Pitts, V. E. (2009). Workplace helping: Interactive effects of personality and momentary positive affect. *Human Performance, 22*, 321–339.

Crant, J. M. (2000). Proactive behavior in organizations. *Journal of Management, 26*, 435–462.

Dalal, R. S. (2005). A meta-analysis of the relationship between organizational citizenship behavior and counterproductive behavior. *Journal of Applied Psychology, 90*, 1241–1255.

Dalal, R. S., Lam, H., Weiss, H. M., Welch, E. R., & Hulin, C. L. (2009). A within-person approach to work behavior and performance: Concurrent and lagged citizenship-counterproductivity associations, and dynamic relationships with affect and overall job performance. *Academy of Management Journal, 52*, 1051–1066.

Deelstra, J. T., Peeters, M. C. W., Zijlstra, F. R. H., Schaufeli, W. B., Stroebe, W., & Van Doornen, L. P. (2003). Receiving instrumental support at work: When help is not welcome. *Journal of Applied Psychology, 88*, 324–331. doi:10.1037/0021-9010.88.2.324

Demerouti, E., Bakker, A. B., Nachreiner, F., & Schaufeli, W. B. (2001). The job demands-resources model of burnout. *Journal of Applied Psychology, 86*, 499–512.

Eatough, E. M., Chang, C., Miloslavic, S. A., & Johnson, R. E. (2011). Relationships of role stressors with organizational citizenship behavior: A meta-analysis. *Journal of Applied Psychology, 96*, 619–632.

Fay, D., & Sonnentag, S. (2012). Within-person fluctuations of proactive behavior: How affect and experienced competence regulate work behavior. *Human Performance, 25*, 72–93.

Festinger, L. (1954). *A theory of cognitive dissonance*. Stanford, CA: Stanford University Press.

Fisher, C. D. (2003). Why do lay people believe that satisfaction and performance are correlated? Possible sources of a commonsense theory. *Journal of Organizational Behavior, 24*, 753–777.

Fisher, J. D., Nadler, A., & Whitcher-Alagna, S. (1982). Recipient reactions to aid. *Psychological Bulletin, 91*, 27.

Fleeson, W. (2001). Toward a structure- and process-integrated view of personality: Traits as density distributions of states. *Journal of Personality and Social Psychology, 80*, 1011–1027.

Fleeson, W., & Leicht, C. (2006). On delineating and integrating the study of variability and stability in personality psychology: Interpersonal trust as illustration. *Journal of Research in Personality, 40*, 5–20.

Fox, S., Spector, P. E., Goh, A., Bruursema, K., & Kessler, S. R. (2012). The deviant citizen: Measuring potential positive relations between counterproductive work behaviour and organizational citizenship behaviour. *Journal of Occupational and Organizational Psychology, 85*, 199–220.

Fredrickson, B. L. (2001). The role of positive emotions in positive psychology: The broaden-and-build theory of positive emotions. *American Psychologist, 56*, 218–226.

Fritz, C., & Sonnentag, S. (2009). Antecedents of day-level proactive behavior: A look at job stressors and positive affect during the workday. *Journal of Management, 35*, 94–111.

George, J. M. (1991). State or trait: Effects of positive mood on prosocial behaviors at work. *Journal of Applied Psychology, 76*, 299–307.

George, J. M., & Brief, A. P. (1992). Feeling good-doing good: A conceptual analysis of the mood at work-organizational spontaneity relationship. *Psychological Bulletin, 112*, 310–329.

Glomb, T. M., Bhave, D. P., Miner, A. G., & Wall, M. (2011). Doing good, feeling good: Examining the role of organizational citizenship behaviors in changing mood. *Personnel Psychology, 64*, 191–223.

Goodman, S. A., & Svyantek, D. J. (1999). Person organization fit and contextual performance: Do shared values matter? *Journal of Vocational Behavior, 55*, 254–275.

Gordon, H. J., Demerouti, E., Bipp, T., & Le Blanc, P. M. (2015). The job demands and resources decision making (JD-R-DM) model. *European Journal of Work and Organizational Psychology, 24*, 44–58.

Greenberg, J., Ashton-James, C. E., & Ashkanasy, N. M. (2007). Social comparison processes in organizations. *Organizational Behavior and Human Decision Processes, 102*, 22–41.

Halbesleben, J. R. B., Neveu, J.-P., Paustian-Underdahl, S. C., & Westman, M. (2014). Getting to the "cor": Understanding the role of resources in conservation of resources theory. *Journal of Management, 40*, 1334–1364. doi:10.1177/0149206314527130

Halbesleben, J. R. B., & Wheeler, A. R. (2011). I owe you one: Coworker reciprocity as a moderator of the day-level exhaustion-performance relationship. *Journal of Organizational Behavior, 32*, 608–626.

Halbesleben, J. R. B., & Wheeler, A. R. (2015). To invest or not? The role of coworker support and trust in daily reciprocal gain spirals of helping behavior. *Journal of Management, 41*, 1628–1650.

Higgins, E. T. (1997). Beyond pleasure and pain. *American Psychologist, 52*, 1280–1300.

Hobfoll, S. E. (1989). Conservation of resources: A new attempt at conceptualizing stress. *American Psychologist, 44*, 513–524.

Hulin, C. L., & Judge, T. A. (2003). Job attitudes. In I. B. Weiner (series ed.) & W. C. Borman, D. R. Ilgen, & R. J. Klimoski (vol. eds.), *Handbook of psychology*, vol. *12*: Industrial and organizational psychology (pp. 255–276). Hoboken, NJ: Wiley.

Humphrey, S. E., Morgeson, F. P., & Mannor, M. J. (2009). Developing a theory of the strategic core of teams: A role composition model of team performance. *Journal of Applied Psychology, 94*, 48–61. doi:10.1037/a0012997

Hunter, J. E., & Schmidt, F. L. (2004). *Methods of meta-analysis: Correcting error and bias in research findings* (2nd ed.). Thousand Oaks, CA: Sage.

Ilies, R., Scott, B. A., & Judge, T. A. (2006). The interactive effects of personal traits and experienced states on intra-individual patterns of citizenship behavior. *Academy of Management Journal, 49*, 561–575.

Izard, C. E., & Ackerman, B. P. (2000). Motivational, organizational, and regulatory functions of discrete emotions. In M. Lewis and J. M. Haviland-Jones (Eds.), *Handbook of emotion* (pp. 253–264). New York, NY: Guilford.

Johnson, R. E., Lanaj, K., & Barnes, C. M. (2014). The good and bad of being fair: Effects of procedural and interpersonal justice behaviors on regulatory resources. *Journal of Applied Psychology, 99*, 635–650.

Judge, T. A., Simon, L. S., Hurst, C., & Kelley, K. (2014). What I experienced yesterday is who I am today: Relationship of work motivations and behaviors to within-individual variation in the five-factor model of personality. *Journal of Applied Psychology, 99*, 199–221.

Katz, D., & Kahn, R. L. (1978). *The social psychology of organizations*. New York, NY: Wiley.

Kernis, M. H., Cornell, D. P., Sun, C. R., Berry, A., & Harlow, T. (1993). Theres more to self-esteem than whether it is high or low—the importance of stability of self-esteem. *Journal of Personality and Social Psychology, 65*, 1190–1204.

Klotz, A. C., & Bolino, M. C. (2013). Citizenship and counterproductive work behavior: A moral licensing view. *Academy of Management Review, 38*, 292–306.

Koopman, J., Lanaj, K., & Scott, B. A. (2016). Integrating the bright and dark sides of OCB: A daily investigation of the benefits and costs of helping others. *Academy of Management Journal, 59*, 414–435.

Lanaj, K., Chang, C. H., & Johnson, R. E. (2012). Regulatory focus and work-related outcomes: A review and meta-analysis. *Psychological Bulletin, 138*, 998–1034.

Larson, R., & Csikszentmihalyi, M. (1983). The experience sampling method. In H. T. Reis (Ed.), *Naturalistic approaches to studying social interaction*. San Francisco, CA: Jossey-Bass.

Lazarus, R. S., & Folkman, S. F. (1984). *Stress, appraisal, and coping*. New York, NY: Springer.

Lee, K., & Allen, N. J. (2002). Organizational citizenship behavior and workplace deviance: The role of affect and cognitions. *Journal of Applied Psychology, 87*, 131–142.

LePine, J. A., Erez, A., & Johnson, D. E. (2002). The nature and dimensionality of organizational citizenship behavior: A critical review and meta-analysis. *Journal of Applied Psychology, 87*, 52–65.

Merritt, A. C., Effron, D. A., & Monin, B. (2010). Moral self-licensing: When being good frees us to be bad. *Social and Personality Psychology Compass, 4*, 344–357.

Miner, A. G., & Glomb, T. M. (2010). State mood, task performance, and behavior at work: A within-persons approach. *Organizational Behavior and Human Decision Processes, 112*, 43–57.

Miner, A. G., Glomb, T. M., & Hulin, C. (2005). Experience sampling mood and its correlates at work. *Journal of Occupational and Organizational Psychology, 78*, 171–193.

Mischel, W., & Shoda, Y. (1995). A cognitive-affective system of personality: Reconceptualizing situations, dispositions, dynamics, and invariance in personality structures. *Psychological Review, 102*, 246–268.

Morrison, E. W. (1994). Role definitions and organizational citizenship behavior—the importance of the employees perspective. *Academy of Management Journal, 37*, 1543–1567.

Morrison, E. W., & Phelps, C. C. (1999). Taking charge at work: Extra-role efforts to initiate workplace change. *Academy of Management Journal, 42*, 403–419.

Motowidlo, S. J., & van Scotter, J. R. (1994). Evidence that task performance should be distinguished from contextual performance. *Journal of Applied Psychology, 79*, 475–480.

Ohly, S., & Fritz, C. (2010). Work characteristics, challenge appraisal, creativity, and proactive behavior: A multi-level study. *Journal of Organizational Behavior, 31*, 543–565.

Organ, D. W. (1988). *Organizational citizenship behavior: The good soldier syndrome*. Lexington, MA: Lexington Books.

Organ, D. W., & Ryan, K. (1995). A meta-analytic review of attitudinal and dispositional predictors of organizational citizenship behavior. *Personnel Psychology, 48*, 775–802.

Podsakoff, N. P., Whiting, S. W., Podsakoff, P. M., & Blume, B. D. (2009). Individual- and Organizational-level consequences of organizational citizenship behaviors: A meta-analysis. *Journal of Applied Psychology, 94*, 122–141.

Podsakoff, P. M., MacKenzie, S. B., Lee, J. Y., & Podsakoff, N. P. (2003). Common method biases in behavioral research: A critical review of the literature and recommended remedies. *Journal of Applied Psychology, 88*, 879–903.

Rodell, J. B., & Judge, T. A. (2009). Can "good" stressors spark "bad" behaviors? The mediating role of emotions in links of challenge and hindrance stressors with citizenship and counterproductive behaviors. *Journal of Applied Psychology, 94*, 1438–1451.

Rubin, R. S., Dierdorff, E. C., & Bachrach, D. G. (2013). Boundaries of citizenship behavior: Curvilinearity and context in the citizenship and task performance relationship. *Personnel Psychology, 66*, 377–406. doi:10.1111/peps.12018

Salovey, P., Mayer, J. D., Goldman, S. L., Turvey, C., & Palfai, T. P. (1995). Emotional attention, clarity, and repair: Exploring emotional intelligence using the Trait Meta-Mood Scale. In J. W. Pennebaker (Ed.), *Emotion, disclosure, and health* (pp. 125–154). Washington, DC: American Psychological Association.

Schreurs, B. H. J., Van Emmerik, I. J., Gunter, H., & Germeys, F. (2012). A weekly diary study on the buffering role of social support in the relationship between job insecurity and employee performance. *Human Resource Management, 51*, 259–280.

Scott, B. A., Barnes, C. M., & Wagner, D. T. (2012). Chameleonic or consistent: A multilevel investigation of emotional labor variability. *Academy of Management Journal, 55*, 905–926.

Shockley, K. M., Ispas, D., Rossi, M. E., & Levine, E. L. (2012). A meta-analytic investigation of the relationship between state affect, discrete emotions, and job performance. *Human Performance, 25*, 377–411.

Sonnentag, S. (2003). Recovery, work engagement, and proactive behavior: A new look at the interface between nonwork and work. *Journal of Applied Psychology, 3*, 518–528.

Sonnentag, S., & Starzyk, A. (2015). Perceived prosocial impact, perceived situational constraints, and proactive work behavior: Looking at two distinct affective pathways. *Journal of Organizational Behavior, 36*, 806–824.

Spector, P. E., & Fox, S. (2002). An emotion-centered model of voluntary work behavior: Some parallels between counterproductive work behavior and organizational citizenship behavior. *Human Resource Management Review, 12*, 269–292.

Spence, J. R., Brown, D. J., Keeping, L. M., & Lian, H. (2014). Helpful today, but not tomorrow? Feeling grateful as a predictor of daily organizational citizenship behaviors. *Personnel Psychology, 67*, 705–738.

Spence, J. R., Ferris, D. L., Brown, D. J., & Heller, D. (2011). Understanding daily citizenship behaviors: A social comparison perspective. *Journal of Organizational Behavior, 32*, 547–571.

Smith, C. A., Organ, D. W., & Near, J. P. (1983). Organizational citizenship behavior: Its nature and antecedents. *Journal of Applied Psychology, 68*, 653–663.

Trougakos, J. P., Beal, D. J., Cheng, B. H., Hideg, I., & Zweig, D. (2015). Too drained to help: A resource depletion perspective on daily interpersonal citizenship behaviors. *Journal of Applied Psychology, 100*, 227–236.

Van Dyne, L., & Ellis, J. B. (2004). Job creep: A reactance theory perspective on ocb as overfulfillment of obligations. In J. C. Shapiro, L. M. Shore, S. Taylor, & L. E. Tetrick (Eds.), *The employment relationship: Examining psychological and contextual perspectives* (pp. 181–205). Oxford, England: Oxford University Press.

Van Dyne, L., & LePine, J. A. (1998). Helping and voice extra-role behaviors: Evidence of construct and predictive validity. *Academy of Management Journal, 37*, 765–802.

Vidyarthi, P. R., Liden, R. C., Anand, S., Erdogan, B., & Ghosh, S. (2010). Where do i stand? Examining the effects of leader-member exchange social comparison on employee work behaviors. *Journal of Applied Psychology, 95*, 849–861.

Watson, D., Clark, L. A., & Tellegen, A. (1988). Development and validation of brief measures of positive and negative affect: The PANAS scales. *Journal of Personality and Social Psychology, 54*, 1063–1070.

Weiss, H. M., & Cropanzano, R. (1996). Affective events theory: A theoretical discussion of the structure, causes, and consequences of affective experiences at work. *Research in Organizational Behavior, 18*, 1–74.

Williams, L. J., & Anderson, S. E. (1991). Job satisfaction and organizational commitment as predictors of organizational citizenship and in-role behaviors. *Journal of Management, 17*, 601–617.

Wood, J. V. (1996). What is social comparison and how should we study it? *Personality and Social Psychology Bulletin, 22*, 520–537.

Wu, C., & Parker, S. K. (2012). The role of attachment styles in shaping proactive behaviour: An intra-individual analysis. *Journal of Occupational and Organizational Psychology, 85*, 525–530.

Xanthopoulou, D., Heuven, E., Demerouti, E., Baker, A. B., & Schaufeli, W. (2008). Working in the sky: A diary study on work engagement among flight attendants. *Journal of Occupational Health Psychology, 13*, 345–356.

CHAPTER

25

Multilevel Antecedents of Organizational Citizenship Behavior: A Review and Recommendations for Future Research

Nathan P. Podsakoff, Philip M. Podsakoff, Scott B. MacKenzie, Timothy D. Maynes, Steven W. Whiting, *and* Trevor M. Spoelma

Abstract

Since their introduction into the literature over 30 years ago, the interest paid to organizational citizenship behaviors (OCBs) has dramatically increased. One reason for this is the relatively recent focus placed by researchers on identifying unit-level antecedents of individual-level OCBs. Unfortunately, our understanding of this growing area of research has been limited by the absence of strong and consistent conceptual foundations, and the lack of sufficient attention to appropriate methods for gathering and analyzing multilevel data. Therefore, the purpose of this review is to (a) provide a summary of research examining how unit-level factors influence individual-level OCBs, with particular attention to the mediators and moderators of these effects; (b) offer recommendations designed to provide stronger conceptual grounding for identifying antecedents, mediators, and moderators in this domain; and (c) suggest improvements to the methods and analytical techniques used for testing hypotheses regarding multilevel antecedents of OCB.

Key Words: organizational citizenship behavior, contextual performance, multilevel, unit-level data, data aggregation, individual differences, leader behaviors, climate, mediation, moderation

The concept of organizational citizenship behavior (OCB) has deep roots in the field of management, going back at least to the work of Barnard (1938), who recognized that "it is clear that the willingness of persons to contribute efforts to the cooperative system is indispensable" (p. 84), and to that of Katz and Kahn (1966), who emphasized the importance of "performance beyond role requirements for accomplishments of organizational functions" (p. 338). However, the modern conceptualization began with the work of Organ and his colleagues (Bateman & Organ, 1983; Organ, 1988; Smith, Organ, & Near, 1983) several decades later. Although Organ's (1988) definition of OCB has evolved since then, his original conceptualization was that OCB is "individual behavior that is discretionary, not directly or explicitly recognized by the formal reward system, and that in the aggregate promotes the effective functioning of the organization" (p. 4).

Since its introduction to the field, interest in organizational citizenship behavior has dramatically increased. Indeed, of the over 3,700 articles published in the literature on OCB, over half have been published in just the past 5 years, and over 80% have been published within the past 10 years (Institute for Scientific Information, 2016). The vast majority of these studies have focused on the individual-level antecedents of individual-level OCB. This type of research is depicted by line 3 in Figure 25.1, which depicts a multilevel model of antecedents and outcomes of

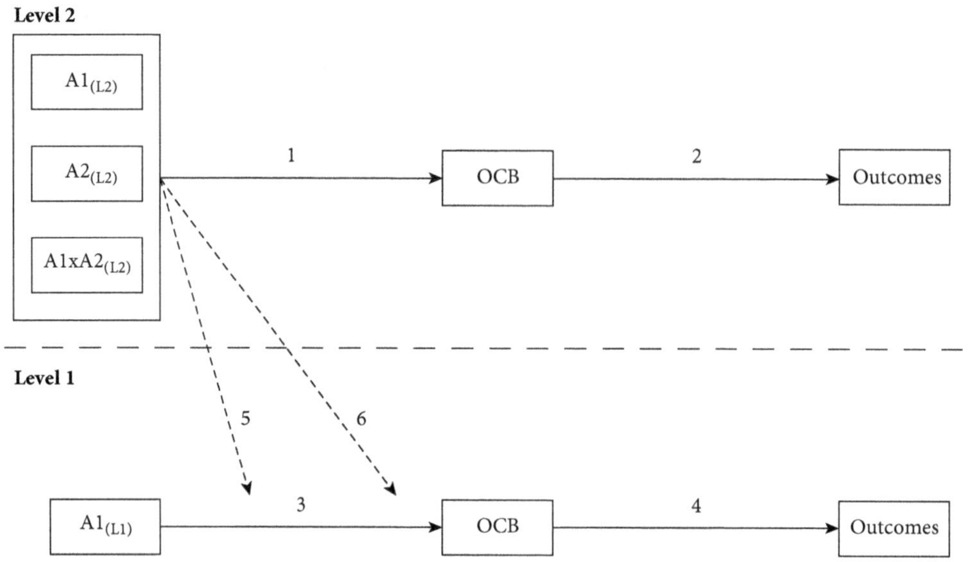

Figure 25.1 Summary of research on organizational citizenship behavior (OCB).

OCB at both the unit level (Level 2) and the individual level (Level 1). This research has generally shown that individual-level OCB is influenced by a number of different attitudinal and dispositional variables, motivational factors, perceptions of leadership characteristics, and environmental variables (see Organ, Podsakoff, & MacKenzie, 2006). A substantial amount of research has also examined the effects of individual-level OCB on individual-level outcomes. This research is depicted by Line 4 in Figure 25.1, and it has demonstrated that individuals who exhibit OCB in organizational settings generally receive higher performance evaluations, are more likely to be promoted, are more likely to receive reward recommendations, and are less likely to leave the organization (Podsakoff, Whiting, Podsakoff, & Blume, 2009). A significant amount of research has also attempted to validate Organ's (1988) general proposition that OCB "in the aggregate and over time" are positively related to a variety of unit-level measures of effectiveness (p. 4). This research is depicted in Figure 25.1 by Line 2. Several meta-analyses of this research (Nielsen, Hrivnak, & Shaw, 2009; Podsakoff et al., 2009; Whitman, Van Rooy, & Viswesvaran, 2010) have shown that unit-level OCBs are positively related to a variety of important organizational outcomes. In addition, researchers have published dozens of empirical articles focusing on unit-level factors that influence unit-level OCB (Line 1 in Figure 25.1).

Finally, researchers have also begun to examine the effects of unit-level factors on individual-level OCB (Line 6 in Figure 25.1), or unit-level moderators of the effects of individual-level antecedents on individual-level OCB (Line 5 in Figure 25.1). Our search identified 68 studies in this domain, all of which contribute to the idea that, "organizations are multilevel systems . . . [and] organizational science is moving toward the development of a paradigm that can bridge the micro-macro gap in theory and research" (Kozlowski & Klein, 2000, pp. 3–4).

Unfortunately, this emerging body of research provides a fragmented understanding of the unit-level antecedents of individual-level OCB, and the theoretical mechanisms through which they work. For example, our review of this literature indicated that researchers have (a) examined almost two dozen different dimensions of OCB and created "general" OCB composite measures using a variety of different subdimensions; (b) explored the effects of well over 100 different unit-level antecedents of OCB in a fairly unsystematic manner; and (c) examined over two dozen potential mediators (and almost as many potential moderators) of the effects of these unit-level antecedents on individual-level OCB. This is unfortunate, because without a comprehensive, coherent summary of the "state of the science" in this area, future research is likely to continue to be conducted in a piecemeal manner, thus inhibiting theory development in this important area of research.

In addition, there are several methodological concerns about the way in which the hypothesized multilevel effects have been tested. Generally speaking, research in this area needs to do a better job of establishing evidence of causality, specifying how lower level data are aggregated to represent higher level constructs, providing evidence that enough between-group variance exists for multilevel modeling, and using the most rigorous analytical procedures available for testing multilevel effects.

Therefore, the purpose of this review is threefold. First, we provide a summary of research on how unit-level factors influence individual-level OCB, with particular attention to the mediators and moderators of these effects. Second, we offer recommendations designed to provide stronger conceptual grounding for identifying antecedents, mediators, and moderators in this domain. Third, we suggest improvements to the methods and analytical techniques used for testing hypotheses regarding the multilevel antecedents of OCB.

Literature Review

To gain a better understanding of the state of research on unit-level antecedents of individual-level OCB, we first conducted a review of the existing literature. For the purposes of this review, we gathered articles examining multilevel antecedents of OCBs in three ways. First, we searched the reference lists of three recent meta-analyses (Nielsen et al., 2009; Podsakoff et al., 2009; Whitman et al., 2010) that report relationships between unit-level OCBs and outcomes. Second, we performed computer-assisted searches using the ISI's *Web of Science* and *ProQuest Dissertation* databases, and the *Google Scholar* search engine. Third, we contacted over 70 authors prominent in the OCB literature requesting in-press or unpublished manuscripts examining the multilevel antecedents of OCBs. These methods led to the identification of a total of 67 empirical studies proposing multilevel models examining the relationships between unit-level antecedents and individual-level OCBs. Studies that used multilevel analytical techniques only to control for nested (nonindependent) data (e.g., supervisor ratings, group membership), but that did not examine any unit-level antecedents, were not included in our review. We coded each study for several relevant characteristics, including sample characteristics, types of OCBs, research design and methods, reported findings, and mediators and moderators of the main effects. All article codes were compared across multiple raters and any discrepancies were discussed until a consensus was reached.

Sample Characteristics

Samples in the studies in our review were drawn from a diverse array of industries, including manufacturing, financial services, health care, professional services, logistics, and entertainment/leisure. A number of studies also reported samples that were drawn from multiple industries. In addition, we found diversity in the countries from which the samples were drawn. About three fifths of the samples were taken from China or Hong Kong (29%) or the United States (29%). Samples were also drawn from Taiwan, Korea, India, England, Lebanon, Canada, Israel, Germany, Kenya, Singapore, and the Netherlands. Although most of the studies we reviewed were published in journals (84%), some came from dissertations or conference presentations (16%). Finally, the average number of Level 2 units was approximately 67 ($M = 67.4$), and on average, about seven ($M = 6.9$) employees were nested in each unit. Finally, the most commonly reported Level 2 units were work groups (49%; employees working for a common supervisor) and teams (26%). Other Level 2 units included bank branches, retail stores, police stations, firms, plants/divisions, and Boy Scout troops.

Types of Organizational Citizenship Behavior

In the 68 studies we reviewed, over two dozen different forms of OCB were examined. This diversity is not uncommon in the OCB literature. Indeed, over the past three decades about 40 different OCB dimensions have been identified in the literature (LePine, Erez, & Johnson, 2002; Organ et al., 2006; Podsakoff, MacKenzie, Paine, & Bachrach, 2000). This proliferation has created some confusion because some dimensions share conceptual content but have different labels, whereas others have similar labels but different content. To reduce the confusion, scholars have searched for a smaller number of factors that underlie the OCB domain. The result of this work is that there are currently three predominant perspectives in the literature regarding the dimensionality of OCB.

The first perspective is that OCB is an aggregate, unidimensional construct. Both LePine et al. (2002) and Hoffman, Blair, Meriac, and Woehr (2007) concluded from their meta-analytic studies that some dimensions of OCB are not entirely distinguishable from each other based on an analysis of the nomological network. Thus, these authors argue for a single-factor model. Consistent with this perspective, a number of the studies in our review used a measure of OCB that was either general or comprised of multiple OCB dimensions (e.g., Chen, Tang, & Wang, 2009; Kehoe & Wright, 2013; Kirkman, Chen, Farh, Chen, & Lowe, 2009; Schuh et al., 2012; Song, Tsui, & Law, 2009).

The second perspective is that there are two general types of OCB that are distinguishable on the basis of who benefits from the behavior (Williams & Anderson, 1991). More specifically, some forms of citizenship behavior benefit the organization in general (OCBO), whereas others benefit individuals within the organization (OCBI). Among the behaviors most commonly identified as OCBI are altruism and courtesy (Organ, 1988); interpersonal facilitation (Van Scotter & Motowidlo, 1996); cooperating with others (Borman & Motowidlo, 1993); and interpersonal harmony (Farh, Earley, & Lin, 1997). Behaviors frequently identified as OCBO include civic virtue, sportsmanship, and conscientiousness (Organ, 1988); organizational loyalty (Graham, 1991); endorsing, defending, and supporting the organization (Borman & Motowidlo, 1993); and protecting the organization (George & Jones, 1997). In our review, a number of studies examined OCBO (e.g., Liao & Rupp, 2005; Yang, Mossholder, & Peng, 2007) and OCBI (e.g., Beeri, 2012; Hu & Liden, 2013; Karam & Kwantes, 2011; Kim, Shin, & Kim, 2012).

The third view, proposed by Van Dyne, Cummings, and Parks (1995), distinguishes between two general types of OCB on the basis of whether the behaviors are affiliation oriented (AOCB) or challenge oriented (COCB). The distinguishing feature is that AOCB tends to solidify/preserve relationships with others in the workplace, whereas COCB potentially damages interpersonal relationships because these behaviors criticize the status quo. The forms of AOCB examined in the studies included in our review were as follows: helping behavior (e.g., Gavin, 1997; Hofmann, Morgeson, & Gerras, 2003; Naumann & Ehrhart, 2011; Ng & Van Dyne, 2005), altruism (e.g., Liao, 2002; Snape & Redman, 2010), and courtesy (e.g., Kidwell, Mossholder, & Bennett, 1997; Liao, 2002). The forms of COCB examined in the studies we reviewed included voice behavior (e.g., Morrison, Wheeler-Smith, & Kamdar, 2011; Tangirala & Ramanujam, 2012), taking charge (e.g., Chen, 2011), and civic virtue (e.g., Wei, Han, & Hsu, 2010).

In our review of the multilevel antecedents of OCB, we adopted the general OCB construct perspective. We took this approach in an attempt to identify more consistent patterns in the findings. The studies in our review examined approximately 120 antecedents and nearly two dozen different forms of OCB. However, there were very few studies that examined the same antecedent and the same form of OCB. This made it difficult to discern any patterns without some form of aggregation. That being said, it is important to recognize that we believe that there is growing evidence that different forms of OCB are distinguishable from each other conceptually and have unique antecedents or consequences (e.g., LePine & Van Dyne, 2001; Van Dyne, Graham, & Dienesch, 1994; Van Dyne & LePine, 1998). Therefore, we encourage researchers to consider the OCBI/OCBO and AOCB/COCB frameworks when conducting multilevel OCB research in the future.

RESEARCH SETTING AND STUDY DESIGN

All the studies we reviewed examined cross-level antecedents of OCB in field, as opposed to laboratory, settings. Given the difficulty of simulating workplace phenomena at units of analysis higher than the individual, this finding is not surprising. Furthermore, 84% of the field studies used a cross-sectional design, compared to 16% that used a lagged design in which the antecedents were gathered at a time period before the OCB measures were gathered.

SOURCES OF ANTECEDENT AND ORGANIZATIONAL CITIZENSHIP BEHAVIOR MEASURES

Obtaining measures of unit-level antecedents from the same source as the measures of OCB can be problematic because doing so may lead to inflated or deflated estimates of the effects of the antecedents on OCB due to same-source biases. Over 72% of the studies in this review obtained (at least some) ratings of the antecedents from a different source than the ratings of OCB. Thus, it appears that the majority of studies in our review were designed in such a way as to limit the impact of common source effects (cf. Podsakoff, MacKenzie, & Podsakoff, 2012).

Multilevel Antecedents and Mediators of Organizational Citizenship Behavior

In our review, we discovered a surprising level of diversity in the unit-level antecedents of OCB that have been examined. Indeed, our search identified over 120 different multilevel antecedents that have been examined in the literature. To identify the patterns in the findings, we first grouped these antecedents into categories based on whether they focused on manager/leader characteristics (e.g., leader demographics, personality, leadership behavior); group characteristics (e.g., group demographics, similarity, socialization, and norms); member perceptions, attitudes, beliefs, and values (e.g., collective efficacy, group trust); climate-related variables (e.g., justice, empowerment, voice, safety); or organizational characteristics (e.g., demographics, structure and strategy, HRM practices). Following this, we aggregated across the different forms of OCB and examined whether the relationship between the antecedent and OCB was positive and significant, negative and significant, sometimes positive and sometimes negative (i.e., "mixed"), or nonsignificant. The results are shown in Table 25.1. Although space limitations preclude us from discussing all of the findings, in the sections that follow we will highlight some of the most important unit-level (Level 2) antecedents of OCB.

MANAGER/LEADER CHARACTERISTICS

Interestingly, manager tenure was found to be positively related to OCB, whereas leader/CEO age was found to be negatively related to OCB. Although this is somewhat counterintuitive, because age and tenure are generally positively correlated, it is possible that the difference in sign is due to the fact that tenure better captures the amount of time the manager has interacted with the subordinates engaging in OCB. Findings regarding leader gender were somewhat unclear with one study (Song et al., 2009) reporting an effect indicating that male leaders were associated with higher levels of OCB, whereas the other study (Schuh et al., 2012) reported a negative relationship between leader gender and employee OCB, but it did not report the way the gender variable was coded.

Undoubtedly, the most widely studied characteristic of managers/leaders was their behavior. Generally speaking, employees exhibit higher levels of OCB when they have transformational leaders (Cohen, Ben-Tura, & Vashdi, 2012; Kirkman et al., 2009) with a strong vision (Choi, 2007) who are open and empowering (Chen, 2011) and authentic in seeking the best for the organization (Hsiung, 2012). The evidence suggests that this happens because at the individual level these leadership behaviors enhance perceptions of procedural justice (Kirkman et al., 2009), identification with the organization (Schuh et al., 2012), relationships with coworkers (Carter, Armenakis, Field, & Mossholder, 2013), and the positive mood of subordinates (Hsiung, 2012); however, at the unit level, these leader behaviors increase the unit's trust in the organization (Li, Bai, & Xi, 2012), its feeling of empowerment, and its sense of obligation to go above and beyond the call of duty (Choi, 2007).

In addition, leaders who are benevolent (Hong, 2008), lead with integrity and morality (Hong, 2008), or who are not authoritarian (Hong, 2008) encourage subordinates to exhibit higher levels of OCB. The findings indicate that this happens primarily because at the individual level these forms of leader behavior enhance employee perceptions of self-efficacy (Hong, 2008) and perceived supervisory support (Hong, 2008), and increase their commitment to their supervisor (Walumbwa et al., 2010).

GROUP CHARACTERISTICS

In this category, the most important determinants of OCB are proximity to the supervisor

Table 25.1 Summary of Unit (Level 2) Antecedents of Organizational Citizenship Behaviors (OCBs) in Multilevel Studies

Categorization of Antecedents		**Level 2 Antecedents (and Study)**	**Unmediated Effect on OCB**	**Level 1 (2-1-1) Mediators**	**Level 2 (2-2-1) Mediators**
Manager/leader characteristics	Demographics	Manager tenure (Anand, 2011)	+		
		Leader/CEO age (Schuh et al., 2012, Study 2; Song et al., 2009)	–		
		Leader/CEO gender (Schuh et al., 2012, Study 2; Song et al., 2009)	+/–		
		Leader disciplinary background breadth (Paik, 2012)	–		
	Personality	Agreeableness, conscientiousness, and neuroticism (Walumbwa & Schaubroeck, 2009)	NS		
	Emotional management	Leader emotional management (Schraub et al., 2014)	+	Affective well-being	
	Leader–member demographic similarity	Leader–member similarity in age, gender, and tenure (Troster & van Knippenberg, 2012)	NS		
		Leader-member similarity in nationality × member team dissimilarity in nationality (Troster & van Knippenberg, 2012)	+	Psychological safety	
		Experienced similarity to supervisor (Gavin, 1997)	NS		
	Transformational/ transactional leadership	Transformational leadership (Carter et al., 2013; Kirkman et al., 2009; Li et al., 2012, 2013; Liang & Tang 2010; Paik, 2012; Schuh, et al., 2012; Song et al., 2009; Walker, 2011)	+	Procedural justice perceptions Employee identification with the organization Relationship quality with coworkers	Aggregate employee trust in the organization [NS—economic exchange norms] [NS—social exchange norms]
		Strong vision (Choi, 2007)	+		Aggregate levels of perceived empowerment Collective levels of felt obligation to engage in OCB

	Authentic leadership (Hsiung, 2012; Wherry, 2012)	+	Positive mood
	Idealized influence (Walumbwa & Schaubroeck, 2009)	NS	
	Transactional leader behavior (Song et al., 2009; Walker, 2011)	Mixed	
	Likelihood of being punished or rewarded for participating in certain behaviors (Schmidt, 2008)	NS	
	Ethical leadership (Walumbwa & Schaubroeck, 2009)	NS	
	Effective leadership behavior (e.g., abusive supervision [reverse scored], emotional control, supportive behaviors, decisiveness; Hui et al., 2007)	NS	
Servant leadership	Servant leadership (Walumbwa, Hartnell, & Oke, 2010)	+	Self-efficacy Commitment to supervisor
Manager consultation	Manager consultation behavior (Tangirala & Ramanujam, 2012)	+	Employee perceived influence on work decisions
Leader openness/ empowerment/ support	Empowering leadership (Chen, 2011)	+	Role-breadth self-efficacy Organization based self-esteem
	Leader openness × member team dissimilarity in nationality (Troster & van Knippenberg, 2012)	+	Affective commitment
Paternalistic leadership	Authoritarian (Hong, 2008: Study 1 & 2) authoritarian leadership (Wang et al., 2010)	–	Self-efficacy Perceived supervisory support
	Benevolence (Hong, 2008: Study 1 & 2)	+	Self-efficacy Dependence on leader for performance Perceived supervisory support
	Moralistic (Hong, 2008: Study 1 & 2)	+	Self-efficacy Dependence on leader for performance Perceived supervisory support

(*continued*)

Table 25.1 Continued

Categorization of Antecedents		Level 2 Antecedents (and Study)	Unmediated Effect on OCB	Level 1 (2-1-1) Mediators	Level 2 (2-2-1) Mediators
	Leader attitudes, moods, values, and beliefs	Leader positive mood (Gavin, 1997)	+		
		Leader organizational identification (Schuh et al., 2012: Study 2)	NS		
	LMX	Unit LMX (Hofmann et al., 2003; Sun et al., 2013; Wherry, 2012)	NS	[NS—OCB as in-role]	Shared perception that engaging in OCB will result in favorable outcomes
		Idiosyncratic deals (Anand, 2011)	+		
Group characteristics	Group demographics	Group size (Anand, 2011; Carter et al., 2013; Chen, 2011; Chen et al., 2009; Choi, 2006, 2007; Chung et al., 2011; Dekas, 2010; Farmer et al., 2015; Gavin, 1997; Hsiung, 2012; Morrison et al., 2011; Paik, 2012; Tuuli & Rowlinson, 2009; Yang et al., 2007)	NS		
		Team longevity group tenure (Dekas, 2010; Paik, 2012)	NS		
		Group density (Chung et al., 2011)	+		
		Team type (Tuuli & Rowlinson, 2009)	+		
		Proximity to supervisor (Gavin, 1997)	+		
	Group personality	Mean extraversion and agreeableness (Gonzalez-Mule et al., 2014)	NS		The mean extraversion direct effect on helping behavior was NS, but the indirect effect through cooperative group norms was significant
		Standard deviation in extraversion (Gonzalez-Mule et al., 2014)	+		Cooperative group norms
		Standard deviation in agreeableness (Gonzalez-Mule et al., 2014)	–		
	Group–member similarity	Group heterogeneity (in gender, ethnicity, location, job level, org. tenure; Dekas, 2010)	NS		
		Experienced similarity toward coworkers (Gavin, 1997; Troster & van Knippenberg, 2012)	NS	[NS—Psychological safety] [NS—Affective commitment]	

	Disciplinary diversity (Paik, 2012)	NS		
Group task characteristics	Disciplinary hierarchy (Paik, 2012)	–		
	Group autonomy (Dekas, 2010)	NS		
	Work unit structure (Aryee et al., 2008)	NS		
	Group task interdependence (Anand, 2011; Chen et al., 2009)	+		Group cohesion
	Goal interdependence (Chen et al., 2009)	+		Group cohesion
	Group workload (Dekas, 2010)	NS		
	Work group hurriedness (Jansen & Kristof-Brown, 2005)	NS		
	Group task conflict (Ng & Van Dyne, 2005; Schraub et al., 2014)	–	Affective well-being	
	Group relationship conflict (Schraub et al., 2014)	NS		
	Group opportunities for non-core activities (Dekas, 2010)	NS		
	Contextual characteristics (perceptions of ergonomics, physical demands, work conditions, equipment use; Chen & Kao, 2011)	+		[NS—collective efficacy]
	Social characteristics (perceptions of social support, initiated interdependence, received interdependence, feedback from others; Chen & Kao, 2011)	+		[NS—collective efficacy]
Group socialization and norms	Socialization emphasis on helping (Gavin, 1997)	NS		
	Descriptive helping norms (Naumann & Ehrhart, 2011); cooperative group norms (Gonzalez-Mule et al., 2014; Ng & Van Dyne, 2005; Shen & Benson, 2014)	+		
	Group OCB (Karam & Kwantes, 2011)	+		
	Prescriptive helping norms (Naumann & Ehrhart, 2011)	NS		
	Team supportive behavior (Hu & Liden, 2013)	NS		
	Group rewards of broad performance contributions (Dekas, 2010)	NS		

(continued)

Table 25.1 Continued

Categorization of Antecedents		Level 2 Antecedents (and Study)	Unmediated Effect on OCB	Level 1 (2-1-1) Mediators	Level 2 (2-2-1) Mediators
Perceptions, attitudes, beliefs, and values	Group perceptions and values	Collective efficacy (Walumbwa et al., 2010)	+		
		Team psychological empowerment (Choi, 2007; Tuuli & Rowlinson, 2009)	+		
		Felt responsibility for change (Choi, 2007)	+		
		Shared moral awareness (Kalshoven et al., 2013)	NS		
		Business values and ethical values (Li et al., 2012)	NS		Aggregate levels of employee trust in the organization
	Feelings toward the group	Group-level affective commitment (Kehoe & Wright, 2013)	+		
		Group cohesion (Chen et al., 2009; Gavin, 1997; Karam, 2011; Kidwell et al., 1997; Ng & Van Dyne, 2005; Schmidt, 2008); group network centralization (Chung et al., 2011)	+		
		Group trust or trust context (Choi, 2006; Li et al., 2012)	+		
		Shared empathic concern (Kalshoven et al., 2013)	+		
		Group positive affective tone (Gavin, 1997; Kim et al., 2012)	NS		
		Group commitment to the supervisor (Walumbwa et al., 2010)	NS		
	Exchange relationships	Social exchange (Song et al., 2009)	NS		
		Group Team Member Exchange (TMX; Farmer et al., 2015; Hu & Liden, 2013; Wech et al., 2009); supportive peer relations (Liang & Tang, 2010)	+	Identification with coworkers	
		Mutual investment (Song et al., 2009)	+		[NS—economic exchange norms] [NS—Social exchange norms]
		Economic exchange (Song et al., 2009)	–		
		Unit outcome favorability (Sun et al., 2013)	NS		
Climate-related variables	Justice climate	Distributive justice climate (Du & Choi, 2010)	–		

	Procedural justice climate (Dekas, 2010; Du & Choi, 2010; Hsiung, 2012; Liao & Rupp, 2005; Morrison et al., 2011; Naumann & Bennett, 2000; Sun et al., 2013; Walumbwa et al., 2010; Yang et al., 2007)	+		
	Procedural justice climate strength (reverse-coded dispersion; Dekas, 2010)	+		
	Group communal climate (trust, fairness, cooperation; Dekas, 2010)	+		
	Organizational-focused informational justice climate, supervisor focused informational justice climate (Liao & Rupp, 2005)	Mixed		
	Organizational focused interpersonal justice climate, supervisor-focused interpersonal justice climate (Liao & Rupp, 2005)	NS		
Empowerment climate	Empowerment/engagement climate (Tuuli & Rowlinson, 2009; Walker, 2011)	+	Empowerment	Aggregate levels of perceived empowerment
Voice climate	Voice climate (Frazier & Fainshmidt, 2012; Morrison et al., 2011)	+	Empowerment	
Safety climate	Psychological safety climate (Tangirala & Ramanujam, 2012; Walumbwa & Schaubroeck, 2009)	+		
Service climate	Service climate (Lam & Mayer, 2014; Walumbwa et al., 2010)	+		
	Organizational climate (Lin & Lin, 2011)	NS		
Other	Autonomy-supportive team climate (Liu & Fu, 2011)	+	Learning	
	Power distance climate group power distance (Chen, 2011; Yang et al., 2007)	NS		
	Innovative climate (Choi, 2007)	+		Aggregate levels of perceived empowerment Collective levels of felt obligation to engage in OCB

(continued)

Table 25.1 Continued

Categorization of Antecedents		Level 2 Antecedents (and Study)	Unmediated Effect on OCB	Level 1 (2-1-1) Mediators	Level 2 (2-2-1) Mediators
		Integrative culture (Song et al., 2009)	+		[NS—economic exchange norms] [NS—social exchange norms]
		Hierarchical culture (Song et al., 2009)	–		Economic exchange norms [NS—social exchange norms]
		Quasi-spot contract (Song et al., 2009)	–		[NS—economic exchange norms] [NS—social exchange norms]
		Instrumental climate (Wang & Hsieh, 2013)	–	Perceived organizational support	
		Independence climate (Wang & Hsieh, 2013)	+	Perceived organizational support	
		Caring climate (Wang & Hsieh, 2013)	+	Perceived organizational support	
Organizational characteristics	Demographics	Organizational size (Chung et al., 2011; Snape & Redman, 2010; Song et al., 2009; Tuuli & Rowlinson, 2009)	+		
		Firm age establishment age (Snape & Redman, 2010; Tuuli & Rowlinson, 2009)	NS		
		Industry and sector type (Chen, Tang, & Wang, 2009); public/private (Snape & Redman, 2010)	NS		
		Country of origin (United States or China; Kirkman et al., 2009)	NS		
	Structure and strategies	Formalization and centralization (Li et al., 2012)	NS		Aggregate levels of employee trust in the organization
		Organizational retrenchment (Beeri, 2012)	NS		

	Organizational reorganization (Beeri, 2012)	–		
	Organizational repositioning (Beeri, 2012)	+		
HRM practices	Pay for performance level (Du & Choi, 2010)	Mixed		
	Higher performance HR practices (Kehoe & Wright, 2013; Snape & Redman, 2010)	+	Discretion in performing work tasks	Group affective commitment
	Commitment-based HR system (Uen et al., 2009)	+	Relational psychological contract	
	HR practices (Wei et al., 2010)	NS	Job satisfaction [NS—Positive psychological climate]	
	Socially responsible HRM practices (Shen & Benson, 2014)	+	Organizational identification	
Other	Span of control (Walumbwa & Schaubroeck, 2009)	NS		

Note: In some cases, authors of the primary studies did not report an unmediated direct effect; in these cases, we reported the effect of the antecedent in the context of the mediated effects analyses. + = the focal relationship was positive; – = the focal relationship was negative; HRM = human resource management; Mixed = the focal relationship has mixed support; NS = the focal relationship was nonsignificant.

(Gavin, 1997), task and goal interdependence (Chen et al., 2009), task conflict (e.g., Schraub, Michel, Shemla, & Sonntag, 2014), physical and social working conditions (Chen & Kao, 2011), descriptive helping norms (Naumann & Ehrhart, 2011), and group OCB (Karam & Kwantes, 2011). The evidence suggests that group task conflict negatively influences individual-level OCB primarily through individual-level feelings of affective well-being (Schraub et al., 2014), and that task and goal interdependence had their positive effects primarily through group-level cohesion (Chen et al., 2009).

PERCEPTIONS, ATTITUDES, BELIEFS, AND VALUES

Several variables in this category were found to be related to OCB. Generally speaking, relative to other groups, groups that felt responsibility for changes in the organization (Choi, 2007), that were empowered to do their work (e.g., Choi, 2007), and believed that they had the ability to perform their tasks (Walumbwa et al., 2010) exhibited higher levels of OCB. In addition, OCB was also higher in groups that were more committed (Kehoe & Wright, 2013), cohesive (e.g., Gavin 1997), trusting (e.g. Choi, 2006), and empathic (Kalshoven, Den Hartog, & De Hoogh, 2013), and that had stronger team exchange relationships (e.g., Wech et al., 2009) and weaker economic exchange relationships (Song et al., 2009). Interestingly, only one of these significant relationships was mediated. Specifically, team member exchange had its effects on OCB because it increased the individual-level identification of employees with their coworkers (Farmer, Van Dyne, & Kamdar, 2015).

ORGANIZATIONAL CLIMATE

Perhaps the most consistently influential determinants of citizenship behavior were various aspects of organizational climate. Aspects of climate that were found to have a positive influence on OCB were procedural justice climate (e.g., Naumann & Bennett, 2000), climate strength (Dekas, 2010), empowerment climate (e.g., Tuuli & Rowlinson, 2009), voice climate (e.g., Frazier & Fainshmidt, 2012), psychological safety climate (e.g., Tangirala & Ramanujam, 2012), service climate (Walumbwa et al., 2010), autonomy-supportive team climate (Liu & Fu, 2011), innovative climate (Choi, 2007), integrative culture (Song et al., 2009), caring climate (Wang & Hsieh, 2013), and independence climate (Wang & Hsieh, 2013). The relationship between empowerment climate and OCB was mediated by employee (Level 1) and group (Level 2) perceptions of empowerment (Tuuli & Rowlinson, 2009); the relationship between voice climate and OCB was mediated by employee (Level 1) perceptions of empowerment (Frazier & Fainshmidt, 2012); the relationship between autonomy-supportive team climate and OCB was mediated by individual-level learning (Liu & Fu, 2011); the relationships between independence climate and caring climate and OCB were mediated by perceived organizational support at the individual level (Wang & Hsieh, 2013); and the relationship between innovative climate and OCB was mediated by group perceptions of empowerment (Choi, 2007) and group-level felt obligation to engage in OCB (Choi, 2007).

Aspects of climate having a negative influence on OCB were distributive justice climate (Du & Choi, 2010), hierarchical culture (Song et al., 2009), quasi-spot contract climate (Song et al., 2009), and instrumental climate (Wang & Hsieh, 2013). Perceived organizational support (Level 1) mediated the relationship between instrumental climate and OCB (Wang & Hsieh, 2013); and economic exchange norms (Level 2) mediated the relationship between hierarchical culture and citizenship behavior (Song et al., 2009).

ORGANIZATIONAL CHARACTERISTICS

Finally, a few organizational characteristics had significant relationships with OCB. Organizational repositioning strategies were positively associated with OCB, whereas reorganization strategies were negatively associated with OCB (Beeri, 2012). In addition, high-performance HR practices and commitment-based HR systems both had positive relationships with OCB; with the former being mediated by unit-level affective commitment (Kehoe & Wright, 2013) and individual-level discretion in performing work tasks (Snape & Redman, 2010); and the latter being mediated by individual-level relational psychological contracts (Uen, Chien, & Yen, 2009).

Multilevel Moderating Effects

Our review of the literature indicated that almost two thirds of the studies examined Level 1 or Level 2 moderators of the effects of different antecedents on individual-level OCB. In the sections that follow, we will first provide a summary of the unit- and individual-level moderators of the relationships between unit-level antecedents and individual-level OCB (Table 25.2). Following this, we will provide a similar summary of the unit-level moderators of the relationships between individual-level antecedents and individual-level OCB (Table 25.3).

In our discussion of these findings, we will attempt to highlight the similarities in the mechanisms through which these moderators produce their effects based on Kerr and Jermier's (1978) substitutes for leadership theory, Mischel's (1973, 1977) situational strength theory, or Tett and Burnett's (2003) trait activation theory. According to Kerr and Jermier, leadership moderators can be classified into three categories: substitutes, neutralizers, and enhancers. Substitutes or neutralizers are moderators that negate or replace the effect of a predictor variable (e.g., leader behavior) by making it unnecessary, redundant, or undesirable. The difference between substitutes and neutralizers is that substitutes negate and replace the impact of the predictor variable, whereas neutralizers counteract the effect of the predictor (effectively making the predictor's influence impossible), but don't replace it. In this sense, the effects of neutralizers are similar to the effects of "strong situations" (Mischel, 1973, 1977). As noted by Tett and Burnett (2003), "Strong situations tend to negate individual differences in response tendencies by their clarity (i.e., everyone construes them the same way) and the severity of extrinsic rewards" (p. 502).

In contrast to substitutes and neutralizers, Howell, Dorfman, and Kerr (1986) described enhancers as moderators that augment the effect of a predictor on a criterion measure. Although Kerr and Jermier (1978) viewed neutralizers and enhancers as two varieties of the same type of moderator, they were not very specific about the mechanisms through which enhancers produce their effects. Fortunately, Tett and Burnett (2003) provide greater insight into these mechanisms in their trait activation theory. They argue that there will be an enhancing effect when a situational variable is relevant to the predictor variable and "presses" people to behave in trait-related ways. In this way, the situational moderator activates, triggers, or provides a cue for the expression of the trait. We would argue that this type of activation, triggering, or cueing mechanism can be applied more broadly to the effects of other types of predictors besides personality traits. Similarly, we also believe that the substitutes and neutralizers can be generalized beyond the leadership domain.

UNIT- AND INDIVIDUAL-LEVEL MODERATORS OF THE RELATIONSHIPS BETWEEN UNIT-LEVEL ANTECEDENTS AND INDIVIDUAL-LEVEL ORGANIZATIONAL CITIZENSHIP BEHAVIORS

As indicated in Table 25.2, 25 of the 82 (30%) moderating effects tested were statistically significant. About half of these tests came from only two studies (Dekas, 2010; Wherry, 2012), and about half of the *significant* moderating effects came from three studies (Dekas, 2010; Li, Chiaburu, Kirkman, & Xie, 2013; Wherry, 2012). Ten (40%) of the significant moderating effects served to enhance the impact of the antecedent on the OCB, 13 (52%) neutralized the impact of the antecedent; none of the moderators substituted for the predictor; and two (8%) moderating effects were not classifiable using the substitutes framework.

In the case of the enhancers, Li et al. (2013) found that followers' proactive personality (Level 1) enhanced the positive relationship between transformational leadership and OCB; Wherry (2012) found that LMX (Level 1) enhanced the positive relationship between authentic leadership and courtesy, and mean LMX (Level 2) enhanced the positive relationship between authentic leadership and altruism; and Kalshoven et al. (2013) reported that shared empathic concern (Level 2) enhanced the positive relationship between ethical leadership and employee courtesy. Dekas (2010) reported that (a) dispersion in group autonomy (Level 2) enhanced the positive relationship between group autonomy and manager-rated OCB; (b) dispersion in group workload (Level 2) enhanced the positive relationship between group workload and peer-rated OCB; (c) dispersion in group workload (Level 2) enhanced the positive relationship between group workload and civic virtue; and (d) dispersion in group opportunities for noncore activities (Level 2) enhanced the positive relationship between group opportunities for noncore activities and employee civic virtue. In addition, Naumann and Ehrhart (2011) found that attraction to the group (Level 1) enhanced the positive relationship between prescriptive helping norms and helping behavior. Finally, Hui, Chiu, Yu, Cheng, and Tse (2007) reported that service climate (Level 2) enhanced the somewhat negative relationship between group perceptions of effective leadership behaviors (e.g., coping effectively with circumstances, rarely abusing power, respecting decisions of subordinates) and OCB directed at internal customers.

Table 25.2 Summary of Individual- or Unit-Level Moderators of the Relationships Between Unit-Level Antecedents and Individual-Level Organizational Citizenship Behaviors (OCBs)

Unit Antecedent Categories		Focal Multilevel Relationship (Level 2 Antecedent → Level 1 OCB)	Moderator (Level 1 or Level 2)	Nature of Moderating Effects
Manager/ leader characteristics	Demographic and personality	Leader–member dissimilarity in nationality → leader-directed voice (Troster & van Knippenberg, 2012)	Member–team dissimilarity in nationality (L1)	NS
		Leader openness → leader-directed voice (Troster & van Knippenberg, 2012)	Member–team dissimilarity in nationality (L1)	NS
	Transformational leadership	Transformational behavior → OCB (Kirkman et al., 2009)	Country (United States/China) (L2)	NS
		Transformational behavior → voice (Liang & Tang, 2010)	Proactive personality (L1)	Proactive personality neutralizes the positive relationship between transformational leader behavior and voice.
		Transformational behavior → OCB and taking charge (Li et al., 2013)	Leader prototypicality (L1)	Leader prototypicality neutralizes the positive relationship between transformational leader behavior and OCB (although the positive relationship between TFL and OCB is NS). Leader prototypicality neutralizes the positive relationship between transformational leader behavior and taking charge (although the positive relationship between TFL and taking charge is NS).
			Follower team identification (L1)	Team identification neutralizes the positive relationship between transformational leader behavior and OCB (although the positive relationship between TFL and OCB is NS). Team identification neutralizes the positive relationship between transformational leader behavior and taking charge (although the positive relationship between TFL and taking charge is NS).
			Follower traditionality (L1)	Follower traditionality neutralizes the positive relationship between transformational leader behavior and OCB (although the positive relationship between TFL and OCB is NS). NS—taking charge

		Follower proactive personality (L1)	Proactive personality enhances the positive relationship between transformational leader behavior and OCB. NS—taking charge
		Follower learning goal orientation (L1)	NS—OCB Follower learning goal orientation neutralizes the positive relationship between transformational leader behavior and taking charge.
Servant and other leadership	Authentic leadership → altruism, courtesy, conscientiousness, sportsmanship, and civic virtue (Wherry, 2012)	LMX (L1)	LMX enhances the positive relationship between authentic leadership and courtesy. All other NS
		Mean LMX (L2)	Group LMX enhances the positive relationship between authentic leadership and altruism. All other NS
	Effective leadership behavior → OCB directed at other employees and OCB directed at customers (Hui et al., 2007)	Service climate (L2)	Service climate enhances the negative relationship between effective leadership and service quality to internal customers. Service climate neutralizes the positive relationship between effective leadership and OCB directed at external customers.
	Mean group ethical leadership → altruism and courtesy (Kalshoven et al., 2013)	Shared empathic concern	NS—altruism Shared empathic concern enhances the positive relationship between ethical leadership and courtesy.
		Shared moral awareness	Shared moral awareness neutralizes the positive relationship between ethical leadership and altruism. Shared moral awareness neutralizes the positive relationship between ethical leadership and courtesy.
Leader empowerment and engagement	Empowering leadership → proactive behavior (Chen, 2011)	Power distance beliefs (L1)	NS
		Power distance climate (L2)	NS
		Power distance beliefs (L1) × Power distance climate (L2)	Nonclassifiable
	Leader empowerment → contextual performance toward employees and contextual performance toward the organization (Walker, 2011)	Transformational leadership (L2)	NS

(continued)

Table 25.2 Continued

Unit Antecedent Categories		Focal Multilevel Relationship (Level 2 Antecedent → Level 1 OCB)	Moderator (Level 1 or Level 2)	Nature of Moderating Effects
Group characteristics	Group demographics	Disciplinary hierarchy → voice (Paik, 2012)	Leader disciplinary background breadth (L2)	Leader disciplinary background breadth neutralizes the negative relationship between disciplinary hierarchy and voice.
			Transformational leadership (L2)	NS
			Team commitment (L1)	NS
			Disciplinary status (L1)	NS
	Group task characteristics	Group autonomy → helping, voice, civic virtue, social participation, peer-rated OCB, and manager-rated OCB (Dekas, 2010)	Dispersion in group autonomy (L2)	Group dispersion enhances the positive relationship between group autonomy and manager-rated OCB. All other NS
		Group workload → helping, voice, civic virtue, social participation, peer-rated OCB, and manager-rated OCB (Dekas, 2010)	Dispersion in group workload (L2)	Dispersion in group workload enhances the positive relationship between group workload and civic virtue. Dispersion in group workload enhances the negative relationship between group workload and peer-rated OCB. All other NS
		Group opportunities for noncore activities → helping, voice, civic virtue, social participation, peer-rated OCB, and manager-rated OCB (Dekas, 2010)	Dispersion in group opportunities for noncore activities (L2)	Dispersion in group opportunities for noncore activities enhances the positive relationship between group opportunities for noncore activities and civic virtue. Manager-rated OCB nonclassifiable. All other NS
	Affect	Peer relations → voice (Liang & Tang, 2010)	Proactive personality (L1)	NS
		Group positive affect→ OCB (Kim et al., 2012)	Group positive affect diversity (L2)	NS
	Socialization and norms	Descriptive helping norms → helping (Naumann & Ehrhart, 2011)	Attraction to the group (L1)	NS
			Role ambiguity (L1)	Role ambiguity neutralizes the positive relationship between descriptive helping norms and helping.

		Prescriptive helping norms → helping (Naumann & Ehrhart, 2011)	Attraction to the group (L1)	Attraction to the group enhances the positive relationship between prescriptive helping norms and helping.
			Role ambiguity (L1)	NS
		Team supportive behavior → OCB (Hu & Liden, 2013)	Team mean LMX (L2)	NS
Perceptions, attitudes, beliefs, and values	Attitudes and perceptions	Collective efficacy → OCB (Walumbwa et al., 2010)	PJ climate (L2)	NS
			Service climate (L2)	NS
		Group commitment to the supervisor → OCB (Walumbwa et al., 2010)	PJ climate (L2)	NS
			Service climate (L2)	NS
Climate-related variables	Justice climate	Procedural justice climate → OCB (Yang et al., 2007)	Group power distance (L2)	Power distance neutralizes the positive relationship between procedural justice climate and OCB.
			Individual power distance (L1)	NS
		Procedural justice climate → helping, voice, civic virtue, social participation, peer-rated OCB, and manager-rated OCB (Dekas, 2010)	Dispersion of procedural justice climate (L2)	All NS
	Communal climate	Communal climate → helping, voice, civic virtue, social participation, peer-rated OCB, and manager-rated OCB (Dekas, 2010)	Dispersion of communal climate (L2)	All NS

Note: LMX = leader member exchange; NS = nonsignificant.

Table 25.3 Summary of Unit-Level Moderators of the Relationships Between Individual-Level Antecedents and Individual-Level Organizational Citizenship Behaviors (OCBs)

Individual Antecedent Categories		**Focal Multilevel Relationship(Level 1 Antecedent → Level 1 OCB)**	**Moderator(Level 2)**	**Nature of Moderating Effects**
Employee factors	Demographics	Follower age → OCB (Schuh et al., 2012)	Leader age	NS
			Leader gender	NS
	Personality and values	Agreeableness → OCBO (Schmidt, 2008)	Group cohesion	NS
			Likelihood of reward	NS
		Agreeableness → prosocial voice, acquiescent voice, and defensive voice (Lee, Diefendorff, Kim, & Bian, 2014)	Participative climate	Participative climate enhances the positive relationship between agreeableness and prosocial voice. Participative climate enhances the negative relationship between agreeableness and acquiescent voice. NS defensive voice
		Extraversion → prosocial voice, acquiescent voice, and defensive voice (Lee, Diefendorff, Kim, & Bian, 2014)	Participative climate	All NS
		Proactive personality → voice (Liang & Tang, 2010)	Transformational leadership	TFL neutralizes the positive relationship between proactive personality and voice.
		Individual positive affect → OCB (Kim et al., 2012)	Group trait positive affect	NS
			Group positive affect diversity	Group positive affect diversity enhances the positive relationship between positive affect and OCB.
			Group trait positive affect × Group positive affect diversity	NS
		Justice orientation → OCBO and OCBS (Liao & Rupp, 2005)	Organization-focused PJ climate	Both NS
			Supervisor-focused PJ climate	Both NS
			Organization-focused IPJ climate	Both NS
			Supervisor-focused IPJ climate	Both NS

		Organization-focused IFJ climate	Justice orientation enhances the positive relationship between organization-focused IFJ climate and OCBS NS OCBO
		Supervisor-focused IFJ climate	Both NS
	Customer orientation → customer-focused voice behavior (Lam & Mayer, 2014)	Service climate	Service climate neutralizes the positive relationship between customer orientation and customer-focused voice.
	Protégé's autonomy orientation → OCB (Liu & Fu, 2011)	Autonomy-supportive team climate	Autonomy climate enhances the positive relationship between autonomy orientation and OCB.
	Power distance orientation → OCB (Kirkman et al., 2009)	Country (United States/China)	NS
	Individual benevolence values → OCBI and OCBO (Arthaud-Day et al., 2012)	Group benevolence values	Both NS
	Individual achievement values → OCBI and OCBO (Arthaud-Day et al., 2012)	Group achievement values	Both NS
	Individual self-direction values → OCBI and OCBO (Arthaud-Day et al., 2012)	Group self-direction values	Group self-direction values enhance the positive relationship between self-direction values and OCBO. Group self-direction values enhance the positive relationship between self-direction values and OCBI.
	Individual power values → OCBI and OCBO (Arthaud-Day et al., 2012)	Group power values	Both nonclassifiable
Attitudes, mood, and perceptions	POS → loyalty-related service-oriented OCBs (Lin & Lin, 2011)	Organizational service climate	Organizational service climate enhances the positive relationship between POS and service- oriented OCB.
	POS → service delivery-related service-oriented OCBs (Lin & Lin, 2011)	Organizational climate	Organizational service climate enhances the positive relationship between POS and delivery-related OCB.

(*continued*)

Table 25.3 Continued

Individual Antecedent Categories	Focal Multilevel Relationship(Level 1 Antecedent → Level 1 OCB)	Moderator(Level 2)	Nature of Moderating Effects
	POS → participation OCBs (Lin & Lin, 2011)	Organizational climate	NS
	POS → helping (Choi, 2006)	Aggregated trust	Aggregated trust neutralizes the positive relationship between POS and helping.
	Job satisfaction → conscientiousness and courtesy (Kidwell et al., 1997)	Cohesiveness	Cohesiveness enhances the positive relationship between job satisfaction and courtesy. NS conscientiousness
	Job satisfaction → voice (Morrison et al., 2011)	Voice climate	NS
	Affective commitment → civic virtue, conscientiousness, and altruism (Cohen et al., 2012)	Group size	Group size enhances the positive relationship between affective commitment and civic virtue. Group size enhances the positive relationship between job satisfaction and conscientiousness. Group size enhances the positive relationship between job satisfaction and altruism.
		Group cohesiveness	Cohesiveness neutralizes the positive relationship between affective commitment and civic virtue. Cohesiveness neutralizes the positive relationship between affective commitment and conscientiousness. NS altruism
		Group size × group cohesiveness	NS civic virtue NS conscientiousness Altruism—the three-way interaction was nonclassifiable.

Continuance commitment → civic virtue, conscientiousness, and altruism (Cohen et al., 2012)	Group size	All NS
Organizational commitment → conscientiousness and courtesy (Kidwell et al., 1997)	Cohesiveness	Both NS
Commitment to the supervisor → OCB (Walumbwa et al., 2010)	Procedural justice climate	Procedural justice climate enhances the positive relationship between commitment and OCB.
	Service climate	Service climate enhances the positive relationship between commitment and OCB.
Positive mood → voice (Hsiung, 2012)	Procedural justice climate	Procedural justice climate enhances the positive relationship between mood and voice.
Conflict-related stress at work → OCB (Karam, 2011)	Group cohesion	Cohesiveness enhances the positive relationship between stress and OCB.
Conflict-related stress at home → OCB (Karam, 2011)	Group cohesion	NS
Identification → voice (Morrison et al., 2011)	Voice climate	Voice climate enhances the positive relationship between identification and voice.
Organizational identification → helping (Shen & Benson, 2014)	Cooperative norms	Cooperative norms enhance the positive relationship between organizational identification and helping.
Outcome favorability → OCB (Sun et al., 2013)	Procedural fairness climate	Procedural justice climate enhances the positive relationship between outcome favorability and OCB.
Perceived fairness → helping (Choi, 2006)	Aggregated trust	Aggregated trust neutralizes the positive relationship between perceived fairness and helping behavior.

(*continued*)

Table 25.3 Continued

Individual Antecedent Categories		Focal Multilevel Relationship(Level 1 Antecedent → Level 1 OCB)	Moderator(Level 2)	Nature of Moderating Effects
		Procedural justice perceptions → OCB (Kirkman et al., 2009)	Country	NS
		Individual empowerment → contextual performance behaviors (Tuuli & Rowlinson, 2009)	Team empowerment	NS
		Self-efficacy → OCB (Chen & Kao, 2011)	Contextual characteristics	Nonclassifiable
			Social characteristics	NS
		Self-efficacy → OCB (Hu & Liden, 2013)	Team supportive behavior	NS
		Self-efficacy → OCB (Walumbwa et al., 2010)	Procedural justice climate	NS
			Service climate	NS
		Individual empowerment → contextual performance toward employees and contextual performance toward the organization (Walker, 2011)	Transformational leadership	Both NS
Job factors	Job characteristics	Task interdependence → OCB (Hu & Liden, 2013)	Team mean LMX	NS
		Job autonomy → customer-focused voice behavior (Lam & Mayer, 2014)	Service climate	Service climate neutralizes the positive relationship between job autonomy and customer-focused voice behavior.
		Individual-level hurriedness → helping (Jansen & Kristof-Brown, 2005)	Work group hurriedness	Nonclassifiable
		Pay for performance → conscientiousness (Du & Choi, 2010)	Procedural justice climate	NS
			Distributive justice climate	NS

		Pay for performance → helping (Du & Choi, 2010)	Procedural justice climate	Procedural justice climate enhances the positive relationship between pay for performance and helping.
			Distributive justice climate	NS
Leader factors	Demographics	Disciplinary embeddedness → voice behavior (Paik, 2012)	Transformational leadership	NS
	Behaviors	Transformational leadership → civic virtue, conscientiousness, and altruism (Cohen et al., 2012)	Group size	All NS
			Group cohesiveness	Group cohesiveness enhances the relationship between TFL and conscientiousness. NS civic virtue NS altruism
			Group size × group cohesiveness	In large groups, cohesiveness is an enhancer of the positive relationship between TFL and all three OCBs (conscientiousness, civic virtue, and altruism). In small groups, cohesiveness is a neutralizer of the positive relationship between TFL and both conscientiousness and altruism. In small groups, cohesiveness is a substitute for the positive relationship between transformational leadership and civic virtue.
		Abusive supervision → interpersonal facilitation and job dedication (Aryee et al., 2008)	Work unit structure	Mechanistic work group structures enhance the negative relationship between abusive supervision and interpersonal facilitation. Mechanistic work group structures enhance the negative relationship between abusive supervision and job dedication.

(*continued*)

Table 25.3 Continued

Individual Antecedent Categories		Focal Multilevel Relationship(Level 1 Antecedent → Level 1 OCB)	Moderator(Level 2)	Nature of Moderating Effects
		Ethical leadership → altruism and courtesy (Kalshoven et al., 2013)	Shared empathic concern	Shared empathic concern enhances the positive relationship between ethical leadership and courtesy. NS altruism
			Shared moral awareness	Shared moral awareness neutralizes the positive relationship between ethical leadership and altruism. Shared moral awareness neutralizes the positive relationship between ethical leadership and courtesy.
		Supervisory guidance → OCB (Dineen, Lewicki, & Tomlinson, 2006)	Supervisory behavioral integrity	Nonclassifiable
		Mentor's autonomy support → OCB (Liu & Fu, 2011)	Autonomy-supportive team climate	Autonomy-supportive team climate enhances the positive relationship between mentor's autonomy support and OCB.
	Leader relations	LMX → voice (Hsiung, 2012)	Procedural justice climate	Procedural justice climate enhances the positive relationship between LMX and voice.
		LMX → OCB (Hu & Liden, 2013)	Team supportive behavior	NS
		LMX → safety OCB role definitions (Hofmann et al., 2003)	Safety climate	Safety climate enhances the positive relationship between LMX and safety OCB role definitions.
		Relationship quality → OCB (Carter et al., 2013)	Change frequency	Change frequency enhances the positive relationship between relationship quality and OCB
		Supervisor-subordinate quanxi → voice behavior (Wang et al., 2010)	Authoritarian leadership	Authoritarian leadership neutralizes the positive relationship between supervisor–subordinate quanxi and voice.

Group factors	Group characteristics	Individual's network centrality → interpersonal citizenship behavior (Chung et al., 2011)	Group density	Group density enhances the positive relationship between individual's network centrality and ICB.
		Relative team member exchange → helping (Farmer et al., 2015)	Group mean TMX	Group mean TMX enhances the positive relationship between relative TMX and helping behavior
		Individual's network transitivity → Interpersonal citizenship behavior (Chung et al., 2011)	Group centralization	Group centralization neutralizes the negative relationship between network transitivity and interpersonal citizenship behavior.
Cultural factors	Cultural perceptions	Perceptions of idiocentrism → OCB (Karam & Kwantes, 2011)	Unit OCB	Nonclassifiable
		Perceptions of allocentrism → OCB (Karam & Kwantes, 2011)	Unit OCB	NS

Note: LMX = leader–member exchange; NS = nonsignificant; TMX = team member exchange.

Turning to the neutralizers, Li et al. (2013) reported that leader protypicality (Level 1) and follower team identification (Level 1) neutralized the positive relationship between transformational leader behavior and both employee OCB and taking charge behavior. They also reported that follower traditionality (Level 1) neutralized the positive relationship between transformational leader behavior and OCB; and that follower learning goal orientation (Level 1) neutralized the positive relationship between transformational leader behavior and taking charge behavior. In addition, Hui et al. (2007) reported that service climate neutralized the positive relationship between effective leadership and OCB directed at external customers; and Kalshoven et al. (2013) found that shared moral awareness (Level 2) neutralized the positive relationship between ethical leadership and both helping and courtesy. Paik (2012) found that leader disciplinary background breadth neutralized the negative relationship between disciplinary hierarchy and employee voice behavior. Yang et al. (2007) reported that group power distance (Level 2) neutralized the positive relationship between procedural justice climate and OCB. Finally, Naumann and Ehrhart (2011) found that role ambiguity (Level 1) neutralized the positive relationship between descriptive helping norms and employee helping behavior.

UNIT-LEVEL MODERATORS OF THE RELATIONSHIPS BETWEEN INDIVIDUAL-LEVEL ANTECEDENTS AND INDIVIDUAL-LEVEL ORGANIZATIONAL CITIZENSHIP BEHAVIOR

As indicated in Table 25.3, 55 of the 118 (47%) moderating effects tested were statistically significant. The majority of the significant moderating effects (34 of 55, or 62%) served as enhancers of the relationship between the antecedent and the OCB, whereas 13 (24%) served as neutralizers, and one (2%) served as a substitute. In addition, there were seven other moderating effects (13%) that were not classifiable.

Several of the enhancers influenced the nature of the relationships between personality variables or employee values and citizenship behaviors. For example, Lee, Diefendorff, Kim, and Bian (2014) found that participative climate enhanced the positive relationship between agreeableness and prosocial voice and the negative relationship between agreeableness and acquiescent voice; Kim et al. (2012) found that group positive affect diversity enhanced the positive relationship between employee positive affect and OCB; Liu and Fu (2011) reported autonomy climate enhanced the relationship between autonomy orientation and OCB; and Arthaud-Day, Rode, and Turnley (2012) reported that group self-direction values enhanced the positive relationship between self-direction values and both OCBI and OCBO. Thus, it appears that fostering a group-level climate where employees either get to participate in the decision-making process or get to make the decisions themselves enhances the effect of several group member characteristics on OCB.

A number of variables also served to enhance the nature of the relationships between employee attitudes, moods, or perceptions and citizenship behaviors. For example, Lin and Lin (2011) found that organizational service climate enhanced the positive relationship between perceived organizational support (POS) and both service-oriented and delivery-oriented OCB; Kidwell et al. (1997) found that group cohesiveness enhanced the positive relationship between job satisfaction and employee conscientiousness behavior; and Cohen et al. (2012) reported that group size enhanced the relationship between employees' affective commitment and their altruism, conscientiousness, and civic virtue. In addition, Walumbwa et al. (2010) reported that both service climate and procedural justice climate enhanced the positive relationship between commitment to the supervisor and OCB; Hsiung (2012) found that procedural justice climate enhanced the relationship between employees' positive moods and their voice behavior; and Sun, Chow, Chiu, and Pan (2013) reported that procedural justice climate enhanced the positive relationship between employees' perceptions of outcome favorability and OCB. Similarly, Morrison et al. (2011) reported that voice climate enhanced the positive relationship between employees' identification with the organization and voice behavior. Taken together, these findings suggest that climates that are fair to employees, that encourage employees to speak up, or that focus on customer service tend to enhance the nature of the relationships between employee attitudes, moods, or perceptions and citizenship behaviors.

The relationships between a number of leader behaviors or characteristics and citizenship behaviors were also enhanced by several variables. For example, Cohen et al. (2012) found that group cohesiveness served as an enhancer of the positive relationship between transformational leadership and conscientiousness; and that, in large groups, cohesiveness is an enhancer of the relationships between transformational leadership and conscientiousness, civic virtue, and altruism. Aryee, Sun, Chen, and Debrah (2008) found that work unit structure moderated the relationship between abusive supervision and OCB. More specifically, these authors reported that mechanistic (as opposed to organic) work unit structures enhanced the negative relationships between abusive supervision and both interpersonal facilitation and job dedication. In addition, Kalshoven et al. (2013) reported that employees' shared moral awareness enhanced the relationship between ethical leadership and courtesy; and Liu and Fu (2011) reported that autonomy-supportive team climates enhanced the positive relationship between mentor's autonomy-supportive behaviors and OCB. Finally, three studies have identified enhancers of the LMX–OCB relationship. Specifically, Hsiung (2012) reported that procedural justice climate enhanced the relationship between LMX and employee voice; and Carter et al. (2013) reported that change frequency enhanced the positive relationship between relationship quality and OCB. Although it is difficult to discern a clear pattern in these moderating effects, it does appear as though positive work climates and cohesiveness were significant enhancers of the relationships between leader behaviors and OCB.

Finally, a few variables enhanced the relationships between some group and organizational characteristics and employee citizenship behaviors. For example, Farmer et al. (2015) reported that group team member exchange (TMX) enhanced the positive relationship between relative TMX and helping behavior; Chung and his colleagues (Chung, Park, Moon, & Oh, 2011) found that the density of social relationships in a group enhanced the positive relationship between an individual's network centrality and interpersonal OCB; and Du and Choi (2010) reported that procedural justice climate enhanced the positive relationship between pay-for-performance systems and helping behavior. These findings suggest that the relationship between organizational characteristics and OCB is more positive in groups that have close social relationships.

Turning our attention to other types of moderators, a few studies have reported variables that serve to neutralize the relationships between employee personality variables or values and individual-level OCB. For example, Liang and Tang (2010) found that transformational leader behaviors neutralized the positive relationship between proactive personality and voice behavior; and Lam and Mayer (2014) reported service climate neutralized the positive relationship between employee customer orientation and customer-focused voice behavior. In the case of employee attitudes and perceptions as predictors, Choi (2006) found that trust neutralized both of the positive relationships between employees' perceptions of organizational support and perceived fairness and helping behavior; and Cohen et al. (2012) found that group cohesiveness neutralized the positive relationships between employee affective commitment and both conscientiousness and civic virtue. In addition, when job factors served as antecedents, Lam and Mayer (2014) reported that service climate neutralized the positive relationship between job autonomy and customer-focused voice behavior. Similarly, in studies where leader behaviors served as antecedents of OCB, Cohen et al. reported that in small groups, cohesiveness neutralized the positive relationship between transformational leadership behaviors and both conscientiousness and altruism; Kalshoven et al. (2013) reported that shared moral awareness neutralized the positive relationships between ethical leadership and both employee helping and courtesy behaviors; and Wang, Huang, Chu, and Wang (2010) reported that authoritarian leadership neutralized the positive relationship between supervisor–subordinate quanxi and employee voice behavior. Finally, we found five moderators that negated and replaced the effect of a predictor variable by substituting for its effects. For example, Cohen et al. reported that in small groups, cohesiveness substituted for the positive relationship between transformational leadership behaviors and civic virtue. These results suggest that transformational leadership behavior, group cohesiveness, and service climate tended to neutralize, or neutralize and replace, the effects of a variety of predictors of OCB.

Future Directions

Conceptual/Theoretical Issues

Although all of the studies in our review were theoretically grounded in one way or another, when taken together, the unsystematic nature of the studies suggests that there is not a predominant theoretical paradigm or framework guiding research in the multilevel OCB literature. In addition, few antecedents or mediators have been examined in more than two studies, and the same is true of moderating variables. One result of this is inconsistent findings across studies. Thus, it appears that researchers in this domain have taken a very broad approach with respect to variable identification and to the application of theoretical frameworks. At the very least, it would seem that this literature would benefit from a more systematic and theoretically grounded approach.

One way to accomplish this is the application of frameworks that have been supported in related research examining the behaviors of individuals operating in groups and teams. The dominant paradigm in this literature is the input-process-output (IPO) model and its contemporary successors (e.g., Ilgen, Hollenbeck, Johnson, & Jundt, 2005). Essentially, this framework is based on the proposition that team inputs (e.g., team member characteristics, leadership, contextual characteristics) influence team processes (e.g., planning, strategy formulation, conflict management) and emergent states (e.g., cohesiveness, group potency), which ultimately lead to team outputs (e.g., effort, performance, efficiency). The IPO literature is comprised of hundreds of empirical and conceptual articles that generally support the underlying tenants of this framework (e.g., Humphrey & Aime, 2014; Ilgen et al., 2005; LePine, Piccolo, Jackson, Mathieu, & Saul, 2008). A brief examination of the research based on this model indicates that it addresses some of the same issues as the multilevel OCB research, and thus it holds promise for this area of inquiry. That being said, there has been very little mention of the IPO model in multilevel OCB studies. In the following sections, we will discuss application of this model to specific conceptual questions that emerged from our review.

Which Antecedents Should Be Given Attention in Multilevel Organizational Citizenship Behavior Studies?

Although our review of the literature indicated that a few antecedents (e.g., group-level authentic leadership, authoritarian leadership, and trust in group members) were consistently related to individual-level OCB, many of the other antecedents either failed to have significant effects or were only examined in one or two studies. At a minimum, these findings suggest that there is a substantial need for replication in this research domain. However, in addition, we think that it might be profitable to look at other group-level antecedents of OCB included in the IPO framework.

Although group composition input variables (e.g., personality, attitudes, values, motives, knowledge, skills, and abilities) are some of the most frequently studied inputs used to predict behavior in teams (e.g., Bell, Villado, Lukasik, Belau, & Briggs, 2011; Mathieu, Maynard, Rapp, & Gilson, 2008), our review indicated that a number of variables in this category have not been studied in the multilevel OCB literature. For example, research taken directly from the IPO literature seems to suggest important connections between team personality composition and citizenship behavior. Using a simulated team environment, Porter and colleagues (2003) reported that team member conscientiousness and emotional stability were positively related to backing-up behavior—a construct similar to helping OCB. Similarly, group member motives seem ripe for examination in this domain. In fact, we were surprised that no studies examined prosocial or instrumental motives because of the theoretical connections between such motives and OCB, and because recent studies report links between prosocial motivation and a variety of OCB dimensions (Grant, 2008; Grant & Mayer, 2009; Rioux & Penner, 2001). Thus, although the evidence supports connections between prosocial and instrumental motives and OCBs at the individual level, we are not aware of any studies that have examined the impact of shared prosocial or instrumental motives on OCBs. Finally, IPO research has identified teamwork orientation as an important determinant of team performance (Bell, 2007). Because teams composed of individuals with a strong preference for teamwork are likely to be more willing to cooperate, we would expect a positive relationship between teamwork orientation and OCB.

In addition to group composition input variables, there are important team input variables identified in the IPO literature that have not been studied in the multilevel OCB literature. Of these, one important variable that has been neglected is the training that individuals receive upon becoming members of the team. For example, Organ et al. (2006) have argued that "There is no reason to assume that people cannot be trained to perform OCBs, just like they can be taught any other form of work behavior. Indeed, Kelley and Caplan (1993) provided evidence that average performers can be trained to be star performers if they are taught to go beyond the explicit requirements of their job and to exhibit greater initiative. People could be trained in a similar manner to perform OCBs" (p. 226). Thus, we would expect that individuals in groups that have been trained to identify opportunities to help coworkers or to voice constructive suggestions for improving the group's performance would exhibit higher levels of OCB.

Finally, at the organizational level, it is notable that we could find no studies that explicitly examined the effects of organizational reward systems on

OCB. This may be an important omission because we believe that reward systems that are based on a combination of group-level and individual-level performance (vs. those solely based on individual-level performance) are more likely to encourage OCB because group members have a personal stake in the performance of others in the group. This would be consistent with the argument made by Podsakoff, Ahearne, and MacKenzie (1997) that "when a portion of one's pay is determined by group effort, OCBs might be expected to be directed at helping and supporting one's peers" or at voicing suggestions to benefit the group (p. 268).

What Mediating Mechanisms Hold the Greatest Promise for Future Research?

Our analysis of the mediating mechanisms that have been examined in the multilevel OCB domain (summarized in Table 25.1) revealed several observations with implications for future research. First, although over half of the studies in this review examined mediators connecting unit-level antecedents to individual-level OCBs, the majority of studies examined mediators that reside at the individual level of analysis. Although this is an important area of study, these findings are not that surprising, given that many of these mediators have already been examined in studies of individual-level antecedents of OCB, whereas our understanding of Level 2 (2-2-1) mediators is much more limited. Acquiring more knowledge of these mechanisms seems to be particularly important, given that one objective of multilevel research is to assess the impact of factors at higher levels on lower level outcomes such as employee OCB. Factors of particular relevance to this area of study include organizational climate variables (e.g., climates focused on the advancement and improvement of the collective), factors associated with shared perceptions or values (e.g., shared perceptions of the value/importance of OCB or a shared concern for the well-being of the collective), and the degree to which the members of collective entities internalize the values of their leader.

Second, we observed that a wide variety of mediators have been examined in the literature and few of their effects have been replicated across studies. One reason why so many different mediators have been examined may be the absence of any overarching theoretical framework for identifying important mediators. Consistent with our discussion in the preceding sections, we believe the IPO framework may provide help in identifying mediating mechanisms that would be fruitful to explore in the multilevel OCB domain. The IPO and IMO models identify three major processes influencing team effectiveness: team processes, emergent states, and blended mediators. Although aspects of each type of process have been examined as mediators in this literature, there are important aspects of each that have been ignored.

For example, in the case of team processes, we could find no studies that examined communication or coordination, even though we would expect that several of the antecedents examined in this literature (e.g., LMX, servant leadership, affective commitment, cohesion, or voice climate) would be expected to influence communication or coordination, which subsequently might be expected to increase OCB. In addition, we were unable to find any study that looked at motivation to perform "above and beyond the call of duty" or "beyond expectations" as a mediator, in spite of the fact that there is evidence that intrinsic motivation mediates the effect of transformational leadership on OCB (Piccolo & Colquitt, 2006) and there are other studies (e.g., Lee & Allen, 2002) that have shown that intrinsic motivation is positively related to some forms of OCB. Finally, we would expect that several of the antecedents identified in the multilevel OCB literature (e.g., leader emotional management, benevolent leadership, cooperative group norms, diversity in group composition factors) would influence the level of relationship conflict (Jehn, 1995), and that individuals on teams with high levels of relationship conflict might perform fewer helping behaviors toward other members, because they fundamentally dislike other members based on personal issues. In contrast, members of teams with high levels of process and task conflict should be more likely to express voice (either destructively or constructively; Maynes & Podsakoff, 2014) about how resources should be allocated and how work should be performed.

In the case of emergent states, one important process that has not been examined in the multilevel OCB literature is shared mental models (SMMs). According to Mathieu, Heffner, Goodwin, Cannon-Bowers, and Salas (2005), a shared mental model is "an organized understanding of knowledge that is shared by team members" (p. 38). Research indicates that SMMs are multidimensional in nature and include aspects of technology, task, team interaction, and the team itself. Although one could develop hypotheses regarding several of these dimensions, it seems likely a strong team SMM ("a shared understanding among team members about how they will interact with one another"; Mathieu et al., 2008, p. 430) would facilitate individual helping and courtesy between team members by increasing coordination and communication across members. Finally, in the blended mediator category, one mediating process that is potentially worthy of investigation is the quantity and quality of information exchange. As in the case of communication, we would expect that the amount and nature of information exchanged among team members might mediate the effect of a number of antecedents, like LMX, servant leadership, TMX, empowerment climate, and justice climate on individual-level OCB.

However, these are only a few examples of how contemporary perspectives on mediators from the IPO model can be integrated into the multilevel OCB research. Other examples would include coordinating the sequencing and timing of interdependent actions within the group (Fleishman & Zaccaro, 1992); tracking team resources and internal and external environmental conditions (Fleishman & Zaccaro, 1992); and the regulation of team member emotions, such as burnout and excitement (Cannon-Bowers, Tannenbaum, Salas, & Volpe, 1995).

What Are the Boundary Conditions of the Multilevel Antecedents of Organizational Citizenship Behavior?

Based on our review, it appears that the most important moderators are various aspects of organizational climate. Research suggests that fostering a group-level climate that permits employees to participate in the decision-making process or to make decisions themselves, is fair to employees, encourages employees to speak up, focuses on customer service, creates a positive work environment, or fosters group cohesiveness enhances the effect of a variety of different predictors (e.g., group member characteristics, team social relationships, attitudes, perceptions, and leader behaviors) on OCB. Although there is some evidence that group cohesiveness can also neutralize the effects of various predictors on OCB, Howell et al. (1986) have argued that this only happens when "group norms run counter to managerial goals" but not when "group norms foster cooperation with management" (p. 90).

Therefore, the general pattern suggests that it might be wise for future research to think about what other aspects of the group's climate or culture ought to be examined. For example, MacKenzie, Podsakoff, and Podsakoff (2011) suggested that a climate of conflict (relationship or task) in a group may moderate the relationship between some antecedents and OCB. Similarly, we would expect that the relationships between antecedents and OCB might be different in groups that share a promotion-focused climate (where advancement, growth, and accomplishment are encouraged) than in groups that share a prevention-focused climate (where security, safety, and responsibility are primary concerns). For example, when group members have a prevention focus, it may serve to neutralize the impact of supervisory support on their voice behavior because they may perceive that voice can upset the status quo or disrupt relationships with their leader or other group members. Finally, with respect to organizational culture, one aspect of culture that may moderate the relationships between antecedents and OCB is Hofstede's (2001) individualism dimension. Taras, Kirkman, and Steel's (2010) meta-analysis indicates that employee individualism is negatively related to both citizenship behavior ($\rho = -.21$) and helpfulness ($\rho = -.20$) at the individual level, and individualism at the group level is negatively related to cooperation in groups ($\rho = -.39$). The latter suggests that individualism at the group level may be an important neutralizer of the effects of other variables that are positively related to OCB because highly individualistic groups are less likely to be cooperative. Given the relationship between individualism and collectivism, one might speculate that collectivism might be an important enhancer of the effects of other variables that are positively related to OCB because highly collectivistic groups are more likely to be cooperative.

Methodological Issues

In addition to the conceptual/theoretical issues, our review also revealed several methodological and analytical shortcomings of prior multilevel research examining the antecedents of OCB. These issues related to (a) the need for better evidence of causality, (b) the nature of the composition model used, (c) meeting the requirements for multilevel modeling, and (d) the analytical procedures used to test the multilevel effects hypothesized. In the following sections we will expand upon each of these issues.

How Can We Obtain Better Evidence of Causality?

About half of the studies included in our review examined 2-1-1 or 2-2-1 mediators in their analysis. This is encouraging because it suggests that researchers in this area are trying to understand the reasons why multilevel antecedents cause OCB. To do this effectively, it is necessary to clearly establish the temporal priority of the antecedent over the mediator and the mediator over the OCB. Unfortunately, temporal priority was not unambiguously established in over 80% of the studies examined in our review because they used a cross-sectional research design which measured the antecedents, mediators, and OCBs all at the same point in time. This limits the ability to make causal statements about the theoretical mechanisms being investigated.

Future research should use research designs that provide stronger evidence of causality by (a) building in appropriate lags between the antecedents, mediators, and OCBs; (b) experimentally manipulating each step of the causal sequence (Spencer, Zanna, & Fong, 2005); or (c) some combination of these methods (e.g., MacKenzie, 1986; Stone-Romero & Rosopa, 2011). An example of (a) is a study by Frazier and Fainshmidt (2012) in which the independent variable (voice climate) was assessed at time 1, the mediating variable (psychological empowerment) was assessed 2 months later, and OCB (voice behavior) was measured 2 weeks after the measurement of the mediator. An example of (b) might be one in which a group-level manipulation is used to establish the causal priority of the hypothesized antecedent (e.g., group workload) over the proposed individual-level mediator (e.g., perceptions of stress) and the ultimate outcome variable (e.g., OCB). Even stronger evidence of the hypothesized causal sequence (c) could be obtained by adding an appropriate time lag between the measurement of the proposed mediator and the ultimate outcome variable or by coupling this study with another study that manipulated the mediator and measured its effect on the outcome variable. Use of any of these alternative designs would provide better evidence for causality and would greatly benefit the literature in this area.

What About the Composition Models?

It was somewhat surprising to find that in a research area focused on the direct and moderating effects of group-level variables, a majority of the studies failed to explicitly specify a composition model. Unfortunately, failing to do so undermines the ability to draw accurate inferences from unit-level research. According to James (1982), a composition model is "the specification of how a construct operationalized at one level of analysis is related to another form of that construct at a different level of analysis" (p. 220). In other words, the composition model determines how data from lower levels are aggregated to represent the higher level construct. Of the composition models identified by Chan (1998), the one that was most commonly used in the studies included in our review is the direct consensus model, although we found examples of the use of the referent shift and dispersion models as well.

For the direct consensus model, the higher level construct is operationally defined as the consensus (i.e., average) among the lower level units. This composition model requires that unit members provide individual ratings of Level 2 variables. Within-group agreement is obviously a necessary prerequisite for this model, and it should be confirmed using an empirical measure of agreement (e.g., ICC1 or R_{wg}; Bliese, 2000). For example, in their study on the relationships between employee perceptions of justice (Level 2) and a number of outcome variables, including OCB, Liao and Rupp (2005) asked group members to rate their personal perceptions of justice, which were aggregated to a mean group value.

The referent shift consensus model is similar to the direct consensus model in that ratings from lower level units are used to create the higher level construct, and consensus among group members is a requirement. However, in this case, members are asked to assess the group as a whole. For example, in their study of the relationship between voice climate (Level 2) and individual voice behavior (Level 1), Frazier and Fainshmidt (2012) worded the voice climate measures "such that the group was the referent" (p. 700). Other studies using this model include Carter et al. (2013), Chen and Kao (2011), and Hofmann et al. (2003).

Finally, the dispersion model uses the within-group variance in attribute scores from the lower level units as the empirical representation of the higher level construct. Thus, in contrast to the other two composition models that use the mean of the lower level observations to represent the higher level construct, and only use the variance to support an assumption of team consensus, the dispersion model uses variance in the lower level observations to represent the higher level construct. For example, Gonzalez-Mule, DeGeest, McCormick, Seong, and Brown (2014) used a dispersion model to examine the relationship between group-level agreeableness and extraversion and OCB and found that low dispersion on agreeableness and high dispersion on extraversion promote the enactment of OCB. Similarly, Dekas (2010) used within-unit variability in employees' perceptions of work group citizenship climate to represent the citizenship climate strength construct.

Thus, although it is encouraging to find that some researchers identified the composition model employed in their studies, the fact that the majority failed to do so indicates that this issue needs more careful consideration in future research. At a minimum, this suggests that researchers need to recognize the important conceptual differences between the composition models and be explicit about which model they are using (cf. Chan, 1998; Kozlowski & Klein, 2000). In addition, for the direct consensus and referent shift models, it is essential to provide empirical verification of the assumption of consensus upon which these models are based (Chan, 1998; Podsakoff, Podsakoff, MacKenzie, Maynes, & Spoelma, 2014). This was not done in many of the studies reviewed.

Analytical Issues

Is a Multilevel Model Appropriate for Your Data?

The first step necessary when conducting a multilevel analysis is to test whether a significant amount of between-group variance is present in the dependent variable (Hofmann, 1997). If a significant (and preferably substantial) amount of between-group variance does not exist in OCB, authors should not attempt to predict this outcome with unit-level antecedents. Unfortunately, many of the studies included in our review did not report an ICC(1) value for their focal OCB variable, nor did they indicate whether there was significant between-groups variance in this outcome. Thus, in these studies, it is not clear that modeling unit-level predictors of the OCB was appropriate. Consistent with expert recommendations, we encourage those conducting multilevel OCB research to report the ICC(1) value for their outcomes and whether the between-groups variance component is significant before conducting analyses.

For the studies in our review that did report this information, we found substantial variability in the magnitude of between-group variance in OCB. Specifically, the ICC(1) values reported in these studies ranged from 1% to 79%, with an average of 29%. This begs the question: What explains the sizable differences in between-group variance across studies? Despite the popularity of multilevel research, our review of this literature indicates that we have very little information about the factors that influence the ICC(1) values we observe (cf. Bliese, 1998). Although it is beyond the scope of this manuscript to examine this topic in greater depth, the increasing trend toward multilevel research in the field of management suggests that this would be a fruitful topic for researchers to explore.

How Should Multilevel Models Be Analyzed?

Every study included in our review used hierarchical linear modeling (HLM). Although there are advantages to this approach, the use of HLM to test multilevel mediation effects has several disadvantages. One is that testing 2-1-1 multilevel mediation effects is not straightforward. Indeed, Zhang, Zyphur, and Preacher (2009) distinguish effects that function between groups from effects that function within groups and show that "when a within-group effect is larger or smaller than a between-group effect, the popularly recommended HLM procedures could produce confounded estimates that are larger or smaller, respectively, than the true mediation effect" (p. 696). Consequently, they recommend that researchers should first develop a strong theory for the hypothesized 2-1-1 mediating effect, and then use group-mean centering and add the group mean at Level 2 (or centered within context with reintroduction of the subtracted means at Level 2). Unfortunately, only 5 of the 23 studies that examined 2-1-1 mediation followed the procedures recommended by Zhang et al. However, as noted by Preacher, Zyphur, and Zhang (2010), using this procedure still has a significant limitation in that "Using group means as proxies for latent cluster-level means implies that the researcher believes the means are perfectly reliable. To the extent that this is not true, relationships involving at least one such group mean will, on average, be biased relative to the true effect" (p. 212). Consequently, it appears that all of the HLM-based tests of 2-1-1 mediation included in our review are likely biased to some extent.

In addition to this problem, testing multilevel mediation using HLM has at least three other major disadvantages. The first is that it cannot accommodate models with multiple mediators. Several of the studies in our review (e.g., Chen & Kao, 2011; Schuh et al., 2012; Wei et al., 2010) actually proposed multiple mediators and were forced to test their hypothesized models in a piecemeal fashion due to this limitation. The second is that HLM cannot accommodate Level 2 outcome variables. As a result, the studies testing

2-2-1 mediation examined in this review had to test the hypothesized indirect effects using a two-step, nonsimultaneous estimation method involving both OLS and HLM. More important, as noted by Preacher et al. (2010), this limitation prevents the examination of several plausible types of cross-level mediating effects, including 1-1-2, 1-2-1, 1-2-2, and 2-1-2. For example, it would not be unreasonable to hypothesize that voice climate strength in a group might influence individual voice behavior, which may subsequently improve group effectiveness (2-1-2 mediation). Unfortunately, such models cannot be tested using HLM. A final disadvantage of HLM is that it cannot control for measurement error in latent variables. Measurement error in a predictor biases estimates of the predictor's effects on criterion variables (cf. Bollen, 1989). Although this bias was not controlled for in any studies included in our review, many reported the results of confirmatory factor analyses of their measures, which revealed the existence of measurement error.

To address these disadvantages, Preacher et al. (2010) proposed the use of a multilevel structural equation modeling (MSEM) paradigm and demonstrated in a simulation study (Preacher, Zhang, & Zyphur, 2011) that under a variety of conditions, MSEM outperforms the two most widely used HLM-based techniques in two-level models. More specifically, they found that MSEM estimates are less biased (while displaying adequate efficiency, convergence rates, and power). In addition, MSEM is flexible enough to accommodate Level 2 outcomes, latent variables with multiple indicators, the evaluation of model fit, extensions to larger models (e.g., with multiple mediators), and various kinds of observed data (e.g., ordinal, nonnormal, count, censored). Therefore, for all the aforementioned reasons, we encourage those with multilevel OCB data to consider statistical software supporting MSEM (e.g., Mplus) as an alternative to HLM.

Conclusions

Although interest in the unit-level antecedents of individual-level OCBs has increased dramatically in the past 5 years, our review of this literature suggests that the rapid growth in this area may have come at the expense of (a) building and using theory with strong foundations, (b) rigorous tests of the hypothesized multilevel effects, and (c) the identification of replicable results regarding the theoretical mechanisms and boundary conditions of these effects. Consequently, we have provided several theoretical, methodological, and analytical recommendations for scholars conducting research in this domain. We hope that these suggestions will assist management scholars in realizing the potential of multilevel research in this area and move the field a step closer to more effectively putting the "organization" (or at least the "unit") into *organizational* citizenship behavior research.

References

Studies included in the literature review are indicated with asterisks.

*Anand, S. (2011). *Multi-level examination of idiosyncratic deals: Antecedents and consequences.* Unpublished doctoral dissertation, University of Illinois at Chicago.

*Arthaud-Day, M. L., Rode, J. C., & Turnley, W. H. (2012). Direct and contextual effects of individual values on organizational citizenship behavior in teams. *Journal of Applied Psychology, 97,* 792–807.

*Aryee, S., Sun, L., Chen, Z. X. G., & Debrah, Y. A. (2008). Abusive supervision and contextual performance: The mediating role of emotional exhaustion and the moderating role of work unit structure. *Management and Organization Review, 4,* 393–411.

Barnard, C. I. (1938). *The functions of the executive.* Cambridge, MA: Harvard University Press.

Bateman, T. S., & Organ, D. W. (1983). Job satisfaction and the good soldier: The relationship between affect and employee "citizenship." *Academy of Management Journal, 26,* 587–595.

*Beeri, I. (2012). Turnaround management strategies in public systems: The impact on group-level organizational citizenship behavior. *International Review of Administrative Sciences, 78,* 158–179.

Bell, S. T. (2007). Deep-level composition variables as predictors of team performance: A meta-analysis. *Journal of Applied Psychology, 92,* 595–615.

Bell, S. T., Villado, A. J., Lukasik, M. A., Belau, L., & Briggs, A. L. (2011). Getting specific about demographic diversity variable and team performance relationships: A meta-analysis. *Journal of Management, 37,* 709–743.

Bliese, P. D. (1998). Group size, ICC values, and group-level correlations: A simulation. *Organizational Research Methods, 1,* 355–373.

Bliese, P. D. (2000). Within-group agreement, non-interdependence, and reliability: Implications for data aggregation and analysis. In K. J. Klein & S. W. J. Kozlowski (Eds.), *Multilevel theory, research, and methods in organizations: Foundations, extensions, and new directions* (pp. 349–381). San Francisco, CA: Jossey-Bass.

Bollen, K. A. (1989). *Structural equations with latent variables.* New York, NY: Wiley.

Borman, W. C., & Motowidlo, S. J. (1993). Expanding the criterion domain to include elements of contextual performance. In N. Schmitt, W. C. Borman, & Associates (Eds.), *Personnel selection in organizations* (pp. 71–98). San Francisco, CA: Jossey-Bass.

Cannon-Bowers, I. A., Tannenbaum, S. I., Salas, E., & Volpe, C. E. (1995). Defining team competencies and establishing team training requirements. In R. Guzzo & E. Salas (Eds.), *Team effectiveness and decision making in organizations* (pp. 333–380). San Francisco, CA: Jossey-Bass.

*Carter, M. Z., Armenakis, A. A., Field, H. S., & Mossholder, K. W. (2013). Transformational leadership, relationship quality, and employee performance during continuous incremental organizational change. *Journal of Organizational Behavior, 34*, 942–958.

Chan, D. (1998). Functional relations among constructs in the same content domain at different levels of analysis: A typology of composition models. *Journal of Applied Psychology, 83*, 234–246.

*Chen, C. V., & Kao, R. (2011). A multilevel study on the relationships between work characteristics, self-efficacy, collective efficacy, and organizational citizenship behavior: The case of Taiwanese police duty-executing organizations. *Journal of Psychology, 145*, 361–390.

*Chen, C. V., Tang, Y., & Wang, S. (2009). Interdependence and organizational citizenship behavior: Exploring the mediating effect of group cohesion in multilevel analysis. *Journal of Psychology, 143*, 625–640.

*Chen, Z. (2011). *A contingency model of empowering leadership on employee proactive behavior: Team power distance climate and individual power distance beliefs as the moderators.* Unpublished doctoral dissertation, Hong Kong University of Science and Technology.

*Choi, J. N. (2006). Multilevel and cross-level effects of workplace attitudes and group member relations on interpersonal helping behavior. *Human Performance, 19*, 383–402.

*Choi, J. N. (2007). Change-oriented organizational citizenship behavior: Effects of work environment characteristics and intervening psychological processes. *Journal of Organizational Behavior, 28*, 467–484.

*Chung, M., Park, J., Moon, H. K., & Oh, H. (2011). The multilevel effects of network embeddedness on interpersonal citizenship behavior. *Small Group Research, 42*, 730–760.

*Cohen, A., Ben-Tura, E., & Vashdi, D. R. (2012). The relationship between social exchange variables, OCB, and performance. *Personnel Review, 41*, 705–731.

*Dekas, K. H. (2010). *Citizenship in context: Investigating the effects of work group climate on organizational citizenship perceptions and behavior.* Unpublished doctoral dissertation, University of Michigan.

*Dineen, B. R., Lewicki, R. J., & Tomlinson, E. C. (2006). Supervisory guidance and behavioral integrity: Relationships with employee citizenship and deviant behavior. *Journal of Applied Psychology, 91*, 622–635.

*Du, J., & Choi, J. N. (2010). Pay for performance in emerging markets: Insights from China. *Journal of International Business Studies, 41*, 671–689.

Farh, J. L., Earley, P. C., & Lin, S. C. (1997). Impetus for action: A cultural analysis of justice and organizational behavior in Chinese society. *Administrative Science Quarterly, 42*, 421–444.

*Farmer, S. M., Van Dyne, L., & Kamdar, D. (2015). The contextualized self: How team-member exchange leads to coworker identification and helping OCB. *Journal of Applied Psychology, 100*, 583–595.

*Frazier, M. L., & Fainshmidt, S. (2012). Voice climate, work outcomes, and the mediating role of psychological empowerment: A multilevel examination. *Group & Organization Management, 37*, 691–715.

Fleishman, E. A., & Zaccaro, S. J. (1992). Toward a taxonomy of team performance functions. In R. W. Swezey & E. Salas (Eds.), *Teams: Their training and performance* (pp. 31–56). Norwood, NJ: Ablex.

*Gavin, M. B. (1997). *Helping behavior in organizations: Examining individual-level and group-level effects.* Unpublished doctoral dissertation, Purdue University.

George, J. M., & Jones, G. R. (1997). Organizational spontaneity in context. *Human Performance, 10*, 153–170.

*Gonzalez-Mulé, E., DeGeest, D. S., McCormick, B. W., Seong, J. Y., & Brown, K. G. (2014). Can we get some cooperation around here? The mediating role of group norms on the relationship between team personality and individual helping behaviors. *Journal of Applied Psychology, 99*, 988–999.

Graham, J. W. (1991). An essay on organizational citizenship behavior. *Employee Responsibilities and Rights Journal, 4*, 249–270.

Grant, A. M. (2008). Does intrinsic motivation fuel the prosocial fire? Motivational synergy in predicting persistence, performance, and productivity. *Journal of Applied Psychology, 93*, 48–58.

Grant, A. M., & Mayer, D. M. (2009). Good soldiers and good actors: Prosocial and impression management motives as interactive predictors of affiliative citizenship behaviors. *Journal of Applied Psychology, 94*, 900–912.

Hoffman, B. J., Blair, C. A., Meriac, J. P., & Woehr, D. J. (2007). Expanding the criterion domain? A quantitative review of the OCB literature. *Journal of Applied Psychology, 92*(2), 555–566.

Hofmann, D. A. (1997). An overview of the logic and rationale of hierarchical linear models. *Journal of Management, 23*(6), 723–744.

*Hofmann, D. A., Morgeson, F. P., & Gerras, S. J. (2003). Climate as a moderator of the relationship between leader-ember exchange and context specific citizenship: Safety climate as an exemplar. *Journal of Applied Psychology, 88*, 170–178.

Hofstede, G. H. (2001). *Culture's consequences: Comparing values, behaviors, institutions, and organizations across nations.* Thousand Oaks, CA: Sage.

*Hong, S. C. C. (2008). *Paternalistic leadership styles and follower performance: Examining mediating variables in a multilevel model.* Unpublished doctoral dissertation, Hong Kong Polytechnic University.

Howell, J. P., Dorfman, P. W., & Kerr, S. (1986). Moderator variables in leadership research. *Academy of Management Review, 11*, 88–102.

*Hsiung, H. (2012). Authentic leadership and employee voice behavior: A multi-level psychological process. *Journal of Business Ethics, 107*, 349–361.

*Hu, J., & Liden, R. C. (2013). Relative leader-member exchange within team contexts: How and when social comparison impacts individual effectiveness. *Personnel Psychology, 66*, 127–172.

*Hui, C. H., Chiu, W. C. K., Yu, P. L. H., Cheng, K., & Tse, H. H. M. (2007). The effects of service climate and the effective leadership behaviour of supervisors on frontline employee service quality: A multi-level analysis. *Journal of Occupational and Organizational Psychology, 80*, 151–172.

Humphrey, S. E., & Aime, F. (2014). Team microdynamics: Toward an organizing approach to teamwork. *Academy of Management Annals, 8*, 443–503.

Ilgen, D. R., Hollenbeck, J. R., Johnson, M., & Jundt, D. (2005). Teams in organizations: From input-process-output models to IMOI models. *Annual Review of Psychology, 56*, 517–543.

Institute for Scientific Information. (June 15, 2016). Web of Science database. https://www.webofknowledge.com/

James, L. R. (1982). Aggregation bias in estimates of perceptual agreement. *Journal of Applied Psychology, 67,* 219–229.

*Jansen, K. J., & Kristof-Brown, A. L. (2005). Marching to the beat of a different drummer: Examining the impact of pacing congruence. *Organizational Behavior and Human Decision Processes, 97,* 93–105.

Jehn, K. A. (1995). A multimethod examination of the benefits and detriments of intragroup conflict. *Administrative Science Quarterly, 40,* 256–282.

*Kalshoven, K., Den Hartog, D. N., & De Hoogh, A. H. B. (2013). Ethical leadership and follower helping and courtesy: Moral awareness and empathic concerns as moderators. *Applied Psychology: An International Review, 62,* 211–235.

*Karam, C. M. (2011). Good organizational soldiers: Conflict-related stress predicts citizenship behavior. *International Journal of Conflict Management, 22,* 300–319.

*Karam, C. M., & Kwantes, C. T. (2011). Contextualizing cultural orientation and organizational citizenship behavior. *Journal of International Management, 17,* 303–315.

Katz, D., & Kahn, R. L. (1966). *The social psychology of organizations.* New York, NY: Wiley.

*Kehoe, R. R., & Wright, P. M. (2013). The impact of high-performance human resource practices on employees' attitudes and behaviors. *Journal of Management, 39,* 366–391.

Kelley, R., & Caplan, J. (1993). How Bell Labs creates star performers. *Harvard Business Review, 71,* 128–139.

Kerr, S., & Jermier, J. M. (1978). Substitutes for leadership: Their meaning and measurement. *Organizational Behavior and Human Performance, 22,* 375–403.

*Kidwell, R. E., Mossholder, K. W., & Bennett, N. (1997). Cohesiveness and organizational citizenship behavior: A multilevel analysis using work groups and individuals. *Journal of Management, 23,* 775–793.

*Kim, S. Y., Shin, Y., & Kim, M. S. (2012). Cross-level interactions of individual trait positive affect, group trait positive affect, and group positive affect diversity. *Asian Journal of Social Psychology, 16,* 197–206.

*Kirkman, B. L., Chen, G., Farh, J., Chen, Z. X., & Lowe, K. B. (2009). Individual power distance orientation and follower reactions to transformational leaders: A cross-level, cross-cultural examination. *Academy of Management Journal, 52,* 744–764.

Kozlowski, S. W. J., & Klein, K. J. (2000). A multi-level approach to theory and research in organizations: Contextual, temporal, and emergent processes. In K. J. Klein & S. W. J. Kozlowski (Eds.), *Multilevel theory, research, and methods in organizations: Foundations, extensions, and new directions* (pp. 3–90). San Francisco, CA: Jossey-Bass.

*Lam, C. F., & Mayer, D. M. (2014). When do employees speak up for their customers? A model of voice in a customer service context. *Personnel Psychology, 67,* 637–666.

*Lee, G. L., Diefendorff, J. M., Kim, T.-K., & Bian, L. (2014). Personality and participative climate: Antecedents of distinct voice behaviors. *Human Performance, 27,* 25–43.

Lee, K., & Allen, N. J. (2002). Organizational citizenship behavior and workplace deviance: The role of affect and cognitions. *Journal of Applied Psychology, 87,* 131–142.

LePine, J. A., Erez, A., & Johnson, D. E. (2002). The nature and dimensionality of organizational citizenship behavior: A critical review and meta-analysis. *Journal of Applied Psychology, 87,* 52–65.

LePine, J. A., Piccolo, R. F., Jackson, C. L., Mathieu, J. E., & Saul, J. R. (2008). A meta-analysis of teamwork processes: Tests of a multidimensional model and relationships with team effectiveness criteria. *Personnel Psychology, 61,* 273–307.

LePine, J. A., & Van Dyne, L. (2001). Voice and cooperative behavior as contrasting forms of contextual performance: evidence of differential relationships with big five personality characteristics and cognitive ability. *Journal of Applied Psychology, 86,* 326–336.

*Li, N., Chiaburu, D. S., Kirkman, B. L., & Xie, Z. (2013). Spotlight on the followers: An examination of moderators of relationships between transformational leadership and subordinates' citizenship and taking charge. *Personnel Psychology, 66,* 225–260.

*Li, P. P., Bai, Y., & Xi, Y. (2012). The contextual antecedents of organizational trust: A multi-dimensional cross-level analysis. *Management and Organization Review, 8,* 371–396.

*Liang, J., & Tang, J. (2010). A multi-level study on employee voice: Evidence from a chain of retail stores. *Frontiers of Business Research in China, 4,* 541–561.

*Liao, H. (2002). *A cross level analysis of citizenship behavior in work groups.* Unpublished doctoral dissertation, University of Minnesota.

*Liao, H., & Rupp, D. E. (2005). The impact of justice climate and justice orientation on work outcomes: A cross-level multifoci framework. *Journal of Applied Psychology, 90,* 242–256.

*Lin, J. S., & Lin, S. (2011). Moderating effect of organizational climate on the relationship of organizational support and service-oriented organizational citizenship behaviors. *African Journal of Business Management, 5,* 582–595.

*Liu, D., & Fu, P. (2011). Motivating protégés' personal learning in teams: A multilevel investigation of autonomy support and autonomy orientation. *Journal of Applied Psychology, 96,* 1195–1208.

MacKenzie, S. B. (1986). The role of attention in mediating the effect of advertising on attribute importance. *Journal of Consumer Research, 13,* 174–195.

MacKenzie, S. B., Podsakoff, P. M., & Podsakoff, N. P. (2011). Challenge-oriented organizational citizenship behaviors and organizational effectiveness: Do challenge-oriented behaviors really have an impact on the organization's bottom line? *Personnel Psychology, 64,* 559–592.

Mathieu, J. E., Heffner, T. S., Goodwin, G. F., Cannon-Bowers, J. A., & Salas, E. (2005). Scaling the quality of teammates' mental models: equifinality and normative comparisons. *Journal of Organizational Behavior, 26,* 37–56.

Mathieu, J. E., Maynard, M. T., Rapp, T., & Gilson, L. (2008). Team effectiveness 1997–2007: A review of recent advancements and a glimpse into the future. *Journal of Management, 34,* 410–476.

Maynes, T. D., & Podsakoff, P. M. (2014). Speaking more broadly: An examination of the nature, antecedents, and consequences of an expanded set of employee voice behaviors. *Journal of Applied Psychology, 99,* 87–112.

Mischel, W. (1973). Toward a cognitive social learning reconceptualization of personality. *Psychological Review, 80,* 252–283.

Mischel, W. (1977). The interaction of person and situation. In D. Magnusson & N. S. Endler (Eds.), *Personality at the crossroads: Current issues in interactional psychology* (pp. 333–352). Hillsdale, NJ: Lawrence Erlbaum Associates.

*Morrison, E. W., Wheeler-Smith, S. L., & Kamdar, D. (2011). Speaking up in groups: A cross-level study of group voice climate and voice. *Journal of Applied Psychology, 96,* 183–191.

*Naumann, S. E., & Bennett, N. (2000). A case for procedural justice climate: Development and test of a multilevel model. *Academy of Management Journal, 43*, 881–889.

*Naumann, S. E., & Ehrhart, M. G. (2011). Moderators of the relationship between group helping norms and individual helping. *Small Group Research, 42*, 225–248.

*Ng, K. Y., & Van Dyne, L. (2005). Antecedents and performance consequences of helping behavior in work groups: A multilevel analysis. *Group & Organization Management, 30*, 514–540.

Nielsen, T. M., Hrivnak, G. A., & Shaw, M. (2009). Organizational citizenship behavior and performance: A meta-analysis of group-level research. *Small Group Research, 40*, 555–577.

Organ, D. W. (1988). *Organizational citizenship behavior: The good soldier syndrome.* Lexington, MA: Lexington Books.

Organ, D. W., Podsakoff, N. P., & MacKenzie, S. B. (2006). *Organizational citizenship behavior: Its nature, antecedents, and consequences.* Thousand Oaks, CA: Sage.

*Paik, Y. (2012). *Redefining multidisciplinary teams: An institutional approach.* Unpublished doctoral dissertation, University of Maryland.

Piccolo, R. F., & Colquitt, J. A. (2006). Transformational leadership and job behaviors: The mediating role of core job characteristics. *Academy of Management Journal, 49*, 327–340.

Podsakoff, N. P., Podsakoff, P. M., MacKenzie, S. B., Maynes, T. D., & Spoelma, T. (2014). Consequences of unit-level organizational citizenship behaviors: A review and recommendations for future research. *Journal of Organizational Behavior, 35*, S87–S119.

Podsakoff, N. P., Whiting, S. W., Podsakoff, P. M., & Blume, B. D. (2009). Individual- and organizational-level consequences of organizational citizenship behaviors: A meta-analysis. *Journal of Applied Psychology, 94*, 122–141.

Podsakoff, P. M., Ahearne, M., & MacKenzie, S. B. (1997). Organizational citizenship behavior and the quantity and quality of work group performance. *Journal of Applied Psychology, 82*, 262–270.

Podsakoff, P. M., MacKenzie, S. B., Paine, J. B., & Bachrach, D. G. (2000). Organizational citizenship behaviors: A critical review of the theoretical and empirical literature and suggestions for future research. *Journal of Management, 26*, 513–563.

Podsakoff, P. M., MacKenzie, S. B., & Podsakoff, N. P. (2012). Sources of method bias in social science research and recommendations on how to control it. In S. T. Fiske, D. L. Schacter, & S. E. Taylor (Eds.), *Annual review of psychology* (Vol. 63, pp. 539–539). Palo Alto, CA: Annual Reviews.

Porter, C. O. L. H., Hollenbeck, J. R., Ilgen, D. R., Ellis, A. P., West, B. J., & Moon, H. (2003). Backing up behaviors in teams: The role of personality and legitimacy of need. *Journal of Applied Psychology, 88*(3), 391–403.

Preacher, K. J., Zhang, Z., & Zyphur, M. J. (2011). Alternative methods for assessing mediation in multilevel data: The advantages of multilevel SEM. *Structural Equation Modeling, 18*, 161–182.

Preacher, K. J., Zyphur, M. J., & Zhang, Z. (2010). A general multilevel SEM framework for assessing multilevel mediation. *Psychological Methods, 15*, 209–233.

Rioux, S. M., & Penner, L. A. (2001). The causes of organizational citizenship behavior: A motivational analysis. *Journal of Applied Psychology, 86*, 1306–1314.

*Schmidt, J. (2008). *Personality, group context, and performance behavior in university football teams.* Unpublished doctoral dissertation, University of Calgary.

*Schraub, E. M., Michel, A., Shemla, M., & Sonntag, K. (2014). The roles of leader emotion management and team conflict for team members' personal initiative: A multilevel perspective. *European Journal of Work and Organizational Psychology, 23*, 263–276.

*Schuh, S. C., Zhang, X., Egold, N. W., Graf, M. M., Pandey, D., & van Dick, R. (2012). Leader and follower organizational identification: The mediating role of leader behaviour and implications for follower OCB. *Journal of Occupational and Organizational Psychology, 85*, 421–432.

*Shen, J., & Benson, J. (2014). When CSR is a social norm: How socially responsible human resource management affects employee work behavior. *Journal of Management, 42*, 1723–1746.

Smith, C. A., Organ, D. W., & Near, J. P. (1983). Organizational citizenship behavior: Its nature and antecedents. *Journal of Applied Psychology, 68*, 655–663.

*Snape, E., & Redman, T. (2010). HRM practices, organizational citizenship behaviour, and performance: A multi-level analysis. *Journal of Management Studies, 47*, 1219–1247.

*Song, L. J., Tsui, A. S., & Law, K. S. (2009). Unpacking employee responses to organizational exchange mechanisms: The role of social and economic exchange perceptions. *Journal of Management, 35*, 56–93.

Spencer, S. J., Zanna, M. P., & Fong, G. T. (2005). Establishing a causal chain: Why experiments are often more effective than mediational analyses in examining psychological processes. *Journal of Personality and Social Psychology, 89*, 845–851.

Stone-Romero, E. F., & Rosopa, P. J. (2011). Experimental tests of mediation models: Prospects, problems, and some solutions. *Organizational Research Methods, 14*, 631–646.

*Sun, L., Chow, I. H. S., Chiu, R. K., & Pan, W. (2013). Outcome favorability in the link between leader-member exchange and organizational citizenship behavior: Procedural fairness climate matters. *Leadership Quarterly, 24*, 215–226.

*Tangirala, S., & Ramanujam, R. (2012). Ask and you shall hear (but not always): Examining the relationship between manager consultation and employee voice. *Personnel Psychology, 65*, 251–282.

Taras, V., Kirkman, B. L., & Steel, P. (2010). Examining the impact of *Culture's Consequences*: A three-decade, multilevel, meta-analytic review of Hofstede's cultural value dimensions. *Journal of Applied Psychology, 95*, 405–439.

Tett, R. P., & Burnett, D. D. (2003). A personality trait-based interactionist model of job performance. *Journal of Applied Psychology, 88*, 500–517.

*Tröster, C., & van Knippenberg, D. (2012). Leader openness, nationality dissimilarity, and voice in multinational management teams. *Journal of International Business Studies, 43*, 591–613.

*Tuuli, M. M., & Rowlinson, S. (2009). Empowerment in project teams: A multilevel examination of the job performance implications. *Construction Management and Economics, 27*, 473–498.

*Uen, J., Chien, M. S., & Yen, Y. (2009). The mediating effects of psychological contracts on the relationship between human resource systems and role behaviors: A multilevel analysis. *Journal of Business and Psychology, 24*, 215–223.

Van Dyne, L., Cummings, L. L., & Parks, J. M. (1995). Extra-role behaviors: In pursuit of construct and definitional clarity (A bridge over muddied waters). In L. L. Cummings & B. M. Staw (Eds.), *Research in organizational behavior* (Vol. 17, pp. 215–285). Greenwich, CT: JAI Press.

Van Dyne, L., Graham, J. W., & Dienesch, R. M. (1994). Organizational citizenship behavior: Construct redefinition, measurement, and validation. *Academy of Management Journal, 37*, 765–802.

Van Dyne, L. & LePine, J. A. (1998). Helping and voice extra-role behaviors: Evidence of construct and predictive validity. *Academy of Management Journal, 41*, 108–119.

Van Scotter, J. R., & Motowidlo, S. J. (1996). Interpersonal facilitation and job dedication as separate facets of contextual performance. *Journal of Applied Psychology, 81*, 525–531.

*Walker, C. T. (2011). *Psychological climate for engagement and the role of leader behavior patterns in fostering employee engagement and performance behaviors.* Unpublished doctoral dissertation, University of Connecticut.

*Walumbwa, F. O., Hartnell, C. A., & Oke, A. (2010). Servant leadership, procedural justice climate, service climate, employee attitudes, and organizational citizenship behavior: A cross-level investigation. *Journal of Applied Psychology, 95*, 517–529.

*Walumbwa, F. O., & Schaubroeck, J. (2009). Leader personality traits and employee voice behavior: Mediating roles of ethical leadership and work group psychological safety. *Journal of Applied Psychology, 94*, 1275–1285.

*Wang, L., Huang, J., Chu, X., & Wang, X. (2010). A multilevel study on antecedents of manager voice in Chinese context. *Chinese Management Studies, 4*, 212–230.

*Wang, Y.-D., & Hsieh, H.-H. (2013). Organizational ethical climate, perceived organizational support and employee silence: A cross-level investigation. *Human Relations, 66*, 783–802.

*Wech, B. A., Kennedy, K. N., & Deeter-Schmelz, D. R. (2009). A multi-level analysis of customer contact teams. *Journal of Services Marketing, 23*, 436–448.

*Wei, Y., Han, T., & Hsu, I. (2010). High-performance HR practices and OCB: A cross-level investigation of a causal path. *International Journal of Human Resource Management, 21*, 1631–1648.

*Wherry, H. M. (2012). *Authentic leadership, leader-member exchange, and organizational citizenship behavior: A multi-level analysis.* Unpublished doctoral dissertation, University of Nebraska.

Whitman, D. S., Van Rooy, D. L., & Viswesvaran, C. (2010). Satisfaction, citizenship behaviors, and performance in work units: A meta-analysis of collective construct relations. *Personnel Psychology, 63*, 41–81.

Williams, L. J., & Anderson, S. E. (1991). Job satisfaction and organizational commitment as predictors of organizational citizenship and in-role behaviors. *Journal of Management, 17*, 601–617.

*Yang, J., Mossholder, K. W., & Peng, T. K. (2007). Procedural justice climate and group power distance: An examination of cross-level interaction effects. *Journal of Applied Psychology, 92*, 681–692.

Zhang, Z., Zyphur, M. J., & Preacher, K. J. (2009). Testing multilevel mediation using hierarchical linear models: Problems and solutions. *Organizational Research Methods, 12*, 695–719.

CHAPTER

26 Helping in Organizations: A Review and Directions for Future Research

Mark G. Ehrhart

Abstract

Helping has long been a central component of organizational citizenship behavior (OCB), and yet our knowledge of the full spectrum of helping processes in organizations is limited. Most helping research in the OCB literature has focused on individuals' tendencies to help across situations, including antecedents and outcomes of those general tendencies. Integrating across a number of related literatures on such topics as prosocial behavior, help seeking, feedback/advice seeking, and favor exchange, this chapter presents an integrative framework of helping processes organized around the key decisions of whether to seek help and whether to help when asked, as well as whether to offer help and whether to accept offered help. An exploration of the factors associated with these decisions identifies a number of topics that have not received full attention in the OCB literature, which can be studied across various types of help and levels of analysis.

Key Words: organizational citizenship behavior, helping behavior, altruism, help seeking, prosocial behavior

Helping behavior has consistently been central to the idea of what makes for a good organizational citizen; as described by Podsakoff, MacKenzie, Paine, and Bachrach (2000), "Helping behavior has been identified as an important form of citizenship behavior by virtually everyone who has worked in this area" (p. 516). As interest in organizational citizenship behavior (OCB) has increased (Podsakoff, Whiting, Podsakoff, & Blume, 2009), so has interest in helping behavior. Spitzmuller and Van Dyne (2013) reported that the number of publications on helping in the management and applied psychology literatures during 2010 was over three times the number published in 2001. Given that helping has received so much attention in the literature, it would be expected that we should have a fairly strong understanding of helping processes in organizations; unfortunately, that is not entirely the case. Thus, the goal of this chapter is to show that there is much more to helping than has typically been addressed in OCB research, and thus there is still much work to be done to understand the who, what, when, why, and how of helping in organizations.

As depicted in Figure 26.1, this chapter is framed around key questions about helping behavior that have been considered in the research literature. The circles in the framework represent decision points for either the help seeker or help giver, and the framework is focused on two key decisions that apply to most episodes of helping: the decision to seek help or not and the corresponding decision to give help or not. The framework also includes two less-studied decisions when there is no request for help: the decision to offer help and the subsequent decision to accept that offer or not.

The chapter begins with the general question of whether there are different types of help, as this question has implications for almost all other aspects of the helping process (as shown at the base of Figure 26.1). The next set of questions covered are toward the center of the framework, pertaining

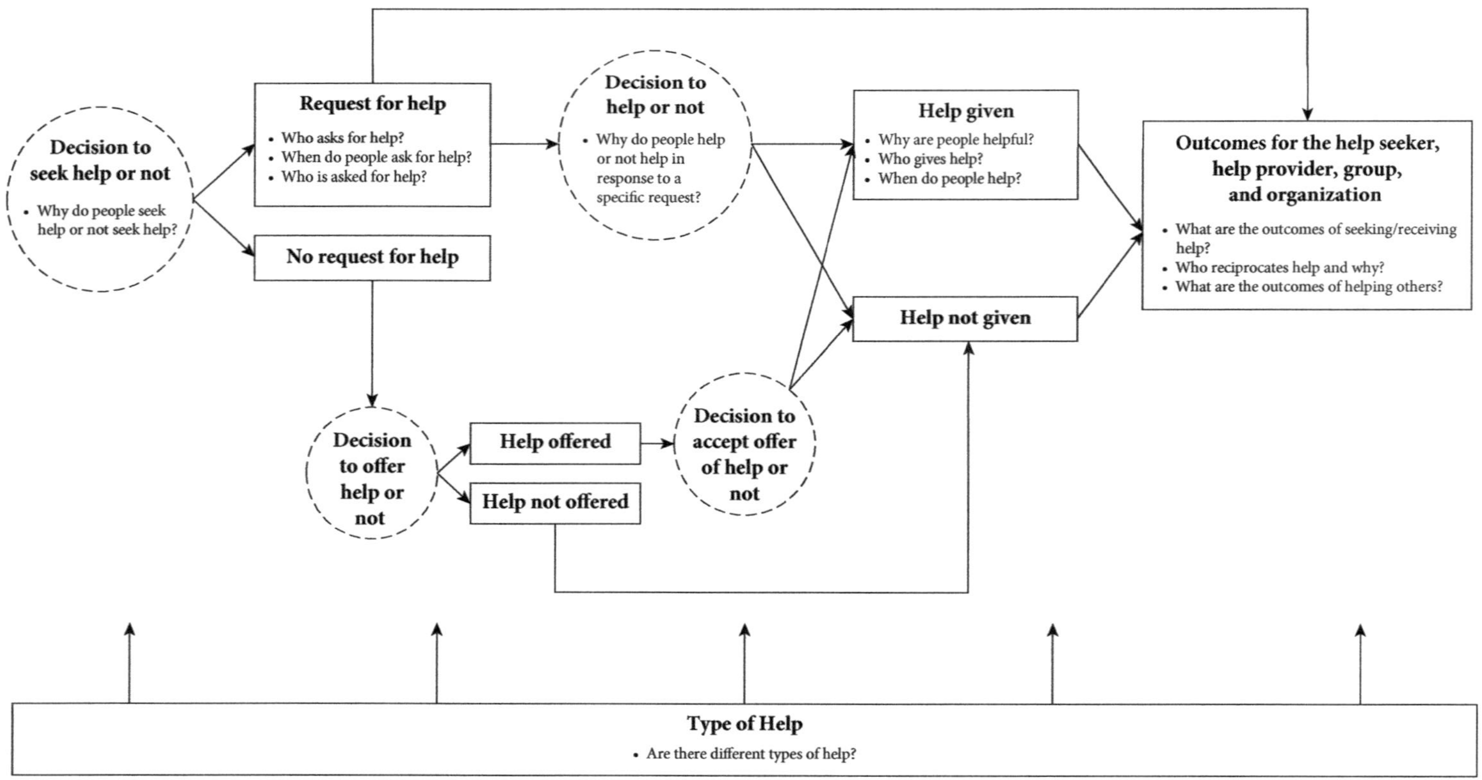

Figure 26.1 A theoretical framework of helping processes in organizations

to the help that is given (the why, who, and when of helping), as this has been the primary focus of the current OCB literature. The chapter then shifts to the decision to seek help or not (i.e., the why, who, and when of help seeking), as well as the decision for the help provider to give help or not. Finally, the chapter discusses the outcomes of helping, including the outcomes of help seeking/receiving, reciprocation, and the outcomes of helping across multiple levels of analysis. The chapter closes with suggestions for future research based on the review and framework. Throughout, the chapter draws from not only the OCB literature but also the literatures on prosocial behavior, help seeking, feedback seeking, advice seeking, information seeking, favor exchange, organizational support, social networks, team processes, intergroup relations, and bystander intervention. By demonstrating the variety of perspectives on helping across these literatures, the hope is to stimulate further research and thinking on helping in the OCB literature.

Are There Different Types of Help?

The starting point for the chapter is the help itself. In the OCB literature, helping was originally referred to as altruism (Smith, Organ, & Near, 1983). Organ (1988) distinguished it from behaviors related to preventing work-related problems, referred to as courtesy, but these behaviors were later grouped under the general category of helping behavior, along with ideas of peacemaking and cheerleading (Organ, Podsakoff, & MacKenzie, 2006; Podsakoff et al., 2000). In recent years, helping typically has been treated as a monolithic concept; it is already a category of the more general concept of OCB, and it is rarely broken down more specifically than that. Nevertheless, the reality is that the broad idea of helping encompasses a variety of types of help and can be discussed in terms of a number of characteristics. In addition, the type of help has implications for almost all of the other issues discussed in this chapter, as depicted in Figure 26.1.

One primary distinction that has been made with regard to types of help is between instrumental help and emotional help. As described by Bamberger (2009), instrumental help (which often includes informational help) tends to be more tangible and task related. In contrast, emotional help tends to be personal and less task related. Similar distinctions have been made between job-related and non-job-related support (Bowling, Beehr, & Swader, 2005) and between task assistance and social and emotional support (Mor Barak, Travis, Pyun, & Xie, 2009). In the OCB literature, the focus tends to be on instrumental help (see Settoon & Mossholder, 2002, for one exception). For instance, items from one of the most commonly used helping measures in the OCB literature specifies helping with heavy workloads and work-related problems (Podsakoff, MacKenzie, Moorman, & Fetter, 1990). That being said, some helping items are less clear, only mentioning being "ready to lend a helping hand" (Podsakoff et al., 1990, p. 121). The Williams and Anderson (1991) scale for the very closely related concept of OCB targeted toward other individuals (or OCB-I) also has more of a mix of items, with some clearly being task focused and others seemingly more along the lines of emotional help (e.g., "Takes the time to listen to coworkers' problems and worries" and "Takes a personal interest in other employees").

Another distinction can be made between help that is prompted by a request for help versus help that is not. Research has suggested that the large majority of helping interactions are prompted by a request for help (Burke, Weir, & Duncan, 1976; Kaplan & Cowen, 1981; Nadler, 1991). Requests for help are the primary focus of the literature on help seeking (Bamberger, 2009) and closely tied to the related literatures on advice seeking (Bonaccio & Dalal, 2006; Nebus, 2006), feedback seeking (Anseel, Beatty, Shen, Lievens, & Sackett, 2015; Ashford, Blatt, & VandeWalle, 2003), and information seeking (Borgatti & Cross, 2003), which are integrated throughout this chapter. Despite most help resulting from a direct response to a helping request, it is also possible that the help may be offered without such a request. For example, help may be offered in response to a recognized need in others without the recipient actually making the request (i.e., a coworker is aware of his or her peer's heavy workload and makes an offer of assistance). Research has shown that proactively providing help to others without a request for assistance develops as early as 2 years of age (Warneken, 2013). The responses of those who receive help are likely to differ depending on whether the help was in response to a request; this issue is discussed more in the section on the outcomes of receiving help. Along these lines, the characteristics of individuals who are willing to offer help without a request may be different from those who help as a direct result of a request.

Helping can also be categorized as to whether it is autonomy-oriented help or dependency-oriented help. In short, autonomy-oriented help involves giving the help recipient the tools he or she needs to solve similar problems in the future, whereas dependency-oriented help involves the help giver solving the problem for the help recipient (Nadler, 2002). Thus, with dependency-oriented help, the help recipient has received a short-term benefit but will need similar support from a help giver should a similar problem occur in the future. Which kind of help the help recipient receives may depend on the type of help he or she requests from the help giver (Komissarouk & Nadler, 2014), contextual factors such as pay structure (Bamberger & Levi, 2009), and the attributions of the help giver (Nadler & Chernyak-Hai, 2014), among other things.

A number of other categorization schemes for helping have been discussed in the research literature. For instance, Spitzmuller and Van Dyne (2013) distinguished between reactive helping for which the interest is in benefitting others and fulfilling their needs, and proactive helping, which is given to fulfill the helper's own motives and thus is self-interested. McGuire (1994) identified four types of helping behaviors: (1) casual helping (relatively low cost to the helper), (2) substantial personal helping (higher cost to the helper), (3) emotional helping (intangible help based on close relationship), and (4) emergency helping (response to an acute need with high cost to the helper). Gross and McMullen (1983) made the distinction between necessary help (when a problem cannot be solved alone) and convenient help (when a problem can be solved alone, but help would make things go more quickly). Bolger and colleagues (Bolger & Amarel, 2007; Bolger, Zuckerman, & Kessler, 2000) have distinguished between support that recipients are aware of (visible support) and support that is outside of their awareness or not interpreted as support (invisible support). Cain, Dana, and Newman (2014) discussed giving versus giving in, such that giving represents willing engagement in prosocial behaviors, whereas giving in represents the engagement in prosocial behaviors in response to social pressure or obligation.

Research on advice giving and advice taking from the decision-making literature has distinguished among several types of advice, which can be considered under the general concept of helping. Specifically, Dalal and Bonaccio (2010) identified five types of assistance decision makers may receive from advisors: (1) recommend for (advising the decision maker to take a particular course of action), (2) recommend against (advising the decision maker to avoid or not take a particular course of action, (3) information (providing information about the alternatives available to the decision maker without endorsing a specific choice), (4) decision support (suggesting alternative processes the decision maker may use for making the decision), and (5) social support (providing general socioemotional support and sympathy targeted toward the decision maker). Across two policy-capturing studies, they found that decision makers generally preferred information assistance as compared to the alternatives, and that the context (e.g., the type of decision to be made), characteristics of the advisor (e.g., expertise/credibility), and characteristics of the decision maker (e.g., gender and personality) influenced the preferred type of assistance.

The approaches thus far are categorizations of different types of help, but an alternative perspective is to view help as varying across a number of dimensions. Pearce and Amato (1980) proposed three dimensions of helping: (1) planned and formal versus spontaneous and informal, (2) serious versus nonserious, and (3) direct versus indirect. Help may also vary in its quality or the extent to which it is viewed as actually being helpful for the recipient. In other words, some help results in more benefits than other help, and the level of benefits that result will impact the recipient's gratitude and response (Malhotra, 2004; Wood, Brown, & Maltby, 2011). Along similar lines, some help may be more difficult, more challenging, or more costly for the help provider than other help (Bartlett & DeSteno, 2007; Fritzsche, Finkelstein, & Penner, 2000). When it is clear that the help provider went substantially out of his or her way to provide the help or incurred substantial costs in order to provide the help, then the recipient is more likely to feel obligated and indebted to the help provided (Greenberg, 1980). Help can be assessed on its ego-centrality (how central it is to self-worth) or how visible (i.e., public or private) the help is (Nadler & Halabi, 2015). As another example, the beneficiaries of the help may vary (Bamberger, 2009). Although much of the OCB literature on helping focuses on the extent to which one person helps other individuals, it is also possible that the help may benefit an entire work group or larger organizational entity. In fact, the category of OCB-O, or organizational citizenship behavior targeted toward the organization as a whole (Williams & Anderson, 1991), could be reframed as individual helping behavior with the recipient being the organization as a whole. Finally and most recently, Golan and Bamberger (2015) identified three dimensions of helping behaviors in their qualitative research: (1) awareness (recognition of the existence of the problem), (2) activity (actively offering help versus passively participating when approached for help), and (3) responsiveness (the degree to which the helper acknowledges the need in a timely manner). Various configurations of these dimensions were then discussed in terms of possible helping behaviors. As is clear from this discussion, there are multiple possibilities for judging characteristics of help that is given. The general point is that not all help is the same, and the characteristics of the help may have important implications for whether it is performed and the extent of its impact.

Why Are People Helpful?

This question and the following two (who gives help and when people help) cover the most commonly researched ground in the OCB literature and are grouped into "help given" in Figure 26.1. Note that although the framework in Figure 26.1 is primarily focused on specific episodes of help (i.e., specific requests for help and decisions to help or not help), most of the literature on predictors of OCB addresses overall tendencies across time. That is, the literature typically addresses predictors of the general tendency to help, rather than predictors specific to a particular request or situation. In addition, issues of motivation and other individual difference predictors are often grouped together in reviews of the OCB literature, but they are treated separately here in order to highlight the importance of understanding what motivates individuals to help and to parallel the help-seeking literature, which typically addresses the question of why people seek help as an independent issue.

When considering why individuals are helpful, it is difficult to avoid a discussion of the extent to which individuals' motives are altruistic, particularly since the term used for helping behavior early in the OCB literature was altruism (Organ, 1988; Smith et al., 1983). The problem, as noted by Organ (1997), was that the label for the behavior implied the motive behind the behavior. Furthermore, it may be more realistic to treat altruism as a continuum or to recognize that altruistic motive and egoistic motives can occur simultaneously, rather than to treat altruistic motives and egoistic motives as mutually exclusive (Krebs, 1991). Moving beyond the altruism issue, this section focuses on other motives that are commonly discussed or studied in the helping literature for why people tend to be helpful or not.

Perhaps the most cited motive behind the performance of helping (and OCB in general) is an exchange motivation, typically discussed in terms of social exchange (Organ, 1988; Organ et al., 2006). The nature of social exchange is that each party acts in the other's best interests over time in a trust-based relationship (Blau, 1964). Accordingly, employees will go above and beyond the call of duty to benefit the organization, their leader, or their coworkers when they feel as though those parties would do the same in return. There is evidence to suggest that the resulting OCB is target-specific, such that individuals reciprocate positive treatment from coworkers by performing helping behaviors targeted toward coworkers, with a similar pattern for leaders (Kamdar & Van Dyne, 2007; Lavelle, Rupp, & Brockner, 2007). An exchange motivation may not apply for all workers; Lester, Meglino, and Korsgaard (2008) found that job satisfaction was related to OCB only for those low in other orientation, a finding they attributed to individuals high in other orientation being less exchange oriented.

In one of the first studies to explicitly attempt to measure the motives for performing OCB, Rioux and Penner (2001) identified three categories of motives: prosocial values (motivated by helping and forming positive relationships), organizational concern (motivated by pride and loyalty toward the organization), and impression management (motivated by being viewed positively by others). In general, helping behavior was more strongly predicted by prosocial values than organizational concern, and both were more strongly related to helping than impression management (which was not related to any of the OCB dimensions). Subsequent research has clarified that impression management motives may play more of a role as a moderator by strengthening the positive relationship between prosocial motives and helping (Grant & Mayer, 2009) or for specific subgroups of employees (e.g., those with lower status, Bowler & Brass, 2006, or those who are extraverted, Chiaburu, Stoverink, Li, & Zhang, 2015).

In a recent qualitative study focused on task-related helping behavior at work, Taber and Deosthali (2014) identified five categories of motives. The first was "helping others contributes to the team or organization," which included ideas of felt responsibility to the team or organization as well as specific ideas of complying with helping norms in the organization and the intertwined success of the individual with the success of their coworkers. The second category was "helping others is a personal value," which captured the idea that individuals help because it is part of their trait makeup and doing so satisfies their basic needs or motives. The third category, "helping others is contingent," involved the idea that helping behavior would be performed so long as certain conditions were met, such as if the help provider had relevant knowledge, if it would not harm the help provider's job performance, or if characteristics of the help seeker or the help request met certain standards. The fourth category, "helping others has an expectation or reciprocity," was focused on receiving benefits to oneself in the future in exchange for helping, whether that was narrowly targeted toward the person to be helped or more generally from others as part of a broad "just world hypothesis." The final category was "helping others is a job responsibility," which aligned with the literature on role definitions (e.g., Morrison, 1994) that has found that people are more likely to help when they view helping as part of their job.

Other literatures provide additional insights about what may motivate helping behavior. For instance, in the volunteering literature, Clary and colleagues (1998) identified six motives for volunteering: values (opportunity to express altruistic or humanitarian values), understanding (learning and self-development), social (relationships with others), career (career preparation or career-relevant skills), protective (guilt reduction for being more fortunate), and enhancement (improving one's self-esteem). In the social psychology literature, Weinstein and Ryan (2010) applied self-determination theory (Deci & Ryan, 2000) to the study of prosocial behavior to discuss how individuals may help others out of their own personal choice in line with their values and interests (autonomous motivation) versus out of pressure from others or other externally-imposed reasons (controlled motivation). This distinction maps onto Cain et al.'s (2014) categories of "giving" and "giving in" discussed in the previous section. Also from the social psychology literature comes the idea of competitive altruism, in which individuals act altruistically (i.e., help others) to gain a reputation for being generous and putting the group first, which enhances their status within the group (Hardy & Van Vugt, 2006). Finally, the literature on intergroup relations suggests that the motivation for helping may depend on who is being helped, such as whether it is the in-group or the out-group (Lorenz, Warner, & VanDeursen, 2015; Nadler, Harpaz-Gorodeisky, & Ben-David, 2009; Stürmer, Snyder, Kropp, & Siem, 2006).

Who Gives Help?

The question of who is more likely to perform OCB is likely the most researched question in the OCB literature. Because reviews of individual differences and attitudes as predictors of OCB are readily available (e.g., Organ et al., 2006; Organ & Ryan, 1995; Podsakoff et al., 2000; Spitzmuller, Van Dyne, & Ilies, 2009), this section will provide a relatively brief overview of the research findings with a specific focus on the results for helping behavior. Note that this discussion is closely tied to the previous section on motives for performing helping behavior, as the presence of each antecedent typically can be explained in terms of one of the underlying motives discussed earlier.

With regard to individual difference predictors of helping or OCB in general, one of the most consistent predictors has been the Big Five dimension of agreeableness (Podsakoff et al., 2000; Organ & Ryan, 1995), even after accounting for job satisfaction (Ilies, Fulmer, Spitzmuller, & Johnson, 2009). As noted by Organ et al. (2006), individuals high in agreeableness may be more likely to help because of their prosocial tendencies and their desire to decrease the levels of discomfort experienced by their coworkers. Moreover, although individuals low in agreeableness vary in their OCB according to their transient mood, those high in agreeableness are more stable in their performance regardless of their mood (Ilies, Scott, & Judge, 2006). These findings are in line with the social psychology literature, which has found that individuals high in agreeableness are more likely to help across situations, group memberships, and levels of costs associated with helping (Graziano, Habashi, Sheese, & Tobin, 2007). Several individual differences closely related to agreeableness have also been associated with helping behavior, including empathy (McNeely & Meglino, 1994; Settoon & Mossholder, 2002) and perspective taking (Kamdar, McAllister, & Turban, 2006). The social psychological literature on the empathy-altruism hypothesis is also relevant here, although that literature focuses on empathy in specific situations targeted at specific individuals, rather than dispositional differences (see review by Batson, Ahmad, & Lishner, 2009).

The other major category of predictors studied in research focusing on who is more likely to perform helping behavior or OCB more generally is employee attitudes. The role of attitudes has been a central question going back to the earliest empirical research on organizational citizenship, when a focus on OCB as a criterion was viewed as a way of understanding how job satisfaction may impact employee performance (Bateman & Organ, 1983) and is closely tied to the social exchange motives discussed previously (i.e., when individuals are satisfied with their work and feel like they are treated fairly, they will perform OCB in exchange). Meta-analyses have confirmed the usefulness of attitudinal variables such as satisfaction, fairness, and commitment for predicting helping behavior (Podsakoff et al., 2000) and that attitudes tend to be more strongly related to OCB than in-role performance (Hoffman, Blair, Meriac, & Woehr, 2007; Organ & Ryan, 1995). One interesting direction in more recent research has been to investigate how individual difference predictors like personality work together with attitudinal variables to predict OCB. For instance, Ilies et al. (2009) showed that the effects of agreeableness on OCB-I were partially mediated by job satisfaction. In other words, the effect of agreeableness on helping is likely due in part to the tendency for agreeable people to be more helpful toward their coworkers, but also in part due to agreeable people being more satisfied in their jobs, and performing more helping behavior as a result. In another example, Lester et al. (2008) found that the relationship between satisfaction and OCB was moderated by other orientation, such that the relationship was more positive when other orientation was low. They explained these findings in terms of individuals high in other orientation being less likely to act out of rational, self-interested judgments associated with social exchange.

When Do People Help?

In contrast to the previous section that focused on characteristics of individuals as predictors of helping, this section focuses on various aspects of the context that contribute to the performance of helping behavior. Context is defined broadly to include all aspects of the work or work environment outside of the individual. Past reviews of the OCB literature have used such categories as task/job characteristics, leadership, group characteristics, organizational characteristics, and cultural context (Organ et al., 2006), although this section will discuss relational characteristics to distinguish attributes of a relationship with another individual coworker from leadership or group characteristics. Because this literature is reviewed in depth elsewhere (Organ et al., 2006; Podsakoff et al., 2000; Spitzmuller et al., 2009), this section will provide only brief highlights from each of these general categories based on these past reviews.

A number of task- or job-related characteristics have been shown to be related to employee helping behavior (or OCB-I). For instance, task feedback (the degree to which the task itself provides information on the employee's performance), intrinsically satisfying tasks (the extent to which performance of the task provides satisfaction independent of extrinsic rewards), and task interdependence (the extent to which the task requires interaction, information, or other resources from a coworker) have been shown to be positively related to helping (Pearce & Gregersen, 1991; Podsakoff et al., 2000). In contrast, task routinization (the degree to which tasks are routine or repetitive) and job/task demands (i.e., role overload) have been shown to be negatively related to helping (Jex & Thomas, 2003; Podsakoff et al., 2000). In addition, combinations of various positive task characteristics, labeled as "task scope," have been shown to be positively related to levels of helping behavior (Farh, Podsakoff, & Organ, 1990). There is evidence that job attitudes such as job satisfaction and organizational commitment or a covenantal relationship with the organization at least partially mediate the relationship between task/job characteristics and helping behavior (Cardona, Lawrence, & Bentler, 2004; Organ et al., 2006; Van Dyne, Graham, & Dienesch, 1994).

Leadership has been heavily studied as a predictor of helping behavior. The meta-analysis by Podsakoff et al. (2000) showed that a variety of behaviors associated with transformational leadership, including articulating a vision, providing an appropriate role model, fostering acceptance of group goals, high performance expectations, and intellectual stimulation, were all positively related to helping behavior. Moreover, transactional behavior such as providing rewards or punishments were shown to be related to helping (positively and negatively, respectively). In addition, they showed that leader supportive behaviors and the task-related behavior of role clarification were positively related to helping, whereas the task behavior of specification of procedures was negatively related to helping. Finally, they and Ilies, Nahrgang, and Morgeson (2007) showed strong effects for the quality of the leader-member exchange (or LMX) as a predictor of helping behavior. Ilies et al. (2007) also showed that LMX was a stronger predictor of helping behavior than it was of organizationally-directed citizenship behaviors (i.e., OCB-O), in line with the literature on social exchange and helping cited previously. A number of other leader-related variables have also been shown to be related to helping behavior, including ethical leadership (Mayer, Kuenzi, Greenbaum, Bardes, & Salvador, 2009), servant leadership (Ehrhart, 2004), and authentic leadership (Hirst, Walumbwa, Aryee, Butarbutar, & Chen, in press), along with negative leader behavior like abusive supervision (Zellars, Tepper, & Duffy, 2002).

In addition to the relationship with one's supervisor, relationships with coworkers have also been shown to be related to helping behavior. For instance, Anderson and Williams (1996) showed that the quality of the working relationship with a coworker was related to increased levels of helping behavior from that coworker (in addition to being related to decreased perceptions of the costs of seeking help from that individual). Other relationship variables, such as similarity (Van der Vegt & Van De Vliert, 2005) and friendship (Bowler & Brass, 2006), have also been shown to predict helping behavior. The topic of coworker relationships is particularly relevant for the application of social network approaches to helping. For example, Venkataramani and Dalal (2007) found that helping was predicted by the strength of the positive affective relationship between two parties, the existence of common-third party affective relationships (both positive and negative), and the help recipient's centrality in both the positive and negative affective relationship network.

Moving beyond characteristics of individual relationships with other coworkers, characteristics of the group have also been shown to be related to helping behavior. For instance, group cohesiveness (the extent to which members are attracted to their group and want to remain part of it) is related to increased levels of helping behavior (Ng & Van Dyne, 2005), as is team-member exchange (TMX, the quality of the relationships among team members; Kamdar & Van Dyne, 2007). In contrast, increased levels of conflict in the group are associated with decreased helping (Ng & Van Dyne, 2005). Another factor that can decrease helping in groups is the presence of a "bad apple"; Raver, Ehrhart, and Chadwick (2012) found that groups with at least one member low in agreeableness tended to have lower mean helping behaviors. The group characteristics perhaps most directly related to helping is the group norm for helping behavior (Ehrhart & Naumann, 2004); in fact, one of the motives identified by Taber and Deosthali (2014) for why individuals perform helping behavior was because it was part of the expectations for group members. Along these lines, Ng and Van Dyne (2005) showed that cooperative group norms were related to individual helping behavior, although Naumann and Ehrhart (2011) found that similar relationships between group helping norms and individual helping were present only when group members were highly attracted to the group or when ambiguity was low.

Characteristics of the organization as a whole can also play a role in the extent to which individuals help their coworkers. For instance, the extent to which the individual perceives that they supported by the organization (perceived organizational support, or POS) is related to helping behavior, although it is more strongly related to OCB directed toward the organization as a whole than OCB directed toward individuals (Rhoades & Eisenberger, 2002), in line with exchange-based theories. Although Podsakoff et al. (2000) did not find that organizational formalization or organizational inflexibility were significantly related to helping in their meta-analysis, they did find that rewards outside of the leader's control were negatively related to helping. Perhaps clarifying these findings, Bamberger and Levi (2009) found that helping was significantly lower under equity-oriented group-based pay structures versus equality-oriented pay structures or mixed structures. Thus, the nature of reward systems in the organization appears to play a role in encouraging (or discouraging) helping (see Mossholder, Richardson, & Settoon, for more on how HR systems might predict helping). Finally, Organ et al. (2006) highlighted organizational constraints (or barriers to effective job performance) as a factor in the performance of helping. Jex, Adams, Bachrach, and Sorenson (2003) found that organizational constraints were negatively related to helping for workers low in affective organizational commitment, but actually positively related to helping for those high in commitment, perhaps because such constraints give highly committed employees more opportunities to help each other out.

A final contextual antecedent to helping behavior is national culture. Over the past two decades, the study of OCB across cultures has increased markedly, in line with the broader global expansion of organizational behavior research (Gelfand, Erez, & Aycan, 2007; Tsui, Nifadkar, & Ou, 2007). Two early and particularly influential articles studying OCB across cultures were by Farh, Earley, and Lin (1997) and Lam, Hui, and Law (1999). Specifically with regard to helping, both studies found support for helping as a dimension of OCB across cultures, and Lam et al. (1999) found that the extent to which helping was considered in-role was similar in Hong Kong, Japan, Australia, and the United States. In addition, Farh et al. (1997) found evidence that the relationship between justice and helping varied across cultures, particularly with regard to traditionality. In follow-up research examining the dimensionality of OCB in China, Farh, Zhong, and Organ (2004) also found evidence for helping as an OCB dimension, although they noted that Chinese employees may have a broader conceptualization of helping to include both work-related and non-work-related helping. Other examples of organizational research with specific implications for the cross-cultural understanding of helping include Perlow and Weeks's (2002) research on differences in the framing of helping between engineers in the United States and India; Meyer, Stanley, Herscovitch, and Topolnytsky's (2002) meta-analyis showing that affective and normative commitment were more strongly related to helping in studies outside of North America; Bachrach, Wang, Bendoly, and Zhang's (2007) research on cross-cultural differences between the United States and China in the importance of OCBs (including helping) in performance evaluations; and Choi's (2009) research on the predictors of group-level helping in a Korean sample. Also relevant is research on cross-cultural differences in prosocial behavior, such as Luria, Cnaan, and Boehm (2015).

Why Do People Seek Help or Not Seek Help?

In contrast to the previous sections that focused primarily on the help provider's perspective, in what follows the focus will be on individuals who ask for or seek help. In Figure 26.1, these questions are covered under the decision to seek help or not and the request for help. As noted previously, most incidents of helping are the direct result of a request for help (Burke et al., 1976; Kaplan & Cowen, 1981; Nadler, 1991). The literature on help seeking addresses a variety of topics, such as who asks for help, when do individuals ask for help, and who is asked for help. Much of that literature is founded on a core idea regarding why people seek help or not: the relative ratio of the costs and benefits of seeking help.

There are a number of benefits to seeking help from another individual. Many of these can be placed into three general categories: task accomplishment, task-related learning, and building relationships (Chan, 2013; Lee, 1997, 2002). When an individual seeks help, it is typically to solve a problem or to complete a task, and thus moving past that hurdle is the primary goal for the help being sought. However, there are other benefits as well. By observing the help provider or by receiving knowledge on how to complete the task, the help recipient can learn how to solve such issues on his or her own in the future (Lee, 1997, 2002; Nebus, 2006). In addition, seeking help can strengthen the relationship between the help provider and help recipient, resulting in stronger informal network ties (Lee, 1997, 2002), which can have important implications for individual and group performance (Balkundi & Harrison, 2006; Cross & Cummings, 2004; Wong, 2008). Finally, seeking help from others can have the added benefits of reducing uncertainty for the help seeker as well as saving face (Hofmann, Lei, & Grant, 2009).

At the same time, there are a number of costs to seeking help. As noted by Nebus (2006), although there could be monetary costs associated with seeking help, the opportunity costs related to the time required for help seeking are likely more salient and influential (see also Fritzsche et al., 2000). The literature on help seeking has mostly focused on its social costs. Lee (1997, 2002) proposed three social costs to help seeking: (1) the admission of incompetence (the help seeker is acknowledging that he or she does not have the skills or ability to solve the problem on his or her own); (2) the acknowledgment of inferiority (the help seeker is acknowledging that the help-seeking target is superior to himself or herself in some way); and (3) the acknowledgment of dependence on the help-seeking target (the help seeker is not independent; he or she requires the help of someone else to solve the problem or accomplish the task). In addition, Lee (1997, 2002) highlighted how these three social costs have important implications for the help seeker's self-esteem and public image (see also Fisher, Nadler, & Whitcher-Alagna, 1982; Gross & McMullen, 1983). Similar repercussions have been identified in the feedback-seeking literature, described in terms of damage to the ego and to the public image (Ashford et al., 2003; Morrison, 2002). Other authors have identified additional possible ways to categorize costs for seeking help. For instance, Lim, Teo, and Zhao (2013) distinguished between intrapersonal costs associated with failing to meet your own aspirations and interpersonal costs associated with failing to meet others' expectations. Nebus (2006) discussed three categories related to seeking advice: (1) social costs, such as the expectation of returning the favor; (2) psychological costs, such as feeling embarrassed for asking for help; and (3) institutional costs, such as possibly violating organizational norms based on the act of asking for help or on who is asked for help. The psychological costs discussed by Nebus (2006) overlap with the work of Lee (1997, 2002) and the implications for help seeking for one's self-esteem. The idea of social costs of feeling indebted to the help provider raises the issue of reciprocation, which will be addressed later in this chapter. In addition, the role of norms is a central concept for how helping can become embedded as typical behavior in work units, which is discussed elsewhere in this chapter as an antecedent to helping behavior and an avenue to explain helping behavior's relationship with unit and organizational effectiveness.

As individuals decide whether to seek help, they weigh the potential benefits against the potential costs (Chan, 2013; Hofmann et al., 2009; Nadler, 1991). The literature on feedback seeking has emphasized a similar cost-benefit analysis (e.g., Anseel et al., 2015; Ashford et al., 2003; VandeWalle & Cummings, 1997). In the social networking literature, this idea was formalized in Nebus's (2006) advice network generation theory. In that model, the interaction between the perceived value of approaching a possible help provider and the value the help seeker would expect to gain from that individual is balanced against the interaction between the perceived costs of approaching a possible help provider and his or her perceived accessibility. Thus, across a number of literatures, the balance between the benefits and costs is central for understanding the decision to seek or not seek help, as well as for understanding who asks for help, when individuals ask for help, and who is asked for help, which are discussed in the next sections.

Who Asks for Help?

The personal predictors of help-seeking behavior have received extensive attention, especially in the social psychology (e.g., Nadler & Halabi, 2015) and clinical psychology (e.g., Wills & DePaulo, 1991) literatures. Although an extensive review of that literature is beyond the scope of this chapter, three of the most commonly studied help seeker attributes will be highlighted here (self-esteem, gender, and achievement goal orientation), along with a brief overview of the various other characteristics that have been studied. Building from the previous section, the common thread throughout much of this literature is the role that these characteristics play in the perception of the costs and benefits of help seeking.

Perhaps the most commonly discussed characteristic of help seekers described in the literature is self-esteem, in line with the ego-related costs of help seeking discussed previously. The findings in this area have been mixed. There is evidence showing that individuals high in self-esteem are less likely to seek help (e.g., Nadler, 1986; Tessler & Schwartz, 1972; Wills & DePaulo, 1991), particularly under conditions when the ego is threatened (Nadler, 1987). The explanation for these findings is that the costs of seeking help, particularly with regard to concerns about inferiority, are higher for those with high self-esteem, in addition to the tendency for individuals high in self-esteem to avoid the social costs involved with being indebted to others (Chan, 2013; Nadler, Mayseless, Peri, & Chemerinski, 1985). In contrast to the idea that high self-esteem is associated with less help seeking, there is also research to suggest that individuals higher in self-esteem seek *more* help (Nadler, 1983). Such findings have come from research on students seeking help for academic performance (Karabenick & Knapp, 1991) as well as in organizational research on feedback-seeking behavior (Ashford, 1986). The explanation for this finding is that individuals low in self-esteem will perceive higher costs for help seeking because admitting incompetence will damage their already fragile ego (Chan, 2013). Adding to this mix of findings, other research has not found support for a relationship between self-esteem and help/feedback seeking (Anseel et al., 2015; Cleavenger, Gardner, & Mhatre, 2007). Chan (2013) explained these disparate findings by suggesting that the relationship between self-esteem and help seeking is curvilinear, such that the different costs of help seeking at both very low and very low levels of self-esteem tend to reduce the frequency of such behaviors. However, at intermediate levels, those costs are minimized (see also Butler & Neuman, 1995).

Gender is another characteristic that has received some attention in the literature on help seeking. In general, women show a stronger willingness to seek help than men across a variety of situations (Nadler & Halabi, 2015), including in managerial (Rosener, 1990) or entrepreneurial roles (Studdard & Munchus, 2009), or when experiencing health or mental health problems (Galdas, Cheater, & Marshall, 2005). Explanations for these differences are typically tied to gender roles (Nadler, 1991). Gender roles for women are associated with more communal characteristics, such as being nurturing, kind, and interpersonally sensitive, whereas the characteristics for men are more agentic, including being aggressive, dominant, and independent (Eagly, 1987; Eagly, Wood, & Diekman, 2000).

Differences in gender roles are linked to differences in perceptions of the costs of help seeking. Specifically, being viewed as incompetent, inferior, and/or dependent is more contrary to the male role than the female role. Thus, the costs of help seeking are typically going to be viewed as higher for men than for women (Lee, 1997). Some research suggests that these findings extend to the gender stereotype of the occupation (Lee, 2002) and may vary depending on the individual's identification with the gender role (Nadler, Maler, & Friedman, 1984) or the nature of the problem (Wills & DePaulo, 1991). In addition, the context may affect the role of gender in help seeking. For instance, Lee (1997) found that men were more likely to seek help when there were collectivistic norms as opposed to individualistic norms. This research highlights the interplay between personal and contextual characteristics in guiding perceptions of the costs of help seeking.

The final example of the characteristics of help seekers highlighted here is achievement goal orientation. Nadler (1991) discussed the tension for instrumentally motivated individuals between wanting to ask for help to make progress toward goal achievement and not wanting to ask for help to avoid being perceived as incompetent. How this tension is handled and its implications for the perception of costs of help seeking are strongly influenced by the goal orientation of the individual. Individuals with a learning or mastery orientation are focused on developing competence, learning new skills, and task mastery (Elliot & Church, 1997; VandeWalle & Cummings, 1997). In contrast, individuals with a performance orientation can be distinguished in terms of the motivation to gain favorable assessments of their competence from others (performance-approach) versus the motivation to avoid unfavorable assessments of competence from others (performance-avoid; Elliot & Church, 1997). These goal orientations have significant implications for perceptions of the costs and benefits of help seeking. Specifically, individuals with a learning orientation will tend to focus on the benefits of help seeking in terms of learning new materials and gaining mastery, whereas the costs of help seeking in terms of being viewed as incompetent or inferior will be particularly salient to individuals with a performance orientation (Chan, 2013; VandeWalle & Cummings, 1997). In addition, the costs for individuals high in performance orientation will be even more salient when the individual's performance is more visible, such that the impact on the individual's public image is heightened (Chan, 2013; Williams & Williams, 1983). Research evidence on the role of goal orientation has supported this general pattern, both in terms of help seeking (e.g., Butler, 2007; Komissarouk & Nadler, 2014; Newman, 1998) and feedback seeking (Anseel et al, 2015; VandeWalle & Cummings, 1997), including the specific role of perceived benefits and costs as a mediator of the relationship between goal orientation and help/feedback seeking (VandeWalle & Cummings, 1997). In addition, research suggests that goal orientation is not only related to levels of help seeking, but the type of help that is sought, such that mastery orientation predicts preference for autonomous help and work avoidance predicts expedient help (Butler, 2007; see also related research on promotion versus prevention focus by Komissarouk & Nadler, 2014).

Although these three characteristics have been highlighted here, there are a number of other characteristics that have been addressed in the literature. For instance, older individuals will generally be less likely to seek help because maintaining independence becomes more central to the ego with age (Nadler, 1991). In fact, in the feedback-seeking literature, age, organizational tenure, and job tenure have all been negatively associated with feedback-seeking behavior (Anseel et al., 2015). The social costs of seeking help will also be more salient to shy individuals, and self-conscious individuals will seek to avoid the negative evaluations associated with help seeking (Nadler, 1991). When individuals are more anxious, they are more likely to seek advice, but they also have trouble recognizing the quality of the advice or potential conflicts of interest (Gino, Brooks, & Schweitzer, 2012). Individuals high in self-monitoring will avoid help seeking due to the status-related costs (Flynn, Reagans, Amanatullah, & Ames, 2006). Individual high in social competence are more willing to seek help (Chan, 2013; Ryan & Pintrich, 1998), likely because the perceived psychological costs of feeling embarrassed by asking for help (Nebus, 2006) are lower for these individuals. Individuals high in need for power will be less likely to seek help in order to avoid the social cost of being indebted to the other person (Chan, 2013). Finally, help seeking is more likely for those higher in attachment anxiety and less likely for those higher in attachment avoidance (Wu, Parker, & De Jong, 2013), as well as more likely for those with a dependent personality (Nadler & Halabi, 2015; Sroufe, Fox, & Pancake, 1983).

When Do People Ask for Help?

Beyond the personal characteristics that influence whether an individual seeks help, there are also a number of contextual variables that play a role. Note that this section does not address the target of the helping requests (i.e., who is asked for help); that issue is addressed in the next section. The two primary categories of contextual characteristics that have been found in the literature are task characteristics and work group/organizational characteristics.

One of the first studies to focus on task characteristics in the help-seeking literature was by Nadler (1987). He studied the ego centrality of the task, which was experimentally manipulated by telling participants that the task was (or was not) associated with intelligence. He found when the task was ego central, help-seeking levels were lower, which he explained in terms of the costs of seeking help related to being viewed as inferior to others. Similarly, Lee (2002) found that help seeking was less likely when tasks were more central to the organization's core competence. Again, the explanation for this finding was in terms of the increased costs associated with being viewed as incompetent and inferior on such core tasks. Another issue related to tasks is the extent of the task demands or the severity of the problems one is having. Bamberger (2009) suggested that the evidence for instrumental help is in line with a curvilinear relationship, such that increased need is associated with increased help seeking up to a point, and then concerns of being viewed as incompetent begin to outweigh the benefits of seeking help (similar to the relationship with self-esteem described previously). Such a curvilinear relationship helps to explain the unexpectedly positive relationship between task demands and perceived costs of help seeking found by Anderson and Williams (1996). Finally, the extent to which the task requires interdependence among workers has been shown to play a role in help seeking. For instance, Anderson and Williams (1996) found that task interdependence has a direct positive relationship with help-seeking behavior. In such cases, the instrumental benefits of help seeking will be higher, overcoming any possible costs.

Other contextual variables found to predict help seeking would best be characterized as group or organizational characteristics. The most well-developed literature on the work environment is captured by research on organizational climate and culture (Ehrhart, Schneider, & Macey, 2014), and such variables play a critical role in help-seeking behavior. One key layer of culture is the behavioral norms in the organization (Rousseau, 1990). Help-seeking behaviors will be more likely to occur when such behaviors are viewed as typical and expected in the organization or work group (Ashford et al., 2003; Ashford & Northcraft, 1992; Bamberger, 2009), as the costs of seeking help are lowered in such environments. Similarly, the extent to which the organizational culture is characterized by individualistic or collectivistic norms can impact help seeking (Lee, 1997), as the costs of being viewed as dependent on others will be higher when the norms are more individualistic (Chan, 2013). With regard to climate, Bamberger's (2009) model of work-based help seeking highlights the relevance of the general supportive climate in the organization for help seeking, as well as very specific climates like a privacy regulation climate and a peer intervention climate, which are particularly relevant when workers are seeking help for personal issues they may be dealing with (e.g., substance abuse treatment; Bennett & Lehman, 2001). Related to issues of climate is the role of the organization's policies and procedures in encouraging or preventing help seeking (Chan, 2013). Given that common definitions and models of climate incorporate the role of policies and procedures (Ehrhart et al., 2014; Ostroff, Kinicki, & Muhammad, 2012), a focus on their impact on help seeking would be useful.

A variety of other group or organizational characteristics have been considered in the help-seeking literature. For instance, building on the work on achievement goal orientation discussed in the previous section, researchers have also highlighted how the context can be task involving, in which learning goals are activated, or ego involving, in which performance goals are activated (Chan, 2013; Newman, 1998; Nicholls, 1984). As noted by Chan (2013), an ego-involving context makes it more likely that workers will view help seeking as indicative of incompetence, decreasing the likelihood of such behaviors, whereas a task-involving context will focus attention on instrumental goals and the benefits of help seeking. Leadership is another contextual factor in help seeking; as indicated in Ashford et al.'s (2003) review of the feedback-seeking literature, task-oriented behaviors can highlight the benefits of the help/feedback received (VandeWalle, Ganesan, Challagalla, & Brown, 2000) and relationship-oriented behaviors can decrease the perception of some of the costs associated with help/feedback seeking (e.g., image costs; Madzar, 1995). The role of the leaders may be particularly important given their critical role in establishing the norms and climate in their work units (Ehrhart & Naumann, 2004; Ehrhart et al., 2014). The level of uncertainty or ambiguity in the environment could also play a role in help seeking. There is evidence from the feedback-seeking literature the level of uncertainty or change in the environment heightens the instrumental motive for feedback (Ashford, 1988; Ashford & Cummings, 1985), but meta-analytic evidence has not supported this relationship (Anseel et al., 2015). Anseel et al. (2015) noted that the lack of results could be due to the reciprocal relationship between feedback seeking and uncertainty, such that uncertainty increases feedback seeking but feedback seeking then reduces uncertainty. Other group or organizational characteristics that have been addressed in the help-seeking literature include national culture (including how cultural diversity could increase the need for help seeking but also create additional costs related to communication differences; Ashford et al., 2003), occupational role (particularly how the gender stereotype of the job can highlight typical gender norms, as discussed previously; Lee, 2002), and the presence of others in the context (such that higher visibility could heighten the social costs of help seeking, although the presence of others with similar problems could decrease those threats; Bamberger, 2009).

Who Is Asked for Help?

A critical question in the help-seeking literature is who is targeted for help requests, and one of the most studied characteristics of individuals who are targets of help seeking is ability or expertise. In general, individuals with higher levels of ability or expertise are more likely to be asked for help (Chan, 2013; Hofmann et al., 2009; Morrison & Vancouver, 2000; Nadler et al., 2003; Nebus, 2006; Vancouver & Morrison, 1995). These findings are in line with the idea that such individuals are going to maximize the benefits of help seeking, whether it be in terms of task accomplishment, task-related learning, or building relationships (i.e., networking). The problem is that the costs of asking for help are typically higher for such individuals as well, particularly since higher expertise is commonly associated with higher levels of status and thus increased concerns about the impact of one's image. The result of such complexity is that the relationship between ability/expertise and help seeking is nuanced and dependent on a variety of other relational and contextual variables. For example, Hofmann et al. (2009) found a three-way interaction between target expertise, trust, and accessibility predicting the likelihood of seeking help from the target. Specifically, they found that when the target is low in expertise, accessibility and trust are positively associated with more help seeking, such that the highest levels of help seeking result when both accessibility and trust are high. In this case, the benefits of help seeking are lower, but the costs are also lower with increasing accessibility and trust. When expertise is high, then trust or accessibility needs to be high for help seeking to occur, although both are not necessary. However, help seeking is least likely to occur when the target is neither accessible nor trustworthy. In this case, even though the benefits of seeking help are higher, at least some of the costs of help seeking need to be mitigated through higher accessibility or trust in order for help-seeking levels to be maximized.

Closely related to the role of expertise in help seeking is the relationship between social proximity or status and help seeking. Multiple authors have highlighted the inconsistency in the research findings in this area (Bamberger, 2009; Nadler, 1991; Nadler & Halabi, 2015). In some research, individuals have been shown to seek more help from individuals of equal status rather than unequal status (e.g., Lee, 1997, 2002). The thinking guiding this research is that the costs of seeking help from individuals of equal status will be lower than seeking help from those of higher or lower status. In other research, the potential helper's similarity to the recipient is negatively associated with help seeking (e.g., Nadler, 1987; Nadler & Fisher, 1986; Nadler, Fisher, & Streufert, 1976). The thinking behind this research is that when similarity is high, asking help from that individual represents a larger threat to the help seeker because he or she would have to acknowledge his or her inferiority to a comparable other (i.e., comparison stress is higher; Nadler & Fisher, 1986). Several explanations for these differences in findings have been suggested. One is the nature of the other individual in terms of the level of intimacy shared, such that help seeking is more likely to be high with an equal-status target with whom the help seeker shares an intimate relationship because the target will be less likely to be a comparison other for the help seeker and is less of a threat in terms of evaluating the help seeker as incompetent or inferior (Bamberger, 2009; Nadler, 1991). Another explanation is the extent to which the context is evaluative or competitive (Nadler & Halabi, 2015), such that a nonevaluative context has lower costs associated with being viewed as dependent or inferior to the help giver. Finally, the type of help may play a role. Nadler (1991) described a two-stage process in which it is initially useful to have an individual high in social proximity for gathering information about the problem and thinking about possible solutions, but once the problem is well defined, the costs of being dependent on a close other increase.

Although the literature on the targets of help seeking has been dominated by issues of expertise and social proximity, other characteristics have also been addressed. These include having high task interdependence with the target of the help-seeking request (Anderson & Williams, 1996), the lack of other options for seeking help or feedback (Walsh, Ashford, & Hill, 1985), the quality of the relationship with the target of help/feedback seeking (Anseel et al., 2015), and future opportunities to reciprocate the help (Greenberg & Shapiro, 1971). From a group relations perspective, individuals are more likely to help members of their in-group (Flippen, Hornstein, Siegal, & Weitzman, 1996; Levine, Prosser, Evans, & Reicher, 2005), although they may go to the out-group for help when doing so will disconfirm a negative stereotype of their own group (Wakefield, Hopkins, & Greenwood, 2014). Erdogan, Bauer, and Taylor (2015) highlighted how work group members with a high-quality relationship with the supervisor (i.e., high leader-member exchange, or LMX) offer potential benefits for help seeking because they are more likely to have access to resources but also additional costs because their close relationship with the leader could increase the salience of the costs associated with image. Their research showed that employees high in LMX were more central in the group's advice network when they had a low tendency to gossip and a strong tendency to help others.

One model that captures a number of these issues comes from Nebus's (2006) advice network generation theory. This theory focuses on who individuals choose to contact when they are in need of task-related advice, which includes the cost-benefit analysis that underlies much of the help-seeking literature, as described previously. Nebus identified four general issues that contribute to whether an individual will contact a particular person for advice (from his Figure 4 on p, 624). The first is the perceived value of contacting the individual, which is influenced by the expertise of the potential help provider and the cognitive trust in that individual (i.e., the general perception that the target is competent and a high performer, independent of his or her expertise in a particular area). The second category is the expectation of obtaining value from that particular individual, or the expectation that the target will be willing to share knowledge with or provide help. This expectation is influenced by such factors as affective trust in the individual (i.e., sharing an emotional bond), an obligation of reciprocation (due to position or past help provided by the help seeker to the target), having mutual friends, the previous responsiveness of the individual, and the homophily of the help seeker and potential help giver (i.e., demographic similarity). The third category is the perceived cost of targeting that particular individual, which is influenced by monetary costs, time duration to receive a response, social costs, psychological costs, and institutional costs (as described previously). Finally, the fourth consideration is the perceived accessibility of the target and the risk of exceeding costs, which are determined by the target's psychic distance (i.e., differences in language, culture, education, etc.), geographic distance, organizational separation (e.g., by level or division), and the frequency of contact with the individual.

Why Do People Help or Not Help in Response to a Specific Request?

Once there is a request for help, the potential helper must decide how to respond (the second major decision depicted in the framework in Figure 26.1). A variety of factors have been studied to understand how individuals respond when presented with an opportunity to help, and some of the issues here overlap with those discussed previously for what motivates people to be generally helpful. To distinguish this section from that one, the focus here will primarily be on those issues related to how individuals respond to a specific help request.

Much in the same way that help seekers weigh the benefits and costs of requesting help (as discussed previously), the targets of help-seeking requests similarly weigh the benefits and costs when responding to a help request. Although the social psychological literature on bystander intervention (Fischer et al., 2011) typically focuses on emergency situations and does not necessarily address a helping request, per se, it does provide insights into the issues that potential help givers take into account when deciding whether to provide help or not. One model from this literature that specifically addresses the costs and rewards of helping is the arousal: cost-reward model (Dovidio, Piliavin, Gaertner, Schroeder, & Clark, 1991; Piliavin, Dovidio, Gaertner, & Clark, 1981). This model proposes that seeing another person in need causes an unpleasant emotional arousal that the perceiver is motivated to reduce. This part of the model proposes that the "clarity, severity, and duration of need" and the potential helper's "physical and psychological closeness to the person in need" (Dovidio et al., 1991, p. 90) are critical in determining the level of arousal and thus the potential helper's likelihood of helping. At the same time, whether the potential helper acts to help is influenced by cost-reward analysis. Possible costs include effort, time required, or discomfort/danger (Dovidio et al., 1991; Fritzsche et al., 2000), and possible rewards include praise, admiration, and effectively making a difference to the person in need (Dovidio et al., 1991). This model also includes costs of not helping, which include personal costs of feeling bad or looking bad to others, as well as costs to the victim depending on the severity of the consequences if they do not receive help. As a result, one implication of the model is that when costs to the potential helper are high, they may reduce the arousal by reinterpreting the situation in a way that minimizes the costs of not helping (e.g., focusing on the responsibility of the person in need for the problem or whether others are in a better position to help).

Some literature on helping or help seeking is in line with the idea of the cost-benefit analysis. For instance, individuals may be more likely to respond favorably to a help request when it is relatively easy to do so (Bartlett & DeSteno, 2007; Fritzsche et al., 2000) because the costs of providing "easy" help are relatively low. As another example, Van Der Vegt, Bunderson, and Oosterhof (2006) found that group members were more committed to and more likely to help those with high levels of expertise. Even though expert members may need help the least, the possibility that the expert would feel obligated to help in return in the future provides a clear benefit to the help giver. Finally, the extent to which the help is perceived to fall outside the help-seeking target's role, the request is perceived to be urgent, and the relative resources between the help seeker and target may increase the perception of the costs associated with providing help (Flynn, 2006).

In addition to weighing the costs and benefits of helping, there are several other relevant issues that have been identified in the literature related to how individuals respond to help requests. The verbal strategies of the help seeker are relevant; for instance, Lee (1999) identified three general categories of such strategies that can be used in help seeking: other-enhancing strategies (elevating the target of the helping request or degrading oneself), minimizing strategies (attempting to reduce the imposition of the request), and task-orienting strategies (focusing on achievement of goal). She found that the use of more strategies was related to providing higher quality information and the help seeker being viewed as more likeable although not more competent. Another issue is the pressure on the target for help and how busy he or she is; Wallaert, Ward, and Mann (2014) found that when individuals are cognitively distracted, they are more likely to respond to pressure to help if those cues are more salient than cues to not help. Why the person is asking for help and his or her in-group versus out-group status are additional factors. Lorenz et al. (2015) showed that the help seeker's stated goal and whether he or she was in the in-group or out-group influence responses to help requests such that the help provider gave more help to the in-group when the goals were power-oriented/instrumental (i.e., solving a specific problem to achieve tangible benefits) and more help to the out-group when the goals were value-oriented/ideological (i.e., supporting personal beliefs or principles). From the teams literature, backing-up behavior (a form of helping) is less likely to occur when the potential help provider does not see the need for help as legitimate (Porter et al., 2003). Finally, in contrast to the previous research reviewed about experts being targets for help seeking, when nonexperts are asked for help, they may not be able to because they simply do not have the necessary skills or resources to do so (Taber & Deosthali, 2014).

A very closely related question to whether people help or not when they have the opportunity or when they are asked is the question of what type of help they give when they do help. In recent research by Nadler and Chernyak-Hai (2014), the status of the help seeker (high versus low) was related to differences in the attributions made about the causes of the need for help (unstable and external for high status individuals versus stable and internal for low status individuals). As a result, high-status individuals were given autonomy-oriented help and low-status individuals were given dependency-oriented help, which can be seen as further reinforcing the current status of both groups. Such research provides an excellent example of the insights that can be gained by differentiating among specific types of help that are given.

Who Reciprocates Help and Why?

The issue of reciprocation is closely tied to the more general idea of helping, as any act of helping raises the question of whether it will be reciprocated. Indeed, the decision to help someone or not can be affected by the help giver's assessment of the likelihood or value of the reciprocation (Van der Vegt et al., 2006). In Figure 26.1, reciprocation is included as a possible outcome of the help given, and this section provides an overview of issues addressed in the literature on reciprocation (including the literature on favor reciprocation), covering such topics as why people reciprocate or not, who is more likely to reciprocate, and what are the outcomes of reciprocating or not.

In general, when individuals receive help, they feel some sense of obligation to reciprocate, which could be based on obligation as part of social exchange (Gouldner, 1960) or because the feelings of indebtedness they experience represent a tension that increases the motivation to reciprocate to remove or reduce the tension (Greenberg, 1980; Greenberg & Shapiro, 1971; Greenberg & Westcott, 1983). In fact, the likelihood of an individual giving help is strongly impacted by whether that individual received help from the other individual in the past (Gross & Latané, 1974). In addition, the more help that was given or the more costly or difficult it was for the help giver, the higher the indebtedness and the increased likelihood of reciprocation (DePaulo, Brittingham, & Kaiser, 1983; Greenberg, 1980). Nevertheless, recent research has identified a number of factors that influence these reciprocation processes and the extent to which individuals reciprocate and, if so, how much.

One major factor that comes into play is the perception of the helping recipient of the help giver's intentions or motives. Ames, Flynn, and Weber (2004) examined the effects of whether help was perceived to be given on the basis of affect (specifically, positive feelings toward the recipient), role (i.e., as part of the help giver's formal duties and obligations in the organization), or cost-benefit calculation (i.e., based on the benefits for the help giver relative to the costs). In general, help recipients' attitudes toward future reciprocation were more positive when the help received was perceived to be based on affect rather than due to role or cost-benefit analysis, although the relative negative reaction to cost-benefit analysis disappeared when the magnitude of the help given was large. More recently, Belmi and Pfeffer (2015) examined the role of the organizational context on perceptions of motives for helping and norms for reciprocity. Their results revealed that the obligation to reciprocate was lower in an organizational setting than a personal setting, which could be explained by individuals tending to be more calculative and more likely to base decisions of reciprocation on the help giver's anticipated future usefulness in organizational settings. Across both of these studies, the results indicate that individuals will be more likely to reciprocate when they judge the help giver as acting out of personal character or sincerely held emotions toward the helping target rather than out of obligation or to gain future benefit.

Several other factors besides motives have been investigated in the literature that shed light on helping reciprocation processes. For instance, how the help is perceived seems to vary between the giver of the help and the receiver of the help (Flynn, 2006), an effect that changes over time as help providers tend to increase in the perceptions of the value of the help, whereas help receivers tend to decrease in their perceptions of the help (Flynn, 2003b). This finding has clear implications for whether help is reciprocated and, if so, to what extent. Going beyond exchange-based explanations for reciprocation, researchers have shown that affective states (Lyons & Scott, 2012), norms for politeness (Flynn, 2006), and both state- and trait-based gratitude (Bartlett & DeSteno, 2007; Emmons & McCullough, 2003; Grant & Gino, 2010) are related to reciprocation. Relatedly, Flynn and Brockner (2003) found that favor recipients' commitment to their relationship with the favor provider was more influenced by the giver's interactional justice when providing the favor than the benefit provided to the recipient. In other words, how the help was given was actually more important than the extent of the help itself. Other research has focused on individual attributes related to reciprocation. For instance, some individuals may be more sensitive to reciprocating in kind based on their exchange ideology (Eisenberger, Huntington, Hutchison, & Sowa, 1986), reciprocity beliefs (Eisenberger, Lynch, Aselage,& Rohdieck, 2004), or personal norm of reciprocity (Perugini, Gallucci, Presaghi, & Ercolani, 2003). In contrast, other individuals are high in reciprocation wariness, such that they are concerned about being taken advantage of or exploited in social relationships (Cotterell, Eisenberger, & Speicher, 1992; Eisenberger, Cotterell, & Marvel, 1987). Furthermore, characteristics such as other orientation (Korsgaard, Meglino, Lester, & Jeong, 2010) or relative standing in the organization (Buunk, Doosje, Jans, & Hopstaken, 1993) may also play a role in how reciprocation processes are perceived.

On a final note regarding reciprocation, a number of outcomes have been associated with levels or reciprocation or imbalances in reciprocation. The results are not straightforward. For instance, individuals tend to experience negative affect, stress, and other negative emotional states when reciprocity is not balanced (Bowling et al., 2004; Nahum-Shani, Bamberger, & Bacharach, 2011), and this is particularly the case for those high in exchange orientation and low in communal orientation (Buunk et al., 1993). In contrast, Mueller and Kamdar (2011) found that reciprocating help diminished performance in terms of creativity, which they attributed time and energy costs of giving help as well as a potential tendency to discount divergent information from a dependent or less competent other. The results from Flynn (2003a) introduce even more complexity to understanding the outcomes of reciprocation. He found that individuals who tended to give more favors than they received experienced status benefits, but that such an imbalanced exchange also had productivity costs. However, he also found that generous individuals may experience increased benefits in both status and productivity if the frequency of exchange is high. Thus, although research as a whole suggests that balanced exchanges have positive benefits, being indebted or generous may have differential outcomes depending on characteristics of the individuals and the situation involved.

What Are the Outcomes of Help-Seeking/Receiving Help?

This section and the next address the two major categories of outcomes associated with helping processes besides reciprocation: the outcomes for seeking/receiving help (this section) and for giving help (the next section). Some of the information covered previously is related to these two topics. For instance, the material on the benefits and costs of help seeking addresses similar issues, although that literature typically focuses on the perceptions of the benefits and costs and how those perceptions impact whether individuals seek help or not (rather than the actual outcomes of help seeking). In addition, the previous section on reciprocation essentially addresses one possible outcome of receiving help: providing help back to the help provider (e.g., Halbesleben & Wheeler, 2015). In this section, the focus will be on examples of research addressing actual (versus perceived) outcomes of receiving help beyond the reciprocation of help.

Several positive benefits of help seeking have been identified in the literature, including increased creativity (Mueller & Kamdar, 2011), reduced errors (Stone & O'Gorman, 1991), improved newcomer job performance (Morrison, 1993), and higher peer-rated performance (Wu et al., 2013). Although a recent meta-analysis did not find a relationship between feedback seeking and performance, it did find that feedback seeking was related to job satisfaction, relationship-building behavior, networking, and socialization behaviors (Anseel et al., 2015). Receiving help is positively associated with job satisfaction, perceived coworker support, and trust, and negatively associated with turnover intentions (Halbesleben & Wheeler, 2015; Regts & Molleman, 2013). Perceived support from a variety of sources (e.g., the organization, supervisor, coworkers) has been shown to have a number of positive benefits (Ng & Sorensen, 2008; Riggle, Edmondson, & Hansen, 2009). Research on social networks also supports the positive implications for team performance when members seek advice from each other; several studies have found positive relationships between the density a team's advice network and team performance (Balkundi & Harrison, 2006; Wong, 2008; Zhang & Peterson, 2011).

Of course, the outcomes of help seeking and receiving help are not necessarily so clear cut, and a number of variables have been found that moderate the outcomes of help seeking or that result in negative outcomes. As previously described, the creative benefits of help seeking can be undercut by the amount of help given in reciprocation (Mueller & Kamdar, 2011). The positive effects of receiving help on job satisfaction are weaker or nonsignificant for individuals low in communion striving or when task interdependence is low (Regts & Molleman, 2013). Similarly, the benefits of feedback seeking on job performance are moderated by attachment anxiety, such that there is no relationship found for those low in attachment anxiety (Wu et al., 2013). Geller and Bamberger (2012) found no overall main effect of help seeking on performance; however, there was a positive effect for those who were oriented toward seeking autonomous help and for those oriented against seeking dependent help. Dalal and Bonaccio (2010) found that recipients' responses to different types of advice varied depending on such issues as the type of decision and the characteristics of the recipient (e.g., agreeableness and gender). Barnes and colleagues (2008) found that the receipt of backing-up behavior in a team-based task resulted in decreased task work in a subsequent task, but only when the dependency of the help recipient was highlighted by another person advocating for the need for help on the first task.

The response to received help may depend on whether it was offered by the helper or requested by the recipient, with some research showing that *offered* help had a more positive response than *requested* help (Broll, Gross, & Piliavin, 1974). At the same time, when help is imposed by another person (i.e., given without a request), it is likely to result in a threat to the self-esteem on the help recipient (Deelstra et al., 2003; Schneider, Major, Luhtanen, & Crocker, 1996), in line with findings that invisible support that occurs outside the recipient's awareness has more positive effects than visible support (Bolger & Amarel, 2007; Bolger et al., 2000). Support can also cause increased strain (e.g., physical symptoms, emotional exhaustion) when the support highlights stressful aspects of the work environment (Beehr, Bowling, & Bennett, 2010). In contrast to the literature suggesting that individuals are viewed as less competent when they seek help (e.g., Lee, 1997, 2002), Brooks, Gino, and Schweitzer (2015) showed that individuals can be perceived as *more* competent when seeking help when the task is difficult, when the perceiver is the target of the help request, and when an expert is the target of the help request. Finally, Nadler et al. (2003) found that help seeking had a curvilinear relationship with performance evaluations, such that very low levels (indicating habitual reluctance to ask for help) and very high levels (indicating habitual reliance on others) were both associated with lower performance relative to moderate levels of help seeking. They also found that the effects were moderated by the expertise of the help-seeking target, such that performance was rated higher when the target of the helping request was more knowledgeable.

One model that captures some of the complexity involved with the outcomes of seeking and receiving help is Fisher et al.'s (1982) threat-to-self-esteem model of recipient reactions to aid. At the core of their model is the idea that help received can be interpreted in one of two ways: as predominantly threatening or predominantly supportive. The interpretation then determines the response, with threatening interpretations leading to such outcomes as negative affect, negative evaluations of the help giver and the help, low reciprocity, low help seeking, high refusal of help to others, and high subsequent self-help. In contrast, supportive interpretations lead to more positive outcomes, such as positive affect, positive evaluations of the help giver and help, high reciprocity, high help seeking, low refusal of help to others, and low subsequent self-help. Furthermore, they describe the conditions that influence the interpretation of the help received, in alignment with the previous discussion of the costs and benefits of help seeking. For instance, the nature of the help given may highlight the support and concern of the help giver, or it may highlight the help recipient's inferiority and dependency. In addition, the help should align with relevant societal values to avoid being viewed as threatening, such as maintaining the recipient's independence and self-reliance in a US context, as well as being consistent with general principles of fairness. Finally, the extent to which the help is instrumental in meeting the recipient's aids without creating dependency is more likely to be viewed as supportive as opposed to threatening. Although this model was not developed specifically for workplace settings, the general principles could easily be expanded to the study of the outcomes of help received in organizations.

What Are the Outcomes of Helping Others?

The outcomes of helping have been found to be generally positive across a number of literatures and levels of analysis. For instance, a meta-analysis by Podsakoff et al. (2009) found that OCB-I was positively related to overall job performance ratings, reward allocation decisions, reward recommendations, and actual rewards, and negatively related to absenteeism, turnover intentions, and actual turnover. Thus, individuals' helping behavior appears to be valued by managers, and employees who help their coworkers are less likely to exhibit withdrawal behaviors. Extending this finding, Grant, Parker, and Collins (2009) found that self-rated anticipatory helping was positively related to supervisor performance evaluations, but only when either prosocial values were high or negative affect was low. In other words, supervisors are likely to value helping when they judge the intentions as being benevolent. Employees' helping behaviors have also been shown to be related to improved mood at work, particularly for extraverts (Glomb, Bhave, Miner, & Wall, 2011). The literature on volunteering (see review by Rodell, Breitsohl, Schröder, & Keating, 2016) suggests that it is associated with higher levels of need satisfaction in terms of providing both a sense of accomplishment and a sense of belonging, and it is also associated with higher levels of well-being (Mojza, Sonnentag, & Bornemann, 2011). Perhaps most strikingly, volunteering has been shown to have a positive impact on mortality

(Brown, Nesse, Vinokur, & Smith, 2003; Moen, Dempster-McClain, & Williams, 1992; Oman, Thoresen, & McMahon, 1999). Research on prosocial behavior outside of the organizational context has also identified a number of positive outcomes for those who help. For instance, in the review by Penner, Dovidio, Piliavin, and Schroeder (2005), they highlighted such positive benefits as improved self-esteem, academic achievement, personal efficacy, prosocial attitudes, well-being, psychological health, and physical health, as well as decreased negative affect and depression. Hypothesized reasons for the positive effects of prosocial behavior include that they distract from an individual's own stress and negative emotions, provide a sense of meaning and value, improve perceived competence (i.e., self-esteem and self-efficacy), improve mood (augmenting positive moods and alleviating negative moods), and enhance social integration a sense of community (Midlarsky, 1991).

In line with Organ's (1988) original conceptualization of OCB having its impact after "summing across time for a single person and also summing across persons in the group, department, organization" (p. 6), it is not surprising that research has revealed a number of positive benefits of helping for group and organizational effectiveness. For instance, the Podsakoff et al. (2009) meta-analysis revealed that unit-level OCB was significantly related to overall unit performance, unit productivity, unit efficiency, unit costs, customer satisfaction, and unit turnover. Nielsen, Hrivnak, and Shaw (2009) performed a similar analysis but distinguished among the specific dimensions of OCB and found that unit-level helping was positively related to unit performance. Also of note was their finding that the relationship between OCB and unit performance was stronger when the items used a unit referent, indicating that the effects of helping may be stronger when it becomes normative in the group (for more on the differences between average levels of OCB and OCB norms, see Ehrhart & Naumann, 2004; Ehrhart & Raver, 2014; Raver, Ehrhart, & Chadwick, 2012). Related to these findings, the effects of norms for helping appear to go beyond the effects of other group process variables like cohesion, relationship conflict, and leadership (Ehrhart, Bliese, & Thomas, 2006), are particularly strong in groups with high task interdependence (Bachrach, Powell, Collins, & Richey, 2006; Nielsen, Bachrach, Sundstrom, & Halfhill, 2012), are mediated by group cohesion (Lin & Peng, 2010), and may be due to individuals with more expertise helping those who are less expert (Van der Vegt et al., 2006). In addition, the literature on backing-up behaviors in a team setting supports the idea that helping is beneficial for team performance (Porter et al., 2003).

Although there are a number of positive benefits associated with helping behavior, there are potential negative consequences as well. Perhaps the most commonly discussed negative outcome of performing OCB in general and helping behavior in particular is that it distracts from an individual's core job responsibilities (Bergeron, 2007; Bolino, Turnley, & Niehoff, 2004). Indeed, Bergeron, Shipp, Rosen, and Furst (2013) found that time spent on OCB (using a composite measure) was negatively related to career outcomes such as salary increases and advancement speed. Furthermore, they found that time spent on task performance was negatively correlated with time spent on OCB, suggesting that time spent on one detracts from time spent on the other. Research on backing-up behavior in teams also supports the potentially negative consequences of neglected taskwork, as Barnes et al. (2008) found that a backup provider's neglected taskwork was negatively correlated with team performance. Also related to this idea is Mueller and Kamdar's (2011) finding that giving help was negatively related to creativity, which they at least in part attributed to the idea that helping others diminishes time available for creative tasks.

Helping behavior may have additional negative consequences beyond the implications for productivity. For instance, helping behavior may be associated with employee stress (Bolino et al., 2004; Li, Kirkman, & Porter, 2014; Organ & Ryan, 1995). Halbesleben, Harvey, and Bolino (2009) found that OCB-I was associated with higher levels of work–family conflict. Other research has suggested that it may be specifically the pressure to perform OCB or helping that results in stress. In line with this idea, Bolino, Turnley, Gilstrap, and Suazo (2010) found that citizenship pressure was associated with work–family conflict, work–leisure conflict, job stress, and intentions to quit, and Vigoda-Gadot (2007) found that compulsory citizenship behavior was positively related to stress, burnout, and intentions to leave. In related research, responding to help requests has been shown to deplete regulatory resources, with depletion rates being higher for workers higher in prosocial motivation, possibly because those are the employees who care the most about the quality of their help and who will use more resources when helping (Lanaj, Johnson, & Wang, 2016).

In addition to stress and resource depletion, helping behavior may have negative repercussions for coworker relationships. Because helping behavior is associated with increased status within a group (Hardy & Van Vugt, 2006), employees may compete with each other to be seen as the most committed, ideal employee (Bolino & Turnley, 2003; Bolino et al., 2004). Related to this idea, research by Parks and Stone (2010) showed that unselfish group members were just as unpopular as selfish members, which they showed could potentially be explained by social comparison (that they make other group members look bad) or because they are a group norm violator (i.e., they threaten the stability of the group). Coworkers may also grow to resent coworkers who they perceive to be helpful only for impression management purposes (Bolino et al., 2004).

Two lines of research have been particularly useful in shedding light on the complexity in understanding the outcomes of helping behavior: research that simultaneously examines the positive and negative outcomes of helping behavior, and research that has identified curvilinear relationships between helping behavior and task performance. With regard to the former, Koopman, Lanaj, and Scott (2016) used experience sampling to show that daily helping was associated with both increased positive affect and decreased work goal progress. Furthermore, increases in positive affect were associated with higher job satisfaction and affective commitment, and decreases in work goal progress were associated with higher emotional satisfaction and lower job satisfaction and affective commitment. Thus, helping appears to have positive and negative consequences simultaneously. With regard to curvilinear relationships with performance, Flynn (2003a) found that balance of favor exchange had an inverted U-shaped relationship with productivity, such that productivity peaked when favor exchange was balanced but declined as employee generosity (giving more than taking) increased. Similarly, Rapp, Bachrach, and Rapp (2013) found that helping behavior had a curvilinear relationship with task performance, such that there was a positive relationship up to moderate levels of helping, but no additional benefits for more helping behavior beyond that point. Thus, although helping may be beneficial up to a point, it may be possible to help too much, such that very high levels detract from one's core responsibilities. Notably, the evidence also suggests that high levels of helping may not be as harmful for everyone, particularly those who exchange favors/help with coworkers at high rates of frequency (Flynn, 2003a) or those who have strong time management skills (Rapp et al., 2013). Along similar lines, it could be that the time horizon is important to take into account when evaluating the possible negative consequences of helping. Although helping may have short-term negative consequences, there may be long-term benefits associated with building a strong social network and a reputation for being trustworthy (Grant, 2013).

What Should Future Research Address?

This review has demonstrated that despite the ample literature on helping behavior, research on the topic is spread across multiple fields that consider different aspects of the helping process and even use different terminology. As a result, cross-field and cross-topic communication has been limited, which has hindered broader progress in the area. With regard to the OCB literature in particular, work on helping has tended to focus on the overall helpfulness of individuals over time, the individual and contextual characteristics that predict overall helpfulness, and the outcomes of helping in organizations. Although these topics are critical to our understanding of helping behavior in organizations, in light of the framework in Figure 26.1, there are a number of aspects of helping processes that have been understudied. To advance the study of helping within the field of OCB, I propose the following directions for future research, organized by three major themes followed by a briefer listing of additional possibilities.

Types of Help

One of the notable findings in this review pertains to the variety of ways that help has been conceptualized and discussed in the literature. Such varieties of helping are not typically considered in the OCB literature, even though the antecedents and outcomes of different types of help are likely to vary. More needs to be known about the types of help and characteristics of help, and how taking them into account could impact some of the traditionally supported findings in the OCB literature. To illustrate, two examples will be briefly presented here: instrumental help versus emotional help, and the quality of the help.

One notable differentiation in the helping literature is between task-related instrumental help and personal, emotional help (Bamberger, 2009). Individuals' willingness to seek help may vary depending on whether it is instrumental or emotional help they seek, and that willingness may vary depending on the individual's personality and other characteristics (i.e., some individuals may be more willing to seek instrumental help, whereas others may be more willing to seek emotional help). In terms of who is asked for help, the potential helper's expertise and capability should be more important for instrumental help, whereas the potential helper's interpersonal skills and personality should matter more for emotional help. When considering whether to make an offer of help, the primary concern with instrumental help may be the self-esteem implications for the person in need, whereas with emotional help the concern may be the appropriateness for the workplace (based on the workplace's industry, culture, etc.). Moving to the decision to give help, the potential benefits and costs will likely be viewed differently based on the type of help. Drawing from the arousal: cost-reward model (Dovidio et al., 1991), the unpleasantness experienced by the potential helper may be higher for emotional help. At the same time, the norms in the organization may be that instrumental help is more acceptable than emotional help. In terms of who is willing to help, personality predictors may vary between the types of help, perhaps with agreeableness having a stronger relationship with emotional help given and conscientiousness having a stronger relationship with instrumental help. The motive behind the help could also vary, with emotional help being driven by the relationship with the other individual and empathy, and instrumental help being driven by the desire to help the organization or because it is part of one's job (Taber & Deosthali, 2014). Finally, with regard to outcomes, it is possible that instrumental help may have a stronger relationship with performance evaluations or group or organization effectiveness, whereas emotional help may be more closely tied to group processes like increased cohesion and decreased relationship conflict.

Another useful example is the quality of the help or the extent to which the help recipient views the help as beneficial. Although this issue has implications for who is asked for help (because individuals would prefer higher quality help that will actually be beneficial), its effects are more likely to be seen for the outcomes of helping. Some of the positive benefits of receiving help in terms of improved performance, creativity, and work quality would likely be ameliorated if the quality of the help received is low. Low-quality help could also damage relationships with peers, resulting in lower quality relationships and decreased trust. Of course, the helper's motivation may come into play as well; if the quality is low but the helper's intentions are viewed as sincere, the implications would be different than if the quality is perceived to be low due to the helper's disinterest or lack of effort. The implications for the help recipient's self-esteem could vary based on the quality of help; the help recipient may actually receive an ego boost in seeing that others struggle with the same task, especially if his or her efforts are sincere. The quality of the help should have direct implications for reciprocation, with higher quality help resulting in higher levels of indebtedness and thus a higher likelihood of reciprocation (DePaulo et al., 1983; Greenberg, 1980). Along those lines, low-quality help could result in downward spirals that result in reduced norms for helping in the work unit; if the help is low quality, then it is less likely to be reciprocated, and the initial helper will be less likely to help again in the future, and so on. In general, the positive implications for the group will be less likely to materialize if the quality of help is low, and it could actually detract from group performance if others have to "undo" problems created by the well-intentioned but flawed help provided, not to mention the wasted productivity and time.

In addition to these two examples, there are a number of other variations that were reviewed in the types of help section, which should have implications across the stages shown in Figure 26.1. Given that many of these distinctions for the type of help originated in nonorganizational literatures, one challenge for future research will be to determine which distinctions are relevant for organizations, or at least which have the strongest potential effects and thus deserve more research attention.

Help Seeking, Requests for Help, and Offering Help

In the framework in Figure 26.1, some helping processes have received less attention than others in the organizational literature. For example, given the size of the literatures on both OCB and help seeking, it is surprising that little research has integrated these two literatures. As pointed out previously, most helping in organizations begins with a request for help, so a complete understanding of helping behavior would seem to necessitate an understanding of help seeking, such as the cost-benefit analysis that occurs. Although a number of possible benefits and costs have been suggested in the literature (e.g., Lee, 1997, 2002; Nebus, 2006), many of these have not been empirically investigated in work contexts, and the relative prioritization of these costs and benefits for different workers in different contexts is not well understood. Research is particularly needed to understand when higher self-esteem is positively versus negatively related to help seeking (Chan, 2013). The organizational context is likely to also play a critical role; moving beyond supportive or relational climates (Bamberger, 2009; Mossholder et al., 2011), the role of strategic climates in the organization should be relevant as well. For instance, in a climate for customer service, seeking help in problems with a customer should yield benefits in terms of advancing the organization's service goals (Chan, 2013), but the potential costs of appearing incompetent on tasks that are core to the organization's competence are high. Perhaps it is the combination of a strategic climate and a supportive climate (such as a climate for psychological safety; Baer & Frese, 2003) that maximizes the likelihood of help seeking on critical organizational tasks. The outcome of the help request is also an important issue; in particular, we do not know much about what happens when help is refused in terms of consequences for the help seeker, the target of the help request, their relationship, and the work unit as a whole (see Williamson, Clark, Pegalis, & Behan, 1996, for an example of research related to this topic).

Another issue that is not well understood pertains to help that is offered without a specific request. The characteristics of those who offer help when it is not requested are likely to differ from those who help solely in response to a request, as is the response from the potential help recipient. An offer of help signals that the potential helper is being proactive and anticipating the needs of the potential help recipient, which would seem to be perceived positively (e.g., Broll et al., 1974), except that an offer of help could also be viewed as a threat to self-esteem (Deelstra et al., 2003; Schneider et al., 1996). In addition, we know little about what distinguishes people who are willing to accept offers of help from those who are not. This is particularly of interest in light of research that individuals tend to overvalue their own perspective and discount the opinions of others (Harvey & Fischer, 1997; Yaniv, 2004; Yaniv & Kleinberger, 2000). A number of costs and benefits are likely to come into play. For instance, the validity of the need could play a role; if the help is viewed as unnecessary, then the benefits would likely be low, and the offer is more likely to be refused. The self-esteem of the potential help recipient is likely to be a factor in how the costs and benefits are perceived, especially since the offer is likely to be instinctively viewed as a threat initially. Nevertheless, in line with Fisher et al.'s (1982) threat-to-self-esteem model, offers of help that are interpreted as supportive should result in different reactions than those interpreted as threatening. For example, an offer of help within the context of a close, communal relationship (Nadler & Halabi, 2015) or from someone who is highly trusted (Sniezek & Van Swol, 2001) is less likely to be viewed as threatening. A final issue involves the implications for when an offer of help is refused; this could be attributed to the target's ego or stubbornness, or it could be taken more negatively as a personal slight or a judgment of the help offerer's (lack of) competence. Such attributions have implications for the relationship between the individuals, as well as for the group's dynamic and helping norms.

Levels of Analysis

The framework in Figure 26.1 does not explicitly differentiate levels of analysis, but there are multiple levels implied. OCB research has tended to study the individual (or between-person) level, but there are opportunities for research by shifting the level of analysis up (i.e., to the dyad, unit, or organizational level) or down (i.e., to the within-person level and specific episodes of helping).

With regard to the shift up, progress has been made in understanding helping in groups and teams, particularly in terms of outcomes (Nielsen et al., 2009; Podsakoff et al., 2009). Relatively less is known about how group norms develop. Leadership appears to play a critical role, whether it be servant leadership (Ehrhart, 2004), ethical leadership (Mayer et al., 2009), leader emphasis on teamwork (Pearce & Herbik, 2004), or leader supportiveness (Choi, 2009). Research on other types of OCB has found an effect for the leader's role modeling of OCB (Yaffe & Kark, 2011), but the relative effects of leadership style versus leader behavioral role modeling have not been investigated. The role of upper-level leadership deserves more attention; Choi (2009) found that the transformational leadership of top management was related to group-level helping, and Mayer et al. (2009) found that the effects of top management ethical leadership on group-level helping were mediated by supervisor ethical leadership. Research has also shown that issues related to group composition can be problematic for group helping norm development (Choi, 2009; Raver et al., 2012); future research should address how to overcome such challenges, especially with regard to the role of leadership.

There are a number of other factors that could play a role in the development, maintenance, and change of group helping norms. Although there is evidence to suggest that the presence of helping behaviors in groups precedes the recognition of the behavior as normative (Raver et al., 2012), research has not addressed whether certain individuals (e.g., those with higher status or higher network centrality) have stronger effects on the formation of helping norms, nor the potential reciprocal relationship between groups norms and individual helping (Ehrhart & Naumann, 2004; Li et al., 2014). Future research should also consider the distinction between descriptive and prescriptive OCB norms (Ehrhart & Naumann, 2004; Naumann & Ehrhart, 2011), and whether helping norms can become *too* prescriptive, such that employees feel forced to help and possibly perform counterproductive behaviors in response. Future research should also examine how helping norms can change; Grant and Patil's (2012) framework for the role of minority influence provides a useful first step in this direction. In addition to norms for helping behavior, research should consider norms for help seeking (i.e., how acceptable is it to ask for help?) and norms for offering help (i.e., how acceptable is it to offer help?). Finally, the organizational level of analysis also deserves more attention, perhaps by studying organizational-level helping norms as a layer of organizational culture (Rousseau, 1990; Schein, 2010) or the relative influence of organizational versus group norms.

In terms of lower levels of analysis, the focus on helping episodes that is common in literature on other helping-related topics, like help seeking, is relatively limited in the OCB literature. In contrast to studying individuals' general helpfulness over time and across situations, a within-person approach highlights how individuals may respond differently to individual helping episodes based on a variety of variables. The chapter by Scott, Matta, and Koopman in this handbook provides a thorough review of the literature on within-person approaches to studying OCB in general, so that will not be repeated here. Nevertheless, it is notable that although some articles in their review did include a specific focus on helping or OCB-I (e.g., Conway, Rogelberg, & Pitts, 2009; Halbesleben & Wheeler, 2011; Ilies et al., 2006; Koopman et al., 2016; Trougakos, Beal, Cheng, Hideg, & Zweig, 2015), most of the literature in this area has investigated OCB in general (aggregating across OCB dimensions), rather than specific dimensions of OCB. Such an approach is likely to miss important differences, especially in light of their finding that almost half of the variance in OCB-I was explained by within-person variance, which was more than what was found for OCB-O. As an example, Ilies et al. (2006) initially found that both job satisfaction and positive affect had intraindividual effects on OCB, but when analyzing OCB-I separately from OCB-O, found that only positive affect was an intraindividual predictor of OCB-I.

This chapter has raised a number additional specific issues that are likely to manifest in any given helping episode that also contribute to the within-person variation in helping. Such issues include the nature of the specific problem (such as whether it is task related or personal), the effort required to provide the help, the presence of a request for help or not, the person targeted for a helping request, whether the help is visible to others, and whether help is part of an ongoing exchange between the parties. Research using experience sampling methodologies that takes into account as many of these episode-specific factors would provide a deeper understanding of how helping dynamics play out in organizational settings. Adding even more complexity, research can extend the within-person approach to study helping episodes from a longitudinal, dynamic perspective, such as in Halbesleben and Wheeler's (2015) research on spirals of support, or look at how group-level variables combined with between-person variables to affect within-person helping.

Additional Topics for Future Research

In addition to pursuing research on the previous three topics, there are a number of other issues that are worthy of research attention. Several very interesting findings with regard to *curvilinear relationships* were uncovered in this review, including between self-esteem and help-seeking behavior (Chan, 2013), between the need for help and help seeking (Bamberger, 2009), between helping seeking and performance evaluations (Nadler et al., 2003), between favor exchange and productivity (Flynn, 2003a), and between helping behavior and performance (Rapp et al., 2013). Such findings add complexity and insight beyond simplistic "either-or" or "more is better" thinking and, in particular, may be critical for understanding the simultaneous positive and negative effects of helping (Koopman et al., 2016).

Much in the same way that help seeking is typically studied independently from helping behavior, *reciprocation processes* are typically distinct from studies of helping in the OCB literature. This is unfortunate, since any act of helping immediately raises numerous issues related to reciprocation. For instance, was the help given as reciprocation or not? Will the help result in future reciprocation? If help is not reciprocated, what are the implications of the lack of reciprocation for helping between the members of the dyad and, furthermore, for the effectiveness of the overall group? Increased integration between the reciprocation and OCB literatures is needed.

Although some helping studies have integrated *social networking*, there are still numerous potential directions for future research. For instance, most social networking research related to helping focuses on advice networks, which is a very specific type of help, but other types of helping merit attention with regard to social networking. In addition, helping could be investigated as a dependent variable in research on other types of networks, such as friendship or communication networks. In line with the earlier discussion on levels of analysis, one benefit of social networking approaches is that they allow for analyses across the individual, dyadic, and unit levels.

The *visibility of the help* is not well understood, and it could have implications in several different ways. For instance, the social costs to the self-esteem of the help recipient are likely to be higher when others are present when the help is requested and/or provided (Bamberger, 2009), and research has shown that help that is "invisible," or outside of the recipient's awareness, has more positive effects (Bolger & Amarel, 2007; Bolger et al., 2000). At the same time, visibility would appear to be generally desirable on the part of the help provider. To achieve some of the benefits of helping others, such as praise or admiration (Dovidio et al., 1991), the help would need to be visible, much in the same way visibility would be desirable when motivated by impression management (Grant & Mayer, 2009; Rioux & Penner, 2001). There are exceptions in both cases; individuals can actually be perceived as more competent when seeking help (Brooks et al., 2015), and the potential help provider may try to avoid visibility if the request for help is going to be denied (Dovidio et al., 1991). More research is needed on how these various concerns are balanced within a helping episode.

There have been a number of recent developments in the literature on *volunteering* (Rodell et al., 2016), which raises the question of the similarities and differences between the antecedents and outcomes of helping others at work versus helping others outside of work. For instance, Rodell (2013) examined whether employees were more likely to volunteer when experiencing high job meaningfulness (an enhancement effect) or low job meaningfulness (a compensation effect). The helping literature has typically taken an enhancement perspective, but it should consider whether helping others may be an "escape" from a job that lacks meaning. Another question is whether employees who volunteer are also those employees who help their coworkers, or whether some employees are willing to help those outside the organization (volunteering) but not their own coworkers.

These future directions only scratch the surface of the opportunities for new insights and knowledge that can be gained by integrating across the various perspectives on helping that have been addressed in this review. Although helping behavior has received much attention in the OCB literature, there is still much work to do.

References

Ames, D. R., Flynn, F. J., & Weber, E. U. (2004). It's the thought that counts: On perceiving how helpers decide to lend a hand. *Personality and Social Psychology Bulletin, 30*(4), 461–474.

Anderson, S. E., & Williams, L. J. (1996). Interpersonal, job, and individual factors related to helping processes at work. *Journal of Applied Psychology, 81*(3), 282–296.

Anseel, F., Beatty, A. S., Shen, W., Lievens, F., & Sackett, P. R. (2015). How are we doing after 30 years? A meta-analytic review of the antecedents and outcomes of feedback-seeking behavior. *Journal of Management, 41*(1), 318–348.

Ashford, S. J. (1986). Feedback-seeking in individual adaptation: A resource perspective. *Academy of Management Journal, 29*(3), 465–487.

Ashford, S. J. (1988). Individual strategies for coping with stress during organizational transitions. *Journal of Applied Behavioral Science, 24*(1), 19–36.

Ashford, S. J., Blatt, R., & VandeWalle, D. V. (2003). Reflections on the looking glass: A review of research on feedback-seeking behavior in organizations. *Journal of Management, 29*, 773–799.

Ashford, S. J., & Cummings, L. L. (1985). Proactive feedback seeking: The instrumental use of the information environment. *Journal of Occupational Psychology, 58*(1), 67–79.

Ashford, S. J., & Northcraft, G. B. (1992). Conveying more (or less) than we realize: The role of impression-management in feedback-seeking. *Organizational Behavior and Human Decision Processes, 53*, 310–334.

Bachrach, D. G., Powell, B. C., Collins, B. J., & Richey, R. G. (2006). Effects of task interdependence on the relationship between helping behavior and group performance. *Journal of Applied Psychology, 91*(6), 1396–1405.

Bachrach, D. G., Wang, H., Bendoly, E., & Zhang, S. (2007). Importance of organizational citizenship behaviour for overall performance evaluation: Comparing the role of task

interdependence in China and the USA. *Management and Organization Review*, *3*(2), 255–276.
Baer, M., & Frese, M. (2003). Innovation is not enough: Climates for initiative and psychological safety, process innovations, and firm performance. *Journal of Organizational Behavior*, *24*(1), 45–68.
Balkundi, P., & Harrison, D. A. (2006). Ties, leaders, and time in teams: Strong inference about network structure's effects on team viability and performance. *Academy of Management Journal*, *49*(1), 49–68.
Bamberger, P. (2009). Employee help-seeking: Antecedents, consequences and new insights for future research. *Research in Personnel and Human Resources Management*, *28*(1), 49–98.
Bamberger, P. A., & Levi, R. (2009). Team-based reward allocation structures and the helping behaviors of outcome-interdependent team members. *Journal of Managerial Psychology*, *24*(4), 300–327.
Barnes, C. M., Hollenbeck, J. R., Wagner, D. T., DeRue, D. S., Nahrgang, J. D., & Schwind, K. M. (2008). Harmful help: The costs of backing-up behavior in teams. *Journal of Applied Psychology*, *93*(3), 529–539.
Bartlett, M. Y., & DeSteno, D. (2007). Gratitude and prosocial behavior: Helping when it costs you. *Psychological Science*, *17*, 319–325.
Bateman, T. S., & Organ, D. W. (1983). Job satisfaction and the good soldier: The relationship between affect and employee "citizenship." *Academy of Management Journal*, *26*(4), 587–595.
Batson, C. D., Ahmad, N., & Lishner, D. A. (2009). Empathy and altruism. In S. J. Lopez & C. R. Snyder (Eds.), *The Oxford handbook of positive psychology* (2nd ed., pp. 417–426). New York, NY: Oxford University Press.
Beehr, T. A., Bowling, N. A., & Bennett, M. M. (2010). Occupational stress and failures of social support: When helping hurts. *Journal of Occupational Health Psychology*, *15*(1), 45–59.
Belmi, P., & Pfeffer, J. (2015). How "organization" can weaken the norm of reciprocity: The effects of attributions for favors and a calculative mindset. *Academy of Management Discoveries*, *1*(1), 35–55.
Bennett, J. B., & Lehman, W. E. (2001). Workplace substance abuse prevention and help seeking: Comparing team-oriented and informational training. *Journal of Occupational Health Psychology*, *6*(3), 243–254.
Bergeron, D. M. (2007). The potential paradox of organizational citizenship behavior: Good citizens at what cost? *Academy of Management Review*, *32*(4), 1078–1095.
Bergeron, D. M., Shipp, A. J., Rosen, B., & Furst, S. A. (2013). Organizational citizenship behavior and career outcomes: The cost of being a good citizen. *Journal of Management*, *39*(4), 958–984.
Blau, P. M. (1964). *Exchange and power in social life*. New York, NY: Wiley.
Bolger, N., & Amarel, D. (2007). Effects of social support visibility on adjustment to stress: Experimental evidence. *Journal of Personality and Social Psychology*, *92*(3), 458–475.
Bolger, N., Zuckerman, A., & Kessler, R. C. (2000). Invisible support and adjustment to stress. *Journal of Personality and Social Psychology*, *79*(6), 953–961.
Bolino, M. C., & Turnley, W. H. (2003). Going the extra mile: Cultivating and managing employee citizenship behavior. *Academy of Management Executive*, *17*(3), 60–71.
Bolino, M. C., Turnley, W. H., & Niehoff, B. P. (2004). The other side of the story: Reexamining prevailing assumptions about organizational citizenship behavior. *Human Resource Management Review*, *14*(2), 229–246.
Bolino, M. C., Turnley, W. H., Gilstrap, J. B., & Suazo, M. M. (2010). Citizenship under pressure: What's a "good soldier" to do? *Journal of Organizational Behavior*, *31*(6), 835–855.
Bonaccio, S., & Dalal, R. S. (2006). Advice taking and decision-making: An integrative literature review, and implications for the organizational sciences. *Organizational Behavior and Human Decision Processes*, *101*(2), 127–151.
Borgatti, S. P., & Cross, R. (2003). A relational view of information seeking and learning in social networks. *Management Science*, *49*(4), 432–445.
Bowler, W. M., & Brass, D. J. (2006). Relational correlates of interpersonal citizenship behavior: A social network perspective. *Journal of Applied Psychology*, *91*(1), 70–82.
Bowling, N. A., Beehr, T. A., Johnson, A. L., Semmer, N. K., Hendricks, E. A., & Webster, H. A. (2004). Explaining potential antecedents of workplace social support: Reciprocity or attractiveness? *Journal of Occupational Health Psychology*, *9*(4), 339–350.
Bowling, N. A., Beehr, T. A., & Swader, W. M. (2005). Giving and receiving social support at work: The roles of personality and reciprocity. *Journal of Vocational Behavior*, *67*(3), 476–489.
Broll, L., Gross, A. E., & Piliavin, I. (1974). Effects of offered and requested help on help seeking and reactions to being helped. *Journal of Applied Social Psychology*, *4*(3), 244–258.
Brooks, A. W., Gino, F., & Schweitzer, M. E. (2015). Smart people ask for (my) advice: Seeking advice boosts perceptions of competence. *Management Science*, *61*(6), 1421–1435.
Brown, S. L., Nesse, R. M., Vinokur, A. D., & Smith, D. M. (2003). Providing social support may be more beneficial than receiving it results from a prospective study of mortality. *Psychological Science*, *14*(4), 320–327.
Burke, R. J., Weir, T., & Duncan, G. (1976). Informal helping relationship in work organizations. *Academy of Management Journal*, *19*, 370–377.
Butler, R. (2007). Teachers' achievement goal orientations and associations with teachers' help seeking: Examination of a novel approach to teacher motivation. *Journal of Educational Psychology*, *99*(2), 241–252.
Butler, R., & Neuman, O. (1995). Effects of task and ego achievement goals on help-seeking behaviors and attitudes. *Journal of Educational Psychology*, *87*(2), 261–271.
Buunk, B. P., Doosje, B. J., Jans, L. G., & Hopstaken, L. E. (1993). Perceived reciprocity, social support, and stress at work: The role of exchange and communal orientation. *Journal of Personality and Social Psychology*, *65*(4), 801–811.
Cain, D. M., Dana, J., & Newman, G. E. (2014). Giving versus giving in. *Academy of Management Annals*, *8*(1), 505–533.
Cardona, P., Lawrence, B. S., & Bentler, P. M. (2004). The influence of social and work exchange relationships on organizational citizenship behavior. *Group & Organization Management*, *29*(2), 219–247.
Chan, M. E. (2013). Antecedents of instrumental interpersonal help-seeking: An integrative review. *Applied Psychology: An International Review*, *62*, 571–596.
Chiaburu, D. S., Stoverink, A. C., Li, N., & Zhang, X-A. (2015). Extraverts engage in more interpersonal citizenship when motivated to impression manage: Getting along to get ahead? *Journal of Management*, *41*(7), 2004–2031.

Choi, J. N. (2009). Collective dynamics of citizenship behaviour: What group characteristics promote group-level helping? *Journal of Management Studies, 46*(8), 1396–1420.

Clary, E. G., Snyder, M., Ridge, R. D., Copeland, J., Stukas, A. A., Haugen, J., & Miene, P. (1998). Understanding and assessing the motivation of volunteers: A functional approach. *Journal of Personality and Social Psychology, 74*, 1516–1530.

Cleavenger, D., Gardner, W. L., & Mhatre, K. (2007). Help-seeking: Testing the effects of task interdependence and normativeness on employees' propensity to seek help. *Journal of Business and Psychology, 21*(3), 331–359.

Conway, J. M., Rogelberg, S. G., & Pitts, V. E. (2009). Workplace helping: interactive effects of personality and momentary positive affect. *Human Performance, 22*(4), 321–339.

Cotterell, N., Eisenberger, R., & Speicher, H. (1992). Inhibiting effects of reciprocation wariness on interpersonal relationships. *Journal of Personality and Social Psychology, 62*(4), 658.

Cross, R., & Cummings, J. N. (2004). Tie and network correlates of individual performance in knowledge-intensive work. *Academy of Management Journal, 47*(6), 928–937.

Dalal, R. S., & Bonaccio, S. (2010). What types of advice do decision-makers prefer? *Organizational Behavior and Human Decision Processes, 112*(1), 11–23.

Deci, E. L., & Ryan, R. M. (2000). The "what" and "why" of goal pursuits: Human needs and the self-determination of behavior. *Psychological Inquiry, 11*(4), 227–268.

Deelstra, J. T., Peeters, M. C., Schaufeli, W. B., Stroebe, W., Zijlstra, F. R., & van Doornen, L. P. (2003). Receiving instrumental support at work: When help is not welcome. *Journal of Applied Psychology, 88*(2), 324–331.

DePaulo, B. M., Brittingham, G. L., & Kaiser, M. K. (1983). Receiving competence-relevant help: Effects on reciprocity, affect, and sensitivity to the helper's nonverbally expressed needs. *Journal of Personality and Social Psychology, 45*(5), 1045–1060.

Dovidio, J. F., Piliavin, J. A., Gaertner, S. L., Schroeder, D. A., & Clark, R. D., III (1991). The arousal: cost-reward model and the process of intervention: A review of the evidence. In M. S. Clark (Ed), *Review of personality and social psychology: Prosocial behavior* (Vol. *12*, pp. 86–118). Thousand Oaks, CA: Sage.

Eagly, A. H. (1987). Reporting sex differences. *American Psychologist, 42*(7), 756–757.

Eagly, A. H., Wood, W., & Diekman, A. B. (2000). Social role theory of sex differences and similarities: A current appraisal. In T. Eckes & H. M. Trautner (Eds.), *The developmental social psychology of gender* (pp. 123–174). New York, NY: Psychology Press.

Ehrhart, M. G. (2004). Leadership and procedural justice climate as antecedents of unit-level organizational citizenship behavior. *Personnel Psychology, 57*(1), 61–94.

Ehrhart, M. G., Bliese, P. D., & Thomas, J. L. (2006). Unit-level OCB and unit effectiveness: Examining the incremental effect of helping behavior. *Human Performance, 19*(2), 159–173.

Ehrhart, M. G., & Naumann, S. E. (2004). Organizational citizenship behavior in work groups: A group norms approach. *Journal of Applied Psychology, 89*(6), 960–974.

Ehrhart, M. G., & Raver, J. L. (2014). The effects of organizational climate and culture on productive and counterproductive behavior. In B. Schneider & K. Barbera (Eds.), *The Oxford handbook of organizational climate and culture* (pp. 153–176). New York, NY: Oxford University Press.

Ehrhart, M. G., Schneider, B., & Macey, W. H. (2014). *Organizational climate and culture: An introduction to theory, research, and practice.* New York, NY: Routledge.

Eisenberger, R., Cotterell, N., & Marvel, J. (1987). Reciprocation ideology. *Journal of Personality and Social Psychology, 53*(4), 743–750.

Eisenberger, R., Huntington, R. H., Hutchison, S., & Sowa, S. (1986). Perceived organizational support. *Journal of Applied Psychology, 71*(3), 500–507.

Eisenberger, R., Lynch, P., Aselage, J., & Rohdieck, S. (2004). Who takes the most revenge? Individual differences in negative reciprocity norm endorsement. *Personality and Social Psychology Bulletin, 30*(6), 787–799.

Elliot, A. J., & Church, M. A. (1997). A hierarchical model of approach and avoidance achievement motivation. *Journal of Personality and Social Psychology, 72*(1), 218–232.

Emmons, R. A., & McCullough, M. E. (2003). Counting blessings versus burdens: an experimental investigation of gratitude and subjective well-being in daily life. *Journal of Personality and Social Psychology, 84*(2), 377–389.

Erdogan, B., Bauer, T. N., & Taylor, S. (2015). Management commitment to the ecological environment and employees: Implications for employee attitudes and citizenship behaviors. *Human Relations, 68*, 1669–1691.

Farh, J. L., Earley, P. C., & Lin, S. C. (1997). Impetus for action: A cultural analysis of justice and organizational citizenship behavior in Chinese society. *Administrative Science Quarterly, 42*(3), 421–444.

Farh, J. L., Podsakoff, P. M., & Organ, D. W. (1990). Accounting for organizational citizenship behavior: Leader fairness and task scope versus satisfaction. *Journal of Management, 16*(4), 705–721.

Farh, J. L., Zhong, C. B., & Organ, D. W. (2004). Organizational citizenship behavior in the People's Republic of China. *Organization Science, 15*(2), 241–253.

Fischer, P., Krueger, J. I., Greitemeyer, T., Vogrincic, C., Kastenmüller, A., Frey, D., Heene, M., Wicher, M., & Kainbacher, M. (2011). The bystander-effect: A meta-analytic review on bystander intervention in dangerous and non-dangerous emergencies. *Psychological Bulletin, 137*(4), 517–537.

Fisher, J. D., Nadler, A., & Whitcher-Alagna, S. (1982). Recipient reactions to aid. *Psychological Bulletin, 91*(1), 27–54.

Flippen, A. R. Hornstein, H. A., Siegal, W. E., & Weitzman, E. A. (1996). A comparison of similarity and interdependence as triggers for in-group formation. *Personality and Social Psychology Bulletin, 22*, 882–893.

Flynn, F. J. (2003a). How much should I give and how often? The effects of generosity and frequency of favor exchange on social status and productivity. *Academy of Management Journal, 46*(5), 539–553.

Flynn, F. J. (2003b). What have you done for me lately? Temporal adjustments to favor evaluations. *Organizational Behavior and Human Decision Processes, 91*(1), 38–50.

Flynn, F. J. (2006). How much is it worth to you? Subjective evaluations of help in organizations. *Research in Organizational Behavior, 27*, 133–174.

Flynn, F. J., & Brockner, J. (2003). It's different to give than to receive: Predictors of givers' and receivers' reactions to favor exchange. *Journal of Applied Psychology, 88*(6), 1034–1045.

Flynn, F. J., Reagans, R. E., Amanatullah, E. T., & Ames, D. R. (2006). Helping one's way to the top: Self-monitors achieve status by helping others and knowing who helps whom. *Journal of Personality and Social Psychology, 91*(6), 1123–1137.

Fritzsche, B. A., Finkelstein, M. A., & Penner, L. A. (2000). To help or not to help: Capturing individuals' decision policies. *Social Behavior and Personality: An International Journal, 28*(6), 561–578.

Galdas, P. M., Cheater, F., & Marshall, P. (2005). Men and health help-seeking behaviour: Literature review. *Journal of Advanced Nursing, 49*(6), 616–623.

Gelfand, M. J., Erez, M., & Aycan, Z. (2007). Cross-cultural organizational behavior. *Annual Review of Psychology, 58*, 479–514.

Geller, D., & Bamberger, P. A. (2012). The impact of help seeking on individual task performance: The moderating effect of help seekers' logics of action. *Journal of Applied Psychology, 97*(2), 487–497.

Gino, F., Brooks, A. W., & Schweitzer, M. E. (2012). Anxiety, advice, and the ability to discern: Feeling anxious motivates individuals to seek and use advice. *Journal of Personality and Social Psychology, 102*(3), 497–512.

Glomb, T. M., Bhave, D. P., Miner, A. G., & Wall, M. (2011). Doing good, feeling good: Examining the role of organizational citizenship behaviors in changing mood. *Personnel Psychology, 64*(1), 191–223.

Golan, M. E., & Bamberger, P. A. (2015). Mapping the emergent choreography of assistance: The dynamics of dyadic peer helping relations in organizations. *Academy of Management Discoveries, 1*(2), 124–149.

Gouldner, A. W. (1960). The norm of reciprocity: A preliminary statement. *American Sociological Review, 25*(2), 161–178.

Grant, A. M. (2013). *Give and take: A revolutionary approach to success.* New York, NY: Viking Press.

Grant, A. M., & Gino, F. (2010). A little thanks goes a long way: Explaining why gratitude expressions motivate prosocial behavior. *Journal of Personality and Social Psychology, 98*(6), 946–955.

Grant, A. M., & Mayer, D. M. (2009). Good soldiers and good actors: Prosocial and impression management motives as interactive predictors of affiliative citizenship behaviors. *Journal of Applied Psychology, 94*(4), 900–912.

Grant, A. M., Parker, S., & Collins, C. (2009). Getting credit for proactive behavior: Supervisor reactions depend on what you value and how you feel. *Personnel Psychology, 62*(1), 31–55.

Grant, A. M., & Patil, S. V. (2012). Challenging the norm of self-interest: Minority influence and transitions to helping norms in work units. *Academy of Management Review, 37*(4), 547–568.

Graziano, W. G., Habashi, M. M., Sheese, B. E., & Tobin, R. M. (2007). Agreeableness, empathy, and helping: A person × situation perspective. *Journal of Personality and Social Psychology, 93*(4), 583–599.

Greenberg, M. S. (1980). A theory of indebtedness. In K. J. Gergen, M. S. Greenberg, & R. H. Willis (Eds.), *Social exchange: Advances in theory and research* (pp. 3–26). New York, NY: Plenum Press.

Greenberg, M. S., & Shapiro, S. P. (1971). Indebtedness: An adverse aspect of asking for and receiving help. *Sociometry, 34*(2), 290–301.

Greenberg, M. S., & Westcott, D. R. (1983). Indebtedness as a mediator of reactions to aid. In J. D. Fisher, A. Nadler, & B. DePaulo (Eds.), *New directions in helping* (Vol. *1*, pp. 85–112). New York, NY: Academic Press.

Gross, A. E., & Latané, J. G. (1974). Receiving help, reciprocation, and interpersonal attraction. *Journal of Applied Social Psychology, 4*(3), 210–223.

Gross, A. E., & McMullen, P. A. (1983). Models of the help-seeking process. In B. M. DePaulo, A. Nadler, & J. D. Fisher (Eds.), *New directions in helping* (Vol. *2*, pp. 45–70). New York, NY: Academic Press.

Halbesleben, J. R., Harvey, J., & Bolino, M. C. (2009). Too engaged? A conservation of resources view of the relationship between work engagement and work interference with family. *Journal of Applied Psychology, 94*(6), 1452–1465.

Halbesleben, J. R., & Wheeler, A. R. (2011). I owe you one: Coworker reciprocity as a moderator of the day-level exhaustion–performance relationship. *Journal of Organizational Behavior, 32*(4), 608–626.

Halbesleben, J. R., & Wheeler, A. R. (2015). To invest or not? The role of coworker support and trust in daily reciprocal gain spirals of helping behavior. *Journal of Management, 41*(6), 1628–1650.

Hardy, C. L., & Van Vugt, M. (2006). Nice guys finish first: The competitive altruism hypothesis. *Personality and Social Psychology Bulletin, 32*(10), 1402–1413.

Harvey, N., & Fischer, I. (1997). Taking advice: Accepting help, improving judgment, and sharing responsibility. *Organizational Behavior and Human Decision Processes, 70*(2), 117–133.

Hirst, G., Walumbwa, F., Aryee, S., Butarbutar, I., & Chen, C. J. (in press). A multi-level investigation of authentic leadership as an antecedent of helping behavior, *Journal of Business Ethics.*

Hoffman, B. J., Blair, C. A., Meriac, J. P., & Woehr, D. J. (2007). Expanding the criterion domain? A quantitative review of the OCB literature. *Journal of Applied Psychology, 92*(2), 555–566.

Hofmann, D. A., Lei, Z., & Grant, A. M. (2009). Seeking help in the shadow of doubt: The sensemaking processes underlying how nurses decide whom to ask for advice. *Journal of Applied Psychology, 94*, 1261–1274.

Ilies, R., Fulmer, I. S., Spitzmuller, M., & Johnson, M. D. (2009). Personality and citizenship behavior: The mediating role of job satisfaction. *Journal of Applied Psychology, 94*(4), 945–959.

Ilies, R., Nahrgang, J. D., & Morgeson, F. P. (2007). Leader-member exchange and citizenship behaviors: a meta-analysis. *Journal of Applied Psychology, 92*(1), 269–277.

Ilies, R., Scott, B. A., & Judge, T. A. (2006). The interactive effects of personal traits and experienced states on intra-individual patterns of citizenship behavior. *Academy of Management Journal, 49*(3), 561–575.

Jex, S. M., Adams, G. A., Bachrach, D. G., & Sorenson, S. (2003). The impact of situational constraints, role stressors, and commitment on employee altruism. *Journal of Occupational Health Psychology, 8*(3), 171–180.

Jex, S. M., & Thomas, J. L. (2003). Relations between stressors and group perceptions: Main and mediating effects. *Work & Stress, 17*(2), 158–169.

Kamdar, D., McAllister, D. J., & Turban, D. B. (2006). "All in a day's work": How follower individual differences and justice

perceptions predict OCB role definitions and behavior. *Journal of Applied Psychology, 91*(4), 841–855.
Kamdar, D., & Van Dyne, L. (2007). The joint effects of personality and workplace social exchange relationships in predicting task performance and citizenship performance. *Journal of Applied Psychology, 92*(5), 1286–1298.
Kaplan, E. M., & Cowen, E. L. (1981). Interpersonal helping behavior of industrial foremen. *Journal of Applied Psychology, 66*, 633–638.
Karabenick, S. A., & Knapp, J. R. (1991). Relationship of academic help seeking to the use of learning strategies and other instrumental achievement behavior in college students. *Journal of Educational Psychology, 83*(2), 221–230.
Komissarouk, S., & Nadler, A. (2014). "I" seek autonomy, "we" rely on each other: Self-construal and regulatory focus as determinants of autonomy-and dependency-oriented help-seeking behavior. *Personality and Social Psychology Bulletin, 40*, 726–738.
Koopman, J., Lanaj, K., & Scott, B. A. (2016). Integrating the bright and dark sides of OCB: A daily investigation of the benefits and costs of helping others. *Academy of Management Journal, 59*(2), 414–435.
Korsgaard, M. A., Meglino, B. M., Lester, S. W., & Jeong, S. S. (2010). Paying you back or paying me forward: Understanding rewarded and unrewarded organizational citizenship behavior. *Journal of Applied Psychology, 95*(2), 277–290.
Krebs, D. L. (1991). Altruism and egoism: A false dichotomy? *Psychological Inquiry, 2*(2), 137–139.
Lam, S. S., Hui, C., & Law, K. S. (1999). Organizational citizenship behavior: Comparing perspectives of supervisors and subordinates across four international samples. *Journal of Applied Psychology, 84*(4), 594–601.
Lanaj, K., Johnson, R. E., & Wang, M. (2016). When lending a hand depletes the will: The daily costs and benefits of helping. *Journal of Applied Psychology, 101*(8), 1097–1110.
Lavelle, J. J., Rupp, D. E., & Brockner, J. (2007). Taking a multifoci approach to the study of justice, social exchange, and citizenship behavior: The target similarity model. *Journal of Management, 33*(6), 841–866.
Lee, F. (1997). When the going gets tough, do the tough ask for help? Help seeking and power motivation in organizations. *Organizational Behavior and Human Decision Processes, 72*(3), 336–363.
Lee, F. (1999). Verbal strategies for seeking help in organizations. *Journal of Applied Social Psychology, 29*(7), 1472–1496.
Lee, F. (2002). The social costs of seeking help. *The Journal of Applied Behavioral Science, 38*(1), 17–35.
Lester, S. W., Meglino, B. M., & Korsgaard, M. A. (2008). The role of other orientation in organizational citizenship behavior. *Journal of Organizational Behavior, 29*(6), 829–841.
Levine, M., Prosser, A., Evans, D., & Reicher, S. (2005). Identity and emergency intervention: How social group membership and inclusiveness of group boundaries shape helping behavior. *Personality and Social Psychology Bulletin, 31*(4), 443–453.
Li, N., Kirkman, B. L., & Porter, C. O. (2014). Toward a model of work team altruism. *Academy of Management Review, 39*(4), 541–565.
Lim, V. K., Teo, T. S., & Zhao, X. (2013). Psychological costs of support seeking and choice of communication channel. *Behaviour & Information Technology, 32*(2), 132–146.
Lin, C. C. T., & Peng, T. K. T. (2010). From organizational citizenship behaviour to team performance: The mediation of group cohesion and collective efficacy. *Management and Organization Review, 6*(1), 55–75.
Lorenz, M. M., Warner, R. H., & VanDeursen, M. J. (2015). Stated goals and their influence on helping behavior toward ingroups and outgroups. *Journal of Applied Social Psychology, 45*(9), 498–508.
Luria, G., Cnaan, R. A., & Boehm, A. (2015). National culture and prosocial behaviors results from 66 countries. *Nonprofit and Voluntary Sector Quarterly, 44*, 1041–1065.
Lyons, B. J., & Scott, B. A. (2012). Integrating social exchange and affective explanations for the receipt of help and harm: A social network approach. *Organizational Behavior and Human Decision Processes, 117*(1), 66–79.
Madzar, S. (1995). Feedback seeking behavior: A review of the literature and implications for HRD practitioners. *Human Resource Development Quarterly, 6*(4), 337–349.
Malhotra, D. (2004). Trust and reciprocity decisions: The differing perspectives of trustors and trusted parties. *Organizational Behavior and Human Decision Processes, 94*(2), 61–73.
Mayer, D. M., Kuenzi, M., Greenbaum, R., Bardes, M., & Salvador, R. B. (2009). How low does ethical leadership flow? Test of a trickle-down model. *Organizational Behavior and Human Decision Processes, 108*(1), 1–13.
McGuire, A. M. (1994). Helping behaviors in the natural environment: Dimensions and correlates of helping. *Personality and Social Psychology Bulletin, 20*, 45–46.
McNeely, B. L., & Meglino, B. M. (1994). The role of dispositional and situational antecedents in prosocial organizational behavior: An examination of the intended beneficiaries of prosocial behavior. *Journal of Applied Psychology, 79*(6), 836–844.
Meyer, J. P., Stanley, D. J., Herscovitch, L., & Topolnytsky, L. (2002). Affective, continuance, and normative commitment to the organization: A meta-analysis of antecedents, correlates, and consequences. *Journal of Vocational Behavior, 61*, 20–52.
Midlarsky, E. (1991). Helping as coping. In M. S. Clark (Ed.), *Review of personality and social psychology: Prosocial behavior* (Vol. *12*, pp. 238–264). Thousand Oaks, CA: Sage.
Moen, P., Dempster-McClain, D., & Williams, R. M., Jr (1992). Successful aging: A life-course perspective on women's multiple roles and health. *American Journal of Sociology, 97*(6), 1612–1638.
Mojza, E. J., Sonnentag, S., & Bornemann, C. (2011). Volunteer work as a valuable leisure-time activity: A day-level study on volunteer work, non-work experiences, and well-being at work. *Journal of Occupational and Organizational Psychology, 84*, 123–152.
Mor Barak, M. E., Travis, D. J., Pyun, H., & Xie, B. (2009). The impact of supervision on worker outcomes: A meta-analysis. *Social Service Review, 83*(1), 3–32.
Morrison, E. W. (1993). Longitudinal study of the effects of information seeking on newcomer socialization. *Journal of Applied Psychology, 78*(2), 173–183.
Morrison, E. W. (1994). Role definitions and organizational citizenship behavior: The importance of the employee's perspective. *Academy of Management Journal, 37*(6), 1543–1567.
Morrison, E. W. (2002). Information seeking within organizations. *Human Communication Research, 28*, 229–242.

Morrison, E. W., & Vancouver, J. B. (2000). Within-person analysis of information seeking: The effects of perceived costs and benefits. *Journal of Management, 26*(1), 119–137.
Mossholder, K. W., Richardson, H. A., & Settoon, R. P. (2011). Human resource systems and helping in organizations: A relational perspective. *Academy of Management Review, 36*(1), 33–52.
Mueller, J. S., & Kamdar, D. (2011). Why seeking help from teammates is a blessing and a curse: A theory of help seeking and individual creativity in team contexts. *Journal of Applied Psychology, 96*(2), 263–276.
Nadler, A. (1983). Personal characteristics and help-seeking. In B. M. DePaulo, A. Nadler, & J. D. Fisher (Eds.), *New directions in helping* (Vol. *2*, pp. 303–340). New York, NY: Academic Press.
Nadler, A. (1986). Self-esteem and the seeking and receiving of help: Theoretical and empirical perspectives. *Progress in Experimental Personality Research, 14*, 115–163.
Nadler, A. (1987). Determinants of help seeking behaviour: The effects of helper's similarity, task centrality and recipient's self esteem. *European Journal of Social Psychology, 17*, 57–67.
Nadler, A. (1991). Help-seeking behavior: Psychological costs and instrumental benefits. In M. S. Clark (Ed.), *Review of personality and social psychology: Prosocial behavior* (Vol. *12*, pp. 290–311). Thousand Oaks, CA: Sage.
Nadler, A. (2002). Inter–group helping relations as power relations: Maintaining or challenging social dominance between groups through helping. *Journal of Social Issues, 58*(3), 487–502.
Nadler, A., & Chernyak-Hai, L. (2014). Helping them stay where they are: Status effects on dependency/autonomy-oriented helping. *Journal of Personality and Social Psychology, 106*(1), 58–72.
Nadler, A., Ellis, S., & Bar, I. (2003). To seek or not to seek: The relationship between help seeking and job performance evaluations as moderated by task-relevant expertise. *Journal of Applied Social Psychology, 33*(1), 91–109.
Nadler, A., & Fisher, J. D. (1986). The role of threat to self-esteem and perceived control in recipient reaction to help: Theory development and empirical validation. *Advances in Experimental Social Psychology, 19*, 81–122.
Nadler, A., Fisher, J. D., & Streufert, S. (1976). When helping hurts: Effects of donor-recipient similarity and recipient self-esteem on reactions to aid. *Journal of Personality, 44*(3), 392–409.
Nadler, A., & Halabi, S. (2015). Helping relations and inequality between individuals and groups. In M. Mikulincer, P. R. Shaver, J. F. Dovidio, & J. A. Simpson (Eds.), *APA handbook of personality and social psychology, Volume 2: Group processes* (pp. 371–393). Washington, DC: American Psychological Association.
Nadler, A., Harpaz-Gorodeisky, G., & Ben-David, Y. (2009). Defensive helping: Threat to group identity, ingroup identification, status stability, and common group identity as determinants of intergroup help-giving. *Journal of Personality and Social Psychology, 97*(5), 823–834.
Nadler, A., Maler, S., & Friedman, A. (1984). Effects of helper's sex, subjects' androgyny, and self-evaluation on males' and females' willingness to seek and receive help. *Sex Roles, 10*(5–6), 327–339.
Nadler, A., Mayseless, O., Peri, N., & Chemerinski, A. (1985). Effects of opportunity to reciprocate and self-esteem on help-seeking behavior. *Journal of Personality, 53*, 23–35.
Nahum-Shani, I., Bamberger, P. A., & Bacharach, S. B. (2011). Social support and employee well-being the conditioning effect of perceived patterns of supportive exchange. *Journal of Health and Social Behavior, 52*(1), 123–139.
Naumann, S. E., & Ehrhart, M. G. (2011). Moderators of the relationship between group helping norms and individual helping. *Small Group Research, 42*(2), 225–248.
Nebus, J. (2006). Building collegial information networks: A theory of advice network generation. *Academy of Management Review, 31*, 615–637.
Newman, R. S. (1998). Students' help seeking during problem solving: Influences of personal and contextual achievement goals. *Journal of Educational Psychology, 90*, 644–658.
Ng, K. Y., & Van Dyne, L. (2005). Antecedents and performance consequences of helping behavior in work groups: A multilevel analysis. *Group & Organization Management, 30*(5), 514–540.
Ng, T. W., & Sorensen, K. L. (2008). Toward a further understanding of the relationships between perceptions of support and work attitudes: A meta-analysis. *Group & Organization Management, 33*(3), 243–268.
Nicholls, J. G. (1984). Achievement motivation: Conceptions of ability, subjective experience, task choice, and performance. *Psychological Review, 91*(3), 328–346.
Nielsen, T. M., Bachrach, D. G., Sundstrom, E., & Halfhill, T. R. (2012). Utility of OCB organizational citizenship behavior and group performance in a resource allocation framework. *Journal of Management, 38*(2), 668–694.
Nielsen, T. M., Hrivnak, G. A., & Shaw, M. (2009). Organizational citizenship behavior and performance: A meta-analysis of group-level research. *Small Group Research, 40*(5), 555–577.
Oman, D., Thoresen, C. E., & McMahon, K. (1999). Volunteerism and mortality among the community-dwelling elderly. *Journal of Health Psychology, 4*(3), 301–316.
Organ, D. W. (1988). *Organizational citizenship behavior: The good soldier syndrome.* Lexington, MA: Lexington Books.
Organ, D. W. (1997). Organizational citizenship behavior: It's construct clean-up time. *Human Performance, 10*(2), 85–97.
Organ, D. W., & Ryan, K. (1995). A meta-analytic review of attitudinal and dispositional predictors of organizational citizenship behavior. *Personnel Psychology, 48*(4), 775–802.
Organ, D. W, Podsakoff, P. M., &. MacKenzie, S. B. (2006). *Organizational citizenship behavior: Its nature, antecedents, and consequences.* Thousand Oaks, CA: Sage.
Ostroff, C., Kinicki, A. J., & Muhammad, R. S. (2012). Organizational culture and climate. In N. W. Schmitt & S. Highhouse (Eds.), *Handbook of psychology, Vol. 12: Industrial and organizational psychology* (2nd ed., pp. 643–676). Hoboken, NJ: Wiley.
Parks, C. D., & Stone, A. B. (2010). The desire to expel unselfish members from the group. *Journal of Personality and Social Psychology, 99*(2), 303–310.
Pearce, J. L., & Gregersen, H. B. (1991). Task interdependence and extrarole behavior: A test of the mediating effects of felt responsibility. *Journal of Applied Psychology, 76*(6), 838–844.
Pearce, C. L., & Herbik, P. A. (2004). Citizenship behavior at the team level of analysis: The effects of team leadership, team

commitment, perceived team support, and team size. *The Journal of Social Psychology, 144*(3), 293–310.
Pearce, P. L., & Amato, P. R. (1980). A taxonomy of helping: A multidimensional scaling analysis. *Social Psychology Quarterly, 43*, 363–371.
Penner, L. A., Dovidio, J. F., Piliavin, J. A., & Schroeder, D. A. (2005). Prosocial behavior: Multilevel perspectives. *Annual Review of Psychology, 56*, 365–392.
Perlow, L., & Weeks, J. (2002). Who's helping whom? Layers of culture and workplace behavior. *Journal of Organizational Behavior, 23*(4), 345–361.
Perugini, M., Gallucci, M., Presaghi, F., & Ercolani, A. P. (2003). The personal norm of reciprocity. *European Journal of Personality, 17*(4), 251–283.
Piliavin, J. A., Dovidio, J. F., Gaertner, S. L., & Clark, R. D., III (1981). *Emergency intervention*. New York, NY: Academic Press.
Podsakoff, N. P., Whiting, S. W., Podsakoff, P. M., & Blume, B. D. (2009). Individual-and organizational-level consequences of organizational citizenship behaviors: A meta-analysis. *Journal of Applied Psychology, 94*(1), 122–141.
Podsakoff, P. M., MacKenzie, S. B., Moorman, R. H., & Fetter, R. (1990). Transformational leader behaviors and their effects on followers' trust in leader, satisfaction, and organizational citizenship behaviors. *The Leadership Quarterly, 1*(2), 107–142.
Podsakoff, P. M., MacKenzie, S. B., Paine, J. B., & Bachrach, D. G. (2000). Organizational citizenship behaviors: A critical review of the theoretical and empirical literature and suggestions for future research. *Journal of Management, 26*(3), 513–563.
Porter, C. O., Hollenbeck, J. R., Ilgen, D. R., Ellis, A. P., West, B. J., & Moon, H. (2003). Backing up behaviors in teams: the role of personality and legitimacy of need. *Journal of Applied Psychology, 88*(3), 391–403.
Rapp, A. A., Bachrach, D. G., & Rapp, T. L. (2013). The influence of time management skill on the curvilinear relationship between organizational citizenship behavior and task performance. *Journal of Applied Psychology, 98*(4), 668–677.
Raver, J. L., Ehrhart, M. G., & Chadwick, I. C. (2012). The emergence of team helping norms: Foundations within members' attributes and behavior. *Journal of Organizational Behavior, 33*(5), 616–637.
Regts, G., & Molleman, E. (2013). To leave or not to leave: When receiving interpersonal citizenship behavior influences an employee's turnover intention. *Human Relations, 66*(2), 193–218.
Rhoades, L., & Eisenberger, R. (2002). Perceived organizational support: A review of the literature. *Journal of Applied Psychology, 87*(4), 698–714.
Riggle, R. J., Edmondson, D. R., & Hansen, J. D. (2009). A meta-analysis of the relationship between perceived organizational support and job outcomes: 20 years of research. *Journal of Business Research, 62*(10), 1027–1030.
Rioux, S. M., & Penner, L. A. (2001). The causes of organizational citizenship behavior: A motivational analysis. *Journal of Applied Psychology, 86*(6), 1306–1314.
Rodell, J. B. (2013). Finding meaning through volunteering: Why do employees volunteer and what does it mean for their jobs? *Academy of Management Journal, 56*(5), 1274–1294.
Rodell, J. B., Breitsohl, H., Schröder, M., & Keating, D. J. (2016). Employee volunteering: A review and framework for future research. *Journal of Management, 42*, 55–84.
Rosener, J. (1990). How women lead. *Harvard Business Review, 68*(6), 119–125.
Rousseau, D. M. (1990). Assessing organizational culture: The case for multiple methods. In B. Schneider (Ed.), *Organizational climate and culture* (pp. 153–192). San Francisco, CA: Jossey-Bass.
Ryan, A. M., & Pintrich, P. R. (1998). Achievement and social motivational influences on help seeking in the classroom. In S. A. Karabenick (Ed.), *Strategic help seeking: Implications for learning and teaching* (pp. 117–139). Mahwah, NJ: Lawrence Erlbaum.
Schein, E. H. (2010). *Organizational culture and leadership* (4th ed.). San Francisco, CA: Jossey-Bass.
Schneider, M. E., Major, B., Luhtanen, R., & Crocker, J. (1996). Social stigma and the potential costs of assumptive help. *Personality and Social Psychology Bulletin, 22*(2), 201–209.
Settoon, R. P., & Mossholder, K. W. (2002). Relationship quality and relationship context as antecedents of person-and task-focused interpersonal citizenship behavior. *Journal of Applied Psychology, 87*(2), 255–267.
Smith, C. A., Organ, D. W., & Near, J. P. (1983). Organizational citizenship behavior: Its nature and antecedents. *Journal of Applied Psychology, 68*, 653–663.
Sniezek, J. A., & Van Swol, L. M. (2001). Trust, confidence, and expertise in a judge-advisor system. *Organizational Behavior and Human Decision Processes, 84*(2), 288–307.
Spitzmuller, M., & Van Dyne, L. (2013). Proactive and reactive helping: Contrasting the positive consequences of different forms of helping. *Journal of Organizational Behavior, 34*(4), 560–580.
Spitzmuller, M., Van Dyne, L., & Ilies, R. (2009). Organizational citizenship behavior: A review and extension of its nomological network. In J. Barling & C. L. Cooper (Eds.), *The SAGE handbook of organizational behavior: Vol. 1 Micro perspectives* (pp. 106–123). Thousand Oaks, CA: Sage.
Sroufe, L. A., Fox, N. E., & Pancake, V. R. (1983). Attachment and dependency in developmental perspective. *Child Development, 54*, 1615–1627.
Stone, N. J., & O'Gorman, M. E. (1991). Trained helping behaviors and group performance. *Psychological Reports, 68*(3c), 1291–1298.
Studdard, N. L., & Munchus, G. (2009). Entrepreneurial firms' acquisition of knowledge using proactive help-seeking behaviour. *International Journal of Entrepreneurial Behavior & Research, 15*, 242–261.
Stürmer, S., Snyder, M., Kropp, A., & Siem, B. (2006). Empathy-motivated helping: The moderating role of group membership. *Personality and Social Psychology Bulletin, 32*(7), 943–956.
Taber, T. D., & Deosthali, K. (2014). Analysis of self-reported motives for task-related helping: Implications for an integrated theory of helping. *Journal of Business and Psychology, 29*(3), 343–366.
Tessler, R. C., & Schwartz, S. H. (1972). Help seeking, self-esteem, and achievement motivation: An attributional analysis. *Journal of Personality and Social Psychology, 21*(3), 318–326.
Trougakos, J. P., Beal, D. J., Cheng, B. H., Hideg, I., & Zweig, D. (2015). Too drained to help: A resource depletion perspective on daily interpersonal citizenship behaviors. *Journal of Applied Psychology, 100*(1), 227–236.
Tsui, A. S., Nifadkar, S. S., & Ou, A. Y. (2007). Cross-national, cross-cultural organizational behavior research: Advances,

gaps, and recommendations. *Journal of Management, 33*(3), 426–478.

Van der Vegt, G. S., Bunderson, J. S., & Oosterhof, A. (2006). Expertness diversity and interpersonal helping in teams: Why those who need the most help end up getting the least. *Academy of Management Journal, 49*(5), 877–893.

Van der Vegt, G. S., & Van de Vliert, E. (2005). Effects of perceived skill dissimilarity and task interdependence on helping in work teams. *Journal of Management, 31*(1), 73–89.

Van Dyne, L., Graham, J. W., & Dienesch, R. M. (1994). Organizational citizenship behavior: Construct redefinition, measurement, and validation. *Academy of Management Journal, 37*(4), 765–802.

Vancouver, J. B., & Morrison, E. W. (1995). Feedback inquiry: The effect of source attributes and individual differences. *Organizational Behavior and Human Decision Processes, 62*(3), 276–285.

VandeWalle, D., & Cummings, L. L. (1997). A test of the influence of goal orientation on the feedback-seeking process. *Journal of Applied Psychology, 82*(3), 390–400.

VandeWalle, D., Ganesan, S., Challagalla, G. N., & Brown, S. P. (2000). An integrated model of feedback-seeking behavior: Disposition, context, and cognition. *Journal of Applied Psychology, 85*(6), 996–1003.

Venkataramani, V., & Dalal, R. S. (2007). Who helps and harms whom? Relational antecedents of interpersonal helping and harming in organizations. *Journal of Applied Psychology, 92*(4), 952–966.

Vigoda-Gadot, E. (2007). Redrawing the boundaries of OCB? An empirical examination of compulsory extra-role behavior in the workplace. *Journal of Business and Psychology, 21*(3), 377–405.

Wakefield, J. R. H., Hopkins, N., & Greenwood, R. M. (2014). Help-seeking helps: Help-seeking and group image. *Small Group Research, 45*(1), 89–113.

Wallaert, M., Ward, A., & Mann, T. (2014). Ask a busy person: Attentional myopia and helping. *Journal of Applied Social Psychology, 44*(7), 505–510.

Walsh, J. P., Ashford, S. J., & Hill, T. E. (1985). Feedback obstruction: The influence of the information environment on employee turnover intentions. *Human Relations, 38*(1), 23–46.

Warneken, F. (2013). The development of altruistic behavior: Helping in children and chimpanzees. *Social Research, 80*(2), 431–442.

Weinstein, N., & Ryan, R. M. (2010). When helping helps: Autonomous motivation for prosocial behavior and its influence on well-being for the helper and recipient. *Journal of Personality and Social Psychology, 98*(2), 222–244.

Williams, L. J., & Anderson, S. E. (1991). Job satisfaction and organizational commitment as predictors of organizational citizenship and in-role behaviors. *Journal of Management, 17*(3), 601–617.

Williams, K. B., & Williams, K. D. (1983). A social-impact perspective on the social inhibition of help-seeking. In B. M. DePaulo, A. Nadler, & J. D. Fisher (Eds.), *New directions in helping* (Vol. *2*, pp. 187–204). New York, NY: Academic Press.

Williamson, G. M., Clark, M. S., Pegalis, L. J., & Behan, A. (1996). Affective consequences of refusing to help in communal and exchange relationships. *Personality and Social Psychology Bulletin, 22*(1), 34–47.

Wills, T. A., & DePaulo, B. M. (1991). Interpersonal analysis of the help-seeking process. In C. R. Snyder & D. R. Forsyth (Eds.), *Handbook of social and clinical psychology* (pp. 350–375). Elmsford, NY: Pergamon.

Wong, S. S. (2008). Task knowledge overlap and knowledge variety: The role of advice network structures and impact on group effectiveness. *Journal of Organizational Behavior, 29*, 591–614.

Wood, A. M., Brown, G. D., & Maltby, J. (2011). Thanks, but I'm used to better: A relative rank model of gratitude. *Emotion, 11*(1), 175–180.

Wu, C. H., Parker, S. K., & De Jong, J. P. (2013). Feedback seeking from peers: A positive strategy for insecurely attached team-workers. *Human Relations, 67*(4), 441–464.

Yaffe, T., & Kark, R. (2011). Leading by example: The case of leader OCB. *Journal of Applied Psychology, 96*(4), 806–826.

Yaniv, I. (2004). The benefit of additional opinions. *Current Directions in Psychological Science, 13*(2), 75–78.

Yaniv, I., & Kleinberger, E. (2000). Advice taking in decision making: Egocentric discounting and reputation formation. *Organizational Behavior and Human Decision Processes, 83*(2), 260–281.

Zellars, K. L., Tepper, B. J., & Duffy, M. K. (2002). Abusive supervision and subordinates' organizational citizenship behavior. *Journal of Applied Psychology, 87*(6), 1068–1076.

Zhang, Z., & Peterson, S. J. (2011). Advice networks in teams: The role of transformational leadership and members' core self-evaluations. *Journal of Applied Psychology, 96*(5), 1004–1017.

CHAPTER

27 From Barriers to Drivers: Understanding Different Approaches to Getting Systematic Upward Voice in Organizations

Ethan R. Burris, Evan A. Bruno, James R. Detert, *and* Andrea E. Caldwell

Abstract

For the last four decades, scholars have noted the importance of getting employees to speak up. Most scholars have focused their attention on the barriers preventing employees from voicing their ideas, with the prominent theory and findings revealing that when employees do not feel it is safe or worthwhile to speak up, they will withhold their voice and stay silent. Given the increasing understanding that voice is indeed importantly related to key organizational outcomes, in this chapter, we will review a growing, though currently not well-integrated, literature about the various ways to encourage employees to speak up. That is, rather than pointing out the barriers for why employees are compelled to withhold their ideas, we seek to shift the focus to evaluating the efficacy of different approaches to getting voice.

Key Words: employee voice, organizational change, leadership, social factors, voice interventions

Because leaders—those with more authority to make critical decisions—do not always have access to timely information about market trends, operational issues, or barriers to efficiency, the upward flow of ideas and suggestions from employees can often be critical to an organization's efforts to stay ahead of its competitors, to serve its stakeholders well, and to otherwise function effectively (Pfeffer, 1998). Therefore, employee voice, defined as improvement-oriented communication about specific problems or ideas, can improve the chances that companies can identify and address existing dysfunctions, as well as seize opportunities (Van Dyne & LePine, 1998). Managers who solicit voice can gather input from their personnel and subsequently implement changes that could improve operational functioning, increase job satisfaction, and enhance overall company performance (Argote & Ingram, 2000; Argyris & Schon, 1978; Dooley & Fryxell, 1999; Morrison & Milliken, 2000). Providing opportunities for employees to voice suggestions, as well as increasing their willingness to do so, can therefore empower organizations with sharper insight into the front lines of their businesses and can increase their ability to operate successfully.

Yet despite the numerous positive organizational outcomes that can result from voice, employees do not always feel comfortable or even able to speak up in their organizations. Previous research has identified that sometimes employees feel the conditions are not favorable for giving suggestions to those above them (Milliken, Morrison, & Hewlin, 2003; Morrison & Milliken, 2000). Other research has identified that some managers, in fact, may feel threatened by voice because it can challenge the ideas and processes that they personally endorse and may even find ways to suppress voice (Burris, 2012; Fast, Burris, & Bartel, 2014). Thus, these managers and their respective organizations can fail to benefit from employee voice. Conversely, larger, more catastrophic business failures such as the demise of Enron may also be averted by promoting and responding more effectively to voice within a company (Morrison, 2011).

Despite the demonstrated desirability of voice in organizations and a broad range of research into impediments that prevent employees from speaking up or their managers from being receptive to voice, we know little about possible avenues to materially change these employee and managerial perceptions about voice behavior, the level of the behavior itself, or the outcomes of actual voice attempts. Thus, we seek in this chapter to begin to expand the focus among researchers from identifying barriers to and documenting the outcomes of different levels or types of voice to also helping shape and then evaluate the efficacy of different approaches organizations take to actually get more voice.

If voice is not present at desirable levels, then something must happen to effect change at some level within the organization. To help understand what types of interventions may prove fruitful in changing employee voice behavior, we draw on the organizational change literature. Specifically, we posit that—rather than discovering via trial and error which intervention strategies work for increasing voice—practitioners and researchers alike can draw from research on organizational change to design interventions that are more likely to be effective in general and appropriately apply this understanding to the challenges of maximizing voice frequency and impact. To that end, we hope this chapter provides a useful impetus for future research into the strategies that managers can employ in order to cultivate voice in their teams and organizations.

First, we will examine the dimensions of voice behaviors, differentiate voice from other related constructs, and outline its unique properties that interventions must target to produce changes in this employee behavior. Specifically, in order to explore how employees, managers, and top management teams can effectively facilitate (and capitalize on) voice behaviors, interventions must target the cognitions that lead to voice (or lack thereof), as well as the individual and organizational antecedents that affect these cognitions. We will subsequently outline principles of effective change management strategies that managers and organizations can implement in order to qualitatively change these employee cognitions to ultimately increase employee voice. Finally, we conclude with a discussion of some of the conditions that might determine which of the proposed strategies may be particularly relevant and effective in a given situation.

Voice Dimensions and Differentiation from Other Constructs: What Does the Behavior Look Like?

The term "voice" appears to have entered the social science lexicon with Hirschman's (1970) publication of the Exit, Loyalty, and Voice framework, which described voice within or toward an organization versus exit from one's relationship with it as the two primary active choices for those who see an organization lacking in some regard. For employees, Hirschman defined voice as any employee response to job dissatisfaction that aimed to improve work conditions within that organization. Today, scholars usually characterize voice as speaking up (1) in a discretionary way, (2) within the organization, (3) with improvement-oriented ideas, and (4) to others perceived as potentially able to help affect change; thus, usually supervisors (Burris, 2012; Morrison, 2011). We clarify that voice does not include communication that solely criticizes a practice, policy, or decision; rather, it must include an improvement-oriented aspect (Burris, 2012). In that vein, voice is considered a challenging, promotive, and prosocial organizational citizenship behavior (Van Dyne, Cummings, & McLean Parks, 1995): Voice is *challenging* because it questions the status quo (Grant, 2013; Tangirala & Ramanujam, 2008; Van Dyne, Ang, & Botero, 2003), *promotive* because it attempts to improve something within the organization, and *prosocial* because it implies the development of ideas to benefit the organization or some collective rather than just the speaker (Grant & Mayer, 2009). For example, one study determined that over 90% of suggestions involved potential improvements to working conditions or outcomes for employees other than just the speaker (McClean, Burris, & Detert, 2013).

Recently, scholars have proposed more nuanced conceptualizations and measures of voice (e.g., Burris, 2012; Farrell, 1983; Liang, Farh, & Farh, 2012; Maynes & Podsakoff, 2014; Van Dyne et al., 2003). For example, *promotive* voice, which aims to improve work practices and processes by speaking up with new opportunities for improvement, has been distinguished from *prohibitive* voice, which involves speaking up to express concern about existing organizational practices with the intent of stopping them (Liang et al., 2012). However, we view these two types of voice simply as different ways to frame ideas that are, broadly speaking, improvement oriented. Maynes and Podsakoff (2014) offered a different typology wherein they distinguish between *constructive, supportive, defensive*, and *destructive* voice. *Constructive* voice is the voluntary expression of opinions focused on changing current aspects of an organization in place, similar to Liang and colleagues' (2012) notion of *promotive* voice. *Supportive* voice is the voluntary expression of support for worthwhile work-related policies or that which defends work processes that are unfairly being criticized. Maynes and Podsakoff (2014) also identified two types of unhelpful voice—*defensive* (voluntary expression of opposition to change even when the proposed changes have merit) or *destructive* (voluntary expression of hurtful or debasing opinions regarding work) voice. Finally, Burris (2012) distinguished between *challenging* and *supportive* voice, arguing that challenging voice aims to change the status quo, whereas supportive voice tries to preserve it. Although supportive voice can be useful, it is often not as difficult to elicit because it is less threatening to targets. Thus, for the purposes of this chapter on voice interventions, we focus on the constructive and challenging forms of voice, as these types of voice have arguably the greatest potential to improve organizational functioning yet can often be most difficult to encourage employees to express because of the potential risks to those who engage in these types of voice.

Voice is also related to a number of other constructs, most notably silence—the intentional withholding of ideas or information (Detert & Edmondson, 2011; Kish-Gephart, Detert, Treviño, & Edmondson, 2009; Milliken et al., 2003; Morrison & Milliken, 2000). Note that this position treats voice and silence not as terms describing opposite ends of the same construct, but instead as distinct constructs, such that an individual can simultaneously engage in high or low levels of both voice and silence (Detert, Burris, & Harrison, 2010; Van Dyne et al., 2003). For example, if an employee readily speaks up about many work-related ideas, but intentionally withholds her opinions about others or at other times, she should be said to be exhibiting both significant voice and silence. Similarly, if employees do not have any ideas to bring forward, they can be low in voice without any necessary implication that they are withholding ideas (i.e., engaging in silence). Indeed, some research has found that employees often exhibit both high levels of voice and silence (Detert et al., 2010). Silence thus merits its own study. For example, if there is a culture of withholding ideas in an organization, this "climate of silence" is an important phenomenon to understand, in part because the collective withholding of information can severely inhibit organizational success by resulting in a lack of critical analysis and ideas from employees (i.e., collectively high levels of withholding can affect individual voice), less effective change processes, and ultimately less effective decision making (Morrison & Milliken, 2000).

Voice is also similar to the constructs of issue selling, taking charge, whistleblowing, and principled organizational dissent. *Issue selling* refers to the specific tactics that employees can use to garner top management attention for larger scale or higher significance issues (Dutton & Ashford, 1993). For example, the issue selling literature examines how to frame issues such that they are deemed of most interest and priority to intended targets, when it would be best to sell an issue, how to do so in ways that most skillfully manage both speakers' and targets' emotions, and a host of other considerations that affect the likelihood of success voicing an improvement or idea upward (Ashford & Detert, 2015; Dutton, Ashford, O'Neill, & Lawrence, 2001; Dutton, Ashford, Lawrence, & Miner-Rubino, 2002; Sonenshein, 2006). In many ways, voice and issue selling are highly overlapping constructs, though research on issue selling typically examines the dynamics at the individual issue level of analysis, whereas voice research typically examines employee behavior across many issues (Morrison, 2014). Voice has also been distinguished from other forms of speaking up, such as whistleblowing and principled organizational dissent. *Whistleblowing*—disclosing illegal or immoral practices to those outside the organization who could take action (Miceli & Near, 1992)—and *principled organizational dissent*—a protest or effort to change an organization's status quo based on objections to current policies or practices (Graham, 1986)—might be classified as speaking up about very specific types of issues in an extra-role capacity, but none are as comprehensive a construct as voice (Van Dyne et al., 1995).

A Framework to Encourage Employee Voice

Employees often have some desire to seek improvements that would benefit themselves, others, and their organization. Indeed, the motivation for voice most frequently stems from dissatisfaction with the status quo and the identification of a better path forward for the organization (Hirschman, 1970). Whereas this describes the initial, necessary conditions of motivation to speak up, the voice literature has identified two primary countervailing cognitions that can prevent employees from speaking up with improvement-oriented suggestions.

Specifically, *perceived risks* and *perceived efficacy*, both of which can be heavily affect-laced, appear to be the primary cognitions that affect an employee's decision to speak up. These cognitions are influenced by numerous antecedents, classified broadly as either *contextual* or *individual* (Morrison, 2011). Taken together, the impetus to speak up and the cognitions and antecedents form a sort of voice calculus: If the perceived costs are high enough, they may overwhelm the desire of an employee to voice. Although the mediation implied in this framework (see Figure 27.1) is not often tested, this antecedents-cognitions-behavior model is a simple way of understanding voice and classifying possible voice interventions.

It follows that, rather than voice barriers, one might also begin examining the voice calculus through the desire to voice at all. However, research to date has relied on the assumption that a member of an organization has some desire to voice. While investigation into interventions to increase motivation, belonging, and other constructs related to employees buying into to their organization are potentially relevant, the widespread nature of barriers and disruptors of voice leads to the logical conclusion that investigating these more immediate and accessible factors is the best path forward.

Cognitions/Perceptions

Perceived risks (versus lack of, and thus perceived safety) are employees' beliefs about what they might lose or suffer as a consequence of speaking up. The potential risks of speaking up can involve social consequences (e.g., being ostracized, losing social capital, damaging one's reputation) and career consequences (e.g., losing compensation or promotion opportunities, or getting fired) (Burris, Detert, & Romney, 2013; Detert & Edmondson, 2008; Dutton et al., 2002; Milliken et al., 2003; Ryan & Oestreich, 1991). Being ostracized, for instance, can be as subtle as not being included in a group lunch invitation during the work week or as severe as having many coworkers become unwilling to communicate with someone anymore. In either case, the anticipated reaction of others could affect the perceived social risks of speaking up. Speaking up about a questionable practice or speaking out against a supervisor's policy may also have adverse immediate evaluation effects and ripple effects on the employee's longer term career trajectory (Seibert, Kraimer, & Crant, 2001). The perceived risks of speaking up in a given situation, and the weighting of those risks, may be vastly different to each employee based on personal circumstance. For instance, the prospective consequence of losing a promotion may tip the calculation away from the decision to voice for one employee but hardly affect the choice of another who cares much less about that outcome. Also worth noting is that it is an employee's perception or estimation of consequences, and not objective certainty, that defines the risk assessment and thus subsequently affects behavior.

The mental calculus surrounding the choice of speaking up or remaining silent often involves perceived social risks, such as concerns about disrupting interpersonal relationships with colleagues or managers (LePine & Van Dyne, 1998; Milliken, Morrison, & Hewlin, 2003). Additionally, the

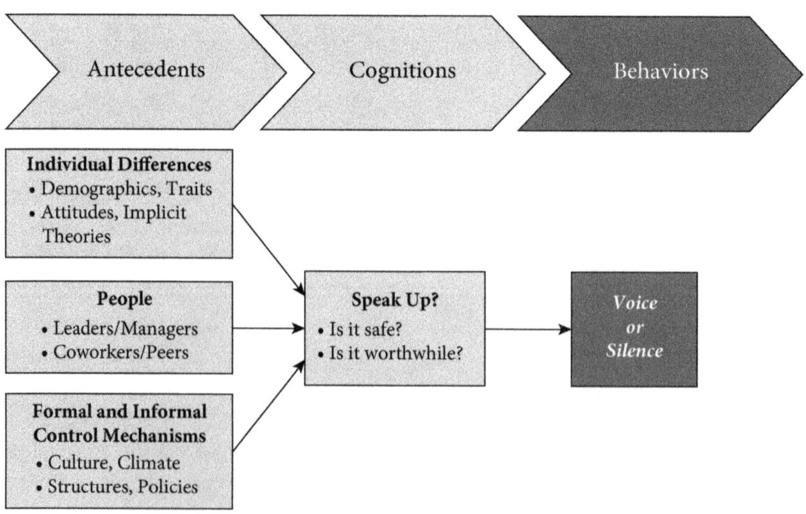

Figure 27.1 Framework for understanding the barriers to voice.

hierarchical direction of the intended voice may play a role, as perceived risks of voice may be more salient when directed at a person in authority as opposed to peers. When the costs are perceived to be too high in such a scenario, employees may engage in "defensive" or "quiescent" silence (i.e., deliberatively withholding information from those in power due to concerns about negative repercussions) (Kish-Gephart et al., 2009; Pinder & Harlos, 2001; Van Dyne et al., 2003).

Risk perceptions can also involve emotional and less conscious implicit beliefs. That is, a powerful emotion like fear may overpower the rational evaluation of costs (Kish-Gephart et al., 2009). For instance, socially acquired beliefs about the dangers of speaking up (e.g., never speak up to the boss in public or speaking up will have negative career consequences) can trump evidence to the contrary, such as when others in the organization may actually be rewarded—not punished—for speaking up (Detert & Edmondson, 2011). An employee may never have actually experienced (or seen someone else experience, for that matter) a negative career consequence such as demotion or firing for speaking up, and yet he or she may still hold the belief that voicing a suggestion upward will lead to such punishment. Although not always rational, such beliefs still have a potent effect on employees' voice decisions.

Perceived efficacy (versus futility) is the second cognition or perception that factors heavily into a decision to speak up or remain silent. Early discussion of this belief was in reference to a particular type of silence—namely, "acquiescent silence," which described failure to speak up based in the perception that doing so was futile rather than because one did not have anything to say (Milliken et al., 2003; Pinder & Harlos, 2001; Van Dyne et al., 2003). Conversely, employees speak up more to the extent that employees see a positive impact stemming from the ideas raised (Maynes & Podsakoff, 2014). The perception of futility (or conclusion that voice has a very low probability of success) is also addressed in the issue selling literature, where scholars utilize the theoretical notion that the amount of effort exerted toward a cause is positively related with the perceived likeliness of success (Vroom, 1964) to make their case. Specifically, researchers have argued and found that motivation to sell an issue is related to the issue sellers' perception of the probable level of success (Ashford, Rothbard, Piderit, & Dutton, 1998; Dutton & Ashford, 1993). Augmenting these findings, a large portion of employees who reported not speaking up in one voice study cited futility as the cause. For instance, when the potential voice target was their direct boss, futility was cited approximately 1.8 times more frequently than fear by respondents who reported withholding input (Detert & Treviño, 2010). And, in a nationally representative sample in a different study, perceptions of futility were seen as a stronger factor than perceptions of safety in preventing employees from speaking up (Detert et al., 2010). As a prominent but as of yet understudied cognition that can significantly affect employees' mental calculus for speaking up, future investigation into *perceived efficacy* is warranted, especially in the context of voice interventions that would have to alter different factors than those influencing perceived risks.

Both *perceived risks* and *perceived efficacy* will factor prominently in our discussion of possible interventions to elicit voice in the workplace, as they have a significant impact on employees' willingness to actually speak up: the lower the perceived risks and higher the perceived efficacy, the higher the likelihood of voice behavior (Morrison, 2011). Thus, an intervention should keep these concepts in the forefront of its structure.

Antecedents

Many factors contribute to employee overall judgments of the risks and efficacy in speaking up. Ranging from studies focusing on individual personality to ambient stimuli, the literature on the antecedents of employee voice beliefs and behaviors continues to grow. In this section, we categorize the various antecedents of voice into individual (e.g., personality) and contextual (e.g., managerial and organizational) factors. As noted earlier, whether explicitly studied as such or not, the majority of these factors are proposed to have an indirect effect on voice through the two mediating cognitions of perceived risks and efficacy.

Individual Level

There are many factors at the individual level that may impact whether or not a particular employee is likely to engage in voice behavior. Significant variations in voice behavior may result from personality traits (LePine & Van Dyne, 2001) and demographic differences such as gender, ethnicity, education, and tenure (LePine & Van Dyne, 1998; Van Dyne & LePine, 1998). Beyond these characteristics, individuals' willingness to speak up may depend on their underlying beliefs about speaking up or their feelings about their job, team, and/or organization

(Burris, Detert, & Chiaburu, 2008; Crant, Kim, & Wang, 2011; Detert & Edmondson, 2011; LePine & Van Dyne, 2001; Liang et al., 2012; Seibert et al., 2001; Tangirala, Kamdar, Venkataramani, & Parke, 2013; Tangirala & Ramanujam, 2008).

To begin, employees are more or less predisposed to engage in voice behaviors based on their personalities. For example, LePine and Van Dyne (2001) explored the relationships between Big Five personality characteristics and voice behavior and found that individuals who are higher in extraversion and conscientiousness are more likely to engage in voice, while individuals who are more agreeable tend to voice less. Crant and colleagues (2011) confirmed that both extraversion and conscientiousness predict higher levels of voice, and also discovered that proactive personality is positively associated with voice. These studies suggest that employees who look to appease upper management or are otherwise predisposed to agreeableness may be less likely to voice (possibly due to higher perceptions of risk, or fewer tendencies to hold or express critical viewpoints), while those who are more proactive and outgoing might be more likely to exhibit voice behaviors as they seize the opportunities available to them. Furthermore, individuals who have a higher duty orientation (i.e., sense of moral and ethical obligation at work) are more likely to voice, while the opposite is true for individuals who have a higher achievement orientation (i.e., drive to get ahead professionally) (Tangirala et al., 2013). As such, employees with a duty orientation may view it as their job and obligation to raise concerns or suggestions for improvement, while those who are achievement oriented tend to be more focused on getting ahead and thus believe that challenging the status quo could interfere with that objective. Similarly, another individual-level factor that contributes to employees' likelihood to engage in voice is the extent to which they self-monitor or adapt their behavior so that others view them positively (Fuller, Barnett, Hester, Relyea, & Frey, 2007). Low self-monitors are relatively consistent in their voice behavior; high self-monitors, on the other hand, may voice more or less in response to cues from the organizational environment or specific supervisors. Those who want to ensure that they are viewed positively by their peers and managers may be less likely to volunteer suggestions to change the status quo as that may affect the way they are viewed.

In addition to personality traits, employees' attitudes about their jobs, organizations, and work groups also impact their voice behavior. Employees who are more satisfied with their jobs and have high levels of investment tend to engage in higher levels of voice behavior because they care about the organization and have the motivation to improve it (Rusbult, Farrell, Rogers, & Mainous, 1988). In addition, felt obligation and organization-based self-esteem may affect the calculations of the risk involved in both promotive and prohibitive voice (Liang et al., 2012). Felt obligation (i.e., feeling personally obligated to drive change) tends to lead primarily to promotive voice as individuals feel some sense of duty to speak up despite perceived risks. Additionally, organization-based self-esteem has a positive relationship with voice behavior, though somewhat weaker than felt obligation.

The degree of control that employees believe they have over their jobs and work-related outcomes, known as their sense of personal control, also affects their voice behavior. Tangirala and Ramanujam (2008) found a curvilinear relationship between personal control and voice, indicating that voice is lower both when employees have very low and very high perceptions of autonomy and impact at work. Having little control likely corresponds to a sense of futility in initiating change, whereas having a high degree of control may spur individuals to simply implement the change rather than seek permission from authorities to enact the change. Voice behavior has also been associated with employees' intent to leave the organization (Farrell, 1983; McClean et al., 2013). For example, in one study, psychological detachment (as measured by the employee's intent to leave) led to lower levels of employee voice; conversely, psychological attachment (measured as affective commitment) did not significantly predict voice (Burris et al., 2008). At the group level, however, employees who have both higher psychological attachment to their work group (measured as work group identification, possibly reflecting the impetus to speak up side of the voice calculation) as well as the ability to personally impact the group's decision (likely affecting perceived efficacy) tend to engage in more voice behavior (Burris et al., 2008; Morrison et al., 2011). Presumably, feeling some attachment to that organization gives employee a sense of agency in making change, or willingness to bear the risks to enact the change despite any possible repercussions.

In addition to these general dispositions, employees' general beliefs and knowledge also guide their voice behavior. For instance, employees hold various implicit theories about the risks and appropriateness of speaking up that seem to be only marginally related to their current environment but nonetheless drive their cognitive voice calculations within it (Detert & Edmondson, 2011). For example, employees may implicitly believe that that one should withhold speaking up if supervisors identify with the status quo, employees do not have data or solutions, and/or that speaking up would embarrass the boss in front of other employees or higher level leaders. These commonly held theories about voice (which lead individuals to assess quickly the riskiness of voice based on past experiences) can be difficult to counteract because the perceived risks are not likely to be particularly conscious nor tested for their accuracy or applicability in a given context (Detert & Edmondson, 2011).

Contextual Level

Although individual personality, attitudes, and implicit beliefs can have a significant impact on employee voice behaviors, the context in which employees work can also significantly impact employees' risk and efficacy perceptions. In fact, contextual features related to the targets of voice and the larger organization can in some cases dwarf the influence of personality on employee voice behavior (Detert & Burris, 2007).

Factors related to the targets of voice—specifically their relationship with the speaker, as well as their attitudes and behaviors—are one primary influence on risk and efficacy perceptions. Managers in particular have been shown to play a key role in determining the amount of voice behavior that occurs to them directly and more generally within work groups (Burris et al., 2008; Botero & Van Dyne, 2009; Dutton et al., 2002; Liu, Tangirala, & Ramanujam, 2013). For instance, leader–member exchange was found to correlate positively with voice behavior in several studies (Botero & Van Dyne, 2009; Burris et al., 2008). These relationship effects can also be connected to employee perceptions of a manager's behaviors. For example, a manager's openness to ideas (in the eyes of employees) and change orientation can increase both general voice behavior patterns and specific episodes of issue selling (Dutton & Ashford, 1993; McClean et al., 2013). Beyond being open to voice, which includes showing a willingness to take action when approached with voice (Detert & Burris, 2007), managers can increase voice behavior by proactively asking employees for ideas (Tangirala & Ramanujam, 2012). While employee perception of a manager's openness to ideas can increase voice, behaviors such as abusive supervision or actively discouraging ideas can reduce voice and significantly affect employee perception of the safety or likely efficacy of speaking up, especially when employees feel detached at work (Burris et al., 2008).

An individual manager's influence within the organization can also impact how willing his or her team members are to engage in voice. Work group members speak up more when their managers participate in decision making with those above them and when they have access to the organization's resources to effect change (McClean et al., 2013). When lower level managers work with higher level managers in decision making, the lower level managers' direct reports feel that their voice will be considered, and they voice more. Access to resources—such as those used for training, marketing, and process implementation—can increase a manager's ability to implement change and therefore can also enhance employee efficacy perceptions. Moreover, the degree to which a particular management team signals its willingness to change can affect employees' feelings about their needs likely being met through voice. These factors increase employee satisfaction as well as improve the likelihood that positive change will result from an employee's decision to voice, hence decreasing the likelihood that futility perceptions will develop.

Given that employee voice efficacy beliefs increase when management is seen as willing and able to act on voice, these characteristics of management teams help to increase voice behavior among employees. In addition, both smaller groups and self-managed teams tend to have higher levels of voice behavior than teams that are larger and that have an official leader (LePine & Van Dyne, 1998), perhaps because both efficacy and risk perceptions are affected in positive ways by smaller size and lack of official hierarchy. Thus, a manager's approach to team building can also affect the quantity of voice.

How managers perceive their employees' reasons for and intentions in speaking up can also affect subsequent voice behavior. Managers may believe that employees are self-interested and untrustworthy or view voice as a form of negative feedback (Fast et al., 2014; Morrison & Milliken, 2000). If managers act on these beliefs, they may suppress voice and create climates in which employees withhold voice. Furthermore, managers' perceptions of how constructive employees are trying to be also impacts voice and its consequences (Whiting, Maynes, Podsakoff, & Podsakoff, 2012). For example, managers who are more efficacious in their role may be more comfortable and less threatened by employees challenging them to make improvements, thus responding more positively to employees who voice and explicitly soliciting them for feedback (Fast et al., 2014).

Beyond individual and supervisor characteristics, other factors can also affect the general climate for speaking up. Some of these factors—such as top management characteristics and organizational structure and policies—can affect employee interactions and have a significant impact on climate (Morrison & Milliken, 2000). Many salient top management team characteristics are similar to those discussed previously as managerial antecedents, including openness to suggestions and change orientation, as well as access to resources or mechanisms to act on voice behavior (McClean et al., 2013; Morrison & Phelps, 1999). Strong voice climates facilitated by top management can increase voice behavior among individuals who might otherwise not speak up, especially if the environment so clearly signals that it is psychologically safe that inhibiting factors are overridden. Lowering power distance perceptions conveyed by an organization's structure and policies can also have a positive impact on voice behavior. For example, Dutton and colleagues (2002) found that female managers were more likely to engage in issue selling in organizations with a traditionally low power distance between middle and top management.

Strong climates of silence may perpetuate beliefs that speaking up will harm one's career or not affect the desired change (Detert & Edmondson, 2011; Morrison & Milliken, 2000). A climate of silence can result from employees' low levels of psychological safety (i.e., higher perceived risks; Kish-Gephart et al., 2009; Liang et al., 2012) and correspondingly high fear of repercussions. Over time, this fear can lead to a state of habituated silence (Kish-Gephart et al., 2009). Such climates can have many causes, such as a cultural value orientation of power distance (e.g., higher power distance perceptions have been shown to be negatively correlated with voice; Botero & Van Dyne, 2009) or shared stereotypes about human tendencies (e.g., finance or economics-based jobs where assumptions that employees are untrustworthy or self-interested may be widespread; Morrison & Milliken, 2000; Pfeffer, 1997). Whether encouraging or inhibiting voice, climates influence, and sometimes override individual-level factors predicting, the risks and efficacy of speaking up in a particular environment.

Summary

The literature on the antecedents and the mediating cognitions leading to voice behavior is rich and continues to grow. Up to this point, unfortunately, most research stops short of showing that these factors can be materially altered by conscious attention and action by managers or others. That is, we have little evidence about the impact of specific interventions designed to influence the levers just described. Hence, we turn next to a consideration of what things, specifically, might be done to actually alter levels of voice in organizations.

Introduction to Voice Intervention Discussion

The field of organizational development and organizational change (collectively referred to henceforth as ODC) provides a lens for understanding and identifying strategies and tactics that managers can employ to change the level and type of employee voice in their teams and organizations. As shown in Figure 27.2, the particular framework we utilize here has four subdimensions, each of which we will review briefly and then explicitly tie to possible voice interventions.

An Organizational Development and Organizational Change Framework

In light of our focus on the employee as the enactor of voice behavior and the cognitions that produce or inhibit that behavior, we base our examination of ODC-based interventions on a framework that focuses on the method and impact of change on an individual target. This model of planned organizational change, developed and later supported by Porras and colleagues (Porras & Hoffer, 1986; Porras & Silvers, 1991; Robertson, Roberts, & Porras, 1993), consists of "four identifiable, interrelated components: (a) a change intervention that alters (b) key organizational target variables that then impact (c) individual organizational members and their on-the-job behaviors resulting in changes in (d) organizational outcomes" (Porras & Silvers, 1991, p. 52). Porras and colleagues acknowledged that the model itself is limited, in that it precludes the impact of the external environment and the possibility of reverse impact (such as organizational outcomes affecting change within the organization instead of change creating the outcome). However, if "behavior is influenced by characteristics of an organization's internal environment—that is, its system elements—then altering the system elements

Physical Setting:
captured by the characteristics of the space in which organizational activities take place. This includes the configuration (e.g., size, relative location), the physical ambiance (e.g., light, noise), and design (e.g., furniture, architecture) of the space

- **Potential Voice Interventions:** use equal furnishings or seating arrangements to lower the status differential between manager and employee; increase proximity of offices between desired voicer and the recipient of voice

Technology:
comprised of all factors associated with transformation of organizational inputs into outputs, both tangible (e.g., tools, equipment) and intangible (e.g., job and work flow design)

- **Potential Voice Interventions:** proactively suggest improvements in order to encourage employees to do the same via accessible and user-friendly online suggestion systems, close the feedback loop when employees do use suggestion systems

Social Factors:
include aspects of the organization's culture (e.g., values, norms, and rituals), the characteristics of both individuals and groups, and the interaction patterns and processes within the organization

- **Potential Voice Interventions:** starting off a meeting with a suggestion and following up on them, pointing out that people don't actually get fired for speaking up (to combat implicit assumptions associated with speaking up)

Organizing Arrangements:
the formal structures and systems that are in place to facilitate coordination and control, including strategies and goals, organizational structure, administrative policies and procedures, rewards systems (e.g., pay, evaluation, benefits), and ownership

- **Potential Voice Interventions:** integrate expectations regarding voice behavior into performance measures and establish rewards for employees who engage in meaningful voice, sharing of profits related to improvements with contributing employees

Figure 27.2 Types of voice interventions.

should lead to altered behavior on the job" (Porras & Hoffer, 1986, p. 480). Thus, focusing on the organization's internal elements allows for interventions that voice researchers might design in order to promote or reward voice behavior.

The model from Porras and colleagues outlines four major subsystems of the organization that an intervention might target: physical setting, technology, social factors, and organizing arrangements. This model aligns with our focus on the antecedents and cognitions that impact voice by emphasizing that lasting change within an organization arises from changes to individual cognitions and behaviors in response to aspects of these four elements. Other theories, such as cognitive theory, support this perspective that in order to change behavior, one must first change beliefs; individuals act the way that they do because of how they think about the situation in which they find themselves (Cameron & Green, 2008).

The *physical setting* is captured by the characteristics of the space in which organizational activities take place. This includes the configuration (e.g., size, relative location), the physical ambiance (e.g., light, noise), and design (e.g., furniture, architecture) of the space. *Technology* is comprised of all factors associated with transformation of organizational inputs into outputs, both tangible (e.g., tools, equipment) and intangible (e.g., job and work flow design). *Social factors* include aspects of the organization's culture (e.g., values, norms, and rituals), the characteristics of both individuals and groups, and the interaction patterns and processes within the organization. Finally, *organizing arrangements* are the formal structures and systems that are in place to facilitate coordination and control. These arrangements include strategies and goals, organizational structure, administrative policies and procedures, reward systems (e.g., pay, evaluation, benefits), and ownership.

Physical Setting

The entire field of environmental psychology addresses the relationships that human beings have with their physical environment. Aspects of a physical environment can influence people's beliefs about both a place as well as the people within that place, which in turn influences their behaviors (Bitner, 1992; Pfeffer, 1982). The impact of the physical environment has been studied within organizations as influencing managerial and employee behavior. Two elements of the organizational environment are particularly pertinent to voice: physical structure (e.g., building size and design, physical location, open vs. closed concept) and symbolic artifacts (e.g., type and style of furniture, colors [of walls, carpets, etc.], photographs and objects on desks or walls in an office) (Davis, 1984).

Collectively, these physical aspects affect workers' beliefs and behaviors, including cooperation, satisfaction, motivation, and perception of status (Bitner, 1992; Oldham & Brass, 1979; Pinto, Pinto, & Prescott, 1993). For example, in a study of small, not-for-profit hospitals, Pinto and colleagues (1993) found that perceived physical proximity significantly influenced cross-functional cooperation. Another interesting intervention investigating the effect of spatial design of a workplace found that employee satisfaction and internal motivation decreased significantly following adoption of an open-floor office design (Oldham & Brass, 1979). A more recent study found that office redesign can be an effective strategy for organizational change: Employees moved to a redesigned space had more favorable perceptions of culture and work-related attitudes (McElroy & Morrow, 2010). Similarly, physical structure and symbolic artifacts seem to have significant potential as the focus of interventions designed to increase voice in workplaces.

First, addressing the physical design of a building may have significant effects on employee voice behavior. The physical distance separating people (i.e., whether they are in the same office, on the same floor, etc.) can impact their interaction patterns and formation of relationships (Davis, 1984). In regard to voice, managers who are physically distant from their employees may struggle to create the impression of openness (Detert & Burris, 2007). For example, front-line employees at a US-based call center reported that they did not frequently speak up about problems or suggestions for improvement because their manager's office was on a different floor (Detert & Burris, 2016). To speak up, employees not only had to go to his floor but also had to walk through four closed doors and past three secretaries. Similarly, when Ken Freeman took over as the Dean of the Boston University School of Management, he recognized the impact that physical proximity could have on collaboration (Martin & Detert, 2014). The prior dean's office (i.e., the office space officially designed for the dean) was located on a high floor of the building, far away from the school's day-to-day student, faculty, and staff traffic. Freeman was concerned that being so far away might make him less accessible, so he relocated his office to the heavily trafficked second floor of the building at the beginning of his second year. This central location, near undergraduate classrooms and the building's in-house Starbucks, significantly reduced what had been a physical barrier between the dean and those who might like to speak with him.

These examples suggest excellent starting points for interventions focused on physical design and proximity as antecedents to voice behavior. It seems straightforward to propose that interventions such as relocating the boss into a more central location and reducing physical barriers to access can increase voice behavior. On a more nuanced level, one might also design an intervention to relocate office spaces for key voice targets near places in the building where informal, comfortable conversations are more likely to occur (e.g., bathrooms or water coolers).

Second, modifying symbolic artifacts in a work environment can change perceptions of underlying organizational values and thus influence related behaviors in that environment (Rafaeli & Vilnai-Yavetz, 2004). These effects occur because artifacts can impact sensory and emotional reactions that in turn influence sensemaking and behavioral reactions. For example, furnishings in an office can influence an employee's perceptions of his or her status in relation to other employees (Bitner, 1992). Associations with specific offices may also have an impact on employee beliefs and behavior. For instance, in a field experiment of equity and workplace status, employees in an underwriting firm were randomly reassigned to a temporary office while their offices were refurbished. Those reassigned to the permanent offices of higher status coworkers raised their performance, while those reassigned to lower status offices lowered their performance (Greenberg, 1988). This suggests that merely providing a different type or size of physical office space, or other physical changes that signal higher status or power, might lead employees to believe speaking up is less risky or more worthwhile and hence be more willing to do so.

The size, arrangement, and décor of a manager's office are also "ambient stimuli" (Hackman, 1992) that can subtly create a psychological distance between the "boss" and everyone else (Detert & Burris, 2016). For example, a power difference is clearly conveyed, with no words needed, when the boss's chair is clearly larger, more comfortable, and more expensive than the one for visiting subordinates. Such cues can reinforce implicit theories of voice and be sufficient reasons by themselves for employees to withhold ideas (Detert & Edmondson, 2011). Other aspects of a physical setting that can send power, status, and psychological distances cues include seating arrangements during a meeting (e.g., does the manager sit at the head of a rectangular table?), how people dress (e.g., does the manager wear far more expensive or formal clothing every day?), and special perks (e.g., does the manager have a fancy office, designated parking space, or private bathroom?). Returning to the previous example, when Ken Freeman moved from his large and far-removed office to a new office at the Boston University School of Management, he chose one that was much smaller and that had a front wall made entirely of glass so that anyone who walked by could see him.

The contrasts in this and other anecdotal stories serve as useful starting points but not scientific foundations for drawing conclusions about the role that physical setting factors play in encouraging or inhibiting voice. We suggest that managers and researchers work together to systematically target aspects of the organization's physical setting in order to decrease the distance (both actual and psychological) between themselves and their employees. For example, a manager could come out from behind his or her large executive desk to sit at a side table next to an employee during a one-on-one meeting in order to create a less hierarchical or adversarial dynamic. Other potential interventions include ensuring that managers are in the same location (i.e., geographically and within the building) as their subordinates, that they keep their doors open, that they sit in comparable chairs at the same or lower height than subordinates, and that they display humanizing pictures of themselves in their office. By making themselves more accessible and approachable, managers may be able to create the impression that they are open to employee ideas for improvement and that they want employees to feel safe in coming to them with problems.

Technology

"Technology" refers to a diverse subsystem, consisting of a multitude of workplace components ranging from the physical (e.g., equipment, machinery, IT materials and tools) to the conceptual (e.g., job design, work flow design, technical procedures, or even technical expertise of employees) (Porras & Hoffer, 1986). The most relevant application of the technology subsystem for voice interventions seems to be the use of technological tools such as online employee suggestion programs designed to increase communication.

Online employee suggestion programs are a common form of attempts to elicit voice from employees via technological methods, but many—as often implemented—may not be a good basis for a voice intervention involving the technology subsystem. In particular, despite their clear intention to increase voice behavior, employee voice suggestion programs utilizing technology as a medium can backfire in the broader sense if they also increase perceptions of risk and/or perceived futility. For instance, if an online suggestion program is introduced as anonymous, the implicit acknowledgement of need for anonymity may unintentionally yet nonetheless remind people that it is not safe to attach one's name to constructive challenges. Likewise, asking employees to submit problems or ideas online but then failing to follow up on what may be hundreds or thousands of suggestions may confirm futility beliefs because so little gets done (or reported as done) based on what gets submitted.

The specific methods of implementing a technological tool like the employee suggestion program may be of particular interest to voice interventions. How employee suggestion programs are managed and acted upon seems to have an impact of the effectiveness of such systems. For example, Piezunka and Dahlander (2015) find that opening suggestion programs up broadly to both employees and external customers can convey a sense of openness to feedback, yet the crowded field of ideas actually narrows the attention of firms such that they only implement a small few ideas. Oftentimes, companies may initiate suggestion programs as a face-saving or cursory gesture without the true intention of implementing voice or addressing cultural issues surrounding the lack of voice. Future interventions involving technology implementations would do well to compare the set-up and follow-through aspects (or lack thereof) that seem to have a significant impact on the voice calculus.

Implementing suggestion systems can be a tool to increase the safety and efficacy of voice, but it is imprudent to rely solely upon technological means to elicit voice. There is likely a stark difference in companies using technology in order to address the root issues versus those using technology to address the presenting problem. For instance, a proactive suggestion system must involve some sort of tackling of the psychological safety issue by providing an avenue for voice and encompass human action that addresses the ideas submitted so that perceptions of futility do not arise. Often, the perception that anonymity is needed or the lack of follow-up to suggestions can be a sign of a cultural issue or norm that is impacting employee voice behaviors, which will be covered next in *social factors*.

Social Factors

Social factors reflect the "human side" of an organization and comprise all of the characteristics and processes related to its social systems (Robertson et al., 1993). A key aspect of this is the organization's culture, which includes its values, norms, stories, myths, history, rituals, and symbols (Denison, 1996; Schein, 2010). Additional social factors include informal networks of communication, decision making, and status; interaction processes between groups and individuals; and individual attributes such as attitudes, beliefs, and skills (Porras & Hoffer, 1986). Collectively, these social factors impact workers' beliefs and behaviors, including group performance and commitment, respect, and trust in management (Golembiewski, Hilles, & Daly, 1987; Porras & Silvers, 1991; Leiter, Laschinger, Day, & Oore, 2011). For instance, approval or disapproval from colleagues can be a key determinant of what is defined as desirable or undesirable behavior in an organization (Cameron & Green, 2008). Thus, social factors can be a potent focal point for change interventions centered on risk calculations involving potential social ostracism or other cultural cues contributing to perceptions that speaking up is futile.

We see at least three distinct types of social factor–related interventions for increasing voice. First, researchers can target particular interaction processes in order to facilitate organizational change. For instance, narrowly focused team-building interventions have been found to have a positive effect on group performance (Porras & Silver, 1991). Dvir and colleagues (2002) studied the effects of training workshops that developed transformational leadership behaviors among a set of military leaders. Followers under leaders who went through the training displayed significantly more extra effort, self-efficacy in completing tasks, and active engagement, all of which translated into increased performance. In another example, Martin, Liao, and Campbell (2013) manipulated whether leaders displayed directive versus empowering leader behaviors over a period of 10 weeks. Employees displayed significantly more proactive behaviors, which then translated into increased unit performance, when leaders displayed more empowering behaviors. These studies suggest that developing interventions targeted toward leader behaviors, like transformational leadership which has been shown to influence voice (Detert & Burris, 2007) and empowerment, can change how employees engage proactive, discretionary behaviors like voice.

Second, the quality of employees' interactions with their managers can influence the extent to which they engage in voice (Burris et al., 2008; Dutton et al., 2002; Liu et al., 2013). An individual manager's interactions within the organization can also influence the voice behavior of his or her direct reports, with employees voicing more to managers who are engaged in the decision-making process (McClean et al., 2013), potentially enhancing the sense of voice efficacy. Thus, a voice intervention targeting social factors such as manager interaction might investigate what specific leader behaviors drive this phenomenon. For instance, where futility is understood to be a major barrier to voice because the boss never seems to change anything, might an intervention designed to increase manager upward participation in the decision-making process, and clear communication of that to subordinates, have an effect on voice behavior of the employees?

Finally, more pervasive challenges may require interventions that are targeted broadly at an organization's culture and processes. For example, a high level of burnout among the human resources staff at a large company was reduced by multilevel interventions directed at the organization's culture (Golembiewski et al., 1987). Golembiewski and colleagues focused first on the interaction of management with employees and sought suggestions for how to include organization members in diagnosis and prescription of the core issues. They then implemented suggested changes (such as career progression plans and more transparency), locking in a "clearer psychological contract between HR employees and the organization" (Golembiewski et al., 1987, p. 306), shifting to a more open culture of transparency that ultimately reduced burnout and turnover rates. Furthermore, a study of a 6-month intervention program utilizing facilitated training and practice scenarios to target key criteria of the CREW framework (Civility, Respect, and Engagement at Work) demonstrated significant improvements in coworker civility, respect, job satisfaction, management trust, and absences (Leiter et al., 2011; Osatuke et al., 2009). Interventions designed to affect the cultural norms regarding transparency, civility, or respect may have a significant effect on an employee's voice calculus. For example, increasing the level of respect managers demonstrate toward their employees through a CREW-like intervention may increase trust between the manager and employees to the point that the risk and futility aspects of employee voice calculus decrease and voice behavior increases.

Aspects of an organization's culture may influence employee voice behavior across the entire organization—that is, by many or most people in the organization toward many different types of voice targets. For instance, some organizations may have a "climate of silence" in which employees collectively withhold ideas (Morrison & Milliken, 2000). In such environments, direct boss-to-subordinate interventions may not be sufficient. In addition, managers at multiple levels may need to introduce new rituals to enhance a sense of voice efficacy (e.g., starting off every meeting getting new suggestions *and* closing the loop on how she or he followed up on ones from the prior meeting), routinely dispel existing myths to reduce fear cognitions (e.g., pointing out that people do not actually get fired for speaking up), visibly speak up to senior leaders to demonstrate that this is not just espoused but regularly enacted by management, or even hire and promote employees who may be more predisposed to voice behaviors based on their personality characteristics (e.g., people higher in extraversion and conscientiousness, as suggested by LePine & Van Dyne, 2001). Managerial actions, when repeated and reinforced, can lead to cultural change and address social factors that may lead to increased senses of fear and futility and decreased voice behavior such as in a climate of silence scenario.

Given the interpersonal and interdependent nature of social factors, related interventions may need to be targeted at various levels within the organization, from employees to lower and middle managers to top executives. However, it is important to acknowledge that changing social systems within an organization often may not be possible without also addressing *organizing arrangements*.

Organizing Arrangements

Organizing arrangements are the factors that an organization formally defines in order to establish the level of control and coordination required for structured activity (Robertson et al., 1993). These include the formal structure of the organization; administrative policies and procedures; organizational goals and strategies; administrative systems related to budgeting, cost control, and information management; and rewards systems (Porras & Hoffer, 1986). For instance, a longitudinal study of top managers at 10 organizations determined that control systems such as those just listed are critical levers in driving organizational change, as they can be used to formalize beliefs; define and measure important outcomes; and establish new strategic agendas, timelines, and targets (Simons, 1994). Interventions targeting organizing arrangements thus seem likely to have significant promise in influencing employee voice levels because the formality of organizing arrangements can provide employees with clear, if unspoken, guidance on what is and is not expected behavior. An organization can incorporate voice efficacy training for employees, voice receptivity training for leaders, administrative policies to promote voice, or even establish rewards for employees who engage in meaningful voicing behaviors. Future voice interventions might also include such levers as incentives or administrative policies and budgets in attempts to affect employees' beliefs about risk and efficacy, as well as about the strategic importance of voice within the organization.

Employees can be socialized to engage in higher voice behaviors through large-scale intervention processes such as training and coaching. For instance, an educational intervention leveraging scenarios, personal reflection, and peer support groups was found to significantly increase voice behaviors among registered nurses by increasing the subjects' perception of their ability to speak up (Sayre, McNeese-Smith, Searle Leach, & Phillips, 2012). Interventions may be able to combine increases in efficacy perceptions with new administrative policies to establish new strategic directives that drive a culture of voice throughout the organization. That is, coaching employees in effective voicing tactics may be significantly augmented with follow-up policies such as enacting policies that foster a sense of receptiveness to voice within the organizations or incorporation of voice behavior into an employee's annual review. An example of such an intervention might be training for the employees to increase voice efficacy perceptions and then following up with training for leadership to start demonstrating behaviors that reduce the risk perceptions of their employees. The company would then be putting its money where its mouth is: Allocating budget resources could be a strong signal to employees that an organization is committed to changing the voice culture.

On their own, reward systems are also an organizational arrangement that can effectively impact change in an organization's voice culture. Reward systems are concerned with both defining and evaluating employee performance as well as distributing rewards (e.g., bonuses, promotions, salary increases, etc.; Kerr & Slocum, 1987). After all, if the way to secure higher paychecks and faster promotions appears to be to remain silent, then it would be "folly" to hope that employees would nonetheless routinely challenge the status quo (Kerr, 1977). Research related to organizing arrangements has also explored the impact of gainsharing and employee ownership. When considering the mental calculus of eliciting voice, much of our focus to this point has been on positive action; that is, on interventions designed to encourage voice by reducing fear and futility perceptions. Another way to look at intervention design is to consider affecting the other side of the equation by increasing the perceived risks or costs of *not* speaking up. With regard to organizing arrangements, gainsharing provides an excellent foundation for exploring this option. Gainsharing interventions (i.e., the policy of sharing profits with employees) have been found to lead to positive results (i.e., higher productivity, more cooperation) when they represent components of a larger, long-term program (Porras & Silvers, 1991). Employee ownership, and in particular both the financial benefits and opportunities to influence organizational outcomes that are associated with ownership, can strongly impact employee attitudes toward the organization (Klein, 1987).

One prominent example of gainsharing that may usefully be considered when designing voice interventions is the Scanlon Plan (first introduced by Joseph Scanlon at his steel manufacturing plant in the 1940s; Davenport, 1950; Schuster, 1984). At its roots, the Scanlon Plan involves the creation of a true worker–management partnership focused on mutual trust and organizational buy-in, both literally and figuratively. The premise is that after establishing rapport, management and labor can both benefit—in quality of work as well as revenue or results sharing—from increased improvement-oriented suggestions from employees (Driscoll, 1979; Schuster, 1984). Most often referenced with regard to unions, some lessons regarding interventions may also be gleaned from the most successful empirical studies of the Scanlon Plan, especially in terms of interventions centered on formal organizing arrangements designed to elicit improvement-oriented voice. For example, in the Scanlon Plan, employees benefit from the positive results of their suggestions. In one intervention, a large manufacturing plant managed to keep turnover and production output at previous levels, despite an industry-wide downturn during that same period (Schuster, 1984). The intervention involved paying consistent bonuses in order to generate over 2,400 employee suggestions in an 8-year period (about 70% of which were implemented). Not only an impressive demonstration of the value of increasing voice behavior, the Scanlon Plan also shows how formal organizing arrangements can be tailored to align rewards with behaviors. In terms of the voice calculus previously discussed, rewards and incentives may be utilized to decrease fear and futility perceptions but also to increase the actual costs of not speaking up. Within the Scanlon Plan framework, workers felt that their suggestions would be heard and acted upon (Schuster, 1984). And because bonuses were tied directly to organizational improvements, they also understood the costs of silence.

In organizational research involving voice interventions, researchers may want to consider the reward structure as a prominent organizational arrangement target. Such interventions can include arrangements in addition to or other than revenue sharing or financial bonuses and also focus on other motivators such as public recognition, reward lunches, or extra time to work on projects that intrinsically motivate employees. In many cases, the rewards associated with speaking up might be determined by, fittingly, seeking employee suggestions (as in Golembiewski et al., 1987). Asking for this feedback and then following up on the data by implementing tailored reward systems would serve the dual purpose of decreasing the perception of futility in the voice calculus while also incentivizing employees to speak up.

Choosing Among Interventions

Leveraging organizational change and development theories provides a theoretical basis for categorizing the types of change efforts organizations might employ to increase voice by reducing barriers. However, there is as yet limited basis for recommending which specific interventions would be most efficacious in producing tangible changes in employee voice behavior in a given situation. In the remaining portion of the chapter, therefore, we offer several preliminary rationales for selecting voice interventions in specific types of situations. Specifically, we describe four contextual factors that likely make some types of interventions much more effective and others perhaps wholly insufficient: the extent to which *fear versus futility is the main driver* of employee silence, the *severity of fear and futility* perceptions, the *level of commitment from top management*, and whether the primarily goal of trying to stimulate more voice is to get a *small number of "big ideas" or an increased overall flow of voice* (see Figure 27.3).

Although fear and futility are the two primary mechanisms limiting employee voice (Morrison, 2014), and are likely often positively correlated, some of the factors that lead employees to experience fear versus futility in the workplace are substantively different (Kish-Gephart et al., 2009;

Guidelines for Selecting Among Intervention Types

ODC Subdimension	Physical Setting	Technology	Social Factors	Organizing Arrangements
Primary Cognitive Barrier:	*Fear*	*Futility*	*Fear*	*Futility*
Severity:	*Low*	*Moderate*	*Moderate*	*High*
Commitment from Top:	*Low*	*Moderate*	*Moderate*	*High*
Type of Voice Recommended:	*Voice Flow*	*Big Idea*	*Voice Flow*	*Voice Flow*

Figure 27.3 Choosing among voice interventions.

Morrison, 2014; Ryan & Oestrich, 1998). When workplaces are characterized primarily by fear, there are often social norms in place that explicitly encourage silence. For instance, beliefs in hierarchy (Morrison & Milliken, 2000) or outright punishments for speaking up like ostracism or ridiculing employees who voice (Milliken et al., 2003) are obvious social factors that can spur fear. In such cases, developing interventions around more appropriate social norms for how to respond to voice could prove worthwhile. Leaders could be taught to model a level of vulnerability by disclosing recent mistakes, learning from those events, and subsequent changes being made going forward, and then invite others to speak up with questions or concerns around similar issues (Edmondson, 2012). If fear of speaking up is not so overt, and instead based in more subtle cues that collectively establish and reinforce a strong power hierarchy (Detert & Burris, 2016; Kish-Gephart et al., 2009), changes to physical arrangements may be in order. For example, instituting meetings to solicit feedback to settings outside of the powerholder's office or changing a room layout to reduce status differences (e.g., using circular tables instead of rectangular tables where the leader is at the head of the table) may be effective in reducing fear. In contrast, offering additional avenues for voice through technology solutions like an online employee suggestion system or organizational arrangements like incentives to speak up are not as likely to fundamentally change perceptions of fear as these change interventions do not directly target how managers behave to solicit or respond to voice. Instead, technology- and organizational arrangements-based interventions seem better suited for addressing perceptions of futility because they offer additional mechanisms for getting and/or responding to voice or for helping align organizational incentives such that voice feels more worthwhile.

A second consideration we recommend for matching interventions to situations is the severity of the problem—that is, the pervasiveness of fear and futility beliefs and associated withholding of voice. For example, in an environment where the fear of repercussions as a result of speaking up and the sense of futility associated with speaking up are relatively low, but more voice is still desired, an intervention targeting physical arrangements (e.g., where meetings occur or how furniture is set up) may be sufficient to prompt more voice. These arrangements simply give more access to leaders and reduce even the more subtle barriers to honest information flow. Yet, as safety and futility concerns increase, more significant efforts, requiring greater resources and managerial time commitment, are likely necessary. For example, if many employees are currently somewhat afraid to speak up, a technology solution may allow them to do so anonymously, whereas simply changing a seating arrangement would not. Similarly, it is hard to imagine a moderate fear problem being significantly eliminated just because a boss meets employees outside his or her own office; instead, real behavior changes in the leader are likely necessary. Finally, if the barriers to voice are most severe, developing overt incentives to spur employees to speak up and to get managers to actually listen to and implement suggestions made may be necessary.

Another consideration in selecting voice interventions is the level of commitment from top management around improving the culture of employee voice. With limited support from top management, developing change interventions that require the coordination of many organizational routines and incentive systems (e.g., performance management, compensation, work process flows) may not be feasible (Detert & Treviño, 2010). Instead, utilizing less resource-intense interventions such as changes to physical arrangements at a local level (e.g., where and how meetings are held in smaller units) may be most viable. After all, among the worst things one can do is to *increase* futility perceptions by overpromising changes to the environment for voice that cannot ultimately be implemented due to insufficient support from the top. If, however, there is significant support from top management, reinforcing the desired changes through social factors like recognition programs or a set of explicit incentives and changes in routines is likely to produce the most robust changes in employee attitudes and behaviors (Beer, Eisenstat, & Foote, 2009).

Finally, although the literature on employee voice has typically considered the overall flow of ideas (Detert, Burris, Harrison, & Martin, 2013) or frequency with which input is offered (Van Dyne & LePine, 1998), the leaders of an organization may actually not be particularly interested in increasing the total volume of voice but, rather, in getting the few "big" ideas that could qualitatively change the game for the organization (Piezunka & Dahlander, 2015). Where quality, not volume, is the key goal, using technology solutions to cast a wide net to capture and sort as many employee ideas as possible seems to fit the desire to search for a few, high-potential ideas to implement. In contrast, using technology to seek the best new ideas (or the most alarming problems) likely does comparatively little to change the day-in, day-out flow of ideas among employees and between employees and their most proximal managers. Knowing there is an "annual competition" for best ideas or a "safety valve" for blowing the whistle is not as efficacious in changing how employees feel about speaking up to their direct bosses, who may or may not show through physical arrangements, social factors, and organizational arrangements that it is safe and worthwhile to speak up routinely.

Conclusions

The need for intervention studies designed to increase voice within organizations as a next step in the evolution of this literature is readily apparent: Researchers have identified many antecedent correlates of critical voice cognitions and behaviors, but to date they have done little documentation of organizational efforts to actually manipulate these factors and measure the improvements. Similarly, the organizational change literature is rife with calls for a more nuanced and detailed exploration of exactly how interventions play out (Martins, 2011; Porras & Silvers, 1991). Our chapter has introduced a framework for different types of interventions to increase employee voice by drawing from research on organizational change. Through examining physical setting, technology, social factors, and organizing arrangements, we have identified several possible avenues for interventions. Yet, although we have offered some preliminary thoughts, much research is needed to clearly delineate the conditions under which each type of intervention will be most efficacious in producing changes in voice behavior. Given the overwhelming evidence of the positive impact voice behaviors can have on an organization, discovering ways to increase it seems like an indisputable next objective for the field, especially given the possibility that successful interventions might have the chance to directly improve the daily work life of employees and corporate performance.

References

Argote, L., & Ingram, P. (2000). Knowledge transfer: A basis for competitive advantage in firms. *Organizational Behavior and Human Decision Processes, 82*(1), 150–169.

Argyris, C., & Schon, D. A. (1978). *Organizational learning: A theory of action perspective*. Reading, MA: Addison-Wesley.

Ashford, S. J., & Detert, J. R. (2015). Get the boss to buy in. *Harvard Business Review*. January–February, 72–79.

Ashford, S. J., Rothbard, N. P., Piderit, S. K., & Dutton, J. E. (1998). Out on a limb: The role of context and impression management in selling gender-equity issues. *Administrative Science Quarterly, 43*, 23–57.

Beer, M., Eisenstat, R. A., & Foote, N. (2009). *High commitment high performance: How to build a resilient organization for sustained advantage*. Hoboken, NJ: John Wiley & Sons.

Bitner, M. J. (1992). Servicescapes: The impact of physical surroundings on customers and employees. *The Journal of Marketing, 56*, 57–71.

Botero, I. C., & Van Dyne, L. (2009). Employee voice behavior interactive effects of LMX and power distance in the United States and Colombia. *Management Communication Quarterly, 23*(1), 84–104.

Burris, E. R. (2012). The risks and rewards of speaking up: Managerial responses to employee voice. *Academy of Management Journal, 55*(4), 851–875.

Burris, E. R., Detert, J. R., & Chiaburu, D. S. (2008). Quitting before leaving: The mediating effects of psychological attachment and detachment on voice. *Journal of Applied Psychology, 93*, 912–922.

Burris, E. R., Detert, J. R., & Romney, A. C. (2013). Speaking up vs. being heard: The disagreement around and outcomes of employee voice. *Organization Science, 24*(1), 22–38.

Cameron, E., & Green, M. (2008). *Making sense of leadership*. London: Kogan Page.

Crant, J. M., Kim, T. Y., & Wang, J. (2011). Dispositional antecedents of demonstration and usefulness of voice behavior. *Journal of Business and Psychology, 26*, 285–297.

Davenport, R. (1950). Enterprise for every man. *Fortune, 41*, 51–58.

Davis, T. R. V. (1984), The influence of the physical environment in offices. *Academy of Management Review, 9*(2), 271–83.

Denison, D. R. (1996). What is the difference between organizational culture and organizational climate? A native's point of view on a decade of paradigm wars. *Academy of Management Review, 21*(3), 619–654.

Detert, J. R., & Burris, E. R. (2007). Leadership behavior and employee voice: Is the door really open? *Academy of Management Journal, 50*(4), 869–884.

Detert, J. R., & Burris, E. R. (2016). Can your employees really speak freely? *Harvard Business Review*, January–February, 80–87.

Detert, J. R., Burris, E. R., & Harrison, D. A. (2010). Debunking four myths about employee silence. *Harvard Business Review, 88*(6), 26.

Detert, J. R., Burris, E. R., Harrison, D. A., & Martin, S. R. (2013). Voice flows to and around leaders: Understanding when units are helped or hurt by employee voice. *Administrative Science Quarterly, 58*(4), 624–668.

Detert, J. R., & Edmondson, A. C. (2008). *The nature and sources of implicit theories of voice*. Presented at the Academy of Management Annual Meeting in Anaheim, CA.

Detert, J. R., & Edmondson, A. C. (2011). Implicit voice theories: Taken-for-granted rules of self-censorship at work. *Academy of Management Journal, 54*, 461–488.

Detert, J. R., & Treviño, L. K. (2010). Speaking up to higher-ups: How supervisors and skip-level leaders influence employee voice. *Organization Science, 21*, 249–270.

Dooley, R. S., & Fryxell, G. E. (1999). Attaining decision quality and commitment from dissent: The moderating effects of loyalty and competence in strategic decision-making teams. *Academy of Management Journal, 42*(4), 389–402.

Driscoll, J. W. (1979). Working creatively with a union: Lessons from the Scanlon Plan. *Organizational Dynamics*, *8*(1), 61–80.

Dutton, J. E., Ashford, S. J., O'Neill, R. M., & Lawrence, K. A. (2001). Moves that matter: Issue selling and organizational change. *Academy of Management Journal*, *44*, 716–736.

Dutton, J. E., Ashford, S. J., Lawrence, K. A., and Miner-Rubino, K. (2002). Red light, green light: Making sense of the organizational context for issue selling. *Organization Science*, *13*(4), 355–369.

Dutton, J. E., & Ashford, S. J. (1993). Selling issues to top management. *Academy of Management Review*, *18*, 397–428.

Dvir, T., Eden, D., Avolio, B. J., & Shamir, B. (2002). Impact of transformational leadership on follower development and performance: A field experiment. *Academy of Management Journal*, *45*(4), 735–744.

Edmondson, A. C. (2012). *Teaming: How organizations learn, innovate, and compete in the knowledge economy*. Boston, MA: Harvard Business School Press.

Farrell, D. (1983). Exit, voice, loyalty, and neglect as responses to job dissatisfaction: A multidimensional scaling study. *Academy of Management Journal*, *26*(4), 596–607.

Fast, N. J., Burris, E. R., & Bartel, C. A. (2014). Managing to stay in the dark: managerial self-efficacy, ego defensiveness, and the aversion to employee voice. *Academy of Management Journal*, *57*(4), 1013–1034.

Fuller, J. B., Barnett, T., Hester, K., Relyea, C., & Frey, L. (2007). An exploratory examination of voice behavior from an impression management perspective. *Journal of Managerial Issues*, *19*, 134–151.

Golembiewski, R. T., Hilles, R., & Daly, R. (1987). Some effects of multiple OD interventions on burnout and work site features. *The Journal of Applied Behavioral Science*, *23*(3), 295–313.

Graham, J. W. (1986). Principled organizational dissent: A theoretical essay. *Research in Organizational Behavior 8*, 1–52.

Grant, A. M. (2013). Rocking the boat but keeping it steady: The role of emotion regulation in employee voice. *Academy of Management Journal*, *56*(6), 1703–1723.

Grant, A. M., & Mayer, D. M. (2009). Good soldiers and good actors: prosocial and impression management motives as interactive predictors of affiliative citizenship behaviors. *Journal of Applied Psychology*, *94*(4), 900.

Greenberg, J. (1988). Equity and workplace status: A field experiment. *Journal of Applied Psychology*, *73*, 606–613.

Hackman, J. R. (1992). Group influences on individuals in organizations. In M. D. Dunnette (Ed.), *Handbook of industrial and organizational psychology* (pp. 1455–1525). Palo Alto, CA: Consulting Psychologists Press.

Hirschman, A. O. (1970). *Exit, voice, and loyalty. Responses to decline in firms, organizations, and states.* Cambridge, MA: Harvard University Press.

Kerr, J., & Slocum, J. W. (1987). Managing corporate culture through reward systems. *The Academy of Management Executive*, *1*(2), 99–107.

Kish-Gephart, J., Detert, J. R., Treviño, L. K., & Edmondson, A. C. (2009). Silenced by fear: Psychological, social, and evolutionary drivers of voice behavior at work. In B. M. Staw & A. P. Brief (Eds.), *Research in organizational behavior* (pp. 163–193). Greenwich, CT: JAI.

Klein, K. J. (1987). Employee stock ownership and employee attitudes: A test of three models. *Journal of Applied Psychology*, *72*(2), 319.

Leiter, M. P., Laschinger, H. K. S., Day, A., & Oore, D. G. (2011). The impact of civility interventions on employee social behavior, distress, and attitudes. *Journal of Applied Psychology*, *96*(6), 1258.

LePine, J. A., & Van Dyne, L. (1998). Predicting voice behavior in work groups. *Journal of Applied Psychology*, *83*(6), 853–868.

LePine, J. A., and Van Dyne, L. (2001). Voice and cooperative behavior as contrasting forms of contextual performance: Evidence of differential relationships with Big Five personality characteristics and cognitive ability. *Journal of Applied Psychology*, *86*, 326–336.

Liang, J., Farh, C., & Farh, L. (2012). A two-wave examination of the psychological antecedents of voice behavior. *Academy of Management Journal*, *55*, 71–92.

Liu, W., Tangirala, S., & Ramanujam, R. (2013). The relational antecedents of voice targeted at different leaders. *Journal of Applied Psychology*, *98*(5), 841.

Martin, S. L., Liao, H., & Campbell, E. M. (2013). Directive versus empowering leadership: A field experiment comparing impacts on task proficiency and proactivity. *Academy of Management Journal*, *56*(5), 1372–1395.

Martin, S. R. & Detert, J. R. (2014). *Organizational change in academia: A case study of Dean Ken Freeman and the Boston University School of Management.* Unpublished teaching case.

Martins, L. L. (2011). Organizational change and development. In Zedeck, S. (Ed.), *APA handbook of industrial and organizational psychology* (pp. 601–728). Washington, DC: APA.

Maynes, T. D., & Podsakoff, P. M. (2014). Speaking more broadly: An examination of the nature, antecedents, and consequences of an expanded set of employee voice behaviors. *Journal of Applied Psychology*, *99*, 87–112.

McClean, E. J., Burris, E. R., & Detert, J. R. (2013). When does voice lead to exit? It depends on leadership. *Academy of Management Journal*, *56*, 525–548

McElroy, J. C., & Morrow, P. C. (2010). Employee reactions to office redesign: A naturally occurring quasi-field experiment in a multi-generational setting. *Human Relations*, *63*(5), 609–636.

Miceli, M. P., & Near, J. P. (1992). *Blowing the whistle: The organizational and legal implications for companies and employees.* New York, NY: Lexington Books.

Milliken, F. J., Morrison, E. W., & Hewlin, P. F. (2003). An exploratory study of employee silence: Issues that employees don't communicate upward and why. *Journal of Management Studies*, *40*(6), 1453–1476.

Morrison, E. W. (2011). Employee voice behavior: Integration and directions for future research. *The Academy of Management Annals*, *5*(1), 373–412.

Morrison, E. W., & Milliken, F. J. (2000). Organizational silence: A barrier to change and development in a pluralistic world. *Academy of Management Review*, *25*(4), 706–725.

Morrison, E. W., & Phelps, C. C. (1999). Taking charge at work: Extrarole efforts to initiate workplace change. *Academy of Management Journal*, *42*(4), 403–419.

Morrison, E. W. (2014). Employee voice and silence. *Annual Review of Organizational Psychology and Organizational Behavior*, *1*, 173–97.

Oldham, G. R., & Brass, D. J. (1979). Employee reactions to an open-plan office: A naturally occurring quasi-experiment. *Administrative Science Quarterly*, 24, 267–284.

Pfeffer, J. (1982). *Organizations and organization theory.* Boston, MA: Pitman.

Pfeffer, J. (1998). *The human equation: Building profits by putting people first*. Cambridge, MA: Harvard Business Press.
Piezunka, H., & Dahlander, L. (2015). Distant search, narrow attention: How crowding alters organizations' filtering of suggestions in crowdsourcing. *Academy of Management Journal, 58*(3), 856–880.
Pinder, C. C., & Harlos, K. P. (2001). Employee silence: Quiescence and acquiescence as responses to perceived injustice. In K. M. Rowland & G. R. Ferris (Eds.), *Research in personnel and human resources management*, Vol. *20* (pp. 331–369). New York, NY: JAI Press.
Pinto, M. B., Pinto, J. K., & Prescott, J. E. (1993). Antecedents and consequences of project team cross-functional cooperation. *Management Science, 39*(10), 1281–1297.
Porras, J. I., & Hoffer, S. J. (1986). Common behavior changes in successful organization development efforts. *The Journal of Applied Behavioral Science, 22*(4), 477–494.
Porras, J. I., & Silvers, R. C. (1991). Organization development and transformation. *Annual Review of Psychology, 42*(1), 51–78.
Rafaeli, A., & Vilnai-Yavetz, I. (2004). Emotion as a connection of physical artifacts and organizations. *Organization Science, 15*(6), 671–686.
Robertson, P. J., Roberts, D. R., & Porras, J. I. (1993). Dynamics of planned organizational change: Assessing empirical support for a theoretical model. *Academy of Management Journal, 36*(3), 619–634.
Rusbult, C. E., Farrell, D., Rogers, G., & Mainous, A. G. (1988). Impact of exchange variables on exit, voice, loyalty, and neglect: An integrative model of responses to declining job satisfaction. *Academy of Management Journal, 31*(3), 599–627.
Ryan, K. D., & Oestreich, D. K. (1991). *Driving fear out of the workplace: How to overcome the invisible barriers to quality, productivity and innovation*. San Francisco, CA: Jossey-Bass Publishers.
Sayre, M. M., McNeese-Smith, D., Leach, L. S., & Phillips, L. R. (2012). An educational intervention to increase "speaking-up" behaviors in nurses and improve patient safety. *Journal of Nursing Care Quality, 27*(2), 154–160.
Schein, E. H. (2010). *Organizational culture and leadership* (Vol. *2*). Hoboken, NJ: John Wiley & Sons.
Schuster, M. (1984). The Scanlon Plan: A longitudinal analysis. *Journal of Applied Behavioral Science, 20*, 23–38.
Seibert, S. E., Kraimer, M. L., & Crant, J. M. (2001). What do proactive people do? A longitudinal model linking proactive personality and career success. *Personnel Psychology, 54*, 845–874.
Simons, R. (1994). How new top managers use control systems as levers of strategic renewal. *Strategic Management Journal, 15*(3), 169–189.
Sonenshein, S. (2006). Crafting social issues at work. *Academy of Management Journal, 49*(6), 1158–1172.
Tangirala, S., & Ramanujam, R. (2008). Exploring nonlinearity in employee voice: The effects of personal control and organizational identification. *Academy of Management Journal, 51*(6), 1189–1203.
Tangirala, S., & Ramanujam, R. (2012). Ask and you shall hear (but not always): Examining the relationship between manager consultation and employee voice. *Personnel Psychology, 65*(2), 251–282.
Tangirala, S., Kamdar, D., Venkataramani, V., & Parke, M. R. (2013). Doing right versus getting ahead: The effects of duty and achievement orientations on employees' voice. *Journal of Applied Psychology, 98*(6), 1040.
Van Dyne, L., & LePine, J. A. (1998). Helping and voice extra-role behaviors: Evidence of construct and predictive validity. *Academy of Management Journal, 41*(1), 108–119.
Van Dyne, L., Ang, S., & Botero, I. C. (2003). Conceptualizing employee silence and employee voice as multidimensional constructs. *Journal of Management Studies, 40*(6), 1359–1392.
Van Dyne, L., Cummings, L. L., & McLean Parks, J. (1995). Extra-role behaviors: In pursuit of construct and definitional clarity (a bridge over muddied waters). *Research in Organizational Behavior, 17*, 215–285.
Vroom, V. H. (1964). *Work and motivation*. New York: Wiley.
Whiting, S. W., Maynes, T. D., Podsakoff, N. P., & Podsakoff, P. M. (2012). Effects of message, source, and context on evaluations of employee voice behavior. *Journal of Applied Psychology, 97*, 159–182.

CHAPTER

28

Rethinking Organizational Citizenship Behavior in Service Organizations: Its Nature and Conceptualization

Anit Somech *and* Anat Drach-Zahavy

Abstract

This chapter focuses on the phenomenon of organizational citizenship behavior (OCB) in the context of service organizations. Specifically, our aim was to challenge the common approach to OCB by delineating the unique characteristics of service organizations. The chapter begins by capturing the distinctive features of services: their intangibility, inseparability, and heterogeneity. Next, we argue that these characteristics compel service organizations to rely primarily on their employees' OCBs. Paradoxically, the more committed managers are to service delivery, the less control they have over service quality compared with their counterparts in manufacturing. We then discuss how service characteristics shape the nature of OCB in this unique context and propose an integrated typology for better understanding OCB in service organizations.

Key Words: service organizations, OCB, emotion-oriented citizenship behavior, ECB, customer service

The service sector in the United States has grown from 73% of the workforce in 1980 to 86% of today's workforce, employing nearly 133 million workers (Bureau of Labor Statistics, 2012). This sector currently accounts for 60% of world GDP and dominates economies in most countries (Raub & Liao, 2012). Whereas manufacturing organizations focus on maximizing production efficiency, service organizations aim to maximize the quality of service for customers.

Scholars agree that services can be characterized by three well-documented features: intangibility, heterogeneity, and inseparability. The first feature, intangibility, refers to the inability to assess the value gained from engaging in an activity using any tangible evidence. Intangibility is often used to describe services that offer no tangible product that the customer can purchase, see, taste, or touch (Palmer Jr et al., 2001). The intangibility of services means that precise specifications concerning standardized quality can rarely be set. "Most services cannot be counted, measured, inventoried, tested, and verified in advance of sale to assure quality" (Parasuraman, Zeithaml, & Berry, 1985, p. 45). Moreover, due to the intangibility of services, managers often face challenges in evaluating service quality (Zeithaml, 1981) and customers, too, have more difficulty evaluating service quality than a product's quality. The second feature of services is heterogeneity, which means that service behavior might vary from one frontline employee to another, from customer to customer, and from one encounter to another. Therefore, assuring uniformity of service behaviors is challenging (Raub & Liao, 2012). Moreover, heterogeneity might lead to significant discrepancies between what the organization intends to deliver and what the customer receives. Finally, the third feature of services, the inseparability of services, refers to the inability to divorce the supply or production of the service from its consumption (Zeithaml, 1981). Consequently, the quality of services is typically shaped "on the spot," that is, during the service provider–customer encounter. Simply put, service quality is a coproduction between the service provider and the customers' inputs, and so quality evaluations are not made solely on the outcome of a service but rather involve also evaluations of the service delivery process itself.

Thus, frontline service employees operate in an uncertain work environment that is characterized by highly diverse and dynamic customer needs and expectations, as well as by customer involvement in the coproduction of the service delivery process (Raub & Liao, 2012). Therefore, the in-role behaviors of service employees, as well as their extra-role behaviors (OCBs), are essential for organizational success (Borucki & Burke, 1999; Johnson, 1996; Liao & Chuang, 2004), yet, paradoxically, service organizations face difficulties specifying the required range of prescribed work roles (Griffin, Neal, & Parker, 2007). In addition, the capacity of managers to control, monitor, and reward frontline employees' behavior is limited. This means that service organizations must not only rely on their employees' willingness to "go the extra mile" but also that the boundaries between in-role and extra-role behaviors are often blurred (Morrison, 1994).

Moreover, the unique characteristics of service, namely the intangibility, heterogeneity, and inseparability, call for a comprehensive context-sensitive exploration of the OCB phenomena as it unfolds in the day-to-day routines of service-sector organizations. First, since service is typically a dyadic phenomenon, occurring between the frontline service employee and the customer, interpersonal factors, and especially emotions might shape its quality. Yet most common typologies of OCB ignore the emotions as an integral part of citizenship behaviors. Second, the role of customers not only as targets of OCB but also as agents that can exhibit OCBs has typically been disregarded by OCB researchers in general organizations. This chapter aims to narrow this void in the literature by introducing an integrative approach for OCBs in service organizations.

The Conceptualization and Nature of Organizational Citizenship Behavior in Service Organizations

Definitions of Organizational Citizenship Behavior in Service Organizations

OCB research in the service context was initially grounded in theories that aimed at developing a general concept of OCB without a reference to a specific context. Although the vast majority of the studies in the early phases of OCB research were actually conducted in service (or sales) settings (e.g., Bateman & Organ, 1983; Smith, Organ, & Near, 1983; Williams & Anderson, 1991), these studies embraced general definitions of employee OCBs. This line of research referred mainly to Organ's seminal work and applied his approach to the service context. For example, based on Organ's work (1988), Kim, Park, and Chang (2011) defined OCB in the service sector as "an individual behavior that is discretionary, not directly or explicitly recognized by the formal reward system which, in the aggregate, promotes the effective functioning of the organization" (p. 86). Others (e.g., Sun, Aryee, & Law, 2007) referred to a later definition of OCB (Organ, 1997) according to which OCBs are "contributions to the maintenance and enhancement of the social and psychological context that supports task performance" (p. 560). This line of research typically treated OCBs as a context-free phenomenon, assuming that the same behaviors are required in order to benefit the organization regardless of the unique characteristics of the service context. Yet some nuances can, albeit, be identified, especially if customer satisfaction is focused on as an important component of organizational effectiveness. For example, Schneider, Ehrhart, Mayer, Saltz, and Niles-Jolly (2005) focused on OCBs in service organizations, and emphasized their contribution for improving customers' satisfaction, as an important component of organizational effectiveness in service organizations. The authors believed that "employees engage not only in role-prescribed behaviors toward customers, but also in behaviors that go above and beyond the call of duty to promote the highest levels of customer satisfaction" (p. 1019). A more context-specific conceptualization was developed by Bettencourt and colleagues (1997), defining service-oriented OCB (SOCB) as discretionary behaviors of contact employees when serving customers that extend beyond the formal requirements. This definition was the first to recognize the unique context of service organizations, by focusing on the citizenship behaviors that typically unfold during the frontline service employee–customer encounter.

To conclude, it seems that most definitions of OCB in service organizations mimic the classical definitions developed in the field, arguing that OCBs are not simply those behaviors that happen to occur within an organization, but rather are those that are directed to or are seen as benefiting the organization (Van Dyne, Cummings, & Parks, 1995).

Yet, with regard to the service sector, benefiting the organization is closely related to boosting customer satisfaction. Therefore, SOCB is aimed directly and indirectly to the benefit of the customers.

Dimensionality of Service Employees' Organizational Citizenship Behavior

Although the general definitions of OCB used in research on service employees' OCB are largely similar to the definitions of this kind of behavior in any kind of occupational sector, it is our goal to use the existing body of research on service-oriented OCBs to provide some insights into how scholars have implicitly defined it with respect to its dimensions. Specifically, three main approaches were identified: grouping OCBs according to (1) the content of the OCB; (2) the target of the OCB; and (3) the agent of the OCB (see Table 28.1).

ORGANIZATIONAL CITIZENSHIP BEHAVIOR CONTENT

Scholars who defined service-oriented OCB initially adopted existing typologies to describe the various types of behaviors defined as OCBs. For example, Dimitriades (2007), Hopkins (2002), and Morrison (1996) used Organ's (1988) typology that consists of five dimensions, as follows: (1) Altruism: behaving in a way that demonstrates selflessness and concern for the welfare of others; (2) Conscientiousness: exhibiting commitment to high levels of work quality and completion; (3) Sportsmanship: choosing not to complain or act in negative ways; (4) Courtesy: taking actions that help prevent problems from occurring, or taking advance actions to mitigate a problem; and (5) Civic virtue: adopting a posture of "responsible, constructive involvement in the political or governance process of the organization" (Organ et al., 2006). This approach posits that these five categories of behaviors capture many of the discretionary behaviors that are important for attaining service quality (Morrison, 1996). Morrison explained how the five dimensions of OCB could be displayed not only within the organization (as demonstrated in the general OCB literature) but also toward external customers (a unique characteristic of service organizations). For example, altruism directed at external customers can take the form of helping a customer with a problem even though doing so is not strictly within the employee's job-related duties, thereby creating an overall sense of goodwill and enhancing the customer's experience of service quality. Similarly, conscientiousness behavior toward clients might occur, for example, when a call center employee goes far and beyond his or her formal duties in an attempt to solve a customer's problem. To summarize, OCBs in service organizations can promote service quality directly, by focusing on the customer–provider encounter, or indirectly, by focusing on the encounter between the employee and his or her counterparts within the organization. Whereas it is obvious why OCBs that focus on customers directly can improve service quality and customer satisfaction, OCBs within the organization can enhance service quality either by creating an overall environment that customers experience as more friendly or because the positive climate among employees is likely to spill over into their interactions with customers (Morrison, 1996; Schneider et al., 2005).

Although this approach has merit for better understanding OCBs in service organizations, several authors suggested that traditional OCBs might not be appropriate for service organizations since such organizations may have special prerequisites for OCB dimensions that relate to dealing with customers (Borman & Motowidlo, 1993; Ma & Qu, 2011). A more context-specific approach, called service-oriented OCB (SOCB) was suggested by Van Dyne et al. (1994) and Bettencourt, Gwinner, and Meuter (2001). This approach identifies those citizenship behaviors that best promote service quality and customer satisfaction. Furthermore, it focuses only on the behaviors of frontline customer employees that derive from their unique position as boundary spanners of the firm (Bettencourt et al., 2001). Three dimensions were identified: loyalty, participation, and service delivery. Loyalty OCBs are defined as "acting as advocates to outsiders not only of the organization's products and services but also of its image" (Bettencourt et al., 2001, p. 29). Contact employee participation OCBs are defined as "taking individual initiative, especially in communications, to improve service delivery by the organization, coworkers, and oneself" (p. 29). And finally, service-delivery OCBs refer to "behaving in a conscientious manner in activities surrounding service delivery to customers" (p. 30). According to this approach, customer-contact employees are crucial to the organizational success; they directly interact with customers and can thus shape the customers' image of the organization (Schneider & Bowen, 1993). Customer-contact employees can be the first to provide information on customer needs and requirements, service failures, and suggested improvements in service (e.g.,

Table 28.1 Review of the Organizational Citizenship Behavior Typologies for Service Organizations

Typology	Focus	Typology's Dimensions	Originally Developed by	Examples
Five-dimensional OCB typology	Content	a. *Conscientiousness/Discretionary behaviors*: Behaviors that go well beyond minimum role requirements regarding customer service. b. *Altruism*: Informal helping behaviors that are critical for ensuring customer service quality. c. *Civic virtue*: A Behavior that indicates willingness to responsibly participate in the life of the organization. d. *Sportsmanship*: A behavior demonstrating tolerance of less than ideal circumstances without complaining. e. *Courtesy*: Efforts to prevent work-related problems with others. (Morrison, 1996, pp. 497–498)	Morrison, 1996;Organ, 1997	Morrison, 1996;Webber & Klimoski, 2004; Dimitriades, 2007; Hopkins, 2002; Ma & Qu, 2011
Three-dimensional SOCB typology	Content	a. *Loyalty*: Reflects allegiance to the organization through the promotion of its interests and image to outsiders. b. *Participation*: Employee participation in the development and governance of the organization. c. *Service Delivery*: Employee conscientiousness in role performance. Performing service delivery to customers in a conscientious manner. (Bettencourt, Gwinner, & Meuter, 2001, pp. 29–30)	Van Dyne, Graham, & Dienesch, 1994;Bettencourt, Gwinner, & Meuter, 2001	Bettencourt, Gwinner, & Meuter, 2001;Coyle-Shapiro, Morrow, & Kessler, 2006; Dimitriades, 2007; Sun, Aryee, & Law, 2007; Lin, Hung, & Chiu, 2008; Wang, 2009; Tang & Tang, 2012; Chou & Lopez-Rodriguez, 2013
Two dimensional OCB typology	Content	a. *Helping*: **Affiliative-promotive** behavior directed towards improving relationships at work and focusing on harmony between employees. b. *Voice*: **challenging-promotive** behavior geared towards suggesting modifications of the status quo and bringing about constructive change. (Raub, 2008, p. 180)	Van Dyne & LePine, 1998	Binnewies, Sonnentag, & Mojza, 2009Raub, 2008

Table 28.1 Continued

Typology	Focus	Typology's Dimensions	Originally Developed by	Examples
Three-dimensional SOCB typology	Target	a. *OCB-O*: behaviors that benefit the organization in general b. *OCB-I*: behaviors that immediately benefit specific individuals and indirectly through this means contribute to the organization. (Williams & Anderson, 1991, pp. 601–602) c. *OCB-C*: Service oriented OCB targets customers. (Ma & Qu, 2011, p. 682)	Williams & Anderson, 1991;Ma & Qu, 2011	Ma & Qu, 2011
Two proposed types of customer behavior	Agent	a. *Customer coproduction behaviors*: Expected and required behaviors for the successful production and/or delivery of service.(Groth, 2005, pp. 10–11) b. *Customer citizenship behavior (CCB)*: Voluntary and discretionary behaviors that are not required for the successful production and/or delivery of the service but that, in the aggregate, help the service organization overall. (Groth, 2005, p. 11).	Groth, 2005	Groth, 2005

OCB, organizational citizenship behavior; SOCB, service-oriented organizational citizenship behavior.

Coyle-Shapiro, Morrow, & Kessler, 2006; Jiang, Sun, & Law, 2011).

ORGANIZATIONAL CITIZENSHIP BEHAVIOR TARGET

A different approach to classifying OCB focuses on the target of the OCB in service organizations (e.g., Ma & Qu, 2011). Three OCB target groups have been identified: OCB toward an individual coworker (OCB-I), OCB toward the organization as a whole (OCB-O), and OCB toward the customer (OCB-C). The two former dimensions were designated by Williams and Anderson (1991) for studying OCBs in general: OCB-I refers to behaviors that immediately benefit particular individuals and thus indirectly contribute to the organization, while OCB-O refers to behaviors that benefit the organization as a whole. An employee OCB-I could be helping a colleague who has a heavy workload, whereas an OCB-O might include volunteering for unpaid tasks or making innovative suggestions to improve the organization. The third dimension, OCB-C, has particular relevance for service organizations and focuses on employee behaviors that promote the interests and needs of customers (Ma & Qu, 2011). This dimension refers to behaviors that immediately benefit a particular customer and/or contribute to the organization's quality of service—for example, being exceptionally courteous and respectful to customers or following customer service guidelines while initiating innovative suggestions for improving service quality in the organization.

The two categorizations (according to content or target) are interrelated. Indeed, the classification of OCB-O relies heavily on the content-based classification according to conscientiousness, sportsmanship, and civic virtue dimensions (Organ, 1988), while OCB-I contains the two dimensions of altruism and courtesy (Ma & Qu, 2011; N. P. Podsakoff, Whiting, Podsakoff, & Blume, 2009). The remaining dimension, OCB-C, seems to capture all five aspects of Organ's typology (1988), specifically targeted toward the customer.

ORGANIZATIONAL CITIZENSHIP BEHAVIOR AGENT

Most research conducted on OCB in service contexts, similar to the research in general organizations, focused almost exclusively on employees rather than on customers. Service organizations are gradually involving customers in the process of service delivery (Bowen, Gilliland & Folger, 2000; Schneider & Bowen, 1985). As Groth (2005) noted, "This gap in the literature is surprising, given that organizations increasingly conceptualize customers as 'partial employees' and human resources of the organization and view effective management of customers as a strategic advantage" (p. 8). OCB research to date has focused only on behaviors that are directed at customers, but it has stopped short of examining behaviors of customers actively participating in service delivery (Bettencourt & Brown, 1997). Based on a definition of employee OCB proposed by Podsakoff and MacKenzie (1997), Groth (2005) defined customer's citizenship behavior (CCB) as voluntary and discretionary behaviors displayed by customers that are not required for the successful delivery of the service, but which help the overall service organization. Groth (2005) suggested that the conceptual distinction between in-role behaviors (i.e., task performance) and extra-role behaviors (i.e., citizenship behavior) can be extended to customers who participate in service delivery. For example, hospital patients who "speak up" and communicate safety problems to staff, or bank customers who raise valuable new ideas for service improvement.

To summarize, scholars have gradually acknowledged that the OCB research in the service sector should reflect the unique characteristics of service organizations (e.g., Bettencourt et al., 2001; Schneider et al., 2009); they conclude that OCB develops within a context and so requires the identification of unique content and target dimensions. Nevertheless, several issues in the definition and dimensionality of SOCB remained unsolved. First, Bettencourt and colleagues (2001) pioneered the development of an OCB conceptualization that is unique to the sector service and consists of the dimensions: loyalty, participation, and service delivery. Yet scholars agree that the concept should be updated to consider and include more current trends (Moon, Van Dyne, & Wrobel, 2005). It makes sense that specific aspects of the nature of frontline employees' work, as well as recent changes in the work environment, should lead to changes in the nature of OCB as well. For example, SOCB should capture not only compliant behaviors, which maintain the status quo of the organization, but also more proactive behaviors that challenge the current organizations' routines. Second, although Groth (2005) called attention to the importance of customers as OCB agents, elaboration is still needed for what exactly customers do and to whom they direct their discretionary behaviors. Given the idea that OCB is a construct that develops within a context, that is, depending on the nature of the work and the organization's characteristics, SOCB should address not only the distinctive features of the service employees' work but also of the customers' OCB. Third, research regarding the emotional aspects of OCB is scarce. This is surprising because service delivery is a social behavior that comprises at least two interaction partners (the service frontline employee and the customer). Furthermore, colleagues and other interaction partners are frequently present when an interaction is taking place (Coté, 2005; Van Kleef, 2009) and so a comprehensive theory of OCB in the service sector should consider how the various agents regulate each other's emotions for the benefit of the organization.

Toward a Comprehensive Conceptualization of Organizational Citizenship Behavior in Service Organizations

Our model for service employees' citizenship behavior suggests that the contextual characteristics of service organizations lead to a three-facet model: content (OCB and emotional citizenship behavior or ECB); target (the individual coworker, the customer, and the organization as a whole); and agent (the employee and the customer) (see Figure 28.1). By integrating these three facets, our model aims to capture the full range of OCBs, delineating those distinctive behaviors that are well suited to the service context. In the following, we start by focusing on the OCB dimension of the content facet (the first facet) and detail the three subcategories of OCBs, according to the three distinct targets (the second facet): the individual coworker, the customer, and the organization as a whole. Each of these subcategories refers to behaviors that might be performed by two distinct agents (the third facet): employees and/or customers. Then, we will describe the ECB dimension of the content facet in a similar manner.

The Facets of Organizational Citizenship Behavior

The OCB facet of the content dimension refers to an array of behaviors that are not part of the

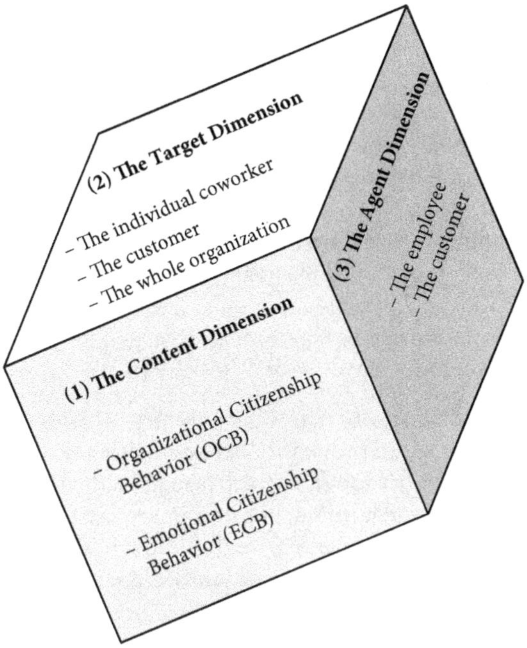

Figure 28.1 A Three-Facet Model for OCB in Service Organizations

formal obligations of the agent (employee or customer) but rather aim to contribute directly to the smooth functioning of the organization and to enhance its effectiveness. This dimension consists of more protective behaviors, behaviors that "protect organizational values, norms, and rules and prevent undesirable or unethical behavior" (Moon et al., 2005) but includes also a range of promotive behaviors, which are "proactive, adaptive, and move the organization in new directions." In accordance with the three targets and the two agents mentioned earlier, OCB dimension refers to three major subcategories, performed by two distinct agents: employees and customers.

1. *OCB toward individual coworkers.* This category represents voluntary behaviors that are directed at helping staff accomplish their tasks and duties. It comprises proactive interpersonal acts of devoting time, energy, or expertise, as well as protective behaviors that are expected to help maintain a positive work climate among staff. This category seems to capture Organ's (1998) dimensions of altruism and courtesy, and Williams and Anderson's (1991) dimension of OCB-I. Such behaviors may be performed both by employees and by customers (Groth, 2005). Examples of these types of employee OCBs are orienting new workers on how to interact with customers, even though it is not formally required; providing professional advice; or refraining from complaining about colleagues' behaviors or undesirable situations. As for customers' OCBs, these may include, for example, waiting patiently on a long queue; notifying management about outstanding service performance by a specific frontline employee; or drawing attention to safety issues so as to protect staff from hazards.

2. *OCB toward the organization as a whole.* The second category of OCBs, also performed by employees and customers alike, pertains to a more impersonal form of voluntary behaviors that do not provide immediate aid to any one specific person but rather aim to benefit the organization as a whole. It comprises proactive acts of active involvement in the organization, as well as protective behaviors that reflect extreme obedience to the organization's regulations and procedures. This category seems to capture Williams and Anderson's (1991) dimension of OCB-O, Organ's (1998) dimensions of conscientiousness, sportsmanship, and civic virtue, and Bettencourt, Gwinner, and Meuter's (2001) dimensions of loyalty and participation. Examples of employees' OCB toward the organization are strictly following work procedures; volunteering for roles that are not a part of the job description; suggesting innovative ideas to improve service delivery; or speaking up about service or safety shortcomings. Customers may similarly adapt to the organization's existing rules and work practices; speak up and suggest improvements in service or safety delivery; or speak in favor of the organization by word of mouth.

3. *OCB toward the customer.* This category refers to behaviors that are intentionally aimed at improving the quality of service toward customers and can be performed by employees and customers alike. Although OCB toward coworkers and the organization also benefits the quality of service, this category refers to behaviors directed at a specific customer at a specific service encounter. This category reflects Bettencourt, Gwinner, and Meuter's (2001) dimension of service delivery, and Ma and Qu's (2011) dimension of OCB-C. Examples of employee OCB toward customers include investing extra effort to help a customer and/or providing any assistance not included in the employee's formal duties; strictly complying with safety norms and procedures to prevent harm to customers; and devoting extra time to customers despite work overload. As for customers' OCB, a customer may familiarize another customer with

the organization's norms and procedures; provide such customer with constructive advice; or may give up on his or her turn in the favor of another customer.

Emotion-Oriented Citizenship Behavior

The second content facet of the content dimension is emotion-oriented citizenship behavior (ECB), which refers to a range of intentional, emotion-oriented extra-role behaviors. These behaviors are either emotions displayed by agents (i.e., employees and/or customers) or behaviors aimed at regulating the emotions of targets (i.e., an employee, the organization as a whole, and/or customers), thereby contributing to the psychological and social environment and consequently to the organizational effectiveness. Although emotions play a growing role in the study of organizations in general (Niven, Totterdell, Stride, & Holman, 2011), and of service organizations in particular (e.g., Hochschild, 1983; Pugh, 2001), they are only rarely manifested in any conceptualization of OCB (for exceptions, see Somech & Oplatka, 2014). Emotions have been considered in the OCB literature solely as an antecedent of citizenship behaviors (e.g., George, 1990), yet the examination of emotion-oriented behaviours as a specific facet of OCB has lagged far behind. This is surprising as organizations are social entities that consist of interpersonal encounters in which emotions play a critical role (Coté, 2005). Furthermore, emotions are perhaps not so easy to enforce, monitor, or reward, and it is, therefore, fundamental that this repertoire of ECB be identified.

Although scholars in the service sector have yet to address the emotional aspect of OCB directly, a review of the literature reveals two streams of research that can serve as a foundation for identifying ECBs in service organizations. The first stream of research focuses on theoretical concepts such as *emotional labor* and *emotional management*. These concepts refer to the deliberate management of one's emotional display by employees or customers as part of the work role (i.e., agents) to manage the encounter (Ashforth & Humphrey, 1993; Grandey, 2000; Kammeyer-Mueller, Wanberg, Rubenstein, & Song, 2013). Such management of emotions so as to create a publicly observable facial and bodily display aims to reframe the emotions of agents, thereby contributing to the psychological and social environment of the organization. The second stream, referred to as *emotion regulation*, focuses on emotion-focused behaviors that agents (employees or customers) may exhibit to initiate, enhance, or maintain the target's affect, cognitions, or behaviors (K. Niven, Totterdell, & Holman, 2009). Indeed, scholars agree that the nature of the service cannot be fully understood if we ignore the emotional aspect of human interaction, and especially the task of tending to customer needs (e.g., Niven et al., 2009, 2011).

Similar to the first content facet of OCB, ECB also consists of three major subcategories: ECB toward staff, the organization as a whole, or toward the customer, as performed by employees or customers.

1. *ECB toward individual coworkers.* This category of ECBs refers to behaviors that are above and beyond that which is required by the formal job description, but that aim to create positive emotions among staff. Although scholars in the field of service have addressed the issue of responding to customers' emotional needs (e.g., Mann & Chicago, 2005), these emotional-oriented behaviors might also be displayed and expressed internally, toward staff within the organization, and can be performed both by employees and by customers (Groth, 2005). Examples of employee ECBs are supporting a colleague in distress; helping a colleague to release tension and handle personal crises; supporting a colleague; showing sympathy; and making a colleague feel special and cared for. Examples of customer ECBs are expressing empathy toward the distress of a service employee; complementing an employee for his or her good service; and using humor to reduce stress and embarrassment during the encounter.

2. *ECB toward the organization as a whole.* The second category pertains to a more impersonal form of voluntary emotion-oriented behaviors that contribute to the organization's social environment and enhance the positive atmosphere in the organization. Employee ECBs toward the organization include behaviors such as expressing vigor and enthusiasm in the work environment; expressing positive affect during the workday; and exhibiting enjoyment at work. Customers may similarly express positive emotions of enthusiasm, excitement, and appreciation toward the organization as a whole.

3. *ECB toward the customer.* This category refers to voluntary behaviors focused at creating positive emotions in customers. Employee ECBs toward customers involve the establishment of meaningful and positive relationships that enhance the customers' well-being. Such ECBs include attentive

behaviors and sensitivity to customers' emotional needs; communicating concern; and exhibiting empathy and understanding. This range of behaviors can also be performed by customers toward other customers, thereby making them feel better.

To summarize, given the idea that OCB develops within a context, the concept of SOCB should be conceptualized according to the unique characteristics of service organizations and the distinctive features of the roles of the service encounter counterparts, namely frontline employees and customers. Our classification of SOCB in service organizations revealed two main content facets: organizational citizenship behavior (OCB) and emotion-oriented citizenship behavior (ECB). Each of the two content facets contains three subcategories that refer to the three targets of SOCBs: the staff, organization as a whole, and customers, as performed by two distinct agents: employees and customers. This conceptualization is closely linked to the unique characteristics of service organizations, emphasizing two novel ideas. First, emotions play a crucial role in service encounters and should, therefore, be manifested in any conceptualization of OCB in service organizations. Second, the growing recognition of customers' involvement in coproducing the service delivery process (Larsson & Bowen, 1989; Lengnick-Hall, 1996) highlights their concomitant role as both agents and targets of OCB.

Service-Oriented Organizational Citizenship Behavior Research: Theoretical Frameworks, Antecedents, and Consequences

The seminal theoretical work by Morrison (1996) sparked a growing research interest in OCB in service organizations. This line of research, which is still in its infancy, is heavily inspired by the common OCB models developed for nonservice sectors. These models were typically grounded in two theoretical frameworks: the cognitive and affective explanation for exhibiting SOCBs. Further research also identified the antecedents and consequences of SOCB.

Theoretical Frameworks for Understanding Service-Oriented Organizational Citizenship Behavior

Like the study of OCB in general organizations, researchers studying OCB in the service sector consistently embedded their research within the widespread cognitive and affective frameworks, with the former more common than the latter. The first approach focuses on cognitive explanations that lie mainly in the field of social exchange theory (Blau, 1964). For example, Bettencourt and Brown (1997) demonstrated the critical impact of the workplace fairness perceptions of contact employees on job satisfaction and on their pro-social service behaviors (helping behaviors directed toward customers and fellow employees). The notion of fairness underlies the norm of reciprocity in that people seek to balance their inputs and outcomes in relation to others (Eyvind, Knut-Andreas, & Are, 2012; Flynn, 2003). Ma and Qu (2011) relied on social exchange principles and reciprocity norms to show that individuals will attempt to reciprocate with those who benefit them (leaders, coworkers, and customers).

The second theoretical approach, the affective explanation, is based on the social-psychological assertion that individuals are more likely to engage in OCBs when they are in a positive mood (George, 1991). For example, Jiang et al. (2011) described how employees who are in a good mood (satisfaction) may be more likely to perceive situations and customers in a more positive light, thereby increasing their SOCB. Jain and colleagues (2012), in their study on OCB in schools, showed how the positive and negative affectivity of employees served as an explanatory mechanism that drives SOCB. Increased attraction to others and a generally favorable outlook may predispose individuals to exhibit behaviors that benefit school members, enhance organizational outcomes, or both. Furthermore, a positive mood can lead to increased social awareness, so that teachers will be more willing to display prosocial behaviors and may, therefore, exhibit OCB as a means of protecting or prolonging their positive emotional state (S. Williams & Shiaw, 1999). The affective explanation also suggests that people who are in a good mood are more helpful because being helpful is self-reinforcing or enables them to maintain their positive mood (George, 1991). All in all, research is lacking with respect to theories that have been developed to capture the unique characteristics of the service sector and that consider the mechanisms that motivate customers and frontline employees to engage in SOCB.

To conclude, the aforementioned review reflects the gradual change taking place in the study of SOCB toward embracing more context-specific models, especially regarding the consequences and antecedents of SOCB, but to a much lesser degree also in regard to the motives to engage in citizenship behavior within the service sector. Nevertheless, the challenge of understanding the emic nature of the service context and the question of generalization across sectors still remains to be solved.

The Antecedents of Service-Oriented Organizational Citizenship Behavior

Reviewing the literature reveals that most of the previous studies adapted common models that were developed within nonservice organizations into the service context. Although scholars frequently used specific typologies of service OCB, they often chose to investigate the typical antecedents that were previously examined in the context of general organizations. Antecedents represented personal employee variables such as personality traits (Wang, 2009), job attitudes (e.g., Lin, Hung, & Chiu, 2008), and organizational variables (e.g., Sun et al., 2007). For example, Lin, Hung, and Chiu (2008) examined the impact of distributive justice, procedural justice, personal cooperativeness, the need for social approval, and organizational commitment on three dimensions of SOCBs (loyalty, service delivery, and participation). In addition, Raub (2008) used a sample from the Swiss hotel industry to demonstrate that OCBs are negatively affected by a centralized organization structure. Studies from this line of research support the generalizability of OCB antecedents to service organizations.

A second trend of research on OCB in service organizations considered the unique characteristics of the service context. At the individual level, these studies investigated unique personal characteristics that are highly relevant to the service context such as service orientation and employees' customer knowledge (Bettencourt et al., 2001); at the organizational or unit level, these studies examined antecedents such as service climate and service-focused behavior (Schneider et al., 2005; Wang, 2009). For example, Schneider and colleagues sampled 55 supermarket departments and showed that the service-focused behavior of unit leaders is positively related to service climate, which in turn promotes customer-focused OCB and customer satisfaction. Surprisingly, however, the least investigated levels of antecedents were the provider–customer dyad level and customer characteristics. An exception to this is Ma and Qu (2011), who explored the customer–employee exchange, among others things, and found that the quality of the relationships between customer and employees motivated SOCB.

The Consequences of Service-Oriented Organizational Citizenship Behavior

Similar to the OCB research conducted in general organizations, less research focused on the consequences of SOCB. Yet in those studies that did explore the consequences of OCB, scholars focused mainly on service-specific outcomes such as customer loyalty (Webber & Klimoski, 2004) and customer satisfaction (Bettencourt & Brown, 1997; Jain, Malhotra, & Guan, 2012; Schneider et al., 2005). For example, Jain, Malhotra, and Guan (2012) investigated 125 medical salespeople and found that SOCB had a significant positive impact on customer loyalty. This line of research highlights a possible trickle-down effect of employee OCB on customer OCB. Put simply, the tendencies of employees to go beyond and above their prescribed role is frequently followed by enhanced customer satisfaction and loyalty. It is important to note that in the Jain et al. study, customer behaviors were not labeled as customer OCBs.

Theoretical Implications

The present conceptualization and inquiry into SOCBs has enduring value in today's focus on service organizations. The three proposed facets in the conceptualization of SOCB (content, target, and agent) reflect the unique characteristics of service organizations. The first facet, content, posits that beyond the conventional studied behaviors of OCB, emotions, as an integral part of the service provider–customer encounter, set the stage for a new array of service-oriented citizenship behaviors. The second facet, the target, highlights the customer as the main target of SOCB, above the common targets of the coworker and the organization as a whole. Finally, the third facet stresses the role of customers, as internal stakeholders of the organization, in engaging in discretionary behaviors for the benefit of the organization. The model assembles together concepts previously studied in three somewhat distinct lines of research: OCB research, emotional regulation research, and the service research. Each of these distinct lines of research has developed and used different vocabularies, and has studied different models, thereby limiting the possibility of transfer of knowledge across disciplines. As a result, there appear to be redundant and overlapping conceptualizations with no mutual enrichment of these research fields. The proposed conceptualization serves to bridge these gaps in the literature.

The model also raises questions regarding theoretical boundaries: What are the boundaries between prescribed in-role behaviors and discretionary extra-role behaviors? And what are the boundaries between the internal and external stakeholders of the organization? For example, when is the expression of positive emotions during a service provider–customer encounter considered in-role behavior and when is it considered extra-role behavior? This question is complex due to the intangible, heterogeneous, and inseparable nature of service. Such blurred boundaries may also present another challenge that faces service organizations: Certain SOCBs have the potential to benefit the organization in the short term, at the expense of long-term benefits. For example, physicians can exhibit "good soldier" behavior by reducing the number of diagnostic tests they order, thus saving organizational costs, or they may suggest a variety of diagnostic tests which go above and beyond the organization's standards, for the benefit of the patients. Although the former may contribute to the organization's efficiency in the short term, the latter can promote organizational effectiveness in the long term, by preserving customer loyalty.

Finally, our three-facet conceptualization of SOCB highlights the dyadic nature of SOCB, which unfolds in any individual encounter. The employee's SOCB might affect the customer's engagement in SOCB and vice versa. Put simply, SOCB should not be considered to be an isolated event in which the employee plays an active role toward improving service quality, but rather as a reciprocal phenomenon in which both counterparts share active roles in shaping each other's citizenship behavior. For example, if a service frontline employee invests extra efforts serving a customer, the customer may reciprocate by exhibiting extra gratitude and appreciation, thereby creating an accelerated cycle of SOCBs.

Future Research

The literature review presented herein reveals that OCB scholars have gradually adopted more context-specific conceptualizations and measures of SOCB. Yet most previous research has taken a more deductive approach by borrowing common OCB measures and adapting them to the specific context of service (e.g., Bettencourt et al., 2001). Research yearns for a more inductive, bottom-up approach that will gather information from various stakeholders—managers, employees, and customers—about their perspectives regarding SOCB. Such an approach will contribute to the development of a comprehensive conceptualization and of measures that will be sensitive to the unique characteristics of the concept of SOCB. This approach will also shed light on the boundaries between in-role and extra-role SOCB. These distinctions are, of course, difficult to define in general OCB (Belogolovsky & Somech, 2010; Morrison, 1996) and are even more complicated in the context of the service sector. As noted, the nontangibility, heterogeneity, and inseparability that characterize service organizations might challenge organizations to specify the required range of prescribed work roles (i.e., in-role behaviors; Griffin et al., 2007), let alone extra-role behaviors. In-depth interviews as well as observations of contact employees during their daily work routines can provide richer insights into SOCB.

A second goal for further research pertains to the development of context-specific models that will afford better understanding of the unique antecedents, mediators, moderators, and outcomes of SOCB. As described in the literature review, scholars have begun to identify context-specific variables, particularly with regard to the consequences of SOCB, such as service quality, customer satisfaction, and customer loyalty. Similar approaches/efforts should be applied also to the identification of the motives of SOCB. Do the two typical explainatory mechanisms offered for why agents engage in OCBs—affect and/or exchange—also apply for the case of service organizations? Is one mechanism more salient in the service sector than the other? Should we identify unique motives for engaging in SOCB? In addition, further research should integrate the type of the organization (i.e., organizations from the service/manufacturing sector) as a moderator variable, thereby enhancing our understanding with respect to the ethic and emic nature of SOCB.

A third, methodological issue for further research concerns the quandary about the best source for evaluating employee and customer SOCB. Traditional OCB literature commonly uses supervisors' evaluations of employee OCB, although in service organizations, this approach might fall short of capturing the full range of SOCB. As mentioned earlier, the capacity of managers to monitor frontline behavior is limited in service organizations. A multisource evaluation of SOCB is, therefore, warranted that will include customers, coworkers, and managers as potential raters, since each of these raters may experience different arrays of behaviors.

Integrating these different perspectives may limit potential biases in measuring SOCB and provide a more accurate and comprehensive measure of the phenomenon.

Fourth, most previous SOCB studies used a retrospective pattern of evaluation that assumed that the SOCB of a contact employee is relatively stable and consistent across time, situations, and customers (Groth, Hennig-Thurau, & Walsh, 2009). Due to the heterogeneous nature of service delivery, however, employees may vary in their level of SOCB from customer to customer and from encounter to encounter. We recommend that future research analyzes also encounters between service providers and customers as the unit of analysis. Such an approach will enable the examination of the *consistency* of service providers' SOCB, as well as fluctuations in the behavior of specific providers across encounters (Groth et al., 2009; Liu, Prati, Perrewé, & Brymer, 2010). It will also lead to more accurate reporting because SOCBs will be measured as they are implemented and experienced by employees and clients with respect to a specific encounter, instead of being collated into an average (Golfenshtein & Drach-Zahavy, 2015; Groth et al., 2009).

Fifth, the common approach to understanding OCB in general, and OCB in the service sector in particular, is to analyze it on the individual level. From that viewpoint, OCB is a personality trait or a social response to the behavior or attitude of superiors or to other motivation-based mechanisms in the workplace (e.g., Christ, Van Dick, Wagner, & Stellmacher, 2003; Zeinabadi, 2010). The individual approach, however, overlooks the possibility that SOCB can be further understood as a team or an organizational phenomenon. Such an alternative approach requires the consideration of different measurement methods such as a direct consensus model and reference-shift model (Chan, 1998). The former refers to within-group agreement to index consensus and justifies aggregation from individual- to group-level analysis; the latter refers to a higher level referent: the group or the organization level. One exception was the study conducted by Schneider et al. (2005), in which service unit leaders were asked to evaluate their unit's customer-focused OCB.

Finally, existing studies of SOCB fail to draw on the dynamic transactions between employees and customers. For example, an employee who exhibits service delivery performance that is above and beyond the standard may impact the customer's willingness to reciprocate by demonstrating customer OCB. Hence, SOCB is both a cause and an outcome, creating a trickle-down effect. Because agent SOCB may evolve over time and may likely be led by, be delayed by, or coevolve with target SOCB, it is critical to track behaviors over time. Moreover, process research can more readily uncover the causal mechanisms that shape SOCB, enabling the field to move away from simple contingencies to a deeper understanding of the complex and evolutionary role of SOCB (Santos & Eisenhardt, 2005). To summarize, research craves new methodologies that focus on multisource (e.g., managers, employees, customers), multilevel (e.g., encounter, individual, group), multitool (e.g., surveys, diaries, observations, and interviews) methods.

References

Ashforth, B. E., & Humphrey, R. H. (1993). Emotional labor in service roles: The influence of identity. *Academy of Management Review, 18*(1), 88–115. doi: 10.5465/AMR.1993.3997508

Bateman, T. S., & Organ, D. W. (1983). Job satisfaction and the good soldier: The relationship between affect and employee "citizenship". *Academy of Management Journal, 26*(4), 587–595.

Belogolovsky, E., & Somech, A. (2010). Teachers' organizational citizenship behavior: Examining the boundary between in-role behavior and extra-role behavior from the perspective of teachers, principals and parents. *Teaching and Teacher Education, 26*(4), 914–923. doi: 10.1016/j.tate.2009.10.032

Bettencourt, L. A., & Brown, S. W. (1997). Contact employees: Relationships among workplace fairness, job satisfaction and prosocial service behaviors. *Journal of Retailing, 73*(1), 39–61. doi: http://dx.doi.org/10.1016/S0022-4359(97)90014-2

Bettencourt, L. A., Gwinner, K. P., & Meuter, M. L. (2001). A comparison of attitude, personality, and knowledge predictors of service-oriented organizational citizenship behaviors. *Journal of Applied Psychology, 86*(1), 29–41. doi: 10.1037/0021-9010.86.1.29

Binnewies, C., Sonnentag, S., & Mojza, E. J. (2009). Feeling recovered and thinking about the good sides of one's work. *Journal of Occupational Health Psychology, 14*(3), 243–256.

Blau, P. (1964). *Exchange and power in social life*. New York, NY: Wiley.

Borman, W. C., & Motowidlo, S. M. (1993). Expanding the criterion domain to include elements of contextual performance. In N. Schmitt & W. C. Borman (Eds.), *Personnel selection in organizations* (pp. 71–98). San Francisco, CA: Jossey-Bass.

Borucki, C. C., & Burke, M. J. (1999). An examination of service-related antecedents to retail store performance. *Journal of Organizational Behavior, 20*(6), 943–962. doi: 10.1002/(SICI)1099-1379(199911)20:6<943::AID-JOB976>3.0.CO;2-9

Bowen, D. E., Gilliland, S. W., & Folger, R. (2000). HRM and service fairness: How being fair with employees spills over to customers. *Organizational Dynamics, 27*(3), 7–23. doi: 10.1016/S0090-2616(99)90018-9

Bureau of Labor Statistics. (2012). Occupational outlook handbook, 2012–2013. Retrieved from http://www.bls.gov/ooh/
Chan, D. (1998). Functional relations among constructs in the same content domain at different levels of analysis: A typology of composition models. *Journal of Applied Psychology, 83*(2), 234–246. doi: 10.1037/0021-9010.83.2.234
Christ, O., Van Dick, R., Wagner, U., & Stellmacher, J. (2003). When teachers go the extra mile: Foci or organizational identification as determinants of different forms of organizational citizenship behavior among schoolteachers. *British Journal of Educational Psychology, 73*, 329–341. doi: 10.1348/000709903322275867
Chou, Y. S., & Lopez-Rodriguez, E. (2013). An empirical examination of service-oriented organizational citizenship behavior: The roles of justice perceptions and manifest needs. *Managing Service Quality, 23*(6), 474–494.
Coté, S. (2005). A social interaction model of the effects of emotion regulation on work strain. *Academy of Management Review, 30*(3), 509–530. doi: 10.5465/AMR.2005.17293692
Coyle-Shapiro, J. A. M., Morrow, P. C., & Kessler, I. (2006). Serving two organizations: exploring the employment relationship of contracted employees. *Human Resource Management, 45*(4), 561–583. doi: http://dx.do.org/10.5334qpd-49-4-249
Dimitriades, Z. S. (2007). The influence of service climate and job involvement on customer-oriented organizational citizenship behavior in Greek service organizations: A survey. *Employee Relations, 29*(5), 469–491. doi: 10.1108/01425450710776290
Eyvind, E., Knut-Andreas, C., & Are, T. (2012). The strength of accountability and teachers' organisational citizenship behaviour. *Journal of Educational Administration, 50*(5), 612–628. doi: 10.1108/09578231211249844
Flynn, F. G. (2003). How much could I give and how often? The effects of generosity and frequency of favor exchange on social status and productivity. *Academy of Management Journal, 46*(5), 539–553.
George, J. M. (1990). Personality, affect, and behavior in groups. *Journal of Applied Psychology, 75*(2), 107–116. doi: 10.1037/0021-9010.75.2.107
George, J. M. (1991). State or trait: Effects of positive mood on prosocial behaviors at work. *Journal of applied Psychology, 76*(2), 299–307.
Golfenshtein, N., & Drach-Zahavy, A. (2015). An attribution theory perspective on emotional labour in nurse–patient encounters: A nested cross-sectional study in paediatric settings. *Journal of Advanced Nursing, 71*(5), 1123–1134. doi: 10.1111/jan.12612
Grandey, A. A. (2000). Emotional regulation in the workplace: A new way to conceptualize emotional labor. *Journal of Occupational Health Psychology, 5*(1), 95–110. doi: 10.1037/1076-8998.5.1.95
Griffin, M. A., Neal, A., & Parker, S. K. (2007). A new model of work role performance: Positive behavior in uncertain and interdependent contexts. *Academy of Management Journal, 50*(2), 327–347. doi: 10.5465/AMJ.2007.24634438
Groth, M. (2005). Customers as good soldiers: Examining citizenship behaviors in internet service deliveries. *Journal of Management, 31*(1), 7–27. doi: 10.1177/0149206304271375
Groth, M., Hennig-Thurau, T., & Walsh, G. (2009). Customer reactions to emotional labor: The roles of employee acting strategies and customer detection accuracy. *Academy of Management Journal, 52*(5), 958–974. doi: 10.5465/AMJ.2009.44634116
Hochschild, A. R. (1983). *The managed heart: Commercialization of human feeling*. Berkeley: University of California Press.
Hopkins, K. M. (2002). Organizational citizenship in social service agencies. *Administration in Social Work, 26*(2), 1–15. doi: 10.1300/J147v26n02_01
Jain, A. K., Malhotra, N. K., & Guan, C. (2012). Positive and negative affectivity as mediators of volunteerism and service-oriented citizenship behavior and customer loyalty. *Psychology & Marketing, 29*(12), 1004–1017. doi: 10.1002/mar.20582
Jiang, J. Y., Sun, L. Y., & Law, K. S. (2011). Job satisfaction and organization structure as moderators of the effects of empowerment on organizational citizenship behavior: A self-consistency and social exchange perspective. *International Journal of Management, 28*(3), 675–693.
Johnson, J. W. (1996). Linking employee perceptions of service climate to customer satisfaction. *Personnel Psychology, 49*(4), 831–851. doi: 10.1111/j.1744-6570.1996.tb02451.x
Kammeyer-Mueller, J., Wanberg, C., Rubenstein, A., & Song, Z. (2013). Support, undermining, and newcomer socialization: Fitting in during the first 90 days. *Academy of Management Journal, 56*(4), 1104–1124. doi: 10.5465/amj.2010.0791
Kim, T., Park, S., & Chang, K. (2011). Antecedents of organizational citizenship behaviours among part-time employees of service organizations in Korea. *Pacific Business Review, 17*(1), 85–101. doi: 10.1080/13602381.2010.495198
Larsson, R., & Bowen, D. E. (1989). Organization and customer: managing design and coordination of services. *Academy of Management Review, 14*(2), 213–233. doi: 10.5465/AMR.1989.4282099
Lengnick-Hall, C. A. (1996). Customer contributions to quality: A different view of the customer-oriented firm. *Academy of Management Review, 21*(3), 791–824. doi: 10.5465/AMR.1996.9702100315
Liao, H., & Chuang, A. (2004). A multilevel investigation of factors influencing employee service performance and customer outcomes. *Academy of Management Journal, 47*(1), 41–58.
Lin, C.-P., Hung, W.-T., & Chiu, C.-K. (2008). Being good citizens: Understanding a mediating mechanism of organizational vommitment and social network ties in OCBs. *Journal of Business Ethics, 81*(3), 561–578. doi: 10.1007/s10551-007-9528-8
Liu, Y., Prati, L. M., Perrewé, P. L., & Brymer, R. A. (2010). Individual differences in emotion regulation, emotional experiences at work, and work-related outcomes: A two-study investigation. *Journal of Applied Social Psychology, 40*(6), 1515–1538. doi: 10.1111/j.1559-1816.2010.00627.x
Ma, E., & Qu, H. (2011). Social exchanges as motivators of hotel employees' organizational citizenship behavior: The proposition and application of a new three-dimensional framework. *International Journal of Hospitality Management, 30*(3), 680–688. doi: http://dx.doi.org/10.1016/j.ijhm.2010.12.003
Mann, S., & Chicago. (2005). A health-care model of emotional labour: an evaluation of the literature and development of a model. *Journal of Health Organization and Management, 17*(4/5), 304–317. doi: http://dx.doi.org/10.1108/14777260510615369
Moon, H., Van Dyne, L., & Wrobel, K. (2005). The circumplex model and the future of organizational citizenship behavior research. In D. L Turnipseed (Ed.), *Handbook*

of Organizational Citizenship Behavior (pp. 3–23). New York: Nova Science.

Morrison, E. W. (1994). Role definitions and organizational citizenship behavior: The importance of the employee's perspective. *Academy of Management Journal, 37*(6), 1543–1567. doi: doi: 10.2307/256798

Morrison, E. W. (1996). Organizational citizenship behavior as a critical link between HRM practices and service quality. *Human Resource Management, 35*(4), 493–512. doi: 10.1002/(SICI)1099-050X(199624)35:4<493::AID-HRM4>3.0.CO;2-R

Niven, K., Totterdell, P., & Holman, D. (2009). A classification of controlled interpersonal affect regulation strategies. *Emotion, 9*(4), 498–509. doi: 10.1037/a0015962

Niven, K., Totterdell, P., Stride, C., & Holman, D. (2011). Emotion regulation of others and self (EROS): The development and validation of a new individual difference measure. *Current Psychology, 30*(1), 53–73. doi: 10.1007/s12144-011-9099-9

Organ, D. W. (1988). *Organizational citizenship behavior: The good soldier syndrome*. Lexington, MA: Lexington Books.

Organ, D. W. (1997). Organizational citizenship behavior: Its construct clean- up time. *Human Performance, 10*(2), 85–97. doi: 10.1207/s15327043hup1002_2

Organ, D. W., Podsakoff, P. M., & MacKenzie, S. B. (2006). *Organizational citizenship behavior: Its nature, antecedents, and consequences*. Thousand Oaks, CA: SAGE.

Palmer, H. C. Jr, Armistead, N. S., Elnicki, D. M., Halperin, A. K., Ogershok, P. R., Manivannan, S., & Evans, K. (2001). The effect of a hospitalist service with nurse discharge planner on patient care in an academic teaching hospital. *The American Journal of Medicine, 111*(8), 627–632. doi: http://dx.doi.org/10.1016/S0002-9343(01)00976-7

Parasuraman, A., Zeithaml, V. A., & Berry, L. L. (1985). A conceptual model of service quality and its implications for future research. *Journal of Marketing, 49*(4), 41–50.

Podsakoff, P. M., & MacKenzie, S. B. (1997). Impact of organizational citizenship behavior on organizational performance: A review and suggestion for future research. *Human Performance, 10*(2), 133–151. doi: 10.1207/s15327043hup1002_5

Podsakoff, N. P., Whiting, S. W., Podsakoff, P. M., & Blume, B. D. (2009). Individual- and organizational-level consequences of organizational citizenship behaviors: A meta-analysis. *Journal of Applied Psychology, 94*(1), 122–141. doi: 10.1037/a0013079

Pugh, S. D. (2001). Service with a smile: Emotional contagion in the service encounter. *Academy of Management Journal, 44*(5), 1018–1027. doi: 10.2307/3069445

Raub, S. (2008). Does bureaucracy kill individual initiative? The impact of structure on organizational citizenship behavior in the hospitality industry. *International Journal of Hospitality Management, 27*(2), 179–186. doi: http://dx.doi.org/10.1016/j.ijhm.2007.07.018

Raub, S., & Liao, H. (2012). Doing the right thing without being told: Joint effects of initiative climate and general self-efficacy on employee proactive customer service performance. *Journal of Applied Psychology, 97*(3), 651–667. doi: 10.1037/a0026736

Santos, F. M., & Eisenhardt, K. M. (2005). Organizational boundaries and theories of organization. *Organization Science, 16*(5), 491–508. doi: http://dx.doi.org/10.1287/orsc.1050.0152

Schneider, B., & Bowen, D. E. (1985). Employee and customer perceptions of service in banks: Replication and extension. *Journal of Applied Psychology, 70*(3), 423–433. doi: 10.1037/0021-9010.70.3.423

Schneider, B., & Bowen, D. E. (1993). The service organization: Human resources management is crucial. *Organizational Dynamics, 21*(4), 39–52. doi: http://dx.doi.org/10.1016/0090-2616(93)90032-V

Schneider, B., Ehrhart, M. G., Mayer, D. M., Saltz, J. L., & Niles-Jolly, K. (2005). Understanding organization-customer links in service settings. *Academy of Management Journal, 48*(6), 1017–1032. doi: 10.5465/AMJ.2005.19573107

Schneider, B., Macey, W. H., Lee, W. C., & Young, S. A. (2009). Organizational service climate drivers of the American Customer Satisfaction Index (ACSI) and financial and market performance. *Journal of Service Research, 12*(1), 3–14. doi: 10.1177/1094670509336743

Smith, C. A., Organ, D. W., & Near, J. P. (1983). Organizational citizenship behavior: Its nature and antecedents. *Journal of applied psychology, 68*(4), 653–663.

Somech, A., & Oplatka, I. (2014). *Organizational citizenship behavior in schools: Examining the impact and opportunities within educational systems.* New York, NY: Routledge.

Sun, L. Y., Aryee, S., & Law, K. S. (2007). High-performance human resource practices, citizenship behavior, and organizational performance: A relational perspective. *Academy of Management Journal, 50*(3), 558–577. doi: 10.5465/AMJ.2007.25525821

Tang, T. W., & Tang, Y. Y. (2012). Promoting service-oriented organizational citizenship behaviors in hotels: The role of high-performance human resource practices and organizational social climates. *International Journal of Hospitality Management, 31*(3), 885–895.

Van Dyne, L., Cummings, L. L., & Parks, J. M. (1995). Extra-role behaviors-in pursuit of construct and definitional clarity (a bridge over muddied waters). *Research in organizational behavior: An annual series of analytical essays and critical reviews, 17*, 215–285.

Van Dyne, L., Graham, J. W., & Dienesch, R. M. (1994). Organizational citizenship behavior: Construct redefinition, measurement, and validation. *Academy of Management Journal, 37*(4), 765–802. doi: 10.2307/256600

Van Dyne, L., & LePine, J. A. (1998). Helping and voice extra-role behaviors: Evidence of construct and predictive validity. *Academy of Management Journal, 41*(1), 108–119.

Van Kleef, G. A. (2009). How emotions regulate social life the emotions as social information (EASI) model. *Current Directions in Psychological Science, 18*(3), 184–188. doi: 10.1111/j.1467-8721.2009.01633.x

Wang, M.-L. (2009). What makes a good citizen in service settings? *The Service Industries Journal, 29*(5), 621–634. doi: 10.1080/02642060902720055

Webber, S. S., & Klimoski, R. J. (2004). Client–project manager engagements, trust, and loyalty. *Journal of Organizational Behavior, 25*(8), 997–1013. doi: 10.1002/job.294

Williams, L. J., & Anderson, S. E. (1991). Job satisfaction and organizational commitment as predictors of organizational citizenship and in-role behaviors. *Journal of Management, 17*(3), 601–617. doi: 10.1177/014920639101700305

Williams, S., & Shiaw, W. T. (1999). Mood and Organizational Citizenship Behavior: The Effects of Positive Affect on Employee Organizational Citizenship Behavior Intentions. *Journal of Psychology, 133*(6), 656–668. doi: 10.1080/00223989909599771

Zeinabadi, H. (2010). Job satisfaction and organizational commitment as antecedents of Organizational Citizenship Behavior (OCB) of teachers. *Procedia—Social and Behavioral Sciences, 5*, 998–1003. doi: http://dx.doi.org/10.1016/j.sbspro.2010.07.225

Zeithaml, V. A. (1981). How consumer evaluation processes differ between goods and services. *Marketing of Services, 9*(1), 25–32.

CHAPTER

29 Implicit Trait Policies About Prosocial Professionalism

Stephan J. Motowidlo, Harrison J. Kell, Michelle P. Martin, *and* Kamalika Ghosh

Abstract

Prosocial elements of organizational citizenship behavior, contextual performance, citizenship performance, extra-role behavior, and organizational spontaneity are driven largely by beliefs about the importance of prosocial behavior for work effectiveness. These beliefs are a person's prosocial implicit trait policy (ITP). We discuss recent theoretical and empirical work that develops the concept of prosocial ITP and tests hypotheses about relations between (a) prosocial ITPs; (b) their trait antecedents in agreeableness, benevolent values, social vocational interests, and emotional intelligence; and (c) their consequences for prosocial performance. Because prosocial action is especially critical in occupations that involve providing services and help to others, we focus primarily on management and administration, voluntary community service, medical practice, and legal practice. We review studies performed to develop measures of prosocial ITPs and test their relations with basic traits and prosocial performance. We also describe an effort to develop a generic measure of prosocial ITP.

Key Words: prosocial, organizational citizenship behavior, contextual performance, citizenship performance, organizational spontaneity, extra-role behavior

This chapter argues that prosocial elements of organizational citizenship behavior (Smith, Organ, & Near, 1983), contextual performance (Borman & Motowidlo, 1993), citizenship performance (Borman, Penner, Allen, & Motowidlo, 2001), extra-role behavior (Van Dyne, Cummings, & Parks, 1995), and organizational spontaneity (George & Brief, 1992) are driven largely by beliefs about the importance of prosocial behavior for work effectiveness. These beliefs are a person's prosocial implicit trait policy (ITP) (Motowidlo, Hooper, & Jackson, 2006a, 2006b). We discuss recent theoretical and empirical work that develops the concept of prosocial ITP and tests hypotheses about relations between (a) prosocial ITPs; (b) their trait antecedents in agreeableness, benevolent values, social vocational interests, and emotional intelligence; and (c) their consequences for prosocial performance. Because prosocial action is especially critical in occupations that involve providing services and help to others, we focus primarily on management and administration, voluntary community service, medical practice, and legal practice. The form of prosocial expressions varies from one occupation to another, but they all involve providing help to others. After a brief explanation of concepts that guide this work, we review studies done to develop measures of prosocial ITPs for managers, community service volunteers, doctors, and lawyers and test their relations with basic traits and prosocial performance. We also describe an effort to develop a generic measure of prosocial ITP potentially applicable to all these professions, and perhaps others as well.

Conceptual Background

Prosocial Professionalism

Brief and Motowidlo (1986) defined prosocial organizational behavior as "behavior which is (a) performed by a member of an organization,

(b) directed toward an individual, group, or organization with whom he or she interacts while carrying out his or her organizational role, and (c) performed with the intention of promoting the welfare of the individual, group, or organization toward which it is directed" (p. 711). Their definition encompasses prosocial acts that are organizationally *functional* by facilitating the organization's mission and organizationally *dysfunctional* by impeding its mission. George and Brief (1992) took issue with the notion that prosocial acts could be either organizationally functional or dysfunctional. They promoted a different idea, organizational spontaneity, which includes prosocial acts such as helping coworkers, protecting the organization, making constructive suggestions, developing oneself, and spreading goodwill, but only in forms that "facilitate the accomplishment of organizational goals" (p. 311).

This definitional disagreement about whether prosocial behavior should necessarily be defined as organizationally functional or whether prosocial actions can have either functional or dysfunctional consequences for the organization foreshadows the main theme that underlies prosocial professionalism and the concept of prosocial implicit trait policy in this chapter.

Because professional services involve helping others, prosocial action is an essential aspect of effective professional job performance. By the same token, antisocial action that hurts others in either blatant or subtler ways is an aspect of ineffective professional performance.

We frame prosocial and antisocial professionalism as aspects of effective and ineffective job performance in four different professional roles: management and administration, voluntary community service, medical practice, and legal practice. The way prosocial action contributes to professional effectiveness is very different from one occupation to another, but we hope to show that underlying all of them is the fundamental idea that helping others is effective professional job performance and hurting others is ineffective professional job performance.

Thus, like George and Brief (1992), our concern here is with expressions of prosocial behavior that are organizationally functional. We are also concerned with expressions of antisocial behavior that are organizationally dysfunctional. There is still ample room, however, for people to disagree on just how effective prosocial action is and just how ineffective antisocial action is. Some people might believe that what is generally regarded as prosocial and effective in a particular profession is actually ineffective, or that what is generally regarded as antisocial and ineffective is actually effective. That disagreement about the effectiveness or ineffectiveness of prosocial and antisocial work behavior is the cornerstone of our argument about the nature of individual differences in prosocial ITPs, as measured by situational judgment tests (SJTs).

Situational Judgment Tests

Written forms of situational judgment tests (SJTs) typically describe problematic work situations and present alternative actions for dealing with them (Motowidlo, Dunnette, & Carter, 1990). They instruct applicants to select response options they would most and least likely perform, identify the best and worst response options, or rate response options' effectiveness. They are usually scored by comparing applicants' responses to subject matter experts' (SMEs') judgments about the response options' effectiveness. When scored this way, SJTs measure procedural knowledge about effective action in the work situations they describe (Clevenger, Pereira, Wiechmann, Schmitt, & Harvey, 2001; McDaniel & Nguyen, 2001; Motowidlo, Borman, & Schmit, 1997; Motowidlo, Hanson, & Crafts, 1997; Weekley & Jones, 1999). An example of an SJT item appears next:

> You and someone from another department are jointly responsible for coordinating a project involving both departments. This other person is not carrying out his share of the responsibilities. You would . . .
>
> (a) Discuss the situation with your manager and ask him to take it up with the other person's manager.
>
> (b) Remind him that you need his help and that the project won't be completed effectively without a full team effort from both of you.
>
> (c) Tell him that he is not doing his share of the work, that you will not do it all yourself, and that if he does not start doing more, you'll be forced to take the matter to his manager.
>
> (d) Try to find out why he is not doing his share and explain to him that this creates more work for you and makes it harder to finish the project.
>
> (e) Get someone else from his department to help with the project.

Although SJTs traditionally present multiple response options for each situational stem, Motowidlo, Crook, Kell, and Naemi (2009) described a different format that presented only a single response option per situational stem. They noted that if an SJT format is designed to force respondents to choose response options they would most and least likely carry out or that are most and least effective, then obviously the format must provide multiple response options per SJT item. But if the response format is designed to ask respondents to rate response options for the level of effectiveness they portray (e.g., Chan & Schmitt, 2002), multiple response options are no longer necessary and, in fact, SJT items can present only a single response option each.

Implicit Trait Policy

Motowidlo et al. (2006a, 2006b) introduced the concept of implicit trait policy (ITP) to explain how people form judgments about the effectiveness of SJT response options. They proposed that people base those judgments implicitly on the personality traits the response options express. Thus, ITPs are "policies" like those studied in the policy-capturing literature (Karren & Barringer, 2002) except that instead of attempting to explain how people make evaluative judgments about matters such as job search, compensation, employee discipline, job analysis, employment interviews, and so on, ITPs concern evaluations in the form of judgments about the effectiveness of response options in SJT items. The policies that ITPs attempt to capture are about how people use information about personality traits expressed in response options when forming these evaluative judgments.

Prosocial ITPs vary across individuals, as explained by Motowidlo's (2003) notion of "dispositional fit." The point here is that while ability, experience, and conscientiousness facilitate the acquisition of all kinds of knowledge and skill, a different mechanism is involved in the acquisition of knowledge about effective interpersonal behavior. When the most effective responses to interpersonal situations are prosocial responses, the notion of dispositional fit argues that people who are highly prosocial are more likely to "know" that prosocial responses are more effective. Having more knowledge in this case means that people weigh prosocial cues in SJT response options more heavily when judging whether an SJT response option is effective. This knowledge is a person's prosocial ITP.

One major aspect of the overall theory that guides this work is the prediction that people who correctly believe, and therefore know, that prosocial behavior is effective and antisocial behavior is not are more likely to behave prosocially. This knowledge is their prosocial ITP. Therefore, the theory predicts that prosocial ITPs incline people to behave prosocially.

A second major aspect of the overall theory is that people with certain traits are more likely to develop prosocial ITPs. Adopting George's (1992) definition, "Prosocial behavior is helping behavior; it is behavior that is performed with the intent to aid or benefit another individual" (p. 197), we focus on traits that we expect are antecedents of prosocial ITP because they are related conceptually and/or empirically to helping behavior. They include *agreeableness*, which is often mentioned as an important determinant of prosocial behavior in general and volunteerism in particular (Graziano, Habashi, Sheese, & Tobin, 2007; Penner, Dovidio, Piliavin, & Schroeder, 2005; Snyder & Dwyer, 2013); *values for benevolence*, which, according to Schwartz (2012), "emphasize voluntary concern for others' welfare (helpful, honest, forgiving, responsible, loyal, true friendship, mature love)" (p. 7); *social vocational interests*, which are presumed to orient people toward vocational activities that involve personal service, teaching, and helping others (Holland, 1985); and *emotional intelligence*, which seems to incline people to criticize others less frequently (Brackett, Rivers, Schiffman, Lerner, & Salovey, 2006), behave less aggressively (Brackett, Mayer, & Warner, 2004), engage in less conflict with others (Lopes et al., 2011), and help others more frequently (Lopes, Salovey, Côté, & Beers, 2005). Thus, we expect that people who are agreeable, benevolent, interested in social vocational pursuits, and emotionally intelligent are more likely to learn and believe that prosocial action is professionally effective and that antisocial action is professionally ineffective. Of the Big Five personality traits, we singled out agreeableness as one that is most clearly associated with helping behavior. We expect the other four personality traits are not so directly associated with helping behavior. This provides an opportunity to test the discriminant validity of our measures of prosocial ITP because they should be more strongly correlated with agreeableness than with conscientiousness, extraversion, openness, or emotional adjustment.

As mentioned, SJTs that are intended to measure procedural knowledge are usually scored by comparing a person's responses to SMEs' judgements about the response options' effectiveness. People get higher SJT scores for procedural knowledge when their judgments of response option *effectiveness* correspond more closely to SMEs' judgments. Measuring prosocial ITP instead of procedural knowledge with an SJT requires a shift in scoring strategy. People get higher SJT scores for prosocial ITP when their judgments of response option effectiveness correspond more closely to the response options' *prosociality*. This means response options must first be scaled according to how prosocial or antisocial they are. This process does not require SMEs who are necessarily familiar with the job targeted by the SJT because it involves judgments about psychological traits expressed by specific behaviors, not how effective or ineffective those behaviors are in a particular work context. Consequently, psychologists or doctoral students in psychology can serve as SMEs for the purpose of providing judgments about response option prosociality. The mean of such judgments can serve as response options' prosociality scores.

The correspondence between response options' prosociality scores and someone's ratings of response option effectiveness is the magnitude of the effect of response option prosociality on an individual's ratings of response option effectiveness. That effect size reflects someone's implicit policy about the importance of prosocial expression for response option effectiveness, or their prosocial ITP. It can be calculated in various ways depending on the specific format of SJT items.

If the SJT format for either multiple-response or single-response SJT items calls for *ratings* of response option effectiveness, one possibility would be to calculate the correlation between an individual's effectiveness ratings and response options' prosociality scores across all response options. That correlation coefficient is the prosocial ITP score.

If response options have been developed specifically to be either extremely prosocial or extremely antisocial, the correlation just described is essentially a point-biserial correlation and can be approximated simply by the difference between mean effectiveness ratings a person gives to the prosocial response option minus the mean effectiveness ratings the person gives to the antisocial response options. Thus, people would get higher prosocial ITP scores if they gave high effectiveness ratings to the prosocial response options and low effectiveness ratings to the antisocial response options.

If the SJT format requires people to *choose* from among multiple alternative response options one they would most likely perform and one they would least likely perform, or one they think is best and one they think is worst, the prosocial ITP score can be calculated by subtracting the mean prosociality scores for options chosen as least likely or worst from the mean prosociality scores for options chosen as most likely or best.

Regardless of SJT format and the statistic used to represent ITP scores, people score higher when their ratings or response option choices correspond to those of experts—that is, when they identify response options that experts consider prosocial as "effective" and when they identify response options that experts consider antisocial as "ineffective."

The remainder of this chapter reviews studies in which we developed SJTs to measure prosocial ITPs and used them to test hypotheses about relations between prosocial ITPs; their antecedents in agreeableness, social vocational interests, benevolent values, and emotional intelligence; and their consequences for prosocial performance in real or simulated work settings.

Prosocial Professionalism in Management and Administration

Prosocial behaviors that involve helping others appear in various forms in discussions about performance requirements of management and administrative jobs. For instance, they appear in the form of performance dimensions such as (a) guiding, directing, and motivating subordinates and providing feedback; training, coaching, and developing subordinates; and maintaining good working relationships with superiors, peers, and subordinates (Borman & Brush, 1993); (b) consulting, supporting, recognizing, and developing (Yukl, Gordon, & Taber, 2002); (c) consideration, support, person-centered (Campbell, 2012); and (d) compassion and sensitivity (Conway, 2000). Thus, although management and administrative jobs often involve more technical matters such as planning and organizing, administration and paperwork, decision making/problem solving, and monitoring and controlling resources (Borman & Brush, 1993), because these positions also require close and frequent interactions with superiors, peers, subordinates, and others, prosocial actions are frequently required for management effectiveness and antisocial actions will frequently detract from management effectiveness.

Several studies of prosocial ITP in management and administration used agreeableness as a proxy for prosociality. Agreeableness is a broader trait than prosociality because it includes facets such as trusting, forgiving, soft-hearted, and tolerant, which do not necessarily involve helping others directly. However, since agreeableness also includes other trait facets that do involve helping others more directly, such as courteous, flexible, good-natured, and cooperative (Barrick & Mount, 1991), results of these studies can be interpreted as preliminary tests of the hypotheses that prosocial ITP is associated with traits related to prosociality and with prosocial performance.

Motowidlo et al. (2006a) described two studies in which SJTs that were developed to predict managers' interpersonal and problem-solving performance (Motowidlo et al., 1990) were rescored to produce measures of ITP for agreeableness. The first study used an SJT that was a preliminary version of the SJT developed by Motowidlo et al. (1990). It had 64 situational stems with 5–7 response options each. Six doctoral students rated all response options for the level of agreeableness they expressed. Their mean ratings served as the response options' agreeableness scores. Three hundred and eighty-three undergraduates completed the SJT by rating each response option for the level of effectiveness it represented. They also completed measures of personality. An ITP score for agreeableness was computed for each student by calculating the correlation between his or her effectiveness ratings and response options' agreeableness scores across the set of response options in the SJT. That correlation was the student's ITP for agreeableness score. Agreeableness ITP scores measured in this way correlated .18 ($p < .01$) with agreeableness, .10 ($p < .05$) with conscientiousness, .05 (N.S.) with extraversion, .12 ($p < .05$) with openness, and –.02 (N.S.) with adjustment.

The second study used a 30-item SJT with five response options per stem that Motowidlo et al. (1990) developed to predict management performance. Four hundred and fifty-eight undergraduates completed this SJT by choosing one response option per stem they would most likely carry out and one response per stem they would least likely carry out. They also completed measures of personality. Using the same ratings of response options' agreeableness that were developed for the first study, students' ITP scores for agreeableness were calculated by summing the agreeableness scores for all response options they would most likely carry out and subtracting agreeableness ratings for all response options they would least likely carry out. Their agreeableness ITP scores correlated .35 ($p < .01$) with agreeableness, .20 ($p < .01$) with conscientiousness, .21 ($p < .01$) with extraversion, .16 ($p < .01$) with openness, and .11 ($p < .05$) with adjustment.

Motowidlo and Beier (2010) reported a third study with an SJT rescored to measure ITP for agreeableness. Six doctoral students rated response options for the level of agreeableness they expressed, and their mean ratings served as response options' agreeableness scores. Motowidlo and Beier rescored SJTs that were completed by 164 managers who participated in the original validity study reported by Motowidlo et al. (1990) by summing the agreeableness scores for all response options managers indicated they would most likely carry out and subtracting agreeableness scores for all response options they indicated they would least likely carry out. In the original validity study, managers' supervisors rated their job performance on four interpersonal dimensions: leadership, assertiveness, flexibility, and sensitivity. Two of these are especially relevant for our present purposes because they include prosocial behavior. They are *flexibility* (negotiating with others; working for compromise solutions when appropriate to resolve disagreement; showing willingness to revise own views when faced with new information); and *sensitivity* (showing sensitivity to the needs and feelings of others, helping others resolve sensitive interpersonal problems, pitching in to help others). We summed supervisors' performance ratings on these two dimensions to form a measure of managerial prosocial performance. The correlation between managers' agreeableness ITP scores and their prosocial performance scores is .22 ($p < .05$).

Motowidlo et al. (2006b) reported three other studies that used SJTs that were specially developed to measure ITP for agreeableness. In the first study, they developed 5 situational stems and 5 to 10 response options per stem. About half the response options were intended to describe agreeable actions and half were intended to describe disagreeable actions. An example of an SJT item with six response options appears next:

> You are in charge of a meeting with six people from other departments. One of them has a very blunt way of announcing that something that was just said is stupid or that somebody's idea just won't work. By the time the meeting is half over, he has done this twice in connection with remarks made by two different participants. You should . . .
>
> (a) during a break or after the meeting, explain to him that you appreciate his point of view, but

that his comments are hurting the other coworkers (agreeable).

(b) during the meeting, tell him to keep his rude comments to himself or he won't have a job anymore (disagreeable).

(c) during a break or after the meeting, tell him that his comments were hurting group participation, and ask him to phrase his criticisms differently (agreeable).

(d) during the meeting, ask him to leave the meeting (disagreeable).

(e) during a break or after the meeting, tell him that you don't want to hear any more comments from him unless they are positive (disagreeable).

(f) address the group as a whole and state that it is important to keep comments constructive (agreeable).

Ninety-six undergraduates completed this SJT by rating all response options for effectiveness. They also completed measures of agreeableness, conscientiousness, and extraversion. Motowidlo et al. (2006b) computed agreeableness ITP scores by summing students' effectiveness ratings for all agreeable response options and subtracting their effectiveness ratings for all disagreeable response options. The agreeableness ITP score correlated .32 ($p < .01$) agreeableness, .20 ($p < .05$) with conscientiousness, and .09 (N.S.) with extraversion.

The second study used a different set of situational stems that were originally developed for an SJT to predict nontechnical performance in a government agency. Motowidlo et al. (2006b) identified 19 stems that seemed to provide opportunities for someone to respond either agreeably or disagreeably. Then, for each situational stem, they wrote three response options to describe agreeable actions and three to describe disagreeable actions. One hundred undergraduates completed the SJT by rating all response options for effectiveness. They also completed the measures of agreeableness and conscientiousness. ITP scores for agreeableness were computed by summing effectiveness ratings for agreeable response options and subtracting effectiveness ratings for disagreeable response options. ITP scores correlated .31 ($p < .01$) with agreeableness and 15 (N.S.) with conscientiousness.

The third study used both SJTs developed in the first two studies. Ninety-nine undergraduates completed both SJTs, which were scored as before to yield two scores for agreeableness ITP. The two ITP scores correlated .71 ($p < .01$) with each other. Students also completed measures of agreeableness and extraversion and participated in seven role-play simulations. They were cast in the role of a manager interacting with people at work. Their role-play performance was recorded and rated by four research assistants for the level of agreeableness students showed. Agreeableness ITP developed in the first study correlated .07 (N.S.) with agreeableness and .08 (N.S.) with extraversion. Agreeableness ITP developed in the second study correlated .11 (N.S.) with agreeableness and .05 (N.S.) with extraversion. Agreeableness shown in their role-play performance correlated .23 ($p < .05$) with ITP scores developed in the first study and .40 ($p < .01$) with ITP scores developed in the second study.

Combined results (mean correlations weighted by sample size) across these studies of prosocial professionalism in management and administration provide support for several predictions generated by the theory that guides this work. They show that prosocial ITPs measured by SJTs about managerial work predict prosocial performance in simulated and real work settings ($r = .26$) and are correlated as expected with agreeableness ($r = .26$). Furthermore, weighted mean correlations with the other Big Five traits are lower ($r = .05$ for adjustment, .14 for openness, .10 for extraversion, and .16 for conscientiousness), providing evidence for discriminant validity. These results suggest that agreeable managers and administrators are more likely to know that prosocial action is effective and that managers and administrators who know this are more likely to behave prosocially.

Prosocial Professionalism in Voluntary Community Service

Millions of American adults volunteer to teach children and adults how to read, visit homebound people, counsel people with personal problems, and minister to people in hospitals. Because volunteers must deliberately choose to engage in these helpful activities, sustained over periods of months or even years, without remuneration, several studies have examined the motivational bases of decisions to volunteer (e.g., Clary et al., 1998; Clary & Snyder, 1999) and personality traits correlated with decisions to volunteer (e.g., Bekkers, 2005; Mitchell & Shuff, 1995; Penner, 2002).

Although these studies explain why some people are more likely to volunteer than others, they do not explain why some volunteers are more *effective* than others. Volunteering effectively is largely a matter of helping effectively. Thus, according to the central premise of this chapter, volunteers' prosocial ITPs should predict their effectiveness in dealing with clients and others during the course of their voluntary community service.

Two studies tested hypotheses about relations between SJT scores that were deliberately saturated with prosocial ITP elements, self-reported agreeableness, and job performance of community service volunteers.

In the first study (Motowidlo et al., 2009), 26 administrators and supervisors working in various volunteer agencies participated in meetings conducted to elicit critical incidents of volunteer performance. They were asked to think of an occasion when they saw a volunteer work with someone who needed help, and the volunteer was either especially effective or especially ineffective in helping that person. This produced 100 critical incidents of volunteer helping performance. Another group of 13 administrators and supervisors rated the incidents for effectiveness. Because of the instructions given to people who provided the incidents, the distribution of effectiveness ratings across incidents was markedly bimodal. Most incidents were either very effective or very ineffective.

> Examples of effective and ineffective incidents appear next:
>
> This volunteer worked with a client who had no family in state and whose family out of state disowned him because he had AIDS. When the client died, the volunteer helped to plan the funeral, notified the family, packed up the client's possessions, and attended the funeral.This volunteer was walking by the information desk in a hospital after her shift was over. She overheard someone in a wheelchair ask the person assigned to the information desk to take her to another location in the hospital. Rather than have the desk attendant leave her post, this volunteer offered to take her where she wanted to go herself.When this volunteer went to the medical records section to pick up a patient's chart, he was told the chart would not be ready for another few minutes. The volunteer complained loudly, became verbally aggressive, and expressed anger at having to wait.When this volunteer was assigned to monitor children in a church nursery, she sat on a table, watched without interacting with them, and paid no attention to children who were crying.
>
> Seven research assistants rated the incidents for the level of agreeableness they expressed (Motowidlo, Martin, & Crook, 2013). Incidents' agreeableness ratings corresponded closely with their effectiveness ratings; effective incidents were mostly agreeable and ineffective incidents were mostly disagreeable.

Motowidlo et al. (2009) identified 25 effective incidents and 25 ineffective incidents to form a 50-item, single-response SJT. They administered this SJT and a personality test to 87 volunteers in a community service agency. The volunteers completed the SJT by rating the incident items for effectiveness. Three supervisors were available to rate the volunteers' performance on work effort, professionalism, and personal skill. Ratings on the three dimensions were summed to form a single performance composite.

Motowidlo et al. (2013) scored the SJT by summing volunteers' effectiveness ratings for effective incidents and subtracting their effectiveness ratings for ineffective incidents. Because the incidents that SMEs judged to be effective were mostly agreeable while incidents that SMEs judged to be ineffective were mostly disagreeable, scoring the SJT this way produces an index of procedural knowledge that is heavily saturated with ITP for agreeableness. This SJT score correlated .28 ($p < .05$) with agreeableness, .39 ($p < .01$) with conscientiousness, .01 (N.S.) with extraversion, .09 (N.S.) with openness, .37 ($p < .01$) with adjustment, and .12 (N.S.) with the performance composite. Although the correlation with the performance composite did not reach statistical significance, because the limited availability of supervisors forced each of them to rate a large number of volunteers, this may have made it more difficult for them to differentiate reliably between performance levels of individual volunteers.

The second study was designed to replicate the first but with a special effort to assure that performance ratings would be acceptably reliable (Crook et al., 2011). The same single-response SJT was administered to 120 volunteers in a community service agency along with a personality test. Each volunteer was rated on work effort, professionalism, and personal skill by *two* supervisors, except for seven volunteers who were rated by only one supervisor. Ratings were summed across raters and performance dimensions for each volunteer. The interrater reliability estimate for the performance composite was .72.

The SJT score, which, as mentioned, is saturated with ITP for agreeableness, correlated .28 ($p < .01$) with agreeableness, .27 ($p < .01$) with conscientiousness, .15 (N.S.) with extraversion, .28 ($p < .01$) with openness, .20 ($p < .05$) with adjustment, and .22 ($p < .05$) with the performance composite.

These results with community service volunteers largely reinforce results obtained with ITP measures based on managerial and administrative content. Prosocial ITP for volunteers predicts volunteers' performance (r = .18) and agreeableness is again correlated with prosocial ITP (r = .28). Results for discriminant validity are not as strong as they were in the managerial context. Weighted mean correlations are .32 for conscientiousness, .09 for extraversion, .20 for openness, and .27 for adjustment.

Prosocial Professionalism in Medical Practice

Discussions about professionalism in the medical literature acknowledge that there is more to being a good doctor than technical proficiency. The nontechnical side of medical practice has been the subject of intensive scrutiny recently because of widespread concern in the medical community that the public's image of the medical profession has deteriorated over the past 20 years (Stevens, 2001). This is often attributed to the growing intrusion of commercial interests in medical practice (Hafferty, 2004) that threaten physicians' professional autonomy. To restore and maintain public esteem for the medical profession (Hafferty, 2004, 2006), the medical community focused attention on the concept of "medical professionalism."

In an effort to define medical professionalism, the American Association of Medical Colleges (AAMC) and the National Board of Medical Examiners (NBME) sponsored a conference to which they invited 25 experts in medical practice and education (National Board of Medical Examiners, 2002). Conference attendees defined several categories of medical professionalism. Three are especially relevant for our purposes because they describe expressions of benevolence, caring, and consideration for patients and their families that go beyond the technical aspects of medical care: *Caring and Compassion* (treats the patient as an individual, taking into account lifestyle, beliefs, personal idiosyncrasies, support system; communicates bad news with sincerity and compassion); *Respect* (respects patient's rights and dignity; knocks on door; introduces self; drapes patients appropriately; shows respect for the patient's privacy; demonstrates tolerance to a range of behaviors and beliefs); and *Responsibility and Accountability* (arrives on time; accountable for deadlines; completes assignments and responsibilities on time).

Thus, there is a general consensus in the medical profession that prosocial actions like these represent effective medical practice. Among individual physicians, however, there may still be disagreement about this. Some physicians might feel they do not have time to spend on such niceties or perhaps that such expressions of caring and compassion do not fit their notions about a physician's professional role and status. The concept of prosocial ITP can therefore be applied to capture physicians' policies about the utility of prosocial action for medical effectiveness. And since the medical community at large values prosocial expressions like these in medical practice, physicians who believe they have utility are "correct" and consequently have more prosocial knowledge about how they should behave as medical practitioners.

Kell, Martin, and Motowidlo (2011; Ghosh, Motowidlo, & Nath, 2015; Kell, Motowidlo, Martin, Stotts, & Moreno, 2014) reported the development of a single-response SJT to measure prosocial ITP in the form of knowledge about the importance of prosocial and antisocial actions in these categories of medical professionalism. They interviewed nurses about occasions when they saw a doctor interact with a patient in a way they thought was especially effective or especially ineffective. After collecting judgments from other nurses about the level of effectiveness represented in these incidents, Kell et al. (2014) identified 200 incidents that described prosocial or antisocial examples of high or low levels of caring and compassion, respect, or accountability. They form the preliminary test of prosocial knowledge about medical professionalism, which was labeled Opinions about Physicians' Interactions with Patients (OPIP). Examples of incidents describing effective prosocial and ineffective antisocial behavior for each of the three categories of professionalism appear next:

Caring and Compassion: When a 10-year-old with a broken arm needed surgery, the anesthesiologist introduced herself to the parents and then knelt down to the child's eye level to introduce herself to the child. A woman had an ultrasound to confirm that her baby died before birth. The physician looked at the monitor and said, "Yep, it's a fatal demise. See, there's the collapsed skull," then walked out of the room without speaking to the patient. *Respect:* A woman had her first appointment with an obstetrician. The physician performed a thorough exam and waited until the patient was fully dressed before discussing results of the exam. When the physician learned that a patient who had a stroke had not been doing her exercises, he yelled at the patient for several minutes. *Responsibility and*

Accountability: When staff at one hospital said a patient had leukemia while staff at another hospital said he did not, the physician went through all of the patient's medical records, formed a team to investigate the matter, and developed a detailed plan to address the situation. A patient recently diagnosed with cancer came in for a minor procedure. The surgeon was delayed. When called by the nurses, he said he would be there in 30 minutes, but he did not arrive until 4 hours later.

One hundred and fifty students in their third or fourth year of medical school completed the OPIP by rating its items according to the levels of effectiveness they depict. Their effectiveness ratings for antisocial items were subtracted from their effectiveness ratings for prosocial items to form a measure of their prosocial ITP or knowledge about the utility of prosocial action in medical practice.

In their third year of medical school, students cycle through a series of rotations (i.e., clerkships) of approximately 1–2 months in each of several clinical areas. At the end of their clerkship in each area, faculty members evaluate their performance. For this study, only their evaluations for their Family Medicine clerkship were available. The evaluation form used for this purpose asks for ratings on 10 dimensions of technical and nontechnical medical performance.

A principal component analysis on the 10 evaluation ratings produced two components. The five technical dimensions loaded primarily on the first component: assessment and organizational skills, clinical problem solving, technical skills, knowledge in subject area, and mastery of principles of family practice. The five nontechnical or professional dimensions loaded primarily on the second component: relationships with patients, professional relationships, educational attitudes, initiative and interest, and attendance and dependability. To further tease apart technical and professional aspects of the performance ratings, we computed a component score for each.

The prosocial ITP score correlated –.06 (NS) with the technical component score and .19 (p < .05) with the professional component score. Since prosocial ITP should predict prosocial professionalism, it should be correlated with the professional component score, but not necessarily with the technical component score.

Data from this study were used to identify a smaller subset of items for a shorter test that might also prove to be more valid. Correlations between SJT knowledge items and the professional component score were used to identify 20 items describing effective professionalism and 20 items describing ineffective professionalism with the best item-criterion correlations. These 40 items make up the shortened version of the OPIP used in subsequent studies reported here.

In a second study along these lines, Kell et al. (2014) administered the 40-item OPIP and a personality test to 208 medical students in their third year of study. Faculty evaluations of students' clerkship performance were available for both primary care areas (family medicine, internal medicine, pediatrics) and secondary care areas (obstetrics/gynecology, neurology, psychiatry, surgery). Because secondary care physicians do not typically develop relationships with patients that are as long-lasting as they are with primary care physicians, the interpersonal and communication aspects of prosocial knowledge are likely to be more relevant for primary care physicians. Thus, the main focus for medical students' performance in this study is on their primary care performance. We summed the ratings across performance dimensions for the three primary care areas to form an overall composite of clinical performance in primary care. Students' scores for their performance in standardized role-plays with actors simulating patients needing medical consultation were also available. Prosocial ITP measured by the OPIP correlated .31 (p < .01) with agreeableness, .11 (N.S.) with conscientiousness,–.11 (N.S.) with extraversion, .04 (N.S.) with openness, .08 (N.S.) with adjustment, .22 (p < .01) with clinical performance in primary care, and .20 (p < .05) with performance in the role-play simulations.

Ghosh et al. (2015) reported a study in which they administered the OPIP to 196 Indian medical students in their third, fourth, and fifth years of study. At the end of each year of study, students complete a 2-hour practical examination, which involves patient–physician interactions in various forms of hands-on clinical performance. Prosocial ITP measured by the OPIP correlated .25 (p < .01) with clinical performance measured in these practical examinations.

Martin-Raugh, Kell, and Motowidlo (2016) reported two studies with undergraduates in role-plays simulating physicians' interactions with patients and others. In the first study 102 undergraduates completed the OPIP, a personality test, and a test of values. Then they participated in nine role-play simulations, which took about 1 minute each. The role-plays cast them in the role of a physician dealing with patients and others in challenging interpersonal situations. The role-plays were recorded and later rated by six doctoral students for students' prosocial performance in caring and compassion and respect shown to others. Ratings were combined across dimensions and raters for each student to form composite scores for prosocial performance. Prosocial ITP measured by the OPIP correlated .33 ($p < .01$) with agreeableness, .07 (N.S.) with conscientiousness, .11 (N.S.) with extraversion, .00 with openness, .03 (N.S.) with adjustment, .37 ($p < .01$) with benevolent values, and .22 ($p < .05$) with prosocial performance in the simulations.

In the second study, Martin-Raugh et al. (2016) administered the OPIP to another sample of 199 undergraduates along with measures of personality and emotional intelligence. Students then participated in the same role-play simulations that cast them as physicians dealing with patients and others. The role-plays were recorded. Three doctoral students rated undergraduates' performance for caring and compassion and three other doctoral students rated their performance for respect. Ratings were summed over dimensions and raters to produce a single score for prosocial performance for each student. Prosocial ITP measured by the OPIP correlated .27 ($p < .01$) with agreeableness, .20 ($p < .01$) with conscientiousness, .05 (N.S.) with extraversion, .15 ($p < .05$) with openness, .06 (N.S.) with adjustment, .22 ($p < .01$) with the understanding part of emotional intelligence, .41 ($p < .01$) with the management part of emotional intelligence, and .21 ($p < .01$) with prosocial performance in the role-play simulations.

Finally, 150 undergraduates participated in a study in which they completed the 40-item OPIP and measures of personality, benevolent values, social vocational interests, and emotional intelligence. Prosocial ITP measured by the OPIP correlated .33 ($p < .01$) with agreeableness, .13 (N.S.) with conscientiousness, .04 (N.S.) with extraversion, .08 (N.S.) with openness, .01 (N.S.) with adjustment, .35 ($p < .01$) with benevolent values, .35 ($p < .01$) with social vocational interests, .32 ($p < .01$) with emotional intelligence in the form of emotional understanding, and .30 ($p < .01$) with emotional intelligence in the form of emotional management.

Overall, these results with prosocial ITP in the medical context further support findings obtained in managerial and volunteer professional contexts. Prosocial ITP predicts prosocial performance in medical settings ($r = .22$) and is correlated as expected with individual differences in agreeableness ($r = .31$), benevolent values ($r = .36$), social interests ($r = .36$), the understanding component of emotional intelligence ($r = .26$), and the management component of emotional intelligence ($r = .36$).

Prosocial Professionalism in Legal Practice

In his address to the American Law Institute in 1971 on "The Necessity for Civility," the Honorable Warren E. Burger, who was then Chief Justice of the United States Supreme Court, said, "The essence of the matter is that if the rights of individuals or society as a whole are to be protected, it can be accomplished only in a judicial environment of calm, orderly civility" (p. 216). His address marks the beginning of a civility movement (Aspen, 1998; Glist, 2000) that has preoccupied many lawyers, jurists, legal scholars, and other commentators (Dickson & Jackson, 1994) over the past 44 years. Many legal professionals are certainly deeply concerned about incivility in the legal profession and are convinced that lawyers' uncivil behavior has dysfunctional consequences for society, the legal profession, practicing attorneys, and the clients they serve.

Hallmarks of lawyers' incivility include rudeness, aggressiveness, abusiveness, uncooperativeness, intimidation, threats, dishonesty, deceit, and trickery in relations between legal professionals (Aspen, 1991). Some negative consequences of incivility that have been widely discussed are these: feelings of dissatisfaction among many lawyers and judges who find that professional relations in legal practice are becoming less congenial and more abrasive (Aspen, 1991; Browe, 1994; Tomain & Watts, 2002); overloading of trial dockets because lawyers' tactical delays and unnecessary argumentative skirmishes burn up court time and generate additional unnecessary information for the courts to process (Browe, 1994); negative stereotypes about the legal profession and the public's loss of respect for lawyers (Daicoff, 1997; Kelly, 1998; Lyon, 2008); and increased legal costs for clients because lawyers' incivility adds unnecessary time to legal proceedings (Aspen, 1994; Browe, 1994).

Despite the potential for negative consequences like these, incivility might actually produce some favorable consequences—favorable, that is, for the lawyers who practice with incivility. Some lawyers may choose to practice with incivility because they believe uncivil words and actions are justified in the pursuit of zealous advocacy and will have utility for accomplishing their clients' objectives. Some lawyers, for example, may believe that some forms of incivility disadvantage opponents by depriving them of time to process information and develop counterarguments; bully opponents into taking courses of action not in their best interests; deprive opponents of information that might help their case; confuse, distract, or put opponents off balance so they will be less effective in making their own case; or misinform opponents in ways that weaken their case.

It is abundantly clear, however, that even if some lawyers practice with incivility, the wider professional standard encourages lawyers to be civil. Bar associations in many, if not all, states developed creeds that exhort lawyers to behave civilly in their professional dealings. For instance, in 1989, the Supreme Court of Texas and the Criminal Court of Criminal Appeals promulgated "The Texas Lawyer's Creed—A Mandate for Professionalism." According to that document,

The conduct of a lawyer should be characterized at all times by honesty, candor, and fairness. In fulfilling his or her primary duty to a client, a lawyer must be ever mindful of the profession's broader duty to the legal system.

The Supreme Court of Texas and the Court of Criminal appeals are committed to eliminating a practice in our State by a minority of lawyers of abusive tactics which have surfaced in many parts of our country. We believe such tactics are a disservice to our citizens, harmful to clients, and demeaning to the profession.

The abusive tactics range from lack of civility to outright hostility and obstructionism.

The Texas Lawyer's Creed urges lawyers to endorse practices such as these:

> "I will advise my client that civility and courtesy are expected and are not a sign of weakness." "I will advise my client of proper and expected behavior." "I will be courteous, civil, and prompt in oral and written communications." "I can disagree without being disagreeable. I recognize that effective representation does not require antagonistic or obnoxious behavior." "I will treat counsel, opposing parties, the Court, and members of the Court staff with courtesy and civility."

Thus, civility in legal practice is an important prosocial aspect of legal professionalism in much the same way that caring and compassion, respect, and accountability in medical practice are important prosocial aspects of medical professionalism. In both cases, prosocial professionalism as defined by professional organizations can be construed as a professional requirement that goes beyond technical requirements of the profession, and just as caring and compassion, respect, and accountability enhance a doctor's professional effectiveness, civility enhances a lawyer's professional effectiveness. Also like the medical profession, although professional legal standards promote the importance of prosocial action for professional effectiveness, some lawyers practice their profession with apparent indifference to these standards. This suggests that lawyers vary in their beliefs about the utility of civility for lawyering effectiveness and, therefore, in their prosocial ITPs.

We conducted two studies designed to measure prosocial ITPs in legal practice and to identify personal characteristics associated with prosocial ITPs.

We interviewed 49 attorneys and 10 judges about occasions when they saw an attorney interact with another attorney, a judge, or a client in a way that struck them as especially professional and effective or especially unprofessional and ineffective. The interviews produced 546 incidents from which we selected 207 that seemed to describe examples of civil or uncivil attorney conduct.

Five persons, including two experienced lawyers, one psychologist, and two doctoral students in psychology, independently read the incidents and determined whether each illustrated a civil or an uncivil action. All five persons agreed on 77 actions that describe civil actions and 96 actions that describe uncivil actions.

To shorten the list of actions for the next stage of the study, we asked 50 undergraduates to rate each of the 207 actions for the level of effectiveness it represented. After summing effectiveness ratings for the civil action and subtracting effectiveness ratings for the uncivil actions, we identified 50 civil actions with the highest item-total correlations and 50 uncivil actions with the highest item-total correlations.

Finally, 113 law students who were enrolled in a Professional Responsibility class rated the effectiveness of these 100 actions. After summing their effectiveness ratings for the civil items and subtracting their effectiveness ratings for the uncivil items, we identified 20 civil actions and 20 uncivil actions with the best item-total correlations. They make up the single-response SJT for prosocial ITP in legal practice, which is entitled "Opinions About Attorneys' Conduct" (OAC). Two examples of civil actions from the OAC appear next followed by two examples of uncivil actions:

When an attorney was injured and could not represent his client in court, another attorney completed his representation in trial free of charge.

When his opposing counsel asked for documents pertaining to their case, the attorney assembled the documents, organized them by category, prepared a summary sheet listing all the documents by category, and sent them neatly packaged in a box.

When a potential client approached the attorney for legal help and told him she had already spoken with another attorney about her case, the attorney responded, "That guy never won a case in his whole life."

When his opposing counsel called him to ask how information would be collected during the discovery period, the attorney told her that things would be done his way and if she did not like it, she would just have to deal with it.

We administered the OAC to 148 undergraduates with instructions to rate each of the 40 attorney actions listed there for the level of effectiveness it described. They also completed measures of personality, benevolent values, social vocational interests, and emotional intelligence. We scored the questionnaire by summing effectiveness ratings for civil actions and subtracting effectiveness ratings for uncivil actions to produce an ITP score for prosocial professionalism in legal practice.

Prosocial ITP measured by the ITP correlated .27 ($p < .01$) with agreeableness, .15 (N.S.) with conscientiousness, .05 (N.S.) with extraversion, .08 (N.S.) with openness, .02 (N.S.) with adjustment, .28 ($p < .01$) with benevolent values, .29 ($p < .01$) with social vocational interests, .22 ($p < .01$) with the management form of emotional intelligence, and .15 (N.S.) with the understanding form of emotional intelligence. These results are generally consistent with results reported for prosocial professionalism in management/administration, volunteerism, and medical practice.

Generic Prosocial Professionalism

Examples of prosocial professionalism described for managers, community service volunteers, physicians, and lawyers portray actions that, on the surface, at least, appear very different from occupation to occupation. For two reasons, however, we suspect that the apparent behavioral differences may obscure what is a fundamental commonality in these various ways to help others while performing a professional service. First, Martin (2011) reported a study done to test the hypothesis that prosocial ITP measured by single-response SJTs generalizes across occupational domains. She administered three single-response SJTs that were developed for different occupations to 152 undergraduates. One consisted of prosocial and antisocial items about physicians' actions, another about human factors engineers' actions, and a third about community service volunteers' actions. Correlations between the three SJTs ranged from .28 to .52, with a mean of .38 indicating substantial overlap across SJTs. Second, when 147 undergraduates completed prosocial ITP measures for both medical practice (OPIP) and legal practice (OAC), the two prosocial ITP scores correlated .56 ($p < .01$). This overlap in prosocial ITPs across occupational domains suggests it might be possible to develop a context-independent SJT (Krumm et al., 2015) measure of generic prosocial ITP that might predict prosocial performance in a variety of social contexts besides those represented in the content of the SJT items.

Motowidlo, Ghosh, Mendoza, Buchanen, and Lerma (in press) conducted two studies to test the feasibility of developing such an instrument. In the first study, they selected items for the SJT by reviewing items used in previous studies of single-response SJTs for physicians (Ghosh et al., 2015; Kell et al., 2014), lawyers (Yu et al., 2012), human factors engineers (Kortum & Motowidlo, 2006; Motowidlo et al., 2013), and community service volunteers (Crook et al., 2011; Motowidlo et al., 2009). Five doctoral students in psychology rated the items for the degree to which the actions they described were either prosocial or antisocial. Prosocial actions were defined as actions that express agreeableness, benevolence, compassion, caring, respect, generosity, courtesy, civility, cooperativeness, and tact. Antisocial actions were defined as actions that express disagreeableness, malevolence, coldness, indifference, disrespect, selfishness, rudeness, incivility, uncooperativeness, and insensitivity. Based on these ratings, Motowidlo et al. identified 101 items that were rated as either especially high or especially low in prosociality.

They administered this preliminary set of SJT items to 396 undergraduates who rated them for effectiveness. They computed a total score by summing effectiveness ratings for prosocial items and subtracting effectiveness ratings for antisocial items. Then they identified five prosocial items and five antisocial items for each occupational group with the strongest item-total correlations. These 40 items make up the final version of the SJT measure entitled "Opinions About Professional Conduct"

(OPC). Students also completed measures of personality, benevolent values, social vocational interests, and emotional intelligence.

Generic prosocial ITP measured by the OPC correlated .32 ($p < .01$) with agreeableness, .18 ($p < .01$) with conscientiousness, .08 with extraversion, .13 ($p < .05$) with openness, .04 (N.S.) with adjustment, .31 ($p < .01$) with benevolent values, .22 ($p < .01$) with social vocational interests, .32 ($p < .01$) with the understanding part of emotional intelligence, and .35 ($p < .01$) with the management part of emotional intelligence.

In the second study, Motowidlo et al. (in press) administered the OPC to 131 undergraduates along with measures of personality and emotional intelligence. Students also participated in five role-plays in which another student needed help and the participant could choose whether and how much to help and in five other role-plays in which someone was acting inconsiderately and the participant could choose whether and how to confront that person about his or her inconsideration. Role-plays were recorded and scored for prosociality by four researchers. Generic prosocial ITP correlated .22 ($p < .01$) with agreeableness, .20 ($p < .05$) with conscientiousness, .22 ($p < .01$) with extraversion, .14 (N.S.) with openness, .08 with adjustment, .20 ($p < .05$) with the understanding part of emotional intelligence, .42 ($p < .01$) with the management part of emotional intelligence, .24 ($p < .01$) with prosocial performance in situations where others need help, and –.02 (N.S.) with prosocial performance in situations where others acted inconsiderately.

Results of these two studies of generic prosocial ITP are consistent with results reported for the four separate professional contexts in showing that prosocial ITP is correlated with agreeableness ($r = .30$) and less so with the other Big Five traits ($r = .18$ with conscientiousness, .11 with extraversion, .13 with openness, and .05 with adjustment). It is also correlated as before with benevolent values ($r = .31$), social interests ($r = .22$), the understanding component of emotional intelligence ($r = .29$), and the management component of emotional intelligence ($r = .37$).

Summary and Conclusions

Mean correlations, with prosocial ITP for various professional contexts, weighted by sample size, are shown in Table 29.1. It shows that agreeableness correlates with prosocial ITP for managers, volunteers, physicians, lawyers, and a generic combination of professions with an overall correlation of .28 (N = 2,677). This supports the hypothesis that beliefs about the utility of agreeable and prosocial behavior are shaped in part by individual differences in agreeableness. Agreeable people are more likely to believe that agreeable and prosocial action is professionally effective and that disagreeable and antisocial action is professionally ineffective. This is true across all professional settings.

Correlations with other personality traits in the Big Five show support for discriminant validity. Overall correlations between prosocial ITP and conscientiousness, extraversion, openness, and adjustment range from .07 to .17 (N = 2,382–2,578) and are substantially lower than the overall correlation with agreeableness, as expected. Thus, our strategy for developing and scoring SJTs to target beliefs specifically about the utility of agreeable and prosocial action successfully pinpoints the intended prosociality construct.

Correlations between prosocial ITP and other traits related to helping behavior provide further support for convergent validity. Table 29.1 shows that, overall, prosocial ITP in various professional contexts correlates .32 (N = 796) with benevolent values, .26 (N = 694) with social vocational interests, .26 (N = 1,024) with the understanding part of emotional intelligence, and .35 (N = 1,024) with the management part of emotional intelligence.

The consistency of these results across professional settings supports the hypothesis that these various measures of prosocial ITP share a common underlying construct. Although expressions of prosocial action vary markedly from profession to profession, they all involve helping others and for that reason share common trait antecedents in agreeableness, benevolent values, social vocational interests, and emotional intelligence.

Table 29.1 also shows that prosocial ITPs are also correlated with prosocial performance across professional contexts with an overall correlation of .21 (N = 1,456).

All in all, results of these studies support the idea that ITPs that represent beliefs about the utility of prosocial action in professional contexts are shaped in part by trait antecedents in agreeableness, benevolent values, social vocational interests, and emotional intelligence and lead to behavioral prosocial expressions of performance in real or simulated work and interpersonal settings.

Future research may benefit from the implementation of longitudinal designs to study the malleability of prosocial ITPs. Although the effect of individuals' basic traits on their prosocial ITPs has been examined, less is known about other constructs or types of experiences that affect how these ITPs

Table 29.1 Mean Correlations With Prosocial Implicit Trait Policy Weighted by Sample Size Across Occupational Contexts

	Occupational Context					
	Managers	Volunteers	Physicians	Lawyers	Generic	Overall
Agreeableness	.26	.28	.31	.27	.30	.28
	(1,136)	(207)	(659)	(148)	(527)	(2,677)
Conscientiousness	.16	.32	.14	.15	.18	.17
	(1,037)	(207)	(659)	(148)	(527)	(2,578)
Extraversion	.10	.09	.01	.05	.11	.08
	(1036)	(207)	(659)	(148)	(527)	(2,577)
Openness	.14	.20	.08	.08	.13	.12
	(841)	(207)	(659)	(148)	(527)	(2,382)
Adjustment	.05	.27	.05	.02	.05	.07
	(841)	(207)	(659)	(148)	(527)	(2,382)
Benevolent values			.36	.28	.31	.32
			(252)	(148)	(396)	(796)
Social interests			.36	.29	.22	.26
			(150)	(148)	(396)	(694)
EI: Understanding			.26	.15	.29	.26
			(349)	(148)	(527)	(1,024)
EI: Management			.36	.22	.37	.35
			(349)	(148)	(527)	(1,024)
Prosocial performance	.26	.18	.22		.11	.21
	(263)	(207)	(855)		(131)	(1,456)

Note: Sample sizes appear in parentheses.

develop over time. Motowidlo and Beier (2010) suggested a theoretical model where both cognitive ability and individuals' general life experiences act as antecedents of prosocial knowledge in the form of ITPs, but these particular elements of the model have not yet been empirically tested. Future research may examine whether individuals higher in cognitive ability are higher in prosocial ITPs than those lower in ability, and it may explore the types of experiences that affect individuals' evaluations of the effectiveness of prosocial expressions in different situations. If particular types of experiences provide opportunities for learning about prosocial and antisocial expressions, perhaps prosocial ITPs are amenable to training interventions. Researchers may examine the efficacy of training interventions on ITP formation and application to real-world situations.

References

Aspen, M. E., & Tuite, C. H. (1991). *Interim Report of the Committee on Civility of the Seventh Federal Judicial Circuit*, Chicago, Ill: The Committee.

Aspen, M. E. (1998). A response to the civility naysayers. *Stetson Law Review, 28*, 253–266.

Barrick, M. R., & Mount, M. K. (1991). The Big Five personality dimensions and job performance: A meta-analysis. *Personnel Psychology, 44,* 1–26.
Bekkers, R. (2005). Participation in voluntary associations: Relations with resources, personality, and political values. *Political Psychology, 26,* 439–454.
Borman, W. C., & Brush, D. H. (1993). More progress toward a taxonomy of managerial performance requirements. *Human Performance, 6,* 1–21.
Borman, W. C., & Motowidlo, S. J. (1993). Expanding the criterion domain to include elements of contextual performance. In N. Schmitt & W. C. Borman (Eds.), *Personnel selection in organizations* (pp. 71–98). San Francisco, CA: Jossey-Bass.
Borman, W. C., Penner, L. A., Allen, T. D., & Motowidlo, S. J. (2001). Personality predictors of citizenship performance. *International Journal of Selection and Assessment, 9,* 52–69.
Brackett, M. A., Mayer, J. D., & Warner, R. M. (2004). Emotional intelligence and its relation to everyday behaviour. *Personality and Individual Differences, 36,* 1387–1402.
Brackett, M. A., Rivers, S. E., Shiffman, S., Lerner, N., & Salovey, P. (2006). Relating emotional abilities to social functioning: A comparison of self-report and performance measures of emotional intelligence. *Journal of Personality and Social Psychology, 91,* 780–795.
Brief, A. P., & Motowidlo, S. J. (1986). Prosocial organizational behaviors. *Academy of Management Review, 11,* 710–725.
Browe, K. P. (1994). A critique of the civility movement: Why Rambo will not go away. *Marquette Law Review, 77,* 751–784.
Campbell, J. P. (2012). Behavior, performance, and effectiveness in the twenty-first century. In S. W. J. Kozlowski (Ed.), *The Oxford handbook of organizational psychology (Vol. 1,* pp. 159–194). New York: Oxford University Press.
Chan, D., & Schmitt, N. (2002). Situational judgment and job performance. *Human Performance, 15,* 233–254.
Clary, E. G., & Snyder, M. (1999). The motivations to volunteer: Theoretical and practical considerations. *Current Directions in Psychological Science, 8,* 156–159.
Clary, E. G., Snyder, M., Ridge, R. D., Copeland, J., Stukas, A. A., Haugen, J., & Miene, P. (1998). Understanding and assessing the motivations of volunteers: A functional approach. *Journal of Personality and Social Psychology, 74,* 1516–1530.
Clevenger, J., Pereira, G. M., Wiechmann, D., Schmitt, N., & Harvey, V. S. (2001). Incremental validity of situational judgment tests. *Journal of Applied Psychology, 86,* 410–417.
Conway, J. M. (2000). Managerial performance development constructs and personality correlates. *Human Performance, 13,* 23–46.
Crook, A. E., Beier, M. E., Cox, C. B., Kell, H. J., Hanks, A. R., & Motowidlo, S. J. (2011). Measuring relationships between personality, knowledge, and performance using single-response situational judgment tests. *International Journal of Selection and Assessment, 19,* 363–373.
Daicoff, S. (1997). Lawyer, know thyself: A review of empirical research on attorney attributes bearing on professionalism. *American University Law Review, 46,* 1337–1427.
Dickson, B. E., & Jackson, J. B. (1994). Professionalism in the practice of law: A symposium on civility and judicial ethics in the 1990s: Renewing lawyer civility. *Valparaiso University Law Review, 28,* 531–541.
George, J. M. (1992). The role of personality in organizational life: Issues and evidence. *Journal of Management, 18,* 185–213.
George, J. M., & Brief, A. P. (1992). Feeling good-doing good: A conceptual analysis of the mood at work-organizational spontaneity relationship. *Psychological Bulletin, 112,* 310–329.
Ghosh, K., Motowidlo, S. J., & Nath, S. (2015). Technical knowledge, prosocial knowledge, and clinical performance of Indian medical students. *International Journal of Selection and Assessment, 23,* 59–70.
Glist, A. O. (2000). Enforcing courtesy: Default judgments and the civility movement. *Fordham Law Review, 69,* 757–785.
Graziano, W. G., Habashi, M. M., Sheese, B. E., & Tobin, R. M. (2007). Agreeableness, empathy, and helping: A person X situation perspective. *Journal of Personality and Social Psychology, 93,* 583–599.
Hafferty, F. (2004). Toward the operationalization of professionalism: A commentary. *American Journal of Bioethics, 4,* 28–30.
Hafferty, F. (2006). The elephant in medical professionalism's kitchen. *Academic Medicine, 81,* 906–914.
Holland, J. L. (1985). *Making vocational choices: A theory of vocational personalities and work environments.* Englewodd Cliffs, NJ: Prentice Hall.
Karren, R. J., & Barringer, M. W. (2002). A review and analysis of the policy-capturing methodology in organizational research and practice. *Organizational Research Methods, 5,* 337–361.
Kell, H. J., Martin, M. P., & Motowidlo, S. J. (April, 2011). *Medical students' knowledge about medical professionalism predicts their professionalism performance.* Poster session presented at the meeting of the Society for Industrial and Organizational Psychology, Chicago, IL.
Kell, H. J., Motowidlo, S. J., Martin, M. P., Stotts, A. L., & Moreno, C. A. (2014). Testing for independent effects of prosocial knowledge and technical knowledge on skill and performance. *Human Performance, 27,* 311–327.
Kelly, P. J. (1998). A return of professionalism. *Fordham Law Review, 66*(2091).
Kortum, P. T., & Motowidlo, S. J. (2006). It takes more than technical knowledge to be an effective human factors professional. *Proceedings of the Human Factors and Ergonomics Society 50th Annual Meeting.*
Krumm, S., Lievens, F., Huffmeier, J., Lipnevich, A. A., Bendels, H., & Hertel, G. (2015). How "situational" is judgment in situational judgment tests? *Journal of Applied Psychology, 100,* 399–416.
Lopes, P. N., Nezlek, J. B., Extremera, N., Hertel, J., Fernández-Berrocal, P., Schütz, A., & Salovey, P. (2011). Emotion regulation and the quality of social interaction: Does the ability to evaluate emotional situations and identify effective responses matter? *Journal of Personality, 79,* 429–467.
Lopes, P. N., Salovey, P., Côté, S., & Beers, M. (2005). Emotion regulation abilities and the quality of social interaction. *Emotion, 5,* 113–118.
Lyon, P. K. (2008). 20 reasons why people don't respect lawyers the way they used to. *The Practical Lawyer,* April, 19–21.
Martin, M. P. (2011). *The generalizability of knowledge as measured by a single-response situational judgment test across domains* (Unpublished master's thesis). Rice University, Houston, Texas.
Martin-Raugh, M. P., Kell, H. J., & Motowidlo, S. J. (2016). Prosocial knowledge mediates effects of agreeableness and emotional intelligence on prosocial behavior. *Personality and Individual Differences, 90,* 41–49.

McDaniel, M. A., & Nguyen, N. T. (2001). Situational judgment tests: A review of practice and constructs assessed. *International Journal of Selection and Assessment, 9*, 103–113.

Mitchell, C. W., & Shuff, I. M. (1995). Personality characteristics of hospice volunteers as measured by Myers-Briggs Type Indicator. *Journal of Personality Assessment, 65*, 521–532.

Motowidlo, S. J. (2003). Job performance. In W. C. Borman, D. R. Ilgen, & R. J. Klimoski (Eds.), *Handbook of psychology: Industrial and organizational psychology* (Vol. *12*, pp. 39–53). New York: Wiley.

Motowidlo, S. J., & Beier, M. E. (2010). Differentiating specific job knowledge from implicit trait policies in procedural knowledge measured by a situational judgment test. *Journal of Applied Psychology, 95*, 321–333.

Motowidlo, S. J., Borman, W. C., & Schmit, M. J. (1997). A theory of individual differences in task and contextual performance. *Human Performance, 10*, 71–83.

Motowidlo, S. J., Crook, A. E., Kell, H. J., & Naemi, B. (2009). Measuring procedural knowledge more simply with a single-response situational judgment test. *Journal of Business and Psychology, 24*, 281–288.

Motowidlo, S. J., Dunnette, M. D., & Carter, G. W. (1990). An alternative selection procedure: The low-fidelity simulation. *Journal of Applied Psychology, 75*, 640–647.

Motowidlo, S. J., Ghosh, K., Mendoza, A. M., Buchanen, A. E., & Lerma, M. N. (in press). *A context-independent situational judgment test to measure prosocial implicit trait policy, Human Performance.*

Motowidlo, S. J., Hanson, M. A., & Crafts, J. L. (1997). Low-fidelity simulations. In D. L. Whetzel & G. R. Wheaton (Eds.), *Applied measurement methods in industrial psychology* (pp. 241–260). Palo Alto, CA: Consulting Psychologists Press.

Motowidlo, S. J., Hooper, A. C., & Jackson, H. L. (2006a). A theoretical basis for situational judgment tests. In J. A. Weekley & R. E. Ployhart (Eds.), *Situational judgment tests: Theory, measurement, and application* (pp. 57–82). Erlbaum, NJ: Lawrence Erlbaum.

Motowidlo, S. J., Hooper, A. C., & Jackson, H. L. (2006b). Implicit policies about relations between personality traits and behavioral effectiveness in situational judgment items. *Journal of Applied Psychology, 91*, 749–761.

Motowidlo, S. J., Martin, M. P., & Crook, A. E. (2013). Relations between personality, knowledge, and behavior in professional service encounters. *Journal of Applied Social Psychology, 43*, 1851–1861.

National Board of Medical Examiners (2002). *Embedding professionalism in medical education: Assessment as a tool for implementation*. Philadelphia, PA: Author.

Penner, L. A. (2002). Dispositional and organizational influences on sustained volunteerism: An interactionist perspective. *Journal of Social Issues, 58*, 447–467.

Penner, L. A., Dovidio, J. F., Piliavin, J. A., & Schroeder, D. A. (2005). Prosocial behavior: Multilevel perspectives. *Annual Review of Psychology, 56*, 365–392.

Schwartz, S. H. (2012). An overview of the Schwartz Theory of Basic Values. *Online Readings in Psychology and Culture, 2*(1). http://dx.doi.org/10.9707/2307-0919.1116.

Smith, C. A., Organ, D. W., & Near, J. P. (1983). Organizational citizenship behavior: Its nature and antecedents. *Journal of Applied Psychology, 68*, 453–463.

Snyder, M., & Dwyer, P. C. (2013). Altruism and prosocial behavior. In H. Tennen & J. Suls (Eds.), *Handbook of psychology: Personality and social psychology* (Vol. 5, pp. 467–485). Hoboken, NJ: Wiley.

Stevens, R. A. (2001). Public roles for the medical profession in the United States: Beyond theories of decline and fall. *The Millbank Quarterly, 79*, 327–353.

Tomain, J. P., & Watts, B. G. (2002). Between law and virtue. *University of Cincinnati Law Review, 71*, 585–627.

Van Dyne, L., Cummings, L. L., & Parks, J. M. (1995). Extra role behaviors: In pursuit of construct and definitional clarity (a bridge over muddied waters). In L. L. Cummings & B. M. Staw (Eds.), *Research in organizational behavior* (Vol. *17*, pp. 215–285). Greenwich, CT: JAI.

Weekley, J. A., & Jones, C. (1999). Further studies of situational tests. *Personnel Psychology, 52*, 679–700.

Yu, A., Martin, M. P., & Motowidlo, S. J. (2012). Knowledge about Legal Professionalism. Poster session presented at the 120th annual convention of the American Psychological Association in Orlando, FL.

Yukl, G. A., Gordon, A., & Taber, T. (2002). A hierarchical taxonomy of leadership behavior: Integrating a half century of behavior research. *Journal of Leadership and Organizational Studies, 9*, 15–32.

CHAPTER

30 Prosocial Behavior in Retirement

Ulrike Fasbender, Mo Wang, *and* Yujie Zhan

Abstract

With the increase of the proportion of the population reaching retirement age in relation to that of working age, extensive research has been conducted to understand the retirement process and to promote older adults' well-being in retirement. In this chapter, we aim to link the theoretical concepts of retirement to the research literature on prosocial behavior. First, we provide an overview of the current conceptualizations of prosocial behavior and retirement. Second, we introduce three main areas of prosocial behavior engagement in retirement (i.e., prosocial behavior in postretirement employment, in the family context, and in the community). Third, we present a comprehensive model of the antecedents and outcomes of prosocial behavior in retirement, covering factors at the micro, meso, and macro levels. Finally, we offer suggestions to advance future research investigating prosocial behavior in retirement.

Key Words: retirement, prosocial behavior, bridge employment, family care, organizational citizenship behavior volunteering, well-being, health

Changing population compositions, as often represented by age pyramids, are the consequence of low birth rates and increased life expectancies across the 28 member states of the European Union and other highly developed economies. As such, the proportion of older people in the total population will grow in the upcoming decades (Eurostat, 2015). In particular, with the baby boomer generation (born approximately 1946–1964) reaching retirement, the share of people of retirement age in relation to those of working age will significantly increase (Eurostat, 2015). For example, as one of the world's leading economies, Germany will face a dramatic upward trend from 16% (12.7 million; old-age dependency ratio, 25; median age, 38.0) of people aged 65 years and older in 1995 to 21% (17.3 million; old-age dependency ratio, 35; median age, 45.6) in 2015 to 30% (23.2 million; old-age dependency ratio, 56; median age, 48.6) in 2035 (Federal Statistical Office of Germany, 2015a). A number of other developed countries will follow this direction assuming continued low birth rates, low immigration rates, and long life expectancy of newborns. On the one hand, economic studies note that this trend will in turn lead to an increased burden on people of working age providing social expenditure related to a range of services required by the people of retirement age. On the other hand, this trend provides a great potential for older people to engage in prosocial behavior in retirement from which many individuals, families, communities, and society as a whole will benefit.

Conceptualizations of Prosocial Behavior

Despite Charles Darwin's (1859) widely recognized principle on the "survival of the fittest," in which the most selfish people would be the ones to survive, there is widespread evidence of prosocial behavior in humankind (Dovidio, Piliavin, Schroeder, & Penner, 2010). Prosocial behavior refers to a broad category of benefiting others' behaviors, which involves an interaction between the person giving assistance (i.e., helper or benefactor) and one or more person(s) receiving help (i.e., recipient). There are certain subcategories that are important to understanding the phenomenon of prosocial behavior, namely helping, altruism, and cooperation. In short, *helping* is about people contributing to other people's well-being (Dovidio et al., 2010). Because this wide definition of helping involves several helping scenarios, Pearce and Amato (1980) derived a classification of three relevant dimensions. First, one can distinguish *formal and planned* (e.g., volunteering in a charity project) versus *informal and spontaneous* helping (e.g., giving way to someone). Second, one can distinguish helping related to the *seriousness* of the problem (e.g., giving change to allow someone to make a phone call versus providing help to someone having a heart attack). Third, helping can be distinguished in *indirect* (e.g., donating to a charity for children in need) versus *direct* behavior (e.g., rescuing a child from drowning). Although the concepts of helping and altruism are related to each other, *altruism* refers more precisely to helping behaviors in which the benefactor does *not anticipate to benefit* from his or her own helping behavior. Furthermore, in contrast to helping and altruism, which primarily refer to aid provided from one person to another, *cooperation* refers to jointly coordinated behaviors along with a *common goal.* Because cooperators interact as benefactors and recipients at the same time, the cooperative exchange leads to the *expectation of reciprocal benefit* from their joint efforts. In addition, cooperation is based on more or less *equal relationships.* In a typical helping relationship one person is in need, and the other person offers relevant resources to satisfy this need. As a consequence, the benefactor might perceive having power over the recipient, who in turn might have a feeling of indebtedness toward the benefactor. However, due to the absence of power hierarchy and the presence of common goals, cooperative exchange might facilitate a variety of positive outcomes, such as interpersonal relationships and group cohesiveness.

Conceptualizations of Retirement

From a historical perspective, the concept of retirement is a rather novel phenomenon that has continuously changed over the last century. Long before the Industrial Revolution and the introduction of social security, people continued working as long as they were able to before reaching the stage of complete physical exhaustion and work disability (Shultz & Wang, 2011). In 1889, the first social security system was introduced by Otto von Bismarck, Germany's chancellor at that time. Although the actual life expectancy was under 45 years, the initial retirement age was set at 70, indicating a limited use for the majority of people. The ratio between retirement age and life expectancy has inverted since then. In Germany, the current retirement age has been recently increased from 65 to 67, while the average life expectancy for newborn boys is about 78 years and for newborn girls about 83 years (Federal Statistical Office of Germany, 2015b). Since the beginning of the 21th century, retirement institutions and policies have started to shift dramatically due to population aging and economic uncertainty. Particularly in highly developed economies, demographic and economic changes have caused a political shift from supporting early retirement toward extending working lives and promoting active aging in society (Fasbender & Deller, 2016; Fraccaroli & Deller, 2015).

From a psychological perspective, retirement is a complex phenomenon, "not just a single event but rather a temporal process that unfolds over time" (Wang, Olson, & Shultz, 2013, p. 159). Retirement is related to a wide variety of factors that influence the planning and decision-making process during the retirement transition. To address the complexity in which the retirement process takes place, Szinovacz (2013) provided a multilevel model of retirement. This contextual approach has its origin in sociological research, assuming a reciprocal interplay between societal-, organizational-, and individual-level factors. In particular, at the macro level, retirement can be thought of as an institution based on cultural norms and values and their integration in various societal support systems. At the meso level, organizational policies and practices are integrated in the work environment, reflecting implicit forms of retirement expectations and images. Furthermore, at the micro level, retirement reflects individual pathways capturing different elements in the transition from work to retirement, such as retirement planning and decision making. Due to its comprehensive approach, the model can be used as an overarching theoretical framework for the conceptualization of the retirement process (Wang & Shi, 2014).

Different macro-level factors influence the individual retirement process (Szinovacz, 2013). Among these factors are economic and labor market conditions. As highlighted by Fasbender, Wang, Voltmer, and Deller (2016), older people are often withheld as hidden reserve in the labor market, in particular under poor economic conditions with low labor demand. In addition, legal issues are directly linked to the retirement process. For example, the pension eligibility age suggests a concrete timeline for many older people to determine their proximity to formal retirement entry (Ekerdt, Hackney, Kosloski, & DeViney, 2001). Also, cultural norms and values encourage the retirement transition and possibly portray rather positive attitudes toward retirement, which in turn facilitate retirement planning and the decision to retire early (Hershey, Henkens, & Van Dalen, 2007). Cultural norms can also influence behavioral arrangements after formal retirement entry. One example of prosocial behavior is "active aging," which has been introduced by the World Health Organization in the 1990s and subsequently promoted by political institutions, such as the European Union (Jensen & Principi, 2014). The concept of active aging refers to a broad approach of late-life engagement in society, including voluntary activities as well as labor market participation. Certain images of older people are created to promote inclusion, health, and well-being outcomes, and at the same time, individuals are implicitly expected to behave in a suggested manner, which, in turn, encourages prosocial behavior among older people (e.g., engaging in volunteering activities in the community).

At the meso level, there are different contextual factors influencing the individual retirement process, including the work context (i.e., job and organizational factors) and the life context (i.e., family and social networks). Among the relevant job and organizational factors are different human resource management policies and practices, work design characteristics, and work-related attitudes. Furthermore, individuals' decisions whether to engage in prosocial behavior in retirement are linked to their significant others (Wang & Shi, 2014). As such, family and social network factors are highly relevant in providing material and immaterial support, offering role modeling opportunities and anchoring points, and providing a socially desirable context (Szinovacz, 2013).

At the micro level, there are several individual factors that influence the planning and decision making during the retirement process. Among these factors are demographics, health and financial resources, personality, and values, as well as attitudes toward retirement (Wang & Shi, 2014). A combination of these factors generates the immediate personal context of the retirement process, often by incorporating cumulative effects (Szinovacz & Davey, 2005; van Solinge & Henkens, 2007; Wang & Shi, 2014). For example, people with a low socioeconomic status accumulate not only less human capital, such as knowledge and skills, but also are more prone to health issues, which in turn influences the structural opportunities during the later retirement process. Taken together, these multilevel factors impact the individual retirement process and, as a consequence, help understand how much effort people are able and willing to invest in prosocial behavior in retirement.

The Organization of the Chapter

The central objective of this chapter is to systematically review research literature on prosocial behavior in retirement. Building from the review, we also attempt to link traditional theoretical concepts of retirement to the current research literature on prosocial behavior. In relating prosocial behavior to retirement, we introduce three main areas of engagement, namely prosocial behavior in postretirement employment, in the family context, and in the community. Given that the context is crucial for individuals' day-to-day, activity-related decision making, it is important to examine prosocial behavior in these different activity contexts. Relying on Szinovacz's (2013) multilevel model of retirement, we also attempt to reveal the antecedents and outcomes in the three areas of prosocial behavior in retirement, as can be seen in Figure 30.1. In addition, we aim to provide directions for future research that guide further investigation of prosocial behavior in retirement.

Prosocial Behavior in Postretirement Employment

Prosocial behavior in the workplace refers to a set of behaviors directed to benefit others and to maintain the social system of a work organization (Chiaburu, Smith, Wang, & Zimmerman, 2014; Ilies, Nahrgang, & Morgeson, 2007; Sonnentag & Grant, 2012), including organizational citizenship behaviors (OCBs) and generative behaviors, such as mentoring and sense giving. As one form of work, postretirement employment refers to paid work after formally entering retirement (i.e., after mandatory retirement age or receiving pension/social security; Fasbender, Deller, Wang, & Wiernik, 2014). The understanding of the concept and the boundaries of retirement have changed in contemporary society. Although retirement has traditionally been defined as withdrawal from work, it has now been redefined as a late career development stage (Kim & Hall, 2013; Wang & Shi, 2014). As such, postretirement employment includes work-related

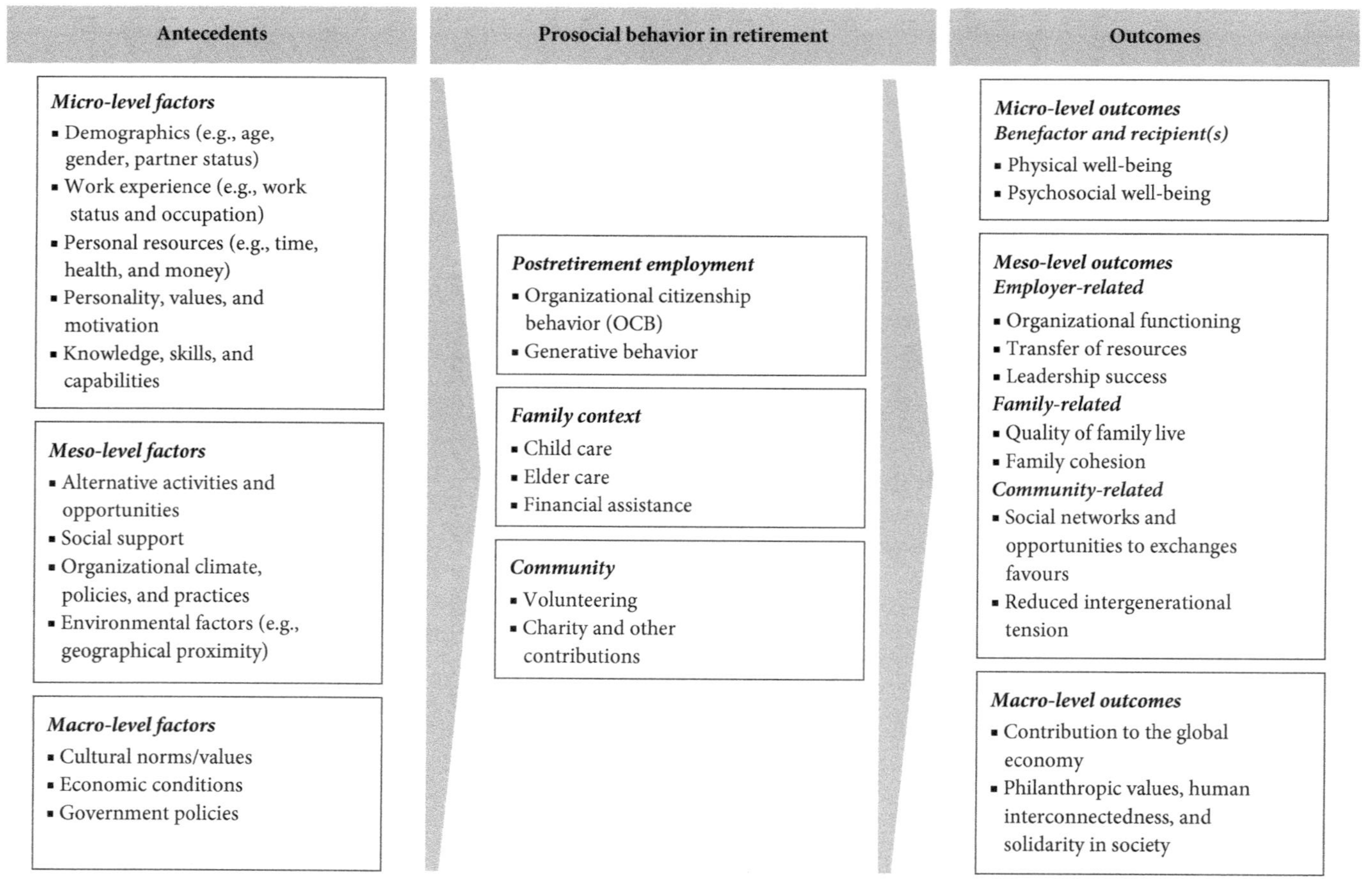

Figure 30.1 Antecedents and outcomes of prosocial behavior in retirement.

activities within the career field as well as work in a different field (Gobeski & Beehr, 2009; Wang, Zhan, Liu, & Shultz, 2008). Furthermore, it can be distinguished in different employer forms, such as continuing to work for the same employer, working for another employer, and being or becoming self-employed (Wang, Adams, Beehr, & Shultz, 2009; Zhan, Wang, & Yao, 2013).

Organizational Citizenship Behavior

OCB has a comprehensive tradition in organizational psychology and management research, which has increasingly developed over the last three and a half decades (LePine, Erez, & Johnson, 2002; Podsakoff, MacKenzie, Paine, & Bachrach, 2000). A first conceptualization was noted by Barnard (1938), who highlighted workers' "willingness to cooperate" as a distinctive work behavior that goes beyond ordinary job performance. After some decades, Katz (1964) has broadened the idea differentiating in-role and extra-role behaviors and emphasizing the importance of "innovative and spontaneous behaviors" at work. Inspired by these earlier approaches, Organ (1988) provided a formal definition of OCB as "'individual behavior that is discretionary, not directly or explicitly recognized by the formal reward system, and that in the aggregate promotes the effective functioning of the organization. By discretionary, we mean that the behavior is not an enforceable requirement of the role or the job description, that is, the clearly specifiable terms of the person's employment contract with the organization; the behavior is rather a matter of personal choice, such that its omission is not generally understood as punishable" (p. 4). Although Organ's original conceptualization (1988) emphasized that OCB is typically not rewarded by the organization, more recent conceptualizations acknowledge that OCB may be recognized during performance evaluations (Johnson, Holladay, & Quinones, 2009; Organ, 1997).

Furthermore, the dimensional structure of the OCB construct has been extensively discussed in the research literature (Dalal, 2005). In their early research, Smith, Organ, and Near (1983) suggested a two-dimensional construct, including OCB directed toward the interpersonal benefit (OCBI) and OCB directed toward the organizational benefit (OCBO). The distinction between OCBI and OCBO as different measures of performance (different from in-role behaviors) has been empirically supported by Williams and Anderson (1991). More elaborated taxonomies of OCB have been developed (e.g., Organ, 1988; Podsakoff, MacKenzie, Moorman, & Fetter, 1990), extending the construct to five dimensions of OCB, namely altruism, civic virtue, conscientiousness, courtesy, and sportsmanship. A meta-analysis investigated this five-dimensional structure of OCB (LePine et al., 2002). The authors state that the five dimensions are highly intercorrelated and "that there are no meaningful differences in relationships with predictors across dimensions" (LePine et al., 2002, p. 62), questioning the relevance of the five-dimensional structure. In addition, Organ and Paine (1999) argue that the two-dimensional structure is the most stable and seems to underlie the more complex structures of OCB (Dalal, 2005).

Generative Behavior

Against the backdrop of global population aging and the upcoming exit of the baby-boomer generation from the workforce, the role of generative behavior in postretirement employment becomes increasingly important. The term *generativity* can be traced back to Erikson's (1950, 1964) developmental theory (namely eight stages of man or human strength and the cycle of generations), introducing the concept of generativity as essential during the late stages of human development.

> The fashionable insistence on dramatizing the dependence of children on adults often blinds us to the dependence of the older generation on the younger one. Mature man [or woman] needs to be needed, and maturity needs guidance as well as encouragement from what has been produced and must be taken care of. Generativity, then, is primarily the concern in establishing and guiding the next generation, although there are individuals who, through misfortune or because of special and genuine gifts in other directions, do not apply this drive to their own offspring.
> *(Erikson, 1950, pp. 266–267)*

Erikson (1950) describes generativity not only as an essential need of older people but also relates the concept to the mutual dependence between older and younger people. Furthermore, Erikson (1964) introduces different outcomes for generative behaviors, benefits for recipients (i.e., the people being taught), the benefactor (i.e., fulfillment of self-identity), and the society (i.e., intergenerational knowledge transfer).

> And man [or woman] needs to teach, not only for the sake of those who need to be taught and not only

for the fulfillment of his [or her] identity, but because facts are kept alive by being told, logic by being demonstrated, truth by being professed.
(Erikson, 1964, p. 131)

Following Erikson's developmental theory, McAdams and de St Aubin (1992) related generativity to the conscious personality that represents (a) people's needs and values of self-perceptions, (b) goals, intentions, and plans, and (c) actual generative behavior (Clark & Arnold, 2008). With regard to postretirement employment, generative behavior refers to an intergenerational transfer of resources, such as knowledge exchange, mentoring, sense giving, training, and development from older to younger workers (Fasbender et al., 2016; Mor-Barak, 1995; Zacher, Schmitt, & Gielnik, 2012).

Antecedents of Prosocial Behavior in Postretirement Employment

To date, there is no empirical study directly investigating OCB in postretirement employment. However, different studies indicated a relationship between age and OCB (e.g., Avanzi, Cortini, & Crocetti, 2012; Gyekye & Haybatollahi, 2015; Wagner & Rush, 2000). For example, a study from Avanzi et al. (2012) investigating the role of teachers' age on job identity and OCB revealed that older teachers showed higher levels of identity commitment and organizational identification but lower levels of group identification compared to their younger colleagues, which in turn was related to OCB. In addition, a meta-analysis from Dalal (2005) found that job satisfaction and organizational commitment were positive predictors of OCB, supporting the assumption that age might be related with OCB through different underlying mechanisms. Other psychological states related to organizations were also found to predict OCB. For example, organizational justice and positive affect were found to be positive predictors, while negative affect was found to be a negative predictor of OCB (Dalal, 2005). Social exchange theory (Thibaut & Kelley, 1959) and the norm of reciprocity (Gouldner, 1960) have been used as explanatory mechanisms, emphasizing OCB as employees' response to working conditions, workplace processes, interactions, and outcomes perceived as fair or satisfying (Dalal, 2005).

Particularly relevant with regard to the role of age in OCB is the socioemotional selectivity theory (e.g., Carstensen, 2006), which postulates changing motivational priorities with aging resulting in behavior consequences. However, instead of chronological age, the theory highlights perceived future time remaining as a more accurate measure of motivational development, especially at increasingly older ages (Carstensen, 2006). According to this theory, people select goals or priorities as a function of future time perspective. When people perceive future time as unlimited, they prioritize the acquisition of new information and expanding social networks. However, when people perceive future time as increasingly limited, they prioritize feelings and emotional well-being, and focus on the moment rather than on the future (Carstensen, Isaacowitz, & Charles, 1999; Lang & Carstensen, 2002). As people get older, they are more likely to perceive future time as limited and as a result should be more likely to engage in socioemotional behaviors in the workplace, such as helping coworkers or avoid complaining in order to maintain positive interpersonal relationships at work. Older workers also appear to prioritize positive work experiences and goals related to emotion regulation (Hertel & Zacher, in press). A range of empirical studies by Bal and colleagues (Bal, De Lange, Jansen, & Van Der Velde, 2013; Bal, Jansen, van der Velde, de Lange, & Rousseau, 2010; Bal & Smit, 2012) supported age-related differences in dealing with emotional events. For instance, a longitudinal study (Bal et al., 2013) revealed that older workers reacted less intensely in terms of their job satisfaction and job performance when experiencing certain negative emotional events, such as psychological contract breach. Supporting the importance of socioemotional goals of older people at work, a meta-analysis (Ng & Feldman, 2010) reported positive relationships between age and affective commitment, job involvement, interpersonal and organizational trust, loyalty, and organizational identification.

Further discussing the antecedents of OCB in postretirement employment, the socially constructed roles (e.g., younger vs. older workers, female vs. male workers) might be relevant predictors of actual citizenship behavior. As such, Kidder and Parks (2001) discuss social identity theory with regard to gender role anchoring the importance of social context in which behavioral decision making takes place. Referring to gender role stereotypes, the authors distinguish instrumental versus expressive behaviors. While feminine or expressive behaviors typically indicate concern for others (e.g., empathy, interpersonal orientation, perspective taking, and helping others), masculine or instrumental behaviors typically indicate confidence, independence, proactivity, and competitiveness. The authors argue that a mechanism of self-selection occurs as a result of a job-role and sex-role spillover, indicating that people choose their job role (e.g., tasks and responsibilities) according to their perceived gender role. With regard to the dimensions of OCB, Kidder and Parks (2001) propose altruism and courtesy to be female behaviors and sportsmanship and civic virtue to be male behaviors. Empirical support for this proposition was found from a recent study by Chiaburu, Sawyer, Smith, Brown, and Harris (2014), investigating role-congruent perceptions of civic virtue across gender. The authors noted that only when gender stereotypes were activated, observers expected less civic virtue from target female employees than from their male counterparts. As all employees take multiple roles, a similar argument regarding pervasiveness and spillover of role stereotypes could occur for older versus younger workers (or the role as postretirement worker in particular). Different cross-sectional studies noted that older people are often perceived as warm but incompetent (e.g., Australia, Hong Kong, New Zealand, Philippines, and the United States, Harwood et al., 1996; Costa Rica, Japan, Israel, and South Korea, Cuddy, Norton, & Fiske, 2005; and 26 European countries, including Germany, France, and the United Kingdom, Shiu, Hassan, & Parry, 2015). The stereotypical view of warmth could lead to higher expectations of OCB (e.g., altruistic behavior) from older workers, which in turn could lead to self-selection of tasks and responsibilities that are more likely to elicit OCB in postretirement employment. As a result, it is conceivable that the opportunity for performing OCB plays a significant role for older people engaging in postretirement employment.

Regarding generative behavior, there are several studies with regard to postretirement employment, often investigating generativity striving as a central motivation for engaging in postretirement employment. Relying on the socioemotional selectivity theory (Lang & Carstensen, 2002), many researchers have argued that the motivation for generativity increases with age (e.g., Dendinger, Adams, & Jacobson, 2005; Kooij, de Lange, Jansen, & Dikkers, 2013; Zhan, Wang, & Shi, 2015). As older people usually perceive future time as limited, they prioritize social goals that are emotionally meaningful, including generative behaviors as well as feelings of emotional intimacy and social embeddedness (Kooij et al., 2013). For example, Zhan et al. (2015) describe the transition from work to retirement as work role loss, which manifests "as losing one's work-related social worth and status, social relationships and contact, and opportunities to nurture younger generations" (p. 2), indicating the opportunity for generative behavior in postretirement employment. As a result, generativity striving can be found as one of the major antecedents for generative behavior in postretirement employment.

Prosocial Behavior in the Family Context

Prosocial behavior between generations has been an enduring characteristic of solidarity in the family context (Brubaker, 1990). Along with demographic trends, technological, and societal changes, there are also changes within families (e.g., diversification of family formation and household structures, changing transition timing within the family context) that cause structural fragility and larger dependence on the voluntary commitment of family members (Harper, 2004; Lowenstein, 2005; Wolf, 2001). Therefore, family can be seen as a point of departure with regard to the challenges that arise from demographic changes in society (Lowenstein, 2005). Prosocial behavior in the family context includes *direct* (i.e., child care and elder care) and *indirect* helping behaviors (i.e., financial assistance) that benefit the members of one's own family. In some circumstances, indirect helping behaviors can be a substitute for direct helping behaviors (e.g., paying for the external care).

Child Care and Elder Care

Within the family context, child care refers to caring for grandchildren and caring for children with chronic or disabling conditions. The shift from a high-mortality and high-fertility society toward a low-mortality and low-fertility society has resulted in a shift from a horizontal (i.e., within one generation) toward a vertical (i.e., between different generations) linkage in the family context (Harper, 2005). As a consequence, older people's role of caring for younger generations has increased in contemporary society (Harper, 2005). Responsibilities in child care contain acting as a family anchor (transferring attitudes and values) and replacement of partner or parent (e.g., disciplinarian, guide, facilitator, listener, or teacher; Harper & Ruicheva, 2010). Furthermore, elder care contains different areas of caring activities. To begin with, elder care refers to the caring for parents (or spouse's parents). Increased longevity has generated a larger number of living generations within one family (i.e., up to five living generations; Lowenstein, 2005; Morgan,

1983). Thus, it is possible that people entering formal retirement with 65 years would be likely to have parents at the age of about 85 years, who are in need of familial care. Furthermore, elder care refers to the caring for one's spouse. In addition, caring in the family context can include helping more distant relatives (e.g., caring for aunts and uncles or nieces and nephews) or even significant friends (Feinberg, 2014).

Financial Assistance

Within the family context, financial assistance refers to different kinds of monetary help to support family members. Financial assistance flows upward and downward between the different living generations within one family (Morgan, 1983). Therefore, retirees can be both benefactor and recipient of financial assistance. However, as this chapter focuses primary on prosocial behavior in retirement in terms of giving help to others, financial assistance is highlighted from the benefactor side. As such, retirees may use their pension or other sources of income (e.g., remuneration from postretirement employment) to support their children and grandchildren or their parents (and spouse's parents). With regard to time, financial assistance can include one-time or short-term support (e.g., paying for medical treatment), medium-term support (e.g., disbursing study enrollment fees), and long-term support (e.g., paying for permanent elder care facility).

Antecedents of Prosocial Behavior in the Family Context

At the micro level, prosocial behavior in the family context is influenced by the personal resources that retirees are able to offer. Among the most important resources are health, time, and money. People's physical functioning has been found to be the most powerful predictor for giving elder care (Lowenstein, Katz, & Gur-Yatish, 2007). Also, time seems to be a highly relevant resource for undertaking caring activities in retirement. Research literature suggests that different care responsibilities influence the decision to retire early and also the perception of retirement transitions as involuntary. As such, Lumsdaine and Vermeer (2014) have found that the need for caring for grandchildren is associated with early retirement among women. Furthermore, Szinovacz and Davey (2005) found that retired men who cared for their parents were more likely to perceive retirement as forced, reflecting the restricted choice that often goes along with caring responsibilities.

While health and time resources are particularly important for direct helping behaviors, such as child and elder care, monetary resources are necessary for providing financial assistance to family members. In turn, personal resources may be affected by different individual factors. Retired couples are more likely to provide financial assistance compared to retired singles or divorcees due to higher levels of economic well-being (Choi, 2003; Harper, 2004). However, due to income disparities between men and women, it is likely that divorced men are in a more favorable position than divorced women and, thus, they are better able to provide financial assistance to their family members. Also, work status can be relevant for personal resources that facilitate prosocial behavior in the family context. Whereas nonworking retirees are likely to have more time to devote to direct helping behaviors, working retirees are more likely to indirectly help their family members by providing financial assistance (Choi, 2003). Different occupations (e.g., between preretirement and postretirement) may also influence personal resources in retirement. Whereas manual workers are likely to suffer from demanding working conditions, nonmanual workers may have higher health resources. Furthermore, workers with managerial responsibilities are likely to have higher monetary resources compared to workers without managerial responsibilities.

At the meso level, one can argue that often the nature of situations (in contrast to the nature of humans) determines when people are ready to help and when they are not (Dovidio et al., 2010). Therefore, the familial formation and related structures play a major role for prosocial behavior in the family context. To begin with, geographical proximity between family members (i.e., benefactor and recipient) seems to be relevant for direct helping behaviors because it might rule out possible hindrances that occur due to lower levels of mobility in retirement. Supporting this argumentation, a cross-national study found geographical proximity to be positively related to elder care in the family context (Lowenstein et al., 2007). In addition, the study revealed familial norms (i.e., the willingness to sacrifice in order to fulfill care responsibilities) and familial solidarity (i.e., feelings of emotional intimacy, similarity, and proximity) to be positively related, while family-state balance (i.e., attitude toward family versus state responsibility) to be negatively associated with elder care in the family. Furthermore, research has indicated that often different family members share direct and indirect helping behaviors in the family (e.g., shared caregiving responsibilities for elder parents; Checkovich & Stern, 2002), highlighting the importance of family cohesion.

At the macro level, the role of public services influences prosocial behaviors in the family context. The availability, accessibility, quality, and costs of public services determine the state solidarity that either complements or substitutes familial solidarity (Lowenstein, 2005). However, the role of public services varies largely between countries. While Scandinavian countries are known for direct governmental involvement through supplying generous public services, many other European countries rely on state insurance-based arrangements, whereas liberal regimes, such as the United States, are known for their limited state solidarity (Lowenstein, 2005). As a result, countries with distinctive public services may replace prosocial behavior in the family context up to a certain degree. However, beyond public services as a means of state solidarity, cultural norms and values determine familial solidarity, which in turn shapes role expectations of family members. Role expectations (e.g., for being a grandmother or grandfather) to take responsibility with emerging dependency in the family (e.g., birth of a grandchild) are largely socially constructed. As a consequence, prosocial behavior in the family context "is the widening concern for what has been generated by love, necessity, or accident; it overcomes the ambivalence adhering to irreversible obligation" (Erikson, 1964, p. 131).

Prosocial Behavior in the Community

Prosocial behavior in the community also includes *direct* (i.e., volunteering activities) and *indirect* helping behaviors (i.e., charity and other contributions) that benefit the members of a community. Emphasizing on different contexts of prosocial behavior in retirement, the community context provides formal structures of helping behaviors that are usually represented in nonprofit organizations (i.e., community sector). By focusing on education, environment, and social services, the community sector is increasingly central to the health and well-being outcomes in society. In the following paragraphs, we introduce volunteering activities, charities, and other contributions and discuss their antecedents based on the multilevel framework of retirement.

Volunteering Activities

Volunteering activities refer to productive but unpaid engagement in society. Based on the general conceptualization of prosocial behavior, volunteering describes the relationship between the volunteer as benefactor, who provides time and other resources to one or more recipient(s). In the past, policymakers often neglected the economic potential of volunteering activities. For example, aggregate indicators (e.g., gross domestic product) rely on traditional definitions of productive activity in estimating economic performance. Ignoring many volunteering activities that produce social benefits in society leads to a substantial underestimation of the true productivity of a country (Dosman, Fast, Chapman, & Keating, 2006). Nevertheless, the rate of older people engaging in volunteering activities has continuously increased for last three decades (Morrow-Howell, 2010). In addition, policymakers have more recently discovered the societal gain of volunteering activities, which has been accentuated with the "Year of Volunteering" in 2011 or the "European Year of Active Aging and Intergenerational Solidarity" in 2012. This reflects the meaning of personal productivity and societal responsibility (Fasbender et al., 2016).

Charity and Other Contributions

Charity and other contributions refer to giving money and goods to the unfortunate, as a humanitarian act. Often charitable giving is associated with a religious practice (e.g., giving one tenth of one's income to the community). However, charitable giving is also prevalent in atheist cultures. Current research revealed that people have "mental budgets for philanthropy" (Sussman, Sharma, & Alter, 2015, p. 130), which is malleable (LaBarge & Stinson, 2014). As such, mental accounting is a psychological process that explains how people allocate their monetary resources to those in need (LaBarge & Stinson, 2014). In addition to monetary resources, charitable contributions also contain the donation of food, clothes, and household goods or even biological resources (e.g., biological tissue, blood, and organ donation). Complementary to charitable giving is the process of gathering contributions from others (e.g., from individuals, businesses and organizations, and governmental institutions), including fundraising activities (e.g., crowd funding, handheld collection) or selling material resources (e.g., charity shops) to invest in philanthropic projects.

Antecedents of Prosocial Behavior in the Community

There is a vast amount of literature on prosocial behavior in the community as retirement has been identified as an important life stage that offers many older people the opportunity to engage in society. At the micro level, there are two opposing theories that have dominated debates on what drives older people to become active in society, when considering retirement from a life course perspective. On the one hand, disengagement theories state that older people become more fragile, less active, and less social, turning toward voluntary retirement and turning away from engagement in society (Jensen, Lamura, & Principi, 2014). On the other hand, activity and continuity theories state that older people maintain their activity patterns and, hence, past prosocial behavior predicts future prosocial behavior (Dury et al., 2015). As a result, retirement satisfaction is preconditioned by continuing earlier lifestyles and remaining active (Atchley, 1989; Jensen et al., 2014). However, there are differences between people; whereas some people disengage, others continue to be active. A resource perspective has been used to explain who engages in the community, with higher levels of individual human and social capital leading to higher involvement (Morrow-Howell, 2010). One type of such important resource is good health, which affects whether people are likely to engage in the community (e.g., Li & Ferraro, 2005; Morrow-Howell et al., 2014). Furthermore, financial resources were found to facilitate prosocial behavior in the community because higher income helps to cover extra costs that are associated with volunteering (e.g., food, lodging, and transportation costs; Morrow-Howell, 2010). Also, higher levels of education have been found to support prosocial behavior in the community because certain skills and capabilities can open up more opportunities to engage in the community (e.g., Choi, Burr, Mutchler, & Caro, 2007; Morrow-Howell et al., 2014). With regard to the motivational orientation of retirees, socioemotional selectivity theory has been used to predict the type of activity. It appears that older people are more motivated by emotional gratification and the desire to stay active in helping others, whereas younger and middle-aged people are rather motivated by instrumental aspirations (e.g., development of knowledge and skills; Morrow-Howell, Hong, McCrary, & Blinne, 2012). In addition, older people tend to engage more in religious communities, health services, and social services and choose relational activities (e.g., being a friendly visitor, mentor, or tutor) over educational and recreational tasks (Morrow-Howell, 2007).

At the meso level, organizational factors influence prosocial behavior in the community beyond individual choice. To begin with, the community climate suggests two different mechanisms for older people's involvement in the community. First, self-selection, which can also be seen as an individual-level factor, influences whether people join a community or not (Cemalcilar, 2009). Second, social assimilation influences whether people will be absorbed and welcomed by the members of a community (Fitzpatrick, 1966). The latter mechanism is partly driven by older people's personality and value orientation in accordance with the community climate (Choi et al., 2007). Also, perceptions of how attractive older people are to organizations depends on what older people have to offer to the community (Jensen et al., 2014). In this context, images of older people are often associated with declining cognitive and physical abilities (Jensen et al., 2014). However, social-gerontological studies have identified different strengths (e.g., emotional stability, life experience and maturity, independence, social understanding) and weaknesses (e.g., less flexible, physically weaker, slower and more anxious in learning new skills and competencies) of older people, suggesting that older people are neither better nor worse compared to their younger counterparts (Griffiths, 2007; Henkens, 2005). Therefore, it is particularly relevant to identity a fit between older people's individual strengths and the organizational demands that are related to prosocial behavior in the community. Strategies for good practice in recruitment, employability, and retention of older people engaging in prosocial behavior in the community are needed throughout the entire volunteer cycle. For example, marketing strategies that create a meaningful image of volunteers and emphasize the strengths- and resources-based options to engage could help attracting older people.

In addition, retention strategies are important because high rates of turnover and decreasing productivity (e.g., due to deterioration in physical and mental health) are costly. As such, training and development opportunities help increasing volunteer commitment, in particular under unclear role specification (Morrow-Howell, Hong, & Tang, 2009; Tang, Choi, & Morrow-Howell, 2010; Wilson, 2012). Furthermore, retention strategies also include providing a certain scope of action and work flexibility. As older people often engage in diverse activities, including familiar responsibilities and interpersonal exchange (e.g., personal leisure, physical exercise, and postretirement employment) in addition to their engagement in the community, organizations need to provide flexibility that allows older people to combine their different activities. Recent research by Dury et al. (2015) found that other activities, in particular, personal leisure including adult education (e.g., reading books, taking part in courses, using the Internet) and household chores (e.g., gardening, repairs in the house), increase the likelihood to be or become a volunteer. Also, postretirement employment can function as a "trampoline for volunteering" because it allows retirees to have higher economic and social resources compared to their nonworking counterparts (Jensen et al., 2014, p. 33). This, however, is a tradeoff between time and other resources. In addition to organizational factors that help recruiting and retaining older people, environmental factors may also influence prosocial engagement in the community. For example, people who live in urban areas have higher access to formal organizations that are in need of voluntary helpers (Choi, 2003). Furthermore, research has revealed a positive change in community activity by taking part in systematic programs (e.g., volunteer program in elementary schools; Morrow-Howell et al., 2012), suggesting that opportunities to engage in the community may influence older people's actual engagement.

At the macro level, governments and policymakers impact prosocial behavior in the community in two major ways, namely in the legal framework setting and culture steering. In some countries, prosocial engagement in the community has become a cornerstone of society, as can be seen, for example, when in 2011 the UK's Prime Minister David Cameron declared volunteering a central element of his vision for a "Big Society" (Jensen et al., 2014). The increased importance of prosocial behavior in the community has been partly explained by market or government failure, indicating that prosocial engagement has become a key instrument in satisfying demands for public goods, which have not been addressed by the market system (Salamon & Anheier, 1996). Recognizing this increased importance, the legal framework can stimulate prosocial engagement by creating (or adjusting) administration, laws, and regulations that are associated with the fundamental rights and obligations under which prosocial engagement takes place in organizational structures (Jensen et al., 2014). Policymakers can, for example, reduce bureaucratization and formal requirements for nonprofit organizations in the community sector (Goss, 2010). Also, policymakers are able to reinforce regulations by providing financial incentives to organizations that promote certain types of engagement, including types that are most favorable to older people or by allowing tax deductions for people who engage in the community. Policies set the framework for prosocial behavior in the community and at the same time, create culture, values, and a belief system that shape individuals' identities, preferences, and the way prosocial engagement works. Culture steering is a top-down process from government officials toward the nation that communicates visions (e.g., "Active Aging" or "Big Society") that are often advanced by benchmarking, best practices, and codes of conduct allowing self-reflexive practices in society (Jensen et al., 2014).

Outcomes of Prosocial Behavior in Retirement

Along the multilevel framework of retirement, prosocial behavior has several positive outcomes for individuals on the micro level; for employers, families, and communities at the meso level; and for society on the macro level. At the micro level, prosocial behavior in retirement benefits both the benefactor and the recipient, albeit in some areas it is more beneficial to the benefactor (e.g., mortality; Brown, Nesse, Vinokur, & Smith, 2003). Several studies have highlighted prosocial behavior as a source of physical and psychosocial well-being in retirement (e.g., Guo, Pickard, & Huang, 2008; Kahana, Bhatta, Lovegreen, Kahana, & Midlarsky, 2013; Morrow-Howell, Hinterlong, Rozario, & Tang, 2003). For example, the longitudinal study from Kahana et al. (2013) revealed that a prosocial orientation (i.e., altruistic attitudes, volunteering behavior, and informal helping behavior) facilitates psychosocial well-being (i.e., positive affect and life satisfaction) in retirement. Furthermore, the individual benefits of prosocial behavior in retirement include maintained or increased physical health (i.e., fewer doctor-diagnosed conditions, functional independence, lower mortality) and cognitive health (i.e., executive function, memory, and mental status) (Anderson et al., 2014; Gonzales, Matz-Costa, & Morrow-Howell, 2015). These positive outcomes have often been explained by role theory as prosocial behavior may substitute role losses experienced due to retirement. However, contrary to those positive findings are studies that reveal negative effects of prosocial behavior, in particular in the family context (see meta-analysis from Pinquart & Sörensen, 2003). With regard to role theory, two alternative hypotheses, role extension and role overload, have been discussed addressing prosocial behavior in the family context. While the role extension hypothesis argues that caregiving for family members (e.g., for the spouse) facilitates the benefactor by having greater social networks and more opportunities to exchange favors within the community, the role overload hypothesis argues that caring for family members requires high levels of commitment, time, and effort that prevent social exchange outside the family (Choi et al., 2007). Role overload has also been discussed for OCB and task performance, suggesting a dual nature of role overload comprising both challenge and hindrance aspects (see meta-analysis from Eatough, Chang, Miloslavic, & Johnson, 2011). Furthermore, the findings of Weinstein and Ryan (2010) highlight the importance of self-determination for prosocial behavior in retirement. In particular, prosocial behavior in retirement can have many different positive psychosocial and physical well-being outcomes when it is carried out as an autonomous or volitional act along one's role preference.

At the meso level, prosocial behavior in retirement is related to a range of positive outcomes, which can be differentiated into employer-related, family-related, and community-related outcomes. Although little is known about the role of prosocial behavior in postretirement employment, research revealed positive employer-related outcomes in more general (preretirement) work settings. For example, research revealed that OCB can improve the performance and functioning of work teams (Nielsen, Hrivnak, & Shaw, 2009). Furthermore, OCB has been found to contribute to lower levels of withdrawal-related behaviors, such as absenteeism and employee turnover, which in turn help organizations reduce recruitment and job training costs (Podsakoff, Whiting, Podsakoff, & Blume, 2009). Also, research explored that OCB helps increasing organizational productivity, efficiency, and customer satisfaction (Podsakoff et al., 2009). In addition, current research suggested that opportunities to engage in generative behavior facilitate the improvement in the quality of intergenerational contact at work, which in turn helps to reduce age bias and turnover intentions (Henry, Zacher, & Desmette, 2015). Furthermore, research showed that generative behavior among older leaders helps maintaining leadership success (i.e., follower satisfaction with leader, follower perceptions of leader effectiveness, and follower extra effort) through higher levels of leader–member exchange (Zacher, Rosing, Henning, & Frese, 2011).

Among the family-related outcomes are quality of family life and family cohesion. Different kinds of prosocial behavior in the family context, such as child care and elder care, can be highly stressful on a day-to-day basis (Fingerman, Pillemer, Silverstein, & Suitor, 2012; Guo et al., 2008). In addition, for the elderly, solely depending on other people's support can cause anxiety, guilt, or even tendencies for suicide (Brown et al., 2003). Nevertheless, research has shown that relying on familial care is less (and partly nonsignificantly) related to the psychological quality of life among the elderly compared to the use of formal care services for elder people (i.e., use of professional services at home and use of community services; Lowenstein et al., 2007). In addition, familial solidarity (i.e., feelings of emotional intimacy, similarity, and proximity) was found to support the psychological quality of life among the elderly (Lowenstein et al., 2007). Furthermore, it is likely that sharing care responsibilities (e.g., by offering social support) helps to reduce possible negative outcomes and at the same time to facilitate family cohesion and quality of family life (Chiou, Chang, Chen, & Wang, 2009; Sebern, 2005).

Furthermore, prosocial behavior in retirement offers several community-related outcomes. To begin with, active and direct engagement in the community helps to foster social inclusion as part of strong and cohesive communities that often build bridges into society (i.e., to neighborhood, companies, and governments; Jones, 2006; Kawachi & Berkman, 2014). Also, prosocial behavior in retirement might also help reduce intergenerational tension through establishing regular contact between young and old community members (see meta-analysis from Pettigrew & Tropp, 2006). Furthermore, additional income, transfer of knowledge, and other relevant resources contributed by benefactors, as well as additional services that cannot be covered by paid workers (e.g., pastoral services), can support the delivery of high-quality services to community members.

At the macro level, it can be expected that prosocial behavior in retirement makes a significant contribution to the economy all around the world. According to the Johns Hopkins Comparative Nonprofit Project that measured the economic size of the nonprofit sector across 37 countries, prosocial behavior contributes with (conservatively estimated) $400 billion to the global economy (International Labour Organization, 2011). Furthermore, the project revealed that approximately 140 million people engage in some kind of direct helping behavior each year, which equals the population size of Russia, half of the United States, or Germany and the United Kingdom together. As older people value the contribution to the public good more highly and also are more likely to behave altruistically compared to their younger counterparts (Freund & Blanchard-Fields, 2014), it can be assumed that prosocial behavior among retirees plays a major role for the world economy. Apart from financial indicators, it is likely that prosocial behavior in retirement helps strengthen philanthropic values, human interconnectedness, and solidarity in society.

Future Research Directions

The literature on prosocial behavior in retirement is still in its infancy. The proposed model of prosocial behavior in retirement needs to be examined and validated by future empirical studies. In examining the antecedents and outcomes of retirees' prosocial behavior, future research should pay particular attention to several issues.

Dynamics of Prosocial Behavior in Retirement

Although existing literature has largely described prosocial behavior as a static behavioral participation, people's participation in prosocial behavior should be dynamic in nature. First, as people age and go through different life and career stages, they may start participating in certain types of prosocial behaviors. As discussed, the socioemotional selectivity theory provides a theoretical foundation for the potential developmental change in prosocial behavior during later life stages. Furthermore, as people transition from employment to retirement, their past experience from engaging in prosocial behavior may have implications on their prosocial behavior in retirement. As for prosocial behavior in postretirement employment (e.g., OCBs and generative behaviors), it is reasonable to expect some continuity from preretirement to postretirement. As for prosocial behavior in the family context or in the community, people may experience role transitions as they start engaging in non-employment-related prosocial behaviors. Thus, the amount of time they spend on these behaviors as well as the motives driving them to these behaviors may change as people move into retirement and move across different retirement phases (e.g., from the initial honeymoon phase to later stability phase; Atchley, 1976). Also, such dynamics may be different for those who have been engaging in family and community prosocial behaviors for a long time before retiring versus older adults who only start engaging in these behaviors when they retire. For example, as suggested by Morrow-Howell (2010, p. 462), the dynamics of starting and stopping volunteer services "may be different for those volunteers who grow old versus older adults who become first-time volunteers."

In addition, the dynamics of prosocial behavior in retirement may also be manifested in the day-to-day fluctuations. As discussed, personal resources (e.g., health, money, etc.) are one of the micro-level antecedents of prosocial behavior in retirement. Although one's monetary resources tend to be stable, health status is likely to vary over time, especially for older adults. Different from younger adults, older adults face increased health risks in daily life because the decline in their physical strength, cognitive functioning, and immune system makes them more physically vulnerable on a daily basis (Wang, Olson, & Shultz, 2013). Related to health, older adults may experience more fluctuations in the amount of psychological energy available for prosocial behavior. Prior research has suggested that the lack of personal resources relates to fewer prosocial behaviors in the workplace (e.g., Cropanzano, Rupp, & Byrne, 2003; Ng & Feldman, 2012) and in the family context (Lowenstein et al., 2007). Therefore, it is meaningful to explore the day-to-day fluctuations of retirees' participation in prosocial behavior.

Adaptive Nature of Prosocial Behavior in Retirement

As reviewed earlier in this chapter, existing research has suggested a wide range of positive outcomes of engaging in prosocial behavior. When examining the prosocial behavior in the retirement context, we call for research effort in understanding the adaptive nature of prosocial behavior; in other words, how and why prosocial behavior in retirement facilitates active and successful aging.

Multiple mechanisms may exist simultaneously in explaining the adaptive nature of prosocial behavior in retirement. For example, prosocial behavior may promote well-being for older adults based on mechanisms specified by the role theory. This is because prosocial activities help buffer the threat of role loss due to retirement, keeping people physically and cognitively active and satisfying their needs related to self-worth, social belongingness, and generativity, and so on. Alternatively, prosocial behavior may promote well-being based on mechanisms specified by the social exchange perspective. Older adults who take caregiving responsibilities and older adults who volunteer in community or charity activities are likely to receive social support from others in their social network, which has been shown to promote older workers' life satisfaction.

It is also important to note that prosocial behaviors in different areas may vary in nature and vary in their potential impacts on older adults. For instance, compared to prosocial behavior in the employment and community context, family-related prosocial behavior (i.e., caregiving and financial assistance) might be less discretionary and less able to substitute the lost work role identity. Furthermore, the outcome may differ for those who participate in multiple types of prosocial behaviors across employment, family, and community contexts versus those who devote themselves to one type of prosocial behavior. Therefore, a comprehensive understanding of the adaptive nature of prosocial behavior in retirement requires future research to examine the differences between prosocial behaviors and to examine how each type of prosocial behavior influences individual well-being.

Social Norms, Culture, and Retirement Institution as Boundary Conditions

In this chapter, we propose antecedents of prosocial behavior in retirement at different levels, which may explain unique variance of retirees' prosocial behavior, respectively. Moreover, these antecedents are likely to work interactively in influencing older adults' decision making in participating in prosocial behavior. Specifically, depending on the macro-level factors such as retirement institution as well as social norms and cultural values related to prosocial behavior for older adults, people may respond in different ways to micro-level and meso-level antecedents and may subsequently experience different outcomes of engaging in prosocial behavior.

For example, the norms about grandparenting vary widely across cultures. In cultures that value familial solidarity and expect grandparents to take care of grandchildren, older adults' personal or work characteristics may not be as important when it comes to making the decisions about when and where they will participate in grandparenting in retirement. Furthermore, the retirement policies and social security system may function as boundary conditions in predicting older adults' participation in postretirement employment because these policies may relate to the need and opportunities of working in retirement.

Measurement Issues

Future research on prosocial behavior in retirement should also pay attention to two measurement issues. First, future research should carefully decide the rating source of prosocial behavior. Given that prosocial behavior in retirement could take a variety of forms and occur in different areas of life, the choice of rating source should be consistent with the specific form of prosocial behavior of interest. For instance, working colleagues might be the best source of prosocial behavior in the postretirement employment context, whereas close family members might be the best source of prosocial behavior in the family and community context. As suggested by the meta-analytic results, the relationship between variables is much stronger when rating sources are the same rather than different (e.g., between OCB and performance, Nielsen et al., 2009). However, using different rating sources for prosocial behavior and its antecedents or outcomes will help reduce the common method bias.

Second, future research should differentiate between age and retirement as a life stage. What variables to measure in one study should be based on the research questions and theoretical foundation. For example, when applying developmental theories to suggest a continuous change in people's behavior and well-being, age could be a good proxy of the aging process. When applying theories that suggest discontinuity across life stages (e.g., preretirement and postretirement) and when studying how people change their prosocial behavior as they move into retirement, only using age may not be appropriate. Instead, researchers may measure whether the participants have retired and/or how far away the participants are from retirement.

Conclusion

Due to workforce aging and the increase of the proportion of the population reaching retirement age, interest among researchers in retirement process and retiree well-being has increased dramatically. In this chapter, we focus our attention on prosocial behaviors in retirement, which is a relatively understudied topic that is related to the well-being of retirees and the society at large. Based on the current conceptualization of retirement and an overview of the current research literature on prosocial behavior, we specify different types of prosocial behavior in retirement in three main areas: postretirement employment, family context, and community. Furthermore, we present a comprehensive multilevel model covering the antecedents and outcomes of prosocial behavior in retirement. We call for more research effort examining this multilevel model, and we also highlight several future directions to advance research on this topic.

References

Anderson, N. D., Wagner, L. M., Dawson, D. R., Binns, M. A., Cook, S. L., Abosh, B., . . . Al, A. E. T. (2014). The benefits associated with volunteering among seniors: A critical review and recommendations for future research. *Psychological Bulletin, 140*, 1505–1533.

Atchley, R. C. (1976). *The sociology of retirement.* New York, NY: Halsted Press.

Atchley, R. C. (1989). A continuity theory of normal aging. *The Gerontologist, 29*, 183–190. http://doi.org/10.1093/geront/29.2.183

Avanzi, L., Cortini, M., & Crocetti, E. (2012). When age matters: The role of teacher aging on job identity and organizational citizenship behaviours. *Revue Internationale de Psychologie Sociale, 25*, 179–210.

Bal, P. M., De Lange, A. H., Jansen, P. G. W., & Van Der Velde, M. E. G. (2013). A longitudinal study of age-related differences in reactions to psychological contract breach. *Applied Psychology: An International Review, 62*, 157–181. http://doi.org/10.1111/j.1464-0597.2012.00524.x

Bal, P. M., Jansen, P. G. W., van der Velde, M. E. G., de Lange, A. H., & Rousseau, D. M. (2010). The role of future time perspective in psychological contracts: A study among older workers. *Journal of Vocational Behavior, 76*, 474–486. http://doi.org/10.1016/j.jvb.2010.01.002

Bal, P. M., & Smit, P. (2012). The older the better! Age-related differences in emotion regulation after psychological contract breach. *Career Development International, 17*, 6–24. http://doi.org/10.1108/13620431211201300

Barnard, C. (1938). *The functions of the executive.* Cambridge, MA: Harvard University Press.

Brown, S. L., Nesse, R. M., Vinokur, A. D., & Smith, D. M. (2003). Providing support may be more beneficial than receiving it: Results from a prospective study of mortality. *Psychological Science, 14*, 320–327. http://doi.org/10.1111/1467-9280.14461

Brubaker, T. H. (1990). Families in later life: A burgeoning research area. *Journal of Marriage and the Family, 42*, 959–981. http://doi.org/10.2307/351841

Carstensen, L. L. (2006). The influence of a sense of time on human development. *Science, 312*, 1913–1915. http://doi.org/10.1126/science.1127488

Carstensen, L. L., Isaacowitz, D. M., & Charles, S. T. (1999). Taking time seriously: A theory of socioemotional selectivity. *American Psychologist, 54*, 165–181.

Cemalcilar, Z. (2009). Understanding individual characteristics of adolescents who volunteer. *Personality and Individual Differences, 46*(4), 432–436. http://doi.org/10.1016/j.paid.2008.11.009

Checkovich, T. J., & Stern, S. (2002). Shared caregiving responsibilities of adult children with elderly parents. *The Journal of Human Resources, 37*, 441–478. http://doi.org/10.2307/3069678

Chiaburu, D. S., Sawyer, K., Smith, T. A., Brown, N., & Harris, T. B. (2014). When civic virtue isn't seen as virtuous: The effect of gender stereotyping on civic virtue expectations for women. *Sex Roles, 70*, 183–194. http://doi.org/10.1007/s11199-014-0346-z

Chiaburu, D. S., Smith, T. a., Wang, J., & Zimmerman, R. D. (2014). Relative importance of leader influences for subordinates' proactive behaviors, prosocial behaviors, and task performance. *Journal of Personnel Psychology, 13*, 70–86. http://doi.org/10.1027/1866-5888/a000105

Chiou, C. J., Chang, H. Y., Chen, I. P., & Wang, H. H. (2009). Social support and caregiving circumstances as predictors of caregiver burden in Taiwan. *Archives of Gerontology and Geriatrics, 48*, 419–424. http://doi.org/10.1016/j.archger.2008.04.001

Choi, L. H. (2003). Factors affecting volunteerism among older adults. *Journal of Applied Gerontology, 22*, 179–196. http://doi.org/10.1177/0733464803251814

Choi, N. G., Burr, J. A., Mutchler, J. E., & Caro, F. G. (2007). Formal and informal volunteer activity and spousal caregiving among older adults. *Research on Aging, 29*, 99–124. http://doi.org/10.1177/0164027506296759

Clark, M., & Arnold, J. (2008). The nature, prevalence and correlates of generativity among men in middle career. *Journal of Vocational Behavior, 73*, 473–484. http://doi.org/10.1016/j.jvb.2008.09.002

Cropanzano, R., Rupp, D. E., & Byrne, Z. S. (2003). The relationship of emotional exhaustion to work attitudes, job performance, and organizational citizenship behaviors. *Journal of Applied Psychology, 88*, 160–169. http://doi.org/10.1037/0021-9010.88.1.160

Cuddy, A. J. C., Norton, M. I., & Fiske, S. T. (2005). This old stereotype: The pervasiveness and persistence of the elderly stereotype. *Journal of Social Issues, 61*(2), 267–285. http://doi.org/10.1111/j.1540-4560.2005.00405.x

Dalal, R. S. (2005). A meta-analysis of the relationship between organizational citizenship behavior and counterproductive work behavior. *Journal of Applied Psychology, 90*, 1241–1255. http://doi.org/10.1037/0021-9010.90.6.1241

Darwin, C. R. (1859). *On the origin of species by means of natural selection, or the preservation of favoured races in the struggle for life.* London: John Murray.

Dendinger, V. M., Adams, G. A., & Jacobson, J. D. (2005). Reasons for working and their relationship to retirement attitudes, job satisfaction and occupational self-efficacy of bridge employees. *International Journal of Aging & Human Development, 61*(1), 21–35.

Dosman, D., Fast, J., Chapman, S. A., & Keating, N. (2006). Retirement and productive activity in later life. *Journal of Family and Economic Issues, 27*, 401–419. http://doi.org/10.1007/s10834-006-9022-y

Dovidio, J. F., Piliavin, J. A., Schroeder, D. A., & Penner, L. A. (2010). *The social psychology of prosocial behavior* (Reprint). Mahwah, NJ: Erlbaum.

Dury, S., Donder, L. D., Witte, N. D., Brosens, D., Smetcoren, A.-S., Regenmortel, S. V., & Verte, D. (2015). Is volunteering in later life impeded or stimulated by other activities? *Research on Aging*, 1–25. http://doi.org/10.1177/0164027515574777

Eatough, E. M., Chang, C.-H., Miloslavic, S. A., & Johnson, R. E. (2011). Relationships of role stressors with organizational citizenship behavior: A meta-analysis. *Journal of Applied Psychology, 96*, 619–632. http://doi.org/10.1037/a0021887

Ekerdt, D. J., Hackney, J., Kosloski, K., & DeViney, S. (2001). Eddies in the stream: The prevalence of uncertain plans

for retirement. *Journal of Gerontology: Social Sciences, 56B*, 162–170.
Erikson, E. H. (1950). *Childhood and society*. New York, NY: W. W. Norton.
Erikson, E. H. (1964). *Insight and responsibility*. New York, NY: Norton.
Eurostat. (2015). Population structure and ageing. Retrieved June 26, 2015, from http://ec.europa.eu/eurostat/statistics-explained/index.php/Population_structure_and_ageing
Fasbender, U., & Deller, J. (2016). Post-retirement career planning. In N. Pachana (Ed.), *Encyclopedia of geropsychology*. Heidelberg: Springer.
Fasbender, U., Deller, J., Wang, M., & Wiernik, B. M. (2014). Deciding whether to work after retirement: The role of the psychological experience of aging. *Journal of Vocational Behavior, 84*, 215–224. http://doi.org/10.1016/j.jvb.2014.01.006
Fasbender, U., Wang, M., Voltmer, J.-B., & Deller, J. (2016). The meaning of work for post-retirement employment. *Work, Aging and Retirement, 2*, 12–23. doi:10.1093/workar/wav015
Federal Statistical Office of Germany. (2015a). 13th coordinated population projection for Germany. Retrieved June 26, 2015, from https://www.destatis.de/bevoelkerungspyramide/
Federal Statistical Office of Germany. (2015b). Lebenserwartung für Jungen knapp 78 Jahre, für Mädchen rund 83 Jahre Statistisches Bundesamt. Retrieved June 26, 2015, from https://www.destatis.de/DE/PresseService/Presse/Pressemitteilungen/2015/04/PD15_143_12621pdf.pdf?__blob=publicationFile
Feinberg, L. F. (2014). Recognizing and supporting family caregivers: The time has come. *Public Policy & Aging Report, 24*, 65–69. http://doi.org/10.1093/ppar/pru007
Fingerman, K. L., Pillemer, K. A., Silverstein, M., & Suitor, J. J. (2012). The baby boomers' intergenerational relationships. *Gerontologist, 52*, 199–209. http://doi.org/10.1093/geront/gnr139
Fitzpatrick, J. P. (1966). The importance of "community" in the process of immigrant assimilation. *International Migration Review, 1*, 5–16. http://doi.org/10.2307/3002231
Fraccaroli, F., & Deller, J. (2015). Work, aging, and retirement in Europe: Introduction to the special issue. *Work, Aging and Retirement, 1*, 237–242. http://doi.org/10.1093/workar/wav017
Freund, A. M., & Blanchard-Fields, F. (2014). Age-related differences in altruism across adulthood: Making personal financial gain versus contributing to the public good. *Developmental Psychology, 50*, 1125–1136. http://doi.org/10.1037/a0034491
Gobeski, K., & Beehr, T. (2009). How retirees work: Predictors of different types of bridge employment. *Journal of Organizational Behavior, 30*, 401–425. http://doi.org/10.1002/job.547
Gonzales, E., Matz-Costa, C., & Morrow-Howell, N. (2015). Increasing opportunities for the productive engagement of older adults: A response to population aging. *The Gerontologist, 55*, 252–261. http://doi.org/10.1093/geront/gnu176
Goss, K. A. (2010). Civil society and civic engagement: Towards a multi-level theory of policy feedbacks. *Journal of Civil Society, 6*, 119–143. http://doi.org/10.1080/17448689.2010.506370
Gouldner, A. W. (1960). The norm of reciprocity: A preliminary statement. *American Sociological Review*. http://doi.org/10.2307/2092623
Griffiths, A. (2007). Healthy work for older workers: Work design and management factors. In W. Loretto, S. Vickerstaff, & P. White (Eds.), *The future for older workers: New perspectives* (pp. 121–137). Bristol, England: Policy Press.
Guo, B., Pickard, J., & Huang, J. (2008). A cultural perspective on health outcomes of caregiving grandparents. *Journal of Intergenerational Relationships, 5*(4), 25–40. http://doi.org/10.1300/J194v05n04_03
Gyekye, S. A., & Haybatollahi, M. (2015). Organizational citizenship behaviour: An empirical investigation of the impact of age and job satisfaction on Ghanaian industrial workers. *International Journal of Organizational Analysis, 23*, 285–301. http://doi.org/10.1108/IJOA-08-2012-0586
Harper, S. (2004). Families in ageing societies: A multidisciplinary approach. In S. Harper (Ed.), *Families in ageing societies* (pp. 1–24). Oxford, England: Oxford University Press. http://doi.org/10.1093/0199251169.001.0001
Harper, S. (2005). Grandparenthood. In M. L. Johnson (Ed.), *The Cambridge handbook of age and ageing* (pp. 422–428). Cambridge, England: Cambridge University Press.
Harper, S., & Ruicheva, I. (2010). Grandmothers as replacement parents and partners: The role of grandmotherhood in single parent families. *Journal of Intergenerational Relationships, 8*, 219–233. http://doi.org/10.1080/15350770.2010.498779
Harwood, J., Giles, H., Ota, H., Pierson, H. D., Gallois, C., Ng, S. H., . . . Somera, L. (1996). College students' trait ratings of three age groups around the Pacific Rim. *Journal of Cross-Cultural Gerontology, 11*, 307–317. http://doi.org/10.1007/BF00115798
Henkens, K. (2005). Stereotyping older workers and retirement: The managers' point of view. *Canadian Journal on Aging, 24*, 353–366. http://doi.org/10.1353/cja.2006.0011
Henry, H., Zacher, H., & Desmette, D. (2015). Reducing age bias and turnover intentions by enhancing intergenerational contact quality in the workplace: The role of opportunities for generativity and development. *Work, Aging and Retirement, 1*, 243–253. http://doi.org/10.1093/workar/wav005
Hershey, D. A., Henkens, K., & Van Dalen, H. P. (2007). Mapping the minds of retirement planners: A cross-cultural perspective. *Journal of Cross-Cultural Psychology, 38*, 361–382. http://doi.org/10.1177/0022022107300280
Hertel, G., & Zacher, H. (in press). Managing the aging workforce. In C. Viswesvaran, N. Anderson, D. S. Ones, & H. K. Sinangil (Eds.), *The SAGE handbook of industrial, work, & organizational psychology* (2nd ed., Vol. 3). SAGE.
Ilies, R., Nahrgang, J. D., & Morgeson, F. P. (2007). Leader-member exchange and citizenship behaviors: A meta-analysis. *Journal of Applied Psychology, 92*, 269–277. http://doi.org/10.1037/0021-9010.92.1.269
International Labour Organization. (2011). *Manual on the measurement of volunteer work: General report to the International 18th Conference of Labour Statisticians*. Geneva, Switzerland.
Jensen, P. H., Lamura, G., & Principi, A. (2014). Volunteering in older age: A conceptual and analytical framework. In A. Principi, P. H. Jensen, & G. Lamura (Eds.), *Active ageing: Voluntary work by older people in Europe* (pp. 21–44). Bristol, England: Policy Press.
Jensen, P. H., & Principi, A. (2014). Introduction: Enhancing volunteering in later life in Europe. In A. Principi, P. H. Jensen, & G. Lamura (Eds.), *Active ageing: Voluntary work by older people in Europe* (pp. 3–20). Bristol, England: Policy Press.
Johnson, S. K., Holladay, C. L., & Quinones, M. A. (2009). Organizational citizenship behavior in performance

evaluations: Distributive justice or injustice? *Journal of Business and Psychology, 24*, 409–418. http://doi.org/10.1007/s10869-009-9118-0

Jones, K. S. (2006). Giving and volunteering as distinct forms of civic engagement: The role of community integration and personal resources in formal helping. *Nonprofit and Voluntary Sector Quarterly, 35*, 249–266. http://doi.org/10.1177/0899764006287464

Kahana, E., Bhatta, T., Lovegreen, L. D., Kahana, B., & Midlarsky, E. (2013). Altruism, helping, and volunteering: Pathways to well-being in late life. *Journal of Aging and Health, 25*, 159–187. http://doi.org/10.1177/0898264312469665

Katz, D. (1964). The motivational basis of organizational behavior. *Behavioral Science, 9*(2), 131–146.

Kawachi, I., & Berkman, L. F. (2014). Social capital, social cohesion, and health. In L. F. Berkman, I. Kawachi, & M. M. Glymour (Eds.), *Social epidemiology* (2nd ed., Vol. 116, pp. 290–319). Oxford, England: Oxford University Press. http://doi.org/10.1093/med/9780195377903.003.0008

Kidder, D. L., & Parks, J. M. (2001). The good soldier: Who is s(he)? *Journal of Organizational Behavior, 22*, 939–959. http://doi.org/10.1002/job.119

Kim, N., & Hall, D. T. (2013). Protean career model and retirement. In M. Wang (Ed.), *The Oxford handbook of retirement* (pp. 102–116). New York, NY: Oxford University Press.

Kooij, D. T. A. M., de Lange, A. H., Jansen, P. G. W., & Dikkers, J. S. E. (2013). Beyond chronological age: Examining perceived future time and subjective health as age-related mediators in relation to work-related motivations and well-being. *Work & Stress, 27*, 88–105. http://doi.org/10.1080/02678373.2013.769328

LaBarge, M. C., & Stinson, J. L. (2014). The role of mental budgeting in philanthropic decision-making. *Nonprofit and Voluntary Sector Quarterly, 43*, 993–1013. http://doi.org/10.1177/0899764013489776

Lang, F. R., & Carstensen, L. L. (2002). Time counts: Future time perspective, goals, and social relationships. *Psychology and Aging, 17*, 125–139. http://doi.org/10.1037/0882-7974.17.1.125

LePine, J. a, Erez, A., & Johnson, D. E. (2002). The nature and dimensionality of organizational citizenship behavior: A critical review and meta-analysis. *Journal of Applied Psychology, 87*, 52–65. http://doi.org/10.1037//0021-9010.87.1.52

Li, Y., & Ferraro, K. F. (2005). Volunteering and depression in later life: Social benefit or selection processes? *Journal of Health and Social Behavior, 46*, 68–84. http://doi.org/10.1177/002214650504600106

Lowenstein, A. (2005). Global ageing and challenges to families. In M. L. Johnson (Ed.), *The Cambridge handbook of age and ageing* (pp. 403–412). Cambridge, UK: Cambridge University Press.

Lowenstein, A., Katz, R., & Gur-Yatish, N. (2007). Cross-national variations in elder care: Antecedents and outcomes. In A. Szinovácz, Maximiliane, and Davey (Eds.), *Caregiving contexts: Cultural, familial, and societal implications* (pp. 93–112). New York, NY: Springer.

Lumsdaine, R. L., & Vermeer, S. J. C. (2014). Retirement timing of women and the role of care responsibilities for grandchildren. *NBER Working Paper, 20756*, 1–55.

McAdams, D. P., & de St Aubin, E. (1992). A theory of generativity and its assessment through self-report, behavioral acts, and narrative themes in autobiography. *Journal of Personality and Social Psychology, 62*, 1003–1015.

Mor-Barak, M. (1995). The meaning of work for older adults seeking employment: The generativity factor. *The International Journal of Aging and Human Development, 41*, 325–344.

Morgan, L. A. (1983). Intergenerational financial support: Retirement-age males, 1971–1975. *The Gerontologist, 23*, 160–166.

Morrow-Howell, N. (2007). A longer worklife: The new road to volunteering. *Generations, 31*(1), 63–67.

Morrow-Howell, N. (2010). Volunteering in later life: Research frontiers. *Journals of Gerontology—Series B Psychological Sciences and Social Sciences, 65*, 461–469. http://doi.org/10.1093/geronb/gbq024

Morrow-Howell, N., Hinterlong, J., Rozario, P. A., & Tang, F. (2003). Effects of volunteering on the well-being of older adults. *Journals of Gerontology, Series B: Psychological Sciences and Social Sciences, 58*, 137–145. http://doi.org/10.1093/geronb/58.3.S137

Morrow-Howell, N., Hong, S.-I., McCrary, S., & Blinne, W. (2012). Changes in activity among older volunteers. *Research on Aging, 34*, 174–196. http://doi.org/10.1177/0164027511419371

Morrow-Howell, N., Hong, S. I., & Tang, F. (2009). Who benefits from volunteering? Variations in perceived benefits. *The Gerontologist, 49*, 91–102. http://doi.org/10.1093/geront/gnp007

Morrow-Howell, N., Putnam, M., Lee, Y. S., Greenfield, J. C., Inoue, M., & Chen, H. (2014). An investigation of activity profiles of older adults. *Journals of Gerontology, Series B: Psychological Sciences and Social Sciences, 69*, 809–821. http://doi.org/10.1093/geronb/gbu002

Ng, T. W. H., & Feldman, D. C. (2010). The relationships of age with job attitudes: A meta-analysis. *Personnel Psychology, 63*, 677–718. http://doi.org/10.1111/j.1744-6570.2010.01184.x

Ng, T. W. H., & Feldman, D. C. (2012). Employee voice behavior: A meta-analytic test of the conservation of resources framework. *Journal of Organizational Behavior, 33*, 216–234. http://doi.org/10.1002/job.754

Nielsen, T. M., Hrivnak, G. a., & Shaw, M. (2009). Organizational citizenship behavior and performance: A meta-analysis of group-level research. *Small Group Research, 40*, 555–577. http://doi.org/10.1177/1046496409339630

Organ, D. W. (1988). *Organizational citizenship behavior: The good soldier syndrome*. Lexington, MA: Lexington Books.

Organ, D. W. (1997). Organizational citizenship behavior: It's construct clean-up time. *Human Performance, 10*, 133–151. http://doi.org/10.1207/s15327043hup1002_2

Organ, D. W., & Paine, J. B. (1999). A new kind of performance for industrial and organizational psychology: Recent contributions to the study of organizational citizenship behavior. *International Review of Industrial and Organizational Psychology, 14*, 337–368.

Pearce, P. L., & Amato, P. R. (1980). A taxonomy of helping: A multidimensional scaling analysis. *Social Psychology Quarterly, 43*, 363–371. http://doi.org/10.2307/3033956

Pettigrew, T. F., & Tropp, L. R. (2006). A meta-analytic test of intergroup contact theory. *Journal of Personality and Social Psychology, 90*, 751–783. http://doi.org/10.1037/0022-3514.90.5.751

Pinquart, M., & Sörensen, S. (2003). Associations of stressors and uplifts of caregiving with caregiver burden and depressive mood: A meta-analysis. *Journals of Gerontology, Series*

B: Psychological Sciences and Social Sciences, 58, 112–128. http://doi.org/10.1093/geronb/58.2.P112

Podsakoff, P. M., MacKenzie, S. B., Moorman, R. H., & Fetter, R. (1990). Transformational leader behaviors and their effects on followers' trust in leader, satisfaction, and organizational citizenship behaviors. *Leadership Quarterly, 1*, 107–142. http://doi.org/10.1016/1048-9843(90)90009-7

Podsakoff, P. M., MacKenzie, S. B., Paine, J. B., & Bachrach, D. G. (2000). Organizational citizenship behaviors: A critical review of the theoretical and empirical literature and suggestions for future research. *Journal of Management, 26*, 513–563. http://doi.org/10.1016/j.leaqua.2003.12.003

Podsakoff, N. P., Whiting, S. W., Podsakoff, P. M., & Blume, B. D. (2009). Individual- and organizational-level consequences of organizational citizenship behaviors: A meta-analysis. *Journal of Applied Psychology, 94*, 122–141. http://doi.org/10.1037/a0013079

Salamon, L. M., & Anheier, H. K. (1996). Social origins of civil society: Explaining the non-profit sector cross-nationally. *Working Papers of the Johns Hopkins Comparative Nonprofit Sector Project, 22*, 1–41.

Sebern, M. (2005). Shared care, elder and family member skills used to manage burden. *Journal of Advanced Nursing, 52*, 170–179. http://doi.org/10.1111/j.1365-2648.2005.03580.x

Shiu, E., Hassan, L. M., & Parry, S. (2015). The moderating effects of national age stereotyping on the relationships between job satisfaction and its determinants: A study of older workers across 26 countries. *British Journal of Management, 26*, 255–272. http://doi.org/10.1111/1467-8551.12091

Shultz, K. S., & Wang, M. (2011). Psychological perspectives on the changing nature of retirement. *American Psychologist, 66*, 170–179. http://doi.org/10.1037/a0022411

Smith, C. A., Organ, D. W., & Near, J. P. (1983). Organizational citizenship behavior: Its nature and antecedents. *Journal of Applied Psychology, 68*, 653–663. http://doi.org/10.1037/0021-9010.68.4.653

Sonnentag, S., & Grant, A. M. (2012). Doing good at work feels good at home, but not right away: When and why perceived prosocial impact predicts positive affect. *Personnel Psychology, 65*, 495–530. http://doi.org/10.1111/j.1744-6570.2012.01251.x

Sussman, A. B., Sharma, E., & Alter, A. L. (2015). Framing charitable donations as exceptional expenses increases giving. *Journal of Experimental Psychology: Applied, 21*, 130–139.

Szinovacz, M. E. (2013). A multilevel perspective for retirement research. In M. Wang (Ed.), *The Oxford Handbook of Retirement* (pp. 1–27). Oxford, England: Oxford University Press

Szinovacz, M. E., & Davey, A. (2005). Predictors of perceptions of involuntary retirement. *The Gerontologist, 45*, 36–47. http://doi.org/10.1093/geront/45.1.36

Tang, F., Choi, E., & Morrow-Howell, N. (2010). Organizational support and volunteering benefits for older adults. *The Gerontologist, 50*, 603–612. http://doi.org/10.1093/geront/gnq020

Thibaut, J., & Kelley, H. (1959). *The social psychology of groups*. New York, NY: Wiley.

Van Solinge, H., & Henkens, K. (2007). Involuntary retirement: The role of restrictive circumstances, timing, and social embeddedness. *Journals of Gerontology, Series B: Psychological Sciences and Social Sciences, 62*, 295–303.

Wagner, S., & Rush, M. (2000). Altruistic organizational citizenship behavior: Context, disposition, and age. *Journal of Social Psychology, 140*, 379–391.

Wang, M., Adams, G., Beehr, T., & Shultz, K. (2009). Career issues at the end of one's career: Bridge employment and retirement. In S. G. Baugh & S. E. Sullivan (Eds.), *Maintaining focus, energy, and options through the life span* (pp. 135–162). Charlotte, NC: Information Age Publishing.

Wang, M., Olson, D., & Shultz, K. (2013). *Mid and late career issues: An integrative perspective*. New York, NY: Psychology Press.

Wang, M., & Shi, J. (2014). Psychological research on retirement. *Annual Review of Psychology, 65*, 209–233. http://doi.org/10.1146/annurev-psych-010213-115131

Wang, M., Zhan, Y., Liu, S., & Shultz, K. S. (2008). Antecedents of bridge employment: A longitudinal investigation. *Journal of Applied Psychology, 93*, 818–830. http://doi.org/10.1037/0021-9010.93.4.818

Weinstein, N., & Ryan, R. M. (2010). When helping helps: Autonomous motivation for prosocial behavior and its influence on well-being for the helper and recipient. *Journal of Personality and Social Psychology, 98*, 222–244. http://doi.org/10.1037/a0016984

Williams, L. J., & Anderson, S. E. (1991). Job satisfaction and organizational commitment as predictors of organizational citizenship and in-role behaviors. *Journal of Management*. http://doi.org/10.1177/014920639101700305

Wilson, J. (2012). Volunteerism research: A review essay. *Nonprofit and Voluntary Sector Quarterly, 41*, 176–212. http://doi.org/10.1177/0899764011434558

Wolf, D. A. (2001). Population change: Friend or foe of the chronic care system? *Health Affairs, 20*(6), 28–42. http://doi.org/10.1377/hlthaff.20.6.28

Zacher, H., Rosing, K., Henning, T., & Frese, M. (2011). Establishing the next generation at work: Leader generativity as a moderator of the relationships between leader age, leader-member exchange, and leadership success. *Psychology and Aging, 26*, 241–252. http://doi.org/10.1037/a0021429

Zacher, H., Schmitt, A., & Gielnik, M. M. (2012). Stepping into my shoes: Generativity as a mediator of the relationship between business owners' age and family succession. *Ageing and Society, 32*, 673–696. http://doi.org/10.1017/S0144686X11000547

Zhan, Y., Wang, M., & Shi, J. (2015). Retirees' motivational orientations and bridge employment: Testing the moderating role of gender. *Journal of Applied Psychology*, (Advanced Online Publication). http://dx.doi.org/10.1037/a0038731

Zhan, Y., Wang, M., & Yao, X. (2013). Domain specific effects of commitment on bridge employment decisions: The moderating role of economic stress. *European Journal of Work and Organizational Psychology, 22*, 362–375. http://doi.org/10.1080/1359432X.2012.762763

CHAPTER

31 Research on Organizational Citizenship Behavior: Where Do We Go From Here?

Philip M. Podsakoff, Scott B. MacKenzie, *and* Nathan P. Podsakoff

Abstract

The purpose of this chapter is to highlight some of the most valuable suggestions for future organizational citizenship behavior (OCB) research made by the authors of this handbook. It is organized by section, beginning with future research issues related to the conceptual nature of OCB. Following this, we examine new directions for research on the consequences and antecedents of OCB. Next, we highlight promising ideas related to the mediating mechanisms and boundary conditions of the antecedents and consequences of OCBs that could be investigated in future research. Finally, we call attention to several methodological issues and problems that have implications for future research.

Key Words: conceptualization of OCB, antecedents of OCB, mediating mechanisms, boundary conditions, methodological considerations, future OCB research

It has been 30 years since Organ (1988) presented the first systematic examination of the nature, antecedents, and consequences of organizational citizenship behavior (OCB), and a dozen years since Organ, Podsakoff, and MacKenzie (2006) provided a comprehensive review of the OCB literature. As indicated by the chapters in this handbook, research in this area has grown rapidly in the interim period, and we have acquired a substantial amount of additional knowledge about these behaviors. In this chapter, we will highlight issues that we believe deserve attention in the future. Generally speaking, we will address these topics in the order that they appeared in the previous sections of the handbook. First, we will discuss some of the conceptual issues related to the definition of organizational citizenship behaviors and how they differ from other behaviors. Next, we will explore research issues related to the consequences of OCBs. Following this, we will turn our attention to future directions for research on the antecedents of citizenship behaviors and the theoretical mechanisms that account for their effects. Once this is done, we will focus on the boundary conditions that influence the strength of the relationships between OCBs and their antecedents and their consequences. Finally, in the last section of this chapter, we will discuss several methodological issues that need additional attention in future research.

Conceptual Issues That Need To Be Addressed in Future Research

Despite 30 years of research on OCB, there is still some controversy over its definition. In his influential book, Organ (1988) proposed that OCBs are discretionary forms of behavior that are often not directly recognized by the formal reward system, but that in the aggregate promote the effectiveness of the organization. Indeed, in the introductory chapter of this book, Organ (2018) reiterated this view, by arguing that, fundamentally, "OCB is about the types of discretionary behavior and contributions that are not explicitly associated with the specific job requirements"; and that they can further be defined as "behaviors that sustain or enhance the cooperative system of the organization but are not systematically or generally recorded in the formal system of the organization or tied in any consistent way to specific rewards" (p. 7).

Subsequent research has raised doubts about several aspects of this definition, particularly with respect to whether employees view OCBs as discretionary (cf. N.P. Podsakoff, Morrison, & Martinez, 2018a), and whether these behaviors are included as an explicit part of the formal organizational reward system (e.g., Allen & Rush, 1998, 2001; Kiker & Motowidlo, 1999; Orr, Sackett, & Mercer, 1989; Park, 1986; Shore, Barksdale, & Shore, 1995; Van Scotter, Motowidlo, & Cross, 2000). Although these criticisms have merit, we agree with Organ (2018) that

> Ultimately, we must concede that there is often a fine line between what is construed as OCB and what would be described as "doing one's job." Rather, we do well to think in terms of a continuum, anchored on one end by "pure productivity" that can be measured objectively and rewarded on a formulaic basis, and an opposite pole representing "pure OCB" that defies quantification or a contractual expression. Between those poles are contributions that represent more or less semblance to "individual productivity" or "going beyond what is required." (p. 10)

Indeed, from our perspective, we believe that regardless of where OCBs fall on this continuum, prior to Organ's (1988) work and the 4,900 plus subsequent studies on this topic by others, they were largely neglected aspects of employee job performance worthy of examination in their own right. Having said this, there is clearly evidence indicating that individuals differ on the extent to which they perceive OCBs as discretionary (Morrison, 1994; N. P. Podsakoff et al., 2018a), and this is important because, as noted by Organ (2018),

> if individuals vary in the extent to which they include OCB in their personal definition of the job and thus proceed to practice it in the process of discharging what they view as incumbent upon them, then we would still be interested in how this enlarged, subjectively viewed sense of job comes about and what contributions derive from it. (p. 10)

For this reason, N. P. Podsakoff, Podsakoff, MacKenzie, Maynes, Whiting, and Spoelma (2018b) have noted that future research should examine how individual differences (e.g., mood and affect, stress), group characteristics (e.g., group climate, norms and behavioral cues), job characteristics (e.g., job descriptions, task interdependence), organizational characteristics (e.g., reward/incentive systems, socialization and training programs), and cultural characteristics (e.g., individualism/collectivism, power distance) influence OCB role perceptions. Related to this, Newton and LePine (2018) note that it is important for future research to improve our understanding of how OCBs relate to the role perceptions of supervisors as well as subordinates, and whether the perspectives of supervisors and subordinates differ with respect to the in-role or extra-role status of OCBs.

Another profitable area for future research is on the distinction between OCB and other, related constructs. Carpini and Parker (2018) emphasize the need for future research to fit OCBs into a broader conceptual framework of work-related constructs in order to facilitate a more rigorous testing of nomological relationships and reveal redundancies between constructs. They suggest using the Griffin, Neal, and Parker (2007) performance model as an organizing framework for this purpose. However, from our perspective, whether this particular model is used or not, it is important for future research to avoid the "jangle fallacy" (Carpini & Parker, 2018; Kelley, 1927; Newton & LePine, 2018), "which occurs when two ostensibly distinct psychological constructs appear different by virtue of their names but in essence represent the same basic phenomena" (Carpini & Parker, 2018, p. 37). Indeed, Newton and LePine (2018) argue that citizenship behavior is distinct from job engagement, and that future research should recognize the differences between these constructs. Similarly, Dalal and Carpenter (2018) make the case that although previous research has attempted to lump OCB and CWB together at opposite ends of a single continuum, closer examination of these constructs reveals that future research should view them as separate constructs. They provide several recommendations for the directions this research might take, including (a) whether there are some personality traits that relate to OCB but not to CWB (or vice versa), or that relate positively (or negatively) to both OCB and CWB; (b) identifying distinct ways in which employees learn about norms regarding OCB and CWB in their organizations; and (c) how the cultural context influences the extent to which employees consider behaviors to be forms of OCB or CWB. Finally, Li, Frese, and Haidar (2018) call for future research examining the biological roots of OCB, and how different brain chemicals may help to distinguish between helping and proactive behaviors.

In addition to distinguishing OCBs from other previously recognized behaviors, several authors in this handbook have called for future research examining new forms of OCB. For example, Newton and LePine (2018) identified role flexibility/adaptability as a potential new form of OCB that may be worth examining. Similarly, building on the research of Sandberg and Grant (2015), Allen and Jang (2018) suggest that office "housework" may be another neglected form of OCB. They note that because women are more likely to take on office housework tasks "that help keep an office running (taking meeting notes; planning office parties), but that do not pay off" (Allen & Jang, 2018, p. 235), a consideration of office housework as part of OCB could help explain why the objective career outcomes of women continue to lag behind those of men. Finally, Ehrhart (2018) calls for future research that takes a closer look at new types of helping behavior. More specifically, he suggests that it may be useful to recognize the differences between instrumental helping behavior and emotional helping behavior, because they are likely to have unique antecedents and outcomes for the individual involved. However, since previous research (LePine, Erez, & Johnson, 2002; Organ et al., 2006; P. M. Podsakoff, MacKenzie, Paine, & Bachrach, 2000) has identified between 30 and 40 different forms of OCB, when investigating these new forms of OCB, it is imperative to carefully define them. We have provided an extensive set of recommendations for developing a good conceptual definition (P. M. Podsakoff, MacKenzie, & Podsakoff, 2016), and we encourage researchers to follow these guidelines.

A final conceptual issue that needs to be addressed in future research was noted in the chapter by Ehrhart (2018). He noted that "Work on helping has tended to focus on the overall helpfulness of individuals over time, the individual and contextual characteristics that predict overall helpfulness, and the outcomes of helping in organizations. Although these topics are critical to our understanding of helping behavior in organizations . . . there are a number of aspects of helping processes that have been understudied" (Ehrhart, 2018, p. 494). His episodic model of helping processes in organizations identifies more than a dozen new questions to be addressed in future research: (a) Why do people seek help or not seek help? (b) Who asks for help?, (c) When do people ask for help?, (d) Who is asked for help?, (e) Why do people help or not help in response to a specific request?, (f) How do people decide whether to offer help or not?, (g) How do people decide whether to accept an offer to help or not?, (h) Why are people helpful?, (i) Who gives help?, (j) When do people help?, (k) What are the outcomes of seeking/receiving help?, (l) Who reciprocates help, and (m) What are the outcomes of helping others? In our view, Ehrhart's episodic helping model has tremendous heuristic value for generating hypotheses on helping behavior, and it has the potential to influence research for years to come.

Additional Consequences To Be Explored in Future Research

The positive consequences of OCBs have long been recognized in the literature (Allen & Rush, 1998; MacKenzie, Podsakoff, & Fetter, 1991, 1993; MacKenzie, Podsakoff, & Podsakoff, 2018; Motowidlo & Van Scotter, 1994; Organ et al., 2006; N. P. Podsakoff, Podsakoff, MacKenzie, Maynes, & Spoelma, 2014; N. P. Podsakoff, Whiting, Podsakoff, & Blume, 2009; P. M. Podsakoff, Ahearne, & MacKenzie, 1997; P. M. Podsakoff, MacKenzie, & Hui, 1993; P. M. Podsakoff et al., 2000; Van Scotter et al., 2000; Walz & Niehoff, 2000; Werner, 1994). At the individual level, these outcomes include more positive performance outcomes, promotions, higher salary recommendations, training recommendations, rewards, awards, and lower levels of intentions to leave the organization, absenteeism, and actual turnover. At the group or organization level, these outcomes include unit/organizational performance (e.g., military combat unit effectiveness, school achievement, number of tasks completed, quantity produced, quality produced), improving business processes (e.g., product quality, unit efficiency, corporate innovation, meeting benchmarks, decreased response times, decreased food waste), customer measures (e.g., perceived service quality, customer satisfaction, sales growth, market performance), and financial measures (e.g., sales revenue, profitability, return on assets, Tobin's Q, reduced operating costs).

In addition to this, the Fasbender, Wang, and Zhan (2018) chapter draws attention to a number of additional beneficial effects of OCBs that have not previously been recognized in the literature. These authors propose a comprehensive model of the antecedents, and the micro-, meso-, and macro-level outcomes of prosocial behavior in retirement. Among the positive effects of OCB are physical well-being, psychosocial well-being, quality of family life, family cohesion, social networks and opportunities to exchange favors, contributions to the global economy, and solidarity in society. These authors note that prosocial behavior in retirement facilitates active and successful aging by producing these outcomes, and they call for research to better understand this phenomenon. They suggest multiple mechanisms that may account for these effects.

For example, prosocial behavior may promote well-being for older adults based on mechanisms specified by role theory. This is because prosocial activities help buffer the threat of role loss due to retirement, keeping people physically and cognitively active and satisfying their needs related to self-worth, social belongingness, generativity, and so on. Alternatively, prosocial behavior may promote well-being based on mechanisms specified by the social exchange perspective. Older adults who take caregiving responsibilities and older adults who volunteer in community or charity activities are likely to receive social support from others in their social network, which has been shown to promote older workers' life satisfaction(Fasbender et al., 2018, p. 572).

Although the earlier discussion suggests that there are many beneficial effects of OCBs, several chapters in this book have highlighted the potential dark side of these behaviors. For example, the Lennard and Van Dyne (2018) chapter proposes several detrimental effects of positively intended helping behavior on the self-esteem, job attitudes, work feelings, and work behaviors of the recipient. They suggest that the effects of helping on the recipient's self-esteem may be moderated by the recipient's attributions (a) of the helper's empathy; (b) of what the helper thinks about the personal adequacy of the recipient; and (c) of the demands of the situation. They then go on to say that the recipient's self-esteem should mediate the impact of the interaction between the helping behavior and the recipient's attributions on the recipient's work attitudes, feelings, and behaviors, which should subsequently influence the recipient's work performance. These are intriguing possibilities which merit further examination and testing in future research.

Scott, Matta, and Koopman's (2018) chapter extends the discussion of the interplay between the helper and recipient of help by calling attention to the importance of whether the person providing help is a "core" or a "noncore" employee. They note that prior research indicates that some employees may be considered "core" or "more tightly linked to the overall performance of the team" (Humphrey, Morgeson, & Mannor, 2009, p. 49), than other ("noncore") employees, and they argue that when a "noncore" employee helps a "core" employee, it may benefit the organization; but when a "core" employee spends time helping "noncore" employees, it may result in an overall net loss in productivity for the organization. Although prior research has shown that helping behavior is positively related to effectiveness at the unit/organizational level (MacKenzie et al., 2018; Organ et al., 2006; N. P. Podsakoff et al., 2014; P. M. Podsakoff et al., 2000), this is an interesting proposition which suggests that future research on OCB should attempt to identify who is doing the helping, and how this might impact the individuals involved in the behavior as well as the organization.

Of course, not all outcomes of OCB will be positive in nature. For example, Bolino, Klotz, and Turnley (2018) argue that unintended negative consequences are possible at multiple levels, and that these harmful effects are more likely to occur when: (a) they result in resource depletion and undermine employee well-being, (b) employees feel compelled or pressured to engage in such behaviors, or (c) such behaviors become an expected part of the job. Based on this idea, they raise a number of interesting questions for future research, including: Is it the pressure to perform OCBs that is most harmful, or are OCBs most harmful when enacted at very high levels, regardless of the reason they are performed? Do unintended consequences build up and worsen over time, or do they ebb and flow over time? And, if employees who experience citizenship fatigue reduce their levels of OCB at a later date, do they eventually return to performing OCBs once they have time to recover? We agree with Bolino et al. (2018, p. 197) that "Answering these questions would provide the foundation for a more comprehensive conceptual model that might explain when, why, and how OCBs can have unintended consequences that can harm organizational effectiveness over time."

Bergeron, van Esch, and Thompson (2018) note that OCBs may sometimes be unrelated or negatively related to economic rewards and call for future research on the extent to which individuals may engage in OCBs at work for reasons beyond pure economic goals, including job and career satisfaction, doing meaningful work, wanting to make a prosocial difference, growth and development, and maintaining a state of well-being. Beyond this, they call for research on whether personal connections developed from OCBs allow individuals to feel more fulfilled, have higher job satisfaction, or have less work–life conflict; as well as whether performing OCBs lead to a more grateful attitude, which positively impacts emotions toward work and life. These authors suggest in conclusion that answering these questions is important because it is possible that the nonutilitarian benefits of OCB may compensate for some of its potential costs.

Finally, the fact that OCBs have been found to have both positive and negative effects suggests that an important priority for future research would be to examine the relative impact of these two types of effects on organizational-level outcomes. Assuming that the positive consequences usually outweigh the negative consequences, another key question for future research is what can be done to diminish the frequency of the negative consequences without diminishing the frequency of the positive consequences? Both of these topics deserve attention. It would also be important for future research to examine whether managers weight OCBs in evaluations in a manner that reflects their impact on unit performance. This is important, because there is some evidence to suggest that they do not (P. M. Podsakoff & MacKenzie, 1994). Indeed, P. M. Podsakoff and MacKenzie (1994) found that the relative effects of different types of OCBs on managerial evaluations were inconsistent with their effects on unit performance. Although it is not readily apparent why managers would tend to undervalue or overvalue different forms of citizenship behavior, it is possible that they simply do not realize the impact that different forms of OCBs have on unit performance. This would be an interesting topic for future research to investigate because, if these findings are replicated, "organizations might want to take steps to ensure that their managers are made aware of the actual influence of various forms of OCB on unit performance, and perhaps change the method of employee evaluations so that the weights managers attach to different forms of OCB reflect the impact of these behaviors on actual unit performance" (P. M. Podsakoff & MacKenzie, 1994, p. 360).

New Directions for Research on the Antecedents of Organizational Citizenship Behaviors

One of the most prolific areas of OCB research has been the search for its antecedents. For example, in their examination of the predictors of citizenship behaviors at the unit level, N. P. Podsakoff et al. (2018b) identified over 120 different antecedents, which they grouped into the following categories: (a) manager/leader characteristics (e.g., leader demographics, personality, leadership behavior); (b) group characteristics (e.g., group demographics, similarity, socialization, and norms); (c) member perceptions, attitudes, beliefs, and values (e.g., collective efficacy, group trust); (d) climate-related variables (e.g., justice, empowerment, voice, safety); or (e) organizational characteristics (e.g., demographics, structure and strategy, HRM practices). At the individual level, employee attitudes, motives, dispositions, personality traits, perceptions, work environments, leader behaviors, leader–member relationships, task characteristics, group characteristics, organizational characteristics, and organizational cultures (Organ et al., 2006) have also been examined. Therefore, in this section, we will focus primarily on some of the newer antecedents identified in the chapters of this handbook.

In their review of the relationships between personality traits and OCBs, Chiaburu, Oh, and Marinova (2018) make several recommendations for future research. First, they recommend that researchers "zoom-in" and examine the individual facets making up each of the Big Five personality dimensions, because research suggests that the individual facets relate to OCBs differently from each other, and from the overall dimension of which they are a part. They also note that it might prove worthwhile to look at profiles of these facets as predictors of OCB. Second, these authors note that prior research has primarily focused on what they call "bright side" personality traits (i.e., positive facets or dimensions), and they recommend focusing on what they call "dark-side" traits as well. More specifically, Chiaburu et al. (2018) argue that "Ideally, research should also include both bright- and dark-side personality traits and a multiplicity of the primary OCB types (OCB-O, OCB-I, and OCB-CH) and their constituent behaviors to capture the complexity of both phenomena using linear and nonlinear functions, and joint effects (interactions)" (p. 211). Finally, they note that it also might prove beneficial to examine traits other than the Big Five (e.g., other-oriented empathy, helpfulness, and proactive personality) as predictors of OCB.

Motowidlo, Kell, Martin, and Ghosh (2018) note that personality traits also influence OCBs, in part, through their effects on prosocial implicit trait policies (ITPs). According to them, prosocial ITPs are "beliefs about the importance of prosocial behavior for work effectiveness" (p. 543). Motowidlo et al. find that agreeableness, benevolent values, social vocational interests, and emotional intelligence can lead to behavioral prosocial expressions of performance. They go on to say that future research should focus on developing a better understanding of the ontology of these ITPs. More specifically, they note that

> Although the effect of individuals' basic traits on their prosocial ITPs has been examined, less is known about other constructs or types of experiences that affect how these ITPs develop over time. . . . Future research may examine whether individuals higher in cognitive ability are higher in prosocial ITPs than those lower in ability, and it may explore the types of experiences that affect individuals' evaluations of the effectiveness of prosocial expressions in different situations. If particular types of experiences provide opportunities for learning about prosocial and antisocial expressions, perhaps prosocial ITPs are amenable to training interventions. Researchers may examine the efficacy of training interventions on ITP formation and application to real-world situations. (Motowidlo et al., 2018, p. 555)

The potential importance of factors that influence employees' voice behavior is examined in the Burris, Bruno, Detert, and Caldwell (2018) chapter. They identify individual differences (demographics, traits, attitudes, etc.), people characteristics (e.g., leader, peer, and coworker characteristics), and organizational control mechanisms (e.g., culture, climate, policies, and structure) that influence an employee's beliefs about whether it is safe and worthwhile to speak up. Building on a model developed by Porras and colleagues (Porras & Hoffer, 1986; Porras & Silvers, 1991) that identifies four major subsystems of the organization that an intervention might target (physical setting, technology, social factors, and organizing arrangements), Burris et al. identify a number of voice interventions that organizations might implement to encourage voice behavior. We think that these are interesting ideas, which should be tested in future research (Burris et al., 2018, Figure 27.2):

- *Physical setting interventions*: use equal furnishings or seating arrangements to lower the status differential between managers and employees; increase the proximity of offices between desired voicer's and the recipient's of voice.
- *Technology interventions*: proactively suggest improvements in order to encourage employees to do the same via accessible and user-friendly online suggestion systems, close the feedback loop when employees do use suggestion systems.
- *Social factors interventions*: start off meetings with suggestions and follow up on them, point out that people don't actually get fired for speaking up (to combat implicit assumptions associated with speaking up).
- *Organizing arrangements interventions*: integrate expectations regarding voice behavior into performance measures and establish rewards for employees who engage in meaningful voice, share profits related to improvements with contributing employees.

As noted earlier, Ehrhart (2018) identified two new forms of helping behavior (instrumental helping and emotional helping). He also called for future research to examine whether their antecedents may be different. For example, he speculated that personality predictors may vary between these types of help (i.e., with agreeableness having a stronger relationship with emotional help given and conscientiousness having a stronger relationship with instrumental help). Similarly, emotional help may be driven by the relationship with the other individual and empathy, and instrumental help may be driven by the desire to help the organization or because it is part of one's job. Finally, he argued that the potential helper's expertise and capability could be more important when deciding whom to ask for instrumental help, whereas the potential helper's interpersonal skills and personality could matter more when deciding whom to ask for emotional help; and the primary concern when deciding whether to make an offer of instrumental help may be the self-esteem implications for the person in need, whereas when deciding to make an offer of emotional help, the primary concern may be the appropriateness of the behavior in the workplace based on its culture.

In their chapter about the effects of employee–organizational relationships on OCB, Coyle-Shapiro, Diehl, and Chang (2018) suggest two interesting possibilities for future research. First, they call for an integration of social exchange theory and conservation of resources theory to better understand the consequences of OCB for future engagement in OCB. More specifically, they suggest that future research should examine the extent to which employees become unable to sustain OCB over time, because of a draining effect based on the conservation of resources model or an unwillingness to sustain OCBs over time, possibly because of a nonreciprocation effect based on social exchange theory. Second, related to this, Coyle-Shapiro et al. suggest that future research should examine whether employees engage in proactive reciprocation, whereby they engage in OCB to ensure continuity or future delivery of inducements, as well as reactive reciprocation, where they merely reciprocate inducements received.

Although Kristof-Brown, Li, and Schneider (2018) found substantial evidence that person–environment (PE) fit relates to OCB, they suggested that future research should be conducted which includes P and E, as well as PE fit, in order to determine whether it is actually PE fit and not P or E causing the effects. In addition, they note that, because they failed to find any studies comparing PE fit with leadership or pay practices or climate and culture, future research should explore the relative impact of these predictors on OCBs.

Finally, based on their examination of the relationships between job embeddedness and OCB, Holtom and Sekiguchi (2018) call for future research in three areas. First, they call for research to explore how job embeddedness may affect the activation of different motives which promote OCBs; and whether the different foci of job embeddedness (e.g., organizational embeddedness or occupational embeddedness) or the different dimensions of job embeddedness (e.g., links, fit and sacrifice) activate different motives for exhibiting OCBs. They speculate that (a) individuals with high levels of organizational embeddedness and low levels of occupational embeddedness might engage in more OCBOs than those with low levels of organizational embeddedness and high levels of occupational embeddedness; and (b) individuals with high levels of organizational links would exhibit more OCBIs than those with few links. To investigate these issues, they argue that future empirical research needs to measure the different motives for OCBs and examine whether they play a mediating role in the relationship between job embeddedness and OCBs. Second, Holtom and Sekiguchi call for a finer grained analysis of the effect of job embeddedness on OCB because prior research has examined the effect of job embeddedness on aggregate OCB, but not on its many subdimensions. Third, based on the work of Hom, Mitchell, Lee, and Griffeth (2012) on proximal withdrawal states, Holtom and Sekiguchi posit that employees who enthusiastically remain in an organization due to a strong desire to stay (affective forces) may be likely to exhibit a wide range of OCBs. However, employees who stay reluctantly (also known as dissatisfied stayers) may be prone to counterproductive work behaviors (CWBs), may suggest fewer workplace improvements, and may engage in fewer discretionary behaviors on behalf of the organization.

Examining Mediating Mechanisms of the Antecedents and Consequences of Organizational Citizenship Behavior

In their chapter on the multilevel antecedents of OCB, N. P. Podsakoff et al. (2018b) reported that over two dozen potential mediators of the effects of unit-level antecedents on individual-level OCB have been examined in this literature. Because a majority of the mediators were individual-level mediators, they suggested that future research should attempt to better understand unit-level mediators such as organizational climate (e.g., climates focused on the advancement and improvement of the collective); shared perceptions or values (e.g., shared perceptions of the value/importance of OCB or a shared concern for the well-being of the collective); and the degree to which the members of collective entities internalize the values of their leader. N. P. Podsakoff et al. also noted that research in this area has been fairly unsystematic, in that most mediators have been examined in only one or two studies. Therefore, they suggested that the input-process-output (IPO) framework may provide help in identifying mediating mechanisms that would be fruitful to explore in future research. The IPO model identifies three major processes influencing unit effectiveness: team processes, emergent states, and blended mediators. For example, in the case of team processes, they note that it might be beneficial to examine communication or coordination, because several of the antecedents examined in this literature (e.g., leader–member exchange, servant leadership, affective commitment, cohesion, or voice climate) would be expected to influence communication or coordination, which subsequently might be expected to increase OCB.

Similarly, in the case of emergent states, they note that one important process that has not been examined is shared mental models (SMMs). They suggest that a strong team SSM ("a shared understanding among team members about how they will interact with one another"; Mathieu, Maynard, Rapp, & Gilson, 2008 , p. 430) would facilitate individual helping and courtesy between team members by increasing coordination and communication across members. Finally, in the blended mediator category, N. P. Podsakoff et al. suggest that one mediating process worthy of future investigation is the quantity and quality of information exchange. As in the case of communication, they speculate that the amount and nature of information exchanged among team members might mediate the effect of a number of antecedents, like leader–member exchange, servant leadership, group–team member exchange, empowerment climate, and justice climate on individual-level OCB.

In their chapter on consequences of OCB, MacKenzie et al. (2018) concluded that, although many mediators of the effects of OCB on individual- and unit-level outcomes have been suggested, relatively few of them have been empirically examined. Bolino et al. (2017) made this same observation in their chapter. So to facilitate future research in this area, MacKenzie et al. organized the different unit-level mediators that have been suggested in the literature (many of which have never been tested) and highlight the mechanisms through which these mediators might be related to different forms of OCB. These mechanisms include factors that (a) affect the group's ability to successfully accomplish the task to which they are assigned (e.g., attracting and retaining talented people, learning from others on the team, realizing the beneficial effects of task conflict); (b) enhance resources or improve the efficiency of the group's task performance (e.g., freeing up resources for more productive purposes, enhancing managerial productivity, optimizing resource allocations); (c) enhance the group's willingness to expend effort to perform the task (e.g., team potency, collective self-efficacy, team spirit); (d) enhance the group's shared perceptions of its routines, practices, procedures, rewards, standards, norms, and goals (e.g., development of team norms, team shared vision, supportive/trusting climate); and (e) help the group to manage and regulate its social interactions (e.g., reduce the need to devote scarce resources to maintenance functions, enhance team cohesiveness, managing interdependencies between members of the team). Investigating these categories of mediating mechanisms would be a worthwhile direction for future research at the unit level.

Finally, Bergeron et al. (2018) recommended that future research needs to examine the mediators of the effects of OCB on career outcomes. They identified a number of potential mediators that should be investigated, including the following: attribution of motive, leader–member exchange, building social capital, exhibiting OCB invites mentoring from supervisors, and signaling of competence to build reputation.

Examining Boundary Conditions

Moderators of the Effects of Organizational Citizenship Behavior on Its Consequences

In their chapter on the consequences of OCB, MacKenzie et al. (2018) reviewed research on the moderators of the impact of OCB and found that although many moderators had been suggested, relatively few had been empirically tested. So, to aid future research, they suggested a broad set of potential moderators of the impact of OCBs on unit- and individual-level outcomes, grouped these moderators into categories (individual, group, supervisor, task, organizational, and cultural/environmental characteristics), and speculated about their potential impact on the relationships between three prototypical forms of OCB (helping, sportsmanship, and voice) and unit- and individual-level outcomes. At the unit level, they hypothesized that the impact of all three prototypical forms of OCB may be generally strengthened by some moderators (e.g., task interdependence) and weakened by other moderators (e.g., spatial distance among group members); and still other moderators (e.g., organizational formalization or inflexibility) may influence the impact of only some forms of OCB but not others. Similarly, at the individual level, they hypothesized that the impact of all three prototypical forms of OCB may be generally strengthened by some moderators (e.g., altruistic/prosocial motives) and weakened by other moderators (e.g., negative affectivity); still other moderators (e.g., collectivism or power distance) may influence the impact of only some forms of OCB but not others.

Other researchers have advanced some of the same hypotheses. For example, several authors in this handbook (e.g., Allen & Jang, 2018; Earley & Calic, 2018; Organ, 2018; N. P. Podsakoff et al., 2018b) have suggested that future research should examine the moderating effect of cross-cultural factors (e.g., individualistic/collectivistic, power distance, gender egalitarianism) on the relationship between OCBs and their consequences; and several authors (e.g., Bellairs & Halbesleben, 2018; Bolino et al., 2018) suggest that a person's motive for exhibiting OCB may also be an important moderator of the effects of OCBs. Beyond this, Bergeron et al. (2018) suggest that future research should examine the moderating effects of the OCB target (individual vs. group; high-status vs. low-status individuals) and the amount of resources on the relationship between OCB and its consequences; and Allen and

Jang (2018) suggest that the potential moderating effects of gender on the relationship between OCB and career outcomes has important implications and is ripe for further investigation. Thus, even though these hypotheses are highly speculative and lack a solid theoretical foundation based on the literature, testing these potential moderators of the effects of OCB on individual- and unit-level outcomes may be a worthwhile endeavor for future research.

Nonlinear Effects of Organizational Citizenship Behavior on Its Consequences

Finally, given that prior research has increasingly found that OCB can have curvilinear effects on important outcomes (e.g., MacKenzie, Podsakoff, & Podsakoff, 2011; Munyon, Hochwarter, Perrewé, & Ferris, 2010; Rapp, Bachrach, & Rapp, 2013; Rubin, Dierdorff, & Bachrach, 2013), several authors in this handbook (e.g., Bolino et al., 2018; Chiaburu et al., 2018; Ehrhart, 2018; MacKenzie et al., 2018) have called for future research to adopt conceptualizations and models that go beyond simple linear relationships and effects when examining the consequences of OCB. For example, in his review, Ehrhart (2018) highlighted several interesting findings with regard to curvilinear relationships between OCB and its antecedents and consequences (i.e., between self-esteem and help-seeking behavior, between the need for help and help seeking, between helping seeking and performance evaluations, between favor exchange and productivity, and between helping behavior and performance). Furthermore, he emphasized that "Such findings add complexity and insight beyond simplistic 'either-or' or 'more is better' thinking, and in particular, may be critical for understanding the simultaneous positive and negative effects of helping" (p. 497). We agree, and hope that the discussions in this handbook facilitate research on these curvilinear effects.

Moderators of the Effects of Unit-Level Antecedents on Organizational Citizenship Behavior

N. P. Podsakoff et al. (2018) reviewed research examining the moderators of the relationships between unit-level antecedents and individual-level OCBs and found that some of them enhanced (i.e., strengthened) these relationships and some of them neutralized (i.e., weakened) them. The individual-level (Level 1) moderators that were found to enhance these relationships were followers' proactive personality, leader–member exchange, and attraction to the group; and the unit-level (Level 2) moderators that enhanced these relationships were service climate, mean leader–member exchange, shared empathic concern, and dispersion in group autonomy, workload, and opportunities for noncore activities. The individual-level moderators (Level 1) that were found to neutralize these relationships were role ambiguity, leader prototypicality, and follower team identification, traditionality, and learning goal orientation; and the unit-level moderators (Level 2) that neutralized these relationships were service climate, shared moral awareness, leader disciplinary background breadth, and group power distance.

Moderators of the Effects of Individual-Level Antecedents on Organizational Citizenship Behavior

N. P. Podsakoff et al. (2018b) also reviewed research examining the unit-level moderators of the relationships between individual-level antecedents and individual-level OCBs. Once again, some moderators were found to enhance (i.e., strengthen) these relationships and some neutralized (i.e., weakened) them. Turning first to the enhancers, the unit-level moderators that were found to enhance the nature of the relationships between employee attitudes, moods, or perceptions and citizenship behaviors were participative climate, autonomy climate, group positive affect diversity, and group self-direction values. The moderators that were found to enhance the relationships between leader behaviors or characteristics and citizenship behaviors were group cohesiveness, autonomy-supportive team climates, procedural justice climate, work unit structure (i.e., mechanistic vs. organic), group shared moral awareness, and change frequency. The moderators that were found to enhance the relationships between group and organizational characteristics and employee citizenship behaviors were group–team member exchange, the density of social relationships in a group, and procedural justice climate. With respect to the neutralizers, the unit-level moderators that were found to neutralize the relationships between employee attitudes, moods, or perceptions and citizenship behaviors were organizational service climate, procedural justice climate, voice climate, group cohesiveness, and group size. The moderators that were found to neutralize the relationships between employee personality variables or values and employee citizenship behavior were transformational leadership, service climate, trust, and group cohesiveness. The moderators that were found to neutralize the relationships between job factors and OCBs were service climate, group cohesiveness, shared moral awareness, and authoritarian leadership.

Although it is difficult to discern a clear pattern in the moderating effects of unit-level and individual-level antecedents on OCB, it does appear that future research on the enhancers and neutralizers of these relationships is needed. In particular, future research should focus on why these moderators have their effects and attempt to fit them into a broader theoretical framework.

Methodological Concerns To Be Addressed in Future Research

Item Content Issues

We now turn our attention to methodological concerns that should be addressed in future OCB research. One issue originally raised by Dalal (2005) is the use of reverse-scored items for measuring some forms of OCB. A reverse-scored item can be problematic when it is content valid for more than one construct. For example, several authors in this handbook (Carpini & Parker, 2018; Dalal & Carpenter, 2018; Rosen, Johnson, Chang, Yochum, & Passantino, 2018) note that one of Williams and Anderson's (1991) reverse-scored OCBO items (i.e., "takes undeserved breaks") is highly similar in content to an item that was subsequently used by Bennett and Robinson's (2000) to measure counterproductive work behavior (i.e., "taken an additional or longer break than is acceptable at your workplace"). This similarity undermines the discriminant validity of the constructs they measure (Dalal & Carpenter, 2018; Rosen et al. 2018).

Another problem raised by several authors (Carpini & Parker, 2018; Dalal & Carpenter, 2018; Rosen et al. 2018) is the use of antithetical items to measure some forms of OCB (after reverse-scoring). As noted by Dalal and Carpenter (2018), "OCB scales contain several antithetical items, intended to measure the absence or avoidance of OCB. These antithetical items are subsequently reverse-scored when calculating an overall OCB scale score" (p. 76). For example, Smith, Organ, and Near's (1983) generalized compliance scale included the following antithetical items: "does not take unnecessary time off work"; "does not take extra breaks"; and "does not spend time in idle conversation." Other examples include Van Dyne, Graham, and Dinesch's (1994) antithetical loyalty items (e.g., "does not tell outsiders this is a good place to work," "does not defend organization when employees criticize it," "does not go out of way to defend organization against outside threats") and antithetical functional participation items (e.g., "avoids extra duties and responsibilities at work," "does not work beyond what is required"). As noted by Carpini and Parker (2018), antithetical items are problematic because they are "inconsistent with the operational definition of individual performance advanced by Campbell et al. (1993). Given [that] . . . antithetical items are about refraining from certain behavior and therefore are, in fact, the lack of the target behavior, these items might not accurately represent the performance construct" (p. 38).

Thus, future research should avoid the use of antithetical items and be careful when using reverse-scored items to measure OCBs. These are distinct problems, although they are often conflated in the literature because antithetical items are almost always reversed-scored, even though not all reverse-scored items are antithetical. Indeed, in Dalal's (2005) meta-analysis where he reported that the correlation between OCB and counterproductive work behavior was significantly larger when "antithetical" items were included in the OCB scale ($r = -.66$) than when they were not included ($r = -.19$), it is impossible to determine whether the studies coded as "antithetical" were examples of "the absence or avoidance of OCB" that were reverse-scored, rather than merely reversed-scored items. The reason this is unclear is that none of the "antithetical" items he provided as examples in his paper captured "the absence or avoidance of OCB," and he failed to report the specific criteria used to identify the studies coded as having "antithetical" items.

Direction of Causality

Several authors (Cropanzano, Rupp, Thornton, & Shao, 2018; Holtom & Sekiguchi, 2018; Moorman, Brower, & Grower, 2018; Piccolo, Buengeler, & Judge, 2018; N. P. Podsakoff et al., 2018b; Scott et al., 2018; Somech & Drach-Zahavy, 2018) called for future research to more carefully examine the direction of causality between OCBs and their antecedents and consequences. For example, Cropanzano et al. (2018) noted that "since the very early days of justice and OCB research, it has been more or less assumed that the former causes the latter (e.g., by Bateman & Organ, 1983; Smith et al., 1983). Although this is no doubt true some of the time (e.g., Skarlicki & Latham, 1996, 1997), it strikes us that the alternative needs to be put to a direct test. It could be that individuals who perform high levels of OCB engender better treatment from their peers and supervisors" (p. 274).

Similarly, Moorman et al. (2018) noted that "Even though research on trust and OCB has mostly supported the unidirectional, simple relationship where increases in trust prompt increases in OCB performance, we believe there is value in thinking about how trust and OCB mutually influence one another, creating a reinforcing spiral. Trust promotes OCB; OCB performance promotes trust; and the occurrence of each reinforces the continued and growing occurrence of the other. This is a virtuous spiral when it occurs in the positive direction and more like a death spiral when it occurs in the negative direction" (p. 288). Therefore, it is important for future research to use research designs that provide stronger evidence of causality. As noted by N. P. Podsakoff et al. (2018b), this can be done by experimentally manipulating each step of the hypothesized causal sequence (cf. Spencer, Zanna, & Fong, 2005), building in appropriate time lags between OCB and its presumed antecedents and consequences, or through some combination of these two methods (e.g., MacKenzie, 1986; Stone-Romero & Rosopa, 2011).

Source of Organizational Citizenship Behavior Ratings

Several authors (Chiaburu et al., 2018; Dalal & Carpenter, 2018; Rosen et al., 2018; Scott et al., 2018; Somech & Drach-Zahavy, 2018; Fasbender et al., 2018) noted that an important issue for future research is resolving the question of who is the best source for OCB ratings. The question is whether OCB ratings should be obtained from the person exhibiting the OCB or from an observer of the OCB. Unfortunately, it is not clear which source is the most accurate, and there is currently no consensus regarding the best source, or combination of sources, for OCB ratings.

As noted by Rosen et al. (2018), the main advantage of self-reports is that "individual employees possess the greatest knowledge of their own behaviors and, therefore, self-ratings of OCBs are likely to be the most accurate among the various sources considered in prior research" (p. 406). However, Rosen et al. note several disadvantages of self-reports: (a) "self-ratings are often viewed as problematic because social desirability biases and self-enhancement motives have the potential to lead individuals to over report behaviors that are viewed favorably by others"; and (b) "self-ratings of OCB may be impacted by common rater effects (i.e., those effects that result from implicit theories, consistency motifs, acquiescence/disacqueiscence biases, and/or mood states of a particular rater), which have the potential to inflate the magnitude of observed correlations between OCBs and other self-reported constructs" (p. 406).

In contrast, Rosen et al. note that the main advantage of obtaining ratings from someone other than the persons exhibiting the OCB (e.g., supervisors, peers, subordinates) is that the ratings are unlikely to be distorted due to social desirability biases or self-enhancement motives. However, the disadvantages are that (a) "a single source other than the self is unlikely to be able to accurately report on the total amount of OCB enacted by a particular individual"; (b) "they are subject to the halo effect . . . (e.g., a supervisor assumes that an employee who is above average in task performance is also above average in terms of helping behaviors directed towards coworkers)"; and (c) "rater's implicit theories might also serve to inflate observed correlations among behavioral reports."

In view of these advantages and disadvantages, Rosen et al. (and others) offer several recommendations for future OCB research. First, to ensure validity, it is essential for raters to have the opportunity to observe the OCB being rated. For example, supervisors may be better positioned to provide ratings of voice behavior, and peers may be better positioned to rate helping behavior, because they are the recipients of these behaviors. A similar point was made by Fasbender et al. (2018) in their discussion of prosocial behavior, "Given that prosocial behavior in retirement could take a variety of forms and occur in different areas of life, the choice of rating source should be consistent with the specific form of prosocial behavior of interest. For instance, working colleagues might be the best source of prosocial behavior in the postretirement employment context, whereas close family members might be the best source of prosocial behavior in the family and community context" (p. 572). Second, when possible and appropriate, we recommend that multiple sources be used to obtain ratings of each type of OCB. This would improve our understanding of the extent these ratings converge, and it may permit measurement error from these sources to be controlled. Third, and related to this, we would also recommend that when possible and appropriate, the sources of OCB ratings should be different from the sources for ratings of their antecedent and consequences. This would help to control some forms of common method bias (e.g., implicit theories, consistency bias, acquiescence bias, etc.). Finally, when it is not possible or appropriate to obtain ratings of

OCB, its antecedents, and its consequences, from different sources, efforts should be made to minimize the threat of common method bias. As we have argued elsewhere (e.g., MacKenzie & Podsakoff, 2012; P. M. Podsakoff, MacKenzie, & Podsakoff, 2012), the researcher's goal should be to reduce the plausibility of method bias as a rival explanation for the hypothesized relationships by thoughtfully assessing the research setting in order to identify the most likely causes of method bias, and then taking concrete steps to mitigate these problems first by procedures designed to prevent their occurrence, and then with statistical controls.

Event Sampling Methodology

Until recently, research on OCBs has examined factors that explain between-person differences in these behaviors. However, several authors in this handbook (e.g., Dalal & Carpenter, 2018; Ehrhart, 2018; Rosen et al., 2018; Scott et al., 2018) have suggested that future research in this area would benefit from the use of event sampling methodology (ESM) in order to reveal the dynamic processes that explain within-person variation in OCBs. For example, Ehrhart (2018) has noted that a within-person approach would be useful to "highlight how individuals may respond differently to individual helping episodes based on a variety of variables" (p. 497). In addition, Dalal and Carpenter (2018) note that much of the theory regarding the relationship between affective states and OCB pertains more to the manner which within-person fluctuations in affect and OCB happen over time rather than between-person fluctuations in these variables.

However, ESM involves the use of systematic or random prompts to obtain observations from individuals over time, and, as noted by Scott et al. (2018) and Rosen et al. (2018), this methodology presents several challenges for OCB research. First, because people are being asked for responses multiple times, sometimes several times per day, ESM researchers frequently rely on abridged or shortened scales, or randomly select a subset of items from a larger scale, in order to reduce the burden on respondents. However, once items are eliminated, it creates deficiency in the measures of OCB (Rosen et al., 2018; Scott et al., 2018). In response to this, Rosen et al. (2018) recommend that ESM researchers examining OCBs should

> take steps to ensure that the measures of OCB that they use are appropriate for examining the phenomenon, as a potential criticism of this research is that because the ESM measures are different from the scales used in more traditional studies of OCB, then they may not be assessing the same construct. Therefore, as with more traditional studies, it is important for ESM researchers to provide a full description of their scales. If they are abridged versions of previously developed scales, then authors need to report which items were dropped and why. For new and abridged scales, authors ought to provide evidence supporting the validity of the measures that they use in order to ensure that what they are measuring does, in fact, represent OCB. (p. 412)

Another issue raised by Scott et al. is that because in a typical ESM study the same people are being asked to respond repeatedly to the same (or similar) questions, common method bias is a concern. One solution for this would be to obtain ratings from different raters at different points in time. However, Scott et al. (2018) note that this may not be practical "because independent raters such as supervisors may have limited observational opportunities" (p. 427). Another potential solution that Scott et al. (2018) note is the use of mean-centering of the responses within individuals. However, to our knowledge, there is no empirical evidence that this procedure actually controls for common method biases. In view of the fact that neither of these potential solutions is likely to be feasible and/or effective, future research should investigate other ways to control for method biases in ESM studies.

Social Network Analysis

In addition to the interest in using intraindividual techniques, another area that seems particularly fruitful is the use of network concepts and analytic techniques. Several scholars have applied concepts from the network literature to the study of several dimensions of OCBs. For example, Bowler and Brass (2006) applied a social network analysis perspective to the study of helping behavior, finding that the strength of employee friendships at work was positively related to both the performance and receipt of interpersonal citizenship behaviors. In addition, Venkataramani and Tangirala (2010) have reported that employee workflow centrality was positively related to the exhibition of voice behavior. In other words, the more critical employees were to the task-related interaction networks of their work groups, the more frequently they spoke up with recommendations for improving work processes and productivity. Detert, Burris, Harrison, and Martin (2013) have also applied the concept of "voice flows" to examine the nature and the impact of voice behavior in groups. Having said that, we are not aware of any studies of citizenship behaviors that use social network analyses, such as UCINET (Borgatti, Everett, & Freeman, 2002). Brass (2018) has explained several network concepts that may be important in the context of OCB research and has discussed how social network methods and analyses may be implemented to study citizenship behavior. Given the dramatic increase in attention paid to social networks, this seems like a potentially fruitful area for future study.

Multilevel Organizational Citizenship Behavior Research

Several authors in this handbook have called for more systematic multilevel research on OCB in the future (e.g., Chiaburu et al., 2018; Cropanzano et al., 2018; Ehrhart, 2018; Moorman et al., 2018; N. P. Podsakoff et al., 2018b; Somech & Drach-Zahavy, 2018). For example, Ehrhart (2018) suggests that multilevel methods could be used to enhance our understanding of how group norms develop, are maintained, and change over time. Moorman et al. (2018) have argued that OCB and trust are multilevel phenomena and that their interpersonal-, group-, and organizational-level determinants should be examined in future research. A similar point has been made by Cropanzano et al. (2018) in terms of the organizational justice–OCB relationships. Finally, Somech and Drach-Zahavy (2018) have noted that although research on OCB in the service sector has focused on the individual level, future research needs to examine these behaviors at the team and organizational levels as well.

However, as noted by N. P. Podsakoff et al. (2018b), there are two major methodological considerations that need to be taken into account when conducting multilevel studies in the future. The first is that researchers need to carefully consider what composition model is appropriate for their research because the composition model determines how data from lower levels are aggregated to represent the higher level construct. N. P. Podsakoff et al. (2018b) report that of the composition models identified by Chan (1998), the one that was most commonly used in multilevel OCB research is the direct consensus model, although they found examples of the use of the referent shift and dispersion models as well. However, N. P. Podsakoff et al. noted that the majority of multilevel studies failed to indicate the nature of the composition model used. This suggests that in future research, researchers need to recognize the conceptual differences between these composition models, be explicit about the one they are using, and provide empirical evidence to support their model choice.

The second important issue to consider in future multilevel OCB research is how to analyze the data. Traditionally, hierarchical linear modeling (HLM) has been used. However, there are three important disadvantages to this. First, HLM fails to control for measurement error, which is known to exist in the measures of OCB, its antecedents, and consequences. Failure to control for measurement error biases estimates and can result in inferential errors when testing hypotheses. Second, HLM can't accommodate multiple mediators in a single model. This is a problem because many mediators have been proposed in the literature. Third, as noted by Preacher, Zyphur, and Zhang (2010), because Level 2 outcomes cannot be accommodated using HLM, several plausible types of cross-level mediating effects cannot be examined, including 1-1-2, 1-2-1, 1-2-2, and 2-1-2. Therefore, as recommended by N. P. Podsakoff et al. (2018b), future research should use multilevel structural equation modeling with latent variables as an alternative to HLM.

Conclusion

Research on the topic of OCBs has grown rapidly since Organ and his colleagues (Bateman & Organ, 1983; Organ, 1988; Smith et al., 1983) first introduced the term into the literature. Despite this, it is obvious from the chapters in this handbook that there are still a substantial number of issues that are in need of additional research in the future. We are encouraged by this fact, and we hope that the suggestions in this chapter are helpful in generating new directions for OCB research.

References

Allen, T. D., & Jang, S. (2018). Gender and organizational citizenship behavior. In P. M. Podsakoff, S. B. MacKenzie, and N. P. Podsakoff (Eds.), *The Oxford handbook of organizational citizenship behavior* (pp. 221–238). Oxford, UK: Oxford University Press.

Allen, T. D., & Rush, M. C. (1998). The effects of organizational citizenship behavior on performance judgments: A field study and a laboratory experiment. *Journal of Applied Psychology, 83*, 247–260.

Allen, T. D., & Rush, M. C. (2001). The influence of ratee gender on ratings of organizational citizenship behavior. *Journal of Applied Social Psychology, 31*, 2561–2587.

Bateman, T. S., & Organ, D. W. (1983). Job-satisfaction and the good soldier—The relationship between affect and employee citizenship. *Academy of Management Journal, 26*, 587–595.

Bellairs, T., & Halbesleben, J. (2018). What are the motives for employees to exhibit citizenship behavior? A review of prosocial and instrumental predictors of OCB. In P. M. Podsakoff, S. B. MacKenzie, and N. P. Podsakoff (Eds.), *The Oxford handbook of organizational citizenship behavior* (pp. 239–254). Oxford, UK: Oxford University Press.

Bennett, R. J., & Robinson, S. L. (2000). Development of a measure of workplace deviance. *Journal of Applied Psychology, 85*, 349–360.

Bergeron, D. M., van Esch, C., & Thompson, P. S. (2018). Citizenship behavior and objective career outcomes: A review and agenda for future work. In P. M. Podsakoff, S. B. MacKenzie, and N. P. Podsakoff (Eds.), *The Oxford handbook of organizational citizenship behavior* (pp. 149–168). Oxford, UK: Oxford University Press.

Bolino, M. C., Klotz, A. C., & Turnley, W. H. (2018). The unintended consequences of organizational citizenship behaviors for employees, teams, and organizations. In P. M. Podsakoff, S. B. MacKenzie, and N. P. Podsakoff (Eds.), *The Oxford handbook of organizational citizenship behavior* (pp. 185–202). Oxford, UK: Oxford University Press.

Borgatti, S. P., Everett, M. G., & Freeman, L. C. (2002). *UCINET for Windows: Software for social network analysis*. Harvard, MA: Analytic Technologies.

Bowler, W. M., & Brass, D. J. (2006). Relational correlates of interpersonal citizenship behavior: A social network perspective. *Journal of Applied Psychology, 91*, 70–82.

Brass, D. J. (2018). A social network perspective on organizational citizenship behavior. In P. M. Podsakoff, S. B. MacKenzie, and N. P. Podsakoff (Eds.), *The Oxford handbook of organizational citizenship behavior* (pp. 317–330). Oxford, UK: Oxford University Press.

Burris, E. R., Bruno, E. A., Detert, J. R., & Caldwell, A. (2018). From barriers to drivers: Understanding different approaches to getting systematic upward voice in organizations. In P. M. Podsakoff, S. B. MacKenzie, and N. P. Podsakoff (Eds.), *The Oxford handbook of organizational citizenship behavior* (pp. 507–525). Oxford, UK: Oxford University Press.

Campbell, J. P., McCloy, R. A., Oppler, S. H., & Sager, C. E. (1993). A theory of performance. In N. Schmitt & W. C. Borman (Eds.), *Personnel selection in organizations* (pp. 35–69). San Francisco, CA: Jossey-Bass.

Carpini, J. A., & Parker, S. K. (2018). The bigger picture: How does OCB fit within a broader conceptualization of work performance? In P. M. Podsakoff, S. B. MacKenzie, and N. P. Podsakoff (Eds.), *The Oxford handbook of organizational citizenship behavior* (pp. 19–42). Oxford, UK: Oxford University Press.

Chan, D. (1998). Functional relations among constructs in the same content domain at different levels of analysis: A typology of composition models. *Journal of Applied Psychology, 83*, 234–246.

Chiaburu, D. S., Oh, I-S., & Marinova, S. (2018). Five-factor model of personality traits and organizational citizenship behavior. In P. M. Podsakoff, S. B. MacKenzie, and N. P. Podsakoff (Eds.), *The Oxford handbook of organizational citizenship behavior* (pp. 203–220). Oxford, UK: Oxford University Press.

Coyle-Shapiro, J., Diehl, M-R., & Chang, C. (2018). The employee-organization relationship and organizational citizenship behavior. In P. M. Podsakoff, S. B. MacKenzie, and N. P. Podsakoff (Eds.), *The Oxford handbook of organizational citizenship behavior* (pp. 331–352). Oxford, UK: Oxford University Press.

Cropanzano, R., Rupp, D. E., Thornton, M. A., & Shao, R. (2018). Organizational justice and organizational citizenship. In P. M. Podsakoff, S. B. MacKenzie, and N. P. Podsakoff (Eds.), *The Oxford handbook of organizational citizenship behavior* (pp. 255–283). Oxford, UK: Oxford University Press.

Dalal, R. S. (2005). A meta-analysis of the relationship between organizational citizenship behavior and counterproductive work behavior. *Journal of Applied Psychology, 90*, 1241–1255.

Dalal, R. S., & Carpenter, N. (2018). The other side of the coin? Similarities and differences between organizational citizenship behavior and counterproductive work behavior. In P. M. Podsakoff, S. B. MacKenzie, and N. P. Podsakoff (Eds.), *The Oxford handbook of organizational citizenship behavior* (pp. 69–89). Oxford, UK: Oxford University Press.

Detert, J. R., Burris, E. R., Harrison, D. A., & Martin, S. R. (2013). Voice flows to and around leaders: Understanding when units are helped or hurt by employee voice. *Administrative Science Quarterly, 58*, 624–668.

Earley, P. C., & Calic, G. (2018). A cultural perspective on organizational citizenship behavior. In P. M. Podsakoff, S. B. MacKenzie, and N. P. Podsakoff (Eds.), *The Oxford handbook of organizational citizenship behavior* (pp. 387–399). Oxford, UK: Oxford University Press.

Ehrhart, M. G. (2018). Helping in organizations: A review and directions for future research. In P. M. Podsakoff, S. B. MacKenzie, and N. P. Podsakoff (Eds.), *The Oxford handbook of organizational citizenship behavior* (pp. 475–505). Oxford, UK: Oxford University Press.

Fasbender, U., Wang, M., & Zhan, Y. (2018). Prosocial behavior in retirement. In P. M. Podsakoff, S. B. MacKenzie, and N. P. Podsakoff (Eds.), *The Oxford handbook of organizational citizenship behavior* (pp. 559–576). Oxford, UK: Oxford University Press.

Griffin, M. A., Neal, A., & Parker, S. K. (2007). A new model of work role performance: Positive behavior in uncertain and interdependent contexts. *Academy of Management Journal, 50*, 327–347.

Holtom, B. C., & Sekiguchi, T. (2018). Exploring the relationship between job embeddedness and organizational citizenship behavior. In P. M. Podsakoff, S. B. MacKenzie, and N. P. Podsakoff (Eds.), *The Oxford handbook of organizational citizenship behavior* (pp. 371–385). Oxford, UK: Oxford University Press.

Hom, P., Mitchell, T., Lee, T., & Griffeth, R. (2012). Reviewing employee turnover: Focusing on proximal withdrawal states and an expanded criterion. *Psychological Bulletin, 138*, 831–858.

Humphrey, S. E., Morgeson, F. P., & Mannor, M. J. (2009). Developing a theory of the strategic core of teams: A role composition model of team performance. *Journal of Applied Psychology, 94*, 48–61.

Kelley, E. L. (1927). *Interpretation of educational measurements*. Yonkers, NY: World.

Kiker, D. S., & Motowidlo, S. J. (1999). Main and interaction effects of task and contextual performance on supervisory reward decisions. *Journal of Applied Psychology, 84*, 602–609.

Kristof-Brown, A. L., Li, C. S., & Schneider, B. (2018). Fitting in and doing good: A review of person-environment fit and OCB research. In P. M. Podsakoff, S. B. MacKenzie, and N. P. Podsakoff (Eds.), *The Oxford handbook of organizational citizenship behavior* (pp. 353–370). Oxford, UK: Oxford University Press.

Lennard, A., & Van Dyne, L. (2018). Helping that hurts intended beneficiaries: A new perspective on the dark side of helping organizational citizenship behavior. In P. M. Podsakoff, S. B. MacKenzie, and N. P. Podsakoff (Eds.), *The Oxford handbook of organizational citizenship behavior*(pp. 169–184). Oxford, UK: Oxford University Press.

Li, W-D., Frese, M., & Haidar, S. (2018). Distinguishing proactivity and citizenship behavior: Similarities and differences. In P. M. Podsakoff, S. B. MacKenzie, and N. P. Podsakoff (Eds.), *The Oxford handbook of organizational citizenship behavior* (pp. 55–68). Oxford, UK: Oxford University Press.

LePine, J. A., Erez, A., & Johnson, D. E. (2002). The nature and dimensionality of organizational citizenship behavior: A critical review and meta-analysis. *Journal of Applied Psychology, 87,* 52–65.

MacKenzie, S. B. (1986). The role of attention in mediating the effect of advertising on attribute importance. *Journal of Consumer Research, 13,* 174–195.

MacKenzie, S. B., & Podsakoff, P. M. (2012). Common method bias in marketing: Causes, mechanisms, and procedural remedies. *Journal of Retailing, 88,* 542–555.

MacKenzie, S. B., Podsakoff, P. M., & Fetter, R. (1991). Organizational citizenship behavior and objective productivity as determinants of managerial evaluations of salesperson's performance. *Organizational Behavior and Human Decision Processes, 50,* 123–150.

MacKenzie, S. B., Podsakoff, P. M., & Fetter, R. (1993). The impact of organizational citizenship behavior on evaluations of salesperson performance. *Journal of Marketing, 57,* 70–80.

MacKenzie, S. B., Podsakoff, P. M., & Podsakoff, N. P. (2011). Challenge-oriented organizational citizenship behaviors and organizational effectiveness: Do challenge-oriented behaviors really have an impact on the organization's bottom line? *Personnel Psychology, 64,* 559–592.

MacKenzie, S. B., Podsakoff, N. P., & Podsakoff, P. M. (2018). Individual—and organizational-level consequences of organizational citizenship behaviors. In P. M. Podsakoff, S. B. MacKenzie, and N. P. Podsakoff (Eds.), *The Oxford handbook of organizational citizenship behavior* (pp. 105–147). Oxford, UK: Oxford University Press.

Mathieu, J. E., Maynard, M. T., Rapp, T., & Gilson, L. (2008). Team effectiveness 1997-2007: A review of recent advancements and a glimpse into the future. *Journal of Management, 34,* 410–476.

Moorman, R., Brower, H. H., & Grover, S. (2018). Organizational citizenship behavior and trust: The double reinforcing spiral. In P. M. Podsakoff, S. B. MacKenzie, and N. P. Podsakoff (Eds.), *The Oxford handbook of organizational citizenship behavior* (pp. 285–296). Oxford, UK: Oxford University Press.

Morrison, E. W. (1994). Role definitions and organizational citizenship behavior: The importance of the employee's perspective. *Academy of Management Journal, 37,* 1543–1667.

Motowidlo, S. J., Kell, H. J., Martin, M. P., & Ghosh, K. (2018). Implicit trait policies about prosocial professionalism. In P. M. Podsakoff, S. B. MacKenzie, and N. P. Podsakoff (Eds.), *The Oxford handbook of organizational citizenship behavior* (pp. 543–558) Oxford, UK: Oxford University Press.

Motowidlo, S. J., & Van Scotter, J. R. (1994). Evidence that task-performance should be distinguished from contextual performance. *Journal of Applied Psychology, 79,* 475–480.

Munyon, T. P., Hochwarter, W. A., Perrewé, P. L., & Ferris, G. R. (2010). Optimism and the nonlinear citizenship behavior—job satisfaction relationship in three studies. *Journal of Management, 36,* 1505–1528.

Newton, D. W., & LePine, J. A. (2018). Organizational citizenship behavior and engagement: "You gotta keep 'em separated." In P. M. Podsakoff, S. B. MacKenzie, and N. P. Podsakoff (Eds.), *The Oxford handbook of organizational citizenship behavior* (pp. 43–54) Oxford, UK: Oxford University Press.

Organ, D. W. (1988). *Organizational citizenship behavior: The good soldier syndrome.* Lexington, MA: Lexington Books.

Organ, D. W. (2018). The roots of OCB. In P. M. Podsakoff, S. B. MacKenzie, and N. P. Podsakoff (Eds.), *The Oxford handbook of organizational citizenship behavior* (pp. 7–18). Oxford, UK: Oxford University Press.

Organ, D. W., Podsakoff, P. M., & MacKenzie, S. B. (2006). *Organizational citizenship behavior: Its nature, antecedents and consequences.* Thousand Oaks, CA: Sage.

Orr, J. M., Sackett, P. R., & Mercer, M. (1989). The role of prescribed and nonprescribed behaviors in estimating the dollar value of performance. *Journal of Applied Social Psychology, 74,* 34–40.

Park, O. S. (1986). *Beyond cognition in leadership: Prosocial behavior and affect in managerial judgment.* Unpublished doctoral dissertation, Pennsylvania State University.

Piccolo, R. F., Buengeler, C., & Judge, T. A. (2018). Leadership [is] OCB: Review of a self-evident link. In P. M. Podsakoff, S. B. MacKenzie, and N. P. Podsakoff (Eds.), *The Oxford handbook of organizational citizenship behavior* (pp. 297–316). Oxford, UK: Oxford University Press.

Podsakoff, N. P., Morrison, E. W., & Martinez, T. M. (2018a). The role of a good soldier: A review of research on OCB role perceptions and recommendations for the future. In P. M. Podsakoff, S. B. MacKenzie, and N. P. Podsakoff (Eds.), *The Oxford handbook of organizational citizenship behavior* (pp. 91–104). Oxford, UK: Oxford University Press.

Podsakoff, N. P., Podsakoff, P. M., MacKenzie, S. B., Maynes, T. D., & Spoelma, T. M. (2014). Consequences of unit-level organizational citizenship behaviors: A review and recommendations for future research. *Journal of Organizational Behavior, 35,* S87–S119.

Podsakoff, N. P., Podsakoff, P. M., MacKenzie, S. B., Maynes, T. D., Whiting, S. W., & Spoelma, T. M. (2018b). Multilevel antecedents of organizational citizenship behavior: A review and recommendations for future research. In P. M. Podsakoff, S. B. MacKenzie, and N. P. Podsakoff (Eds.), *The Oxford handbook of organizational citizenship behavior* (pp. 435–473). Oxford, UK: Oxford University Press.

Podsakoff, N. P., Whiting, S. W., Podsakoff, P. M., & Blume, B. D. (2009) Individual-and organizational-level consequences of organizational citizenship behaviors: A meta-analysis. *Journal of Applied Psychology, 94,* 122–141.

Podsakoff, P. M., Ahearne, M., & MacKenzie, S. B. (1997). Organizational citizenship behavior and the quantity and quality of work group performance. *Journal of Applied Psychology, 82,* 262–270.

Podsakoff, P. M., & MacKenzie, S. B. (1994). Organizational citizenship behavior and sales unit effectiveness. *Journal of Marketing Research, 31,* 351–363.

Podsakoff, P. M., MacKenzie, S. B., & Hui, C. (1993). Organizational citizenship behaviors and managerial evaluations of employee performance: A review and suggestions for future research. In G. R. Ferris and K. M. Rowland

(Eds.), *Research in personnel and human resources management* (Vol. 11, pp. 1–40). Greenwich, CT: JAI Press.

Podsakoff, P. M., MacKenzie, S. B., Paine, J. B., & Bachrach, D. G. (2000). Organizational citizenship behaviors: A critical review of the theoretical and empirical literature and suggestions for future research. *Journal of Management, 26,* 513–563.

Podsakoff, P. M., MacKenzie, S. B., & Podsakoff, N. P. (2012). Sources of method bias in social science research and recommendations on how to control for it. *Annual Review of Psychology, 63,* 539–569.

Podsakoff, P. M., MacKenzie, S. B., & Podsakoff, N. P. (2016). Recommendations for creating better concept definitions in the organizational, behavioral, and social sciences. *Organizational Research Methods, 19,* 159–203.

Porras, J. I., & Hoffer, S. J. (1986). Common behavior changes in successful organization development efforts. *The Journal of Applied Behavioral Science, 22,* 477–494.

Porras, J. I., & Silvers, R. C. (1991). Organization development and transformation. *Annual Review of Psychology, 42,* 51–78.

Preacher, K. J., Zyphur, M. J., & Zhang, Z. (2010). A general multilevel SEM framework for assessing multilevel mediation. *Psychological Methods, 15,* 209–233.

Rapp, A. A., Bachrach, D. G., & Rapp, T. L. (2013). The influence of time management skill on the curvilinear relationships between organizational citizenship behavior and task performance. *Journal of Applied Psychology, 98,* 668–677.

Rosen, C. C., Johnson, R. E., Chang, C-H., Yochum, E., & Passantino, L. (2018). Review and recommended best practices for measuring and modeling. In P. M. Podsakoff, S. B. MacKenzie, and N. P. Podsakoff (Eds.), *The Oxford handbook of organizational citizenship behavior* (pp. 401–416). Oxford, UK: Oxford University Press.

Rubin, R. S., Dierdorff, E. C., & Bachrach, D. G. (2013). Boundaries of citizenship behavior: Curvilinearity and context in the citizenship and task performance relationship. *Personnel Psychology, 66,* 377–406.

Sandberg, S., & Grant, A. M. (2015, February 6). Madam C.E.O., Get Me a Coffee. *The New York Times.* Retrieved from http://www.nytimes.com/2015/02/08/opinion/sunday/sheryl-sandberg-and-adam-grant-on-women-doing-office-housework.html.

Scott, B. A., Matta, F. K., & Koopman, J. (2018). Within-person approaches to the study of organizational citizenship behaviors: Antecedents, consequences, and boundary conditions. In P. M. Podsakoff, S. B. MacKenzie, and N. P. Podsakoff (Eds.), *The Oxford handbook of organizational citizenship behavior* (pp. 417–434). Oxford, UK: Oxford University Press.

Shore, L. M., Barksdale, K., & Shore, T. H. (1995). Managerial perceptions of employee commitment to the organization. *Academy of Management Journal, 38,* 1593–1615.

Skarlicki, D. P., & Latham, G. P. (1996). Increasing citizenship behavior within a labor union: A test of organizational justice theory. *Journal of Applied Psychology, 81,* 161–169.

Skarlicki, D. P., & Latham, G. P. (1997). Leadership training in organizational justice to increase citizenship behavior within a labor union. *Personnel Psychology, 50,* 617–633.

Smith, C. A., Organ, D. W., & Near, J. P. (1983). Organizational citizenship behavior—Its nature and antecedents. *Journal of Applied Psychology, 68,* 653–663.

Somech, A., & Drach-Zahavy, A. (2018). Rethinking organizational citizenship behavior in service organizations. In P. M. Podsakoff, S. B. MacKenzie, and N. P. Podsakoff (Eds.), *The Oxford handbook of organizational citizenship behavior* (pp. 527–541). Oxford, UK: Oxford University Press.

Spencer, S. J., Zanna, M. P., & Fong, G. T. (2005). Establishing a casual chain: Why experiments are often more effective than mediational analyses in examining psychological processes. *Journal of Personality and Social Psychology, 89,* 845–851.

Stone-Romero, E. F., & Rosopa, P. J. (2011). Experimental tests of mediation models: Prospects, problems, and some solutions. *Organizational Research Methods, 14,* 631–646.

Van Dyne, L., Graham, J. W., & Dienesch, R. M. (1994). Organizational citizenship behavior: Construct redefinition, measurement, and validation. *Academy of Management Journal, 37,* 765–802.

Van Scotter, J. R., Motowidlo, S. J., & Cross, T. C. (2000). Effects of task performance and contextual performance on systemic rewards. *Journal of Applied Psychology, 85,* 526–535.

Venkataramani, V., & Tangirala, S. (2010). When and why do central employees speak up? An examination mediating and moderating variables. *Journal of Applied Psychology, 95,* 582–591.

Walz, S. M., & Niehoff, B. P. (2000). Organizational citizenship behaviors: Their relationship to organizational effectiveness. *Journal of Hospitality & Tourism Research, 24,* 301–319.

Werner, J. M. (1994). Dimensions that make a difference: Examining the impact of in-role and extra-role behaviors on supervisory ratings. *Journal of Applied Psychology, 79,* 98–107.

Williams, L. J., & Anderson, S. E. (1991). Job-satisfaction and organizational commitment as predictors of organizational citizenship and in-role behaviors. *Journal of Management, 17,* 601–617.

INDEX

Note: Figures and tables are indicated by an italic "*f*" or "*t*" following the page number. Endnote entries are indicated by an italic "*n*" and note number following the page number.

D

E

P

Q

R

T